WORD
SMART BASIC

Word Smart Basic WORD SMART JUNIOR 1·2권 통합본

지은이 C. L. Brantley
펴낸이 임상진
펴낸곳 (주)넥서스

초판 1쇄 발행 2001년 8월 25일
초판 42쇄 발행 2015년 3월 20일

2판 1쇄 발행 2015년 10월 25일
2판 12쇄 발행 2022년 12월 15일

3판 1쇄 발행 2023년 10월 25일
3판 2쇄 발행 2023년 10월 30일

출판신고 1992년 4월 3일 제311-2002-2호
주소 10880 경기도 파주시 지목로 5
전화 (02)330-5500 팩스 (02)330-5555

ISBN 979-11-6683-635-0 13740

출판사의 허락 없이 내용의 일부를
인용하거나 발췌하는 것을 금합니다.

가격은 뒤표지에 있습니다.
잘못 만들어진 책은 구입처에서 바꾸어 드립니다.

www.nexusbook.com

전미 PARENTS' CHOICE AWARD© 수상에 빛나는 혁신적인 주니어 어휘집!

WORD SMART

BASIC

WORD SMART JUNIOR

1·2권 통합본

C. L. Brantley 지음

넥서스

NEVER BEFORE!

전미 PARENTS' CHOICE AWARD®를 수상한 『WORD SMART JUNIOR』 I + II 권을 하나로 묶어 편역한 『WORD SMART BASIC 한국어판』은 미국에서 대학 강의를 수학할 수 있는 기준이 되는 필수어휘 1300개를 STORY READING과 연계하여 반복 습득하는 혁신적인 어휘 교재입니다. (독자의 학습 성향과 성격에 따라 STORY편을 먼저 읽고 즐기셔도 좋습니다.)

여는글

모국어 외에 다른 나라말을 배우고 습득한다는 것은 대단한 노력과 정성을 요하는 일이다. 외국어를 거대한 산맥으로 비유하자면 어휘는 그 산맥을 이루는 하나하나의 산줄기에 해당할 것이다.

통합적인 외국어 학습을 지향하는 시대적 흐름에서 어느 부분이 가장 중요한가 하는 것은 우문일 수도 있다. 하지만 어휘가 외국어 학습에 있어서 상당한 부분을 차지하고 있고 보다 발전된 단계의 외국어를 구사하기 위해서는 어휘학습이 필수과정이라는 것 또한 간과할 수 없는 사실이다.

그래서 많은 이들이 어휘학습에 시간을 투자한다. 하지만 우리 주변에서 마음먹은 대로 어휘학습에 성공한 사례를 찾아보기는 쉽지 않다. 그 이유는 뭘까?

첫째, 잘못된 학습방법이 문제다. 대부분의 학습자들이 어휘를 익힐 때 단어와 발음기호, 뜻 하나만 외우고 끝내버리는데 이는 효과적인 어휘 학습방법이라 할 수 없다. 어린아이가 모국어를 배울 때를 생각해보자. 모국어는 어휘만을 따로 떼서 배우지 않는다. 그 어휘가 쓰이는 예문을 많이 들으면서, 또 글을 읽을 수 있기 시작하면서부터는 많은 텍스트들을 접하면서 각각의 어휘가 지니고 있는 원래의 의미는 물론이고 독특한 뉘앙스까지도 익히게 되는 것이다. 많은 학습자들이 이런 사실을 간과하는 것이 효과적인 어휘학습의 주요 실패 요인이다.

둘째, 기존에도 문맥 중심의 어휘학습을 강조하면서 예문과 함께 단어를 익힐 것을 주장한 어휘책은 많았다. 하지만 실제로 책을 살펴보면 안의 예문들이 실생활에서 쓰이는 말과 너무 떨어져 있거나 학습자의 흥미를 만족시키기에는 역부족인 딱딱한 것들이 대부분이었다. 게다가 어휘는 어렵게 공부하고 이해하기 어려운 긴 예문을 읽어야 향상된다는 근거 없는 편견도 효과적인 어휘학습을 저해한 한 요인이었다.

셋째, 어휘는 어떤 분야보다도 반복학습이 중요하다. 그러나 익힌 어휘를 바로바로 확인할 수 있는 시스템이 완벽하게 갖추어져 있는 책이 없어 어렵게 어휘를 익히고도 활용하지 못하고 사장시켜버리는 경우가 많았다.

이런 문제점들 때문에 영어학습자들은 자신이 원하는 바대로 어휘학습을 할 수가 없었던 것이다. 이것을 해결한 책이 바로 이 『WORD SMART BASIC』이다. 이 책은 기존의 어휘책들이 가지고 있었던 여러 가지 문제점들을 파악해 해결점을 제시하면서 효과적인 학습이 이루어지도록 해준다. 무엇보다도 『WORD SMART BASIC』의 STORY 내용은 기존의 어휘책에 나와 있는 진부하고 딱딱한 예문과는 달리 한번 잡으면 손을 놓을 수 없을 정도로 기발하다.

책 처음에 나오는 WORDS에서 익힌 어휘들이 STORY에 빠짐없이 들어가 있으면서도 그 내용이 어떤 이들이 읽더라도 입가에 미소를 띨 만큼 흥미롭고 재미있다는 점은 이 책에서 가장 높이 살 부분이다. 어휘를 공부한다는 압박감 없이 소설을 읽듯 죽 읽어나가다 보면 이 책만이 가지고 있는 특유의 시스템을 통해 어휘가 체득되는 경험을 하게 되는 것이다.

학습자 여러분에게 말하고 싶은 것은 이 책을 공부하는데 많은 것이 필요하지는 않다는 점이다. 일단 모르는 단어가 나오더라도 당황하여 멈추지 않고 끝까지 STORY를 즐기려고 하는 자세만 되어 있다면 그것으로 충분하다. 그러다 보면 어느 순간 자신도 모르게 향상된 어휘실력에 깜짝 놀라게 될 것이다.

무엇보다도 『WORD SMART BASIC』의 STORY 내용은 기존의 어휘책에 나와 있는
진부하고 딱딱한 예문과는 달리 한번 잡으면 손을 놓을 수 없을 정도로 기발하다.

이 책의 구성

이 책은 미국 Junior들이 SAT를 준비하기 위해 기본적으로 알아야 할 핵심어휘를 익히게 해주는 『WORD SMART JUNIOR』의 Ⅰ·Ⅱ권을 통합한 책으로 PART A와 PART B로 구성되어 있다. 각 PART는 뒤의 STORY에 나오는 단어들을 미리 익히는 'WORDS', 뉴욕 출신의 도시적인 아이 브리지트와 신비한 프랑스 소녀 바베트, 흐트러진 머리모양의 천재소년 바너비, 그리고 화려한 과거를 자랑하는 거대한 검은 수코양이 보리가드의 모험담을 따라 펼쳐지는 8개의 'STORY', 다시 한번 앞서 배운 단어들을 확실히 이해하도록 도와주는 다양한 형식의 'QUIZ'로 구성되어 있다.
흥미진진한 이야기를 통해 총 1300여개의 어휘를 배울 수 있다는 것이 이 책의 가장 큰 장점으로 그 외에 다음과 같은 특징을 지니고 있다

1. 흥미진진한 STORY로 익히는 혁신적인 단어학습 지향
어휘를 익혀야 하는 필요성은 느끼지만 기존의 어휘학습 방법과는 다르게 공부하고자 하는 모든 이들을 위한 책이다. 영어뿐 아니라 다른 외국어를 공부할 때도 어휘학습에 있어서 가장 효과적인 방법은 단순히 어휘를 공부하는 것에서 끝나는 것이 아니라 예문을 통해 확인하고 체득하는 것이다. 그러나 기존의 어휘책들이 지루하고 딱딱한 예문으로 학습동기 유발에 실패했던 것이 사실이다. 『WORD SMART BASIC』은 개성 있는 네 명의 주인공들이 겪는 흥미진진하고 다양한 모험담을 생생한 예문으로 구성해 한 권의 이야기책을 읽으면서 동시에 어휘가 습득되도록 하고 있으며 이 점은 다른 책과는 비교할 수 조차 없는 이 책만이 가지고 있는 최대의 장점이다.

2. WORDS-STORY-QUIZ로 이어지는 최적의 학습능률 시스템 구현
예문으로 어휘를 익히는 것 외에 어휘학습에서 중요한 요소 중의 하나가 바로 반복하는 것이다. 이 책은 스토리 속에 나오는 필수 단어를 상세한 영어해설과 참신한 예문으로 미리 학습하고, 스토리를 읽으면서 앞에서 익힌 단어를 다시 한번 복습하고, 재미있고 다양한 형식으로 구성된 퀴즈를 풀어보면서 그동안 익혔던 어휘를 한 번 더 확인할 수 있게 구성되어 있어 학습능률과 어휘 메모리에 있어서 최적의 시스템을 구현하고 있다.

3. 잘못 이해하거나 잘못 쓰기 쉬운 단어 · 동의어 · 파생어 총정리
영어를 대하면서 흔히 저지르고 당황해하는 대부분의 경우는 확실히 알고 있는 단어라도 그 단어가 활용된 예문을 이해하지 못할 때이다. 『WORD SMART BASIC』은 사람들이 알고 있지만 잘못 이해하고 있거나 실수를 범하는, 더러 다른 단어와 혼동하기도 하는 단어들을 묶어서 보여주고 동의어와 파생어들을 충분히 제시한다. 또 앞에서 나온 어휘와는 별도로 본문에 나온 단어들 중 학습자들이 반드시 알고 있어야 하는 중요 단어들을 정확한 영어사전식 정의, 알찬 예문과 해석으로 정리해 더 효율적인 어휘학습을 할 수 있도록 편의를 제공하고 있다.

[STORY LINE]

PART A

제1장 뉴욕 출신의 브리지트는 파리 루브르 박물관으로 부모와 여행을 왔다가 길을 잃어 버리고 신비의 소녀 바베트와 천재소년 바너비, 수코양이 보리가드와 운명적인 만남을 갖는다.

제2장 돌풍이 이는 가운데 낯선 곳에 떨어진 일행들. 알고 보니 코끼리 제국을 뒤엎으려는 재칼들에게 붙잡히게 되는데 .

제3장 재칼 일당의 혁명이 성공적으로 마무리 된 후 공간 이동을 당한 주인공들은 악명 높은 우주 히피 워블리 필스타인과 그의 여자 친구 재니스가 이끄는 악랄한 해적선 '파 아웃'에 승선하게 된다.

제4장 재니스의 도움으로 우주선을 빠져나온 주인공들은 미시시피강에 빠지고 익사직전에 간신히 살아나지만 식인종이라는 이름의 팔 네 개 달린 괴물에게 붙잡히고 만다. 그 식인종을 조종하는 사람은 악당 스네이크와 베르나였다.

제5장 홍수를 일으키려던 음모를 꾸미던 스네이크는 법정에서 유죄 판결을 받고 주인공들은 파리를 향해 가다 신천옹과 부딪쳐 어느 이상한 수도원에 떨어지게 되고 .

제6장 이상한 수도사들의 옛날 이야기를 듣고 그들이 신봉하는 더 괴상한 마법사와의 만남을 뒤로 하고 어느 섬에 도착하게 된다. 거기에서 바너비는 무인도 왕의 사위가 될 것을 부탁받는데 .

제7장 가까스로 왕과 공주로부터 도망친 일행들은 항해도중 바위에 부딪쳐 아주 이상한 동굴 속으로 들어가게 되는 데 그 곳은 다름 아닌 위조범들의 소굴이었다.

제8장 위조의 대가 폭스 할아버지한테 인정을 받지 못했던 레오나르도, 주인공들의 노력으로 레오나르도는 할아버지의 인정을 받아 파리의 미술학교로 공부하러 오고 브리지트는 잃어버린 부모님과 해후한다.

PART B

제1장 뉴욕에서 다시 만난 네 주인공들. 뉴욕 양키즈 야구 시합을 보러 7회가 진행 중인 야구장에 간다. 그러나 갑자기 들려오는 소리, "양키즈를 내놓을 테냐, 목숨을 내놓을 테냐."

제2장 열 개의 기다란 촉수에 초록색 머리, 늘어진 귀가 달려 있는 거대한 고르가스가 양키즈의 유명한 투수 레프티 잼비시에게 '너클볼' 다루는 능력을 알려달라고 떼를 쓴다.

제3장 주인공들의 기지로 고르가스에게서는 벗어나지만 교활한 고르가스는 이들을 17세기로 보내고 이들은 킬 선장이 이끄는 스페인 해적선에 떨어지게 된다. 자칭 고르가스보다 더 지혜롭다고 주장하는 바르가스를 알게 되면서 주머니쥐 포포를 만나게 된다.

제4장 스쿠너 선을 타고 가다 도착한 곳은 거대한 상아색 탑. 거기에는 계속해서 움직이는 도서관과 동물들의 말까지 다양하게 구사할 수 있는 보그스 박사가 살고 있었다. 그리고 그는 주인공들이 이 세계를 구해야 한다고 말을 하는데 .

제5장 주인공들은 온갖 공룡들이 모여 있는 운명의 화산에 도착하여 아름다운 지구행성을 파괴하려는 고르가스를 다시 만나게 된다.

제6장 공룡들은 고르가스의 음모를 알아차리게 되고 나선형 급강하로 주인공들은 1926년 루이지애나의 한 법정에 있는 자신들을 발견한다 거기에는 죄인으로 심판을 받는 고르가스와 바르가스가 있었다.

제7장 백년의 시간을 거슬러 2026년에 온 주인공들은 바르가스와 고르가스로부터 보조금을 받아 살인광선을 만들려고 하는 과학자 닐스를 만난다.

제8장 우주선을 타고 지구로 돌아온 주인공들. 몇 십 년 후의 미래에서 온 닐스 덕분에 오몰리 학장은 바너비를 제네바 그룹의 회원으로 추천하고 양키즈 경기가 진행 중이던 7회로 돌아가 야구 경기를 보면서 집으로 돌아온 것을 즐거워한다.

새로 나온 단어들을 익히는 최선의 방법은 그것들을 문맥 속에서 읽거나 듣는 것이다.

이 책의 활용법

『WORD SMART BASIC』의 목적은 중요한 어휘를 문맥 속에서 읽게 함으로써 가능한 한 즐겁게 학습하도록 하는 데 있다. 이 책은 꼭 어떤 식으로 공부해야 한다고 못박을 수는 없지만 두 가지 방법을 제안할 수 있다.

첫 번째는 WORDS를 익히고 그 어휘가 쓰인 STORY를 읽으면서 앞의 어휘를 복습하고 각 STORY마다 달려 있는 QUIZ를 풀어봄으로써 확실하게 배운 단어를 익히는 방법이다. 두 번째는 STORY를 읽고 QUIZ를 풀면서도 확실한 개념이 서지 않은 어휘들을 WORDS를 보면서 확인하고 익히는 방법이다.

두 가지 방법 중 어느 것을 택하더라도 명심해야 할 것은 어휘는 반드시 문맥 속에서 익혀야 한다는 사실이다. 새로 나온 단어들을 익히는 최선의 방법은 그것들을 문맥 속에서 읽거나 듣는 것이다. 마지막으로 본문에 볼드체로 표시된 것은 앞의 WORDS에 나온 단어들을 나타내고 이탤릭체로 표시되어 있는 것은 본문 아래 학습자들의 편의를 돕기 위해 달아 놓은 어구를 나타낸 것이다.

- 앞부분에 있는 단어 해설을 읽으며 1차 어휘학습을 한다
- 어휘 학습이 끝나면 STORY를 읽는다.
- STORY를 읽어가다 모르는 단어가 나오더라도 멈추지 않는다
- 장이 끝날 때마다 퀴즈를 풀어 학습한 어휘를 확인한다.
- 모르는 문제가 나오면 앞의 단어 해설을 찾아 반복 학습한다.
- 그래도 외워지지 않는 단어는 노트정리 등을 통해 반드시 자기 것으로 만든다.

새로운 단어를 공부하는 법

놀이에서 찾은 어휘 공부법

아이들은 주위 사람들이 말하는 것을 흉내냄으로써 새로운 어휘를 배운다. 세 살배기 아기는 자신의 흥미를 끄는 새로운 단어를 듣게 되면, 그 단어에 익숙해질 때까지 하루나 이틀 동안 그 단어를 반복적으로 사용한다. 아이는 문맥에서, 실험과 실수를 반복하며 단어의 의미를 파악한다.

아이들은 어른보다 새로운 단어를 배우는 시간이 훨씬 빠르다. 주위 환경에서 언어를 빨아들이듯 습득하는 마법과도 같은 능력은 아동기를 지나면 점점 쇠퇴하는 듯하다. 그러나 이처럼 아이들이 처음으로 언어를 배우는 과정은 어른들에게도 어휘력을 강화시키는 데 유효한 방법이다.

어휘는 사용할 때만이 유용성을 갖는다

맨 처음 아이들이 말을 배울 때처럼 어른들도 마찬가지로 계속 중얼거리면서 반복해야 한다. 철저한 연습과 규칙적인 훈련을 해야만 새로운 단어를 자신의 것으로 만들 수 있다.

새로운 어휘를 습득하는 데는 동기부여도 중요하다. 시험을 앞둔 학생이라면 어렵게 생각되는 단어를 확실히 알 때까지 계속 반복하여 암기해야 한다. 글쓰기나 말하는 기술을 높이려는 목표도 어휘 공부의 중요한 동기가 될 수 있다.

어쨌든 자신의 어휘력을 향상시키려면 아이들이 새로운 단어를 배울 때처럼 일상생활 속에서 자꾸 반복하여 사용해야 한다.

읽고, 읽고, 또 읽어라!

어렵고 복잡한 어휘를 습득하는 가장 좋은 방법은 무엇보다 열의를 갖고 반복해서 읽는 것이다. 그러다 보면 두뇌를 자극하게 되고 이해력도 향상된다. 광범위한 독서를 꾸준히 하다 보면 어느새 자신의 어휘 실력이 향상되어 있을 것이다. 새로운 단어를 자꾸 접하다 보면 전염되듯 익숙해지는데, TV보다는 확실히 독서가 좋은 방법이다. 「Time」지를 비롯하여 좋은 글이 많이 실린 여러 종류의 잡지나 신문 역시 많은 도움이 된다.

문맥에만 의존하는 방법의 위험성

문맥 속에서 그 단어가 어떻게 사용되는지를 파악하는 것도 중요하지만, 단어의 뜻을 유추할 때 문맥에만 의존하게 되면 함정에 빠질 우려가 있다. 노련한 저자나 연사라도 부적절한 언어를 사용하거나 아니면 강조나 극적인 효과를 위해 의도적으로 틀린 단어를 사용하는 일도 가끔 있기 때문에 반드시 정확한 의미로 단어를 사용했다고는 단정할 수 없다.

그보다 중요한 것은 대부분의 단어들이 서로 다른 뜻을 함께 갖거나 의미상 미묘한 차이가 있다는 점이다. 그래서 문맥을 통해 추정한 단어의 뜻이 다른 경우에도 그대로 적용된다고 단정할 수는 없다.

또한 문맥은 그 자체로 잘못 해석될 수도 있다. 단어가 빠진 문장이 주어지고 그것을 채워야 할 때 문맥에 맞는 단어를 선택하더라도 본래의 정답과는 거리가 멀어지는 경우가 있다. 이럴 때 사전이 필요하다.

두꺼운 책

어휘공부를 끝내야겠다는 의욕에 사로잡혀 사전을 들고 앉아 첫 페이지부터 읽기 시작한다. 그러나 이 방식으로 시작한 학생들의 대부분은 첫 페이지를 좀처럼 넘기지 못하고 포기하기 쉽다. 사실 이 방법으로 새로운 단어를 공부한다는 것은 불가능하다. 보다 쉽고 효과적인 방법인 이 책으로 시작해보자.

학생이라면 항상 사전을 휴대해야 한다

어딜 가든 작은 휴대용 사전을 꼭 갖고 다니자. 모르는 단어를 접했을 때 현장에서 바로 찾아보면 더 오래 기억에 남을 것이다. 하지만 최고의 사전일지라도 항상 정확한 것만은 아니다. 권위 있는 사전을 접할 수 있다면 다시 한 번 그 뜻을 확인해두는 것도 좋다. 이 책에서 쓰인 어법과 단어의 정의는 『The American Heritage Dictionary』 『Webster's Third New International Dictionary』 『Webster's Seventh New Collegiate Dictionary』 『The Random House College Dictionary』 등을 참조했다. 사전 찾는 것을 귀찮게 여기거나 어렵게 생각하지 마라.

WORD SMART의 단어는 왜 사전과 다른가

우선 이 책은 사전이 아니다. 부피가 큰 사전보다 이해하기 쉽게 만들려고 애썼다. 일차적으로 사전에 기초하고 있지만 그만큼 복잡하고 자세하지는 않다. 대신 기본 단어의 뜻을 정의하고 때로는 관련 단어를 충분히 다뤘다. 그리고 무엇보다 중요한 것은 단어의 실제 활용방법을 보여주기 위해 적어도 한 개 이상의 예문을 제시했다는 것이다.

이 책을 읽기 위하여

사전이나 단어 숙어 사전을 통해 어휘를 공부하는 것은 좋은 방법이지만, 시간이 너무 많이 걸린다. 이러한 난제를 해결하는 데 적절한 책이 바로 『WORD SMART BASIC』이다.

『WORD SMART BASIC』의 주요 섹션은 핵심 단어들만—교육용 어휘를 마스터할 수 있게 도와주는—엄선했다. 다년간 수천 명의 학생들과 공부하는 과정을 통해 어떤 방법이 능률적이고 그렇지 않은지를 터득했다.

시작하기 전에, 명심해야 할 것

새로운 언어를 공부하는 것은 다이어트를 하는 것과 같다. 정말 쉬운 방법이란 없다. 몸무게를 줄이고자 한다면, 반드시 적게 먹고 운동을 많이 해야 한다. 안일한 생각이나 작은 약약으로 되는 것이 아니다.

지적 어휘를 습득하고자 할 때도 많은 노력이 필요하다. 이러한 학습법을 통해 많은 사람들이 상당한 성공을 거두었으며, 여타의 방법보다 더 효과적이라고 생각한다. 물론 저절로 얻어지는 것은 없다. 모두 값진 노력의 대가인 것이다.

지난 수년간 학생들을 지켜보면서 성공적인 몇 가지 방법을 소개하고자 한다. 각자에게 가장 적합한 방식을 선택하여 활용하기 바란다.

방법1 : 기억증진에 관한 요령

arithmetic이라는 단어를 암기하기 위해 "A Rat In The House Might Eat Tom's Ice Cream"이라는 문장을 외운다. 아주 기초적이고 우스꽝스러운 이 문장에서 각 단어의 첫 글자를 따면 arithmetic이 되는 것이다. 철자나 역사적 사건의 연대를 암기하는 방법도 있다.

기억력 증진법은 어떻게 작용하는가

모든 기억력 증진법은 같은 방식으로 작용한다. 자신이 기억하려는 것과 이미 알고 있는 다른 어떤 것이나 기억하기 쉬운 것을 연관시켜 생각한다. 일정한 형태나 운율은 기억하기 쉽기 때문에 기억력 증진법 중의 하나로 이용된다.

방법2 : 보는 것이 기억하는 것이다

새로운 단어의 생생한 영상을 머리 속에 남기는 것 또한 기억술의 한 방법이다. 여기서 강조하는 것은 철자의 동일시나 재치 있는 약자가 아니라 머리 속에 연상되는 그림을 의미한다. 예를 들어보자. abridge라는 단어는 짧게 줄이거나 압축한다는 의미이다. 이 단어를 생각할 때, 순간적으로 어떤 이미지가 떠오르는가? 답은 간단하다. 바로 a bridge(다리)이다. '다리'와 abridge의 의미(짧게 만들다, 압축하다)를 연결시켜줄 그림을 만들 필요가 있다. 공룡이 다리 한가운데를 물어뜯었다면? 폭탄이 다리 위에서 폭발했다면? 어 그림을 선택하느냐 하는 것은 전적으로 여러분에게 달려있다.

머리 속의 이미지가 비정상적일수록 더 잘 기억된다

정상적인 것은 평범하고 재미가 없다. 따라서 비정상적이고 우스꽝스러운 것보다 기억하기 어렵다.

방법3 : 어원에 의한 실마리

영어에는 수십만 개의 단어가 있지만 같은 어원에서 갈라져 나와 의미상 관계가 있는 그룹으로 나눌 수 있는 것들이 많이 있다. 비슷한 어원을 갖고 있는 단어로 분류할 수 있다면, 훨씬 쉽게 단어를 암기할 수 있을 것이다. 예를 들면,

mnemonic: device to help you remember something.
amnesty: a general pardon for offenses against a government(an official "forgetting")
amnesia: loss of memory

이 세 단어는 기억을 의미하는 mne를 공통적으로 갖고 있다.

어원연구의 강점

어원을 풀이하는 방법으로 단어를 공부하는 방법이 효과가 있는 이유는 어원이 실제로 단어의 뜻과 관련이 깊기 때문이다. (그런 의미에서 이미지 연상방법과는 대립되는 방법이다.)

어원 연구는 수세기에 걸친 역사가 있는 단어의 이야기에 빠져들게 만들고 같은 뿌리를 가진 단어들에 흥미를 갖게 한다.

어원공부의 함정

어원은 단어에 대해서 무엇인가를 말해주는 것이기는 하지만 단어의 정의를 직접 제시하는 것은 아니다. 그리고 어원을 오해하는 경우도 있다.

예를 들면, verdant라는 단어를 보고 verify, verdict, verisimilitude, veritable와 같이 진실이나 사실을 의미하는 어원을 갖고 있다고 추정한다. 그러나 verdant는 초록색을 의미하는 프랑스의 고어 vert에서 유래한 것이다. pedestrian, pedal, pedestal, pedometer, impede, expedite에서 ped는 발과 관련된 것을 의미하지만 pediatrician는 소아과 의사를 의미한다.

어원연구는 어휘 공부에 유익한 도구이기는 하지만, 모르는 단어의 의미를 단정하기에는 위험한 도구이기도 하다.

방법4 : 손으로 쓰거나 그림을 그리거나 도표 만들기

많은 사람들은 손으로 직접 쓰면서 더 쉽게 새로운 정보를 기억한다. 글씨를 쓰는 물리적인 동작이 머리 속에 각인되는 것을 돕는 듯하다. 아마도 글씨를 쓰면서 단어에 대해 어떤 느낌을 형성하는 것 같다.

보조 기억장치나 영상 이미지, 그리고 어원이 생각난다면, 적어두어라. 그림을 그리거나 도표를 만들 수도 있을 것이다.

방법5 : 플래시카드와 공책에 모두 적어두기

플래시카드란 앞면에는 단어를 적고 뒷면에는 그 단어의 뜻을 적어놓은 단순한 카드이다. 글자를 처음 배울 때나 처음으로 외국어를 공부할 때 흔히 이용한다. 이 카드를 이용하여 서로 퀴즈를 내면서 자투리 시간을 이용하면 공부를 게임처럼 할 수 있다.

또한 카드 뒷면 한쪽 귀퉁이에 우리가 앞서 해온 기억술에 관한 방법들을 첨가하면 카드를 꺼내볼 때마다 재미도 있고 공부도 더 잘 될 것이다. 이제 카드를 주머니에 넣어두고 버스를 탈 때나 음악을 들을 때처럼 남는 시간을 최대한 이용하기 바란다. 물론 플래시 카드보다는 어휘 자체를 일상생활에서 자꾸 사용해보는 것이 기억에 더 오래 남고 공부가 된다는 것은 말할 나위 없다.

노트의 이용에 관하여

학생들은 새로운 단어를 접하면 언제나 노트에 적어둔다. 한 페이지 가득 단어를 공부하는 동안에 두뇌에 기록될 것이다.

잡지를 뒤적거리다 공부하고 있는 단어를 발견하게 되면, 노트에 그 문장을 적어둘 수도 있다. 문맥 속에서 단어가 활용되고 있는 새로운 예를 얻는 것이다.

이전에 배운 단어를 자신이 정리한 노트 속에서 다시 보게 되면 성취감을 느낀다고 한다. 어휘에 관한 정리노트는 스스로 진전되고 있다는 명백한 증거이다.

단어 공부를 위한 게임 방법 ─ 단계적 접근법

1단계: 문맥에서 단어의 의미를 추론한다

문맥은 간혹 오답을 만들기도 하지만, 추론은 사고의 연마를 돕고 글을 읽을 때 이해력을 높일 수 있다.

2단계: 사전을 찾는다

대부분의 사람들은 이 단계를 건너뛰고 싶어하지만 어휘의 정확한 의미를 알기 위해서는 반드시 통과해야 하는 과정이다.

3단계: 스펠링을 써본다

단어의 스펠링을 써보고 변화형도 함께 알아둔다. 단어의 스펠링을 보면 비슷한 단어나 관계가 있는 단어들도 연상될 것이다.

4단계: 큰 소리로 말해본다

독백으로가 아니라 다른 사람에게 말해야 한다.

5단계: 주요한 뜻을 읽는다. 부차적인 뜻풀이까지 자세히 읽어야 한다.

사전의 풀이는 중요한 순서에 따라 쓰여졌다. 그러나 단어를 완전하게 이해하기 위해서는 부수적인 뜻풀이까지 모두 읽어보는 것이 좋다.

6단계: 시간이 허락하면, 동의어의 쓰임과 뜻까지도 비교해본다.

7단계: 자신이 이해한 언어로 뜻을 풀이한다.

8단계: 문장 속에서 배운 단어를 활용해 본다.

단어의 뜻을 이해했다면 적절한 문장을 만들어본다. 단어의 암기력을 높이는 연상법 등을 활용하는 문장도 괜찮다.

9단계: 그 단어에 기억력을 강화시키는 연상장치나 머리 속의 이미지, 그밖의 암기를 돕는 방법을 고안하여 연결해본다.

8단계를 거치면서 이미 암기된 단어라도 연상 기억술을 통해 확고하게 기억하는 것이 좋다.

10단계: 플래시카드를 작성하고 노트에 정리한다.
특히, 단기간에 많은 양의 어휘를 습득하고자 할 때는 이 방법이 매우 효과가 있다.

11단계: 기회가 닿는 대로 그 단어를 사용한다.
과감하게 반복적으로 사용하라. 새로 알게 된 지식을 굳건히 하지 않는다면, 결코 자신의 것이 될 수 없을 것이다.

마지막으로 덧붙이고 싶은 말은 항상 의구심을 갖도록 한다. 아무리 알고 있는 단어라고 해도 방심해서는 안 된다. 정말로 확실하게 알고 있는지 되짚어보기 바란다. 자신은 익숙한 단어라고 확신하지만, 사실은 부정확하게 알고 있기 때문에 종종 황당한 실수들이 발생한다. 자, 이제 시작해보자. 욕심 내지 말고 한번에 조금씩만 도전하면, 많은 것을 얻게 될 것이라는 사실을 기억하라.

 CONTENTS

여는 글

이 책의 구성과 특징

이 책의 활용법

새로운 단어를 공부하는 법

PART A

WORDS	21
Chapter 1 The Fateful Meeting 숙명적인 만남	161
Chapter 2 The End of the Elephant Empire 코끼리 제국의 몰락	175
Chapter 3 Space Hippies Freak Out 괴상한 우주 히피들	197
Chapter 4 Curtains for Caspar 캐스퍼의 최후	219
Chapter 5 Monks are Weird, but Wizards are Weirder 이상한 수도사들, 더 이상한 마법사들	239
Chapter 6 Heir We Go Again 이번엔 후계자라니	261
Chapter 7 The Cave of the Counterfeiters 위조범들의 소굴	277
Chapter 8 That's a Big Museum 박물관 한번 크네	293
Translation & Answer 해석과 정답	301

PART B

WORDS	373
Chapter 1 Seventh Inning Snatch 7회 때의 납치	513
Chapter 2 Knuckleballs and Tentacles 너클볼과 촉수	529
Chapter 3 Popo the Bandicoot 주머니쥐 포포	545
Chapter 4 Dr. Borges and the Library of the Infinite Fiction 보그스 박사와 무한한 허구의 도서관	563
Chapter 5 Volcano of Doom 운명의 화산	577
Chapter 6 Judge, Jury, and Jailer 재판관, 배심원 그리고 교도관	593
Chapter 7 Showdown 2026 최후의 대결 2026	607
Chapter 8 Like the Cheshire Cat 체셔 고양이처럼	625
Translation & Answer 해석과 정답	637

PART A

A

ABDICATE [ǽbdəkèit] v. to give up the throne, or some other sort of right or power   (왕위, 권리를) 포기하다, 양위하다

King Edward VIII of England had to *abdicate* because he wanted to marry an American divorcée.
영국 왕 에드워드 8세는 미국인 이혼녀와 결혼하기 원해서 왕위를 포기해야 했다.

My social studies teacher made me *abdicate* my position as Student Council president in front of the whole class after she caught me cheating.
우리 사회 선생님은 내가 시험에서 부정행위하는 걸 적발하자 후로 전체 학급 앞에서 학생회장 자리를 포기하도록 만들었다.

ABRUPT [əbrʌ́pt] adj. unexpected; quick   뜻밖의; 빠른

Susan was zooming down Pineapple Street on her bike, when a fallen tree in the middle of the road caused her to make an *abrupt* stop.
수잔은 자전거를 타고 파인애플가를 신나게 달리고 있었는데, 길 한가운데 나무 한 그루가 쓰러져 있어서 급정거했다.

Aunt Gloria had been talking non-stop for at least an hour when I brought her endless yammering to an *abrupt* end by pouring ice water down her dress.
글로리아 이모는 적어도 한 시간 동안을 쉼없이 얘기하고 있었는데, 내가 이모의 드레스에 얼음물을 쏟는 바람에 끝없는 수다를 뚝 그치게 만들었다.

ABSTRACT [ǽbstrǽkt] adj. not solid, like something you can touch or see, but more like an idea, thought, or theory   추상적인

Our country's government is based on *abstract* concepts like "justice."
우리나라 정부는 "정의"같은 추상적인 개념들에 그 기초를 두고 있다.

"Wishing me a happy birthday is fine," reasoned Whiney William, "but how about giving me something a little less *abstract*, like a five pound-box of taffy?"
"생일 축하의 말을 해주는 거 좋지." 위니 윌리엄이 이런식으로 말했다. "헌데 좀 덜 추상적인 걸 주는 건 어때? 5파운드짜리 태피 한 상자처럼 말야."

ABSURD [əbsə́:rd/-zə́:rd] adj. against common sense; ridiculous   상식에 어긋나는; 우스꽝스러운

The rumor that Jimi Hendrix was born with a guitar in his hand is *absurd*.
지미 헨드릭스가 손에 기타를 들고 태어났다는 소문은 말도 안 된다.

When I asked Gary why his cat Fluffy was shaved completely bald, he told me some *absurd* story about a dangerous gang of furcutting "cat whackers."
게리에게 그의 고양이 플러피의 털을 왜 전부 깎아 버렸는지 물었더니, 털을 깎는 "고양이 피롭히는 사람들"이라는 위험한 갱단에 대한 좀 우스꽝스러운 얘길 들려주었다.

ACCLAIM [əkléim] v. to show approval by cheering, praising, or applauding 환호하다, 갈채하며 인정하다

I think Mr. Witherspoon will *acclaim* my latest book report as the greatest piece of writing he'd seen since my essay on the joys of bubble wrap.
위더스푼 씨는 내가 최근에 쓴 독후감을 버블랩을 가지고 노는 즐거움에 대한 작문이래로 가장 잘된 글이라고 인정해 줄 것이다.

When the dinosaur movie *Jurassic Park* first opened in theaters, the special effects were *acclaimed* by both audiences and critics.
공룡 영화 '쥬라기 공원'이 처음 극장에서 개봉됐을 때 관객과 비평가들 모두 특수 효과에 환호했다.

ACCOMPLICE [əkámplis/əkóm-] n. someone who helps another person do something wrong or against the law 공범자

Police have arrested the jewel thief, but are still looking for his *accomplice*, who drove the getaway car.
경찰은 보석 강도는 체포했지만, 도주용 차를 운전했던 그의 공범은 아직도 잡지 못했다.

ACQUAINTANCE [əkwéintəns] n. someone you know or have met, but who is not a close friend 그냥 아는 사람

Even though we have lived in this neighborhood for years, our neighbors seem more like *acquaintances* than friends.
우린 몇 년간을 이 동네에서 살아왔지만 이웃들은 친구라기보다는 그냥 아는 사람 정도인 것 같다.

Scott had several *acquaintances* at camp he was looking forward to seeing again.
스콧은 캠프에서 또다시 만나보고 싶은 사람을 서너 명 알게 됐다.

ACUTE [əkjúːt] adj. sharp; intense; keen 날카로운; 격렬한; 예민한

My sense of hearing is so *acute*, I can tell the ice cream man is coming from ten blocks away.
난 청각이 아주 예민해서 아이스크림 장사가 10블록 떨어진 곳에서 오고 있는 소리도 구분할 수 있다.

Jean's *acute* hunger pangs caused her to steal Cheezies from Bonnie.
진은 피로울 정도로 극심한 허기를 느껴 보니의 치즈를 훔쳤다.

ADAMANT [ǽdəmənt] adj. firm in one's position; stubborn 확고한, 단호한; 완고한

Tanya was *adamant* in her refusal to wear the frilly pink dress her grandmother picked out for her.
타냐는 할머니가 골라 주신 주름잡힌 분홍 드레스를 단호하게 입지 않겠다고 했다.

Lefty Lucas was an *adamant* supporter of the pitcher's rights in the pitcher/catcher baseball controversy of 1899.
왼손잡이 투수 루카스는 1899년 투수/포수 야구 논쟁에서 투수의 권리를 확고하게 지지했다.

AD-LIB [ǽd lib] v. to make up something as you go along, without preparation 즉석에서 만들다

Wolfgang was supposed to play Ebenezer Scrooge in the play, but he forgot his lines and had to *ad-lib* the whole first act.
볼프강은 연극에서 에벤에셀 스크루지 역을 맡기로 돼 있었는데, 대사를 잊어버려서 1막 전체를 즉흥적인 대사로 해야 했다.

The president forgot to bring a copy of his speech to the rally, but he spoke so well that no one realized he was *ad-libbing*.
대통령은 깜빡하고 대회장에 연설 원고를 안 가져왔지만, 연설을 너무나 잘해서 아무도 그가 즉흥적으로 연설을 하고 있는 줄 몰랐다.

ADORN [ədɔ́ːrn] v. to decorate 장식하다

The queen *adorned* herself with diamond earrings and a ruby necklace.
여왕은 다이아몬드 귀걸이와 루비 목걸이로 치장했다.

He *adorned* himself with earrings, a boa, and a purple velvet hat.
그는 귀걸이, 긴 모피 목도리, 자줏빛 벨벳 모자로 치장했다.

ADVERSE [ædvə́ːrs] adj. not favorable; going against the direction you want 불리한; 거스르는, 반대의

The snake oil I took to cure my baldness had some *adverse* effects: my toenails fell out and my face turned blue.
대머리를 치료하기 위해 만병통치약을 발랐는데 역 효과가 나서, 발톱이 빠지고 얼굴이 퍼렇게 변했다.

We were going to have a big barbecue out in the back yard, but *adverse* weather conditions forced us to stay inside and play Go Fish.
우린 뒤뜰에서 바베큐 파티를 거창하게 열려고 했는데, 기상 조건이 안 좋아 어쩔 수 없이 실내에 머물면서 고피쉬(카드 게임의 일종)를 했다.

ADVOCATE [ǽdvəkèit] v. to be in favor of 지지하다

Charles won a landslide victory as student council president because he *advocated* longer lunch hours and a four-day school week.
찰스는 학생회 회장 선거에서 압승을 했는데, 점심시간을 더 늘리고 주 4일 등교를 지지했기 때문이다.

Do you *advocate* using doggie biscuits as rewards when teaching puppies to do tricks?
넌 강아지들에게 재주부리는 걸 가르치면서 보상으로 강아지 비스킷 주는 걸 찬성하니?

AESTHETIC [esθétik/iːs-] adj. having to do with beauty or a sense of beauty 미의; 미적 감각이 있는

The reason Mario doesn't like the new race car was more *aesthetic* than practical: he just hates it because it's orange.
마리오가 새 경주용차를 맘에 안 들어 하는 이유는 실제적인 것보다는 미적인 것으로, 그는 그게 오렌지색이라서 싫어할 뿐이다.

Even though the radish salad you made is *aesthetically* pleasing, I can't eat it because it tastes terrible.
네가 만든 무 샐러드는 미적으로는 보기 좋지만, 맛이 형편없어서 못 먹겠다.

AFFRONT [əfrʌ́nt] v. to insult or n. an insult 모욕하다 / 모욕

Bertha was *affronted* when Mary pointed at her feet and yelled, "Those things are as big as Buicks!"
버사는 메리가 자신의 발을 가리키며 "발이 자동차 만하네!" 하고 소리치자 모욕감을 느꼈다.

When the waiter seated us in the kitchen, then ignored us all night, we took it as an *affront*.
웨이터가 우릴 부엌 자리에 앉히고는 밤새 무시했을 때 우린 그걸 모욕으로 받아들였다.

AGENDA [ədʒéndə] n. a list of things to do 의사일정, 일의 목록

While we were traveling through Europe, our daily *agenda* was usually made up of shopping, visiting museums, and eating at famous restaurants.
유럽을 여행하는 동안 우리의 하루 일정은 주로 쇼핑하고 박물관에 들르고 유명 식당에서 식사하는 것으로 이루어졌었다.

Zach wanted to sleep all day Saturday, but his mother had a different *agenda* in mind. She made him wash the car, mow the lawn, and catch up on his homework.
제크는 토요일 내내 자고 싶었지만, 어머니는 다른 일정을 염두에 두고 계셨다. 어머니는 그에게 세차하고 잔디를 깎고 밀린 숙제를 하도록 시키셨다.

AGHAST [əgǽst/əgάːst] adj. very shocked; horrified   깜짝 놀란; 겁에 질린

Melissa was *aghast* at how much weight John had gained over the winter holidays.
멜리사는 존이 겨울방학 동안 얼마나 살이 쪘는지를 알고 깜짝 놀랐다.

Dad was *aghast* when he got an electricity bill for five hundred dollars.
아빠는 5백 달러에 달하는 전기요금 청구서를 받고 기겁하셨다.

AGITATE [ǽdʒitèit] v. to shake up; to upset someone or shake up their feelings   뒤흔들다; 선동하다, 교란하다

To make his famous "Flying Pickle Punch," Danny poured milk, cranberry juice, and pickle relish into his thermos, and *agitated* the mixture until it was completely blended.
대니는 자신의 유명한 "날으는 피클 펀치"를 만들기 위해 보온병에 우유, 크랜베리 주스, 피클 소스를 넣은 다음, 완전히 섞일 때까지 혼합물을 흔들었다.

We could tell the cat was *agitated* by the presence of two snarling German shepherds in the living room.
거실에서 으르렁거리는 독일산 셰퍼드 두 마리가 나타나자 고양이가 흥분 되었다는 걸 알 수 있었다.

ALIAS [éiliəs] n. a fake name used to hide someone's identity   가명

The train and bank robber Jesse James used the *alias* "Mr. Howard" in the small town where he and his wife lived.
열차 및 은행 강도 제시 제임스는 자신과 아내가 살던 작은 마을에서 "하워드 씨"라는 가명을 사용했다.

Many criminals like to make up *aliases*, like "the Green Goblin" or "the Shah of Shoplifting," because their real names are too boring.
많은 범죄자들이 "푸른 도깨비"나 "들치기의 왕"같은 가명을 즐겨 만드는데, 자신들의 진짜 이름이 너무 평범해서다.

ALLAY [əléi] v. to lessen or calm   줄이거나 진정시키다

Carrie thought she could *allay* her little brother's fear of kindergarten by sitting in class with him every day.
캐리는 유치원에 대한 남동생의 두려움을 자신이 날마다 교실에 함께 앉아 있으면 누그러뜨릴 수 있을 거라고 생각했다.

Before aspirin was invented, people used to drink willow bark tea to *allay* headaches.
아스피린이 만들어지기 전에는 사람들이 두통을 진정시키기 위해 버드나무 껍질 차를 마시곤 했다.

ALLEVIATE [əlíːvièit] v. to relieve; lessen; allay   (고통을) 경감하다; 줄이다; 진정시키다

There are many medicines you can take to *alleviate* the symptoms of a cold, but the best cure is bed rest and daytime television.
감기 증세를 완화시키기 위해 복용할 수 있는 약은 많지만, 최선의 치료법은 충분히 쉬고 낮에는 텔레비전을 보는 것이다.

In order to *alleviate* the stress she feels at work, Mom goes to the gym and lifts weights for a couple of hours before coming home at night.
엄마는 직장에서의 스트레스를 줄이기 위해 밤에 집에 오시기 전, 체육관에 들러 두어 시간 동안 역기를 드신다.

ALLURE [əlúər] v. to attract or n. attraction   유혹하다 / 유혹

The ads for the movie *Plot B from Outer Mongolia* were so *alluring* that I went to see it the day it opened.
영화 '외몽고에서의 음모 B'에 대한 광고가 상당히 마음을 끌어서 개봉 첫날에 보러 갔다.

Basil was supposed to be doing his algebra homework, but the *allure* of his Funboy handheld rocket-blaster game was too much for him to resist.
배질은 대수학 과제를 해야 했는데, 펀보이의 포켓용 로켓 폭파 게임의 유혹이 너무 커 물리칠 수가 없었다.

ALOOF [əlúːf] adj. distant or removed, as if you were keeping yourself apart from things going on around you   무관심한, 쌀쌀한

We all tried to make friends with the French girl who moved to our neighborhood, but she acted so *aloof* it was hard to talk to her.
우리 모두는 이웃에 이사 온 프랑스 여자애와 사귀어 보려고 애썼지만, 그 애가 너무 멀리하려고 해 말을 걸기가 어려웠다.

Joey always gets crushes on girls who are *aloof*: the more they don't know he exists, the more he likes them.
조이는 늘 쌀쌀한 여자애들한테 훌딱 반한다. 그들이 자신의 존재를 모를수록 더 좋아한다.

ALTERNATE [ɔ́ːltərnèit/ǽl-] v. to switch back and forth, or do in turns or [ɔ́ːltərnət/ǽl-] adj. in place of another   교차시키다, 교대하다 / 대신하는

Tallulah was such a great actress she could *alternate* between laughing and crying very easily.
탈룰라는 대단히 훌륭한 여배우여서 웃음과 울음을 아주 쉽게 교차시킬 수 있었다.

I usually drive down Main Street to get to school, but I had to take an *alternate* route this morning because the St. Vitus Day parade was blocking that street.
나는 보통 차를 몰고 메인 가를 지나 등교하는데, 오늘 아침엔 성 바이터스 퍼레이드로 길이 차단되는 바람에 다른 길로 와야 했다.

AMATEUR [ǽmətʃùər/-tʃər/-tər] n. a person who takes part in an activity for fun, not as a job or for money or adj. having to do with an amateur   아마추어, 비전문가 / 아마추어의

Dr. Jensen has gotten so good at golf, even the professional players have a hard time believing he's an *amateur*.
젠슨 박사의 골프 실력은 아주 뛰어나, 프로 선수들마저도 그가 아마추어란 사실을 믿기 어려워한다.

After many discussions, the city council decided that an *amateur* bridge builder's competition was not such a good idea after all, and voted to hire a professional engineer for the job.
시의회는 많은 토론 끝에, 아마추어 교량 건축자끼리 경쟁을 시켜 선정하는것은 좋은 아이디어가 아니라는 결론을 내리고는, 전문기술자를 그 일에 고용하기로 했다.

AMBASSADOR [æmbǽsədər] n. a high-ranking government official who represents his or her country in another country   대사

Joseph Kennedy, President John F. Kennedy's father, was the American *ambassador* to England in the late 1930s.
존 F. 케네디 대통령의 아버지인 조셉 케네디는 1930년대 후반 미국의 주영 대사였다.

People who have many years of experience at settling arguments and keeping peace between countries are usually the best *ambassadors*.
국가 간의 분쟁을 해결하고 평화를 유지시키는 데 다년간의 경험을 가진 사람들이 일반적으로 최적임의 대사들이다.

[Note] An *embassy* [émbəsi] is the building where an ambassador and his or her staff work.
embassy는 '대사관' 을 의미

AMBIGUOUS [æmbígjuəs] adj. unclear in meaning 모호한, 불분명한

The directions we got from the man at the gas station were so *ambiguous* we wound up even more lost than we were before.
주유소 남자에게서 들은 방향 지시가 너무 애매해서 우린 그 전보다 훨씬 심하게 길을 잃었다.

She wouldn't come out and say so, but I could tell Martha didn't like my new haircut because she was deliberately *ambiguous* when I asked her what she thought.
마사는 드러내 놓고 그렇게 말하려고는 하지 않았지만, 내가 그녀에게 생각을 물었을 때 일부러 애매하게 말한 걸 보니 새로 자른 내 머리를 싫어한다는 걸 알 수 있었다.

AMOROUS [æmərəs] adj. feeling love, or having to do with love 사랑을 느끼는, 사랑의

Michael almost died of embarrassment when his teacher read the class a very private, *amorous* note he was trying to pass to his girlfriend during class.
마이클은 수업 시간에 자기 여자 친구에게 건네려던 지극히 사적인 연애 쪽지를 교사가 전체 학급에게 읽어 주자 창피해 죽을 지경이었다.

Of all the cartoon characters I have ever seen, there is none more romantic than Pepe le Pew, the *amorous* skunk who tries to seduce every female cat he meets.
지금까지 내가 본 만화 캐릭터 중에서 마주치는 암컷 고양이마다 꼬시려고 애쓰는 바람둥이 스컹크, Pepe le Pew보다 더 로맨틱한 캐릭터는 없었다.

ANARCHY [ǽnərki] n. the lack of any system of government or confusion caused by lack of authority or organization 무정부 상태, 무질서

During the French Revolution, the king and queen and many royal advisers were killed, which caused France to fall into a state of *anarchy*.
프랑스 혁명 동안 왕과 왕비 그리고 많은 왕실 보좌관들이 살해당해 프랑스는 무정부 상태가 됐다.

Although Russia has an official government, most people there feel they are living in *anarchy* because laws are not enforced and everyone must fend for himself.
러시아에도 공식적인 정부가 있지만, 그곳 국민의 대부분은 자신들이 무정부 상태에서 살고 있다고 느끼는데, 법이 시행되지를 않고 모두가 스스로를 돌봐야 하기 때문이다.

The substitute teacher left an orderly classroom to get a drink of water, and returned to find *anarchy*: spitballs were flying, desks were overturned, and loud screeching noises were coming from the back of the room.
대리 교사는 물을 한잔 마시려고 정숙한 교실을 나섰는데, 돌아와 보니 난장판이 돼 있었다. 종이를 씹어서 훅 부는것들이 날아다니고 책상이 뒤집어져 있고, 커다란 비명 소리가 교실 뒤에서 들려오고 있었다.

ANCESTOR [ǽnsestər] n. a family relation who came before you 선조, 조상

Many scientists believe the *ancestors* of the Native Americans came to North America from Asia thousands of years ago.
많은 과학자들은 아메리칸 인디언의 조상들은 수천 년 전 아시아에서 북아메리카로 왔다고 생각한다.

The Jeffersons have lived in Virginia since their *ancestors* travelled here from England almost four hundred years ago.
제퍼슨 가는 그들의 선조가 거의 4백 년 전 영국에서 버지니아로 이주한 이래 줄곧 이곳에서 살아왔다.

ANESTHETIC [ænəsθétik] n. a drug that causes the sense of touch to be numbed 마취제

The dentist injected an *anesthetic* into my gums before he started pulling out my teeth.
치과의사는 내 이를 뽑기 전 잇몸에 마취제를 주사했다.

Polly wished that her mother had given her some kind of *anesthetic* before trying to dig the splinter out of her foot.
폴리는 어머니가 그녀의 발에서 가시를 빼내려고 하기 전에 마취제를 좀 놓았으면 좋았을 텐데라고 생각했다.

ANIMOSITY [æ̀nəmásəti/-mɔ́s-] n. open hatred 악의, 증오, 원한

The *animosity* between the English and French, who were at war on and off throughout the Middle Ages, dates back to the Battle of Hastings in 1099.
중세 시대를 통틀어 이따금 전쟁을 치렀던 영국과 프랑스 간의 원한은 1099년 헤이스팅즈 전투로 거슬러 올라간다.

There was much *animosity* between Bunny and Betty, even before Bunny set Betty's Barbies on fire.
버니가 베티의 바비인형을 불태우기 전부터도 둘 사이에는 깊은 원한이 있었다.

ANTICIPATE [æntísəpèit] v. to expect; see in advance; look forward to 기대하다; 예상하다; 고대하다

Professor Zoltag did not *anticipate* such a large turnout for his slide-show presentation of "Those Amazing Leeches."
졸탁 교수는 자신의 "놀랄 만한 거머리들"이라는 슬라이드쇼 발표회에 그렇게 많은 사람들이 오리라고는 미처 생각 못 했다.

[Note] The noun form of anticipate is *anticipation* [æntìsəpéiʃən], which usually means happy expectation.
명사형은 anticipation인데, 보통 '행복한 기대'를 뜻한다.

- Sammy licked her lips in *anticipation* of the double scoop of Kandy Korn Krunch ice cream her grandfather was buying for her.
  새미는 할아버지가 사주실 캔디콘 크런치 아이스크림 더블콘을 기대하면서 입맛을 다셨다.

ANXIETY [æŋzáiəti] n. a feeling of worry about something 걱정

The thought of playing a tuba solo in front of the whole stadium caused Mort a great deal of *anxiety*.
모트는 경기장에 모인 그많은 사람들 앞에 나가 튜바 솔로 연주를 할 생각에 걱정이 이만저만이 아니었다.

I had a moment of *anxiety* before I jumped out of the airplane, but my parachute opened just fine.
비행기에서 뛰어내리기 전에 한순간 걱정을 했지만, 내 낙하산은 제대로 펼쳐졌다.

APATHY [ǽpəθi] n. lack of emotion or interest 냉담, 무관심

Apathy is often blamed for low voter turnout.
투표율이 저조하면 무관심을 탓하는 경우가 많다.

When Marie Antoinette, queen of France, was told that her people were starving she supposedly said, "Let them eat cake." Her *apathy* in the face of such suffering sparked the French Revolution.
프랑스 여왕 마리 앙뜨와네뜨는 자신의 백성이 굶어 죽는다는 얘길 들었을 때 "케이크를 먹이라"고 말했다고 한다. 백성들이 굶주려 그렇게 고통을 받는데도 그런 식으로 냉담하게 대하자 프랑스 혁명이 촉발되었다.

[Note] The word *apathetic* [æ̀pəθétik] is the adjective form of apathy.
형용사는 apathetic

- It's hard to understand how people can be *apathetic* about pollution when their own drinking water might be filled with dangerous waste.
  자기가 마시는 물이 위해한 폐기물로 가득 차 있을지 모르는데도 사람들이 어떻게 오염에 대해 무관심할 수 있는지 이해하기 힘들다.

APPEASE [əpíːz] v. to calm or satisfy 진정시키다, 충족시키다

The babysitter tried rocking, feeding, changing, and burping the crying baby, but nothing would *appease* him.
아이 돌보는 사람은 아이를 살살 흔들어 주고, 우유를 먹여 주고, 기저귀를 갈아주고, 트림까지 시켰지만, 어떻게 해도 아이가 진정되지 않았다.

No amount of buried treasure would *appease* the pirate's lust for gold.
매장된 보물이 아무리 많아도 해적의 황금욕을 채워 주진 못했다.

APPREHEND [æprihénd] v. to arrest or to understand 체포하다; 이해하다

The police *apprehended* the person who was painting mustaches on all the city's statues.
경찰은 도시에 있는 모든 동상에 콧수염을 그리고 다니는 자를 체포했다.

Everyone thought the professor was brilliant, but few students could *apprehend* his theories.
모두들 그 교수가 뛰어나다고 생각했지만, 그의 이론을 이해할 수 있는 학생은 거의 없었다.

APPRENTICE [əpréntis] n. a person who works closely with an expert in order to learn his trade or craft 도제, 견습생

The watchmaker's *apprentice* started out cutting glass for watch crystals, but is now learning how to make the tiny gears that run the hands.
시계 제조인의 견습생은 시계의 뚜껑 유리용 유리를 자르는 일에서 시작했지만, 지금은 시계 바늘을 가게 하는 작은 톱니바퀴 만드는 법을 배우고 있다.

Josh got a good job as an *apprentice* to a tailor.
조쉬는 재단사의 견습생이라는 괜찮은 일자리를 얻었다.

APPROXIMATE [əpráksəmət/-rɔ́k-] adj. nearly exact or [əpráksəmèit/-rɔ́k-] v. to make a best guess 대략의, 거의 정확한 / 근접하다, ~와 비슷하다

The famous diver plunged into the ocean from a cliff *approximately* six stories high.
이름난 잠수부는 거의 6층 높이의 절벽에서 바다 속으로 뛰어들었다.

The *approximate* speed of light is 186,000 miles per second.
대략적인 빛의 속도는 초속 18만6천 마일이다.

Can you *approximate* the age of a person by listening to her voice?
넌 어떤 사람의 나이를 그 목소리만 듣고 짐작할 수 있니?

APTITUDE [æptətùːd/-tjùːd] n. a natural ability or quickness in learning 타고난 재능, 소질

Keisha's *aptitude* for languages led her to become a translator at the United Nations.
케이샤는 언어에 대한 타고난 재능으로 UN의 통역사가 되었다.

Hakeem Olajuwon's *aptitude* for basketball helped him become a big star, even though he didn't start playing until he was seventeen.
하킴 올라주원은 17세가 돼서야 운동을 시작했는데도, 농구에 대한 소질을 타고나 빅스타가 될 수 있었다.

AROUSE [əráuz] v. to awaken or excite 깨우다, 자극하다

Paul Revere *aroused* the sleeping Minutemen by riding through town yelling, "The British are coming! The British are coming!"
폴 리비어는 말을 타고 마을을 다니며 "영국군이 온다! 영국군이 온다!"고 소리쳐서 잠자고 있던 민병들을 깨웠다.

We could tell the dog was *aroused* by the thought of getting leftover steak bones: he was drooling and whining.

우린 개가 스테이크 뼈 남은 걸 얻어먹으려는 생각에 흥분돼 있음을 알 수 있었다. 그 개는 침을 질질 흘리고 낑낑거렸다.

ARRAY [əréi] n. an organized group or a very large number or v. to dress up   조직된 그룹, 아주 큰 수 / 잘 차려 입히다

The *array* of studies linking smoking and lung cancer cannot be ignored.

흡연과 폐암의 상관관계를 다룬 수많은 연구 논문들을 무시할 수는 없다.

When you graduate, you'll find an *array* of colleges to choose from.

네가 졸업을 하면 선택할 수 있는 대학이 아주 많을 것이다.

The girls *arrayed* themselves in white dresses and floral wreaths for the spring dance.

여자아이들은 봄 댄스파티에 가려고 하얀 드레스를 입고 화관을 걸었다.

ARTICULATE [ɑːrtíkjulət] adj. spoken clearly, or able to speak clearly or [ɑːrtíkjulèit] v. to say or explain verbally   명료한, 명료하게 말할 수 있는 / 똑똑히 발음하다, 명료하게 표현하다

The jury was impressed by the *articulate*, well-dressed lawyer.

배심원은 표현이 명료하고 옷을 잘 차려입은 변호사에게서 깊은 인상을 받았다.

Despite my *articulate* explanation of how space travel works, my grandmother still wouldn't believe that a man had walked on the moon.

우주여행이 어떻게 이뤄지는지에 대해 내가 명료하게 설명해 드렸는데도 우리 할머니는 여전히 인간이 달에 발을 디뎠다는 사실을 믿지 않으시려 했다.

Buster felt horrible about running over his sister's bicycle, but he couldn't seem to *articulate* his feeling to her.

버스터는 여동생의 자전거를 치고는 끔찍한 기분이 들었지만, 동생에게 자신의 감정을 제대로 표현하지 못하는 듯 했다.

ASCETIC [əsétik] adj. self-denying, rejecting the pleasures of life, often as a show of religious devotion   고행의, 금욕적인

Cole never went to parties, never bought new clothes, never laughed, and insisted on sleeping next to the recyclables on the floor in the kitchen. For the son of a millionaire, he sure had *ascetic* tastes.

코올은 파티에 가는 일도 없었고, 새 옷을 사는 일도 없었고, 웃지도 않았고, 부엌 바닥의 재활용품 옆에서 잠자기를 고집했다. 그는 백만장자의 아들이면서 정말로 금욕적인 취향을 가졌었다.

I paid the interior decorator thousands of dollars, and the only furniture he bought for my apartment was a single bed, a wooden stool, and a frying pan. He says the *ascetic* look is very popular in New York these days.

나는 실내 장식가에게 수천 달러를 들였는데, 그가 내 아파트에 사온 가구라고는 싱글 침대, 나무 의자, 프라이팬 하나가 전부였다. 그의 말로, 요즘 뉴욕에서는 금욕적인 디자인이 대유행이란다.

ASPIRE [əspáiər] v. to desire strongly to achieve some goal   열망하다

All her life, little Squeaky Fromm *aspired* to be a respected political activist.

꼬마 스퀴키 프롬은 평생에 걸쳐 훌륭한 정치적 활동가가 되기를 열망했다.

"*Aspiring* after wealth is fine, Grover," said June, "but spending all your money on lottery tickets probably isn't the best way to achieve your goal."

"부를 갈망하는 건 좋아, 그로버." 준이 말했다. "하지만 있는 돈을 다 복권 사는 데 쓰는 건 네 목표를 이루는 최상의 방법이 아닐 거야."

명사형은 aspiration인데, 복수 형태가 일반적

- He had *aspirations* of becoming a rocket scientist.
  그는 로켓 과학자가 되기를 열망했었다.

ASTONISH [əstániʃ/-tɔ́n-] v. to fill with wonder, to amaze 깜짝 놀라게 하다

Barney and Betty were *astonished* when their baby Bam Bam lifted the pet dinosaur over his head.
바니와 베티는 그들의 아기 뱀뱀이 애완 공룡을 머리 위로 들어올리자 깜짝 놀랐다.

The Great Bardolini *astonishes* his audiences with magic tricks like escaping from handcuffs and pulling pigeons out of his hat.
마술사 바돌리니는 수갑을 풀고 탈출하는 묘기와 모자에서 비둘기를 꺼내는 등의 마술로 관객을 놀래킨다.

ASTUTE [əstú:t/-tjú:t] adj. showing good judgement and quick understanding 기민한, 빈틈없는

Sherlock Holmes solved the crime by making the *astute* observation that the mud in the front yard was not the same color as the mud on the dead man's shoes.
셜록 홈즈는 앞뜰에 있는 진흙이 죽은 남자의 신발에 묻은 것과 색깔이 다르다는 걸 빈틈없이 관찰해 범죄를 해결했다.

Most people know that fortune tellers don't really see into the future. They are just very *astute* judges of character.
대부분의 사람들은 점쟁이가 정말로 미래를 보는 게 아니란 걸 안다. 그들은 단지 기민하게 성격을 판단하는 것이다.

ATROCIOUS [ətróuʃəs] adj. very evil; bad; cruel 극악한, 잔인한

More and more teenagers are being sent to adult prisons for *atrocious* crimes like murder and rape.
점점 더 많은 십대들이 살인과 강간 같은 흉악 범죄를 저질러 성인 감옥으로 보내진다.

명사형은 atrocity

- After World War II, many Nazis were forced to stand trial for the *atrocities* they committed.
  제2차 세계대전이 끝난 후 많은 나치당원들이 그들이 자행한 잔학 행위로 인해 법정에 세워졌다.

AUDACITY [ɔːdǽsəti] n. boldness, daring; sometimes a disrespectful boldness or outspokenness 대담, 배짱; 때로는 무례할 정도의 대담 혹은 솔직함

Until that fateful day when the famous marshal Wyatt Earp rode into Tombstone, no one had the *audacity* to stand up to the fierce Clanton gang.
이름난 보안관 와이어트 어프가 툼스톤 속으로 말을 타고 들어간 운명의 날까지, 사나운 클랜튼 갱단에 대항할 만한 배짱을 가진 사람은 하나도 없었다.

In the story "The Emperor's New Clothes," a little boy is the only one with the *audacity* to point out that the emperor is parading around town completely naked.
"벌거벗은 임금님"을 보면, 임금이 완전히 벌거벗은 채 마을을 행진하고 있다는 사실을 지적할 만한 용기를 가진 사람은 꼬마 남자아이 뿐이다.

AUGMENT [ɔːgmént] v. to increase or make larger 증가시키다, 증대시키다

The opera singer's weak voice had to be *augmented* with microphones.
그 오페라 가수는 목소리가 가냘퍼서 마이크로 소리를 키워야만 했다.

Waiters rely on tips to *augment* their small salaries.
웨이터들은 박봉을 늘리기 위해 팁에 의존한다.

AUSTERE [ɔːstíər] adj. having a serious, stern appearance or personality; very plain and simple 엄한; 간소한, 간결한

Though life at the orphanage was *austere*, Little Orphan Annie kept her spirits up because she knew one day she would be rescued by an old bald millionaire who would spoil her rotten.
고아원에서의 생활은 엄격했지만 꼬마 고아 애니는 언젠가 자신에게 정말 잘 대해 줄 늙은 대머리의 백만장자가 나타나 구원해 줄 것을 알았기에 언제나 힘을 냈다.

The children were a bit afraid of Miss Thumbscrew because her dark clothes and unsmiling face made her seem so *austere*.
아이들은 섬스크루 양을 좀 무서워했는데, 그녀의 어두운 옷과 무뚝뚝한 얼굴 때문에 아주 엄해 보였기 때문이다.

AUTHORITARIAN [əθɔ̀rətɛ́riən/əθɑ̀r-] adj. having to do with a system of government or power in which the freedoms of the people are threatened or taken away by one person or a small group of people who have all the control and who are not held responsible to the people (See dictator) 권위주의의, 독재주의의

Under the former *authoritarian* government, the people of Haiti were often arrested, thrown in jail, or even killed with no explanation.
이전 독재 정부 하에서 아이티 국민들은 체포당해 투옥되고 심지어는 이유없이 살해당하는 일이 흔했다.

Even though it paid well and gave him a chance to travel, Elmer found life in the military too *authoritarian* for him.
군 생활을 하면 보수도 좋고 여행할 기회도 많았지만 엘머는 그것이 자신에게는 너무 권위적이라는 걸 알게 됐다.

AUTONOMOUS [ɔːtánəməs/-tɔ́n-] adj. self-ruling; existing independently 자율적인; 자주적인

Many American Indian reservations in the United States have *autonomous* governments, police forces, and legal systems.
미국에 있는 많은 아메리칸 인디언 보호 거주지에는 자율적인 정부와 경찰 그리고 사법제도가 있다.

"Now that you're out of college, in your own apartment, and are more-or-less *autonomous*," Mr. March told her son, "it is time you learned to do your own laundry."
마치 씨는 아들에게 말했다. "이제 넌 대학도 나왔고, 네 아파트도 생겼고, 어느 정도 독립이 됐으니, 네 빨래는 네가 직접 하는 걸 배워야겠구나."

AVAIL [əvéil] n. use or advantage 효용, 이익

Huey tried every argument he could think of to convince his parents, but to no *avail*: they refused to let him get his scalp tattooed.
휴이는 부모님을 설득하기 위해 생각해 낼 수 있는 대로 온갖 논리를 펴 봤지만, 아무 소용이 없었다. 부모님은 그가 머리 가죽에 문신 새기는 것을 허락하지 않으셨다.

"I hope you have more luck with this than I did," said Lucy. "I've been trying to untangle these necklaces for an hour, but to no *avail*."
루시가 말했다. "네가 이걸 하는 데 나보다 운이 좋아야 할 텐데. 난 한 시간 동안 이 목걸이를 풀려고 애썼지만 헛수고였거든."

AVERSION [əvə́ːrʒən/-ʃən] n. a strong dislike 혐오

While she was pregnant, Alicia had an *aversion* to chicken.
앨리시아는 임신하자 닭고기를 아주 싫어했다.

I have an *aversion* to men who wear pinky rings or berets.
난 새끼손가락에 반지를 끼었거나 베레모를 쓴 남자를 혐오해.

AWKWARD [ɔ́:kwərd] adj. clumsy; embarrassing; hard to deal with   서투른; 당황하게 하는; 다루기 힘든

Ben has always been an *awkward* boy, constantly knocking things over and tripping over his own feet.
벤은 언제나 행동이 굼뜨고 어리석게 구는 아이로 끊임없이 물건들을 쳐서 넘어뜨리고 자기 발에 걸려 넘어진다.

An *awkward* silence fell over the room when the chairman of the board got up to speak and everyone saw that his fly was unzipped.
이사회 의장이 연설하기 위해 일어났는데 모두들 그의 바지 지퍼가 열려 있는 걸 보자 그 방은 거북스러운 침묵에 휩싸였다.

B

BAFFLE [bǽfl] v. to confuse 당황하게 하다, 혼란시키다

I am *baffled* by this jigsaw puzzle. All the pieces are the same color!
이 그림 맞추기 퍼즐은 헷갈려. 조각이 전부 똑같은 색이잖아!

Your ability to stay up playing video games all night and still come to school in the morning is truly *baffling*.
비디오게임을 하느라 밤을 새고도 아침에 등교하는 네 능력은 정말 이해가 안돼.

BANAL [bənǽl/bəná:l] adj. humdrum; dull 평범한; 지루한

"Aunt Flora," sighed Kit, "every time you come over, you make the same *banal* comment about how much I've grown. It's starting to bore me."
키트는 한숨을 지었다. "플로라 이모, 이모는 오실 때마다 내가 얼마나 컸는지 똑같이 지루한 말씀만 하세요. 지겨워지려고 한다구요."

The parole board was not impressed by Stan's *banal* speech about how crime doesn't pay.
가석방 심사위원들은 범죄를 저질러봐야 본인에게 아무런 이익이 되지않는다는 것을 느꼈다는 스탠의 판에박힌 말에 감동을 받지 못했다.

BANE [bein] n. a cause of ruin or harm 파멸이나 해악의 원인

The unstoppable roaches were the *bane* of the otherwise spotless kitchen.
막을 수 없는 바퀴벌레들이 부엌에서 유일한 해악의 원인이었다.

The actor's stuttering problem was the *bane* of his career.
그 배우는 말을 더듬는 문제가 그의 배우생활을 망친 원인이었다.

BARRAGE [bərá:ʒ/bǽra:ʒ] n. an overwhelming quantity (usually having to do with words) 압도적인 양(주로 말과 관련됨)

The president wasn't able to handle the *barrage* of questions from reporters.
대통령은 기자들의 질문 공세에 대처할 수 없었다.

Keanu didn't expect such a *barrage* of insults from the audience at his one-man show "I Am a Thespian Genius."
키아누는 자신의 1인극 "난 천재 배우"에서 관객들로부터 그렇게 모욕이 쏟아질 줄은 몰랐다.

BASE [beis] adj. low; crude; without honor or decency 낮은; 조잡한, 거친; 천한, 비열한

Some *base* thief stole the ring off the dead man's hand during the funeral.
비열한 도둑은 장례식이 치러지는 동안 죽은 남자의 손에서 반지를 빼갔다.

"You will never win my heart with such *base* suggestions and bad language," said the young lady.
아가씨가 말했다. "그런 비열한 암시와 욕설로는 제 마음을 빼앗지 못할 거예요."

BECKON [békən] v. to signal with a nod or wave; to lure   고갯짓이나 손짓으로 알리다; 유혹하다

Silently, the ghost *beckoned* Scrooge to look at his own tombstone.
유령은 말없이 몸짓으로 스크루지에게 자신의 묘비를 쳐다보라고 했다.

Scarlett's smile seemed to *beckon* me to come over and introduce myself.
스칼렛의 미소는 날 보고 와서 인사를 하라는 것처럼 보였다.

The beautiful cake practically *beckoned* me to dip my finger in the frosting.
그 케이크는 너무 예뻐서 난 하마터면 손가락을 케이크에 입힌 당의에 집어넣을 뻔 했다.

BEHOLDEN [bihóuldən] adj. indebted   신세를 진

The Clampetts didn't like to be beholden to anybody, but after their crops failed and they ran out of firewood, they finally accepted donations from the church.
클램펫 부부는 누구에게든 신세지는 걸 싫어했지만, 흉작이 되고 땔나무도 바닥나자 마침내 교회의 원조를 받았다.

Mike was beholden to his neighbors for taking care of his daughter while he was in the hospital.
마이크는 병원에 입원해 있는 동안 그의 딸을 보살펴 준 이웃들에게 신세를 졌다.

BEHOOVE [bihú:v] v. to be required or proper for; to be good or worthwhile for   (~하는 것이) 의무다; (~하는 것이) 좋거나 할 만하다

It *behooves* young ladies and gentlemen not to use bad language unless they are very, very angry.
아가씨와 신사들은 정말 정말 화가 난 경우가 아니라면 나쁜 말을 쓰지 말아야 한다.

It would *behoove* you to learn to play the guitar early so you can get really good at it, join a band, and be extra-popular in college.
기타 연주에 아주 능숙해지고 밴드에 들어가고 대학에서 특별히 유명해지려면 기타를 일찍 배우는 게 좋을 것이다.

BELLIGERENT [bəlídʒərənt] adj. warlike; fond of war or conflict; hostile   전쟁의; 전쟁이나 충돌을 좋아하는; 적대적인

By repeatedly moving his troops near Iraq's border with Kuwait, Saddam Hussein is showing he has *belligerent* intentions.
사담 후세인은 쿠웨이트와 맞닿은 이라크의 국경 부근으로 군대를 여러 차례 이동시킴으로써 전쟁을 일으키려는 의도가 있음을 보여주고 있다.

As often happens when he's had too much pie for dessert, Hank became *belligerent* shortly after dinner.
행크는 디저트로 파이를 너무 많이 먹고 나면 종종 그렇듯이, 저녁을 먹고 나자마자 적대적으로 되었다.

BENEVOLENT [bənévələnt] adj. kind; full of goodness   친절한; 아주 선량한

The *benevolent* king opened his castle to people who needed shelter and gave bread to the hungry.
친절한 왕은 살곳이 필요한 사람들에게 자신의 성을 개방하고 배고픈 이들에게 빵을 주었다.

If it weren't for the *benevolent* donations from people across the country, Janet's parents wouldn't have been able to pay for the operation she needed.
전국의 사람들로부터 온 인정 어린 기부금이 없었더라면 재닛의 부모님은 재닛의 수술비를 충당하지 못했을 것이다.

BENIGN [bináin] adj. harmless; gentle 무해한, 양성의; 친절한

The huge dog looked frightening, but the owner assured us it was completely *benign*.
그 거대한 개는 겁나게 생겼지만, 주인은 아주 온순하다고 우릴 안심시켰다.

Kurt went to the doctor because he had a weird lump on his neck, but it turned out to be *benign*.
커트는 목에 이상한 혹이 나서 병원에 갔는데, 양성인 것으로 밝혀졌다.

BIGOT [bígət] n. a person who is intolerant of people who are different from himself, in religion, race, or belief 편견을 가진 사람; 고집쟁이

While they were on their honeymoon in Acapulco, Jerry kept sneering at the language and customs of the Mexican people, and Midge realized she had married a *bigot*.
제리와 미지가 아카풀코로 신혼여행을 갔을 때, 제리는 멕시코인들의 말과 풍습을 연신 비웃어 대자, 미지는 편견이 심한 사람과 결혼했다는 걸 깨달았다.

[Note] The word *bigotry* [bígətri] is used to describe the attitude or behavior of a bigot.
bigotry는 bigot의 태도나 행동을 묘사하는 말

- Since the Civil Rights movement of the 1960s, Americans have made great strides toward ending *bigotry* in our country; unfortunately, we still have a long way to go before all people are truly considered equal.
1960년대의 민권 운동 이래로 미국인들은 우리나라에서 편견을 없애는 데 장족의 진보를 했다. 하지만 안타깝게도 모든 사람이 진정으로 평등한 대접을 받으려면 아직 갈 길이 멀다.

BINGE [bindʒ] n. a period of excessive activity; a spree 과도한 열중; 흥청망청

Whenever Toby got depressed he would head for the mall and go on an all-day shopping *binge*.
토비는 우울해질 때면 쇼핑몰에 가서 온종일 정신없이 쇼핑을 하곤 했다.

To celebrate her birthday, Michelle treated herself and her friends to an all-you-can-eat ice cream *binge*.
미셸은 자기의 생일을 축하하기 위해 친구들과 아이스크림을 실컷 사먹었다.

BLACKMAIL [blǽkmèil] n. the act of forcing someone to give you money or other favors by threatening to expose some secret you know about them or v. to subject someone to blackmail 협박, 갈취 / 협박하다, 갈취하다

The butler immediately thought of *blackmail* when he found the box of pictures of Lord Periwinkle dressed as a ballerina.
집사는 페리윙클경이 발레리나 복장으로 찍은 사진 박스를 발견하고서 이내 협박을 해야겠다고 생각했다.

The judge had been *blackmailed* for years by a woman he once had an affair with, but her demands for money finally got to be too much, and he confessed to his wife.
판사는 예전에 관계를 가졌던 여자에게 몇 년 동안 협박을 당했었지만, 그녀가 요구하는 돈이 결국 너무 많아지자 아내에게 털어놓았다.

BLATANT [bléitənt] adj. totally obvious 너무 빤한

Junior, who was standing with a slingshot in his hand, told a *blatant* lie about how his baby sister threw a rock through the neighbor's window.
주니어는 손에 고무총을 들고 서서는, 막내 여동생이 이웃집 창문으로 돌을 어떻게 던졌다느니 하는 빤한 거짓말을 했다.

In a *blatant* attempt to stay up past 11 o'clock, Tim made up a story about having to watch "Sports Center" for a grade in gym class.
팀은 11시가 넘도록 잠을 안 자려고 속 보이는 시도를 하면서 체육 수업에서 성적을 받기 위해 "스포츠 센터"를 봐야 한다고 이야기를 꾸며댔다.

BLEAK [bli:k] adj. gloomy; dark and depressing   어두운; 어둡고 침울한

The cruise in the Caribbean was supposed to be fun, but bad weather made the whole week chilly and *bleak*.
카리브 해에서의 유람선 여행이 재미있어야 했는데, 악천후로 그 주 내내 춥고 침울한 분위기였다.

The chances of Dad giving me thirty-five dollars for tickets to see *Nine Inch Nails* are *bleak*.
아빠가 내게 '나인 인치 네일스' 공연 티켓을 사라고 35달러를 줄 가망은 거의 없다.

BLUNDER [blʌ́ndər] v. to make a big mistake or n. a big mistake   큰 실수를 저지르다 / 큰 실수

The lab assistant was worried the chemist would discover that his *blunder* in measuring the saline had ruined the year-long experiment.
연구실 조교는 자신이 염수를 측정하면서 큰 실수를 저질러 화학자의 1년에 걸친 실험을 망쳐 놓았단 사실을 화학자가 알게 될까 봐 걱정이었다.

David had almost convinced his mother to let him go to Jim's party when he *blundered* by telling her that Jim's parents were out of town.
데이빗은 어머니를 설득해 짐의 파티에 갈 뻔했는데, 짐의 부모님이 여행을 가셨다고 말해 버리는 바람에 큰 실수를 저질렀다.

BODE [boud] v. to be a sign of something to come   어떤 일이 일어나리라는 징조가 되다

The Houston Oilers' decision to trade quarterback Warren Moon *boded* trouble for their run-and-shoot offense.
휴스턴 오일러스에서 쿼터백 워렌 문의 트레이드를 결정한 것은 런앤슛 공격에 대해 걱정한다는 징조였다.

The fact that Clark falls asleep whenever the lights are turned off does not *bode* well for his desire to be a film projectionist.
클락이 불이 꺼져 있기만 하면 잠들어 버린다는 사실은 그가 영화 영사기사가 되고 싶어 하는 데에 좋은 징조가 아니다.

BOHEMIAN [bouhí:miən] n. a person whose lifestyle is unusual or "on the edge"; often a person who has artistic or intellectual interests and doesn't share the same values as the rest of society or adj. having to do with the characteristics of a bohemian   방랑적인 사람; 자유분방한 사람형. 자유분방한

The folks at the Glen Ridge apartment complex suspected that the people in 15J were a couple of *bohemians* when the woman who lived there told her neighbor she didn't believe in marriage, and the man said that organized religion was responsible for the greatest evils in history.
글렌 리지 아파트 단지의 사람들은 15J호에 사는 사람들이 보헤미안 커플이 아닌가 생각했는데, 거기 살고 있는 여자는 이웃에게 자신은 결혼 제도를 인정하지 않는다고 말했고, 남자는 제도권 종교가 역사상 가장 큰 죄악들에 대해 책임이 있다고 말했기 때문이다.

Clare tried to put up with her father's *bohemian* lifestyle, but the endless flow of poets and painters sleeping in the living room and the late-night shouting matches about philosophy got on her nerves so much that she went to live with her mother in Palm Beach.
클레어는 아버지의 자유분방한 생활 방식을 참으려고 애썼지만, 시인과 화가들이 쉴 새 없이 몰려와 거실에서 잠을 자고 한밤중에 철학에 대해 시끄럽게 논쟁을 벌이자 너무나 신경질이 나서 어머니와 함께 지내려고 팜비치로 갔다.

[Note] The word *bohemian* comes from Bohemia, a region in which used to be Czechoslovakia, and originally referred to the gypsies who lived there and their unusual lifestyle.
bohemian은 구 체코슬로바키아의 한 지역인 보헤미아(Bohemia)에서 온 단어로, 원래는 그곳에 살던 집시들과 그들의 유별난 생활 방식을 가리켰다.

BOISTEROUS [bɔ́istərəs] adj. rough; noisy and undisciplined   거친; 떠들썩하고 규율이 없는

Minnie hated visiting her uncle's house because her *boisterous* cousins always wound up accidentally hurting her.
미니는 삼촌댁에 가는 걸 싫어했는데, 거친 사촌들이 언제나 잘못해서 그녀를 다치게 했기 때문이다.

When the New York Rangers won the hockey championship, the *boisterous* fans throughout the city cheered and honked their horns.
뉴욕 레인저스가 하키 선수권을 획득하자 떠들썩한 팬들이 도시 전체에서 환호를 하고 경적을 울려 댔다.

BOVINE [bóuvain] adj. cow-like; dull 소같은; 우둔한

Josh, who didn't have a clue what the teacher was talking about, just sat there with a *bovine* expression on his face.
조쉬는 교사가 무슨 얘기를 하는지 전혀 알아듣지 못한 채 소같은 표정을 하고서 거기에 그냥 앉아 있었다.

BRISK [brisk] adj. quick; lively; stimulating 민첩한; 활기있는; 자극하는

I was practically falling asleep on my books, so I took a *brisk* walk around the block to wake myself up.
난 책을 읽다가 잠이 들 뻔해서 졸음을 쫓으려고 빠른 걸음으로 블록을 한바퀴 돌았다.

The old sea captain loved the salt air and the *brisk* wind off the waves.
나이든 선장은 파도에서 전해지는 소금기있는 공기와 활기찬 바람을 사랑했다.

BROACH [broutʃ] v. to bring something up for the first time (이야기를) 꺼집어내다, 제기하다

The police sergeant *broached* the theory that the fire that burned down the dry cleaners was started by someone with too much starch in his collar.
경사는 세탁소를 전소시킨 불은 자신이 맡긴 옷의 칼라에 풀이 엄청나게 칠해지자 그사람이 지른 것이라는 가설을 처음 제기했다.

"I know in my heart that I must drop out of college to become a trapeze artist," confided Emo to his grandfather. "I just don't know how to *broach* the idea with my parents."
에모는 할아버지께 말씀드렸다. "전 대학을 그만두고 그네 타는 곡예사가 될 거예요. 부모님께 그 생각을 어떻게 꺼내야 할 지 모르겠어요."

BUREAUCRACY [bjuərákrəsi/-rɔ́k-] n. an administration, as in a business or government, in which following strict rules and procedures becomes more important than the task at hand, and action becomes slow and complicated 관료주의적 행정

All I wanted to do was transfer out of French class and into Spanish class, but the school's *bureaucracy* held up my request for a month.
내가 원했던 건 프랑스어 반에서 나와 스페인어 반으로 들어가는 게 전부였는데, 학교의 관료주의적 행정이 내 요구를 한 달이나 지연시켰다.

After filling out six forms, waiting in five lines, and wasting three hours, I was beginning to believe that the company's *bureaucracy* was designed to keep people from returning items by wearing down their will to live.
여섯 개의 서식을 기입하고, 줄을 다섯 번이나 기다리고, 세 시간을 낭비하고 나자, 내게는 회사의 관료주의적 행정이 계획적으로 사람들에게 버틸 의지를 다 소모시켜서 반품을 못하도록 한다는 생각이 들기 시작했다.

C

CALIBER [kǽləbər] n. quality or the diameter of a bullet   품질; (총의) 구경

"No doubt about it," said the doctor, "the bullet that hit this clown's nose was a 22-*caliber*."
의사가 말했다. "틀림없이 이 광대의 코를 명중한 총탄은 22구경이었어요."

When I travel, I will only stay in hotels on the highest *caliber*.
난 여행을 할 때 최고 수준의 호텔에서만 묵는다.

Vinnie was the greatest quarterback in the state when he was in high school, but, as he quickly learned, the football players in college are of a much higher *caliber*.
비니는 고등학교 시절 주에서 가장 훌륭한 쿼터백이었지만, 오래지 않아 대학에 있는 미식축구 선수들 기량이 훨씬 더 뛰어나다는 걸 알았다.

CALLOUS [kǽləs] adj. uncaring; unfeeling   무정한; 무감각한

Ike was finally getting used to his new home town when his classmate's *callous* joke about his "funny accent" made him feel lonelier and more homesick than ever.
아이크는 마침내 새 고향에 적응해 가고 있었는데, 동급생이 그의 "우스운 억양"을 듣고 무정하게 놀려대서 전보다 더 외로워지고 향수에 젖게 됐다.

Old man Jones is the richest landlord in town, and the most *callous*: he throws people out on the street even if they're only one day late on the rent.
존스 노인은 마을에서 가장 부유한 집주인이자 가장 무정한 사람이다. 그는 사람들이 하루라도 임대료를 늦게 지불하면 거리로 내쫓는다.

CAMOUFLAGE [kǽməflɑ̀ːʒ] n. the act of hiding yourself or your equipment, especially for military purposes, by making yourself blend in with the natural surroundings; a disguise or v. to hide or disguise through camouflage   위장 / 위장하다

Black and green face paint, palmetto leaves, and green uniforms are all part of the *camouflage* soldiers use when fighting in the jungle.
흑색과 녹색 얼굴 페인트, 종려나무 잎, 초록 유니폼은 모두 병사들이 정글에서 싸울 때 사용하는 위장물들이다.

Brian tried to *camouflage* his magazines by putting notebook binders around them.
브라이언은 잡지들을 노트 바인더로 둘러서 숨기려고 했다.

CANDID [kǽndid] adj. open and straightforward   솔직하고 거리낌 없는

Mrs. Shields was determined to make her daughter a star, until a famous movie director was *candid* enough to tell her that acting was not one of her daughter's talents.
쉴즈 부인은 자신의 딸을 인기 배우로 키울 작정이었지만, 유명한 영화감독이 그녀의 딸에게는 연기의 재능이 없다고 노골적으로 말해 버렸다.

I would appreciate your *candid* opinion of my painting.
제 그림에 대해 솔직한 의견을 말씀해 주시면 감사하겠습니다.

CANINE [kéinain/kǽn-] adj. of or like a dog, or having to do with dogs 개의, 개같은

The detective had an almost *canine* ability to track down criminals.
그 탐정은 범인들을 추적해서 잡아내는 데 개에 버금가는 능력이 있었다.

Suddenly, through the mist, a strange, *canine* creature, far too large to be a wolf, emerged and bared its bloody fangs to the unfortunate tourists.
느닷없이 안개를 뚫고, 늑대라고 하기에도 너무 큰 이상하게 생긴 개같은 동물이 나타나 운이 나빴던 관광객들에게 피묻은 송곳니를 드러냈다.

CANNIBAL [kǽnəbəl] n. a person who eats human flesh 식인종

The survivors of the airplane crash in the mountains became *cannibals* when they ate the dead passengers in order to survive.
산맥 속에 갇힌 비행기 사고 생존자들은 살아남기 위해 식인종이 되어 사망한 승객들을 먹었다.

[Note] *Cannibalism* [kǽnəbəlìzəm] n. is the practice of being a cannibal.
cannibalism은 '사람 고기를 먹는 풍습'

- The explorer was unaware that *cannibalism* was part of the tribe's tradition until he figured out he was to be the main course, not the guest of honor, at the feast that night.
  탐험가는 그날 밤 향연에서 자신이 주빈이 아니라 본 요리가 될 거란 사실을 알고 나서야 사람 고기를 먹는 풍습이 그 부족 전통의 일부라는 걸 깨달았다.

CAPACITY [kəpǽsəti] n. the ability to hold or contain; ability to do something, mental ability 용적, 수용량; 재능, 정신력

The stadium has a seating *capacity* of sixty thousand.
경기장에는 6만 명을 수용할 만한 좌석이 있다.

Elmo has no *capacity* for math of any kind.
엘모는 어떤 종류의 수학에도 재능이 없다.

The trunk of the car was filled to *capacity* with enough firewood to last all month.
차 트렁크에는 한달 꼬박 버틸 만큼 충분한 양의 땔나무가 가득 들어 있었다.

CAPTIVE [kǽptiv] n. a prisoner or adj. held under restraint 죄수, 포로 / 감금되어 있는

Senorita Flores was held *captive* by the pirates after they attacked her father's ship and took her along with the family jewels.
플로어즈양은 해적들이 그녀 아버지의 배를 공격해 가족들이 가지고 있던 보석과 함께 그녀를 데려간 후 포로로 붙잡혀 있었다.

The creative writing teacher tried to free the *captive* imaginations of her students.
글짓기 담당 교사는 학생들의 억압된 상상력을 풀어 주려고 애썼다.

CARCINOGEN [kɑːrsínədʒən] n. a substance that causes cancer 발암 물질

Chemicals called "nitrites," found in hot dogs and bacon, are known to be *carcinogens*.
핫도그와 베이컨에서 발견되는 "아질산염"이라는 화학물은 발암 물질로 알려져 있다.

[Note] *Carcinogenic* [kɑːrsənóudʒénik] adj. means cancer-causing.
carcinogenic은 '발암성의'

- Nuclear radiation is highly *carcinogenic*.
  원자력 방사선은 암을 유발할 확률이 아주 높다.

CARICATURE [kǽrikətʃùər/-tʃər] n. a picture of a person or thing in which certain features are exaggerated for comic effect   풍자 그림

The *caricatures* of President Clinton we see in the newspapers often make him look chubbier than he really is.
신문에서 보는 클린턴 대통령의 풍자화에는 그가 실제보다 살쪄 보이게 나올 때가 많다.

CASUALTY [kǽʒuəlti] n. a person killed or injured during an accident, or killed, injured, or taken prisoner during a military action   사상자, 전시의 인적 손해

One reason the Vietnam War was so unpopular was that the number of civilian *casualties* was very high.
베트남 전쟁이 그렇게 평판이 좋지 못한 이유 하나는 민간인 사상자 수가 아주 많았기 때문이다.

Officials say the number of *casualties* from last night's earthquake could be as high as three hundred.
당국에 따르면 어젯밤 지진으로 인한 사상자 수가 3백 명에 달할지도 모른다고 한다.

CENSOR [sénsər] v. to prevent from making public any material (such as movies, books, letters, or speech) that is considered harmful or n. a person who censors   검열하다, 검열하여 삭제하다 / 검열관

In the early days of Hollywood, movie stars like Mae West and W. C. Fields were often in trouble with studio *censors* because their scripts were too "spicy."
헐리우드 초창기에 메이 웨스트와 W.C. 필즈 같은 인기 배우들은 종종 그들의 각본이 너무 "음란"하다는 이유로 스튜디오 검열관과 말썽이 생겼다.

In some situations, the military is allowed to *censor* soldiers' letters to protect national security.
어떤 상황에서는 군대가 국가의 기밀을 보호하기 위해 군인들의 편지를 검열하는 것이 허용된다.

CHAFE [tʃeif] v. to irritate by rubbing; to warm by rubbing   문질러서 염증을 일으키다; 비벼서 따뜻하게 하다

The criminal complained to the police that his handcuffs were *chafing* his wrists.
범죄자는 수갑 때문에 손목이 까졌다고 경찰에게 투덜거렸다.

Bob's feet were bright red and stinging with cold after his day of sledding, so he *chafed* them with his hands.
밥은 썰매를 타고 난 뒤 추위로 발이 새빨개지고 따끔거려서 손으로 비벼 따뜻하게 했다.

CHAGRIN [ʃəgrín/ʃǽgrin] n. a feeling of shame or regret   수치심, 후회

I was overcome with *chagrin* when I learned that my sister had been saving her allowance for months to buy me a Christmas present, and I hadn't even bothered to get her a card.
여동생이 내게 크리스마스 선물을 사주려고 몇 달 동안 용돈을 모아 왔다는 걸 알고 부끄러워 어쩔 줄 몰랐다. 그런데, 난 동생에게 카드 하나도 쓸 생각을 안 했었다.

Much to my *chagrin*, I overslept the day I was supposed to take the SAT, which means I won't be able to apply for college this year.
너무나 후회스럽게도 난 대학 예비고사를 보기로 되어 있는 날에 늦잠을 잤다. 따라서 올해에는 대학에 응시할 수가 없는 것이다.

CHAOS [kéias/-ɔs] n. complete confusion and disorder   완전한 혼란과 무질서

As the audience filed in for the opening night of the play, they had no idea that the backstage area was in a state of total *chaos*: the leading man was drunk and no one could find the severed head they needed for Act V.
관객들은 연극이 개막되는 날 밤에 줄지어 들어왔을 때 무대 뒤가 완전히 아수라장인 것을 몰랐다. 주연 남자 배우는 술에 취해 있었고 5막에 필요한 절단된 머리를 찾을 수가 없었다.

We tried to find our friend Bruno at the Zombies concert, but since the club was in complete *chaos*, we didn't meet up until after the show.

우린 '좀비스' 콘서트에서 친구 브루노를 찾아보려고 했는데, 클럽이 너무나 혼란스러워 쇼가 끝나고 나서야 만날 수 있었다.

CHIC [ʃi(ː)k] adj. stylish; fashionable 세련된; 최신 유행의

Shannon's new hairstyle is very *chic*.

섀넌의 새로운 머리 모양은 아주 세련됐다.

Lance just got back from Paris with a French girlfriend and a *chic* wardrobe.

랜스는 프랑스인 여자 친구와 함께, 최신 유행의 옷을 입은 채 파리에서 막 돌아왔다.

CIVIL [sívəl] adj. polite 공손한, 예의바른

If you can't be nice to your brother, at least be *civil*.

네 오빠에게 잘 대해 주지 못하겠으면 최소한 예의는 갖춰라.

During the 1970s, relations between the United States and the Soviet Union were tense but *civil*.

1970년대에 미국과 소련의 관계는 팽팽했지만 정중했다.

CIVILIAN [sivíljən] n. a person who is not in the military or adj. having to do with civilian life 일반 민간인 / 민간의

After thirty years in the navy, the admiral was looking forward to being a *civilian* again.

해군에서 30년을 보낸 해군 제독은 다시 민간인이 되기를 고대하고 있었다.

I didn't recognize the major in his *civilian* clothes.

난 육군 소령을 민간복 차림이라서 못 알아봤다.

CLAMOR [klǽmər] n. loud, sustained noise or v. to make a clamor 떠들썩함, 아우성 / 떠들어대다

The students were alarmed by the *clamor* coming from the teacher's lounge, where the faculty members were meeting.

학생들은 직원회의가 열리고 있는 교사 휴게실에서 시끄러운 소리가 들려오자 깜짝 놀랐다.

After waiting for over an hour, the fans started *clamoring* for Ozzy Ozbourne to come on stage and start his concert.

팬들은 한 시간 이상을 기다리고 나자 오지 오스본에게 무대로 나와 공연을 시작하라고 떠들어대기 시작했다.

CLERGY [klə́ːrdʒi] n. a group of people whose job is to serve their religion (like priests, rabbies, or ministers) 성직자

In the Middle Ages it was common for sons of wealthy parents to enter the *clergy*, because priests could become very powerful.

중세 시대에 부유한 부모를 둔 아들은 성직자가 되는 것이 일반적이었는데, 성직자가 되면 막강한 권력을 쥘 수 있었기 때문이다.

In times of family trouble or confusion, many people turn to a member of the *clergy* for advice and comfort.

가족간에 문제나 혼란스러운 일이 생기면 많은 사람들은 성직자를 찾아가 조언과 위안을 구한다.

CLICHÉ [kli(:)ʃéi] n. an overused expression that has lost its original impact 진부한 표현, 판에 박힌 문구

After a crushing 72-0 defeat at the hands of the Paramus Pythons, the football coach told his team, "It's not whether you win or lose, it's how you play the game." The players didn't find much comfort in that *cliché*.

패러머스 파이슨스 팀에게 72대 0으로 박살난 후 미식축구 코치는 선수들에게 말했다. "너희가 이기느냐 지느냐의 문제가 아니라 어떻게 경기를 펼치느냐다." 하지만 선수들은 그 진부한 표현에서 위안을 얻지 못했다.

COMMEND [kəménd] v. to praise 칭찬하다

The mayor *commended* the men and women for their work as volunteer firefighters.
시장은 자원 봉사 소방관으로 활약한 남녀들을 칭찬했다.

COMPETENT [kámpətənt/kɔ́m-] adj. capable; able to do something passably well 유능한; 자격이 있는

All the designers at La Boutique are *competent* dressmakers, but Sylvia is a fashion genius who can make anyone look good.
라 부띠끄에 있는 디자이너들은 모두 유능한 재단사지만, 실비아는 그 누구라도 근사해 보이게 만들 수 있는 패션 천재다.

Mark is a *competent* drummer, and a pretty good bass player, but he really excels on the tuba.
마크는 유능한 드러머에 꽤 훌륭한 베이스 주자지만, 정말로 탁월한 것은 튜바 연주다.

COMPILE [kəmpáil] v. to put together into one set 편집하다, 수집하다

Detective O'Reilly *compiled* a list of all the people who had entered or left the art museum on the day of the robbery.
오릴리 형사는 박물관에 강도가 들었던 날 그곳에 들어오고 나갔던 모든 사람들의 명단을 작성했다.

The library managed to *compile* a complete collection of first-edition Ernest Hemingway novels.
도서관에서는 어니스트 헤밍웨이 소설의 초판들을 완벽하게 수집해 놓았다.

COMPLACENT [kəmpléisnt] adj. overly pleased with oneself 자기만족의

Ted Kennedy has been a senator for so long that he seems *complacent* even during election years.
테드 케네디는 아주 오랫동안 상원의원을 지내서인지 선거가 있는 해인데도 걱정이 없는 것 같다.

Sportswriters claimed that the Cincinnati Bengals were able to beat Dallas because winning the Super Bowl two years in a row had made the Cowboys *complacent*.
스포츠 기자들은 수퍼볼 2연승을 거둔 댈러스 카우보이즈가 자기만족에 빠졌기 때문에, 신시내티 벵갈스가 댈러스를 이길 수 있다고 말했다.

COMPLIANCE [kəmpláiəns] n. acting according to a rule, order, or demand (규율, 명령, 요구 등에의) 응낙, 순종

Compliance with a strict moral code is required of all students at Brigham Young University.
브리검 영 대학의 모든 학생들은 엄격한 도덕률을 따라야 한다.

[Note] The verb form of compliance is comply [kəmplái].
동사형은 comply

- "Unless the city *complies* with my demands for a monster truck and ten cases of Mello Yello," cried the mad bomber, "I'll blow up every playground in the city!"
미친 폭파범이 소리쳤다. "시당국이 거대한 트럭 한 대와 멜로 옐로 열 상자를 가져오라는 내 요구에 응하지 않으면, 도시에 있는 모든 운동장을 날려버리겠다!"

COMPREHEND [kàmprihénd/kɔ̀m-] v. to understand 이해하다

Darius was speaking so quickly and waving his arms around so wildly, it was impossible to *comprehend* what he was trying to say.
대리어스는 말을 너무 빨리 하고 팔을 너무 과격하게 흔드는 바람에 그가 무슨 얘길 하려는 건지 이해할 수 없었다.

Most Americans have read our country's Constitution, but many do not truly *comprehend* it.
미국인들 대부분은 우리 나라의 헌법을 읽었지만 많은 이들이 그 내용을 제대로 이해하지 못한다.

COMRADE [kámræd/-rid/kɔ́mreid] n. a friend who shares your activities 동료

Dad went all out and bought imported beer and cashew nuts because his old army *comrades* were coming over.
아빠는 오랜 전우가 찾아올 거라면서 밖에 나가시더니 수입 맥주와 캐슈 열매를 사오셨다.

CONCEAL [kənsíːl] v. to hide 숨기다

Frank was jealous when he saw Josephine with her new boyfriend at the party, but he *concealed* his true feeling by cracking jokes and flirting with every girl he met.
프랭크는 파티에서 조세핀이 새로운 남자 친구와 있는 걸 보고 질투가 났지만, 본심을 숨기면서 만나는 여자들마다 농담을 지껄이고 시시덕거렸다.

The diamonds were *concealed* in a cooler full of ice.
다이아몬드들은 얼음으로 가득 채워진 아이스박스 속에 숨겨져 있었다.

CONCEIT [kənsíːt] n. vanity; an exaggerated sense of your own worth, importance, or abilities 허영심; 자만, 자부심

"Our band leader's *conceit* knows no limits," complained Ruth. "He criticizes us all the time, but he can't even play one instrument."
루스는 투덜거렸다. "우리 밴드 리더의 자만심은 끝이 없다니까. 끊임없이 우릴 흠잡지만, 자기는 악기 하나도 연주할 줄 몰라."

[Note] *Conceited* [kənsíːtid] is the adjective form of conceit.
형용사형은 conceited

■ Nancy was beautiful and rich, but she was so *conceited* no one could stand to be with her for more than a couple of hours.
낸시는 아름답고 부유했지만, 허영심이 지나쳐 어느 누구도 그녀와 두 시간 이상 있는 걸 참아 낼 수 없었다.

CONCILIATORY [kənsíliətɔ̀ːri/-təri] adj. tending to smooth over differences and calm hostilities 달래는, 회유적인

The little league coach used his most *conciliatory* tone of voice to stop the fight between the pitcher and the catcher.
리틀 야구단 코치는 최대한 달래는 어조로 투수와 포수 간의 싸움을 중단하라고 말했다.

After his son dropped out of medical school to become a clown, Mr. Hobnob refused to have any contact with him, but at the family reunion, he took a more *conciliatory* attitude and actually let his son make a balloon dog for him.
합납 씨는 아들이 어릿광대가 되겠다며 의대를 그만둔 후로 아들과는 어떤 접촉도 하지 않았지만, 가족 모임에서는 좀더 부드러운 태도를 취했고 자신에게 풍선으로 개를 만들어 주게 했다.

CONCLUDE [kənklúːd] v. to bring to an end; to determine through reasoning 끝내다; 결론을 내리다

Every episode of the old television show "The Beverly Hillbillies" *concluded* with the words, "ya'll come back now, y'hear?"

"비벌리 힐빌리"라는 오래된 텔레비전 연속극은 매 회가 "시방 돌아올 거지유?"라는 말로 끝났다.

After a thorough examination of the victim, Quincy *concluded* that a blow to the head with a blunt instrument was the cause of death.

퀸시는 희생자의 시신을 철저히 살펴본 뒤 무딘 도구로 머리를 강타 당해 죽었다는 결론을 내렸다.

CONDENSE [kəndéns] v. to shorten (usually referring to a book or story) or to make smaller or more concentrated 요약하다, 줄이다, 압축하다

The author had to *condense* her short story so it could be published in the magazine.

작가는 자신의 단편소설을 잡지에 싣기 위해서는 그 길이를 줄여야 했다.

The aluminum cans we brought to the recycling center were sent through the crushing machine and *condensed* to a fraction of their original size.

우리가 재활용 센터로 가져온 알루미늄 캔은 분쇄기로 들어가서 원래 크기에서 한 조각만 하게 작아졌다.

CONDONE [kəndóun] v. to forgive or ignore 용서하다, 묵과하다

The police chief was accused of *condoning* the fact that his officers were taking bribes from local businesses.

경찰서장은 그의 경관들이 지방 기업들로부터 뇌물을 수수해 온 사실을 묵과한 혐의로 기소되었다.

"I may *condone* your talking in class and your tardiness," said the teacher, "but cheating is something I will never tolerate."

교사가 말했다. "난 너희가 교실에서 떠들거나 지각하는 건 용서할지 몰라도, 시험에서 부정행위를 하는 것은 절대 용납하지 않을 거야."

CONSPICUOUS [kənspíkjuəs] adj. easily noticed; obvious 눈에 잘 띄는; 명백한

William was trying to spy on his sister at the fair, but by dressing all in black and wearing sunglasses, even though it was night, he made himself *conspicuous*.

윌리엄은 마을 축제가 열리는 유원지에서 누이동생을 감시하려고 했지만, 밤인데도 온통 까만 옷에 선글라스를 끼는 바람에 자신이 눈에 띄게 됐다.

The undercover cop was a bit *conspicuous* because everyone could see he had a gun stuffed down his pants.

그 위장 근무하는 형사는 바지 춤에 총이 꽂혀 있는 것이 누구에게나 보였기 때문에 눈에 띄었다.

CONSPIRACY [kənspírəsi] n. a secret plan or the act of creating a secret plan to do something illegal 음모, 모의

Many people believe that Lee Harvey Oswald, the man accused of killing President John F. Kennedy, was part of a huge communist *conspiracy*.

많은 이들은 존 F. 케네디 대통령의 암살자로 고발됐던 리 하비 오스왈드는 거대한 공산주의자 조직 음모의 일부였다고 생각한다.

The police discovered the doctor and his patients were involved in a *conspiracy* to get money from insurance companies by sending in claims for fake illnesses.

경찰은 의사와 환자들이 병을 조작해 지불 청구를 하는 방법으로 보험사로부터 돈을 뜯어내려는 음모에 가담하고 있다는 사실을 알아냈다.

CONTAMINATE [kəntǽmənèit] v. to pollute or make unclean 오염시키다, 더럽히다

The Mississippi River has been *contaminated* for years by industries that dump waste into its waters.
미시시피 강은 수년간 물속으로 폐기물을 쏟아 부은 기업들 때문에 오염됐다.

The air around Bhopal, India, was *contaminated* by an accident at a nearby chemical plant.
인도 보팔 부근의 공기는 인접한 화학 공장에서 일어난 사고로 오염됐다.

CONTEMPLATE [kántəmplèit/kɔ́n-] v. to think about carefully; to ponder 곰곰이 생각하다, 심사숙고하다

Raoul enjoyed sitting on the beach, *contemplating* the meaning of life.
라울은 해변에 앉아 인생의 의미에 대해 곰곰이 생각하는 걸 좋아했다.

When you hear about someone dying of a heart attack at the age of twenty-five, it makes you *contemplate* your own lifestyle and health.
누군가가 25세의 나이로 심장마비에 걸려 죽어 간다는 얘기를 들으면 자신의 생활 방식이나 건강에 대해 깊이 생각하게 된다.

CONTEMPT [kəntémpt] n. scorn; a feeling you have for anything that is worthless, disgraceful, low 경멸, 멸시

After she discovered that her boyfriend had lied to her about owning a Corvette, Melinda felt nothing but *contempt* for him.
멜린다는 남자 친구가 스포츠카 코르벳을 가지고 있다고 한 건 거짓말이었음을 알고 나자 그에게 경멸감을 느낄 뿐이었다.

Benedict Arnold, a traitor to the American Revolution, has been an object of *contempt* for over 200 years.
미국 독립전쟁의 반역자였던 베네딕트 아놀드는 2백년이 넘도록 경멸의 대상이다.

CONTENT [kəntént] adj. happy, satisfied or [kántent/kɔ́n-] n. a feeling of happiness 행복한, 만족한 / 만족

Whiskers the cat was *content* just to lie in the patch of sun under the window for hours.
고양이 위스커스는 몇 시간 동안 창문 밑 해가 비치는 자리에 누워 있는 것만으로도 행복했다.

Grandpa told us he had the swimming pool put in his backyard so we could "splash around to our hearts' *content*."
할아버지는 "우리가 신나서 첨벙거리며 다닐" 수 있도록 뒤뜰에 수영장을 만들 거라고 말씀하셨다.

CONVALESCE [kànvəlés/kɔ́n-] v. to get well after an illness (병을 앓고 난 뒤) 건강을 회복하다

After a dangerous case of pneumonia last winter, grandmother went to a warm beach resort to *convalesce*. She's been there ever since.
할머니는 지난 겨울 위독한 폐렴을 앓고 나신 후 건강 회복을 위해 따뜻한 해변 리조트로 가셨다. 그 이후로 계속 거기 계신다.

CONVENIENT [kənvíːnjənt] adj. easy to use; close by; well-suited to a particular purpose 편리한; 가까운; 손쉽고 편리한

Babs never used to eat ice cream, but since Milky Miracles opened a store right next to her office, it's just too *convenient* to pass up.
밥스는 아이스크림을 먹는 일이 거의 없었는데, 그녀의 사무실 바로 옆에 밀키 미라클스가 가게를 여는 바람에 너무 가까워 무시할 수가 없다.

My friend Timmy says he doesn't recycle his bottles, cans, and newspapers because sorting his trash and taking it to the recycling center is not as *convenient* as just throwing everything into one bag and leaving it on the curb for the garbage collectors.

내 친구 티미는 병이나 캔, 신문 등을 재활용하지 않는다는데, 쓰레기를 분류해서 재활용 센터까지 가지고 가느니 그냥 전부 한 봉지에 넣어서 쓰레기 수거인이 가져가도록 길에 내놓는 게 편하기 때문이라고 말한다.

CORPSE [kɔ:rps] n. a dead, usually human, body 시체

The medical student fainted when the doctor began to dissect the *corpse*.

그 의대생은 의사가 시신을 해부하기 시작하자 기절했다.

COUNTERFEIT [káuntərfìt] adj. fake, made to look real in order to fool people or v. to fake or n. a fake 위조의 / 위조하다 / 위조품

Paula was arrested for giving a *counterfeit* twenty dollar bill to an A & P supermarket.

폴라는 A&P 슈퍼마켓에서 20달러짜리 위조지폐를 낸 혐의로 체포됐다.

The art dealer gave us a certificate that proved that painting we bought was a real Da Vinci, but both the certificate and the painting turned out to be *counterfeits*.

미술품 상은 우리가 구입한 그림이 다빈치의 진품임을 입증하는 증서를 주었지만, 알고 보니 증서와 그림 둘 다 위조된 것이었다.

The beautiful widow *counterfeited* grief over the death of her very rich, very old husband, but the rest of the family knew she didn't really care.

아름다운 미망인은 갑부의 늙은 남편이 죽자 대단히 슬픈 척했지만, 나머지 가족은 그녀가 실제로는 개의치 않았다는 걸 알고 있었다.

COUP D'ÉTAT [ku: deitá:/-detá] n. the overthrow of a government 쿠데타

[Note] This phrase is often shortened to *coup* [ku:], which means either coup d'état or a successful, strong action.

coup로 줄여서 쓰기도 하며, 그럴 경우엔 '쿠데타' 혹은 '대히트', '대성공'을 뜻한다.

The Cambodian government of Prince Sihanouk was overthrown in a bloody *coup d'état*.

시아누크 공이 이끌던 캄보디아 정부는 유혈 쿠데타로 전복됐다.

Putting a man on the moon before the Soviets was seen as a major scientific *coup* for the Americans.

소련을 앞질러 달에 인류를 보낸 것은 미국인들에게 중요한 과학적 쾌거로 비쳤다.

COVET [kʌ́vit] v. to crave, often to crave something someone else has 열망하다, 남이 가진 것을 턱없이 탐내다

The Academy Award is an honor *coveted* by most Hollywood actors.

아카데미상은 헐리우드 배우 대부분이 열망하는 영예다.

CRISIS [kráisis] n. a dangerous or difficult event or situation, a turning point 위기, 고비, 분기점

The rash of burglaries, muggings, and assaults forced the mayor to admit that the downtown area was in a state of *crisis*.

다발적인 주택 침입 절도, 노상강도, 폭력 행위로 시장은 도심 지역이 위기에 놓여 있다는 것을 인정할 수밖에 없었다.

Americans felt a *crisis* of faith in their government during the Watergate scandal, in which President Nixon was accused of ordering a burglary.

미국인들은 워터게이트 스캔들 기간 동안 정부의 신뢰감에 대해 위기를 느꼈는데, 그 사건에서 닉슨 대통령은 불법 침입을 명한 혐의로 고소당했다.

The American colonists had been unhappy for a long time with the taxes the British government was forcing them to pay, but the tea tax brought the situation to a *crisis*, and started talk of a revolution.

미국에 이주해서 살던 사람들은 오랫동안 영국 정부가 세금 납부를 강요하자 불만이 많았었는데, 차에 대한 세금으로 그 상황은 분기점을 맞았고, 혁명에 대한 이야기가 나오게 됐다.

CULPRIT [kʌ́lprit] n. a person guilty of a crime or fault 범죄자, 범인

"We suspect our school mascot was kidnapped by students from our rival high school," announced the principal, "but we haven't yet found the *culprits*."

교장은 발표했다. "우리 학교의 마스코트는 라이벌 학교의 학생들이 훔쳐 간 것 같지만, 아직 범인들을 잡지는 못했습니다."

The FBI said it was close to nabbing the main *culprit* in the counterfeiting ring that had made over two million dollars in fake bills.

연방수사국은 2백만 달러가 넘는 위조지폐를 만들어 낸 위조 도당 가운데 주요 범인을 검거하기 직전이라고 말했다.

CULT [kʌlt] n. a system of religion; a religious group that has an unusual lifestyle and set of beliefs, usually led by one person or a small group of people who demand the complete obedience of the followers; a strong devotion to something 종교 제도; 이교, 숭배자 집단; 대단한 헌신

Thousands of years ago, most people were part of nature-worshiping *cults* that paid tribute to the gods and goddesses of trees, water, and weather.

수천 년 전에 대부분의 사람들은 나무, 물, 날씨의 신들에게 공물을 바치는 자연숭배 집단에 속했었다.

The leaders or religious *cults* are often very passionate and convincing, but are sometimes dangerous because they can use their influence to force their followers to do whatever they want.

소수파 종교 집단의 지도자들은 흔히 아주 정열적이고 설득력이 있지만, 추종자들에게 자신들이 원하는 것은 무엇이든 하도록 강요하기 위해 영향력을 행사할 수 있으므로 위험할 때가 있다.

The *cult* of physical perfection in the United States has caused many young girls and boys to think they need plastic surgery in order to be attractive.

미국에서 완벽한 몸매에 대한 숭배는 많은 소년, 소녀들에게 매력적인 모습을 만들기 위해 성형수술을 받아야 한다고 생각하도록 만들었다.

CUMBERSOME [kʌ́mbərsəm] adj. hard to carry, bear, or manage 주체스러운, 성가신

The luggage is too *cumbersome* for you to handle alone.

가방이 너 혼자 들기에는 너무 버겁다.

Hans complained that the Lincoln Town Car was too *cumbersome* for driving in the narrow German streets.

한스는 좁다란 독일 골목에서 링컨 타운 카를 운전하기 힘들다고 투덜거렸다.

CURSORY [kə́ːrsəri] adj. quick and not thorough 마구잡이의, 빠르지만 철저하지 못한

The teacher got so behind in his grading, he only had time to give each paper a *cursory* reading.

교사는 채점할 것이 너무 밀려서 각 답안지를 대충 훑어볼 시간 밖에 없었다.

It only took a *cursory* look under the hood for the mechanic to tell that the car had serious engine trouble.

정비공은 후드 아래를 쓱 보기만 하고는 차에 심각한 엔진 문제가 있다고 말했다.

CURT [kəːrt] adj. brief, sometimes rudely brief, in speech or action 간략한, 퉁명스러운

Marvin gave his dinner guests a *curt* greeting, then went back to the den to watch the end of the hockey game.
마빈은 저녁 손님들에게 대충 인사를 하고는 하키 경기의 뒷부분을 보기 위해 서재로 돌아갔다.

On her last day of work, Claudia said a few *curt* good-byes, then hurried out of the building.
클로디아는 근무 마지막 날, 작별 인사 몇 마디를 짤막하게 하고는 서둘러 건물을 나갔다.

CYNIC [sínik] n. a person who believes that most people are selfish and no good 빈정대는 사람, 냉소적인 사람

Harvey showed what a *cynic* he was when he commented that profits from the church bake sale would probably be used to pay for the minister's vacation in the Bahamas.
하비는 가정에서 구운 케이크를 교회에서 판매한 이익금이 아마도 목사의 바하마 휴가비로 사용될 거라고 말하면서 자신이 얼마나 냉소적인 사람인지를 보여주었다.

[Note] The adjective form of cynic is *cynical* [sínikəl], which means distrustful.
형용사 cynical은 '의심 많은', '냉소적인'

- Voters are *cynical* when the politicians they elect do not keep their campaign promises.
  유권자들은 선출된 정치인들이 자신들의 선거 공약을 지키지 않으면 냉소적인 반응을 보인다.

D

DABBLE [dǽbl] v. to splash around in water; to do some activity without serious intentions   물을 튀기다; 취미 삼아 해보다

The grown-ups lounged on the lawn furniture while the kids *dabbled* in the kiddie pool.
아이들이 풀에서 물장난을 치고 있을 때 어른들은 잔디 위 의자에 드러누워 있었다.

"Before I became an accountant I *dabbled* in music," sighed Herb. "I was even in a band during one semester in college."
허브는 한숨을 지으며 말했다. "난 회계사가 되기 전 취미로 음악을 했었지. 대학에서 한 학기 동안 밴드 활동도 했어."

DEBACLE [deibá:kl/-bǽkl/də-] n. a disaster or downfall   재난, 몰락, 큰 실패

The movie *Ishtar* was a *debacle* for the studio: it went millions of dollars over budget and was a flop in the theaters.
영화 '이슈타르' 는 영화사에게 실패작이었다. 수백만 달러의 빚을 졌고 극장 상영에서도 실패였다.

Springfield's production of the ballet *Swan Lake* was the worst *debacle* ever to hit the theaters: dancers tripped over each other, the set fell down, and the orchestra stopped playing twenty minutes into the show.
스프링필드의 '백조의 호수' 발레 공연은 지금까지 극장을 강타한 재난 중 최악이었다. 무용수들은 서로의 발에 걸려 넘어졌고, 무대 장치도 넘어졌으며, 오케스트라는 공연 중에 20분 동안 연주를 멈추었다.

DEBAUCHERY [dibɔ́:tʃəri] n. overindulgence in food, drink, or other pleasures   방탕, 탐닉

Nowadays, people do not tolerate *debauchery* in their public officials. They want politicians who are faithful to their wives and don't stay out partying all night.
요즈음 사람들은 공무원들의 방탕을 그대로 두지 않는다. 그들은 아내에게 충실하고 밤새 나가서 진탕 놀아 대지 않는 정치인들을 원한다.

The Roman emperors led lifestyles of great *debauchery*, spending their days and nights feasting and drinking wine.
로마 황제들은 밤낮 할 것 없이 잔치를 열고 술을 마시면서 극심하게 방탕한 생활을 보냈다.

DEBRIS [dəbrí:/déibri:/déb-] n. the broken pieces of something that has been destroyed   파편, 잔해

After the mysterious explosion under the World Trade Center in New York, investigators spent weeks sorting through the *debris* looking for clues that might lead them to the bomber.
뉴욕의 세계무역센터 지하에서 원인 모를 폭발 사고가 난 후 수사관들은 폭파범을 알려줄지 모를 단서를 찾기 위해 몇 주 동안 파편을 가려냈다.

The high winds from the hurricane scattered *debris* up and down the Florida coastline.
태풍이 몰고 온 세찬 바람때문에 플로리다 해안선을 따라 나뭇가지등이 어지럽게 흩어져있다.

DECAPITATE [dikǽpətèit] v. to cut the head off 목을 베다

Henry VIII, the King of England, accused his wife of treason and had her *decapitated*.
영국 왕 헨리 8세는 자신의 아내를 반역죄로 기소해 목을 베었다.

The townspeople were hopping mad when they found out that the statue of their founding father had been *decapitated* by some hoodlum.
건달들이 마을창립자 동상의 목을 벤 사실을 알게 된 마을 사람들은 화가 나 펄쩍 뛰었다.

DECEASED [disíːst] adj. dead or n. the dead person or people 사망한 / 고인

The traveling cat food salesman was unaware that the Smithereen's pet was *deceased*. If he had known, he wouldn't have knocked on the door and asked, "Is your cat as healthy as he could be?"
고양이 먹이 방문판매원은 스미더린네 애완동물이 죽었다는 걸 몰랐다. 그가 알았더라면 문을 노크하고 "사모님의 고양이는 더할 나위 없이 건강한가요?"라고 묻지 않았을 것이다.

The church was filled with the friends and family of the *deceased*.
교회는 고인의 친구들과 가족으로 꽉 메워졌다.

DECOY [díːkɔi/dikɔ́i] n. person or thing used to lure someone into a trap 유인하는 것(사람), 미끼

Police knew mobster Bruce "Buzzsaw" Parker was a big Madonna fan, so they hired her to act as a *decoy*, knowing he would try to meet her when his men told him she was in his favorite restaurant.
경찰은 "버즈소"라 불리는 조폭 단원 브루스 파커가 마돈나의 열렬한 팬이라는 사실을 알았다. 그래서 그가 좋아하는 식당에 그녀가 있다고 부하가 얘기하면 만나보려 할 거란 사실을 알고 그녀를 고용해 미끼 역할을 하게 했다.

DEEM [diːm] v. to hold as opinion, believe 생각하다, 간주하다

Karen *deemed* Shelly's inability to throw a softball more than twenty feet a major problem for a third baseman.
카렌은 쉘리가 소프트볼을 20피트 이상 못 던지는 것은 3루수에게 있어 중대한 문제라고 생각했다.

I will do whatever the doctor *deems* necessary to recover from my flu.
의사가 내 독감을 치료하는 데 필요하다고 생각하는 건 뭐든 하겠다.

Betty's short black dress was *deemed* inappropriate for the afternoon tea party at her great aunt's house.
베티의 짧은 검은 드레스는 대고모 댁의 오후 티파티에 입고 가기엔 부적당한 것 같았다.

DEFECT [díːfekt/diːfékt] n. a flaw or [difékt] v. to abandon one country to take refuge in or become a citizen of another 결함, 흠 / 망명하다

The clothes the store sold had minor *defects*, but no one cared because they were so inexpensive.
그 가게에서 파는 옷은 사소한 흠들이 있었지만, 워낙 저렴했기 때문에 아무도 개의치 않았다.

Margaret's eyes had rare *defects* that made it impossible for her to cry.
마가렛은 눈에 희귀한 결함이 있어서 울 수가 없었다.

Many famous citizens of the Soviet Union *defected* to the United States during the Cold War.
냉전 기간 동안 소련에서 많은 유명 인사들이 미국으로 망명해 왔다.

DEFERENCE [défərəns] n. respectful submission to another person's wishes; respectful politeness 복종; 존경, 경의

In *deference* to the guest of honor, who was a vegetarian, no meat was served at the party.
파티에서는 채식주의자인 주빈을 존중하는 뜻으로 고기가 제공되지 않았다.

The Vargas family spoke English with each other most of the time, but at dinner they spoke only in Spanish, out of *deference* to their grandmother, who didn't understand English.
바르가스 가족은 대부분의 시간 동안 영어로 얘기를 나눴지만, 저녁을 먹을 때는 스페인어로만 얘기했는데, 영어를 못하시는 할머니를 존중하는 뜻에서였다.

Cal almost never wore anything but ripped jeans and tank tops, but he would put on a shirt and tie when he visited home, in *deference* to his mother.
칼은 거의 언제나 찢어진 청바지와 탱크탑만 입었지만 집에 갈 때는 어머니에 대한 존경의 표시로 셔츠를 입고 넥타이를 맸다.

DEGRADE [digréid] v. to disgrace or dishonor 지위를 낮추다, 품위를 떨어뜨리다

Carmen was so stuck up, she wouldn't pump her own gas because she said it *degraded* her.
카멘은 아주 거만해서 주유도 직접 하지 않았는데, 자신의 품위를 떨어뜨리기 때문이란다.

You only *degrade* yourself by spreading hurtful gossip about other people.
다른 사람에 대해 고통을 주는 뒷말을 퍼뜨리는 건 네 자신의 격을 떨어뜨릴 뿐이다.

Pierre found it *degrading* to work behind a deli counter after he had been head chef at *Le Chat Pendu*, a fancy French restaurant.
피에르는 근사한 프랑스 식당 르 샤 빵뒤에서 수석 요리사로 일하다가 조제 식품점 카운터 뒤에서 일하는 것은 자존심이 상한다는 걸 알았다.

DEJECTION [didʒékʃən] n. depression, the condition of being in low spirits 낙담, 우울

The girls couldn't hide their *dejection* after failing to make the cheerleading squad.
여자아이들은 치어리더 팀에 들어가는 데 실패한 이후 낙담해 있는 걸 숨길 수 없었다.

DELIBERATE [dilíbərət] adj. on purpose or [dilíbərèit] v. to consider or think carefully about 고의의 / 숙고하다

Homer made a *deliberate* attempt to knock over the soda can castle I spent all day building.
호머는 내가 하루 종일 걸려 만들어 놓은 소다캔 성 위로 일부러 넘어지려고 했다.

The jury needed only ten minutes to *deliberate* before deciding that Sister Mary Margaret was not guilty of armed robbery.
배심원은 메리 마가렛 수녀가 무장 강도짓을 저지른 게 아니라는 평결을 내리기 전 숙고하는 데에 10분밖에 걸리지 않았다.

Grant spent three days *deliberating* over whether sky blue or robin's egg blue was a better color for his bedroom walls.
그랜트는 3일에 걸쳐 자신의 침실 벽에 하늘색이 더 좋을지 청록색이 더 좋을지 곰곰이 생각했다.

DELIRIOUS [dilíəriəs] adj. uncontrollably excited 미쳐 날뛰는, 열중한

Miss Burkina Faso was so *delirious* when she won the Miss World pageant, she ran around kissing the other 278 contestants, blew 500 kisses to her friends in Ouagadougou, and completely forgot to do the usual walk-and-wave downstage.
미스 버키나파소는 미스 월드에 당선됐을 때 너무나 흥분한 나머지 다른 278명의 경쟁자들에게 키스를 하며 뛰어다녔고, 와가두구에 있는 친구들에게 500번의 키스를 보냈으며, 으레 무대 앞에서 손 흔들며 걷는 것은 까맣게 잊어버렸다.

DENOUNCE [dináuns]   v. to condemn openly or publicly   비난하다

Prince Sergei Radzievsky was *denounced* by the members of high society when it was discovered that he was not actually heir to the Polish throne.
세르게이 라지에프스키 왕자가 사실은 폴란드의 왕위 계승자가 아니라는 사실을 알게 된 상류사회 사람들은 그를 비난했다.

The principal called an assembly to *denounce* the use of violence in settling fights between students.
교장은 학생들 간의 싸움을 해결하는 데 폭력을 사용하는 것을 비난하기 위해 회의를 소집했다.

DENSE [dens]   adj. thick; crowded together   빽빽한; 밀집한, 조밀한

The cat had a hard time creeping through the tall, *dense* weeds around the house.
고양이는 집 주변의 크고 울창한 잡초를 헤치고 기어가느라 힘이 들었다.

Because the population is so *dense*, pollution is usually worse in big cities.
대도시는 인구가 너무 조밀해서 일반적으로 오염이 더 심하다.

DEPLETE [diplí:t]   v. to use up or empty   다 써 버리다, 고갈시키다

By driving cars everywhere instead of walking or biking, we are *depleting* our supplies of gas and oil.
우리는 걷거나 자전거를 타지 않고 어딜 가든 차를 몰고 다니면서 가스와 석유의 비축량을 바닥내고 있다.

Irving developed a gambling habit late in life, and in two short years he managed to *deplete* the life savings he had spent fifty years accumulating.
어빙은 늦은 나이에 도박에 맛을 들여서 단 2년 만에, 50년 평생을 모아 온 저축을 탕진했다.

DEPRAVITY [diprǽvəti]   n. evilness; complete moral corruption   악행; 타락, 부패

After he was fired as the minister at First Baptist, Reverend Foster just gave up on life — and the afterlife. His *depravity* knew no limits; there was not a sin he didn't commit.
포스터 목사는 제1 침례교에서 목사직을 파면 당한 후 인생을, 그리고 사후 세계까지 포기해 버렸다. 그의 타락에는 한계가 없었고, 저지르지 않은 죄가 하나도 없을 정도였다.

When Dana Plato was arrested on drug and armed robbery charges, the public was shocked at her *depravity*.
다나 플라토가 마약 복용과 무장 강도 혐의로 체포됐을 때 국민들은 그 여자의 타락에 충격을 받았다.

DERIDE [diráid]   v. to jeer at; to tease or laugh at in a mean way   비웃다, 조롱하다; 야비한 방법으로 놀리거나 비웃다

The cruel students *derided* Jill for stuttering during her book report presentation.
잔인한 학생들은 질이 독후감을 발표하면서 더듬거리는 걸 보고 비웃었다.

Duke *derided* the French custom of kissing both cheeks as a form of greeting. He thought it was "sissified."
듀크는 인사의 의미로 양 볼에 키스를 하는 프랑스식 풍습을 비웃었다. 그는 그것을 "계집애들이나 하는 짓"이라고 생각했다.

DESCENT [disént]   n. the act of coming down; family background   강하, 하락; 가계, 혈통

Lillian found it easy to climb up Eagle Peak, but the *descent* was difficult and frightening.
릴리안에게 독수리 봉에 오르는 것은 쉬웠지만, 내려오는 것은 어렵고 무서웠다.

My friend Ali O'Malley is of Iranian and Irish *descent*: his mother is from Teheran and his father is from Tipperary.
내 친구 앨리 오맬리는 이란과 아일랜드계다. 어머니는 테헤란 출신이시고, 아버지는 티퍼러리 출신이시다.

DESPICABLE [déspikəbl/dispí-] adj. deserving contempt 경멸할 만한

The landlord's attempt to force tenants out of the apartment building by turning off the heat in the middle of January was *despicable*.
집주인이 거주자들을 아파트에서 나가게 하려고 1월 중순에 난방을 꺼버린 것은 비열한 처사였다.

DETER [ditə́:r] v. to prevent someone from doing something, usually through fear or doubt (겁먹어서 혹은 의심돼서) 못하게 하다, 그만두게 하다

Farmer Fred put up an electrified fence to *deter* cattle from wandering away.
프레드 농부는 소들이 나돌아다니지 못하도록 전기가 통하는 울타리를 놓았다.

When people go on vacation, they try to *deter* theft by using a device that turns the lights and television on and off so it will look as though they are at home.
사람들은 휴가를 떠날 때 전기와 텔레비전이 켜졌다 꺼졌다 하는 장치를 사용해 도둑을 막는다. 그렇게 하면 사람이 집에 있는 것처럼 보인다.

DETEST [ditést] v. to hate 혐오하다

"I absolutely *detest* these fancy dinner parties," complained Mr. Vanderhooven. "There's never any ketchup for my steak!"
"이런 고상한 체 하는 저녁 파티는 질색이야." 밴더후벤 씨가 투덜거렸다. "스테이크에 뿌릴 케첩도 없다니까!"

DEVOUR [diváuər] v. to eat something completely and greedily 게걸스럽게 먹다

Kristin *devoured* the entire lasagna right out of the pan while her friends were in the kitchen looking for plates and forks.
친구들이 부엌에서 접시와 포크를 찾고 있는 동안 크리스틴은 접시에 있는 라자냐를 모조리 퍼먹었다.

After soccer practice, the boys and girls are so hungry they *devour* everything their parents give them at dinner, including the cauliflower.
축구 연습이 끝나면 아이들은 배가 너무 고파 부모님이 저녁으로 차려 준 음식을 있는 대로, 꽃양배추까지도 먹어 치운다.

DIALECT [dáiəlèkt] n. a variation in a language spoken in a certain location or by a certain group of people; a dialect has its own pronunciations for words and uses for words 방언, 특정 그룹의 통용어

In the *dialect* spoken in the South, people say they are "fixin' to do something" to mean they are about to do something.
남부에서 쓰는 방언에서는 막 뭔가를 하려고 한다는 뜻으로 "fixin' to do something"이라고 말한다.

Connor spoke in an Irish *dialect* I found hard to understand.
캐너는 내가 이해하기 힘든 아일랜드 방언으로 말했다.

DICTATOR [díkteitər] n. an absolute ruler, especially one in control of a country without the free consent of the people 독재자

Adolf Hitler was a German *dictator* from 1934 to 1945, and leader of a depraved movement to kill off everyone he decided was "inferior" to the so-called "true Germans."
아돌프 히틀러는 1934년부터 1945년까지 독일의 독재자였는데, 소위 "순수 독일인"에 비해 열등하다고 자신이 판단하는 사람을 모조리 없애기 위한 악랄한 운동을 이끌었다.

Gail was a great reporter for the school newspaper, but when she became editor-in-chief, the power must have gone to her head because she started acting like some kind of *dictator* — she even renamed the paper "Gail's Gazette."

게일은 뛰어난 교내 신문 기자였지만, 편집장 자리에 오르자 권력이란 것에 흥분된 모양이었다. 무슨 독재자처럼 행세하기 시작했기 때문인데, 신문을 "게일 신문" 으로 개명까지 했다.

DIDACTIC [daidǽktik/di-] adj. used for teaching purposes; inclined to teach too much, or in a preachy way 교훈적인; 지나치게 남을 가르치려고 드는

Aesop's Fables are *didactic* stories that use animals as characters, but are meant to demonstrate human faults like vanity and greed.

이솝우화에는 동물들이 주인공으로 등장하지만 허영과 탐욕같은 인간의 결점을 보여주기 위해 지어진 교훈적 이야기다.

"Whenever we go to an art museum, Ted becomes so *didactic*!" said Sid. "He gives a whole art history lecture on every painting and sculpture we pass, and bothers everyone around him."

시드가 말했다. "우리가 미술관에 갈 때면 언제나 테드는 우릴 가르치려고 들어! 그 앤 지나가는 그림과 조각품마다 미술사 총강의를 하면서 주변 사람들을 성가시게 해."

DIGNITARY [dígnətèri/-təri] n. a high-ranking person 고위 인사

The ambassador threw a big party for all the foreign *dignitaries* who had come to the conference.

대사는 회의에 참석했던 외국 고위 인사들을 위해 성대한 파티를 열었다.

DIGNITY [dígnəti] n. noble, honorable character; formal, noble action or speech 존엄, 품위; 품위 있는 행동이나 말

While Prince Charles and Princess Diana have hurled insults at each other and exposed all sorts of embarrassing secrets, Queen Elizabeth has tried to preserve the *dignity* of the British throne.

찰스 왕세자와 다이애나 왕세자비가 서로에게 모욕을 퍼붓고 온갖 종류의 난처한 비밀들을 폭로하는 동안 엘리자베스 여왕은 영국 왕위의 존엄을 유지하려고 애썼다.

The governor took her defeat in the election with great *dignity*, and made a speech urging everyone to support the new administration.

주지사는 대단히 품위있게 선거에서의 패배를 받아들였고, 모든 이에게 새로운 정부를 지지해 줄 것을 당부하는 연설을 했다.

DIGRESS [digrés/dai-] v. to stray from the main topic 본 주제에서 옆으로 빠지다

Grandpa was trying to tell us about his cruise in the Caribbean, but he kept *digressing* to talk about his days in the navy.

할아버지는 카리브 해에서의 유람선 여행에 대해 얘기해 주시려고 했지만, 계속 해군 시절 얘기를 하시며 옆길로 빠지셨다.

I was reading an article on the rise of tourism in Australia, but it was filled with *digressions* on the mating rituals of kangaroos and the eating habits of koalas, so I got bored and stopped reading.

호주 관광산업의 번창에 대한 기사를 읽고 있었는데, 거기엔 캥거루의 짝짓기 의식과 코알라의 식습관에 대한 여담만 가득했다. 그래서 지겨워졌고 읽는 걸 그만두었다.

DILEMMA [dilémə] n. a situation that forces a person to choose between two equally bad options 진퇴양난, 딜레마

Norm was faced with a *dilemma*: if he went on strike with the other workers, he could lose his job, but if he didn't go on strike, the owner of the plant would probably never do anything about the dangerous working conditions.

노움은 딜레마에 직면했다. 다른 노동자들과 함께 파업에 들어간다면 일자리를 잃을 수도 있지만, 파업에 가담하지 않는다면 공장주는 위험한 근무 조건에 대해 어떤 조치도 취하지 않을 것이다.

When the teacher accused him of stealing hall passes from her desk, Lyle was faced with the *dilemma* of accepting the blame and being expelled, or telling her that he saw Rocky take them and being beaten up by Rocky and his gang after school.

교사가 라일에게 자기 책상에서 홀패스(수업에 빠질 수 있는 허가증)를 훔쳐 갔다고 비난했을 때, 라일은 비난을 감수하고 쫓겨날 것인가, 아니면 록키가 그것들을 가져가는 걸 보았다고 말한 다음 방과 후에 록키와 그 패거리한테 두들겨 맞을 것인가 하는 진퇴양난에 빠졌다.

DILIGENT [dílədʒənt] adj. painstaking; constant in effort to achieve something; hardworking   근면한; 수고를 아끼지 않는; 열심히 일하는

Vince realized that even after twelve years of *diligent* practice on the parallel bars, he could never hope to win an Olympic gold medal in that event.

빈스는 12년 동안 부지런히 평행봉 연습을 하고 난 뒤에도 그 종목으로 올림픽 금메달의 획득을 기대할 수 없다는 걸 깨달았다.

Professor Hardihar rewarded his assistant's *diligent* research and record-keeping by giving her the weekend off.

하디하 교수는 그의 조교가 조사와 기록 관리를 열심히 한 것에 대한 보답으로 주말을 쉬게 해주었다.

DISCERNMENT [disɔ́:rnmənt] n. sharpness of judgement and understanding   통찰력

When Uma's fifth husband turned out to be a thief, just like the other four, her mother urged her to use a little more *discernment* the next time she decided to get married.

우마의 다섯 번째 남편 역시 앞의 네 명과 똑같은 도둑임이 밝혀졌을 때 그녀의 어머니는 다음번에 결혼을 결심할 때는 좀더 통찰력을 가지라고 촉구했다.

The basketball scout from Duke University showed great *discernment* in recruiting talented players.

듀크 대학에서의 농구부 스카우트 당당자는 재능있는 선수들을 보충하는 데 있어 대단한 통찰력을 보여주었다.

DISCIPLINE [dísəplin/-plín] n. a branch of learning   학문의 분야, 학과

History and art can be seen as related *disciplines* because most major events and advances in civilization are interpreted or reflected through art.

역사와 예술은 관련된 학문으로 볼 수 있는데, 문명 속에서 가장 중요한 사건과 진보는 예술을 통해 해석되고 반영되기 때문이다.

"I'm afraid I don't have an opinion on ancient Egyptian burial rites," said the physics professor. "My knowledge is limited to one *discipline*."

물리학 교수가 말했다. "유감이지만 난 고대 이집트 매장 의식에 대해 별다른 의견이 없군. 내 지식은 한 학문에만 한정돼 있어서 말야."

DISCLOSE [disklóuz] v. to make known or to reveal   알리다, 드러내다

My mother refused to *disclose* the contents of any of the boxes under the Christmas tree.

어머니는 크리스마스트리 밑에 있는 상자 중 어떤 것도 내용물을 알려주시지 않았다.

It is considered impolite to ask a woman to *disclose* her age or weight, unless, of course, you work for the Department of Motor Vehicles.

여성에게 나이나 체중을 물어보는 것은 무례한 일로 간주됩니다. 물론 당신이 차량 관리국 직원이 아니라면 말이죠.

DISCORD [dískɔ:rd] n. disagreement; lack of harmony between people or things   불일치; 불화, 의견 충돌

The Barrett family house was filled with *discord* because no one could agree on where they should go for summer vacation.

버렛 가족의 집은 여름휴가를 어디로 갈 것인지에 대해 아무도 의견일치를 보지 못해 불협화음으로 가득 찼다.

It is hoped that the new peace agreement will end the decades of *discord* that existed between the Israelis and Palestinians.

새로운 평화 협정이 이스라엘 사람들과 팔레스타인 사람들 사이에 존재했던 수십년 동안의 불화를 마감시켰으면 한다.

DISCRIMINATE [diskrímənèit] v. to tell the difference between or to show prejudice 식별하다, 분간하다; 차별하다

The skilled artist was able to *discriminate* between very similar shades of color.
숙련된 미술가는 아주 비슷한 색깔의 농도를 구분할 수 있었다.

When deciding how to sentence a criminal, a judge must *discriminate* different levels of guilt.
범죄자에게 어떤 판결을 내릴 것인가 결정할 때 판사는 죄의 서로 다른 정도를 분간해야 한다.

Some flight attendants have accused the airlines they work for of *discriminating* against people who are overweight.
일부의 여객기 승무원들이, 살이 많이 찐 사람들을 차별대우한다는 이유로 자신들의 항공사를 고소했다.

DISDAIN [disdéin] n. a feeling of contempt for anything considered beneath oneself; scorn 경멸감, 경멸

The princess agreed to kiss the frog in order to get her golden ball back, but she did it with *disdain*.
공주는 자신의 황금공을 돌려받기 위해 개구리에게 입 맞춰 주겠다고 했지만, 경멸감을 느끼며 그렇게 했다.

Bridget gave me a look of *disdain* when I told her I'd give her five dollars if she'd let me copy her homework.
브리지트에게 그녀의 숙제를 베끼게해 주면 5달러를 주겠다고 말하자 그녀는 경멸하는 표정으로 나를 봤다.

DISORIENT [disɔ́ːriənt] v. to confuse or cause to lose one's bearings 방향감각을 잃게 하다, 어리둥절하게 하다

Right after he wakes up from a nap, Andrew is usually so *disoriented* that he bumps into things and isn't sure what time it is or where he is.
앤드류는 낮잠에서 깨고 난 직후엔 대체로 너무 어리둥절해서 여기저기 부딪히고 지금이 몇 시인지 여기가 어디인지도 잘 모른다.

The long subway ride got me so *disoriented* that when I got up to the street I felt completely lost.
지하철을 오래 탔더니 방향감각을 잃어버려서 거리로 나와 섰을 때 완전히 길을 잃은 것 같았다.

DISPARAGE [dispǽridʒ] v. to try to discredit something or lower its importance; to belittle or speak of something as inferior 비난하다; 얕보다, 깔보다

Environmental activists *disparage* the attempts of big business to avoid anti-pollution laws.
환경 운동가들은 반오염 법규를 기피하려는 대기업의 시도를 비난한다.

Ingrid is such a jealous person, she tries to *disparage* everyone else's work to make herself feel better about her own.
잉그리드는 질투심이 너무 심해서, 다른 사람의 작품을 모조리 헐뜯어 스스로 자기 것이 더 낫다고 생각하려 든다.

DISPARATE [díspərət/dispǽ-] adj. completely different 완전히 다른

When the cook found out that people from India, Ireland, Italy, and Israel were coming to the dinner, she was concerned that she wouldn't be able to come up with a menu to please their *disparate* tastes.
요리사는 인도, 아일랜드, 이탈리아 그리고 이스라엘 출신의 사람들이 저녁 식사를 하러 온다는 얘길 듣자, 그들의 각기 다른 입맛을 만족시켜 줄 메뉴를 생각 해내지 못할 거라며 걱정했다.

It's unusual to find someone with the *disparate* experiences of metal welding, professional balloon sculpting, and accounting on his resumé.
이력서에 금속 용접, 전문적인 풍선 모형 만들기, 회계라는 전혀 다른 경력을 기재한 사람을 찾기란 흔한 일이 아니다.

DISPASSIONATE [dispǽʃənət] adj. not affected by emotions 감정적이 아닌, 냉정한

Child custody cases are difficult to decide, even for the most *dispassionate* judge.
자녀 양육권 문제에 관한 소송은 가장 냉정한 판사에게조차 판결 내리기가 어렵다.

The reporter wrote a *dispassionate* story about the mass murderer's gruesome death in the electric chair.
기자는 집단 살인범이 전기의자에서 섬뜩하게 사형 당한 데 대한 냉정한 글을 썼다.

DISREGARD [dìsrigáːrd] v. to ignore or pay no attention to 무시하다, 신경 쓰지 않다

If you choose to *disregard* the posted speed limit, you should be prepared to get a speeding ticket.
게시되어 있는 속도제한을 무시한다면 과속 딱지를 떼일 각오를 해야 한다.

We *disregarded* the flash flood warning and wound up having to leave our car and run for high land as the street filled with water.
우린 돌발 홍수 경고를 무시했다가 결국 거리에 물이 가득 찼을 때 차를 버리고 고지로 뛰어가야 했다.

DISSENT [disént] n. disagreement 의견 차이, 이의

Until the bombing of Pearl Harbor, there was *dissent* in America over becoming involved in the war with Japan.
진주만 폭격이 있기 전까지는 일본과의 전쟁에 개입할 것인가를 두고 미국 내에서 의견 차이가 있었다.

The demonstrators held up signs expressing their *dissent* with the government's civil rights policy.
시위자들은 정부의 민권 정책에 대해 이의를 나타내는 표지판을 들고 있었다.

DIVERSE [divə́ːrs/dáivəːrs/daivə́ːs] adj. different; of various kinds 다른; 다양한 종류의

The best way to stay healthy is to get plenty of exercise and make sure your diet is made up of *diverse* foods.
건강을 유지하는 최선책은 운동을 많이 하고 반드시 다양한 종류의 음식을 섭취하는 것이다.

My taste in music is *diverse*; I like everything from country to rock to classic.
내 음악 취향은 다양해. 컨트리 음악에서부터 록음악, 그리고 클래식에 이르기까지 모두 좋아하지.

DOGMATIC [dɔ(ː)gmǽtik/dɑg-] adj. characterized by holding to certain beliefs or principles in an arrogant or stubborn way 독단적인

Pat spent so much of her time working for women's rights that she became rather *dogmatic* about it, and started calling all men sexist.
패트는 너무 많은 시간을 여성의 권리를 위해 일하다 보니 상당히 독단적이 되어, 모든 남자들을 성차별주의자라고 부르기 시작했다.

Copernicus, a Polish astronomer of the 1500s, believed the earth revolved around the sun, but his theory upset and enraged the *dogmatic* priests who had believed for hundreds of years that it was the other way around.
1500년대의 폴란드 천문학자였던 코페르니쿠스는 지구가 태양 주위를 돈다고 믿었지만, 그의 이론은 수백 년 동안을 그 반대라고 믿어 왔던 독단적인 성직자들을 당황하게 하고 화나게 했다.

DOMAIN [douméin/də-] n. an area of control or authority; a field in which someone is skilled 영토, 세력 범위; 능숙한 분야

The count's *domain* stretched from the Transylvanian mountains to the shores of Lake Blud.
백작의 영토는 트란실바니아 산맥에서부터 블러드 호의 기슭까지 뻗쳐 있었다.

"You're in luck!" cried Ernie the fix-it man. "Broken vacuum cleaners are in my *domain*."

"참 운이 좋네요" 만능 수리공 어니가 소리쳤다. "망가진 진공청소기는 제 전문이거든요."

DON [dɑn/dɔn] v. to put on (clothes) 입다, 쓰다

Cowboy Jake *donned* his hat and vest, kissed Maggie good-bye, and rode off into the sunset.

카우보이 제이크는 모자를 쓰고 조끼를 입은 다음 매기에게 작별의 키스를 하고는 일몰 속으로 말을 타고 갔다.

DORMITORY [dɔ́ːrmətɔ̀ːri/-tri] n. a residence hall with living facilities for many people 기숙사

Oliver stayed in the *dormitory* on campus his first year in college, but moved to an apartment off-campus when he got tired of having to walk all the way down the hall to use the bathroom.

올리버는 대학 1학년 때 학교 기숙사에 있었는데, 화장실을 쓰려면 복도를 한참 걸어가야 하는 것에 짜증이 나 학교 밖의 아파트로 이사했다.

DOTE [dout] v. to show excessive love or fondness 애지중지하다, 홀딱 빠지다

We tried to tell Willie that he was making a fool of himself by *doting* on Samantha so much, but he just shrugged and went off to buy her another dozen roses.

우린 윌리에게, 그가 사만다에게 그렇게 홀딱 빠져서 스스로 바보 노릇을 하고 있는 거라고 말하려고 했지만, 그는 그저 어깨를 으쓱하더니 그녀에게 줄 또 다른 장미다발을 사겠다며 나가 버렸다.

Lisa absolutely *doted* on her pony, Princess.

리사는 그녀의 조랑말 프린세스를 애지중지했다.

DUB [dʌb] v. to make someone a knight by tapping him on the shoulder with a sword; to nickname (누군가의 어깨를 칼로 가볍게 치고) 나이트 작위를 주다; 별명을 붙이다

Sir Laurence Olivier was *dubbed* by Queen Elizabeth II.

로렌스 올리비어 경은 엘리자베스 2세 여왕에게 나이트 작위를 받았다.

The dog was named Theodore, but Ralph *dubbed* him "Hog" because of his fondness for bacon.

개의 이름은 테오도르였지만, 랄프는 그에게 베이컨을 좋아한다고 해서 "돼지"라는 별명을 붙였다.

DUBIOUS [djúːbiəs/dúː-] adj. doubtful; inclined to doubt; questionable 의심스러운; 의심을 품는, 믿지 못하는

Dad seemed *dubious* about letting me go on the field trip to the state prison.

아빠는 날 주 교도소로 견학을 보내는 데 마음을 못 놓으시는 것 같았다.

Arthur was excited about his investment in Here Today Reality – he was sure he would triple his money in just a few months – but the whole set-up looked *dubious* to me.

아서는 'Here Today Reality'에 투자를 하고선 흥분했고, 몇 달만 지나면 자신의 돈이 세 배로 불어날 거라 장담했지만, 그런 장사꾼들이 하는 짓 전부가 나에게는 의심스러워 보였다.

DUPE [djuːp/duːp] v. to fool or trick or n. someone who is tricked 속이다 / 속는 사람

Thousands of people were *duped* into buying "gravity boots" because the ads promised that by hanging themselves upside down for an hour a day they could stop the aging process.

수천 명의 사람들이 속아서 "중력 부츠"를 구입했는데, 광고에서 하루에 한 시간 동안 거꾸로 매달려 있으면 노화 진행을 막을 수 있다고 장담했기 때문이다.

Carl was just a *dupe* the bombers used to unknowingly bring the briefcase full of dynamite aboard the plane.

칼은 다이너마이트가 가득 찬 서류 가방을 모르는 채로 비행기에 들고 타게 만들려고 폭파범들이 이용한 '밥'에 불과했다.

DUPLICATE [djúːplikət/duː-] v. to make a copy of; to do again or repeat   복사하다; 반복하다

The artist was asked to *duplicate* Leonardo Da Vinci's masterpiece, "La Gioconda."
화가는 레오나르도 다 빈치의 걸작 "모나리자"를 복제해 달라는 부탁을 받았다.

Scientists have to *duplicate* their experiments in order to make sure their results are accurate.
과학자들은 그들의 실험 결과의 정확성을 기하기 위해 실험을 반복해서 해야 한다.

DURABLE [djúərəbl/dú-] adj. sturdy; tough; lasting   튼튼한; 오래 가는

"I just can't find jeans that are *durable* enough for Tony," whined Mrs. Vance. "He wears them out as fast as I can buy them."
밴스 부인은 푸념했다. "토니가 입을 만한 튼튼한 진바지를 못 찾겠어요. 그 앤 바지를 사주자마자 해지게 만들거든요."

The doghouse Dad built wasn't the most stylish structure, but it was *durable* enough to withstand ten years of rain, heat, and snow.
아빠가 지은 개집은 그리 멋진 건조물은 아니었지만, 10여년 정도 비와 열과 눈을 견뎌 낼 만큼 튼튼했다.

DUSK [dʌsk] n. that point in the evening just before dark, when the sky has almost gone black; near darkness   어스름, 황혼

Mom told us to be home by *dusk*.
엄마는 우리에게 해가 지기 전에 집에 들어오라고 했다.

I could barely see the raccoon in the forest at *dusk*.
해질녘 숲 속에서 그 미국 너구리를 간신히 볼 수 있었다.

E

EARMARK [íərmɑ̀ːrk] v. to set aside for a certain purpose 특정 용도에 지정하다

The funds raised by the bake sale were *earmarked* for new uniforms for the school band.
집에서 구운 케이크 판매로 거두어진 기금은 학교 밴드의 새 유니폼을 맞추는 비용으로 지정됐다.

Lyle had *earmarked* the money he won in the lottery for a down payment on a private jet.
라일은 복권 당첨으로 번 돈을 개인용 제트기의 계약금으로 떼 놓았다.

EARNEST [ə́ːrnist] adj. showing seriousness and sincerity 진지한, 진심인

Mark showed an *earnest* desire to patch things up with his brother, who hadn't spoken to him in five years.
마크는 5년 동안 말을 안하고 지낸 남동생과 관계를 수습하려는 진지한 바람을 보여주었다.

The kids made an *earnest* attempt to train the stray dog, but finally had to admit that it would never make a good pet.
아이들은 길 잃은 개를 열심히 훈련시켜 보려고 했지만, 결국엔 좋은 애완견이 되지는 못할 거라고 인정해야 했다.

EAVESDROP [íːvzdrɑ̀p/-drɔ̀p] v. to listen secretly to a private conversation 엿듣다

Tommy hid in the closet to *eavesdrop* on the conversation his parents were having about what to get him for his birthday.
토미는 벽장 속에 숨어서 자기 생일 선물로 무엇을 사줄지에 대해 부모님이 나누고 있는 대화를 엿들었다.

Ilsa caught her sister with her ear against the bathroom wall, *eavesdropping* on the telephone conversation their brother was having in the next room.
일자는 오빠가 옆방에서 통화하는 내용을 엿들으면서, 여동생의 귀를 잡아 욕실 벽에 댔다.

EBB [eb] v. to fade away; to flow back 사라지다; 조수가 빠지다

Only after the high tides from the storm began to *ebb* were we able to figure out how much damage had been caused.
폭풍으로 인한 만조가 빠지기 시작한 이후에야 우린 얼마나 많은 피해가 발생했는지 알아낼 수 있었다.

As the day dragged on and his strength began to *ebb*, the marathon runner began to wonder what point there was in running twenty-six miles when he had a perfectly good car.
낮은 지루하게 계속되고 힘은 빠지기 시작하자, 마라톤 주자는 자기에게는 완벽하게 좋은 차가 있는데 26마일을 달린다는 것이 무슨 의미가 있는지 의아해지기 시작했다.

ECCENTRIC [ikséntrik/ek-] adj. odd or out of the ordinary in appearance, behavior, or action   별난, 평범하지 않은

Mr. Farmer was pretty normal except for his *eccentric* habit of dressing in a long black robe and wizard's hat, and riding his motorcycle through town early in the morning.
파머 씨는 길고 검은 겉옷과 마법사 모자 차림으로 이른 아침 오토바이를 몰고 마을을 다니는 괴상한 버릇만 빼고는 아주 정상이었다.

We all complimented the hat Susie had made out of staples and empty toilet paper rolls, but in truth we thought it was kind of *eccentric*.
수지가 스테이플러 알과 다 쓴 화장실용 두루마리 화장지로 만든 모자를 보고 모두 칭찬을 했지만, 사실 우린 좀 괴상하다고 생각했다.

ECSTASY [ékstəsi] n. overwhelming joy   무아경, 황홀경

Oliver was in *ecstasy* over the fancy dessert selection at the restaurant.
올리버는 식당에서 신기하고 맛있는 디저트를 보고 황홀했다.

Marisa Tomei was in *ecstasy* over winning an Oscar for her role in *My Cousin Vinny*.
마리사 토메이는 '내 사촌 비니' 에서의 역으로 오스카상을 받고 좋아서 어쩔 줄 몰랐다.

[Note] The adjective form of ecstasy is *ecstatic* [ekstǽtik].
형용사는 ecstatic

- Cole was *ecstatic* when he found out that he had passed chemistry.
  코울은 화학 시험을 통과했다는 사실을 알고 황홀할 지경이었다.

EGO [íːgou/égou] n. awareness of yourself as an independent person; self-confidence, sometimes to the point of arrogance   자아; 자부, 자만

Babies are very attached to their mothers because they have not yet developed *egos*.
아기들은 아직 자아가 개발되지 않았기 때문에 엄마에게 강하게 애착한다.

The little boy hurt my *ego* by saying my new hair-do made me look like Ronald McDonald.
꼬마 남자애가 내 새로운 머리 모양을 보고 로널드 맥도널드 같다고 말하면서 내 자존심에 상처를 줬다.

Even though everyone thinks he's a brilliant piano teacher, I had to quit taking lessons from Mr. Legato because his *ego* was so huge he would only let me play music he had written himself.
모두들 레가토 씨가 훌륭한 피아노 교사라고 생각하지만, 난 그에게 레슨 받는 걸 그만두어야 했는데, 그의 자만심이 너무 대단해 자기가 작곡한 곡만 연주하라고 시켰기 때문이다.

ELOQUENT [éləkwənt] adj. having the power of forceful, persuasive, or elegant speech or writing; marked by persuasive or masterful expression   능변인; 설득력 있는

Martin Luther King, Jr. was an *eloquent* leader in the civil rights movement who gained support for his cause through his speeches and actions.
마틴 루터 킹 주니어는 민권 운동의 설득력 있는 지도자로, 연설과 행동을 통해 자신의 주장에 대한 지지를 얻었다.

Abraham Lincoln's "Gettysburg Address," given to honor the soldiers who died in the Battle of Gettysburg, is one of the most *eloquent* speeches in American history.
아브라함 링컨이 게티즈버그 전투에서 전사한 군인들을 기리기 위해 했던 "게티즈버그 연설" 은 미국 역사에서 가장 설득력 있는 연설 중 하나다.

ELUDE [ilúːd] v. to escape or avoid through skill or cunning; to escape the understanding   교묘하게 피하다; 이해되지 않다

The spy *eluded* his attackers by cleverly disguising himself as former British Prime Minister Margaret Thatcher.
스파이는 전 영국 수상 마가렛 대처로 교묘하게 변장함으로써 공격자들을 피했다.

Yvette was winking and gesturing at her father to let him know he had a long strip of toilet paper stuck to his shoe, but he just stared at her and said, "I'm afraid the meaning of all that head jerking *eludes* me, dear."

이베트는 아버지에게 신발에 화장실 휴지 긴 조각이 붙어 있다는 걸 알려주려고 윙크를 하고 몸짓을 했지만, 아버지는 그녀를 빤히 쳐다보고는 "머리를 홱 움직이는 게 다 무슨 뜻인지 모르겠구나, 얘야." 라고 말했다.

Elmer *eluded* his creditors by always answering the phone with a thick Hungarian accent and pretending not to understand English.

엘머는 항상 심한 헝가리 억양으로 전화를 받고 영어를 모르는 척함으로써 채권자들을 피했다.

EMBARGO [imbáːrgou/em-] n. an order by a government forbidding the shipment of certain goods or all goods to another country   출항 금지, 통상 정지

The U.S. trade *embargo* on Iraq is causing the common people to go without food and medicine, while the leader of the country still lives in high style.

이라크에 대한 미국의 수출입 제제 조치는, 국가 지도자는 여전히 호화로운 생활을 하는 가운데 일반 국민들만 식약품 없이 지내도록 만들고 있다.

In the 1980s, many countries used trade *embargos* on South Africa to compel that country to give up its racist practices.

1980년대에는 많은 나라들이 인종차별 관행을 포기하도록 강요하기 위해 남아프리카에 통상 정지 명령을 이용했다.

EMERGE [imə́ːrdʒ] v. to rise up (from under water, usually); to come forth or come into existence   (물 밖으로) 올라오다; 나타나다, 드러나다

The divers finally *emerged* from the dark waters after several hours of looking for the sunken treasure supposedly left by the pirate known as "Swamp Rat."

잠수부들은 "늪 쥐"라고 알려진 해적이 두고 간 것으로 추정되는 가라앉은 보물을 찾느라 몇 시간을 보낸 뒤 마침내 어두운 물 밖으로 나왔다.

Eleanor Roosevelt *emerged* as a strong political force in her own right.

엘리노어 루즈벨트는 자신의 권리로 강력한 정치적 힘을 드러냈다.

After repeated questioning and threats, the truth about how all the pots got covered in melted plastic began to *emerge*.

계속적인 심문과 협박 후에 어떻게 그 많은 돈 전부가 녹은 플라스틱 속에 감추어져 있는지에 대한 진실이 드러나기 시작했다.

ENDORSE [indɔ́ːrs/en-] v. to give approval or support   찬성하다, 지지하다

The school board does not *endorse* the use of physical punishment.

교육 위원회는 체벌을 가하는 것에 찬성하지 않는다.

Texas billionaire Ross Perot *endorsed* Bill Clinton during the 1992 presidential election.

텍사스의 백만장자 로스 페로는 1992년 대통령 선거 때 빌 클린턴을 지지했다.

Celebrities are often used to *endorse* products in television commercials.

유명 인사들은 종종 텔레비전 광고에 나와 상품을 선전하는 데 이용된다.

ENGROSS [ingróus/en-] v. to absorb the complete attention of   집중시키다, 몰두시키다

At first, Marlon didn't want to watch the nature show about the insect world, but he was soon *engrossed* by the close-ups of a spider sucking the blood out of a fly.

처음에 말론은 곤충 세계에 대한 자연 다큐멘터리물을 보고 싶지 않았는데, 파리의 피를 빨아먹는 거미의 근접 촬영을 보고 이내 푹 빠져들었다.

Valerie was so *engrossed* by the detective novel she was reading, she didn't even notice that the kids she was supposed to be babysitting were setting fire to the curtains.

발레리는 탐정소설을 읽는 데 너무 열중해서 봐주기로 한 애들이 커튼에 불을 지르고 있는 것도 몰랐다.

ENIGMA [inígmə] n. a person or occurrence that is puzzling or hard to explain 수수께끼

The disappearance of Amelia Earhart's airplane over the Pacific Ocean has remained an *enigma* for almost sixty years.
에밀리아 이어하트의 비행기가 태평양 상공에서 실종된 것은 거의 60년 동안 수수께끼로 남아 있다.

Mr. Jones is a bit of an *enigma* — either he doesn't remember his past, or he refuses to tell any of us about it.
존스 씨는 좀 수수께끼 같은 인물이다. 자신의 과거를 기억하지 못하는 건지 우리에게 얘기를 안 하려는 건지 모르겠다.

How the ancient monument of Stonehenge was made is an *enigma*.
고대 유적인 스톤헨지가 어떻게 세워졌는지는 수수께끼다.

ENSUE [insú:/en-] v. to come after; to result from 뒤이어 일어나다; ~이 결과로 일어나다

When the manager told the crowd that supermodel Cindy Crawford would not be appearing at the bookstore to sign her latest calendar, a riot *ensued*.
신디 크로포드가 최근 자신이 모델로 나온 달력에 사인을 하러 서점에 오기로 한 것이 취소됐다고 매니저가 군중에게 말하자 소동이 뒤따랐다.

"We must not let anger *ensue* from our defeat," said the coach. "We must be good sports."
코치가 말했다. "우린 졌다고 해서 화를 내서는 안 된다. 우린 패배를 인정할 줄 아는 신사가 돼야한다."

EN ROUTE [à:n rú:t] adv. on the way 도중에

The car ran out of gas *en route* to the fishing hole.
낚시터로 가는 중 차의 기름이 떨어졌다.

We'll pick up some chips and ice cream *en route* to the party.
우리가 파티에 가는 길에 포테이토칩과 아이스크림을 좀 사 갈게.

ENVY [énvi] n. jealousy over someone else's possessions or accomplishments or v. to be jealous of someone else's possessions or accomplishments 질투 / 질투하다

When I saw Anne's beautiful new car I was filled with *envy*.
앤의 근사한 새 차를 보았을 때 난 질투심에 휩싸였다.

I don't *envy* famous people because everybody wants something from them and they can't go anywhere without being chased by photographers.
난 유명인들이 부럽지 않아. 모두들 그들에게서 뭔가를 얻으려 하고, 어디엘 가든 사진기자들이 쫓아다니잖아.

EPHEMERAL [ifémərəl] adj. lasting a very short time 명이 짧은, 순식간의

Bilbo enjoyed the *ephemeral* beauty of his garden at twilight.
빌보는 황혼녘에 정원의 순간적인 아름다움을 즐겼다.

For Ned, Yolanda was nothing but an *ephemeral* attraction, a short and sweet summer romance — but Yolanda was convinced that Ned was the man she would marry.
네드에게 있어 올란다는 그저 잠깐 동안의 매력으로, 짧고 달콤한 여름의 로맨스에 불과했지만, 올란다는 네드가 결혼할 만한 남자라고 확신했다.

EQUILIBRIUM [ì:kwəlíbriəm/ék-] n. balance or stability 평형, 안정

The medicine Walt was taking affected his *equilibrium*, making it difficult for him to walk.
월트가 복용하는 약이 그의 평형감각에 영향을 줘서 걷는 것을 힘들게 만들었다.

Husbands and wives keep *equilibrium* in their relationships by sharing household chores.
남편들과 아내들은 집안일을 나눠 함으로써 안정된 관계를 지속시킨다.

The stock market crash of 1929 upset the country's financial *equilibrium* for over ten years.
1929년 주식시장의 대폭락은 10년 이상 나라의 재정 안정을 뒤흔들어 놓았다.

ERADICATE [irǽdəkèit] v. to wipe out; destroy completely   뿌리째 뽑다; 박멸하다

I believe Dad would stop at nothing to *eradicate* the stink-weed in our yard.
아빠는 우리 마당에서 악취나는 풀을 뿌리 뽑기 위해서라면 어떤 것도 주저하지 않을 것이다.

Genghis Khan refused to stop fighting until the enemy army was completely *eradicated*.
징기스칸은 적군이 완전히 박멸될 때까지 싸움을 멈추지 않으려 했다.

ESSENCE [ésns] n. the basic, necessary part of something; the thing that makes it what it is   본질; 실체

"Good music is the *essence* of a successful party," claimed the DJ.
DJ는 주장했다. "좋은 음악은 성공적인 파티의 본질이에요."

"The *essence* of good eggnog is plenty of nog, and very little egg," insisted Mrs. Tippler, rather confusingly.
티플러 부인은 좀 헷갈리게 강조했다. "좋은 에그노그의 본질은 충분한 노그와 아주 약간의 달걀이에요."

ESTIMATE [éstəmèit] v. to make a rough calculation or [éstəmət/-mèit] n. a rough calculation   어림하다, 추정하다 / 어림, 견적

Dan *estimated* that dinner for four at Taco Fandango would cost about thirty-five dollars.
댄은 타코 판당고에서 네 명이 저녁 식사를 하려면 35달러쯤 들겠다고 어림잡았다.

The mechanic gave me a written *estimate* of what it would cost to repair the brakes on my car.
정비사는 내 차의 브레이크를 수리하려면 얼마나 들지에 대해 견적서를 써 주었다.

ETIQUETTE [étikit/-kèt] n. the accepted rules of polite behavior   에티켓, 예의범절

According to Malaysian *etiquette*, it is very rude to expose the soles of your feet to another person.
말레이시아인의 에티켓에 따르면 다른 사람에게 발바닥을 드러내는 것은 대단한 실례다.

Good *etiquette* requires you to send a thank-you note if someone has given you a gift or done you a special favor.
누군가 당신에게 선물을 주었거나 특별한 호의를 베풀었다면 감사의 편지를 보내는 것이 좋은 에티켓입니다.

Thirty years ago, *etiquette* required men to stand up whenever a woman entered a room or came to a table, and remain standing until she was seated.
30년 전의 에티켓으로는, 여자가 방에 들어오거나 테이블로 다가올 때면 언제나 남자는 일어서야 하고, 여자가 앉을 때까지 그대로 서 있어야 했다.

EUPHONY [júːfəni] n. pleasant sounds (usually in speech or writing, a pleasant sounding of words)   듣기 좋은 음조

People said Mike Donohue had the gift of the gab because of the *euphony* of his speech.
사람들은 마이크 도노후가 말할 때의 듣기 좋은 음조 덕에 말재주를 가졌다고 말했다.

Many people rely on the *euphony* of the poetry of Keats to win their sweethearts.
많은 사람들은 연인의 마음을 사로잡기 위해 키이츠 시의 아름다운 음조에 의존한다.

EVADE [ivéid] v. to escape or get around something through cleverness 교묘하게 피하다

Trudy tried to *evade* her parents' questions about her grades by changing the subject whenever they brought it up.
트루디는 부모님이 성적 문제를 꺼낼 때마다 주제를 바꾸면서 질문을 피하려고 애썼다.

During the Vietnam War, many men *evaded* the draft by moving to Canada.
베트남 전쟁 동안 많은 남자들이 징병을 피해 캐나다로 이사했다.

EXCAVATE [ékskəvèit] v. to dig out, remove by digging out, or form a hole by digging 파내다, 파서 구멍을 만들다

When Joey found a dinosaur bone behind his house, scientists came and *excavated* the entire back yard, looking for any more prehistoric remains.
조이가 집 뒤에서 공룡뼈를 발견했을 때 과학자들이 와서는 뒤뜰 전체를 파내 선사시대의 유물을 더 찾으려 했다.

A huge lot behind the hotel was *excavated* to make room for an Olympic-size swimming pool.
호텔 뒤편의 거대한 부지가 올림픽 경기장 만한 수영장을 만들기 위해 파헤쳐졌다.

EXCEPTION [iksépʃən] n. an instance of not sticking to rules or conditions; someone or something for whom rules or conditions are not applied or do not apply 예외; 예외가 되는 것 혹은 사람

"I don't usually eat dessert." Madge claimed, "but since it's my birthday, I'll make an *exception* and have the chocolate cake."
매지는 말했다. "난 보통은 디저트 안 먹지만, 오늘은 내 생일이니까 예외로 초콜릿 케이크를 먹겠어."

Most people think that lizards aren't very lovable, but my pet iguana Bobo is an *exception*.
대부분의 사람들은 도마뱀이 그리 매력적이지 못하다고 생각하지만, 내 애완용 이구아나 보보는 예외다.

EXCURSION [ikskə́:rʒən/-ʃən] n. a short trip made for fun or a certain purpose 짧은 여행, 소풍

We stuck to the main highways for most of our cross-country drive, but we made an *excursion* to Memphis to see Graceland, the former home of Elvis Presley.
우린 국토 횡단 드라이브의 대부분을 주요 간선도로로 달렸지만, 엘비스 프레슬리의 고향 그레이스랜드를 보기 위해 멤피스에 잠깐 들렀다.

Val was from a small town in Missouri, but she was always dressed in the latest fashions because she and her mother went on monthly shopping *excursions* to St. Louis.
밸은 미주리의 작은 마을 출신이었지만 항상 최신 유행의 옷을 입었는데, 그녀와 엄마가 매달 세인트루이스로 쇼핑 여행을 다녔기 때문이다.

EXHAUST [igzɔ́:st] v. to use up or wear out completely 다 써 버리다, 기진맥진하게 하다

The overuse of cars will eventually *exhaust* the world's supply of fossil fuels.
자동차의 과도한 이용은 결국 전 세계 화석연료의 비축량을 바닥낼 것이다.

"All this bickering is beginning to *exhaust* my patience, boys," said Dad.
"이런 말다툼이 내 인내력을 소모시키기 시작하는구나, 얘들아." 아빠가 말했다.

[Note] People often say "*exhausted*" [igzɔ́:stid] to mean very tired.
'아주 피곤한' 의 의미로 exhausted를 쓴다.

- He was *exhausted* after the football game.
  그는 미식축구 경기가 끝난 후 기진맥진했다.

- After a long week at work, I'm too *exhausted* to go out.
  기나긴 한 주의 근무가 끝나면 난 너무 지쳐서 외출도 할 수 없다.

EXODUS [éksədəs] n. the departure of a lot of people   대이동

The story in the newspaper about a leak at our town's nuclear power plant caused an *exodus*.
신문에 우리 마을 원자력 발전소에서 방사능이 누출되었다는 기사가 실리자 사람들이 대거 이사 했다.

Neighboring countries had a hard time providing shelter for the *exodus* of refugees fleeing the war in Rwanda.
인접 국가들은 르완다의 내전을 피해서 대이동하는 망명자들에게 피난처를 제공하느라 힘이 들었다.

EXPEDIENT [ikspí:diənt] adj. suitable for a certain purpose; serving one's own desires   편리한; 사리를 꾀하는

The swimmer decided that cutting her hair very short was more *expedient* than wearing a swimming cap or having to wash and style it all the time.
그 수영하는 사람은 수영 모자를 쓰거나 매번 빨아서 스타일을 맞추어야 하는 것보다 머리를 아주 짧게 자르는 것이 더 편하겠다고 결론 내렸다.

Oscar was not a popular manager because when it came time to make decisions, he always did what was *expedient* rather than what was best for the department in the long run.
오스카는 인기있는 부장이 못됐는데, 결정을 내릴 때가 되면 긴 안목으로 봐서 부서에 가장 이로울 일보다는 자신에게 유리한 일을 했기 때문이다.

EXPEDITE [ékspədàit] v. to speed up the progress of   진척시키다, 촉진시키다

Mr. Johnson's teaching assistant alphabetized the papers from all his classes in order to *expedite* the grading process.
존슨 씨의 조교는 채점 과정을 신속히 하기 위해 모든 수강생들의 시험지를 알파벳순으로 표시했다.

Paying by credit card often *expedites* the delivery of orders you make over the phone.
신용카드로 지불하면 전화로 주문한 물건의 배달이 빨라질 때가 있다.

EXPEDITION [èkspədíʃən] n. a trip made by a group for a purpose   목적을 가지고 단체로 떠나는 여행, 원정(대)

The explorer Ponce de Leon led an *expedition* to the Bimini Islands in search of the Fountain of Youth.
탐험가 퐁스 드 레옹은 젊음의 샘을 찾아 비미니 제도로 원정대를 이끌고 갔다.

Ernest went on a hunting *expedition* through northern Africa.
어니스트는 북 아프리카 전역으로 수렵 원정을 떠났다.

EXPLICIT [iksplísit] adj. clearly shown or said, with nothing left out   명백한, 적나라한

We weren't allowed to see the movie about the Salem witch trials in school because the scenes of women being burned at the stake were too *explicit*.
우리 학교에서는 수업시간에 살렘 마녀재판에 대한 영화를 못 보게 했는데, 여자들을 화형에 처하는 장면이 너무 적나라했기 때문이다.

Ronald is a good worker, but he doesn't really think for himself, so you have to give him *explicit* instructions.
로널드는 훌륭한 일꾼이지만, 스스로는 전혀 생각을 하지 않는다. 그러니 그에게는 분명한 지시를 내려 줘야 한다.

EXPLOIT [ikspl5it] v. to use something to the greatest advantage; to use selfishly or wrongly 최대한으로 이용하다; 부당하게 이용하다

Graham *exploited* the unlimited supply of blackberries on his land by starting a major blackberry shipping company.
그레이엄은 검은 딸기 선적 회사를 차려서 자신의 땅에서 나는 한없이 많은 검은 딸기를 최대한 활용했다.

Illegal immigrants are often *exploited* by companies that want very cheap labor and know they can control immigrants by threatening to send them back to their country.
불법 이민자들은, 아주 값싼 노동력을 원하고 고국으로 돌려보낸다고 협박하면 그들을 통제할 수 있다는 사실을 아는 회사들에게 흔히 착취를 당한다.

EXTOL [ikstóul] v. to praise very highly 격찬하다, 극구 칭찬하다

Joan of Arc, a young peasant girl who led the French into battle against the English and was burned at the stake for her trouble, was *extolled* for her courage and devotion to the church, and was declared a saint after her death.
프랑스 국민을 영국인과 맞서 싸우도록 이끌고 화형에 처해진 시골 소녀 잔 다르크는 용기와 교회에 대한 헌신으로 찬양받았고, 죽음 후 성인으로 추서되었다.

I saw a well-known senator on a late-night television show *extolling* the health benefits of turnip juice.
심야 TV쇼에서 유명한 상원 의원이 나와 순무 주스가 건강에 좋다며 극구 칭찬하는 걸 봤다.

EXTRAORDINARY [ikstrɔ́:rdənèri/ikstrɔ́:dənəri] adj. out of the ordinary; remarkable 이상한, 비상한; 주목할 만한, 두드러진

After the afternoon showers had ended, I saw the most *extraordinary* thing — a triple rainbow!
오후에 소나기가 그친 뒤 난 너무나 이상한 것, 바로 3중 무지개를 봤다!

Angie has the *extraordinary* ability to add up long columns of numbers in her head.
앤지는 머릿속으로 큰 숫자들을 덧셈하는 비상한 능력이 있다.

F

FACET [fǽsit]　n.　one way of looking at an issue or one piece of an issue; a flat surface on a cut gemstone　일면; 잘라진 보석의 한 면

> We must consider every *facet* of this problem before deciding what to do.
> 우리는 무엇을 할지 결정하기에 앞서 이 문제의 모든 면을 고려해야 한다.

> A marquise-shaped diamond has many *facets*, which make it glisten in the light.
> 보석 모양의 다이아몬드에는 여러 면이 있는데, 그래서 빛을 받으면 반짝거린다.

> Mike's quick temper is not one of the best *facets* of his personality.
> 마이크의 급한 성미는 그의 성격에서 그리 좋은 면은 아니다.

FACTION [fǽkʃən]　n.　a group within a larger group, usually a group that has interests or goals that aren't shared by the rest of the organization　도당, 당파

> One *faction* of the student council was in favor of starting a student strike, but the rest of us knew it wasn't a good idea.
> 학생회의 한 파는 학생들의 동맹파업을 시작하는 데 찬성했지만, 나머지는 좋은 생각이 아니란 걸 알고 있었다.

> The terrorist acts of a few violent *factions* have given the world a biased view of Islam.
> 소수의 폭력적 당파들의 테러 행위는 전 세계에 이슬람교에 대한 편견을 심어 주었다.

FALTER [fɔ́ːltər]　v.　to hesitate in action; to lose confidence or drive; to move unsteadily or stumble　주춤하다; 망설이다; 비틀거리다

> My faith in the accuracy of my car's speedometer began to *falter* after I got my third speeding ticket.
> 세 번째 과속 딱지를 떼인 후로 자동차 속도계의 정확성에 대한 믿음이 흔들렸다.

> The old professor *faltered* as he walked onto the stage to accept his award.
> 노교수는 수상하기 위해 무대 위를 걸어가던 중 비틀거렸다.

> Wilma's desire to become an ambassador *faltered* when she learned that only two percent of U.S. ambassadors are women.
> 대사가 되고자 하던 윌마의 소망은 미 대사 중 겨우 2퍼센트가 여성이라는 사실을 알게 되자 주춤하게 됐다.

FAMINE [fǽmin]　n.　a widespread, extreme shortage of food　식량 부족, 기근

> In the mid-1980s, a large group of popular musicians got together to raise money to help the victims of *famine* in Ethiopia.
> 1980년대 중반 유명한 대중 음악인들 다수가 에티오피아의 기근 희생자들을 돕기 위해 기금을 모으려고 한데 뭉쳤다.

The repeated failure of potato crops in Ireland in the 1840s led to what's known as the Irish potato *famine*, which caused many people to starve to death and led many others to leave their homeland to come to America.

1840년대 아일랜드에서 감자 흉작이 잇따르자 아일랜드 감자 기근이라 알려진 일이 일어났는데, 그 일로 인해 많은 사람들이 아사했고 다른 많은 이들은 고향을 떠나 미국땅으로 가야 했다.

FANATIC [fənǽtik]   n.   a person who is completely, unreasonably devoted to a cause, person, or belief
열광자, 광신자

Some people think the Buddhist monks who set themselves on fire to protest war are *fanatics*.
일부의 사람들은 전쟁에 저항하기 위해 자기 몸에 불을 지르는 불교 승려들을 광신자라고 생각한다.

When it comes to the New York Giants, Lee is a complete *fanatic*: he knows every player, goes to every game, and regularly fights with people who say the team will never make it to Super Bowl again.
뉴욕 자이언츠에 관해서라면 리가 완전히 골수팬이지. 모르는 선수가 없고, 매 경기마다 보러 가고, 그 팀이 다시는 슈퍼볼에 못 오를 거라고 말하는 사람하고는 죽어라고 싸우거든.

FATIGUE [fətíːg]   n.   extreme tiredness or   v.   to tire out   극도의 피로 / 피곤하게 하다

Tom digs ditches for a living, so *fatigue* usually keeps him from wanting to go out after work.
탐은 막노동을 해서 생계를 꾸리기 때문에 퇴근을 하면 너무 피곤한 나머지 대체로 어디 외출할 생각을 못한다.

After boxing up everything I owned, loading it into my car, driving for three days, then unloading everything in my new apartment, I felt very *fatigued*.
내 물건을 전부 상자에 담아 차에 실은 다음 3일 동안 차를 몰고 가서 새 아파트에 짐을 풀고 나자 난 너무 피곤했다.

FEIGN [fein]   v.   to pretend or give false appearance   가장하다, 꾸미다

Brian had found the mountain bike in his parents' closet a month before his birthday, but he *feigned* surprise when they gave it to him.
브라이언은 그의 생일 한 달 전에 부모님 옷장 속에서 산악자전거를 발견했지만, 부모님이 그것을 주셨을 때 놀라는 척했다.

Mary *feigned* a stomachache to get out of going to school.
메리는 학교에 안 가려고 배가 아픈 척했다.

FELINE [fíːlain]   adj.   cat-like   고양이 같은; 교활한, 음흉한

There was something *feline* and mysterious about her slanting green eyes.
그녀의 비스듬히 쳐다보는 초록 눈 속엔 뭔가 음흉하고 수수께끼 같은 것이 있었다.

My little sister has an almost *feline* ability to sneak up on people.
내 여동생은 거의 고양이처럼 몰래 사람들에게 다가간다.

FERVOR [fə́ːrvər/fə́ːvər]   n.   great warmth or strength of feeling   열정, 열렬

Our country's 200th anniversary was celebrated with patriotic *fervor*.
건국 2백 주년은 열렬한 애국심으로 경축되었다.

Even at a young age, Margaret showed great *fervor* when discussing the subject of women's rights.
마가렛은 어린 나이 때에도 여성의 권리에 대해 토론할 때면 대단한 열정을 보여주었다.

FEUD [fju:d] n. a bitter, sometimes long-lasting quarrel or v. to have a feud 불화, 숙원 / 반목하다

During the Middle Ages, the counts of Europe were constantly *feuding* with each other over land or money, probably because they had nothing better to do since television hadn't yet been invented.
중세 시대에 유럽의 백작들은 땅이나 돈을 두고 끊임없이 서로 다투었는데, 아마 텔레비전이 아직 발명되기 전이라 달리 할 일이 없었기 때문인 것 같다.

The Hatfields and McCoys had a famous family *feud* that lasted for generations.
햇필드 가와 맥코이 가의 여러 세대에 걸쳐 지속된 집안 간의 반목은 유명했다.

FICKLE [fíkl] adj. having changeable or inconstant feelings 변하기 쉬운, 변덕스러운

Loren is a *fickle* friend: one day she stands up for you, the next day she's gossiping behind your back.
로렌은 변덕스런 친구야. 하루는 네 편을 든다면, 다음 날엔 네 뒤에서 험담을 하고 있을 거야.

Don Juan was a famous Spaniard whose *fickle* heart and romantic skill let him from one love affair to another throughout his life.
돈 주앙은 변덕스런 마음과 연애 기술로 평생 동안 이 여자 저 여자와 관계를 가졌던 이름난 스페인 사람이었다.

FIDELITY [fidéləti/fai-] n. loyalty; faithfulness 충성; 성실

When a man and woman get married, they swear an oath of *fidelity* to each other.
남자와 여자가 결혼할 때엔 서로에게 충실할 것을 서약한다.

No one questioned the soldier's *fidelity* to his commanding officer.
그 군인이 자신의 지휘관에게 충성할 것을 의심하는 이는 아무도 없었다.

FINESSE [finés] n. delicacy and skill in performing a task 기교, 솜씨

The grandmother had enough *finesse* to change her sleeping grandson out of his clothes and into his pajamas without waking him up.
할머니는 자고 있는 손자를 깨우지 않고서 옷을 벗기고 잠옷을 입힐 수 있는 기교를 가지셨었다.

A good brain surgeon must have patience and *finesse*.
훌륭한 뇌 수술 전문의라면 인내심과 기교가 있어야 한다.

FLIMSY [flímzi] adj. weak; not effective; thin; light 연약한; 효과 없는; 얇은; 가벼운

The construction of those beach houses was so *flimsy*, it's no wonder they were torn apart by the first storm that hit them.
해변의 집들은 구조가 너무 취약해 첫 번째 폭풍이 강타했을 때 허물어진 건 당연하다.

Tanya, who was freezing to death in her *flimsy* evening gown, wished she'd checked the weather report before going out.
타냐는 얇은 이브닝 가운만 입고 추워서 얼어 죽을 것 같아, 나오기 전 일기예보를 봤어야 하는데 하며 후회했다.

FLIPPANT [flípənt] adj. disrespectful; showing a lack of seriousness 무례한; 경솔한

George used to anger his boss by passing notes and making *flippant* remarks during the weekly department meetings.
조지는 매주 부서 회의를 할 때면 쪽지를 돌리고 무례한 말을 하면서 상사를 열받게 하곤 했다.

"This is no time to be *flippant*, Vinnie," said Irene. "Losing the cable television will be the least of our worries if we don't get out of here before the hurricane hits."

아이린이 말했다. "경솔하게 행동할 시간이 없어요. 허리케인이 강타하기 전에 여기서 빠져나가지 않으면 우선 텔레비전을 못 보는 건 아무 것도 아니라구요."

FOE [fou] n. enemy 적, 원수

On the television show "Star Trek," the Klingons are the *foes* of Captain Kirk and his crew.
TV 프로 "스타트렉"을 보면 클링온은 커크 함장과 승무원들의 적이다.

In many of Arthur Conan Doyle's detective novels, Sherlock Holmes must match wits with his old *foe*, Professor Moriarty.
아서 코난 도일의 탐정소설을 여러 편 보면, 셜록 홈즈는 오랜 원수 모리아티 교수와 기지를 겨루게 된다.

Sugar and sticky desserts are the *foes* of healthy teeth.
설탕과 끈적거리는 디저트는 건강한 치아의 적이다.

FORBEARANCE [fɔːbɛ́ərəns/fɔːr-] n. restraint; tolerance 인내, 자제; 관용

I praised Hal for his *forbearance* in not punching the bully who was calling him names.
난 깡패가 자기에게 욕을 하는데도 주먹을 날리지 않은 할의 인내심을 칭찬해 주었다.

When the two kids were found guilty of stealing a car and running it into a tree, their parents begged the judge to show some *forbearance* by giving the boys a light sentence.
두 아이가 차를 훔쳐 몰고 가다 나무에 박은 것에 대해 유죄판결을 받았을 때, 그 부모들은 판사에게 관용을 베풀어 가벼운 선고를 내려 달라고 간청했다.

FORFEIT [fɔ́ːrfit] v. to give up a right or possession as a penalty for a mistake or offense (벌로서) 상실하다, (자격 등을) 잃다

We need at least eight players to show up before six o'clock, or we *forfeit* the softball game and the other team wins.
6시전에 최소한 8명의 선수가 나타나지 않으면, 우린 소프트볼 경기 출전 자격을 박탈당하고 다른 팀이 이기게 된다.

If he can't pay back his bank loan, the farmer will have to *forfeit* his land.
농부는 은행 융자를 상환하지 못하면 그의 땅을 차압당할 것이다.

FORGERY [fɔ́ːrdʒəri] n. a fake or copy or the act of making such a fake or copy 위조, 위조품

The theft at the art museum wasn't discovered for weeks, because the thieves had replaced the paintings they stole with clever *forgeries*.
미술관의 절도는 몇 주 동안 일어난 지도 몰랐었는데, 절도범들이 훔친 그림을 교묘한 위조 작품과 바꿔 놓았기 때문이다.

Izzy made a *forgery* of his report card and replaced all the Ds with Bs so he wouldn't get in trouble with his parents.
이지는 부모님에게 혼나지 않도록 성적표를 위조해 D를 모두 B로 바꾸어 놓았다.

FORGO [fɔːrgóu] v. to do without or give up ~없이 지내다, 포기하다

Barbara and Bernie decided to *forgo* their usual summer vacation so they could use the money to buy a motorcycle.
바바라와 버니는 오토바이 사는 데 돈을 쓰려고 매년 가던 여름휴가를 안 가기로 했다.

Uncle Evan had to *forgo* his after-dinner cigar because the restaurant didn't allow smoking of any kind.
이반 삼촌은 식후 담배를 포기해야 했는데, 식당에서 어떤 식의 흡연이든 금했기 때문이다.

FORSAKE [fəséik/fər-] v. to give up, leave, or renounce someone or something 버리다, 저버리다

No one could believe that Mr. Holden would *forsake* his wife and children to follow his dream of being a circus clown.
홀든 씨가 서커스 광대가 되겠다는 꿈을 좇아 아내와 아이를 버리려 한다는 것을 아무도 믿을 수 없었다.

Mrs. Richter said she wouldn't take her husband back unless he quit gambling and hanging around the pool halls and swore to *forsake* his sinful ways.
리히터 부인은 남편이 도박하는 것과 당구장에서 죽치는 것을 그만두고 죄짓는 길을 버리기로 맹세하지 않는 한 받아 주지 않겠다고 말했다.

FOUL [faul] adj. offensive to the senses; disgusting; unclean; evil 구역질나는; 불결한; 악랄한

There was a *foul* smell coming from Shawn's gym locker.
숀의 체육관 라커에서는 역겨운 냄새가 났다.

The mass murderer was sentenced to the electric chair for his *foul* crimes.
대량 학살자는 악랄한 범죄에 대해 전기의자 사형을 선고받았다.

Don't use *foul* language in front of your teacher.
선생님 면전에서 음란한 언어를 쓰지 마라.

FRAUD [frɔːd] n. a trick or other dishonest action used to gain something; an impostor or swindler 기만, 사기; 사기꾼, 협잡꾼

The woman who dressed as a nun and called herself "Sister Margaret" had managed to collect almost ten thousand dollars in donations for the so-called Holy Mother of Munificence orphanage, when it was discovered that the whole thing was a *fraud*, and that she was actually an escaped convict named Maggie "the Ax" McGill.
수녀 차림을 하고 자신을 "마가렛 수녀"라고 얘기한 여자가 소위 아낌없이 주는 성모마리아 고아원을 위해 만 달러 가까운 기부금을 모았는데, 알고 보니 그 모두가 사기였고, 실상 그녀는 탈주범으로 "도끼"라 불리는 매기 맥길이었다.

The government tries to protect citizens from *fraud* by monitoring advertisements to make sure false claims are not made.
정부는 허위 선전을 막기 위해 광고를 모니터하면서 시민들이 사기 당하지 않게 보호한다.

FRIGID [frídʒid] adj. very cold in temperature; lacking warmth of feeling; without enthusiasm 몹시 추운; 쌀쌀한; 냉담한, 무뚝뚝한

Dad's proposal that we get rid of the television so that we would all use our time more productively got a *frigid* response from the rest of the family.
아빠는 우리가 시간을 좀더 생산적으로 쓰기 위해 텔레비전을 없애자고 제안했는데, 나머지 가족의 반응은 냉담했다.

There was an unusual wave of *frigid* weather in late April last year.
작년 4월말에는 예년 같지 않게 한파가 몰려왔었다.

FUTILE [fjúːtl/-tail] adj. having no effect; useless 효과 없는; 무익한

The fly made several *futile* attempts to get out of the spider's web.
파리는 몇 차례 거미줄에서 빠져나오려고 해봤지만 소용이 없었다.

All our efforts to get the engine started again were *futile*: it was dead and we were stuck.
엔진에 다시 시동을 걸어 보려고 아무리 애써도 소용없었다. 엔진은 멈춰 버렸고 우린 꼼짝 할 수 없었다.

G

GALLANT [gǽlənt] adj. stylish and dashing; brave and noble   멋있고 당당한; 용감한

All the girls were shocked to see Pam, the class brain, with such a *gallant* escort at the prom.
학급의 수재인 팸이 댄스파티에 멋진 남자 파트너를 데리고 온 것을 보고 모든 여자아이들은 충격을 받았다.

The Polish people put up a *gallant* resistance to the much stronger German forces.
폴란드 국민들은 훨씬 더 강력한 독일군에 맞서 용감하게 저항했다.

GALLIVANT [gǽləvæ̀nt] v. to wander around looking for fun things to do   건들건들 돌아다니다

David was always out *gallivanting* instead of doing school work, so no one was surprised when he failed eighth grade.
데이빗은 언제나 학교 공부는 안 하고 건들거리며 나다녀서, 그가 8학년에서 낙제했을 때 아무도 놀라지 않았다.

GALLOWS [gǽlouz] n. a structure or framework with two uprights and a crossbeam, built for the purpose of executing people by hanging   교수대

As he stood on the *gallows* before being executed by the British, Nathan Hale said, "I only regret that I have but one life to lose for my country."
나단 헤일은 영국군에게 사형 당하기 전 교수대에 올랐을 때 "내 조국을 위해 내놓을 목숨이 단 하나 뿐이라는 게 안타까울 뿐이오."라고 말했다.

"You'd better get back on your horse and ride on," said the gambler to the gunfighter. "If the sheriff sees you here, you'll be swinging from the *gallows* by sundown."
"말에 올라 사라지는 게 좋을 거다." 도박사가 총잡이에게 말했다. "여기서 어정거리다가 보안관 눈에 띄면 일몰 즈음엔 교수대에 매달려 있게 될 테니까."

GAPE [geip/gæp] v. to stare with an open mouth   입을 벌리고 멍하니 쳐다보다

The audience *gaped* at the amazing performance of the trapeze artists.
관중들은 공중 그네 곡예사의 놀라운 공연에 입을 쩍 벌리고 바라봤다.

Tourists in New York City often *gape* at the strange people and sights they see on the streets.
뉴욕 시를 찾아온 관광객들은 거리에서 만나는 이상한 사람들과 광경에 입을 벌리고 쳐다볼 때가 많다.

GARNISH [gɑ́:rniʃ] v. to decorate, usually food   (주로 음식을) 장식하다

The cook *garnished* the plate of fish with bright lemon slices and parsley.
요리사는 생선 요리를 산뜻한 레몬 조각과 파슬리로 장식했다.

My mother *garnished* my birthday cake with strawberries and cream.
어머니는 내 생일 케이크를 딸기와 크림으로 꾸미셨다.

GAVEL [gǽvəl] n. small mallet used by a judge to call a court to order 망치, 의사봉

The judge pounded his *gavel* when a fight broke out in the courtroom.
판사는 법정에서 싸움이 일어나자 의사봉을 탕탕 두드렸다.

GENETIC [dʒənétik] adj. having to do with heredity or physical traits inherited from parents and relatives
유전적인

Our physical features — from the color of our eyes to our height — are largely decided by our *genetic* makeup.
눈동자의 색부터 키에 이르기까지 우리의 신체적 특징은 대개 유전적 기질로 결정된다.

Folks here in Harrisonburg think it must be something *genetic* that makes all the Clampett boys grow up to be plumbers.
여기 해리슨버그의 사람들은, 클램핏가 아이들이 모두 커서 배관공이 되는 것은 틀림없이 뭔가 유전적인 거라고 생각한다.

GENOCIDE [dʒénəsàid] n. the deliberate attempt to kill off an entire group of people 인종 말살

During World War II, the Nazis killed at least six million Jews — one of the most horrible acts of *genocide* in modern history.
제2차 세계대전 동안 나치는 최소 6백만 명의 유대인을 살해했는데, 이는 현대사에서 가장 끔찍한 인종 말살 중 하나다.

Many people consider Christopher Columbus a great explorer and a great man, but others point out that he and his men were guilty of the brutal *genocide* of the Arawak Indians, the friendly, peaceful natives that greeted him after his first journey across the Atlantic.
많은 이들은 크리스토퍼 콜럼버스가 위대한 탐험가이자 대단한 인물이라고 생각하지만, 어떤 이들은 첫 번째 대서양 횡단 여행을 마치고 찾아온 그를 반겨 주었던 친절하고 평화로운 원주민들, 즉 아라와크 인디언들을 그와 그 일행이 잔인하게 인종 말살한 죄가 있다고 지적한다.

GEYSER [gáizər/-sər] n. a hot spring in the earth that sprays boiling water and steam into the air 온천,
간헐천

Old Faithful is a famous *geyser* located in Yellowstone National Park.
올드페이스풀은 옐로우스톤 국립공원에 위치한 유명한 간헐천이다.

GHOSTWRITER [góustràitər] n. a person who writes something for another person, but who doesn't take credit for writing it 대필 작가

The basketball star hired a *ghostwriter* to write his life story.
그 농구 스타는 대필 작가를 고용해 자신의 자서전을 쓰게 했다.

Most presidents have *ghostwriters* who create their speeches.
대부분의 대통령에게는 그들의 연설문을 작성해 주는 대필 작가가 있다.

GLOAT [glout] v. to show great pleasure, sometimes in a mean-spirited or unkind way 아주 흡족해 하다,
(남의 불행을) 고소해 하다

Lydia *gloated* about her promotion so much that her co-workers began to hate her.
리디아는 승진한 것을 너무 흡족해 해서 동료들이 그녀를 미워하기 시작했다.

It's not good sportsmanship to *gloat* over your victories.
승리에 너무 만족하는 것은 훌륭한 운동가 정신이 아니다.

GLUTTON [glʌ́tn]   n. someone who eats way too much   대식가

When she found him with mustard all over his tie and his hand stuck in the candy machine, Marge decided she'd better duck out the back door before people found out that the *glutton* was her date.
마지는 넥타이에 겨자를 범벅한 채 사탕 기계 속에 손을 넣고 있는 그를 보고는, 그 먹보가 자기의 데이트 상대라는 걸 사람들이 알게 되기 전에 뒷문 밖으로 몸을 피해야겠다고 결심했다.

GOATEE [goutíː]   n. a small beard that doesn't cover the cheek area and is trimmed to a point below the chin   (턱밑의) 염소수염

Spike Lee has a *goatee*.
스파이크 리는 염소수염을 길렀다.

GORE [gɔːr]   v. to stab with a horn or tusk or   n. blood from a wound   뿔이나 엄니로 찌르다 / 상처에서 나온 피

The toreador was *gored* to death by the bull.
기마 투우사는 황소 뿔에 받혀 죽었다.

There's too much blood and *gore* in horror movies nowadays.
요즈음의 공포 영화에는 피 흘리는 장면이 너무 많이 나온다.

GORGE [gɔːrdʒ]   n. a narrow passage between high cliffs or   v. to stuff yourself with food or eat greedily   골짜기 / 포식하다, 게걸스럽게 먹다

Some of the oldest human remains known to scientists were found in Olduvai *Gorge*, in the African country of Tanzania.
과학자들에게 알려진 가장 오래된 사람들 유골의 일부가 탄자니아라는 아프리카 나라의 올두바이 골짜기에서 발견됐다.

After sticking to his diet for two months and losing fifteen pounds, Ira *gorged* himself on spaghetti and meatballs every night for a week, and gained every pound back.
이라는 2개월간 다이어트에 매달려 15파운드를 뺀 후, 일주일 동안 밤마다 스파게티와 미트볼을 정신없이 먹어 대더니 몸무게가 그대로 늘어났다.

GOUGE [gaudʒ]   v. to scoop out or cut out   파내다, 잘라 내다

Henrietta was suspended from school for trying to *gouge* out her classmate's eye with a ballpoint pen.
헨리에타는 볼펜으로 동급생의 눈을 후벼 파려고 하다가 정학 당했다.

The bandit used a stick to *gouge* out a little hole in the ground in which to bury his loot.
강도는 훔친 물건을 묻으려는 땅에 조그만 구멍을 파기 위해 막대기를 사용하였다.

GOUT [gaut]   n. a disease in which uric acid salts are deposited in the joints of legs, feet, and hands, causing pain and discomfort   통풍(痛風)

When you read old British novels, you will find many characters, usually rich old men, who complain of having *gout*.
오래된 영국 소설들을 읽으면 많은 인물을 만날 수 있는데, 으레 통풍에 걸려 투덜거리는 부유한 노인들이 나온다.

GRAVE [greiv]   adj. serious, somber; important; critical   엄숙한, 침울한; 중요한; 위험한

The *grave* expression on the doctor's face as he came out of the operating room told us that the news wasn't good.
의사가 수술실에서 나올 때 그 얼굴에 비친 심각한 표정은 좋지 않은 소식임을 말해 주었다.

"The situation is *grave*, guys," said Bob. "We're out of cheezy noodles already, and it isn't even halftime."

밥이 말했다. "상황이 심각해, 얘들아. 치즈 국수가 벌써 다 떨어졌어. 아직 반도 안 지났는데 말야."

[Note] the noun form of *grave* is *gravity* [grǽvəti].

명사형은 gravity

- No one understood the *gravity* of Lyle's condition until doctors told us that even though he seemed healthy, he was slowly going blind.
  라일이 건강해 보이지만 서서히 시력을 잃어 가고 있다고 의사가 말해 줬을 때에야 우린 그의 상태가 심각하다는 걸 알았다.

GRIEVE [gri:v] v. to cause to be sad or to feel sad; to mourn   몹시 슬프게 하다; 슬퍼하다

The news of his parents' planned divorce *grieved* Paul terribly.
폴은 부모님이 이혼하실 계획이라는 소식에 너무나 슬퍼했다.

"So what if you lost the tennis championship?" said Mo the coach. "There's no sense *grieving* like this."
코치인 모가 말했다. "네가 테니스 선수권을 잃었다 하더라도 그게 무슨 대단한 일이냐? 이렇게 한탄하는 건 무분별한 일이야."

GRIMACE [gríməs/griméis] n. a twisted sort of expression on the face caused by pain or disgust or v. to make a grimace   찌푸린 얼굴 / 얼굴을 찌푸리다

I tried to sing "Happy Birthday" to my boyfriend, but I was so off-key he *grimaced* in spite of himself.
난 남자 친구에게 생일 축하 노래를 불러 주려 했는데, 음정이 너무 맞지 않아서 남자 친구가 자기도 모르게 얼굴을 찌푸렸다.

Daniel tried a bite of liver in order to please his mother, but as soon as it hit his tongue, his face twisted up into a *grimace* and he had to spit it out.
대니얼은 어머니를 기쁘게 해 드리려고 간을 한 입 먹어 보려 했지만, 간이 혀에 닿자마자 얼굴이 찌푸려졌고 뱉어낼 수밖에 없었다.

GROSS [grous] adj. without deductions; very easy to see   모두 합친, 총체의; 분명한

Chris's *gross* pay is two thousand dollars a month, but after all the state and federal income taxes are deducted, he's only left with $1,400.
크리스의 총수입은 한 달에 2천 달러지만, 주 소득세와 연방 소득세를 공제하고 나면 겨우 천4백 달러가 남는다.

When Marie handed in her algebra test, she was sure she had done well, but when she got it back she was shocked at the number of *gross* errors she had made.
마리는 대수학 시험지를 제출할 때엔 잘 치렀다고 확신했지만, 돌려받고 나서는 분명하게 틀린 문제의 개수를 보고는 충격을 받았다.

GRUFF [grʌf] adj. rough; harsh; unfriendly   거친; 불친절한

When football coach Paul "Bear" Bryant barked out orders in his *gruff* voice, no one dared disobey.
미식축구 감독인 "곰"이란 별명의 폴 브라이언트가 거친 목소리로 우렁차게 명령을 내리자 아무도 감히 불복종하지 못했다.

Miranda was put off by her grandfather's *gruff* manner and stern face.
미란다는 할아버지의 거친 태도와 엄한 표정에 정이 떨어졌다.

GUILE [gail] n. skillful trickery; cunning   교묘한 속임수; 교활함

The spy used her *guile* to persuade enemy officers she was in love with them, then tricked them into telling her military secrets.
스파이는 교활하게도 적군의 장교들로 하여금 그녀가 그들을 사랑한다고 믿게 만든 다음, 그들을 속여 군사기밀을 말하게끔 만들었다.

The traveling salesman had enough *guile* to sell ice cubes to the Eskimos.
방문 판매원은 에스키모에게 얼음을 팔 수 있을 정도로 아주 간사했다.

GULLIBLE [gʌ́ləbl] adj. easy to fool or mislead   잘 속는

The charming saleslady actually convinced the *gullible* woman that her special thigh cream would "melt the pounds away."
매력적인 판매원은 잘 속는 여자에게 자신의 특수 허벅지 크림을 바르면 "살이 녹아 없어질" 거라며 확신시켰다.

On the first day of junior high, Wally had his lunch stolen because he was *gullible* enough to give it to a kid who said he was the student council lunch inspector.
중학교에 입학한 첫날 월리는 도시락을 도둑맞았는데, 그는 너무 잘 속아서 학생회에서 나온 도시락 조사관이라고 말하는 아이에게 자신의 도시락을 줘 버렸기 때문이다.

GUST [gʌst] n. a sudden, strong wind; a sudden, strong burst of something like rain, smoke, or even an emotion   돌풍; 돌발, 격발

A *gust* of wind blew the umbrella out of my hands.
돌풍이 불어와 손에 들고 있던 우산이 날아갔다.

Mr. and Mrs. Hutchins thought they had their daughter calmed down, but when they tried to leave her with her kindergarten teacher, she let loose another *gust* of tears and protests.
허친스 부부는 딸을 진정시켰다고 생각했지만, 유치원 교사에게 맡겨 놓고 가려 하자 아이는 또다시 울음을 터뜨리며 떼를 썼다.

GUSTO [gʌ́stou] n. great enjoyment, usually in eating or drinking   마음껏 즐김

The Thanksgiving dinner smelled so good we ate with *gusto*.
추수감사절 저녁 식사가 너무나 향긋해서 우린 아주 맛있게 먹었다.

GYRATE [dʒaiəréit/dʒáiəreit] v. to move in a circular motion or circular path   회전하다

Elvis Presley was a rock 'n' roll singer who drove teenage girls crazy by *gyrating* his hips when he sang.
엘비스 프레슬리는 노래할 때 엉덩이를 빙빙 돌려 십대 여자아이들을 미치게 만든 로큰롤 가수였다.

The earth *gyrates* on its axis.
지구는 축을 중심으로 회전한다.

H

HALLOWED [hǽloud] adj. seen or respected as holy 신성시되는, 신성한

Jerusalem is a very important city for Jews, Christians, and Muslims, all of whom think of it as a *hallowed* place.
예루살렘은 유대교인들, 기독교인들, 이슬람교도들에게 아주 중요한 도시로, 그들 모두 그곳을 신성한 곳으로 여긴다.

In his "Gettysburg Address," President Lincoln said that the battlefield outside Gettysburg was *hallowed* ground because of the brave sacrifices made by the soldiers who fought and died there.
링컨 대통령은 "게티즈버그 연설"에서 게티즈버그 외곽의 싸움터는 군인들이 그곳에서 싸우다 죽으며 용감한 희생을 했기에 신성한 땅이라고 말했다.

HALLUCINATE [həlú:sənèit] v. to see, hear, or sense things that aren't really there 환각을 일으키다

Irene's fever was so high she began to *hallucinate*, screaming that there were bats in her bedroom and spiders crawling on her arms.
아이린은 열이 너무 높아서, 침실에 박쥐가 있고 팔 위로 거미가 기어 다닌다고 소리치며 환각 증세를 보였다.

[Note] The noun form of hallucinate is *hallucination* [həlù:sənéiʃən].
명사형은 hallucination

- On Halloween night, Oscar claimed he saw a ghost, but we think it was just a *hallucination* brought on by eating too much candy.
  할로윈데이 밤에 오스카는 유령을 보았다고 주장했지만, 우리 생각에 그건 사탕을 너무 많이 먹어서 환각을 일으킨 것에 불과하다.

HAMPER [hǽmpər] v. to prevent the progress of; hold back; interfere with 막다, 방해하다

The prisoner tried to escape by running across the field, but he was *hampered* by the fifty-pound iron ball attached to his leg with a chain.
죄수는 들판을 가로질러 도망치려 했지만, 쇠사슬과 함께 그의 발에 붙어 있는 50파운드 무게의 쇠공 때문에 방해를 받았다.

Clara couldn't climb the tree because she was *hampered* by her high heels, her tight dress, and her fear of bark.
클라라는 하이힐을 신고 딱 붙는 드레스를 입은 데다 나무껍질이 무서워서 나무에 올라갈 수 없었다.

HARASS [hərǽs/hǽrəs] v. to bother or attack repeatedly 괴롭히다, 귀찮게 하다; 쉴 새 없이 공격하다

It turned out that some crazy fan of actress Erin Moran was the one *harassing* actor Scott Baio with phone calls and threatening letters.
여배우 에린 모런의 열성적인 팬은 바로 남자 배우 스콧 바이오를 전화와 협박 편지로 괴롭혔던 사람으로 밝혀졌다.

The confused activist for vegetable rights was arrested for *harassing* people in the supermarket.
정신이 혼란한 야채 권리 운동가가 슈퍼마켓에서 사람들을 괴롭혔다는 이유로 체포됐다.

HAUGHTY [hɔ́ːti] adj. proud in a snobby way   오만한, 건방진

The rich girl was so *haughty* she wouldn't dream of going to the dance at the public school or hanging out with people who didn't come from her neighborhood.
그 부잣집 여자애는 워낙 거만해서 공립학교에서 열리는 댄스파티에 가거나 자기 마을 출신이 아닌 사람들과 어울릴 생각은 하지도 않았다.

HAZARDOUS [hǽzərdəs] adj. risky; full of danger   모험적인; 위험한

Many of the settlers didn't survive the *hazardous* journey through the desert and across the mountains.
개척자들 가운데 많은 수가 사막을 통과하고 산맥을 가로지르는 위험한 여행에서 살아남지 못했다.

Only the bravest skiers attempt *hazardous* course at Icicle Canyon.
가장 용감한 스키어들만이 아이시클 협곡의 위험한 코스에 도전한다.

HEARTY [hɑ́ːrti] adj. friendly and cheerful; nourishing and satisfying; strong   친절하고 쾌활한; 영양 있는, 배부른; 건장한, 원기 왕성한

When Ron saw his old grade-school friend, he greeted him with a *hearty* handshake and a pat on the back.
론은 옛날 초등학교 친구를 보자 애정 어린 악수를 나누고 등을 토닥이며 인사했다.

After a day of sledding, there's nothing like a *hearty* bowl of beef stew.
썰매를 타고 난 후엔 영양가 있는 비프스튜 한 그릇만 한 게 없다.

Life on the farm had made Olaf *hearty* and healthy.
농장에서의 생활이 올래프를 원기 왕성하고 건강하게 만들었다.

HEATHEN [híːðən] n. a term used mainly by Christians to describe someone who is not of their faith; a barbarian; an uncivilized person   이교도; 미개인, 야만인

The church sent missionaries to South America to convert the *heathens* to Christianity.
교회에서는 이교도들을 기독교로 개종시키려고 남미로 선교사들을 파송했다.

HEED [hiːd] v. to give close attention to or n. close attention   주의하다 / 주의, 조심

Everyone we met told us not to drive up Mt. Slippy right after a snowstorm, but unfortunately we didn't *heed* their warnings.
우리가 만나는 사람마다 눈보라가 친 직후엔 슬리피 산에 차를 몰고 오르지 말라고 했는데, 불행히도 우린 그들의 경고를 귀담아듣지 않았다.

You would be wise to *heed* the words of old Jedediah, because rumor has it he's over two hundred years old and knows how to talk to animals.
제디디아 노인의 말씀에 유의하는 게 좋을 거야. 소문에, 그 분은 2백 살이 넘었고 동물과 말하는 법도 아신대.

Lon paid no *heed* to his mother when she told him his eyes would stick that way if he kept crossing them.
론은 자꾸 눈을 사시로 뜨면 그렇게 고정돼 버릴 거라는 어머니의 말씀에 주의를 기울이지 않았다.

HEIR [ɛ́ər] n. someone who is legally entitled to inherit the title or property of another   상속인, 후계자

Prince Charles is *heir* to the British throne.
찰스 왕자는 영국 왕위의 계승자다.

Marvin is *heir* to the Fluffo Marshmallow Company fortune, which his grandfather started building eighty years ago with one marshmallow cart on the Lower East Side of New York.
마빈은 플러포 마시멜로 회사 재산의 상속자인데, 그것은 그의 할아버지가 80년 전 뉴욕 이스트사이드에서 마시멜로 한 수레를 가지고 시작한 회사다.

[Note] A woman who is legally entitled to inherit a title or property is called an *heiress* [ɛ́əris].
여자의 경우는 heiress라 한다.

HEIRLOOM [ɛ́ərlùːm] n. a possession passed down from one generation to the next   대대로 전해 내려오는 소유물, 가보

The gold watch Neil got for his graduation was a family *heirloom* that had been bought by his grandfather's grandfather.
닐이 졸업 선물로 받은 금시계는 그의 고조부가 구입하셨던 가보였다.

HERALD [hérəld] v. to announce the coming of or n. someone who announces the coming of something   예고하다, 고지하다 / 사자, 보고자

When the new principal replaced recess with a required study hall, we knew it was the *herald* of a dark and joyless time for the students of Shadowvale Middle School.
새로 부임한 교장이 휴게 시간을 필수 자습 시간으로 대체했을 때 우린 그것이 셰도우베일 중학교의 학생들에게 어둡고 쓸쓸한 시간의 예고라는 걸 알았다.

The dogs' barking always *heralds* my father's return home from work.
개들이 짖어대면 언제나 아버지가 퇴근해서 집에 오셨다는 뜻이다.

HERESY [hérəsi] n. an opinion that isn't in line with the accepted view on a subject, especially religion   이설, 이교, 이단

In the Middle Ages, it was dangerous to challenge the teachings of the Roman Catholic Church because *heresy* was punishable by death.
중세 시대에는 로마 카톨릭 교회의 가르침에 도전하는 것은 위험한 일이었는데, 이단은 죽음으로 응징 당할 수 있었기 때문이다.

Many gourmet cooks consider it *heresy* to put ketchup on steak or put ice cubes in wine.
고급요리 전문 요리사들은 스테이크에 케첩을 얹거나 와인에 얼음 조각을 넣는 것은 이단이라 생각한다.

[Note] A person accused of heresy is called a *heretic* [hérətik].
이단자, 이교도는 heretic

HESITATE [hézətèit] v. to pause in uncertainty before acting; to be slow in acting   주저하다, 머뭇거리다

Tom *hesitated* to call his father for money more than three times in one month.
탐은 아버지에게 한 달에 세 번 이상 돈을 달라고 전화하려니 망설여졌다.

When I got to the edge of the diving board, I *hesitated* because I had never jumped off the high board before.
다이빙대 끝에 이르게 되자 한번도 높은 대에서 뛰어내린 적이 없던 터라 머뭇거려졌다.

HOARD [hɔːrd] v. to gather and store for future use   저장하다, 모아 두다

My parents *hoard* canned foods in the cellar because if there's ever a war, they want to be sure they'll have enough to eat.
부모님은 지하실에 통조림을 비축해 놓으시는데, 혹시 전쟁이 일어나면 먹을 것이 충분하도록 하기 위해서다.

Squirrels *hoard* their nuts and berries so they can get through the winter.
다람쥐들은 겨울을 나기 위해 견과류와 나무 열매를 저장한다.

HOAX [houks]　n. something designed to fool people; a deception　속임수; 속임

The circus claimed to have a three-headed horse in one of its tents, but it turned out to be a *hoax*.
서커스는 텐트 중 하나에 머리 세 개 달린 말이 있다고 주장했지만, 알고 보니 속임수였다.

The Piltdown Skull, supposedly the skull of a new kind of human, was "discovered" in England in 1911, but was later uncovered as a *hoax* perpetrated by a geology professor at Oxford University.
새로운 종의 인류 두개골로 추정되는 필트다운 두개골이 1911년 영국에서 "발견"됐지만, 나중에 옥스퍼드 대학의 어느 지질학 교수가 저지른 속임수임이 밝혀졌다.

HOMAGE [hámidʒ/hɔ́m-]　n. special honor or respect　경의, 충성

The Vietnam Memorial Wall is a *homage* to the veterans of the Vietnam War.
베트남 참전 용사 추모벽은 베트남 전에 참전했던 퇴역 군인들에게 경의를 표하는 것이다.

The school paid *homage* to the well-loved coach by naming the football field after him.
학교는 축구장 이름을 많이 사랑받는 코치의 이름으로 지어 그에게 경의를 표했다.

HONE [houn]　v. to sharpen or make more effective　날카롭게 하다; 향상시키다

The camper *honed* his knife on a whetstone.
캠핑하는 사람은 숫돌에 칼을 갈았다.

Many famous chefs have *honed* their skills at the Cordon Bleu cooking school in Paris.
많은 유명 요리사들은 파리의 꼬르동 블루 요리 학교에서 요리 솜씨를 갈고 닦았다.

HORIZONTAL [hɔ̀ːrəzántl/hár-/hɔ̀rizɔ́ntl]　adj. parallel to the ground; flat　지평선 상의; 수평의, 평평한

The library was well stocked but hard to use because all the books were stacked *horizontally*, so you couldn't pull a book off the shelf without disturbing the books on top of it.
도서관에는 소장 도서가 많지만 이용하기는 힘든데, 모든 책이 수평으로 쌓여 있어서 책꽂이에서 한 권을 꺼내려면 그 위의 책들을 치워야 하기 때문이다.

The Christmas tree was too tall to fit through the door upright, so we carried it through *horizontally*.
크리스마스트리가 너무 높아 문으로 똑바로 세운 채 들어올 수 없어서 수평으로 눕혀서 옮겼다.

HOSTILE [hástl/-tail/hɔ́stail]　adj. showing ill will toward, as an enemy would　적대하는

The unpopular governor didn't realize how *hostile* the audience was until they started booing and throwing rotten eggs at him.
인기 없는 주지사는 청중들이 그에게 야유를 퍼붓고 상한 달걀을 던지자 그제서야 그들이 자기에게 얼마나 적대적인지 깨달았다.

Ever since Dad accused him of breaking our lawn mower when he borrowed it last spring, our neighbor, Mr. Hathaway, has been *hostile* toward our whole family.
이웃집의 해서웨이 씨는, 아빠가 작년 봄 우리 집 잔디 깎는 기계를 빌려 가더니 고장 냈다며 그를 나무란 이래로 우리 집 식구 모두에게 적대적이었다.

[Note]　The noun form of hostile is *hostility* [hastíləti/hɔs-].
명사형은 hostility

- The old ethnic *hostility* between the Serbians and the Bosnian Muslims erupted into a bloody war.
세르비아인과 보스니아 이슬람교도 사이의 해묵은 민족적 적개심은 유혈전으로 폭발했다.

HUMBLE [hʌ́mbl] adj. modest; meek; not boastful or proud   수수한; 유순한; 겸손한

Even after all the Olympic gold medals she won, Bonnie is still very *humble* and down-to-earth.
보니는 그 많은 올림픽 금메달을 따고 난 후에도 여전히 아주 겸손하고 현실적이다.

Janice was so *humble* when she found out she had won first place at the science fair, she kept saying she truly felt many of the other projects were more deserving than hers.
재니스는 과학 박람회에서 자신이 1등상을 땄다는 걸 알았을 때 너무 겸손해서, 연신 다른 프로젝트들이 자기 것보다 더 상을 탈 만하다고 말했다.

[Note] The noun form of humble is *humility* [hju:míləti].
명사형은 humility

- It is wise to show a little *humility* when you become rich and famous.
부유하고 유명해지면 조금이라도 겸손함을 보이는 것이 현명하다.

HYPOCHONDRIAC [hàipəkándriæk/-kɔ́n-] n. someone who imagines he is ill or worries about getting sick too much   심기증 환자

Marcel was a *hypochondriac*: he wore a scarf all summer, was deathly afraid of drafts, and went to the doctor at least once a week, complaining of chills and aches.
마셀은 심기증 환자였다. 여름 내내 스카프를 매고 다녔고, 죽을 것처럼 바람을 무서워했으며, 일주일에 적어도 한번씩은 병원에 가서 오한과 통증을 호소했다.

HYPOCRITE [hípəkrit] n. someone who tells other people what virtues or beliefs to have, but doesn't uphold or act on those beliefs herself; someone who doesn't "practice what she preaches"   위선자

Our English teacher, Mr. Unger, is such a *hypocrite* – he won't accept our papers after the due date, but he always turns in his lesson plans late.
우리 반 영어 교사 엉거 선생님은 대단한 위선자다. 우리 과제물은 마감 날짜가 지나면 절대 안 받으면서, 그는 항상 수업 계획서를 늦게 제출한다.

[Note] The adjective form of hypocrite is *hypocritical* [hìpəkrítikəl].
형용사형은 hypocritical

- We all thought it was *hypocritical* of the senator to push for school prayer when he hadn't been to church in years.
그 상원 의원은 자기는 수년 동안 교회에도 안 다녔으면서 학교에 기도 시간을 만들려고 하는 걸 보고 우리 모두 위선적이라 생각했다.

HYSTERICAL [histérikəl] adj. having extreme, uncontrollable, sometimes irrational emotion (often laughter or crying); having to do with such an emotion   극도로 흥분한, 이성을 잃은; 히스테리성의

The child became *hysterical* when we took his blanket away so we could wash it.
그 아이는 우리가 그의 담요를 빨기 위해 빼 가자 히스테리를 부렸다.

Hysterical laughing is sometimes a reaction people have when they get very bad news or become very upset.
히스테리성의 웃음은 아주 나쁜 소식을 들었거나 대단히 화가 났을 때 취하는 반작용일 때가 있다.

I

IDEAL [aidíːəl] adj. seen as the standard of perfection; perfect 이상적인; 완벽한

The sky was gray, the air was chilly, I had nothing clean to wear; it was an *ideal* day to stay in bed and read.
하늘은 흐리고 공기는 차갑고 입을 만한 깨끗한 옷도 없고, 침대에 누워 책읽기에 딱 좋은 날이었다.

Moist, hot conditions are *ideal* for growing orchids.
습도와 온도가 높은 상태는 난초를 키우기에 이상적인 조건이다.

"This light cotton dress is *ideal* for outdoor summer parties," said the sales clerk.
판매사원이 말했다. "이 가벼운 면 드레스는 여름의 야외 파티에 딱이죠."

IDENTICAL [aidéntikəl/id-] adj. exactly alike; exactly the same 동일한, 꼭 같은

Margery was embarrassed when she got to the prom and saw that three other girls were wearing dresses *identical* to hers.
마저리는 졸업댄스파티에 가서 그녀 말고 세 명의 여자애가 그녀와 똑같은 옷을 입고 있는 걸 보고 창피했다.

"That's so weird," thought Paco. "Those two cake molds are *identical*."
파코는 생각했다. "그거 참 이상하다. 케이크 틀 두 개가 똑같네."

IDIOM [ídiəm] n. a phrase or expression whose meaning cannot be understood from the meanings of the individual words; a phrase whose meaning has little to do with the literal meaning of the words 관용구, 숙어

"To fly off the handle" is an *idiom* that means to lose one's temper.
"To fly off the handle"은 "화를 내다"란 의미의 숙어다.

Most languages have *idioms* that are hard to translate literally.
대부분의 언어에는 글자 그대로 옮기기 어려운 숙어가 있다.

IDIOSYNCRASY [ìdiəsíŋkrəsi] n. a unique trait or habit someone has 특징, 기벽

Ernie has this strange *idiosyncrasy* of always going to the bathroom before leaving any building.
어니에겐 이상한 특징이 있는데, 어떤 건물이든 그곳을 나서기 전에 꼭 화장실에 간다.

Wearing a dyed green carnation on his coat was one of Oscar Wilde's *idiosyncrasies*.
코트에 녹색으로 물들인 카네이션을 꽂고 다니는 것은 오스카 와일드의 기벽 가운데 하나였다.

ILLEGIBLE [ilédʒəbl] adj. very hard or impossible to read   읽기 어려운

"My mother wrote me an excuse for being absent from school, but rain smeared the ink and made it *illegible*," said Clarisse. "Honest."
클라리스는 말했다. "어머니가 결석한 이유를 써 주셨는데, 빗물에 잉크가 번져서 읽을 수가 없었어요. 정말이에요."

Doctors are known for having *illegible* handwriting.
의사들의 필체는 알아보기 힘든 것으로 알려져 있다.

IMMACULATE [imǽkjulət] adj. spotless; perfectly clean   오점 없는; 완벽하게 깨끗한

The cook insisted on keeping the kitchen *immaculate*.
요리사는 부엌을 완전히 깨끗하게 유지할 것을 강조했다.

No one dared to accuse the police chief of planting evidence because his record was *immaculate*.
아무도 경찰서장을 증거 은닉 혐의로 고소하지 못했는데, 그의 경력엔 오점이 하나도 없었기 때문이다.

IMMORTAL [imɔ́:rtl] adj. living forever; having fame that lasts forever   불사의, 불멸의; 불후의 명성을 지닌

Elvis Presley may be dead (at least most people think so) but his legend is *immortal*.
엘비스 프레슬리는 죽었을지 모르나 (적어도 대부분의 사람은 그렇게 생각한다) 그의 전설은 영원하다.

As long as they get plenty of blood and avoid sunlight and wooden stakes, vampires are *immortal*.
흡혈귀는 풍부한 피를 섭취하고 햇빛과 나무 막대기만 피하면 죽지 않는다.

IMMUNITY [imjú:nəti] n. ability to resist disease; freedom from certain restrictions or punishments   면역(성); 면제, 특전

Once you catch the chicken pox, your body builds up a natural *immunity* to it, so you can never catch it again.
한번 수두에 걸리고 나면 몸에는 수두에 대한 자연 면역성이 생겨 다시는 걸리지 않는다.

The district attorney granted Jimmy Scoffo *immunity* from prosecution in exchange for his testimony against the crime boss known as "The Hammer."
지방 검사는 지미 스코포가 "망치"라고 알려진 조폭 두목에 대해 반대 증언을 해준 대가로 그의 기소를 면제해 줬다.

IMPAIR [impέər] v. to lessen in strength or ability; to weaken   (힘이나 능력을) 줄게 하다; 약화시키다

The bride's heavy veil *impaired* her vision and caused her to fall into one of the pews as she tried to walk down the aisle.
신부는 두꺼운 베일을 써서 시야가 가려지는 바람에 복도를 따라 걸으려 하다가 좌석으로 넘어졌다.

Cough and cold medicines can *impair* your ability to operate a wrecking crane, bulldozer, car, or other large machine.
기침약이나 감기약은 건물 해체 기중기나 불도저, 자동차, 그 밖의 큰 기계를 작동하는 능력을 약화시킬 수 있다.

IMPARTIAL [impá:rʃəl] adj. fair; not favoring one side over another   공평한, 편견이 없는

In the United States, you have the right to a fair and *impartial* jury if you must stand trial.
미국에서는 부득이 재판을 받아야 할 경우 공정하고 편견 없는 배심원단을 요구할 권리가 있다.

Umpires are supposed to be *impartial*, but many people think they give the benefit of the doubt to more famous pitchers.
심판은 공정해야 하지만, 많은 사람들은 그들이 의심되는 점이 생기면 더 유명한 투수들에게 이롭도록 판정한다고 생각한다.

IMPROMPTU [imprámptu:/-prɔ́mptju:] adj. said or done without preparation 즉흥적인

When we found out it was Gary's birthday, we threw together an *impromptu* celebration for him.
우린 그 날이 게리의 생일이란 걸 알고 다함께 즉석 파티를 열어 주었다.

In the age of television, it is dangerous for political candidates to make *impromptu* remarks because any little mistakes they make can be broadcast on the news that night.
텔레비전의 시대에서 선거에 입후보한 정치인들이 즉흥적인 말을 하는 것은 위험한데, 어떤 사소한 잘못이라도 그날 밤 뉴스에 방송될 수 있기 때문이다.

IMPUDENT [ímpjudnt] adj. disrespectfully or offensively bold 뻔뻔한, 건방진

The *impudent* teenager laughed at the police when they arrested him, and boasted that he would never go to jail because he was a juvenile.
뻔뻔한 십대는 경찰이 자기를 체포하자 비웃었고, 자기는 청소년이므로 감옥에 가지 않을 거라며 큰소리쳤다.

[Note] The noun form of impudent is *impudence* [ímpjúdəns].
명사형은 impudence

- Barney got a slap on the face for having the *impudence* to call his father an old gas bag in front of several dinner guests.
바니는 저녁 손님들이 몇 명 있는 앞에서 자기 아버지를 보고 버릇없이 늙은 허풍선이라고 불러서 뺨을 맞았다.

INADMISSIBLE [ìnədmísəbl] adj. not permitted to enter; not admissible; often used in court to describe information or evidence that will not be allowed in the trial 들어올 수 없는; 용납할 수 없는; (법정에서 증거로) 인정할 수 없는

The judge decided that the bloody knife was *inadmissible* as evidence because it was discovered during an unlawful search by the police.
판사는 피 묻은 칼을 증거로 인정할 수 없다는 결정을 내렸는데, 그것은 경찰의 비합법적인 수색을 통해 발견됐기 때문이다.

The accused murderer's confession was *inadmissible* because he was not informed of his rights at the time of his arrest.
고소당한 살인범의 자백은 인정될 수 없었는데, 그는 체포될 당시 자신의 권리에 대해 듣지 못했기 때문이다.

INCENTIVE [inséntiv] n. something that promotes action or provides motivation 자극, 장려금, 보상물

As an *incentive* for finishing the term papers early, the teacher promised five extra-credit points on each paper that was handed in before the due date.
학기말 과제물을 일찍 끝내도록 자극하기 위해 교사는 마감 이전에 제출하는 과제마다 5점의 가산점을 주겠다고 약속했다.

The speed with which I lost weight and developed muscle was all the *incentive* I needed for continuing my exercise program.
나는 체중이 줄고 근육이 발달되는 속도에 고무되어 운동 프로그램을 계속했다.

INCESSANT [insésnt] adj. unending; continuous 끊임없는, 연속적인

Woody found it hard to sleep in the country because of the *incessant* chirping of the crickets outside his window.
우디는 창 밖에서 끊임없이 울어대는 귀뚜라미 때문에 시골에서 잠을 자기란 어렵다는 걸 알았다.

"I could never live in Seattle," said Tex. "I hear the rain is almost *incessant* up there."
텍스가 말했다. "난 시애틀에서는 죽어도 못 살아. 거기선 거의 쉬지 않고 빗소리가 들려."

INCOGNITO [inkɑgníːtòu/-kɔgni-] adv. or adj. having one's identity hidden to avoid notice; with one's identity hidden to avoid notice 익명의 / 익명으로

The prince learned a great deal about his country by traveling *incognito* for a year.
왕자는 일년 동안 신분을 숨기고 여행 다니면서 자신의 나라에 대해 아주 많은 걸 알게 됐다.

Rumor has it that Mick Jagger made an *incognito* appearance at this nightclub yesterday to see his friend's band play.
소문에 따르면 믹 재거가 어젯밤 이 나이트클럽에 변장을 하고 와서는 친구의 밴드가 연주하는 걸 봤다고 한다.

INCOHERENT [ìnkouhíərənt/-hér-] adj. confused, not logically put together; unable to think or express yourself clearly 논리가 맞지 않아 혼란스러운; 조리가 서지 않는

Mrs. Meyer, who was abducted by aliens last week, used to write long letters to the military about spaceships landing in her backyard; unfortunately, the letters were so *incoherent*, no one knew what she was saying until it was too late.
지난 주 외계인들에게 납치당한 메이어 부인은 그 동안 자신의 뒤뜰에 우주선이 내려온다는 내용의 장문 편지들을 군부에 보냈었다. 하지만 불행히도, 편지들은 도무지 논리가 일관되지 않아서 그녀가 말한 내용을 이해했을 땐 이미 너무 늦어 있었다.

After the seventh brutal sack of the game, the quarterback was dazed and *incoherent*.
쿼터백은 게임에서 일곱 번째 난폭한 백 태클을 당한 후 어리벙벙한 채 정신을 못 차렸다.

INDEFINITE [indéfənit] adj. not clear; not clearly defined; vague 불분명한; 애매한, 막연한

Our plans for our summer vacation are still pretty *indefinite* – all we know is we want to go some place warm and sunny.
우리의 여름휴가 계획은 아직 불확실하다. 우리가 아는 거라고는 따뜻하고 햇볕이 잘 드는 곳으로 가고 싶다는 것뿐이다.

If you look hard enough, you can see the *indefinite* outlines of reindeer hoofprints in the snow on the roof.
열심히 보면 지붕 위 눈 속에 순록 발굽의 희미한 윤곽을 볼 수 있다.

INDICT [indáit] v. to accuse of wrongdoing; in law, a formal accusation based on the findings of a grand jury 비난하다, 고발하다; 대배심의 평결에 기초한 정식 기소

The article in *The Daily Gazette indicted* the entire airline industry for endangering passengers by lowering safety standards.
'데일리 가제트' 지의 기사는 안전 기준을 낮춤으로써 승객을 위험에 빠뜨렸다고 항공업 전체를 비난했다.

Harry "the Horse" Hooperman was *indicted* thirty-six times for crimes ranging from fraud to grand theft, but he was never convicted.
"말"이라 불리는 해리 후퍼맨은 사기에서부터 중절도에 이르는 범죄로 36번이나 기소됐지만 유죄를 선고받은 적은 한번도 없었다.

INDIFFERENT [indífərənt] adj. not caring or having an interest 무관심한

The cat seemed *indifferent* to the can of tuna we opened for her.
고양이는 우리가 참치 캔을 열어 줬는데도 무관심한 것 같았다.

Eleanor was *indifferent* to the flowers and candy her boyfriends kept sending her.
엘리노어는 남자 친구가 계속해서 보내오는 꽃이며 사탕에 무관심했다.

INEDIBLE [inédəbl] adj. not fit to be eaten 먹을 수 없는

The pot roast was burned so badly it was *inedible*.
냄비에 볶은 고기가 너무 심하게 타서 먹을 수가 없었다.

[Note] The opposite of inedible is *edible* [édəbl].
반대말은 edible

- There are many varieties of *edible* mushrooms in these woods, but be careful — some of the mushrooms you'll find are poisonous.
이 숲에는 많은 종류의 식용 버섯이 있지만, 조심해야 돼. 발견하는 버섯 중 일부는 유독할 수 있으니까.

INEPT [inépt] adj. awkward; lacking skill 서투른; 기술이 부족한

Clancey did his friend a favor by hiring his son as a file clerk, but the boy kept losing things and was so *inept*, in general, that he had to be let go two weeks after he started.
클랜시는 친구에 대한 호의로 그 아들을 문서 정리원으로 고용했지만, 그 애는 자꾸 이것저것을 잃어버렸고, 전반적으로 너무 서툴러 2주 만에 해고당해야 했다.

Kate was such an *inept* cook, she never failed to burn or break something every time she was in the kitchen.
케이트는 너무 미숙한 요리사여서 부엌에 들어가기만 하면 뭔가를 태우거나 깨 먹었다.

INEVITABLE [inévətəbl] adj. unavoidable, inescapable; certain to happen 피할 수 없는; 필연적인

For most people, falling down a lot is an *inevitable* part of learning to ski.
대부분의 사람들에게, 스키를 배울 때 여러 번 넘어지는 건 피할 수 없는 부분이다.

Taxes and death are both *inevitable*.
세금과 죽음은 모두 필연적인 것이다.

INFAMOUS [ínfəməs] adj. having a terrible reputation; shocking or shamefully bad 악명 높은; 수치스러운, 파렴치한

Nero was *infamous* Roman emperor known mostly for playing his lyre and reciting poetry while watching a fire, which he caused, burn down most of Rome.
네로는 주로 불구경을 하면서 수금을 켜고 시를 읊었다고 알려진 악명 높은 로마 황제였는데, 그 불은 그가 지른 것으로 로마의 거의 대부분을 전소시켰다.

Jesse James was an *infamous* train and bank robber in the late 1800s.
제시 제임스는 1800년대 후반의 파렴치한 열차 및 은행 강도였다.

Japanese pilots began their *infamous* bombing attack on the U.S. Pacific fleet in Pearl Harbor at 7:53 on a Sunday morning.
일본의 비행기 조종사들은 일요일 오전 7시 53분에 진주만의 미국 태평양 함대에 악랄한 폭격을 가하기 시작했다.

INHABIT [inhǽbit] v. to live in ~에 살다

Many different kinds of plants and animals *inhabit* the world.
지구상에는 많은 다양한 종류의 동식물들이 서식한다.

We have yet to discover any other *inhabited* planets in our solar system.
우린 아직 우리의 태양계에서 사람이 살고 있는 또 다른 행성을 발견하지 못했다.

INHERIT [inhérit]   v. to receive from someone else   물려받다

When his uncle died, Pat *inherited* his valuable stamp collection.
팻은 삼촌이 돌아가셨을 때 그 분의 귀중한 우표 수집물을 물려받았다.

Colleen *inherited* her red hair from her mother's side of the family.
콜린의 빨강 머리는 가족 중 엄마 쪽에서 물려받은 것이다.

INHIBIT [inhíbit]   v. to hold back; restrain   제지하다; 금하다

Tina's braces *inhibited* her from smiling.
티나는 치열 교정기 때문에 웃지 못했다.

The giant centerpiece *inhibited* the dinner conversation because no one could see across the table.
거대한 중앙부 장식 때문에 테이블 건너편을 볼 수 없어서 저녁 식사를 하며 대화할 수가 없었다.

INITIAL [iníʃəl]   adj. first; having to do with the beginning   처음의, 최초의

The astronauts landed successfully on their *initial* attempt.
우주비행사들은 첫 번째 시도에서 성공적으로 착륙했다.

The *initial* results of our poll show that most people prefer chocolate over vanilla ice cream, but more opinions must be gathered before we can draw any definite conclusions.
우리가 실시한 여론조사의 처음 결과는, 대부분의 사람들이 바닐라 아이스크림보다 초콜릿 아이스크림을 더 좋아한다는 것을 보여주지만, 확실한 결론을 내리려면 좀더 많은 의견을 수렴해야 한다.

INNATE [inéit]   adj. inborn; possessed since birth; existing as a necessary part of something   타고난; 본질적인

Martha has an *innate* musical ability. She can pick up almost any instrument and play it without ever taking lessons.
마사에게는 천부적인 음악적 재능이 있다. 그녀는 거의 어떤 악기든 잡기만 하면 레슨을 받지 않고도 연주할 수 있다.

Cats have an *innate* dislike of being thrown into water.
고양이는 물에 빠지는 것을 선천적으로 싫어한다.

INNOVATE [ínəvèit]   v. to do or introduce for the first time   혁신하다; (새로운 것을) 받아들이다, 시작하다

For years, scientists have worked on *innovating* new, safer, cleaner sources of energy to help us stop polluting the environment.
수년 동안 과학자들은 환경오염을 막기 위해 새롭고 더 안전하고 더 깨끗한 에너지원을 도입하려고 연구해 왔다.

[Note] The noun form of innovate is *innovation* [ìnouvéiʃən], which is either the act of introducing something new, or the new thing itself.
명사형은 innovation으로, '혁신' 또는 '새로 도입한 것' 을 뜻한다.

- The electric can opener was an *innovation* that helped millions of left-handed people open cans more easily.
  전기 깡통 따개는 수백만 명의 왼손잡이들이 더 쉽게 캔을 따도록 도와준 혁신적인 물건이었다.

INSATIABLE [inséiʃəbl]   adj. impossible to satisfy   만족시키기 불가능한

The student had an *insatiable* desire to learn.
그 학생은 끝없이 배우고자 했다.

I have an *insatiable* appetite.
나의 식욕은 도무지 만족을 모른다.

The pirate had an *insatiable* thirst for rum.
그 해적의 럼주에 대한 갈망에는 만족이 없었다.

INSIPID [insípid]   adj. lacking flavor; dull or uninteresting   맛이 없는; 무미건조한, 재미없는

Grandma's "oatmeal" was actually more like an *insipid*, watery mush.
할머니의 "오트밀"은 오트밀이라기보다 맛없고 묽은 죽 같았다.

The movie about a figure skater who falls in love with a hockey player was so predictable and *insipid* that I left in the middle.
하키 선수와 사랑에 빠지는 피겨 스케이트 선수에 대한 영화는 내용이 너무 빤하고 무미건조해 중간쯤에 나와 버렸다.

INSTIGATE [ínstəgèit]   v. to provoke; to stir up   자극하다, 선동하다

The surprising verdict in the much-publicized trial *instigated* a riot in the streets that lasted for several days.
널리 알려진 재판에 의외의 평결이 내려지자 거리마다 폭동이 일어나 며칠간 계속됐다.

The deadly fire at the Coconut Grove nightclub *instigated* the development of many new fire safety practices and laws.
'코코넛 그로브' 나이트클럽에서 발생한 치명적인 화재는 새로운 화재 안전 관례와 법규들의 제정을 자극했다.

INSUBORDINATE [ìnsəbó:rdənət]   adj. disobedient; not obeying orders   순종하지 않는

The *insubordinate* employee, who talked to the press even after strict orders not to, was fired.
언론에 얘기를 하지 말라는 엄격한 금지 명령이 내려진 후에도 명령을 따르지 않은 직원이 해고당했다.

Insubordinate behavior is not tolerated in the military.
군대에서 불복종이란 허용되지 않는다.

INTERROGATE [íntərəgèit]   v. to examine a person by asking questions, especially for official reasons   심문하다

The police *interrogated* the suspect for two hours before they managed to get any information out of her.
경찰은 두 시간 동안 용의자를 심문해 겨우 정보를 얻어냈다.

INTERFERE [ìntərfíər]   v. to get in the way as if to block or stop something; to meddle   방해하다; 간섭하다

Donny and Daisy were having an ugly argument, but I didn't try to do anything about it because I think it's best not to *interfere* in fights between brothers and sisters.
도니와 데이지는 사나운 논쟁을 벌이고 있었지만, 난 형제 자매들 간의 싸움에는 끼어들지 않는 게 최선이라고 생각해 아무 조치도 취하지 않았다.

When I told the man in the seat in front of me that his talking was *interfering* with my enjoyment of the movie, he dumped his popcorn on my head.
앞자리에 앉은 남자에게 그의 말소리 때문에 나의 영화 보는 즐거움이 방해받는다고 말하자 그는 내 머리에다 들고 있던 팝콘을 쏟았다.

INTERVENE [ìntərvíːn] v. to come between two things or events; to come between two things to change the course of action   사이에 끼이다; 개입하다

A stranger on the street was brave enough to *intervene* in a struggle between a mugger and a woman who was fighting to keep her purse from being stolen.
거리에 있던 낯선 사람은 용감하게도, 강도와 핸드백을 뺏기지 않으려고 저항하고 있는 여자 사이의 싸움에 끼어들었다.

The United States sometimes sends its military to *intervene* in foreign wars.
미국은 때때로 외국끼리의 전쟁에 개입하기 위해 군대를 파견한다.

INTOXICATE [intάksikèit/-tóksi-] v. to make someone lose full control over their mental or physical abilities, especially through chemicals or alcohol; to fill with excitement   취하게 하다; 흥분시키다

The driver of the car that hit the cyclist was so *intoxicated* he could barely stand up straight.
자전거 탄 사람을 치이게 한 자동차 운전자는 술에 잔뜩 취해서 똑바로 설 수조차 없었다.

The ocean breeze and the clear, starry night *intoxicated* the romantic young girl.
바다에서 불어오는 산들바람과 맑고 별이 총총한 밤은 로맨틱한 소녀를 흥분시켰다.

INTROVERT [íntrəvèːrt] n. a person who keeps to him or herself; a shy person   내성적인 사람; 숫기 없는 사람

Kelly is such an *introvert*, she would rather sit in her room and read than go out to the movies or hang out with friends.
켈리는 워낙 내성적이라서 친구들과 영화를 보러 가거나 어울려 다니는 것보다는 방에 앉아 책 읽는 걸 더 좋아한다.

Ben goes out to parties with us, but he's too much of an *introvert* to meet new people or get involved in conversations.
벤은 우리와 함께 파티에 가기는 하지만, 숫기가 너무 없어서 새로운 사람과 인사를 하거나 대화에 끼질 못한다.

IRK [əːrk] v. to annoy; to bother   짜증나게 하다; 귀찮게 하다

Nothing *irks* me more than people who hum when they chew their food.
나를 가장 짜증나게 하는 건 음식을 씹으면서 콧노래를 하는 사람들이다.

Karen was *irked* when the customer service person at Toast-o-Matic put her on hold for the third time.
카렌은 '토스토매틱'의 고객 서비스 담당자가 세 번이나 통화를 기다리게 하자 불쾌해졌다.

IRONY [áiərəni/áiərni] n. using words to express something different from or opposite to the literal meaning of the words used; when what you say is the opposite of what you mean; a conflict between what is expected and what actually happens   반어(법); 예상외의 결과

Saying "What a dump!" when entering a huge, beautiful mansion is an example of *irony*.
크고 멋진 대저택에 들어가면서 "웬 쓰레기 더미야!"라고 말하는 건 반어의 한 예다.

When Megan came home covered in mud with holes in her jeans, her mother said she was "pretty as a picture," but the *irony* of the statement was lost on Megan.
메건이 바지 여기저기에 구멍이 나고 진흙을 뒤집어 쓴 채 집에 들어왔을 때 어머니가 그녀에게 "아주 어여쁘다"고 말했는데, 메건은 반어적인 그 말을 이해하지 못했다.

[Note] The adjective form of irony is *ironic* [airάnik/-rɔ́n-].
형용사는 ironic

- It's *ironic* that Gayle, who has no sense of smell, got a job selling perfume.
  후각이 둔한 게일이 향수 장사를 한다는 건 뜻밖의 일이다.

IRRELEVANT [iréləvənt] adj. having nothing to do with the matter at hand 관련이 없는, 부적절한

We were having a great class discussion about the play *Hamlet*, when Joey asked an *irrelevant* question about Danish cooking.
우리가 희곡 '햄릿' 에 대해 열심히 학급 토론을 하고 있을 때 조이가 엉뚱하게도 덴마크 요리에 대해 질문을 했다.

A person's race or sex is *irrelevant* to how smart they are.
어떤 사람의 인종이나 성은 그가 얼마나 똑똑한가와는 상관이 없다.

Your height, weight, and marital status are considered *irrelevant* pieces of information on a resumé.
키와 몸무게 그리고 기혼이나 미혼이냐는 이력서 상의 정보로 부적절한 부분이다.

IRREPARABLE [irépərəbl] adj. impossible to repair 수선할 수 없는, 돌이킬 수 없는

The accident caused *irreparable* damage to the car.
그 교통사고는 자동차에 수리할 수 없는 손상을 입혔다.

The broken wing on the statue of the angel was *irreparable*.
천사 상의 부러진 날개는 고칠 수 없었다.

ITINERARY [aitínəreri/-nərəri] n. a schedule of places to visit on a trip 여행 스케줄, 여정

While we were in Italy, our *itinerary* was mostly made up of trips to cathedrals and museums.
이탈리아에 있는 동안 우리의 여정은 대부분 대성당과 박물관에 가는 것으로 이루어졌다.

Cleavon and Patricia spent a month in Southeast Asia without any sort of *itinerary*—they just drifted around and did whatever they felt like doing.
클리번과 파트리샤는 동남아시아에서 어떤 여행 스케줄도 없이 한 달을 보냈다. 그들은 그냥 되는대로 돌아다니면서 아무거나 하고 싶은 걸 했다.

J

JEOPARDY [dʒépərdi] n. danger; risk of harm   위험

Frequent hurricanes put Howard's beach house in *jeopardy*.
빈번한 허리케인이 하워드의 해변 주택을 위험하게 만들었다.

[Note] The verb form of jeopardy is *jeopardize* [dʒépərdaiz], meaning to put at risk or endanger.
동사형은 jeopardize로, '위태롭게 하다'

■ Howard *jeopardized* his whole life savings by betting everything he owned on a horse race.
하워드는 가진 돈을 모두 경마에 걸어서 평생 동안의 저축을 위태롭게 했다.

JIHAD [dʒihá:d] n. a Muslim holy war against non-Muslims   회교 옹호를 위한 성전(聖戰)

The Ayatollah Khomeni, former religious leader of Iran, declared a *jihad* against non-believers.
이란의 전 종교 지도자 아야톨라 호메니는 불신자들에 대항하는 지하드를 선언했다.

A *jihad* is very much like the Christian Crusades that happened in the Middle Ages, except that if you die fighting for the forces of the *jihad*, you supposedly go straight to heaven.
지하드는 중세 시대에 일어났던 기독교 십자군과 아주 흡사한데, 지하드 군대를 위해 싸우다 죽으면 아마 곧장 하늘나라로 올라가게 되는 것만 다르다.

JURISDICTION [dʒùərisdíkʃən] n. the power to interpret or enforce the law in a certain area; range of power or control   사법권; 관할권, 관할구역

A police officer from New York could not arrest someone in California because California is not under her *jurisdiction*.
뉴욕의 경찰관은 캘리포니아에 있는 사람을 붙잡을 수 없는데, 캘리포니아는 그 여자의 관할권이 아니기 때문이다.

The Supreme Court of Alabama has *jurisdiction* over the entire state.
앨라배마 대법원은 앨라배마 주 전체에 대해 사법권을 갖고 있다.

"The yard is not under my *jurisdiction*," said the housekeeper when her employer told her the grass needed cutting. "You should speak to the gardener."
"마당은 제 관할구역이 아닌데요." 주인이 잔디를 깎아야겠다고 하자 가정부가 말했다. "정원사에게 말씀하셔야죠."

K

KOWTOW [kàutáu] v. to kneel and touch your forehead to the ground to show respect; to show exaggerated respect or obedience 무릎을 꿇고 절하다; 비굴하게 아부하다

The insecure manager expected all his employees to fetch his coffee, do personal favors for him, and basically *kowtow* to him in every way.
심리상태가 불안정했던 부서장은 직원들이 모두 자기에게 커피를 타다 주고, 개인적인 부탁을 들어주고, 어떤 식으로든 비굴하게 아부할 것을 기대했다.

In China, it was customary to *kowtow* before any member of the royal family.
중국에서는 왕실 사람이면 누구에게나 무릎을 꿇고 절하는 것이 관습이었다.

KUDOS [kúːdɑːs/kjúːdɔs] n. praise, glory (seen as singular) 칭찬, 영예

The children received *kudos* from their parents for getting straight As.
아이들은 올 A를 받고서 부모님에게 칭찬을 들었다.

L

LABYRINTH [lǽbərinθ]   n. a maze; something confusing in design or construction   미로; 복잡하게 뒤얽힌 것

According to Greek mythology, the Minotaur, a creature half-man and half-bull, was kept in a *labyrinth* on the island of Crete.
그리스 신화에 따르면 반은 사람에 반은 소의 몸을 한 미노타우로스는 크레타 섬의 미로 속에 갇혀 있었다.

LACERATION [læ̀səréiʃən]   n. a jagged tear or wound   갈갈이 찢음, 찢어진 상처

Rene fell off her skateboard onto a broken drain pipe and got a nasty *laceration* on her leg.
르네는 깨진 하수관 위에서 스케이트보드를 타다 넘어져 다리에 심한 상처가 생겼다.

The tree branch whipped back unexpectedly in the wind and gave Charlie several *lacerations* on his face and neck.
나뭇가지가 바람이 불자 갑자기 뒤로 휘둘리는 바람에 찰리의 얼굴과 목 몇 군데가 찢어졌다.

LAMENT [ləmént]   v. to grieve over or regret deeply   몹시 슬퍼하다, 깊이 후회하다, 안타까워하다

The children all *lamented* the end of summer vacation.
아이들은 여름방학이 끝나자 모두들 안타까워했다.

Some people spend so much time *lamenting* the state of our country that they don't have enough time left over to vote.
어떤 사람들은 나라의 사정을 한탄하느라 너무 많은 시간을 보내 투표하러 갈 시간이 없다.

LANGUISH [lǽŋgwiʃ]   v. to become weak or feeble; to be neglected   약해지다; 무시되다

In the book *The Count of Monte Cristo*, Edmond Dantés is thrown into a terrible prison and is left to *languish* there for many years.
몽테크리스토 백작이라는 책을 보면 에드몽 당테스는 끔찍한 감옥에 갇혀 수년 동안 그곳에 있으면서 초췌해진다.

The poor dog *languished* in the dry heat of the Arizona desert.
불쌍한 개는 애리조나 사막의 건조한 열 속에 방치되었다.

LAPSE [læps]   v. to fall back into worse or lower conditions; to become invalid or inactive   나쁜 길로 빠지다; 실효하다, 소멸하다

After going almost a month without so much as saying "ain't," Moe *lapsed* into his former bad grammar habits.
모는 한 달 가까이 "ain't"란 말조차 하지 않고 지내더니, 그 후로는 이전의 좋지 못한 문법 습관으로 다시 돌아갔다.

It seemed like my cold was getting better, but then I *lapsed* into pneumonia.
감기가 나아지는 것 같더니만 폐렴에 걸리고 말았다.

Dad let the insurance policy on the car *lapse* because he wanted to sell it.
아빠는 차를 팔고 싶어서 차에 대한 보험을 취소했다.

[Note] *Lapse* can also be used as a noun to mean a slip or failure.
명사로 쓰이면 '실수' 나 '실패' 를 의미

- "I must be having a memory *lapse*," said George. "I can't remember my telephone number."
  조지가 말했다. "기억 상실증에 걸리려나 봐. 내 전화번호도 생각이 안나."
- It must have been a *lapse* of good sense that caused Roger to leave the stove on when he left the house.
  로저가 난로를 켜 놓은 채로 집을 나선 것은 분별력에 이상이 생겼던 모양이다.

LAUDABLE [lɔ́:dəbl] adj. praiseworthy 칭찬할 만한

Your efforts to get the school to recycle paper and cans are *laudable*.
학교에서 종이와 깡통을 재활용하게 만들려는 네 노력은 칭찬할 만하다.

Sylvester made *laudable* improvements in his grades this year.
실베스터는 올해 칭찬할 만큼 성적이 올랐다.

LAVISH [lǽviʃ] adj. very generous; very plentiful 아낌없이 주는; 풍부한

There was a *lavish* buffet at the birthday party—so much food, in fact, that much of it was wasted.
생일 파티에 아주 많은 뷔페 음식이 있었다. 사실은 음식이 너무 많아서, 많은 양이 버려졌다.

When it came to his grandchildren, Grandfather was *lavish* with his money, and bought them practically anything they wanted.
손자들에 관해서라면 할아버지는 돈을 아끼지 않으셨고 원하는 건 거의 뭐든지 사주셨다.

LAX [læks] adj. not careful; not firm; loose 주의 깊지 못한; 엄격하지 못한; 느슨한

Max had been *lax* in his kitchen cleaning chores, and soon all sorts of gunk began to build up in the oven and in the vegetable drawer of the refrigerator.
맥스는 부엌에서 자질구레한 것들을 청소하는 데 꼼꼼하지 못했고, 곧 온갖 종류의 오물이 오븐 안과 냉장고의 야채 칸에 쌓이기 시작했다.

When Arnold stopped lifting weights, his muscles became *lax* within a few months.
아놀드가 역기 드는 걸 그만두자 그의 근육은 몇 달 사이에 풀어졌다.

LEGACY [légəsi] n. something left to someone in a will; something passed on to future generations 유산

Part of Howard's *legacy* to his granddaughter was a trust fund set up to pay for her college education.
하워드가 손녀딸에게 물려준 유산 중 일부는 그녀의 대학 교육비를 충당하기 위해 모아 둔 신탁 자금이었다.

Democracy as a system of government is our *legacy* from the ancient Greeks.
민주주의라는 정치 체제는 고대 그리스인들에게 물려받은 유산이다.

LENIENT [lí:niənt] adj. tolerant; flexible where rules are concerned; permissive 너그러운; 관대한

The kids liked Rhonda as their sitter because she was more *lenient* than the others and would let them eat popsicles and stay up past ten.
아이들은 자기들을 돌봐주는 론다를 좋아했는데, 그녀는 다른 사람들보다 너그러워 그들에게 아이스케이크도 먹게 해주고 10시가 넘어도 잠자리에 들지 않아도 되게 해주었다.

"Since this is the first time you've been arrested, I've decided to be *lenient*," said the judge. "But if you're ever caught knocking over mailboxes again, you're going to jail!"

판사가 말했다. "당신이 검거된 건 이번이 처음이니 관용을 베풀어주기로 결정했소. 하지만 또다시 우체통을 뒤집어엎었다가 걸리면 감옥행이오!"

LEST [lest] conj. for fear that ～할까 봐, ～하지 않게

It is important to keep studying history *lest* we repeat our past mistakes.
과거의 잘못을 반복하지 않기 위해 계속해서 역사를 공부하는 것은 중요하다.

Keep your voice down, *lest* your parents wake up and find us raiding the refrigerator.
목소리 좀 낮춰. 부모님이 깨셔서 우리가 냉장고 뒤지는 걸 들키지 않게.

[Note] Don't worry. *Lest* is not used too much in conversation or writing anymore, but you'll find it often in older books.
Lest는 회화나 글에서 이제는 더 이상 많이 쓰이지 않고 오래된 책에서만 볼 수 있다.

LEVEE [lévi] n. a high bank of earth, rock, or other material built up along the side of a river to keep it from flooding 제방

We had a picnic out on the *levee* beside the Mississippi River.
우린 미시시피 강가의 제방으로 소풍을 갔다.

After ten days of heavy rain, the river began to rush over the top of the *levee* and flooded over one-third of the town.
열흘 동안 폭우가 내리자 제방 꼭대기 위로 강물이 쏟아져 나와 마을의 3분의 1을 침수시켰다.

LIAISON [liːeizɔ́ŋ/líəzɑn/liéizɑn] n. a contact person between two units of an organization; an improper romantic connection 연락원; 남녀의 사통(私通)

Doug worked as a *liaison* between the advertising department and the budget department to make sure spending on commercials didn't get out of control.
덕은 광고부와 예산부 사이의 연락원으로, 광고에 대한 지출이 감당할 수 없을 정도가 되지 않도록 했다.

The queen's *liaison* with the king's best general was the source of gossip around the palace.
여왕이 왕의 총애하는 장군과 관계를 갖는 것은 궁정 곳곳에서 가십 거리였다.

LIMB [lim] n. a part of an animal body that is not the head or trunk, like arms, legs, or wings; a large tree branch 사지, 날개; 큰 가지

Most ballet dancers have long, graceful *limbs*.
발레 댄서들은 대부분 팔다리가 길고 우아하다.

We hung the swing off one of the lower *limbs* of the tree.
우리는 나무의 아래쪽에 있는 큰 가지 중 하나에 그네를 맸다.

LIMBO [límbou] n. in Roman Catholicism, a place between heaven and hell that serves as the eternal resting place of the souls of babies who died before baptism and of good people who died before the birth of Christ; a state of being neglected, forgotten, or put aside 지옥의 변방 (천국과 지옥 사이의 장소로, 세례를 받기 전에 죽은 아기들이나 그리스도가 탄생하기 전에 죽은 착한 사람들의 영혼을 위한 영원한 안식처); 망각, 보류

The completion of the giant hotel has been in *limbo* for ten years, ever since the construction company ran out of money.
거대한 호텔의 완공은 건설회사의 자금이 바닥난 이래 10년 동안 보류돼 왔다.

We were making arrangements to go on a vacation in the Bahamas this June, but the plans are in *limbo* now because Dad might not be able to get off work.

우린 올 6월에 바하마로 휴가 떠날 준비를 하고 있었는데, 아빠가 휴가를 못 내실 지도 몰라서 그 계획은 보류된 상태다.

According to Catholicism, on the Day of Judgement, the souls of the prophets, like Moses, will be accepted out of *limbo* and into heaven.

천주교에 따르면 심판의 날에 모세를 비롯한 선지자들의 영혼은 천국과 지옥의 변방에서 나와 천국으로 들여보내질 것이다.

LISTLESS [lístlis] adj. without energy or interest 생기 없는, 관심 없는

The school usually overheated the classrooms during the winter, which made the teachers and students sleepy and *listless*.

겨울이면 그 학교에선 보통 교실 난방을 너무 지나치게 해서 교사와 학생들을 졸립고 나른하게 만들었다.

The rainy, dark day made me *listless* and depressed.

비가 오고 어두컴컴한 날 때문에 무기력하고 우울해졌다.

LITERAL [lítərəl] adj. sticking to the exact meaning of a word or words, as in a translation; sticking to the exact meaning of a word or words, rather than a hidden or implied meaning 글자대로의; 단어의 정확한 의미에 구애된

Sometimes it's hard to give a *literal* translation of foreign phrases because there isn't always an exact match for the words in English.

때때로 외국어 구를 직역한다는 건 어려운데, 정확하게 들어맞는 영어 단어가 늘 있는 것이 아니기 때문이다.

You'll miss the meaning of many songs and poems if you stick to the *literal* meaning of every word.

모든 단어마다 글자대로의 뜻에 매달리면 여러 노래와 시들의 의미를 놓칠 것이다.

[Note] The word *literally* [lítərəli] is the adverb form of literal, and it means exactly literal, or without exaggeration.

부사형은 literally로, '글자 뜻대로', '과장 없이', '정말로'의 의미

- There were *literally* hundreds of thousands of protesters in front of the Capitol building in Washington, D.C.

  워싱턴 DC의 국회 의사당 건물 앞에 글자 그대로 수십만 명의 항의자가 있었다.

- "You shouldn't take me so *literally*," said Billie's father. "When I said dinner would be ready in a minute, I didn't mean exactly sixty seconds."

  빌리의 아버지가 말했다. "내 말을 그렇게 글자 뜻대로 이해하면 안 되지. 저녁 식사가 1분이면 준비될 거라는 얘긴 정확히 60초를 의미한 게 아니었어."

LOAF [louf] v. to be lazy; to spend time doing nothing, or very little 게으르다; 하는 일 없이 빈둥거리다

"I can't believe you just *loafed* around the house all day when you were supposed to be painting the kitchen," huffed Maggie.

매기가 호통을 쳤다. "세상에, 부엌에 페인트칠을 하기로 해 놓고선 온종일 집에서 빈둥거리다니."

Dad loves to spend the weekends *loafing* around the yard in his cut-off shorts.

아빠는 주말이면 반바지 차림으로 마당에서 놀며 지내는 걸 아주 좋아한다.

LOATHE [louð] v. to hate intensely; to despise 몹시 싫어하다; 경멸하다

I *loathe* the sight of water beetles, but my cat thinks they're fun to play with.

난 물방개를 보기만 해도 너무 싫은데, 우리 집 고양이는 어울려 노는 게 재미있는 모양이다.

Mom keeps making me eat fried liver, even though she knows I *loathe* it.

엄마는 내가 간 튀김을 질색하는 줄 아시면서 계속 먹게 만드신다.

When Barney found out his best friend had snitched on him, a feeling of *loathing* swept over him.
바니는 가장 친한 친구가 그를 고자질했다는 걸 알고 나서 혐오감에 휩싸였다.

LOCALE [loukǽl/-káːl] n. a place, especially having to do with events related to it; a setting 현장, 장소; 배경

A dark alley is probably not a good *locale* for a birthday party.
어두운 골목은 생일 파티를 하기에 적당한 장소는 아닐 것이다.

Boston is the *locale* in the television show "Cheers."
보스턴은 TV 프로 "치어스"의 배경이다.

LONGEVITY [lɑndʒévəti/lɔn-] n. long life; the length of a life 장수; 수명

Tortoises, which can live for over a hundred years, are famous for their *longevity*.
백년 이상 살 수 있는 거북이들은 장수로 유명하다.

Humans have an average *longevity* of seventy-five years.
인간의 평균 수명은 75세다.

I had no idea when I bought this toaster fifty years ago that it would have such amazing *longevity*.
난 50년 전 이 토스터를 살 때 이렇게 놀랄 정도로 오래갈 줄은 몰랐다.

LOOT [luːt] v. to rob by open force, as in a war, raid, or riot or n. the stuff stolen through looting 약탈하다 / 약탈품, 전리품

During the electrical blackout, thieves broke shop windows and *looted* stores throughout the city.
정전이 일어난 동안 도둑들은 도시 곳곳에서 상점 유리를 깨고 물건을 약탈해 갔다.

For some reason, crowds celebrating the Chicago Bulls NBA championship got carried away and started *looting* the stores in their own hometown.
무슨 이유에선지 시카고 불스의 NBA 우승을 축하하던 군중들이 정신을 잃고는 자신들이 살고있는 지역의 상점들을 약탈하기 시작했다.

The pirates returned to their ship with bags of *loot* after their midnight raid on the island town.
해적들은 한밤중에 섬 마을을 습격한 후 약탈품 가방들을 매고 배로 돌아왔다.

[Note] *Loot* is also a slang term for money.
속어로는 '돈'을 의미한다.

LUCID [lúːsid] adj. clear and easy to understand; rational and mentally sound; clear and bright 명쾌한; 제정신인; 맑고 밝은

Captain Dan, the airplane pilot, gave the passengers a *lucid* explanation of how air travel works.
비행기 조종사 댄 기장은 승객들에게 비행기 여행이 어떻게 이루어지는지 명쾌하게 설명해 줬다.

Lottie had witnessed the burglary, but because she was so old and her memory failed so often, the judge decided she was not *lucid* enough to give testimony.
로티는 절도 행위를 목격했었지만, 그녀는 너무 늙었고 기억력도 너무 자주 깜빡거렸기 때문에 판사는 그녀가 증언을 하기에는 정신 상태가 정상이 아니라는 결정을 내렸다.

The night sky was so *lucid*, you could see millions of stars.
밤하늘이 너무 맑아서 수백만 개의 별이 보일 정도였다.

LUCRATIVE [lú:krətiv] adj. profitable 돈이 벌리는

Poker can be very *lucrative* for people who know what they're doing; unfortunately, most people don't.
포커는 그 방법을 아는 사람에겐 아주 유리할 수 있지만, 불행히도 대부분은 알지 못한다.

Even though Sasha dreamed of being a violinist, he took a job as a banker because it was more *lucrative*.
사샤는 바이올리니스트가 꿈이었지만, 돈을 더 많이 벌 수 있는 은행가를 직업으로 택했다.

LULL [lʌl] v. to cause to sleep; to soothe and calm 잠재우다; 달래다, 가라앉히다

The mother *lulled* her baby by rocking it and softly humming a song.
어머니는 아기를 살살 흔들어 주고 부드럽게 콧노래를 흥얼거려 주면서 달랬다.

The sound of the waves *lulled* the sunbather to sleep.
파도 소리가 일광욕하는 사람을 잠들게 했다.

[Note] *Lull* can also be used as a noun to be a period of calm or quiet.
명사로도 쓰여 '일시적인 고요' 를 뜻한다.

- Most businesses experience a *lull* between Christmas and New Year's Day because a lot of people are on vacation.
  상점들은 대부분 크리스마스와 새해 첫날 사이에 많은 사람들이 휴가를 떠나기 때문에 일시적으로 잠잠해진다.

LUMINOUS [lú:mənəs] adj. shining, full of light 빛나는

The reflection of the moon made the lake *luminous*.
호수에 달이 비쳐 반짝였다.

Elizabeth's eyes were *luminous* in the candlelight.
엘리자베스의 두 눈이 촛불로 빛났다.

LURCH [lə:rtʃ] v. to move suddenly and unsteadily 갑자기 불안하게 움직이다

As I was coming to a stop at a red light, my foot slipped off the brake, and the car *lurched* forward and almost hit a woman in the crosswalk.
빨간 불을 보고 멈추려고 했는데 발이 브레이크에서 미끄러졌고, 차가 앞으로 홱 움직여서 횡단보도에 서 있는 여자를 칠 뻔했다.

We shot the monster three times and thought it was going to fall down, but instead it *lurched* toward us, so we screamed and ran.
괴물을 총으로 세 번이나 쏘고 나서 이젠 쓰러지겠구나 생각했는데, 그러기는커녕 괴물이 우리 쪽으로 성큼 다가와 우린 소리를 지르며 도망쳤다.

LURE [luər/ljuər] v. to attract or tempt or n. an attraction or temptation 유혹하다 / 유혹

The trainer *lured* the dog into the cage with a steak bone.
조련사는 뼈다귀를 들고서 개를 우리 안으로 유인했다.

Old Salty the sailor tried to settle down and lead a normal life, but in the end, he couldn't resist the *lure* of the sea.
뱃사람 올드 솔티는 정착해서 평범한 삶을 살려고 해보았지만, 결국 바다의 유혹을 뿌리칠 수 없었다.

The *lure* of Lee's meatball sandwich was too much for Kristin to stand, so she sneaked over and took it while he was out of the room.
크리스틴은 리가 만든 미트볼 샌드위치의 유혹을 물리칠 수가 없어서, 그가 방에서 나갔을 때 슬쩍 가서 먹었다.

LYNCH [lintʃ]　v.　to execute someone by hanging without benefit of a trial　린치를 가하다(재판 과정 없이 교수형에 처하다)

The accused horse thief was captured by an angry mob, who *lynched* him before the sheriff could get there to stop them.

성난 폭도는 말 도둑으로 고발당한 사람을 붙잡아, 보안관이 와서 저지하기 전에 그를 교수형에 처했다.

M

MACHO [máːtʃou/mǽ-] adj. having an exaggerated sense of manliness; overly aggressive; virile; dominant 지나치게 남자다운 체하는; 너무 적극적인; 남자다운; 두드러진

John was so *macho*, he wouldn't be caught dead cooking because he considered it "women's work."
존은 너무 남자다운 체를 해, 요리는 "여자들의 일"이라고 생각해서 절대로 하지 않으려고 하거든.

I don't like going to the gym anymore because it's full of all those *macho* men flexing their huge muscles and talking about sports.
난 더 이상 체육관에 가고 싶지 않아. 왜냐면 거기엔 거대한 근육에 힘을 주고 스포츠 얘기를 하면서 남자다워 보이려는 사람들 밖에 없거든.

In his movies, Clint Eastwood usually plays very *macho* characters, like gun-fighting cowboys and tough detectives.
클린트 이스트우드는 그의 영화에서 주로 총잡이 카우보이나 강인한 형사처럼 아주 남자다운 역할로 나온다.

MALICE [mǽlis] n. bad will toward others; the desire to hurt others 악의, 앙심

Holly told everyone her sister Polly was a bed-wetter out of *malice*.
홀리는 앙심을 품고 모두에게 폴리가 오줌싸개라고 말했다.

I know a kid who was so full of *malice*, he would shove a firecracker into a turtle's shell just to watch it explode.
악의가 가득했던 아이가 있었는데, 그 앤 거북이 등딱지 안에 폭죽을 쑤셔 넣고 폭발하는 걸 지켜보곤 했다.

[Note] The adjective form of malice is *malicious* [məlíʃəs].
형용사형은 malicious

- Polly was angry at her sister for spreading the *malicious* rumor that she wet her bed.
  폴리는 그녀가 자면서 오줌을 싼다고 심술궂은 소문을 퍼뜨린 여동생에게 화가 났다.

MALIGNANT [məlígnənt] adj. having ill will, malicious; deadly 악의 있는; 악성의

Cal was having *malignant* thoughts about running over his brother's bike with a car.
캘은 자동차로 동생의 자전거를 치려는 심술궂은 생각을 하고 있었다.

Diabetes can be a *malignant* disease if it is not treated.
당뇨병은 치료하지 않으면 악성 질병이 될 수 있다.

MANIPULATE [mənípjuleit] v. to control with skill; to influence in a clever way 솜씨 있게 다루다; 교묘하게 다루다, 조종하다.

Years of practice made it easy for Victor to *manipulate* the complex controls on the wrecking crane.
몇 년 동안 연습한 덕에 빅터는 건물 해체 기중기의 복잡한 제어 장치를 조종하는 것이 수월했다.

Rasputin was a Siberian monk who used his personal and religious power to *manipulate* the last monarchs of Russia to suit his evil purposes.

라스푸틴은 시베리아의 수도사로, 개인적이고 종교적인 힘을 이용해 러시아 말기의 역대 군주들이 자신의 사악한 의도에 따르도록 조종했다.

MANSLAUGHTER [mǽnslɔ̀:tər] n. the crime of killing a person without meaning to, as through negligence 과실치사

Rich was convicted of *manslaughter* for killing a person while driving drunk, and is serving five years in prison.

리치는 음주운전을 하다가 사람을 치어 죽인 데 대해 과실치사 판결을 받아서, 5년을 복역할 것이다.

In certain cases of extreme emotional distress, a person who shoots or stabs someone to death may be charged with *manslaughter* instead of murder because it could be argued they didn't know what they were doing at that time.

극도로 감정적인 고뇌 속에서 총을 쏘거나 칼로 찔러 누군가를 죽게 한 사람은 살인보다는 과실치사로 고발될 수도 있는데, 그 당시에는 스스로 뭘 하고 있는지 자신도 몰랐다고 주장할 수 있기 때문이다.

MANUAL [mǽnjuəl] adj. having to do with the hands or being operated by hand 손의; 수동의

Gregory had such *manual* skill, we knew he would either be a great surgeon or a great magician.

그레고리는 손재주가 아주 좋아서 우린 그가 훌륭한 외과 의사나 대단한 마술사가 될 줄 알았다.

Most of the controls in the car are electric, but you have to roll down the windows *manually*.

차 속의 제어 장치 대부분은 전기로 움직이지만, 창문은 손으로 돌려서 내려야 한다.

In a car with a *manual* transmission, you have to shift gears yourself; an automatic transmission shifts gears for you.

수동 변속기 자동차에서는 기어를 직접 바꾸어야 하지만, 자동 변속기는 운전자 대신 기어를 바꾸어 준다.

MARTIAL LAW [má:rʃəl lɔ:] n. military rule over a civilian population in times of emergency, such as during a war or after the collapse of the civilian government 계엄령

The country was still under *martial law* after three attempts at democratic elections had failed or resulted in bloody riots.

그 나라는 민주 선거를 치르려는 세 차례의 시도가 실패로 끝나거나 유혈 폭동으로 번지고 난 후 그대로 계엄령 하에 있었다.

The general overthrew the president, declared himself the supreme ruler, and declared *martial law* over the entire country.

장군은 대통령을 타도하고 스스로를 최고 지도자라고 선언한 다음, 나라 전체에 계엄령을 선포했다.

MARVEL [má:rvəl] n. a thing of wonder or v. to be filled with wonder 놀라운 일, 경이 / 놀라다, 이상하게 여기다

The laptop computer is a *marvel* of modern technology.

노트북 컴퓨터는 현대적 과학기술로 이루어진 경이다.

The audience *marvelled* at the juggler's ability to juggle a bowling ball, a flaming torch, a knife, and a live chicken all at the same time.

관중들은 요술쟁이가 볼링공, 횃불, 칼 그리고 살아 있는 닭을 한꺼번에 던져 돌리는 걸 보고 감탄했다.

MATERNAL [mətə́:rnl] adj. motherly; having to do with the mother or motherhood 어머니다운; 어머니의

One of the strongest *maternal* instincts is the desire to protect children from harm.

가장 강력한 모성 본능 가운데 하나는, 아이를 다치지 않게 보호하려는 욕구다.

"Stop being so *maternal*," snapped Jim at his girlfriend. "I can pick out my clothes without your help."

짐은 여자 친구에게 날카롭게 말했다. "그렇게 엄마처럼 굴지 좀 마. 내 옷은 네가 안 도와줘도 내가 고를 수 있어."

All the neighborhood kids loved Mrs. Wallace, a kind, *maternal* woman who always gave them cookies, and who always smelled of cinnamon and vanilla.

그 동네 아이들은 모두 월러스 부인을 좋아했는데, 부인은 친절하고 어머니 같은 여자로, 언제나 아이들에게 쿠키를 주고, 늘 계피와 바닐라 냄새를 풍겼다.

MATRIARCH [méitrià:rk] n. a woman who rules a family, clan, tribe, or other organization 여자 가장, 여자 족장

Isadora, the founder of the first theater in Greenville, was the *matriarch* of the town's artistic society.

그린빌에 최초의 극장을 설립한 이사도라는 그 마을 예술가 사회의 여장부 격이었다.

In ancient times, many tribes were ruled by *matriarchs*, who passed their power on to their daughters and granddaughters.

고대에는 많은 부족을 여자 족장이 다스렸는데, 그들은 딸이나 손녀에게 권력을 물려주었다.

MECCA [mékə] n. the center of a certain interest or activity 메카, 특정한 관심이나 활동의 중심지

New York City is a *mecca* for people who want to be stage actors.

뉴욕 시티는 연극배우를 꿈꾸는 사람들의 메카다.

Hollywood is the international movie *mecca*.

헐리우드는 세계적인 영화 메카다.

Silicon Valley is a *mecca* for innovation in the field of computer technology.

실리콘 밸리는 컴퓨터 기술 분야에서 기술 혁신의 중심지다.

MEDIA [mí:diə] n. plural of medium [mí:diəm] a way of giving information to large numbers of people (medium의 복수) 매개물, 매체

Movies are a good *medium* for telling stories.

영화는 이야기를 들려주는 훌륭한 매체다.

The Internet is a *medium* that gives computer owners access to huge amounts of information.

인터넷은 컴퓨터 이용자를 막대한 양의 정보로 안내해 주는 매체다.

[Note] The plural, *media*, is used to refer to those groups that usually report news events: radio, television, newspapers, and magazines. Remember, the word *media* is plural (even though it doesn't have an "s" on the end of it), so make sure you use the right verb with it.

media는 라디오, TV, 신문, 잡지 같은 '대중 전달 매체'를 뜻하기도 한다. 끝에 "s"가 없지만 복수형임을 유념

- The *media* were tracking the Senator like bloodthirsty lions, waiting to pounce on any mistake he might make.

  대중매체는 상원 의원이 무슨 잘못이라도 할라치면 와락 덤벼들려고 기다리는 피에 굶주린 사자처럼 그를 쫓고 있었다.

- The *media* were accused of turning the trial into a circus.

  대중매체는 재판을 서커스처럼 바꾸어 놓는다는 비난을 받았다.

MEDIATE [mí:dièit] v. to settle an argument by working with all sides; to bring about an agreement between different sides (협정을) 성립시키다; (쟁의를) 조정하다, 중재하다.

President Jimmy Carter *mediated* an important peace treaty between Egypt and Israel.

지미 카터 대통령은 이집트와 이스라엘 간의 중요한 평화 조약을 중재했다.

Recently, former president Jimmy Carter *mediated* the dispute between the U.S. government and the government of Haiti, and helped us avoid a war.
최근에 지미 카터 전 대통령은 미국 정부와 아이티 정부간의 논쟁을 중재해서 전쟁을 피할 수 있도록 해주었다.

My big brother Ned *mediated* a fight I was having with my friend over who could play the video game first, and helped us work out a way to share it.
우리 큰 형 네드는 누가 비디오게임을 먼저 할 것인가를 놓고 나와 친구가 싸우고 있는 걸 중재해서 같이 하는 방법을 만들게끔 도와주었다.

MEDITATE [médətèit] v. to think deeply about something   숙고하다

Albert Einstein spent a lot of time *meditating* about the nature of time and space.
앨버트 아인슈타인은 많은 시간을 시간과 공간의 본질에 대해 숙고하며 보냈다.

Carol couldn't figure out why the model plane she put together didn't fly as it was supposed to, so she sat in her room to *meditate* on the problem.
캐롤은 자신이 조립한 모형 비행기가 왜 예상대로 날지 않는지 알아낼 수 없었다. 그래서 방에 앉아 그 문제를 곰곰이 생각했다.

MEDLEY [médli] n. a mixture, a musical arrangement that uses pieces of different songs   혼성곡, 메들리; 잡동사니

The restaurant makes a dish called "Seafood *Medley*," which is a mixture of shrimps, scallops, mussels, and lobsters.
그 식당에는 "해산물 메들리"라는 요리가 있는데, 새우, 가리비, 홍합, 바다 가재의 혼합 요리다.

The pianist played a *medley* of songs of Cole Porter.
피아니스트는 코울 포터의 노래를 메들리로 연주했다.

MELEE [méilei/mélei] n. a confused fight among a number of people   난투, 혼전

There was some kind of *melee* in the school cafeteria this afternoon, but no one is sure what it was about.
오늘 오후 학교 식당에서 난투가 있었는데, 무엇 때문인지는 아무도 확실히 모른다.

Sara, who was on her way home from the market, got hit in the head with a brick when she stumbled onto a *melee* that had broken out over who had the right to use a certain parking space.
시장에서 집으로 돌아가는 길이던 사라는, 어떤 주차 구역을 두고 그 이용권이 누구에게 있나를 놓고 벌어진 난투극에 휩싸여, 머리에 벽돌을 맞았다.

MEMENTO [məméntou] n. something that serves as a reminder of something past; a souvenir   추억 거리; 기념품

Valerie bought a pair of mouse ears as a *memento* of her trip to Disneyland.
발레리는 디즈니랜드를 여행한 기념으로 생쥐 귀 한 쌍을 샀다.

The whole time he was stationed in Korea, Sgt. York kept a pressed magnolia blossom in the front pocket of his uniform as a *memento* of his home in Mississippi.
요크 하사는 한국에 배치돼 있는 동안 미시시피의 고향의 기념물로 군복 앞주머니에 목련꽃 눌린 것을 넣고 다녔다.

MENACE [ménis] n. something that threatens to cause danger or harm   위험한 것, 골칫거리

The fire ants were a *menace* to all the people who were trying to have a picnic on the grass.
쏘는 개미는 잔디밭에서 소풍을 즐기려는 사람들에게 골칫거리였다.

Armed gangs are a *menace* to the safety of our neighborhoods.
무장한 폭력단들이 우리 동네의 안전을 위협한다.

MENTOR [méntɔːr] n. a wise teacher and adviser 훌륭한 교사, 조언자

When I first started working at Bumbleby & Bumbleby, I knew nothing about the honey business, but luckily my boss became my *mentor*, and she showed me all the ins and outs of the company.
범블비&범블비 사에서 처음 근무를 시작할 때 나는 벌꿀 사업에 대해 아무 것도 몰랐지만, 운 좋게도 나의 상사가 훌륭한 조언자가 되어서, 회사에 대해 자세한 것들을 알려주었다.

My father's business partner was always a *mentor* to me. I'd turn to him for advice and support.
아버지의 사업 파트너는 언제나 내게 훌륭한 스승이셨다. 난 조언과 도움이 필요할 땐 그 분께 의지했다.

MERIT [mérit] n. excellence; something that entitles a person to a reward or recognition or v. to deserve 장점, 우수: 공적: 공로 / 마땅히 받을 만하다

Her writing professor told Marcia her short story had *merit*.
마샤의 작문 교수는 그녀의 단편소설이 뛰어나다고 말했다.

Colin has many *merits*, but neatness is not one of them.
콜린은 장점이 많지만, 깔끔한 면은 없다.

The actor's wonderful performance *merits* the praise of the critics and the applause of the audience.
그 배우의 뛰어난 연기는 비평가의 칭찬과 관객들의 박수갈채를 받을 만하다.

METAMORPHOSIS [mètəmɔ́ːrfəsis] n. a complete change in appearance or attitude 변형, 변질

When the wicked, selfish Grinch sees that stealing all the presents in Whoville doesn't ruin Christmas, and that the Whos still seem happy even without gifts, he goes through a *metamorphosis*, and turns into a pretty nice guy.
사악하고 이기적인 그린치는 후빌에 있는 모든 선물을 훔쳤는데도 크리스마스가 망쳐지지 않고, 마을 사람들이 선물 없이도 행복해 하는 듯한 모습을 보고는, 변형 작용을 겪어서 아주 멋진 남자로 변신한다.

In one weird short story by Franz Kafka, Gregor Samsa goes to sleep as a human, goes through some *metamorphosis* in the night, and wakes up as a giant insect.
프란츠 카프카의 기이한 단편소설에서는, 그레고르 잠자가 잠이 들 때는 사람인데, 밤중에 어떤 변형을 일으켜 깨어날 때는 거대한 벌레가 되어 있다.

MILITANT [mílətənt] adj. fiercely aggressive or warlike, especially for a cause 전투적인, 호전적인

Millicent was *militant* about her objection to testing products on animals, and would go into stores and break as many bottles of perfume or hair dye as she could before security guards stopped her.
밀리슨트는 동물에 대한 제품 테스트에 대해 과격한 반응을 보여, 여러 상점에 들어가서는 경비원이 저지하기 전까지 향수병과 염색약병을 닥치는 대로 깨부수곤 했다.

Militant protesters chanted slogans and held up signs calling for the Congress to repeal the Eighteenth Amendment.
투쟁적인 항의자들은 국회에 수정헌법 18조인 금주법을 폐지하라고 요구하면서 슬로건을 외치고 피켓을 들었다.

MIMIC [mímik] v. to imitate; to copy closely in speech or expression 모방하다; 흉내 내다

Wanda didn't realize she was doing it, but after about a week in Scotland she started to *mimic* the accents of Scottish people.
완다는 자기가 그러는 줄 깨닫지 못했지만, 스코틀랜드에서 일주일쯤 지나자 스코틀랜드인의 억양을 따라하기 시작했다.

Sam can *mimic* the calls of birds so well, they sometimes answer him or fly close to him.
샘은 새들의 우짖는 소리를 아주 잘 흉내 낼 수 있어서, 어떤 때는 새들이 그에게 대답을 하거나 가까이로 날아온다.

MIRAGE [mirá:ʒ] n. an illusion usually seen in the desert that looks like a body of water or a city; something that has no substance or isn't real 신기루; 망상

After being stranded in the desert for three days without water, Baldwin saw a pool of water up ahead of him and went running toward it, but it turned out to be nothing more than a *mirage*.
물도 없이 3일 동안을 사막에서 꼼짝 못하고 지낸 후 볼드윈은 자기 앞에 물웅덩이가 보이자 뛰어갔는데, 알고 보니 그저 신기루일 뿐이었다.

Blanche's beauty was a *mirage* created with clever lighting, makeup, and memories.
블랑슈의 아름다움은 교묘한 조명과 화장 그리고 기억 장치로 만들어진 환상에 불과했다.

MISCELLANEOUS [mìsəléiniəs] adj. made up of different things, subjects, or qualities 잡다한, 갖가지의, 다방면의

The book entitled *Reading Matter* is made up of *miscellaneous* poems, stories, songs, and observations.
'Reading Matter' 란 제목의 책은 갖가지 시와, 소설, 노래, 관찰기로 이루어져 있다.

His shelves are filled with books, compact discs, and *miscellaneous* knicknacks.
그의 책꽂이에는 책과, CD 그리고 잡다한 장식 소품들이 가득 차 있다.

"You have such a *miscellaneous* collection of CDs." remarked Judy when she noticed Evan seemed to have every sort of music imaginable.
"넌 아주 다양한 방면의 CD를 모았구나." 에반에게 상상할 수 있는 온갖 종류의 음악이 있는 것처럼 보이자 주디가 말했다.

MODERATE [mádərət/mɔ́d-] adj. not extreme; medium; not severe; mild 적당한; 중간의; 온건한; 온화한

The new Chinese restaurant charges *moderate* prices, but the food is fantastic!
새로 생긴 중국 식당은 가격은 보통인데 음식은 환상적이야!

Most of the year, the accountants have a *moderate* workload, but they get really busy in the spring.
회계사들은 일년 중 대부분은 일의 양이 적당하지만, 봄에는 정신없이 바빠진다.

"We can expect *moderate* temperatures for the rest of the week, with a chance of rain on Friday," said Buff Shiney, our local weatherman.
"이번 주 동안은 포근할 것으로 예상되며, 금요일에 비 올 확률이 있습니다." 우리 지역의 기상 예보원 버프 샤이니의 말이었다.

MODEST [mádist/mɔ́d-] adj. not like a show-off, not overly proud; not too large or fancy 겸손한; 수수한, 적당한

"Wilma was just being *modest* when she said her grades were okay," boasted her mother. "She's made straight As since she was in first grade."
윌마의 어머니가 우쭐하며 말했다. "윌마가 자기 성적이 괜찮은 정도라고 말한 건 그저 겸손한 거였죠. 그 앤 1학년 때부터 줄곧 A만 받았거든요."

All the other girls wore bright gowns with beads and sequins and bows to the prom, but Eula preferred her *modest* white dress.
다른 여자애들은 모두 졸업댄스파티에 가려고 구슬과 금속 조각에 나비 리본까지 달린 번쩍이는 가운을 입었지만, 울라는 그보다는 수수한 하얀 드레스를 입었다.

The Jones family lives in a *modest* home in a nice part of town.
존스 가족은 부자 동네에서 수수한 집을 짓고 산다.

MOMENTUM [mouméntəm] n. speed of motion 움직이는 속도, 힘, 추진력

The steam engine started out slowly, but gradually built up *momentum*.
증기 엔진은 천천히 출발했지만 점점 가속이 붙었다.

When we headed down the hill on our bikes, it was as though we were flying, but we lost *momentum* as the ground leveled out.

우린 자전거를 타고 언덕을 내려갈 때 꼭 날아가는 것 같았는데, 땅이 평탄해지자 속도를 잃었다.

MONOGAMY [mənágəmi/mɔnɔ́g-] n. the condition of having only one mate for life; having one marriage at a time; having only one sexual partner 일부일처

Biologists say that *monogamy* is not uncommon in the animal world, and that animals like wolves and eagles mate for life.

생물학자들 얘기로는, 동물 세계에서 일부일처는 일반적인 것인데, 이리와 독수리 같은 동물은 평생 동안 짝을 바꾸지 않는다고 한다.

[Note] The adjective form of monogamy is *monogamous* [mənágəməs/mɔnɔ́g-].

형용사는 monogamous

- Marriage is a *monogamous* relationship between a man and woman.
  결혼은 한 남자와 한 여자 사이의 일부일처 관계다.

MONOTONY [mənátəni/-nɔ́t-] n. boring repetition; lack of variation 지루한 반복; 단조로움

I usually pass the time by looking out the car window when we take trips, but the *monotony* of the flat, treeless North Dakota landscape had me bored and restless in five minutes.

난 우리가 여행을 갈 때면 보통 자동차 창 밖을 내다보며 시간을 보내는데, 노스다코타 주에서는 단조롭고 나무도 없는 풍경이 지루하게 반복돼 5분만 지나면 따분하고 안절부절 못하게 되었다.

"Every day for the past six months we've had candy for breakfast, ice cream for lunch, and waffles for dinner," cried Lyle. "The *monotony* is driving me crazy."

라일은 소리 질렀다. "우린 지난 6개월 동안을 매일같이 아침에는 사탕, 점심에는 아이스크림, 저녁에는 와플을 먹었어. 맨날 똑같아서 지겨워 죽을 지경이라구."

MORBID [mɔ́:rbid] adj. overly interested in death and decay; gruesome 병적인, 병적으로 음울한; 무시무시한

Harold was a *morbid* little boy who liked to visit funeral parlors.

해롤드는 장의사에 찾아가는 걸 좋아했던 음울한 소년이었다.

We thought using a coffin as a coffee table was kind of *morbid*.

우린 관을 커피 테이블로 사용하는 건 좀 섬뜩하다고 생각했다.

Barbara got some sort of *morbid* enjoyment out of pretending to drown herself in the swimming pool.

바바라는 수영장에 빠져 죽는 시늉을 하면서 일종의 병적인 즐거움을 가졌다.

MOTIVE [móutiv] n. something that causes or leads someone to act a certain way 동기

It seems greed was Mrs. Boswell's *motive* for killing her husband, who had left her several million dollars in his will.

보스웰 부인이 남편을 살해한 동기는 탐욕인 것 같다. 그녀의 남편은 유언으로 부인에게 수백만 달러를 남겼었다.

Mr. Creases said his love of children was his only *motive* in donating all the money needed for a new youth center.

크리시즈 씨는 새로운 청소년 센터를 짓기 위해 필요한 돈 전액을 기부하는 동기는 오로지 아이들에 대한 사랑이라고 말했다.

MUTATE [mjú:teit/mju:téit] v. to change form 변화하다

In the movie, *The Thing*, aliens take over the bodies of humans, and just when you least expect it, people who look normal start to *mutate* into horribly disgusting, slimy monsters.

영화 'The Thing' 에서 외계인들은 인간의 신체를 지배하는데, 전혀 예상치 못한 때에 정상적으로 보이는 사람들이 끔찍할 정도로 역겹고 불쾌한 괴물로 변하기 시작한다.

Exposure to gamma rays caused Dr. Bruce Banner to *mutate* into in Incredible Hulk.
브루스 배너 박사는 감마선에 노출되자 무시무시한 헐크로 변했다.

[Note] A *mutant* [mjú:tnt] is a living thing that has gone through mutation.
mutant는 '돌연변이체', '변종'을 의미

- The petting zoo at the circus was full of *mutants*: two-headed horses, a hippopotamus with wings, and goats with six legs.
서커스의 애완동물원에는 돌연변이들이 가득했다. 머리 둘 달린 말, 날개 달린 하마, 다리가 여섯 개인 염소들이 있었다.

MUTINY [mjú:təni] n. rebellion against authority, especially on a ship at sea (특히 항해중인 배에서의) 폭동, 반란

In the late 1700s, Fletcher Christian, an officer aboard H.M.S. Bounty, led a famous *mutiny* against the cruel Captain Bligh.
1700년대 말 플레처 크리스천은 영국 해군 함정 바운티호에 승선한 장교로, 잔인한 블라이 선장에 대항해 유명한 반란을 주도했다.

Rumor has it the girls at the Sylvia Smithers Academy staged a *mutiny* against the outdated dress code, and all showed up to class in jeans on Monday.
소문에 따르면, 실비아 스미더스 아카데미의 여학생들이 구식의 복장 규정에 맞서 반란을 꾀하고, 월요일에 모두들 청바지 차림으로 수업에 들어왔다.

MYTH [miθ] n. a traditional tale usually used to explain why the world is the way it is, or how the world was created; a story that is not really true, but is often repeated 신화; 전설, 미신

The existence of the Loch Ness monster in Scotland is thought of as a *myth* by most people, although many others have spent years trying to prove the existence of the giant beast.
스코틀랜드에 네스호 괴물이 산다는 것은, 많은 사람들이 수년 동안 그 거대한 짐승의 존재를 증명하려 애써 왔지만, 대부분의 사람들은 미신이라고 생각한다.

According to an ancient Roman *myth*, Echo was a young girl who loved a very handsome, but vain, young man who didn't return her love, so she wasted away until nothing was left of her but her voice.
고대 로마 신화에 따르면, 에코는 아주 잘생겼지만 자만심이 강한 젊은 남자를 사랑했던 어린 소녀로, 그는 그녀의 사랑을 받아 주지 않았고, 그래서 그녀는 쇠약해져 오직 목소리만 남게 되었다.

N

NAIVE [nɑːíːv] adj. inexperienced; innocent in the ways of the world 경험이 없는; 세상 물정을 모르는, 순진한

Kelly's brother told her someone had put poison in the Halloween candy and that she better give hers to him so he could get rid of it, and she was so *naive* she didn't realize he just wanted her candy for himself.
켈리의 오빠는 그녀에게 누군가 할로윈 사탕에 독약을 넣었다면서 자기가 갖다 버릴 테니 달라고 했는데, 그녀는 너무나 순진해 오빠가 그저 동생의 사탕을 차지하려고 그러는 줄 알아차리지 못했다.

"Don't be so *naive*," said Mrs. Woolard to her husband as the hitchhiker drove away in their car. "We're in the middle of nowhere. I doubt he's just gone to run an errand."
"어쩜 그렇게 세상을 몰라요?" 히치하이커가 그들의 차를 몰고 가 버리자 울러드 부인이 남편에게 말했다. "우린 어딘지도 모르는 곳에 있어요. 그 사람이 그저 볼 일 보러 갔을 리가 없어요."

NAVIGATE [nǽvəgèit] v. to plan a course and steer through it 조종하다, 운전하다, 항해하다

It takes an expert kayaker to *navigate* the rough waters of this river.
이 강의 거친 물살을 헤쳐 가려면 노련한 카약 조종사가 필요하다.

Hundreds of years ago, sailors used to *navigate* their ships using the stars to guide them.
수백 년 전의 선원들은 별들의 안내를 받으며 배를 운전하곤 했다.

NEGLIGENT [néglidʒənt] adj. not showing proper care or concern; neglectful 무관심한, 부주의한; 태만한

Jack was a *negligent* pet owner: he never bathed his dogs, and sometimes let them go for days without food.
잭은 애완동물을 키우는 데 너무 태만했다. 개들을 목욕 한번 안 시켰고, 어떤 땐 며칠 동안 먹을 것도 주지 않았다.

Samantha was supposed to take care of her friend's sea monkeys while she was on vacation, but she was so *negligent*, most of the sea monkey tribe died by the time her friend returned.
사만다는 친구가 휴가를 떠나 있는 동안 친구의 애완용 새우들을 돌봐 주기로 했지만, 그녀는 너무 무관심해서 친구가 돌아올 때쯤엔 새우 가족 대부분이 죽어 버렸다.

NICHE [nitʃ/niːʃ] n. a hollowed out space in a wall; a place or position that suits someone or something well 벽감(조각상 등을 놓기 위한 벽의 움푹한 곳); 적소(適所)

The little statue of Peter Pan was displayed in a *niche* in the entry hall of the theater.
작은 피터 팬 상이 극장으로 들어가는 복도의 벽감에 전시돼 있었다.

Nelson the shoemaker had a lot of competition until he found his *niche* as a maker of ballet slippers.
제화업자 넬슨은 발레용 덧신 제조라는 틈새 시장을 찾기까지 숱한 경쟁을 했다.

Pauline had a hard time settling into college and making friends until she found her *niche* in the art department.
폴린은 대학 생활에 적응하고 친구들을 사귀는 데 어려움을 겪다가 미술부에서 딱 맞는 자리를 찾게 됐다.

NOCTURNAL [nɑktə́:rnl/nɔk-] adj. having to do with night; most active at night; happening at night
밤의, 야간의; 야행성의; 밤에 일어나는

Witches are known for their *nocturnal* meetings, which are called covens.
마녀들은 밤에 모이는 것으로 알려져 있는데, 마녀의 집회라고 부른다.

The moon is best seen in the *nocturnal* sky, but sometimes you can see it during the day as well.
달은 밤하늘에서 가장 잘 보이지만, 가끔은 낮에도 볼 수 있다.

My cat is a *nocturnal* animal: she sleeps all day, and scampers around the house all night.
우리 집 고양이는 야행성이다. 낮이면 계속 잠만 자고, 밤새도록 집 주변을 장난치며 뛰어다닌다.

NOMAD [nóumæd] n. a person who wanders from place to place; a person who belongs to a group of people who move around to find food for themselves and their livestock 방랑자; 유목민

Danny's mother wondered when her son would give up being a *nomad* and find himself a nice girl to settle down with.
대니의 어머니는 아들이 언제쯤 떠돌이 생활을 청산하고 좋은 아가씨를 만나 정착을 하게 될지 궁금했다.

Most of the Native Americans who lived in the North American plains were *nomads* who moved from season to season.
북미 대륙 평원에 거주했던 아메리칸 인디언들은 대부분 계절마다 옮겨 다니는 유목민들이었다.

[Note] The adjective form of nomad is *nomadic* [noumǽdik].
형용사는 nomadic

- The Gypsies are a *nomadic* group of people, known for their dancing and their wily ways, who first came to Europe from India 600 years ago.
  집시들은 춤과 꾀로 유명한 방랑자 무리로, 600년 전에 처음으로 인도에서 유럽에 건너왔다.

NOMINATE [námənèit/nɔ́m-] v. to propose someone as a candidate for an elected office (후보로) 지명하다

I *nominated* Betsy as our student council representative.
베시를 학생회 대표로 지명했다.

NONCHALANT [nɔnʃələnt/nɑ̀:nʃɑ́:lənt] adj. cool and unconcerned 무관심한

George didn't want Melanie to know he liked her, so whenever she spoke to him, he tried to act as *nonchalant* as possible.
조지는 자기가 멜라니를 좋아한다는 걸 그녀가 알게 하고 싶지 않아서, 그녀가 말을 걸어올 때면 가능한 한 무관심하게 행동하려 애썼다.

Trey, who was dressed up as a giant lizard, realized a moment too late that this wasn't a costume party after all, but he somehow managed to be completely *nonchalant* as he strolled toward the punch bowl, dragging his tail behind him.
왕도마뱀 차림을 하고 온 트레이는 뒤늦게서야 가장 무도회가 아니란 걸 알았지만, 전혀 아랑곳하지 않는 듯 애쓰면서 뒤에 달린 꼬리를 질질 끌며 펀치볼 쪽으로 느릿느릿 걸어갔다.

NOTORIOUS [nouthɔ́:riəs/nə-] adj. having a bad reputation that is widely known 악명 높은

Mrs. Jacobson was *notorious* for falling asleep at dinner parties, sometimes even before the main course arrived.
제이콥슨 부인은 저녁 파티 도중에 잠드는 걸로 악명이 높았는데, 가끔은 본 요리가 미처 나오기 전에도 그랬다.

Doc Holiday was a *notorious* gambler of the Old West.
독 홀리데이는 서부 개척 시대의 악명 높은 도박꾼이었다.

NOVEL [nɑ́vəl/nɔ́v-] adj. new and different 새로운, 진기한

Adam had a *novel* approach to mopping: he strapped sponges to his feet and skated across the kitchen floor.
아담은 새로운 걸레질을 시도했다. 발에다 스펀지를 끈으로 잡아맨 다음 부엌 바닥을 가로질러 스케이트를 탔다.

Millions of empty plastic milk jugs were going to waste until someone came up with the *novel* idea of using them as planters.
다 마신 플라스틱 우유병 수백만 개가 그대로 버려질 뻔했는데, 누군가 그것을 식물 재배 용기로 사용하자는 진기한 아이디어를 생각해 냈다.

NOVICE [nɑ́vis/nɔ́v-] n. a beginner 무경험자, 초보자

The ski resort has small hills called "bunny slopes" for *novices*.
스키 리조트에는 초보자들을 위한 "토끼 비탈"이라는 이름의 작은 언덕이 있다.

After Luigi dropped the fourth batch of dough on his head, he was forced to admit that he was a *novice* in the art of pizza crust twirling.
루이지는 밀가루 반죽을 네 번째 자기 머리 위로 떨어뜨리고 난 후 어쩔 수 없이 피자 크러스트 반죽을 돌리는 데엔 풋내기임을 인정했다.

 O

OASIS [ouéisis] n. a small area in the desert that has plants and water; a place or thing that is a pleasant change or relief 오아시스; 위안처, 휴식처

The weary travelers decided to rest themselves and their camels at the *oasis*.
지친 여행객들은 오아시스에서 낙타와 함께 쉬기로 결정했다.

Sandra's office was an *oasis* of calm in an otherwise tense and frantic company.
산드라의 사무실은 긴장되고 정신없는 회사에서 유일하게 평온한 오아시스 같은 존재였다.

OBESE [oubíːs] adj. very overweight 지나치게 살찐

According to her doctor, Kim is *obese*, and must lose weight if she wants to avoid health problems.
의사에 따르면 킴은 너무 살이 쪄서 건강상의 문제가 생기지 않으려면 몸무게를 빼야만 한다.

The man was so *obese* he had to be buried in a piano crate because a regular coffin wasn't big enough for him.
그 남자는 너무 뚱뚱해 보통 관은 크기가 맞지 않아서 피아노 운반 상자에 넣어져 묻혀야 했다.

OBJECTIVE [əbdʒéktiv] adj. not influenced by emotion or personal opinion 객관적인

Mothers are rarely *objective* about their children's abilities, and usually think their sons and daughters are the smartest, cutest, most talented kids in the world.
어머니들은 자식들의 재능에 대해 객관적이기 힘들어서 자기 자식이 세상에서 가장 똑똑하고 가장 예쁘고 가장 재능 있다고 생각하는 게 보통이다.

Elaine was *objective* enough about her appearance to realize she would never be Miss America.
일레인은 자신의 외모에 대해 충분히 객관적이어서 결코 미스아메리카 감은 못 된다는 걸 알았다.

OBLIGATION [àbləgéiʃən/ɔ̀b-] n. a duty, or something you've promised to do; a debt owed for a favor 의무, 책무; 은혜, 신세

"After all your grandfather has done for you, you have an *obligation* to go see him in the hospital," scolded Jim's mother.
"할아버지가 너한테 그만큼 해주셨는데 당연히 병원으로 문병을 가야지." 짐의 어머니가 꾸짖었다.

When Iggy broke Pop's electric can opener, he felt an *obligation* to buy him a new one.
이기는 팝의 전기 깡통 따개를 고장내고는 새 걸 사 줘야겠다는 의무감을 느꼈다.

OBLITERATE [əblítəreit] v. to destroy completely 흔적을 없애다, 말소하다

The sand castle was *obliterated* by the rising tide.
모래성은 밀물에 의해 완전히 없어졌다.

Kelly completely *obliterated* her opponent when she checkmated him at chess in five minutes.
켈리는 체스에서 5분만에 외통장군을 불러 상대를 완전히 제압했다.

OBLIVIOUS [əblíviəs] adj. unaware; unmindful 알아차리지 못하는; 염두에 두지 않는, 관심 없는

The substitute teacher was *oblivious* to the whispering and notepassing that was going on in his classroom.
대리 교사는 교실에서 아이들이 쑥덕거리고 쪽지를 돌리고 있는 걸 눈치 채지 못했다.

Sharon was madly in love with Stan, but he was *oblivious* to her affection.
섀런은 스탠을 미친 듯이 사랑했지만, 그는 그녀의 애정에 무관심했다.

OBSCURE [əbskjúər] adj. hard to see or understand; not well known 분명치 않은; 알려지지 않은

The scientist found a stone tablet with ancient writing on it, but many of the letters were too *obscure* to make out.
과학자는 고대의 글이 써 있는 석판을 발견했지만, 글자 대부분이 너무 흐려서 알아볼 수 없었다.

Shawn has an irritating habit of quoting *obscure* movies and books none of us have ever heard of.
숀은 우리가 들어본 적도 없는, 유명하지도 않은 영화나 책을 인용하는 버릇이 있어서 짜증난다.

OBSOLETE [àbsəlí:t/óbsəli:t] adj. out of date, no longer useful; no longer in use 진부한, 시대에 뒤떨어진; 더 이상 안 쓰이는

When the light bulb was invented, oil lamps became *obsolete*.
백열전구가 발명되자 기름 램프는 구식이 됐다.

Because our language changes and grows, new words are always being added to the dictionary, while other words become *obsolete* and are dropped.
우리의 언어는 변화하고 성장하기 때문에 언제나 새로운 단어가 사전에 추가되고, 반면에 다른 단어들은 안 쓰이게 되어 제외된다.

OBTRUSIVE [əbtrú:siv] adj. forced and obvious 강제적인; 눈에 띄는

Cal kept clearing his throat and coughing in the most *obtrusive* way, trying to get his girlfriend, who was sitting in the front of the theater, to turn around and see him.
캘은 계속해서 최대한 억지로 헛기침을 하면서 극장 앞에 앉아 있는 여자 친구가 몸을 돌려 자기를 보게 하려고 애썼다.

The president's daughter wanted, more than anything, to have a normal birthday party, but it was hard to have fun with two huge, *obtrusive* security guards at every door.
사장의 딸은 다른 무엇보다도 평범한 생일 파티를 열고 싶었지만, 큰 덩치의 눈에 거슬리는 경비원이 문마다 둘씩 서 있는 상태에서 즐겁게 지내기는 힘들었다.

OMEN [óumən/-men] n. something that is believed to be a sign of events to come, or sign of good or bad luck 조짐, 징조

Many cultures consider the appearance of a raven to be a bad *omen* that predicts death or bad luck.
많은 문화권에서는 갈가마귀가 나타나면 죽음이나 불운을 예시하는 나쁜 징조라고 생각한다.

When the general tripped and fell on his face getting out of his jeep, the soldiers took it as a bad *omen* for the battle they would face the next day.
장군이 지프에서 내리면서 발을 헛디뎌 푹 엎어지자, 군인들은 다음 날 치르게 될 전투에 대한 불길한 징조라고 생각했다.

OMIT [oumít]   v. to leave out   빼다, 생략하다

When my high school did a production of the play *A Streetcar Named Desire*, we had to *omit* certain scenes that our parents and teachers thought were too adult for us.
고등학교에서 연극 '욕망이란 이름의 전차' 를 공연할 때 우리는 부모님이나 선생님이 우리에게 너무 성인용이라고 생각하는 장면 몇 군데를 빼야만 했다.

"Please tell me all about the party, and don't *omit* a single detail," said Jeannie, who was eager to hear some good gossip.
"파티에 대해서 전부 말해 줘. 단 하나라도 빼놓지 말고." 지니가 재미있는 뒷말을 듣고 싶어서 안달하며 말했다.

OMNIPOTENT [ɑmnípətənt/ɔm-]   adj. having the ability to control everything   전능한, 절대력을 가진

In the George Orwell book *1984*, the people's lives are ruled by an *omnipotent* dictator named "Big Brother."
조지 오웰의 소설 '1984' 를 보면 사람들의 생활은 "빅 브라더" 라는 이름의 절대 권력자에게 지배당한다.

Christians, Jews, and Muslims all believe in the existence of one, *omnipotent* god.
기독교인, 유대인, 이슬람교도는 모두 유일하고 전능한 신의 존재를 믿는다.

OPAQUE [oupéik]   adj. not letting light pass through; not transparent   (빛이) 통하지 않는; 불투명한

Betty prefers *opaque* tights to sheer stocking because she has a lot of freckles on her legs.
베티는 다리에 잡티가 많아서 비치는 스타킹보다는 속이 안 보이는 타이츠를 더 좋아한다.

We decided the windows in the bathroom should be *opaque* so no one could look in and see us taking baths.
우리가 목욕하는 걸 아무도 들여다보지 못하도록 욕실 창문을 불투명하게 달기로 했다.

OPTIMISM [ɑ́ptəmizm/ɔ́p-]   n. an ability to look on the bright side of things and believe that everything will work out for the best   낙관주의

The *optimism* and excitement Frank felt on the opening of his restaurant, Frank's Fry House, soon faded as days went by with no customers.
프랭크는 자신의 식당 '프랭크 프라이 하우스' 를 열 때 낙관하며 흥분했지만, 며칠 동안 손님이 전혀 오지 않자 곧 시들해졌다.

[Note] The adjective form of optimism is *optimistic* [àptəmístik/ɔ̀p-].
형용사는 optimistic

Even though it looked as though she would lose the election, Anne stayed *optimistic* and refused to give up until all the votes were counted.
앤은 선거에서 실패할 것처럼 보였지만 계속 낙관을 하며 모든 표가 헤아려질 때까지 포기하지 않으려 했다.

ORATOR [ɔ́(:)rətər/á̄r-]   n. someone who gives formal speech; a public speaker   웅변가; 연설자, 강연자

The revered Martin Luther King, Jr. was a gifted *orator* whose speeches on civil rights moved many people to take a stand against bigotry.
존경받는 마틴 루터 킹 주니어 목사는 타고난 웅변가로, 민권에 대한 그의 연설은 많은 이들에게 감동을 주어 편견에 맞서 저항하도록 만들었다.

We had no idea Damon was such a good *orator* until we saw him at the city council meeting, where his speech on homeless puppies brought tears to the eyes of many in the audience.
우린 데이먼을 시의회 모임에서 보고서야 그가 대단한 연설가임을 알았는데, 집 없는 강아지에 대한 그의 연설은 많은 청중들을 울렸다.

ORTHODOX [ɔ́:rθədɑ̀ks/-dɔ̀ks] adj. sticking to traditional, accepted beliefs or expectations 전통적인, 보수적인

The wedding was completely *orthodox*, except for the fact that the couple wrote their own vows.
결혼식은 신랑 신부가 자신들의 서약을 쓴 것만 빼고는 완전히 전통식이었다.

The critic's taste in art was a bit too *orthodox* for him to appreciate the new paintings at the modern art gallery.
그 비평가의 예술적 취향은 다분히 보수적이어서 현대 미술관에 있는 새로운 그림들을 높이 평가하지 않았다.

OSTRACIZE [ástrəsaiz/ɔ́s-] v. to banish or cut off from a group or society 추방하다, 배척하다

People with AIDS are often *ostracized* by neighbors and friends who are ignorant about the nature of the disease.
에이즈에 감염된 사람들은 그 병의 특징에 대해 잘 모르는 이웃들이나 친구들에게 배척당하는 일이 흔하다.

Mr. Weltkrieg was *ostracized* by the town when it was discovered he was a notorious war criminal.
월트크리그 씨가 악명 높은 전범이라는 사실이 알려지자 마을에서는 그를 추방했다.

OVERT [óuvə:rt/ouvə́:rt] adj. open and obvious 공공연한, 명백한

After weeks of trying to get Cindy to notice him, Elmo decided more *overt* steps were necessary, so he sent her a dozen roses and asked her on a date.
몇 주 동안 신디에게 자신의 존재를 알리려고 애쓴 엘모는 좀더 노골적인 조치가 필요하다고 생각해, 그녀에게 장미꽃 다발을 보내고 데이트 신청을 했다.

Horace made an *overt* attempt to walk out of the lunchroom with an entire tray of desserts, but he was stopped before he got to the door.
호러스는 공공연하게 디저트가 담긴 접시를 통째로 들고 구내식당을 나오려고 했지만 문에 이르기 전에 저지당했다.

OVERWHELM [òuvərwélm] v. to overpower; to affect deeply 압도하다; 지대한 영향을 끼치다

Tulane University's football team was simply *overwhelmed* by Florida State, and they lost the game 72 to 3.
튤레인 대학 미식축구 팀은 플로리다 주립 대학에 완전히 압도당해 72대 3으로 패했다.

Myra was *overwhelmed* with gratitude when she found out her whole neighborhood had chipped in some money to help her pay her hospital bills.
마이러는 마을 사람들 전체가 그녀의 병원비 납부를 도와주려고 조금씩 돈을 모았다는 사실을 알고 고마워서 어찌할 바를 몰랐다.

OZONE LAYER [óuzoun lèiər] n. a layer of the gas ozone high above the surface of the Earth; it helps shield the world from too much radiation from the sun 오존층

Scientists say that our overuse of chemicals called "chlorofluorocarbons" has caused holes in the *ozone layer* above the arctic poles.
과학자들에 따르면, 우리가 "클로로플루오로카본"이라는 화학물질을 남용해 극지방 상공의 오존층에 구멍이 생겼다고 한다.

P

PACIFIST [pǽsəfist] n. someone who is against violence as a way of settling problems; someone who refuses to fight in a war because of the belief that war and killing are wrong   평화주의자; 반전주의자

William is a *pacifist* who spent time in jail for refusing to report to the draft board during the Vietnam War.
윌리엄은 베트남 전쟁 동안 징병 위원회에 신고하기를 거부해 복역했던 평화주의자다.

Some religions, like the *Society of Friends*, require their members to be *pacifists*.
'Society of Friends' 같은 일부 종교는 신도에게 반전주의자가 될 것을 요구한다.

PALLOR [pǽlər] n. extreme paleness of the skin, as from fright or sickness   창백

Macbeth's face took on such a *pallor*, you would think he had seen a ghost.
맥베드의 얼굴은 너무 창백해서 유령을 본 얼굴이라고 생각할 정도였다.

Years of working long hours in the city gave Cindy bad headaches and a sickly *pallor*.
신디는 도시에서 몇 년 동안 늦게까지 일하다 보니 심한 두통을 얻었고 병자같이 창백해졌다.

PANACHE [pənǽʃ/-nάːʃ] n. grand, dramatic style or manner   당당한 차림이나 태도

The count always leaves a room with great *panache*: he kisses the hand of his hostess, bows deeply, turns into a bat, and flies out the window.
백작은 언제나 아주 거창하게 방을 나선다. 안주인의 손에 키스를 하고, 깊숙이 고개를 숙인 다음, 박쥐로 변해 창문 밖으로 날아간다.

Bela always wore a cape – even during the summer – because he thought it gave him some *panache*.
벨라는 늘 어깨 망토를 걸치고 다녔다. 심지어 여름에도 그랬는데, 그러면 좀 당당해 보인다고 생각했기 때문이다.

PANDEMONIUM [pæ̀ndəmóuniəm] n. a wild uproar   대혼란, 아단법석

What started as a minor food fight between two students turned into a *pandemonium* of flying cakes and clattering trays before teachers could do anything about it.
두 학생 간의 사소한 음식 다툼으로 시작된 것이 교사들이 어떻게 손을 써 보기도 전에 케이크가 날아다니고 접시들이 달가거리는 대혼란으로 변했다.

When the football team won its first game in five years, the fans rushed onto the field and the whole stadium was in a state of *pandemonium*.
미식축구팀이 5년 만에 처음으로 우승하자 팬들이 경기장으로 뛰어들었고 운동장 전체가 아수라장으로 변했다.

PANTOMIME [pǽntəmaim] n. face and body gestures used to express a message or v. to make face and body gestures to express a message 몸짓, 손짓 / 몸짓(손짓)으로 나타내다

When we were on vacation in China, we had to communicate mainly through *pantomime*, since the only things we knew how to say in Chinese were "I am an American" and "Where is the embassy?"
휴가차 중국에 갔을 때 주로 몸짓을 통해 의사소통을 해야 했는데, 우리가 중국어로 할 수 있는 말은 "전 미국 사람이에요"와 "대사관이 어디죠?" 밖에 없었기 때문이다.

My grandfather flapped his arms at the Italian desk clerk and pretended things were stinging his behind in an attempt to *pantomime* the fact that there was a nest of wasps in his hotel room.
우리 할아버지는 이탈리아 접수계원 앞에서 팔을 날개처럼 퍼덕이며 뭔가에 엉덩이가 쏘이는 시늉을 했는데, 호텔 방에 말벌 둥지가 있다는 사실을 몸짓으로 알리기 위해서였다.

PARALLEL [pǽrəlèl] adj. running in the same direction, but never crossing; similar or along the same lines 평행의; 같은 방향의, 비슷한

Main Street is usually so full of traffic that I often take Second Street, which runs *parallel* to Main, whenever I want to go downtown.
난 도심지로 나가고 싶을 때면 메인 가는 보통 교통이 너무 혼잡하기 때문에 같은 방향으로 뻗어 있는 2가로 갈 때가 많다.

PARANOID [pǽrənɔ̀id] adj. abnormally concerned about one's safety or security; having the feeling that everyone is against you or "out to get you" 편집증의, 피해망상적인

My great aunt was so *paranoid*, every night she made me check in all the closets and under the bed to make sure a crazy killer was not hiding, waiting for her to go to sleep.
우리 대고모님은 피해망상이 심해 밤마다 나를 시켜 모든 옷장 속과 침대 밑을 살펴보게 하셨는데, 미치광이 살인자가 당신이 잠들기를 기다리며 숨어 있는 게 아닌지 확인하기 위해서였다.

General Augusto was convinced that all his conversations were being recorded through hidden microphones, that his food was being poisoned, and that secret police were following him, but his doctor told him he was being *paranoid*.
아우구스토 장군은 자신이 얘기하는 건 모두 숨겨진 마이크로 녹음되고 있고, 그가 먹는 음식에는 독이 들어 있고, 비밀경찰이 그를 미행하고 있다고 확신했지만, 의사는 그가 피해망상에 걸려 있다고 말했다.

PARAPLEGIC [pæ̀rəplíːdʒik] adj. having the lower half of the body paralyzed, usually through injury to the spinal cord or n. a person who is paralyzed from the waist down 하반신 마비의 / 하반신 마비 환자

Since his terrible car accident Bud has been *paraplegic*.
버드는 끔찍한 자동차 사고로 하반신이 마비됐다.

Bud had a hard time adjusting to life as a *paraplegic* because he was so active and athletic before his accident.
버드는 하반신 마비 환자로서의 생활에 적응하느라 애를 먹었는데, 사고가 나기 전 그는 너무나 활동적이고 운동을 즐겼기 때문이다.

PASSIVE [pǽsiv] adj. not active; receiving action, but not returning any; giving no resistance 수동적인, 소극적인; 무저항의, 순순히 따르는

It amazed me that Amy could stay completely *passive* while her brother tried to tickle the soles of her feet.
에이미의 오빠가 그녀의 발바닥을 간지럽히는데도 꼼짝하지 않고 있는 걸 보고 놀랐다.

The dog was *passive* as the children tied its ears above its head and dressed it up in doll's clothing.
개는 아이들이 머리 위로 두 귀를 묶고 인형 옷을 입히는 데도 가만히 있었다.

PATHOLOGICAL [pæ̀θǝládʒikǝl/-lɔ́dʒ-] adj. having to do with, or caused by, a disease or mental disorder 병리학의, 병적인

Steve is a *pathological* liar, which means he can't control his tendency to lie.
스티브는 병적인 거짓말쟁이로, 거짓말하는 버릇을 억제할 수가 없다.

Sylvia's mood swings are so extreme they might be considered *pathological*.
실비아는 감정의 기복이 너무 심해서 병적으로 여겨질 정도다.

PATRIARCH [péitriɑ̀ːrk] n. the father or leader of a tribe, family, or group; an old, respected man 가장, 족장, 지도자; 원로

Old Mr. Jenkins, one of our town's founders and certainly its *patriarch*, was much more powerful than the mayor and town council combined.
나이든 젠킨스 씨는 우리 시의 설립자 가운데 한 분이자 원로로 시장과 시의회를 합쳐 놓은 것보다 훨씬 더 막강했다.

PATRONIZE [péitrǝnaiz/pǽt-] v. to be a supporter or customer of; to talk down to someone 후원하다; 단골이 되다; 무시하다

Eva *patronized* only the most exclusive, expensive stores on Rodeo Drive.
에바는 로데오 로에 있는 가장 고급스럽고 가장 비싼 상점들만 이용했다.

"Don't *patronize* me," my grandmother yelled at the waiter. "I may be old, but that doesn't mean I'm stupid."
"날 어린애로 취급하지 말라고." 할머니가 웨이터에게 소리쳤다. "내가 늙었는지는 몰라도 그렇다고 멍청한 건 아니야."

[Note] A *patron* [péitrǝn] is a person who supports a group or activity, or a regular customer.
patron은 '후원자', '단골손님'을 의미

- Isabella Stewart Gardner was a *patron* of the arts.
  이사벨라 스튜어트 가드너는 미술의 후원자였다.

PAUPER [pɔ́ːpǝr] n. a very poor person 극빈자; 가난뱅이

Nothing makes rich men into *paupers* faster than a bad gambling habit.
부자를 가난뱅이로 만드는 가장 빠른 길은 심한 도박 벽이다.

PENDING [péndiŋ] adj. not yet occurring or happening soon or prep. while awaiting 임박한 / ~하는 동안에

The *pending* peace talks brought an air of optimism to the wartorn country.
임박한 평화 회담은 전쟁으로 파괴된 나라에 낙관의 기류를 실어다 주었다.

His *pending* meeting with the principal made Jimmy nervous.
교장과의 면담이 임박해지자 지미는 초조했다.

Pending a full safety inspection of its rides, the carnival was closed down.
놀이 기구에 대해 전면적인 안전 검사를 하는 동안 놀이 공원은 폐쇄됐다.

PENSIVE [pénsiv] adj. in deep, serious thought or showing deep thought 생각에 잠긴, 곰곰이 생각하는; 시름에 젖은

Harold was a *pensive* and quiet boy who would spend hours just staring out a window.
해롤드는 창 밖을 내다보며 몇 시간을 보내곤 하던, 생각이 많고 조용한 아이였다.

Even though my mother said nothing was wrong, I could tell by the *pensive* expression on her face that she was worried about my father's plane landing safely in the snowstorm.
비록 어머니는 아무 일도 없다고 하셨지만, 얼굴에 나타난 시름에 잠긴 표정으로, 아버지의 비행기가 눈보라 속에 무사히 착륙할지 걱정하고 계심을 알 수 있었다.

PERCEPTIVE [pərséptiv] adj. having sharp insight, or the ability to notice small details 지각력이 있는, 지각이 예민한

The detective Hercule Poirot was *perceptive* enough to notice that the candlestick holder had been moved about one foot to the left since the last time he had been in the study.
에르큘 포와로 탐정은 지각력이 뛰어나 촛대 받침이 지난 번 서재에서 봤을 때보다 왼쪽으로 1피트 정도 옮겨져 있다는 걸 알아차렸다.

Her parents thought they were being very sneaky, but Clara was a *perceptive* girl, and realized right away they were planning a surprise party for her.
클라라의 부모님은 그들이 몰래 하고 있다고 생각했지만, 클라라는 지각이 예민한 아이여서 부모님이 자신을 위해 깜짝 파티를 준비하고 있다는 걸 바로 알아차렸다.

PERJURY [pə́:rdʒəri] n. the unlawful act of lying while under oath to tell the truth 위증

Mr. Thompson knew his wife was guilty, so to protect her he committed *perjury* by telling the jury he was the one who had shot the stranger.
탐슨 씨는 아내에게 죄가 있다는 걸 알고서, 아내를 보호하기 위해 판사에게 낯선 사람을 쏜 건 자기라고 말함으로써 위증죄를 저질렀다.

PERPENDICULAR [pə̀:rpəndíkjulər] adj. crossing or meeting at a right angle 직각을 이루는

Church Street is *perpendicular* to Varick Street.
처치 가는 배릭 가와 직각을 이루며 교차한다.

The table legs are *perpendicular* to the tabletop.
테이블 다리는 테이블 표면과 직각이다.

PERSECUTE [pə́:rsikjù:t] v. to bother, harass, or attack regularly 괴롭히다, 정기적으로 공격하다

All the popular kids at school *persecuted* Warren terribly by stealing his lunch money, calling him a geek, snapping his suspenders, and generally making his life a nightmare.
학교에서 인기 있는 아이들 모두가 워렌을 지독하게 괴롭혔는데, 점심 값을 빼앗고, 변태라고 부르고, 멜빵을 확 잡아채고, 전반적으로 그의 생활을 악몽처럼 만들었다.

Many immigrants came to the United States because they were being *persecuted* for their religious beliefs in Europe.
많은 이주민들이 유럽에서 종교적 믿음 때문에 괴롭힘을 당해 미국으로 왔다.

PERSEVERE [pə̀:rsəvíər] v. to hold on or keep on in a course of action or a belief 인내하다, 끈기있게 버티다

In spite of harsh weather and food shortages, the pioneers *persevered* and made it to their destination.
험악한 날씨와 식량 부족에도 불구하고 개척자들은 끈기있게 버텨 목적지에 도달했다.

If you want to be a famous writer, you must *persevere*, no matter how many times your work is rejected.
유명한 작가가 되고 싶다면 작품이 얼마나 많이 퇴짜를 맞는다 해도 끈기있게 버텨야 한다.

PERTINENT [pə́:rtənənt]　adj.　related to the matter at hand; relevant　관계있는; 적절한

Clancey irritated his teacher by always asking questions that weren't *pertinent* to the class discussion.
클랜시는 늘 학급 토론과 관계없는 질문을 해서 선생님을 짜증나게 했다.

Weather and traffic conditions are *pertinent* factors to consider when planning a car trip.
날씨와 교통 상황은 자동차 여행을 계획할 때 고려해야 할 적절한 요인들이다.

PESSIMISM [pésəmizm]　n.　a tendency to stress the bad side of things　비관주의

Our coach was always so full of *pessimism* about our chances of winning that it was hard for us to get fired up, and we usually lost.
코치는 언제나 우리가 우승할 가능성에 대해 너무 비관적이어서 우린 동기를 부여받지 못했고 그래서 대개 지고 말았다.

[Note]　The adjective form of pessimism is *pessimistic* [pèsəmístik].
형용사는 pessimistic

- Geraldine was *pessimistic* about her chances of becoming president.
제럴다인은 자신이 사장이 될 가능성에 대해 비관적이었다.

PHILANTHROPY [filǽnθrəpi]　n.　the love of humankind that is often shown through generosity and charity　박애, 자선

The fact that Mr. Moneybags left most of his money to charity is a great example of his *philanthropy*.
머니백스 씨가 자기 재산 대부분을 자선단체에 남겼다는 사실은 그의 박애심을 보여주는 본보기다.

[Note]　Someone known for philanthropy is a *philanthropist* [filǽnθrəpist].
'자선가', '박애주의자'는 philanthropist

- The princess was widely known as a *philanthropist* and activist for the underprivileged.
공주는 가난한 사람들을 위한 자선가와 활동가로 널리 알려져 있었다.

PINNACLE [pínəkl]　n.　the peak or highest point of something　정상, 정점

Mike Tyson was at the *pinnacle* of his career as a heavyweight boxer when he was thrown in prison for attacking a young beauty queen.
마이크 타이슨은 젊은 미인대회 여왕을 폭행해서 감옥에 들어갈 당시 헤비급 선수로서 정상에 올라 있었다.

I planted a little American flag at the *pinnacle* of the mountain.
나는 산꼭대기에 조그만 성조기를 꽂았다.

PIOUS [páiəs]　adj.　showing religious devotion, commitment and respect　신앙심이 깊은, 독실한

Mary was a *pious* woman who would never think of skipping church on Sunday.
메리는 주일에 교회를 빠진다는 건 상상도 못할 독실한 여자였다.

We always knew William was *pious*, but we never thought he would decide to become a priest.
윌리엄의 신앙심이 깊다는 건 늘 알고 있었지만 성직자가 될 결정을 하리라고는 전혀 생각 못했다.

PITTANCE [pítns]　n.　a very small amount of money　얼마되지않는 돈

It was hard for Bob Crachit to take care of his family on the *pittance* Mr. Scrooge paid him.
밥 크래칫은 스크루지 씨가 주는 얼마 되지않는 돈으로 자신의 가족을 돌보기가 힘들었다.

"One million dollars is a *pittance* to him," said the kidnapper. "I'm sure he'll pay much more for the return of his daughter."

유피범이 말했다. "백만 달러가 그에겐 껌 값이야. 딸을 돌려주는 대가라면 훨씬 더 많이 줄 거라구."

PLACATE [pléikeit/plǽk-/pləkéit] v. to calm the anger of, especially by giving something (특히 뭔가를 주어서) 달래다, 진정시키다

Bonnie screamed and cried when her mother left the room, so the babysitter *placated* her by letting her play with her special squeaky bunny toy.

보니는 어머니가 방을 나가자 소리치며 울고불고했는데, 베이비시터가 찍찍 소리 나는 토끼 인형을 가지고 놀게 해주어 그녀를 진정시켰다.

The angry townspeople were not *placated* by the police chief's vow to bring the hoodlums to justice - they wanted immediate action.

성난 읍민들은 폭력배들을 법에 비추어 처단하겠다는 경찰서장의 맹세에도 누그러지지 않았다. 그들이 원하는 건 즉각적인 행위였다.

PLAINTIVE [pléintiv] adj. sorrowful 구슬픈, 애처로운

Wanda finally gave in to the dog's *plaintive* whines and gave her some table scraps.

완다는 마침내 개가 애처롭게 낑낑거리는 것에 굴복해서 먹다 남은 음식을 좀 주었다.

The streets were filled with the slow, *plaintive* song of the saxophone player.

거리마다 색소폰 연주자의 느리고도 구슬픈 노랫소리가 가득했다.

PLATONIC [plətánik/plei-/-tɔ́n] adj. not physically passionate; mainly friendly or spiritual 육체적으로 격렬하지 않은; 우애적인, 정신적인

"My relationship with Candace is strictly *platonic*!" Martin insisted to his jealous girlfriend.

"캔더스와 내 관계는 순전히 정신적인거야!" 마틴이 시샘하는 여자 친구에게 강조했다.

Everyone thought that Chris and Marie were boyfriend and girlfriend, but it turned out they just had a very intense, *platonic* relationship.

모두들 크리스와 마리가 사귀는 사이라고 생각했는데, 알고 보니 그들은 그저 아주 친밀한 정신적 관계를 갖는 것뿐이었다.

PLEA [pli:] n. an urgent request; in law, the accused criminal's answer to the charges 탄원, 다급한 부탁; 항변

Sandra's *plea* for a raise in her allowance was ignored.

용돈을 올려 달라는 산드라의 간청은 무시됐다.

Herman's lawyers encouraged him to enter a *plea* of "not guilty."

허먼의 변호인단은 그에게 "무죄" 항변을 하라고 독려했다.

PLIGHT [plait] n. a dangerous or difficult situation 곤경

Quentin was moved by the *plight* of the wounded bird, so he took it in and nursed it back to health.

퀜틴은 부상당한 새가 곤경에 처한 걸 보고 마음이 흔들려, 데리고 들어와서는 건강해질 때까지 간호해 줬다.

The *plight* of the baby whale which had accidentally wound up in the Delaware River was broadcast on the news every night until it was rescued.

뜻하지 않게 델라웨어 강에 갇히게 된 새끼 고래의 딱한 처지가 고래가 구조될 때까지 매일 밤 뉴스에 보도되었다.

POLYGAMY [pəlígəmi] n. the crime of being married to more than one person at the same time 중혼죄

It took ten years for Eldridge's wives, one living in Utah, one in Kentucky, and another in Oregon, to realize they were married to a *polygamist*.

한 사람은 유타 주에, 한 사람은 켄터키 주에, 또 한 사람은 오리건 주에 살고 있는 일드리지의 부인들은 10년이 지나서야 자신들이 여러명의 여자와 결혼한 남자와 살고있다는 걸 알게 됐다.

POMPOUS [pámpəs/pɔ́m-] adj. self-important; overly full of a sense of importance or dignity 자부심이 강한, 자만심 강한; 과시하는, 화려한

It's a shame that winning the Little Miss Apple Blossom beauty contest turned Margery into such a *pompous* girl.

마저리가 리틀 미스 사과꽃 미인대회에서 우승하더니 아주 거만한 아이로 변한 건 유감스러운 일이다.

The student council president's speech at graduation was so *pompous* that all the seniors rolled their eyes and giggled.

학생회장의 졸업식 연설은 너무 거창해서 모든 졸업생들이 눈동자를 굴리며 낄낄거렸다.

POTENT [póutnt] adj. powerful 힘센, 강력한

The doctor gave me a very *potent* medicine for my insomnia—two pills put me to sleep in ten minutes.

의사가 내 불면증에 대해 아주 강력한 약을 줘서, 두 알 먹었더니 10분이 지나 잠들었다.

European settlers often faced *potent* opposition from the Native Americans who were being forced off their land.

유럽에서 온 이주자들은 자신들의 땅에서 강제로 쫓겨나는 아메리칸 인디언들에게 강한 저항을 받는 경우가 흔했다.

PRAGMATIC [prægmǽtik] adj. practical 실용적인, 실제적인

Mom had a *pragmatic* solution to our fight over the last piece of pie: she sliced it in half.

엄마는 마지막 파이 한 조각을 가지고 우리가 싸우는 것에 실제적인 해법을 갖고 계셨다. 엄마는 그걸 반으로 자르셨다.

PRECARIOUS [prikέəriəs] adj. dangerously unstable 위태로운

The way Mona had the tray of glasses balanced on her head looked pretty *precarious*.

모나가 머리 위에 유리컵 쟁반을 올려놓고 균형 잡는 건 아주 위태로워 보였다.

The peace between the two countries was *precarious* at best: one false move on either side, and the war could start up again.

두 나라 간의 평화는 가장 좋아 봐야 위태로운 상태였다. 어느 쪽에서라도 까딱하다가는 다시 전쟁이 터질 수 있었다.

PREDOMINANT [pridámənənt/-dɔ́m-] adj. strongest or greatest; most common or most represented 막강한, 탁월한; 주된, 두드러진

During the 1980s, the San Francisco Forty-Niners were the *predominant* football team.

1980년대 에는 샌프란시스코 포티나이너스가 막강한 미식축구팀이었다.

Tulips are the *predominant* flowers in my garden.

튤립이 우리 정원에서 주된 꽃이다.

predominantly는 mostly, 즉 '주로'란 의미

- His hair is *predominantly* black, with a few flecks of gray.
  그의 머리카락은 주로 검은데, 군데군데 하얀머리가 있다.

PREJUDICE [prédʒudis] n. a judgement made about someone or something before the facts are known; unfair judgements or beliefs about a race, religion, or group 선입관; 편견

Melvin had a *prejudice* against opera music because his father always made fun of it, so he refused to go on the field trip to see *Carmen*.
멜빈은 오페라 음악에 대해 선입관이 있었는데, 그의 아버지가 늘 오페라 음악을 비웃었기 때문이다. 그래서 그는 카르멘을 관람하는 현장학습 여행에도 가지 않으려고 했다.

Zoe's belief that all used-car salespeople are dishonest is an example of *prejudice*.
조가 중고차 판매원은 모두 부정직하다고 생각하는 건 편견의 본보기다.

PREMATURE [prìːmətʃúər/prémətʃər] adj. too early; happening before the usual time 때 이른, 시기상조의; 때 아닌

When Edson failed his English exam and wound up getting an "F" in the course, his father realized that his sending out graduation invitations had been *premature*.
에드슨이 영어 시험에서 낙제해 그 과목에서 F를 받게 되자 아버지는 졸업 초대장을 발송하는 건 시기상조라는 걸 알게 됐다.

Don't you think that deciding you hate a book after reading only two pages is a little *premature*?
책을 겨우 두 쪽 읽어본 후에 싫다고 결정짓는 건 좀 이르지 않니?

PREOCCUPIED [priːákjupaid/-ɔ́k-] adj. distracted or caught up in thought 몰두한, 여념이 없는

Olivia was so *preoccupied* with thoughts of her weekend trip to the beach that she didn't even hear her teacher call on her.
올리비아는 해변으로 주말 여행 떠날 걸 생각하느라 여념이 없어서 선생님이 부르는 소리도 못 들었다.

"I apologize for not giving you my full attention," said Beth's piano teacher, "but I'm a little *preoccupied* with problems of my own today."
베스의 피아노 선생님이 말했다. "제대로 신경을 못 써 줘서 미안해요. 오늘은 개인적인 문제로 좀 정신이 없어요."

PRESTIGE [prestíːʒ] n. honor or high standing 영예, 위신

Being the football quarterback gave Penn great *prestige* among his classmates.
펜이 미식축구 쿼터백이라는 건 급우들 사이에서 대단히 위신서는 일이었다.

형용사는 prestigious

- The Congressional Medal of Honor is one of the most *prestigious* awards an American can receive.
  의회 명예 훈장은 미국인이 받을 수 있는 가장 영예로운 상 중의 하나다.

PREVALENT [prévələnt] adj. common; in wide existence 일반적인; 널리 퍼진

Blond hair is *prevalent* in the Scandinavian countries.
금발머리는 스칸디나비아 국가들에서 흔하다.

Tuberculosis is a disease that is much more *prevalent* in cities than in the country.
결핵은 시골보다는 도시에서 훨씬 더 유행하는 병이다.

PREVIOUS [príːviəs] adj. coming before in order 앞의, 이전의

Ms. Spurlock went back to the *previous* day's lesson to review some topics that gave the students difficulty.
스퍼록 씨는 전날 수업으로 돌아가 학생들이 어려워했던 몇 가지 주제를 다시 살폈다.

In the *previous* episode of "Star Trek," Mr. Spock had been kidnapped, but this time it was Captain Kirk who was in danger.
"스타트렉" 지난 회에서는 스팍이 납치당했었지만, 이번 회에서는 커크 선장이 위험에 처했다.

PRIME [praim] adj. first in quality, value, or degree (품질, 가치, 등급에서) 제1의

"My *prime* concern is the safety of the children," said the fire chief.
소방서장이 말했다. "제가 가장 걱정하는 건 아이들의 안전입니다."

Dr. Jonas Salk's *prime* accomplishment was the development of a polio vaccination in the 1950s.
조나스 소크 박사의 최고 업적은 1950년대에 소아마비 백신을 개발한 것이었다.

PRIOR [práiər] adj. coming before in time or order (시간이나 순서상) 이전의, 앞의

"I'm afraid I can't come to your dance recital," said Dinah. "I have a *prior* engagement."
디나가 말했다. "안됐지만 네 무용 발표회에 못 가겠어. 선약이 있거든."

[Note] *Prior to* means before.
prior to는 before, 즉 '~에 앞서', '~전에'의 의미

- *Prior to* the game, Troy tripped and reinjured his thumb, so he was unable to play.
  경기가 시작되기 전 트로이는 넘어져서 엄지손가락을 또 다치는 바람에 출전할 수 없었다.

PROCRASTINATE [proukrǽstənèit/prə-] v. to delay or put off doing something 지연시키다, 늑장부리다

Emily would use any excuse to *procrastinate* when it came to doing her homework.
에밀리는 숙제에 관해서라면 무슨 핑계를 대서라도 미루려고 했다.

Every year, Andy said he wanted to go to clown school, but he *procrastinated* until it was too late to send in an application.
해마다 앤디는 서커스 학교에 가고 싶다고 했지만, 늑장을 부리는 바람에 원서를 써 보내기엔 너무 늦어 버렸다.

PRODIGAL [prádigəl/prɔ́d-] adj. reckless; wasteful; overly generous 무모한; 낭비하는; 아낌없이 주는

Roy made *prodigal* use of the money he won in the lottery: he went to the racetrack and lost it all in one day.
로이는 복권에서 딴 돈을 아무렇게나 썼다. 경마장에 가더니 하루만에 몽땅 잃고 만 것이다.

Mrs. Finney was *prodigal* when it came to buying gifts for her children and grandchildren.
피니 부인은 아이들과 손자들의 선물을 사는 데라면 돈을 아낌없이 썼다.

PROFOUND [prəfáund] adj. deep; thorough; deeply felt 깊은; 철저한; 의미심장한

Ever since she was bitten by a dachshund at the age the three, Lillian has had a *profound* dislike of dogs.
릴리안은 세 살 때 닥스훈트에게 물린 이래로 개라면 질색을 했다.

Voltaire was a philosopher known for his *profound*, but sometimes cynical observations on life.
볼테르는 인생에 대해 심오하지만 때로는 냉소적인 발언으로 알려진 철학자였다.

PROFUSE [prəfjúːs] adj. plentiful; extravagant   풍부한; 낭비하는

My eyes began to water as I stood in the elevator with Dennis because he had made rather *profuse* use of aftershave that evening.
데니스와 엘리베이터에 서 있자니 눈물이 나기 시작했는데, 그날 밤 그가 면도 후 로션을 좀 과하게 발랐기 때문이다.

The neighbors were annoyed by the crowds attracted to the *profuse* display of Christmas lights in Mr. Kringle's lawn.
크링글 씨 집 잔디에 크리스마스 등을 너무 많이 달아 놓아 사람들이 몰려오는 바람에 이웃 사람들은 짜증이 났다.

PROPAGANDA [prɑ̀pəgǽndə/prɔ̀p-] n. material or information distributed to a large number of people, often repeatedly, for the purpose of winning them over to a certain belief, this information is usually one-sided, often unfair, and sometimes untrue   선전, 선전 방법 (특히 정부에서 여론에 영향을 주기 위해 계획적으로 퍼뜨리는 정보)

During times of war, most countries use *propaganda* to keep the civilian population supportive.
전시에는 대부분의 나라에서 일반 민간인들의 협력을 계속 받기 위해 선전 방법을 사용한다.

Many extreme political groups use *propaganda*—scary television commercials, alarming speeches, and sometimes outright lies—to push people into voting a certain way without knowing all the facts.
많은 과격한 정치 집단들은 무서운 TV 광고, 놀라게 하는 연설, 때로는 공공연한 거짓말 등의 선전 활동을 하는데, 사람들로 하여금 모든 사실을 알지 못한 채 특정한 방향으로 투표하도록 만들기 위해서다.

PROSAIC [prouzéiik] adj. dull and unimaginative   무미건조한, 평범한

Cameron's attempts at romance are so *prosaic*, it's no wonder he can never keep a girlfriend.
카메론이 연애를 시도하는 건 너무 무미건조하다. 그가 여자 친구를 못 사귀는 건 당연하다.

Up until the time he met the magician and learned to turn himself into any animal he wanted, Lorenzo led the *prosaic* life of a small-town paper boy.
로렌조는 마술사를 만나 어떤 동물이든 원하는 대로 자신의 몸을 바꾸는 법을 배울 때까지는 소도시의 신문 배달원으로 평범하게 살았다.

PROSE [prouz] n. ordinary speech or writing, as opposed to poetry   산문

The language in Zola's novels was so beautiful that it sounded more like music than *prose*.
졸라의 소설 속 언어는 너무나 아름다워서 산문이라기보다는 음악 같았다.

The exciting story of the battle at the Alamo was made boring by the book's dull, straightforward *prose*.
흥미진진한 앨라모 전투 이야기가 책에서는 단조롭고 직설적인 산문체로 지루해졌다.

PROTRUDE [proutrúːd/prə-] v. to stick out   내밀다, 내뻗다

The man's shoe *protruded* from under the curtain he was trying to hide behind.
남자는 커튼 뒤에 숨으려고 했는데, 신발이 커튼 밑에서 삐져나와 있었다.

Stella's tongue *protruded* every time someone said hello to her, which was quite rude on her part.
스텔라는 누군가 인사를 할 때면 혀를 쭉 내밀었는데, 그럴 때면 그녀는 상당히 무례해 보였다.

PROVINCIAL [prəvínʃəl] adj. not sophisticated, as if from a small town; narrow-minded   시골풍의, 세련되지 못한; 편협한

It was easy to see Joe was not from the city because of his country accent and his *provincial* clothing.
조가 도시 출신이 아니라는 건 쉽게 알 수 있었는데, 시골 억양과 세련되지 못한 옷차림 때문이었다.

Antoinette was embarrassed by her date's *provincial* habit of asking for ketchup with his steak.
앙트와네트는 데이트 상대가 스테이크에 뿌려먹게 케첩을 달라고 하는 촌스러운 습관을 보고 창피했다.

The French think Americans have *provincial* attitudes about showing nudity on television.
프랑스인들은 미국인들이 TV에서 나체를 보여주는 것에 대해 편협한 태도를 갖는다고 생각한다.

PROVOCATIVE [prəvάkətiv/-vɔ́k-] adj. tending to stir up feeling, excitement, or action   도발하는, 흥분시키는, 자극하는

The new scientific evidence showing that eating a pound of chocolate a day will make you live to 100 was so *provocative* that sales of chocolate skyrocketed the day after the research was made public.
하루에 초콜릿 1파운드를 먹으면 100세까지 살 수 있다는 새로운 과학적 입증은 너무나 자극적이어서 그 연구가 발표된 바로 다음 날 초콜릿 판매량이 급등했다.

Annie got a standing ovation for her *provocative* version of the song "I'm Just a Girl Who Can't Say No."
애니는 "난 No라고 말할 수 없는 그런 여자일 뿐예요"를 자극적으로 노래해 기립 박수를 받았다.

PROXIMITY [prɑksíməti/prɔ́k-] n. the state of being near; nearness   근접

The *proximity* of Jacob's apartment to his job made it possible for him to walk to work.
제이콥의 아파트는 직장과 가까워 걸어 다닐 수 있었다.

At the air show, we saw several planes flying in close *proximity* to each other.
에어쇼에서 비행기 몇 대가 서로 가깝게 날아가는 걸 보았다.

The *proximity* of the beautiful beach made it hard for Matthew to stay inside and study.
매튜는 아름다운 해변이 가까이 있다 보니 안에 들어앉아 공부하기가 힘들었다.

PSEUDONYM [súːdənim/sjúːdənim] n. a false name used by an author   필명

In the 1800s, women authors sometimes chose male *pseudonyms*. George Eliot's real name was Mary Ann Evans, and George Sand's real name was Lucie Dudevant.
1800년대에 여류작가들은 이따금 남자의 필명을 썼다. 조지 엘리엇의 본명은 메리 앤 에반스였고, 조르주 상드의 본명은 루시 뒤드방이었다.

PSYCHOLOGICAL [sàikəlάdʒikəl/-lɔ́dʒ-] adj. having to do with the mind and emotions or the study of the mind and emotions   심리적인, 심리학의

After many tests proved that there was nothing wrong with her legs, doctors decided that Mary's illness was *psychological*, not physical.
많은 테스트를 통해 메리의 다리에 아무 이상이 없음이 밝혀지자 의사들은 그녀의 질병이 신체적인 것이 아니라 심리적인 것이라는 결론을 내렸다.

Dr. Skinner conducted several *psychological* experiments on dogs to learn more about human behavior.
스키너 박사는 인간의 행동에 대해 더 알아내기 위해 개를 가지고 몇 가지 심리적 실험을 했다.

Q

QUALM [kwɑːm/kwɔːm] n. a sudden, disturbing feeling; a pang of conscience. This word is usually used in the plural 메스꺼움; 양심의 가책 (복수형태가 일반적)

I'm having *qualms* about leaving the kids all alone for five days.
5일 동안 애들만 따로 두려니 양심에 가책이 느껴진다.

Cody had no *qualms* about feeding his sister's prized fish to the cat.
코디는 누나가 가장 아끼는 애완용 물고기를 고양이에게 먹이면서도 아무런 가책이 없었다.

QUANDARY [kwɑ́ndəri/kwɔ́n-] n. a state of uncertainly or doubt 당황, 난처한 처지

Celeste was in a *quandary* as to what to do with all the leftovers from last night's dinner.
셀리스티는 어젯밤 저녁 식사에서 남은 음식을 어떻게 처리해야 할지 난감했다.

QUERY [kwíəri] n. a question 질문

The vice president was caught off guard by *queries* from the press about his policy on war in Burkina Faso, a country he had never heard of.
부통령은 기자단들에게 생전 들어보지도 못한 버키나 파소라는 나라의 전쟁에 대한 정책에 관한 질문을 받고는 속수무책이었다.

The grandfather was embarrassed by his four-year-old granddaughter's *query* about where babies come from.
할아버지는 네 살 된 손녀가 아기는 어디서 나오는 거냐고 묻자 당황했다.

QUIRK [kwəːrk] n. some odd part of a person's behavior 기벽

Ian always mixes together all the food on his plate before he eats it. It's just one of his *quirks*.
이안은 접시에 있는 모든 음식을 먹기 전에 항상 뒤섞는다. 그건 그저 그의 기벽 중 하나다.

QUOTA [kwóutə] n. a number or amount set as an acceptable standard 몫, 할당량

When Sunny worked at the basket weaving factory, each weaver had a *quota* of twenty baskets a day.
써니가 바구니 직조 공장에서 일할 때 각 직조공들의 할당량은 하루에 바구니 스무개였다.

The government sometimes sets *quotas* on the number of immigrants the United States will accept from different countries.
미국 정부는 때때로 다른 나라에서 받아들이는 이민자의 수를 할당한다.

 R

RADICAL [rǽdikəl] adj. extreme; revolutionary 과격한, 급진적인; 혁명적인

Justine made a *radical* change in her appearance by shaving her head and losing 150 pounds.
저스틴은 머리를 밀고 150파운드의 체중을 빼서 외모를 확 바꾸었다.

Ross had proposed a *radical* method for keeping the U.S. out of entanglements in messy foreign wars: he suggested we build a huge wall all the way around the country and cut off all long-distance telephone conversation with outside countries.
로스는 성가신 외국 전쟁에 미국이 얽히는 걸 피하기 위한 급진적 방법을 제안했다. 나라 온 둘레에 거대한 벽을 쌓고 외국과의 장거리 전화 대화를 중단할 것을 제안한 것이다.

RAPPORT [ræpɔ́:r/rə-] n. a good relationship or connection 좋은 관계, 화합

It's important for a teacher to develop a *rapport* with his students.
교사는 학생들과 좋은 관계를 발전시키는 것이 중요하다.

Everyone in the department thought Jane should bring their complaints to the boss since she had the best *rapport* with him.
부서의 사람들은 모두 제인이 상사와 사이가 가장 좋으므로 그녀가 그들의 불평거리를 상사에게 전달해야 한다고 생각했다.

REAP [ri:p] v. to gain as a result of effort 수확하다, (노력의 결과를) 얻다

If you start exercising when you are young, you will *reap* the health benefits later in life.
젊은 나이에 운동을 시작하면 나이가 들어서 건강의 이익을 얻을 것이다.

The inventor had no idea that he would *reap* such riches from his simplest creation: the paper clip.
발명가는 종이 집게라는 아주 간단한 물건을 만들어 그렇게 많은 부를 얻게 될 줄 몰랐다.

REBUTTAL [ribʌ́tl] n. a counter-argument; presentation of a side of an issue different from one already presented 반론, 반박

In the debate, Mike made an angry *rebuttal* to the accusation that he had stolen public funds.
논쟁이 벌어지는 동안 마이크는 자신이 공금을 횡령했다는 비난에 대해 강하게 반박했다.

The newspaper article attacking Mr. McBain for poor management of the strained-banana disaster at the baby food plant was unfair because the reporter had never called Mr. McBain for a comment or a *rebuttal*.
유아식 공장의 바나나 압착 공정 사고를 잘못 처리했다며 맥베인 씨를 공격한 신문 기사는 불공평했다. 왜냐하면 그에게는 어떤 설명이나 반론의 기회도 주지 않았기 때문이다.

RECLUSE [riklúːs/rékluːs] n. a person who lives alone, away from society 은둔자

The once-famous movie star gave up her career at the age of thirty and became a *recluse*, living in a small house on a faraway island.
한때 유명 영화배우였던 여자는 서른살에 배우라는 직업을 버리고 은둔자가 되어 멀리 떨어진 섬의 작은 집에서 살았다.

RECONCILE [rékənsail] v. to bring friendship or good relations back; to settle or bring into agreement
화해시키다; 조정하다, 일치시키다

On yesterday's episode of the "Susie Snoop Show," a mother and daughter who hadn't spoken in ten years were *reconciled*.
어제 방송된 "수지 스눕 쇼"에서는 10년 동안 말을 안하고 지낸 엄마와 딸이 화해했다.

The two countries decided to give up war and *reconcile* their differences through negotiation.
두 나라는 전쟁을 그만두고 협상을 통해 의견 차를 조정하기로 했다.

[Note] The noun form of reconcile is *reconciliation* [rèkənsiliéiʃən].
명사형은 reconciliation

- Mr. and Mrs. Semper made several attempts at *reconciliation*, but finally decided it was best if they got divorced while they still had some unbroken dishes.
  셈퍼 부부는 몇 차례 화해를 시도했지만, 결국엔 아직 깨지지 않은 접시가 조금 남아 있을 때 이혼하는 게 최선이라고 결정했다.

RECOUNT [rikáunt] v. to tell in detail 자세히 말하다

The tribal storyteller can *recount* the entire history of his clan, all the way back to its beginning several hundred years ago.
부족의 만담가는 수백 년 전까지 거슬러 올라가는 일족의 전 역사를 자세히 말할 수 있다.

The book *I, Claudius recounts* the final years of the corrupt Roman Empire.
'나, 클라우디우스' 라는 책은 타락한 로마제국의 마지막 몇 해를 상세히 말해 준다.

RECTIFY [réktəfai] v. to correct or make right 수정하다, 교정하다

When the president of the college noticed that the plaque under the statue of the founder had a spelling error on it, he decided to *rectify* the mistake, and ordered a new plaque immediately.
학장은 설립자 동상 밑의 명판에 철자가 하나 잘못된 걸 발견하고는 수정하기로 결정하고 즉시 새로운 명판을 만들라고 지시했다.

The children thought the sun revolved around the earth until their astronomy teacher *rectified* their mistake.
아이들은 천문학 교사가 잘못을 바로잡아 주기 전까지 태양이 지구 주위를 돈다고 생각했다.

RECUR [rikə́ːr] v. to happen again; to happen repeatedly 재발하다; 반복되다

After the playoffs, I had a *recurring* nightmare about a sad-faced clown dressed in a Los Angeles Lakers uniform.
플레이오프가 끝난 뒤, 나는 슬픈 얼굴의 광대가 LA 레이커스 유니폼을 입고 있는 악몽을 계속해서 꾸었다.

Selena showed me the meadow where the reported alien visitations had *recurred* over the years.
셀레나가 내게 수년 동안 계속해서 외계인이 나타났다고 전해지는 목초지를 보여주었다.

REDUNDANT [ridʌ́ndənt] adj. made up of more words than necessary; unnecessarily wordy; unnecessarily repetitive (표현이) 잉여적인; 말이 많은, 장황한; 불필요하게 반복되는

When Mrs. Flipper yelled, "I want an immediate explanation and I want it right now!" no one had the guts to tell her she was being *redundant*, since "immediate" and "right now" mean the same thing.
플리퍼 부인이 "즉각적인 해명을 해줘요. 지금 당장 해줘요!" 라고 소리쳤을 때 어느 누구도 "즉각적인" 과 "지금 당장" 이 똑같은 의미로 그녀가 중복된 표현을 쓰고 있다는 걸 말할 용기가 없었다.

The editor removed several *redundant* paragraphs from the textbook.
편집자는 교재에서 중복된 단락을 몇 개 없앴다.

Asking someone to repeat something again is *redundant*.
누군가에게 뭔가를 또다시 반복하라고 요구하는 것은 불필요하다.

REFUGE [réfju:dʒ] n. a place of safety or shelter 피난처, 은신처

Several African countries set aside land as a *refuge* for the elephants, which were being killed off by hunters who wanted their tusks for ivory.
아프리카 몇 개국은 코끼리들의 은신처로 별도의 땅을 두었는데, 코끼리는 상아를 얻으려고 엄니를 노리는 사냥꾼들에게 죽임을 당하고 있다.

For Sarah, the attic was a *refuge* from her loud, rough brothers.
사라에게 다락방은 시끄럽고 거친 오빠들로부터의 피난처였다.

REGIME [rəʒí:m/rei-] n. the ruling system of government 제도, 체제

Many Romanians died at the hands of their own government during the cruel *regime* of Nicolae Ceausescu, the former communist ruler.
많은 루마니아인들이 전 공산주의 지도자 니콜라이 차우셰스쿠의 잔인한 체제 동안 정부의 손에 죽어 갔다.

The arts flourished and England prospered during the Queen Elizabeth I's *regime*.
엘리자베스 1세 체제에 예술이 융성하고 영국이 번영을 누렸다.

Albania is still under the control of a strict, communist *regime*.
알바니아는 아직도 엄격한 공산주의 체제 하에 놓여 있다.

REHABILITATE [rì:həbíləteit] v. to restore to health or usefulness (건강이나 쓰임새를) 회복하다, 복귀시키다

Supposedly, the aim of our prison system is to *rehabilitate* criminals so that when they get out, they can be productive members of society.
우리가 교도소를 운영하는 목적은 범죄자들이 출소했을 때 생산적인 사회 구성원이 될 수 있도록 재활 교육을 시키는 것이다.

The athlete spent months doing special exercises, hoping to *rehabilitate* his knee.
운동선수는 무릎이 회복되길 바라며 몇 달 동안 특수 운동을 했다.

REIMBURSE [rì:imbə́:rs] v. to pay back 상환하다, 갚다

"If you pick up a pizza on the way here to watch the game, I'll *reimburse* you for it," offered Pete.
"경기 보러 여기로 오는 길에 피자를 사오면 내가 돈 줄게." 피트가 제안했다.

Sid wanted to be *reimbursed* for the cost of the long distance phone calls he made on behalf of the company.
시드는 회사일로 자신이 거는 장거리 전화에 대해 비용을 상환 받기 원했다.

RELENTLESS [riléntlis] adj. harsh; severe; unending 거친; 엄한; 끝없는

We were lost at sea for days, our boat tossed and battered by *relentless* wind and rain.
우리 며칠 동안 바다에서 조난을 당했는데, 거친 비바람에 배가 흔들리고 부서졌다.

The police officer was *relentless* when it came to hunting down criminals: he wouldn't rest until he got his man.
그 경찰관은 범죄자를 추적하여 잡는 데 가차 없었다. 그는 범인을 잡을 때까지 쉬질 않았다.

RELEVANT [réləvənt] adj. having something to do with the matter at hand (당면한 문제와) 관련된, 적절한

I think Mary's age is *relevant* to the question of whether or not she would be a good trapeze artist, but everyone else disagrees with me.
나는 메리의 나이가 뛰어난 그네 곡예사가 될 수 있는가와 관련이 있다고 생각하는데, 다른 사람들은 모두 나와 의견을 달리한다.

It seems as though some of my classmates like to raise their hands and make comments even if they have nothing *relevant* to say.
우리 반 아이들 몇 명은 관련된 얘기를 할 것도 없으면서 손을 들고 의견을 말하는 것 같다.

RELINQUISH [rilíŋkwiʃ] v. to give back; to give up; to abandon 돌려주다; 포기하다; 버리다

Endless bombing raids forced the army to *relinquish* its camp and retreat.
끝없는 폭격으로 육군은 진지를 버리고 퇴각해야 했다.

When a new Miss America is selected, the old Miss America must *relinquish* her crown and title.
새로운 미스 아메리카가 당선되면 이전의 미스 아메리카는 자신의 왕관과 타이틀을 돌려주어야 한다.

RELUCTANT [rilʌ́ktənt] adj. unwilling 마음 내키지 않는

The magician asked Otto to come up on stage and assist him, but Otto was shy and *reluctant*.
마술사는 오토에게 무대로 나와 도와 달라고 했지만, 오토는 부끄러워서 내켜 하지 않았다.

Ernie was *reluctant* to leave the beach because he was only halfway through building his sand castle.
어니는 모래성을 겨우 반 밖에 못 지어서 해변을 떠나고 싶지 않았다.

REMINISCE [rèmənís] v. to remember and tell stories about past events 추억하다

When we moved back to Alabama, my parents were eager to spend time *reminiscing* with their old friends.
우리가 앨라배마로 돌아왔을 때 부모님은 옛 친구 분들과 추억을 나누며 시간 보내기를 간절히 원하셨다.

I don't mind the fact that my grandmother likes to *reminisce*, but she tells the same stories over and over again.
할머니가 추억에 잠기는 걸 좋아하신다는 게 싫진 않지만 할머니는 똑같은 말씀만 계속해서 하신다.

RENDEZVOUS [rɑ́:ndəvù:/-dei-/rɔ́ndi-] n. a meeting at a certain time and place or v. to meet at a certain time and place (시간과 장소를 정한) 만남 / (약속 장소에서) 만나다

Colette and Pierre decided that the cafe by the river was the perfect spot for a *rendezvous*.
콜레트와 피에르는 가장 적당한 약속 장소로 강변에 있는 카페를 정했다.

The spies decided to *rendezvous* at midnight under the bridge so they could exchange the secret information.
스파이들은 비밀 정보를 교환하기 위해 자정에 다리 밑에서 만나기로 했다.

RENOUNCE [rináuns] v. to give up formally; to reject 포기하다; 거절하다; 관계를 끊다

Claude *renounced* his father when it was discovered he had sold secret military information to the enemy.
클로드는 아버지가 적에게 군사기밀을 팔았다는 것을 알고 아버지와 관계를 끊었다.

Mrs. Evans told her husband she would only take him back if he *renounced* gambling forever.
에반스 부인은 남편에게 그가 영원히 도박을 포기한다면 다시 받아주겠다고 말했다.

RENOWNED [rináund] adj. famous 유명한

Natalia is a *renowned* concert pianist.
나탈리아는 유명한 콘서트 피아니스트다.

Jimmy Carter is *renowned* for his diplomatic negotiation skills.
지미 카터는 외교상의 협상 수완으로 유명하다.

Tracy is *renowned* throughout school for being able to blow gigantic bubbles with her gum.
트레이시는 교내에서 껌으로 커다란 풍선을 불 수 있는 것으로 유명하다.

REPENT [ripént] v. to regret or feel bad about 후회하다, 유감스럽게 여기다

Irving *repented* after cheating on the test.
어빙은 시험에서 부정행위를 하고 난 후 후회했다.

Elizabeth *repented* her mean treatment of the new girl at school.
엘리자베스는 학교에서 전학 온 아이에게 짓궂게 대한 것을 후회했다.

REPRIEVE [riprí:v] n. temporary safety from danger; cancellation of punishment 위험의 일시적 모면; 집행 유예

Calvin awoke with a sense of doom because he realized he'd forgotten to study for the big test, but nature granted him a *reprieve* in the form of a huge snowstorm that caused school to be cancelled.
캘빈은 중요한 시험을 앞두고 공부하는 걸 잊어버렸음을 깨닫고는 잠에서 깨며 끝장났다고 생각했지만, 자연이 거대한 눈보라로 휴교가 되게 만들어 그를 구제해 주었다.

Theodore was about to be executed by the firing squad when his life was saved by a last-minute *reprieve* from the governor.
테오도르는 총살형에 처해질 뻔했는데, 주지사가 마지막 순간에 사면해주어 목숨을 구했다.

REPRIMAND [réprəmænd/-mɑ̀:nd] v. to scold or n. a strong scolding 꾸짖다 / 비난, 질책

Hugo, the bus driver, was sternly *reprimanded* by his boss when he was found sleeping in the baggage compartment.
버스 운전기사 휴고는 수화물 칸에서 잠을 자다 발각되는 바람에 상사에게 호되게 꾸중을 들었다.

Mr. Philips, the chemistry teacher, received a written *reprimand* from the principal for teaching his students how to make a bomb with soapflakes and olive oil.
필립스 화학 선생님은 학생들에게 비누와 올리브유로 폭탄 만드는 법을 가르쳤다는 이유로 교장에게 징계문을 받았다.

REPULSIVE [ripʌ́lsiv] adj. disgusting, off-putting 불쾌한, 혐오스러운

That dog is cute from a distance, but it has a *repulsive* odor.
저 개는 멀리서 보면 귀엽지만 불쾌한 냄새가 난다.

Nick makes a really *repulsive* face by flipping his eyelids inside out and rolling his eyes back into his head so all you can see are the whites.
닉은 눈꺼풀을 뒤집고 눈동자를 굴려 흰자만 보이도록 머릿속에 집어넣어 정말 혐오스러운 얼굴을 만든다.

RESERVE [rizə́:rv] v. to save for later; to order for use later 남겨 두다; 예약해 두다

I want a glass of milk before bedtime, but I'll *reserve* enough so you can have cereal for breakfast.
자기 전에 우유 한 잔 마시고 싶어요. 하지만 당신이 아침으로 시리얼을 먹을 수 있을 만큼은 남겨 둘게요.

That restaurant is so popular that you have to call and *reserve* a table two months in advance if you want to eat there.
저 식당은 아주 유명해서 거기서 식사하려면 두 달 전에 전화해 자리를 예약해야 한다.

[Note] When people say a person is *reserved*, that means the person holds himself back, or is shy and says little. A person who is *reserved* has *reserve*.
사람을 보고 reserved라 하면, '삼가는', '수줍은', '말수가 적은' 이란 의미. be reserved는 have reserve와 같은 표현

RESIGNATION [rèzignéiʃən] n. the act of quitting or a notice that one is quitting; acceptance of something difficult 사직, 사표; 포기, 체념

Nancy's boss refused to accept her *resignation* and offered to double her salary if she would stay and keep working.
낸시의 상사는 그녀의 사표 수리를 거부했고, 계속 남아 일을 해주면 월급을 두 배로 주겠다고 제안했다.

Brian was so upset by the vice president's unfair accusations that he went back to his desk, typed up his *resignation*, left it on his boss's desk, and went home.
브라이언은 부사장의 불공평한 질책에 너무 화가 나 책상으로 돌아가서 사직서를 작성한 다음 상사의 책상 위에 올려놓고 집에 가 버렸다.

After fighting about it for two weeks, Harvey sighed with *resignation* and said, "Okay, we'll sell that television."
하비는 2주 동안 그 문제로 싸운 후 체념의 한숨을 쉬며 말했다. "좋아, 텔레비전을 파는 거야."

The soldiers could hear the *resignation* in the general's voice as he announced that the president had relieved him of duty and put another general in charge.
대통령이 자신을 해임하고 그 자리에 다른 장군을 임명했다는 소식을 전하는 장군의 목소리에서 군인들은 체념을 읽을 수 있었다.

RESOLUTE [rézəlù:t] adj. firm and determined 단호한, 굳게 결심한

In a calm and *resolute* voice, Mindy said, "Give me a full refund right now, in cash, or I will have the police in here to arrest you so fast it will make your head spin."
민디가 조용하지만 단호한 목소리로 말했다. "지금 당장 전액을 상환해. 현금으로 말야. 안 그러면 경찰을 여기로 불러서 널 당장 체포시키겠어. 그럼 넌 정신 못 차릴 거라구."

Ted had grown from a shy little boy into a confident man: his head held high, his step *resolute*, his handshake firm, and his smile warm.
테드는 숫기 없는 꼬마에서 자신만만한 남자로 자라났다. 고개는 꼿꼿하고 발걸음은 단호하며 악수는 힘있고 미소는 따뜻했다.

RESOLVE [rizálv/-zólv] v. to commit oneself, or make a firm decision; to find a solution 자신과 약속하다, 결심하다; 해결하다

In an effort to make better grades, Linda *resolved* to spend no less than two hours every night doing homework.
린다는 좀더 나은 성적을 얻기 위해 매일 밤 숙제하는 데 두 시간씩이나 할애하기로 결심했다.

It's a sign of maturity to be able to *resolve* problems on your own.
문제를 네 스스로 풀 수 있다는 것은 성숙했다는 표시다.

[Note] The word *resolution* [rèzəlúːʃən] means a firm agreement you make with yourself.
resolution은 자신과 맺는 굳은 약속, 즉 '결의', '결심'을 의미

- When people talk about making New Year's resolutions, they are promising themselves that they will start or stop doing something.
새해 다짐(New Year's resolutions)에 대해 이야기하는 것은 뭔가를 시작하거나 그만둘 거라는 약속을 스스로에게 하는 것이다.

RESUME [rizúːm/-zjúːm] v. to start again 다시 시작하다

After I came back from the restroom, we *resumed* our discussion.
화장실에서 돌아온 후 우리는 토론을 다시 시작했다.

Our game of chess had dragged on so long we decided to quit for the day and *resume* tomorrow.
체스 게임이 너무 질질 끌려서 오늘은 그만하고 내일 다시 하기로 했다.

RETORT [ritóːrt] v. to make a quick and witty answer or n. a quick, witty answer 말대꾸하다, 응수하다 / 말대꾸

When the man in the restaurant asked, "What's this fly doing in my soup?" his waiter *retorted*, "It looks like the backstroke."
식당에서 남자가 "이 파리가 내 수프에서 뭘 하고 있는 거요?" 하고 묻자 웨이터는 "배영을 하고 있나 보네요" 라고 대꾸했다.

Winston Churchill, the former prime minister of Great Britain, was known for his clever *retorts* as well as his leadership.
영국의 전 수상 윈스턴 처칠은 지도력만큼이나 재치 있는 말대꾸로도 유명했다.

REVEL [révəl] v. to take great pleasure; to have noisy, festive fun 매우 기뻐하다; 잔치를 베풀다, 마시며 흥청거리다

Will *revelled* in the millions of dollars he won in the lottery.
윌은 복권이 당첨되어 생긴 수백만 달러로 흥청거렸다.

Jealous Joan *revelled* in the misfortune of her co-worker.
질투심 많은 조안은 동료가 불행한 일을 당하자 너무 좋아했다.

When the New York Mets won the World Series, all the New York City *revelled* for days.
뉴욕 메츠가 월드 시리즈에서 우승하자 뉴욕 시 전체가 며칠 동안 축제 분위기였다.

[Note] *Revelry* [révəlri] is loud partying.
revelry는 '떠들썩한 파티'

- Marco is so rich he can afford not to work and to spend his days and nights in endless *revelry*.
마르코는 돈이 아주 많아 일은 하지 않고 밤낮 없이 파티를 벌이며 지낼 수 있다.

REVERE [rivíər] v. to respect highly; to honor 매우 존경하다, 숭배하다

Before the end of World War II, the Japanese people *revered* their emperor as a god.
제2차 세계대전이 끝나기 전 일본인들은 천황을 신처럼 숭배했다.

The Chief Justice of the Supreme Court is *revered* for his fairness and wisdom.
대법원장은 공정함과 지혜로 존경받는다.

[Note] To be *reverent* [révərənt] is to be respectful. To be *irreverent* [irévərənt] is to be slightly disrespectful.

reverent는 '경의를 표하는', '숭상하는', irreverent는 '무례한', '불손한'

- It was *irreverent* for Joey to call the eighty-year-old bank president "gramps."
  조이가 80세 된 은행장을 "영감탱이"라 부른 것은 좀 무례했다.

RIGOROUS [rígərəs] adj. strict; harsh 엄한, 엄격한; 혹독한

Actress Demi Moore hired a personal trainer and started a *rigorous* exercise schedule to get into top shape for her next movie.
여배우 데미 무어는 다음 영화에 대비해 최고의 몸매를 만들려고 개인 트레이너를 고용해 엄격한 운동 스케줄을 시작했다.

When Tina found out that she had to go to practice three times a week, she decided that the life of a cheerleader was too *rigorous* for her.
티나는 일주일에 세 번씩 연습하러 가야 한다는 사실을 알고 치어리더의 생활은 자신에게 너무 혹독하다고 생각했다.

RISQUÉ [riskéi/rískei] adj. very close to being shocking or indecent 충격적인, 음란한

The school board wouldn't let us see the 1960s movie version of *Romeo and Juliet* because they thought some of the love scenes were too *risqué*.
학교이사회는 우리에게 1960년대에 영화로 만들어진 '로미오와 줄리엣'을 못 보게 했는데, 그 이유는 러브신 일부가 너무 외설적이라고 생각해서다.

Grandpa was about to tell a story about an exotic dancer he knew during the war, but, much to our disappointment, Mom told him it was too *risqué* for us kids to hear.
할아버지는 전시에 알았던 이국적인 무용수에 대해 말씀하시려고 했는데, 실망스럽게도 엄마는 할아버지에게 그 이야기가 우리 같은 아이들이 듣기엔 너무 외설스럽다고 말했다.

RITE [rait] n. a ceremony; an act or series of acts performed by custom 의식; 관습, 관례

Many different cultures have *rites* of passage that boys and girls must go through in order to be considered men and women.
많은 다른 문화에는 소년과 소녀가 성인으로 여겨지기 위해 겪어야 하는 통과의례가 있다.

The tradition of dancing around a Maypole on the first day of May is an ancient *rite* of spring.
5월의 첫날 5월제 기둥을 춤추며 도는 전통은 봄을 맞는 고대의 관습이었다.

RUSTIC [rʌ́stik] adj. having to do with the country or country life 시골의, 시골풍의

Even though he was a rich, big-city lawyer, Harold liked having *rustic* furniture and decorations in his apartment.
해롤드는 부자에 대도시 변호사였지만 자신의 아파트는 시골풍으로 가구를 놓고 장식하길 좋아했다.

The restaurant was brand-new, but it was built to look old-fashioned and *rustic* - the wooden tables looked faded and weatherbeaten, drinks were served out of mason jars, and there were a lot of antlers hanging on the walls.
그 식당은 최근에 개업했지만, 구식에 시골풍으로 지어졌는데, 나무 테이블은 빛이 바래고 비바람에 시달린 듯했으며, 술은 유리 단지에서 따라주었고, 벽에는 사슴뿔이 잔뜩 걸려 있었다.

S

SABOTAGE [sǽbətɑːʒ] n. an attempt to slow down or stop a cause or activity by destroying property or disrupting work or v. to commit sabotage 파괴 행위, 방해 행위(기물을 파손하거나 일을 망쳐서 어떤 활동을 늦추거나 막으려는 시도) / 사보타주하다, 고의로 파괴하다, 방해하다

When Dad discovered that some important parts of the lawn mower were missing, he immediately accused us of *sabotage*.
아빠는 잔디 깎는 기계의 중요 부품 몇 개가 없어진 걸 알고는 곧 우리가 일부러 망가뜨려 놓았다며 나무랐다.

Jake dreaded going back to boarding school so much that he tried to *sabotage* the family car.
제이크는 기숙학교로 돌아가는 게 너무나 두려워 부모님 차를 일부러 망가뜨리려 했다.

Computer viruses are a new and dangerous form of *sabotage*.
컴퓨터 바이러스는 새롭고 위험한 형태의 파괴행위다.

SARCASTIC [sɑːrkǽstik] adj. ironic, sneering, or intended to hurt someone's feelings 반어적인; 빈정대는

Ian's *sarcastic* sense of humor upsets lots of people, but I think he is very funny.
이안의 반어적인 유머 감각은 많은 사람들을 당황하게 하지만 나는 그가 아주 재미있는 사람 같다.

When Bonnie admitted she didn't know the capital of California, Les made the *sarcastic* comment: "I'm sure you'll make the state a fine senator some day."
보니가 캘리포니아의 주도를 모른다고 시인하자 레스는 "넌 분명히 언젠가 캘리포니아주 출신 상원 의원으로 아주 훌륭하신 분을 뽑을 거야." 라며 빈정거렸다.

SCANTY [skǽnti] adj. barely sufficient or not enough in term of amount 부족한, 불충분한

Sally's father wouldn't let her out of the house in such a *scanty* dress.
샐리의 아버지는 샐리가 그처럼 노출이 심한 옷을 입은 채로는 집밖에 못 나가게 했다.

The supply of apples on our tree is so *scanty* this year, I doubt I'll have enough for more than a couple of pies.
올해 우리 나무에 열린 사과가 너무 적어서 파이 2-3개 이상을 만들 만큼이나 될지 모르겠다.

SCOFF [skɔːf/skɑf/skɔf] v. to express contempt; to mock 경멸하다; 비웃다, 조롱하다

The children *scoffed* at my idea that we should turn the television off and go outside to play.
아이들은 텔레비전을 끄고 밖에 나가서 놀자는 내 아이디어를 비웃었다.

"You've done nothing but *scoff* at every idea I've had so far," said Lillian to Mick. "Since you're so smart, why don't you go get that elephant off our car by yourself?"
릴리안이 미크에게 말했다. "넌 지금껏 내가 내놓은 아이디어를 비웃기만 했어. 넌 아주 똘똘하니까 가서 혼자 힘으로 차에 있는 코끼리를 꺼내 보지 그래?"

SCRUPULOUS [skrú:pjuləs] adj. extremely careful 꼼꼼한, 철저한

Eugene was *scrupulous* in keeping his room clean: he never so much as left a sock on the floor.
유진은 방청소를 꼼꼼하게 했다. 바닥에 양말 한 짝도 절대 두지 않을 정도였다.

Ferns are delicate plants that need *scrupulous* care and attention.
양치류는 철저한 보살핌과 주의를 요하는 예민한 식물이다.

SCRUTINY [skrú:təni] n. close observation; careful watching or study 정밀한 조사; 세심한 관찰이나 연구

Simon's room appeared neat at a glance, but closer *scrutiny* would show that he had just shoved everything under his bed.
사이먼의 방은 얼핏 보면 깔끔해 보였지만 가까이서 자세히 보면 침대 밑에 온갖 것을 쑤셔 넣었다는 걸 알 수 있었다.

The editor was known for his *scrutiny*: he never missed a single mistake.
그 편집자는 세심하게 보는 것으로 유명했다. 그는 단 하나의 실수도 놓치는 법이 없었다.

SECT [sekt] n. a number of people that form their own special group within a larger group 분파, 종파, 학파, 당파

The Baptist church can be considered a Protestant *sect* because it shares many beliefs with other Protestant churches, but has some of its own practices, too.
침례교는 다른 신교들과 공유하는 신앙이 많아 신교의 한 종파로 여겨질 수 있지만, 침례교만의 고유한 관습도 있다.

The Hasidism are the members of a Jewish *sect* that stresses the power of mysticism and prayer.
하시디즘은 신비주의와 기도의 힘을 강조하는 유대교의 한 분파다.

SEDATE [sidéit] adj. calm and dignified; quiet 고요하고 위엄 있는; 조용한

Nothing – not even loud noises, big dogs, or squirts from my water gun – could disturb the fat, *sedate* cat.
큰 소음이나 커다란 개, 내 물총에서 뿜어 나오는 물줄기, 그 어떤 것도 비대하고 위엄있는 고양이를 방해할 수 없었다.

The principal was scared our prom would get too wild and out of hand, but it turned out to be so *sedate* you could have mistaken it for a meeting of the bridge club.
교장 선생님은 우리의 졸업 댄스파티가 너무 소란하고 통제 불능이 될까 봐 겁먹었지만, 실제로는 너무나 조용해서 브리지 클럽의 모임이라고 착각할 수 있을 정도였다.

SEDENTARY [sédntèri/-təri] adj. requiring a lot of sitting; used to sitting a lot and not getting much exercise 앉아 있는, 앉아 일하는; 잘 앉는

Even though Kristin eats constantly and has a *sedentary* lifestyle, she is as skinny as a toothpick.
크리스틴은 끝없이 먹어 대고 잘 앉아 있는 생활을 하면서도 바싹 말랐다.

If you don't like *sedentary* work, truck driving is not for you.
앉아 일하는 것을 좋아하지 않으면 트럭 운전은 부적합하다.

SERENE [sərí:n] adj. peaceful and calm 평화롭고 고요한

The lake looked so beautiful and *serene* in the early morning light.
호수는 이른 아침 햇빛을 받아 너무나 아름답고 고요해 보였다.

Even though children were yelling and fighting all around her, Mrs. Dolittle looked happy and *serene*.
아이들이 사방에서 소리 지르고 싸우고 하는데도 두리틀 부인은 행복하고 평화로워 보였다.

SERVILE [sə́:rvil/-vail] adj. like a slave or servant; submissive 노예의, 하인 같은; 비굴한, 굴종적인

Mona was alarmed by the *servile* attitude her boyfriend's mother had toward him and her husband. She did all the laundry, cooked all the meals, and fetched them something to drink whenever they wanted.
모나는 남자 친구의 어머니가 아들과 남편에게 하인처럼 행동하는 걸 보고 깜짝 놀랐다. 그녀는 빨래도 혼자 다 했고 요리도 혼자 다 했으며, 그들이 원할 때면 언제든 마실 것을 갖다 주었다.

Veronica was a beautiful but mean-spirited girl who demanded *servile* obedience from her boyfriend.
베로니카는 아름다웠지만 비열한 아이로, 자신의 남자 친구에게 비굴한 복종을 요구했다.

[Note] The noun form of servile is *servility* [sə:rvíləti].
명사형은 servility

- Mona told her boyfriend he'd better not expect *servility* from her.
  모나는 남자 친구에게 자신이 굴종하기를 기대하지 말라고 했다.

SHREWD [ʃru:d] adj. clever 영리한; 약삭빠른

Clara is *shrewd* shopper: she always finds the best bargains and never pays full price.
클라라는 물건을 살 때 야무지다. 항상 제일 싼 물건을 찾아내기 때문에 제 가격을 다 주는 법은 없다.

Shrewd poker players can tell whether or not you have a good hand by the look on your face.
포커를 잘 치는 사람은 상대의 표정을 보고 패가 좋은지 아닌지를 분간할 수 있다.

SIESTA [siéstə] n. a nap taken after the midday meal 낮잠

In Spain and Italy, many stores are closed for a couple of hours in the afternoon while the owners take their *siestas*.
스페인과 이탈리아에서는 많은 상점들이 오후 두어 시간 정도 주인이 낮잠을 자는 동안 문을 닫는다.

I wish *siestas* were a common practice in America.
낮잠이 미국에서도 일반적인 일이 됐으면 좋겠다.

SIMILAR [símələr] adj. alike but not exactly the same 비슷한

Spanish and Italian are *similar* languages because they both came from Latin.
스페인어와 이탈리아어는 비슷한 언어인데, 둘 다 라틴어에서 유래됐기 때문이다.

Larry's car is *similar* to Mo's: they both drive blue Ford Mustangs, but Larry's is couple of years older than Mo's.
래리의 차는 모의 차와 비슷하다. 둘 다 파란색 포드 머스탱을 모는데, 래리의 차가 모의 것보다 2년쯤 더 됐다.

SIMULTANEOUS [sàiməltéiniəs/sìm-] adj. happening at the same time 동시에 일어나는

The flash of lightning and the crash of thunder were almost *simultaneous*.
번개의 번쩍임과 천둥의 쾅 소리가 거의 동시에 일어났다.

The umpire had a hard call to make: the runner slid home and *simultaneously* the catcher tagged him.
심판은 판정을 내리기가 어려웠다. 주자가 홈으로 슬라이딩함과 동시에 포수가 그를 태그아웃 시켰다.

SKEPTIC [sképtik] n. a person who doubts the truth of something 의심이 많은 사람, 회의론자

"I'm afraid I'm a *skeptic* when it comes to so-called true love," said Ida.
이다가 말했다. "안타깝지만 난 소위 진실한 사랑이라는 것에 대해선 회의적이야."

[Note] A skeptic is *skeptical* [sképtikəl].

skeptical은 '회의적인', '의심 많은'

- The rest of the town was convinced that the Magnificent Mario could predict the future, but Saul was *skeptical*.
  훌륭한 마리오가 미래를 예언할 수 있다고 마을 사람들 모두 확신했지만 사울만은 의심했다.

SKIRMISH [skə́:rmiʃ]   n. a minor battle between small groups   사소한 싸움, 충돌

Except for a few *skirmishes*, the town was finally peaceful after three years of war.
그 마을은 몇 번의 사소한 충돌을 빼고는 3년간의 전쟁 이후 마침내 평화로워졌다.

Several *skirmishes* between rival gang members broke out during the Icey Dogg concert.
아이시 독이 공연하는 동안 경쟁 관계의 깡패들끼리 몇 차례 작은 싸움을 벌였다.

SLANDER [slǽndər/slá:n-]   v. to spread false, bad rumors about someone; to tell lies about someone publicly or   n. a false statement spread publicly to damage a person's reputation   헛소문을 퍼뜨리다; 중상하다, 명예를 훼손하다 / 중상

The coach *slandered* his quarterback by calling him a shoplifter on national television.
코치는 국영 TV에 나와 자기 팀의 쿼터백을 좀도둑이라 부르며 중상했다.

The quarterback said he would not put up with such *slander*, and sued the coach for five million dollars.
쿼터백은 그런 중상모략을 참을 수 없다면서 코치를 상대로 500만 달러의 손해배상 소송을 걸었다.

SMIRK [smə:rk]   n. the annoying smile of a person who is too happy with himself or   v. to smile annoyingly out of self-satisfaction   (자기만족에서 나오는) 능글맞은 웃음 / 능글능글 웃다, 히죽히죽 웃다

Gregory *smirked* at the rest of the students when the teacher announced that he had made a perfect score on the test and the rest of them had failed.
그레고리는 선생님이 자기만 시험에서 만점을 받고 나머지 학생들은 낙제했다고 발표하자 나머지 아이들을 보며 히죽거렸다.

Priscilla told Gregory he'd better wipe that *smirk* off his face or she'd do it for him.
프리실라는 그레고리에게 능글맞은 웃음을 지우라면서, 그렇지 않으면 자기가 지워주겠다고 말했다.

SNIDE [snaid]   adj. cruel and sarcastic   잔인한, 교활한, 빈정거리는

Sylvia was reduced to tears by Monty's *snide* comment that her dress looked like a tent.
실비아는 몬티가 그녀의 드레스를 보고 잔인하게도 텐트 같다고 말하자 울음을 터뜨렸다.

SOLEMN [sáləm/sɔ́l-]   adj. very serious   매우 진지한, 엄숙한

I could tell by Mom's *solemn* expression that she was not pleased with my report card.
엄마의 엄숙한 표정을 보고 엄마가 내 성적에 만족하지 못하신다는 걸 알 수 있었다.

Police officers must take a *solemn* oath to uphold the law.
경찰관은 법질서를 유지하겠다는 진지한 맹세를 해야 한다.

SOLICIT [səlísit] v. to try to get; to ask for repeatedly 간청하다; 계속 조르다

Terry's mother found him *soliciting* donations of scrap metal from the neighbors for a time travel machine he planned on building.
테리의 어머니는 테리가 타임머신 기계를 지으려고 이웃들에게 고철을 달라고 부탁했다는 사실을 알았다.

Pamela *solicited* her parents and grandparents for contributions to the class party.
파멜라는 부모님과 할아버지, 할머니께 학급 파티에 기부금을 내달라고 계속 졸라댔다.

SOLITARY [sálətèri/sɔ́litəri] adj. existing or living alone; being the only one 혼자의; 유일한, 단 하나의

Jed lived a *solitary* existence in the backwoods of Kentucky.
제드는 켄터키 벽지에서 혼자 살았다.

There was a *solitary* tree left standing after the storm.
폭풍이 지나간 뒤 서 있는 나무는 단 한 그루였다.

SOPHISTICATED [səfístəkèitid] adj. having experience, education, upbringing to be worldly; pleasing to the tastes of worldly people 세상 물정에 밝은, 세련된

Lena left the farm an innocent young girl and came back six months later a *sophisticated* movie star.
레나는 순진무구한 소녀로 농장을 떠났다가 6개월 후에 세련된 영화배우가 되어 돌아왔다.

Her taste had become so *sophisticated*, she no longer liked hot dogs and soda, but preferred champagne and caviar.
그녀는 입맛이 너무 세련되어져서, 더 이상은 핫도그와 탄산수를 좋아하지 않고 샴페인과 캐비어를 더 좋아했다.

Lena traded in her simple cotton dress for a *sophisticated* silk gown and expensive furs.
레나는 수수한 면 드레스를 세련된 실크 가운과 값비싼 모피로 바꾸었다.

SPECULATE [spékjəlèit] v. to wonder or think deeply on 이상하게 여기거나 깊이 생각하다

The neighbors were forced to *speculate* about what the giant pile of mud was doing in Mr. Sampson's backyard; he refused to tell them what it was for.
이웃들은 샘슨 씨 뒷마당에 있는 거대한 진흙 더미가 어디에 쓰이는 건지 궁금해졌는데, 그는 그것의 용도를 말해 주지 않았다.

[Note] The noun form of speculate is *speculation* [spèkjuléiʃən], which means the act of speculating or the opinion formed after speculating.
명사형은 speculation으로, '심사숙고' 혹은 '심사숙고한 후의 의견'을 의미

- Everyone had his own *speculations* about Mr. Sampson's mud pile, but I knew he was using it to hide a giant dinosaur egg.
  모두들 샘슨 씨의 진흙 더미에 대해 각자의 의견을 냈지만, 난 그것을 커다란 공룡 알을 숨기는 데 사용한다는 걸 알았다.

SPONTANEOUS [spɑntéiniəs/spɔn-] adj. happening without apparent cause; sudden and impulsive
자발적인, 자연적인; 갑작스럽고 충동적인

When something just bursts into flames without any noticeable reason, it's called *spontaneous* combustion.
이렇다 할 이유 없이 뭔가가 확 타오르면 자연발화라고 한다.

After twenty years of driving to and from work the same way, Mr. Peabody, while pulling out of his driveway this morning, made a *spontaneous* decision to take the scenic route to the office.
20년간 똑같은 길로 출퇴근했던 피바디 씨는 오늘 아침 차를 몰고 나오면서 경치가 좋은 길로 출근해야겠다고 충동적으로 결심했다.

The noun form of spontaneous is *spontaneity* [spÀntəníːəti/spɔ̀n-].
명사형은 spontaneity

- Going to school at the convent, with all its rules and schedules, was hard to Peggy. She longed for more freedom and *spontaneity*.
온통 규율과 시간표로 짜여진, 수녀원에서 운영하는 학교에 다니는 것은 페기에게 어려운 일이었다. 그녀는 더 자유롭고 자발적인 것을 원했다.

SPOUSE [spaus/spauz] n. a husband or wife 배우자

Everyone in the company was invited to bring his or her *spouse* to the office holiday celebration.
회사 직원 모두가 회사에서 여는 기념파티에 각자의 배우자를 데려오도록 초대받았다.

SQUANDER [skwÁndər/skwɔ́n-] v. to spend or use up wastefully 낭비하다, 탕진하다

Danny *squandered* his huge inheritance on fast women and slow horses.
대니는 자신의 막대한 유산을 행실이 좋지 못한 여자들과 둔한 말들에게 다 써 버렸다.

Let's not *squander* the last days of summer vacation sitting around inside!
집안에 가만히 앉아서 여름휴가의 마지막 날을 낭비하지 말자!

SQUEAMISH [skwíːmiʃ] adj. easily shocked or sickened 쉽게 충격을 받거나 메스꺼워지는

Stacy is too *squeamish* to sit through a horror movie that has a lot of blood in it.
스테이시는 충격을 잘 받아서 유혈 장면이 많은 공포 영화를 끝까지 못 본다.

Olivia might have made a good doctor except for the fact that she was *squeamish*, and fainted at the sight of blood.
올리비아는 피만 보면 토하기를 잘하고 기절하는 것만 아니면 훌륭한 의사가 됐을지도 모른다.

STAGNANT [stǽgnənt] adj. not moving or flowing; not changing 움직임 없는, 흐르지 않는; 변화가 없는

Because of the lack of rain, the river stopped flowing into the little pond, and the water became *stagnant*.
가뭄 때문에 작은 연못으로 흘러드는 강물이 멈춰 물이 흐르지 않았다.

Life in Dullsville was stale and *stagnant*: everyone did exactly the same thing every day, and you always knew what people were about to say to you before they even opened their mouths.
덜스빌에서의 생활은 생기가 없고 변화가 없었다. 모두들 매일같이 똑같은 일만 했고, 상대방이 입을 열기도 전에 무슨 말을 할지 알 수 있을 정도였다.

STAMINA [stǽmənə] n. endurance; the ability to keep doing something without getting tired 인내; 지구력, 체력

To be a marathon runner, you have to build up enough strength and *stamina* to run twenty-six miles.
마라톤 선수가 되려면 26마일을 달릴 만큼의 힘과 지구력을 키워야 한다.

"I used to be able to drive all day and night without stopping," mumbled Dad. "But since I turned forty, I don't even have enough *stamina* to drive eight hours without resting."
아빠가 중얼거렸다. "난 멈추지 않고 하루 종일 운전을 할 수 있었지. 하지만 마흔이 넘으니까 쉬지 않고서는 8시간 운전할 만한 체력도 안돼."

STEALTH [stelθ] n. the ability to move or do something quietly and secretively, without being noticed 몰래 하기, 몰래 하는 능력

Cats use their *stealth* to sneak up and pounce on mice and birds.
고양이는 기척을 느끼지 못하게 움직이는 능력을 쥐나 새에게 살금살금 다가가 와락 덮칠 때 사용한다.

"The burglar we are hunting is a man or woman of incredible *stealth*," said the inspector. "Those diamonds were stolen right out from under our noses!"
수사관이 말했다. "우리가 쫓고 있는 강도는 놀라울 정도로 몰래 움직이는 사람이야. 다이아몬드는 우리 바로 눈앞에서 도둑맞은 거라구."

STIMULATE [stímjulèit] v. to stir up, excite, or boost the activity of something 자극하다, 흥분시키다, 부추기다

Thomas found that going for a short jog *stimulated* his creativity.
토마스는 짧은 시간 조깅을 하면 독창력이 자극 받는다는 것을 알았다.

"I've just had the most *stimulating* conversation with a man who just got back from a mountain climbing expedition," gushed Fenella.
피넬라가 신이 나 말했다. "방금 등산 원정에서 돌아온 사람과 정말 흥분되는 대화를 나눴어."

My aunt Kate drinks tea after dinner because she says it *stimulates* digestion.
케이트 숙모는 식사 후 차를 마시는데, 그러면 소화가 촉진된다고 하신다.

STRENUOUS [strénjuəs] adj. demanding great effort and energy 분투를 요하는, 격렬한

Ice hockey is a *strenuous* sport.
아이스하키는 격렬한 스포츠다.

"I know I said we should get outside and do something," said Roger, "but I was thinking of something a little less *strenuous* than mountain biking up the Matterhorn."
로저가 말했다. "그래, 우린 나가서 뭔가를 해야겠다고 내가 말했지. 하지만 산악자전거를 타고 마터호른에 오르는 것보다는 좀 덜 힘든 걸 생각했던 거야."

After he had his appendix removed in an operation, Brian had to avoid *strenuous* exercise for a couple of weeks.
브라이언은 맹장 수술을 받은 후 몇 주 동안 격렬한 운동을 피해야 했다.

STUDIOUS [stjú:diəs/stú:-] adj. devoted to study 공부에 힘쓰는

Larry is a very serious, *studious* boy, but for some reason he makes nothing but Cs in school.
래리는 아주 진지하고 공부에 힘쓰는 소년인데, 어떤 이유에서인지 학교에서 C만 받는다.

After one semester in college, Carl decided he wasn't cut out for the *studious* lifestyle and decided to quit and go get a job.
칼은 대학에서 한 학기가 끝나자 공부에 열중하는 생활이 자기에게 안 맞는다는 결정을 내리고는, 학교를 그만두고 직장을 구하기로 결심했다.

SUBCONSCIOUS [sʌbkɑ́nʃəs/-kɔ́n-] adj. below the level of awareness 잠재의식의

George misplaces his catcher's mitt every week before baseball games, and his mother thinks it's because he has a *subconscious* desire to quit the team, but doesn't want to admit it.
조지는 매주 야구 경기 전에 포수 글러브를 어디 두었는지 잊어버리는데, 그의 어머니는 그가 무의식중에 팀을 탈퇴하고 싶어 하지만 그것을 인정하지 않으려 하기 때문이라고 생각한다.

Steven is always getting in trouble at school, but the principal doesn't think he's a bad kid, just someone with a *subconscious* need for attention.
스티븐은 항상 학교에서 말썽을 일으키지만, 교장은 그를 나쁜 아이라 생각하지 않고, 그저 잠재의식적으로 주목을 끌고 싶어 한다고 생각한다.

SUBDUE [səbdjúː/-dúː] v. to conquer; to bring under control; to lessen in strength 정복하다; 진압하다, 억제하다; 완화하다

The Aztec tribe was easily *subdued* and quickly destroyed by the Spanish forces led by the explorer Hernando Cortes.
아즈텍 족은 탐험가 에르난도 코르테스가 이끄는 스페인 군대에게 손쉽게 정복당해 급속히 무너졌다.

The police *subdued* the crowd of angry people who were marching to city hall demanding the resignation of the mayor.
경찰은 시장의 사임을 요구하며 시청으로 행진해 가는 성난 군중을 진압했다.

[Note] The word *subdued* can also be used to mean quiet and understated, or low in intensity.
subdued는 '조용한', '말수가 적은', '부드러운' 의 의미로도 쓴다.

- The flowers and *subdued* lighting created a very romantic atmosphere.
  꽃들과 부드러운 조명이 아주 낭만적인 분위기를 자아냈다.
- Dad likes *subdued*, conservative ties, not bright, floral ones.
  아버지는 밝고 꽃무늬 있는 넥타이 말고 차분하고 수수한 넥타이를 좋아하신다.

SUBSEQUENT [sʌ́bsikwənt] adj. happening or coming after, later, or next 다음의, 그 후의

I was completely confused by all the characters and events in the first chapter of *The Emu Enigma*, but *subsequent* chapters cleared things up for me.
'Emu Enigma' 의 첫 장에서는 등장인물과 사건들로 너무나 혼란스러웠지만 다음 장들에서 모든 것이 분명해졌다.

Ansel's plans for Thanksgiving included a turkey feast, a *subsequent* nap, and an afternoon of football viewing.
엔젤의 추수감사절 계획에는 칠면조 연회를 열고 그 후에 낮잠을 잔 다음 오후에 미식축구를 보는 것이 포함돼 있었다.

SUBTLE [sʌ́tl] adj. slight; not obvious 약간의, 미세한; 불분명한

Whenever Penelope leaves a room, she leaves the *subtle* scent of her perfume in the air.
페넬로프는 방을 나갈 때마다 공기 중에 희미한 향수 냄새를 남겨 놓는다.

"Even the most *subtle* change in the temperature of this room could ruin my experiment!" screamed the scientist.
"이 방의 아주 미세한 온도 변화도 내 실험을 망칠 수 있단 말이야!"라고 과학자가 소리쳤다.

Jane's make-up is very *subtle*.
제인은 화장을 아주 살짝 한다.

SUCCUMB [səkʌ́m] v. to give in or give up; to be overpowered 굴복하다; 압도당하다

Carlo and I begged for weeks before Dad finally *succumbed* and let us get a puppy.
카를로와 나는 아빠가 마침내 두 손을 들고 강아지 기르는 것을 허락할 때까지 몇 주를 졸라댔다.

Even though everyone else in the office was sick with the flu, Lee refused to let his body *succumb* to the illness.
사무실의 다른 사람은 모두 독감으로 아파할 적에도 리는 독감에 굴복하지 않았다.

SUITOR [súːtər] n. a man who woos a woman or tries to win her affection 구혼자, 구애자

Penelope had so many *suitors* calling her all the time, her father finally got her her own phone line.
페넬로프에게 항상 너무 많은 구애 전화가 걸려 오자 그녀의 아버지는 마침내 그녀에게 전화선을 따로 갖게 했다.

My aunt Charlene has a very charming *suitor* who brings her flowers and plays his banjo for her.
우리 살렌 이모는 꽃을 가져다주고 밴조도 연주해 주는 아주 매력적인 구혼자를 만났다.

SUPERFICIAL [sù:pərfíʃəl] adj. on the surface; concerned only with what's on the surface; shallow 표면상의; 외면의, 겉면의; 얕은, 피상적인

Amazingly, Allan fell all the way down the rocky hill and only wound up with a few *superficial* cuts.
놀랍게도 앨런은 울퉁불퉁한 언덕 꼭대기에서 밑으로 굴러 떨어졌는데도, 외관상으로 몇 군데 상처만 입었다.

I told Amanda that judging people by how they dress or wear their hair is very *superficial*.
나는 아만다에게 사람을 옷차림이나 머리 모양으로 판단하는 것은 너무 피상적이라고 말했다.

After a *superficial* examination the doctor told me I had no broken bones, but the X-rays showed I had two cracked ribs.
겉모습만 살펴본 의사는 내게 뼈가 부러지지 않았다고 했지만, 엑스레이 검사를 받아 보니 늑골 두 군데에 금이 가 있었다.

SUPERNATURAL [sù:pərnǽtʃərəl] adj. having to do with or being outside or beyond what can be explained by the laws of nature; beyond what is normal, natural or explainable 초자연적인; 불가사의한, 신비한

Even though countless people have reported seeing them, ghosts are considered *supernatural* beings.
수없이 많은 이들이 유령을 봤다고 말해 왔지만, 유령은 초자연적인 존재로 간주된다.

Superman uses his *supernatural* powers, like flying and seeing through walls, to protect the innocent and fight the bad guys.
슈퍼맨은 날아다니거나 벽을 투시하는 것 같은 불가사의한 힘을 이용해, 죄없는 사람들을 보호하고 나쁜 사람들과 싸운다.

SUPERSTITION [sù:pərstíʃən] n. a belief that a certain act or event foretells or predicts another event even though the two things have no logical relation 미신

Believing that putting a hat on a bed will bring bad luck is a *superstition*.
침대 위에 모자를 올려놓으면 재수가 없다고 믿는 것은 미신이다.

There is a *superstition* that if the palm of your right hand itches, you'll be getting some money soon, but if the palm of your left hand itches, you'll be getting into a fight.
오른쪽 손바닥이 가려우면 곧 돈이 생길 것이고, 왼쪽 손바닥이 가려우면 곧 싸움에 말려들게 된다는 미신이 있다.

[Note] A person who has superstitions is *superstitious* [sù:pərstíʃəs].
superstitious는 '미신적인', '미신에 사로잡힌'

- Professional athletes are often *superstitious*: they believe using a certain bat, or eating a certain dish for dinner, or listening to a certain song before a game will help them win.
프로 운동선수는 미신을 믿는 경우가 많다. 경기 전에 특정한 배트를 쓰거나 저녁으로 특정한 음식을 먹거나 혹은 특정한 음악을 들으면 우승하도록 도와준다고 믿는다.

SUSCEPTIBLE [səséptəbl] adj. easily affected; sensitive 영향 받기 쉬운; 민감한

Lonny is *susceptible* to colds: he gets sick if he so much as gets his feet wet in the rain.
로니는 추위에 민감하다. 비가 와서 발이 젖기만 하면 병이 난다.

Rudy found it hard to stay on a diet because he was *susceptible* to the temptation of dessert.
루디는 다이어트를 계속하기가 어렵다는 걸 깨달았는데, 후식의 유혹에 쉽게 넘어가기 때문이다.

SUSPICION [səspíʃən] n. the act of believing something with little proof 혐의, 의심

My lunch had disappeared, and I had a strong *suspicion* that the dog was the sandwich thief.
점심 식사가 없어졌었는데, 나는 개가 샌드위치 도둑이라고 강하게 의심했다.

[Note] Someone who is full of suspicion is *suspicious* [səspíʃəs].

'의심 많은' 은 suspicious

- My old Uncle Herman is *suspicious* of anyone from the big city.
  나이 든 우리 허먼 삼촌은 대도시에서 온 사람이면 누구든 의심한다.

SYMPATHY [símpəθi] n. the ability to understand or share another person's feelings; pity or sorrow for another person's unhappiness   공감, 동감; 동정, 연민

Yolanda's friends called to express their *sympathy* when they heard about the accidental death of her goldfish.

욜란다의 친구들은 욜란다의 금붕어가 뜻하지 않게 죽었다는 소식을 듣고 위로하기 위해 전화했다.

When my parents told me we were moving to another state, I was sad to leave my friends. My teacher said she felt *sympathy* for me because she moved around a lot as a kid, and knew how hard it was.

부모님이 우리가 다른 주로 이사 간다고 하셨을 때 나는 친구들을 떠나게 되는 것이 슬펐다. 선생님도 어릴 적에 이사를 많이 다녀서 그것이 얼마나 힘든지 이해하기 때문에 나와 공감한다고 하셨다.

[Note] To show or feel sympathy is to *sympathize* [símpəθaiz].

'동정하다', '동감하다' 는 sympathize

- It was hard for us to *sympathize* with the rich boy who was complaining and crying because his parents wouldn't buy him another new pony.
  부잣집 꼬마 애가 자기부모님이 조랑말 한마리를 더 안 사주신다고 불평하며 우는 것을 보고 동정하기는 어려웠다.

SYNOPSIS [sinápsis/-nɔ́p-] n. a short outline of a story or topic   개요, 강령

A good book report should be more than just a *synopsis* of the plot.

훌륭한 독후감이란 단순히 줄거리를 요약하는 것이어서는 안된다.

Tim missed the first few minutes of the movie because he was getting popcorn, so Nancy whispered a quick *synopsis* when he got back to his seat.

팀이 팝콘을 사느라 영화의 처음 몇 분을 못 봐서, 낸시는 그가 자리로 돌아오자 귓속말로 재빨리 개요를 말해 주었다.

SYNTHETIC [sinθétik] adj. not of natural origins; artificial; not natural   합성의, 인조의; 자연적이 아닌

"I'm sorry to tell you this, but you paid $10,000 for a necklace made of *synthetic* rubies," said the jeweler.

"말씀드리기 좀 곤란하지만, 만 달러 주고 사신 목걸이는 인조 루비로 만들어진 겁니다." 라고 보석상이 말했다.

Wool and cotton are natural fabrics, but nylon and polyester are *synthetic*.

모와 면은 천연 직물이지만, 나일론과 폴리에스테르는 합성섬유다.

 T

TANTALIZE [tǽntəlaiz] v. to tempt someone with something, but keep it out of reach   애타게 하다, 감질나게 하다

I was *tantalized* by the beautiful pies locked in the rotating display case.
회전 진열 상자 안에 넣어져 있는 아름다운 파이를 보고 애가 탔다.

"It's cruel to *tantalize* the dog with that drumstick when you know you're not going to give him any of it," huffed Dinah.
다이나가 화를 내며 말했다. "개에게 닭다리를 줄 것도 아니면서 감질나게 하다니 잔인해."

TARNISH [táːrniʃ] v. to dull the shine of; to stain or disgrace   흐리게 하다, 녹슬게 하다; 더럽히다, 욕보이다

Exposure to the wind and rain had *tarnished* the brass lamppost.
놋쇠로 된 가로등 기둥이 비바람에 노출돼 녹슬어 버렸다.

Peter's record of straight As was *tarnished* by one D in chemistry.
피터의 올 A 성적이 화학에서 D를 맞는 바람에 훼손됐다.

TEDIOUS [tíːdiəs/-dʒəs] adj. long, slow, and boring   지루한, 지겨운

Making spaghetti sauce from fresh tomatoes is such a *tedious* task.
신선한 토마토로 스파게티 소스를 만드는 것은 너무 지겨운 일이다.

Dorian's explanation of why the sky is blue was so *tedious*, I lost track of what he was saying.
도리안이 하늘이 파란 이유에 대해 설명하는데 너무 지루해서 무슨 말을 하고 있는지 도중에 놓쳐 버렸다.

TEMPERATE [témpərət] adj. mild; moderate; restrained   온화한; 적당한; 절제하는

The weather was *temperate* during the first week in March, but snowstorms hit us again in the middle of the month.
3월 첫 주 동안은 날씨가 온화했지만 중순이 되자 또다시 눈보라가 불어 닥쳤다.

The harsh, fiery old headmaster of the academy finally retired, and the students were glad to see a younger, more *temperate* man take his place.
거칠고 사납고 늙은 학원 교장이 마침내 은퇴하고, 그 보다 젊은 온건한 사람이 교장으로 오자 학생들은 기뻐했다.

TENEMENT [ténəmənt] n. a run-down, often overcrowded, apartment building   허름하고 좁은 아파트

At the beginning of the 1900s, many Europeans came to the United States with very little money and were forced to live in *tenements* in big cities like New York and Chicago.
1900년대 초에 많은 유럽인들이 거의 무일푼으로 미국에 건너와 뉴욕이나 시카고 같은 대도시의 허름한 아파트에서 살 수 밖에 없었다.

146

TENTATIVE [téntətiv] adj. not final or firm; unsure   시험적인, 임시의; 불확실한

We set a *tentative* appointment for Marcy to get braces on her teeth, but we will have to delay it if she gets a chance to play the flute on television.
마시가 치열 교정기를 달도록 진료 약속을 임시로 해 두었는데, 그녀가 TV에 출연해 플루트 연주를 하게 된다면 약속을 미뤄야 할 것이다.

The baby took three or four *tentative* steps before falling down on his padded behind.
아기는 뒤뚱뒤뚱 서너 걸음 걷더니 푹신한 엉덩이로 방아를 찧으며 넘어졌다.

THWART [θwɔːrt] v. to keep from happening; to block or prevent   저지하다, 방해하다

Bad weather *thwarted* our plans for a wheelbarrow race to the Dairy Queen.
악천후 때문에 데어리 퀸까지의 일륜차 경주 계획에 차질이 생겼다.

Thank goodness, we have superheroes like the Tick around to *thwart* the evil plots of fiendish criminals!
고맙게도 우리에겐 틱 같은 수퍼영웅이 있어 극악한 범죄자들의 사악한 음모를 저지할 수 있다.

TIMID [tímid] adj. shy; easily scared   숫기 없는; 겁 많은

The little girl was too *timid* to come out from behind her mother's legs to say hello.
꼬마 여자애는 수줍음을 너무 많이 타서 엄마 다리 뒤에서 나와 인사도 할 수 없었다.

Dexter was so *timid* he was frightened by the sound of the doorbell ringing.
덱스터는 겁이 너무 많아서 초인종 소리에도 깜짝 놀랐다.

TOLERANCE [tάlərəns/tɔ́l-] n. the practice of respecting the beliefs of others; the ability to endure or put up with something   관용, 포용; 참을성, 내구력

Tolerance of different religion is one of the most important tenets of the United States government.
다른 종교에 대한 포용은 미국 정부의 가장 중요한 신조 가운데 하나다.

Mimi has no *tolerance* for heat: she sweats and turns almost purple whenever the temperature goes over seventy degrees.
미미는 더운 것을 못 참는다. 온도가 화씨 70도(섭씨 23도)를 넘어서면 땀을 흘리며 얼굴이 거의 보라색이 된다.

[Note] Someone who has tolerance is *tolerant*.
　　　'관대한', '참을성 있는' 은 tolerant

- A *tolerant* parent tolerates, or puts up with, more than a strict parent would.
  참을성 있는 부모는 엄격한 부모보다 관대하다.

- Not many parents will *tolerate* bad behavior.
  나쁜 행동을 참고 넘어가는 부모는 그리 많지 않다.

TORMENT [tɔːrmént] v. to cause great pain; to annoy   고통을 주다; 괴롭히다

The mean little boy *tormented* grasshoppers by tearing their legs off.
잔인한 꼬마 애가 메뚜기들을 다리를 떼어내며 괴롭혔다.

After we had been driving for about thirty minutes, I began to be *tormented* by the thought that I had forgotten to turn off the oven before we left.
차를 몰고 30분쯤을 가고 나자 오븐을 안 끄고 나왔다는 생각이 떠올라 골치가 아프기 시작했다.

TOXIC [táksik/tɔ́k-] adj. poisonous 독성의

The dye used on these Christmas tree ornaments is *toxic*, so parents should be careful to keep small children from putting them in their mouths.
크리스마스트리 장식에 쓰는 물감에는 독성이 있으므로, 부모들은 어린 아이들이 입에 넣지 않도록 주의해야 한다.

The river used to be full of fish, but they were all killed by the *toxic* chemicals dumped into the water by the plastics plant.
예전에는 강에 물고기가 가득했었는데, 플라스틱 공장이 강물에 쏟아 버린 독성 화학약품 때문에 모두 죽고 말았다.

TRANSCRIBE [trænskráib] v. to write or type a copy of 복사하다, 베끼다

Dorothy liked the speech so much, she *transcribed* every word.
도로시는 그 연설이 너무 좋아서 한 자도 빠짐없이 받아 적었다.

[Note] Once you have transcribed something, you have a *transcript* [trænskript].

transcript는 '베낀 것', '사본', '대본'

- You can often buy *transcripts* of television shows by sending a request to the network.
  방송국에 요청하면 텔레비전 프로의 대본을 구입할 수 있다.

TRANSPOSE [trænspóuz] v. to reverse or switch in placement or order (위치나 순서를) 바꾸어 놓다

Melvin was a fast typist, but often *transposed* the letter of words, so that "fort" became "frot" and "bird" became "brid."
멜빈은 타이핑이 빨랐지만 종종 철자의 순서를 바꾸어 놓아서 "fort"가 "frot"가 되고 "bird"가 "brid"가 되었다.

TRAUMA [trɔ́:mə/tráu-] n. a serious shock with lasting effects (영구적인 영향을 미치는) 심한 충격

For little children, being left with a babysitter for the first time can be a *trauma*.
어린아이들을 처음으로 베이비시터에 맡겨두고 나가버리는 것은 아이들에게는 큰상처가 될 수 있다.

[Note] An experience that causes trauma is *traumatic* [trɔ:mǽtik/trɔ:-/trau-].

형용사 traumatic은 '잊을 수 없이 충격적인'

- For Maggie, missing an episode of her favorite soap opera "As Time Drags on" is a *traumatic* experience.
  매기에게는 자신이 가장 좋아하는 드라마 "As Time Drags on"의 한 회를 못 본 것은 잊지 못할 충격이다.

[Note] If you've had a trauma, you have been *traumatized* [trɔ́:mətaiz/tráu-].

traumatize는 '충격을 주다', be traumatized는 '충격을 받다'

- Being shut in the clothes dryer overnight had *traumatized* the cat.
  빨래 건조기 속에 밤새 갇혀 있었던 것은 고양이에게 영구적인 충격을 주었다.

TRITE [trait] adj. uninteresting because of overuse; stale 흔한; 진부한

The phrase "pretty as a picture" is too *trite* to do justice to Allison's good looks.
"그림처럼 아름답다"는 표현은 앨리슨의 미모를 제대로 나타내기엔 너무 진부하다.

Candy and roses are *trite* Valentine's Day gifts.
사탕과 장미는 흔해빠진 밸런타인데이 선물이다.

TURBULENT [tə́:rbjulənt] adj. stirred up or disturbed (바람 등이) 휘몰아치는, 격한

The thunderstorm and *turbulent* winds made air travel impossible.
뇌우와 휘몰아치는 바람으로 비행기 운항이 불가능했다.

The civil rights movement, the women's rights movement, and the widespread objection to the Vietnam War made the 1960s a *turbulent* decade in American history.

민권 운동과 여성 인권 운동, 베트남 전에 대한 광범위한 반대 등은 1960년대를 미국 역사에서 격동의 세기로 만들었다.

TYCOON [taikúːn] n. a wealthy, powerful business person 실업계의 거물

Donald Trump – who owns casinos, hotels, apartment buildings, and other properties worth millions and millions of dollars – is a real estate *tycoon*.

카지노, 호텔, 아파트 빌딩, 그 외에 어마어마한 가치의 토지를 소유한 도널드 트럼프는 부동산 재벌이다.

Mr. Franklin, who owns the paper mill and several other businesses in our town, is a local *tycoon*.

우리 마을에서 제지 공장과 몇 가지 다른 사업체를 갖고 있는 프랭클린 씨는 지역 거물이다.

TYRANT [táiərənt] n. a ruler with total, unrestricted control who is often harsh and cruel 폭군, 전제군주

Jane was okay as a co-worker, but when she was promoted and took charge of our department she became a complete *tyrant*, firing people for no reason and forcing everyone to work seven days a week.

제인은 동료로 일할 때는 괜찮았는데, 승진을 하고 우리 부서를 책임지게 되더니 완전히 폭군으로 돌변해, 아무 이유 없이 사람들을 해고하고 모두에게 일주일 내내 근무하도록 강요했다.

[Note] A tyrant enforces and expresses *tyranny* [tírəni], which is absolute or oppressive power exerted by a government or ruler.

'전제정치', '학정', '횡포' 는 tyranny

- Before she had the chance to fire me, I told Jane I refused to put up with her *tyranny* and I quitted.

  제인이 해고할 기회를 잡기 전에 내가 먼저 그녀의 횡포를 더 이상 못 참겠다고 말하고 그만두었다.

U

ULCER [ʌ́lsər] n. a sore in or on the body, usually in a moist area 궤양

Ignatius had a painful *ulcer* on the inside of his cheek that kept him from enjoying his Thanksgiving dinner.
이그네이셔스는 볼 안쪽의 궤양으로 통증이 심해 추수감사절 저녁 식사를 즐길 수가 없었다.

Aubrey's stressful job gave him a stomach *ulcer* that hurt him whenever he ate.
오브리는 일에서 오는 스트레스 때문에 위궤양이 생겨서 식사를 할 때마다 고통스러웠다.

ULTERIOR [ʌltíəriər] adj. beyond what is seen or admitted 이면의, 배후의, 마음 속의

Ben said he was just trying to be useful when he helped Dad change the oil on the car, but he had an *ulterior* motive: he knew the faster he could get the oil changed, the sooner his father would leave town for the weekend, and the sooner he could invite all his friends over for a party.
벤은 그저 아빠가 자동차 오일 교환하는 걸 도와드리려는 것뿐이라고 했지만, 그에겐 딴 심산이 있었다. 아버지가 오일을 빨리 교환하게 되면 주말 여행을 더 빨리 떠나실 테고, 그러면 더 빨리 친구들을 불러 파티를 열 수 있었기 때문이다.

In the story of Hansel and Gretel, the witch gives the hungry children some food, but her *ulterior* plan is to fatten them up so she can eat them.
헨젤과 그레텔의 이야기에서 마녀는 배고픈 아이들에게 음식을 주지만, 그녀의 속셈은 아이들을 잡아먹을 수 있도록 살찌우려는 데 있다.

UNANIMOUS [juːnǽnəməs] adj. having the same opinion; in complete agreement 동의하는; 만장일치의

After fifteen long rounds, the judges made the *unanimous* decision that Cesar Chavez had won the boxing match.
기나긴 15라운드의 권투경기가 끝나자 심판들은 만장일치로 세자르 차베스가 복싱 경기를 이겼다는 판정을 내렸다.

The students were *unanimous* in their objection to their teacher's cruel and unusual decision to give them a test the day they got back from their winter break.
학생들은 겨울방학이 끝나고 개학하는 날 시험을 치르겠다는 선생님의 무자비하고 유별난 결정에 반기를 들자는 데 동의했다.

UNBEKNOWNST [ʌ̀nbinóunst] adv. without the knowledge of 알려지지 않은, 미지의

"If someone fed Fido the leftover steak, it was *unbeknownst* to me," claimed Edgar.
에드거가 주장했다. "누가 파이도에게 스테이크 남은 걸 먹였는지 모르지만 난 모르는 일이야."

UNBRIDLED [ʌnbráidld] adj. uncontrolled; wild 억제되지 않은; 거친

Nancy had an *unbridled* affection for Vince—there was nothing she wouldn't do for him, and she couldn't bear being apart from him.
낸시는 빈스에게 억누를 수 없는 애정을 느꼈다. 그를 위해서라면 못할 일이 하나도 없었고, 그와 떨어져 지낸다는 것은 참을 수 없는 일이었다.

UNCONSCIOUS [ʌnkánʃəs/-kɔ́n-] adj. not awake; not aware 의식을 잃은; 깨닫지 못하는

After she fell off the jungle gym and hit her head, Isabella was *unconscious* for five minutes.
이사벨라는 정글짐에서 떨어져 머리를 부딪친 후에 5분 동안 의식을 잃었다.

Neville, who thought he was the life of the party, was *unconscious* of the fact that everyone was bored to tears by his silly jokes.
네빌은 일행 중 자기가 가장 인기 있다고 생각하면서, 자신의 유치한 농담에 모두들 지겨워 죽을 지경인 줄 몰랐다.

UNCOUTH [ʌnkú:θ] adj. crude; unrefined; unmannerly 거친; 세련되지 못한; 무례한

After he ate the pudding with his fingers, wiped his mouth on the tablecloth, belched loudly, then spat into his water glass, Cedric's mother moaned, "How could I have possibly raised such an *uncouth* son?"
세드릭이 손으로 푸딩을 집어먹고 식탁보에 입을 닦은 다음 큰 소리로 트림을 하고 물 컵 안에 침을 뱉고 나자, 어머니가 한탄하듯 말했다. "어떻게 내가 저렇게 세련되지 못한 아들을 키웠을까?"

"Your manners were fine," Kyle's friend assured him, "but flicking your cigarette ashes in the antique vase and calling their modern art collection 'finger paintings' was a little *uncouth*."
카일의 친구가 카일에게 확실히 말했다. "네 매너는 좋았는데, 골동품 꽃병에다 담뱃재를 떨고 그들의 현대 미술품을 보고 '손가락으로 그린 그림'이라고 말한 건 좀 무례했어."

UNDERMINE [ʌndərmáin] v. to weaken by wearing away or attacking the foundation 밑을 파다, 손상시키다

Greg's midnight ice cream feasts were *undermining* the effects of his diet and exercise program.
그레그가 한밤중에 아이스크림을 몰래 먹는 것이 다이어트와 운동 프로그램의 효과를 약화시켰다.

Sylvia's boss *undermined* her authority by contradicting instructions she gave and overriding rules she made for her department.
실비아의 상사는 그녀가 내린 지시를 반박하고 그녀가 부서를 위해 만든 규정을 무시함으로써 실비아의 위신을 깎아내렸다.

UNEASY [ʌní:zi] adj. nervous and unsure 불안한, 걱정되는

Amanda's mother was *uneasy* about letting her stay by herself for the evening, even though she was eleven years old.
아만다의 어머니는 아만다가 열한 살이나 됐는데도, 그녀를 저녁에 혼자 두기가 불안했다.

Caroline is *uneasy* driving by herself late at night.
캐롤라인은 밤늦게 혼자 차를 몰고 가는 것이 걱정된다.

"I have the *uneasy* feeling that someone is watching us," said Shaggy.
"누군가 우리를 보고 있는 것 같아 불안해."라고 섀기가 말했다.

UNFOUNDED [ʌnfáundid] adj. having no factual support; not backed up by facts 근거 없는, 사실무근의

"All those stories about me skinny-dipping in the hotel fountain are completely *unfounded*," said Monica. "No one can prove a thing."
모니카는 말했다. "제가 호텔 분수에 알몸으로 들어갔다는 얘기는 모두 사실무근이에요. 아무도 증명할 수 없다구요."

Reports of aliens landing in the cornfields have proved to be *unfounded* - no trace of any such landings

can be found.
옥수수 밭에 외계인들이 내려왔다는 보도는 사실무근으로 밝혀졌다. 어떠한 착륙의 흔적도 찾아볼 수 없다.

UNKEMPT [ʌ̀nkémpt] adj. messy; untidy 어질러진; 단정치 못한

Evelyn, who had stayed up late studying and slept in her clothes, showed up for the exam looking sleepy and *unkempt*.
밤늦게까지 공부하다가 옷을 입은 채로 잠들어 버린 이블린은 졸립고 단정치 못한 모습으로 시험 장소에 나타났다.

Marian keeps the top down on her convertible whenever she drives somewhere, so her hair tends to be *unkempt*.
메리언은 어디로 차를 몰고 가든지 컨버터블의 지붕을 걷어 놓기 때문에 머리가 쉽게 흐트러진다.

The security guard was very embarrassed when he found out that the *unkempt* man in the shabby jacket he had just thrown out was, in fact, Albert Einstein, the famous scientist and guest speaker.
경비원은 자기가 쫓아낸 허름한 재킷의 너저분한 남자가 사실은 유명한 과학자요 초청된 연사인 앨버트 아인슈타인이라는 걸 알고 매우 당황했다.

UNWIELDY [ʌnwíːldi] adj. hard to carry or manage because of shape or size. (부피가 커서) 다루기 힘든

The box of posters wasn't heavy, it was just so large and *unwieldy* it was hard for one person to carry alone.
포스터 상자가 무겁지는 않았는데, 부피가 너무 커서 혼자 나르기엔 힘들었다.

Brandon was used to driving a small sports car, so he found the bus kind of *unwieldy*.
브랜든은 소형 스포츠카를 모는 데 익숙해져 있어 버스같이 큰 차는 운전하기가 좀 어렵다는 걸 알았다.

UPHEAVAL [ʌphíːvəl] n. a sudden, strong disturbance 갑작스러운 대소동, 격변

The assassination of President John F. Kennedy caused a great *upheaval* across the country.
존 F. 케네디 대통령의 암살은 나라 전체에 대격변을 일으켰다.

Our neighborhood was thrown into a state of *upheaval* when the fifth pet in one week was found with all its fur mysteriously shaved off.
우리 마을은 일주일 안에 다섯 번째 애완동물이 불가사의하게 털이 모두 깎여 나간 채 발견되자 대소동에 빠졌다.

UPHOLSTERY [ʌphóulstəri] n. the materials used to stuff and cover furniture 가구속을 채우거나 덮는 것

We had to have the cat de-clawed because she was destroying the *upholstery* on the couch and chairs.
고양이가 소파와 의자의 속을 방석을 못 쓰게 만들어서 고양이 발톱을 없애 버려야 했다.

"All true luxury cars have leather *upholstery*," declared Mario.
마리오가 우겼다. "진짜 고급차에는 시트가 가죽으로 되어 있다니까."

V

VACATE [véikeit/vəkéit] v. to empty; to leave or exit 비우다; 떠나다, 빠져나가다.

The people *vacated* the burning building as quickly as possible.
사람들은 화재가 난 건물에서 가능한 한 빨리 빠져나갔다.

Nothing can *vacate* an auditorium fast than my aunt Myrtle playing her accordion and singing her polka version of "You Light up My Life."
머틀 이모가 아코디언을 연주하고 "당신은 내 삶을 비추어요"를 폴카 버전으로 부르는 것보다 더 빨리 객석을 텅 비게 만들 수 있는 건 아무 것도 없다.

Tommy and his roommates were ordered to *vacate* their apartment after the landlord got several complaints about their loud band practices.
토미와 룸메이트들은 시끄러운 밴드 연습 소리에 집주인이 몇 번 불평을 한 후 아파트를 비워 달라는 요구를 받았다.

VACILLATE [vǽsəlèit] v. to change your opinion or course of action back and forth 마음이 동요하다, 주저하다, 망설이다

We all waited in the living room while, upstairs, Vicki *vacillated* between wearing flats or high heels.
우리 모두 거실에서 기다리는 동안 비키는 위층에서 굽이 없는 신발과 하이힐 중 어느 것을 신을까 고민하고 있었다.

"We don't have time to stand here *vacillating* between chocolate cake and coconut cake," said Tina. "The surprise party is supposed to start in ten minutes!"
티나는 말했다. "우린 여기 서서 초콜릿 케이크를 먹을지 코코넛 케이크를 먹을지 망설일 시간이 없어. 깜짝 파티는 10분 후에 시작이란 말야!"

VAGRANT [véigrənt] n. a person who wanders from place to place with no permanent home or adj. wandering 방랑자, 유랑자 / 방랑하는, 떠돌아다니는

When he was in his early twenties, my uncle lived as a *vagrant* musician, playing his tuba for money in cities across the country.
우리 아저씨는 20대 초반에 전국의 도시들을 돌며 튜바를 불어 돈을 버는 떠돌이 음악가 생활을 했다.

At night, *vagrants* come and sleep on the park benches.
밤이 되면 부랑자들이 공원 벤치에 와서 잠을 잔다.

VAGUE [veig] adj. unclear; not definite or precise 흐릿한, 분명치 않은; 애매한, 막연한

Patrick saw the *vague* shape of a person coming towards him through the fog, but by the time he realized it was Count Dracula, it was too late to run.
패트릭은 안개를 뚫고 다가오는 흐릿한 사람의 형체를 보았는데, 그것이 드라큘라 백작임을 깨달았을 때엔 도망가기에 너무 늦어 있었다.

Paula was *vague* about her plans for the weekend, so we suspected she had some sort of secret meeting.
폴라가 자신의 주말 계획에 대해 애매하게 말해서 우리는 무슨 비밀스런 만남이 있는 게 아닌가 짐작했다.

Stan's teacher told him some of the arguments in his report were too *vague*, and that he should use examples to back up his points.

교사는 스탠에게 리포트의 주장 일부가 너무 모호하며, 논점을 뒷받침해줄 예를 더 들어야겠다고 말했다.

VAIN [vein]   adj.   useless; having no effect   쓸모없는; 헛수고의

We were forced to call a tow truck after several *vain* attempts to push the car out of the deep mud.

우리는 깊은 진창 속에서 차를 빼내려고 몇 차례 헛수고를 하고 난 뒤 하는 수 없이 견인 트럭을 불렀다.

[Note] *Vain* also means conceited, or overly pleased with one's looks or abilities.

vain에는 '자만심이 강한', '허영적인', '뽐내는' 이란 의미도 있다.

- Jon was so *vain*, he thought every girl who smiled or said hello to him had a crush on him.

  존은 허영심이 대단해 자기를 보고 웃거나 인사를 건네는 여자애들은 모두 자기에게 홀딱 빠져 있다고 생각했다.

- Everyone thought Eugenia was *vain* because she was always admiring herself in the mirror.

  모두들 유지니아가 자만심이 강하다고 생각했는데, 그녀는 항상 거울을 보며 자신의 모습에 감탄하기 때문이다.

VANDAL [vǽndl]   n.   someone who destroys or harms another person's property on purpose   다른 사람의 소유물에 대한 고의적인 파괴자

The statue of George Washington was spray-painted purple by a group of young *vandals*.

과격한 젊은이 집단이 조지 워싱턴의 동상을 자주색으로 칠해 버렸다.

[Note] To act like a vandal is to *vandalize* [vǽndəlaiz].

vandalize는 '(공공시설 등을) 고의적으로 파괴하다'

- The teenagers were accused of *vandalizing* several statues around town.

  십대들이 마을 여기저기에 있는 동상 몇 개를 파손시킨 혐의로 고소되었다.

VANQUISH [vǽŋkwiʃ]   v.   to defeat or destroy totally   패배시키다, 정복하다; 극복하다

Tina *vanquished* her fear of water by taking swimming lessons at the YMCA.

티나는 YMCA에서 수영 레슨을 받아 물에 대한 공포감을 떨쳐 버렸다.

Napoleon's army was finally *vanquished* in the disastrous battle at Waterloo.

나폴레옹의 군대는 마침내 참혹한 워털루 전투에서 완전히 패하고 말았다.

VEER [viər]   v.   to swerve   방향을 바꾸다

I had to *veer* to the left to avoid running into the fallen tree in the road.

길에 쓰러져 있는 나무로 돌진하는 것을 피하기 위해 왼쪽으로 방향을 바꾸어야 했다.

The car *veered* dangerously close to the cliff.

차는 절벽 거의 끝까지 와서 방향을 틀었다.

VELOCITY [vəlásəti/-lɔ́s-]   n.   speed   속도

Nolan Ryan could throw a baseball at a *velocity* of over one hundred miles per hour.

놀런 라이언은 시속 백 마일 이상의 속도로 야구공을 던질 수 있었다.

Driving at high *velocities* is especially dangerous when the roads are wet.

도로가 젖어 있을 때 고속으로 차를 모는 것은 정말 위험하다.

VENERABLE [vénərəbl] adj. worthy of respect, usually because of age or position   존경할 만한; 유서 깊은

The Sacred Heart Academy is a *venerable* Catholic school for girls.
세이크리드 하트 아카데미는 유서 깊은 가톨릭계 여학교다.

The *venerable* minister was loved by everyone in the church, even though he had started to give the same sermon several weeks in a row and often forgot what he was talking about in the middle of a sentence.
존경할 만한 목사는 몇 주 동안 연달아 똑같은 설교를 했었고 종종 설교 도중 무슨 얘기를 하고 있는지 잊어버리는 수도 있었지만 교회의 모든 신도들에게 사랑을 받았다.

VERDICT [və́:rdikt] n. the jury's decision at the end of a trial; a judgment   배심원의 평결; 판결; 의견

"What's your *verdict*?" asked aunt Faye, after we sampled her latest pecan pie recipe.
페이 이모가 최근 요리법으로 만든 피칸 파이를 우리가 시식하고 나자 이모는 "맛이 어떠니?"라고 물었다.

The jury took two days to reach a *verdict* of "guilty" in the Hawlsey murder trial.
배심원단이 홀시의 살인 재판에서 "유죄" 평결을 내리기까지 이틀이 걸렸다.

VERIFY [vérəfai] v. to prove or determine the truth or accuracy of something   증명하다, 확인하다

Most employers will *verify* the information you put on your application before hiring you.
대부분의 고용주들은 당신을 고용하기 전에 지원서에 기재된 내용을 확인할 것이다.

The FBI tried to *verify* reports of an invasion of space aliens in Omaha.
FBI는 우주인들이 오마하를 침공했다는 보도의 사실 여부를 확인하려고 애썼다.

Before the radio station would give him the tickets he won, Roy had to *verify* his identity by showing the DJ his school ID card.
로이는 라디오 방송국에서 자신이 따낸 티켓을 받기 전에 DJ에게 학생증을 보여주고 신분을 입증해야 했다.

VERSATILE [və́:rsətl/-tail] adj. useful for many purposes; capable of many things   다목적의, 다용도의; 다재다능한, 만능의

Keenan is a *versatile* actor: he can be a villain, a hero, or a comedian.
키넌은 만능 배우다. 악한도 될 수 있고, 영웅 혹은 코미디언도 될 수 있다.

This new white shirt is very *versatile*: it goes with all my other clothes, and I can wear it on casual and dressy occasions.
이 새로 산 흰 셔츠는 아주 다목적이다. 내 다른 옷들과도 잘 어울리고, 편안한 자리에도 정장을 하는 자리에도 입을 수 있다.

VERTICAL [və́:rtikəl] adj. upright; standing up on end, rather than flat on a side   곧추 선; 수직의, 세로의

Most libraries stack their books in *vertical* rows.
대부분의 도서관에서는 책을 세워서 꽂아 놓는다.

The suit was black with thin *vertical* white stripes.
양복은 검은 바탕에 세로로 가느다란 흰 줄무늬가 있었다.

VICE VERSA [váis və́:rsə/váisi-/-və:sə] adv. the other way around; in reverse order   반대로(도 같음); 역순으로

Kathy borrows Bobby's bike whenever she needs it, and *vice versa*.
캐시는 필요할 때마다 바비의 자전거를 빌리고 바비 역시 그렇게 한다.

"It's the man's job to ask a woman for a date, not *vice versa*," said my grandfather.
"여자에게 데이트를 신청하는 것은 남자의 일이야. 반대의 경우는 안 되지." 라고 할아버지가 말씀하셨다.

VIGOROUS [vígərəs] adj. strong and full of energy; done with a lot of energy   정력적인, 원기 왕성한; 활발한, 격심한

After six months' good care at the stable, the horses were healthy and *vigorous*.
말들을 마구간에서 여섯 달간 잘 보살폈더니 건강하고 원기 왕성해졌다.

The pitcher's trainer gave his arm a *vigorous* rubdown after he pitched nine tough innings.
투수 트레이너는 투수가 9이닝 동안 호투하고 나자 그의 팔을 힘차게 마사지 해주었다.

VIRULENT [vírələnt] adj. very harmful; infectious; mean   매우 해로운; 전염성의; 비열한

Doctors are urging everyone to get a flu shot this season because an especially *virulent* strain of the disease has been going around.
의사들이 이번 계절에는 특히 전염성 강한 바이러스가 돌고 있기 때문에 독감 예방접종을 맞으라고 강력히 권하고 있다.

Susie started screaming the most *virulent* insults she could think of when she saw her best friend holding hands with her boyfriend outside the movie theater.
수지는 가장 친한 친구가 자신의 남자 친구와 손을 잡고 극장에서 나오는 걸 보고 생각해 낼 수 있는 가장 심한 욕을 퍼붓기 시작했다.

VIVACIOUS [vivéiʃəs/vai-] adj. lively and full of spirit   활기 있는, 활발한

Belle is usually a giggling, *vivacious* girl, but for some reason she is feeling sad today.
벨은 평상시에 잘 웃고 활달한 아이인데, 오늘은 어쩐 일인지 우울해 한다.

Vivian decided to play something light and *vivacious* at her piano recital.
비비안은 피아노 독주회에서 가볍고 쾌활한 곡을 연주하기로 했다.

VOLITION [voulíʃən] n. a conscious act or choice; the power of independent choice   의지, 결단; 의지력, 결단력

Her parents were stunned when Michelle, of her own *volition*, offered to share the last piece of cake with her sister.
미셸이 자진해서 케이크 마지막 조각을 여동생과 나누어 먹겠다고 하자 부모들은 어안이 벙벙했다.

Farley had about as much *volition* as a jellyfish: he simply did what he was told.
팔리는 의지가 정말 약했다. 그저 남이 하라는 대로만 했다.

VOLUNTARY [váləntèri/vɔ́ləntəri] adj. done by free choice   자발적인

Participation in the school blood drive is completely *voluntary*: no one will force anyone to give blood.
학교에서 헌혈 캠페인에 참여하는 것은 완전히 자발적이다. 아무도 누구에게 헌혈을 강요하지 않을 것이다.

Brad made the *voluntary* decision to give up playing on the football team in order to pay more attention to his school work.
브래드는 학업에 더 힘쓰기 위해 미식축구팀에서 운동하는 것을 그만둬야겠다고 스스로 결정했다.

VULNERABLE [vʌ́lnərəbl] adj. open to harm, injury, or attack   상처 입기 쉬운, 공격받기 쉬운

Homes without locks on the windows are *vulnerable* to burglary.
창문에 자물쇠가 없는 집에는 강도가 들기 쉽다.

Achilles, the great Greek hero, had only one spot on his body that was *vulnerable* to knives, swords, or arrows: the back of his heel.

위대한 그리스 영웅 아킬레스는 몸에서 칼이나 검, 화살에 상처 입기 쉬운 단 한 곳이 있었는데, 바로 발 뒤꿈치였다.

W

WALLOW [wάlou/wɔ́l-] v. to roll around, as in water or mud; to give in to a state of mind or way of life
뒹굴다; 빠지다, 탐닉하다

The hippopotamus *wallowed* happily in the muddy bank of the river.
하마는 질퍽한 강둑에서 행복한 듯 뒹굴었다.

"I wish you'd quit *wallowing* in self-pity," said Nell to Bea. "I assure you your bangs will grow out eventually."
넬이 비에게 말했다. "자기 연민에서 그만 빠져나왔으면 좋겠어. 네 앞머리는 다시 자랄 거라구."

WARRANT [wɔ́(:)rənt/wάr-] n. official permission; official written permission   공식적인 허가, 면허; 허가증, 면허증, 영장

The police needed a *warrant* from the judge before they could search the warehouse owned by the suspected cheese thieves.
경찰이 치즈 절도 용의자가 소유한 창고를 수색하려면 판사로부터 영장을 발급받아야 했다.

The teachers have the *warrant* of the school board to use strict discipline in the classrooms.
교사들은 학교 이사회로부터 교실 내에서 엄격한 징계를 내려도 된다는 허가를 받았다.

[Note] *Warrant* can also be a verb meaning to deserve or to call for.
warrant는 '~를 받을 만하다' 또는 '요구하다' 라는 동사로도 쓰인다.

- Does coming home fifteen minutes late really *warrant* such strong punishment?
  집에 15분 늦게 들어오는 것이 그렇게 심하게 혼날 만한 일인가요?

WARY [wέəri] adj. on guard; cautious   경계하는, 방심하지 않는; 조심성 있는

Evelyn made a slow, *wary* search of the dark, abandoned house.
에블린은 천천히 조심스럽게 어둡고 버려진 집을 찾았다.

Be *wary* of people who come up and offer to carry your bags in the airport—they might try to rob you.
공항에서 너한테 다가와 가방을 들어주겠다는 사람을 경계해. 강도질을 하려고 할 수도 있어.

WEARY [wíəri] adj. tired; worn down   피곤한; 기진맥진한

The long walk from his broken-down car to the gas station had made Fred *weary*.
프레드는 차가 고장나 버려 주유소까지 먼 길을 걸어가느라 녹초가 됐다.

After years of wars and battles, the soldier grew *weary* of fighting and longed for peace.
몇 년 동안 전쟁과 싸움이 계속되자 군인들은 싸움에 지쳐 갔고 평화를 열망했다.

"I'm *weary* of all this arguing," snapped Mom. "Either shut up or speak nicely to each other."
엄마가 매섭게 말했다. "이런 언쟁은 지긋지긋해. 입을 다물든지 부드럽게 말하든지 해."

WINCE [wins] v. to flinch or start from shock, pain, or embarrassment 주춤하다, 움찔하다

Zach *winced* as his mother tried to pull the piece of glass out of his foot.
재크는 어머니가 그의 발에 박힌 유리 조각을 빼려고 하자 움찔했다.

Hearing the tape of myself singing in the shower made me *wince*.
샤워하면서 내가 부른 노래의 녹음테이프를 듣고는 움찔했다.

WITNESS [wítnis] n. a person who saw or heard an event and can tell others about it or v. to see or hear an event 목격자 / 목격하다

There were seven *witnesses* to the car accident.
교통사고를 목격한 사람이 일곱 명이었다.

Jack was sitting on a bench across the street, and *witnessed* the whole accident.
잭은 길 건너편의 벤치에 앉아 있다가 사건의 전모를 목격하게 됐다.

WOO [wu:] v. to try to get the affection or favor of 구애하다, 얻으려고 노력하다

Percy *wooed* Gwendolyn with poetry, flowers, and soft music.
퍼시는 시와 꽃과 부드러운 음악으로 겐돌린에게 구애했다.

The grocery store tried to *woo* shoppers with sales and giveaways.
식품점은 염가 판매와 경품으로 손님을 끌려고 애썼다.

Y, Z

YIELD [ji:ld] v. to surrender or give over; to provide or give forth 양보하다, 항복하다; 산출하다, (결과물을) 내다

A yellow traffic light means you should slow down and *yield* the right of way to traffic from another direction.
노란 신호등은 속도를 줄이고 다른 방향에서 오는 차량에게 통행권을 내줘야 한다는 의미다.

The Texan rebels at the Alamo refused to *yield* to the much stronger forces of the Mexican Army.
앨라모 요새의 텍사스 반군은 훨씬 더 강한 멕시코 군대에게 항복하기를 거부했다.

This year, my garden *yielded* several baskets full of tomatoes.
올해 우리 정원에는 몇 광주리 가득차게 토마토가 열렸다.

ZEAL [zi:l] n. enthusiasm for a cause or goal 열심, 열성, 열의

"I've never seen someone file papers with such *zeal*," Ms. Roth told her assistant.
로스 부인은 자신의 비서에게 말했다. "난 당신처럼 열심히 서류를 정리하는 사람은 처음 봤어."

Bruno poisoned the rats with great *zeal*.
브루노는 쥐를 독살시키는 데 정말 열심이었다.

The Fateful Meeting

숙명적인 만남

Allow me to introduce myself. My name is Beauregard, a gentleman cat from a long line of South Carolina aristocrats. My **ancestors**, from my father way on back of my great-great-great-great-great-great grandfather Lucius, have *resided* in the homes of the finest families of the South. We are known as much for our perfect manners, grace, and all-round **gentility**, as we are for our size (I, myself, stand nearly four and a half feet tall when I walk on my rear **limbs**). Our good breeding is also obvious by our beautifully kept, *glossy* coats. Mine is completely black, and I spend a good deal of time each morning *grooming* and smoothing it to perfection (one never knows who one might meet).

That afternoon, I was as happy and **content** as can be, taking a well-earned nap on the softest, sunniest patch of grass in the Bois de Boulogne, a large and beautiful park in Paris. As for what I was doing in France, well I am forced to admit that I was a bit wild in my youth, and my family thought it best that I take a long trip until some of the scandals died down. Yes, it's true, I've always been one to go out **carousing** until all hours, eating catnip and singing loudly with my tomcat friends, and chasing young lady cats around. Those were the days! I remember one beautiful cat named Felinia. She and I used to... well, that's a story for another time. Let's just say my folks thought it best that I do my **gallivanting** on foreign soil.

But I **digress**. As I said, I was taking my afternoon **siesta**, which ordinarily I wouldn't have interrupted for anyone or anything. But I knew that little girl was in trouble from the minute I laid eyes on her. She was trying to act calm and **nonchalant**, just *smacking* on her bubble gum and *strolling* through the Bois as though she didn't give a hoot about anything in the world, but she wasn't fooling anyone but herself. She wasn't from Paris, you could tell that from the New York Yankees cap she wore backwards on her braided head. I couldn't see anyone that looked like her parents around, so I just put two and two together and figured she was lost.

RESIDE v. to live (in or at a place) for a long time; to dwell   살다, 거주하다
This family has resided in Richmond for 100 years.
이 가문은 리치몬드에서 100년 동안 거주해왔다.

GLOSSY adj. smooth and shiny; highly polished   매끄럽고 빛나는; 광택이 나는
The beautiful, glossy coat of the cat shone as it lay in the sunlight.
햇빛을 받으며 누워있을 때 고양이의 아름답고 광택이 나는 털이 반짝 빛났다.

GROOM v. to feed, rub down, brush, and generally take care of (a horse or dog)   (말이나 개 따위를) 돌보다, 손질하다
A dog with long hair needs grooming often.
털이 긴 개는 자주 손질을 해줄 필요가 있다.

SMACK v. to open (the lips) quickly so as to make a sharp sound   입맛을 다시는 소리를 내다
He smacked his lips over the thought of cake.
그는 케이크를 생각하면서 입맛을 다셨다.

STROLL v. to walk in a slow leisurely way   한가로이 거닐다, 산책하다
We were strolling about under the trees.
우리는 나무 밑을 여기저기 한가로이 거닐고 있었다.

Well, this little girl was so full of anxiety you could practically see the worry coming out her ears, so, today, I decided to make an exception, and interrupt my siesta. She had *plopped* herself down on a bench and was sort of kicking her feet around in the dirt. I was just about to go up to her to see if I could do anything to help, when Babette came along and the two struck up a conversation. I was somewhat curious, as cats can be, and a little worried, so I decided to stick around to make sure they were alright. Of course, I hadn't the slightest suspicion that later that day I would be involved in a plot to overthrow the Elephant Empire...

"You're an American," said Babette, matter-of-factly.

Bridget jumped a little. She wasn't expecting to hear someone talk to her in English, and she definitely wasn't expecting to run into someone like Babette: black hair, black clothes, black sunglasses that **concealed** most of her face. In fact, the bright red lipstick she wore was the only thing that added any color to her outfit. Bridget usually thought lipstick and all that "girlie" stuff was silly—she was a tomboy, herself—but this girl didn't seem silly at all. Actually, she was very grown up and **sophisticated**.

"Yep, I'm American," replied Bridget, trying to look casual. "So what?"

"What are you doing here?" asked Babette.

"I'm just sitting on a bench minding my own business. You got a problem with that?" *growled* Bridget. She didn't mean to seem **gruff** or unfriendly, but for some reason she didn't want this strange, older girl to know she was afraid.

"I have no problem," said the French girl. "I am simply curious. Where is your family?"

Bridget *heaved* a sigh and stared down into the dirt. "I lost them," she *mumbled*.

PLOP v. to make a sound like that of an object striking water without a splash; to cause (something) to plop, or to fall with a plop 풍덩 떨어뜨리다(떨어지다)
The noise of the frog as he plopped into the water, startled the ducks.
개구리가 물속으로 풍덩 떨어지면서 내는 소리에 오리들이 놀랐다.

GROWL v. to complain angrily; to grumble 투덜거리다, 불평하다
The sailors growled about the poor food.
선원들은 형편없는 음식에 대해 불평했다.

HEAVE v. to give (a sigh or groan) with a deep, heavy breath or with effort (탄성, 앓는 소리를) 괴로운 듯이 내다, 발하다
Please don't heave a sigh at such a thing.
제발 그런 일에 한숨쉬지 마라.

MUMBLE v. to speak or say something unclearly and usually quietly, so that people cannot hear what is said 불분명하게 말하다
He always mumbles when he's embarrassed.
그는 창피하면 항상 말을 얼버무린다.

"Oh, I see. You are an orphan. You lost them in an accident?"

"No, not in an accident. In the Louvre. Accidentally in the Louvre. I mean, we went to that stupid art museum, and I lost them. I mean, they lost me. Or we lost each other. Anyway, they're not here," said Bridget. She bit her lower lip. She knew she was **babbling** a bunch of nonsense, and she didn't want to blow her cool.

"Ah," said Babette, her eyebrows appearing above her sunglasses.

Who is this girl? thought Bridget. What's all this "ah" stuff? She had had about enough of this conversation.

"Hey, just who are you and what do you want?" demanded Bridget. "Can't you see I'm busy **loafing**? Talking with you is *messing up* my plans to sit around doing nothing all day."

"Why don't I help you find them?" Babette replied. She had an odd way of not responding to what people said.

Bridget was **baffled**. She just couldn't figure this out. Why would this girl, who wasn't even an **acquaintance** of hers, much less a friend, want to help her? Besides, Bridget didn't like owing people favors. She especially didn't want to be **beholden** to some mysterious French girl she'd only just met. On the other hand, she probably knew Paris well, and Bridget had to admit that finding her parents wasn't a bad idea.

While Bridget was *puzzling* over this **quandary**, Babette repeated her offer, "Come, let us go find your family."

"Back off, Frenchie," *snapped* Bridget. "Who says I need your help?"

"My name is Babette, and you are obviously in need of assistance. We can go search for your family now, if you will get up and come with me." She didn't seem to mind Bridget's **hostile** tone of voice. In fact, she seemed completely **oblivious** to it.

MESS v. (mess up의 형태로 쓰여) to spoil 망치다, 엉망으로 하다
It will mess up the whole analysis.
그것이 전체 분석을 엉망으로 만들 것이다.

PUZZLE v. to make (somebody) think hard; to perplex 어찌 줄 모르게 하다; 당황하게 하다
The sudden fall in the value of the dollar has puzzled financial experts.
달러 가치의 갑작스런 하락으로 투자 전문가들은 당황하게 됐다.

SNAP v. to speak or say (something) in a sharp (usually angry) voice (화난 듯이) 툭 내뱉다
He never speaks calmly, just snaps all the time.
그는 차분하게 말하는 법이 없다. 항상 툭 내뱉는다.

Bridget could tell there was no way to change Babette's mind. She was obviously **adamant**, and **circumstances** being as they were, it seemed the best thing she could do was to take her up on the offer. But Bridget, being a New Yorker and naturally **reluctant** to trust people, still wondered if Babette had some **ulterior** motive for wanting to help her. Was she a space alien *disguised* as a human looking for someone to do *weird* experiments on? Was she one of those people who kidnaps children and sells them to the gypsies? Bridget decided to ask her straight out.

"Why do you want to help me?"

"Frankly, I am quite bored and have nothing better to do," sighed Babatte.

Bridget *grinned*. Now that was an answer she could believe. This Babette might be as cool as she looked after all. She got up and offered her hand to the other girl.

"My name's Bridget," she said, "Let's get going."

Babette shook her hand and they started walking away.

"How did you know I was American, anyway?" asked Bridget, as they rounded a curve in the path and headed for the street.

"You are, well, **conspicuous**. You stick out, you see? Your hat, your blue jeans—these are very American clothes. Your hat is very nice, especially. Very **chic**. All the most stylish Parisians want to wear these hats."

"Thanks. You're pretty chic yourself," said Bridget. "I'll tell you what. If you find my parents, you can have the hat. Deal?"

"Deal," said Babette. It seemed like she was smiling, but it was hard to tell what was going on behind those dark sunglasses.

DISGUISE v. to make somebody/something look or sound different from normal 변장하다
The raiders disguised themselves as security guards.
그 침입자들은 경비원으로 변장했다.

WEIRD adj. unconventional, unusual or bizarre 이상한
I found some of her poems a bit weird.
나는 그녀의 시들이 약간 이상하다는 것을 알아냈다.

GRIN v. to smile broadly, so as to show the teeth, expressing amusement, foolish satisfaction, contempt, etc. 싱긋 웃다
He grinned at me, as if sharing a secret joke.
그는 비밀스런 농담을 주고받는 것처럼 내게 싱긋 웃었다.

The two new friends walked out on to the busy sidewalk to begin their mission. And if they had paused to look over their shoulders, they would have seen that they were not alone. A gigantic, elegant black cat was following right behind them.

Bridget and Babette had been walking along in silence for a while when suddenly, Babette came to an **abrupt** stop in front of what looked like an apartment building. In fact, it was such a *run-down*, ugly apartment building, it might have been safe to call it a **tenement**.

"We must go in here," she said.

"Well... um, okay, I guess," said Bridget, **hesitantly**. She didn't like the look of the place at all. "What is this building, anyway?"

"It is a **dormitory** for all the science students at the university," Babette replied as she opened the door. "It is where all the young geniuses live—when they are not in their *laboratories*, that is. We are here to see my friend Barnaby. He is American, like you. It is my belief he may be able to help us find your parents."

"Great," chirped Bridget, as they walked into the building, followed by Beauregard the cat. "Let's find him."

"I must warn you, Barnaby has his **quirks**. Just odd little habits, of course, but some people are *put off* by them," Babette calmly explained as they walked up the stairs.

"What kind of quirks?" asked Bridget, who was becoming more nervous and **uneasy** about this whole thing with each step they took.

RUN-DOWN adj. in a very poor condition because it has not been repaired or looked after (건물 등의) 상태가 좋지 않은
The building is getting run-down.
건물이 점점 누추해지고 있다.

LABORATORY n. room or building used for (especially scientific) research, experiments, testing, etc. 실험실
There was a big explosion in the laboratory.
실험실에서 큰 폭발이 있었다.

PUT v. (put off의 형태로 쓰여) to cause to change one's mind and not do or have something that they were intending to do or have 막다, 단념시키다
Nothing would put her off once she had made up her mind.
일단 그녀가 마음을 먹으면 어느 것도 그녀를 막을 수 없다.

"Nothing to worry about, really. His most noticeable **idiosyncrasy** is his hair. He has hair unlike any other person's—it is his trademark. He is also the most brilliant person I know. He entered the university when he was only ten years old. A 'boy wonder,' I believe they called him. But he is still so young, and he is excitable. Ah," she said, stopping in front of plain wooden door. "Here is his room. Knock, please."

Bridget gave the door a couple of **tentative** taps with her right hand. She was almost *grateful* there was no response.

"He's not in. Let's go," she said.

Babette smiled and started beating the door with both her fists. "Don't be so **timid** about it. Barnaby! Barnaby!" she yelled. "Open this door at once!"

Just then the door *jerked* open and a strange looking boy *poked* his head out. His hair was bushy, long, and pale, and stuck a couple of feet off his head in every direction like a crazy lion's mane. Beneath that wild mop, his face was that of any ordinary boy. To call him **unkempt** would be putting it mildly. It looked like birds had nested in his hair, and his lab coat looked as though it had never been anywhere near a washing machine. The "boy wonder" seemed **bewildered** at first, as if two girls and a giant cat had never paid him a visit before, but after a few seconds, he smiled widely and flung the door open.

"Hey, Babette!" he cried, **beckoning** her into the room with a wave of his hand. "Come in here, quick. You have to see my latest experiment."

The place was filled with bubbling test tubes, strangely colored liquids, a bunch of dead insects, and a huge **array** of vegetable plants—everything from alfalfa to yams.

GRATEFUL adj. feeling or showing appreciation for something good done to one, for something fortunate that happens, etc.; thankful 고마워하는; 감사하는
I am grateful to you for your help.
네가 도와줘서 고마워.

JERK v. (cause something/somebody to) move with a short sudden action or a series of short uneven actions 갑자기 움직이다
She jerked her head towards the door.
그녀는 문 쪽으로 머리를 확 돌렸다.

POKE v. to put or move something in a specified direction, with a sharp push; to thrust 쑥 내밀다; 찌르다
He poked his head round the door to see if she was in the room.
그는 그녀가 방안에 있는지 보려고 문 안쪽으로 머리를 쑥 내밀었다.

"As you can see from all my little green friends here, my experiment is **botanical** in nature. Yes, Babette, I have long been tortured by the **plight** of plants, the innocent vegetable in particular," he **lamented**. "Oh, how the poor plants suffer! They have such beauty but, unfortunately, no legs or arms, so they can't fight off these cruel and **despicable** bugs!" He smashed his hand down on a pile of dead *mealy* bugs. "Until now, there was no choice but to spray these lovely vegetables with poisons so **toxic** they polluted the soil and **contaminated** the waters. But no more! My invention will do away with these poisons. They simply won't be needed anymore—they will be completely **obsolete**! At last we will... hey," he paused suddenly, "who let that cat in here?"

All eyes turned to the cat which was, it appeared, sleeping in the doorway.

"I have seen this cat before," said Babette. "He chases pigeons in the Bois de Boulogne and makes **amorous** advances toward every female cat he sees. Oh, he is so ridiculous, yet so harmless."

They all giggled, and the cat seemed to grumble in his sleep.

"Yes, well, er, as I was saying, at last we will defeat the creeping killers," Barnaby muttered.

"Man, something smells **foul** in here," said Bridget, wrinkling up her face. "What stinks?"

"Aha! You see? It works!" cried Barnaby, clapping his hands.

Bridget looked puzzled. "Are you *nuts* or something?"

"Not at all, not at all. Allow me to explain. What you smell are gym socks. Dirty gym socks that have been worn for an entire semester without a wash and left in a locker. You don't like the smell, eh?" asked Barnaby, smiling. He paused for a moment. "Well, let me tell you something. Bugs hate the smell. But it goes beyond a simple **aversion** to the smell of gym socks. They **detest** the smell so much they can't bear to come near it. It also **inhibits** the growth of some plant *fungi*, but it doesn't stop it altogether. Those socks even killed these mealy bugs," he said, wiping his hand off on his lab coat. "Yes, the day of the bug is over. No longer will these pests destroy crops and cause **famines**."

MEALY adj. as if dusted with flour; pale 밀가루로 덮인 듯한; 창백한
I only know two sorts of boys. Mealy boys, and vigorous boys.
나는 두 종류의 소년들만 알고 있다. 창백한 아이들과 혈기왕성한 아이들.

NUTS n. foolish, eccentric or mad person 바보, 괴짜, 미치광이
He drives like a nuts – he'll kill himself one day.
그는 미치광이처럼 운전하는데 언젠가는 그러다 죽게 될 것이다.

FUNGUS n. any of various types of plant without leaves, flowers or green colouring matter, growing on other plants or decaying matter 진균류, 균 복수형은 fungi
Mildew and mushrooms are fungi.
곰팡이와 버섯은 진균류이다.

"Preventing starvation is a wonderful cause. But surely, Barnaby, there are not enough disgusting gym socks in the world to keep insects off all the crops," offered Babette.

"An **astute** observation. You're as sharp as ever. No, unfortunately, there aren't enough socks to go around. So I've been trying to capture the **essence** of the disgusting gym sock, the thing that makes it *tick*. Is it the odor of foot? The sweat? The toenail *grime*? Once I discover this, I can use a variety of ingredients to create a **synthetic** spray that has the same effect as the real thing. It will be very **potent**. Oh, yes. No one will doubt its power. But it will not be poison."

Bridget rolled her eyes. Barnaby seemed a little full of himself, and **pompous** people always really **irked** her. "Look, my name's Bridget and Babette here thinks you can help me find my parents."

"So you've lost your parents, huh? I know exactly how you feel. Yes, you have my **sympathy**. I once lost my parents for an entire year. Or, rather, it seems I forgot to call them for an entire year while I was studying tropical bird songs in the Amazon rainforest. So you could say they lost me, I suppose. It's upsetting either way. Yes." Barnaby scratched his head. Bridget wasn't sure, but it looked as though he had pulled a wristwatch out of his bushy hair. Or maybe he already had a wristwatch. "Time to check the solution!" he cried.

The young scientist *scurried* over to a large beaker full of bubbling, smoking, grayish liquid and carefully calculated the temperature, all the while mumbling to himself. Then he filled an eyedropper full of bubbling blue liquid from another beaker and added it to the gray *muck*. Next, he **agitated** the unholy mixture by picking up the beaker and giving it a shaking so **vigorous** it made him break out in a sweat.

"Ladies," he announced, "you are about to witness scientific history!" With that he began a countdown. "Ten, nine, eight, seven, six..."

Barnaby never reached the end of his countdown. Around "four" a terrible rumbling began. Then an explosion. Then, a horrible, horrible smell.

TICK n. unpleasant or contemptible person 싫은(귀찮은) 녀석
I don't want to live with such a terrible tick.
나는 그런 끔찍스런 녀석과 함께 살고 싶지 않다.

GRIME n. dirt, especially in a layer on a surface 때
Soap and water removed only a little of the grime on the coal miner's hands.
비누와 물은 석탄광부의 손에 묻은 때를 조금밖에 없애주지 못했다.

SCURRY v. to run with short quick steps 허겁지겁 달려가다
The rain sent everyone scurrying for shelter.
비가 오자 모든 사람들이 허겁지겁 피할 곳을 찾아 달려갔다.

MUCK n. dirt; filth; anything disgusting 흙; 오물
Don't come in here with your boots all covered in muck.
부츠에 흙을 잔뜩 묻힌 채 여기 들어오지 마라.

"Quick! We must **vacate** the building at once! Out! Out!" shrieked Barnaby.

The girls and the cat were all too happy to **comply**. They ran out the door and down to the street. There they stopped to catch their breath (which they had been holding for a couple of minutes).

"Oh, what a stupid **blunder**!" *gasped* Barnaby. "How could I have made such a mistake?"

"There, there," said Babette, not very convincingly.

"It was my **ego** that made me do it. My foolish pride! I thought I was smarter than the great Vogelstellenstein, a scientist **renowned** the world over for his brilliantly simple discoveries! How I **envy** his genius! It was he who suggested cigar smoke as an insect *repellent*. Naturally, since cigar smoke is a **carcinogen**, I thought it was best not to encourage farmers to smoke in their fields, **lest** they develop lung cancer. How was I to know gym socks could be worse than cigars?" Barnaby seemed near tears.

"Look, don't *sweat* it. Um, I mean, quit worrying about it," said Bridget.

"Yes, I suppose you're right," he said, changing moods abruptly. "After all, I'm only an **amateur** when it comes to botany. My true profession is physics. Still, I do enjoy **dabbling** in the other sciences. But this little accident doesn't **bode** well for me. It's the third explosion I've caused this week, and the university said they'd have me sent home if I continued to destroy their property. I guess my announcement of my great discovery was **premature**. I must do many more tests to **verify** the results so that I can be absolutely certain they are correct. In the meantime, I should probably go try to straighten up."

"Nonsense," snapped Babette. "We have a more important matter to take care of. Let the university sort through all the broken glass and **debris**. We must find Bridget's parents."

"I apologize. Of course. Where do we begin?" asked Barnaby.

"I thought you were supposed to know that," said Bridget. She stared down at her sneakers sadly. This whole thing was beginning to seem hopeless.

GASP v. to take one or more quick breaths with open mouth, because of surprise or exhaustion 헐떡거리다, 숨이 막히다
I gasped in/with astonishment at the magician's skill.
나는 마법사의 솜씨에 놀라서 숨이 막혔다.

REPELLENT n. chemical that repels insects 살충제
Rub some of this mosquito-repellent on your legs.
다리에 모기약을 좀 바르세요.

SWEAT v. to be in a state of great anxiety 걱정하다, 고민하다
They all want to know my decision but I think I'll let them sweat a little, i.e. by not telling them yet.
그들 모두 내 결정을 알고 싶어하는데, 나는 그 사람들이 좀 고민하게 내버려 둘거야, 즉 아직 말을 안해줄거야.

"Come, Bridget, there is no need for such **dejection**," said Babette. "Barnaby is always full of good ideas."

"Naturally!" agreed Barnaby. "Now, let's see. If you want to cover a lot of ground, the best way is in the air! What we need is some kind of hot-air balloon. I could design one by tomorrow morning."

Bridget *perked* up at this idea. "A hot-air balloon, huh? Why didn't you say so? Let me show you two little trick I picked up back home."

With that, Bridget began chewing her gum, her jaws and cheeks pumping furiously. Then she slowly blew a large pink bubble, bigger than a beach ball, toward the sky. And, to Babette and Barnaby's (and Beauregard's) amazement, she began to lift off the ground!

"Oh, my, you Americans are incredible!" cried Babette.

"How **convenient**," remarked Barnaby. "A hot-air balloon you can carry in your mouth!"

With a loud smack, Bridget sucked her gum back into her mouth and plopped back down in front of them. "How about it, guys? I can't look down very well while I do that. But if you hold onto me, you can look for me."

"Sounds fascinating," said Barnaby.

Babette agreed. So Bridget took a deep breath and began to create a blimp of a bubble. As she rose into the air, her two friends grabbed on—Barnaby on the right leg, Babette on the left—and they began their ascent.

But just as they became airborne, Barnaby let out a *squeal*.

"Aaaiieee! That cat just jumped on my leg!"

"So we have a **feline** *stowaway*, eh?" said Babette. "Careful, then, Barnaby. The last thing we need is to drop a hundred-pound cat on some innocent Parisian."

Soon, the four of them were floating above the rooftops of the city, eagerly searching for the misplaced parents. Unfortunately, they didn't notice the angry black clouds forming overhead.

PERK v. to become cheerful, lively or vigorous, especially after illness or depression 활기를 되찾다
He looked depressed but perked up when his friends arrived.
그는 의기소침해 보였는데 친구들이 도착하자 활기를 되찾았다.

SQUEAL n. high-pitched cry or sound, longer and louder than a squeak (often indicating terror or pain) 비명(소리)
There were squeals of excitement from the children.
아이들로부터 흥분의 비명이 터져 나왔다.

STOWAWAY n. person who hides himself in a ship or aircraft before its departure, in order to travel without paying or being seen 무임 승선자
There were seven stowaways in that ship.
그 배에는 무임 승선자가 7명 있었다.

You can see what I mean about those kids needing help, now, can't you? That Barnaby, for instance. He certainly knows how to put words together, but being **articulate** doesn't necessarily mean you have common sense. And Babette—well, she's obviously just out for a bit of excitement. She's not **naive**, that's for sure, but even the most *worldly-wise* girl needs looking after now and again. Bridget? She seemed tough enough, all right, but I figured she just might have gotten a little big for her *britches*, if you'll pardon the expression.

And as for me, well, a **trauma** like that frightening gym sock explosion should have been enough to **deter** me from any further involvement with that bunch of crazy kids. The decision to jump on Barnaby's leg was pretty **spontaneous**. I just saw them floating away, and the next thing I knew, I was floating away with them. It wasn't long after takeoff that I realized we might be in trouble. The sun was setting and the air was unusually **sultry** for a fall day, sticky and hotter than the fourth of July. A **gust** of wind blew some damp air into my face, which I was grateful for at first. But then another gust came, and I realized it had started to rain—big, fat, heavy raindrops. Then, all at once, everything let loose. The air became so **turbulent** it felt as though we were riding a roller coaster. The rain came down in buckets. I was reminded of the **monsoons** of southern Asia, those winds that brought such heavy rain. How well I remember the lazy evenings I used to spend in Bangkok, waiting out the storms with a beautiful, exotic... but I **digress**. Back to the subject.

The winds *swirled* around us faster and faster, until they built up such **velocity** I feared we would be thrown far off course. But there was nothing I could do but hold on tight (and hope Barnaby held on tight) and wait for the storm to die down. When it finally did, I almost wished we were still high in the air being whipped by wind and water. We had landed safely in a grassy field, but our relief quickly gave way to fear. We were immediately surrounded and taken prisoner—the helpless **captives** of the jackal army.

WORLDY-WISE adj. experienced and knowledgeable about life   세상 경험이 있는
He had a friend called Clive who was younger but far more worldly-wise.
그에게는 클리브라는 나이는 어리지만 세상 경험은 훨씬 많은 친구가 있다.

BRITCHES n. (too big for one's britches의 형태로 쓰여) overestimating oneself too cocky   건방진, 자만심에 가득 찬
Before the mike and camera, he spoils them with praise; behind the scenes, he boxes their ears when they get too big for their britches.
마이크와 카메라 앞에서 그는 그들을 칭찬해서 우쭐거리게 하지만, 무대 뒤에서는 자만심에 가득 차 있으면 그들의 따귀를 때렸다.

SWIRL v. (cause air, water, etc. to) move or flow with twists and turns and with varying speed   소용돌이치다
The log was swirled away downstream by the current.
물살에 따라 통나무가 하류로 소용돌이치며 내려갔다.

Relationships

Decide what relationship the following pairs of words have to each other. If they mean close to the same thing, make "S." If they have opposite meanings, mark "O."

1. anxiety :: uneasiness
2. hesitant :: reluctant
3. chic :: unkempt
4. carousing :: gallivanting
5. sophisticated :: naive
6. suspicion :: trust
7. quirk :: idiosyncrasy
8. premature :: tardy
9. amateur :: dabbler
10. despicable :: foul
11. acquaintance :: close friend

Relationships

Decide what relationship the following pairs of words have to each other. If they mean close to the same thing, make "S." If they have opposite meanings, mark "O."

1. gruff :: hostile
2. conspicuous :: concealed
3. tentative :: timid
4. oblivious :: astute
5. inhibits :: assists
6. bewildered :: baffled
7. potent :: weak
8. toxic :: contaminated
9. abrupt :: sudden
10. comply :: disobey
11. tenement :: mansion

Fill in the Blank

For each sentence below, choose the word that best completes the sentence.

1. Mark was the happiest guy at the party when the girl he had been staring at all evening finally noticed him and _____ him to come over to her.
   a. babbled   b. loafed   c. beckoned   d. agitated

2. When the little girl dropped her ice cream cone in the dirt, the ice cream man felt _____ for her and gave her another one for free.
   a. sympathy   b. envy   c. dejection   d. aversion

3. Sally hadn't planned on traveling to the beach for the weekend, but the weather was so beautiful she made the _____ decision to hop into her car and head for the shore.
   a. amorous   b. vigorous   c. pompous   d. spontaneous

4. The invention of compact disc players made turntables and vinyl records practically _____ .
   a. obsolete   b. renowned   c. synthetic   d. articulate

5. Barry got a reputation for being the coolest kid in school because he always acted _____ , no matter what was happening to him or around him.

   a. content   b. nonchalant   c. adamant   d. turbulent

6. "I agree, much stricter punishments are needed to _____ cheating in the classrooms," said the principal, "but spanking the students is against the law."

   a. irk   b. vacate   c. deter   d. verify

7. Until the recent article in *National Geographic*, people didn't know about the _____ of the blue-tongued skinks, the little lizards who are hunted down and killed by the hundreds every day so their skins can be used for belts and wallets.

   a. essence   b. ego   c. gentility   d. plight

Q U I C K   Q U I Z   **4**

Matching

Match each word on the right with a word on the left that has a meaning that's close to the same.

1. siesta	a. speed
2. ancestors	b. indebted
3. convenient	c. nap
4. blunder	d. foretell
5. beholden	e. warm
6. sultry	f. handy
7. ulterior	g. starvation
8. array	h. sleeping quarters
9. velocity	i. plant-related
10. detest	j. forefathers
11. botanical	k. hate
12. bode	l. collection
13. dormitory	m. mistake
14. famine	n. other

Q U I C K   Q U I Z   **5**

Matching

Match each word on the right with a word on the left that has a meaning that's close to the same.

1. carcinogenic	a. difficulty
2. lest	b. situation
3. exception	c. seasonal winds
4. limbs	d. for feat that
5. circumstance	e. trash
6. quandary	f. cancer-causing
7. digress	g. stray
8. captives	h. prisoners
9. gust	i. special case
10. feline	j. upsetting experience
11. monsoons	k. legs and arms
12. trauma	l. blast
13. debris	m. cat-like

The End of the Elephant Empire

코끼리 제국의 몰락

2

It was no ordinary army of jackals that had taken us prisoner. These soldiers wore metal armor and helmets that made them a most frightening pack of dogs. That is, I think Barnaby, Babette, and Bridget were frightened. I, of course, am a cat. And cats, as everyone knows, feel a certain, shall we say, **animosity** toward most creatures of the **canine** *persuasion*. I felt nothing but **contempt** for these *puny* pups. One on one, I could have handled any of them easily. But since we were greatly outnumbered, and our wrists and ankles were tied up, I decided to keep myself in check. Besides, I had a feeling we wouldn't be prisoners for long.

"I never learned about any place like this in geography class," said Bridget, shaking her head. "Boy, when things go wrong..."

"Something tells me we're not in France any more," agreed Barnaby.

"I could ask them where we are, if you like," offered Babette.

"Yeah, if you spoke 'dog' you could," *snorted* Bridget.

"They're jackals, actually, and I did pick up a working knowledge of their language while I was on safari last year. Their poetry is excellent, although somewhat primitive."

Bridget tried to think of a clever **retort**, but all she could say was, "Yeah, right. And I hear they're all portrait painters in their spare time. 'Dogs Playing Pool' by Fido is one of my favorite pieces."

Barnaby *snickered*.

"There's no need to be **sarcastic**," replied Babette calmly, turning away from her companions. Then she made some odd growling noises, followed by a short bark and a couple of whimpers, apparently in the direction of the guard behind her. She got no response.

PERSUASION n. kind; sort; description 종류; 계급
The house was filled with pets of every persuasion.
그 집은 온갖 종류의 애완동물로 가득 차 있었다.

PUNY adj. small, weak and underdeveloped 작고 약하고 덜 발달된, 보잘 것 없는
What a puny little creature!
얼마나 작고 보잘 것 없는 동물이냐!

SNORT v. to show contempt, defiance, anger, or other feeling by snorting 코웃음 치며 경멸의 뜻을 나타내다
He snorted at the suggestion.
그는 그 제안에 코웃음을 치며 경멸의 뜻을 나타냈다.

SNICKER v. to laugh in a suppressed, especially unpleasant way; to snigger 낄낄거리며 웃다
We snickered at the obscene pictures.
우리는 그 외설스러운 그림을 보고 낄낄거리며 웃었다.

"They don't seem to understand you," Barnaby commented.

Babette ignored him, and repeated her "question" to the guard.

"Save it, sister," barked the dog suddenly, in English. "Your accent is hurting my ears. And pick up your smart aleck friend there. Kind of **awkward**, isn't she? She's *tripped* over her own feet."

Bridget had, indeed, fallen over from the sheer shock of hearing the dog speak. Babette helped her up, but she remained *stunned*, and just stood there, **gaping** at the jackal.

"Close your mouth, kiddo," said the jackal. "And let me give you a word of advice. You're in the animal kingdom now. This is our **domain**. And as long as you're on our turf, you would do well to be a little more respectful and a little less **impudent**. For example, I didn't like the way you knocked our artistic abilities just now. You shouldn't **disparage** things you know nothing about, and from what's come out of your mouth so far, that's a lot. Do I make myself clear?"

Bridget continued to stare.

"Do you **comprehend** what I have just told you? Quit giving me that **bovine** stare. You look as dumb as a cow," he *snarled*.

"Yes. I'm very sorry," stuttered Bridget.

"That's better. Now look, we have nothing against you humans personally. But too bad you have that cat with you. We absolutely **loathe** cats, *sneaky* little devils, mostly spies. And you should have known better than to land in the middle of a troop movement."

"But we didn't mean to come here!" *blurted* Barnaby. "We just ran into **adverse** weather conditions above Paris, and..."

TRIP v. to catch one's foot on something and stumble or fall 걸려 넘어지다
I tripped over, dropping the tray I was carrying.
나는 걸려 넘어져서 들고 있던 쟁반을 떨어뜨렸다.

STUN v. to daze or shock (somebody), e.g. with something unexpected 어리벙벙하게 하다, 대경실색케 하다
She was stunned by the news of his death.
그 여자는 그의 사망 소식에 대경실색했다.

SNARL v. to speak in an angry bad-tempered voice 무서운 어조로 말하다, 호통 치다
'Get out of here,' he snarled at us.
'여기서 나가' 라고 그는 우리에게 무서운 어조로 말했다.

SNEAKY adj. done or acting in a secret or deceptive way 비열한
This sneaky girl was disliked by the rest of the class.
이 비열한 소녀를 학급의 모든 아이들이 싫어했다.

BLURT v. to say something suddenly and tactlessly 불쑥 말하다
He blurted out the bad news before I could stop him.
그는 내가 말리기도 전에 나쁜 소식을 불쑥 말해버렸다.

"Oh yeah? Then how do you explain the cat?" yipped the jackal. "But as I was saying, we really have nothing against you; even the cat might not be so bad. We've hired cats as spies now and then ourselves. But you have to understand, the situation here is *tense*. Until a few days ago, the jackal army was united in the revolution. We were working to overthrow the Elephant Empire and hold free, democratic elections open to every animal that **inhabits** this region, from *antelopes* to zebras. But General Horace got greedy. He decided to turn the revolution into some kind of holy war, a jackal **jihad**, if you will. 'All creatures must come under submission to the word of Dog,' he said. "Well, that's the last thing we needed, to get rid of one **authoritarian** government only to replace it with an even crazier dictatorship."

The jackal shook his head in disgust.

"Well, our Colonel Cano spoke up against the idea right away. But as it turned out, Horace wasn't prepared to accept any form of **dissent** or disagreement, and he planned to have Cano executed. So, that same night, Cano and all of us broke off to form our own **faction**. We're hoping other animal armies will help us carry out the revolution and keep Horace out of *power*."

"And where are you taking us?" asked Babette.

"We're taking you back to camp. Colonel Cano will want to meet you," he replied.

"Thanks for the information," said Bridget, who had somehow regained the ability to speak. "By the way, my name is Bridget, and this is Babette and Barnaby."

"I am Lieutenant Lassiterius. Folks call me Lassie for short."

Bridget thought it best not to make a joke.

TENSE adj. anxious, strained   긴장한, 절박한
The situation was very tense.
상황이 매우 절박했다.

ANTELOPE n. an animal with long legs and horns, which looks like a deer   영양
Antelopes live in Africa and Asia.
영양은 아프리카와 아시아에 산다.

POWER n. control over other people or over events or activities   권력
They haven't had that power before.
전에 그들은 그런 권력을 가진 적이 없었다.

When they reached camp, they saw many soldiers gathered around, as if waiting for something to happen. At first they were quiet and patient, but after five minutes or so, they started barking and stomping their feet, **clamoring** for whatever it was they were waiting for. Finally, a big, important-looking jackal with grayish fur appeared at the front of the room, and with one sharp bark, he silenced the **boisterous** crowd. From the way he looked, so noble and powerful, so full of **dignity**, Barnaby, Bridget, and Babette correctly assumed it was Cano.

He began speaking in Jackal, and you didn't have to understand the words to know that Cano was a gifted **orator** who knew how to hold an audience. He barked, growled, leaped around, and yipped his way to such a stirring climax that all the jackals, including Lassie, began to *howl* with excitement.

"I'd follow him anywhere," sighed Lassie. Then, suddenly, he let out a bark in the colonel's direction.

Cano's ears *pricked* up as he noticed Lassie. He came right over.

"It's **unanimous**!" cried Cano. "We voted, and every single jackal has agreed to fight 'til the end to keep Horace out of power."

"I told you not to doubt our loyalty, sir," said Lassie. "That was some speech you just gave."

"Well, to tell the truth, I hadn't planned on giving a speech. It was just one of those **impromptu**, spur-of-the-moment things, you know? I **ad-libbed** the whole thing."

"Well, it was pretty amazing for a speech you made up as you went along. You were speaking from the heart, and we're with you. We'll teach that *wacko* a lesson," the lieutenant replied.

"I believe **fanatic** is more accurate than wacko, Lassie. He's not crazy, he's just, well, let's just say he's dangerously full of enthusiasm and **zeal**."

HOWL v. to make a howl; to weep loudly 소리를 길게 뽑으며 짖다: 울부짖다
The baby howled all night.
아기가 밤새 울었다.

PRICK v. (prick up one's ear의 형태로 쓰여) to stand up straight or point sharply towards a sound 귀를 쫑긋 세우다
The dog's ears were pricked up straight.
개귀가 쫑긋 섰다.

WACKO(=wacky) n. an eccentric or crazy person 괴팍스러운(별난, 이상한) 사람
Dear old wacko, would you like to walk through the streets of the city tomorrow giving away money?
친애하는 피짜여, 내일 돈을 거저 나눠주면서 시내를 걸어보지 않겠습니까?

"Anyway, look what we found on patrol today, Colonel," said Lassie, jerking his head toward the prisoners.

"I see, I see," said the jackal. "A few humans and... hey! Beauregard, you old son of gun, what are you doing here?"

Cano had *trotted* over to the cat and seemed very glad to see him.

"You know him?" asked Lassie and Barnaby. They were both **astonished**, but for different reasons.

"Know him?" laughed the colonel, "Why, back in the old days, Beau and I used to run the *undercover* division of..."

Just then the cat growled softly in Cano's ear.

"Yes, well, um, whoops! Heh, heh. What was I saying?" the colonel continued *clumsily*. "I, uh, must be mistaken. I've never seen this sorry old cat before. Take them all to my tent for questioning."

Babette, Barnaby, and Bridget exchanged perplexed looks. The situation was getting weirder and weirder.

On their arrival at the tent, Cano ordered that they be untied and Lassie began to loosen the ropes.

"Thanks, man, those things were beginning to **chafe** my wrists," said Bridget. "Hey!" she shouted to the colonel. "You got anything to eat?"

TROT v. to move at a pace faster than a walk but slower than a gallop; to run with short steps 빠른 걸음으로 가다; 총총 걸음으로 걷다
The children were trotting along beside their parents.
아이들이 부모 옆에서 총총 걸음으로 걷고 있었다.

UNDERCOVER adj. working or done in secret 위장하고 근무하는
The jeweler was an undercover agent of the police.
그 보석상은 경찰의 위장 근무 요원이었다.

CLUMSILY adv. awkwardly and ungracefully in movement or shape 어색하게, 꼴사납게
The boy clumsily bumped into all the furniture.
소년은 꼴사납게 모든 가구들과 부딪쳤다.

"Remember the talk we had about respect, Bridget?" snarled Lassie. "It would **behoove** you to behave with a little more **deference** toward the colonel. After all, he is in control of your fate right now."

"Oh, come now," laughed Cano. "These people are welcome here. In fact, they should be treated as foreign **dignitaries**, honored and important visitors from the human world. Bridget is hungry, we should have a feast for her! Lassie, go out and tell everyone that tonight we'll be having a party to celebrate the arrival of new friends and to revel in the certain defeat of Horace and the end of the Empire!"

The travelers began to wonder if Cano was always so full of **optimism**, but as soon as Lassie left to make arrangements for the *feast*, he let out a heavy sigh.

"I don't know how much the *lieutenant* has told you, but we are facing serious *odds*. The situation actually looks pretty **bleak**," he said.

"I can see that," said Babette. "You plan a **coup d'état** against the Empire, and a **feud** develops within your ranks. A very difficult situation, indeed. Can you not find support outside of jackal army?"

"I have considered the possibility," replied the colonel, "but we animals have never had strong alliances. The jackals are the only group that has an army to speak of. Until recently, we were the royal guards of the Elephant Emperor himself."

Cano shook his head and continued, "The ostriches, for example, could be a great help. They seem to favor democracy, and their speed and size make them valuable friends. But, unfortunately, they are known for their **apathy**. They're happy to bury their heads in the sand and not bother with anything."

FEAST n. a large and special meal to which several people are invited 잔치, 연회
I won't go to her wedding feast.
그녀의 결혼 피로연에는 안 갈 거야.

LIEUTENANT n. a person who holds a junior officer's rank in the army, navy, or air force 중위
He served as a lieutenant in U.S. Army in Far East.
그는 극동에서 미 육군 중위로 복역했다.

ODDS n. quarreling; disagreeing 다툼; 불화
The two brothers were often at odds.
두 형제는 종종 다투었다.

"The pandas, strong and fierce as they look, are all **pacifists**. That's right—they don't believe in war for any reason. It's against their religion. On the other hand, the warthogs, nasty-looking creatures, are definitely **belligerent** enough to join us. They like fighting. *Waging* war is how they get their jollies. But when they don't have a war to fight, they tend to kill each other. No, it's best to *steer* clear of them. Still, there is some hope. We have **solicited** the aid and advice of the Reptile Republic. It looks as though they are willing to help us. We got word that King Cobra is sending an **ambassador** to our camp tonight—a high-ranking lizard, I believe—to see if there is anything they can do. The reptiles have much to teach us. They have lived outside the Empire for many years now. Frankly, I think the elephants are a little afraid of them," Cano chuckled.

"Tell us more about this Horace character," demanded Bridget. "He sounds much worse than the Emperor."

"You're right there," agreed the colonel. "Horace is the worst kind of **tyrant** imaginable. He expects more than obedience from his animals—he wants them to be absolutely **servile**, slavishly satisfying his every *whim*. It's been like that for years, and the elephants have always backed him up. He even issued an order that all soldiers must fall to their knees and bow before him, **revere** him as if he were some kind of god! That was the last straw for me. I refuse to **kowtow** to anyone, not even the Emperor, and especially not Horace! I went through basic training with him, for goodness sake!"

"You said it, Colonel," said Bridget.

Cano took a deep breath. "Horace actually does think of himself as some kind of god—the **omnipotent** kind, at that. You know, all-powerful, all-seeing. But really he's just totally **paranoid**. He was always imagining that there were secret plots and **conspiracies** against him."

WAGE v. to begin and carry on (a war, campaign, etc.) 수행하다
No country wants to wage a nuclear war.
어떤 나라도 핵전쟁을 하고 싶어하지 않는다.

STEER v. (steer clear of의 형태로 쓰여) to keep away from; to avoid ~을 피하다, ~에 관계하지 않다
Steer clear of him until he calms down.
그가 진정할 때까지 그를 피해라.

WHIM n. sudden desire or idea, especially an unusual or unreasonable one; caprice 변덕, 일시적인 생각
She has a whim for gardening but it won't last long.
그녀는 일시적인 기분으로 정원을 가꾸고 있지만 오래 가지는 않을 것이다.

"If he's such a rotten guy, why did you go along with him on this whole coup d'état thing?" asked Bridget.

"That's a good question," replied Cano, "and I can only respond with the tired old **cliché**, 'desperate times require desperate measures.' I knew Horace was a *kook*, but I thought that continuing to live under the harsh rule of the elephants was worse. It wasn't until after we declared our freedom that I found out how truly evil he was. He's an absolute **bigot**."

"A bigot?" gasped Barnaby.

"I honestly don't know how I didn't figure it out before. I guess before we broke away from the elephants, he kept his **prejudices** to himself. Now he is much more **overt** about his hatred of all other creatures, even ones he's never even met. He feels jackals are the only worthy animals. It's extremely *disturbing*. To think, not so terribly long ago he was my friend, and now he is my most dangerous **foe**."

Cano sighed again, and stared off into the distance as if **contemplating** all the events that had led him up to this moment. Soon, he was completely lost in thought.

"Um, maybe we should go wash up **prior** to eating," offered Barnaby, wanting to leave the colonel alone with his thoughts.

"Yes, how rude of me," said Cano, snapping out of it. "You'll find a guest tent outside to the right. Everything you need is there. We'll come get you when the feast is ready."

"*Cool*. See you later, Cano," said Bridget.

"Thank you, Colonel," said Babette.

And with that, they left the tent. But the cat stayed behind.

KOOK n. peculiar, eccentric or crazy person   미치광이
He must be a kook.
그는 미치광이임에 틀림없다.

DISTURBING adj. causing worry or anxiety; alarming; disquieting   불온한, 불안하게 하는; 교란시키는
Because of the disturbing sound, the silence of the evening was disappeared.
혼란스런 소리 때문에 저녁때의 조용함이 사라졌다.

COOL adj. pleasant; fine   좋은
Her guy's really cool.
그녀 남자 친구는 정말 멋져.

I should explain about Colonel Cano and myself. It's true, we were *comrades-in-arms* back when I was working undercover for the Elede agency of disparate experiences—traveling with the circus, selling encyclopedias, organizing labor unions, and yes, even spying for the Empire. You see, at the time, humans were guilty of atrocious acts of violence against elephants. Hunters would kill them by the hundreds, rip their tusks out for ivory, and leave their bodies to rot. Animals all around the world decided to fight against this senseless cruelty.

Cano and I got together at a meeting of the United Animal Nations and came up with a completely new, *off-beat*, altogether **radical** idea. We would take our story to the **media**: newspapers, television, radio, the works. We took pictures of the horrors ourselves: elephants lying tuskless in the jungles. Then we went off into the human world and tried to blend in as pets, waiting for the opportunity to put out plan into action.

Of course, it was easy for me. I was used to **cohabiting** with humans, and besides, pet cats usually get to act as mean and *persnickety* as they want, and no one thinks twice about it. Cano had more of a problem. He was a jackal, and a soldier, and he didn't have much **tolerance** for the whole stick-fetching, tail-wagging routine dogs are expected to put on. But he put up with it somehow.

Finally, I managed to slip a videotape of the elephant hunts to a major television channel. One of the station managers saw it and things just sort of took off from there. There was a huge public outcry. Many countries got together and imposed **sanctions** against other countries that supported the ivory trade—that is, they refused to do business with them or help them in any way. Some even called for **embargos**, refusing to import any ivory at all. Cano and I were mighty pleased with our **audacity**. It sure took a lot of *guts* and daring to do what we did.

After that, we went our separate ways. I didn't see Cano again—until now. I had no idea the elephants had come back so strongly—too strongly, it seems. I sure didn't like seeing my old friend so upset. After the kids left, we had a talk and reminisced about old times. I told him not to blow my cover, that I was watching over theses kids, but I didn't want them to know it. And I told him I'd help him in any way I could. Well, he took me at my word. We spent the next hour working out a plan to take care of Horace and the Emperor once and for all.

COMRADE-IN-ARMS n. fellow soldier 전우
They'd long been comrades-in-arms in the Labour Party.
그들은 오랫동안 노동당에서 전우로 지냈다.

OFF-BEAT adj. unusual; unconventional 특이한; 자유로운
Her style of dress is definitely off-beat.
그녀의 드레스 스타일은 매우 특이하다.

PERSNICKETY(=pernickety) adj. worrying too much about details or unimportant things; fussy 좀스러운, 지나치게 소심한; 성미가 까다로운
It is clear that the planning, no matter how grandiose, is also much too persnickety.
그 계획은 아무리 웅대하다 해도 또한 너무 좀스러운 것이 사실이다.

GUTS n. courage and determination 용기, 배짱
I like a man with plenty of guts.
나는 배짱이 두둑한 사람을 좋아한다.

"Boy, I'm so hungry," said Bridget, who was resting comfortably on some cushions in the guest tent. "I hope dinner's ready soon. I plan to **gorge** myself until I can't eat another bite."

"I wouldn't go planning an eating **binge** so soon," warned Barnaby. "After all, we have no idea what jackals eat. And whatever it is, it's likely to be *raw*."

"Yikes, I hadn't thought of that," said Bridget, springing upright. "What are we going to do? Are we going to *starve*, or what?"

"Hmmm," replied Barnaby, scratching his bushy head. "We'll just have to put our minds to it and see what we can come up with. Well, what do you know?"

"What?" asked Bridget.

"Look what I found! These must have gotten lodged in my hair that time I blew up the vending machine in the library!"

Sure enough, Barnaby had somehow managed to pull four candy bars, a bag of potato chips, and some bright orange crackers out of his hair. Ordinarily, Bridget would have been surprised at such an event, but with everything that had happened in the past couple of days, she hardly *batted* an eyelash.

"Wow! Can I have some?" she asked.

"Sure. Help yourself."

As Bridget began to **devour** the candy bars greedily, Babette spoke from the other side of the tent.

RAW adj. not cooked 날 것의
You can eat carrots cooked or raw.
당근을 익혀서도 날 것으로도 먹을 수 있다.

STARVE v. to suffer greatly from lack of food and sometimes die 굶주리다, 굶어죽다
When the rescuers arrived, the survivors were starving.
구조원들이 도착했을 때 생존자들은 이미 굶어죽어 가고 있었다.

BAT v. (not bat an eyelid의 형태로 쓰여) not to show any surprise or feeling 눈 하나 깜짝하지 않다
The condemned man listened to his sentence without batting an eyelid.
그 사형수는 눈 하나 깜짝하지 않고 판결을 들었다.

"That is an amazing head of hair you have, Barnaby," she said.

"It suits me, I think," he agreed. "You sure have been awfully quiet and **pensive**. What have you been thinking about?"

"I have been thinking about these poor jackals. You see, the French people know what it is to live under the rule of emperors and dictators. It is something you Americans, thankfully, have not had to bear," she said, *munching* thoughtfully on a potato chip.

"What's your point?" asked Bridget, her mouth full of candy.

"My point is, I feel **sympathy** for them. I think we should help them."

Barnaby and Bridget sat quietly for a few seconds, and were about to reply when Lassie came in through the tent flap.

"Thanks, but no thanks," he said. "I hope you don't think I was **eavesdropping**, but I couldn't help hearing what you said about helping us. We don't need anything from you. Colonel Cano has it all figured out."

"I was only...," started Babette.

"I know, I know. Look, I didn't come to argue. I came to tell you the feast is on. Come on out!"

Babette, Bridget, and Barnaby emerged from the tent to find the camp lit up like a carnival. Torches glowed all around. Seven female jackals were doing the dance of the seven *wails*—they **gyrated** until they were too dizzy to stand up, then let out seven heartbreakingly **plaintive** howls. And Cano, in his finest *cape*, sat at the head of a long, low table, a gigantic, wrinkled-up old lizard on one side and a gigantic cat on the other.

MUNCH v. to chew (something) with much movement of the jaw 우적우적 씹어먹다
The horse munched its oats.
그 말은 귀리를 우적우적 씹어 먹었다.

WAIL n. shrill cry, especially of pain or grief 비탄, 울부짖음
The child burst into loud wails.
그 아이는 거세게 울부짖기 시작했다.

CAPE n. a short cloak 짧은 망토
Waving a red cape, Delgado provoked the bull to attack.
빨간 망토를 흔들며 델가도는 소가 공격하도록 자극했다.

"My friends!" he called when the three humans appeared. "Come join us!"

The three travelers joined their host, and introductions were made.

"This is Ambassador Sangfroid, a respected and **venerable** statesman from the Reptile Republic," said Cano. "He has traveled all the way from the **Chateau** Guécot to be with us tonight."

"Actually, it's not really a chateau. More like a large *dungeon* than a small castle. But I suppose it will have to serve as the reptile **embassy** for the time being, until the jackals can come up with more suitable office space," said the lizard.

Babette and Bridget *squirmed* uncomfortably at his rudeness. Barnaby was too busy examining the food to notice what was going on.

"Of course," said Cano, good-naturedly. "Please, help yourself to some food."

"You must be mad, Colonel," replied the lizard with complete **disdain**. "I can't stand to smell this boot camp slop, much less eat it."

"Hey!" cried Bridget. "The colonel doesn't have to sit here and have his food **scoffed** at by some *stuck-up*, **haughty** Gila monster!"

"Foolish child, I am an iguana."

"A pretty **obese** iguana, if you ask me," snapped Bridget. "Maybe it's best if you don't eat anything. Looks like you could afford to skip a few meals."

"Well, I never!" huffed the ambassador, who got up to leave.

"Actually, I think Ambassador Sangfroid looks very strong and distinguished at his current size," said Babette, trying to **appease** the offended lizard.

DUNGEON n. dark underground room or cell to keep prisoners in; large, strongly fortified tower of a medieval castle   지하 감옥; 누각
Beneath the castle I could discern vast dungeons.
성 밑에서 나는 거대한 지하 감옥을 알아볼 수 있었다.

SQUIRM v. to feel embarrassment, discomfort, or shame   거북해서 몸을 비비꼬다, 창피스럽게 느끼다
It made him squirm to think how he'd messed up the interview.
자신이 얼마나 인터뷰를 엉망으로 만들었는지 생각하자 그는 창피해졌다.

STUCK-UP adj. snooty, proud and unfriendly   거만한, 불친절한
I don't like him. He is very stuck-up.
난 그 사람 싫어. 너무 거만해.

It seemed to work, because he sat back down and **resumed** the conversation he had been having with Colonel Cano before the three humans arrived. He completely ignored Bridget. Bridget, in turn, ignored him. She turned toward the female jackals and feigned great interest in their weird dance steps.

"As I was saying, Colonel, the Reptile Republic is completely **autonomous**—totally independent. We are free to make alliances as we choose. But of course we must choose wisely."

"Surely you can't think that *siding* with Horace is wise. And your people hate the Emperor as much as we do," argued Cano.

"That's true, but at least the Emperor keeps order. If and when you *topple* his government, what happens then? We reptiles don't want to live next to a country in a state of **anarchy**. Without an organized system of government, you'll have **chaos** on your hands—complete disorder. Bedlam!" cried the lizard.

"Surely, Sangfroid, you don't think we went into this without a plan," Cano replied. "We have a well-thought-out **agenda**. We have already sent a letter to the Emperor asking him to **abdicate** the *throne* and set up free and democratic elections. He refused to **relinquish** control, as we thought he would, so we wrote a declaration stating that all animals should have equal say in the government and that we refused to recognize the Emperor as our ruler. Naturally, he **denounced** us as traitors and immediately began releasing false reports about us to the media. Of course, these reports were nothing but **propaganda** designed to frighten the other animals into thinking we were dangerous. But, as you surely understand, we have no choice but to fight for our rights!"

SIDE v. (side with의 형태로 쓰여) to support somebody in a quarrel or argument 편들다
The daughters sided with their mother.
딸들은 엄마 편을 들었다.

TOPPLE v. (cause (somebody/something)) to fall from power or authority; to overthrow 권력에서 물러나게 하다; 전복시키다
The coup d'état toppled the dictator from his position.
쿠데타로 독재자는 자리에서 쫓겨났다.

THRONE n. royal authority or power 왕위, 권력
Queen Elizabeth II succeeded to the throne in 1952.
엘리자베스 2세 여왕은 1952년에 왕위를 계승했다.

"Please forgive my **skepticism**, Colonel, but so many revolutions fail that I think we have a right to be doubtful," said the lizard. "That is why we are prepared to offer you limited support. We can give you a unit of light lizards trained in electronic **sabotage** to damage the elephant computer networks and telephone lines. These lizards have the natural ability to **camouflage** themselves. Their skins change color to match their surroundings, so they are rarely *detected*."

"I am grateful for your help, Ambassador," said Cano.

Just then, some awful *racket*—yowling and crashing—started on the edge of the camp.

"What on earth is that?" yelled the colonel. "Lassie, can you see what's going on?"

"It seems to be some sort of *brawl*, sir," replied the lieutenant. "Probably a fight over one of those wail dancers. I'll go check it out."

It was a brawl. And soon the brawl turned into a skirmish. Then the **skirmish** turned into a **melee**. And before Cano's men realized what was happening, they were under full-scale attack by the forces of General Horace and his jackals!

"To arms, to arms!" ordered Cano. "Fight for your lives!"

"Much as I'd like to help, I'm afraid I have to be going," said Sangfroid sheepishly. "The **gout** in my leg has been acting up, swelling something awful, so I wouldn't be much good anyway. Ta ta!"

With that, the ambassador scurried off as quickly as a fat lizard with gout can scurry.

"Don't worry, Colonel," yelled Bridget over the battle noise. "We'll help you!"

DETECT v. to notice or know something even when it is not very obvious 알아차리다, 인지하다
These animals seem able to detect a shower of rain falling five miles away.
이 동물들은 5마일 떨어진 곳에서 소나기가 내리는 것도 알아채는 것 같다.

RACKET n. loud noise; uproar or noisy disturbance 시끄러운 소리; 소동
What a racket the children are making!
아이들이 얼마나 시끄럽게 구는지!

BRAWL n. noisy quarrel or fight 싸움
Did you see a drunken brawl in a bar?
술집에서 술 취해서 일어난 싸움을 봤니?

In fact, Babette and Barnaby were busy doing just that. Babette, it appeared, had a few more tricks up her sleeve than speaking fluent Jackal. She was running around, karate-chopping dogs like some kind of crazed ninja. And Barnaby kept pulling stink bombs, firecrackers, and other explosives out of his hair and hurling them at the enemy. Bridget pulled out her bubble gum and began stretching it into a huge *lasso*, with which she captured several of Horace's soldiers and *yanked* them to the ground.

But the enemy jackals were **relentless**. They fought on and on, refusing to give up. But Cano's soldiers wouldn't **yield** either, and finally, after several hours of battle, they got the upper hand. Beauregard even managed to capture General Horace himself.

Then they heard the footsteps. Heavy, loud footsteps.

"Oh, no, the elephants are coming in from the north!" cried Cano, more with exhaustion than fear. "Judging from the sound of their footsteps, they're about a mile from camp!" That means they'll be here in **approximately** ten minutes."

"At least **stealth** isn't one of their advantages," Bridget commented. "You can't exactly *sneak* up on someone with footsteps as loud as that."

"That's no help right now, Bridget," said Babette. "We have just **subdued** Horace's soldiers, and already we are under attack again. Cano's jackals are tired, many are wounded. We are at our most **vulnerable**. We can no longer defend ourselves!"

Bridget was shocked to see how upset Babette was getting. She had been so cool until now.

LASSO n. long rope with a noose at one end, used for catching horses and cattle 올가미 줄
A cowboy's lasso made of nylon is used especially for catching steers and horses.
나일론으로 된 카우보이 올가미는 특히 수송아지와 말을 잡는데 사용된다.

YANK v. to pull with a sudden motion; to jerk; to tug 홱 잡아당기다
She yanked the rope and it broke.
그녀가 갑자기 로프를 잡아당기자 밧줄이 끊어졌다.

SNEAK v. to move in a stealthy, sly way 몰래 다가가다
The man sneaked about the barn watching for a chance to steal the cow.
그 남자는 암소를 훔칠 기회를 보면서 헛간 근처로 몰래 다가갔다.

"Hey, don't give up yet! We've still got ten minutes!"

"Nine," said Cano.

"Okay, nine," said Bridget. "Anything could happen. There was a **similar** situation in New York during the '86 World Series. It looked like the Mets were going to lose for sure, but the first baseman totally choked, made an error, and we were saved."

"What *is* she talking about?" groaned Cano.

"Well, maybe that's not the greatest example," said Bridget. "All I'm saying is, it ain't over 'til it's over."

"So what do you suggest we do, oh *perky* one?" asked Barnaby, his eyebrows raised into high, confronting arches.

"Well, first of all I think we should get a bunch of green paint, a can of root beer, a few bushels of cotton, and some dry toast. Then..."

But Bridget didn't get a chance to finish outlining her plan. From the east came the sound of two-footed galloping and what seemed like the *throaty* quaking of enormous ducks. From the west, came a rumbling sea of black and white. And from the south, a really *revolting* snorting noise and a **repulsive** piggish odor.

Bridget, Barnaby, and Babette looked around wildly, fearing for their lives, but Cano leaped with excitement.

"It's the ostriches! And the warthogs! And even the pacifist pandas!" he cried. "We're saved!"

PERKY adj. (too) full of self-confidence; cheeky 자신만만한; 건방진
That child is a bit too perky!
그 아이는 너무 으스대!

THROATY adj. sounding hoarse; low-pitched and resonant 목 쉰; 묵직한. 목 안쪽에서 나오는
Her throaty cough irritates my nerves.
그녀가 쉰 목소리로 내는 기침이 내 신경에 거슬린다.

REVOLTING adj. disgusting; repulsive 불쾌한, 혐오감을 일으키는
A revolting odor hung heavy in the air.
공기 중에는 불쾌한 냄새가 짙게 퍼져 있었다.

The allied armies arrived at the camp, gathered around Cano, and pledged their support to him just as the elephants began to arrive. A huge wall of gray legs, like granite columns, thundered into view, stopped, then broke into neat formation to make way for the chief, the father of their clan, the **patriarch** of the *pachyderms*—the Elephant Emperor himself.

The two forces, a hodgepodge of birds, dogs, hogs, and bears on one side and the giant elephant on the other, faced each other uncomfortably. Finally, the emperor spoke.

"Cano," he *boomed*. "Are you the one responsible for stirring this whole thing up? Did you **instigate** this rebellion?"

"Yes, but as you can see, I'm not the only one who's tired of your rigid, **dogmatic** rule," yelled Cano.

"I've had about enough of all this," replied the emperor. "All of you, go on home. Cano, if you and your soldiers turn yourselves in, you will not be harshly punished. I am prepared to be **lenient**."

"You just don't get it, do you?" said the colonel. "This isn't a childish *prank*. We don't want an emperor anymore. We want democracy! We want democracy!"

The crowd behind Cano began cheering and chanting in their *assorted* languages.

"Hmmph," said the elephant, frowning, "I have my doubts about this whole thing, but just because I am **dubious** doesn't mean you are wrong."

"You mean, you will step down?" asked Cano, both shocked and hopeful.

PACHYDERM n. any of various types of thick-skinned, four-footed animal   후피 동물
The elephant, hippopotamus, and rhinoceros are pachyderms.
코끼리, 하마, 무소는 후피 동물이다.

BOOM v. to make a deep hollow resonant sound   우렁찬 목소리로 외치다, 울리다
The headmaster's voice boomed (out) across the playground.
교장 선생님의 목소리가 운동장을 건너 우렁차게 울렸다.

PRANK n. playful or mischievous trick   장난.
On April Fools' Day people often play pranks on each other.
만우절에 사람들은 종종 서로 장난을 친다.

ASSORTED adj. arranged by kinds; classified   분류된, 구분된
She served assorted cakes.
그녀는 케이크를 다양하게 제공했다.

"Well, I should warn you, a dictatorship such as ours has certain advantages over democracy," said the elephant. "For one thing, we have no **bureaucracy**—no confusing lines of authority, no piles of paperwork, no useless officials to *bog* things down. What I say goes, and that's that. It's very efficient."

"But it's not fair!" argued the colonel. "We must have a say in our own government!"

The crowd mumbled agreement. The emperor stood for a moment in deep thought. Not a sound was heard throughout the camp. Several minutes passed before he spoke again.

"Okay, then, you shall have your elections. I certainly don't want a bunch of ungrateful, unhappy subjects. We might as well get the ball rolling immediately. Cano, I guess you and your army are in charge. The country will have to be under **martial law** until an election can be arranged," he said.

The animals, realizing that they had won without fighting a single battle, cheered with joy. The emperor, recognizing that it was useless to stand in the way of democracy, let out a sigh of **resignation**. Then some serious partying began.

Babette pointed out to Barnaby, Bridget, and Beauregard that touring a country immediately after a revolution, however *bloodless*, is usually not wise. Everything is in a state of **upheaval** and confusion, and it's impossible to find a hotel room. It was agreed that they should take this opportunity to thank their hosts and be on their way.

They began walking back to the clearing they had landed in. But as soon as they reached the open field, a blinding flash of rainbow-colored light and a great whooshing of air *engulfed* them, and they promptly disappeared from the face of the planet.

BOG v. (cause to) become stuck and unable to make progress 수렁에 빠지다, 일을 망치다
Our discussions got bogged down in irrelevant detail.
우리의 토론은 엉뚱한 사소한 일에 빠져 진척이 안 되었다.

BLOODLESS adj. very pale in colour 창백한
She has flat dark hair and bloodless cheeks.
그녀의 머리는 단조로운 검은색에 빰은 창백하다.

ENGULF v. to swallow up; to overwhelm; to submerge 집어삼키다; 압도하다; 가라앉히다
A wave engulfed the small boat.
파도가 작은 배를 집어삼켰다.

Relationships

Decide what relationship the following pairs of words have to each other. If they mean close to the same thing, make "S." If they have opposite meanings, mark "O."

1. abdicate :: relinquish
2. animosity :: contempt
3. deference :: imprudence
4. foe :: comrade
5. gorge :: devour
6. anarchy :: chaos
7. melee :: skirmish
8. lenient :: authoritarian
9. tolerance :: bigotry
10. impromptu :: ad-libbed
11. zeal :: apathy
12. reminisce :: forget

Relationships

Decide what relationship the following pairs of words have to each other. If they mean close to the same thing, make "S." If they have opposite meanings, mark "O."

1. pacifists :: belligerent
2. dissenting :: unanimous
3. radical :: traditional
4. servile :: haughty
5. disdain :: scoff
6. dogmatic :: flexible
7. disparage :: praise
8. paradnoid :: trusting
9. autonomous :: independent
10. pensive :: boisterous
11. feigning :: pretending

Fill in the Blank

For each sentence below, choose the word that best completes the sentence.

1. It was obvious that Lance felt _____ toward the girls' softball team because even before he saw them, he had made up his mind that they were lousy players.

   a. audacity   b. reverence   c. prejudice   d. dignity

2. The kids called Marlon "dog-face" because his pointed teeth, shaggy hair, and his habit of hanging his tongue out of his mouth gave him a sort of _____ look.

   a. canine   b. bovine   c. plaintive   d. awkward

3. Cassie was being _____ when she said, "I can't wait to go have my wisdom teeth pulled. It will be more fun than Disneyland!"

   a. sarcastic   b. adverse   c. fanatic   d. overt

4. During the student council elections, my opponent handed out tons of pamphlets filled with lies and twisted stories about me and my plans as student council president, but most students knew it was just a bunch of _____ , and I won the election anyway.

    a. agenda   b. embargo   c. propaganda   d. media

5. The military overthrew the government in a bloody _____ .

    a. jihad   b. coup d'état   c. feud   d. upheaval

6. During the holiday, Margie _____ donations of canned goods from her neighbors for her school food drive.

    a. solicited   b. comprehended   c. contemplated   d. denounced

7. Sheldon was not usually a troublemaker, but when the lunchroom served gruel for the fourth day in a row, he _____ a riot in the cafeteria, and led a crowd of students to the secret supply of chocolate pudding the cook had been keeping for herself.

    a. sabotaged   b. clamored   c. gaped   d. instigated

8. Genghis Khan was a powerful _____ who ruled with an iron fist and crushed anyone who tried to disobey or disagree with him.

    a. ambassador   b. orator   c. tyrant   d. patriarch

9. Mr. Spalding, our social sciences teacher, is a _____ old man who has taught at our school for forty years and is respected and liked by the whole town.

    a. vulnerable   b. omnipotent   c. disparate   d. venerable

10. Ambassador Black hosted a big party at the American _____ in Tokyo.

    a. domain   b. embassy   c. chateau   d. bureaucracy

11. Jacob was _____ in his efforts to get Samantha to date him—he called her and sent her flowers every day for six months, until she finally gave in.

    a. repulsive   b. dubious   c. atrocious   d. relentless

12. Mindy sent me a Valentine's Day card that said "Roses are red, violets are blue, sugar is sweet, and so are you," which I thought was pretty _____ , but it was nice of her anyway.

    a. similar   b. clichéd   c. obese   d. bleak

Q U I C K   Q U I Z   9

Matching

Match each word on the right with a word on the left that has a meaning that's close to the same.

1. retort	a. delight
2. astonish	b. hate
3. loathe	c. rub
4. inhabit	d. live with
5. faction	e. bow
6. camouflage	f. reply
7. chafe	g. hide
8. behoove	h. surprise
9. dignitary	i. secret plot
10. revel	j. important person
11. kowtow	k. live in
12. prior	l. benefit

13. conspiracy   m. group
14. cohabit   n. before

Q U I C K   Q U I Z   (10)

Matching

Match each word on the right with a word on the left that has a meaning that's close to the same.

1. sanction   a. overhear
2. binge   b. doubter
3. eavesdrop   c. conquer
4. gyrate   d. revolve
5. appease   e. punishment
6. resume   f. military rule
7. skeptic   g. spree
8. yield   h. give in
9. approximately   i. acceptance
10. stealth   j. calm
11. subdue   k. begin again
12. martial law   l. sneakiness
13. resignation   m. about

Space Hippies Freak Out

괴상한 우주 히피들

Barnaby, Babette, Bridget, and Beauregard lay flat on their backs, staring up at a large mirrored ball that was spinning and casting multicolored light all around them. The smell of *incense* hung heavy in the air. They were all feeling a little **disoriented**. After all, thirty seconds ago they had been standing in a grassy field. Now they had no idea where they were or what was going on.

"Is this Hell?" whispered Bridget, to no one in particular.

"I think it's a disco," responded Babette.

Suddenly a voice thundered all around them.

"Aw, man, Janice! You've gone and done it again. I keep telling you that isn't a disco ball—it's a highly sensitive *teleportation* device!"

The four friends sat up and stared at each other in wonder. This was all very unusual.

"You cats just hang loose for a sec," continued the voice. "I'll be right there."

"Cats?" questioned Barnaby. "But there's only one cat."

"That's just an old hippie expression," said Bridget. "It just means 'guys.' Do you think...?"

But Bridget's question was answered before she asked it. Through the door walked a hippie so hippie-ish he was practically a **caricature** of himself: long hair, a *scraggly* **goatee** on his chin, granny glasses, and a flowing Indian robe.

"Peace," he said, making a V-shaped sign with the fingers of his right hand.

INCENSE n. (smoke from a) substance that produces a pleasant smell when burnt, used especially in religious ceremonies 향, 향내
The room was filled with the smell of the incense.
그 방은 향냄새로 가득 차 있었다.

TELEPORTATION n. moving over a long distance at a short time 공간이동
In SF movies the teleportation device is very often used.
공상 과학 영화에서 공간이동 기법은 매우 자주 사용된다.

SCRAGGLY adj. rough, untidy or irregular 터부룩한, 들쭉날쭉한
The field was filled with scraggly weeds.
들판은 들쭉날쭉한 잡초들로 가득 차 있었다.

Now, you'll have to admit, this was an extraordinary turn of events. I think I ought to give you some background information to help clear things up. As you may have guessed, we were all feeling a bit fatigued after our battle with the jackal fanatics. But even though we were worn out, we were all still *eager* to get back to Paris and commence our search for Bridget's parents. The last thing we needed was to have our plans thwarted yet again. Only this time, it was a spaceship, not bad weather, that threw a wrench in things.

That's right, we were "beamed up" against our will, right off the ground and into a spaceship. And not just any spaceship, either. We suddenly found ourselves aboard the **infamous** pirate ship, the *Far Out*, captained by the **notorious** space hippie, Wobbly Philstein. At one time, everyone in America knew his name, and knew about the pranks he and his followers pulled on politicians they didn't like. The worst was when he somehow managed to dye the Speaker of the House bright red from head to toe as some sort of protest against the Speaker's plans to cut spending on education and public television. The FBI was never exactly sure who the **culprit** was in this crime, but Wobbly kind of gave himself away when he got on television and asked the Speaker whether he was "better red than dead or better dead than well read." That statement alone made him a prime suspect. Later, the FBI even discovered he had a *tattoo* of Big Bird on his arm, and that he was a known watcher of "Masterpiece Theater."

So the FBI named Wobbly the number one most wanted man in America, and a manhunt **ensued** the likes of which the country had never seen. Police officers, Secret Service agents, even regular citizens were searching every barn, barrel, and basement for the hippie. But he was too **crafty** for them, and managed to **elude** his pursuers for months.

The rumor *cropped* up that Wobbly was planning to **defect** to Holland, a country known as a **refuge** for misunderstood **bohemians**, a place where hippies, artists, musicians, and other uninsured free spirits with kooky or **eccentric** habits could feel safe. Later, however, it was revealed that Wobbly had been in Mexico all along, building a spaceship out of old tour buses. Destination: Far Out. Yes, he and his followers blasted off, and the authorities were forced to give up their hunt. Outer space, unfortunately, does not fall under the FBI's **jurisdiction**.

EAGER adj. hoping to have or do something very much 몹시 바라는
The majority are moderate, and eager to express their opinions.
대다수가 온건주의자로, 자신의 의견을 표현하고 싶어한다.

TATTOO n. a picture, design, or motto tattooed on the skin 문신
His chest was covered in tattoos.
그의 가슴은 문신들로 덮여 있었다.

CROP v. (crop up의 형태로 쓰여) to appear or happen, especially unexpectedly 갑자기 나타나다, 생기다
All sorts of difficulties cropped up.
모든 종류의 어려운 점들이 갑자기 나타났다.

Gradually, the frenzy over Wobbly **ebbed**, and things returned to normal. Many even suspected his spaceship fell apart during takeoff, and that Wobbly and his *buddies* were now probably **deceased**. But they were obviously wrong, because there he was, standing in front of us, very much alive.

"I am Captain Wobbly Philstein," announced the hippie. "You can call me Captain Wobbly if you want, but plain Wobbly is cool, too, if you don't *dig* the military thing."

"I'm Bridget, and this is Babette and Barnaby," Bridget replied. "And this cat apparently is a spy named Beauregard, but he doesn't talk to humans."

Barnaby and Babette giggled.

"You aren't from the government, are you?" Wobbly asked suspiciously.

"No," said Bridget.

"Well, then everything's *groovy*! Welcome aboard the *Far Out*. Come on and meet the rest of the crew."

The kids followed Wobbly down a long hall that looked like the inside of a bus. Only a few candles were glowing, so the light was **dim**. There seemed to be someone in there playing the sitar, but the air was so **dense** with incense it was impossible to be sure. It was very peaceful.

Then they passed into another room, which also looked like the inside of a bus. Only this room, unlike the **previous** room, was in a state of **pandemonium**. All sorts of music were being played **simultaneously**, resulting in a terrible *jumble* of noises. Men, women, and children were swirling and dancing around the room, banging tambourines and finger cymbals in a kind of spiritual frenzy. And one guy was actually swinging by his heels from a chandelier, his face completely covered with hair and beads. Babette barely had time to admire the orange velour **upholstery** on the *beanbag* chairs before a group of spinning girls *whisked* her into their dance.

BUDDY n. friend 친구
He and I were buddies at school.
그와 나는 학교 때 친구였다.

DIG v. to understand 이해하다
I don't dig modern jazz.
나는 현대 재즈를 이해하지 못한다.

GROOVY adj. attractive or excellent; fashionable or modern 매혹적인, 멋진
Do you want a groovy car?
멋진 자동차를 원하니?

JUMBLE n. a muddle; mixed-up mess; state of confusion 뒤범벅
My desk was in such a jumble I couldn't find anything.
내 책상은 너무나 뒤범벅이라서 아무 것도 찾을 수가 없었다.

BEANBAG n. (beanbag chair로 쓰여) a chair filled with pellets which takes on the shape of the person sitting in it 쿠션 의자
It is easy to be authoritarian from an office armchair; difficult when sprawled on a beanbag; impossible on a waterbed.
사무실 의자에서 권위적이 되는 것은 쉽지만, 쿠션 의자에 쭉 뻗고서는 권위적이 되기가 힘들고, 물침대 위에서는 불가능하다.

WHISK v. to go or take (somebody/something) away quickly and suddenly 휙 가져(끌어)가다
The waiter whisked away the food before we had finished.
우리가 식사를 마치기도 전에 웨이터가 음식을 급히 가져 가버렸다.

"Is this some kind of religious **cult**?" shouted Bridget over the racket. "If so, I'm telling you right now, I will not let you shave my head."

"No, we're not a cult," Wobbly yelled back. Then he shouted over to a woman with long blond hair who had her back to them, "Hey, Janice, cool it, will you? We've got *company*, remember?"

Janice turned around. She was very beautiful. She had a daisy painted on her cheek, and her face looked calm and **serene**, especially her peaceful blue eyes. She smiled at the visitors, then stood up on her seat and held her hands out in some sort of gesture to the crowd. She looked like a queen. In fact, it was clear she was the **matriarch** of the merry band of hippies, because they all quieted down when they noticed what she was doing, then stood as if awaiting orders.

"Hey, everybody, looks like we have some more Dead-heads aboard," she announced.

"What do you mean?" asked Barnaby, rather alarmed. "We are not dead, and neither are our heads."

"Naw, man," said a hippie in dark sunglasses standing next to him, "the Dead is a band. As in the Grateful Dead, you dig? We're **en route** to the shows on Alpha C."

"The Grateful Dead play on other planets?" asked Babette.

"Where do you think they got the *inspiration* for their song 'Space'? Man, they've been coming out here for years."

"I always knew there was some explanation," mumbled Bridget. Then she turned toward Wobbly. "The show sounds fun, but we really have to get back. I've misplaced my parents."

"Count yourself lucky. I had to blast off into space in order to misplace mine," replied Wobbly.

COMPANY **n.** a group of guests or people who are together in one place for social purposes 동료, 일행
You are selfish. That's why you have no company to help you when you are in trouble.
네가 이기적이니까 어려울 때 도와줄 동료가 없는 거야.

INSPIRATION **n.** ideas which make somebody enthusiastic and encourage somebody to do something 고무, 고취
I have derived inspiration from Freud.
나는 프로이드로부터 영감을 얻었다.

Bridget looked down sadly at the brown shag carpet.

"Hey, I'm sorry, man," said Wobbly, seeing that his joke had not been appreciated. "I didn't mean to be **flippant** about something that's got you so low. But you see, it's like this: I can't beam you back down right now. The teleporter is stuck in 'up', and I can't fix it myself."

"Can't you land us somewhere on the Earth? We could pick a hidden spot no one would be able to sneak up and arrest you," Bridget offered.

"No can do, sister. The *Far Out* probably wouldn't survive a **descent** through the Earth's atmosphere. And if the descent didn't get us, going back up probably would. We could try to position ourselves over one of the holes in the **ozone layer**, but that would only help a little. There are plenty of other layers of gas ready to burn this bus up."

"You mean I'm stuck here? I'm going to live out my life as some sort of space **vagrant**—no home, no family, no money?" wailed Bridget. Her lower lip began to tremble and her eyes *welled* up with tears.

"Hey, don't *knock* it, man. The wandering life of a **nomad** is full of adventure. There's nothing like the freedom of pulling up stakes and moving on whenever you feel like it," *raved* Wobbly. "Of course, being a **pauper** isn't all that much fun. Which reminds me... you kids don't have any money, do you? I'll **reimburse** you as soon as we get to Alpha C."

At that point Bridget lost it. She sat down and began sobbing loudly.

"Hey, man, what's all this **lamenting** about?" asked Wobbly kindly. "I said I'd pay you back."

Janice, who had been talking with Babette and Barnaby over by the ship's controls, made her way over to Bridget.

WELL v. to flow or rise like water from a well   (물 따위가) 흘러나오다
Blood was welling (out) from the wound.
상처에서 피가 흘러 나오고 있었다.

KNOCK v. to find fault; to criticize   흠잡다; 비난하다
The newspapers are too fond of knocking the England team.
신문들은 영국 팀 비난하는 것을 너무 좋아한다.

RAVE v. to talk wildly or furiously as if in a fever or mad   열심히 떠들다
The patient began to rave incoherently at the nurses.
그 환자는 간호사들에게 횡설수설 열심히 떠들기 시작했다.

"Nice work, Wobbly," said Janice. "First, I accidentally beam them up, and now you make them cry."

The captain shrugged helplessly and wandered off.

"Your name's Bridget, right?" asked Janice in a soft, comforting voice.

Bridget nodded. She even stopped crying quite so hard. There was something nice and **maternal** about Janice, and it made her miss her own mother a little less.

"Don't let Wob upset you, honey," she said. "I know he seems cold and **dispassionate**, but he's really not uncaring. We'll get you back home, I promise. We're actually stopping at a space station on the way to the show to do a little shopping and pick up *supplies*. I'm sure we can fit a trip to the mechanic into our **itinerary**. We'll get that disco ball fixed."

Bridget nodded and managed a small smile.

"There, now, that's better," said Janice. "Say, I know what you need. You need to do a little yoga."

"Um, I don't know...," Bridget hesitated. She was **wary** of strange Indian exercises that didn't involve running, jumping, or sweating.

"It'll help you center yourself. Right now you're all out of balance. Yoga can restore your **equilibrium**."

Bridget was **vacillating**. On the one hand, Janice was so cool that she wanted to go along with her, but on the other hand, the whole yoga thing seemed dangerous. What if she got into one of those twisted-up positions and couldn't get out?

SUPPLY n. thing that is supplied; stock or store of things provided or available 공급품, 필요한 물품들
Helicopters dropped supplies for the stranded villagers.
헬리콥터는 오도 가도 못하게 된 주민들에게 필요한 물품들을 떨어뜨려 주었다.

"Don't sweat it, honey," Janice assured her. "I'm about to teach my daily yoga class now anyway. Unfortunately, life on a remodeled tour bus can be pretty **sedentary**, and we all know that sitting around all the time isn't very healthy. That's why we do yoga. Kind of works the *kinks* out. Join in if you want, but only if your decision is completely **voluntary**. I'm not forcing you."

The fact that other people were going to join her kind of took the pressure off, so Bridget decided to try it. She **donned** the *baggy* muslin trousers Janice loaned her, and they were ready to begin.

The first exercise was more like sleeping than stretching. Janice told everyone to "get **horizontal**," and they all just lay down flat on the floor. After concentrating on breathing for a while, Janice told the class to stay on their backs but lift their legs up into a **vertical** position, straight up in the air, **perpendicular** to the floor.

"Then," she said, "when you're ready, lift your lower back off the floor, supporting it with your hands, and stretch your legs out over your head, so your knees are close to your face and your legs are **parallel** to the carpet. This pose will **stimulate** the flow of blood to the brain."

"I think it's definitely working," groaned Bridget. "My head's about to explode."

"Hmmm," said Janice. "Maybe this is too hard for a **novice**. Since you're a beginner, I'll start you off with something less **strenuous**. Bring your legs down, and I'll show you how to **meditate**."

Bridget *wriggled* out of her pose and sat up. Janice came over and sat down cross-legged in front of her.

KINK n. a short twist or curl in a rope, thread, hair, or wire   꼬임, 엉클림
There was a kink in a cable.
밧줄이 꼬여 있었다.

BAGGY adj. hanging loosely; baglike   헐렁한
The clown had baggy trousers.
광대는 헐렁한 바지를 입고 있었다.

WRIGGLE v. to avoid (doing) an unpleasant task by being cunning or by making excuses   요리조리해서 빠져나가다
It's your turn to take the dog for a walk. Don't try to wriggle out of it.
네가 개 데리고 산책 나갈 차례야. 요리조리해서 빠져나갈 생각하지 마.

"Meditation," explained Janice, "is basically just deep thought. But in yoga, you don't meditate on a particular problem or concrete issue. It's much more **abstract**, you know? You just think, but not about anything solid. Just close your eyes and let your mind relax. Understand?"

Bridget nodded. Janice helped her get into the correct position.

"Now then, as you do this, weird ideas may come into your head. Don't fight them, they're just **subconscious** thoughts that you're not aware of all the time because they're hidden away in your mind. One time when I was meditating, I got so caught up I began to **hallucinate**. I opened my eyes and found myself floating in an endless sea of non-dairy *whipped* topping with chocolate *sprinkles* falling on my head, and a great maraschino cherry moon shining and **luminous** overhead. It was so cool."

Janice smiled in a vague sort of way. Bridget was a little concerned, although finding herself in a bowl of whipped topping didn't sound all that bad.

"I mean, I wasn't really there. I was just seeing things, dig? Anyway, I don't think that will happen to you," Janice assured her.

Bridget closed her eyes and began her meditation, and Janice went back to the rest of the class. Over by the control panel, Babette, Barnaby, and Wobbly were having a conversation.

"Captain Wobbly, I must say, I **marvel** at your mechanical abilities," said Barnaby. "It's truly amazing that you managed to build such a fine spaceship out of ordinary buses."

"Yeah, well, it could have been a fine ship, but the *feds* were breathing down my neck, you know what I'm saying? I had to hurry," said Wobbly. "For one thing, it's not that easy to **navigate**. The *Mayflower* was probably easier to steer than this baby. But the thing that burns me most is the transmission."

WHIP v. to stir rapidly with a fork or some other instrument (포크 등으로) 휘젓다
Whip the ingredients (up) into a smooth paste.
재료들이 부드럽게 되도록 휘저어라.

SPRINKLE v. to scatter in drops or tiny bits (액체, 분말 등을) 뿌리다
He sprinkled sand on the icy sidewalk.
그는 얼어붙은 보도 위에 모래를 뿌렸다.

FED n. member of the Federal Bureau of Investigation(FBI) 미연방 수사관
The cops and the feds swooped down and caught the terrified Waxey with a pound of heroin.
경찰과 연방 수사관은 헤로인 1파운드를 가지고 겁에 질려 있는 왁시를 덮쳐서 잡았다.

"You mean the gears?" asked Babette, somewhat shocked. "A spaceship with gears? I expected 'hyperdrive' and 'warp factors' and things like that."

"You've got to work with what you have," replied Wobbly. "And for the *Far Out*, that meant a **manual** transmission. I was trying to build an automatic transmission for her back in Mexico, but I ran out of time. So until I get the parts I need, gears are shifted the old-fashioned way— by hand."

"Hmmm, automatic transmission," *mused* Barnaby, scratching his head and pondering the problem. "You'd need a timing belt, for starters, right?"

Suddenly, something fell out of Barnaby's hair and under the captain's seat.

"Barnaby!" gasped Babette. "Don't tell me you had a timing belt stuck in your hair!"

"Well, not exactly a timing belt," said Wobbly, who had pulled the object out from under his seat. "More like the latest issue of *Women and Men of Science*: *The Swimsuit Edition*. There are some pretty **risqué** pictures in here."

"I only read it for the articles," said Barnaby, blushing slightly. "I like to keep up on what my *colleagues* are doing. Give it back!"

Barnaby leaped at the magazine, but the captain held it out of his reach. The two *scuffled* over the magazine until Wobbly suddenly cried, "Hey, my contact!"

"You wear contacts?" asked Barnaby, who lost interest in the magazine for the time being. "But doesn't that make your granny glasses a bit **redundant**? I mean, what do you need glasses for if you wear contacts?"

MUSE v. to think about something carefully   곰곰이 생각하다
The eminent science fiction author William Tenn once mused about the possibilities of genetic manipulation.
저명한 공상과학소설 작가인 윌리엄 텐은 이전에 유전자 조작에 대해 생각했었다.

COLLEAGUE n. person with whom one works, especially in a profession or business   동료
David is a colleague of mine.
데이비드는 내 동료야.

SCUFFLE v. to struggle or fight in a rough, confused manner   싸우다
Somewhere in the darkness two rats scuffled.
어둠 속 어딘가에서 쥐 두 마리가 싸우고 있었다.

Wobbly paid no attention to his question. He was busy trying to find his contact lens in the dense brown shag.

"Got it!" he *chirped*, after a couple of minutes. "Man, that was close. Now, what were we talking about?"

"Your life story," said Babette, seizing the chance to change the subject. "You were going to tell us how you became such a scandalous hippie, and how you met Janice, and how you decided to get married and blast off into space together."

"Well, first of all, Janice is not my **spouse**," replied the hippie.

"Oh, I am so disappointed," frowned Babette.

"How come?"

"Ah, well, it seemed so romantic," she sighed dreamily. "Two outlaw hippies, chased from the Earth, finding love among the stars."

"You'll have to forgive her. She's French," whispered Barnaby.

"Hey, man, don't get me wrong," he told Babette. "I mean, she's not my girlfriend. Our relationship is strictly **platonic**, but I do like her just fine. But we *outlaws* can't get tied down, dig? Wild, **unbridled** affections only get you in trouble. Besides, that whole idea of settling down with one person your whole life is so middle-class and outdated. **Monogamy** is for *squares*, man!"

"Hmmph," huffed Babette, crossing her arms over her chest.

"I can see we aren't connecting on this topic," said Wobbly. "Maybe I should tell you about how we got where we are. Actually, it started back when I was teenager. My mother, who was a hippie herself, said to me, 'Bob, I want you to be rich.'"

CHIRP **v.** to make the short, sharp sound made by some small birds and insects; to speak in a manner in some respect like the chirping of birds 짹짹 울다, 지저귀다; 즐거운 듯이 말하다
The crickets chirped outside the house.
집 밖에서 귀뚜라미들이 울어댔다.

OUTLAW **n.** a person who has done something illegal and who is hiding from the authorities 무법자
He led a bands of outlaws in his country.
그는 자기네 나라에서 무법자 무리들을 이끌었었다.

SQUARE **n.** a person who is out of touch with new ideas, styles, etc.; conventional or old-fashioned person 고지식한 사람; 유행에 뒤진 사람
I'm basically a bit of a square.
나는 근본적으로 약간 고지식한 사람이다.

"I thought your name was Wobbly. Why did she call you Bob?" asked Barnaby.

"Well, that happened when I was born. Supposedly, she wanted to name me Bob Weir Philstein, but she got confused. She was way out of it when it came time to fill out the birth *certificate*, and when they asked her what she wanted the name to be, she just kept saying, 'Wob Beer, Wob Beer.' She **transposed** the 'b' and the 'w.' At least, that's the best explanation we could come up with. Anyway, she always called me Bob."

"So, as I was saying, she wanted me to be a very rich and powerful businessman—a **tycoon**, if possible. Let's face it, being a hippie isn't that **lucrative**, and she decided someone better start making some money, or she'd wind up old and homeless. Man, was I sad. I didn't want to leave the *commune* and I seriously doubted I had the **capacity** to be successful in business. As I set out for New York City, I was afraid. Afraid I'd be laughed at. Afraid I'd be *fired*. Afraid I'd never be *hired* at all."

"As it turned out, my fears were completely **unfounded**. New York was a *boom* town. I was hired right away, and I discovered I had a real **aptitude** for business. It just came naturally. Soon I was a millionaire. Man, I mean, I was rolling in bread..."

"Rolling in bread?" whispered Barnaby to Babette. "What does that mean?"

"I have no idea," she whispered back. "It's another one of those hippie **idioms**. At least, I don't think he actually rolled around with loaves of bread. We will have to ask Bridget."

"But my wealth had a price," continued Wobbly. "First of all, the stress gave me stomach **ulcers**—open sores in my stomach."

Babette and Barnaby **winced** at the thought of such a horrible thing, almost as if they felt pains in their own stomachs.

CERTIFICATE n. a written or printed statement that may be used as proof of some fact 증명서
A birth certificate gives the date and place of a person's birth and the names of his parents.
출생증명서에는 그 사람의 생일, 출생지, 부모의 이름이 있다.

COMMUNE n. a group of people, not all of one family, living together and sharing property and responsibilities 공동 생활체
An abandoned lumber town has been turned into a little commune by a bunch of hippies.
버려졌던 벌목꾼들의 마을이 히피 집단들로 인해 공동 생활체로 변했다.

FIRE v. to dismiss (an employee) from a job 해고하다
He was fired for stealing money from the till.
계산대 서랍에서 돈을 훔친 죄로 그는 해고되었다.

HIRE v. to pay for the use of (a thing) or the work or services of (a person) 고용하다, 쓰다
The storekeeper hired a boy to deliver groceries.
가게 주인은 식품 배달을 위해 소년을 고용했다.

BOOM n. sudden increase; period of prosperity 갑작스런 증가; 호경기
The land speculation has changed our village into a boom town.
땅 투기로 인해 우리 마을이 신흥 도시로 바뀌었다.

"But the worst was that I had given up all the values that were important to me. Yes, for money I was willing to **forsake** every social and political cause I once held sacred. Man, I even worked for a company whose only purpose was to **deplete** our country's natural supply of kale. If they keep it up, there will be no more kale in the United States by the year 2010!"

Barnaby and Babette stared at each other, obviously shaken.

"That was the last straw. I had to do something. The country was going down the tubes, man, and I had to stop it. I became active, dedicated, **militant** in service to the cause. That's when the pranks began."

"I wrapped the White House with recycled toilet paper. I *dumped* a truckload of *compost* on the floor of the Senate. And, as you may have heard, I turned the Speaker of the House bright red with vegetable dye. Sure, some people said I was nothing more than a **vandal**, but these were hardly acts of senseless spray painting and destruction of property."

"By the time of the red dye prank, I already had a following of several dozen. But my life was changed forever when I met Janice."

"Aha!" cried Babette. "I knew it. You are crazy about her. You **dote** on her, admit it!"

"Back off, Babette," said Wobbly. "I'm no love *sap*. I do owe her a lot, though. Before I met her, I was full of anger. My pranks were getting more and more dangerous. I was even starting to have violent thoughts. Janice chilled me out, helped me become more **moderate**. But by that time, the government already wanted me dead, and I was getting tired of spending all my time **evading** capture, so we beat it down to Mexico, followed by tons of like-minded hippies. It was an **exodus**, man; whole populations picked up and left the country. The government folks probably thought we were doing them a favor. Anyway, the rest you already know. Whoa, man, we're already at the mall! We'd better slow down."

DUMP v. to put (something unwanted) in a place and leave as rubbish 쏟아 놓다
Some people just dump their rubbish in the river.
강에 쓰레기를 쏟아 넣는 사람들이 있다.

COMPOST n. mixture of decayed organic matter, manure, etc. added to soil to improve the growth of plants 퇴비
The plants need much compost.
그 식물들은 퇴비가 많이 필요하다.

SAP n. a silly, stupid person; fool 어리석은 사람; 바보
He would talk all the way back from school about what a sap she was.
그는 학교에서 돌아오는 길 내내 그녀가 얼마나 어리석은지에 대해 말하곤 했다.

Wobbly jammed his foot onto the clutch and shifted clumsily into first gear. The whole ship **lurched** forward. Bridget, deep in her meditations, fell over sideways. Beauregard, which had been **lulled** into a deep sleep by the incense and sitar music in the other room, came in to see what had so rudely awakened him. He fixed an angry stare on the captain.

"Sorry, man," said Wobbly with a little wave of his hand.

Bridget, suddenly awake, was full of excitement. "I've got it!" she cried.

Janice and a couple of other people from the yoga class came over and helped her up.

"Did you have some kind of vision?" Janice asked.

"The perfect counterplay to the pick-and-roll! Somebody get me some paper—I've got to sketch this out and send it to the New York Knicks!"

"A basketball formation? How **profound**. How deep. What an important insight into the meaning of life," said one of the hippies in a **snide**, mocking tone.

"I'd wipe that self-satisfied **smirk** off my face if I were you, Ralph," **cautioned** Janice. "Should I tell everyone what your great insight was? It was rather **prosaic**, if I remember. Totally *dullsville*. Boring. Something along the lines of 'Oswald acted alone,' right?"

Ralph grumbled and walked off.

"Let's go see what Wobbly's up to," suggested Janice. "I think we're almost at the mall."

Janice brought up the idea of stopping at the mechanic's shop, getting the disco ball fixed, and returning Barnaby, Babette, Bridget, and Beauregard to the Earth before heading to the shows. Wobbly didn't take to the idea immediately.

DULLSVILLE n. a condition of utter boredom; something very dull   지루함; 단조롭고 따분한 것
That movie was real dullsville.
그 영화는 정말 지루한 것이었다.

"But, baby," he *whined*, "we've got a **rendezvous** with Stan the Fruit Man in less than four hours. If we don't meet him when we're supposed to, we won't have any RSGs for the shows!"

"RSGs?" asked Bridget.

"Red seedless grapes," said Janice. "Great snack food. **Ideal** for Dead shows. Anyway, look, Wob, that's a pretty **flimsy** excuse for kidnapping. You know you can get some grapes at the stadium. We have no right to drag these kids to three days of Dead shows. If they decided to come of their own **volition**, that would be another story. But they obviously want to go back to the Earth, and we should help them, so unless you can come up with a stronger reason than your desire for snack food, I suggest we return them to their planet."

Wobbly unhappily agreed, and pulled the *Far Out* into the airlock of a spaceship service station. He honked the horn, and a stooped-over, gray-haired man in *greasy* coveralls came shuffling out. Wobbly, Janice, and the kids jumped out of the ship.

"Yeah?" asked the man, whose coveralls had the name "Bruce" *sewn* on the breast pocket.

"Our teleportation device is stuck in 'up.' We need to get these kids back to the Earth right away. Do you think you could help us, um, Bruce?" asked Janice as sweetly as possible.

"My name's not Bruce," grumbled the mechanic. But fortunately, he agreed to take a look at the disco ball.

After only a **cursory** examination of the broken ball, he came right back out and announced that all his attempts to fix it were **futile**.

"Well, there you have it," said Wobbly. "Let's be on our way."

"Hold it, Wob. What do you mean, futile? You barely looked at it!" Janice told the man whose name wasn't Bruce.

WHINE v. to make a long high-pitched complaining cry 우는 소리하다, 푸념하다
She is always whining about trifles.
그녀는 하찮은 일에 늘 불평을 한다.

GREASY adj. covered with grease; slippery 기름 묻은; 미끄러운
He put his greasy fingers on my new dress.
그는 기름 묻은 손을 내 새 드레스에 댔다.

SEW v. to work with a needle and thread 바느질하다, 수놓다
You can sew by hand or with a machine.
손이나 기계로 바느질을 할 수 있다.

"I mean useless. Unsuccessful. There's only one thing that could fix it, and that's..."

"Duct tape?" asked Barnaby.

All eyes turned toward the boy genius, who stood there holding a roll of shiny gray tape. Bridget and Babette exchanged knowing smiles.

"Well, I'll be," said the mechanic. "Boy, give me that tape, and I'll have it fixed up in a *jiff*."

He was true to his word. Within five minutes, they were waving good-bye and heading toward the Earth. Within fifteen minutes, however, the engine had coughed to a stop. Wobbly began banging his head on the steering wheel.

"This is some kind of **omen**, man. A sign, dig? Something's trying to tell us our Dead-head days are over."

"Calm down, Wobbly," said Bridget. "Barnaby here is mainly a physicist, but he's pretty **versatile**. I'll bet he can fix it. He's a genius!"

"Such **optimism**. Such a cheery outlook. Don't you see, it's hopeless?" he moaned.

"Well, I'm not sure I'm such a genius," said Barnaby, trying to sound **humble**, "but since Captain Wobbly seems too upset to fix it himself, I guess I can take a look."

Bridget and Babette followed him to the engine room.

"Hmm," said Barnaby, after examining things for a minute. "It looks like Wobbly's been pretty **lax** about changing the oil in this spaceship. You're supposed to do it every three months. I'd say, judging from all this *clogged*-up goo, that he hasn't it done in, well, a really, really long time."

"Never mind that," said Bridget, "Can you fix it?"

JIFF(=jiffy) n. a very short time; moment 금세
He was on his bike in a jiff, pedaling down the drive.
그는 즉시 자전거에 올라타 페달을 밟으며 집안 차도로 달려갔다.

CLOG v. (cause to) become blocked with thick or sticky material (기름, 먼지 등이 기계의) 움직임을 방해하다
That heavy oil will clog up the machinery and prevent it from working properly.
그 뻑뻑한 기름이 기계를 막아서 기계가 제대로 작동하지 못하게 할 것이다.

"I'm not sure," he replied. "It would take the proper tools and the **finesse** of an expert to *chip* out the clog without damaging the engine."

"Nonsense," said Babette. "It just needs a good whacking."

"Are you crazy?" asked Barnaby. "You can't simply hit a machine and expect it to work."

"Barnaby, we are in the middle of a **crisis** here," said Bridget through clenched teeth. "If we don't fix this engine, we'll be adrift with a bunch of freaked-out hippies forever. God knows what could happen! They might start playing Grateful Dead **medleys** on their guitars! Get the picture?"

"I see. The situation is desperate indeed. Whack away, Babette."

Babette examined the engine for a moment to select a good spot. Then she took a few cleansing breaths and, with a loud "hiyah!" karate-kicked the engine, which promptly sputtered back to life.

Barnaby and Bridget were impressed. They began heaping praise on their French friend, **extolling** her many and varied talents. Finally, they could return to their planet. They went back to the front of the ship to say good-bye.

When they got there, things were not all peace and love, to say the least. The hippies were in the middle of an ugly argument. Sure, a few of them were quietly chanting or meditating, but the **predominant** feeling in the room was definitely anger. And the anger was directed at Wobbly.

"You **hypocrite**! How can you tell us to do one thing while you do something else?" yelled one woman. "You said we should give up our worldly belongings and stop being dependent on money. You said that's the only way we'd be free. And this whole time you've had a million dollars in high-yield bonds invested on the Earth! Admit it—Stan the Fruit Man is your broker!"

CHIP v. to break or cut (a small piece) from the edge or surface of something 잘게 썰다, 깎아내다, 도려내다
We chipped the old plaster (away) from the wall.
우리는 벽에서 오래 된 회반죽을 도려냈다.

"I *resent* your tone, Sunshine," replied Wobbly. "I am your captain. Show me the proper respect, or I'll have to punish you for **insubordination**."

That didn't sit well with the hippies, and Captain Wobbly suddenly had an uprising on his hands, a **mutiny** on the *Far Out*. Somehow, Janice remained calm throughout the fight. She walked over to where Barnaby, Bridget, Babette, and Beauregard were *huddled* in the corner.

"Even space hippies lose their cool sometimes," she explained, "but there's no reason you should have to **witness** such **discord** among people who usually live so peacefully together. Come on, let's go to the transporter room. I think we're within beaming range."

The kids and the cat followed Janice to the room they had first appeared in. She hugged them all, scratched Beauregard's head, and gave them matching love-bead necklaces, **identical** except that each one had its wearer's initial hanging from it.

"Keep these as something to remember us by—**mementos** of your brief **excursion** into space," said Janice.

"We will," said Bridget, who was feeling a little sad at having to leave her new friend.

"Now, then," began Janice, as she approached the teleporter controls, "you all just huddle together in the middle of the floor. I'm not sure how precise this disco ball is, but you'll wind up on the Earth somewhere, at least."

The disco ball began spinning, pink and green and yellow and blue flashing everywhere. Soon Barnaby, Beauregard, Babette, and Bridget were enveloped in a warm, melting feeling.

"Have a nice trip!" yelled Bridget, just as she began to disappear.

"Oh, we will," replied Janice. "We will."

RESENT **n.** to feel bitter, indignant or angry about (something hurtful, insulting, etc.) 혐오하다
I bitterly resent your criticism.
나는 네 비평이 끔찍이도 싫다.

HUDDLE **v.** to curl one's body up into a small space; to crowd or be heaped together, especially in a small space 몸을 움츠리다; 모여 있다.
We all huddled around the radio to hear the news.
우리는 모두 뉴스를 듣기 위해 라디오 주변에 모여 있었다.

Relationships

Decide what relationship the following pairs of words have to each other. If they mean close to the same thing, make "S." If they have opposite meanings, mark "O."

1. infamous :: notorious
2. elude :: evade
3. vagrant :: nomad
4. horizontal :: vertical
5. perpendicular :: parallel
6. abstract :: concrete
7. tycoon :: pauper
8. platonic :: romantic
9. luminous :: dim
10. cursory :: thorough
11. sedentary :: active
12. dispassionate :: caring
13. lulled :: soothed
14. novice :: beginner
15. futile :: useless

Relationships

Decide what relationship the following pairs of words have to each other. If they mean close to the same thing, make "S." If they have opposite meanings, mark "O."

1. militant :: moderate
2. volition :: free will
3. bohemian :: eccentric
4. pandemonium :: serenity
5. aptitude :: capacity
6. discord :: harmony
7. wary :: cautious
8. flippant :: respectful
9. simultaneously :: separately
10. jurisdiction :: control
11. ebbed :: decreased
12. ideal :: perfect
13. prosaic :: profound
14. omen :: sign
15. humble :: proud

Fill in the blank.

For each sentence below, choose the word that best completes the sentence.

1. All my careful plans and hopes for a happy outdoor jamboree were _____ by an unexpected snowstorm.

    a. disoriented   b. fatigued   c. thwarted   d. ensued

2. Donating blood is a completely _____ action, strongly encouraged but not required.

   a. extraordinary   b. crafty   c. voluntary   d. itinerary

3. Dad kept _____ on the issue of whether or not to have a swimming pool in the back yard, but after months of going back and forth, he finally decided to go ahead.

   a. vacillating   b. hallucinating   c. stimulating   d. meditating

4. After college, Andy decided he wanted to be a juggler, but his mother advised him to take a more _____ job so he could make enough money to pay off his loans and get his own apartment.

   a. strenuous   b. subconscious   c. lax   d. lucrative

5. The president of Acme, Inc. decided to throw a big office picnic, and told all his employees that their _____ and children were also welcome.

   a. culprits   b. cults   c. matriarchs   d. spouses

6. If you must borrow money from friends, be sure to _____ them as soon as you can, or there might be hard feelings.

   a. lurch   b. reimburse   c. forsake   d. lament

7. Mr. Kroft told Timmy he was taking away his issue of *Swimsuits Spectacular* because the pictures were too _____ for a ten-year-old, but we think he just wanted the magazine for himself.

   a. unbridled   b. risqué   c. redundant   d. en route

8. After I got off the Whirl-a-Twirl ride at the fair, it took me a while to regain my _____ and walk straight without feeling dizzy.

   a. upholstery   b. goatee   c. equilibrium   d. monogamy

9. Whenever Penny travels to a new place, she always picks up a little _____ to remind her of her trip.

   a. memento   b. medley   c. idiom   d. ulcer

10. Bruce threatened to _____ to Canada if the American ice hockey teams didn't start performing to his satisfaction.

   a. dote   b. commence   c. wince   d. defect

11. Myra was a(n) _____ for calling her neighbors lazy when she hadn't even left her house or mowed her lawn in over a month.

   a. hypocrite   b. witness   c. vandal   d. exodus

Q U I C K Q U I Z (14)

Matching

Match each word on the right with a word on the left that has a meaning that's close to the same.

1. unfounded	a. shelter
2. refuge	b. unsupported
3. deceased	c. fall
4. dense	d. wonder
5. previous	e. dead
6. descent	f. use up
7. maternal	g. thick
8. don	h. hand-operated

9. marvel
10. navigate
11. manual
12. transposed
13. deplete

i. former
j. reversed
k. steer
l. put on
m. motherly

Q U I C K Q U I Z 15

Matching

Match each word on the right with a word on the left that has a meaning that's close to the same.

1. snide
2. rendezvous
3. versatile
4. optimism
5. finesse
6. crisis
7. extol
8. predominant
9. insubordination
10. mutiny
11. identical
12. excursion

a. skill
b. main
c. praise
d. flexible
e. mean-spirited
f. trip
g. disobedience
h. same
i. date
j. hopefulness
k. uprising
l. dangerous situation

Curtains for Caspar

Caspar

캐스퍼의 최후

Down we went, splash, right into the Mississippi River. I knew it was the Mississippi because there's just no mistaking that muddy water, so opaque it's doubtful sunlight's ever touched its bottom. Needless to say, the situation filled me with chagrin. In the first place, as you may know, cats do not enjoy being thrown into water, even nice warm water. But this water was not nice and warm, it was absolutely frigid. In addition, after our adventure with the space hippies, my fur had taken on the subtle smell of incense. Nothing so obtrusive that you'd notice it right away, of course, just a trace of perfume. I kind of liked it, and then here I was having it rinsed off me by brisk brown currents. Yes sir, I was *fit to be tied*.

It's a good thing Bridget still had her gum, because the waters, which were already flowing quickly, started gaining more and more **momentum**. We soon felt as though we were being *blasted* by a fire hose. I never thought I'd have occasion to praise a child for **incessant** gum chewing (where I'm from, children are frowned on for chewing gum at all, much less all the time), but Bridget had raised her habit to the level of art. She blew an enormous bubble in the shape of a raft, and managed to pull us all aboard.

It was pretty rough sailing for a while. It kind of felt like we were caught in a washing machine spin cycle, but finally we drifted off the main river onto a more peaceful stream and I was able to check out our **locale**. It was Louisiana swampland. Spanish moss hung thickly from the trees, **obscuring** our view of the sky and sun, so that even at midday it seemed like **dusk**. The water gradually stopped flowing altogether becoming *stale* and **stagnant**. There were also plenty of alligators hanging around—every now and then a green, scaly head would **emerge** from the *murky* water, as if to check us out, then sink back below the surface.

FIT n. (fit to be tied의 형태로 쓰여) very angry or annoyed   노발대발하여
I was fit to be tied when three-quarters of an hour had elapsed without any sign of Barney.
45분이 지나도록 바니의 모습이 안 보이자 나는 안절부절 못했다.

BLAST v. to destroy or break apart   폭파하다
The village was blasted by enemy bombs.
적의 폭탄으로 마을이 폭파되었다.

STALE adj. no longer interesting because heard, done, etc. too often before; not new   식상해 있는; 새롭지가 않은
Her performance has become stale.
그녀의 연기는 진부해졌다.

MURKY adj. unpleasantly dark; gloomy   어두운; 음울한
The light was too murky to continue playing.
조명이 너무 어두워 경기를 계속 할 수가 없었다.

I was glad we hadn't drowned, of course, but the situation made me nervous. When we washed ashore, Bridget, Babette, and Barnaby tumbled out of the raft and flopped down on the ground, **exhausted** by our struggle with the rapids. But I was too *edgy* to rest. I had a feeling danger *lurked* behind those trees. And, besides, my fur needed some serious grooming. I took it upon myself to keep watch. Unfortunately, there's only so much one cat can do...

"This is getting ridiculous," said Bridget, sitting up after her rest. "Where are we now?"

"Judging from the plant and animal life, and the amazing size of the cockroaches, I'd say we're in southern Louisiana," replied Barnaby, who was holding up an enormous brown bug by one of its fuzzy hind legs.

"Yuck," Bridget said, wrinkling her face into a **grimace**. "Put that nasty thing down, man."

Barnaby dropped the creature, and it scurried off noisily into the swamp. Babette stretched and sat up, and the three began discussing what they should do next. But their conversation was suddenly cut short by a *blood-curdling* scream.

"Rrrairrow!"

The kids jumped to their feet and spun around. Not three feet behind them was a **monstrous** man, as big as a bear, as bald as an egg, with four huge arms stretched out to grab them, and Beauregard, hissing, *clawing*, and yowling up a storm on top of his head.

"Oh, my God," gasped Barnaby. "What could explain such a **mutation**? What did his parents feed him when he was little? Or perhaps it's **genetic**—maybe his brothers and sisters all have four arms, too."

"This is no time for note-taking, Barnaby. Run!" screamed Bridget, who had already turned to make a dash for it with Babette.

EDGY adj. nervous; easily upset or annoyed   초조한; 쉽게 화를 내는
She's been very edgy recently, waiting for the examination results.
시험 결과를 기다리면서 그녀는 요즘 매우 초조해 있다.

LURK v. to exist unobserved   남의 눈에 띄지 않고 있다. 잠재해 있다
Resentment lurked in his heart.
그의 마음속에는 증오가 도사리고 있었다.

BLOOD-CURDLING adj. filling one with horror; terrifying   소름끼치는; 공포에 찬
Do you like a blood-curdling story?
소름끼치게 무서운 이야기를 좋아하니?

CLAW v. to try to scratch or tear somebody/something with a claw or with one's finger-nails   (발톱이나 손톱으로) 할퀴다
The prisoner clawed at the cell door in desperation.
그 죄수는 절망에 빠져 독방 문을 손톱으로 긁어댔다.

They didn't get very far, though, because standing right behind them were a short, *stocky* man in a dark, pinstriped suit and wide-brimmed hat, and a *peroxide* blond in a short red dress. Ordinarily, that wouldn't be enough to stop two kids fleeing a four-armed monster, but the man happened to have a large gun in his hand-a .44-**caliber**, to be exact. **Circumstances** being what they were, Bridget and Babette stopped running.

By this time, the monster had managed to scoop Barnaby up with one of his arms and had pulled Beauregard off his head with another. He stood, as if awaiting orders, as the boy and the cat struggled uselessly.

"Good boy, **Cannibal**," said the man with the gun.

"He's a cannibal? Don't tell me you're going to feed us to him! I mean, he eats things other than people, right?" Bridget blurted out nervously.

"Enough already with the questions," barked the man. "If anyone's going to do any **interrogating** around here, it's going to be me. And my first question is, what are you doing out here sniffing around our **loot**?"

"Loot?" asked Babette.

"Don't play *dumb* with me! You must know we're the dangerous gangsters that looted Mrs. Peychaud's Praline Palace back in New Orleans. We got away with seven crates of pralines. The whole police department must be after us by now. We *stashed* the loot in our hideout, and you know it. You're after our loot!"

"You like saying 'loot' a lot, don't you?" remarked Bridget.

STOCKY adj. short, strong and solid in appearance   땅딸막한
He is a stocky, round-faced man.
그는 땅딸막하고 얼굴이 둥그란 사람이다.

PEROXIDE n. colourless liquid used as an antiseptic and to bleach hair   과산화수소, 표백제
A peroxide blonde means a woman with hair that has been bleached with peroxide.
머리를 금발처럼 표백한 여자란 과산화수소로 머리를 표백한 여자란 뜻이다.

DUMB adj. stupid   우둔한
If the police question you, act dumb, pretending you don't know anything.
경찰이 물어보거든 아무 것도 모르는 것처럼 바보 시늉을 해라.

STASH v. to store something safely and secretly; to hide something   숨겨 두다
He's got his money stashed (away) in an old suitcase.
그는 자신의 돈을 낡은 가방 안에 숨겨 두었다.

"'Loot' is real gangster talk, kid. So is 'gun', if you get my *drift*. Watch it, or you'll wind up just another nameless **corpse**, floating face down in the Mississippi."

For some reason, Bridget wasn't all that afraid of this guy. He was trying too hard to be **macho**. All that toughness and manliness seemed fake, like an act designed to cover something up. The gun seemed real enough, though, so she decided to keep her mouth shut.

"Ooooh, Verna, these kids are making me really angry! I'd have no **qualms** about shooting them. I figure they got it coming," growled the gangster, waving his gun around.

"Don't kill them yet, Snake," *cooed* Verna in a high, little-girl voice. "We might be able to use them in our plan, don't you think?"

"Say, baby, that's not a bad idea," said Snake, brightening up. "Not bad at all. You kids better be glad Verna's got such a *level* head. Cannibal! Grab these two and take them back to the hideout!"

The possibly people-eating monster gathered up Bridget and Babette with his free arms, and started back through the swamp, followed by Snake and then by Verna, who was slowed down because her six-inch high heels kept sinking into the mud.

The hideout turned out to be a one-room shack furnished with a couple of cots and a few chairs. Snake wasted little time pulling four chairs together and tying Babette, Bridget, Barnaby, and Beauregard up with their backs to each other. And, as soon as his captive audience stopped whining, he began to tell them all the details of his evil plan. Gangsters and villains always tell the good guys all the details of their evil plans. It's practically **inevitable**. Unfortunately, for the captives, Snake found it necessary to **recount** his entire criminal life story before getting around to the plan at hand.

"I'll tell you kids, I've led a life of crime that would put Al Capone's to shame," he began. "Sometimes I'm even shocked by my own **depravity**, my complete and utter wickedness. It started when I **disregarded** my first traffic signal. The light was red, and I ignored it. I just drove right on through. 'Yeah, baby, yeah,' I said to myself, 'This is living. This is freedom!'"

DRIFT n. general meaning or sense; gist 의미; 요점
My German isn't very good, but I got the general drift of what she said.
내 독일어 실력은 형편없지만 그녀가 하는 말의 의미를 대강 이해했다.

COO v. to make a soft murmuring sound like that of a dove; to say in a soft murmur 소곤거리다, 속삭이다
'It will be all right', she cooed soothingly.
'괜찮을 거야' 라고 달래면서 그녀는 속삭였다.

LEVEL adj. mentally well-balanced; sensible; rational 분별력 있는; 지각 있는; 합리적인
He tried to keep a level head in the crisis.
그는 위기 속에서 분별력을 잃지 않으려고 애썼다.

Barnaby, Bridget, Babette, and Beauregard rolled their eyes, but Snake paid them no mind.

"After I got a taste for crime, I just couldn't stop," he continued. "Next I tried **polygamy**. Of course, you're only allowed to be married to one person at a time. I made it my goal to have a wife in every state! I wanted to be the biggest polygamist this country had ever known! I know what you're thinking. 'Fifty women? Is there no limit to this man's **debauchery**? Has he no shame?' I'll tell you: I lost my sense of shame the day I ran that first red light."

"Did you? I mean, did you manage to trick fifty women into marrying you?" asked Barnaby.

"Well, not exactly. *Dames* aren't that easy to **dupe**. I'd try to **lure** them in with fancy dinners and jewelry, but most of them got wise to me before I managed to get them to the altar. Women are creatures of great **discernment**, kid. Try to *pull* a fast one on them, and they see right through it every time."

Over in the corner, Verna was smiling to herself.

"But, anyway, the coppers never wised up, and that's the most important thing. Then I tried my hand at **black-mail**. I got some old pictures of Heather Locklear, the actress, dressed in some very embarrassing outfits from the mid-1970s. You should have seen the collars on some of those shirts! And the *bell-bottoms*! I won't even tell you about her hair. Oh, sure, she begged me not to show them to anyone. 'I was just a kid!' she said. 'I didn't know what I was doing!' But her begging didn't do any good. Sure, I told her, I'd keep the photos to myself—for a price, baby, for a price!"

"Don't tell me she actually paid you off?" said Babette.

"I'm sure she would have, Miss Smarty-Pants, but unfortunately, just as I was about to start **barraging** her with threatening letters and mysterious phone calls, the whole '70s look came back into fashion. Well, as they say, life is a balance sheet—and sometimes debits outweigh credits."

"Hold it one second, uh, Mr. Snake," snapped Bridget. "Life is a balance sheet? What kind of **metaphor** is that for a gangster to be using?"

DAME n. lady; madam 숙녀, 귀부인
Our secrets have been betrayed not by men, but by dames.
우리의 비밀은 남자들이 아니라 여자들로 인해 발각 되었다.

PULL v. (pull a fast one (on somebody)의 형태로 쓰여) to gain an advantage (over somebody) by a trick; to deceive 속이다
Finally it turned out that he pulled a fast one on them.
마침내 그가 그들을 속였다는 것이 밝혀졌다.

BELL-BOTTOMS n. trousers made very wide below the knee 나팔바지
She looked cool in her bell-bottoms.
그녀가 나팔바지 입고 있는 모습이 멋져 보였다.

Snake was visibly *flustered*. Bridget was obviously hitting a sore spot.

"I mean, maybe 'life is a big bank *heist*' or even 'all the world's a cage', but 'balance sheet'?" she continued, gathering confidence. "That's not gangster talk, that's a comparison only an accountant would make! You're a **fraud**! A phony! I knew there was something weird about you. This whole evil plot thing is a **hoax**, isn't it?"

"Okay, kid, you got me," said Snake. "Yeah, I was an accountant. For twenty long years I sat at the same desk at Ingalls & Marks, **languishing** in a sea of numbers, slowly having the life force sucked out of me. And, since you're so smart, you probably figured out that 'Snake' is just a **pseudonym**. My real name is Caspar, but Verna here **dubbed** me Snake because she said Caspar's a name for friendly folks, and I have **malice** in my heart. That's right, baby, mean and evil intentions.

"Why, you ask? I'll tell you why—because I've spent my life *juggling* other people's money, making sure they wouldn't go to jail for tax violations, sometimes even touching up the books, if you know what I mean, while I earned a **pittance** of a salary. Rich businesspeople **exploited** my mathematical abilities, and you know what I got in return, after twenty years? A gold-plated pen. Sure, it was the erasable-ink kind, but still, it wasn't nearly enough!"

"Take it easy, honey," cooed Verna, "you're getting sweat stains on your suit!"

"I can't help it," *huffed* Caspar the Snake. "You kids just will never understand. You can't imagine the **monotony** I had to put up with—doing the same things, saying the same things, eating the same things day in and day out. But I have a newsflash for you—you're wrong about the evil plot. I may have failed as a gangster so far, but I'll get my recognition yet. My name will be remembered throughout the entire world!"

"Oh, yeah, you're a regular **menace** to society, aren't you? What a threat you pose," laughed Bridget. "What do you plan to do, loot another candy store?"

FLUSTER v. to make (somebody) nervous and confused 당황하게 만들다
Don't get flustered!
당황하지 마라!

HEIST n. robbery; burglary 강도, 강탈
Four men were involved in the armored car heist.
남자 네 명이 (현금 수송용) 무장 자동차 강도 사건에 관련되어 있었다.

JUGGLE v. to change the arrangement of something constantly in order to achieve a satisfactory result or to deceive people 속이기 위해 조작하다, 속이다
The government has been juggling (with) the figures to hide the latest rise in unemployment.
정부는 최근의 실업 증가를 감추기 위해 숫자를 조작해 왔다.

HUFF v. to make angry; to offend 벌컥 화를 내다; 화나게 하다
Please don't huff at such a thing.
그런 일에 화내지 마십시오.

Babette and Barnaby chuckled. Surprisingly, even the four-armed monster *sniggered* to himself in the corner.

"Shut up, Cannibal," said Snake. "What if I told you that I plan to blow up the one thing that keeps the city of New Orleans from being flooded over by the Mississippi River? What if I told you I'm going to destroy the **levee**?"

Babette gasped. "But the city of New Orleans is below sea level! If you blow up the levee, nothing will hold back the waters! The entire city will be destroyed!"

"What reason do you have for doing that? What's your **motive**? The innocent people of New Orleans have done nothing to you," reasoned Barnaby.

"In the first place, don't kid yourself about the people of New Orleans," said Snake. "In the second place, I already told you I want to go down in history as the world's most evil gangster. And you kids are going to help me."

"No way, man, I won't be your **accomplice**! I won't help you commit such a crime!" yelled Bridget, struggling against the ropes that bound her.

"Oh, yes, you will. I'm afraid you don't have a choice," laughed Snake. "See, to blow up the levee, I need to use a whole boatload of dynamite. And a boatload of dynamite is the kind of thing that might **arouse** the suspicion of a watchful river cop. I can't afford to have any coppers nosing around and spoiling things for me now, can I? That's where you come in. I'm going to put you in an even bigger boat full of even more explosives. You'll be a **decoy**, see? The river cops will be so busy questioning you, they won't even notice my **modest** little boat quietly sailing along the edge of the levee. And by the time they figure it out, it'll be too late!"

Snake began to laugh a crazy villain laugh, then he turned abruptly and walked out of the cabin. Verna, who had been standing quietly in a corner, was *fidgeting* nervously.

SNIGGER v. to laugh in a half-suppressed unpleasant way   낄낄 웃다
The guests sniggered at her shabby appearance.
손님들은 그녀의 초라한 행색을 보고 낄낄 웃었다.

FIDGET v. to make small restless movement, thus annoying other people   안절부절 못하다
It's bad manners to fidget about at the table.
식탁에서 안절부절 못하는 것은 나쁜 예절이다.

"Verna, you can't really be in favor of this. You don't seem like the kid of woman who would **advocate** the senseless destruction of an entire town!" pleaded Bridget.

"That shows what you know!" *squeaked* Verna in her high voice. "Until I met Caspar, I mean Snake, I was just another substitute teacher. I wanted to make it in show business, but all the movie producers told me I didn't stand a chance because of my voice. Snake gave me the confidence to pursue my dreams. He says as soon as we're rich, he'll buy a studio and make me a big star!"

"Yeah, that'll happen," muttered Bridget.

"Ooooh, you kids think you're so smart!" *twittered* Verna, stomping her high-heeled foot. "I'm going to help Snake with the boats. Cannibal, keep an eye on them."

And, with that, she turned and stormed out. Finally more or less alone, Bridget, Babette, and Barnaby tried to figure out some way to stop the would-be gangsters.

"Well," said Babette, "the first thing I need to do is get out of these ropes. My legs have fallen asleep."

"Good luck," said Bridget, looking over her shoulder at her own bound wrists. "I've been twisting my hands around, trying to work on these knots. They're tied pretty tight. And the rope is so rough, I think I've given myself a couple of **lacerations**. Maybe if we... hey!"

Babette was standing, free of her ropes, in front of her. She was shaking out her legs.

SQUEAK v. to make a short high-pitched cry or sound; to say something in a squeaking voice 찍찍거리듯 말하다
'Let go of me!' he squeaked nervously.
'나를 풀어줘!' 그가 신경질적으로 찍찍거리듯 말했다.

TWITTER v. to talk rapidly in an excited or a nervous way 흥분해서 말하다
What is he twittering (on) about?
그는 무엇에 대해 흥분해서 말하고 있는 거니?

"Mmm, that's better," she said.

"Babette, how did you get out so fast?" asked Barnaby.

"A little trick I picked up in China. Also, I am double-jointed in every joint," she replied.

Cannibal grunted suddenly and began *lurching* toward Babette.

"Watch out!" cried Bridget. "The monster's behind you!"

"Do not worry. I have a **theory** about this monster."

"I sure hope it's right, whatever it is," said Bridget, closing her eyes to keep from seeing Babette get eaten.

"You are not a monster at all, are you?" Babette asked, turning to face Cannibal.

The giant four-armed man hesitated for a second or two, then shook his head and let out a sigh.

"Indeed, no, young lady. At least, not on the inside," he said in a high-class British accent.

If they hadn't already been sitting, Bridget and Barnaby would have fallen over from shock.

"It can talk!" observed Barnaby.

"Naturally, dear boy" he replied, as politely as possible. It's hard to be **civil**, after all, when people are referring to you as "it." But Cannibal was obviously a person of good breeding. Looking to Babette, he asked, "If I may inquire, how could you tell I am not the dumb beast Snake and Verna think I am?"

"Actually, it was your breath. While you were carrying me, I caught a *whiff* of it. It smells like Earl Grey tea. Not a drink I would think people-eating monsters favor too much," said Babette, smiling.

LURCH v. to lean suddenly; to stagger 비틀거리며 걷다
A drunken man was lurching along the street.
술 취한 남자가 길을 따라 비틀거리며 걷고 있었다.

WHIFF n. faint smell or puff of air or smoke 냄새
Can you catch a whiff of perfume in this room?
이 방에서 향수 냄새를 맡을 수 있니?

The giant laughed. "No, I suppose not. Allow me to **commend** you on your sharp powers of observation. You are very **perceptive** indeed! I had just finished my tea when you children arrived. I'm afraid we weren't introduced properly. My name is Rupert."

He extended his lower right hand and Babette shook it.

"I am Babette, and these are my friends, Bridget, Barnaby, and Beauregard, our cat companion."

"Let me ask you something, Rupert," snapped Bridget. "Do you really think you're going to get away with destroying New Orleans? A guy like you is pretty hard to miss. The police will **apprehend** you and the rest of your gang before you can say 'crumpet'!"

"Please, you mistake me, Bridget," protested Rupert, gesturing with all four arms. "This is the first I heard of this terrible plot. I had no idea what they were up to."

Bridget looked doubtful.

"Really, you must believe me. It was a mistake," he said sadly. "I am a lonely man— misunderstood, *shunned*, and **ostracized** even in my home town. I wandered around the world trying to make friends, but people ran from me in horror. I became a complete **introvert**, shy and unwilling to talk to other people. I have been living the **solitary** life of a **recluse**, all by myself in this hut in the swamp, starved for contact with other human beings. When Snake and Verna arrived, I was overjoyed. I was willing to put on the act they seemed to expect of me, **pantomiming** and grunting like Frankenstein's monster, as long as they would stay and keep me company. I see now that it must end. But what can we do? I am strong, but Snake has a gun."

"Well, I have an idea," said Babette. "First of all, Rupert must sneak out the back. When Snake comes…"

SHUN v. to keep away from; to avoid 기피하다
She shuns being photographed.
그 여자는 사진 찍히는 것을 기피한다.

Just then, Snake opened the door. He had changed out of his gangster clothes, and into a fishing outfit, yellow *slicker* and all. He still had his gun, though, and it was pointed straight at Babette.

"Yeah, sweetheart?" he asked. "I'm all ears. Tell me what you're going to do."

Babette stood frozen to the ground, speechless.

"I thought so," he sneered. "Cannibal, you've been very bad. Tie the girl back up."

Fortunately, he hadn't come into the room in time to hear Rupert speaking. Babette gave her new friend a little nod that told him it was okay to tie her up again. Her plan had been spoiled, and there was no sense in letting Snake find out that Rupert had turned against him.

Once she was secured in her chair, Snake picked up his speech where he had left off.

"It's show time, kids," he announced with a laugh. "The boats are loaded and we're off to *dampen* New Orleans. I **estimate** our sailing time will be about three hours, so we'd better get a move on if we're going to make it before dark. I'm going to *stuff* dynamite in every crack, **crevice**, and *cranny* along that little old levee."

Through the door of the hut came Verna, also dressed in fishing *gear*.

"What do you think, Snake" she asked, modeling her new outfit.

"Very convincing," he replied. "Now remember our **aliases**—we are Myra and Blake Turner, two ordinary people out to catch a mess of catfish."

"I thought your alias was Snake," said Bridget.

"That just shows what you know about gangsters," said Snake. "Snake is my pseudonym, but for special crimes, you have to use special aliases, see? Now, Cannibal, pick up these kids and put them in the big boat outside."

SLICKER n. long loose waterproof coat   비옷, 방수복
Fishermen used to wear slickers.
어부들은 예전에는 비옷을 입었다.

DAMPEN v. to make (something) damp   적시다
I always dampen shirts before ironing them.
나는 다리미질을 하기 전에 항상 셔츠를 적신다.

STUFF v. to fill something tightly (with something); cram something (with something)   쑤셔 넣다
Don't stuff him with silly ideas.
그에게 어리석은 생각들을 쑤셔 넣지 마라.

CRANNY n. small cavity or opening, e.g. in a wall   틈
I looked in all the nooks and crannies of our house for the misplaced letter.
나는 잃어버린 편지를 찾으려 집안 모든 구석과 틈들을 살펴보았다.

GEAR n. equipment, clothing, etc. needed for an expedition, a sport, etc.   장비, 차림
All his camping gear was packed in the rucksack.
배낭에 모든 캠핑 장비를 담았다.

Rupert obeyed, lifting all four captives and their chairs off the ground. It was a little difficult to get them through the door all tied together like that, but he managed without bumping them too much. In a matter of minutes, they were sitting on a boat, surrounded by piles of dynamite.

"We're going to *tow* you kids until we're almost there," explained Snake, "then we'll cut you loose and send you down the river ahead of us. And that's the last you'll hear from us until... KA-BOOM!"

Snake laughed, Verna *tee-heed*, and Rupert frowned. The three of them got into smaller boat, started the motor, and slowly pulled out into the water.

Several hours later, after they had been cut loose and sent on down the river, Babette finally thought it was safe to untie herself and her friends.

"I only hope Rupert can stop them in time without getting himself shot," she **fretted**, pacing up and down the boat. "We must try to attract the attention of the police and tell them what is happening."

"But how will we convince them that we aren't the ones up to no good?" asked Barnaby. "Why should they believe us, when we are completely surrounded by dynamite?"

"We must make them understand how **grave** the danger is," replied Babette, who was *flapping* her arms wildly in an effort to attract the attention of a passing *patrol* boat.

She succeeded in *hailing* it, but unfortunately, Barnaby was right. No matter how hard they tried to convince the police that the city was in **jeopardy**, the police refused to believe them.

"Please," begged Bridget, "we're wasting time. You have to stop Snake now or you'll have a **catastrophe** on your hands!"

The two river cops who had come aboard looked at each other and smiled.

TOW v. to pull (something) along with a rope, chain, etc. 묶은 채 끌고 가다
If you park your car here the police may tow it away.
여기에 차를 주차하면 경찰이 끌고 갈지도 모른다.

TEE-HEE(=te-hee) v. to titter; to snicker; to snigger; to giggle 히히 웃다
Don't tee-hee at the mistakes of others.
다른 사람의 실수를 보고 히히 웃지 마라.

FLAP v. to move, swing, wave, etc. up and down or from side to side, usually making a noise 흔들다
The bird flapped its wings and flew away.
새는 위아래로 날개를 흔들다가 날아 가버렸다.

PATROL n. going round to check that all is secure and orderly 순찰
The army makes hourly patrols of the area.
군대는 그 지역을 한 시간마다 순찰한다.

HAIL v. to call out in order to attract attention 불러 세우다
After our car stalled, we hailed passing cars to beg a ride.
우리 차 엔진이 멈춘 후에 우리는 얻어 타려고 지나가는 차들을 불러 세웠다.

"Now you must think we're awfully **gullible**," said one officer. "We weren't born yesterday. Here you are with a boatload of dynamite, and you expect us to think someone else in another boat is trying to blow up the levee. That's a real laugh."

Both cops *chuckled*, which enraged Bridget.

"How can you be so **callous** and insensitive? I'm trying to tell you the entire city is about to be flooded, and you seem completely **indifferent**! Well, if you two won't do something about this, I will!" she cried, running toward the edge of the boat.

Just as she swung her leg over the side and jumped, a huge explosion crashed through the air. When she came to the surface, *clumps* of grass and dirt were falling from the sky and the air was filled with smoke.

"Babette! Barnaby! Beauregard!" she called, treading water. "Answer me! Are you okay? Answer me!"

She heard coughing and *sputtering* not far from her. As the smoke cleared a little, she could see Beauregard swimming toward her. He didn't look at all happy. Two *dunks* in the Mississippi is two dunks too many for most cats.

"Beauregard!" she cried. "Where are the others?"

But her question was answered when a gust of wind cleared the air. At first she was relieved at what she saw: the levee was still there. The city was saved. But lying on the ground, completely motionless, were her friends.

"Oh, no!" she gasped. "Beauregard, quick, we have to get to them!"

They paddled as fast as they could against the current toward the embankment. Bridget gasped as she looked down at the **pallor** of her friends' faces. She was afraid they were dead. She *prodded* Babette, then Barnaby, with her foot.

CHUCKLE v. to laugh quietly or to oneself 낄낄 웃다
He chuckled to himself as he read the newspaper.
그는 신문을 읽으면서 혼자 낄낄거리며 웃었다.

CLUMP n. group or cluster 덩어리, 덤불
The boy hid in a clump of trees.
소년은 나무 덤불 속에 숨었다.

SPUTTER v. to make a series of spitting or popping sounds 푸푸하는 소리를 내다
The engine sputtered feebly for a while and then stopped.
그 엔진은 잠시 동안 약하게 푸푸하는 소리를 낸 다음 멈췄다.

DUNK v. to submerge (somebody/something) briefly in water 적시다, 물속에 넣다
They dunked her in the swimming pool as a joke.
그들은 재미로 그녀를 수영장 물속에 넣었다.

PROD v. to push or poke (somebody/something) with a finger or some other pointed object 찌르다
They prodded the animal through the bars of its cage.
그들은 동물 우리의 울타리 사이로 동물을 찔렀다.

"No, Mom, no!" yelled Barnaby, jumping to his feet. "You can't make me take ballet lessons! Get those tights away from me!"

"Barnaby, get *ahold* of yourself," cried Bridget, shaking her friend by the shoulders. "You must be **delirious** or something. No one is forcing you to wear tights."

"Ow," said Barnaby, rubbing his head.

Babette opend her eyes and sat up carefully. "Barnaby, are you okay?"

"Tights. Tight-fisted fish in a peddle of pickles," he said politely. "I said don't to be glimming my tulip, pilgrim. No, and no again! Time to pay the spleen!" Barnaby shook his fist in the air, then began staggering around as if he were **intoxicated**.

"Well, obviously he's **incoherent**," said Bridget. "He doesn't look seriously hurt, though. You were both knocked **unconscious** by the explosion."

"Explosion!" repeated Babette, pushing herself to her feet. "Quick! We must find Snake and Verna before they escape!"

They didn't have to go far. Not twenty yards away, Snake and Verna were having a knock-down-drag-out fight. Rupert was standing off to one side, watching with great amusement.

"You worm!" *screeched* Verna, scratching at Snake's eyes. "You're nothing but a big failure! You barely made a *dent* in this levee. Some explosives artist you are!"

"I told you, you twit, I was only an **apprentice** explosives artist," he growled, pulling her hair. "I still had a year's worth of study with the Master Blaster before I would have been certified. I told you it would be best if I **honed** my skills by trying some minor explosions first, but you wouldn't wait! Oh, no, you just kept on needling me, and bothering me and **harassing** me until I gave in!"

AHOLD **n.** a hold 잡기
He also passes notes to me during school and if the teacher got ahold of one I would just die in my seat.
그는 또한 수업 중에 나에게 쪽지들을 전달하는데 만일 선생님 손에 하나라도 들어가게 되면 나는 그 자리에 꼼짝 않고 있을 것이다.

SCREECH **v.** to give a harsh high-pitched cry 소리 지르다
The monkeys are screeching in the trees.
원숭이들이 나무에서 소리를 지르고 있다.

DENT **n.** hollow place in surface 움푹 들어간 곳, 홈
Did you see a dent in my car?
내 차에서 홈을 봤니?

"How was I to know you'd be so **inept** you couldn't even dynamite one little levee?" she squeaked, kicking his shins. "The only thing you have any skill for is adding up numbers!"

"That was a really low blow," yelled Snake. "Take that back right now!"

"No, no, no!" she *squealed*, beating her fists into his chest and sobbing. "We're ruined! We're doomed! And it's all your fault!"

Rupert must have finally had enough of this little **spat**, because he decided to **intervene**. He reached on arm over and pulled the upset woman away.

"Now, now, dear, you're getting **hysterical**," he said, holding her firmly about three feet off the ground. She didn't even notice that the man she called Cannibal was speaking to her, so angry and caught up was she in her **vain** attempts to free herself from his grasp. But Rupert was far stronger, and he had no intention of letting her go.

"Oh, officers!" he called to the two river patrolmen who had just wandered through the smoke. "I believe we have here a pair of criminals for you to arrest."

Sensing that he was about to be taken into *custody*, Snake began backing away, trying to lose himself in the smoke. But Babette had her eye on him the entire time.

"Not so fast, Caspar," she said, karate-kicking him across the knees. Then, standing over him with one foot at his throat, she began to feel quite pleased with herself. "Hmmm, let's see, what is that gangster phrase I'm looking for. Oh, yes—it's curtains for you, Caspar baby."

"Don't **gloat** yet, Frenchie," grunted the fallen accountant. "You may think you've won, but there's still going to be a trial, and I have lots of lawyer friends."

SQUEAL v. to make a high-pitched cry or sound; to say something in a squealing voice 우는 소리를 하다; 꿱꿱거리며 말하다
He squealed the words out.
그는 우는 소리로 말했다.

CUSTODY n. imprisonment while awaiting trial 구류, 감금
The magistrate remanded him in custody for two weeks.
치안 판사는 그에게 2주 동안의 구류를 명했다.

"Yeah?" said one of the cops, who had come to handcuff Snake. "Too bad about that. I'm sure plenty of right-minded citizens would like to **lynch** you up right now. Unfortunately, it's our job to make sure an angry mob doesn't string you up before you're tried before a fair and **impartial** jury. But you'll face the **gallows** sooner or later, I'm sure of that."

"Yeah, well don't count your money until the check clears," said Caspar as they led him away with Verna.

"Hey, you don't plan on leaving town any time soon, do you?" one of the cops asked Rupert. "It sure would speed things along if you *testified* against these two."

"I would be happy to **expedite** the proceedings in any way possible," replied the giant.

"Good, then you'd better come down to the station with us. And you kids had better not go anywhere, either," he said as they walked off. "We'll need your testimonies, too."

"Oh, sure," said Babette and Bridget, nodding as convincingly as possible. But as soon as the police were out of sight, all that changed.

"Man, let's get out of here!" said Bridget.

Babette agreed wholeheartedly. After they found Barnaby, who was still wandering around in a daze, and gathered up Beauregard, which was into some serious grooming, they discussed their options—or, more accurately, option.

"The way I see it," said Bridget, "the only way we're going to cover any serious ground and make up for lost time is by traveling by air again. Of course, that's what got us into this mess in the first place. Still, I don't see any way around it. Are you game?"

"Naturally," said Babette. "The situation can't get any worse."

"I almost wish you hadn't said that," replied Bridget with a little laugh.

A few minutes later, they were on their way up again, floating beneath an enormous pink bubble.

TESTIFY v. to give evidence; to declare as a witness, especially in court 증언하다
The teacher testified to the boy's honesty.
선생님은 그 소년의 정직함을 증언했다.

QUICK QUIZ (16)

Relationships

Decide what relationship the following pairs of words have to each other. If they mean close to the same thing, make "S." If they have opposite meanings, mark "O."

1. fraud :: hoax
2. pseudonym :: alias
3. subtle :: obtrusive
4. callous :: indifferent
5. malice :: depravity
6. opaque :: clear
7. introvert :: recluse
8. grimace :: smile
9. debauchery :: sinfulness
10. monotony :: variety
11. stagnant :: moving
12. unconscious :: awake
13. delirious :: clear-headed

QUICK QUIZ (17)

Relationships

Decide what relationship the following pairs of words have to each other. If they mean close to the same thing, make "S." If they have opposite meanings, mark "O."

1. jeopardy :: safety
2. apprentice :: expert
3. cannibal :: vegetarian
4. obscure :: reveal
5. polygamy :: monogamy
6. menace :: threat
7. incessant :: endless
8. dusk :: dawn
9. lure :: attract
10. hysterical :: calm
11. exhausted :: refreshed
12. ostracized :: rejected

QUICK QUIZ (18)

Fill in the Blank

For each sentence below, choose the word that best completes the sentence.

1. Bugsy Blaine, the bank robber, was caught by the police, but his _____ , who was waiting in the getaway car, escaped.

   a. decoy   b. accomplice   c. corpse   d. mutation

2. "We are out of fish today," said the waitress at Cap'n Briney's, "so please _____ everything on the menu except the salad and dessert sections."

   a. recount   b. interrogate   c. disregard   d. commend

3. We thought it was amazingly _____ of Barney to shake hands and sit at the same table with Richard, who was his worst enemy.

   a. modest   b. impartial   c. macho   d. civil

4. I was filled with _____ when I found out that my softball team had to forfeit the game because I didn't show up.

   a. chagrin   b. qualms   c. blackmail   d. lacerations

5. A major league umpire must use great _____ to tell the difference between strikes and balls in important baseball games.

   a. loot   b. momentum   c. discernment   d. pittance

6. Carol realized she had been _____ when she discovered the so-called "organic" cat litter she paid $20 for was nothing but ordinary sand.

   a. duped   b. barraged   c. dubbed   d. lynched

7. The babysitter saw Mark and Melanie beating each other over the head with their dinner plates, but she decided not to _____ , hoping that they could work out their differences themselves.

   a. gloat   b. emerge   c. arouse   d. intervene

Q U I C K   Q U I Z   (19)

Matching

Match each word on the right with a word on the left that has a meaning that's close to to the same.

1. locale	a. inescapable
2. genetic	b. reason
3. inevitable	c. weaken
4. frigid	d. sharp
5. brisk	e. lonely
6. metaphor	f. quick
7. languish	g. approve
8. exploit	h. location
9. levee	i. dike
10. motive	j. capture
11. advocate	k. take advantage
12. perceptive	l. inherit
13. apprehend	m. cold
14. solitary	n. comparison
15. expedite	o. speed up

Q U I C K   Q U I Z   (20)

Matching

Match each word on the right with a word on the left that has a meaning that's close to the same.

1. pantomiming	a. guess
2. estimate	b. disaster
3. crevice	c. unskillful
4. grave	d. crack
5. catastrophe	e. confused
6. gullible	f. paleness
7. pallor	g. hanging tree
8. intoxicated	h. gesturing
9. incoherent	i. sharpened
10. honed	j. easily fooled
11. harass	k. useless

12. inept   l. serious
13. vain   m. drunk
14. gallows   n. bother

Monks are Weird, but Wizards are Weirder

이상한 수도사들, 더 이상한 마법사들

You're probably wondering what happened to Snake and Verna. Well, it's an interesting story. Both of them were **indicted** on charges ranging from conspiracy to start a flood to attempted **manslaughter**, and both entered **pleas** of "not guilty." Lawyers for the *prosecution* got a little nervous that Snake might indeed have some kind of trick up his sleeve, so they granted Verna **immunity** from prosecution in exchange for her testimony—a fancy way of saying that they agreed not to send her to jail if she would agree to *rat* on Snake. And she ratted on him with great **gusto**, calling him all sorts of dirty names and accusing him of practically every unsolved crime in Louisiana—even dragging up some of his underhanded accounting jobs from way, way back. The jury didn't have to spend too much time **deliberating** before deciding on a **verdict** of "guilty on all counts," but no sooner had the judge *pounded* his **gavel** and said "court is *adjourned*," than Snake filed an appeal, accusing Verna of **perjury**. Unfortunately, false statements are **inadmissible** as evidence in a trial.

After all the paperwork was completed and the case was retried, the only thing Snake was *convicted* of was fishing without a license, for which he received the maximum sentence: a very stern **reprimand** from the judge. Imagine, after all that, Snake gets scolded and Verna gets off *scot-free*. Justice truly is blind.

But I should get back to the matter at hand. After we took off from New Orleans, everything went along smoothly for quite some time. We had great hopes of landing in close **proximity** to Paris—that is, until an albatross *collided* with Bridget's bubble and poked a big hole in it. After that, I can only assume we crashed because I don't remember anything except waking up in a very strange place...

PROSECUTION n. the act or process of carrying on a lawsuit 기소, 고발
The prosecution will be stopped if the stolen money is returned.
분실된 돈이 돌아오면 기소는 중단될 것이다.

RAT v. to reveal a secret; to betray somebody 배신하다
She's ratted on us. Here comes the head teacher!
그녀는 우리를 배신했다. 교장 선생님이 오시잖아!

POUND v. to hit (something) with repeated heavy blows 쾅쾅 두드리다
He pounded the door when we were having dinner
저녁을 먹고 있었을 때 그가 문을 쾅쾅 두드렸다.

ADJOURN v. to stop for a time; to postpone 휴정하다; 연기하다
The trial was adjourned until the following week.
재판은 다음 주까지 연기되었다.

CONVICT v. to declare in a law court that somebody is guilty (of a crime) 유죄를 선고하다
She has twice been convicted of fraud.
그녀는 사기죄로 두 번 유죄선고 받았다.

SCOT-FREE adv. without punishment or harm 처벌을 받지 않고
The accused escaped scot-free because of lack of evidence.
그 피의자는 증거 부족으로 처벌을 받지 않고 풀려났다.

COLLIDE v. to strike violently against something or each other 부딪치다
As the bus turned the corner, it collided with a truck.
버스가 모퉁이를 돌다가 트럭과 부딪쳤다.

Bridget slowly opened one eye, then the other, and looked around without moving her head. She couldn't see much, really, just a high, gray, domed ceiling faintly lit by a light source she couldn't see. She tried to sit up, but an **acute** pain shot through her head and she lay back down on her cot.

"You shouldn't try to move," said a calm, deep, man's voice. "You've been very ill. You are beginning to recover."

"Who are you?" groaned Bridget. "Whare am I? Where are my friends?"

"So many questions," said the voice. "You are safe. Your friends are in another room. They, too, are **convalescing** from the illness."

"You make it sound as if we've been here a while," said Bridget. "Just how long have I been lying here?"

"It is impossible to say. Time is a **labyrinth**, full of twists and turns—and sometimes dead ends. You may have been here forever. Perhaps you have not yet arrived. No one can be certain," replied the voice.

Bridget tried to roll her eyes, but it hurt too much. "Look, that's very interesting, but it's a little too **ambiguous** for me. Just tell me what time it was, or what day it was, when we got here, and what time or day it is now, okay?"

"Child, don't you see? Your **query** is meaningless. Time is a **myth**. It doesn't exist, at least not as you think of it. It is a fairy tale for people with weak minds."

"Hmmm," said Bridget. "You said before that it was a maze. Well, if time is a *maze*, I can find my way out, right?"

"Ah, and what is beyond the walls of time? That is the question," boomed the voice.

MAZE n. a network of paths through which it is hard to find one's way 미로
A guide led us through the maze of tunnels in the cave.
안내인은 동굴속 미로 같은 터널을 제대로 통과하도록 우리를 안내했다.

Bridget decided it was high time for some action. She pushed herself up into a sitting position and sat very still for a few seconds. The room seemed to be spinning around and she felt dizzy. Finally, the whirling stopped and she looked around.

The room was very old, like one of those ancient churches her parents had dragged her to before she lost them. The difference was that this place was much more **austere**. There were no brightly colored glass windows, no flowers, no furniture except her cot, nothing to liven up the **solemn** gray room except the plain white candles which *flickered* here and there. A small fire burned in a large stone fireplace.

Sitting cross-legged in the firelight was a small man with a flowing gray beard. He seemed unbelievably old, but somehow also young and full of energy. Bridget stared at him in wonder.

"Does your head hurt much?" he asked, "I can give you something to **alleviate** the pain."

"No, I feel fine," said Bridget, getting off the cot and trying to stand up. "Look, I want to go talk to my friends. Where are they?"

"Child, you must sit!" ordered the old man, lifting his hand in a commanding gesture.

Bridget fell back down on the cot, almost as if the man had given her a *shove*. Something very mysterious was going on here.

"I do not mean to use force," he sighed, "but I cannot **condone** such silly behavior. You have been ill. Your dizzy *spells* are likely to **recur**. You must **heed** my advice, or you will surely hurt yourself. Have a drink of water. Rest a while. Then you may walk about—but *slowly*."

"Yeah, sure," said Bridget.

FLICKER v. to burn or shine unsteadily 깜박이다
All the lights flickered for a moment.
모든 불이 잠시 동안 깜박였다.

SHOVE n. an act of moving forward; push 떼밀기
He gave the boat a shove which sent it far out into the water.
그가 보트를 떼밀자 보트는 물속으로 멀리 갔다.

SPELL n. a period of time of anything 한동안, 계속, 한참
There was a long spell of rainy weather in April.
4월에 오랫동안 비 오는 날씨가 이어졌다.

The old man brought her a glass of cool water, and they sat in silence for a long time. It didn't seem as though he was going to say anything, so Bridget decided to strike up a conversation.

"So, this is where you live, huh?" she remarked. "No offense, but it's kind of **ascetic**. The furnishings are a bit **scanty**—no television, no books, no stereo, no chairs. You don't even have a rug. What is this, a prison or something?"

"This is a monastery. I am a monk," the man answered.

"A monk? That means you belong to some kind of religious **sect**, right?" she asked.

"In a way," he replied. "My brothers and I have devoted our lives to the Eternal."

"You have brothers?"

"Brothers in the spiritual sense," he explained. "We follow no organized religion, however. Our practices are not what most people would consider **orthodox**. I'll admit, we are unusual. When we first came together, other religious men and women accused us of **heresy**. Of course, nowadays I'm told people use that word to describe any idea or opinion that seems strange, but back then heresy was a serious crime. We were forced to withdraw from society—but not before several of our brothers were taken prisoner by the **clergy** of another religion. Those clergymen, supposedly so **pious** and devoted, tortured our brothers to force them to **repent** their so-called sins. But of course it is impossible to regret something if you don't feel it is wrong. Many of them died horrible deaths."

Bridget squirmed uncomfortably. This conversation was getting gloomy and depressing.

"I am sorry," said the monk. "I have a tendency to get a bit **morbid** when I think about the past. You seem to be feeling better. For a while there you were hanging in that *hazy* **limbo** between consciousness and sleep. But now I think you are perfectly **lucid**—no more mixed-up talk about dancing jackals and spaceships, right?"

HAZY **adj.** misty 어렴풋한
We couldn't see far because it was so hazy.
너무 흐려서 멀리 볼 수가 없었다.

He smiled a kind and **benevolent** smile. He was so well-meaning she didn't have the heart to tell him that the dancing jackals and the spaceship were real. She decided to let him think he had cured her.

"Yeah, whew!" she said. "I'm glad I'm more clear-headed now. It's all thanks to you, um, what's your name?"

"You can call me Brother Gruffydd. You are Bridget, I gather. Come, now. I hereby **deem** you healthy enough to walk around. Let us go check on your friends."

Without any visible movement of his legs, Gruffydd was standing. Or, rather, he appeared to be floating just above the ground. Bridget couldn't be sure, because his long white robe covered his feet. He just sort of drifted along ahead of her toward a small door at the opposite end of the room.

On the other side of the door was another room that looked exactly the same as the first. Babette and Barnaby lay stretched out on two simple cots, and another old monk, with a long, flowing, gray beard was sitting in front of another fire. She was about to ask Gruffydd about Beauregard, when she was *toppled* over by a hundred pounds of leaping cat.

Beauregard was obviously happy to see her. He was rubbing his head on her chin, his *purrs* were deafening, and he even gave her face a couple of rough licks.

"Remarkable," said the old monk by the fire. "That cat has been absolutely **listless**. He refused to eat or drink or even move, for that matter. I was beginning to think he was either very lazy or very bored. I guess he just missed you."

"I guess so," agreed Bridget, who had just struggled out from under the affectionate, hairy, hundred pounds. "I'm glad to see he's doing alright. But how are Babette and Barnaby?"

"Ask them yourself," said the monk. He waved his hand, and suddenly, their eyes fluttered open.

TOPPLE **v.** to be unsteady and fall 넘어지다
The pile of books toppled over onto the floor.
책 더미가 바닥으로 무너졌다.

PURR **n.** a low continuous vibrating sound 그르렁거리는 소리
You can hear the contented purrs of the cat.
너는 고양이가 만족스럽게 그르렁거리는 소리를 들을 수 있을 거야.

Babette leaped up from her cot and assumed a fighting pose, her hands up and ready for combat.

"Relax, Babette," urged Bridget. "You're not in any danger."

"That's a relief," she sighed, letting down her guard. "Where are we? How did we get here?"

"We found you while we were out gathering herbs," answered one of the old monks. "You were very weak, and had **succumbed** to some sort of fever. The illness was especially **virulent** in you, much more intense and dangerous than what your companions experienced. We brought you here to make sure you recovered safely."

"That is very kind," Babette replied. "May I ask what sort of place this is? What is your name?"

"My name is Brother Owain. This is Brother Gruffydd," he said, with a small wave toward the floating monk. "You are in our monastery."

Over on his cot, Barnaby began to *moan*.

"Oh, oh!" he groaned, "I'm dying. I'm *paralyzed*. Help! Get a doctor!"

"You are in no danger of dying, my son," said Owain. "You are perfectly healthy."

"You must be mistaken. I have a bandaged foot that is obviously paralyzed. I must see a specialist," insisted Barnaby.

"I'm afraid you had a large *splinter* caught in your heel. We gave you a mild **anesthetic** so we could remove the splinter without hurting you. The feeling will return to your foot in a few minutes," explained the monk.

"I don't need some mad monk telling me I'm not dying! I feel my life just slipping away! It's probably your fault, too! You probably poisoned me with some of those herbs your were just talking about!" yelled Barnaby.

MOAN v. to make a sound, usually expressing regret, pain or suffering 끙끙거리다
The wind was moaning through the trees.
바람이 나무 사이를 누비며 신음소리를 내고 있었다.

PARALYZE v. to affect (somebody) with paralysis 마비시키다
The accident left her paralyzed from the waist down.
그 사고로 그녀는 하반신이 마비되었다.

SPLINTER n. small thin sharp piece of wood, metal, glass, etc. 가시
I've got a splinter in my finger.
내 손가락에 가시가 박혔다.

"Shut up, Barnaby," snapped Bridget. "Quit being such a **hypochondriac**. You are perfectly healthy. I think you should apologize to Brother Owain. He's shown a lot of **forbearance** by not giving you a punch in the nose for being so rude."

"Nonsense, child," said the monk. "Violence has no place here."

"Yes, well, sorry," said Barnaby, pushing himself into a sitting position and feeling a little embarrassed by his outburst. "We scientists have a history of being at odds with men of religion. I think it's a healthy competition, but I'm sorry if I **affronted** you. Thank you for helping us."

Owain nodded his head slightly, but said nothing.

"Where are we?" Barnaby whispered to his friends. "I've had the most amazing memory **lapse**. Last thing I remember, I was standing in a boat talking to some police officers."

"I can explain all that later," Bridget whispered back. "But I think we should figure out what our situation here is. All I can tell so far is that these monks are really old, kind of *spooky*, and that they give **vague** answers to the simplest questions. I asked what time it was, and all I got was some kind of *mumbo-jumbo* about time being a maze."

"I'm sorry if you think we're being unclear," said Owain, which shocked Bridget because she didn't think he could hear her. "We are not used to speaking with people who look at things the way you do. Please ask any questions you like, and we will make an **earnest** attempt to give you **explicit** answers."

Since Bridget and Barnaby were still too surprised at being overheard so easily, Babette decided to ask the first question.

SPOOKY adj. frightening 겁나는
We stayed a night in the spooky old house.
우리는 무시무시한 고가(古家)에서 하룻밤을 지냈다.

MUMBO-JUMBO n. meaningless or unnecessarily complicated language 알아들을 수 없는 말
These government forms are full of such mumbo-jumbo, I can't understand them at all.
이 정부 문서 양식은 알아들을 수 없는 말로 가득 차서 하나도 이해할 수가 없다.

"I hope I may be completely **candid** and honest with you, brothers," said Babette. "Frankly, there is something strange about you both. You seem so very old, yet you do not look it. You have odd, **supernatural** powers, almost like magic. And this place is unlike any monastery I've ever seen. Please tell us how you came here."

"Yeah, what's your story?" asked Bridget.

Both monks chuckled.

"Our story, you ask? Very well, then," said Owain, "I will tell you. Yes, looking at time the way you do, you could say we are very old. Over nine centuries old, in fact."

"Are you **immortal**, then?" asked Babette.

"Oh, no. We are humans just like you, and just like you, we will die eventually. We owe our **longevity** to the many secrets of nature we have learned through the years. We are not **susceptible** to the same illnesses as most people. There are special herbs that grow only here on a little corner of this island. They give us **immunity** to the diseases of the body, and our beliefs help us develop other special powers."

"It all started when Pope Urban II called on the European noblemen to make a long **expedition** to the Holy Land. A 'crusade,' he called it. Our goal was to *reclaim* the **hallowed** city of Jerusalem from the **heathens**, as we used to call anyone who wasn't Jewish or Christian.

"The problem we didn't realize at the time was that Jerusalem was holy to the Muslims, too, and naturally they didn't want to give it up to a bunch of Europeans who just showed up out of nowhere. But we knights were practically burning up with religious **fervor**. We were ready to do anything to **vanquish** the heathens and take back our city (even though, technically speaking, it never had been our city)."

RECLAIM v. to bring back to a useful good condition 교정(개선)하다, 개심 시키다
Society reclaims criminals by teaching them skills.
사회는 기술을 가르쳐서 죄수들을 개선한다.

"You were knights in the First Crusade," Babette observed. "I have always wondered, how did the pope convince you to go to a faraway land to fight people who had simply been minding their own business?"

"It is difficult to understand," Gruffydd offered. "But you should know, Owain and I, and many of our brothers, were not always peaceful men. Before the Crusade, we had **lavish** lifestyles devoted to feasting, chasing women, and fighting each other. We gave in to every **base** human desire. Urban II was an **eloquent** and persuasive pope. Not only did he appeal to our love of battle by promising us a jolly good war, complete with blood, guts, and **gore**, but he said that by fighting for the Holy Land we would be washed clean of all our sins in the process."

"It seemed like a great idea at the time," agreed Owain. "But once we got there, we realized that what was happening was no ordinary war. It was **genocide**. The other crusaders seemed bent on the **eradication** of the entire Muslim population. We like a fight as much as the next knight, but the *slaughter* we saw in Jerusalem and Antioch and Ashkalon left even us **aghast**."

Owain fell silent, as if remembering those long-ago battles.

Gruffydd picked up where he left off. "To make matters worse, the people we were fighting were hardly the *barbarians* we had been told. They had an extremely rich culture, well-developed sciences, medicine, poetry, art, music, and architecture. How **conceited** we Europeans were, to think our way of life was so superior! Compared to them, *we* were the barbarians.

"Even though the war was going well, many of us decided to **desert** the army and **renounce** violence for good. We didn't even know each other at the time, but somehow, separately, we all came to the same decision. We just threw down our arms and wandered off into the desert.

"I wandered along for many days and nights without food or water. Finally, just when I thought I was about to die of thirst, I saw what looked like a palm tree and a pool of water in the distance. And around the pool stood dozens of men in shining white robes."

SLAUGHTER n. the killing of many people at once; massacre 집단 학살
The battle resulted in a frightful slaughter.
전투 결과 무시무시한 대량 학살이 일어났다.

BARBARIAN n. a person belonging to a people or a tribe that is not civilized 야만인
Rome was conquered by the barbarians.
로마는 야만인들에 의해 정복되었다.

"I thought at first I was seeing things, that it was just a **mirage**. But as I got closer, I could see that it was an actual **oasis**. Trees and flowers grew there and the breeze rippled the blue waters of the pond and the robes of these strange men. So shocked was I by their appearance that I almost forgot my thirst. I was covered in dirt and blood and sweat, yet these men seemed to glow from within, and their white clothing was spotless and **immaculate**. They seemed not to notice me as I fell to my knees at the edge of the pool and began *scooping* water to my mouth with my hands. Then I felt a pair of hands shoving me from behind, and I fell soundlessly into the deep blue water."

"It was I who pushed him," said Owain.

"But why?" asked Barnaby. "Were you trying to drown him?"

"No, of course not, don't you see?" replied the monk. "We had all been bathed in those waters. We came there as ugly men, some of us Muslims and some Crusaders, with sick bodies and even sicker hearts. Those waters changed us inside and out. I wanted him to undergo the same **metamorphosis** so he could feel the same overwhelming joy, the same ecstasy as we had."

Owain paused again, but by this time, Babette, Barnaby, and Bridget were so **engrossed** in the story they weren't about to let him stop.

"What happened to you all?" they demanded together.

"It is impossible to explain," answered Gruffydd.

The children grumbled with disappiontment.

"I can tell you bits and pieces. First, I saw a beautiful, mysterious woman who told me things without speaking. I felt burning beams of light that did not hurt me. I held the whole weight of the world in my arms, but I was as light as a *snowflake*," he said.

SCOOP v. to lift something with, or as if with, a scoop   퍼 올리다
He scooped the coins up in his hands.
그는 두 손으로 동전들을 퍼 올렸다.

SNOWFLAKE n. any one of the soft small collections of ice crystals that fall as snow   눈송이
Snowflakes are melting as they reach the ground.
눈송이들은 땅에 닿자마자 녹는다.

"But that's impossible!" said Barnaby. "You can't be heavy and light at the same time. And you can't be burned without pain."

"There are mysteries in the world, my boy, that cannot be broken down and explained by science. Whatever that pool contained is an **enigma** that cannot be logically accounted for, but something that must be experienced and grasped whole.

"Yet in a way, exactly what or who we saw in the water is **irrelevant**. What matters is *how* we were transformed. I was **overwhelmed**, completely overcome, by feelings of happiness and peace. I have no idea how long I remained beneath the surface, but I was returned to the world on a blast of steam and water that shot me many yards into the air, then suddenly disppeared as quickly as it started. A **geyser**, I believe it is called.

"My brothers welcomed me back, and I noticed that I was now one of them—the same glowing skin, the same white robe. So many things had changed within me. I realized that wealth and beauty and fame and many other human achievements are nothing but passing joys, as **ephemeral** as the morning dew that is gone before the day has even begun. We decided to give up the pursuit of glory and devote our lives to helping the needy, healing the sick, and other such acts of **philanthropy**. But, as I told you before, Bridget, people wouldn't accept us. Other monks told terrible lies about our actions and our characters, the most vicious **slander** you can imagine."

"We were forced to withdraw to the island of Cyprus, where you find yourselves now," continued Owain. "After the Crusade, Cyprus became a **mecca** for *misfits*. The war changed people, and many did not wish to return to their old lives. Here we were not bothered by the outside world. But now we know it is time to share our knowledge with others, for the Great and Powerful Oz has spoken to us."

MISFIT n. person not well suited to his work or his surroundings   사회 부적응자
He always felt a bit of a misfit in the business world.
그는 사업상 항상 자신이 약간 사회 부적응자라고 느꼈다.

Bridget gasped with surprise at the monk's last words.

"Hold it, brother," she said. "What do you mean, 'the Great and Powerful Oz'? Hey, Barnaby, Babette, check this out. I think we're actually stuck in Euro-Disney exhibit. We're closer to Paris than we think!"

"Child, you are making less sense than usual," said Gruffydd. "I hope your illness is not returning. But do I understand from what you are saying that you are trying to reach Paris?"

"That's right," said Bridget.

"Well, then, perhaps we should take you to the wizard himself. After all, he descended from the sky. He must have the power to get you home."

"Sure, I've always wanted to meet the Wizard of Oz," she said.

"Come, then," said the monk. "We're off to see the wizard."

"Oh, boy," Bridget muttered under her breath. "Sometimes life is just like a movie."

The two floating monks led the travelers down a long corridor to a huge metal door. Owain knocked three times, turned and said good-bye, then both monks vanished into thin air.

"Remarkable," said Barnaby.

Slowly the metal door swung open. Beyond it was a large room with a domed ceiling. The air was filled with smoke, an amazing laser light show was going on, and strange pictures were being *projected* on the walls, probably by a hidden movie projector.

"Cool," said Bridget. "I haven't seen anything like this since the last Pink Floyd tour."

PROJECT v. to show (a film) on a screen using a film projector   투영(투사)하다, 비추다
Will you be able to project the film for us?
우리를 위해 그 영화를 틀어줄 수 있니?

A voice boomed from some speakers in the ceiling. "I am the Great and Powerful Oz!"

"Can it, *bub*," replied Bridget. "I'm not some thousand-year-old monk. Come out from whatever curtain you're hiding behind."

"Huh?" boomed the voice through the speakers.

"Sir, whoever you are," said Barnaby, "we know the Wizard of Oz is a **fictional** character. You appear to have these monks fooled. We don't especially care about that, but there is an off chance you can help us get back to Paris."

Suddenly, a man in a magician's suit, complete with black cape, appeared through a hidden door. He wasn't very tall. He had black hair and a pencil-thin black mustache. And he was definitely walking on the ground.

"Are you from the publisher's office?" he asked as he walked forward. "At last, my work will be recognized! I knew you'd like the idea. I think the title should be 'How to Live Forever Without Really Trying,' part adventure story, part cookbook. It's such a **novel** idea, don't you agree? It's the newest idea in **prose** since *In Cold Blood!* Why... oh no. You're only children."

The man sighed, greatly disappointed.

"What are you talking about?" asked Bridget. "Who are you, anyway?"

"Well, you might as well know," he said. "It seems my book will never be published anyway. I am the Amazing Mumpo. At least, that was my stage name back when I was a famous magician. I had five shows a week in Las Vegas—and the occasional television special. You're probably too young to remember."

BUB **n.** a childish term for a brother, also used in familiar address to any boy or man   소년, 젊은 친구
Come on, you bubs, let's get going!
이봐, 젊은이들, 가보자고!

Barnaby, Bridget, and Babette had to admit he was right.

"My real name is Milton. Milton Fenlich," he continued, offering his hand for shaking. Introductions were made all around.

"I hope I didn't seem too rude just now," said Milton. "It's just that I've been working on this book for years. I've been **tantalized** by visions of my great work, published in hardcover, attractively displayed in shop windows, and eager customer lining up to buy it. But it's a goal that seems forever out of reach."

"You have no idea how difficult writing a book is. You have to set yourself a schedule and have the **discipline** to stick to it. And you must be **diligent** enough to keep at it. Oh, I worked so hard! But my manuscript has been rejected by every publisher I've sent it to! I'm worthless and so is my book!"

"Come on, there is no need to **wallow** around in a *puddle* of self-pity. Maybe you can fix the book up so they will like it more. Did they say why they rejected it?" asked Babette, feeling sorry for the magician.

"They said my writing was bad. Oh, sure, my sentences may not have the **euphony** of a Shakespearean sonnet, but at least I was getting a point across. Can't they see what a great idea it is? Even if my writing is bad, surely they could hire a **ghostwriter** to do the writing and still credit me as the author. It is my idea, after all."

Milton sighed heavily again. "It's those monks I feel really bad about. You see, I was doing some shows in Greece years ago, and I rented a little airplane to get from island to island. I had just gotten my pilot's licence a couple of weeks earlier. Anyway, I ran into some rough weather one night and *wound up* making an emergency landing here. The monks saw me coming down out of the sky and, well, they thought I was some kind of powerful wizard. Luckily I had all my gear with me, so I went ahead and did my act. It really *wowed* them. Especially the laser show. After that, they kind of **nominated** me 'head holy man.' I figured it was better to be a head holy man than a *cheesy* Vegas magician, so I decided to stay." He chuckled to himself.

PUDDLE n. small pool of water, especially of rainwater on the road   물웅덩이
The children always play in the puddle of rain water.
그 아이들은 항상 빗물 웅덩이에서 논다.

WIND v. (wind up의 형태로 쓰여) to arrive finally in a place; to end up   마침내 ~에 도착하다; ~으로 끝나다
We eventually wound up staying in a little hotel by the sea.
우리는 마침내 바닷가에 있는 작은 호텔에서 묵게 되었다.

WOW v. to fill (somebody) with admiration or enthusiasm   신나게 하다
The new musical wowed them on Broadway.
브로드웨이에서 하는 새 뮤지컬은 사람들을 열광시켰다.

CHEESY adj. of low quality; inferior   값싼; 하급의
I don't like to go to a cheesy restaurant.
나는 싸구려 음식점에 가고 싶지 않다.

"And you know what? These monks actually pay **homage** to me. They bow before me, show me respect, and do anything I say. For example, there's no photocopy machine here, so I had them spend hours **transcribing** copy after copy of my manuscript by hand. Monks have great hand-writing, you know. Except for that Owain guy. His writing is practically **illegible**. Anyway, I keep telling them that they'll be doing the world a service, and they seem to like that idea very much, but I still can't help feeling a little guilty."

"Hey," said Bridget, who didn't like the idea of the magician taking such advantage of the monks. "This book you wrote—I don't suppose it **discloses** all the secrets these monks have spent centuries learning about?"

"What if it does?" replied Milton defensively. "They say they want to help people. And when the world finds out these guys have kept themselves alive for nine hundred years with their little *potions* and teas, people will be beating down the door to get to them."

"But don't you see?" said Babette. "The herbs that they use only grow on a small part of this island. People will come here by the thousands, picking their plants and *roaming* through their halls. These monks are from a time when faith and honor meant something. You will completely destroy their way of life!"

"I don't think they'll *squawk* too much about it when they start getting some money from the book sales," he replied. "Ten percent of the profits will be **earmarked** for donation to the monastery. That should keep them happy."

"How can you be such a **cynic**?" cried Babette. "Not everyone is selfish and greedy like you!"

"Oh yeah? Well, you're just a kid. Wait until you get a little older. You'll find out I'm right," he said.

Babette looked as if she was about to give the magician a swift kick, but Bridget put her hand on her friend's arm to calm her down.

POTION n. a drink, especially one used as a medicine or poison, or in magic (약이나 독이나 마법에서 쓰는) 물약, 소량
The magician displayed his charms and potions.
마법사는 자신의 부적과 약들을 보여주었다.

ROAM v. to walk or travel without any definite aim or destination   어슬렁거리다
He used to roam the streets for hours on end.
그는 몇 시간 동안 계속해서 거리를 어슬렁거리곤 했다.

SQUAWK v. to utter a loud harsh cry   불평하다
The parrot squawked loudly.
앵무새가 큰소리로 울어댔다.

"Listen, Milton, it looks like we disagree on this subject," she said. "We don't want these monks hurt. They've helped us. But our main problem is that we need to get back to Paris as soon as possible. I don't suppose you could help us with that, could you?"

"I'd love to get rid of you kids, but I'm afraid I *dismantled* the plane long ago and used the parts to **augment** my film and laser display. It needed *beefing* up, you know? The Great and Powerful Oz deserves a great and powerful show. No, I'm afraid the only way off this island is by boat, and I don't have one of those either. Anyway, you'd need a compass to keep you pointed in the right direction."

Barnaby began scratching his head. Bridget and Babette looked at each other hopefully. And sure enough, something came tumbling out of his hair. Babette stooped to pick it up.

"Is it a compass?" asked Bridget.

"No, it is a book," she sighed. Barnaby seemed disappointed. "Do not worry, Barnaby. We cannot rely on your hair for everything. At least we have something to read."

Looking down at the cover, however, Babette's face brightened. She gave Bridget a wink, then turned toward Milton.

"Well, we must be on our way," she said. "I hope your writing improves."

"Get lost," muttered the would-be author.

Beauregard, Babette, Bridget, and Barnaby were happy to **oblige**. Once they were back out in the hall, Babette began looking around for the monks.

"Where do you think they are?" she asked. "Owain? Gruffydd? Brothers?"

Suddenly, the two monks appeared, floating ahead of her.

DISMANTLE v. to take (something) to pieces   해체하다
We should dismantle our inefficient tax system.
우리는 우리의 비효율적인 세금 제도를 깨버려야 한다.

BEEF v. to add force or weight to something   강화하다
The new evidence beefed up their case.
새 증거가 그들의 주장을 강화시켜 주었다.

"Yes, child?" said Owain. "I hope the wizard has helped you."

"Well, actually, we prefer to **solve** our own problems. Why don't you three go down to the shore and find us a good place to set sail from," she said to her friends. "I want to say good-bye to the monks."

After thanking the brothers for their help, Bridget, Barnaby, and Beauregard left the dark monastery and walked out into the bright sunlight and down to the shore. Most of the beach was rocky, but they soon found a patch of soft sand where they sat and waited for Babette.

A few minutes later, she came strolling down the beach.

"Are you all ready?" she asked. "Bridget, we'll need another bubble, I suppose. France is west of here, that is all I know."

"Wait a minute, Babette, what did you tell those monks?" asked Barnaby.

"I told them that sometimes the best way to help people is to let them make their own mistakes," she said. "And I told them Milton is no wizard."

"Did they believe you?"

"No. But then I gave them the book: *The Grand Illusion: The History of Motion Pictures from 1918 to the Present*. It should explain Milton's little light show. I do not think he will be head holy man for long."

Everyone was *relieved*. As Bridget prepared to blow her boat, Babette offered one last detail.

"You know, the cover of the book had such a lovely picture on it. An *adorable* little dog and a girl with shiny red shoes. I wonder if you can guess what movie it was from," she demanded with a grin.

Bridget and Barnaby *shrugged*.

"*The Wizard of Oz!*" she answered, laughing. "But of course!"

RELIEVE v. to lessen or remove (pain, distress, anxiety, etc.) (고통, 걱정 따위를) 덜다
This drug will relieve your discomfort.
이 약이 너의 불안감을 없애줄 것이다.

ADORABLE adj. very attractive; delightful; lovable 귀여운
Your dress is absolutely adorable.
네 드레스는 정말 귀엽다.

SHRUG v. to raise (one's shoulders) slightly to express doubt, indifference, ignorance, etc. (의심, 무관심, 무시 등을 나타내기 위해) 어깨를 으쓱하다
I asked her where Sam was, but she just shrugged her shoulders.
나는 샘이 어디에 있냐고 물었는데 그녀는 어깨만 으쓱했다.

Relationships

Decide what relationship the following pairs of words have to each other. If they mean close to the same thing, make "S." If they have opposite meanings, mark "O."

1. ambiguous :: explicit
2. indicted :: accused
3. austere :: solemn
4. lavish :: scanty
5. orthodoxy :: heresy
6. aghast :: shocked
7. eradicate :: vanquish
8. ephemeral :: permanent
9. augment :: increase
10. base :: pious
11. ascetic :: luxurious
12. philanthropy :: genocide
13. prose :: poetry

Relationships

Decide what relationship the following pairs of words have to each other. If they mean close to the same thing, make "S." If they have opposite meanings, mark "O."

1. condone :: approve
2. susceptible :: immune
3. slander :: praise
4. alleviate :: ease
5. enigma :: mystery
6. benevolent :: virulent
7. hallowed :: holy
8. verdict :: decision
9. gusto :: listlessness
10. affronted :: offended
11. vague :: lucid
12. disclose :: hide

Fill in the Blank

For each sentence below, choose the word that best completes the sentence.

1. Sheila refused to _____ smashing all of her brother's model airplanes with the heel of her shoe—she said she'd do it again in a heartbeat.

   a. recur   b. succumb   c. repent   d. renounce

2. I used to think the Amazing Melvin had _____ powers, but now I see he just used tricks and mirrors to fool us into thinking he really could do magic.

   a. supernatural   b. immortal   c. inadmissible   d. immaculate

3. John congratulated his sister on her _____, because it was her moving and persuasive speech that finally made their father give them permission to go to the concert by themselves.

    a. perjury   b. forbearance   c. longevity   d. eloquence

4. My embarrassment was _____ when I discovered my skirt had been tucked into the back of my pantyhose since I came out of the bathroom an hour ago.

    a. acute   b. conceited   c. earnest   d. irrelevant

5. Miriam was _____ in Colonel Thompson's stories about big game hunting in Africa, so she didn't even notice that her date had left with another woman.

    a. overwhelmed   b. disciplined   c. engrossed   d. nominated

6. Until I saw one with my own eyes, I always thought the existence of werewolves was just a silly _____ .

    a. mirage   b. myth   c. geyser   d. oasis

7. David Livingstone led an important _____ to try to find the source of the Nile River.

    a. sect   b. clergy   c. limbo   d. expedition

8. The aliens finally returned Kevin to earth, but he had a huge _____ in his memory, so he couldn't tell us what he'd been doing for the past twelve years.

    a. lapse   b. fervor   c. ecstasy   d. proximity

9. Mary was such a hardened _____ that she believed that most charities were just scams to cheat people out of their money.

    a. anesthetic   b. hypochondriac   c. ghostwriter   d. cynic

10. After Phyllis caught the flu, the mumps, and the chicken pox one right after another, her parents sent her to her grandmother in Florida so she could _____ .

    a. wallow   b. deliberate   c. tantalize   d. convalesce

Q U I C K   Q U I Z (24)

Matching

Match each word on the right with a word on the left that has a meaning that's close to the same.

1. query	a. gloomy
2. mecca	b. question
3. heed	c. accidental killing
4. plea	d. center
5. morbid	e. request
6. deem	f. declare
7. gore	g. abandon
8. manslaughter	h. mallet
9. gavel	i. listen to
10. desert	j. blood

Matching

Match each word on the right with a word on the left that has a meaning that's close to the same.

1. metamorphosis
2. labyrinth
3. novel
4. reprimand
5. diligent
6. euphony
7. heathen
8. homage
9. transcribe
10. illegible
11. earmark

a. maze
b. set aside
c. dedicated
d. transformation
e. respect
f. new
g. pleasant sound
h. unreadable
i. scold
j. non-believer
k. copy

Heir We Go Again

Again 이번엔 후계자라니

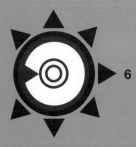

6

Setting sail from Cyprus on a bubble boat went pretty smoothly. It wasn't the fastest way to travel, but Bridget's bubble balloon had proven hazardous to our health recently, and we decided we'd better play it safe. The problem was, we only had a general idea of which direction to take. Barnaby once again showed how diverse his scientific talents were by using his knowledge of *astronomy* for the purpose of nocturnal navigation—that is, steering at night. He knew the names and positions of quite a few of the stars, and when you know where the stars are, you know where you are. More or less, anyway. Bridget, for all her *street-smarts*, and Barnaby, for all his genius, and Babette, for all her worldly wisdom, didn't know enough about plain old geography to figure exactly which way France was.

So, we wound up stopping to ask directions a lot, and it's a good thing Babette was there. She has an **innate** talent for picking up foreign languages. It truly is something you're born with, I think. I can only speak four or five, myself, no matter how hard I try, but Babette hears a few words, and the next thing you know she's chattering away with ease. Anyway, we stopped off at several of the Greek islands, but Babette kept getting conflicting advice, so once again we were left to our own devices. Nevertheless, we seemed to be making reasonable progress until, as we got out to look for food on a very small, deserted island, we were suddenly swept off our feet and left swinging upside down in a net that was hanging from a tree.

"This is making me really dizzy," groaned Bridget, who was struggling mightily to get herself free of the net.

Barnaby was taking a more **passive** approach. "Look, Bridget," he said. "It doesn't do any good to struggle. You're just *tangling* us up more. Just keep still."

But Bridget wasn't the kind of girl who could calmly hang upside down on a strange island.

ASTRONOMY n. scientific study of the sun, moon, stars, planets, etc. 천문학
My favorite subject is astronomy.
내가 가장 좋아하는 과목은 천문학이다.

STREET-SMART adj. (=street-wise) familar with local people and their problems; wise to the ways and needs of people on the street
도시 물정에 밝은
No mayor can function effectively unless he has around him competent and street-smart people who can assume much of his responsibility.
시장은 주변에서 책임져 줄 수 있는 유능하고 도시 물정에 밝은 사람이 없으면 효과적으로 직무를 수행할 수 없다.

TANGLE v. (cause something to) become twisted into a confused mass 엉키게 하다, 혼란시키다
Her hair got all tangled up in the barbed wire fence.
그녀의 머리카락은 철조망에 온통 엉켰다.

"Babette," she said. "Does this net feel very strong to you?"

"Actually, no," replied Babette. "The cords seem very **flimsy**. You are thinking I should try to chop through them?"

"Wait a minute!" cried Barnaby. "We're almost twenty feet in the air! If you chop through the net, we'll fall on our heads."

"What we have here is a **dilemma**, Barnaby," said Bridget. "If we just wait here and do nothing, we'll probably be eaten by the tribe of savages who set this trap. If we cut the net, we fall on our heads. Personally, I vote for falling on our heads. At least there's a chance we can get up and run away."

"I must agree with Bridget," said Babette, who was getting ready to *whack*.

"Hold it a second, Babette!" he yelled. "I admit your argument has its strong points, but I think you should give me time for a **rebuttal** before sending us on a dangerous free fall."

"This isn't a debate, Barnaby," said Bridget. "We're in a serious *jam*! We've got to get out of here on the *double*!"

Just then, a terrible, high-pitched, horsey laugh came from far below them.

"Oh, Father, aren't they quaint?" said a female voice in an odd, sort-of-British accent. "What is that **dialect** they speak? It sounds as though they come from the American colonies! Do let's cut them down!"

Barnaby, Bridget, Babette, and Beauregard heard a snap, and with that, they all came tumbling down.

WHACK v. to strike or beat (somebody/something) vigorously   세게 치다, 탁 때리다
The batter whacked the baseball out of the park.
타자는 야구공을 경기장 밖으로 나가게 세게 쳤다.

JAM n. difficult or embarrassing situation   곤경, 궁지
How am I going to get out of this jam?
어떻게 이 궁지를 벗어날 것인가?

DOUBLE n. (on the double의 형태로 쓰여) quickly; hurrying   신속히, 황급히
The boss wants you-you'd better get upstairs on the double.
사장이 당신을 찾아요. 빨리 위층으로 올라가는 게 좋겠어요.

"See," mumbled Bridget, rubbing her head. "We were going to fall on our heads one way or another."

The horsey laugh broke out again.

"Oh, look, Father, the girl is so **rustic**. Loot at those heavy work pants of hers. She looks like she's straight out of the *backwoods*!"

Bridget looked around to find the source of the voice that had insulted her jeans. When she found it, she wished she hadn't bothered. Standing behind her was a large woman in a *fluffy* pink ball gown with a face so ugly it made Bridget *shudder* to look at her. Next to the woman was an old, fat man in a long purple robe. The man had a very fancy crown on his head.

"Hey, what do you mean by stringing us up like that? Who are you people, anyway?" growled Bridget.

"Dear me, that child is **uncouth**!" huffed the man in the crown. "Girl, were you not raised with any manners? Do you not know the proper way to address a king?"

"Please forgive us. It is just that we were taken by surprise. Good day, your majesties," said Barnaby with a little bow. The fall must have shaken up his hair, because as soon as he bent forward, a box of chocolates fell on the ground.

The woman's eyes grew very round, then very narrow, then she *pounced* on the box, opened it, and devoured every last chocolate.

"Oh, Father," she cooed, sucking caramel out from between her teeth. "I love him, I do! Did you see how he offered me this tribute? He is so **gallant**, so charming, like a knight in shining armor!"

BACKWOODS n. remote or sparsely inhabited region; uncleared or wild regions far away from towns   벽지; 삼림지
The trapper lived in the backwoods far from the city's cares.
그 사냥꾼은 도시의 관리에서 벗어난 벽지에서 살았다.

FLUFFY adj. covered with soft feathery pieces of material shed; like fluff   보풀로 덮인; 보풀 같은
Most animals are soft and fluffy when first born.
대부분의 동물들은 처음 태어나면 부드럽고 보풀로 덮여 있다.

SHUDDER v. to shiver violently with cold, fear, etc.; to tremble   몸서리치다; 떨다
I shudder to think of the problems ahead of us.
나는 우리 앞에 놓인 문제들을 생각하면 몸서리가 쳐진다.

POUNCE v. to jump suddenly and seize something   달려들어 움켜잡다, 덥석 집어들다
The cat pounced upon the mouse.
고양이는 달려들어 쥐를 움켜잡았다.

"I see!" said the king, looking rather pleased. "Young knight, you have won my daughter's heart. What say you marry her? You will be my **heir**, and when I die you will **inherit** the throne and my entire fortune will be yours!"

"Things certainly do happen quickly around here," remarked Babette.

"Silence!" thundered the king. "Well, young knight?"

"Bu... but I... you don't...," said Barnaby, **faltering** and hesitating over his words. "I don't even know her name."

"Ah, you are right. May I present Princess Equinia, daughter of Lyle the Great, King of Littledot," said king with a wave of his hand. "And you are...?"

Barnaby paused for a moment. These two people seemed genuinely crazy, and he didn't want to upset them. They might be dangerous. He decided on a bold strategy: *stall* them.

"Um, my name is Barnaby, Your Highness," he said. "I think I should point out that we hardly know each other. Shouldn't, er, Princess Equinia and I get acquainted before I **broach** the subject of marriage with her?"

"A *courtship*, eh?" said the king with a chuckle. "I've always thought that romance was a rather **provincial** custom. Good for the commoners, but we royals are much too sophisticated for all that hair-pulling and jumping about. Still, the idea has a sort of country charm, and it might please Equinia. Very well, Sir Barnaby. You have my permission to **woo** my daughter."

"Well, you know, it is important to develop a friendly relationship, a good **rapport** before going into marriage," said Barnaby.

"Fine, fine, fine," said the king. "All that will take care of itself."

STALL v. to avoid giving a definite answer of taking action (in order to get more time); to delay 주저하다; 지연시키다
Stop stalling and give me an answer!
시간 끌지 말고 내게 대답을 해다오!

COURTSHIP n. the condition or time of courting in order to marry; wooing 구애 시기; 구애
They married after a brief courtship.
그들은 짧은 구애 시기를 거쳐 결혼했다.

"Oh, goody, goody!" cried the princess, clapping her hands and dancing around. "I have a new **suitor**. Barnaby's my boyfriend! Barnaby's my boyfriend!"

With that, the princess grabbed Barnaby's hand and pulled him after her into the woods. Barnaby tried to resist her yank, but Equinia was several times larger than he. He looked over at his friends desperately, and they tried to come to his aid, but just as they were about to run after him, they were stopped by the edge of a long, sharp blade.

"I wouldn't do that if I were you," said King Lyle, holding his sword out in front of them. "The romantic **liaison** between Equinia and Sir Barnaby is at a very delicate stage. You must leave them alone and not *butt* in or **interfere**."

"But he's not a 'sir' or a knight," said Bridget. "He's our friend, and we're very busy. He's nothing but a scientist."

"A man of science, eh?" said the king. "Splendid. Well, I, too, am a very busy man. You two, I mean three, must come with me to the castle so I can keep watch over you."

The king gestured with his sword, and Beauregard, Babette, and Bridget *reluctantly* followed him through the woods. His castle was an odd building, more like a tower than a royal house. It was round, made of stone, and several stories high. Inside, it was filled with papers and pens. Books lined the walls from floor to ceiling.

"It looks as if you enjoy reading, Your Majesty," Babette commented.

"Actually, the enjoyment has faded," he sighed. "You see, as King of Littledot, it is my duty to make sure that all the reading material in the land is good for my people. New books are sent here, where they are stored **pending** my approval. I'm afraid many have been lying around for quite a long time. I must be so careful! I can't have people reading harmful or misleading material. No, I must personally read and approve everything—nothing goes out unless I **endorse** it."

Bridget opened her mouth to ask about these "people" the king supposedly ruled, but he started talking again.

BUTT v. (butt in (on somebody/something)의 형태로 쓰여) to interrupt (somebody/something) or interfere (in something) 참견하다, 방해하다
Don't butt in like that when I'm speaking.
내가 말하고 있을 때 그렇게 참견하지 말아라.

RELUCTANTLY adv. unwillingly and therefore slowly to co-operate, agree, etc. 어쩔 수 없이, 억지로
After much thought, we reluctantly agreed.
많이 생각한 후에 우리는 어쩔 수 없이 동의했다.

"Of course, not every book is entirely bad or good. If that were the case, my job would be much easier. Instead, I must make changes when necessary. Sometimes books are too depressing, for example, so I do my best to change sad endings to happy ones."

"Sometimes a book means to be good, but it is just too long. In that case, I **condense** the text, boil it down to the essentials. People like short books, after all. I read one book in which a fellow commits a terrible murder early on. Then he worries about it for hundreds of pages, and finally turns himself in near the end. I thought it was much clearer without the middle part, so I decided it should be **omitted**. In my *version*, he commits the murder and goes directly to prison. Much better, don't you think?"

"And sometimes it seems like the author's only purpose is to stir up people's emotions, to get them angry or excited. Believe me, **provocative** literature is the last thing I need in my kingdom. Kings prefer things to be as unexciting and **sedate** as possible. It's amazing how irresponsible authors are sometimes."

"But what you're doing is wrong!" said Bridget. "You're not making the books better, you're **censoring** them—taking out or changing anything that doesn't suit your personal and political goals!"

"Exactly, child!" boomed the king. "It is my royal right to decide what my subjects will read. What's wrong with that?"

"Nothing!" chirped Babette, who then turned and whispered to her friend, "Do not be upset. I strongly suspect the king and his daughter are the only people on this island, so he is harming no one. We should not anger him."

Bridget shrugged, and was silent.

VERSION n. a special form or variant of something   각색, 개작
It's a modern version of an antique.
그것은 고대 양식의 현대판 각색이다.

"So, what are you working on today?" asked Babette.

"I'm glad you asked," said King Lyle eagerly, taking up his pen. "I'm working on a most *frustrating* book. It's about the French Revolution. Terrible war, I'm told. Many nobles were **decapitated**. That's right, the rebels had a machine that would chop their heads right off. Well, that just gave me the willies. The word 'decapitate' should not appear in decent literature. It gives people ideas. So I must go through and **obliterate** the word, wipe out any trace of it, every time it appears in the text—which is far too often, believe me."

King Lyle picked up a book, flipped to a marked page, and *scribbled* hard over one of the offensive words.

"Oh, there are so many of them!" he exclaimed, obliterating another one.

Babette, Bridget, and Beauregard decided to make themselves comfortable for the time being. It looked like they were in for a serious delay.

Things were much more interesting on the other side of the island, which wasn't far away, since it was very small. Barnaby, who was supposed to be wooing Equinia, found instead that it was he who was being wooed quite *outrageously* in a tiny beach bungalow.

"Darling, I adore you," *purred* the princess. "Your fluffy hair has such style, such *oomph*, such **panache**! Your concerned little face is so scholarly! I love men who study a lot. They are so… **studious**!"

Barnaby tried his best to ignore her, but that only seemed to spur her on. Equinia ran to a cupboard and pulled out a plate of cookies.

"Here, my love, I baked these for you myself," she cooed, offering him one.

Barnaby accepted. After all, he was very hungry. He tried biting into it, but it was so hard that he hurt his tooth.

FRUSTRATING adj. annoying; discouraging   좌절감을 주는
I find it frustrating that I can't speak other languages.
나는 다른 언어를 말할 줄 모른다는 데서 좌절감을 느낀다.

SCRIBBLE v. to write (something) very fast or carelessly   휘갈겨 쓰다
She scribbled her name on the envelope.
그녀는 봉투 위에 자신의 이름을 휘갈겨 썼다.

OUTRAGEOUSLY adv. very offensively or immorally; shockingly   난폭하게; 엄청나게
He treated his wife outrageously.
그는 아내를 난폭하게 다루었다.

PURR v. to utter a low, continuous, murmuring sound expressive of contentment or pleasure   만족스런 듯이 말하다
The little girl purred when we gave her some gift.
어린 소녀는 우리가 선물을 주자 만족스런 듯이 말했다.

OOMPH n. energy; enthusiasm; sex-appeal   열정; 매력
Marilyn Monroe had lots of oomph.
마릴린 먼로는 무척 매력적이었다.

"I can't eat them," he said.

"Why not?" asked the princess, looking hurt.

"It's **inedible**," replied Barnaby.

"What do you mean?" she gasped.

"I mean, it can't be eaten," he said, simply.

Equinia frowned a little, but she wasn't put off. She left the hut for a moment, and came back covered in *tacky* necklaces and *gaudy* earrings.

"Do you like me now?" she asked. "See? I have **adorned** myself with jewels to make myself even more attractive."

"There was no need," he replied.

"You mean, you thought I was already pretty without decoration?" she said, falling before him and putting her face near his as if waiting for a kiss.

Barnaby was not a **squeamish** person, not by a long shot, but the thought of kissing Equinia would have turned almost anyone's stomach. He was trying not to be rude, but he couldn't help noticing a huge, skin-colored growth that **protruded** about two inches from her right eyelid. It stuck out so far, in fact, that it seemed to block her line of vision.

"Doesn't that growth **impair** your vision?" he asked.

"What?" yelped Equinia, jumping up.

"That thing on your eyelid. It seems to be interfering with your ability to see," he said. "You should really have a doctor take a look at it. It's probably **benign**, which means there's nothing to worry about. But it could be **malignant**. That's bad. That means it's dangerous."

TACKY adj. in poor taste; shabby or gaudy   초라한; 볼품없는
She was tacky when she was young.
그녀는 젊었을 때 초라하고 볼품없었다.

GAUDY adj. too bright and showy, especially in a vulgar way   촌스럽게 화려한
Look at the gaudy dress!
저 촌스럽게 화려한 드레스 좀 봐!

"How can you be so cruel?" she cried. "First you ignore me, sitting there so cold and **aloof**, and then when you do decide to talk to me, you're mean!"

Barnaby began to feel guilty.

"You don't love me anymore!" she moaned. "My heart is broken into a million pieces, and the damage is **irreparable**. I will never be happy again. I will **grieve** for your lost love forever! Boo hoo hoo!"

Equinia began to weep *appallingly*, which made her even more monstrous. Barnaby tried his best to **placate** her, but he didn't really have the *knack*.

"Don't cry, princess. This has all been a mistake. I never loved you in the first place," he said.

"You're lying. You gave me a box of chocolates on the beach!" she cried. "You're just **fickle**, just like the rest of them. Your feelings come and go like the tides you rode it on."

"What do you mean 'just like the rest of them'?" demanded Barnaby. He suddenly started feeling a little less guilty. There might be a way out of this situation after all.

Just as he was about to ask more, there was a knock at the door. It *creaked* open, and King Lyle poked his head in.

"Hello, children," he said cheerily. "Sir Barnaby, may I have a word with you?"

Barnaby was more than happy to have a **reprieve** from the terrible situation with Equinia, so he got up and followed the king.

"Well, how are things going, dear boy?" he asked, clapping his hand on Barnaby's shoulder. "Have you asked for her hand in marriage yet?"

"Um, no," replied Barnaby.

APPALLINGLY adv. shockingly; extremely badly 끔찍할 정도로
She is appallingly thin.
그 여자는 끔찍할 정도로 말랐다.

KNACK n. skill at performing some special task; ability 솜씨, 재주
I used to be able to skate quite well, but I've lost the knack.
나는 스케이트를 꽤 잘 탈 줄 알았었는데 이제 그 재주를 잃어버렸다.

CREAK v. to make a harsh sound like that of an unoiled door-hinge 삐걱 소리를 내다
The wooden cart creaked as it moved along.
나무로 만든 그 손수레는 움직일 때 삐걱거리는 소리가 났다.

"What's the delay? Stop **procrastinating**. No sense in putting it off. The sooner you get done with it, the sooner we can plan the wedding," he said.

"I'm glad you brought that up, Your Highness," said Barnaby. "The marriage ceremony is a very important **rite**, almost as important as graduation. It shouldn't be taken lightly."

King Lyle looked at Barnaby carefully for a moment, then smiled broadly.

"You're a smart young man, I see," he declared. "You want some **incentive** to marry the princess, as if someday becoming King of Littledot weren't reason enough. Well, come on then. I'll show you what else you'll get in the bargain."

Barnaby was eager to get as far away from Equinia as possible, so he gladly walked with the king through the woods to a *clearing* where dozens of wooden barrels stood stacked.

"You see, Sir Barnaby, I am rich," he said.

"Um, I don't understand," said Barnaby. "What's in them?"

King Lyle motioned Barnaby close to one of the barrels. Then he cut a hole through its side with his sword. Water began pouring out into the sandy dirt.

"Ha ha! It doesn't even matter! I have plenty more. I have an endless supply!" he cried.

Barnaby stuck his hand in the stream of water and brought it to his mouth.

"This is sea water," he said, completely shocked at the utter senselessness of it. "Do you mean you've been **hoarding** barrels of sea water?"

"I don't have to hoard it! I have an endless supply! I hope that sweetens the marriage deal for you!"

CLEARING n. open space from which trees have been cleared in a forest 개척지
They lived in the clearing.
그들은 개척지에서 살았다.

Barnaby was a his wits' end. These people were absolutely mad. He was done being polite and wasting his time with them, even if it meant King Lyle might stick him with his sword.

"Look, the deal's off, Lyle," he said *grimly*. "Your daughter has had many suitors before me, and I'm not about to take their hand-me-downs. She's damaged goods, Pops."

"How dare you **tarnish** my daughter's reputation like that!" yelled the king. "Equinia is a charming, lively, **vivacious** girl. Naturally, she has had many admirers."

"Admirers you trapped for her!" snapped Barnaby.

"I would be **negligent** in my duties as father as king if I did not try to find my daughter a husband," explained the king. "I don't see why my method of doing so is **relevant**."

"It matters a great deal! Men are not animals to be caught and turned into pets!"

"I would have made you a king, not a pet!"

"Well, I'm happy to **forfeit** any claim to the throne in exchange for my liberty," declared Barnaby nobly.

Just then, there was a *rustling* in the bushes behind him, and looking over his shoulder, Barnaby was greatly relieved to see Bridget, Babette, and Beauregard.

"I wish we could stay and **mediate** between you two, and help you reach a friendly agreement, but I'm afraid we don't have time," said Bridget.

"Yes, Barnaby," said Babette. "We have thought about it for a long while, and we have come up with a plan."

"What is the plan?" he asked.

GRIMLY adv. sternly; severely 단호하게, 엄하게
He grimly refused the proposal.
그는 단호하게 그 제안을 거절했다.

RUSTLING n. (instance of the) sound made by something that rustles 급히 움직이는 소리
Can you hear the rustling of the dry leaves?
마른 잎사귀들이 급히 움직이며 내는 소리가 들리니?

"Run to the beach as fast as you can!" she yelled.

Barnaby didn't have to be told twice. It sounded like a great plan to him, and he dashed through the woods after his friends. Of course, King Lyle came running after them, but he was not nearly as fast as they were. Bridget had plenty of time to blow her bubble boat and they were safely offshore by the time King Lyle even got the beach. And there he stood, waving his sword and yelling at them, as they sailed off.

"What a pair of *freaks*!" panted Bridget. After a few minutes, she continued, "Gee, Barnaby, I thought you were a quite, **reserved** type. I never realized you were such a heartbreaker," she said, giggling.

"I think this is a new **facet** of Barnaby's personality," said Babette. "Another side of him, yes?"

"That was my first experience with love," sighed Barnaby, who didn't think it was funny, "and it was a total **debacle**. What a disaster! I used to **covet** the good looks of my classmates who were popular with all the girls. Now I'm glad I don't have what they have. I don't envy them one little bit. Love is *heck*!"

Bridget and Babette rolled their eyes and laughed to themselves. But Beauregard simply nodded his furry black head in silent agreement, and stared sadly out to sea.

FREAK n. person considered abnormal because of his behaviour, appearance, ideas, etc. 괴물
People think she's a freak just because she's religious.
사람들은 그 여자가 종교적이라는 이유만으로 그녀를 괴물로 생각한다.

HECK n. (used to express mild annoyance or surprise or for emphasis) hell 지옥
We had to wait a heck of a long time.
우리는 끔찍이도 오래 동안 기다려야 했다.

Relationships

Decide what relationship the following pairs of words have to each other. If they mean close to the same thing, make "S." If they have opposite meanings, mark "O."

1. begin :: malignant
2. reserved :: vivacious
3. endorse :: approve
4. condense :: expand
5. provocative :: sedate
6. impair :: improve
7. debacle :: disaster
8. uncouth :: gallant
9. passive :: active
10. tarnish :: polish
11. placate :: soothe

Fill in the Blank

For each sentence below, choose the word that best completes the sentence.

1. The people in Smallville had _____ tastes, so they didn't appreciate the experimental theater group from New York that visited their town last month.

   a. squeamish   b. diverse   c. rustic   d. provincial

2. In order to get into the club, Jim had to go through an initiation _____ that involved running through the campus in his underwear.

   a. dilemma   b. liaison   c. rite   d. facet

3. During wartime, soldiers' letters are opened, read, and sometimes _____ to keep secrets from leaking out.

   a. mediated   b. broached   c. censored   d. hoarded

4. Vince seemed to have a(n) _____ athletic ability that made it easy for him to do well at any spot.

   a. innate   b. pending   c. irreparable   d. relevant

5. When his grandfather dies, Manuel will _____ half of his great fortune—the other half goes to his sister, Amelia.

   a. inherit   b. interfere   c. decapitate   d. obliterate

6. Clancey's strange _____ was hard to understand unless you came from the same Irish village as he.

   a. rapport   b. incentive   c. rebuttal   d. dialect

Matching

Match each word on the right with a word on the left that has a meaning that's close to the same.

1. hazardous
2. nocturnal
3. flimsy
4. heir
5. faltering
6. woo
7. suitor
8. omit
9. panache
10. studious

a. at night
b. admirer
c. weak
d. inheritor
e. leave out
f. scholarly
g. dangerous
h. stumbling
i. flair
j. to romance

Matching

Match each word on the right with a word on the left that has a meaning that's close to the same.

1. inedible
2. adorned
3. protrude
4. aloof
5. grieve
6. fickle
7. reprieve
8. procrastinate
9. negligent
10. forfeit
11. covet

a. envy
b. not fit to eat
c. changeable
d. give up
e. cool
f. neglectful
g. relief
h. decorated
i. stick out
j. mourn
k. delay

The Cave of the Counter-feiters

위조범들의 소굴

Well, we hadn't eaten in a while and we still weren't exactly sure how to get back to France, but at least the weather was temperate—mild and dry, with a pleasant light wind blowing us westward. After all the delays and accidents, I was grateful for that much. That, and the fact that Barnaby was still a bachelor. The poor boy had a narrow escape.

I was kind of hoping we'd be picked up by an ocean liner—those cruise ships travel through the Greek islands all the time—but we didn't see anything but water. Everyone was very quiet, probably because we were so weary of traveling. But we all snapped out of it pretty quickly when we noticed that the boat had begun to veer sharply to the left and again speed. We were headed straight toward a big, *craggy* rock that was sticking out of the ocean, and there was nothing we could do to change our course! I thought for sure that this was the end for us, but just before we crashed headlong into it, we were sucked down underwater. We didn't drown, though. No, instead we found ourselves in a very strange cave beneath the surface of the ocean...

A deafening siren **heralded** their arrival. Speakers all over the cave announced: "Intruder alert! Intruder alert! Intruder alert!"

All around them, people were scurrying to hide what they were doing. Desks were slammed shut. Work tables were covered with sheets. Pieces of paper were being chewed up and swallowed. Documents were being *shredded*.

Suddenly, much to their displeasure, Bridget, Barnaby, Babette, and Beauregard saw that once again they had a gun aimed at them. This time, it was an old man in a fancy antique wheelchair who was threatening them. He was a very proper and dignified-looking man, his few gray hairs neatly combed, his red silk jacket neatly pressed, and a fine wool blanket thrown over his legs. He looked like someone from another time and place. Even his gun, a very **ornate** pistol made of polished wood and covered in fancy brass decorations, looked like some kind of family **heirloom**, passed down by a soldier or *duelist* far back in his family's past.

CRAGGY adj. having many crags; rough   바위가 울퉁불퉁 돌출한; 거친
The craggy hill was difficult to climb.
바위가 울퉁불퉁 돌출한 그 언덕은 오르기가 힘들었다.

SHRED v. to tear or cut into small pieces   갈갈이 찢다
Paper is often shredded for use in packing dishes and the like.
접시 같은 것을 싸는 데 쓰기 위해서 종종 종이를 갈갈이 찢는다.

DUELIST n. a person fighting a formal fight   결투자
He was a famous duelist at that time.
그는 당시에 유명한 결투자였다.

"Just what do you think you're doing here?" he demanded. "How much did you see?"

"Nothing!" cried the travelers all at once. "We didn't see anything, honest!"

They all began talking at once, trying to convince the armed man of their harmlessness. But their talking did little to **allay** his suspicions. In fact, all it did was make matters worse.

"I don't believe you," he said simply. "I think this whole innocent kid thing is nothing but a clever act. Apart from his hair, you appear to be normal children, but I'm sure you have all the **guile** to be international spies. That's what you're here for, right?"

"I don't see much to spy on," replied Barnaby innocently, his right hand *twiddling* his hair nervously. He was trying to prove again that he and his friends hadn't seen anything important when they arrived. The man in the wheelchair, however, seemed terribly insulted by the comment.

"Oh, you don't see much, do you?" he yelled. "I'll have you know that this is the finest **counterfeiting** operation in the world! The finest in imitation jewels, *fake* money, **forgeries** of famous artworks, *knock-offs* of designer watches, wallets, purses, furs, and other **miscellaneous** items—they're all made right here in this cave! Not much, indeed!"

"Then we regret not seeing much of it, for we surely would have been impressed," said Babette in the most **conciliatory** tone possible. After all, they seemed to be in a rather **precarious** position, considering that the old man had both a gun and a very short temper.

"I appreciate that, young lady," he said, apparently pleased with her compliment, "but I'm afraid you've caused us a great deal of trouble today. You see, we have daily **quotas** to satisfy. We're supposed to have at least one billion lira in thousand-lira notes ready this evening for some very important organizations in Italy. When you came in, these artists behind me were forced to destroy most of what they worked on so we wouldn't be caught with it."

"But why?" asked Bridget.

TWIDDLE v. to twist or turn (something), especially idly or aimlessly 만지작거리다
She sat twiddling the ring on her finger.
그녀는 손가락에 낀 반지를 만지작거리면서 앉아 있었다.

FAKE n. object (e.g. a work of art) that seems genuine but is not 위조(품)
That's not a real diamond necklace, it's just a fake!
저것, 진짜 다이아몬드 반지 아니예요. 모조품이예요.

KNOCK-OFF n. a copy, usually an unauthorized one and often less expensive than the popular original 복제품
It looked like a work of Renoir but it was really a knock-off.
르누아르의 작품처럼 보였지만 사실은 복제품이었다.

"My dear girl, because making your own money is highly illegal. That means it's against the law. Only governments are allowed to create money. Understand?" the man asked. He spoke very slowly and clearly. Bridget didn't like his tone. She felt that he was talking down to her, and being **patronized** was one thing she really hated.

"Yeah, I get it," she snapped. "Of course I know making fake stuff is against the law. I only meant that it's obvious we're not spies or police officers, so there was no reason to *trash* your whole day's work."

"It was not obvious to me what you were. And it still isn't clear what you are doing here," he replied sharply. "Anyway, I don't have the time right now to decide what to do with you. We must catch up to make our quota. I suppose the most **expedient** thing would be to shoot you, throw you into the ocean, and let that be the end of it. Yes, that would be easiest, to be sure."

The old man paused for a brief, very tense moment, then, to the great relief of Barnaby, Babette, Bridget, and Beauregard, he yelled, "Leonard! Come take these children and this enormous cat to the conference room and make sure they don't get into any trouble until after we ship the lira! We'll decide what to do with them then."

A young man dressed in jeans and a paint-covered T-shirt came forward.

Still trying her best to act friendly, Babette decided to introduce herself and her friends. Leonard, though, didn't respond well. He just gave them a **curt** nod of his head and waved his hand to show that they should walk ahead of him toward a door marked "Conference Room."

The room looked pretty much like any other conference room you might find in a regular office building. There were no windows, the lighting was harsh and bright, and one long light bulb in the corner hummed away quietly, *flickering* every now and then. There were two pots of coffee slowly burning on the coffee maker, filling the room with a bitter smell. There was a whiteboard on one wall and several dry-erase colored markers. Beauregard went to sleep right away, as do many people in conference rooms. Indeed, the only thing that was out of the ordinary was the beautiful white marble conference table.

TRASH v. to treat or discard as worthless 버리다
I trashed many books and magazines.
나는 많은 책과 잡지들을 버렸다.

FLICKER v. to burn or shine unsteadily 깜박거리다
All the lights flickered for a moment.
잠시 동안 모든 불빛들이 깜박거렸다.

"What a lovely table," remarked Babette.

Leonard smiled, walked over to the table, and *rapped* on it with his *knuckles*. Instead of hearing the solid sound of stone, the kids heard a hollow, cheap sound, as if he were knocking on an empty milk jug.

"That's right," said Leonard. "Plastic. It's a fake. Amazing, isn't it?"

They had to agree, it was an amazing likeness.

"It seems impossible," said Barnaby, "to **duplicate** the look and shine of marble so well with plastic. Did you create this?"

Leonard shook his head sadly. "No," he said. "I'm not nearly talented enough. Mr. Faux himself made this table."

"Mr. Faux is the guy with the gun?" asked Bridget.

"The guy with the gun, yes," said Leonard with a little laugh. "But in addition to having a gun, he is also one of the most **acclaimed** artists in the world. You can't imagine the praise, the **kudos** that have been heaped on him. I am proud to be his grandson."

He did look proud. But he looked troubled as well.

"If he's such a great artist, what's he doing hiding in a cave?" demanded Bridget.

"He isn't hiding," growled Leonard. "The public did not understand his genius. He was **persecuted** and **tormented** by the authorities. Police would follow him, arrest him on the flimsiest excuse, sometimes even **confiscate** his art equipment, saying it was 'evidence.' Ha! They just wanted to *crush* his spirit by taking away his supplies."

RAP v. to knock or tap lightly and quickly 톡톡 두드리다
She rapped on the desk.
그 여자는 책상 위를 톡톡 두드렸다.

KNUCKLE n. bone at the finger-joint 손가락 마디
Each finger of a person's hand has three knuckles.
사람들의 손가락은 세 마디로 되어 있다.

CRUSH v. to defeat (somebody/something) completely; to subdue 짓밟다, 진압하다, 꺾다
The rebellion was crushed by government forces.
그 반란은 정부군에 의해 진압되었다.

"He heard about this place from a friend of his in one of the terrible dungeons they threw him in. Apparently, the ancient Greeks found a small underwater cave hundreds of years ago, and they **excavated** it, removing sand and rocks and sometimes **gouging** through stone and *silt* to expand the living space. Since those days, it has been used by many different armies as a secret hiding place. So my grandfather came here, too—to be safe. Surely you can understand that."

"Right," said Bridget. "But why are all those other people here? Are they misunderstood artists, too?"

"Some are," said Leonard. "Most were drawn here by my grandfather's reputation. He is their boss, but he is also their **mentor**. He teaches and guides them. He's a very demanding teacher. Some of the new people here say he's too **didactic**. I have to admit, he does tend to lecture people, but only because he wants them to reach their 'personal **pinnacle**,' as he calls it. The highest point of their talent."

"Well, I guess that's **laudable** enough," said Barnaby. "I mean, you have to give a guy a little credit for pushing people to do their best. But what I want to know is how he got here all by himself. He's **paraplegic**, isn't he?"

"No, his legs aren't paralyzed," said Leonard. "That was just a model of an old Victorian wheelchair he made. He amuses himself with little projects like that. Like the pistol. It's an imitation of an eighteenth-century French dueling pistol."

Bridget and Babette exchanged a quick look, but Leonard was on to them. "It will shoot just as well as a real pistol, though." he added.

Leonard went and poured himself a cup of *stale* coffee. He blew into the styrofoam cup and sighed.

SILT n. very fine particles of earth, sand, clay, or similar matter, carried by moving water   모래보다는 곱고 진흙보다는 거친 입자의 침적토, 침니
The harbor is being choked up with silt.
항구는 침니로 메워지고 있다.

STALE adj. not fresh   싱싱하지 못한, 오래된
They gave us some stale bread.
그들은 우리에게 오래된 빵을 주었다.

"I came here with my grandfather when I was about your age, right after he escaped from prison," he said. "He told me he needed my help, and in exchange he promised to teach me to be a great artist. He knew I **aspired** to be a painter. It was my greatest wish. His offer held such a strong **allure** for me, I couldn't resist. I quit school and left with him on a dark, cold winter evening. I didn't even tell my parents where I was going. I haven't seen them since."

He took a sip of his coffee and looked thoughtfully into the cup. Bridget felt a little depressed, too.

"Well, did he?" she asked.

"Did he what?" said Leonard.

"Did he make you a great artist? Was it worth leaving your parents?"

Leonard shook his head and was silent for a while. If there had been a window in the room, he probably would have stared out of it.

"I am ashamed to say that I failed him," he said finally. "I tried my hardest to copy exactly everything he showed me. I learned to **discriminate** the finest details of a painting. Were the brush strokes made by a left-handed or right-handed person? Was the paint applied with a palette knife or with bare hands? Is that shade of brown burnt sienna or burnt *umber*? I practiced day and night, trying to **mimic** the styles in the paintings Grandfather showed me. I was absolutely **scrupulous**. But my careful attention to detail was absolutely to no **avail**.

"At first, Grandfather told me my work had some **merit**. He'd praise one little thing or another, but I noticed that none of it was ever shipped out. I thought if I **persevered** I might get better, but I could have stuck to it for ten years or a hundred—nothing would have changed. Finally, I asked him to give me a straight, **objective** opinion of my talent. I wasn't prepared for what he had to say."

UMBER n. brown or reddish brown   고동색
My favorite color is umber.
내가 가장 좋아하는 색은 고동색이다.

"He was actually angry at me. He said I put too much of myself into the paintings. A good forgery, he told me, must be **superficial**, nothing but surface detail. My feelings and emotions should never show. I tried to argue with him, but he had caught me. You see, **unbeknownst** to me, he had sneaked into my workroom and discovered that I had been painting on my own. Not copies of anything, either, just whatever I felt like. I only did it for a change of pace, something different... making copies can be so **tedious**."

Leonard kind of drifted off for a minute in his own thoughts. Bridget, Babette, and Barnaby were too confused to offer any help.

"He **derided** my originals cruelly, making fun of them and scoffing at them. He said there was no challenge in painting something you thought up yourself because no one could tell if it was any good if there was nothing to compare it to. Originality, he said is the **bane** of all good counterfeiters. The kiss of death, he said. He told me I must stop wasting my time painting. I cried and cried, but finally he calmed me down. He told me I could stay and help around the office, do little errands and things."

"That's what I've been doing ever since. It's been so **degrading**. The other counterfeiters know I'm a failure, and they treat me like dirt. But I have to put up with it. I'm not fit for anything else."

"That is absolutely **absurd**," said Babette, *stomping* her foot.

"What?" said Leonard, as if shocked out of a dream.

"I mean, what your grandfather, Mr. Faux, said is completely ridiculous," she said, stomping her foot again. "I insist that we go see your paintings immediately."

Leonard was too startled to do or say anything for a minute. Then he objected mildly, saying that his grandfather had told him to keep them in the conference room. But Babette wouldn't take no for an answer.

STOMP v. to walk with very heavy steps e.g. when annoyed about something   쿵쿵거리며 걷다
Michael stomped off home
마이클은 쿵쿵거리며 집에서 걸어나왔다.

"You can watch us just as easily in your workroom. Leave a note on the whiteboard," she said.

"Back in five minutes," he wrote on the board. Then he showed them out another door and all of them, including Beauregard which had been awakened by Babette stomping on his tail, followed him down a long, damp, gray hallway. They came to a little door at the end, and Leonard pulled a key out of his jeans pocket, unlocked the door, and let them in.

The room was large and round, and had a big *skylight* high overhead that let in plenty of natural light. Leonard began explaining how they had built the skylight, but no one was listening. They were too busy admiring the amazing painting that covered every wall. Even Bridget and Barnaby, who weren't big art fans, were impressed. Babette and Beauregard, who were obviously into that sort of thing, were studying the different paintings closely.

Leonard began to *shuffle* nervously from foot to foot. His paintings had never undergone such **scrutiny** before. He was scared he'd be laughed at again.

Finally, Babette came and looked him straight in the eyes. "Leonard," she said, "I think you are a very great artist. Your work is not only moving and powerful, it's **innovative**. You've created something entirely new!"

"That's the problem," said Mr. Faux, who had appeared suddenly in the doorway, without his wheelchair this time. "You see, I had a duty. I promised to make Leonard a great counterfeiter, and I failed to fulfill that **obligation**. Or rather, we failed. He just didn't have it in him. Pity, too, since I wanted to make this entire operation my **legacy** to him when I *pass* on."

"Unfortunately, he's a bad businessman as well as a bad counterfeiter. And one has to be **pragmatic** when it comes to business. You can't let emotions get in the way of taking money, if you'll forgive the *pun*. That's why I'm leaving everything to Ed. Boy, does he have a head for business. You'll never meet a **shrewder** man."

SKYLIGHT n. window in a roof or ceiling 채광 창
We lived in a house with a skylight.
우리는 채광 창이 있는 집에서 살았다.

SHUFFLE v. to walk without lifting the feet completely clear of the ground 발을 질질 끌고 다니다
The prisoners shuffled along the corridor and into their cells.
죄수들은 발을 질질 끌면서 복도를 지나서 자신들의 독방으로 들어갔다.

PASS v. (pass on=pass away의 형태로 쓰여) to die 죽다
His mother passed on last year.
그의 어머니는 작년에 돌아가셨다.

PUN n. humorous use of a word that has two meanings or of different words that sound the same; play on words 말장난
The slogan was a pun on the name of the product.
그 슬로건은 그 제품의 이름을 이용한 말장난이었다.

Leonard looked very pained. Babette looked very angry.

"Mr. Faux, you are a very bad grandfather!" she snapped. "And you are a very bad artist."

Mr. Faux actually looked upset at that, but because she couldn't tell which part of what she'd said had upset him, Babette just kept talking.

"Why don't you encourage him instead of **undermining** his confidence and cutting him down? He is your own flesh and blood!"

Mr. Faux seemed unmoved.

"Leonard is a very talented painter. A great artist, even. Much better than you ever were or could ever hope to be! You're just jealous!" she cried.

Well, that seemed to *hit* home. Mr. Faux turned red in the face. Then purple. Then a sort of grayish-greenish shade. Veins started to pop out on his forehead. Barnaby was beginning to think he had suddenly been struck with a serious illness, but it turned out that Mr. Faux's reaction was more **psychological** than **pathological**.

"All right, all right!" he finally blurted out. "Yes, if you must know, I can't bear to look at these paintings. I knew when I brought him here that Leonard had a strong **aesthetic** sense. He could see and appreciate beauty in anything. But when I saw these paintings, I realized he was more than just a lover of beauty, he was an artistic genius. I almost hated him for that."

HIT v. (hit home의 형태로 쓰여) to have the intended (often painful) effect   정곡을 찌르다
I could see from her expression that his sarcastic comments had hit home.
그녀의 표정에서 그의 비꼬는 말이 정곡을 찔렀다는 것을 알 수 있었다.

Bridget frowned.

"Oh, I see, you don't approve?" he said. "How could you hate your own grandson, you ask? Well, I'll tell you. All I ever wanted as a boy, as a teenager, as a young man, and even as a not-so-young man was to be an artist. I was so **resolute**, absolutely determined that nothing would stop me, not even starvation. I even left my wife and child because I thought they were **hampering** my career. A great artist, I thought, must **forgo** the comforts of home and family."

"I showed my first painting in a gallery when I was twenty years old. I was so excited. Finally, I thought, the world would appreciate my work. I would get all the **prestige** and recognition I deserved. The critics, however, did something worse than attack me. '**Competent** but unoriginal,' they said. Basically, they meant I knew how to paint a horse that looked like a horse, but so what? It was nothing new or impressive."

"I didn't care, though. Their criticism only strengthened my **resolve**. I tried harder, put myself through a **rigorous** schedule or working as a waiter all day to earn a few dimes and painting all night to get ready for another show. A few months later I was ready. You know what the reviews in the papers said that time? '**Banal**.' '**Trite**.' That's right, boring and unoriginal. One critic said my work was '**insipid**,' which means more uninteresting than unoriginal, but you get the picture. The next show got the same reaction. In fact, all the subsequent shows got the same reaction. Banal, trite, insipid, unoriginal. Ergghh!!"

Mr. Faux started to turn red again, but calmed down before going purple.

"I took all sorts of lessons. I asked everyone for advice on how to improve. But they gave only the most **indefinite** answers, like, 'you've just got to feel it' or 'let yourself go'," he continued. "I've always been a person who likes things *clear-cut*, you know? Finally, after many years, I decided to give up. But not without a fight."

CLEAR-CUT adj. not vague; definite   명쾌한
The handsome actor had clear-cut features.
잘 생긴 그 배우는 뚜렷한 용모를 지니고 있었다.

"My burning desire to be an artist turned into an **insatiable** desire for revenge against the entire artistic community, a desire that would never be satisfied! I had **squandered** my youth trying to impress them, but I would spend my older years destroying them. I started making forgeries of the most famous works of art in the world. My copies were so good that even experts had trouble telling the difference. Then I started copying other things, like clothing, money, jewels. I finally found my **niche** in the world of art. I am unoriginal, and good at being unoriginal. I make lots of money being unoriginal, and I don't intend to stop **reaping** the rewards just yet."

With that, Mr. Faux pulled his pistol out of the deep pocket of his red silk jacket and aimed it at the kids.

"Okay, that's enough, Mister," said Bridget, who was tired of hearing all this complaining and whining. "Face it, you're a *flop* as an artist. So what? I can't paint either. But it's not too late for you to be a good grandfather. Look at your choices: you can continue your life of crime, get caught eventually, because all criminals get caught eventually, and live out your days alone in a prison. Or you can give up your evil ways and try to **rectify** all the wrong you have done to your grandson. Get him out of this depressing dump, help him make something of himself, you know?"

Mr. Faux seemed torn and puzzled. He lowered the gun slightly, and seemed to be going through some emotional distress.

Babette chimed in, "Yes, Mr. Faux. Take him away from all this. Take him to Paris, so he can be truly appreciated as an artist. And through his success, you will have success."

Leonard looked longingly at his grandfather. "Could we?" he asked quietly. "Could we really go?"

FLOP **n.** total failure (of a book, play, etc.) 실패
Despite all the publicity, her latest novel was a complete flop.
모든 광고에도 불구하고 그녀의 최근 소설은 완전 실패였다.

Mr. Faux let the gun drop from his hand as tears flooded his eyes. "Of course, dear boy, of course," he said, holding out his arms to his grandson. At that, Leonard rushed to his grandfather and gave him a **hearty** *embrace*. The **calamity** had been avoided.

"Oh," said Babette, clapping her hands together. "It is so good to see that they have **reconciled** their differences."

"Yes, this is certainly a touching scene," said Barnaby.

But Bridget wasn't feeling as happy as her friends. She had wandered off into a corner and was lost in her own little world. When Beauregard came over and tried to *nuzzle* her hip, she was so **preoccupied** she didn't even notice him. When Babette saw her friend looking so troubled, she came over to help, too.

"Bridget, what is it?" she asked.

"Leonard has his grandfather back," she said, looking down at her high-top *sneakers*. "But I guess I'll never get my parents back, will I?"

Babette frowned and wrinkled her forehead in thought.

"Hmmm," she said. "I'm not so sure about that. I know you have every reason to be **pessimistic**, but I do think there is hope. Mr. Faux? Do you and Leonard plan to go to Paris right away?"

Mr. Faux, who was now beaming with joy, looked up and smiled widely. "Yes, of course!" he laughed. "Just as soon as we can arrange transportation."

"But I thought you shipped goods from here," said Barnaby. "Don't you have a boat?"

"Oh, no," he said. "Our customers must pick up their orders personally."

"Oh, dear. You see, we have a problem," Babette explained. "We need to get back to Paris very quickly. Bridget's parents are there, and she needs them. Do you think we can start building a ship right away?"

"Well, I'm not sure I have all the materials I need," Mr. Faux replied, "but we could look into it. I'll do anything I can to help you kids. After all, you gave me back my grandson!"

EMBRACE v. to take (a person, etc.) into one's arms as a sign of affection 포옹하다
She embraced her son before leaving.
그녀는 떠나기 전에 아들을 포옹했다.

NUZZLE v. to press or rub (somebody/something) gently with the nose 코로 문질러대다
The horse nuzzled my shoulder.
말이 내 어깨를 코로 문질러댔다.

SNEAKER (=plimsoll) n. a light canvas shoe with a soft rubber sole, used for games and sports 운동화
He wore old jeans and a pair of sneakers.
그는 낡은 진 바지에 운동화를 신고 있었다.

Poor Bridget. I've never seen a child more depressed. I guess she'd put up a brave front as long as she could. Babette told her to go take a nap, get some rest, and I had to agree that was good advice. By the time she woke up, the situation looked much brighter. Leonard and Barnaby had worked together to draw up the plans for a small submarine. Mr. Faux was busy gathering maps and materials, and Babette was chopping sheet metal with her right hand (that girl packs a wow of a punch). Barnaby's amazing head of hair came in handy again. I swear I will never, so long as I live, forget how he pulled an entire *periscope* from behind his ear.

It didn't take long before all the pieces were ready. The only problem, it seemed, was how to hold them all together, but thanks to Bridget's *resourcefulness* that wasn't a problem for long. While everyone held the stuff up, Bridget pulled her gum out and wrapped it around and around the submarine until it was completely *airtight* and looked like a big pink ball of rubber bands. After packing up some food and art supplies, we were ready to go. Mr. Faux left all the keys with that fellow Ed, and we were off.

Of course, it being Leonard and Barnaby's first attempt at submarine design, there were some minor *hitches*. The controls were awkward and difficult to **manipulate**, and the whole vessel clumsy and **unwieldy**. But all that aside, it looked as though we were headed for Paris at last.

PERISCOPE n. apparatus with mirrors and lenses arranged in a tube so that the user has a view of the surrounding area above, e.g. from a submarine when it is under water   잠망경
Why don't you use a periscope?
잠망경을 사용하지 그러니?

RESOURCEFULNESS n. cleverness at finding ways of doing things   수완이 비상함, 기량이 풍부함
No one can imitate his resourcefulness.
아무도 그의 수완을 흉내낼 수 없다.

AIRTIGHT adj. so tight that no air or gas can get in or out   밀폐된
It's an airtight bottle.
그것은 밀폐된 병이다.

HITCH n. temporary difficulty or problem   장애, 고장
The launch was delayed by a technical hitch.
기술 장애 때문에 발사가 지연되었다.

Relationships

Decide what relationship the following pairs of words have to each other. If they mean close to the same thing, make "S." If they have opposite meanings, mark "O."

1. counterfeit :: forgery
2. persecuted :: tormented
3. innovative :: insipid
4. banal :: trite
5. prestigious :: acclaimed
6. duplicate :: mimic
7. merit :: bane
8. kudos :: praise
9. confiscate :: donate
10. competent :: capable
11. resolute :: determined
12. squander :: waste
13. unwieldy :: graceful
14. pessimistic :: cheerful
15. temperate :: mild

Fill in the Blank

For each sentence below, choose the word that best completes the sentence.

1. Lilian's ball gown was very _____ : it must have taken weeks to sew on all those beads and decorations.

    a. miscellaneous   b. ornate   c. precarious   d. conciliatory

2. Herman's silver belt buckle is a family _____ , first worn by his great-great-great-grandfather Pete on his journey out to California many years ago.

    a. heirloom   b. niche   c. legacy   d. guile

3. In order to keep up with the demand for their goods, the basket weavers set themselves a _____ of ten baskets a day each.

    a. mentor   b. quota   c. pinnacle   d. scrutiny

4. As part of a(n) _____ experiment, my roommate is forcing himself to go without sleep for five days to see how it affects his moods.

    a. psychological   b. pathological   c. aesthetic   d. expedient

5. If you invest you money early, you will _____ great rewards later in life.

    a. preoccupy   b. manipulate   c. undermine   d. reap

6. The other kids in the band _____ my lame attempts to play "Melancholy Baby" on the tuba.

    a. patronized   b. degraded   c. derided   d. discriminated

7. Lila's family loves to hear her sing and play the piano, but a more _____ audience might not think she's as entertaining as her parents do.

    a. paraplegic   b. insatiable   c. didactic   d. objective

Matching

Match each word on the right with a word on the left that has a meaning that's close to the same.

1. herald
2. weary
3. veer
4. allay
5. curt
6. excavate
7. gouge
8. laudable
9. aspire
10. allure
11. scrupulous
12. avail
13. persevere
14. superficial

a. shallow
b. cut out
c. hollow out
d. announce
e. lesson
f. careful
g. tired
h. usefulness
i. swerve
j. brief
k. keep on
l. praiseworthy
m. attraction
n. hope

Q U I C K   Q U I Z   33

Matching

Match each word on the right with a word on the left that has a meaning that's close to the same.

1. unbeknownst
2. tedious
3. absurd
4. obligation
5. pragmatic
6. shrewd
7. hamper
8. forgo
9. resolve
10. rigorous
11. indefinite
12. rectify
13. hearty
14. reconcile

a. crafty
b. reunite
c. not known
d. friendly
e. demanding
f. make right
g. duty
h. vague
i. tiresome
j. ridiculous
k. practical
l. determination
m. hold up
n. do without

That's a Big Museum

박물관 한번 크네

All things considered, that submarine turned out to be pretty *durable*, especially for something held together with bubble gum. It proved to be more than tough enough to withstand our long trip underwater. Leonard and Mr. Faux alternated between steering and navigating. That is, while Leonard steered, Mr. Faux would plot the course, and vice versa. Which was fine by me. I was glad to have a chance to rest, and I know Bridget, Barnaby, and Babette were too.

In fact, I was forced to admit I didn't have the **stamina** I once had as a young cat. Our little adventures had emptied my saved-up energy **reserves**, if you know what I mean. I felt the need for a good long sleep, so I found a *cozy* little corner and was soon off in dreamland.

Next thing I knew, I was being awakened by all sorts of shouts and hand clapping. "Oh, no," I thought, "here we go again," but when I opened my eyes, I was what all the *racket* was about. Believe it or not, we had made it! The submarine had surfaced in the Seine River—in Paris!

"Well, my friends, it is time for us to part," said Mr. Faux, as the travelers stood on the river bank. "I will always be grateful to you, but it is doubtful we will ever meet again. I am a wanted criminal, so I must travel **incognito** to avoid arrest. I will change my name, maybe even disguise my face! You would do well to forget you know me."

"We will never forget you," said Babette, "but we understand your point."

The friends hugged and waved good-bye to Leonard and his grandfather.

"Take care!" called Mr. Faux. "Come, Leonard, we are off to the Louvre."

Bridget jumped.

"The Louvre? Wait, wait!" she cried, running to catch up with them. "Um, I don't suppose we could share a taxi with you, could we?"

DURABLE adj. lasting for a long time 튼튼한
These trousers were made of durable material.
이 바지는 튼튼한 소재로 만들어졌다.

COZY (=cosy) adj. warm and comfortable 아늑한
It really is a nice cozy little house.
그것은 정말 멋지고 아늑한 작은 집이다.

RACKET n. loud noise; uproar or noisy disturbance 소음; 법석
What a racket the children are making!
아이들이 얼마나 법석을 떨어대는지!

"Good idea," said Barnaby. "Let's start our search for your parents at the last place you saw them. Maybe we can pick up some *clues*."

"We should explain," said Babette to Mr. Faux. "Getting back to Paris was an important goal for us, but our **prime** goal is to find Bridget's parents."

"But of course!" said Mr. Faux. "It is the least I can do. But a couple of you will have to keep your heads down. I think you're only allowed four people in one taxi."

And with that, they walked up to the street to hail a cab.

It was a good thing Bridget was such a fast thinker, because they didn't have any money and the walk to the museum would have taken a very long time. After a lengthy ride, Mr. Faux paid the driver. Once again, it was time to say good-bye.

"We are going to overload our senses with art!" declared Mr. Faux, and he and Leonard walked into the museum.

Bridget, Barnaby, Babette, and Beauregard sat outside, trying to come up with a plan.

"The first thing we must do is **speculate** upon every possible course of action your parents could have taken. Think hard," said Barnaby. "They may be in a nearby restaurant, they may be back at your hotel, they may be at the police station. We must **compile** a list of every possible *option*, then follow up on each one."

"That would take a very long time," said Bridget.

"That is a **gross** *understatement*, Bridget," said Babette.

"It would not just take a long time, it would take forever! Bridget's parents could be anywhere by now."

CLUE n. fact or piece of evidence that helps to solve a problem or reveal the truth in an investigation 단서
The only clue to the identity of the murderer was a half-smoked cigarette.
살인자의 신원에 대한 유일한 단서는 반만 타다 남은 담배였다.

OPTION n. power or freedom of choosing; choice 선택권; 선택
He did it because he had no other option.
그는 다른 선택 사항이 없어서 그것을 했다.

UNDERSTATEMENT n. statement that expresses an idea, etc. too weakly 자제된 표현
To say that he was displeased is an understatement.
그가 기쁘지 않았다고 말하는 것은 자제된 표현이다.

"I suppose you have a better idea," snapped Barnaby.

"Yes. I usually don't like calling on adults for help, but I think such action is **warranted** in a situation like this," said Babette. "I think adult assistance is definitely called for."

"What do you suggest, that I turn myself in to the lost and found?" asked Bridget.

"Well, no, I... hey, Bridget—those two people coming out the door," said Babette, pointing toward the museum. "They look a great deal like you, don't they?"

Bridget looked over her shoulder and *squinted*. She could see a man and woman. The man was struggling with some big, **cumbersome** packages, and the woman was looking around anxiously. As they got a little closer, Bridget let out a yelp of happiness.

"Mom! Dad! Mom!" she called, waving her hands above her head.

The woman stopped and looked, then began running toward her full speed.

"Bridget!" she cried, as she scooped her daughter up in her arms. "Bridget, baby, here you are!"

Bridget's mother hugged and kissed her so **profusely** that her face was practically covered in pink lipstick prints. But her mother's **initial** happiness soon gave way to another reaction, which was definitely anger. She put her daughter down and looked her sternly in the eye.

"Bridget, didn't I tell you to wait by the information desk if we got separated?" she demanded. "What are you doing out here? Where have you been?"

Bridget's father finally managed to *waddle* over to them. He put down his many bags and packages and heaved a sigh.

"See?" he said. "I told you she was alright."

SQUINT v. to look or gaze with the eyes partly closed; to look sideways 실눈을 뜨고 쳐다보다, 곁눈질을 하다
The bright sun made him squint at the sky to see the airplane.
밝은 태양 때문에 그는 비행기를 보기 위해 실눈을 뜨고 하늘을 쳐다보았다.

WADDLE v. to walk with short steps and a swaying movement, as a duck does 어기적어기적 걸어오다
A short plump woman came waddling along the pavement.
땅딸막하고 뚱뚱한 여자가 보도를 따라 어기적어기적 걸어오고 있었다.

"How can you be so **complacent**? I can't understand how you keep from worrying about your own daughter. Anything could have happened to her! *Kidnappings* and murders are so **prevalent** these days, and the problem is as wide-spread in Paris as it is in New York!"

"Well, I knew she couldn't have gone far," he said.

Barnaby and Babette giggled at the **irony** of that statement.

"Where have you been?" Bridget's mother repeated.

Bridget was too tired and hungry to give her mother a full **synopsis** of what she'd been up to. Besides, she thought, a summary like that might get her into more trouble. So she decided to answer her mother's question with a question of her own.

"Where have I been? I don't see how that's relevant. I'm the child, and it's your responsibility to keep up with me. I think a more **pertinent** question is where have you been? I've been waiting for you for days!" said Bridget. She felt quite pleased with herself. That gave her mother something to *chew* on.

But Bridget's mother only chewed on it for a couple of seconds before making Bridget sorry she'd ever even thought of talking back.

"My responsibility? I'll tell you about my responsibility, young lady. I told you to wait by the information desk. You chose to ignore me. Based on that, I can only **conclude** that you have no respect for your mother, and it's my responsibility to punish you until you can learn to mind your parents!" she said in that low, *scary* voice she used whenever she was really mad.

"Wait just a minute, honey," said Bridget's father. "There's no sense locking her up and throwing away the key. Maybe she can be **rehabilitated**, you know? Reformed into a good citizen? Bridget, do you promise to be a good daughter from now on and wait where your mother tells you?"

Bridget nodded her head gratefully.

KIDNAPPING n. stealing somebody away by force and illegally, especially in order to obtain money or other demands 유괴
The kidnapping occurred in broad daylight.
대낮에 유괴가 일어났다.

CHEW v. to think something over; to meditate 깊이 생각하다
He chewed the problem over in his mind.
그는 마음속으로 그 문제를 깊이 생각했다.

SCARY adj. causing fright or alarm 무서운
Maxwell Anderson's scary melodrama dealing with a winsome little girl is very popular.
매력적인 어린 소녀를 다루고 있는 맥스웰 앤더슨의 공포 멜로드라마는 아주 인기가 있다.

"There, see?" said her father. "Besides, honey, it does sort of seem like we've been in that museum gift shop for days." He looked down at all the packages around his feet.

"Your mother's been up to her **prodigal** gift buying again," he laughed. "I think she got a present for everyone on our block back home—even the folks she doesn't like!"

Bridget laughed. Her mother smiled and relaxed a bit.

"Well, it's okay to be *extravagant* when you're on vacation," she said. "But we're being rude. Bridget, it looks like you've made some friends."

"Yeah, Mom, these are my very best friends, Barnaby, Babette, and Beauregard," said Bridget.

"Well, since you are my daughter's very best friends, we'd be pleased if you'd join us for lunch. We're starved," she said. "That Louvre is one huge museum. You could spend days in there and not even notice the time passing."

Barnaby and Babette smiled at each other, and accepted her invitation. Then the whole group began walking to a nearby restaurant.

"That's a big black cat," said Bridget's dad, watching Beauregard's long tail *swish* back and forth ahead of him. "Careful he doesn't bring you big bad luck."

"That is one **superstition** I will never have again," said Bridget. "Beauregard is a great cat to have around when you're in trouble."

"Hmm," said Bridget's father, smiling with amusement, "maybe we'll have to buy him a big piece of fish, then, since he's such a good buddy."

"Definitely," said Bridget.

Beauregard's stomach *rumbled* softly in **anticipation** of the wonderful lunch he would soon be eating.

EXTRAVAGANT adj. using or spending too much; wasteful 낭비하는
An extravagant person has extravagant tastes and habits.
낭비하는 사람은 낭비하는 기호와 습관을 갖고 있다.

SWISH v. to swing through the air with a hissing sound; to move with or make this sound; to rustle 획획 소리를 내며 움직이다
She swished across the floor in her long silk dress.
그녀는 긴 비단 드레스로 획획 소리를 내며 마루 위를 지나갔다.

RUMBLE v. to make a deep heavy continuous sound 꼬르륵거리다
I'm so hungry that my stomach's rumbling.
너무 배가 고파서 배속에서 꼬르륵거린다.

And it was a truly wonderful lunch. Babette, Barnaby, Bridget, and Beauregard all ordered huge plates of fish and french fries, and they were so hungry they even ate the parsley **garnish**, which was only meant for decoration, not for eating. In fact, they *gobbled* up everything they could lay their hands on.

"My, what little **gluttons** we have on our hands," said Bridget's mother, smiling. "Please have some dessert. We can't have you going away hungry!"

The children ordered chocolate mousse and ice cream and enjoyed it mightily, and they laughed and talked and told adventure stories for hours. Then they ordered more food, and told more stories. Bridget handed over her Yankees cap to Babette, who managed to look even more chic and mysterious with this new accessory. Everyone was having such a good time, in fact, that they didn't even notice the enormous black cat quietly *slip* out from under the table.

He knew his job was done. Bridget was safely returned to her parents, and Babette and Barnaby were back where they belonged, too. Beauregard took one last look at his human friends and smiled, thinking about all the fun they'd had. Then he walked out of the restaurant, down the block, and off into the beautiful Parisian sunset, perhaps to have a few little adventures of his own.

GOBBLE v. to eat something fast, noisily and greedily 게걸스럽게 먹다
Eat slowly and don't gobble!
천천히 먹지 게걸스럽게 먹지 마라!

SLIP v. to go somewhere quietly or quickly, e.g. in order not to be noticed, or without being noticed 빠져나가다
The thief slipped out by the back door.
도둑은 뒷문으로 빠져나갔다.

Relationships

Decide what relationship the following pairs of words have to each other. If they mean close to the same thing, make "S." If they have opposite meanings, mark "O."

1. prodigal :: profuse
2. initial :: final
3. durable :: flimsy
4. prime :: main
5. pertinent :: relevant
6. garnish :: decoration
7. prevalent :: rare
8. cumbersome :: awkward
9. ironic :: literal
10. superstition :: fact

Matching

Match each word on the right with a word on the left that has a meaning that's close to the same.

1. alternate	a. take turns
2. vice versa	b. justify
3. stamina	c. in reverse
4. reserve	d. in disguise
5. incognito	e. endurance
6. speculate	f. large
7. compile	g. think about
8. gross	h. stored supply
9. warrant	i. put together
10. complacent	j. summary
11. synopsis	k. overeater
12. conclude	l. expectation
13. rehabilitate	m. decide
14. anticipation	n. restore
15. glutton	o. self-satisfied

Translation & Answer

해석 및 정답

p.162

우선 내 소개를 할게. 이름은 보리가드고, 오랜 전통을 지닌 사우스캐롤라이나 귀족 출신의 고양이 신사지. 우리 선조들은 8대조 할아버지인 루시어스부터 우리 아버지에 이르기까지 남부 지방 훌륭한 가문들의 저택에서 살아왔어. 우린 몸집뿐만 아니라(나만 봐도, 뒷다리로 서서 걸을 땐 키가 4피트 반 가까이나 된다구) 완벽한 몸가짐과 기품, 어느 모로 보나 훌륭한 신사 집안으로도 명성이 자자하지. 아름답게 손질된 윤기 흐르는 털을 보더라도 탁월한 혈통을 짐작하고도 남을 거야. 내 털은 새까만 색인데, 아침마다 손질하고 쓰다듬어 완벽한 모양을 만드는 데 꽤 많은 시간을 들인다구(어디서 누굴 만날지 모르는 일이잖아?).

그날 오후 난 더할 수 없이 행복하고 만족스러웠어. 파리의 널따랗고 아름다운 공원 불로뉴 숲에서 너무나 부드럽고 볕이 잘 드는 잔디밭에 누워 누구도 뭐라 하지 않을 낮잠을 자고 있었거든. 내가 프랑스에서 뭘 하면서 지냈냐면, 글쎄 젊은 시절 좀 방종했다는 걸 나도 인정해. 그래서 집안에선 스캔들이 좀 가라앉을 때까지 장기 여행을 떠나는 게 최선이라고 생각했던 거야. 맞아, 사실이야, 난 날이면 날마다 나가서 하루 종일 흥청망청 마셔대고 개박하를 먹고 호색꾼 친구 녀석들과 목청 높여 노래를 불러 대고, 젊은 숙녀 고양이들 뒤꽁무니를 쫓아다녔어. 그때가 좋았는데! 펠리니아라는 아리따운 고양이가 있었어. 그녀와 난 곧잘... 뭐, 그 얘긴 다음에 하기로 하지. 어쨌든 우리 가족들은 내가 이국땅에서 건들거리며 다니는 게 최선이라고 생각한 거야.

얘기가 딴 데로 흘렀군. 아까 말했듯이 난 낮잠을 자고 있었는데, 평소 같으면 그 어느 것도 날 방해하지 않았을 거야. 그런데 조그만 여자애를 본 순간 그녀가 곤경에 처해 있다는 걸 알았지. 여자애는 차분하고 별일 없는 듯 행동하려고 했어. 세상 어떤 것에도 관심 없다는 듯 그저 풍선껌을 씹으며 공원을 한가로이 산책하면서 말야. 그런데 자기만 그렇게 생각했던 거지. 그녀는 파리 출신이 아니었는데, 땋아 내린 머리 위로 뉴욕 양키즈 모자를 거꾸로 쓰고 있는 걸로 알 수 있었지. 주변엔 부모로 보이는 사람이 아무도 없었어. 그래서 요모조모 따져 본 후 그녀가 길을 잃은 거라는 판단을 내렸어.

p.163

이 여자애는 불안한 기색이 역력해 한눈에 봐도 속을 태우고 있음을 알 수 있었지. 그래서 그날 난 예외를 두고 낮잠 자는 걸 그만두기로 한 거야. 그녀는 벤치에 풀썩 주저앉더니 진흙 속에서 발을 이리저리 차고 있었어. 뭐라도 도울 수 있을까 싶어 막 일어나 그녀에게 가려고 하는데, 그때 바베트가 다가오더니 둘이 이야기를 나누기 시작했어. 난 고양이들이 그렇듯, 호기심이 생기기도 하고 걱정이 되기도 해서 가까이에 있으면서 그 애들이 괜찮은지 확인해야겠다 마음먹었지. 물론 그날 이후로 내가 코끼리 제국을 전복시킬 음모에 말려들게 되리라고는 추호도 생각하지 못했던 거야.

"너 미국인이구나." 바베트가 단조로운 투로 말했다.

브리지트는 약간 움찔했다. 그녀는 누군가 자기에게 영어로 말을 걸리라고는 생각 못했고, 더군다나 바베트 같은 사람을 만나게 되리라고는 생각지 못했다. 그녀는 검은 머리에 검은 옷을 입고 검은 선글라스를 끼고 있어 얼굴이 거의 안보였다. 사실상 그녀의 차림 중 눈에 띄는 색이라고는 선명한 붉은 립스틱뿐이었다. 브리지트는 말괄량이 그 자체로, 립스틱이나 "여자애들"하고 다니는 건 죄다 바보 같다고 생각해 왔는데, 이 여자애는 전혀 바보같이 보이지 않았다. 오히려 어른 같았고 세련돼 보였다.

"그래, 난 미국인이야." 브리지트는 무관심한 듯 보이려고 애쓰며 대답했다. "근데 그게 뭐?"

"여기서 뭐하고 있니?" 바베트가 물었다.

"그냥 벤치에 앉아 내 일을 생각하고 있는 거야.

그게 뭐 잘못됐어?" 브리지트가 투덜거렸다. 퉁명스럽거나 불친절해 보이려는 생각은 없었지만, 어쩐지 이 낯설고 나이 많은 아이에게 자신이 겁에 질려 있다는 걸 들키고 싶지 않았다.

"잘못된 건 없어." 프랑스 소녀가 말했다. "그냥 궁금해서. 네 가족은 어디 있는데?"

브리지트는 한숨을 내쉬고는 진흙 속을 빤히 내려다봤다. "잃어버렸어."라고 중얼거렸다.

p.164

"아, 그렇구나. 넌 고아로구나. 사고를 당했니?"

"아니, 사고는 아니야. 루브르에서. 루브르에서 우연히. 그러니까, 그 시시한 박물관에 갔다가 잃어버렸어. 가족들이 날 잃어버린 거지. 아니면 서로 잃어버렸든지. 어쨌든 가족들은 여기 없어."브리지트는 이렇게 말하고, 아랫입술을 깨물었다. 그녀는 쓸데없는 얘기를 지껄였다는 생각이 들었지만, 그렇다고 평정을 잃고 싶진 않았다.

"아," 바베트 선글라스 위로 눈썹을 보이며 말했다.

'이 앤 누구지?' 브리지트는 생각했다. '아'라는 건 무슨 의미야? 그녀는 이런 식의 대화를 더 이상 하고 싶지 않았다.

"이봐, 넌 대체 누구고 원하는 게 뭐야?"브리지트가 물었다. "빈둥거리느라 바쁜 거 모르겠어? 너랑 얘기하느라 온종일 아무것도 안 하고 빈둥거리려는 내 계획에 차질이 생기고 있잖아."

"부모님 찾는 거 내가 도와줄까?"바베트가 대답했다. 그녀에겐 사람들 말에 대꾸를 않는 이상한 버릇이 있었다.

브리지트는 당황했다. 이 말을 어떻게 받아들여야 할지 알 수 없었다. 아는 사람도 아닌데다 친구는 더더욱 아닌 이 아이가 왜 나를 돕겠다는 거지? 게다가 브리지트는 남들에게 신세지는 것을 싫어했다. 특히 방금 만났을 뿐인 어딘지 수수께끼 같은 프랑스 여자애에게 빚을 지고 싶지 않았다. 그러나 한편으론, 이 애는 아마 파리를 잘 알고 있을 테고, 자신의 부모님을 찾는 것도 사실 괜찮은 생각이었다.

브리지트가 이 난처한 상황에서 어쩔 줄 몰라 하고 있자 바베트가 또 제안을 했다. "자, 가서 네 가족을 찾아보자."

"저리 가," 브리지트가 툭 내뱉었다. "누가 너보고 도와 달랬니?"

"내 이름은 바베트야. 그리고 넌 도움이 필요한 게 분명해. 지금 네 가족을 찾으러 갈 수 있어. 일어나서 나랑 같이 간다면 말야." 바베트는 브리지트의 적대적인 말투를 신경쓰는 것 같지 않았다.

아니, 사실은 전혀 눈치 채지 못하는 것 같았다.

p.165

브리지트에겐 바베트의 마음을 바꿀 방법이 없었다. 그녀는 눈에 띄게 단호했고, 지금 자신의 처지도 그렇고, 브리지트가 할 수 있는 최선의 방법은 그 제안에 응하는 것이었다. 하지만 뉴욕 시민에다가 천성적으로 남을 잘 믿지 않는 브리지트는, 바베트가 자신을 도우려 하는 데 무슨 꿍꿍이가 있는 게 아닌지 여전히 의심스러웠다. 저 애는 인간으로 변장한 외계인으로 이상한 실험에 필요한 사람을 찾고 있는 게 아닐까? 아이들을 유괴해 집시에게 팔아넘기는 사람이 아닐까? 브리지트는 대놓고 물어보리라 마음먹었다.

"왜 날 도우려는 거지?"

"솔직히 난 너무 심심한데 별달리 할 일이 없어." 바베트가 한숨지으며 말했다.

브리지트가 싱긋 웃었다. 그건 믿을 수 있는 대답이었다. 이 바베트란 애는 외모처럼 멋진 아이일 것 같았다. 브리지트는 일어나 바베트에게 손을 내밀었다.

"내 이름은 브리지트야. 가자." 브리지트가 말했다.

바베트도 손을 내밀어 악수했고, 둘은 걸어가기 시작했다.

"그런데 내가 미국인인 건 어떻게 알았니?"커브 길을 돌아 거리로 나설 때 브리지트가 물었다.

"넌, 뭐랄까, 두드러져. 눈에 띈다구. 모자며 청바지며, 이런 건 아주 미국적인 차림이잖아. 특히 모자가 아주 멋져. 아주 세련돼 보여. 아주 멋진 파리인들이라면 모두 이런 모자를 쓰고 싶어 하지."

"고마워. 너도 아주 세련됐어."브리지트가 말했다. "있지. 네가 우리 부모님을 찾아 주면 이 모자 줄게. 어때?"

"좋아," 바베트가 대답했다. 그녀는 미소 짓는 듯했지만, 저 어두운 선글라스 뒤로 어떤 표정을 짓고 있는지 알 수 없었다.

새로 사귄 두 친구가 그들의 임무 수행을 시작하기 위해 분주한 보도로 걸어 나갔다. 그들이 잠깐 멈추어 자신들의 어깨 너머를 봤다면 그들 둘만이 아니라는 사실을 알았을 것이다. 거구의 우아한 검은 고양이가 그 뒤를 바짝 쫓아가고 있었다.

브리지트와 바베트는 잠시 동안 말없이 걷고 있었는데, 그때 갑자기 바베트가 아파트 빌딩처럼 생긴 건물 앞에서 우뚝 멈추어 섰다. 사실 그것은 아주 낡고 누추한 아파트 건물로, 시민 아파트라 부르는 게 나을 법했다.

"여기에 들어가야 돼." 바베트가 말했다.

"어... 그래, 그러자." 브리지트가 머뭇거리며 말했다. 그녀는 이 건물의 외관이 전혀 맘에 들지 않았다. "근데 이 건물은 뭐야?"

"자연과학계 학생들을 위한 대학 기숙사야." 바베트가 문을 열면서 대답했다. 젊은 천재들이 모두 여기 살아. 실험실에 없을 땐 말야. 내 친구 바너비를 만나려고 온 거야. 그 애도 너처럼 미국인이야. 그 애가 네 부모님 찾는 걸 도와줄수 있을지 모르니까."

"잘됐다." 브리지트가 들뜬 목소리로 말했고, 둘은 건물 안으로 들어갔는데, 고양이 보리가드도 그 뒤를 따랐다. "그애를 찾아보자."

"미리 말해 두겠는데, 바너비는 기벽이 좀 있어. 그냥 이상한 자잘한 버릇들인데, 어떤 사람들은 그걸 싫어하더라구." 바베트가 계단을 올라가면서 조용히 설명했다.

"어떤 기벽인데?" 브리지트가 물었는데, 그녀는 자신들이 하고 있는 이 모든 일에 대해 점점 초조하고 불안해졌다.

"걱정할 건 없어, 정말로. 제일 눈에 띄는 특이한 것은 머리카락이야. 그 애의 머리 모양은 다른 사람과는 다른데, 그게 트레이드마크지. 그 앤 내가 아는 가장 똘똘한 사람이기도 해. 겨우 열 살의 나이로 대학에 들어갔어. 사람들이 "신동"이라고 불렀을 거야. 그런데 아직 너무 어려서 흥분을 잘해. 아," 민무늬의 나무문 앞에서 걸음을 멈추며 말했다. "여기가 그 애 방이야. 노크해 봐."

브리지트가 오른손으로 조심스럽게 문을 몇 번 톡톡 두드렸다. 그녀는 아무 응답이 없는 것이 고마울 지경이었다.

"안에 없네. 가자." 브리지트가 말했다.

바베트가 미소 짓더니 양주먹으로 문을 힘껏 두드리기 시작했다. "그렇게 겁먹지 마. 바너비! 바너비!" 바베트가 소리 질렀다. "어서 문 열어!"

바로 그때 문이 왹 열리더니 이상하게 생긴 남자아이가 고개를 쑥 내밀었다. 머리는 숱이 많고 긴 데다 옅은 빛깔이었고, 미친 사자의 갈기처럼 사방으로 쭉쭉 뻗쳐 있었다. 그렇게 제멋 대로인 더벅머리 밑에 있는 얼굴은 그냥 평범한 소년의 모습이었다. 아주 약하게 표현하면, 깔끔하지 못하다고 할 수 있었다. 사실은 새들이 날아와 머릿속에 둥지를 튼 것 같았고, 실험실 가운은 세탁기 근처에 가본 적도 없는 것처럼 보였다. 그 "신동"은 두 명의 여자아이와 거구의 고양이가 찾아온 일은 처음인 듯이 처음엔 당황한 것 같았는데, 이내 방실 웃으며 문을 왈칵 열어젖혔다.

"어머나, 바베트!" 그는 소리치며 방으로 들어오라는 손짓을 했다. "들어와, 어서. 내 최근 실험을 봐야지."

방은 거품이 부글거리고 있는 시험관들, 이상한 색깔의 액체들, 죽은 곤충 한 무더기, 자주 개자리에서부터 참마에 이르기까지 죽 널려 있는 온갖 종류의 야채들로 가득 차 있었다.

"여기 내 작은 녹색 친구들을 보면 알겠지만, 내 실험은 사실상 식물학적인 거야. 그래, 바베트, 난 오랫동안 식물들, 특히 무해한 야채들의 불행한 처지를 보고 괴로워." 그는 안타까워했다. "불쌍한 식물들이 얼마나 고생을 하는지! 얘들은 이렇게 아름답지만 불행히도 팔다리가 없어서 이 잔인하고 비열한 벌레들과 싸워 물리칠 수도 없다구!" 그는 손으로 창백하게 죽어 있는 벌레 더미를 세게 내리쳤다. "지금까지는 이 사랑스러운 야채에 농약을 뿌리는 수밖에 없었지. 그건 너무 유독해서 땅을 오염시키고 물을 더럽히는 데 말이야.

하지만 이젠 아니야! 내 발명품이 이런 독약을 없앨 거니까. 그런 건 더 이상 전혀 필요 없을 거야. 완전히 없어질 거라구! 마침내 우리는... 이봐," 그는 갑자기 말을 멈추었다, "누가 고양이를 들어오라고 했지?"

모든 눈이 고양이에게로 쏠렸는데, 고양이는 문간에서 자고 있는 듯했다.

"난 이 고양이 본 적이 있어." 바베트가 말했다. "불로뉴 숲에서 비둘기들을 쫓아다니고 암컷 고양이만 보면 추근거려. 너무어리석어서 그렇지 해롭지는 않아."

모두들 낄낄거리며 웃었고, 고양이는 잠을 자면서 작게 으르렁거리는 듯했다.

"그래, 그러니까, 내가 말한 대로 마침내 우린 비열한 킬러들을 물리치게 될 거야." 바너비가 중얼거렸다.

"야, 여기 냄새 너무 지독해." 브리지트가 얼굴을 찡그리며 말했다. "고약한 냄새는 뭐니?"

"아하! 그렇지? 효과가 있구나!" 바너비가 손뼉을 치며 소리쳤다.

브리지트는 어리둥절해 보였다. "너 정신 나갔니?"

"아니, 전혀 아니야. 내가 설명해 줄게. 네가 맡고 있는 냄새는 운동 양말들이야. 학기 내내 한번도 안 빨고 신어서 라커 속에 남아 있던 더러운 운동 양말들 말야. 냄새 지독하지?" 바너비가 웃으며 물었다. 그는 잠깐 말을 멈추었다. "근데 있지. 벌레들은 냄새를 싫어하거든. 하지만 운동 양말 냄새는 그냥 싫어하는 정도가 아니지. 얘들은 이 냄새를 너무너무 싫어해서 가까이 올 수도 없어. 이 냄새는 또 어떤 식물균들의 생장을 억제하지만, 완전히 멈추게 하지는 않아. 이 양말들이 이 비열한 벌레들을 죽이기까지 했다구." 그는 실험실 가운에 손을 문질러 닦으며 말했다. "벌레의 시대는 이제 끝난 거야. 더 이상 이 해충들이 농작물을 파괴해 식량 부족을 일으키는 일은 없을 거라구."

p.169

"기아를 막는다는 건 참으로 고상한 생각이야. 그런데, 바너비, 이 세상에 메스꺼운 운동 양말이 모든 농작물로부터 곤충의 접근을 막아낼 만큼 많진 않잖아." 바베트가 의견을 제시했다.

"날카로운 지적이야. 너 정말 예리하구나. 그래, 불행하게도 우리 주변에는 그런 양말이 많이 있지는 않지. 그래서 내가 메스꺼운 운동 양말의 본질, 바로 그 양말을 구역질나게 만드는 것이 무엇인지를 포착하려고 애쓰는 중이야. 그게 발냄새일까?

땀일까? 발톱엔 낀 때일까? 일단 그걸 알아내기만 하면 다양한 원료를 이용해 진짜 양말과 똑같은 효과를 지닌 합성 스프레이를 만들어 낼 수 있는 거야. 아주 효과가 좋을 거야. 정말 그래. 아무도 그 힘을 의심치 않을 거라구. 하지만 독성은 없을 거야."

브리지트는 눈동자를 굴렸다. 바너비는 좀 의기양양해 보였는데, 브리지트는 늘 잘난 척하는 사람들에게 짜증이 났다. "있지, 난 브리지트라고 하는데 바베트는 네가 우리 부모님 찾는 걸 도와줄 수 있다고 생각하나 봐."

"그럼 넌 부모님을 잃어버린 거니? 기분이 어떨지 알겠다. 정말 안됐다. 나도 옛날에 꼬박 일 년 동안 부모님을 잃었었어. 아니, 그보다는, 일년 동안 부모님께 전화 거는 걸 잊어버렸던 것 같아. 아마존 다우림 지역의 열대지방 새들의 노래를 연구하고 있었거든. 그러니 부모님께서 날 잃어버리셨다고 할 수도 있겠네. 어느 쪽이든 그건 당황스런 일이지. 그래." 바너비는 머리를 긁적였다. 브리지트는 확실히 보지 못했지만, 그가 자신의 더벅머리에서 손목시계를 꺼내는 것 같았다. 아니면 아까부터 손목시계를 차고 있었던 건지도 모르겠다. "용액을 점검할 시간이야!" 그가 외쳤다.

젊은 과학자 바너비는 부글부글 김을 뿜는 회색 액체가 가득 담긴 큰 비커로 허겁지겁 달려가더니 조심스럽게 온도를 쟀는데, 그러는 내내 혼잣말을 중얼거렸다. 그리고는 다른 비커에 담겨진 부글거리는 푸른 액체를 안약병 같은 데 가득 붓더니 그것을 회색빛 오물에 더했다. 그런 다음, 그는 비커를 집어 들고 그 더러운 혼합물을 흔들었는데, 너무나 힘차게 흔드는 바람에 땀이 날 정도였다.

"숙녀 여러분," 그가 발표했다, "여러분은 과학에 있어서 역사적인 순간을 목격하게 될 것입니다!" 그러더니 카운트다운을 시작했다. "십, 구, 팔, 칠, 육..."

바너비는 카운트다운을 끝까지 하지 못했다. "사"쯤에 이르러 끔찍한 우르르 소리가 나기 시작했다. 그러더니 폭발이 일었고, 그런 다음엔 끔찍하기 이를 데 없는 냄새가 났다.

p.170

"서둘러! 당장 건물에서 나가야 돼! 나가! 나가라구!" 바너비가 소리를 질렀다.

소녀들과 고양이는 너무나 기뻐서 기꺼이 따랐다. 그들은 문밖으로 뛰어나가 길로 달려갔다. 그리고는 멈추어 서서 숨을 헐떡였다(이들은 2분 정도 숨을 참고 있었다).

"아, 바보같이 큰 실수를 저지르다니!" 바너비는 헐떡거렸다. "어떻게 그런 실수를 했지?"

"그래, 그래." 바베트가 별로 수긍을 하지 않으며 말했다.

"그 짓을 하게 만든 건 나의 자만이었어. 바보 같은 자존심이라니! 난 내가 그 위대한 포겔스텔렌슈타인보다 똑똑하다고 생각했어. 놀라울 만큼 단순한 발견들로 세계적 명성을 얻은 과학자 말야. 어떻게 내가 그 사람의 천재성을 탐낼 수가 있지! 그는 담배 연기를 살충제로 쓰자고 제안했던 사람이야. 당연히, 담배 연기에는 발암물질이 있기 때문에, 나는 농부들이 폐암에 걸리면 안 되니까 밭에서 담배 피우는 것을 장려하지 않는 게 최선이라고 생각했어. 운동 양말이 담배보다 더 해로울 수 있다는 걸 내가 어떻게 알았겠어?" 바너비는 거의 울 것 같았다.

"이봐, 걱정 마. 어, 그러니까, 그만 염려하라구." 브리지트가 말했다.

"그래, 네 말이 맞아." 바너비는 금세 기분을 바꾸며 말했다. "어차피 난 식물학이라면 아마추어에 불과해. 내 진짜 전문 분야는 물리학이야. 그래도 재미 삼아 다른 과학 분야에 도전해 보는 건 재미있지. 하지만 이 작은 사고는 나한테 좋은 징조가 아냐. 이 폭발은 내가 이번 주에 세 번째로 일으킨 거고, 학교 당국에선 내가 학교 재산을 계속 파괴시키면 퇴학시키겠다고 했지. 나의 위대한 발견을 발표한다는 건 아직 시기상조였나 봐. 결과를 입증하기 위해 더 많은 실험을 해야겠어. 그 결과들이 옳다는 걸 내가 절대적으로 확신할 수 있도록 말야. 그러려면 가서 정리를 해야겠지."

"말도 안돼." 바베트가 느닷없이 말을 꺼냈다. "우린 더 중요한 일을 처리해야 돼. 깨진 유리며 파편은 모두 학교에서 정리 하라고 해. 우린 브리지트의 부모님을 찾아야 한다구."

"미안. 당연히 그래야지. 어디서부터 시작할까?" 바너비가 물었다.

"그건 네가 알 줄 알았는데." 브리지트가 말했다. 그녀는 슬픈 표정으로 자신의 운동화를 빤히 내려다봤다. 이 모든 상황이 절망적으로 보이기 시작했다.

p.171

"자, 브리지트, 그렇게 낙담할 필요 없어." 바베트가 말했다. "바너비한테는 언제나 좋은 아이디어가 가득하니까."

"그렇고 말고!" 바너비도 맞장구쳤다. "자, 어디 보자. 넓은 땅을 한번에 보려면 공중에서 보는 게 최선이지! 우리한테 필요한 건 일종의 열기구야. 내일 아침까지 내가 설계할 수 있어."

브리지트는 이 아이디어에 활기를 되찾았다. "열기구라구? 진작 얘기하지 그랬어? 내가 미국에서 배워 온 자그마한 요술 두 가지를 보여줄게."

그렇게 말하며 브리지트는 껌을 씹기 시작했는데, 턱과 볼을 사납게 움직여 댔다. 그리고 나서 천천히 하늘을 향해 비치볼보다도 큰 핑크빛의 풍선을 불었다. 그리고는 바베트와 바너비는 (보리가드 까지도) 깜짝 놀라게, 브리지트가 땅 위로 떠오르기 시작하는 것이었다!

"어, 미국인들은 정말 놀라워!" 바베트가 외쳤다.

"정말 편리하겠다." 바너비가 말했다. "열기구를 입안에 가지고 다닐 수 있다니!"

브리지트는 크게 쪽 소리를 내며 껌을 입안으로 빨아들이고는 그들 앞으로 뚝 떨어졌다. "얘들아, 어때? 그러고 있으니까 아래가 잘 안 보이더라. 하지만 너희가 날 붙들고 있으면 나 대신 볼 수 있을 거야."

"그거 정말 재밌겠다." 바너비가 말했다.

바베트도 맞장구를 쳤다. 그리하여 브리지트는 심호흡을 하고 풍선껌으로 된 비행선을 만들기 시작했다. 그녀가 공중으로 떠오르자 두 명의 친구들, 즉 바너비는 오른쪽 다리, 바베트는 왼쪽 다리를 붙들었고, 다함께 하늘로 올라가기 시작했다.

그런데 이들이 막 이륙하게 됐을 때 바너비가 꽥 비명을 질렀다.

"아이! 저 고양이가 내 다리로 뛰어올랐어!"

"그럼 여기 무임 승차 고양이가 있는 거네?" 바베트가 말했다. "조심해, 바너비. 죄없는 파리 사람에게 백 파운드나 되는 고양이를 떨어뜨리는 일은 절대 하면 안 되니까."

잠시 후 이들 넷은 도시의 지붕 위로 떠올라 잃어버린 브리지트의 부모님을 열심히 찾았다. 안타깝게도 이들은 머리 위로 성난 먹구름 떼가 만들어지고 있음을 알아차리지 못했다.

p.172

이제 내가 도움이 필요한 저 아이들에 대해 무슨 얘기를 하는 건지 알겠지? 예를 들면, 바너비 말야. 그 애는 확실히 얘기를 종합할 줄은 알지만, 말에 조리가 있다고 해서 꼭 상식이 많은 건 아니지. 그리고 바베트는, 글쎄, 그 애는 그냥 좀 재미있는 일이 없나 해서 나온 게 분명해. 그 애는 순진하지만은 않아, 그건 확실해, 하지만 제 아무리 세상일에 밝은 아이라도 때로는 보살핌이 필요하지. 브리지트? 그 애는 충분히 강해 보여, 좋아, 하지만 좀 건방진 것 같더라. 표현이 좀 그랬다면 미안.

그리고 나는, 글쎄, 그 무시무시한 운동 양말 폭발 같은 충격은 그런 미친 애들 일에 더 이상 개입하는 걸 단념시키기에 충분했을 거야. 바너비 다리에 뛰어오르겠다는 결심은 아주 무의식적이었어. 그냥 그 애들이 떠오르는 걸 보니까, 내가 할 일은 나도 같이 떠오르는 거였지. 이륙하고 얼마 되지 않아서 우린 궁지에 빠질지도 모른다는 걸 깨달았어. 해는 떨어지고 있었고, 공기는 이상하게 가을날 치고 후덥지근하고 끈적거리는 데다 한여름보다 더웠어. 돌풍이 불어와 얼굴의 축축한 공기를 날려 주었는데, 처음엔 고마웠지. 그런데 또 다른 돌풍이 불어왔고, 비가, 커다랗고 무거운 빗방울이 떨어지기 시작한 걸 알았어. 그러자 순식간에 모든 게 제멋대로가 됐어. 바람이 너무 사납게 불어 꼭 롤러코스터를 타는 기분이었지. 비는 억수같이 쏟아져 내렸어. 남부 아시아의 계절풍이 생각났어. 엄청난 폭우를 몰고 오는 바람 말야. 방콕에서 보냈던 나른한 밤들이 선명하게 떠오르는군. 폭풍우가 멎기를 기다리며, 아름답고 이국적인... 또 딴 길로 빠졌군. 본론으로 돌아가자구. 바람이 우리 주위에서 점점 더 빠르게 소용돌이쳤는데, 진로를 벗어나 멀리 던져질 것 같은 두려움에 떨 정도로 굉장한 속도였어. 하지만 내가 할 수 있는 일이라고는 단단히 붙들고 (그리고 바너비가 꼭 붙들고 있기를 바라고) 폭풍우가 사그라지기를 기다리는 것 뿐이었어. 마침내 폭풍이 멎었을 때 나는 하마터면 우리가 계속 바람과 빗물에 매질 당하면서 공중 높이에 떠 있기를 바랄 뻔했어. 우린 무사히 풀밭으로 내려왔지만, 안도는 이내 두려움으로 바뀌었지. 우린 곧 포위당했고 포로, 즉 재칼 군대의 무기력한 포로로 붙잡히고 만 거야.

p.173

QUICK QUIZ 1
관계짓기
아래의 단어 쌍들이 서로 어떤 관계를 갖는지 판단하세요. 비슷한 의미이면 "S" 반대 의미이면 "O"를 하세요.

1. 걱정 :: 불안
2. 머뭇거리는 :: 마음 내켜 하지 않는
3. 세련된 :: 깔끔하지 못한
4. 술 마시며 흥청거리는 :: 건들건들 돌아다니는
5. 약아빠진 :: 순박한
6. 의심 :: 믿음
7. 기벽 :: 기행
8. 조숙한 :: 더딘
9. 아마추어 :: 재미로 하는 사람
10. 경멸할 만한 :: 비열한
11. 그냥 아는 사람 :: 가까운 친구

QUICK QUIZ 2
관계짓기
아래의 단어 쌍들이 서로 어떤 관계를 갖는지 판단하세요. 비슷한 의미이면 "S" 반대 의미이면 "O"를 하세요.

1. 퉁명스러운 :: 적대적인
2. 눈에 잘 띄는 :: 숨겨진
3. 주저하는 :: 소심한
4. 잘 잊어버리는 :: 빈틈없는
5. 못하게 하다 :: 도와주다
6. 어리둥절한 :: 당황한
7. 힘센 :: 약한
8. 유독한 :: 오염된
9. 뜻밖의 :: 갑작스런
10. 따르다 :: 불복종하다
11. 빈민 아파트 :: 대저택

빈칸 채우기

아래에 있는 각각의 단어들 중에서 가장 완벽한 문장을 만들어 주는 단어를 고르세요.

1. 마크는 파티에서 시종일관 뚫어져라 쳐다본 여자가 마침내 그를 알아보고 자기 쪽으로 오라고 (   ) 최고로 행복한 기분을 느꼈다.
   a. 재잘거리자   b. 배회하자   c. 신호하자   d. 선동하자

2. 꼬마 여자아이가 아이스크림콘을 진흙 속에 떨어뜨리자 아이스크림을 파는 남자는 그녀에게 (   )을/를 느껴 다른 콘을 공짜로 주었다.
   a. 동정   b. 부러움   c. 낙담   d. 혐오

3. 셀리는 주말에 해변으로 여행갈 계획이 없었는데, 날씨가 너무 좋아서 차에 올라타 해변으로 가야겠다고 (   ) 결정을 내렸다.
   a. 호색적인   b. 원기 왕성한   c. 잘난 척하는   d. 즉흥적인

4. CD 플레이어의 발명은 턴테이블과 비닐 레코드를 사실상 (   ) 만들었다.
   a. 폐물이 되게   b. 유명하게   c. 합성으로   d. 명료하게

p.174

5. 배리는 학교에서 가장 멋진 아이라는 명성을 얻었는데, 자기나 자기 주변에 어떤 일이 일어나든지 언제나 (   ) 행동했기 때문이다.
   a. 만족하게   b. 무관심하게   c. 단호하게   d. 사납게

6. "그렇습니다, 교실에서 커닝을 (   ) 위해서는 더 엄격한 처벌이 필요합니다." 교장이 얘기했다. "하지만 학생에게 체벌을 가하는 것은 법에 저촉됩니다."
   a. 지겹게 하기   b. 떠나게 하기   c. 못하게 막기   d. 입증하기

7. '내셔널 지오그래픽'의 최근 기사가 나오기까지 사람들은, 벨트와 지갑에 가죽을 사용할 목적으로 날마다 수백 마리씩 붙잡혀 죽는 작은 도마뱀인 푸른혀도마뱀의 (   )을/를 몰랐다.
   a. 본질   b. 자아   c. 상류계급   d. 곤경

짝짓기

오른쪽의 단어를 비슷한 의미의 왼쪽 단어와 짝지으세요.

1. 낮잠	a. 속도
2. 조상들	b. 신세를 진
3. 편리한	c. 낮잠
4. 큰 실수	d. 예시하다
5. 은혜를 입고 있는	e. 따뜻한
6. 무더운	f. 편리한
7. 이면의, 다른	g. 기아
8. 소집, 정렬	h. 숙소
9. 속도	i. 식물과 관련된
10. 혐오하다	j. 선조들
11. 식물학의	k. 싫어하다
12. 징조이다	l. 수집
13. 기숙사	m. 실수
14. 기아	n. 다른, 그 밖의

짝짓기

오른쪽의 단어를 비슷한 의미의 왼쪽 단어와 짝지으세요.

1. 발암성의	a. 어려움
2. ~하지 않도록	b. 상황
3. 예외	c. 계절풍
4. 팔다리	d. ~할까 두려워서
5. 환경	e. 부스러기
6. 곤경, 난국	f. 암을 일으키는

7. 옆길로 새다   g. 옳은 길에서 빗나가다
8. 포로들   h. 포로들
9. 돌풍   i. 특별한 경우
10. 고양이과의   j. 황당한 경험
11. 계절풍   k. 다리와 팔
12. 충격   l. 돌풍
13. 파편   m. 고양이 같은

2 코끼리 제국의 몰락

p.176

우리를 포로로 잡아간 것은 평범한 재칼 군대가 아니었어. 이 군견들은 자신들을 가장 무서운 개 집단으로 만들어 줄 금속으로 된 갑옷과 헬멧을 착용하고 있었어. 즉, 바너비와 바베트, 브리지트는 공포에 질린 것 같았지. 나야 물론 고양이잖아. 누구나 알듯이 우리 고양이들은 개과에 속하는 모든 것들에게는 어느 정도의, 뭐랄까, 증오심을 느끼지. 나에겐 이 보잘 것 없는 강아지들이 우스울 뿐이었어. 하나씩이라면 누구라도 손쉽게 처리할 수 있었을 거야. 하지만 우린 수적으로 훨씬 불리한 데다 손과 발목이 묶여 있었기 때문에 난 그냥 참기로 마음먹었어. 거기다 우린 그리 오래 포로로 있진 않을 거라는 예감이 왔거든.

"지리학 수업 시간엔 이런 장소를 배운 적 없는데." 브리지트가 고개를 저으며 말했다. "이런, 일이 잘못 되려니까..."

"우리가 있는 곳은 프랑스가 아닌 것 같아." 바너비도 동의했다.

"괜찮다면 여기가 어딘지 저들한테 물어볼게." 바베트가 제안했다.

"그래, 네가 '개' 말을 할 수 있으면 그렇게 해." 브리지트가 코웃음 쳤다.

"저들은 재칼인데, 난 작년에 사파리로 사냥갔을 때 저들 언어에 대해 도움이 될 만한 지식을 좀 얻었어. 저들의 시는 좀 원초적이긴 하지만 아주 훌륭해."

브리지트는 현명한 반박 거리를 생각해 내려 애썼지만 이런 말 밖에 할 수 없었다. "그래 맞아. 쟤들은 여가 시간엔 하나같이 초상화가들이래. 파이도의 "당구치는 개들"은 내가 제일 좋아하는 작품 중 하나지."

바너비가 낄낄거리며 웃었다.

"빈정거릴 것까진 없잖아." 바베트가 친구들에게서 고개를 돌리며 조용히 대답했다. 그리고는 좀 이상한 으르렁거리는 소리를 내더니 짤막하게 짖고 두어 번 낑낑거렸는데, 그녀 뒤에 있는 호위병을 향해 그러는 것 같았다. 하지만 아무 반응이 없었다.

p.177

"저들은 네 말을 이해 못하는 것 같아." 바너비가 말했다.

바베트는 그의 말을 못 들은 척하고 호위병에게 "질문"을 반복했다.

"조용히 해요." 개가 갑자기 짖었는데, 그것은 영어였다. "당신 억양 때문에 귀가 따가워. 저기 있는 똑똑한 친구 좀 일으켜 세워요. 저 친구는 좀 서투네요, 그렇죠? 자기 발에 걸려 넘어졌잖아요."

브리지트는 개가 이야기하는 걸 듣고 너무 놀란 나머지 정말로 넘어졌다. 바베트가 그녀를 일으켜 주었지만, 브리지트는 여전히 어리벙벙한 상태로, 입을 쩍 벌리고 재칼을 멍하니 바라보며 거기에 그냥 서 있었다.

"입 다물어요, 꼬마들." 재칼이 말했다. "충고 하나 하죠. 당신들은 지금 동물의 왕국에 와 있는 거예요. 여긴 우리 영토라구요. 당신들이 우리 땅에 와 있는 한 좀 더 공손하고 덜 건방지도록 처신을 잘해야 할 거예요. 예를 들면, 방금 그런 식으로 우리의 예술적 재능을 깎아내린 건 기분 나빴어요. 아무것도 모르면서 깔보면 안 된다는 거예요. 그리고 지금까지 당신 입에서 나온 거, 그것만으로도 과해요. 내 말 알아듣겠어요?"

브리지트는 계속 빤히 쳐다보았다.

"방금 한 얘기 알아듣겠어요? 소처럼 빤히 쳐다보지 말아요. 암소같이 멍청해 보여요." 그는 호통 치듯 말했다.

"알았어요. 정말 미안해요." 브리지트는 더듬거리며 말했다.

"좀 낫군요. 이봐요, 우린 당신 인간들에게는 개인적으로 감정 없어요. 하지만 유감스럽게도 당신들은 저 고양이와 함께 있군요. 우린 고양이를 무지 싫어해요. 비열한 작은 악마에다가 대부분 스파이거든요. 그리고 군대가 이동하는 한가운데로 착륙하는 건 좋지 못하다는 걸 알았어야죠."

"하지만 우린 여기 올 생각이 없었어요!" 바너비가 불쑥 말했다. "우린 파리 상공에서 뜻하지 않게 사나운 기상 조건을 만난 거예요, 그리고..."

p.178

"어 그래요? 그렇담 고양이는 어떻게 설명할래요?" 재칼이 깨갱거렸다. "하지만 내가 말했듯이 우린 당신들한테 악감정은 없어요. 고양이도 그리 나쁘진 않을지도 모르죠. 우리도 가끔 고양이들을 스파이로 고용했으니까요. 하지만 당신들은 알아야 돼요. 지금 여기 상황은 절박해요. 며칠 전까지 재칼 군대는 다같이 혁명을 수행 중이었어요. 우린 코끼리 제국을 전복시키고 영양에서부터 얼룩말에 이르기까지 이 지역에 거주하는 모든 동물에게 개방되는 자유롭고 민주적인 선거를 치르기 위해 애쓰는 중이었죠. 그런데 호라스 장군이 탐욕을 부렸어요. 그는 혁명을 일종의 신성한 전쟁, 말하자면 재칼 성전으로 바꾸기로 결심했어요. "모든 피조물은 개의 말에 복종해야 한다."고 말했죠. 참, 그런 일은 절대 일어나지 말아야 하는데. 단지 훨씬 더 잔인한 독재 정권으로 교체하기 위해 기존의 독재 정부를 없애는 일은 말예요."

재칼은 넌더리를 내며 고개를 저었다.

"우리의 카노 대령님은 지체하지 않고 그 생각에 반대를 표명하셨어요. 하지만 결국 호라스 장군은 어떤 식의 이의나 불일치도 받아들일 준비가 안 됐어요, 그래서 카노 대령님을 처형할 계획을 세웠어요. 그래서 같은 날 밤, 카노 대령님과 우리 모두는 우리들끼리의 당을 만들기 위해 떨어져 나왔죠. 우린 다른 동물 군대들도 우리가 혁명을 수행하고 호라스를 권좌에서 쫓아내는 걸 도와주길 바라고 있어요."

"그럼 우릴 어디로 데려가는 거죠?" 바베트가 물었다.

"당신들을 데리고 캠프로 되돌아가는 거예요. 카노 대령님께서 만나보고 싶어 하실 거예요." 그가 대답했다.

"알려줘서 고마워요." 어느 정도 말할 능력을 회복한 브리지트가 말했다. "그건 그렇고, 내 이름은 브리지트고, 얘들은 바베트와 바너비예요."

"난 래시테리어스 중위예요. 다들 줄여서 래시라고 불러요."

브리지트는 농담을 안 하는 게 좋겠다고 생각했다.

p.179

캠프에 도착한 이들은 많은 군인들이 둘레에 모여 있는 걸 보았는데, 무슨 일이 일어나길 기다리고 있는 듯했다. 처음에 그들은 조용히 참고 있었지만, 5분쯤이 지나자 짖어 대고 발을 세차게 구르고, 그것이 무엇이든 자신들이 기다리고 있는 것을 달라고 시끄럽게 떠들기 시작했다. 마침내 큰 덩치의 힘 있어 보이는 회색 털의 재칼이 방 앞에 모습을 드러냈고, 한번 날카롭게 짖고 나니 떠들썩하던 군중이 조용해졌다. 그의 외양을 보니 아주 당당하고 강력한 데다 위엄이 가득해, 바너비와 브리지트, 바베트는 그가 카노라는 것을 제대로 짐작할 수 있었다.

그는 재칼어로 이야기하기 시작했는데, 굳이 그 말을 알아들을 수 없어도 카노가 군중을 사로잡는 방법을 알고 있는 타고난 웅변가라는 걸 알아차릴 수 있었다. 그가 짖어 대고 으르렁거리고 이러저리 뛰어다니고 깨갱거리면서 흥분의 절정으로 몰고 가자 래시를 포함한 모든 재칼들이 흥분하며 울부짖기 시작했다.

"난 그 어디라도 저 분을 따라갈 거예요." 래시가 한숨지으며 말했다. 그러고 나서 갑자기 대령이 있는 쪽을 향해 짖었다.

카노가 래시를 알아보자 양 귀가 쫑긋하게 섰다. 그가 이쪽으로 건너왔다.

"만장일치요!" 카노가 외쳤다. "우린 투표를 했고, 하나도 빠짐없이 모든 재칼이 호라스를 권좌에서 쫓아내기 위해 끝까지 투쟁할 것을 찬성했소."

"저희의 충성을 의심치 마시라고 말씀드렸잖습니까, 대령님." 래시가 말했다. "대령님께서는 방금 엄청난 연설을 하신 겁니다."

"글쎄, 사실은, 난 연설을 할 계획이 없었소. 그건 그냥 즉석에서, 순간적인 충동으로 한 그런 거였소. 전부 다 준비 없이 즉흥적으로 한 거였소."

"그냥 즉흥적으로 하신 연설이라니 정말 놀라웠습니다. 대령님은 진심에서 우러나는 말씀을 하셨고, 저희는 이제 대령님 편입니다. 우린 그 괴팍한 호라스를 혼내줄 겁니다." 중위가 대답했다.

"내 생각엔 괴팍한 인물보다는 광신자란 말이 더 정확할 것 같소, 래시. 그 놈은 미친 정도가 아니라, 글쎄, 위험할 정도로 열광과 열의가 가득한 자라고 해 두지."

p.180

"어쨌든 대령님, 오늘 저희가 순찰을 돌던 중 발견한 걸 보십시오." 래시가 포로들을 향해 고개를 홱 돌리며 말했다.

"그래, 그래." 재칼이 말했다. "인간 몇 명과... 이봐! 보리가드, 이 친구야, 여기서 뭐하는 거냐?"

카노는 총총걸음으로 고양이에게 갔는데, 그를 보더니 아주 반가워하는 것 같았다.

"저 자를 아시나요?" 래시와 바너비가 물었다. 그들 둘 다 깜짝 놀랐지만, 그 이유는 서로 달랐다.

"저 자를 아냐고?" 대령이 웃었다. "그러니까, 옛날에, 보와 나는 위장근무를 했었지, 그게..."

바로 그때 고양이가 카노 귀에 대고 조용히 으르렁거렸다.

"그래, 어, 이런! 허허. 내가 무슨 말을 했지?" 대령은 어색하게 말을 이었다. "내가, 어, 실수를 한 모양이군. 난 이 딱한 늙은 고양이를 한번도 본 적이 없는데. 전부 내 텐트로 데려가 심문하도록 하게."

바베트와 바너비 그리고 브리지트는 어리둥절한 표정으로 서로를 쳐다봤다. 상황이 점점 더 이상하고 요상하게 돌아가고 있었다.

텐트에 도착했을 때 카노가 그들을 풀어 주라고 명하자 래시가 밧줄을 풀기 시작했다.

"고마워요, 저 밧줄 때문에 손목이 벗겨지려고 했어요." 브리지트가 말했다. "이봐요!" 브리지트는 대령을 향해 소리 쳤다. "뭐 먹을 거 없어요?"

p.181

"브리지트, 우리가 존경에 대해 얘기했던 거 잊어버렸어요?" 래시가 호통 쳤다. "대령님께는 좀더 경의를 가지고 행동해야 한다구요. 어쨌든 그분이 바로 지금 당신 운명을 손에 쥐고 계세요."

"아, 이보게." 카노가 웃었다. "여기서 이 분들은 환영일세. 사실, 이 분들은 외국 고관들, 인간세계에서 온 명예롭고 중요한 방문객들로 대접을 받아야 하네. 브리지트가 배가 고프니 그녀를 위해 잔치를 베풀어야겠네! 래시, 가서 모두에게 오늘밤 새 친구들의 방문을 환영하고 호라스의 확실한 패배와 코끼리 제국의 최후를 한껏 즐기기 위해 파티를 열 거라고 얘기하게!"

여행객들은 카노가 늘 그렇게 낙관주의로 가득한 건지 궁금해지기 시작했는데, 래시가 잔치 준비를 하기 위해 자리를 뜨자마자 카노가 깊은 한숨을 내쉬었다.

"중위가 당신들한테 얼마나 얘길 했는지 모르겠소만, 우린 지금 심각한 처지에 직면하고 있소. 지금 상황은 사실 아주 비관적인 것 같소." 그가 말했다.

"그런 것 같아요." 바베트가 말했다. "당신은 지금 제국에 대해 쿠데타를 계획하고 있는데, 당신의 군대 안에서 불화가 일고 있잖아요. 정말 아주 어려운 상황이네요. 재칼 군대 외부에서는 도움을 받을 데가 없나요?"

"나도 그 가능성을 생각해봤소." 대령이 대답했다. "하지만 우리 동물들은 지금껏 확고한 동맹 관계를 맺어 본 적이 없소. 군대라고 할 만한 조직을 가지고 있는 집단은 재칼들이 유일하지. 최근까지 우린 코끼리 제국의 왕실 호위병이 었소."

카노는 머리를 가로저은 후 말을 이었다. "예를 들어 타조들이라면 큰 도움이 될 거요. 그들은 민주주의에 찬성하는 것 같고, 그들의 빠른 발과 큰 몸집은 유익한 친구가 될 수 있소. 하지만 불행히도, 그들은 무관심한 걸로 유명하오.

그들은 머리를 모래 속에 파묻는 걸 좋아하고 어떤 것도 걱정하지 않으려고 하지."

p.182

"팬더는 강하고 사나워 보이지만 모두 평화주의자들이오. 맞소. 그들은 어떤 이유에서건 전쟁을 찬성하지 않소. 전쟁은 그들 종교를 거스르는 것이오. 한편, 혹멧돼지는 추하게 생긴 피조물들로, 우리에게 합류할 만큼 분명히 호전적이오. 그들은 싸움을 좋아하지. 전쟁을 수행하는 것이 그들에겐 즐거움을 얻는 방법이오. 하지만 그들은 일으킬 전쟁이 없을 때엔 서로를 죽이는 경향이 있소. 그들과는 관계하지 않는 게 최선이오. 하지만 희망은 있소. 우린 파충류 공화국에게 원조와 조언을 간청했소. 그들이 기꺼이 우릴 도와줄 것 같소. 코브라 왕이 오늘밤 우리 캠프에 사절을 파견할 거란 얘기를 들었소. 아마 고위직에 있는 도마뱀일 거요. 자기들이 할 수 있는 일이 있는지 알아보러 오는 것이오. 파충류는 우리에게 가르쳐줄 것이 많소. 그들은 지금까지 여러 해 동안 제국 밖에서 살아왔소. 솔직히, 코끼리들이 그들을 좀 무서워하는 것 같소." 카노는 껄껄 웃었다.

"이 호라스란 인물에 대해 좀더 얘기해 주세요." 브리지트가 말했다. "그가 코끼리 제국보다 훨씬 더 악랄한 것 같아요."

"맞소." 대령이 동의했다. "호라스는 상상할 수 있는 폭군 가운데 최악이오. 그는 자신의 동물들에게 복종 이상의 것을 기대하지. 자신에게 절대적으로 맹종하고 자기 변덕을 노예처럼 맞춰 주길 바라지. 여러 해 동안 그래 왔고, 코끼리들이 늘 그를 뒷받침 해줬소. 심지어는 모든 군인들에게 자기 앞에서 무릎을 꿇고 절을 하고 마치 자기를 무슨 신이나 되는 듯이 숭배하라는 명령까지 내렸소! 난 더 이상 참을 수가 없었소. 난 누구에게든 비굴하게 아부하는 걸 거부했소, 코끼리 제국에까지, 그리고 특히 호라스에게 말이오! 난 그와 기초 훈련을 함께 받았는데 말이오, 세상에!"

"맞아요, 대령님." 브리지트가 말했다.

카노는 깊은 숨을 몰아쉬었다. "호라스는 사실 자기 자신을 일종의 신이라고 생각하고 있소. 전능한 존재 말이오. 뭐든지 할 수 있고, 뭐든지 볼 수 있다. 하지만 사실 그는 완전히 피해망상증 환자에 불과하오. 늘 자기를 거스르는 비밀스런 음모와 모의가 있다고 상상해 왔소."

p.183

"그가 그렇게 타락한 작자라면 왜 이런 쿠데타에 그와 함께 나섰죠?" 브리지트가 물었다.

"좋은 질문이오." 카노가 대꾸했다. "진부하고 케케묵은 표현으로 밖에 대답할 수가 없소. '지푸라기라도 잡는다.'고 하잖소. 호라스가 미치광이라는 걸 알았지만, 그보다는 코끼리들의 압제 아래서 계속 사는 것이 더 힘든 일이라고 생각했소. 우리가 자유를 선언할 때에서야 그 자가 정말 얼마나 사악한지를 알게 됐소. 그 놈은 완전히 편견에 사로잡힌 놈이오."

"편견에 사로잡힌 놈이오?" 바너비가 헐떡이며 말했다.

"솔직히 전에는 어떻게 그걸 못 알아차렸는지 모르겠소. 우리가 코끼리들로부터 도망쳐 나오기 전에는 그는 자신의 편견을 비밀로 했던 것 같소. 이제 그는 훨씬 더 공공연하게 다른 피조물들에 대해, 심지어는 여태껏 만나본 적이 없는 동물들에 대해서도 증오심을 드러내고 있소. 그는 재칼만이 유일하게 가치 있는 동물이라 생각하지. 그건 정말 불온한 생각이오. 불과 얼마 전까지만 해도 그는 내 친구였는데, 이제는 가장 위험한 원수가 된 거요."

카노는 또 한숨을 쉬었고, 이 순간까지 자신을 몰고 온 모든 사건들을 곰곰이 생각하는 듯 먼 곳을 응시했다. 그러더니 곧 생각에 완전히 몰두했다.

"어, 우린 먹기 전에 세수부터 하러 가야 할 것 같아요." 대령이 혼자 생각에 잠겨 있도록 내버려두길 바라며 바너비가 말했다.

"참, 내가 이렇게 무례하다니." 대령이 생각에 잠겨있다가 깨어나더니 말했다. "밖에 나가면 오른쪽으로 내빈용 텐트가 보일 거요. 필요한 건 모두 거기에 있소. 잔치 준비가 되면 데리러 가겠소."

"좋아요. 이따 봐요, 카노." 브리지트가 말했다.

"고마워요, 대령님." 바베트가 말했다.

이렇게 그들은 텐트를 나왔다. 하지만 고양이는 그대로 남아 있었다.

카노 대령과 나의 관계에 대해 설명을 해야겠군. 맞아, 서커스와 돌아다니고, 백과사전을 팔고, 노동조합을 조직하고, 그래, 심지어는 코끼리 제국의 스파이 노릇을 하는 등 온갖 종류의 일들을 하던 엘리드 에이전시라는 곳에서 내가 첩보 활동을 하고 있을 때 우린 전우였지. 그때 인간들은 코끼리들에게 아주 잔악한 폭력을 저질렀어. 사냥꾼들이 코끼리들을 수백 마리씩 죽여서 상아를 얻으려고 엄니를 빼고, 나머지는 썩도록 내팽개쳐 두곤 했지. 전 세계의 동물들은 이 몰지각한 잔학 행위에 맞서 싸울 것을 결심했어.

카노와 난 국제동물연합의 한 회의에서 만났고 완전히 새롭고 색다르고 전적으로 급진적인 아이디어를 생각해 냈어. 우린 우리의 이야기를 매스미디어, 즉 신문, 텔레비전, 라디오 모든 곳에 알리려고 했지. 우린 직접 참사의 사진을 찍었어. 정글 속에 엄니 없이 누워 있는 코끼리들의 사진 말이야. 그리고는 인간세계로 들어가 애완동물로 섞여 들려고 했지. 우리의 계획을 실행에 옮길 기회를 기다리면서 말이지.

물론, 나한테는 그게 쉬웠어. 난 인간들과 함께 사는 데에 익숙했고, 거기다 애완 고양이는 보통 인간들이 원하는 대로 비열하고 속물적으로 행동하게 되고, 아무도 그것에 대해 재고하지 않아. 카노는 그보다는 문제가 좀 있었지. 그는 재칼이고 군인으로, 으레 개들이 할 거라고 생각하는 나뭇가지를 집어 오고 꼬리를 흔드는 등의 틀에 박힌 행동들에 대해서 참을성이 별로 없었거든. 그래도 그는 그럭저럭 참아 냈어.

마침내, 나는 주요한 텔레비전 방송국에 코끼리 사냥에 대한 비디오테이프를 제보해 주었지. 방송국 매니저 중 하나가 그것을 보았고 그때부터 일이, 말하자면 터지기 시작했어. 대중적인 항의가 엄청나게 일어났어. 많은 나라들이 모여서 상아 무역을 지지하는 다른 국가들에 대해 제재 조치를 가했어.

즉, 그런 나라들과는 거래를 하지 않고 어떤 식으로든 도와주는 것도 거부했어. 일부의 나라들은 어떤 상아도 수입하길 거부하면서 통상 정지를 선언하기까지 했어. 카노와 나는 우리의 대담함에 너무나 기뻐했지. 우리가 한 일을 하려면 정말 많은 용기와 대담성이 필요했거든.

그런 일이 있은 후 우린 각자의 길을 갔지. 다시는 카노를 만나지 못했어. 지금까지 말야. 코끼리들이 그렇게 강해져서 돌아왔을 줄은 꿈에도 몰랐어. 지나치게 강해진 것 같아. 내 오랜 친구가 그렇게 화난 걸 보니 마음이 정말 안 좋았어. 아이들이 떠난 후 우린 이야기를 나누며 옛 시절을 추억했어. 난 그에게 내 정체를 드러내지 말라고 했어. 내가 이 애들을 감시하고 있는 걸 말야. 애들이 알게 하고 싶지 않았거든. 그리고 얘기했어. 가능한 어떤 방법으로든 그를 도와주겠다고. 그는 내 말을 받아들였어. 그리고 나서 우린 호러스와 제국을 단호하게 처리할 계획을 짰어.

"이런, 난 너무 배고파." 내빈용 텐트에서 쿠션에 기대 편히 쉬고 있는 브리지트가 말했다. "저녁이 빨리 준비됐으면 좋겠다. 난 더 이상 한 입도 못 먹게 될 때까지 실컷 먹을 테야."

"난 그렇게 정신없이 먹어 대진 않을 거야." 바너비가 경고했다. "아무튼 우린 재칼들이 뭘 먹는지 모르잖아. 그게 뭐든 간에 아마 날 음식일 거야."

"저런, 난 그 생각은 미처 못 했어." 브리지트가 펄쩍 뛰며 말했다. "우린 어떡하지? 그럼 굶어 죽는 거야 뭐야?"

"음…" 바너비가 덥수룩한 머리를 긁적이며 대답했다. "우린 거기에 정신을 집중하고 뭘 떠올릴 수 있는지 보면 돼. 야, 이것봐라?"

"뭔데?" 브리지트가 말했다.

"내가 찾아낸 걸 보라구! 이것들은 내가 도서관에서 자동판매기를 폭파했을 때 내 머릿속으로 들어왔나 봐!"

아니나 다를까, 바너비는 그의 머릿속에서 캔디바 네 개와 감자칩 한 봉지, 그리고 오렌지 크래커 몇 개를 힘들여 끄집어냈다. 평상시라면 브리지트는 이런 뜻밖의 일을 보고 깜짝 놀랐겠지만, 지난 며칠간 일어났던 모든 일 때문인지 거의 눈 하나 깜짝하지 않았다.

"이야! 좀 먹어도 돼?" 브리지트가 물었다.

"그럼. 갖다 먹어."

브리지트가 캔디바를 게걸스레 먹기 시작할 때 텐트 반대쪽에 있던 바베트가 말했다.

"네 머리 모양 끝내 준다, 바너비." 바베트가 말했다.

"잘 어울리잖아." 그가 맞장구쳤다. "넌 너무 조용하고 생각에 잠긴 것 같은데. 무슨 생각을 하는 거니?"

"이 불쌍한 재칼들에 대해 생각했어. 우리 프랑스인들은 황제와 독재자의 지배 아래서 사는 게 어떤 건지 알고 있어. 너희 미국인들은 다행히 그런 일을 견뎌 낼 필요가 없지." 바베트가 생각에 잠긴 채 감자칩 하나를 우적우적 씹어 먹으며 말했다.

"얘기의 요점이 뭔데?" 브리지트가 한입 가득 캔디를 문 채로 물었다.

"내 말은, 재칼들이 불쌍하다는 거야. 우리가 그들을 도와줘야 한다고 생각해."

바너비와 브리지트는 잠시 아무 말 없이 앉아 있다가, 막 대답을 하려고 했는데 마침 래시가 텐트를 젖히고 들어왔다.

"고맙지만 사양하겠어요." 그가 말했다. "내가 엿들었다고는 생각하지 않았으면 좋겠는데, 당신이 우릴 도와준다고 한 얘기가 저절로 들렸어요. 우린 당신들 도움은 아무것도 필요 없어요. 카노 대령님께서 모든 걸 해결하셨어요."

"난 그냥..." 바베트가 입을 열었다.

"알아요. 있죠, 난 논쟁하러 온 게 아녜요. 잔치가 열릴 거라고 말하려고 온 거예요. 자, 나가자구요!"

바베트와 브리지트, 바너비가 텐트에서 나와 보니 캠프에는 축제가 열리는 듯 불이 밝혀져 있었다. 도처에서 횃불이 타올랐다. 일곱 마리의 암컷 재칼들이 일곱 가지 비탄의 춤을 추고 있었다. 그들은 너무 어지러워 서 있을 수 없을 때까지 뱅글뱅글 돌더니, 그 다음엔 비통할 정도로 애처롭게 짖는 소리를 일곱 번 내뱉었다. 그리고 멋진 망토를 걸친 카노가 기다랗고 낮은 테이블의 상단에 앉아 있었고, 큰 몸집의 주름투성이의 늙은 도마뱀이 한편에, 거구의 고양이가 다른 편에 앉아 있었다.

p.187

"친구들!" 세 사람이 모습을 드러내자 카노가 외쳤다. "이리로 오시게!"

세 명의 여행객은 주인과 합석했고 서로 간의 소개가 이루어졌다.

"이 분은 생프로이드 대사님으로, 파충류 제국에서 오신 훌륭하고 덕망있는 정치인이오." 카노가 말했다. "오늘밤 우리와 함께 하시기 위해 구에꼬 성에서부터 먼 길을 오셨소."

"사실, 여긴 성이라고 할 수가 없네요. 작은 성 보다는 큰 지하 감옥 같군요. 하지만 재칼들이 좀더 적당한 직무 공간을 마련해 줄 때까지 당분간은 여기를 파충류 대사관으로 써야 할 것 같네요." 도마뱀이 말했다.

바베트와 브리지트는 그의 무례함에 기분이 언짢아 어색해졌다. 바너비는 음식을 살펴보느라 정신이 없어서 무슨 일이 일어나고 있는지 알아차리지 못했다.

"물론입니다." 카노가 친절하게 말했다. "자, 음식을 마음껏 드시죠."

"대령, 당신 정신 나갔군요." 도마뱀이 완전히 경멸하는 기색으로 대꾸했다. "이런 신병 훈련소의 저질 음식은 먹기는 커녕 냄새도 못 참겠어요."

"이봐요!" 브리지트가 소리쳤다. "대령님은 여기 앉아서 저런 거만하고 건방진 큰 도마뱀한테 음식때문에 비웃음 당할 필요도 없어요!"

"바보 같은 애야, 난 이구아나야."

"좋아요, 돼지 같은 이구아나." 브리지트가 서슴없이 얘기했다. "당신은 아무것도 안 먹는 게 좋겠어요. 보아하니 몇 끼는 굶어도 끄덕 없겠는걸요."

"그래, 먹나 봐라!" 대사가 발끈 화를 내며 떠나려고 일어났다.

"사실, 제 생각에는 생프로이드 대사님이 지금 체격으로도 아주 강하고 기품 있어 보이는데요." 바베트가 성난 도마뱀을 달래려고 애쓰며 말했다.

p.188

그건 효과가 있어 보였는데, 왜냐면 도마뱀이 다시 자리에 앉더니 세 사람이 나타나기 전 카노 대령과 나누고 있던 대화를 다시 시작했던 것이다. 그는 브리지트를 완전히 무시했다. 브리지트 역시 그를 무시했다. 브리지트는 암컷 재칼들 쪽으로 몸을 돌리고는 그들의 이상한 댄스 스텝을 아주 재미있어 하는 척했다.

"말씀드렸듯이, 대령, 파충류 공화국은 완벽하게 자주적입니다. 완전히 독자적이죠. 우린 우리가 선택하는 대로 마음껏 동맹을 맺을 수 있어요. 물론 현명하게 선택해야겠죠."

"물론 호라스의 편을 드는 것이 현명하다고 생각진 않으시겠죠. 거기다 당신 나라 국민들은 우리만큼이나 코끼리 제

314

국을 싫어하잖습니까." 카노가 주장했다.

"그렇긴 하지만, 적어도 황제는 질서를 유지해 주잖습니까. 당신들이 그 정부를 넘어뜨린다면 어떤 일이 생기는 겁니까? 우리 파충류는 무정부 상태에 빠져 있는 나라와 이웃해 살고 싶지는 않아요. 조직적인 정부 체계가 없으면 당신들은 대혼란을 맞을 겁니다. 완전한 무질서 말입니다. 난장판 말이오!" 도마뱀이 소리쳤다.

"생프로이드, 물론 우리가 계획도 없이 이런 일을 시작했다고 생각하시는 건 아니겠죠?" 카노가 대꾸했다. "우리는 치밀한 계획을 세워 일을 추진하고 있는 겁니다. 이미 황제에게 편지를 보내 왕위에서 물러날 것과 자유롭고 민주적인 선거를 실시할 것을 요구했어요. 우리가 생각했던 대로 그는 지배권을 포기할 것을 거부했고, 그래서 우린, 모든 동물들은 정부 내에서 동등한 발언권을 가질 것과, 황제를 우리의 통치자로 인정하지 않을 것을 표명하는 선언문을 작성했어요. 당연히 그는 우릴 반역자라고 비난했고 곧이어 우리에 대한 거짓된 보고서를 대중매체에 발표하기 시작했어요. 물론 이 보고서들은 다른 동물들에게 겁을 주어 우리를 위험한 존재로 생각하게 만들기 위한 선전에 지나지 않았어요. 하지만 당신도 물론 이해하듯이, 우리에겐 우리의 권리를 위해 싸우는 것 외엔 선택의 여지가 없어요!"

p.189

"제가 회의적으로 생각하는 것을 용서해 주세요, 대령, 하지만 하도 많은 혁명들이 실패를 맛보기 때문에 우린 우려를 할 수 밖에 없어요." 도마뱀이 말했다. "그래서 우리는 제한적인 원조만 제공하려는 거예요. 우린 코끼리들의 컴퓨터 통신망과 전화선에 피해를 줄 수 있도록 전자 파괴 분야의 훈련을 받은 경무장 도마뱀 부대를 보내줄 수 있어요. 이 도마뱀들에게는 타고난 위장술이 있어요. 그들의 피부는 환경에 맞추어 색이 변하죠, 그래서 좀처럼 발견되지 않을 거예요."

"도와주셔서 감사합니다, 대사." 카노가 말했다.

바로 그때, 아주 시끄러운 소리, 울부짖고 와르르 쿵쿵 부서지는 소리가 캠프 언저리에서 들려오기 시작했다.

"대체 무슨 소리요?" 대령이 소리 질렀다. "래시, 무슨 일인지 알겠소?"

"싸움이 일어난 모양입니다." 중위가 대답했다. "비탄 무용수들 중 하나 때문에 일어난 싸움 같습니다. 가서 알아보겠습니다."

그것은 싸우는 소리였는데, 이내 싸움은 작은 접전으로 바뀌었고, 그러더니 작은 접전은 난투로 발전했다. 카노의 부하들은 무슨 일인지 알아차리기도 전에 호라스 장군과 그 재칼들의 군대에게 총공격을 당하고 있었다!

"전투 준비, 전투 준비!" 카노가 명령을 내렸다. "필사적으로 방어하라!"

"도와드리고 싶은 맘 간절하지만, 이만 가봐야겠네요." 생프로이드가 기어 들어가는 목소리로 말했다. "다리의 통풍이 재발돼서 끔찍하게 부어올랐어요. 그래서 어떻게 하든 별로 힘을 못 쓸 거예요. 안녕!"

그러면서 대사는, 통풍을 앓는 뚱뚱한 도마뱀이 달릴 수 있는 한 빨리 허겁지겁 뛰어갔다.

"걱정 마세요, 대령님." 브리지트가 전투의 소음 와중에서 소리쳤다. "우리가 도울게요!"

p.190

그렇지 않아도 바베트와 바너비는 정신없이 그렇게 하고 있었다. 바베트는 재칼어를 유창하게 하는 것 말고도 몇가지 재주를 더 알고 있었다. 그녀는 여기저기 뛰어다니면서 미친 닌자 거북이처럼 재칼들을 가라데 하듯 뻥뻥 찼다. 바너비는 계속 악취탄과 폭죽과 다른 폭발물들을 머리에서 끄집어내 적군을 향해 내던졌다. 브리지트는 풍선껌을 분 다음 그것을 잡아당겨 거대한 올가미 줄을 만들어, 그것으로 호라스의 군인들 몇을 사로잡은 다음 바닥으로 패대기쳤다.

하지만 적군의 재칼들은 가차 없었다. 그들은 계속해서 싸웠고 항복하기를 거부했다. 카노의 군인들 역시 항복하지 않으려 했고, 마침내 몇 시간 동안의 전투 후 카노 군대가 승리했다. 보리가드는 옹케도 호라스 장군을 직접 사로잡았다.

그러고 나자 그들에게 발자국 소리가 들렸다. 무겁고 시끄러운 발자국 소리였다.

"아, 이런, 코끼리들이 북쪽에서부터 오고 있다!" 카노가 두려움보다는 기진맥진한 상태로 외쳤다. "발자국 소리를 들어보니 캠프에서 1마일 쯤 떨어져 있다! 그렇다면 대략 10분 후엔 여기에 당도할 것이다."

"저들은 적어도 몰래 뭘 하는 건 불리하겠는데." 브리지트가 말했다. "저렇게 커다란 발자국 소리로 어떻게도 누군가에게 몰래 다가갈 수가 없어."

"그런건 지금은 아무런 도움도 안돼, 브리지트." 바베트가 말했다. "우린 막 호라스의 군대를 정복했는데, 벌써 또다

315

시 공격을 받게 됐다구. 카노의 재칼들은 지쳤고 많은 수가 부상을 당했어. 우린 지금 가장 공격받기 쉬운 상태에 있다구. 더 이상 우리 자신도 방어할 수가 없어!"

브리지트는 바베트가 얼마나 흥분을 하고 있는지 알고서는 충격을 받았다. 지금까지 너무나 침착하던 그녀였기 때문이다.

p.191

"이봐, 아직 포기하지 마! 우리에겐 아직 10분이 있잖아!"

"9분이오." 카노가 말했다.

"그래요, 9분." 브리지트가 말했다. "어떤 일도 일어날 수 있는 시간이야. 1986년도 월드시리즈 때 뉴욕에서도 비슷한 상황이 있었어. 메츠가 틀림없이 질 것처럼 보였지만, 1루수가 잔뜩 긴장을 해서 실책을 저지르는 바람에 우린 살아난 거야."

"지금 무슨 소리를 하고 있는 거요?" 카노가 투덜거렸다.

"뭐, 가장 적절한 예는 아닐지도 모르겠네요." 브리지트가 말했다. "내 말은 정말 끝날 때까지는 아직 끝난 게 아니라는 얘기예요."

"그럼 우린 뭘 해야 하는 거지, 으스대는 친구?" 바너비가 눈썹을 높이 치켜 올리며 물었다.

"어, 우선, 초록 페인트 한 다발과 루트비어 한 캔, 목화 몇 부셸, 그리고 마른 빵 조금이 필요해. 그런 다음..."

하지만 브리지트에겐 자신의 계획을 간단히 설명할 기회도 채 주어지지 않았다. 동쪽에서부터 두발 달린 동물들이 전속력으로 달려오는 소리와 거대한 오리들이 쉰 목소리로 꽥꽥거리는 듯한 소리가 들려왔다. 서쪽에서는 검고 흰 무리가 우르르 몰려왔다.

남쪽으로부터는 정말 불쾌한 거친 콧바람 소리와 혐오스러운 돼지 같은 냄새가 몰려왔다.

브리지트와 바너비 그리고 바베트는 목숨의 위태로움을 느끼며 정신없이 이리저리 둘러보았는데, 카노는 흥분해서 껑충껑충 뛰었다.

"저건 타조들이다! 그리고 혹멧돼지들이다! 거기다 평화주의자 팬더들도 왔다!" 그는 소리쳤다. "이제 우린 살았다!"

p.192

연합군들이 캠프에 도착해 카노 주변에 모여들더니, 카노에게 도와줄 것을 약속할때 코끼리들이 도착했다. 화강암 기둥 같은 회색 다리들로 이루어진 거대한 벽이 큰소리를 내며 시야에 들어와 멈추어 섰고, 그런 다음 균형 잡힌 대형으로 나뉘더니 그들의 우두머리이자 일당의 아버지이자 후피동물들의 족장, 바로 코끼리 황제에게 길을 내주었다.

두 군대, 즉 새와 개, 돼지, 곰의 뒤범벅은 한쪽에, 거대한 코끼리들은 다른 쪽에 선 채 서로를 불쾌하게 바라보았다. 마침내 황제가 입을 열었다.

"카노," 그는 우렁찬 목소리로 외쳤다. "이 모든 일을 선동한 책임이 있는 자가 당신인가? 자네가 이 반란을 유발시켰나?"

"그렇소, 하지만 당신도 보듯이, 당신의 완고하고 독단적인 통치에 염증을 느낀 건 나뿐이 아니오." 카노는 소리쳤다.

"정말 지긋지긋하군." 황제는 대꾸했다. "당신들 모두, 집으로 돌아가시오. 카노, 자네와 자네 군인들이 자수한다면 엄벌을 내리지는 않겠네. 난 너그러운 사람이니까."

"당신은 이해를 못하는군요." 대령이 말했다. "이건 유치한 장난이 아니오. 우린 더 이상 황제를 원치 않소. 우리가 원하는 건 민주주의요! 우린 민주주의를 원하는 거요!"

카노 뒤편의 군중이 각자 자기들의 언어로 환호하며 떠들기 시작했다.

"흠." 코끼리가 얼굴을 구기며 말했다. "이 모든 일이 의심스럽긴 하지만, 내가 의심을 품는다고 해서 꼭 당신이 틀린 건 아니지."

"그럼, 권좌에서 물러나는 거요?" 카노가 놀라기도 하고 기대에 부풀기도 한 채 물었다.

"글쎄, 경고하겠는데, 우리 같은 독재 정권이 민주주의보다 확실히 유리한 점들이 있지." 코끼리가 말했다. "하나만 들자면, 우리에겐 관료주의가 없지. 헷갈리는 명령 체계도 없고, 서류더미도 없고, 일을 망쳐놓는 도움이 안 되는 공무원들도 없소. 내가 말하면 되는 거고, 그럼 끝나는 거지. 아주 효율적이라구."

"하지만 그건 불공평하오!" 대령이 주장했다. "우리에게도 우리 정부 내에서의 발언권이 주어져야 하오!"

군중도 웅얼웅얼 동의를 했다. 황제는 잠시 깊은 생각에 잠긴 채 서 있었다. 캠프 전체에서 어떤 소리도 들리지 않았다. 몇 분이 지나 그가 다시 입을 열었다.

"좋소, 그렇다면 선거권을 갖도록 하시오. 배은망덕하고 불행한 백성들을 다스리는 건 원치 않소. 지금 바로 시작하는 게 좋겠소. 카노, 자네와 자네 군대가 맡아야 할 것 같소. 선거가 준비될 때까지 계엄령을 선포하겠소." 황제의 말이었다.

단 한 차례의 전투도 치르지 않고 승리를 쟁취했음을 깨달은 동물들은 기쁨으로 환호했다. 민주주의를 가로막아 봐야 소용없다는 걸 알아차린 황제는 체념의 한숨을 내쉬었다. 그리고 나서 시끌벅적한 파티가 시작됐다.

바베트는 바너비와 브리지트, 그리고 보리가드에게, 아무리 무혈혁명이었다 해도 혁명 직후의 나라를 여행하는 것은 현명하지 못한 일임을 지적했다. 모든 것이 격변과 혼란의 상태에 있고, 호텔 방을 찾는 것도 불가능하기 때문이다. 그들은 이 기회를 빌어 주인들에게 고마움을 전하고 갈길을 가자는 데 의견을 일치시켰다.

그들은 자신들이 착륙했던 공터를 향해 걸어갔다. 하지만 드넓은 들판에 도착하자마자 무지개 색깔의 눈부신 빛과 대기의 획 하는 소리가 그들을 집어삼켰고, 그들은 순식간에 지구표면에서 사라졌다.

QUICK QUIZ 6
관계짓기
아래의 단어 쌍들이 서로 어떤 관계를 갖는지 판단하세요. 비슷한 의미이면 "S" 반대 의미이면 "O"를 하세요.

1. 버리다 :: 포기하다
2. 악의, 증오 :: 경멸
3. 존경 :: 뻔뻔함, 무례
4. 적 :: 동료, 동지
5. 포식하다 :: 게걸스레 먹다
6. 무정부상태, 무질서 :: 무질서, 대혼란
7. 난투 :: 작은 접전
8. 너그러운 :: 권위적인
9. 관용 :: 고집불통
10. 즉석에서의 :: 즉흥적인
11. 열성, 열의 :: 냉담, 무관심
12. 추억하다 :: 잊어버리다

QUICK QUIZ 7
관계짓기
아래의 단어 쌍들이 서로 어떤 관계를 갖는지 판단하세요. 비슷한 의미이면 "S" 반대 의미이면 "O"를 하세요.

1. 평화주의자들 :: 호전적인
2. 이의 있는 :: 만장일치의
3. 급진적인 :: 전통적인
4. 비굴한 :: 오만한
5. 경멸하다 :: 비웃다
6. 독단적인 :: 융통성 있는
7. 헐뜯다 :: 칭찬하다
8. 편집적인 :: 믿고 있는
9. 자주적인 :: 독립적인
10. 생각에 잠긴 :: 사나운, 떠들썩한
11. 가장하는 :: 거짓의

빈칸 채우기

아래에 있는 각각의 단어들 중에서 가장 완벽한 문장을 만들어주는 단어를 고르세요.

1. 랜스는 여학생 소프트볼 팀에 대해 (   )을/를 느꼈던 게 분명했다. 왜냐하면 그는 학생들을 만나보기 전부터 그들이 형편없는 선수들일 거라고 단정 지었기 때문이다.
   a. 대담함   b. 존경심   c. 편견   d. 위엄

2. 아이들은 말론을 "멍멍이 얼굴"이라고 불렀는데, 그 이유는 날카로운 이와 텁수룩한 머리, 입 밖으로 혀를 내미는 버릇 때문에 그의 외관이 (   ) 때문이다.
   a. 개 같았기   b. 소 같았기   c. 애처로웠기   d. 어색했기

3. 캐시가 "난 어서 가서 사랑니를 뽑고 싶어. 디즈니랜드 보다 더 재미있을 거야!"라고 말한 것은 (   ) 것이었다.
   a. 반어적인   b. 반대하는   c. 열광하는   d. 명백한

p.195

4. 학생회 선거기간 동안 내 상대는 나와 학생회장으로서의 내 계획에 대한 거짓말과 왜곡된 얘기들로 가득한 팸플릿을 마구 뿌려댔지만, 대부분의 학생들은 그건 그저 (   ) 뭉치라는 걸 알았고, 어쨌든 선거에서 내가 이겼다.
   a. 의사일정   b. 통상정지   c. 흑색선전   d. 대중매체

5. 군대가 유혈 (   )을/를 일으켜 정부를 전복시켰다.
   a. 옹호운동   b. 쿠데타   c. 불화   d. 대변동

6. 휴가기간 동안 마지는 학교의 음식 모으기 운동을 위해 이웃들에게 통조림을 기부해 달라고 (   ).
   a. 간청했다   b. 이해했다   c. 심사숙고했다   d. 비난했다

7. 셸던은 원래 말썽꾸러기가 아니었지만, 구내식당에서 4일을 연달아 오트밀 죽을 제공하자 식당 내에서의 소동을 (   ), 학생 무리를 이끌고 요리사가 몰래 보관해 놓았던 초콜릿 푸딩이 있는 곳으로 갔다.
   a. 고의로 파괴했고   b. 외쳤고   c. 입을 벌리고 멍하니 봤고   d. 선동했고

8. 징기스칸은 강력한 (   )(으)로, 잔인한 통치를 일삼고 자신에게 불복종하거나 이의를 제기하려는 사람은 누구든 억압했다.
   a. 대사   b. 연설자   c. 폭군   d. 족장

9. 스폴딩 씨는 우리 사회과학 선생님이신데, 우리 학교에서 40년간 교편을 잡아오신 (   ) 노인으로, 마을사람 모두가 그분을 존경하고 좋아합니다.
   a. 공격받기 쉬운   b. 전능한   c. 공통점이 없는   d. 덕망있는

10. 블랙 대사는 토교 주재 미국 (   )에서 성대한 파티를 열었다.
    a. 영토   b. 대사관   c. 성   d. 관료정치

11. 제이콥은 사만다와 데이트하려고 (   ) 온갖 노력을 기울였다. 6개월 동안 하루도 빠짐없이 그녀에게 전화를 걸고 꽃을 보내다보니, 마침내 그녀가 마음의 문을 열었다.
    a. 냉정하게   b. 의심하며   c. 극악하게   d. 끝없이

12. 민디가 내게 보낸 발렌타인데이 카드에는 "장미는 붉고, 제비꽃은 푸르고, 설탕은 달콤해요, 마치 당신처럼요."라고 써 있었어. 그건 참 (   ) 것 같았지만, 그래도 어쨌든 좋았어.
    a. 비슷한   b. 진부한   c. 뚱뚱한   d. 차가운

짝짓기

오른쪽의 단어를 비슷한 의미의 왼쪽 단어와 짝지으세요.

1. 말대꾸하다	a. 즐거움
2. 놀라게 하다	b. 싫어하다
3. 혐오하다	c. 문지르다
4. 거주하다	d. ~와 함께 살다
5. 당파	e. 절하다
6. 위장하다	f. 대답하다
7. 벗겨지게 하다	g. 숨다
8. ~하는 것이 의무다	h. 놀라게 하다
9. 고위인사	i. 비밀 계획
10. 환락	j. 중요한 사람
11. 절하다	k. ~에서 살다
12. 전에	l. ~하는 것이 이롭다

13. 음모	m. 집단
14. 동거하다	n. 전에

QUICK QUIZ 10

1. 제재	a. 엿듣다
2. 진탕 떠들기	b. 의심하는 사람
3. 도청하다	c. 정복하다
4. 회전하다	d. 회전하다
5. 달래다	e. 처벌
6. 재개하다	f. 군대의 명령
7. 회의론자	g. 흥청거림
8. 포기하다	h. 포기하다
9. 대개	i. 수락
10. 몰래 하기	j. 가라앉히다
11. 정복하다	k. 다시 시작하다
12. 계엄령	l. 몰래 하기
13. 포기	m. 약

3 괴상한 우주 히피들

p.198

바너비와 바베트, 브리지트 그리고 보리가드는 땅에 등을 대고 누워, 빙빙 돌면서 그들 주위로 온통 여러 빛깔의 빛을 뿌리고 있는 거대한 반사경 볼을 뚫어져라 올려다보고 있었다. 공기 중에는 향냄새가 짙게 퍼져 있었다. 그들 모두는 방향감각을 잃고 좀 어리둥절했다. 불과 30초 전만 해도 이들은 풀이 우거진 들판에 서 있었는데, 지금은 여기가 어디인지, 무슨 일이 일어나고 있는 건지 알 수가 없었다.

"지옥인가?" 브리지트가 특별히 누구에게 묻는다고 할 것 없이 속삭였다.

"디스코텍인 것 같아." 바베트가 대답했다.

이때 갑자기 그들 주변으로 큰 목소리가 울렸다.

"이런, 재니스! 또 그랬구나. 그건 디스코 볼이 아니라고 몇 번을 말했잖아! 그건 고도로 민감한 공간이동 장치라구!"

네 친구는 그대로 앉은 채 놀라서 서로를 빤히 쳐다봤다. 이건 정말 보기 드문 일이었다.

"너희 고양이들, 잠깐만 그냥 늘어져 있어." 그 목소리가 계속해서 말했다. "내가 곧 갈게."

"고양이들?" 바너비가 물었다. "고양이라고는 한 마리뿐인데."

"저건 오래된 히피식 표현일 뿐이야." 브리지트가 말했다. "그냥 '너희들'이란 뜻이야. 네 생각엔…"

하지만 브리지트는 질문을 채 마치기도 전에 대답을 얻었다. 문을 통해 너무나 히피다운 한 히피가 걸어 나왔는데, 실제로는 자기 자신을 풍자한 모습으로, 긴 머리에, 턱에는 터부룩한 염소수염을 기르고, 할머니용 안경을 끼고, 축 늘어진 인디언식 긴 옷을 입고 있었다.

"여러분께 평화를." 그가 오른쪽 손으로 V자를 만들며 말했다.

자, 이야기가 이상하게 바뀌었지? 정황을 제대로 이해할 수 있도록 배경지식을 좀 알려줘야겠군. 충분히 짐작할 수 있겠지만, 그 광적인 재칼 일당과 싸우고 난 뒤 우린 모두 좀 피곤했어. 하지만 비록 기진맥진한 상태였어도 우리 모두는 여전히 파리로 돌아가길 열망했고 그래서 브리지트 부모님을 찾는 일에 착수하려 했지. 우리 계획을 또다시 방해받는 일은 절대 있어서는 안됐지. 다만 이번엔 일을 뒤틀리게 만든 것이 악천후가 아니라 우주선이었어.

그래, 우리의 의지와는 상관없이 우린 "공간이동을 당해" 땅에서 떠나 우주선으로 들어가게 된 거야. 그것도 그냥 아무 우주선이 아니었어. 우린 느닷없이 악명 높은 우주 히피 워블리 필스타인이 이끄는 악랄한 해적선 "파 아웃"에 승선하고 있었던 거야. 한때 미국인이라면 누구나 그의 이름을 알았고, 그와 그의 추종자들이 마음에 안 드는 정치인들을 골라 짓궂게 장난쳤던 걸 알고 있었지. 그 중 최악의 사건은 그가 하원 의장을 머리끝에서 발끝까지 새빨갛게 물들였던 건데, 그 하원 의장이 교육과 공공 텔레비전 방송에 대한 지출을 삭감하려는 계획에 반대하기 위해서였어. 연방수사국은 이 범죄를 저지른 자가 누군지 도저히 밝혀낼 수가 없었는데, 워블리가 자신의 정체를 밝혔어. 그는 텔레비전 프로에 나와서 그 대변인에게 "죽느니 빨개지는 게 나은지 많이 아니라 죽는 게 나은지" 물어보았지. 그 발언 하나로 그는 유력한 용의자가 된 거야. 나중에 연방수사국은 그의 팔뚝에 빅버드 문신이 있음을 발견했고 그가 "명화극장"을 즐겨 봤다는 것도 알아냈지.

그래서 연방수사국은 미국 전역에 워블리를 긴급 지명수배자로 지목했고, 뒤이어 미국 역사상 전대미문의 범인 수사가 이루어졌어. 경관들과 대통령 경호대 요원들, 심지어 평범한 시민들까지 그 히피를 찾기 위해 이곳저곳을 샅샅이 뒤졌어.

하지만 그들에게 그는 너무나 교활했고 몇 달 동안이나 추적자들을 피해 다녔어.

워블리는 네덜란드로 망명할 계획이라는 소문이 일었어. 네덜란드는 오해를 받는 자유분방한 자들의 피난처로 알려진 나라이자 히피들, 예술가들, 음악인들, 그밖에 기이하거나 별난 기질을 가진 불안하고도 자유로운 영혼들이 안전함을 느낄 수 있는 곳이지. 하지만 나중에 알려진 바로는 워블리는 줄곧 멕시코에 머물면서 낡은 관광버스를 가지고 우주선을 만들고 있었지. 행선지는 먼 곳(Far Out)이었어. 그래, 그와 그 추종자들은 우주선을 발사시켰고, 관계당국은 추적을 포기할 수밖에 없었어. 불행히도 우주공간은 연방수사국의 관할권을 벗어나니까.

서서히 워블리에 대한 격분은 사그라졌고, 모든 일은 평소대로 돌아갔어. 많은 사람들은 그의 우주선이 이륙하는 동안 산산조각 났고, 워블리와 그 일당은 아마 죽었을 거라고까지 생각했어. 하지만 그들의 생각은 여지없이 틀렸지. 왜냐면 거기에서 그가 우리 앞에 서 있었으니까. 아주 멀쩡하게 살아서 말야.

"난 워블리 필스타인 함장이다." 히피가 말했다. "원한다면 워블리 함장이라고 불러도 되지만, 군대명칭 같은 걸 모르면 그냥 워블리라고 해도 좋다."

"전 브리지트고 여긴 바베트와 바너비예요." 브리지트가 대답했다. "그리고 이 고양이는 보리가드라는 이름의 스파이 같은데 사람과는 얘기를 하지 않아요."

바너비와 바베트가 낄낄거렸다.

"정부에서 온 건 아니겠지?" 워블리가 의심스러워하며 물었다.

"아니에요." 브리지트가 대답했다.

"좋아, 그렇다면 다 좋아! 파 아웃에 승선한 걸 환영한다. 어서 가서 다른 선원들을 만나보자."

아이들은 워블리를 따라 버스 안처럼 생긴 기다란 복도를 걸어갔다. 거의 양초 몇 개가 타고 있었는데, 그 빛은 희미했다. 저편에서 누군가 시타르를 퉁기고 있는 것처럼 보였는데 공기 중에 짙은 향이 피워져 있어 뚜렷하게 볼 수는 없었다. 아주 평화스러웠다.

그곳을 지나 그들은 다른 방으로 들어갔는데, 그곳 역시 버스의 내부처럼 보였다. 이 방만은 이전의 방과 달리 대단히 혼란스러웠다. 온갖 종류의 음악이 동시에 연주되어 소음들의 끔찍한 뒤범벅을 만들어냈다.

남자들과 여자들, 그리고 아이들이 방안을 빙빙 돌며 춤을 추고, 탬버린과 손가락 심벌즈를 미친 듯이 두들기고 있었다. 한 남자는 샹들리에에 거꾸로 매달려 이리저리 흔들리고 있었는데, 그 얼굴은 머리카락과 수염으로 완전히 뒤덮여 있었다. 바베트가 쿠션의자 위의 오렌지빛 벨루어 깔개를 보고는 미처 감탄을 하기도 전에 한 무리의 뱅뱅 돌던 여자아이들이 그녀를 확 잡아끌어 같이 춤을 추게 만들었다.

p.201

"이건 일종의 종교의식이에요?" 시끌벅적한 가운데서 브리지트가 소리쳤다. "그렇다면 지금 바로 얘기하겠는데, 제 머리는 밀면 안돼요."

"우린 무슨 숭배자 집단이 아니야." 워블리도 소리치며 대답했다. 그러더니 그들에게 등을 돌리고 있던 긴 금발머리의 어떤 여자를 향해 외쳤다. "이봐, 재니스, 좀 진정해. 우리에게 일행이 있잖아."

재니스가 뒤로 돌았다. 그녀는 너무나 아름다웠다. 뺨에는 데이지가 그려 있었고, 얼굴은 차분하고 조용해 보였는데, 특히 푸른 눈이 평온해 보였다. 그녀는 방문객들을 보고 미소짓더니 자리에서 일어나 군중을 향해 일종의 제스처로 손을 쭉 내뻗었다. 마치 여왕 같았다. 사실, 그녀는 왁자지껄한 히피 무리의 여족장임이 분명했는데, 왜냐하면 그들이 그녀의 행동을 알아차리더니 모두 조용해졌고 순서를 기다리는 듯 가만 서 있었기 때문이다.

"여러분, 여기 데드헤드(록그룹 the Grateful Dead의 팬) 몇 사람이 더 승선했나 봐요." 그녀가 말했다.

"그게 무슨 얘기죠?" 바너비가 좀 놀라며 물었다. "우린 죽지 않았어요. 우리 머리도 그렇구요."

"그게 아니야." 바너비 옆에 서 있는 검은 선글라스를 낀 한 히피가 말했다. "데드는 밴드를 말해. 그레이트풀 데드처럼, 알겠어? 우린 알파C에 공연을 하러 가는 길이야."

"다른 행성에서 그레이트풀 데드 공연이라구요?" 바베트가 물었다.

"그들이 그들 노래 '스페이스'에 대한 영감을 어디서 얻은 줄 알아? 그들은 몇 년 동안 여기에 나와 있었다구."

"언제나 무슨 이유가 있을 줄 알았지." 브리지트가 중얼거렸다. 그러더니 워블리 쪽으로 고개를 돌렸다. "공연이 재미있을 것 같지만, 우린 정말 돌아가야 해요. 전 부모님을 잃어버렸어요."

"넌 운 좋은 거야. 난 날 잃어버리게 하려고 우주로 날아와야 했다구." 워블리가 대답했다.

p.202

브리지트는 침울해져서 갈색의 까칠한 카페트를 내려다봤다.

"이봐, 미안하군." 자기의 농담이 먹혀들지 않았다는 걸 안 워블리가 말했다. "경솔한 말로 널 그렇게 침울하게 만들 생각은 아니었어. 하지만 그게 이런 거야. 지금 당장 널 공간이동을 시켜 내려 보낼 순 없어. 공간이동기가 '위'로 고정돼 있는데, 내 손으로 고칠 수가 없거든."

"지구 아무 데라도 내려 보내 줄 순 없나요? 우리가 비밀 장소를 고를 수 있어요. 그럼 아무도 몰래 와서 당신을 잡아가진 못할 거예요." 브리지트가 제안했다.

"아무도 그렇게는 못한다. 파 아웃은 지구 대기를 뚫고 강하하면 살아남지 못할 거야. 내려갈 수 없다면 다시 올라와야겠지. 오존층에 나 있는 구멍 중 하나 위로 자리를 잡아볼 수도 있겠지만, 그건 조금 도움이 될 뿐이야. 이 버스를 태워버릴 준비가 돼 있는 다른 가스층들이 수두룩하니까."

"그럼 전 여기서 꼼짝 못하는 건가요? 남은 평생을 우주 미아로 살아가야 하나요? 집도 없고 가족도 없고 돈도 없이요?" 브리지트가 울부짖듯 말했다. 아랫입술이 떨리기 시작했고 두 눈에선 눈물이 흘러내렸다.

"이봐, 울지 말라구. 방랑자가 되어 돌아다니는 삶은 모험으로 가득해. 있는 곳을 떠나 원하는 곳 어디로든 갈 수 있는 자유, 그만한 건 없다구." 워블리가 열심히 떠들었다. "물론, 거지가 된다는 건 다 좋은 수만은 없지. 그리고 보니... 너희들 돈 가진 거 없니? 알파C에 도착하는 대로 내가 다 갚아줄게."

바로 그 말에 브리지트는 화가 났다. 그녀는 앉아서 소리 높여 흐느껴 울기 시작했다.

"이봐, 뭣 때문에 그렇게 슬픈 거야?" 워블리가 다정하게 물었다. "내가 갚아준다고 했잖아."

우주선의 조종장치 옆에서 바베트, 바너비와 얘길 나누고 있었던 재니스가 브리지트 쪽으로 건너왔다.

p.203

"잘했어요, 워블리." 재니스가 말했다. "처음엔 내가 실수로 얘들을 공간이동 시켰는데, 이젠 당신이 울게 만드는군요."

함장은 어쩔 수 없다는 듯 어깨를 으쓱하더니 저쪽으로 걸어가버렸다.

"네 이름이 브리지트 맞지?" 재니스가 부드럽고 편안함을 주는 목소리로 물었다.

브리지트가 고개를 끄덕였다. 그녀는 그렇게 격하게 울던 것을 뚝 그치기까지 했다. 재니스에게는 뭔가 친절하고 어

321

머니 같은 면이 있었고, 그래서 브리지트는 자신의 엄마가 조금 덜 그리워졌다.

"워블리 때문에 속상해하지 마라, 얘야." 그녀가 말했다. "그 사람이 차갑고 냉정해 보이지만, 정말 인정이 없는 사람은 아니야. 우리가 널 집에 돌려보내 줄게, 약속해. 우린 사실 공연을 하러 가는 길에 우주정거장에 들러서 쇼핑을 좀 하고 물건들을 살 거야. 우리 여행스케줄에다 정비공한테 들르는 걸 넣을 수 있을 거야. 그 디스코 볼을 고치게 할 거야."

브리지트가 고개를 끄덕였고 살짝 웃어보였다.

"자, 그렇게 웃으니까 좋잖아." 재니스가 말했다. "너한테 뭐가 필요한지 알아. 넌 요가를 좀 해야겠어."

"어, 전 모르는데..." 브리지트는 머뭇거렸다. 그녀는 달리지도 않고 뛰어오르지도 않고 땀을 흘리지도 않는 이상한 인도 운동이 내키지 않았다.

"중심을 잡는 데 도움이 될 거야. 지금 넌 균형감각이 전혀 없어. 요가가 네 평형감각을 되찾아줄 거야."

브리지트는 망설이고 있었다. 한편으로는 재니스가 너무 멋있어서 그녀를 따라하고 싶었지만, 또 한편으로는 요가라는 게 위험해 보였다. 그렇게 비비꼬아 올린 자세를 취했다가 다시 못 풀게 되면 어쩌지?

p.204

"걱정 마, 얘야." 재니스가 브리지트를 안심시켰다. "난 지금 매일 요가강습을 하고 있어. 안타깝게도 개조된 관광버스에서 지내는 건 거의 앉아 있는 것인데, 우린 모두 늘상 앉아 있는 게 건강에 안 좋다는 걸 알지. 그래서 우린 요가를 하는 거란다. 몸을 꼬는 게 어느 정도 효과가 있거든. 하고 싶으면 같이 해. 하지만 네 결정은 전적으로 자발적이어야 해. 강요하지는 않을 거야."

다른 사람들이 그녀와 동참하려고 한다는 사실이 브리지트에게 어느 정도 부담감을 덜어줘, 그녀도 한번 해보기로 마음먹었다. 그녀는 재니스가 빌려준 헐렁한 모슬린 바지를 입었고, 이제 그들은 시작할 준비가 되었다.

맨처음의 운동은 스트레칭이라기 보다는 잠을 자는 것 같았다. 재니스가 모두에게 "수평을 취하세요."라고 말하자 사람들 모두 바닥 위에 그냥 누워 있었다. 잠깐 호흡에 집중을 한 후 재니스는 사람들에게 등은 그대로 둔 채 다리를 수직으로 들어올려 공중으로 쭉 뻗어서 바닥과 직각이 되게 만들라고 했다.

"그 다음엔," 재니스가 말했다, "준비됐으면 아래쪽 등을 바닥에서 들어 손으로 받치고, 다리를 머리 위로 뻗으세요. 그러면 무릎이 얼굴 가까이에 닿고 다리는 카페트와 평행이 돼요. 이 자세는 피가 뇌로 흘러가도록 자극하는 거에요."

"정말 효과가 있나 봐요." 브리지트가 끙끙거리며 말했다. "머리가 터질 것 같아요."

"음." 재니스가 말했다. "아마 이건 처음 하는 사람한텐 너무 어려울 거야. 넌 초보자니까 덜 힘든 걸로 시작하도록 해줄게. 다리를 아래로 내려, 그러면 명상하는 방법을 보여줄게."

브리지트는 몸을 움직여 자세를 푼 다음 앉았다. 재니스가 오더니 그녀 앞에 책상다리를 하고 앉았다.

p.205

"명상이란," 재니스가 설명했다, "원래는 그냥 깊은 생각을 말하지. 하지만 요가에서는 특별한 문제나 구체적인 쟁점에 대해 명상을 하는 게 아니야. 그보다 훨씬 추상적인 거야, 알겠니? 그냥 생각을 하는 거지, 어떤 구체적인 것에 대해서가 아니라. 그저 눈을 감고 마음의 긴장을 풀어. 알겠니?"

브리지트는 고개를 끄덕였다. 재니스가 바른 자세를 취할 수 있도록 그녀를 도와주었다.

"자 이젠, 이렇게 하고 나면 별의별 생각들이 네 머릿속으로 들어올지 몰라. 그 생각들과 싸우려고 하지 마. 그것들은 그저 잠재의식적인 생각들로, 네 마음속에 감추어져 있기 때문에 언제나 의식하지 못하는 것들이야. 한번은 내가 명상을 하고 있는데, 그런 생각에 너무 사로잡혀서 환각을 일으키기 시작했어. 눈을 떴는데 내 몸이, 우유 안 넣고 휘저은 크림의 망망대해 속에 둥둥 떠 있는 거야. 초콜릿이 내 머리에 후두둑 떨어지고, 머리 위로는 커다란 마라스키노 체리 달이 반짝반짝 빛나고 있었어. 너무나 근사했지."

재니스는 희미하게 웃어보였다. 브리지트는 휘저어 놓은 크림 사발 속에서 자신을 발견한다는 게 그리 나쁠 것만 같진 않았지만 그래도 좀 걱정이 되었다.

"그러니까, 정말 거기 있었던 건 아니야. 그저 그런 것들이 보였다는 거야, 알겠니? 아무튼 너한테 그런 일이 일어나진 않을 거야." 재니스가 브리지트를 안심시켰다.

브리지트는 두 눈을 감고 명상을 시작했고, 재니스는 다른 수강생들에게 돌아갔다. 제어반 옆에서는 바베트와 바너비 그리고 워블리가 이야기를 나누고 있었다.

"워블리 함장님, 기계를 다루시는 재주가 놀라워요." 바너비가 말했다. "평범한 관광버스를 가져다가 저렇게 멋진 우주선을 만드시다니 정말 굉장해요."

"응, 뭐, 멋진 우주선이 될 수도 있었지만, 연방수사관들이 날 끈질기게 감시하고 있었지. 무슨 얘긴지 알겠니? 난 서둘러야 했어." 워블리가 말했다. "한 가지만 들자면 항해하는 것이 그리 쉽지 않아. 아마 메이플라워 호가 이것보단 조종하기 쉬웠을 거야. 하지만 무엇보다 날 화나게 만드는 건 변속기지."

p.206

"기어 말인가요?" 바베트가 좀 놀라며 말했다. "기어가 달린 우주선이라구요? 전 '하이퍼드라이브'나 '워프 팩터'나 그런 걸 기대했는데."

"가지고 있는 걸로 해야지." 워블리가 대답했다. "파 아웃에 있는 건 수동 변속기였어. 멕시코에 있을 때 자동 변속기를 달려고 했는데 시간이 부족했지. 그래서 필요한 부품을 얻을 때까지는 기어가 구식, 즉 수동으로 변속되지."

"음, 자동 변속기라," 바너비가 머리를 긁적이고 문제를 곰곰이 생각했다. "우선 속도조절 벨트가 필요하겠죠?"

갑자기 바너비 머리카락 속에서 뭔가가 나오더니 선장의 자리 밑에 떨어졌다.

"바너비!" 바베트가 놀라움으로 숨이 막혔다. "설마 네 머릿속에 속도조절 벨트가 붙어 있었던 건 아니지!"

"글쎄, 꼭 속도조절 벨트는 아니고." 워블리가 자리 밑에서 물건을 끄집어낸 후 말했다. "그보다는 '과학자 인명록' 최신호 수영복편인데. 여기 아주 아슬아슬한 사진들이 있군."

"전 기사만 읽었어요." 바너비가 얼굴을 약간 붉히며 말했다. "내 동료들이 무슨 일들을 하는지 잘 알고 있으려고요. 돌려줘요!"

바너비가 잡지를 잡으려고 껑충 뛰었지만 함장이 그의 팔이 닿지 않는 곳에 들고 있었다. 두 사람은 잡지를 놓고 계속 싸우다가 갑자기 워블리가 소리쳤다. "이봐, 내 콘택트!"

"콘택트 렌즈를 끼나요?" 바너비가 잠시 잡지에 대한 흥미를 접어두고 물었다. "그러면 할머니같은 안경은 쓸 필요 없는 거 아니에요? 그러니까, 콘택트 렌즈를 끼면서 안경은 왜 필요한 거예요?"

p.207

워블리는 그의 질문에는 아랑곳하지 않았다. 빽빽한 갈색 털 속에서 콘택트 렌즈를 찾느라 정신이 없었다.

"찾았다!" 몇분이 지난 뒤 워블리가 신이 나서 말했다. "야, 큰일 날 뻔했네. 자, 우리가 무슨 얘길 하고 있었지?"

"함장님의 인생 이야기요." 바베트가 화제를 바꾸어볼 기회를 잡으며 말했다. "어쩌다가 그렇게 악평이 자자한 히피가 되셨는지, 그리고 재니스는 어떻게 만나셨는지, 또 어떻게 결혼할 결심을 하셨고 함께 우주로 날아올 생각을 하셨는지에 대해 얘기해 주시려고 했어요."

"글쎄, 우선 재니스는 내 배우자가 아니란다." 워블리가 대답했다.

"저런, 너무 실망스러워요." 바베트가 얼굴을 찡그렸다.

"왜?"

"아, 뭐, 너무나 로맨틱해 보였거든요." 그녀가 꿈결처럼 안타까워했다. "지구로부터 추격당하며 별들 사이에서 사랑을 찾는 두 명의 추방당한 히피."

"바베트를 용서해 주세요. 쟤는 프랑스 애거든요." 바너비가 속삭이듯 말했다.

"이봐, 날 오해하지 말라구." 워블리가 바베트에게 말했다. "내 말은, 재니스는 내 여자친구가 아냐. 우리 관계는 순전히 정신적인 거야. 하지만, 난 그녀를 좋아하지. 그런데 사회로부터 추방당한 우리들은 어디에 매일 수가 없단다, 알겠니? 거칠고 억제되지 않은 감정은 어려움에 빠지게 할 뿐이야. 게다가 평생을 한 사람과 결혼해서 산다는 생각은 아주 중산계급적이고 시대에 뒤떨어진 사고야. 일부일처는 고지식한 사람들을 위한 거라구!"

"흥." 바베트가 벌컥 화를 내며 가슴 위로 두 팔을 팔짱끼었다.

"이 주제에 대해서는 우리가 통하지 않는구나." 워블리가 말했다. "우리가 어떻게 지금 여기에 와 있는지 말해줘야겠구나. 사실, 그건 내가 십대였을 때로 거슬러 올라가. 히피셨던 우리 어머니는 나한테 '밥, 난 네가 부자였으면 좋겠구나.' 하고 말씀하셨지."

"함장님 이름은 워블리인 줄 알았는데요. 왜 어머니는 밥이라고 부르셨죠?" 바너비가 물었다.

"글쎄, 그렇게 된 건 내가 태어날 때였어. 아마, 어머니는 내 이름을 밥 위어 필스타인이라고 짓고 싶으셨던 모양이야. 헷갈리셨던 모양이야. 출생신고서를 작성할 때가 됐을 때 어머니는 오락가락하셨고, 사람들이 어떤 이름으로 짓길 원하는지 물었을 때 어머니는 계속 '웝 비어, 웝 비어' 라고 말씀하신 거야. 'b' 와 'w' 의 자리를 바꿔서 말야. 최소한, 그게 우리가 생각해낼 수 있는 최선의 설명이지. 어쨌든 어머니는 항상 날 밥이라고 부르셨어."

"그래서, 아까 얘기한 대로, 어머니는 내가 아주 부유하고 힘있는 사업가, 가능만 하다면 실업계의 거물이 됐으면 하셨어. 현실을 직시해봐. 히피라는 건 그리 돈이 벌리는 일이 못돼. 그러니까, 어머니는 누군가 돈을 벌기 시작하는 게 좋겠다고 생각하셨어. 안 그러면 어머닌 늙고 집도 없는 신세가 될 테니까. 이런, 난 슬펐어. 난 히피의 공동생활체를 떠나고 싶지도 않았고, 나한테 사업가로 성공할 능력이 있을지 대단히 의심스러웠거든. 뉴욕시티를 향해 출발했을 때 난 두려웠어. 사람들한테 비웃음을 당할까봐 겁이 났고, 해고당할까봐 겁이 났고, 어디에도 취직을 하지 못할까봐 겁이 났어."

"나중에 와서 보니 그런 두려움들은 완전히 헛된 거였어. 뉴욕은 호경기였지. 난 당장에 취직이 됐고, 사업에 대한 천재적인 소질이 있다는 걸 발견했어. 그냥 자연스럽게 그렇게 된 거야. 곧 난 백만장자가 됐지. 그러니까, 난 빵에 굴러다녔어..."

"빵에 굴러다녀?" 바너비가 바베트에게 속삭였다. "그게 무슨 뜻이야?"

"나도 몰라." 그녀도 속삭이듯 말했다. "히피 언어 중의 하나겠지. 최소한 진짜로 빵 덩어리들과 굴러다녔다는 얘기는 아닐 거야. 브리지트한테 물어보자."

"하지만 내 부에는 대가가 따랐어." 워블리가 계속해서 말했다. "무엇보다, 스트레스 때문에 위궤양에 시달렸지. 속이 마구 쓰렸어."

바베트와 바너비는 그런 끔찍한 걸 생각하면서 질겁했는데, 마치 자기들의 배가 그렇게 아픈 것처럼 보일 정도였다.

"하지만 그중 최악은 나한테 중요했던 모든 가치들을 포기했다는 거였지. 그래, 난 돈을 위해서라면 한때 신성시했던 모든 사회적 운동과 정치적 주장까지 기꺼이 저버렸어. 심지어, 우리나라에서 케일의 자연공급을 바닥나게 하는 것이 유일한 목적인 회사를 위해서도 일을 했지. 계속 그렇게 하면 2010년에 이르러서는 미국이란 나라에 케일은 더 이상 없게 될 거야!"

바너비와 바베트는 정말 놀라서 서로를 빤히 쳐다봤다.

"더 이상은 참을 수가 없었지. 난 뭔가를 해야 했어. 나라는 망하고 있고, 난 그걸 멈춰야만 했던 거야. 난 적극적이고 헌신적이고 투쟁적으로 그 운동에 가담했어. 그때부터 짓궂은 장난을 치기 시작한 거야."

"난 재활용 화장지를 가지고 백악관 건물을 둘렀어. 의사당 건물 바닥엔 퇴비 한 트럭분을 쏟아놓았지. 그리고, 너희들도 들었겠지만, 하원 의장을 야채 물로 새빨갛게 만들어버렸지. 그래, 어떤 사람들은 날 공공시설 파괴자에 불과하다고 말하지만, 이런 행동들은 몰상식한 스프레이 페인팅이나 자산의 파괴행위와는 달라."

"빨간 물 장난을 할 때쯤엔 나한테 이미 수십 명의 추종자들이 생겼어. 하지만 내 인생이 영원히 뒤바뀐 건 재니스를 만났을 때였지."

"아하!" 바베트가 소리쳤다. "그런 줄 알았어요. 선장님은 재니스에게 반했어요. 푹 빠져 있다구요, 맞잖아요!"

"그만둬, 바베트." 워블리가 말했다. "난 사랑 따윈 안 믿어. 하지만 그녀에게 많은 걸 빚졌지. 그녀를 만나기 전에 난 노여움으로 가득차 있었어. 내 장난은 점점 더 위험해지고 있었지. 폭력적인 생각까지 하기 시작했어. 재니스는 나의 분노를 식히고 내가 더 온건해지도록 도와주었어. 하지만 그때 정부에선 이미 날 잡아 없애려고 했고, 난 모든 시간을 체포를 피해 다니며 보내는 데 지쳐가고 있었어. 그래서 우린 멕시코로 도망쳤고, 같은 생각을 가진 히피들이 수없이 우릴 따라왔지. 그건 대이동이었어. 집단 전체가 짐을싸서 미국을 떠난 거야. 정부에선 아마 우리가 자기들한테 호의를 베푼다고 생각했을 거야. 어쨌든, 그 뒷얘기는 벌써 알고 있는 거고. 와, 벌써 상점에 다 왔잖아! 속도를 좀 낮추어야겠군."

p.210

워블리는 급히 발로 클러치를 밟았고 기어를 서투르게 1단으로 변속했다. 우주선 전체가 갑자기 앞으로 쏠렸다. 깊은 명상에 잠겨 있던 브리지트는 옆으로 넘어졌다. 다른 방에서 향과 시타르 음악으로 깊은 잠에 빠져 있던 보리가드는 그렇게 무례하게 자신의 잠을 깨운 게 무엇인지 알아보려고 왔다. 그는 화난 눈으로 함장을 노려보았다.

"미안하네, 친구." 손을 살짝 흔들며 워블리가 말했다.

갑자기 잠에서 깬 브리지트는 흥분으로 가득차 있었다. "난 알았다!" 그녀는 소리쳤다.

재니스와 요가 강습을 듣는 다른 사람들 몇이 와서 브리지트가 일어서는 걸 도와주었다.

"무슨 환상이라도 봤니?" 재니스가 물었다.

"완벽한 픽앤롤 수비였어요! 누가 종이 좀 갖다줘요. 스케치해서 뉴욕 닉스에 보내야겠어요!"

"농구 대형이야? 심오하기도 하지. 정말 심원하구나. 인생의 의미에 대한 얼마나 중요한 통찰력이니." 히피 가운데 하나가 빈정대며 조롱하는 투로 말했다.

"랄프, 내가 당신이라면 얼굴에서 그렇게 독선적이고 능글맞은 웃음은 지워버리겠어요." 재니스가 경고했다. "모든 사람들한테 당신의 대단한 통찰력은 뭐였는지 얘기해줘야 하나요? 제 기억으론 좀 무미건조했는데. 따분함 그 자체였죠. 지루했어요. '오스왈드의 단독범행이었다' 뭐 그런 거였어요, 맞죠?"

랄프는 투덜거리더니 저쪽으로 걸어가버렸다.

"워블리가 무슨 생각을 하는지 가서 보자." 재니스가 제안했다. "상점에 거의 다 온 것 같은데."

재니스는 공연을 하러 가기 전에 정비소에 들러 디스코 볼을 고치게 해서 바너비와 바베트, 브리지트, 그리고 보리가드를 지구로 돌려보내자는 아이디어를 내놓았다. 워블리는 그 생각에 바로 찬성하지 않았다.

p.211

"하지만 재니스," 워블리가 푸념하듯 말했다, "우린 과일장수 스탠과의 랑데부가 4시간도 안 남았어. 예정대로 만나지 못한다면 공연을 하며 먹을 RSG를 구하지 못할 거라구!"

"RSG요?" 브리지트가 물었다.

"씨없는 붉은 포도를 말해." 재니스가 말했다. "아주 맛있는 스낵이지. 데드 공연을 할 때 먹기에 딱이지. 어쨌든, 이 봐요, 워블리, 그건 유괴에 대한 아주 얄팍한 구실이에요. 포도는 공연장에서도 구할 수 있다는 거 알잖아요. 우리에겐 이 애들을 3일간 데드 공연에 억지로 데려갈 권리가 없다구요. 이 애들이 자유의사로 가겠다고 하면 그건 얘기가 달라요. 하지만 아이들은 분명히 지구로 돌아가고 싶어하고, 그러니 우린 애들을 도와줘야 해요. 스낵을 먹고 싶은 것보다 더 설득력있는 이유를 생각해내지 못하면 우린 이 애들을 지구로 돌려보내야 한다고 생각해요."

워블리는 비참한 기분으로 동의했고, 파 아웃을 우주선 정비소의 출입구 속으로 끌고 들어갔다. 그가 경적을 울리자 기름묻은 작업복 차림의 등이 구부정한 회색머리 남자가 발을 질질 끌며 나왔다. 워블리, 재니스 그리고 아이들은 우주선 밖으로 뛰어나왔다.

"무슨 일이죠?" 남자가 물었는데, 그의 작업복에는 가슴 주머니 위에 "브루스"라는 이름이 수놓아져 있었다.

"공간이동 장치가 '위'로 고정이 돼 있는데, 이 애들을 지금 당장 지구로 돌려보내야 해요. 우릴 도와주실 수 있나요, 어, 브루스?" 재니스가 가능한 한 다정하게 물었다.

"내 이름은 브루스가 아니오." 정비공이 투덜거렸다. 하지만 다행히도 그는 디스코 볼을 한번 봐주겠다고 했다.

그는 고장난 볼을 그저 건성으로 쓱 본 후에 바로 나와서는 고치려고 무슨 수를 써봐도 소용없다고 말했다.

"그래, 당신말이 맞아요." 워블리가 말했다. "우린 가던 길을 가자구."

"잠깐만요, 워블리. 소용이 없다니 무슨 뜻이죠? 제대로 보지도 않았잖아요!" 재니스는 브루스가 아니라는 남자에게 말했다.

p.212

"쓸데없단 얘기예요. 성공하지 못한다구요. 그걸 고치는 방법이 단 하나 있는데, 그건..."

"덕 테이프요?" 바너비가 물었다.

모두의 시선이 천재 소년을 향했는데, 그는 번쩍이는 회색 테이프 두루마리를 들고 거기 서있었다. 브리지트와 바베트는 알겠다는 미소를 교환했다.

"어, 내가..." 정비공이 말했다. "얘야, 그 테이프 이리 줘라. 내가 금새 고쳐줄게."

정비공은 그의 말대로 했다. 5분도 되지 않아 그들은 작별인사를 나누며 지구를 향해 가고 있었다. 하지만 15분도 채 되지 않아 엔진이 불연소음을 내며 멈추어섰다. 워블리는 타륜에 머리를 쥐어박기 시작했다.

"이건 일종의 예시야. 징조라구, 알겠어? 뭔가가 우리에게 데드 공연을 하기는 글렀다고 말해주려는 거야."

"진정해요, 워블리." 브리지트가 말했다. "바너비가 주전공은 물리학이지만, 아주 다재다능해요. 틀림없이 고칠 수 있을 거예요. 얘는 천재라구요!"

"참으로 낙관적이구나. 정말 기분좋은 전망이라구. 소용없다는 걸 모르겠니?" 그가 한탄하듯 말했다.

"글쎄, 내가 그 정도로 천재인지는 모르겠지만," 바너비가 겸손해 보이려고 애쓰며 말했다, "워블리 함장님은 너무 화가 나서서 직접 못 고치실 것 같으니, 내가 한번 봐야겠다."

브리지트와 바베트는 그를 따라 엔진실로 갔다.

"음." 바너비가 잠깐 동안 이것저것 살펴본 후 말했다. "워블리 함장님은 이 우주선의 오일을 갈아끼우는 데 아주 소홀했던 것 같아. 3개월에 한번은 갈아줘야 하는데. 이렇게 꽉 막혀서 끈적거리는 걸 보니까, 글쎄, 아주 오래, 진짜 오랫동안 교환을 안한 것 같아."

"그건 신경쓰지 마." 브리지트가 말했다. "고칠 수 있겠어?"

p.213

"모르겠어." 그가 대답했다. "엔진을 손상시키지 않고 막혀 있는 걸 도려내려면 적합한 연장과 전문가의 기술이 필요할 거야."

"말도 안돼." 바베트가 말했다. "그냥 한방에 뻥 치면 되겠네."

"너 미쳤니?" 바너비가 말했다. "기계를 그냥 때린 다음 작동되길 기대할 수는 없어."

"바너비, 우린 지금 위기 한가운데에 봉착했어." 브리지트가 이를 악물며 말했다. "이 엔진을 못 고치면 우린 영원히 괴상한 히피들 떼거리와 떠돌아다녀야 한다구. 무슨 일을 당하게 될지 몰라! 그 사람들은 기타를 치면서 그레이트풀 데드 노래를 메들리로 연주하기 시작할지도 몰라. 알아듣겠어?"

"그래. 정말 절망적인 상황이구나. 힘껏 때려, 바베트."

바베트는 좋은 위치를 선정하기 위해 잠시 엔진을 살펴보았다. 그런 다음 몇차례 호흡을 가다듬었고, 크게 "히야!" 하고 외치며 엔진을 카라테하는 자세로 걷어찼더니, 그 즉시 엔진이 탁탁 소리를 내며 되살아났다.

바너비와 브리지트는 감동을 받았다. 그들은 다양한 재능을 격찬해주며 프랑스 친구를 한껏 추켜세우기 시작했다. 마침내 그들은 지구로 돌아갈 수 있게 된 것이다. 그들은 작별인사를 하기 위해 우주선의 앞쪽으로 돌아갔다.

그들이 그곳에 가보니 평화와 사랑은 온데간데 없었다. 히피들이 한창 사나운 논쟁을 벌이고 있었다. 물론, 그들 가운데 몇 명은 조용히 노래를 부르거나 명상을 하고 있었지만, 방안의 지배적인 감정은 확실히 노여움이었다. 그리고 그 노여움은 워블리를 향한 것이었다.

"이 위선자! 어떻게 우리한텐 이렇게 하라고 말하면서 당신은 딴짓을 할 수가 있지?" 한 여자가 소리쳤다. "당신은 우리한테 세속적인 소유물을 포기하고 돈에 의존하는 걸 그만두라고 했잖아. 그것이 우리가 자유로워지는 유일한 길이라고 했잖아. 이러는 동안 당신은 지구에서 고수익 채권으로 백만 달러를 투자해 놓았단 말이지! 인정해, 과일장수 스탠은 당신 브로커잖아!"

p.214

"당신 말투가 불쾌하군, 선샤인." 워블리가 대꾸했다. "난 여러분 함장이오. 적절한 경의를 표하시오. 그렇지 않으면 반항에 대해 처벌해야 할 거요."

그런 반응은 히피들과는 어울리지 않았고, 워블리 함장은 갑자기 자신의 지배에 대한 봉기, 즉 파 아웃에서의 폭동을 맞게 되었다. 웬일인지 재니스는 싸움 내내 침착함을 유지하고 있었다. 그녀는 바너비, 브리지트, 바베트 그리고 보리가드가 구석에 몸을 움츠리고 있는 곳으로 걸어왔다.

"우주의 히피들조차도 이따금 흥분을 할 때가 있어." 그녀는 설명했다. "하지만 평상시에 아주 평화롭게 어울려 사는 사람들이 그런 불화를 일으키는 걸 목격해야 할 이유는 없지. 자, 전송실로 가자. 지금 우리가 공간이동 구역 안에 있는 것 같아."

아이들과 고양이는 재니스를 따라 자신들이 처음 나타났던 방으로 갔다. 재니스는 그들 모두를 꼭 안아주었고 보리가드의 머리를 긁적여준 다음, 그들에게 목걸이를 주었는데, 각각 착용자의 이름 첫글자가 달아매져 있는 것 말고는 동일했다.

"이걸 갖고 다니면서 우릴 기억하렴. 짧은 우주여행의 기념품이란다." 재니스가 말했다.

"그럴게요." 새로 사귄 친구를 떠나야 한다는 사실에 좀 서글퍼진 브리지트가 말했다.

"자, 그럼," 재니스가 공간이동 조종장치로 다가가며 말문을 열었다. "모두 같이 바닥 가운데 모여 있어. 이 디스코볼이 얼마나 정확할지는 모르겠지만, 적어도 지구 어딘가로는 날아갈 거야."

디스코 볼이 도처에 분홍빛, 초록빛, 노란빛, 파란빛을 번쩍이며 회전하기 시작했다. 이내 바너비, 보리가드, 바베트 그리고 브리지트는 따뜻하고 녹아드는 느낌에 감싸였다.

"즐거운 여행 되세요!" 브리지트가 막 사라지기 시작하면서 소리쳤다.

"어, 그래." 재니스가 대답했다. "그럴게."

p.215

QUICK QUIZ 11

관계짓기

아래의 단어 쌍들이 서로 어떤 관계를 갖는지 판단하세요. 비슷한 의미면 "S" 반대 의미이면 "O"를 하세요.

1. 나쁘기로 이름난 :: 악명 높은
2. 벗어나다 :: 피하다
3. 유랑자 :: 방랑자
4. 수평의 :: 수직의
5. 수직의 :: 평행의
6. 추상적인 :: 구체적인
7. 실업계의 거물 :: 가난뱅이
8. 정신적인 사랑의 :: 열렬한 사랑의
9. 빛나는 :: 흐릿한
10. 피상적인 :: 철저한
11. 앉아 있는 :: 활동적인
12. 냉정한 :: 배려하는
13. 달랬다 :: 위로했다
14. 풋내기 :: 초보자
15. 소용없는 :: 무익한

QUICK QUIZ 12

관계짓기

아래의 단어 쌍들이 서로 어떤 관계를 갖는지 판단하세요. 비슷한 의미이면 "S" 반대 의미이면 "O"를 하세요.

1. 투쟁적인 :: 온건한
2. 의지 :: 자유의지
3. 자유분방한 :: 별난
4. 대혼란 :: 평온
5. 소질 :: 재능
6. 불일치 :: 조화
7. 조심성 있는 :: 신중한
8. 경솔한 :: 공손한
9. 동시에 :: 각각
10. 지배 :: 관리
11. 줄었다 :: 감소했다
12. 이상적인 :: 완벽한
13. 무미건조한 :: 심오한
14. 조짐 :: 징후
15. 겸손한 :: 뽐내는

빈칸 채우기

아래에 있는 각각의 단어들 중에서 가장 완벽한 문장을 만들어주는 단어를 고르세요.

1. 즐거운 야외모임에 대한 나의 철저한 계획과 기대 모두가 예기치 못한 눈보라로 (   ).
   a. 방향감각을 잃었다   b. 피곤해졌다   c. 차질이 생겼다   d. 구해졌다

p.216

2. 헌혈은 완전히 (   ) 행동으로, 열심히 장려는 하지만 의무적인 것은 아니다.
   a. 이상한   b. 교활한   c. 자발적인   d. 여정의

3. 아빠는 뒷마당에 수영장을 만들 건지 말 건지에 대해 계속 (   ), 몇 달 동안 결정을 못 하다가 마침내는 짓기로 결심했다.
   a. 망설였지만   b. 환각을 일으켰지만   c. 자극이 됐지만   d. 명상했지만

4. 앤디는 대학을 졸업한 후 마술사가 되리라 마음먹었지만, 그의 어머니는 그에게 대출금을 다 갚고 아파트를 얻을 수 있을 만큼의 돈을 벌 수 있게 좀더 (   ) 직업을 가지라고 충고했다.
   a. 분투하는   b. 잠재의식적인   c. 느슨한   d. 돈이 벌리는

5. 애크미 사의 사장은 성대한 야유회를 열기로 결정했고, 모든 사원들에게 그들의 (   ) 아이들도 데려오라고 말했다.
   a. 범죄자들과   b. 숭배자집단과   c. 여자족장들과   d. 배우자들과

6. 친구들에게서 돈을 빌려야 한다면 반드시 가능한 한 빨리 (   ). 그렇지 않으면 좋지 않은 감정이 생길 수 있습니다.
   a. 비틀거리세요   b. 갚으세요   c. 저버리세요   d. 슬퍼하세요

7. 크로프트 씨는 티미에게서 열 살짜리가 보기에는 사진들이 너무 (   ) 이유로 그의 '수영복 콜렉션'지를 빼앗아갔는데, 우리 생각엔 그가 그저 잡지를 보고 싶어 한 것 같다.
   a. 굴레를 벗겼다는   b. 외설스럽다는   c. 과다하다는   c. 도중에

8. 나는 놀이공원에서 회전놀이기구를 타고 내린 다음 (   )을/를 되찾아 어지러운 느낌 없이 똑바로 걷는 데 잠깐의 시간이 걸렸다.
   a. 실내 장식업   b. 염소수염   c. 평형   d. 일부일처

9. 페니는 새로운 곳에 여행갈 때마다 자신의 여행을 추억하기 위해 늘 조그만 (   )을/를 가져온다.
   a. 기념품   b. 메들리   c. 숙어   d. 궤양

10. 브루스는 미국의 아이스하키 팀들이 자신의 성에 차게 경기를 펼치지 않으면 캐나다로 (   ) 협박했다.
    a. 홀딱 빠지겠다고 b. 개시하겠다고   c. 주춤하겠다고   d. 망명하겠다고

11. 미라는 한달 넘도록 자기 집 밖으로 나오지도 않고 잔디를 깎지도 않았으면서 이웃사람들을 보고 게으르다고 말하는 (   )였다.
    a. 위선자   b. 목격자   c. 고의적인 파괴자   d. 대이동

짝짓기

오른쪽의 단어를 비슷한 의미의 왼쪽 단어와 짝지으세요.

1. 근거 없는	a. 은신처
2. 피난처	b. 지지되지 않은
3. 사망한	c. 낙하
4. 빽빽한	d. 경이
5. 앞의	e. 죽은
6. 낙하	f. 다 써버리다
7. 어머니의	g. 밀집한, 두꺼운
8. 입다	h. 손으로 조작하는

p.217

9. 놀라운 일	i. 이전의
10. 운전하다	j. 뒤집힌
11. 수동의	k. 조종하다
12. 거꾸로 된	l. 입다
13. 고갈시키다	m. 어머니 같은

짝짓기

오른쪽의 단어를 비슷한 의미의 왼쪽 단어와 짝지으세요.

1. 교활한	a. 기술
2. 회합약속, 랑데부	b. 주요한
3. 융통성 있는	c. 칭찬하다
4. 낙관주의	d. 탄력적인
5. 기교, 솜씨	e. 비열한
6. 위기	f. 짧은 여행
7. 격찬하다	g. 불복종
8. 우세한	h. 같은
9. 반항	i. 약속
10. 반란	j. 기대에 참
11. 동일한	k. 폭동, 봉기
12. 소풍, 짧은 여행	l. 위험한 상황

4 캐스퍼의 최후

p.220

우리는 아래로 내려가 미시시피 강 속으로 첨벙 떨어졌어. 그런 흙탕물은 오해의 여지없이 미시시피 강이라는 걸 알았는데, 너무나 탁해 햇빛이 바닥에 닿은 적이 있을까 의심될 정도였지. 말할 것도 없이 이런 상황은 날 너무나 원통하게 만들었어. 우선, 아마 알겠지만, 우리 고양이들은 물속에 빠지는 걸 좋아하지 않아. 기분 좋게 따뜻한 물이라도 말이야. 하지만 이 물은 기분 좋게 따뜻하지도 않았거니와 지독하게 차가웠어. 거기다, 우주 히피들과의 진기한 경험을 한 후 내 털에는 희미한 향냄새가 배어 있었어. 물론 당장 알아차릴 정도로 거슬리는 냄새가 아니라 그저 흐릿한 향내였어. 난 그게 좋았단 말야. 근데 여기서 찰랑이는 갈색 물결에 그 향이 씻겨나가고 있었던 거지. 그래, 난 노발대발했다구.

다행스럽게도 브리지트는 아직 껌을 갖고 있었어. 안 그래도 빨리 흘러가고 있던 물살에 점점 가속이 붙기 시작했거든. 곧 우린 마치 소방용 호스로 뿜는 물에 얻어맞는 기분이 됐어. 쉴 새 없이 껌을 씹어대는 아이를 내가 칭찬하게 되리라고는 생각도 못했었는데 (내가 태어난 곳에서는 아이들이 껌 씹는 걸 아주 싫어했는데, 하물며 온종일 씹는 건 말할 것도 없지), 브리지트는 자신의 습관을 예술의 경지로 끌어올렸던 거야. 그녀는 뗏목 모양으로 엄청나게 큰 풍선을 불더니, 우리 모두를 끌어올려 그 위에 태웠어.

얼마 동안은 항해하기가 상당히 힘들었어. 마치 세탁기의 회전 사이클에 꼼짝없이 붙들려 있는 것 같았은데, 마침내 본 강을 벗어나 물결이 좀더 고요한 곳으로 떠내려갔고, 그리고 나서 우리가 어디 있는지 확인할 수가 있었어. 그곳은 루이지애나의 늪지였어.

소나무겨우살이가 나무들마다 울창하게 늘어져서 하늘과 태양의 시계를 가리는 바람에, 한낮인데도 해질녘인 것 같았어. 강물은 차츰 세차게 흐르는 걸 멈추더니 힘없이 고여 있었어. 주변에서 어슬렁거리는 악어 떼도 있었는데, 이따금 초록빛의 비늘 덮인 머리가 시커먼 물 밖으로 나와 우리를 점검하는 듯하고는 다시 수면 아래로 가라앉곤 했어.

p.221

물론 난 우리가 익사하지 않았다는 사실만으로 기뻤지만, 이 상황은 내 신경을 곤두세웠어. 우리를 실은 뗏목이 물가로 밀려오자 브리지트, 바베트, 바너비는 허둥지둥 뗏목 밖으로 나와서 땅위에 철퍼덕 쓰러졌어. 급류와 악전고투하며 지쳐버린 거지. 하지만 난 너무 초조해 쉴 수도 없었어. 난 저 나무들 뒤에 도사리고 있는 위험을 감지했던 거야. 거기다 내 털은 심각한 손질이 필요했거든. 난 경계의 끈을 놓지 않았어. 하지만 안타깝게도, 고양이 한 마리가 할 수 있는 일이라곤 별로 없었어...

"이거 갈수록 황당해지는데." 브리지트가 쉬고 난 후 일어나 앉더니 말했다. "지금 여기가 어디야?"

"동식물들과 어마어마한 크기의 바퀴벌레를 보니까 남부 루이지애나에 있는 것 같아." 바너비가 엄청나게 큰 갈색 벌레의 잔털 난 뒷다리 하나를 든 채로 대답했다.

"우웩." 브리지트가 얼굴을 찌푸리며 말했다. "그 더러운 것 좀 내려놔."

바너비가 그 생물을 툭 떨어뜨리자 그것은 요란한 소리를 내며 허둥지둥 늪 속으로 들어갔다. 바베트도 기지개를 켜더니 일어나 앉았고, 세 아이들은 이제 무엇을 해야 할지 논의하기 시작했다. 하지만 그들의 대화는 갑자기 소름끼치는 비명소리에 중단되었다.

"으르렁!"

아이들은 벌떡 일어나 몸을 뒤로 확 돌렸다. 그들 뒤로 3피트도 안 되는 거리에 괴물 같은 남자가 있었는데, 곰처럼 크고, 훌렁 벗겨진 대머리로, 네 개의 거대한 팔을 뻗어 그들을 붙잡으려고 했는데, 보리가드가 쉿쉿 소리를 내며 발톱으로 할퀴고 그의 머리에 올라가 사납게 울부짖었다.

"세상에." 바너비는 놀라움으로 숨이 막혔다. "어떻게 저런 돌연변이가 생길 수 있지? 어렸을 때 부모가 뭘 먹인 거야? 아니, 어쩌면 유전일 수도 있겠다. 형이나 누나도 다 팔이 네 개일지도 몰라."

"필기할 시간 없어, 바너비. 뛰어!" 브리지트가 소리쳤는데, 그녀는 이미 바베트와 함께 달음박질치기 위해 몸을 돌린 상태였다.

p.222

하지만 그들은 그리 멀리 가지 못했는데, 그들 바로 뒤로 까만색의 세로줄 무늬 양복 차림에 테 넓은 모자를 쓴 땅딸막한 남자와 빨간 색 짧은 드레스 차림에 머리를 금발로 표백한 여자가 서 있었다. 보통 그 정도로는 네 팔 괴물에게서 도망치는 두 아이를 멈추어 세우기에 역부족이겠지만, 공교롭게도 남자의 손에는 커다란 권총이 들려 있었는데, 정확히 말하자면 44구경이었다. 상황이 그렇게 되고 보니 브리지트와 바베트는 뛰는 것을 멈추었다.

이때 이미, 괴물은 바너비를 한손으로 들어올리고, 다른 손으로는 머리에서 보리가드를 떼어낸 상태였다. 그는 남자아이와 고양이가 쓸데없이 몸부림치고 있는 동안 명령을 기다리듯 서 있었다.

"잘했다, 식인종." 총을 든 남자가 말했다.

"식인종이라구요? 설마 저 사람에게 우릴 먹이려는 건 아니겠죠?! 그러니까, 저 사람은 사람 말고 다른 걸 먹죠, 그렇죠?" 브리지트가 흥분해서 불쑥 말했다.

"질문은 그만해라." 남자가 호통 쳤다. "여기서 질문이란 걸 할 수 있는 사람은 나뿐이다. 내 첫 번째 질문은, 니들은 여기서, 우리 약탈품 근처에서 냄새를 맡으며 뭘 하고 있는 거냐?"

"약탈품이라구요?" 바베트가 물었다.

"날 놀리려고 하지 마! 너넨 우리가 뉴올리언스에서 페이쇼드 부인의 프랄린 저택을 약탈한 위험한 폭력배라는 걸 모를 리 없어. 우린 프랄린 일곱 바구니를 훔쳐왔어. 지금쯤 틀림없이 전 경찰조직이 우릴 쫓고 있을 거야. 우린 약탈품을 우리 은신처에 숨겨두었는데, 너희도 알 거야. 네 놈들은 우리 약탈품을 쫓고 있다구!"

"아저씬 '약탈품'이라는 말을 좋아하시나봐요." 브리지트가 말했다.

p.223

"'약탈품'은 진짜 폭력배 말이다, 꼬맹아. '권총'도 그렇지, 내 말을 알아듣는다면. 조심해, 안 그럼 미시시피 강에서 고갤 숙인 채 떠돌아다니는, 그저 또 하나의 이름 없는 송장이 될 테니까."

무슨 이유에서인지 브리지트는 이 남자가 그리 무섭지만은 않았다. 그는 남자답게 보이려고 지나치게 애를 쓰고 있었다. 터프함과 남자다움은 꾸며진 것, 뭔가를 은폐하려고 계획된 행동 같았다. 하지만 총은 충분히 진짜처럼 보였고,

그래서 브리지트는 입을 다물고 있기로 마음먹었다.

"우우, 베르나, 이 꼬맹이들이 내 속을 정말 뒤집어 놓는데! 얘들을 쏘아 죽인다 해도 양심의 가책은 없겠어. 없애버려야겠는 걸." 폭력배가 총을 마구 휘두르며 으르렁거렸다.

"아직은 죽이지 마, 스네이크." 베르나가 높고 좀 여자애 같은 목소리로 소곤거렸다. "우리 계획에 이용해 먹을 수 있을지도 몰라, 안 그래?"

"그래, 거 괜찮은 생각인데." 스네이크가 눈을 반짝이며 말했다. "그거 괜찮겠네. 너희들, 베르나가 이렇게 분별이 있는 게 다행인 줄 알아라. 식인종! 이 두 애들 잡아다가 은신처로 데리고 가!"

진짜 식인종인지도 모르는 괴물이 브리지트와 바베트를 자유자재의 팔로 들어올려서는 습지를 지나 돌아가기 시작했고, 스네이크가 그 뒤를 따랐고, 그 뒤로 베르나가 따라왔는데, 베르나는 6인치 높이의 신발 뒤축이 자꾸만 진흙탕 속으로 빠지는 바람에 걷는 속도가 느렸다.

은신처는 간이침대 두 개와 의자 몇 개가 갖추어진 원룸형 오두막집이었다. 스네이크는 지체 없이 의자 네 개를 한데 끌어 다가 바베트, 브리지트, 바너비 그리고 보리가드를 각각의 의자에 등을 대게 해서 묶었다. 그리고는 포로 관객들의 흐느낌이 멈추자마자 자신의 사악한 계획에 대해 상세히 설명하기 시작했다. 폭력배들과 악한들은 늘 착한 사람들에게 자신들의 사악한 계획을 자세히 알려주는 법이다. 실제로 그건 필연적인 것이다. 포로들에게는 불행한 일이지만, 스네이크는 계획에 대해 설명하기에 앞서 범죄자로서의 자신의 삶 전체를 자세히 말해줄 필요가 있음을 느꼈다.

"잘 들어라 얘들아, 난 알 카포네도 부끄러워할 만한 범죄인생을 살았다." 그는 이야기를 시작했다. "가끔은 내 자신의 악행과 완벽하고 철저한 사악함에 내가 놀랄 정도지. 그건 내가 맨 처음 교통신호를 위반했을 때부터 시작됐다. 빨간 불이었는데, 난 그걸 무시했어. 멈추지 않고 그냥 쭉 달린 거야. '그래, 좋아.' 나 자신에게 이렇게 말했지. '이게 살아있는 거야. 이게 자유라구!'"

p.224

바너비와 브리지트, 바베트, 보리가드는 눈동자를 굴렸지만, 스네이크는 신경 쓰지 않았다.

"범죄에 맛을 들인 후에는 멈출 수가 없었어." 그는 계속해서 말했다. "다음번엔 일부다처에 도전했지. 물론, 너희는 한번에 한 사람하고만 결혼하도록 돼 있어. 난 각 주마다 아내 하나씩을 갖는 목표를 세운 거야! 난 이 나라 역사상 가장 위대한 일부다처자가 되고 싶었다구! 너희가 무슨 생각을 할지 알아. '50명의 여자라구? 이 남자의 방탕은 한계가 없는 건가? 부끄럽지도 않나?' 이렇게 생각하겠지. 근데 말이다. 난 맨 처음 빨간 신호를 무시하고 달렸던 날로 수치심이라는 걸 잃어버렸다구."

"정말이에요? 그러니까, 아저씬 50명의 여자를 속여서 결혼하게 만든 거예요?" 바너비가 물었다.

"뭐, 꼭 그렇진 않지. 귀부인들은 속이기가 그리 쉽지 않아. 근사한 저녁과 보석으로 유혹해 보려고 하지만, 결혼식장까지 데려가기 전에 대부분 내 정체를 눈치 채게 되지. 여자들이란 대단한 통찰력을 지닌 존재란다, 얘야. 여자들을 속이려고 해봐라, 그럼 번번이 그걸 꿰뚫어보지"

저쪽 구석에서 베르나가 혼자 웃고 있었다.

"하지만, 어쨌든, 경찰들은 절대 눈치 채지 못했는데, 그게 가장 중요한 점이지. 그래서 난 공갈을 시도했어. 나한테 히더 로클리어의 옛날 사진이 몇 장 있었는데, 그녀는 1970년대 중반에 아주 민망할 정도의 옷차림을 하고 나왔던 여배우지. 너희도 그 셔츠의 칼라를 봤어야 하는데! 나팔바지는 어떻구! 머리모양에 대해선 말도 말아야겠다. 아, 물론, 그녀는 아무한테도 사진을 보여주지 말라고 나한테 간청했지. '난 그저 어린애였어요!' 그녀가 말했어. '내가 뭘 하는지도 몰랐다구요!' 하지만 그녀의 간청은 아무 소용이 없었지. 물론, 난 그녀한테 말했지. 그 사진들은 내가 갖고 있겠노라고. 대가를 받고 말이야!"

"설마, 그녀가 진짜로 아저씨한테 돈을 지불했나요?" 바베트가 말했다.

"틀림없이 그랬을 걸, 똑똑이 아가씨. 하지만 재수 없게도, 내가 막 협박편지와 비밀전화를 그녀에게 퍼붓기 시작하려던 찰나에 70년대의 패션이 다시 유행하게 된 거야. 참, 사람들 말처럼, 인생이란 대차 대조표고, 때로는 차변이 대변을 능가하는 거더군."

"잠깐만요, 어, 스네이크 아저씨." 브리지트가 불쑥 말했다. "인생은 대차 대조표라구요? 그런 말을 폭력배가 하면 무슨 비유죠?"

스네이크는 눈에 띄게 당황했다. 브리지트가 허를 찌른 게 분명했다.

"그러니까, '인생은 커다란 은행 강도다' 아니면 '세상은 전부 하나의 새장이다' 이 정도면 몰라도, '대차 대조표' 라뇨?" 그녀는 점점 자신감에 차 얘기를 계속했다. "그건 폭력배 용어가 아니라 회계사나 만들 법한 비유라구요! 아저씨 사기꾼이에요! 가짜라구요! 처음부터 이상한 게 있다 했어요. 이 사악한 음모는 다 속임수예요, 그렇죠?"

"그래, 얘야, 내가 졌다." 스네이크가 말했다. "그래, 난 회계사였어. 20년 동안 잉갤스&막스의 똑같은 책상에 앉아, 서서히 내게서 생명력을 빨아나가는 숫자의 바다 속에서 시들어가고 있었지. 네가 워낙 똑똑하니 짐작했겠지만, '스네이크'는 그냥 익명이야. 진짜 이름은 캐스퍼인데, 여기 베르나가 스네이크란 이름을 붙여줬다. 캐스퍼는 상냥한 사람들한테나 어울리는 이름이라면서 말야. 난 마음속에 앙심을 품고 있거든. 그래 맞아, 비열하고 사악한 목적을 갖고 있지."

"왜냐고? 그 이유를 말해주지. 난 내 인생을 다른 사람들의 돈을 속여주면서 살았어. 탈세로 감옥에 가는 일이 없도록 만들어주고, 가끔은 장부까지 손을 대고, 무슨 얘긴지 알려나 모르겠지만, 그러면서 난 봉급에서 약간의 수당을 더 받았지. 부유한 사업가들은 내 수리적 재능을 최대한 이용해 먹었는데, 20년 후에 내가 돌려받은 게 뭔 줄 아나? 금도금된 펜 하나였다구! 물론 그건 잉크가 지워지는 종류였지만, 그래도 그 정도로는 어림도 없었어!"

"진정해, 자기야." 베르나가 속삭였다. "당신 양복에 땀자국 나겠어!"

"어쩔 수가 없어." 캐스퍼, 즉 스네이크가 벌컥 화를 냈다. "너희 애들은 절대 이해 못할 거다. 너희들은 내가 참아내야 했던 지루함을 상상도 못할 거야. 날이면 날마다 똑같은 일을 하고, 똑같은 말을 하고, 똑같은 걸 먹고 말이지. 헌데 새로운 걸 알려주지. 사악한 음모에 대해선 너희가 틀렸어. 지금까지는 내가 폭력배로 실패했을지 모르지만, 이제 인정을 받게 될 거라구. 내 이름이 전 세계에 기억될 거야!"

"아, 그래요, 아저씬 단골 사회악이네요, 그렇죠? 대단한 협박을 하시는군요." 브리지트가 웃으며 말했다. "뭘 하실 건가요? 사탕 창고를 하나 더 약탈하시려구요?"

바베트와 바너비가 킬킬거렸다. 놀랍게도, 네 팔 달린 괴물까지 구석에서 혼자 낄낄 웃고 있었다.

"입 다물어, 식인종." 스네이크가 말했다. "뉴올리언스가 미시시피 강물에 잠기지 않게 막아주는 어떤 걸 폭파할 계획이라면 어떻게 할래? 내가 그 제방을 무너뜨려버리겠다고 하면 어쩔 거냐고?"

바베트가 깜짝 놀랐다. "하지만 뉴올리언스는 해수면보다 낮잖아요! 제방을 날려버리면 아무것도 강물을 막을 수가 없다구요! 그럼 도시 전체가 파괴되는 거예요!"

"무슨 이유 때문에 그런 걸 하시는데요? 동기가 뭔데요? 무고한 뉴올리언스 시민들은 아저씨한테 아무 잘못도 안 했어요." 바너비가 설명했다.

"첫째, 뉴올리언스 시민들에 대해서는 모르는 소리다." 스네이크가 말했다. "둘째, 아까도 말했듯이 난 세계에서 가장 악랄한 갱스터로 역사에 남고 싶다. 그리고 너희 꼬맹이들도 날 도와줄 거다."

"말도 안돼요. 난 아저씨와 공범자가 안 될 거예요! 그런 범죄를 저지르는 걸 도울 수 없어요!" 브리지트가 밧줄에 묶여 몸부림치며 소리쳤다.

"아니, 넌 그럴 거다. 안됐지만 네겐 선택의 기회가 없지." 스네이크가 웃었다. "제방을 폭파하려면 말이지, 한배 가득한 다이너마이트를 사용해야 돼. 그런데 한배 가득한 다이너마이트는 주의 깊은 강 경찰의 의심을 살 수 있거든. 이젠 어떤 경찰이든 냄새를 맡고 와서 내 일을 망쳐놓게 할 순 없어. 거기엔 너희가 들어가는 거지. 난 너희를 훨씬 더 많은 폭발물이 가득 실린 훨씬 더 큰 보트에 태울 거야. 너희는 미끼가 되는 거라구, 알겠니? 강 경찰들은 너희를 심문하느라 정신없어서 적당히 자그마한 내 보트가 제방 끝을 따라 유유히 항해하는 건 알아차리지도 못할 거다. 그들이 알아냈을 때엔 너무 늦어버리는 거라구!"

스네이크는 미친 악한처럼 큰소리로 웃기 시작하더니, 갑자기 몸을 돌려 오두막에서 걸어 나갔다. 구석에서 조용히 서 있던 베르나는 긴장감으로 안절부절 못하고 있었다.

"베르나, 아줌마는 이 일을 절대 찬성할 리 없어요. 아줌마는 도시 전체를 무의미하게 파괴하는 일을 지지할 만한 그런 여자 같지가 않아요!" 브리지트가 간청하듯 말했다.

"뭘 모르는 소리!" 베르나가 특유의 날카로운 목소리로 찍찍거리듯 말했다. "캐스퍼, 그러니까 스네이크를 만나기 전까지 난 그냥 평범한 대리교사였다. 난 연예계에 진출해 성공하고 싶었지만, 영화제작자들 모두 내 목소리 때문에 가망이 없다고 말했지. 하지만 스네이크는 내가 꿈을 추구할 수 있도록 자신감을 주었어. 우리가 부자가 되기만 하면 그는 스튜디오를 사서 나를 빅스타로 만들어 줄 거래!"

"네, 그렇겠네요." 브리지트가 투덜거렸다.

"우우, 니들 스스로 아주 똑똑한 줄 아는구나!" 베르나가 높은 굽의 발을 세게 구르며 흥분해서 말했다. "스네이크가 보트 가져오는 걸 도와야겠어. 식인종, 얘들을 잘 지켜."

그러면서 베르나는 몸을 돌려 미친 듯이 뛰어나갔다. 마침내 따로 남게 된 브리지트, 바베트, 바너비는 자칭 갱스터들을 어떻게 저지해야 할지 궁리해 보려고 했다.

"글쎄," 바베트가 입을 열었다, "난 우선 이 밧줄을 풀어야겠어. 다리에 감각이 없어."

"잘 해봐." 브리지트가 어깨 너머로 자신의 묶인 손목을 보며 말했다. "묶인 걸 풀어보려고 손을 이리저리 비틀어봤어. 아주 단단히 묶여 있다구. 밧줄이 너무 까칠해서 몇 군데 까진 것 같아. 아마 우리가... 야!"

밧줄에서 풀려난 바베트가 그녀 앞에 서 있었다. 바베트는 다리를 털고 있었다.

p.228

"음, 한결 낫군." 바베트가 말했다.

"바베트, 어떻게 그렇게 빨리 풀어?" 바너비가 물었다.

"중국에 있을 때 요령을 좀 배웠지. 게다가 난 모든 관절이 이중이거든." 그녀가 대답했다.

식인종이 갑자기 툴툴거리더니 바베트 쪽으로 비틀거리며 걸어오기 시작했다.

"조심해!" 브리지트가 소리쳤다. "괴물이 뒤에 있어!"

"걱정 마. 나한테 이 괴물에 대한 이론이 있지."

"그게 뭐든 간에 제발 맞았으면 좋겠다." 바베트가 잡아먹히는 걸 보지 않으려고 두 눈을 감으며 브리지트가 말했다.

"당신은 전혀 괴물이 아니에요, 그렇죠?" 바베트가 식인종을 쳐다보려고 몸을 돌리며 말했다.

네 팔 달린 거인은 잠시 주춤하더니 머리를 가로저은 다음 한숨을 내쉬었다.

"그래, 아니야, 꼬마 아가씨. 적어도 속마음은 그렇지 않아." 그가 고급스러운 영국식 억양으로 말했다.

이때 브리지트와 바너비가 서 있었더라면 충격을 받고 쓰러졌을 것이다.

"그게 말을 할 수 있네!" 바너비가 말했다.

"물론이지, 꼬마야." 그는 가능한 한 공손한 투로 대답했다. 사람들이 당신을 가리켜 "그것"이라고 한다면 공손하게 대하기 힘든 일이다. 하지만 식인종은 분명히 훌륭한 혈통을 가진 사람이었다. 그는 바베트를 보며 물었다. "물어봐도 될지 모르겠는데, 내가 스네이크와 베르나가 생각하는 것처럼 멍청한 짐승이 아닌 걸 어떻게 알아볼 수 있었니?"

"실은, 그건 당신의 호흡이었어요. 당신이 날 데려오는 동안 숨냄새를 맡았거든. 얼 그레이차 냄새였어요. 그건 사람을 잡아먹는 괴물이 그리 좋아할 음료 같지 않았거든요." 바베트가 미소 지으며 말했다.

p.229

거인도 큰소리로 웃었다. "맞아, 그렇지 않을 거야. 네 날카로운 관찰력을 칭찬해주고 싶구나. 넌 정말 통찰력이 대단해! 너희들이 도착할 때 막 차를 마시고 난 뒤였거든. 이런, 우린 제대로 인사도 안 했구나. 내 이름은 루퍼트야."

그가 밑에 있는 오른쪽 손을 내밀었고 바베트가 악수를 했다.

"난 바베트고, 이쪽은 내 친구들인 브리지트와 바너비, 그리고 우리의 고양이 친구 보리가드예요."

"뭐 좀 물어볼게요, 루퍼트." 브리지트가 불쑥 끼어들었다. "정말 뉴올리언스를 파괴하는 걸 무사히 해낼 거라 생각하나요? 당신 같은 사람은 쉽게 잡혀요. 당신이 입도 뻥긋하기 전에 경찰은 당신과 나머지 일당을 체포할 거라구요!"

"그만해. 넌 날 오해하고 있어, 브리지트." 루퍼트가 네 팔을 모두 들고 항변하듯 말했다. "이런 끔찍한 음모는 나도 처음 들었어. 난 저자들이 무슨 꿍꿍이인지 몰랐다구."

브리지트는 의심을 하는 것 같았다.

"정말이야, 날 믿어야 돼. 그건 오해였어." 그가 애처롭게 말했다. "난 외로운 사람이야. 오해받고 기피되고 우리 고향에서조차도 추방당했어. 친구들을 사귀어 보려고 세계 곳곳을 떠돌아다녔지만, 사람들은 날 보고 공포에 질려 도망쳤지.

난 완전히 내성적인 사람이 됐고, 사람들과 얘기하는 걸 수줍어하고 내켜하지 않게 됐어. 늪 속의 이 오두막에서 완전히 나 혼자가 되어, 외로운 은둔자의 삶을 살아온 거야. 다른 인간들과의 접촉을 갈망하면서 말야. 스네이크와 베르나가 이곳에 왔을 때 난 미칠 듯이 기뻤지. 그들이 내게 기대하는 것 같은 행동을 기꺼이 했어. 프랑켄슈타인의 괴물처럼 몸짓으로 말하고 으르렁거리면서 말야. 그들이 머물며 내 친구가 돼주기만 한다면 기꺼이 하려고 했지. 이젠 그것도 끝이겠구나. 그런데 우리가 뭘 할 수 있니? 난 힘이 세긴 하지만 스네이크는 총을 가졌잖아."

"어, 내게 아이디어가 있어요." 바베트가 말했다. "우선 루퍼트가 뒤에서 몰래 나오는 거예요. 그러다 스네이크가 들어오면…"

p.230

바로 그때 스네이크가 문을 열었다. 그는 갱스터 복장을 벗고 낚시꾼 차림에 노란 비옷을 입고 있었다. 하지만 총은 여전히 갖고 있었는데, 바베트를 향해 똑바로 겨누어져 있었다.

"그래, 아가야?" 그가 물었다. "두 귀를 쫑긋해서 들을게. 뭘 어떻게 할 건지 말해봐."

바베트는 할 말을 잃은 채 자리에 꼼짝 못하고 서 있었다.

"내 그럴 줄 알았지." 그가 코웃음 쳤다. "식인종, 그럼 못쓰지. 여자애를 다시 묶어."

다행히도, 그가 방으로 들어올 때는 루퍼트가 말을 하고 있지 않았다. 바베트는 새로운 친구에게 자길 다시 묶어도 좋다는 뜻으로 고개를 살짝 끄덕여 주었다. 자신의 계획은 이미 수포로 돌아간 상태였고, 스네이크에게 루퍼트가 배신했다는 걸 알리는 건 무분별한 일이었다.

바베트가 의자에 묶이고 나자 스네이크는 아까 중단했던 이야기를 다시 시작했다.

"시작해보자, 얘들아." 그는 웃음을 터뜨리며 말했다. "각 보트마다 짐이 실려 있고 우린 뉴올리언스를 침수시키기 위해 출발하는 거야. 어림짐작으로는, 우리의 항해시간은 대략 세 시간일 거다. 그러니 어두워지기 전에 해내려면 서둘러야겠어. 난 그 오래된 제방을 따라가면서 틈이라는 틈에는 모조리 다이너마이트를 쑤셔 넣을 거야."

오두막 문을 통해 베르나가 들어왔는데, 똑같이 낚시를 떠나는 차림이었다.

"나 어때, 스네이크?" 그녀가 새로 입은 옷을 보이며 말했다.

"아주 그럴 듯해." 그가 대답했다. "이젠 우리의 가명을 기억해라. 우린 마이어와 블레이크 터너로, 메기 떼를 잡으러 온 평범한 두 사람이다."

"당신 가명은 스네이크인 줄 알았는데요." 브리지트가 말했다.

"네가 갱스터들에 대해 뭘 아는지 알겠구나." 스네이크가 말했다. "스네이크는 내 익명이지만, 특별한 범죄에 대해서는 특별한 가명을 써야 하는 거야, 알겠니? 자, 식인종, 이 애들을 들어다 밖에 있는 큰 보트에 실어라."

p.231

루퍼트는 시키는 대로 네 명의 포로와 그들의 의자를 들어올렸다. 애들을 그렇게 한데 묶은 채로 문을 통해 내보내기는 좀 어려웠지만, 루퍼트는 애들을 심하게 부딪치는 일 없이 해냈다. 몇 분이 지나 그들은 보트 위에서, 다이너마이트 더미에 둘러싸인 채 앉아 있었다.

"거기에 거의 닿을 때까지 너희를 묶은 채로 끌고 갈 거야." 스네이크가 설명했다. "그리고는 밧줄을 끊어 풀어주고 우리보다 앞서 강으로 보낼 거야. 그러면 그게 너희가 우리한테 듣게 될 마지막이지. '쾅' 하는 때까지는 말이다."

스네이크가 크게 웃었고, 베르나는 히히 웃었고, 루퍼트는 눈살을 찌푸렸다. 그들 셋은 더 작은 배에 올랐고, 모터를 돌린 후 천천히 물속으로 나아갔다.

몇 시간 뒤, 그들이 밧줄에서 풀려나 강으로 보내진 후, 바베트는 마침내 자신과 친구들이 풀려나자 안심했다.

"루퍼트가 총에 맞는 일 없이 조만간 그들을 저지할 수 있길 바랄 뿐이야." 그녀가 배 안에서 왔다갔다 하며 초조해했다. "우린 경찰의 주의를 끌어서 무슨 일이 벌어지고 있는지 말해야 해."

"하지만 어떻게 우리가 나쁜 짓을 꾸미는 사람들이 아니라고 그들을 확신시킨다지?" 바너비가 물었다. "우리가 다이너마이트에 완전히 둘러싸여 있는데, 그들이 무슨 수로 우릴 믿겠어?"

"그들에게 얼마나 심각하게 위험한 건지 이해시켜야 해." 바베트의 대답이었는데, 그녀는 지나가는 순찰보트의 주의를 끌어보려고 막무가내로 손을 흔들어댔다.

그녀가 순찰보트를 불러 세우는 데는 성공했지만, 불행하게도 바너비가 말한 대로였다. 그들이 아무리 애를 써서 도시 전체가 위험에 빠져 있다고 설득시키려 해도 경찰관들은 그들 말을 믿으려 하지 않았다.

"제발요," 브리지트가 애걸했다, "우린 지금 시간을 낭비하고 있어요. 지금 스네이크를 저지해야 해요. 안 그러면 아저씨들 때문에 대참사가 일어날 거라구요!"

보트에 올라온 강 경찰 두 명은 서로를 쳐다보고는 웃음을 지었다.

p.232

"이제 보니 너희들, 우리가 아주 쉽게 속아 넘어갈 줄 아는 모양이구나." 한 경찰이 말했다. "우린 그렇게 어수룩한 사람들이 아니야. 여기 너희들이 한 배 가득 다이너마이트를 갖고 있으면서, 다른 배에 있는 다른 사람이 제방을 폭파하려 한다고 믿길 바라다니. 정말 웃기는군."

두 경찰관이 낄낄 웃어대자 브리지트가 격분했다.

"어쩜 그렇게 둔하고 무감각할 수 있죠? 도시 전체가 물에 잠기게 될 거라고 얘기하려는데, 아저씬 전혀 관심이 없는 것 같아요! 아저씨 두 분이 이 일에 대해 아무 조치도 취하지 않을 거면 제가 하겠어요!" 브리지트는 보트 끝으로 뛰어가며 소리쳤다.

그녀가 한쪽 다리를 뱃전에 매달린 뒤 막 뛰어내렸을 때 공기를 뚫고 쿵하는 거대한 폭발음이 들려왔다. 그녀가 수면에 닿았을 때 풀과 진흙 덩어리들이 하늘에서부터 쏟아져 내렸고 공기는 연기로 가득 채워졌다.

"바베트! 바너비! 보리가드!" 브리지트가 물 위에 고개를 똑바로 내민 채 소리쳤다. "대답해! 괜찮니? 대답하라구!"

멀지 않은 곳에서 콜록거리는 소리와 푸푸하는 소리가 들렸다. 연기가 조금 걷히고 나자 그녀 앞에서 헤엄치고 있는 보리가드가 보였다. 고양이는 전혀 행복해 보이지 않았다. 미시시피 강에 두 번이나 빠진다는 건 대부분의 고양이에게 너무 많은 횟수다.

"보리가드!" 브리지트가 소리쳤다. "나머지는 어디 있니?"

하지만 그녀의 질문은 한차례의 돌풍이 불어와 공기를 맑게 하자 답이 나왔다. 처음에 그녀는 눈에 보이는 것에 안도했다. 제방이 그 자리에 그대로 있었던 것이다. 도시는 안전하게 됐다. 하지만 땅에 누워 전혀 꼼짝 못하고 있는 친구들이 있었다.

"어, 안돼!" 브리지트는 헐떡거렸다. "보리가드, 빨리, 쟤들한테 가야 돼!"

브리지트와 보리가드는 물살을 거슬러 가능한 한 빨리 제방 쪽으로 헤엄쳐 갔다. 브리지트는 친구들의 창백한 얼굴을 내려다보고는 숨이 막혔다.

친구들이 죽은 게 아닌가 겁이 났다. 그녀는 바베트를, 그 다음엔 바너비를 발로 건드려 보았다.

p.233

"안돼요, 엄마, 싫어요!" 바너비가 벌떡 일어서며 소리쳤다. "나보고 발레 레슨을 받으라구요! 그 꽉 끼는 옷 좀 치워요!"

"바너비, 정신차려." 브리지트가 바너비의 어깨를 흔들며 소리쳤다. "너 헛소리를 하나봐. 아무도 너한테 타이츠 입으라고 안해."

"이크." 바너비가 머리를 긁적이며 말했다.

바베트가 눈을 떴고 조심스럽게 일어나 앉았다. "바너비, 괜찮니?"

"간장공장 공장장은 강공장장이고" 바너비가 공손히 말했다. "저기 저 콩깍지가 깐 콩깍지냐 안 깐 콩깍지냐, 그거 하지 말랬잖아요. 하지 말아요, 제발!"

바너비는 공중에서 주먹을 휘둘러대더니, 술 취한 듯 비틀거리기 시작했다.

"오락가락 하는가봐." 브리지트가 말했다. "하지만 많이 다친 것 같진 않아. 너희 둘 다 폭발 때문에 기절했었어."

"폭발!" 바베트가 일어서면서 반복했다. "빨리! 스네이크와 베르나가 도망가기 전에 찾아야 돼!"

그들은 멀리 갈 필요가 없었다. 20야드도 안되는 거리에 스네이크와 베르나가 이판사판 싸우고 있었다. 루퍼트는 한쪽에 서서 대단히 즐거워하며 지켜보고 있었다.

"이 벌레 같은 자식!" 베르나가 스네이크의 눈을 할퀴며 소리 질렀다. "넌 대실패자에 지나지 않아! 제방에 홈 하나도 못 냈잖아. 폭발물 전문가 좋아하시네!"

"이 멍청아, 난 폭발물 전문가의 견습생이었다고 했지." 그는 베르나의 머리카락을 잡아당기며 화를 냈다. "자격증을 따려면 발파 명인과 일년을 더 공부해야 했다구. 처음에 사소한 폭발을 몇 번 해보고 기술을 연마하는 게 좋겠다고 했는데, 네가 기다려주지 않았잖아! '어, 안돼' 그러면서 계속 날 볶아대고 귀찮게 하고 괴롭히기만 했잖아. 내가 항복할 때까지 말야!"

p.234

"네가 그렇게 바보 같아서 조그만 제방 하나도 다이너마이트로 폭파할 수 없을지 내가 어떻게 알았겠어?" 그녀가 그의 정강이를 걷어차며 찍찍거렸다. "네가 갖고 있는 기술은 고작 숫자를 합계 내는 것뿐이라구!"

"그건 진짜 비열해." 스네이크가 소리 질렀다. "그 말 당장 취소해!"

"싫어, 어림없어!" 그녀가 두 주먹으로 그의 가슴을 때리더니 흐느껴 울며 말했다. "우린 망했어! 우린 끝났다구! 다 네 탓이야!"

루퍼트는 마침내 이런 째째한 말다툼을 참을 수 없었던 모양인지, 끼어들기로 마음먹었다. 그는 한 팔을 뻗더니 화가 난 여자를 떼어놓았다.

"자, 자, 당신은 이성을 잃어가고 있어요." 루퍼트가 땅에서 3피트쯤의 높이로 그녀를 꽉 붙들어 올린 채 말했다. 그녀는 자신이 식인종이라고 불렀던 자가 얘기하고 있는 건지도 모를 정도로 너무나 화가 나 있었고, 꽉 잡혀 있는 데서 헤어나려고 헛수고만을 하고 있었다. 하지만 루퍼트는 훨씬 더 힘이 세었고, 그녀를 놓아줄 생각이 없었다.

"아, 경찰님!" 그가 막 연기를 헤치고 걸어 나온 두 명의 강 순찰대원을 향해 외쳤다. "여기 체포하실 범죄자 한 쌍이 있는 것 같습니다."

자신이 곧 붙잡힐 것을 알아차린 스네이크가 연기 속에 몸을 숨기려고 하면서 물러서기 시작했다. 하지만 바베트가 그에게서 한눈을 팔지 않았다.

"그렇게 빨리 안 될 걸요, 캐스퍼." 바베트가 가라데식 발차기로 그의 무릎을 걷어차며 말했다. 그런 다음, 한쪽 발로 그의 목을 누르고 서서 스스로에게 아주 만족해하기 시작했다. "음, 어디 보자, 갱스터식 숙어가 뭐가 있을까. 아, 그래. 자넨 이제 막 내렸어, 캐스퍼."

"아직은 만족해하지 마라, 프랑스 꼬맹아." 쓰러진 회계사가 툴툴거렸다. "네가 이겼다고 생각할지 모르겠는데, 아직 재판이 남아 있을 거고, 나한텐 변호사 친구들이 많다구."

p.235

"그래요?" 스네이크에게 수갑을 채우려고 다가온 한 경찰관이 말했다. "그거 참 안됐군요. 많은 강직한 시민들은 틀림없이 지금 당장 당신을 목매달고 싶을 텐데. 불행하게도, 공정하고 편견 없는 판사 앞에서 재판을 받기 전에는 어떤 성난 군중도 당신을 목매달아 죽이지 못하게 만드는 것이 우리 일이죠. 하지만 당신은 조만간 교수형을 당할 거요. 그건 내가 장담하죠."

"그래, 뭐, 김칫국부터 마시지는 말라구." 경찰관들이 자신과 베르나를 끌고 가자 캐스퍼가 말했다.

"이봐요, 당신은 조만간 마을을 떠날 계획은 없겠죠?" 경찰관 하나가 루퍼트에게 물었다. "당신이 이 두 작자들에 대해 증언해 준다면 일이 확실히 빨라질 거요."

"가능만 하다면 어떤 식으로든 기꺼이 소송절차를 진척시키겠어요." 거인이 대답했다.

"좋아요, 그럼 저희와 함께 경찰서로 갑시다. 그리고 너희들도 어디로 안 가는 게 좋겠다." 다같이 걸어가면서 경찰관이 말했다. "너희들 증언도 필요할 거야."

"아, 그럼요." 바베트와 브리지트가 최대한 확신을 주려고 고개를 끄덕이며 말했다. 하지만 경찰이 시야에서 벗어나자마자 그들 모두는 안면을 바꾸었다.

"야, 여기서 나가자!" 브리지트가 말했다.

바베트도 전심으로 동의했다. 그들은 여전히 어리벙벙한 상태에서 이리저리 헤매고 있는 바너비를 찾고, 진지하게 털

손질에 열중하고 있는 보리가드까지 한데 모은 후, 자신들의 선택권들, 아니 좀더 정확하게, 선택권에 대해 논의했다.

"내가 보기에는," 브리지트가 말했다, "우리가 상당한 거리도 가면서 잃어버린 시간을 보충하려면 다시 날아서 여행하는 게 유일한 방법인 것 같아. 물론, 애당초 그것 때문에 이런 혼란에 빠지긴 했지만 말야. 하지만 그것 말고 다른 방법은 모르겠어. 그렇게 할래?"

"물론이지." 바베트가 말했다. "여기서 더 나빠지진 않겠지."

"네가 찬성 안 했으면 하고 바랄 뻔했어." 브리지트가 조금 웃으며 대답했다.

몇 분 후 그들은 거대한 분홍빛 풍선 밑에 두둥실 떠서 또다시 올라가고 있었다.

p.236

QUICK QUIZ 16
관계짓기
아래의 단어 쌍들이 서로 어떤 관계를 갖는지 판단하세요. 비슷한 의미이면 "S" 반대 의미이면 "O"를 하세요.

1. 사기 :: 속임
2. 익명 :: 가명
3. 불분명한 :: 명백한
4. 무정한 :: 무관심한
5. 악의 :: 부패, 악행
6. 불투명한 :: 투명한
7. 내성적인 :: 외로운
8. 얼굴을 찌푸리다 :: 미소 짓다
9. 방탕 :: 죄 많음
10. 단조로움 :: 다양함
11. 정체된 :: 움직이는
12. 의식 없는 :: 깨어있는
13. 헛소리를 하는 :: 명석한

QUICK QUIZ 17
관계짓기
아래의 단어 쌍들이 서로 어떤 관계를 갖는지 판단하세요. 비슷한 의미면 "S" 반대 의미면 "O"를 하세요.

1. 위험 :: 안전
2. 견습생 :: 전문가
3. 식인종 :: 채식주의자
4. 가리다 :: 드러내다
5. 일부다처 :: 일부일처
6. 협박 :: 위협
7. 부단한 :: 끝없는
8. 어스름 :: 동틀 녘
9. 유혹하다 :: 유인하다
10. 이성을 잃은 :: 침착한
11. 지친 :: 원기를 회복한
12. 추방당한 :: 거절당한

QUICK QUIZ 18
빈칸 채우기
아래에 있는 각각의 단어들 중에서 가장 완벽한 문장을 만들어주는 단어를 고르세요.

1. 은행강도 벅시 블레인은 경찰에 붙잡혔지만, 도주용 차안에서 기다리고 있던 그의 (   )은/는 도망쳤다.
    a. 미끼   b. 공범자   c. 시체   d. 돌연변이

2. "오늘은 생선이 다 떨어졌어요." 캡틴 브리니즈의 여종업원이 말했다. "그러니 샐러드와 디저트 부분만 빼고 메뉴에 있는 건 모두 (   ) 주세요."
    a. 자세히 말해   b. 심문해   c. 무시해   d. 칭찬해

3. 우리, 바니가 자신의 철천지원수인 리처드와 악수를 하고 한 테이블에 앉은 건 정말 (   ) 생각했다.
    a. 겸손했다고   b. 공정했다고   c. 남성적이었다고   d. 예의바른 행동이었다고

4. 난 내가 나오지 못해 우리 소프트볼 팀이 경기를 놓쳐야만 했다는 걸 알고 (   )에 사로잡혔다.
   a. 억울함   b. 메스꺼움   c. 공갈   d. 찢긴 상처

5. 메이저리그의 심판이라면 중요한 야구경기에서 스트라이크와 볼을 구분하기 위해 대단한 (   )을/를 이용해야 한다.
   a. 약탈품   b. 힘   c. 식별력   d. 약간의 수당

6. 캐롤은 20달러를 주고 구입한 소위 "유기" 고양이 깔짚이 평범한 모래에 불과하다는 걸 알고서 자신이 (   ) 깨달았다.
   a. 속았음을   b. 연발 사격 당했음을   c. 이름 불렸음을   d. 린치 당했음을

7. 아이 돌보는 사람은 마크와 멜라니가 머리 위로 접시를 들고 서로 때리는 걸 봤지만, 그들의 의견차를 스스로 해결할 수 있길 바라며 (   ) 않기로 마음먹었다.
   a. 만족해하지   b. 나타나지   c. 자극하지   d. 개입하지

QUICK QUIZ 19

짝짓기

오른쪽의 단어를 비슷한 의미의 왼쪽 단어와 짝지으세요.

1. 장소	a. 피할 수 없는
2. 유전적인	b. 이유
3. 불가피한	c. 약해지다
4. 쌀쌀한	d. 예리한
5. 민첩한	e. 고독한
6. 은유	f. 빠른
7. 약해지다	g. 찬성하다
8. 이용하다	h. 위치
9. 제방	i. 둑
10. 동기	j. 사로잡다
11. 지지하다	k. 이용하다
12. 지각이 예민한	l. 물려받다
13. 체포하다	m. 냉담한
14. 외로운	n. 비유
15. 진척시키다	o. 가속하다

QUICK QUIZ 20

짝짓기

오른쪽의 단어를 비슷한 의미의 왼쪽 단어와 짝지으세요.

1. 몸짓으로 하는	a. 추측하다
2. 어림짐작하다	b. 재앙
3. 틈	c. 서투른
4. 엄숙한	d. 틈
5. 대참사	e. 혼란스러운
6. 잘 속는	f. 창백함
7. 창백	g. 교수대
8. 술 취한	h. 몸짓으로 하는
9. 흐트러진	i. 날카롭게 된
10. 숫돌로 갈아진	j. 쉽게 속는
11. 괴롭히다	k. 소용없는

12. 서투른	l. 심각한
13. 헛된	m. 술 취한
14. 교수대	n. 귀찮게 하다

p.240

스네이크와 베르나에게 무슨 일이 일어났는지 궁금할 거야. 글쎄, 재미있는 이야기지. 두 사람 모두 홍수를 일으키려는 음모에서 살인미수까지의 혐의로 기소되었는데, 둘 다 "무죄"라고 항변했지. 검찰 측 변호인단은 스네이크가 무슨 꿍꿍이를 숨겨두고 있을지 모른다는 생각에 좀 소심해졌고, 그래서 그들은 베르나에게 증언의 대가로 기소 면제를 해주었지. 그녀가 스네이크를 배신하는 데 찬성하면 감옥에 안 가게 해주겠다는 터무니없는 말이었어. 그녀는 아주 신이 나서 그를 변절했는데, 온갖 종류의 상스러운 욕설을 퍼붓고, 루이지애나에서 사실상 미해결된 모든 범죄에 대해 그를 범인으로 지목했으며, 심지어는 아주 먼 옛날 부정한 회계업무의 일부까지 끄집어내왔어. 배심원단은 오래 숙고할 것도 없이 "모든 점에서 유죄"라는 평결을 내렸는데, 판사가 의사봉을 쾅쾅 두드리면서 "휴정을 선언합니다"라고 말하기가 무섭게 스네이크가 베르나를 위증죄로 고발하는 항소를 제기했어. 안타깝게도 허위 진술은 재판에서 증거로 인정할 수 없으니까.

모든 사무처리가 완료되고 재심이 이루어지고 난 후 스네이크에게 유죄가 선고된 건 단 한 가지, 면허 없이 낚시를 한 것뿐이었어. 스네이크는 그에 대해 최고의 판결을 받았는데, 그건 바로 판사로부터의 아주 따끔한 질책 한마디였어. 생각을 해봐, 그 모든 일이 끝난 뒤, 스네이크는 질책을 받고 베르나는 처벌을 면하게 된 거야. 정말 정의란 게 눈이 멀었지.

그런데 가까이 있는 문제로 돌아가야겠군. 우리가 뉴올리언스에서 이륙하고 난 후 꽤 얼마 동안은 모든 게 순조로웠어. 파리와 아주 가까운 곳에 내릴 거라는 원대한 희망을 안고 있었지. 그러니까, 신천옹 한 마리가 브리지트의 풍선과 부딪혀 큰 구멍을 내기 전까지는 말이야. 그 후로는 우리가 추락했다고 짐작할 수밖에 없어. 왜냐면 아주 이상한 곳에서 깨어난 것 말고는 아무것도 기억이 안 나거든…

p.241

브리지트는 천천히 한쪽 눈을 뜬 다음, 나머지 눈을 마저 뜨고 머리를 움직이지 않은 채 주변을 둘러보았다. 그리 많은 게 보이지는 않았는데, 빛의 출처를 알 수 없이 희미하게 밝혀진, 높다란 회색빛의 둥근 천장만이 보였다. 브리지트는 일어나 앉으려고 했지만, 격렬한 통증이 머리를 뚫고 지나가 다시 간이침대에 드러누웠다.

"움직이려고 하면 안돼." 평온하고 장중한 남자의 목소리였다. "넌 심하게 아팠단다. 이제 회복되기 시작하는 거야."

"누구세요?" 브리지트가 신음하며 말했다. "여기가 어디죠? 제 친구들은 어디 있어요?"

"질문이 많구나." 그 목소리가 말했다. "넌 안전하단다. 네 친구들은 다른 방에 있고. 그 애들도 병에서 회복되고 있지."

"저희가 여기 꽤 있었나 보네요?" 브리지트가 말했다. "제가 여기 얼마동안 누워 있었던 거죠?"

"그건 말할 수 없단다. 시간이란 굴곡으로 가득하고, 때로는 막다른 골목도 나오는 하나의 미로니까. 넌 이곳에 영원토록 있었는지도 몰라. 어쩌면 아직 도착하지 않았을 수도 있고. 아무도 확신할 수가 없지." 그 목소리가 대답했다.

브리지트는 눈동자를 굴려보려고 했지만 눈이 너무 아팠다. "있잖아요, 참 재미있는 말씀이지만, 저한테는 좀 너무 모호하게 들려요. 그냥 그때가 몇 시였고, 아니면 며칠이었고, 저희가 여기 온 게 말이에요, 그리고 지금이 몇 시나 며칠이라고 말씀해 주세요, 네?"

"얘야, 모르겠니? 네 질문은 무의미한 거야. 시간이란 신화에 불과해. 그건 존재하지 않아, 적어도 네가 생각하는 그런 건 아니야. 그건 여린 마음을 가진 사람들을 위한 동화란다."

"음." 브리지트가 말했다. "아까 시간이란 미로라고 하셨죠? 그럼, 시간이 미로라면 전 출구를 찾을 수 있겠네요?"

"아, 그럼 시간의 벽 밖에는 무엇이 있을까? 그것이 문제구나." 그 목소리가 우렁차게 말했다.

브리지트는 지금이 뭔가 행동을 취할 적기라고 판단했다. 그녀는 몸을 일으켜 앉은 자세를 취한 다음 잠깐 동안 꼼짝 않고 앉아 있었다. 방이 빙글빙글 돌고 있는 것 같아 브리지트는 어지러웠다. 마침내 핑핑 돌던 것이 멈추자 그녀는 주위를 둘러보았다.

방은 아주 오래돼 보였는데, 브리지트의 부모님이 그녀를 잃어버리기 전 억지로 데려갔던 옛날 교회 같았다. 교회와 다른 점은 이곳이 훨씬 더 간소하다는 것이었다. 밝게 채색된 유리창도 없었고, 꽃도 없었고, 그녀의 간이침대를 빼고는 가구도 없었으며, 여기저기서 깜박이는 새하얀 양초들 말고는 엄숙하고 어두운 방에 활기를 더해주는 건 아무것도 없었다. 돌로 만든 커다란 벽난로 안에 조그만 불이 지펴져 있었다.

회색 턱수염을 텁수룩하게 늘어뜨린 자그마한 남자가 난로 불빛 속에 책상다리로 앉아 있었다. 그는 믿을 수 없을 정도로 늙어 보였는데, 웬일인지 젊고 에너지로 충만해 보이기도 했다. 브리지트는 놀라서 그를 뚫어져라 쳐다봤다.

"머리가 많이 아프니?" 남자가 물었다. "통증을 완화시킬 뭔가를 줄 수 있어."

"아니오, 괜찮아요." 브리지트가 간이침대에서 나와 일어서려고 애쓰며 말했다. "있잖아요, 가서 제 친구들과 얘기하고 싶어요. 그 애들은 어디 있어요?"

"얘야, 앉아 있어!" 늙은 남자가 명령하는 제스처로 손을 들어올리며 말했다.

브리지트는 마치 그 남자가 자신을 떼밀기라도 한 것처럼 간이침대에 다시 주저앉았다. 아주 신비스러운 뭔가가 여기서 일어나고 있었다.

"무력을 쓸 생각은 없단다." 그는 한숨을 쉬었다. "하지만 그런 어리석은 행동을 묵과할 수는 없어. 넌 앓아왔어. 현기증이 재발할 수도 있어. 내 충고를 명심해야 돼. 안 그러면 틀림없이 다치게 될 거야. 물 한모금 마시고 잠깐 쉬도록 해. 그런 다음에는 걸어도 되지만 천천히 걸어야 해."

"네, 그럴게요." 브리지트가 말했다.

노인은 브리지트에게 냉수 한잔을 가져다주었고, 그들은 한참 동안 말없이 앉아 있었다. 그는 아무 말도 할 것 같지 않았고, 그래서 브리지트는 대화를 시작하기로 마음먹었다.

"그럼, 할아버지는 여기서 사시는 건가요?" 브리지트가 말했다. "기분 나쁘시게 할 생각은 없는데, 좀 금욕적이네요. 가구도 부족하구요. 텔레비전도 없고, 책도 없고, 오디오도 없고, 의자도 없잖아요. 깔개도 하나 없구요. 여긴 뭐예요, 감옥 같은 건가요?"

"여긴 수도원이란다. 난 수도사고." 남자가 대답했다.

"수도사요? 그럼 어떤 종류의 종파에 속하신 거예요, 맞나요?" 브리지트가 물었다.

"어떤 면에서는 그렇지." 남자가 대답했다. "내 형제들과 나는 우리의 생을 하느님께 바쳤단다."

"형제들이 계세요?"

"종교적 의미에서의 형제들 말이다." 그가 설명했다. "하지만 우린 어떤 조직된 종교를 따르지는 않아. 우리의 관습은 대부분의 사람들이 정통이라고 생각하는 게 아니지. 나도 인정하듯이 우린 보통과 달라. 우리가 처음 모였을 때 다른 종교인들은 우릴 이단이라고 비난했지. 물론 요즈음엔 생소해 보이는 생각이나 의견을 말할 때 그런 단어를 쓴다고 하더라만, 그 당시에 이단이라는 말은 중대한 죄악이었어. 우린 어쩔 수 없이 사회에서 물러났는데, 우리 형제 가운데 몇 명이 다른 종교의 성직자 때문에 감옥에 들어가게 되면서였지. 그 성직자들은 아마도 독실하고 헌신적인 사람들일 텐데, 우리 형제들을 고문해서 소위 죄를 회개하라고 강요했어. 하지만 물론, 자기가 잘못했다고 느끼지도 않는 것을 후회한다는 건 불가능하지. 많은 형제들이 끔찍한 죽임을 당했단다."

브리지트는 마음이 불쾌해져 몸을 움찔했다. 대화가 점점 어둡고 침울해져갔다.

"미안하구나." 수도사가 말했다. "지난 일을 생각할 때면 좀 음울해지는 경향이 있어. 넌 좀 좋아진 것 같구나. 얼마 동안 너는 의식과 잠 사이의 어렴풋한 망각 속에 매달려 있었단다. 하지만 이젠 완전히 제정신이 돌아온 것 같구나. 춤추는 재칼과 우주선에 대해 뒤죽박죽이 된 얘기도 더 안하고, 그렇지?"

그는 친절하고 인자한 미소를 지어보였다. 노인의 마음씨가 너무 좋아서, 브리지트는 춤추는 재칼과 우주선이 진짜 있었던 일이라고 말할 용기가 나지 않았다. 브리지트는 노인이 자기를 고쳐준 거라고 생각하도록 그냥 두기로 했다.

"네, 휴!" 브리지트가 말했다. "이제 머리가 더 맑아져서 다행이에요. 다 할아버지 덕분이에요, 그런데 성함이 어떻게 되세요?"

"그러피드 형제라고 부르면 돼. 넌 브리지트지, 아마. 자, 가자. 이젠 걸어도 될 만큼 건강해진 것 같구나. 가서 네 친구들이 어떤지 보자."

다리를 움직이는 것이 보이지도 않았는데 그러피드는 일어났다. 아니, 그보다는 그냥 땅위로 떠오르는 것 같았다. 브리지트는 확실히 알 수 없었는데, 그의 길고 하얀 겉옷이 다리를 덮고 있었기 때문이다. 그는 브리지트보다 앞서 방 반대쪽 끝에 있는 작은 문을 향해 떠가듯이 갔다.

그 문의 다른 쪽으로 처음 방과 똑같이 보이는 또 다른 방이 있었다. 바베트와 바너비가 두 개의 간소한 간이침대 위에 큰대자로 뻗어 있었고, 길고 텁수룩한 회색 수염을 기른 또 다른 늙은 수도사가 또 다른 벽난로 앞에 앉아 있었다. 브리지트가 그러피드에게 보리가드에 대해 물어보려고 할 찰나, 백 파운드는 됨직한 고양이가 껑충 뛰어올라 브리지트는 넘어지고 말았다.

보리가드는 그녀를 보고 아주 기쁜 모양이었다. 머리를 브리지트의 턱에 대고 비벼댔고, 그르렁 소리에 귀청이 터질 것 같았으며, 그녀의 얼굴을 몇 차례 마구 핥아대기까지 했다.

"놀랍구나." 불가에 있는 늙은 수도사가 말했다. "저 고양이는 전혀 생기가 없었단다. 먹지도 마시지도 심지어는 꼼짝하지도 않았지. 난 저 녀석이 아주 게으르거나 몹시 지루해한다고 생각하기 시작했지. 이제 보니 그저 널 그리워한 거였구나."

"그랬나 봐요." 애정 깊고 텁수룩한 백 파운드 고양이 밑에서 겨우 빠져나온 브리지트가 동의했다. "고양이가 괜찮은 걸 보니 기뻐요. 그런데 바베트와 바너비는 어떤가요?"

"직접 물어보렴." 수도사가 말했다. 그가 자신의 손을 흔들었고, 그러자 갑자기 그들의 눈이 확 떠졌다.

p.245

바베트가 간이침대에서 벌떡 일어나더니 두 손을 들고 싸울 준비가 됐다는 듯 전투태세를 취했다.

"진정해, 바베트." 브리지트가 설득하려고 했다. "넌 위험하지 않아."

"그거 다행이군." 그녀는 방어자세를 풀며 한숨을 쉬었다. "여기가 어디지? 어떻게 이런 데 온 거야?"

"우리가 너를 발견한 건 허브를 따려고 밖에 나가셨단다." 늙은 수도사 한 명이 대답했다. "너는 아주 허약한 상태였고 어떤 종류의 열병으로 쓰러졌던 거란다. 그 병은 특히 너한테서 심했는데 다른 친구들이 겪는 것보다 훨씬 더 격렬하고 위험했지. 우린 너를 무사하게 회복시키려고 여기 데려온 거란다."

"정말 친절하시네요." 바베트가 대답했다. "여기가 어떤 곳인지 여쭤봐도 될까요? 성함은 어떻게 되세요?"

"내 이름은 오웨인 형제란다. 이쪽은 그러피드 형제야." 그가 떠 있는 수도사 쪽으로 살짝 손짓하며 말했다. "넌 우리 수도원에 있는 거란다."

바너비가 간이침대 위에서 끙끙거리기 시작했다.

"아, 아!" 그가 신음했다. "나 죽겠어. 몸이 마비됐어. 도와줘! 의사를 불러줘!"

"넌 죽을 위험에 처해있지 않단다, 아가야." 오웨인이 말했다. "넌 아주 건강해."

"잘못 아시는 거예요. 제 발이 붕대에 감겼는데 분명히 마비됐어요. 전문의의 진찰을 받아야 해요." 바너비는 계속 우겼다.

"안됐지만 네 발 뒤꿈치에 큰 가시가 박혀 있었단다. 우리가 가벼운 마취제를 놓아서 아프지 않게 가시를 뺄 수 있었어. 몇 분만 있으면 네 발에 감각이 돌아올 거야." 수도사가 설명해 주었다.

"나보고 안 죽을 거라고 말하는 정신 나간 수도사 따위는 필요 없어요! 난 숨이 끊어져가고 있어요! 그것도 당신 탓일 거예요! 당신이 방금 얘기했던 허브로 내 몸에 독을 넣었을 거예요!" 바너비가 소리쳤다.

p.246

"입 다물어, 바너비." 브리지트가 툭 끼어들었다. "심기증 환자처럼 그러지 좀 말라구. 넌 완벽하게 건강해. 오웨인 형제님께 사과드려야 할 것 같아. 그렇게 무례하게 구는데도 코에 주먹 한방 날리지 않으시고 정말 많이 참으셨다구."

"말도 안 되는 소리구나, 얘야." 수도사가 말했다. "여기서 폭력은 용납되지 않아."

"그래요, 뭐, 죄송해요." 자리에 앉으면서 자신이 격분한 데 대해 좀 무안해진 바너비가 말했다. "우리 과학자들은 역사적으로 종교인들과는 사이가 안 좋거든요. 전 그게 건전한 경쟁이라고 생각하지만, 제가 무례했다면 죄송해요. 저희를 도와주신 것 감사드려요."

오웨인은 가볍게 고개를 끄덕일 뿐 아무 말이 없었다.

"여기가 어디야?" 바너비가 친구들에게 속삭이듯 말했다. "이렇게 기억이 엉망이 된 적은 처음이야. 마지막으로 기억나는 건, 내가 어떤 경찰관들과 얘길 하면서 보트에 서 있었던 거야."

"그건 내가 나중에 다 설명해줄게." 브리지트가 속삭이며 말했다. "하지만 지금 여기서 우리 상황이 어떤 건지 알아내야 할 것 같아. 지금으로서 할 수 있는 얘기는 이 수도사들은 아주 늙은 데다 좀 유령 같다는 것, 그리고 가장 단순한 질문에도 애매한 답을 한다는 거야. 내가 몇 시냐고 물었는데, 시간은 미로라느니 하는 알아들을 수 없는 말만 하더라구."

"우릴 불분명하다고 느낀다면 유감이구나." 오웨인이 말했는데, 자신의 얘기를 알아들으리라고는 생각 못했던 브리지트가 깜짝 놀랐다. "우린 너와 같은 방식으로 사물을 바라보는 사람들과 이야기하는 데 익숙하지가 않단다. 어떤 질문이라도 원하는 대로 하렴. 그러면 명쾌한 대답을 주도록 열심히 애써볼게."

브리지트와 바너비는 자신들의 얘기를 그리 쉽게 엿들었다는 데 너무 놀라 멍하니 있었기 때문에, 바베트가 첫 번째 질문을 하기로 마음먹었다.

p.247

"형제님들, 저는 완전히 솔직하고 정직하게 말씀드리고 싶어요." 바베트가 말했다. "솔직히 말해서, 두 분 다 좀 이상한 점이 있어요. 정말 나이가 많으신 것 같은데, 그렇게 보이지가 않아요. 이상하고 초자연적인 힘, 거의 마법 같은 힘이 있는 것 같아요. 그리고 여긴 제가 보았던 수도원들과도 달라요. 어떻게 여기에 오셨는지 알고 싶어요."

"그래요, 어떤 사연인가요?" 브리지트가 물었다.

두 명의 수도사 모두 싱그레 웃었다.

"우리의 사연을 묻는 거니? 좋아, 그렇다면," 오웨인이 말했다, "내 말해주지. 그래, 네 방식대로 시간이란 걸 본다면 우리가 아주 늙었다고 할 수 있을 거다. 사실은, 9세기도 넘게 살았지."

"그럼 죽지 않으시는 건가요?" 바베트가 물었다.

"아, 아니야. 우리도 너희와 똑같은 인간이란다. 또 너희처럼 똑같이 결국엔 죽게 될 거야. 우린 여러 해를 거치면서 알게 된 여러 가지 자연의 신비 덕에 장수하게 된 거지. 우리는 대부분의 사람들이 걸리는 질병에 감염되지 않아. 여기 이 섬의 작은 모퉁이에서만 자라는 독특한 허브가 있지. 그 허브 덕에 몸에는 질병에 대한 면역이 생기고, 신앙 덕에 다른 특별한 힘이 발달하게 되는 거란다."

"그 모든 일은 교황 우르반 2세가 유럽의 귀족들에게 성지로의 기나긴 원정을 떠나라고 명한 때 시작됐다. 그는 그것을 '십자군'이라고 불렀어. 우리의 목표는 이교도들로부터 신성한 도시, 예루살렘을 되찾는 것이었지. 이교도란 유대인이나 기독교도가 아닌 사람을 부를 때 썼던 말이야."

"그 당시 우리가 미처 깨닫지 못 했던 문제는, 예루살렘은 이슬람교도들에게도 성지였고, 당연히 그들은 어디서인지도 모르게 불쑥 나타난 한 떼의 유럽인들에게 그곳을 포기하지 않으리라는 거였지. 하지만 우리 기사들은 종교적인 열정에 거의 불타올라 있었어. 우린 이교도들을 무찌르고 우리의 도시를 (비록 법적으로 말하자면, 결코 우리의 도시는 아니었지만 말야) 되찾기 위해서라면 무슨 짓이라도 할 준비가 돼 있었지."

p.248

"제1십자군의 기사들이셨군요." 바베트가 말했다. "전 늘 궁금했어요. 어떻게 교황은 당신들을 머나먼 땅까지 가서 그저 자기들 일에 신경 쓰며 살고 있는 사람들과 싸우라고 납득을 시킨 거죠?"

"그건 이해하기 어려울 거다." 그러피드가 말했다. "하지만 이건 알아야 해. 오웨인과 나, 그리고 우리의 많은 형제들이 항상 평화를 애호했던 건 아니야. 십자군이 있기 전에 우리는 잔치를 열고 여자들을 쫓아다니고 서로 싸우는 일에 푹 빠져 무절제한 생활을 하고 있었어. 우린 온갖 속된 인간적 욕망에 굴복했던 거야. 우르반 2세는 언변에 능하고 설득력이 있는 교황이었지. 그는 우리에게 피와 내장과 핏덩어리가 완비된 아주 즐거운 전쟁을 약속함으로써 전쟁에 대한 사랑에 호소했을 뿐 아니라, 성지를 얻기 위해 싸움으로써 그 과정 가운데 우리의 모든 죄가 깨끗이 씻겨질 거라고 말했단다."

"그 당시엔 그것이 훌륭한 생각처럼 보였지." 오웨인이 동조했다. "하지만 일단 그곳에 도착하고 난 우리는, 지금 일어나고 있는 일이 보통의 전쟁이 아니란 걸 깨달았지. 그건 집단학살이었어. 나머지 십자군 전사들은 이슬람교도 전체를 없애버릴 결심을 한 것 같았어. 우리도 뒤에 온 기사들 못지않게 싸움을 좋아하지만, 예루살렘과 안티옥 그리고 아슈켈론에서 목격한 대학살은 우리까지도 혼비백산시켰어."

오웨인은 먼 옛날의 그 전투들을 회상하는 듯 침묵에 잠겼다.

그러피드가 멈추었던 이야기를 다시 이어나갔다. "설상가상으로, 우리가 상대해서 싸운 사람들은 들었던 것과 달리 야만인들이 아니었어. 그들에겐 대단히 풍부한 문화와 잘 발달된 과학, 의학, 시, 미술, 음악 그리고 건축이 있었지. 우리 유럽인들은 우리의 생활방식이 대단히 뛰어난 줄 알고 얼마나 으쓱했었는데! 그들과 비교해보니 야만인들은 바로 우리였어."

"비록 전쟁은 우리에게 유리해져 갔지만, 우리 가운데 많은 이들은 탈영해서 영원히 폭력을 버리기로 마음먹었단다. 그 당시에 우린 서로를 알지도 못했는데, 어쩌다가 제각각 모두 똑같은 결정을 내렸던 거야. 우린 그냥 무기를 버리고 사막 속으로 방랑길을 떠났지."

"나는 먹지도 마시지도 못한 채 숱한 낮과 밤을 혼자 떠돌아다녔지. 마침내 이젠 목말라 죽겠구나 생각하던 차에, 저 멀리에서 야자나무 한 그루와 연못처럼 생긴 게 보였어. 그리고 그 연못 둘레에 반짝이는 흰색 옷을 입은 수십 명의 남자가 서 있었지."

p.249

"처음엔 뭔가가 보이긴 했지만 그저 신기루라고 생각했지. 그런데 가까이 갈수록 그건 진짜 오아시스란 걸 알 수 있었어. 나무들과 꽃들이 그곳에서 자라고 있었고 산들바람이 불어와 연못의 푸른 물과 이상한 남자들의 옷자락을 찰랑거리게 했어. 그들의 모습에 너무 놀란 나머지 난 목마름도 거의 잊어버렸단다. 나는 먼지와 피와 땀으로 뒤범벅된 상태였는데, 이 남자들은 속에서부터 빛이 나오는 것 같았고, 그들의 하얀 옷은 티 하나 없이 깨끗했어. 내가 연못가에 무릎을 꿇고 두 손으로 물을 퍼 올려 입에 넣기 시작하는데도 그들은 날 못 알아보는 것 같았어. 그러다 뒤에서 날 떼미는 손길이 느껴졌는데, 그리고는 난 소리 없이 깊고 푸른 물속으로 빠져들었어."

"그를 떼민 건 바로 나였단다." 오웨인이 말했다.

"하지만 왜요?" 바너비가 물었다. "익사시키려고 하셨나요?"

"아니, 물론 아니지, 모르겠니?" 수도사가 대답했다. "우린 모두 그 물속에서 목욕을 했단다. 우린 추악한 사람들로 그곳에 갔어. 일부는 이슬람교도였고 일부는 십자군 전사들로, 아픈 몸과 그보다 더 상한 심령을 갖고 있었지. 그 물은 우릴 안팎으로 변화시켰단다. 난 그러피드도 그와 같은 변질작용을 경험해서, 우리가 그랬던 것처럼 황홀한 기쁨과 회한을 느낄 수 있길 바란 거야."

오웨인은 또다시 말을 멈추었는데, 이번엔 바베트, 바너비 그리고 브리지트가 이야기에 너무나 사로잡혀서 멈추도록 두지 않으려 했다.

"모두에게 무슨 일이 일어났나요?" 세 명이 한꺼번에 물었다.

"그건 설명하기가 불가능하단다." 그러피드가 대답했다.

아이들은 실망감으로 투덜거렸다.

"자잘한 얘기들은 해줄 수 있지. 우선, 난 아름답고 신비로운 여인을 만났는데, 그녀는 말을 하지 않고 내게 여러 가지를 얘기해 주었지. 난 뜨거운 광선을 느꼈는데 아프지는 않았어. 내 두 손에는 온 세상의 무게가 실려 있었는데, 난 마치 눈송이처럼 가벼워졌지." 그러피드가 말했다.

p.250

"하지만 그건 불가능하잖아요!" 바너비가 말했다. "동시에 무거우면서 가벼울 수는 없다구요. 그리고 고통 없이 몸이 탈수도 없어요."

"세상에는 수수께끼 같은 일이 많단다, 얘야. 그건 과학으로는 분석되거나 설명될 수가 없지. 그 연못 속에 무엇이 들어 있었는지는 논리적으로 설명될 수 없는 수수께끼지만, 그건 분명 완전히 경험되고 손에 잡히는 거였어.

"하지만 어떤 면에선, 그 물 속에서 우리가 정확히 무엇을 혹은 누구를 보았느냐는 상관이 없단다. 문제가 되는 것은 우리가 "어떻게" 변했느냐지. 나는 행복감과 평화로움에 압도당했고, 완전히 정복당했단다. 수면 아래에서 얼마 동안이나 있었는지는 모르겠지만, 증기와 물이 폭발해 날 공중으로 멀리 쏘아서 세상에 돌아왔는데, 그리고는 갑자기 그건 처음에 그랬던 것처럼 순식간에 사라졌어. 그걸 온천이라고 부르는 것 같구나."

"형제들은 내가 돌아오자 반겨주었고, 나도 이제 그들 가운데 하나라는 걸 알게 됐지. 똑같이 빛나는 피부에 똑같이 흰 옷을 입고 말이야. 내 안에 있는 아주 많은 것들이 변해 있었지. 부, 미모, 명성, 그리고 그 밖의 많은 인간적인 성취는 낮이 되기 전에 사라져버리는 아침이슬처럼 덧없는, 잠깐 동안의 즐거움에 불과하다는 걸 깨달았지.

우린 영화의 추구를 단념하고 궁핍한 사람들을 돕고, 병든 사람들을 고쳐주고, 그 외의 다른 자선들을 베푸는 데 우리의 삶을 헌신하기로 마음먹었어. 하지만 아까 얘기한 것처럼, 브리지트야, 사람들은 우릴 받아주지 않으려 했단다. 다른 수도사들은 우리 행동과 성격에 대해 끔찍한 거짓말들을 했는데, 너희가 상상할 수 있는 가장 악랄한 중상이었어."

"우린 어쩔 수 없이 키프로스 섬으로 쫓겨 왔는데, 지금 여기가 그곳이지." 오웨인이 이어서 말했다. "십자군 이후로 키프로스는 사회 부적응자들의 메카가 되었지. 전쟁은 사람들을 바꾸어 놓았고, 많은 이들은 자신들의 옛날 생활로 돌아가고 싶어 하지 않았어. 이곳에서 우린 바깥세상에 시달림을 당하지 않았지. 하지만 이젠 우리의 지식을 다른 이들과 나누어야 할 때라는 걸 알아. '강하고 위대한 오즈님'께서 우리에게 말씀하셨으니까."

p.251

브리지트는 수도사의 마지막 말에 놀라서 숨이 막힐 지경이었다.

"잠깐만요, 형제님." 그녀가 말했다. "무슨 말씀이세요, '강하고 위대한 오즈님'이라뇨? 바너비, 바베트, 이것 좀 봐. 우린 사실 유로-디즈니 전시회에 와 있는 건가봐. 생각보다 파리와 더 가까이 있다구!"

"얘야, 아까보다 분별력이 떨어지는구나." 그러피드가 말했다. "네 병이 재발하는 게 아니어야 할 텐데. 하지만 네 말을 들어보면 너는 파리로 가려고 하는 거니?"

"맞아요." 브리지트가 말했다.

"그렇다면, 우리가 널 마법사님께 데려가야겠구나. 어쨌든 그 분은 하늘에서 내려와 계시거든. 그 분에게는 널 집에 데려다 주실 능력이 있을 거야."

"좋아요, 전 언제나 오즈의 마법사를 만나고 싶었어요." 브리지트가 말했다.

"그럼 가자꾸나." 수도사가 말했다. "우린 마법사님을 만나러 가는 거다."

"아, 이런." 브리지트가 작은 소리로 중얼거렸다. "때로는 인생이 마치 한편의 영화 같구나."

두 명의 떠다니는 수도사가 여행객들을 이끌고 기다란 복도를 지나 거대한 금속문으로 갔다. 오웨인이 문을 세 번 노크하더니 몸을 돌려 작별인사를 한 다음, 두 명의 수도사가 모두 엷은 공기 속으로 사라졌다.

"놀라워." 바너비가 말했다.

천천히 금속문이 활짝 열렸다. 문 너머로 둥근 천장이 달린 커다란 방이 있었다. 공기에는 연기가 자욱했고, 놀랄 만한 레이저 라이트 쇼가 진행 중이었으며, 이상한 그림들이 벽에 투사되고 있었는데, 아마 영사기가 어디 숨겨져 있는 듯했다.

"멋지다." 브리지트가 말했다. "지난 번 핑크 플로이드 공연 이후로 이런 건 처음 봐."

p.252

천장에 있는 스피커에서 어떤 목소리가 울려나왔다. "내가 강하고 위대한 오즈님이시다!"

"이봐요, 그만해요." 브리지트가 대답했다. "난 몇 천 살 먹은 수도사가 아니에요. 어떤 커튼에 숨어 있든지 어서 나오세요."

"어?" 스피커에서 나오는 목소리가 울렸다.

"아저씨, 누구시든지 간에," 바너비가 말했다, "우린 오즈의 마법사가 꾸며진 인물이란 걸 알아요. 아저씨가 이 수도사들을 속이나 보네요. 우린 특별히 그걸 상관하진 않지만, 어쩌면 아저씨가 우리가 파리로 돌아가는 걸 도와줄 수 있을지도 몰라요."

갑자기 검은 망토까지 완비한 마술사 차림의 남자가 비밀의 문을 열고 나타났다. 그다지 크진 않았다. 검은 머리에 아

344

주 얄따란 검은 콧수염을 하고 있었다. 그는 틀림없이 땅위를 걷고 있었다.

"너희는 출판사에서 왔니?" 그가 앞으로 걸어오면서 물었다. "드디어 내 작품이 인정받는구나! 너희들이 그 아이디어를 좋아할 줄 알았어. 제목은 '전혀 애쓰지 않고 영생하는 법'이라고 지을까 해. 반은 모험이야기고, 반은 요리책으로 말야. 정말 색다른 아이디어지? 이건 'In Cold Blood' 이래로 가장 새로운 산문이라구! 이런... 아, 안되겠구나. 너흰 그저 어린애들이지."

남자는 대단히 실망한 듯 한숨을 지었다.

"무슨 말씀이세요?" 브리지트가 물었다. "그건 그렇고, 아저씬 누구세요?"

"글쎄, 너희도 아는 게 좋겠구나." 그가 말했다. "내 책은 아무래도 결코 출판이 될 것 같지 않구나. 내 이름은 굉장한 멈포다. 적어도, 그건 내가 잘나가는 마술사였을 때 예명이었지. 난 라스베이거스에서 일주일에 다섯 차례 공연을 했고, 가끔은 텔레비전 특집에도 나왔어. 너희는 아마 너무 어려서 기억을 못할 거다."

p.253

바너비, 브리지트 그리고 바베트는 그가 옳다는 걸 인정해야만 했다.

"내 본명은 밀튼이야. 밀튼 펜리치." 그는 손을 내밀어 악수를 청하며 말을 이었다. 서로서로 소개가 이루어졌다.

"방금 내가 너무 무례해 보이지 않았으면 좋겠구나." 밀튼이 말했다. "난 이 책을 수년 동안 써왔단다. 난 내 위대한 작품을 상상하며 애가 탔지. 하드커버로 출판돼서 서점 진열창에 눈에 띄게 놓여지고, 열렬한 독자들이 책을 사려고 줄을 서는 것 말야. 하지만 그건 영원히 도달할 수 없어 보이는 목적지야."

"너희는 책을 쓴다는 게 얼마나 어려운 것인지 몰라. 자신을 스케줄에 맞추어야 하고 그것을 충실히 지키기 위해 훈련을 해야 하지. 또 그것을 견디어낼 만큼 충분히 부지런해야 하고. 아, 난 정말 열심히 일했어! 하지만 내 원고는 보냈던 출판사마다 모조리 거절당했어! 난 아무짝에도 쓸모없는 사람이고, 내 책도 마찬가지야!"

"그러지 마세요, 자기연민의 웅덩이에 빠져 몸부림쳐봐야 소용없어요. 어쩌면 출판사에서 더 좋아하게끔 책을 고칠 수 있을 거예요. 출판사에서 거절하는 이유가 뭐랬는데요?" 바베트가 마술사에게 연민을 느끼며 물었다.

"그들은 내 글이 서투르다고 했지. 아, 물론, 내 문장에는 셰익스피어 소네트처럼 듣기 좋은 음조는 없을지 모르지만, 적어도 난 포인트는 분명하다구. 그들은 위대한 아이디어라는 게 뭔지 모르나? 내 글이 서투르다고 해도, 그럼 대필 작가를 고용해 글을 쓰게 하고 나를 작가로 해주면 됐을 텐데. 하지만 그건 내 생각이지."

밀튼은 다시 무겁게 한숨을 쉬었다. "내가 정말 안됐다고 느끼는 건 저 수도사들이야. 난 몇 년 전에 그리스에서 공연을 몇 번 했는데 섬에서 섬으로 이동하기 위해 소형 비행기를 한 대 빌렸어. 막 2주 전에 조종사 면허증을 땄거든. 어쨌든, 어느 날 밤 험악한 날씨를 만났고, 결국 이곳에 비상착륙하게 된 거야. 수도사들이 내가 하늘에서 내려오는 걸 보더니, 글쎄, 날 무슨 능력 있는 마법사라고 생각했던 거야. 운 좋게도 나에겐 마법사 의복이 다 있었고, 그래서 망설임 없이 내 일을 계속했던 거야. 수도사들은 정말 신이 나 어쩔 줄을 모르더라. 특히 레이저 쇼에 말야. 그런 후에 그들은 나를 '최고의 성자'로 지명 같은 걸 했어. 난 값싼 라스베이거스 마술사보다는 최고의 성자가 되는 게 낫겠다고 생각했고, 그래서 머물기로 한 거야." 그는 혼자 낄낄거렸다.

p.254

"근데 있잖아. 이 수도사들은 정말 내게 경의를 표한단다. 내 앞에서 절을 하면서 존경을 표하고, 내가 말하는 건 뭐든지 해. 예를 들면, 여긴 복사기가 없어. 그래서 난 그들을 시켜 몇 시간 동안 내 원고를 손으로 계속 베끼도록 하지. 수도사들은 필적이 아주 좋단다. 그 오웨인이란 남자만 빼고 말야. 그가 쓴 건 거의 알아볼 수가 없어. 아무튼 난 계속해서 그들에게 세상에 대해 봉사하는 게 될 거라고 말하는데, 그들은 그 아이디어를 아주 좋아하는 것 같아. 하지만 그래도 죄책감이 조금 드는 건 사실이란다."

"있죠." 마술사가 수도사들을 그렇게 이용해먹는 것이 맘에 들지 않는 브리지트가 말했다. "아저씨가 쓴 책 말인데요. 그 책에서 이 수도사들이 수세기를 들여 배워온 신비들을 모두 밝히는 건 아니겠죠?"

"그러는 게 어때서?" 밀튼이 방어적으로 대답했다. "그들은 스스로 사람들을 돕고 싶다고 말해. 그리고 이 수도사들이 소식과 차만으로 구백년 동안 생명을 유지해왔다는 걸 세상 사람들이 알게 된다면, 그들을 만나보려고 찾아올 거야."

"하지만 모르세요?" 바베트가 말했다. "그들이 이용하는 허브는 이 섬의 아주 작은 지역에서만 자라는 거예요. 사람들은 수천 명씩 몰려와 그들의 식물을 뽑고 그들의 홀을 어슬렁거릴 거예요. 이 수도사들은 믿음과 명예가 중요한 의미였던 시대의 사람들이에요. 아저씨는 그들의 생활방식을 완전히 파괴할 거라구요!"

"그들이 책 판매로 돈을 좀 벌기 시작하면 그런 것에 대해선 그다지 불평하지 않을 거다." 그는 대답했다. "이익금의 10%가 수도원에 대한 기부금으로 지정될 거야. 그러면 그들은 계속 만족할 거라구."

"아저씨는 어쩜 그렇게 냉소적일 수 있어요?" 바베트가 소리쳤다. "모든 사람이 아저씨처럼 이기적이고 탐욕스럽진 않다구요!"

"어 그래? 넌 어린애에 불과해. 좀더 나이가 들 때까지 기다려라. 내가 옳다는 걸 알게 될 테니." 그가 말했다.

바베트가 마술사를 재빨리 한번 걷어차려는 것처럼 보였는데, 브리지트가 진정하라며 친구의 팔을 잡았다.

p.255

"있잖아요, 밀튼 아저씨, 이 주제에 대해서 우린 의견이 안 맞는 것 같네요." 그녀가 말했다. "저희는 이 수도사들이 다치는 걸 원치 않아요. 그들은 우릴 도와줬으니까요. 하지만 우리에게 중요한 문제는, 가능한 한 빨리 파리로 돌아가야 한다는 거예요. 아저씨가 우릴 도와줄 수 있을 것 같진 않은데, 그렇죠?"

"너희 꼬맹이들을 없애버리고 싶지만, 안타깝게도 비행기는 오래 전에 해체해서 부품을 필름과 레이저 디스플레이를 늘리는 데 써버렸지.

강화할 필요가 있었거든. 강하고 위대한 오즈님은 강하고 위대한 쇼를 보여줄 만하니까. 안타깝게도 이 섬을 떠나는 유일한 길은 배로 가는 건데, 나한텐 배 역시도 없구나. 어쨌든 너희에겐 계속 오른쪽을 가리켜줄 나침반이 있어야겠다."

바너비가 머리를 긁적이기 시작했다. 브리지트와 바베트는 희망에 차서 서로를 쳐다봤다. 아니나 다를까, 그의 머리카락 사이에서 뭔가가 나와 바닥에 떨어졌다. 바베트가 몸을 구부려 그것을 집어 들었다.

"나침반이야?" 브리지트가 물었다.

"아니, 책인데." 바베트가 한숨을 지었다. 바너비도 실망한 것 같았다. "걱정 마, 바너비. 모든 걸 네 머리카락에 의존할 순 없잖아. 적어도 우리한테 읽을거리는 생긴 거야."

그러나 책표지를 내려다보는 바베트의 얼굴이 밝아졌다. 그녀는 브리지트에게 윙크를 했고, 그런 다음 밀튼 쪽으로 고개를 돌렸다.

"저희는 가봐야겠어요." 그녀가 말했다. "아저씨의 글이 나아지길 바래요."

"어서 가버려라." 자칭 작가가 투덜거렸다.

보리가드, 바베트, 브리지트 그리고 바너비는 기꺼이 그 말에 따랐다. 그들이 복도로 다시 나오자마자 바베트는 수도사들을 찾아 두리번거리기 시작했다.

"그들이 어디에 있을까?" 그녀가 물었다. "오웬인? 그러피드? 형제님들?"

그때 갑자기 두 명의 수도사가 붕 떠서 바베트 앞에 나타났다.

p.256

"왜 그러니, 애야?" 오웬인이 말했다. 마법사님이 너를 도와주셨으면 좋겠구나."

"어, 사실은, 저희 문제는 저희가 직접 푸는 게 좋겠어요. 너희들 먼저 해안으로 가서 배를 띄울 만한 적당한 장소를 찾아볼래?" 그녀가 친구들에게 말했다. "난 수도사님들께 작별인사를 하고 싶어."

브리지트, 바너비 그리고 보리가드는 형제들에게 도와준 것에 대해 고마움을 표하고 어두운 수도원을 떠나 밝은 햇빛 속으로 걸어 나가 해안을 향해 갔다. 해변의 대부분은 바위로 돼 있었지만, 곧 부드러운 모래밭을 발견했고, 그곳에 앉아 바베트를 기다렸다.

몇분이 지난 뒤 바베트가 해변으로 천천히 걸어왔다.

"다 준비됐어?" 그녀가 물었다. "브리지트, 우린 또 풍선거품이 필요할 것 같아. 프랑스는 여기서 서쪽이라는 게 내가 아는 전부야."

"잠깐만, 바베트, 수도사들한테는 무슨 말을 했어?" 바너비가 물었다.

"때로는 직접 실수를 하도록 두는 게 사람들을 돕는 최선의 길이라고 말했지." 바베트가 말했다. "그리고 밀튼은 마법사가 아니라고 했어."

"그들이 네 말을 믿었니?"

"아니. 하지만 그리고 나서 그들에게 그 책을 줬어. '위대한 환상: 1918년에서 현재까지의 영화의 역사' 말야. 그걸 보면 밀튼의 어설픈 라이트 쇼를 알게 될 거야. 그가 오랫동안 최고의 성자로 있을 것 같진 않을거야."

모두가 걱정을 덜었다. 브리지트가 보트를 불 준비를 할 때 바베트가 마지막으로 하나를 더 말했다.

"그런데, 책 표지에 너무나 멋진 사진이 있었어. 귀여운 강아지 한 마리와 반들반들한 빨간 신발을 신은 여자애였지. 그게 어떤 영화에서 나온 건지 너희가 알 수 있을지 모르겠네." 그녀는 싱긋 웃으며 물었다.

브리지트와 바너비가 어깨를 으쓱했다.

"오즈의 마법사잖아!" 그녀는 웃으며 대답했다. "다들 알겠지만!"

p.257

QUICK QUIZ 21
관계짓기
아래의 단어 쌍들이 서로 어떤 관계를 갖는지 판단하세요. 비슷한 의미이면 "S" 반대 의미이면 "O"를 하세요.

1. 모호한 :: 명백한
2. 기소했다 :: 고발했다
3. 엄격한 :: 엄숙한
4. 풍부한 :: 부족한
5. 정교 :: 이교
6. 깜짝 놀라 :: 충격을 받아
7. 박멸하다 :: 정복하다
8. 순식간의 :: 영구적인
9. 증가시키다 :: 늘리다
10. 천한 :: 경건한
11. 금욕적인 :: 사치스러운
12. 박애, 자선 :: 대량학살
13. 산문 :: 시, 운문

QUICK QUIZ 22
관계짓기
아래의 단어 쌍들이 서로 어떤 관계를 갖는지 판단하세요. 비슷한 의미이면 "S" 반대 의미이면 "O"를 하세요.

1. 묵과하다 :: 찬성하다
2. 영향 받기 쉬운 :: 면역의
3. 중상하다 :: 칭찬하다
4. 완화하다 :: 진정시키다
5. 수수께끼 :: 신비
6. 인자한, 호의적인 :: 유독한
7. 신성한 :: 성스러운
8. 평결 :: 결정, 판결
9. 즐김 :: 무관심함
10. 모욕했다 :: 화나게 했다
11. 막연한, 흐릿한 :: 맑은, 명쾌한
12. 드러내다 :: 숨기다

QUICK QUIZ 23
빈칸 채우기
아래에 있는 각각의 단어들 중에서 가장 완벽한 문장을 만들어주는 단어를 고르세요.

1. 쉴라는 신발 뒤꿈치로 오빠의 모형비행기들을 전부 박살을 내놓고 (   ) 하지 않았다. 그녀는 속으로 또 그러겠다고 말했다.
   a. 회상하려고   b. 굴복하려고   c. 뉘우치려고   d. 포기하려고

2. 난 굉장한 멜빈이 (   ) 힘을 가진 줄 알았는데, 이제 알고 보니 그저 속임수와 거울을 이용해 자기가 진짜 마술을 부리는 것처럼 우릴 속인 거였다.
   a. 초자연적인   b. 불멸의   c. 용납할 수 없는   d. 흠없는

3. 존은 여동생의 (   )을/를 축하해 주었는데, 마침내 아버지가 그들에게 콘서트에 가도 된다는 허락을 내리게 만든 것은 그녀의 감동적이고도 설득력 있는 말이었기 때문이다.
   a. 위증   b. 인내   c. 장수   d. 유창한 화술

4. 화장실에서 나온 지 한 시간이 지나서 내 치맛자락이 팬티스타킹 속으로 말려들어가 있던 걸 발견했을 때 내 무안함은 (   ).
   a. 심각했다   b. 자부심이 강했다   c. 진지했다   d. 부적절했다

5. 미리엄은 아프리카의 대형수렵에 대한 탐슨 대령의 이야기를 듣느라 (   ) 자신의 데이트 상대가 다른 여자와 나간 것도 알아차리지 못할 정도였다.
   a. 압도당해서   b. 단련돼서   c. 열중해서   d. 지명돼서

6. 나는 내 눈으로 직접 늑대인간을 볼 때까지는 늑대인간의 존재는 그저 어리석은 (   )에 불과하다고 생각했었다.
   a. 신기루   b. 신화   c. 간헐천   d. 오아시스

7. 데이빗 리빙스톤은 나일강의 원천을 찾으려고 했던 중요한 (   )을/를 이끌었다.
   a. 분파   b. 성직자   c. 망각   d. 원정대

8. 외계인들은 마침내 케빈을 지구로 돌려보냈지만, 케빈은 심각한 기억의 (   )이/가 생겨, 지난 12년 동안 뭘 했었는지 말해 줄 수 없었다.
   a. 착오   b. 열정   c. 황홀경   d. 근접

9. 메리는 너무나 단호한 (   )여서, 대부분의 자선기관들은 사람들을 속여 돈을 갈취하는 사기꾼들에 지나지 않는다고 생각했다.
   a. 마취제   b. 심기증 환자   c. 대필작가   d. 냉소가

10. 필리스가 감기, 유행성 이하선염 그리고 수두에 잇따라 걸리고 나자 부모님은 그녀가 (   ) 수 있도록 플로리다의 할머니에게 보냈다.
   a. 몸부림칠   b. 숙고할   c. 애타게 할   d. 건강을 회복할

QUICK QUIZ 24
짝짓기
오른쪽의 단어를 비슷한 의미의 왼쪽 단어와 짝지으세요.

1. 질문	a. 우울한
2. 메카	b. 물음
3. 주의하다	c. 우발적인 살해
4. 청원	d. 중심지
5. 음울한	e. 요청
6. 생각하다, 간주하다	f. 선언하다
7. 핏덩이	g. 그만두다
8. 살인, 과실치사	h. 방망이
9. 망치, 의사봉	i. 귀담아 듣다
10. 버리다	j. 피

QUICK QUIZ 25
짝짓기
오른쪽의 단어를 비슷한 의미의 왼쪽 단어와 짝지으세요.

1. 변형	a. 미로
2. 미궁	b. 챙겨두다
3. 진기한, 새로운	c. 헌신적인
4. 비난하다	d. 변형
5. 근면한, 공들인	e. 존경
6. 듣기 좋은 음조	f. 새로운
7. 이교도, 불신자	g. 기분 좋은 소리
8. 경의	h. 읽을 수 없는
9. 베끼다	i. 질책하다
10. 읽기 어려운	j. 불신자
11. 지정하다	k. 복사하다

p.262

풍선보트를 타고 키프로스를 떠나온 것은 꽤 순조로웠어. 그게 가장 빠른 여행방법은 아니었지만, 최근 들어 브리지트의 거품풍선은 우리의 건강에 위험한 것으로 밝혀졌고, 그래서 우린 안전하게 가야겠다고 마음먹었지. 그런데 문제는, 어느 방향으로 가야 할지에 대해 우린 단지 일반적인 생각만 갖고 있었던 거야. 바너비는 다시 한번 그의 과학적 재능이 얼마나 다양한지 보여주었는데, 야간 항해를 위해, 그러니까 밤에 배를 조종할 때 그의 천문학 지식을 활용했어. 그는 꽤 많은 별들의 이름과 위치를 알고 있었고, 그러니까 별들의 위치를 알면 어디에 있는 건지 알 수 있잖아. 여하튼 어느 정도는 말이야. 도시 물정에 밝은 브리지트, 천재적인 자질을 갖춘 바너비, 처세에 능한 바베트였지만, 이들은 프랑스가 정확히 어느 쪽에 있는지 판단해줄 간단한 옛날 지리에 대해서는 충분히 몰랐던 거야.

그래서 우린 여러 번 멈추어 방향을 물어봐야 했는데, 그때마다 바베트가 있었던 건 참 다행이야. 그녀는 외국어를 배우는 데 천부적인 재능이 있어. 정말 너희는 그런 걸 타고나는 가봐. 난 아무리 열심히 애를 써 봐도 기껏 너 댓 마디를 할 수 있는데, 바베트는 몇 단어만 듣고서 그 다음엔 누워서 떡먹듯이 재잘거리는 거야.

어쨌든, 우린 그리스의 섬 몇 군데에 들렀는데, 바베트가 얻어낸 조언들은 저마다 달랐고, 그래서 우린 또 다시 그냥 우리의 생각대로 하게 된 거야. 그랬지만 우린 무리 없이 전진하고 있는 것 같았어. 그런데 아주 작은 버려진 섬에 음식을 구하러 나갔다가 우린 느닷없이 벌렁 넘어졌고 나무에 매달린 그물 속에 거꾸로 달려 있게 됐지 뭐니.

"너무 어지러워." 브리지트가 그물에서 빠져나오려고 있는 힘을 다해 몸부림치면서 끙끙거렸다.

바너비는 그보다 소극적인 접근법을 취했다. "이봐, 브리지트." 그가 말했다. "몸부림쳐봐야 아무 소용없어. 넌 우릴 더 엉키게 하고 있을 뿐이야. 그냥 가만히 있어."

하지만 브리지트는 이상한 섬에 거꾸로 매달린 채 가만히 있을 타입의 아이가 아니었다.

p.263

"바베트." 그녀가 말했다. "이 그물이 너한테 아주 튼튼한 것 같니?"

"사실 그렇진 않아." 바베트가 대답했다. "끈은 꽤 약해 보여. 나보고 그물을 끊으라는 거야?"

"잠깐만!" 바너비가 외쳤다. "우린 공중에서 거의 20피트 높이에 매달려 있다구! 네가 그물을 끊어버리면 우린 땅에 머리를 박을 거야."

"우린 지금 여기서 딜레마에 빠졌어, 바너비." 브리지트가 말했다. "여기서 그냥 기다리면서 아무것도 안하면 우린 아마 이 덫을 놓은 야만족에게 잡아먹힐 거야. 그물을 자르면 땅에 머리를 박을 거고. 개인적으로 난 땅에 머리를 박는 쪽이 낫겠어. 최소한 일어나서 도망칠 가능성은 있잖아."

"난 브리지트 말에 동의할래." 바베트가 강타를 날릴 준비를 하며 말했다.

"잠깐만, 바베트!" 바너비가 소리쳤다. "네 주장에 장점이 있다는 건 인정하지만, 우릴 나무에서 떨어지게 하기 전에 나한테 반박할 시간은 줘야지."

"이건 논쟁할 게 아니야, 바너비." 브리지트가 말했다. "우린 심각한 곤경에 처해 있다구! 어서 빨리 여기서 빠져나가야 돼!"

바로 그때, 저 아래에서 소름끼칠 정도로 높은 음조의 말 같은 웃음소리가 들렸다.

"아, 아빠, 쟤네들 기묘하지 않아요?" 이상하고 약간은 영국식 억양 같은 여자 목소리가 말했다. "쟤들이 말하는 사투리는 뭐죠? 미국 식민지에서 온 애들 같아요! 베어버려요!"

바너비와 브리지트, 바베트 그리고 보리가드는 툭 하는 소리를 들었고, 그와 동시에 그들 모두 굴러 떨어졌다.

"그것 봐." 브리지트가 머리를 문지르며 중얼거렸다. "우린 어떻게 했어도 머리를 박고 떨어졌을 거라구."

말 같은 웃음소리가 다시 터져 나왔다.

"이것 봐요, 아빠, 여자애는 너무 촌스러워요. 저렇게 무거운 작업용 바지를 입고 있어요. 벽지에서 그대로 나온 애 같아요!"

브리지트는 자신의 진바지를 모욕한 목소리가 어디서 나오는 건지 찾으려고 두리번거렸다. 브리지트가 그 주인공을 발견했을 때 그녀는 굳이 그랬던 것을 후회했다. 그녀 뒤로 분홍색의 보풀보풀한 무도회용 가운을 입고, 쳐다보기에 몸서리가 처질 정도로 너무나 못생긴 얼굴의 커다란 여자가 서 있었다. 그 여자 옆에는 기다란 자주색 옷을 입은 나이 많고 뚱뚱한 남자가 있었다. 그 남자는 머리에 아주 화려한 왕관을 쓰고 있었다.

"이봐요, 왜 우릴 저렇게 매달아 놨어요? 그것도 그렇고, 당신들은 누구죠?" 브리지트가 화를 내며 말했다.

"이런, 버릇없는 아이로구나!" 왕관을 쓴 남자가 버럭 화를 냈다. "얘야, 너는 예의범절도 못 배우고 자랐느냐? 왕을 어떻게 호칭해야 하는지도 모르느냐?"

"저희를 용서해 주세요. 저희는 그저 놀라서 그랬어요. 안녕하세요, 폐하." 바너비가 낮은 목소리로 말했다. 떨어지면서 머리카락이 뒤흔들렸던 모양으로, 앞으로 몸을 숙이자마자 초콜릿 상자가 땅에 떨어졌다.

여자의 눈이 휘둥그레지더니 아주 가늘어졌고, 그런 다음 여자는 초콜릿 상자를 덥썩 집어들어 열더니 초콜릿을 모조리 정신없이 먹어댔다.

"아, 아빠." 그녀가 이 사이에 낀 캐러멜을 핥으며 정답게 속삭였다. "저 사람이 맘에 들어요, 정말로요! 어떻게 이런 증정물을 저한테 바쳤는지 보셨어요? 너무나 씩씩하고, 너무나 매력적이고, 마치 빛나는 갑옷을 입은 기사 같아요!"

"그렇구나!" 왕이 상당히 흡족한 표정으로 말했다. "젊은 기사, 자네가 내 딸애의 마음을 사로잡았군. 이 애와 결혼하는 게 어떻겠나? 자네는 내 후계자가 되는 거고, 내가 죽으면 왕위를 물려받을 거고 내 전 재산이 자네 것이 되는 걸세!"

"일이 정말 순식간에 벌어지는군." 바베트가 말했다.

"조용해라!" 왕이 호통 쳤다. "자, 젊은 기사?"

"하... 하지만 전... 당신이..." 바너비는 주춤하면서 말을 더듬거렸다. "전 따님의 이름조차 모르는데요."

"아, 그렇군. 리틀도트의 왕인 라일 대왕의 딸, 에퀴니아 공주를 소개하겠네." 왕이 손을 흔들며 말했다. "그리고 자네는...?"

바너비는 잠깐 멈칫했다. 이 두 사람은 정말 제정신이 아닌 것 같았는데, 그들을 화나게 하고 싶지는 않았다. 위험한 사람들일지도 몰랐다. 그는 대담한 전략을 펴기로 결심했다. 바로 지연작전이었다.

"어, 제 이름은 바너비입니다, 폐하." 그가 말했다. "저희는 서로를 거의 알지 못한다는 점을 지적해야 할 것 같습니다. 결혼 얘기를 꺼내기 전에, 어, 에퀴니아 공주님과 제가 좀 사귀어봐야 하지 않을까요?"

"구애 말인가?" 왕이 킬킬거리며 말했다. "난 늘 로맨스란 건 좀 촌스러운 풍습이라고 생각해왔네. 평민들에게야 좋지만, 우리 왕족은 그렇게 머리를 잡아당기고 날뛰고 하기에는 너무 세련돼버려서 말이야.

하지만 그것도 어느 정도는 시골풍의 매력이 있고, 에퀴니아가 좋아할지도 모르지. 아주 좋아, 바너비 경. 내 딸에게 구애하는 걸 허락하겠네."

"어, 그러니까, 결혼을 하기 전에 정다운 관계, 좋은 관계를 발전시키는 것이 중요합니다." 바너비가 말했다.

"좋아, 좋아." 왕이 말했다. "다 알아서 잘 될 거네."

"아, 근사해요, 멋져요!" 공주가 박수를 치고 뛰어다니면서 소리쳤다. "새로운 구혼자가 생겼네. 바너비가 내 애인이야! 바너비가 내 애인이라구!"

그러면서 공주는 바너비의 손을 잡더니 숲 속으로 끌고 들어갔다. 바너비는 에퀴니아가 확 잡아당기는 걸 저지하려고 했지만, 그녀가 그보다 몇 배는 더 컸다. 바너비는 절망적인 표정으로 친구들 쪽을 쳐다보았고, 친구들은 그를 도우러

가려고 했는데, 그들이 바너비 쪽으로 막 달려가려고 할 때 기다랗고 날카로운 칼날 끝이 그들을 가로막았다.

"내가 자네들이라면 그러지 않겠네." 라일 왕이 그들 앞에 칼을 든 채로 말했다. "에퀴니아와 바너비 경 사이의 연애는 아주 예민한 단계에 있네. 그들을 내버려두고 참견하거나 방해하지 말게."

"하지만 바너비는 '경'도 아니고 기사도 아니에요." 브리지트가 말했다. "그 앤 저희 친구고, 저희는 아주 바빠요. 그 앤 과학자에 불과하다구요."

"과학을 한다구?" 왕이 말했다. "훌륭하군. 그런데, 나도 만만치 않게 바쁜 사람이네. 자네 둘은, 그러니까 셋은 나랑 같이 성에 가야겠네. 내가 감시할 수 있게 말야."

왕은 칼로 제스처를 취했고, 보리가드와 바베트 그리고 브리지트는 어쩔 수 없이 그를 따라 숲을 헤쳐 갔다. 그의 성은 기이한 건물이었는데, 왕의 거처라기보다는 탑 같았다. 둥근 모양에 돌로 지어졌으며 3-4층 정도의 높이였다. 안에는 종이와 펜이 가득 차 있었다. 책들이 바닥에서 천장까지 벽을 메우고 있었다.

"독서를 즐기시나 보네요, 폐하." 바베트가 말했다.

"사실은, 그 즐거움도 시들해졌네." 그가 한숨지었다. "리틀도트의 왕으로서, 이 나라의 모든 읽을거리가 내 백성들에게 도움이 되도록 하는 것이 내 임무지.

새 책들은 이곳으로 보내져서 내 승인이 떨어질 때까지 보관되네. 안됐지만 많은 책들이 꽤 오랫동안 여기 널려 있다네. 난 아주 조심해야 해! 백성들을 해하거나 오도하는 글을 읽게 하면 안 되니까. 그래서 내가 친히 모든 걸 읽고 승인을 내려야 하지. 내가 승인해주지 않으면 어떤 책도 나갈 수 없다네."

브리지트는 왕이 다스리는 것 같은 이 "백성들"에 대해 물어보려고 입을 열었지만, 그가 다시 얘기하기 시작했다.

p.267

"물론, 모든 책이 완전히 나쁘거나 완전히 좋은 건 아니지. 그렇기만 하다면 내 일은 훨씬 더 쉬울 텐데 말야. 그 보다도 필요할 경우 내가 내용을 바꾸어야 한다네. 예를 들어, 때로는 책들이 너무 우울한 내용인데, 그러면 슬픈 결말을 행복하게 바꾸려고 최선을 다하지."

"어떤 때는 책의 내용은 좋은데 너무 길 때가 있어. 그런 경우는 본문을 줄여서 꼭 필요한 내용으로만 요약을 한다네. 어쨌거나 사람들은 짧은 책을 좋아하니까. 한 녀석이 끔찍한 살인을 저지르게 되는 내용의 책을 읽었지. 그런데 그는 수백 페이지에 걸쳐 자신의 행위를 걱정하다가, 드디어 거의 끝부분에 가서 자수를 한다네. 난 중간 부분이 없으면 훨씬 더 명료할 것 같았고, 그래서 생략을 하기로 했지. 내 각색으로는, 그는 살인을 저지르고 곧바로 감옥에 들어간다네. 그게 훨씬 낫지, 안 그런가?"

"또 가끔은 작가의 의도가 오로지 백성들의 감정을 자극해서 화나거나 흥분하도록 만드는 것일 때가 있지. 정말로, 내 왕국에서는 자극적인 문학이 절대 있어서는 안 된다네. 왕들은 뭐든지 가능한 한 흥분이 안 되고 점잖은 걸 선호하지. 이따금은 작가들이 얼마나 무책임한지 놀랄 정도라구."

"하지만 당신이 하는 일은 잘못된 거예요!" 브리지트가 말했다. "당신은 책을 더 좋게 만드는 게 아니라 검열하는 거잖아요. 당신의 개인적이고 정치적인 목적에 들어맞지 않는 건 뭐든지 빼버리거나 바꾸면서 말예요!"

"바로 그거다, 얘야!" 왕이 우렁차게 말했다. "내 백성들이 무엇을 읽을지 결정하는 건 왕으로서의 내 권리지. 그게 뭐 잘못됐다는 거냐?"

"전혀 아니에요!" 바베트가 명랑하게 말하더니, 친구에게 고개를 돌리고 속삭였다. "흥분하지 마. 이 나라에 백성이라고는 틀림없이 왕과 딸 뿐일 거야. 그러니까 누구에게도 해를 주는 게 아니라구. 우린 그를 화나게 하면 안돼."

브리지트는 어깨를 으쓱했고, 그러더니 조용해졌다.

p.268

"그럼, 오늘은 어떤 책을 읽고 계셨나요?" 바베트가 물었다.

"질문 잘했구나." 라일 왕이 펜을 집어 들면서 흥겨워하며 말했다. "너무나 좌절감을 주는 책을 보고 있단다. 프랑스 혁명에 대한 내용이지. 끔찍한 전쟁이라고 하더라. 많은 귀족들의 목을 베었지. 그래, 반역자들에게는 그들의 목을 쏙 베어 버리는 기계가 있었어. 그건 정말 소름이 끼쳤어. '목을 베다'라는 단어는 점잖은 문학에 나와서는 안 돼. 백성들에게 망상을 갖게 하지. 그래서 난 쭉 읽으면서 그 단어를 없애야 해. 그게 본문에 등장할 때마다 흔적이 남지 않도록 말끔히 지워야 하지. 그런데 너무 자주 나오는구나, 정말."

라일 왕은 책 한 권을 집어 들더니 책장을 홱 넘겨 표시된 페이지를 펼친 다음 그 공격적인 단어들 중 하나 위에 마구 휘갈겨 썼다.

"아, 그 단어가 너무 많아!" 그는 또 하나를 없애면서 소리쳤다.

바베트, 브리지트 그리고 보리가드는 당분간 편하게 있기로 마음먹었다. 그들의 일이 상당히 지연될 것 같았다.

섬의 다른 쪽에서는 상황이 훨씬 더 재미있었는데, 섬이 워낙 작기 때문에 그리 먼 곳도 아니었다. 에퀴니아에게 구애를 하기로 돼 있던 바너비는, 해변의 조그만 방갈로 안에서 아주 난폭하게 구애를 당하는 것은 오히려 자기라는 걸 알게 됐다.

"내 사랑, 자기가 너무너무 좋아." 공주가 만족스러운 듯 말했다. "자기의 텁수룩한 머리칼은 너무나 개성 있고, 너무나 매력 있고, 너무나 당당해 보여! 자기의 근심어린 작은 얼굴은 너무나 학구적이야! 난 공부를 많이 하는 남자들이 좋아. 그들은 너무나... 공부에 열심이잖아!"

바너비는 어떻게든 그녀를 무시하려고 했는데, 그건 오히려 그녀를 자극하기만 하는 것 같았다. 에퀴니아는 찬장으로 뛰어가더니 쿠키 한 접시를 꺼내왔다.

"자, 자기야, 자기 주려고 내가 직접 구운 거야." 그녀가 쿠키 하나를 내밀면서 정답게 속삭였다.

바너비는 쿠키를 받았다. 어쨌거나 그는 몹시 배가 고팠다. 그는 쿠키를 깨물려고 했는데, 쿠키가 너무 딱딱해 이가 아플 정도였다.

p.269

"못 먹겠어." 그가 말했다.

"아니 왜?" 공주가 상심한 표정으로 물었다.

"먹을 수가 없어." 바너비가 대답했다.

"그게 무슨 얘기야?" 그녀가 놀라며 물었다.

"그러니까, 먹을 수가 없다구." 그는 간단하게 대답했다.

에퀴니아는 눈살을 약간 찌푸렸지만 낙담하지는 않았다. 그녀는 잠깐 오두막을 비우더니 볼품없는 목걸이와 촌스럽게 화려한 귀걸이를 주렁주렁 매단 채 돌아왔다.

"이제 내가 맘에 들어?" 그녀가 물었다. "어때? 훨씬 더 매력적으로 보이려고 보석으로 치장했어."

"그럴 필요 없었어." 그가 대답했다.

"그럼, 내가 꾸미지 않아도 원래 예쁘다고 생각한 거야?" 그녀는 이렇게 말하면서 바너비 앞에 털썩 앉더니 마치 키스를 기다리는 듯 얼굴을 그의 얼굴 가까이로 가져갔다.

바너비는 쉽게 놀라는 사람이 아니었지만, 조금도 그렇지 않았지만, 에퀴니아에게 키스할 생각을 한다면 거의 누구라도 기분이 상했을 것이다. 그는 무례하게 행동하지 않으려고 애썼지만, 그녀의 오른쪽 눈꺼풀에서 2인치 가량이나 튀어나와 있는 커다란 살색의 종양을 주목하지 않을 수가 없었다. 실제로, 그것은 너무 많이 뻗어 나와 있어서 그녀의 시야를 가로막을 것 같았다.

"그 종양 때문에 잘 안 보이지 않아?" 그가 물었다.

"뭐라구?" 에퀴니아가 펄쩍 뛰면서 큰소리로 말했다.

"네 눈꺼풀에 있는 것 말야. 그것 때문에 잘 안 보일 것 같아서." 그가 말했다. "꼭 의사의 진찰을 받아야겠어. 아마도 양성, 그러니까 걱정할 건 아니겠지. 하지만 악성일 수도 있으니까. 그건 나쁜 거야. 그러니까 위험하다는 얘기야."

p.270

"어쩜 그렇게 무정할 수가 있지?" 그녀가 소리쳤다. "처음엔 저기서 아주 냉담하고 무관심하게 앉아서 날 무시하더니, 그리고는 나한테 말을 건다 했더니 비열하구나!"

바너비는 죄책감이 들기 시작했다.

"날 더 이상 사랑하지 않는구나!" 그녀가 신음하듯 말했다. "내 가슴은 갈가리 찢어졌고, 그 피해는 배상할 수 없을 정도야. 난 다시는 행복해질 수 없을 거야. 영원히 잃어버린 네 사랑 때문에 마음 아파할 거라구! 엉엉!"

에퀴니아는 끔찍할 정도로 울어대기 시작했는데, 그럴수록 훨씬 더 괴물 같아 보였다. 바너비는 어떻게든 그녀를 달래보려고 했지만, 전혀 그만한 재주가 없었다.

"울지 마, 공주. 이건 다 오해야. 난 처음부터 널 사랑한 게 아니라구." 그가 말했다.

"거짓말 마. 넌 해변에서 내게 초콜릿 한 상자를 줬잖아!" 그녀는 소리쳤다. "넌 정말 변덕스러워, 다른 남자들이랑 똑같아. 네 감정은 네가 타고 온 조수처럼 들락날락한다구."

"무슨 얘기야, '다른 남자들이랑 똑같다'니?" 바너비가 물었다. 그는 갑자기 죄책감이 좀 덜해지기 시작했다. 어쨌든 이 상황에서 빠져나갈 길이 있을지도 몰랐다.

그가 막 더 물어보려고 할 찰나에 누군가 문을 두드렸다. 문이 삐걱거리며 열렸고, 라일 왕이 고개를 삐죽 내밀었다.

"안녕, 얘들아." 그가 명랑하게 말했다. "바너비 경, 잠깐 얘기 좀 나눠도 되겠소?"

바너비는 에퀴니아와의 끔찍한 상황을 잠깐이나마 모면하게 되자 너무나 기뻤고, 그래서 일어나 왕을 따라갔다.

"어, 일이 어떻게 돼가고 있나?" 왕이 바너비의 어깨를 두드리며 물었다. "이제 내 딸애에게 청혼을 했나?"

"어, 아니오." 바너비가 대답했다.

p.271

"왜 그렇게 미루나? 그만 꾸물거리게. 계속 미루는 건 분별없는 일이네. 자네가 빨리 끝낼수록 우린 더 빨리 결혼 계획을 잡을 수 있다구." 왕이 말했다.

"그 얘길 꺼내주시니 다행입니다, 폐하." 바너비가 말했다. "결혼식이란 건 아주 중요한 의식으로, 거의 졸업식만큼 중요합니다. 쉽게 치를 수는 없습니다."

라일 왕은 잠시 바너비를 빤히 쳐다보더니 활짝 웃었다.

"자넨 똘똘한 젊은이로군, 알겠네." 그가 말했다. "자넨 공주와 결혼하는 데 다른 보상물을 원하는군. 훗날 리틀도트의 왕이 되는 건 충분한 설득력이 없나 보구만. 그럼 이리 오게나. 그 계약으로 또 어떤 걸 얻게 될지 내 보여주지."

바너비는 가능한 한 에퀴니아에게서 멀어지고 싶었고, 그래서 기꺼이 왕을 따라 숲을 지나서 수십 개의 나무통이 쌓여 있는 개척지까지 걸어갔다.

"자, 바너비 경, 난 부자라네." 왕이 말했다.

"어, 무슨 말씀이신지..." 바너비가 말했다. "저 안에 뭐가 있는데요?"

라일 왕은 몸짓으로 바너비에게 통들 가운데 하나로 가까이 오도록 했다. 그러더니 칼로 통 옆을 뚫어 구멍을 냈다. 물이 모래진흙 속으로 콸콸 쏟아지기 시작했다.

"하하! 이 정도는 아무것도 아니지! 훨씬 더 많이 있어. 끝없이 공급할 수 있다구!" 그가 소리쳤다.

바너비는 흐르는 물속에 손을 넣은 다음 입으로 가져왔다.

"이건 바닷물이네요." 그는 너무나 몰상식한 일에 완전히 어안이 벙벙해져서 말했다. "바닷물 몇 통을 저장해오셨다는 건가요?"

"그건 저장할 필요가 없어! 끝없이 공급이 되니까! 그것이 결혼 거래에 자네 구미가 당기도록 해줬으면 좋겠네!"

p.272

바너비는 어찌할 바를 몰랐다. 이 사람들은 완전히 미친 것이었다. 그는 비록 라일 왕이 칼로 그를 찌른다고 할지라도, 더 이상 예의를 갖추거나 이들과 시간을 낭비할 수가 없었다.

"이보세요, 거래는 끝났어요, 라일." 그는 단호하게 말했다. "당신 딸은 나 이전에 많은 구혼자들이 있었고, 난 그들의 헌옷을 물려받지는 않을 거예요. 그녀는 망가진 물건이에요, 아저씨."

"감히 내 딸애의 평판을 그런 식으로 더럽히다니!" 왕이 소리쳤다. "에퀴니아는 매력적이고 명랑하고 생기 있는 아이야. 많은 구혼자들이 있었던 건 당연하지."

"당신이 딸을 위해 덫으로 잡아준 구혼자들이죠!" 바너비가 날카롭게 말했다.

"내가 내 딸에게 신랑감을 찾아주려고 애쓰지 않는다면, 그건 아버지와 왕으로서의 임무를 게을리 하는 것이지." 왕이 설명했다. "내가 그렇게 하는 것이 무슨 상관인지 모르겠구나."

"그건 아주 큰 상관이 있어요! 남자란 붙잡혀서 애완용으로 길러지는 동물이 아니니까요!"

"난 자넬 왕으로 만들어줄 거야, 애완동물이 아니라!"

"전 자유를 얻기 위해서라면 왕위에 대한 어떤 권리라도 기꺼이 빼앗기겠어요." 바너비가 당당하게 말했다.

바로 그때, 그의 뒤 덤불 속에서 급히 움직이는 소리가 났는데, 어깨 너머로 브리지트와 바베트, 보리가드의 모습이 보이자 바너비는 크게 안도했다.

"우리가 머물면서 당신 둘을 중재해주고 우호적인 합의에 도달하도록 도와주고 싶지만, 안타깝게도 우린 시간이 없어요." 브리지트가 말했다.

"그래, 바너비." 바베트가 말했다. "우리가 한참 동안 그 문제를 생각해봤고, 계획 하나를 짜냈어."

"무슨 계획인데?" 바너비가 물었다.

p.273

"있는 힘을 다해 해변까지 뛰는 거야!" 그녀가 소리쳤다.

바너비는 다시 들을 필요도 없었다. 그에게 그건 근사한 계획으로 들렸고, 그는 친구들을 따라 숲을 헤치고 돌진했다. 물론, 라일 왕은 그들을 쫓아 뛰었지만, 그는 도저히 그들만큼 빠르지 못했다. 브리지트가 풍선을 불만큼 시간은 충분했고, 라일 왕이 해변에 이르렀을 때에 그들은 무사히 바다로 나가 있었다. 그들이 배를 타고 떠날 때 라일 왕은 그곳에 서서 칼을 휘두르고 그들을 향해 소리를 질렀다.

"정말 괴물 같은 한 쌍이야!" 브리지트가 헐떡이며 말했다. 몇분 후에 그녀는 말을 이었다. "세상에, 바너비, 난 네가 얌전하고 말없는 앤 줄 알았어. 그렇게 남을 애태우게 할 줄은 미처 몰랐는걸." 그녀는 낄낄 웃으며 말했다.

"이게 바너비 성격의 또 다른 일면인가봐." 바너비가 말했다. "그의 또 다른 모습 말야, 그렇지?"

"그건 내게 사랑에 대한 첫 경험이었는데," 바너비는 한숨지었는데, 그게 재밌었다고 생각하진 않았다, "그런데 완전한 대실패였어. 실패작이었다구! 난 우리 반 애들 중에서 모든 여자애들이 좋아하는 잘생긴 외모를 몹시 부러워했었지. 이젠 그들처럼 잘생기지 않아서 다행이야. 그 애들이 눈곱만큼도 안 부러워. 사랑은 지옥이라구!"

브리지트와 바베트는 눈동자를 굴리더니 자기들끼리 웃었다. 하지만 보리가드는 그저 털이 덮인 까만 머리를 끄덕이며 묵묵히 동의하고는, 슬픈 듯 먼 바다를 응시했다.

p.274

QUICK QUIZ 26

관계짓기

아래의 단어 쌍들이 서로 어떤 관계를 갖는지 판단하세요. 비슷한 의미이면 "S" 반대 의미이면 "O"를 하세요.

1. 양성의 ∷ 악성의
2. 말수가 적은 ∷ 활발한
3. 승인하다 ∷ 찬성하다
4. 단축하다 ∷ 팽창시키다
5. 자극하는 ∷ 차분한
6. 손상시키다 ∷ 향상시키다
7. 산사태, 큰 실패 ∷ 재앙, 큰 실패
8. 세련되지 않은 ∷ 화려한
9. 수동적인 ∷ 활동적인
10. 더럽히다 ∷ 닦다, 윤내다
11. 달래다 ∷ 진정시키다

QUICK QUIZ 27

빈칸 채우기

아래에 있는 각각의 단어들 중에서 가장 완벽한 문장을 만들어주는 단어를 고르세요.

1. 스몰빌의 사람들은 (   ) 취향을 지니고 있어, 지난 달 그들 마을을 찾아왔던 뉴욕 출신의 실험적인 극단을 높이 평가하지 않았다.
   a. 신경질적인   b. 다양한   c. 시골풍의   d. 지방특유의

2. 짐은 그 클럽에 들어가기 위해 속옷차림으로 캠퍼스를 돌아야 하는 등의 입문 (   )을/를 치러야만 했다.
   a. 진퇴양난   b. 연락   c. 의식   d. 일면

3. 전시 동안에는 군인들의 편지가 개봉되어 읽히며, 때로는 기밀 유출을 막기 위해 (   ).
   a. 중재된다   b. 구멍이 뚫린다   c. 검열 삭제된다   d. 저장된다

4. 빈스는 어떤 운동이든 잘하는 걸 보니 (   ) 운동능력이 있는 것 같았다.
   a. 천부적인   b. 임박한   c. 돌이킬 수 없는   d. 관련된

5. 매뉴얼은 그의 할아버지가 돌아가시면 할아버지의 막대한 재산 중 반을 (   ), 나머지 반은 여동생 에밀리아에게 돌아갈 것이다.
   a. 물려받고   b. 방해하고   c. 목을 베고   d. 지우고

6. 클랜시의 이상한 (   )은/는 그와 똑같은 아일랜드 시골 출신이라 해도 알아듣기가 어려웠다.
   a. 관계   b. 장려금   c. 반박   d. 사투리

p.275

QUICK QUIZ 28
짝짓기
오른쪽의 단어를 비슷한 의미의 왼쪽 단어와 짝지으세요.

1. 모험적인	a. 밤에
2. 야간의	b. 숭배자, 구혼자
3. 연약한	c. 약한
4. 후계자	d. 상속인
5. 비틀거리는	e. 생략하다
6. 구애하다	f. 학구적인
7. 구혼자	g. 위험한
8. 빼다	h. 비틀거리는
9. 당당함, 화끈함	i. 유능함, 시원시원함
10. 열심히 공부하는	j. 구애하다

QUICK QUIZ 29
짝짓기
오른쪽의 단어를 비슷한 의미의 왼쪽 단어와 짝지으세요.

1. 먹을 수 없는	a. 부러워하다
2. 장식된	b. 먹기에 부적당한
3. 내밀다	c. 변하기 쉬운
4. 냉담한	d. 포기하다
5. 몹시 슬퍼하다	e. 냉정한
6. 변하기 쉬운	f. 부주의한
7. 위험의 일시적 모면	g. 경감, 안심
8. 꾸물거리다	h. 장식된
9. 태만한	i. 내뻗다
10. 상실하다	j. 한탄하다
11. 탐내다, 갈망하다	k. 지체하다

p.278

우린 얼마 동안 먹지도 못했고 프랑스로 돌아가는 방법은 여전히 확신할 수 없었지만, 적어도 날씨만큼은 온화했어. 포근하고 건조한 날씨에, 기분 좋게 살랑거리는 바람이 우릴 서쪽으로 실어다 주었거든. 지연되고 사고가 터지긴 했지만 난 그것에 아주 감사했지. 그것, 그러니까 바너비가 총각으로 남아 있다는 사실 말야. 가엾은 녀석이 구사일생한 거지.

난 우리가 대양 정기선에 발견됐으면 하고 바랬지. 그런 유람선들이 끊이지 않고 그리스 섬들 사이에서 운항되잖아. 하지만 보이는 거라곤 물 밖에 없었지. 모두들 아주 조용했는데, 아마 여행으로 너무 지쳐서였을 거야. 하지만 보트가 급격하게 왼쪽으로 방향을 바꿔어 가속이 붙기 시작했다는 걸 알아차리고는 우리 모두 순식간에 태도가 돌변했지. 우린 바다에서 튀어나와 있는 커다랗고 울퉁불퉁한 바위를 향해 직진하고 있었는데, 진로를 바꾸기 위해 어떤 수도 쓸 수가 없었던 거야! 난, 이젠 정말 우린 끝이구나 생각했지. 그런데 바위에 곤두박질쳐 산산조각나기 직전, 우린 물속으로 가라앉게 된 거야. 하지만 익사진 않았어. 아니, 그 대신 우린 해수면 아래의 아주 이상한 동굴 속에 들어가게 된 거야.

귀청이 터질 듯한 사이렌이 이들의 도착을 알렸다. 동굴 곳곳에 있는 스피커에서는 "침입자 경보! 침입자 경보! 침입자 경보!"를 외쳤다.

그들 사방에서 사람들이 하고 있던 일을 숨기려고 허둥지둥했다. 책상들이 쾅 닫혔다. 작업대들이 시트로 덮였다.

종이들은 꼭꼭 씹어서 삼켜졌다. 서류들은 갈기갈기 찢겨졌다.

갑자기, 너무나 불쾌하게도, 브리지트, 바너비, 바베트 그리고 보리가드는 또 한번 자신들에게 총이 겨누어져 있다는 사실을 알았다. 이번에, 그들을 위협하고 있는 사람은 화려한 구식 휠체어에 몸을 싣고 있는 늙은 남자였다. 그는 아주 단정하고 기품 있어 보이는 남자로, 숱이 얼마 없는 회색 머리는 깔끔하게 빗질돼 있었고, 붉은 색 실크 재킷은 단정하게 다려져 있었으며, 고급스런 모직 담요가 다리 위에 펼쳐져 있었다. 그는 다른 시공에서 온 사람 같았다. 그의 총 마저도, 광택 나는 나무로 만들어졌고 놋쇠 장식물로 덮여 있는 아주 화려한 권총이었는데, 먼 옛날 그의 집안 과거 속에 등장했던 어떤 군인이나 결투에 의해 전해 내려온 일종의 가보처럼 보였다.

p.279

"너희들 여기서 뭐 하는 거냐?" 그가 물었다. "얼마나 본 거지?"

"아무 것도 안 봤어요!" 여행객들이 동시에 입을 모아 소리쳤다. "우린 아무 것도 안 봤어요, 진짜예요!"

그들 모두 무장한 남자에게 자신들은 악의가 없다는 것을 확신시키려고 애쓰며 한꺼번에 이야기를 하기 시작했다. 하지만 그들이 하는 말로는 그의 의심이 좀체 줄어들지 않았다. 사실, 그 모든 건 상황을 더 악화시킬 뿐이었다.

"너희 말을 못 믿겠다." 그가 딱 잘라 말했다. "이렇게 순진한 애들이 어쩌구 하는 건 다 교묘한 짓에 불과하지. 남자애 머리만 빼면 너희는 다 정상적인 애들처럼 보이지만, 교활한 꾀를 써서 국제 스파이 짓을 하려는 게 틀림없어. 그래서 여기 온 거지?"

"스파이 짓을 할 것도 별로 없는 것 같은데요." 바너비가 겁먹은 듯 오른손으로 머리카락을 만지작거리며 순진하게 대답했다. 그는 자신과 친구들이 도착할 때 중요한 건 아무것도 못 봤다는 걸 재차 입증해 보이려고 애썼다. 그러나 휠체어를 탄 남자는 그 말에 대단히 기분이 상한 것 같았다.

"아, 별로 없는 것 같다고?" 그가 소리쳤다. "여기는 세상에서 가장 정교한 위조 작업을 하는 곳이란 걸 알게 해주지! 가장 정교한 모조 보석, 위조지폐, 유명한 수공예 모조품, 유명 디자이너의 시계, 지갑, 핸드백, 모피, 그 밖의 갖가지 물건의 복제품... 이것들 모두가 바로 여기, 이 동굴 안에서 만들어진다구! 정말 별로 안 되는구나!"

"그렇다면 별로 보지 못한 게 후회스럽네요, 정말 감동받았을 텐데 말예요." 바베트가 최대한 달래는 듯한 어조로 말했다. 아무튼 이들은 늙은 남자가 총을 들었을 뿐만 아니라 성미도 아주 급하다는 걸 고려하면서 다소 불확실한 처지에 놓여 있는 것 같았다.

"고맙소, 젊은 아가씨." 바베트의 칭찬에 기분이 좋아진 것 같은 남자가 말했다. "하지만 너희는 오늘 우리에게 상당한 폐를 끼쳤다. 우린 매일 할당량을 채워야 해. 이탈리아의 아주 중요한 기관 몇 곳을 위해 오늘밤까지 천 리라 지폐로 최소한 10억 리라를 준비해 놓아야 하거든. 너희가 들어오는 바람에 내 뒤에 있던 예술가들이 지금껏 작업해 놓은 것 대부분을 어쩔 수 없이 폐기해 버렸어. 적발당하지 않도록 말야."

"그건 왜요?" 브리지트가 물었다.

p.280

"얘야, 그건 네가 가질 돈을 만드는 건 심각한 불법행위이기 때문이다. 그러니까 법에 위배된다는 말이지. 오직 정부만이 돈을 만들어낼 수 있거든. 알겠니?" 남자가 물었다. 그는 아주 천천히 그리고 또렷하게 말했다. 브리지트는 그의 어투가 맘에 들지 않았다. 그가 자신을 무시하면서 말하는 것 같았는데, 그녀가 정말 싫어하는 것이 무시당하는 것이었기 때문이다.

"네, 알아요." 그녀가 툭 말했다. "물론 위조품을 만드는 게 위법이라는 건 저도 알아요. 제 얘긴, 저희는 절대 스파이나 경찰이 아니니까, 하루 종일 일하신 걸 버릴 필요가 없었다는 거예요."

"너희의 정체가 뭔지 분명하지 않았으니까. 그리고 너희가 여기서 뭘 하고 있는지는 아직도 불확실해." 그가 날카롭게 대답했다. "어쨌든 지금 당장은 너희를 어떻게 처리할지 결정할 시간이 없다. 우린 어서 할당량을 채워야 하니까. 너희를 쏘아버리고 바다 속에 던져버린 다음, 그걸로 끝내는 게 최상책일 것 같다. 그래, 그러는 게 가장 손쉽겠구나, 정말."

늙은 남자는 아주 잠깐 숨을 돌리더니, 그리고는 소리를 질렀는데, 바너비, 바베트, 브리지트, 보리가드는 크게 안심할 수 있었다. "레오나드! 와서 이 애들이랑 육중한 고양이를 회의실로 데리고 가서 우리가 리라를 배에 다 실을 때까지 말썽 못 피우도록 해라. 그런 다음 어떻게 처리할지 결정할 거다."

진바지와 페인트로 뒤덮인 티셔츠 차림의 젊은 남자가 다가왔다.

바베트는 여전히 친절하게 대하려고 최대한 애쓰면서 자신과 친구들을 소개하려고 했다. 하지만 레오나드는 반응이 시큰둥했다. 그는 그저 고개를 한번 끄덕할 뿐이었고 손을 들어 "회의실"이라고 표시된 문 쪽으로 자기보다 앞서 걸어가라는 신호를 했다.

그 방은 일반 사무실용 빌딩에서 볼 수 있는 여느 회의실과 아주 흡사했다. 창문은 없었고, 조명은 눈이 부실 만큼 밝았으며, 구석에 있는 기다란 백열전구 하나가 이따금씩 깜박거리며 조용히 윙윙거렸다. 커피 두 주전자가 커피메이커 위에서 서서히 타고 있었는데, 방안을 쓴 냄새로 가득 채웠다. 한쪽 벽에는 칠판이 걸려 있었고, 유색 매직펜도 서너 개 있었다. 회의실에 있으면 사람들이 으레 잠들 듯이, 보리가드도 곧바로 잠이 들었다. 실제로, 보통과 다른 것은 하얀 대리석으로 만든 근사한 회의용 테이블뿐이었다.

p.281

"정말 멋진 테이블이다." 바베트가 말했다.

레오나드는 미소짓더니 테이블 쪽으로 걸어가서는 손가락 마디로 테이블을 톡톡 두드렸다. 그런데 아이들 귀에 들리는 소리는 딱딱한 돌 소리가 아니라, 마치 텅 빈 우유병을 두드리고 있는 듯 공허하고 시시한 소리였다.

"그래." 레오나드가 말했다. "플라스틱이야. 모조품이지. 놀랍지 않니?"

그들은 동의할 수밖에 없었다. 그건 놀라운 유사품이었다.

"불가능할 것 같아요." 바너비가 말했다. "플라스틱으로 대리석의 모양과 윤택을 그렇게 똑같이 만들어내는 게 말이에요. 아저씨가 이걸 만드신 건가요?"

레오나드는 슬픈 듯 고개를 저었다. "아니." 그가 말했다. "나한텐 그만한 재주가 전혀 없단다. 폭스 씨 혼자서 이 테이블을 만들었지."

"폭스 씨라면 총을 갖고 계신 분이오?" 브리지트가 물었다.

"그래, 총을 갖고 계신 분." 레오나드가 살짝 웃으며 말했다. "하지만 총을 갖고 계실 뿐만 아니라 세상에서 가장 인정받는 예술가 중 한분이시기도 하지. 너희는 그 칭찬을, 그 분에게 쌓아올려진 그 명성을 상상도 못 할 거다. 난 그

분의 손자라는 사실이 자랑스럽다."

그는 우쭐한 것 같았다. 하지만 동시에 근심스러운 표정이기도 했다.

"그 분이 그렇게 대단한 예술가시라면, 동굴 속에 숨어서 뭘 하고 계신 거죠?" 브리지트가 물었다.

"그 분은 숨어 계신 게 아니야." 레오나르드가 성내며 말했다. "일반 사람들이 그 분의 천재성을 이해하지 못했어. 그 분은 당국으로부터 학대를 받고 고문을 당했어. 경찰은 그 분을 뒤쫓아서 정말 시시한 구실로 체포하려 했고, 어떤 땐 그 분의 예술장비까지 압수해 그걸 '증거품'이라고 말하려고 했어. 하! 그들은 그 분의 공급품을 빼앗아 그 분의 정신을 짓밟고 싶었을 뿐이야."

p.282

"그 분은 그 자들이 던져 넣은 무시무시한 지하 감옥에서 한 친구 분을 통해 이곳 얘기를 들으셨지. 내가 듣기로는, 고대 그리스인들이 수백 년 전에 수중의 작은 동굴을 발견한 다음 그 굴을 판 거야. 모래와 바위를 제거하고 생활공간을 넓히기 위해서 간혹 돌과 미사까지 둥글게 파내고 말이지. 그때 이후로 이 곳은 여러 많은 군대들의 비밀 은신처로 사용되었지. 그렇게 해서 우리 할아버지도 여기 오신 거야. 안전을 위해서 말야. 물론 너희는 알아들을 수 있겠지."

"그래요." 브리지트가 말했다. "하지만 다른 사람들은 모두 왜 여기 와 있죠? 그들도 인정받지 못한 예술가들인가요?"

"일부는 그렇지." 레오나르드가 말했다. "대부분은 우리 할아버지의 명성을 듣고 여기까지 찾아온 거야. 그 분은 그들에게 보스지만, 동시에 훌륭한 스승이란. 그 분이 그들을 가르치고 이끌어 주시니까. 아주 많은 걸 요구하는 선생님이시지. 여기 새로 온 사람들 일부는 그 분이 너무 가르치시려 든다고 말하지. 그건 나도 인정해. 그 분은 사람들을 훈계하는 경향이 있지. 하지만 그건 단지 그들이, 그 분의 표현대로 '개인의 정점'에 도달하기를 바라시기 때문이야. 그들 재능의 최고점에 말이지."

"뭐, 그건 충분히 훌륭한 일 같네요." 바너비가 말했다. "그러니까, 사람들에게 최선을 다하게끔 밀어주는 데 대해 조금이라도 공로를 인정해 줘야죠. 하지만 제가 궁금한 건, 그 분이 여길 어떻게 혼자 오셨느냐는 거예요. 하반신 마비가 아니신가요?"

"아니, 그 분 다리는 마비된 게 아니다." 레오나르드가 말했다. "그건 그저 옛날 빅토리아 여왕시대의 휠체어 모형을 그 분이 만드는 거야. 그 분은 그런 사소한 것들을 설계하면서 즐거워하시지. 권총도 그래. 그건 18세기 프랑스의 결투용 권총을 모방해서 만드신 거야."

브리지트와 바베트는 잽싸게 눈빛을 교환했는데, 레오나르드는 그걸 놓치지 않았다. "하지만 진짜 권총과 똑같이 발사되는 거야." 그가 덧붙였다.

레오나르드는 가더니 자기가 마시려고 오래된 커피를 한잔 따랐다. 그는 스티로폼 컵 안을 후후 불더니 한숨을 지었다.

p.283

"내가 할아버지를 따라 여기 온 건 너희들 나이 때쯤으로, 할아버지가 감옥에서 탈출하신 직후였지." 그가 말했다. "할아버지는 내 도움이 필요하다고 하셨고, 그 대신 날 위대한 예술가가 되도록 가르쳐 주시겠다고 약속하셨어. 내가 화가가 되길 열망한다는 걸 아셨거든. 그건 내게 최고의 바람이었어. 그 분의 제안은 내게 아주 강력한 유혹이었고, 난 뿌리칠 수 없었지. 난 학교를 그만뒀고, 어느 어둡고 추운 겨울밤에 그 분을 따라 집을 나왔어. 부모님한테 조차 어디에 가는지 얘기하지 않았어. 그때 이후로 부모님을 못 만났지."

그는 커피를 한 모금 마셨고 생각에 잠겨 컵 속을 들여다보았다. 브리지트도 덩달아 조금 울적해졌다.

"그럼, 그 분이 그러셨나요?" 그녀가 물었다.

"그러셨나니, 뭘?" 레오나르드가 물었다.

"당신을 위대한 예술가로 만들어 주셨나요? 부모님을 떠날 만한 가치가 있었나요?"

레오나르드는 고개를 저었고 잠시 침묵에 잠겼다. 그 방안에 창문이 있었다면 아마 창밖을 응시했을 것이다.

"말하기 부끄럽지만, 난 그 분을 실망시켰어." 마침내 그가 입을 열었다. "그 분이 내게 보여주시는 건 뭐든 똑같이 만들려고 있는 힘을 다했지. 그림에서 아주 정교한 세부사항까지 식별해내는 걸 배웠어. 붓놀림이 왼손잡이인가, 오른손잡이인가? 채색은 팔레트 나이프로 했나, 맨손으로 했나? 갈색의 음영이 구운 시에나토인가, 고동색인가? 난 할아버지가 보여주신 그림들의 스타일을 흉내 내려고 애쓰면서 밤낮없이 실습했지. 난 정말 꼼꼼하게 했어. 하지만 세

부적인 것에 대해 정성껏 주의를 기울여도 아무 소용이 없었어."

"처음에 할아버지께선 내 작품이 상당한 가치가 있다고 하셨지. 이것저것을 칭찬해 주셨어. 하지만 난 어떤 작품도 선정돼 나가는 걸 보지 못했지. 난 끈기 있게 노력하면 나아질 거라고 생각했지만, 십년 아니 백년을 거기에만 매달릴 수도 있었을 거야. 그런다 해도 아무것도 변하지 않았을 거고. 마침내 난 그 분께 내 재능에 대해 솔직하고 객관적인 의견을 말씀해 달라고 했지. 그 분이 하셔야 했던 말씀을 받아들일 준비가 안 된 상태에서 말야."

p.284

"그 분은 내게 몹시 화를 내셨어. 내가 그림에 지나치게 몰두한다고 하셨지. 그 분은 말씀하셨어, 훌륭한 위조품이란 피상적인 것, 오직 표면적인 세부묘사여야 한다고. 내 감정과 정서는 절대 보여서는 안 된다. 난 그 분과 논쟁을 하려 했지만 그 분은 이미 내가 한 일을 보셨던 거야. 내가 모르는 사이에 그 분은 내 작업실에 몰래 들어 오셨고, 내 맘대로 색칠하고 있는 걸 보셨어. 어떤 것의 복사품도 아니었고 그저 내가 하고 싶은 대로 했던 거야. 난 단지 페이스의 변화, 즉 뭔가 다른 것을 위해서 그랬지. 복사품만 만들면 너무 지겨워질 수 있으니까."

레오나드는 잠시 혼자의 생각에 빠져 있었다. 브리지트, 바베트 그리고 바너비는 너무 당황해서 어떻게 거들어야 할지 몰랐다.

"그 분은 내가 독창적으로 그린 작품들을 잔인하게 비웃고 놀리고 조롱하셨어. 그 분은, 내가 스스로 생각해낸 걸 그려봐야 의미 없는 일이라고 하셨어. 그것과 비교되는 대상이 없으면 그게 좋은지 어떤지 아무도 말할 수 없다면서. 독창성이라는 건 훌륭한 위조자들에겐 독이라고 하셨지. 죽음의 키스라고 하셨어. 내가 그림을 그리며 시간 낭비하는 것을 그만둬야 한다고 하셨지. 난 울고 또 울었지만 결국 그 분은 날 진정시키셨어. 이곳에 머물면서 사무실 일을 돌보고 사소한 심부름 같은 걸 해도 된다고 하셨거든."

"그게 그때 이후로 내가 해온 일이야. 정말 자존심 상하는 일이었지. 다른 위조자들은 내가 실패자라는 걸 알고, 날 쓰레기 취급하지. 하지만 난 그걸 감수해야 해. 다른 건 아무것도 잘 하지 못하니까."

"그건 정말 말도 안돼요." 바베트가 발을 쿵쿵 구르며 말했다.

"뭐가?" 레오나드가 꿈에서 깨어나 놀란 듯이 말했다.

"그러니까, 당신 할아버지 폭스 씨가 한 얘기는 완전히 웃긴다구요." 그녀가 또 발을 세게 구르며 말했다. "우리가 당장 가서 당신 그림들을 봐야겠어요."

레오나드는 너무 놀라서 잠시 동안 어떤 행동도 어떤 말도 하지 못했다. 그러더니, 그의 할아버지가 그들을 회의실 안에 가둬두라고 하셨다면서 부드럽게 반대했다. 하지만 바베트는 거부의 대답을 받아들이려 하지 않았다.

p.285

"우리는 당신 작업실에서도 쉽게 감시할 수 있잖아요. 칠판에 메모를 남겨두세요." 그녀가 말했다.

"5분 후에 돌아옵니다." 그가 칠판에 썼다. 그리고는 그들에게 다른 방을 가리켰고, 바베트가 꼬리를 세게 밟는 바람에 잠에서 깬 보리가드까지 포함해 그들 모두는 그를 따라 기다랗고 습하고 음침한 복도를 걸어갔다. 그들은 끝에 있는 작은 문에 이르렀고, 레오나드는 진바지 주머니에서 열쇠를 꺼내 문을 열고는 그들을 들여보냈다.

방은 크고 둥글었고, 자연광을 흠뻑 받도록 머리 위로 높이 커다란 채광창이 뚫려 있었다. 레오나드는 그들이 채광창을 어떻게 지었는지 설명하기 시작했지만, 아무도 귀 기울여 듣지 않았다. 그들은 벽 전체를 덮고 있는 놀라운 그림들을 보고 감탄하느라 정신이 없었다. 대단한 미술 애호가가 아닌 브리지트와 바너비 마저도 감동받을 정도였다. 분명히 그런 종류를 좋아하는 바베트와 보리가드는 서로 다른 그림을 가까이에서 자세히 보고 있었다.

레오나드는 초초해하며 발을 질질 끌고 다니기 시작했다. 그의 그림들을 그렇게 뚫어져라 쳐다본 처음이었다. 그는 또다시 비웃음을 당하는 게 아닐까 겁에 질렸다.

마침내, 바베트가 다가오더니 그를 똑바로 쳐다봤다. "레오나드." 그녀가 말했다. "당신은 정말 위대한 예술가인 것 같아요. 당신의 작품은 감동적이고 힘이 있을 뿐 아니라 혁신적이에요. 당신은 전혀 새로운 걸 창조해낸 거예요!"

"그게 문제였다." 폭스 씨가 느닷없이 문간에 모습을 드러냈는데, 이번엔 휠체어가 없었다. "나에겐 의무가 있었다. 난 레오나드를 뛰어난 위조자로 만들겠다고 약속했는데, 그 의무를 이행하는 데 실패했다. 아니 그보다, 우리가 실패한 거지. 그 애 내부엔 그런 게 없었지. 안타까운 일이었다. 내가 죽으면 이 경영 전체를 그에게 유산으로 물려주고 싶었기 때문이다."

"불행히도, 그 앤 위조자로 뿐만 아니라 사업가로도 서툴러. 사업에 관해서라면 실제적이어야 하지. 돈을 위조하는데 있어서는 감정을 개입시키면 안돼. 말장난 같지만 말이다. 그래서 모든 걸 에드한테 물려주려는 거다. 정말, 그 친군 사업에 필요한 두뇌를 가지고 있지. 그보다 더 영리한 사람은 못 찾을 거다."

p.286

레오나드는 몹시 마음이 상한 것 같았다. 바베트는 단단히 화가 난 듯했다.

"폭스 씨, 당신은 정말 나쁜 할아버지예요!" 그녀가 서슴없이 말했다. "그리고 아주 형편없는 예술가예요."

폭스 씨는 그 말에 정말 화가 난 것 같았는데, 바베트는 자신이 말한 어느 부분에 그가 화가 난 건지 알 수 없었기 때문에 그냥 계속 얘기했다.

"레오나드에게서 자신감을 빼앗고 좌절시키는 게 아니라 격려해줘야 하는 거 아닌가요? 당신에게 유일한 혈육이잖아요!"

폭스 씨는 그저 태연해 보였다.

"레오나드는 정말 재능 있는 화가예요. 위대한 예술가라구요. 과거의 당신이나 당신이 바랄 수 있었던 것보다 훨씬 더 뛰어나다구요! 당신은 그저 질투를 하는 거예요!" 그녀가 외쳤다.

그 말이 정곡을 찌른 것 같았다. 폭스 씨의 얼굴이 붉어지더니, 그리고는 자줏빛이 되었다. 그 다음엔 회초록색 같이 됐다. 이마의 혈관이 벌떡거리기 시작했다. 바너비는 그에게 갑자기 심각한 병이 덮친 거라고 생각됐는데, 알고 보니 폭스 씨의 반응은 병적이기보다는 심리적인 것이었다.

"그래, 그래!" 그가 마침내 불쑥 말을 꺼냈다. "좋다, 너희가 알아야겠다면 말하겠는데, 난 이 그림들을 눈 뜨고 볼 수가 없다. 난 레오나드를 여기 데려올 때 그에게 대단한 미적 감각이 있다는 걸 알았다. 그 앤 어떤 것이든 아름다움을 발견하고 감상할 줄 알았지.

하지만 난 이 그림들을 보고 깨달았어. 그 앤 단순한 탐미가 이상이었고, 천재적 예술가란 걸 말이다. 그것 때문에 그 앨 미워했다고 해도 좋다."

p.287

브리지트가 얼굴을 찡그렸다.

"어, 그래, 수긍이 안 가나?" 그가 말했다. "어떻게 자기 손자를 미워할 수 있냐고? 그건 말이다. 꼬마였을 때, 십대였을 때, 젊은이였을 때, 그리고 심지어는 어느 정도 나이가 들었을 때조차 내가 원했던 건 오로지 예술가가 되는 거였다. 난 너무나 단호하고 정말로 결연해서 어떤 것도 날 막을 수 없었다. 배고픔까지도 말이다. 난 내 아내와 아이까지도 내 일에 방해가 되는 것 같아 저버렸다. 난 생각했지, 위대한 예술가는 집이나 가족의 안락함을 포기해야 한다고."

"난 스무 살 때 화랑에서 첫 전시회를 가졌다. 너무나 흥분됐지. 마침내 세상이 내 작품을 알아주겠구나, 생각했다. 충분히 그럴 만한 명성과 인정을 얻을 거라 생각했다. 하지만 평론가들은 날 비난하는 정도가 아니었다. '유능하지만 독창적이지 못한'이라고 말했지. 근본적으로 그 의미는, 내가 말을 말처럼 보이게 그릴 줄 알지만 그래서 어쨌다는 거냐, 이거다. 그건 새롭지도 않고 인상적이지도 못하고 아무것도 아니었지."

"하지만 난 상관하지 않았다. 그들의 비평은 내 결심을 강하게 할 뿐이었다. 난 더 열심히 노력했고, 낮에는 몇 푼이라도 벌기 위해 웨이터로 일하고, 밤에는 또 다른 전시회를 준비하기 위해 그림을 그리는 엄격한 스케줄대로 살아갔지. 몇 달이 지난 뒤 난 준비가 됐다. 신문마다 그때를 어떻게 논평했는지 아나? '진부하다.' '평범하다.' 그래, 따분하고 독창적이지 못했지. 어떤 비평가는 내 작품이 '무미건조하다'고 말했지. 그건 독창적이지 못한 것보다 재미없다는 뜻인데, 너희도 이해할 거다. 다음 번 전시회도 똑같은 반응을 얻은 거지. 사실, 그 다음의 전시회도 모두 똑같은 반응이었다. 진부하고, 평범하고, 무미건조하고, 비독창적이고, 으아!!"

폭스 씨는 다시 열을 내기 시작했지만, 자줏빛 얼굴이 되기 전에 평정을 찾았다.

"나는 온갖 레슨을 다 받았다. 모든 사람한테 어떻게 하면 나아질 수 있는지 조언을 구했지. 하지만 그들은 너무 막연한 대답만 해주었다. '그건 그냥 느껴야 한다'느니 '자신을 놓아줘라'느니 그런 것 말이다." 그는 말을 이었다. "난 언제나 명쾌한 걸 좋아하는 사람이었지. 마침내 몇 년이 지난 뒤, 난 포기하기로 마음먹었다. 하지만 싸우지 않고는 그럴 수 없었다."

"예술가가 되려는 나의 불타는 욕망은 전체 예술가 집단에 대한 끝없는 복수욕, 결코 만족될 수 없는 욕망으로 바뀌었지! 난 그들을 감동시키려고 애쓰며 내 젊음을 탕진했지만, 그 이후의 인생은 그들을 파괴시키는데 쓰려고 한 거다. 세상에서 가장 유명한 예술작품들의 모조를 만들기 시작했다. 내 모조품들은 아주 훌륭해서 전문가들조차 차이를 구분하려면 애를 먹었지. 그리고 나서는 다른 것들, 옷이나 돈, 보석 같은 걸 위조하기 시작했다. 마침내 예술 세계에서 내게 딱 맞는 자리를 찾아낸 거다. 난 비독창적이고, 또 비독창적인 데에 재주가 있지. 많은 돈을 모방해서 만들어내고, 아직은 보답 받는 걸 그만둘 생각이 없다."

그 말과 함께 폭스 씨는 붉은색 실크 재킷의 깊숙한 주머니에서 권총을 꺼냈고 아이들을 향해 겨누었다.

"그래요, 됐어요, 선생님." 온갖 불평과 넋두리를 듣느라 지겨워진 브리지트가 말했다. "현실을 직시하세요, 선생님은 예술가로서 실패자예요. 그런데 그게 뭐요? 그림은 저도 못 그려요. 하지만 좋은 할아버지가 되는 건 아직 늦지 않았어요. 선택사항이 있어요. 계속 범죄생활을 해나가다가 결국 붙잡히시는 거예요. 모든 범죄자들이 결국엔 붙잡히니까요. 그래서 혼자 감옥에 갇혀 여생을 사시는 거예요. 아니면, 사악한 욕망을 버리고, 손자에게 저질러온 모든 잘못을 고치려고 하시는 거예요. 손자를 이 악악적인 쓰레기 더미에서 꺼내 자신을 키워나가도록 도와주세요, 네?"

폭스 씨는 괴롭고도 당황한 것 같았다. 그는 총을 약간 내리더니, 그리고는 감정적인 고뇌에 시달리는 듯했다.

바베트는 끼어들었다. "그래요, 폭스 씨. 손자를 여기서 데리고 나가세요. 파리로 데리고 가세요. 예술가로서 제대로 평가받을 수 있도록 말예요. 그의 성공을 통해 선생님도 성공하시는 거예요."

레오나르드가 갈망하듯 할아버지를 쳐다봤다. "그럴 수 있어요?" 그가 조용히 물었다. "우리가 정말 갈 수 있어요?"

폭스 씨는 손에서 총을 놓았고, 그의 눈에서는 눈물이 흘러넘쳤다. "그렇고 말고, 얘야, 그러자꾸나." 그가 손자에게 두 팔을 뻗으며 말했다. 그걸 본 레오나르드는 할아버지에게 바로 뛰어갔고 할아버지를 꼭 껴안았다. 참사를 피하게 된 것이었다.

"아." 바베트가 손뼉을 치며 말했다. "그들이 서로간의 의견차를 조정한 걸 보니 정말 다행이야."

"그래, 정말 감동적인 광경이야." 바너비가 말했다.

하지만 브리지트는 친구들만큼 행복하지가 않았다. 그녀는 구석으로 걸어가서는 혼자만의 작은 세상에 빠져들었다. 보리가드가 다가와서 그녀의 엉덩이를 코로 문질러댔는데, 그녀는 뭔가에 너무 몰두한 나머지 알아차리지도 못했다. 바베트도 너무나 근심스러운 표정의 친구를 보고는 도와주려고 다가갔다.

"브리지트, 왜 그래?" 그녀가 물었다.

"레오나르드는 할아버지를 되찾았는데." 그녀가 발목까지 올라오는 자신의 운동화를 내려다보며 말했다. "그런데 난 부모님을 다시는 못 찾을 것 같아, 안 그러니?"

바베트는 생각에 잠겨 얼굴을 찡그리고 이마에 주름살을 지었다.

"음." 그녀가 말했다. "아주 자신하지는 못하겠어. 네가 충분히 비관할 만도 하지만, 그래도 희망은 있는 것 같아. 폭스 씨? 선생님과 레오나르드는 지금 바로 파리에 가실 계획인가요?"

폭스 씨는 희색이 만면해서 위를 올려다보고는 활짝 미소 지었다. "그럼, 물론이지!" 그가 웃었다. "차표가 준비되는 대로 당장 가야지."

"여기서 물건을 선적하시는 줄 알았는데요." 바너비가 물었다. "배가 없으신가요?"

"아니, 없다." 그가 말했다. "우리 고객들은 자기가 주문한 걸 직접 가지고 가야 해."

"어, 이런. 저희에게 문제가 있어요." 바베트가 설명했다. "저희는 아주 급하게 파리로 돌아가야 해요. 브리지트의 부모님이 거기 계시고, 브리지트는 그 분들을 만나야 해요. 지금 바로 배를 하나 지을 수 있을까요?"

"글쎄, 필요한 재료가 다 있는지 모르겠구나." 폭스 씨가 대답했다. "하지만 알아볼 수는 있다. 너희를 도울 수 있는 일이라면 뭐든 하겠다. 어쨌거나 너희가 내 손자를 돌려줬으니까!"

가엾은 브리지트. 난 그렇게 의기소침한 아이는 처음 봤어. 그동안 용감한 태도를 보일 만큼 보였던 것 같아. 바베트는 그녀에게 가서 낮잠을 자면서 좀 쉬라고 말했고, 그건 적절한 조언이었지. 그녀가 깨어날 쯤엔 상황이 훨씬 나아져 있었거든. 레오나드와 바너비는 힘을 합쳐 작은 잠수함의 설계도를 작성했어. 폭스 씨는 지도와 재료를 모으느라 분주했고, 바베트는 오른손으로 금속 박판을 잘라내고 있었지 (그녀의 펀치는 감탄사가 나올 정도라구). 바너비의 놀랄 만한 머리는 또다시 여러모로 편리했지. 내가 살아 있는 한은, 그가 어떻게 귀 뒤에서 잠망경을 통째로 끄집어냈는지 절대 잊지 않을 거야.

오래 걸리지 않아 모든 부품이 준비가 됐어. 단 한 가지 문제는, 그들 모두를 어떻게 다 싣느냐인 것 같았는데, 브리지트의 비상한 수완 덕택에 그건 곧 해결되었지. 모두가 잠수함을 올리고 있는 사이, 브리지트는 풍선을 불어서 그걸로 잠수함 둘레를 온통 싸더니, 배가 완전히 밀폐되고, 고무밴드로 된 커다란 분홍색 공처럼 보이게 만들었어. 약간의 음식과 예술작품을 담은 후 우린 출발준비가 됐지. 폭스 씨는 에드라는 그 사람에게 모든 열쇠를 맡겼고, 우린 출발했어.

물론 레오나드와 바너비가 처음으로 시도한 잠수함 설계였기 때문에 몇 가지 사소한 고장이 있었지. 제어장치가 불편하고 조종하기 힘들었으며, 배가 전체적으로 불편하고 다루기 힘들었어. 하지만 그 모든 걸 제쳐두고, 우린 마침내 파리를 향해 가고 있는 것 같았어.

p.291

QUICK QUIZ 30
관계짓기
아래의 단어 쌍들이 서로 어떤 관계를 갖는지 판단하세요. 비슷한 의미이면 "S" 반대 의미이면 "O"를 하세요.

1. 위조 :: 위조
2. 학대하다 :: 고문하다
3. 혁신적인 :: 무미건조한
4. 진부한 :: 평범한
5. 이름난 :: 인정받는
6. 복제하다 :: 모방하다
7. 가치, 장점 :: 독, 파멸의 원인
8. 명성, 칭찬 :: 칭찬
9. 압수하다 :: 기부하다
10. 유능함 :: 능력 있는
11. 단호한 :: 결연한
12. 탕진하다 :: 낭비하다
13. 꼴사나운 :: 우아한
14. 비관적인 :: 명랑한
15. 절제하는, 온건한 :: 온화한

QUICK QUIZ 31
빈칸 채우기
아래에 있는 각각의 단어들 중에서 가장 완벽한 문장을 만들어주는 단어를 고르세요.

1. 릴리안의 무도회 가운은 아주 (   ). 그 구슬과 장식품을 다 수놓는 데 몇 주일은 걸렸을 것이다.
   a. 갖가지였다   b. 화려했다   c. 불확실했다   d. 회유적이었다

2. 허먼의 은색 벨트의 버클은 집안의 (   )(으)로, 그의 5대조인 피트 할아버지가 오래 전 캘리포니아로 여행가실 때 처음 차셨던 것이다.
   a. 가보   b. 적소   c. 유산   d. 교활

3. 바구니 직조공들은 물건 주문에 맞추기 위해 각각 매일 열 바구니씩의 (   )을/를 배정했다.
   a. 선도자   b. 할당량   c. 정점   d. 정밀한 조사

4. (   ) 실험의 일환으로, 내 룸메이트는 5일 동안 억지로 잠을 안 자고 지내면서 그것이 기분에 어떤 영향을 주는지 보고 있다.
   a. 심리학   b. 병리학   c. 심미적   d. 편리한

5. 귀하의 돈을 일찍 투자하시면 노년에 커다란 보상을 (   ) 것입니다.
   a. 선취하실   b. 조종하실   c. 믿을 파실   d. 받으실

6. 밴드부의 다른 아이들이 튜바로 "우울한 아가"를 연주해 보려는 내 서툰 시도를 (   ).
   a. 후원했다   b. 강등시켰다   c. 비웃었다   d. 분간했다

7. 릴라의 가족은 그녀의 노래와 피아노 연주를 아주 즐겨 듣지만, 좀더 (   ) 청중이라면 그녀의 연주가 그녀 부모님이 생각하
는 것만큼 유쾌하다고 느끼지 않을 수도 있다.
     a. 하반신이 마비된   b. 탐욕스러운   c. 교훈적인   d. 객관적인

p.292

QUICK QUIZ 32

짝짓기

오른쪽의 단어를 비슷한 의미의 왼쪽 단어와 짝지으세요.

1. 고지하다	a. 얕은, 피상적인
2. 지친	b. 잘라내다
3. 방향이 바뀌다	c. 구멍을 파다
4. 진정시키다, 완화하다	d. 알리다, 공고하다
5. 간략한, 짧은	e. 적게 하다, 작게 하다
6. 구멍을 파다	f. 주의 깊은
7. 잘라내다	g. 피곤한
8. 칭찬할 만한, 훌륭한	h. 유용함
9. 열망하다	i. 빛나가다
10. 매력, 유혹	j. 간결한, 간단한
11. 꼼꼼한, 조심성 있는	k. 계속하다
12. 이익, 효용	l. 칭찬할 만한
13. 인내하다	m. 매력
14. 표면의, 피상적인	n. 희망하다, 기대하다

QUICK QUIZ 33

짝짓기

오른쪽의 단어를 비슷한 의미의 왼쪽 단어와 짝지으세요.

1. 알려지지 않은	a. 교활한
2. 지루한	b. 화해시키다, 재결합시키다
3. 불합리한, 우스꽝스러운	c. 알려지지 않은
4. 의무	d. 친절한
5. 실용적인	e. 요구가 많은
6. 약삭빠른	f. 바르게 고치다
7. 방해하다	g. 의무
8. ~없이 지내다	h. 애매한
9. 결심	i. 지루한
10. 엄격한	j. 웃기는, 터무니없는
11. 막연한	k. 실제적인
12. 교정하다	l. 결심
13. 애정 어린, 친절한	m. 방해하다
14. 화해시키다	n. ~없이 지내다

8 박물관 한번 크네

p.294

만사를 고려해 볼 때 그 잠수함은 꽤 튼튼했는데, 특히 풍선껌으로 붙여놓은 것 치고는 그랬지. 그것은 긴 수중여행을 견뎌낼 만큼 튼튼한 것 이상이었어. 레오나드와 폭스 씨가 번갈아가면서 조타와 방향지시를 했어. 즉, 레오나드가 키를 잡으면 폭스 씨는 코스를 정했고, 아니면 그 반대로 했지. 어느 쪽도 맘에 들었어. 난 쉴 기회를 가질 수 있어 좋았고, 내가 알기론 브리지트, 바너비, 바베트도 마찬가지였지.

사실, 인정하고 싶진 않지만 내겐 젊은 고양이였을 때만큼 체력이 없었지. 우리가 겪은 이런저런 모험들로 내가 비축해두었던 에너지는 바닥이 났는데, 무슨 얘긴지 알 거야. 난 잠을 좀 충분히 자야겠다고 생각했고, 그래서 아늑한 작은 모퉁이를 발견해 바로 꿈나라 여행을 떠났지.

그 다음으로 생각나는 건, 온갖 환호성과 박수치는 소리로 잠에서 깨어난 거야. "어, 안돼," 난 생각했지, "또 시작이구나." 하지만 눈을 떴을 때 그 법석이 무엇 때문인지 알게 됐어. 믿거나 말거나, 우린 도착했던 거야! 잠수함이 세느 강에 떠올라 있었어, 파리 말이야!

"친구들, 헤어져야 할 시간이구나." 여행자들이 강둑 위에 올라서 있을 때 폭스 씨가 말했다. "너희들 은혜는 잊지 않겠지만, 언제 다시 만날지는 모르겠다. 난 지명수배자고, 그래서 체포를 피하려면 신분을 숨기고 다녀야 한다. 이름을 바꿀 거고, 어쩌면 얼굴까지 변장할 거야. 너희는 날 알고 있는 걸 잊어버리는 게 좋을 거다."

"할아버지를 절대 못 잊을 거예요." 바베트가 말했다. "하지만 어떤 말씀인지는 알겠어요."

친구들은 레오나드와 할아버지를 포옹하고 손을 흔들어 작별인사를 했다.

"조심해라!" 폭스 씨가 소리쳤다. "자, 레오나드, 우린 루브르 박물관으로 출발하자."

브리지트는 깜짝 놀랐다.

"루브르 박물관이오? 잠깐, 잠깐만요!" 그녀가 그들을 따라잡으려고 뛰어가며 소리쳤다. "저, 택시를 같이 타고 가면 안 될까요?"

p.295

"좋은 생각이야." 바너비가 말했다. "네가 부모님을 봤던 마지막 장소에서 찾아보기 시작하자. 아마 몇 가지 단서를 얻을 수 있을 거야."

"설명을 해드려야겠네요." 바베트가 폭스 씨에게 말했다. "파리로 돌아오는 게 저희의 중요한 목적이었지만, 가장 중요한 목적은 브리지트의 부모님을 찾는 거예요."

"물론이다마다!" 폭스 씨가 말했다. "그 정도 해주는 건 아무것도 아니지. 하지만 너희 둘은 머리를 숙이고 있어야겠구나. 택시 한 대에는 네 명만 탈 수 있을 테니까."

그러면서 그들은 택시를 잡기 위해 거리로 나갔다.

브리지트가 머리회전이 그렇게 빠른 건 다행스런 일이었다. 그들에겐 돈이 한 푼도 없었고, 박물관까지 걸어가려면 시간이 아주 오래 걸렸을 것이기 때문이다. 택시를 한참 타고 간 후, 폭스 씨는 기사에게 돈을 지불했다. 또 다시 작별할 시간이었다.

"예술작품을 실컷 보겠구나." 폭스 씨가 말했고, 그와 레오나드는 박물관으로 걸어 들어갔다.

브리지트, 바너비, 바베트 그리고 보리가드는 밖에 앉아서 계획을 짜내보려고 애썼다.

"제일 먼저 해야 할 일은 너희 부모님이 취하셨을 만한 모든 행동 경로를 잘 생각해 보는 거야. 최대한 잘 생각해 봐." 바너비가 말했다. "그 분들은 근처 식당에 계실 수도 있고, 묵었던 호텔로 돌아가 계실 수도 있고, 경찰서에 계실지도 몰라. 가능한 모든 선택사항을 모아 목록으로 만든 다음, 하나씩 추적해야 해."

"그러려면 시간이 너무 오래 걸릴 텐데." 브리지트가 말했다.

"참 자제해서 표현하는구나, 브리지트." 바베트가 말했다. "그냥 오래 걸리는 정도가 아니라 영원히 걸릴 거라구! 브리지트 부모님은 지금쯤이면 어디에나 계실 수 있어."

p.296

"너한테 더 좋은 아이디어가 있는 것 같은데." 바너비가 투덜거리며 말했다.

"그래. 난 원래 어른들한테 도움을 청하는 건 싫어하지만, 이런 상황에서는 그렇게 해도 괜찮을 것 같아." 바베트가 말했다. "어른의 도움이 분명히 필요한 것 같아."

"이건 어떨까, 날 사람 찾기 광고에 내보는 건?" 브리지트가 물었다.

"글쎄, 아니, 난... 브리지트, 저기 두 사람이 문밖으로 나온다." 바베트가 박물관 쪽을 가리키며 말했다. "너랑 아주 닮았는데, 안 그래?"

브리지트는 어깨 너머로 실눈을 뜨고 쳐다봤다. 한 남자와 한 여자가 보였다. 남자는 크고 들기 버거운 가방을 몇 개 들고는 낑낑대고 있었고, 여자는 근심스러운 표정으로 주변을 두리번거리고 있었다. 그들이 좀더 가까이로 오자 브리지트는 행복의 비명을 질렀다.

"엄마! 아빠! 엄마!" 그녀가 머리 위로 두 손을 흔들며 소리쳤다.

여자가 걸음을 멈추고 쳐다보더니, 브리지트를 향해 전속력으로 뛰어오기 시작했다.

"브리지트!" 그녀가 딸을 팔로 안아 들어올리며 소리 질렀다. "브리지트, 내 아가, 여기 있구나!"

브리지트의 어머니는 딸을 꼭 껴안았고 입을 쉴 새 없이 맞추는 바람에 브리지트의 얼굴은 온통 분홍 립스틱 자국의 범벅이 되었다. 하지만 처음에 행복하던 어머니는 이내 또 다른 반응을 보였는데, 그것은 분명한 노여움이었다. 그녀는 딸을 내려놓더니 엄한 표정으로 눈을 쳐다봤다.

"브리지트, 우리가 헤어지게 되면 안내데스크 옆에서 기다리라고 말했잖아?" 그녀가 다그쳤다. "여기서 뭘 하고 있는 거야? 그동안엔 어디 있었던 거고?"

브리지트의 아버지가 마침내 그들에게로 어기적어기적 걸어왔다. 그는 많은 가방과 짐을 내려놓고 한숨을 내쉬었다.

"보라구." 그가 말했다. "브리지트는 무사할 거라고 했잖아."

p.297

"어쩜 그렇게 태평할 수가 있어? 어떻게 하나뿐인 딸을 걱정도 안 하는지 도무지 모르겠어. 무슨 일이라도 일어날 수 있었다구요! 유괴와 살인이 횡행하는 요즘인데, 거기다 그 문제는 뉴욕만큼이나 파리에서도 만연돼 있다구요!"

"멀리는 못 갔을 줄 알았지." 그가 말했다.

바너비와 바베트는 반어적인 그 말에 낄낄 웃었다.

브리지트는 너무나 지치고 배가 고파서 어머니에게 그동안 자신이 겪었던 일을 전체적으로 요약해줄 기운이 없었다. 게다가 그렇게 요약을 했다가는 더 혼나게 될지도 모른다고 생각했다. 그래서 그녀는 어머니의 질문을 자기가 만든 질문으로 대답하기로 했다.

"제가 어디 있었냐구요? 그게 무슨 상관인지 모르겠는데요. 전 어린아이고, 절 놓치지 않는 게 엄마의 책임이잖아요. 엄마가 어디 계셨느냐는 게 더 적절한 질문일 것 같은데요. 전 며칠 동안 엄마를 기다렸단 말예요!" 브리지트가 말했다. 그녀는 스스로 흡족해했다. 그 말은 어머니를 깊이 생각하게 만들었다.

하지만 브리지트의 어머니는 겨우 잠깐 숙고하더니, 브리지트로 하여금 말대꾸하려고 생각했던 걸 후회하게 만들었다.

"엄마의 책임이라구? 꼬마 아가씨, 엄마의 책임에 대해서 말해주지. 엄만 너보고 안내데스크 옆에서 기다리라고 말했다. 엄마 말을 무시한 건 너였어. 거기에 기초해 볼 때 넌 네 엄마를 존중하지 않는다는 결론 밖에 내릴 수 없고, 그래서 네가 부모님 말씀을 따르는 걸 배울 때까지 혼내는 게 엄마의 책임이야!" 그녀는 정말 화가 났을 때 나오는 저음의 무서운 목소리로 말했다.

"잠깐만, 여보." 브리지트의 아버지가 말했다. "아이를 가두어놓고 열쇠를 던져버리는 건 무분별한 처사야. 아마 브리지트는 다시 좋아질 수 있을 거야. 선량한 시민으로 바뀔 거라구. 브리지트, 이제부턴 착한 딸이 되어 네 엄마가 얘기한 데서 기다릴 거라고 약속할래?"

브리지트는 기꺼이 고개를 끄덕였다.

"보라구, 알겠지?" 아버지가 말했다. "거기다, 여보, 우린 어쩐지 며칠 동안 박물관 선물가게에만 있었던 것 같은데." 그가 발 주변의 꾸러미들을 내려다보았다.

"네 엄만 또 선물을 있는 대로 사느라 정신이 없었단다." 그가 웃었다. "집에 가서 우리 블록 사람들 전부한테 줄 선물을 산 모양이야. 자기가 싫어하는 사람들까지 말이다!"

브리지트는 웃었다. 그녀의 어머니도 미소 지으며 좀 누그러졌다.

"휴가 중에 낭비 좀 하는 건 괜찮아." 어머니가 말했다. "그런데 우리가 실례를 범하고 있구나. 브리지트, 친구들을 여럿 사귄 것 같은데."

"네, 엄마, 정말 최고의 친구들 바너비, 바베트 그리고 보리가드예요." 브리지트가 말했다.

"내 딸의 최고의 친구들이라니, 점심 먹으러 같이 가면 좋겠구나. 우린 정말 배가 고프거든." 어머니가 말했다. "루브르는 거대한 박물관이지. 그 안에서 며칠을 보내도 시간가는 줄 모를 거야."

바너비와 바베트는 서로 쳐다보며 웃음 지었고, 어머니의 초대를 받아들였다. 그런 다음 전체 일행은 가까운 식당으로 걸어가기 시작했다.

"큼직한 검은 고양이로구나." 보리가드의 긴 꼬리가 앞에서 휙휙 소리를 내며 앞뒤로 움직이는 걸 보며 브리지트 아빠가 말했다. "액운을 가져다주지 않도록 조심해라."

"그건 말도 안 되는 미신이에요." 브리지트가 말했다. "보리가드는 곤경에 처했을 때 데리고 있을 만한 훌륭한 고양이라구요."

"음." 브리지트 아버지는 즐거운 미소를 띠며 말했다. "그렇게 훌륭한 친구라니, 그럼 큼직한 생선 한 마리를 사줘야겠는걸."

"그렇고말고요." 브리지트가 말했다.

보리가드의 배가 곧 먹게 될 근사한 점심에 대한 기대로 조용히 꼬르륵거렸다.

정말로 근사한 점심식사였다. 바베트, 바너비, 브리지트, 보리가드는 저마다 엄청난 양의 생선과 프렌치 프라이즈 요리를 주문했는데, 너무나 배가 고픈 나머지 식용이 아니라 꾸밈용으로 놓여 있는 파슬리 장식까지 먹어치웠다. 사실 그들은 손댈 수 있는 모든 걸 집어 게걸스레 먹었다.

"아, 대단한 꼬마 대식가들이로구나." 브리지트의 어머니가 웃으며 말했다. "후식도 좀 먹으렴. 배고픈 상태로 가게 할 순 없지."

아이들은 초콜릿 무스와 아이스크림을 주문해서 힘차게 먹어댔고, 몇 시간 동안을 웃고 떠들고 모험이야기를 나누었다. 그리고 나서는 음식을 더 주문했고, 이야기를 더 나누었다. 브리지트는 자신의 양키 모자를 바베트에게 주었는데, 바베트는 새로운 장신구를 쓰고 나니 훨씬 더 세련되고 신비스러워 보였다.

사실은, 모두들 너무나 즐거운 시간을 보내고 있어서 큼직한 검은 고양이가 테이블 밑에서 슬그머니 빠져나가는 걸 눈치 채지 못했다.

보리가드는 자신의 일이 끝났음을 알았다. 브리지트는 무사히 부모님께로 돌아왔고, 바베트와 바너비도 원래 있던 곳으로 돌아왔다. 보리가드는 자신의 인간 친구들을 마지막으로 한번 보고는, 함께 한 즐거웠던 일들을 떠올리며 미소 지었다. 그리고 나서는 식당을 나와 블록을 걸어 아름다운 파리의 일몰 속으로 들어갔다. 아마도 자신만의 자그마한 모험들을 찾아서였을 것이다.

QUICK QUIZ 34

관계짓기

아래의 단어 쌍들이 서로 어떤 관계를 갖는지 판단하세요. 비슷한 의미이면 "S" 반대 의미이면 "O"를 하세요.

1. 낭비하는, 풍부한 ∷ 풍부한, 아낌없는
2. 처음의 ∷ 마지막의
3. 항구적인, 튼튼한 ∷ 얇은, 연약한
4. 제1의, 주요한 ∷ 주요한
5. 적절한, 관계있는 ∷ 관련된
6. 장식물 ∷ 장식(물)
7. 유행하는, 널리 퍼진 ∷ 드문, 진기한
8. 다루기 힘든, 성가신 ∷ 어색한, 다루기 힘든
9. 반어적인 ∷ 글자대로의
10. 미신 ∷ 사실

QUICK QUIZ 35

짝짓기

오른쪽의 단어를 비슷한 의미의 왼쪽 단어와 짝지으세요.

1. 교체하다, 교차하다	a. 교대로 하다
2. 거꾸로, 반대로	b. 정당화하다
3. 체력, 끈기	c. 반대로
4. 보존물, 예비품	d. 변장하여, 위장하여
5. 익명으로, 가명으로	e. 인내
6. 숙고하다	f. 큰
7. 편집하다, 수집하다	g. 생각하다, 사색하다
8. 큰	h. 저장품, 준비품
9. 정당화하다, 보증하다	i. 모으다, 편집하다
10. 자기만족의	j. 요약, 개요
11. 개요	k. 대식가
12. 끝내다, 최종적으로 결정하다	l. 기대
13. 복구하다	m. 결심하다, 결정하다
14. 기대	n. 복구하다, 회복시키다
15. 대식가	o. 자기만족의

QUICK QUIZ 정답

QUICK QUIZ 1
1. S   2. S   3. O   4. S   5. O   6. O   7. S   8. O   9. S   10. S   11. O

QUICK QUIZ 2
1. S   2. O   3. S   4. O   5. O   6. S   7. O   8. S   9. S   10. O   11. O

QUICK QUIZ 3
1. c   2. a   3. d   4. a   5. b   6. c   7. d

QUICK QUIZ 4
1. c   2. j   3. f   4. m   5. b   6. e   7. n   8. l   9. a   10. k   11. i   12. d   13. h   14. g

QUICK QUIZ 5
1. f   2. d   3. i   4. k   5. b   6. a   7. g   8. h   9. l   10. m   11. c   12. j   13. e

QUICK QUIZ 6
1. S   2. S   3. O   4. O   5. S   6. S   7. S   8. O   9. O   10. S   11. O   12. O

QUICK QUIZ 7
1. O   2. O   3. O   4. O   5. S   6. O   7. O   8. O   9. S   10. O   11. S

QUICK QUIZ 8
1. c.   2. a   3. a   4. c   5. b   6. a   7. d   8. c   9. d   10. b   11. d   12. b

QUICK QUIZ 9
1. f   2. h   3. b   4. k   5. m   6. g   7. c   8. l   9. j   10. a   11. e   12. n   13. i   14. d

QUICK QUIZ 10
1. e   2. g   3. a   4. d   5. j   6. k   7. b   8. h   9. m   10. l   11. c   12. f   13. i

QUICK QUIZ 11
1. S   2. S   3. S   4. O   5. O   6. O   7. O   8. O   9. O   10. O   11. O   12. O   13. S   14. S   15. S

QUICK QUIZ 12
1. O   2. S   3. S   4. O   5. S   6. O   7. S   8. O   9. O   10. S   11. S   12. S   13. O   14. S   15. O

QUICK QUIZ 13
1. c   2. c   3. a   4. d   5. d   6. b   7. b   8. c   9. a   10. d   11. a

QUICK QUIZ 14
1. b   2. a   3. e   4. g   5. i   6. c   7. m   8. l   9. d   10. k   11. h   12. j   13. f

QUICK QUIZ 15
1. e   2. i   3. d   4. j   5. a   6. l   7. c   8. b   9. g   10. k   11. h   12. f

QUICK QUIZ 16
1. S   2. S   3. O   4. S   5. S   6. O   7. S   8. O   9. S   10. O   11. O   12. O   13. O

QUICK QUIZ 17
1. O   2. O   3. O   4. O   5. O   6. S   7. S   8. O   9. S   10. O   11. O   12. S

QUICK QUIZ 18
1. b   2. c   3. d   4. a   5. c   6. a   7. d

QUICK QUIZ 19

1. h   2. l   3. a   4. m   5. f   6. n   7. c   8. k   9. i   10. b   11. g   12. d   13. j   14. e   15. o

QUICK QUIZ 20

1. h   2. a   3. d   4. l   5. b   6. j   7. f   8. m   9. e   10. i   11. n   12. c   13. k   14. g

QUICK QUIZ 21

1. O   2. S   3. S   4. O   5. O   6. S   7. S   8. O   9. S   10. O   11. O   12. O   13. O

QUICK QUIZ 22

1. S   2. O   3. O   4. S   5. S   6. O   7. S   8. S   9. O   10. S   11. O   12. O

QUICK QUIZ 23

1. c   2. a   3. d   4. a   5. c   6. b   7. d   8. a   9. d   10. d

QUICK QUIZ 24

1. b   2. d   3. i   4. e   5. a   6. f   7. j   8. c   9. h   10. g

QUICK QUIZ 25

1. d   2. a   3. f   4. i   5. c   6. g   7. j   8. e   9. k   10. h   11. b

QUICK QUIZ 26

1. O   2. O   3. S   4. O   5. O   6. O   7. S   8. O   9. O   10. O   11. S

QUICK QUIZ 27

1. d   2. c   3. c   4. a   5. a   6. d

QUICK QUIZ 28

1. g   2. a   3. c   4. d   5. h   6. j   7. b   8. e   9. i   10. f

QUICK QUIZ 29

1. b   2. h   3. i   4. e   5. j   6. c   7. g   8. k   9. f   10. d   11. a

QUICK QUIZ 30

1. S   2. S   3. O   4. S   5. S   6. S   7. O   8. S   9. O   10. S   11. S   12. S   13. O   14. O   15. S

QUICK QUIZ 31

1. b   2. a   3. b   4. a   5. d   6. c   7. d

QUICK QUIZ 32

1. d   2. g   3. i   4. e   5. j   6. c   7. b   8. l   9. n   10. m   11. f   12. h   13. k   14. a

QUICK QUIZ 33

1. c   2. i   3. j   4. g   5. k   6. a   7. m   8. n   9. l   10. e   11. h   12. f   13. d   14. b

QUICK QUIZ 34

1. S   2. O   3. O   4. S   5. S   6. S   7. O   8. S   9. O   10. O

QUICK QUIZ 35

1. a   2. c   3. e   4. h   5. d   6. g   7. i   8. f   9. b   10. o   11. j   12. m   13. n   14. l   15. k

PART B

A

ABACK [əbǽk] adv. by surprise 놀라서

I was taken *aback* when my grandmother answered the door dressed in her Grim Reaper Halloween costume.
할머니가 할로윈 복장인 저승사자 차림을 하고 문을 열어 줘서 깜짝 놀랐다.

Since nobody knew about my midnight phone calls to Guam, Father was taken *aback* when he received the long-distance bill for $4,700.23.
내가 한밤중에 괌으로 전화 거는 걸 아무도 몰랐기 때문에 아버지는 4천7백달러 23센트에 달하는 장거리 전화 요금 청구서를 받아 보고는 깜짝 놀라셨다.

ABHOR [æbhɔ́ːr/əb-] v. to regard with disgust or hatred 질색하다, 끔찍하게 싫어하다

Mr. Simplet, who refused to change his clothes more than once a year, was *abhorred* by everyone in the neighborhood.
심플리트 씨는 일 년에 한 번 이상 옷을 갈아입지 않아서 이웃 사람들 모두가 끔찍하게 싫어했다.

Juliet *abhorred* the task of cleaning out the bathtub and toilet, but she did it so that she wouldn't be grounded.
줄리엣은 욕조와 변기 청소하는 일이 끔찍하게 싫었지만, 외출 금지를 당하지 않으려고 청소를 했다.

ABIDE [əbáid] v. to tolerate or put up with; to agree to go along with; to remain or stay 참다, 버티다; 따르다, 지키다; 남다, 머물다

I could not *abide* my neighbor's rude manners, so I told him he could no longer borrow my lawn mower.
이웃 사람의 무례한 태도를 참을 수 없어서 더 이상 우리 집 잔디 깎는 기계를 빌려주지 않겠다고 말했다.

Since he would not *abide* by the other children's rules, Brandon was never asked to play Terminators vs. Cowboys again.
브랜든은 다른 아이들의 규칙을 따르지 않으려고 해서 터미네이터스 대 카우보이스의 놀이에 끼지 못했다.

ABOMINABLE [əbɑ́mənəbəl/əbɔ́m-] adj. horrible or unpleasant 끔찍한, 불쾌한

My teacher warned me that my grade on the test was *abominable*, but I had no idea that I could actually score a -80.
선생님은 내 시험 성적이 끔찍할 정도라고 경고했지만, 난 내가 정말 -80점을 맞게 될 줄은 몰랐다.

The salad dressing made by my brother was so *abominable* that we ended up using it to poison rats.
남동생이 만든 샐러드 드레싱의 맛이 너무나 지독해서 우린 결국 쥐를 독살시키는 데 사용했다.

373

ABOUND [əbáund] v. to be plentiful; to be full 풍부하다; 가득 차다

My mind *abounded* with compliments for Samirah's new hair, but I was tongue-tied and unable to voice any of them.
내 마음은 사마이라의 새 머리 모양에 대한 칭찬으로 가득 찼지만, 말문이 막히는 바람에 어떤 말도 할 수 없었다.

Our garden *abounded* with healthy tomatoes each summer so we had plenty of homemade spaghetti sauce all year round.
우리 집 정원에는 여름마다 신선한 토마토가 풍부하게 열려서 일년 내내 집에서 만든 스파게티 소스가 많이 있다.

ABRIDGE [əbrídʒ] v. to reduce; to limit 줄이다; 제한하다

The tough editor took my two hundred page novel and *abridged* it into a three-page pamphlet.
가차없는 편집자는 2백 페이지짜리 내 소설을 가져다가 내용을 줄여서는 세 페이지짜리 팸플릿 하나로 만들어 버렸다.

The new *abridged* dictionary contained none of the medical and scientific terms that had been included in the full-length version.
새로 나온 요약판 사전에는 원판에 포함되어 있던 의학 용어와 과학 용어가 하나도 없었다.

ABYSS [əbís] n. a seemingly bottomless hole or space 심연, 끝없이 깊은 구덩이

We threw a pebble into the *abyss* to see if we could hear it hit the ground, but no sound came back to us.
우린 깊은 구덩이 속에 조약돌을 던져서 바닥에 부딪치는 소리가 들리는지 보려고 했는데, 아무 소리도 되돌아오지 않았다.

Morty Jenkins, whose stomach was like an *abyss*, was able to eat ten large pizzas and still be hungry.
모티 젠킨스의 위는 마치 심연과 같아서 큼직한 피자를 열 개나 먹고서도 여전히 허기를 느꼈다.

ACADEMIC [ækədémik] adj. having to do with school or college 대학의

After years of writing long *academic* papers, Professor Propster had a hard time adjusting to his new job which involved writing snappy advertising slogans.
프랍스터 교수는 몇 년 동안 장문의 대학 논문을 썼던 터라 톡톡 튀는 광고 표어를 제작하는 새 일에 적응하는 데 애를 먹었다.

During her first year at college, Carol had a hard time focusing on her *academic* responsibilities because she was having so much fun with her new friends.
캐롤은 새로 사귄 친구들과 어울려 신나게 노느라 대학에 입학한 첫 해에 대학에서 해야할 일에 제대로 집중하지 못했다.

ACCESS [ǽkses] n. the right to enter or use; the act of entering 접근(이용)할 권리; 접근, 출입, 이용

Since I had *access* to the master set of keys, we were able to go backstage during the concert quite easily.
내게 마스터 키 세트를 이용할 권리가 있어서 우린 콘서트 중에 아주 쉽게 분장실로 들어갈 수 있었다.

Once the man had spoken the secret password, the guard granted him *access* to the hidden military base.
남자가 일단 비밀 암호를 말하자 보초는 그에게 숨겨진 군사기지로 출입하도록 허가해 주었다.

ACCOMMODATE [əkámədèit/əkɔ́m-] v. to help someone; to adjust or adapt; to have room for 편의를 도모하다, 도와주다; 적응하다, 조절하다; 수용하다, 숙박시키다

We tried to *accommodate* our guests as best we could, but some of them still ended up sleeping on the floor of the kitchen.
우린 최선을 다해서 손님들을 접대하려고 했지만, 그래도 몇 사람은 결국 부엌 바닥에서 자게 됐다.

Our new Land Rover was so large that it could easily *accommodate* the entire family as well as a pair of German Shepherds.

새로 구입한 랜드로버는 워낙 커서 독일산 셰퍼드 한 쌍뿐 아니라 가족 전체를 싣는 데도 전혀 어려움이 없었다.

ACCORD [əkɔ́ːrd] v. to grant or give; to be in agreement or n. harmony or agreement 주다, 허용하다; 일치하다 / 조화, 일치

The King *accorded* Duchess Francesca a chest full of gold for saving the prince from drowning in his bowl of soup.

왕은 수프 사발에 빠져 죽을 뻔한 왕자를 구해 준 프란체스카 공작부인에게 금화 한 상자를 주었다.

The negotiations ended after all sides reached an *accord* about how to solve the water shortage problem.

물 부족 문제를 어떻게 해결할 것인가에 대해 모든 편이 의견 일치를 본 후 협상이 끝났다.

ACCUMULATE [əkjúːmjulèit] v. to collect or gain; to increase 모으다; 모이다, 늘어나다

My goal for the next five years is to *accumulate* all the money that I can so I can afford to buy the Australian continent.

향후 5년간의 내 목표는 가능한 한 있는 대로 돈을 모아 오스트레일리아 대륙을 살 수 있을 정도가 되는 것이다.

During our vacation in Europe my family *accumulated* so many souvenirs that we had to buy an extra suitcase to bring them home in.

우리 가족은 유럽에서 휴가를 보내는 동안 하도 기념품을 많이 사서 그것들을 담아 집에 가져오기 위해 가방을 따로 사야 할 정도였다.

ACQUISITION [æ̀kwəzíʃən] n. the act of obtaining something; something added, like an addition to an existing collection 획득, 습득; 추가물

My *acquisition* of the Omar Moreno baseball card meant that I now had the entire starting lineup of the 1979 Pittsburgh Pirates.

오마 모레노의 야구 카드까지 얻게 돼서 이제 난 1979년 피츠버그 파이어리츠의 선발 멤버 전체를 갖게 됐다.

The art collector's most recent *acquisition* was a statue of a ballerina that was sculpted by the French artist Edgar Degas.

미술품 수집가가 가장 최근에 입수한 작품은 프랑스 미술가 에드가 드가가 조각한 발레리나 상이었다.

ADAGE [ǽdidʒ] n. an old saying that is usually considered to be true 격언, 속담

The sight of Kyle moaning and clutching his twisted ankle reminded me of the old *adage*, "Look before you leap."

카일이 삔 발목을 부여잡고 끙끙거리는 걸 보자 "돌다리도 두들겨 보고 건너라"는 오랜 속담이 생각났다.

Uncle Nork firmly believed in the *adage* "Haste makes waste," so he would never complete any task in under three hours.

노크 삼촌은 "서두르면 일을 그르친다"는 격언을 굳게 믿어서 무슨 일이든 세 시간 이내에 끝내는 법이 없었다.

ADJACENT [ədʒéisnt] adj. next to or nearby; lying close by 옆에 있는, 인접한

All the kids in the neighborhood used to play dodgeball in the abandoned field that was *adjacent* to our apartment complex.

동네 아이들 모두가 우리 아파트 단지옆에 있는 공터에서 도지볼 게임을 하곤 했다.

Unfortunately, Tammy's iced tea was *adjacent* to the glass containing Grandpa's dentures and when Tammy reached for her cool, refreshing beverage she ended up drinking teeth.

공교롭게도 태미의 아이스티가 할아버지의 틀니가 담긴 유리잔 옆에 놓여 있었는데, 시원한 청량음료를 마시려고 손을 뻗은 태미는 그만 틀니를 마셔 버렸다.

ADMONISH [ədmániʃ/-mɔ-] v. to scold or criticize in a friendly yet serious way 훈계하다, 주의를 주다, 타이르다

My grandfather *admonished* me every time I forget to call him "Sir."

할아버지는 내가 "님"자 붙이는 걸 잊어버릴 때마다 주의를 주셨다.

Jessica's parents *admonished* her for not calling them to say that she would be home late from the concert because of the traffic jam.

제시카의 부모님은 그녀를 나무랐는데, 도로가 막혀서 콘서트를 보고 집에 늦게 올 거라고 전화하지 않았기 때문이다.

AFFECTED [əféktid] adj. changed or influenced in some way or behaving in an artificial manner 영향을 받은, 병에 걸린; 꾸미는, ~인 체하는

Luckily, the doctors were able to treat the *affected* area of skin with antibiotics, and thereby stop the disease from spreading deeper into the body.

다행히도 의사들은 피부의 감염 부위를 항생제로 치료할 수 있었고, 그 때문에 질병이 몸속으로 더 깊이 퍼지는 것을 막을 수 있었다.

Michael quickly stopped speaking in his *affected* English accent once everyone learned that he was born and raised in New Rochelle, New York.

마이클은 모두들 그가 뉴욕의 뉴로셀에서 태어나 자랐다는 걸 알게 되자 즉시 영국식 악센트로 꾸며서 말하던 것을 그만두었다.

AIL [eil] v. to suffer from sickness; to cause to suffer (병을) 앓다; 괴롭히다

Medieval doctors believed that bleeding their patients helped to cure what *ailed* them.

중세의 의사들은 환자의 피를 흘리게 하면 병을 치료하는 데 도움이 된다고 믿었다.

I went to nurse my *ailing* grandmother in order to help her recover from a bout of the flu.

나는 독감으로 고생하시는 할머니를 간호해 드리러 갔다.

ALCOVE [ǽlkouv] n. a small room that opens into a larger room; no wall separates the two rooms 큰방 입구의 작은방

We hung our insect wings on a peg in the *alcove* and then joined the Halloween party that was in progress in the living room.

우리 곤충 날개들을 작은방 안의 못에 걸어 놓은 다음 거실에서 진행 중인 할로윈 파티에 참석했다.

Visitors were asked to leave their shoes in the *alcove* before proceeding into the holy Mackinut shrine.

방문객들은 매키넛 성지로 들어가기 전에 입구방 안에 신발을 벗어 놓으라는 요청을 받았다.

ALIGHT [əláit] v. to settle down upon gently or to leave or get off something or adj. burning or lit up 내려앉다; (차에서) 내리다 / 불타는, 불이 켜진

The mosquito gently *alighted* upon my brother's cheek and bit him before I could smash it with my hand.

모기가 내가 손으로 내려치기 전에 남동생 뺨 위에 사뿐히 내려앉아 살을 깨물었다.

Realizing that this subway stop was our destination, we *alighted* from the train and headed out into the driving snow.

우리는 이번 지하철역이 우리의 행선지라는 걸 깨닫고는 열차에서 내려 휘몰아치는 눈 속으로 나갔다.

Once the bonfire was *alight*, all of the faces in the crowd seemed to glow with a warm, reddish tinge.
화톳불이 타오르자 모든 군중의 얼굴이 따뜻하고 불그스름한 빛을 띠며 불타는 것 같았다.

ALLEGE [əlédʒ] v. to declare that something is true without offering any proof 증거도 없이 사실이라고 주장하다

Although Olaf *alleged* that he knew nothing about the attempted robbery, the police suspected that he was the Pez Dispenser Burglar.
올래프는 강도 미수에 대해 아무 것도 모른다고 주장했지만 경찰은 그가 "페즈 자판기 강도"라고 생각했다.

While the prosecuting lawyers continue to *allege* that Heidi is guilty, the defense lawyers have already proven in a court of law that she was merely an innocent victim.
검찰측은 줄곧 하이디의 유죄를 강력히 주장했지만, 피고 측 변호인단은 이미 그녀가 무고한 피해자에 불과하다는 것을 법정에서 입증했다.

ALLIANCE [əláiəns] n. a formal agreement between two or more groups to unite 결연, 동맹, 연합

After they formed an *alliance* with the auto workers at Trucker Inc., the windshield technicians demanded higher salaries from their company by threatening its management with a strike.
바람막이 유리 기술자들은 트러커 사의 자동차 제조 노동자들과 결연을 맺은 후, 파업을 하겠다고 경영진을 협박하며 회사 측으로부터 월급 인상을 요구했다.

The *alliance* between the two rebel factions soon fell apart after a bitter dispute over who had to wash the dishes.
누가 설거지를 할 것인가를 두고 격심한 논쟁을 벌인 후 두 반란파 사이의 연합은 이내 깨지고 말았다.

ALLY [əlái/ǽlai] n. a country or person that is united or joined with another for a certain reason 동맹국, 동맹자

France and England, which were political *allies* during the great wars of this century, seem to be completely culturally incompatible.
프랑스와 영국은 이번 세기에 큰 전쟁을 치르는 동안 정치적 동맹국이었지만, 문화적으로 전혀 어울릴 수 없는 것처럼 보인다.

As I continued to push for longer work hours with less pay, I quickly discovered that I had few *allies* among my co-workers.
내가 계속해서 임금은 덜 받고 일은 더 하자는 주장을 밀고 나갈 때 동료들 중에서 내 편이 거의 없다는 걸 금세 알게 됐다.

ALTRUISTIC [æltruːístik] adj. showing concern for the well-being of others 이타적인

The *altruistic* efforts of Mother Theresa of Calcutta have saved thousands of poor people from starvation and disease.
캘커타에서의 마더 테레사의 헌신적인 수고가 수천 명의 가난한 사람들을 기아와 질병에서 구제했다.

Although at first I thanked the old man for his *altruistic* donation of fifty dollars, I soon learned that the money he had given me was fake.
처음엔 50달러를 기부한 노인에게 감사했지만 알고 보니 그가 낸 돈은 위조지폐였다.

AMASS [əmǽs] v. to gather or gain; to increase 모으다; 모이다

Once the general had *amassed* all his troops in the field, he boldly led the charge against the fortress of Count Stoppmenau.
장군은 들판에서 자신의 군대를 소집하고 난 뒤 대담하게 스탑메노 백작의 요새를 향해 진군해 갔다.

The billionaire had *amassed* so much wealth that whenever he sneezed, dimes came out of his nose.
억만장자는 하도 많은 재산을 모아서 재채기만 하면 코에서 10센트 짜리 동전이 쏟아져 나왔다.

ANALOGY [ənǽlədʒi] n. some form of similarity between two things that are otherwise unlike; an explanation that compares one thing to something else that is similar   유사, 비슷함; 유추, 유추법

To help us understand how some sea creatures breathe, our teacher made an *analogy* between gills on fish and lungs in mammals.
선생님은 바다 생물의 호흡법에 대한 우리의 이해를 돕기 위해 물고기의 아가미와 포유동물의 폐를 놓고 유추에 의한 설명을 했다.

Poets have long seen an *analogy* between spring and youth, and between winter and death.
시인들은 이전부터 봄과 젊음, 겨울과 죽음 사이의 유사점을 보아 왔다.

ANALYSIS [ənǽləsis] n. the process of separating something into smaller parts to better understand the properties of the object as a whole   분석

The laboratory completed its *analysis* of the foreign substance that was found on the last space shuttle mission and determined that it was an alien chewing gum.
연구실에서는 지난 우주 왕복선 비행에서 발견된 이물질에 대한 분석을 끝마치고 난 뒤, 그것은 외계인의 껌이라고 단정지었다.

Even after three years of careful *analysis*, I am still confused by the National Basketball Association draft system.
난 3년 동안 NBA의 드래프트제에 대해 철저히 분석해 봤지만, 아직도 뭐가 뭔지 모르겠다.

ANTISOCIAL [æ̀ntisóuʃəl/-tai-] adj. avoiding the company of other people or interfering with society 비사교적인; 반사회적인

The *antisocial* writer threw rocks at anyone who tried to walk up the path to his front door.
사교적이지 못한 작가는 그의 집 앞문에 이르는 길로 올라오려고 하는 사람에게는 누구든 돌을 던졌다.

Marvin's shoplifting habit and bullying behavior are signs of an *antisocial* personality.
마빈의 좀도둑질을 하는 버릇과 약한 아이를 괴롭히는 행동은 반사회적인 성격의 징후들이다.

APPALL [əpɔ́:l] v. to shock or amaze; to horrify   깜짝 놀라게 하다; 질겁하게 하다

Larry's ability to turn his eyelids inside out was truly *appalling*.
래리가 눈꺼풀을 뒤집는 것은 정말 소름이 끼쳤다.

The family was *appalled* to come home after the movie and find that their house had been blown up by a stray missile.
영화를 보고 집에 돌아온 가족은 그들의 집이 빗나간 미사일에 폭격 맞았었다는 걸 알고 깜짝 놀랐다.

APPARITION [æ̀pəríʃən] n. a visible spirit or ghost   유령

My mother didn't believe in the haunted house's *apparition* until she walked into the kitchen one day and saw a shadowy form doing the dishes.
어머니는 흉가에 유령이 나온다는 걸 믿지 않으셨는데, 어느날 부엌에 들어가셨다가 흐릿한 형상이 설거지하고 있는 걸 보셨다.

The *apparition* that I thought was trying to break through my upstairs window to take my soul turned out to be a large piece of cardboard stuck in our tree.
유령이 위층 창문을 깨고 들어와 내 영혼을 빼앗아 가려고 한다고 생각했는데, 알고 보니 커다란 판지가 나무에 끼여 있던 거였다.

APPEND [əpénd] v. to add on to something 덧붙이다, 추가하다

Congressman Debbs *appended* a paragraph to the crime bill that made it illegal to spit on penguins.
뎁스 의원은 펭귄에게 침을 뱉는 것을 불법으로 하는 범죄 법안에 단락 하나를 덧붙였다.

The manager wanted to *append* my contract so that I would have to pay for any food I ate while on duty, but I vowed not to sign the contract if he did.
매니저는 계약서에 내가 일하는 동안 먹는 음식에 대해 값을 치르도록 하는 내용을 추가하려고 했지만, 나는 그렇게 한다면 맹세코 계약서에 서명하지 않겠다고 말했다.

APT [æpt] adj. just right for the occasion or quick to learn 적절한; 총기있는

As the snow began to fall, I discovered that my friend's decision to bring heavy jackets to the ball game was a very *apt* move.
눈이 내리기 시작하자 야구장에 두툼한 재킷을 가져가겠다는 친구의 결정이 아주 적절한 조치였음을 알게 됐다.

My sister's ability to perfectly construct a model of the Eiffel Tower using toothpicks showed that she was an *apt* student of architecture.
이쑤시개를 이용해서 에펠탑의 완벽한 모형을 만들어 낸 여동생의 능력은 그녀가 총기있는 건축학도라는 걸 보여주었다.

ARBITRATE [ɑ́:rbətrèit] v. to agree to have a dispute settled by a third party 중재하다, 중재 재판에 회부하다

Judge Nervil once *arbitrated* a dispute between two neighbors over who had the right to play their stereo the loudest.
너빌 판사는 전축을 가장 크게 틀어 놓을 권리가 누구에게 있는지에 대해 두 이웃 간에 일어난 분쟁을 중재한 적이 있다.

Fearing high legal costs, the two battling companies asked a local fortune teller to *arbitrate* for them.
싸움을 일으킨 두 회사는 법적 비용에 부담을 느껴 지역 점쟁이에게 중재를 부탁했다.

ARDENT [ɑ́:rdnt] adj. greatly passionate or enthusiastic 불타는, 열렬한

Corey was such an *ardent* lover of music that he once duct-taped his head to his stereo speakers.
코리는 열렬한 음악광이어서 한때 머리에 덕 테이프로 스테레오 스피커를 붙이고 다닐 정도였다.

Security guards finally had to go into the stands and throw the *ardent* fan out of the stadium, since the game had ended over three hours ago.
경비원들은 마침내 스탠드로 들어가 열광하는 팬을 운동장 밖으로 끌어내야 했는데, 경기가 끝난 지 세 시간도 더 됐기 때문이다.

ARID [ǽrid] adj. very dry; having little rainfall 건조한, 메마른

The Empty Quarter of the Arabian Desert is so *arid* that no living thing can survive there.
아라비아 사막의 엠티 쿼터는 너무나 메말라 생물이 살아남을 수 없을 정도다.

Crops refused to grow in the *arid* soil and the farmer was forced to go into the used-car business to make a living.
건조한 토양에서 농작물이 자라지 않자 농부는 어쩔 수 없이 생계를 위해 중고차 사업에 뛰어들어야 했다.

ARMADA [ɑ:rmɑ́:də/-méi-] n. a great fleet of warships 함대

Due to faulty navigation, a Finnish *armada* sailed into the wrong harbor and invaded their own country.
핀란드 함대는 그릇된 항법 때문에 잘못된 항구로 들어서서 자신의 나라를 침공했다.

The astronauts watched as the vast *armada* of spaceships stopped outside the space station, rolled down a window, and asked for directions to the Pleiades.

우주비행사들은 거대한 우주선 함대가 우주 정거장 밖에 정차하고 창문을 내린 뒤 플레이아데스로 가는 방향을 묻는 것을 지켜보았다.

ARTERY [ɑ́ːrtəri] n. a tube or vessel within your body that carries blood from the heart or a major road or highway 동맥; 주요 도로, 간선 도로

Luckily for him, Jonathan's botched attempt at knife juggling did not sever any of his *arteries*, although he won't need to shave for a while.

조나단은 서투르게 칼로 저글링을 하려다가 당분간 면도할 일은 없어졌지만 다행히 동맥을 베지는 않았다.

The collision of two semi-trucks carrying manure clogged the main *artery* into town for over six hours, but it seemed like longer.

동물의 거름을 싣고 가던 세미 트럭 두 대가 충돌해 시내로 진입하는 간선 도로가 6시간 넘게 차단됐는데, 정체된 시간은 그보다 더 긴 것처럼 생각되었다.

ASPECT [ǽspekt] n. an element or feature; look or appearance 일면, 양상; 외관, 모양

The fact that people are often forced to parallel park is one of the more annoying *aspects* of driving a car.

종종 별 수 없이 노변에 평행 주차를 해야 한다는 사실은 운전하는 데 있어 더 짜증나는 면 중 하나다.

The warped glass in the old barn windows gave everyone standing outside a distorted *aspect*.

오래된 헛간 창문의 휘어진 유리는 밖에 서 있는 사람들을 비뚤어져 보이게 했다.

ASSAILANT [əséilənt] n. a person who attacks someone else 공격자

Using what I learned in karate class, I was able to defend myself from the *assailant* by giving him a swift kick in the belly.

나는 가라데 수업에서 배운 걸 이용해 공격자의 배를 잽싸게 걷어차서 자기 방어를 할 수 있었다.

The cowardly *assailant* who tried to steal the old woman's purse soon found himself stunned by 10,000 volts of electricity from her Taser.

노파의 지갑을 훔치려고 했던 비열한 공격자는 곧 테이저총의 만 볼트 전기를 맞고 기절했다.

ASSERT [əsə́ːrt] v. to state a viewpoint definitively; to declare or to defend or maintain 단언하다, 강력히 주장하다; 옹호하다, 고집하다

The students organized a boycott of the cafeteria to *assert* their opinion that the food was horrible.

학생들은 음식이 형편없다는 주장을 펼치며 간이식당을 상대로 불매 동맹을 맺었다.

In the town meeting, the Hendersons *asserted* their right to hang from trees in the park and scream at the top of their lungs, claiming that it was freedom of speech.

마을회의에서 헨더슨 부부는 그것이 의사 표현의 자유라고 주장하면서 공원의 나무에 매달려 목청이 터지도록 소리를 지를 수 있는 권리를 옹호했다.

ASSESS [əsés] v. to evaluate; figure out the value or importance of or to charge with a special payment 어림잡다, 평가하다; (세금 등을) 부과하다

The baseball coach could *assess* a player's batting skills by watching him make just one swing.

야구 코치는 단 한 번 스윙하는 것을 보고 그 선수의 타격 실력을 어림잡을 수 있었다.

My public speaking teacher *assessed* me one dollar every time I ended a sentence with "Ya know?"

화술 교사는 내가 말 끝에 "Ya know?"를 붙일 때마다 1달러를 물게 했다.

ASSET [ǽset] n. a worthwhile object or quality that you possess   자산; 이점, 장점

While bravery is an honorable *asset* in any individual, sometimes cowardice is much more useful.
용감한 것은 누구에게나 훌륭한 장점이지만 가끔은 비겁한 것이 훨씬 더 유익할 때가 있다.

My ancient Greek coin, one of only three in the world, was definitely my most valuable *asset*, even though no one else could tell that it was valuable.
내게 있는 고대 그리스 주화는 전 세계에 있는 단 세 개 중의 하나로, 다른 사람은 아무도 귀중한지 모른다 해도 내겐 틀림없이 가장 귀중한 자산이다.

ASTRINGENT [əstríndʒənt] n. a cosmetic that cleans the skin and constricts the pores   수렴성 화장수, 아스트린젠트

The *astringent* I used to get rid of my pimples caused me to break out in an ugly purple rash.
여드름을 없애려고 사용한 아스트린젠트 때문에 보기 흉하게 보라색 뾰루지가 생겼다.

ATMOSPHERE [ǽtməsfiər] n. the mixture of gases that surround a planet and is held by gravity or the mood of a place   대기; 분위기

Scientists speculate that Mars once had an *atmosphere* like the Earth's, but something happened in the distant past to destroy almost all traces of it.
과학자들의 추측으로는, 화성에도 지구와 같은 대기가 있었는데, 먼 옛날 어떤 일이 일어나 거의 흔적도 없이 사라져 버렸다.

With its flashing lights, people in cages, and incredibly loud music, Zyggy's Fruit Stand had just the right *atmosphere* for our festive mood.
번쩍거리는 불빛, 자리에 앉아 있는 사람들, 엄청나게 시끄러운 음악이 어우러져 '지기스 프룻 스탠드'는 축제 분위기에 딱 들어맞는 분위기를 연출했다.

ATROPHY [ǽtrəfi] n. the wasting or withering away of parts of the body   위축, 쇠약, 퇴화

The severe frostbite caused Ellen's smallest toe to *atrophy*, although the rest of her foot remained healthy.
엘렌은 심한 동상에 걸려 다른 발가락들은 괜찮은데, 새끼발가락을 못 쓰게 됐다.

Janice was so lazy that her leg muscles *atrophied* to the point where she couldn't get up off the sofa without the help of a crane.
재니스는 너무 게을러 크레인의 도움 없이는 소파에서 일어설 수도 없을 지경으로 다리 근육이 위축돼 버렸다.

AUDIBLE [ɔ́:dəbl] adj. loud enough to be heard   들리는, 들을 수 있는

The signal coming from the radio tower in Antarctica was a little fuzzy but still *audible*.
남극대륙의 무전탑에서 송신되는 신호는 소리가 좀 탁하지만 그래도 들을 수 있었다.

Much to my dismay, Clumsy Clyde's whisper of "I love you" in my ear was *audible* to the entire class.
클럼지 클라이드가 내 귀에 대고 "사랑해" 하고 속삭인 것을 학급 아이들 전체가 듣는 바람에 너무나 당황했다.

AUTHENTIC [ɔ:θéntik] adj. genuine and true; not fake   진짜의, 진품의

The art expert concluded that the painting was an *authentic* Van Gogh and not a forgery.
미술품 전문가는 그 그림이 반 고흐의 진품이며 위조품이 아니라는 결론을 내렸다.

I thought I'd found an *authentic* copy of the Declaration of Independence in our attic, but then I noticed that it had the word "suckers" in it.
난 우리 집 다락방에서 진짜 독립선언서의 사본을 발견한 줄 알았는데, 가만 보니 그 안에 "잘 속는 사람들"이라는 단어가 있었다.

AVANT-GARDE [æ̀vant gárd/à-] *adj.* ahead of the times by being new and different, especially in the arts 전위적인, 첨단적인

A symphony composed of alarm clocks, airplane engines, and clanging pots and pans was too *avant-garde* for audiences in the 1920s.
자명종, 비행기 엔진, 땡그렁거리는 냄비 소리로 구성된 교향곡은 1920년대 청중에게는 너무 전위적이었다.

The popular *avant-garde* coffee shop served thimbles full of thick, weird coffee at fifty dollars per drop.
인기 있는 전위적 커피숍은 걸쭉하고 이상한 커피를 골무에 담아서 한방울에 50달러씩 팔았다.

AWE [ɔ:] *n.* a feeling of wonder usually felt in the presence of something magnificent or majestic 두려움, 경외

I felt an incredible sense of *awe* while standing at the edge of the Grand Canyon, and then my brother sneezed on my hiking boots.
그랜드캐니언의 절벽의 끝에 서 있자니 굉장한 경외심이 들었는데, 그때 오빠가 내 하이킹 부츠에 대고 재채기를 했다.

The other jugglers watched in *awe* as Jerry the Three-Handed Dude juggled thirty hacksaws at one time.
'세 손의 멋쟁이' 제리가 한번에 30개의 쇠톱을 들고 저글링할 때 다른 저글러들은 두려움을 느끼며 쳐다봤다.

AWRY [ərái] *adv.* turned or twisted out of shape 구부러져, 비뚤어져, 잘못되어

Eleanor called room service for an iron when she discovered that her evening gown was all *awry* after it had been stuffed in a suitcase for three weeks.
엘리노어는 이브닝 가운을 3주 동안 가방 속에 쑤셔 넣어 두어 온통 구겨져 있는 걸 보고는 다리미를 구하러 룸서비스를 불렀다.

My plans to skip school went *awry* when my mother saw my foot sticking out from under my bed.
학교를 땡땡이치려던 내 계획은 어머니가 침대 밑으로 삐져나와 있는 내 발을 보시는 바람에 실패로 돌아갔다.

B

BALEFUL [béilfəl] adj. evil or harmful; threatening or wretched and miserable 해로운, 악의 있는; 위협적인; 비참한, 불쌍한

The *baleful* look I received from the python told me that my idea to pick up the snake and hug it was not a good one.
비단뱀의 위협적인 표정을 보고, 뱀을 집어 들어 껴안으려는 내 생각은 좋은 게 아님을 알 수 있었다.

The child let out a *baleful* moan when the three scoops of chocolate ice cream slipped off the cone and fell into the dirt.
아이는 3단짜리 초콜릿 아이스크림이 콘에서 미끄러져 진흙 속에 떨어지자 불쌍하게 신음했다.

BALK [bɔːk] v. to stop in the middle of something and refuse to proceed 갑자기 서다

Much to the dismay of all the passengers, the pilot *balked* at landing the plane at the airport, and instead informed us that he was going to fly forever.
조종사가 공항에 비행기를 착륙시키던 중 갑자기 멈추더니 자신은 영원히 날아다닐 거라고 알리자 승객들은 모두 깜짝 놀랐다.

I was about to ask Richard to the dance, but I *balked* at the last minute and talked about particle physics instead.
나는 리처드에게 댄스파티에 가자고 말하려다가 마지막 순간에 생각을 바꿔서 소립자 물리학에 대해 얘기했다.

BANDY [bǽndi] v. to throw back and forth; to exchange 주고받다

The two political candidates *bandied* threats and insults most of the night, and then finally started swinging punches at each other.
두 후보는 그날 밤 거의 내내 위협과 모욕을 주고받더니, 마침내 주먹을 휘두르기 시작했다.

The crowd at the basketball game *bandied* around a giant beach ball, which kept falling into the court and interrupting the game.
농구 경기장 관중들이 커다란 비치볼을 서로 던졌는데, 공이 계속 코트로 떨어져 경기를 방해했다.

BEAM [biːm] v. to send a signal or to smile proudly 신호를 보내다; 밝게 미소 짓다

We used a large reflecting mirror and a Bic lighter to *beam* a message in Morse code to the rescue ship waiting in the harbor.
우리는 커다란 반사경과 빅 라이터를 이용해 항구에 정박해 있는 구조선에 모스 부호로 된 메시지를 보냈다.

Father *beamed* with pride when he learned that all three of his daughters had been accepted into Yale University, but when he found out the cost of its tuition, he cried.
아버지는 딸 셋 모두가 예일대에 합격했다는 사실을 알고 뿌듯한 미소를 지었지만, 등록금 액수를 알고 나자 울음을 터뜨렸다.

BEARING [béəriŋ] n. the way in which you walk or handle yourself or the knowledge of your general location (usually bearings) 태도; 방위

King Stephanouspolous carried himself with such regal *bearing* down the stairs that no one had the nerve to tell him that his pants were unzipped.
스테파누스폴러스 왕이 너무나 당당한 태도로 계단을 내려왔기 때문에 아무도 감히 그의 바지 지퍼가 열렸다고 말할 용기를 내지 못했다.

After we got our *bearings* from the mountain peak and the angle of the shadows, we knew we could find our campground again.
우리는 산꼭대기와 그림자의 각도로 우리의 방위를 파악하고 나자 캠프장을 다시 찾을 수 있다는 걸 알았다.

BELLOW [bélou] v. to yell in a deep voice 고함지르다, 호통 치다

The foreman at the cheese factory had to *bellow* in order to be heard over the loud noises coming from the huge cheese-shaping machines.
치즈 공장의 주임은 치즈의 모양을 뜨는 거대한 기계들에서 나오는 시끄러운 소음을 뚫고 목소리가 들리도록 하기 위해 고함을 질러야 했다.

To me, the love call of a walrus sounds more like the *bellow* of a drunken sailor than a romantic love song, but then again I'm not a walrus.
내가 듣기에 해마의 러브콜은 로맨틱한 러브송이라기보다는 술 취한 선원의 고함소리 같지만, 어쨌든 난 해마는 아니다.

BERTH [bə:rθ] n. a built-in bed on a ship or a train (배나 기차의) 침대

The train did not have enough *berths* for all the passengers who wanted to sleep, so I was forced to take a nap in the luggage compartment.
열차에는 잠을 자려는 승객 모두에게 돌아갈 침대가 충분치 않아서, 난 어쩔 수 없이 수하물 칸에서 선잠을 자야 했다.

BESIEGE [bisí:dʒ] v. to surround a city in order to conquer it; to swamp or overwhelm (도시를) 포위하다; 쇄도하다, 압도하다

The invaders *besieged* the city of Carthage and vowed to keep fighting until all their demands were met.
침략자들은 카르타고를 포위하고 그들의 모든 요구가 충족될 때까지 싸울 것을 맹세했다.

Our office was *besieged* with phone calls after a local news station reported that we were giving away free turkeys for Thanksgiving.
지역 방송국이 우리 회사에서 추수감사절용 칠면조를 무상으로 배포한다고 보도하자 사무실에 전화가 쇄도했다.

BESTOW [bistóu] v. to present a gift or honor (선물이나 영예를) 주다, 수여하다

The National Committee of Birdwatchers *bestowed* the Grand Hoot Prize on Dr. Feldspar for his achievements in owl stalking.
'조류관찰 전국 동호회'는 올빼미를 몰래 추적한 공로로 펠드스파 박사에게 '훌륭한 올빼미 상'을 수여했다.

In honor of the time she spent there in college, Lydia *bestowed* a gift of $50,000 on Zubazz University.
리디아는 자신이 대학에서 보낸 시간을 영예롭게 생각해 주바즈 대학에 5만달러 상당의 선물을 제공했다.

BEWILDER [biwíldər] v. to confuse greatly 당황하게 하다, 어리둥절하게 하다

The skinny, short taxi driver was *bewildered* when fourteen different people approached him and asked if he was Arnold Schwarzenegger.
비쩍 마르고 키가 작은 택시 운전기사는 14명의 각각 다른 사람이 자신에게 다가와 아놀드 슈워제네거가 아니냐고 묻자 어리둥절했다.

We *bewildered* our dog by spinning her around in circles while shining a strobe light at her and playing industrial music. Obviously, we were bored.

우리 집 개에게 플래시 라이트를 비추고 전자악기 음악을 연주하면서 주위를 뱅뱅 돌자 개는 어쩔 줄 몰라했다. 우린 정말 따분했었다.

BIAS [báiəs] n. a personal leaning or point of view in one direction or v. to cause to have bias or be biased 성향, 편견 / 한쪽으로 치우치게 하다, 편견을 갖게 하다

Since she was unable to overcome her *bias* against livestock, Griselda was fired from her job as a cowgirl.

그리셀다는 가축에 대한 편견을 극복할 수 없어서 소몰이자리에서 해고됐다.

We suspect some sort of *bias* on the part of our teacher, because all the girls in my class receive As and all the boys fail.

우리 반 선생님에게 일종의 편견이 있는 게 아닌가 의심스럽다. 여자아이들은 모두 A를 맞고 남자아이들은 전부 낙제했기 때문이다.

The Texan judges were *biased* against all the contestants from New York City.

텍사스 주의 심사 위원들은 뉴욕 시에서 온 대회참가자들 모두에게 편견을 가졌다.

BIPARTISAN [baipá:rtəzn] adj. made up of two political parties 2당의

The *bipartisan* committee was able to write up a contract that was satisfactory to both the Democrats and the Republicans.

2당 위원회는 민주당원과 공화당원 모두에게 만족스러운 계약서를 작성할 수 있었다.

It was going to be another strictly *bipartisan* election until Pete Newlywick, the world's wealthiest man, decided to run as an independent candidate.

또다시 완전한 2당 선거가 치러질 뻔했는데, 세계 최고의 갑부 피트 뉼리윅이 무소속 후보로 출마하겠다고 나섰다.

BLASÉ [blɑːzéi] adj. bored or uninterested due to constant exposure 지루한, 무관심한

The fans screamed wildly after Ponsky hit the home run, but the *blasé* expression on the sports announcer's face did not change at all.

폰스키가 홈런을 치자 팬들은 미친 듯이 소리를 질렀는데, 아나운서의 지루한 표정은 전혀 변함이 없었다.

During the climactic end of the movie, when most of the audience was cheering wildly, the *blasé* movie critic got up to get a root beer.

영화의 절정이 끝나갈 때 대부분의 관객들은 미친 듯 갈채를 보냈지만 시큰둥한 영화평론가는 일어나더니 루트비어를 마시러 갔다.

BLEARY [blíəri] adj. blurred and indistinct, usually by tears; fuzzy and vague (눈물, 피로 등으로) 흐려진; 흐릿한, 모호한

Stephon's *bleary* eyes and rumpled clothes were evidence that he had not slept for the past five days.

스티본의 흐려진 두 눈과 구겨진 옷은 그가 지난 5일간 잠을 못 이루었다는 증거였다.

The chocolate stains left on the map by my little brother made the directions so *bleary* that I soon got lost.

남동생이 지도에 묻혀 놓은 초콜릿 얼룩 때문에 방향이 아주 흐릿해져서 나는 곧 길을 잃었다.

BLOAT [blout] v. to swell up 부풀다

Eating an entire large triple-decker combo pizza all by myself caused my stomach to *bloat* and my belt to break.

3층짜리 라지 콤보 피자 한 판을 혼자서 다 먹었더니 배가 볼록 튀어나와 벨트가 끊어졌다.

Our schnauzer Rex became *bloated* immediately after eating the Alka-Seltzer tablets someone had left on the bathroom counter.

우리집 슈나우처 강아지 렉스는 누군가 욕실 카운터 위에 놓아둔 위장약을 먹고 나더니 곧바로 통통 부어올랐다.

BLOCKADE [blɑkéid/blɔk-] v. to surround a place so that nothing can get in or out 봉쇄하다, 차단하다 / 봉쇄

The army of intelligent rats tried to *blockade* the city so that no news of their revolution could escape, but some cats escaped with the news anyway.

총명한 쥐 군대는 그들의 혁명에 대한 소식이 새나가지 못하도록 도시를 봉쇄하려 했지만, 몇몇 고양이가 어떻게든 도망쳐서는 소식을 전했다. 도망쳤다.

The *blockade* of Tyre soon caused a massive shortage of food within the city.

티루스의 봉쇄는 이내 도시 내의 심각한 식량 부족을 가져왔다.

BOG [bɑg/bɔ(:)g] v. to be slowed down or hindered or n. a damp, muddy place filled with decaying plants, somewhat like a swamp 지체되다, 방해받다 / 습지, 늪

I got so *bogged* down by reading the hundreds of footnotes in Henry's research paper that I forgot what the paper itself was about.

헨리의 논문에 달린 수백 개 달린 각주를 읽느라 자꾸 흐름이 끊겨 논문 자체가 무슨 내용인지 잊어버릴 정도였다.

Our tennis shoes were so slimy after walking across the *bog* that we had to just throw them away.

우리의 테니스 신발은 늪을 가로질러 걷고 난 뒤 진흙투성이가 돼 그냥 내버려야 했다.

BOMBARD [bɑmbáːrd/bɔm-] v. to continuously strike at a place, usually using some kind of explosive; to fire at repeatedly 포격하다, 폭격하다; 퍼붓다

During World War II, citizens of London hid underground while German planes *bombarded* the city above.

제2차 세계대전 동안 런던 시민들은 독일군 비행기들이 공중에서 도시에 폭격을 가하자 지하로 숨었다.

My teacher *bombarded* me with so many different questions that I instantly regretted having raised my hand.

선생님이 내게 너무 많은 질문을 퍼부어서 난 곧바로 손을 들었던 걸 후회했다.

BORE [bɔːr] v. to drill into something, creating a hole (구멍을) 뚫다

Since he knew that there was oil underneath him, Donald was determined to *bore* into the earth until he discovered it.

도널드는 자기 밑에 석유가 있다는 걸 알고서 찾아낼 때까지 땅 속을 파기로 마음먹었다.

We *bored* holes into the flat piece of oak so we could place legs in them and create a table.

우리는 오크 판자에 구멍을 뚫고 그 안에 다리를 넣어 테이블을 만들었다.

BOUNTY [báunti] n. a reward for performing a special action or plentiful goods or wealth 사례금, 보상금; 풍부한 물건이나 재산

Once the millionaire offered a $10,000 *bounty* for the capture of the bluejay that stole her diamond necklace, people everywhere began climbing trees to look for it.

백만장자가 자신의 다이아몬드 목걸이를 훔쳐 간 큰어치를 포획하면 만 달러를 사례하겠다고 하자 도처의 사람들이 그것을 찾으려고 나무에 기어오르기 시작했다.

The peanut crops this year yielded so much *bounty* that we knew we would be able to eat peanut butter and jelly sandwiches for the rest of our lives.
올해 땅콩 수확량이 아주 많아서 앞으로 평생 동안 땅콩버터와 젤리 샌드위치를 먹을 수 있을 정도였다.

BOUQUET [boukéi/bu-] n. a group of flowers or a pleasant odor, especially from wine or liquor 꽃다발; (포도주 등의 특별한) 향

When he saw the wild flowers blooming by the roadside, Prakash stopped the car and picked a *bouquet* to give to his wife.
도로변에 활짝 핀 들꽃을 본 프래캐쉬는 차를 세우고는 아내에게 주려고 꽃 한 다발을 뽑았다.

The wine expert inhaled, enjoying the *bouquet* of the expensive champagne.
포도주 전문가는 값비싼 샴페인의 독특한 향을 음미하며 들이마셨다.

BRAMBLE [brǽmbl] n. a shrub or plant with many thorns 가시나무

I ripped my shirt in over thirty different places when I tried to walk into the *brambles* to retrieve my baseball.
야구공을 찾아오려고 가시나무 속으로 걸어 들어가려다 셔츠가 서른 군데 이상 찢어졌다.

The rabbit used to hide underneath the *brambles* where foxes couldn't go, until the real estate company sold the land and bulldozed the rabbit's hiding place.
토끼는 여우가 들어올 수 없는 가시나무 밑으로 몸을 숨기곤 했는데, 부동산 회사가 그 땅을 팔고 토끼의 은신처를 불도저로 파내버렸다.

BRETHREN [bréðrən] n. a group of relatives; associates within the same organization 친척; 같은 신자, 동료, 조합원, 동업자

The annual family picnic attracted so many of my *brethren* that we ran out of potato salad in under thirty minutes.
매년 갖는 가족 소풍에 하도 많은 친척이 와서 감자 샐러드가 30분도 안돼 동이 났다.

After Pinkerton and his work crew were fired unjustly, the rest of the miners went on strike in a show of support for their *brethren*.
핑커튼과 그의 반원 전체가 부당하게 해고당하자 나머지 광부들은 동료들에 대한 지지를 보여주기 위해 파업에 돌입했다.

BUCCANEER [bʌ̀kəníər] n. a pirate 해적

When the *buccaneers* had stormed the ship and taken the regular crew hostage, they stole all the rum that they could carry.
해적들은 배를 습격하고 정규 승무원들을 인질로 잡아 둔 다음 가져갈 수 있는 술을 모조리 훔쳐 갔다.

When I was young I heard the call of the sea and wanted to be a fierce *buccaneer*, but I ended up being an accountant instead.
난 어렸을 때 바다가 부르는 소리를 듣고 사나운 해적이 되고 싶었지만, 결국엔 그 대신 회계사가 되었다.

BUNGALOW [bʌ́ŋgəlòu] n. a small cottage with only one story 방갈로(자그마한 목조 단층집)

I left my *bungalow* on the beach and moved into a mansion after I won the lottery.
난 복권에 당첨된 다음 해변의 방갈로를 떠나 대저택으로 이사했다.

We thought the *bungalow* in the middle of the forest was a perfect spot to relax, but we soon found out that a family of three bears had leased the property through the summer.
우린 숲 한가운데에 있는 방갈로가 완벽한 휴양지라고 생각했는데, 이내 알고 보니 곰 세 마리 가족이 여름 내내 그 곳을 임대했었다.

BURLY [bə́ːrli] adj. very stocky and muscled   탄탄하고 근육질인, 체구가 억센

The *burly* police officer enjoyed towing away cars with his bare hands and a piece of rope.
억센 체구의 경찰관은 맨손과 밧줄 하나로 차를 견인하는 걸 재미있어했다.

The last time David started a fight, his *burly* opponent threw him out a window.
데이빗이 최근에 일으킨 싸움에서 그의 억센 상대가 데이빗을 창 밖으로 던져버렸다.

BURNISH [bə́ːrniʃ] v. to rub a surface until it's smooth and shiny   닦다, 광내다

Grandpa used to *burnish* his favorite brass spittoon so much that we could easily see our reflections in it.
할아버지는 당신이 아끼는 놋쇠 타구를 너무 열심히 광내서 우리 얼굴이 그대로 비칠 정도였다.

The marble banister was *burnished* by the many hands that slid along it over the years.
대리석 난간은 수년 동안 계단을 오르내리는 손들로 문질러져 빤질빤질 윤이 났다.

BUSTLE [bʌ́sl] v. to hurry around; to walk around busily or n. lots of activity   서두르다: 부산하게 움직이다 / 야단법석, 소란

Eager to impress his new neighbors, Charles *bustled* around the kitchen for an entire afternoon preparing his favorite dish, Mongolian Clams.
찰스는 새로운 이웃 사람들에게 좋은인상을 심어주려고 자신이 제일 좋아하는 요리, 몽고 대합조개를 준비하느라 오후 내내 정신없이 부엌을 왔다갔다했다.

The boss was greatly impressed by the *bustle* in the mail room, although in fact most people were simply hurriedly ordering lunch.
사장은 우편물실이 분주하자 크게 감동을 받았는데, 사실 그들 대부분은 그저 점심을 주문하느라 정신없었던 것이었다.

C

CACHE [kæʃ] n. a hidden supply of goods 감추어 둔 물건

I thought the attic would be a good place to hide my extra cookies, but some squirrels discovered my *cache* and ate them all.
난 다락방이 남은 쿠키를 숨기기에 적당한 장소라고 생각했는데, 청설모들이 감추어 둔 물건을 발견해 전부 먹어버렸다.

The rebels found the *cache* of arms that were hidden in the mountains by the government and used the weapons to shoot down birds for their lunch.
반역자들은 정부가 산속에 숨겨 둔 무기들을 찾아내 점심으로 먹을 새를 사냥하는 데 사용했다.

CACKLE [kǽkl] v. to laugh in a high-pitched, unpleasant manner 깔깔거리며 웃다

The woman *cackling* in the front row bothered the comedian so much that he refused to tell any more jokes.
앞줄에 앉아 깔깔거리는 여자 때문에 너무 짜증이 난 코미디언은 더이상 농담을 안 하려고 했다.

Kristin and John were happily married but had few friends because whenever they laughed, Kristin would *cackle* and John would snort.
크리스틴과 존은 행복한 결혼 생활을 했지만 친구는 별로 없었는데, 웃을 때마다 크리스틴은 낄낄거리고 존은 코웃음을 쳤기 때문이다.

CAJOLE [kədʒóul] v. to influence someone by using flattery or lies 감언이설로 속이다, 꾀다

We attempted to *cajole* our mother into letting us stay up late by telling her that she was undoubtedly the most perfect human being who ever existed.
우린 어머니에게 밤샘 허락을 받아 내려고 어머니가 이 세상에서 가장 완벽한 사람임에 틀림없다고 아첨을 했다.

The foreign exchange student *cajoled* the teacher into letting him bake souvlaki instead of taking the final exam.
외국인 교환학생은 교사를 꾀어 자신에게 학기말 시험을 치르게 하는 대신 수블라키 굽는 것을 시키도록 했다.

CANDIDATE [kǽndədèit/-dit] n. a person running for an award or political office 후보자

By informing voters that her opponent was no more than an ignorant clump of dirt, Laura Jackson proved that she was the better *candidate* in the race for Governor.
로라 잭슨은 유권자들에게 그녀의 경쟁 후보는 무식한 진흙 덩어리에 불과하다고 알리면서 자신이 더 나은 주지사 감임을 증명해 보였다.

Strangely enough, for once the *candidate* with the most political experience won the election instead of the candidate that had heaping bags of money to spend.
이상하게도 이번만은, 산더미 같은 돈자루가 있는 후보 대신 정치 경험이 가장 많은 후보가 당선되었다.

CANNY [kǽni] adj. careful and shrewd; cautious 신중한, 빈틈없는

The mouse in our kitchen had the *canny* ability to avoid all of the traps we'd set and still find food for its entire family.
우리 집 부엌의 쥐는 우리가 놓아둔 모든 덫을 신중하게 피해 갔고 여전히 자신의 가족에게 먹일 음식을 찾아낸다.

We took Bruce along on the camping trip with us because of his *canny* ability to always discover a source of fresh water.
우리는 캠핑 여행을 가면서 브루스를 데려갔는데, 신선한 물이 어디서 나오는지 어김없이 찾아내는 그의 빈틈없는 능력 때문이었다.

CARCASS [ká:rkəs] n. the remains of a dead animal 사체

Judging by the nasty smell coming from that raccoon *carcass*, I'd say the animal fought a wolf about two days ago and lost.
미국 너구리의 사체에서 풍기는 역겨운 냄새를 맡아보니, 그것은 이틀쯤 전에 이리와 싸움이 붙어서 패한 것 같다.

The *carcass* of the cow had been in the desert sun for so long that only its bones remained.
암소의 사체가 사막의 태양에 너무 오래 방치돼서 뼈밖에 남아 있지 않았다.

CATACLYSM [kǽtəklizm] n. a terrible disaster; a violent change in the earth 끔찍한 재난; 지각의 격변

The town of Greenville, California nicknamed itself "The Unluckiest Place on the Earth" after a series of *cataclysms*, including two earthquakes and a typhoon, hit the town in one summer.
캘리포니아 주의 그린빌은 한 여름에 두 차례의 지진과 한 차례의 태풍을 포함한 일련의 재앙이 마을을 강타하고 난 뒤 스스로 "지구상 가장 불행한 곳" 이란 별명을 붙였다.

The island of Krakatoa was destroyed by a *cataclysmic* volcanic eruption in 1883.
크라카토아 섬은 1883년 무시무시한 화산 폭발로 파괴되었다.

CAVALCADE [kæ̀vəlkéid] n. a procession of notable events or people 화려한 행렬, 퍼레이드

We decided to call our school talent show "The *Cavalcade* of Laughs," since every single student planned on doing a comedy routine.
우리 학교의 탤런트 쇼를 "웃음의 퍼레이드" 라 짓기로 했는데, 학생들 하나하나가 코미디 연기를 할 계획이었기 때문이다.

A colorful band of polka lovers danced down the streets behind the marching *cavalcade* of accordion players.
일단의 화려한 폴카 애호가들이 아코디언 연주자들의 행렬을 뒤따르며 거리에서 춤을 추었다.

CAVORT [kəvɔ́:rt] v. to jump and leap about playfully 신나게 뛰놀다

When we learned that school had been canceled for two weeks, my friends and I rushed outside to *cavort* in the waist-high snow.
친구들과 나는 2주 동안 휴교된다는 사실을 알고 허리까지 올라오는 눈 속에서 뛰어놀기 위해 밖으로 뛰쳐나갔다.

Our family *cavorted* in the cool waters of the Pacific Ocean until someone yelled "shark!"
우리 가족이 태평양의 시원한 물속에서 신나게 헤엄치고 있을 때 누군가 "상어다!" 하고 소리쳤다.

CELESTIAL [səléstʃəl] adj. having to do with the stars or sky 하늘의, 천체의

According to my astrologist, whenever three *celestial* objects - for instance, Mars, Jupiter, and Venus - line up, I'll break out with acne.
점성가 말에 따르면 세 개의 천체, 예를 들면 화성, 목성, 금성 같은 것이 한 줄로 늘어서게 되면 내 몸에 여드름이 솟는다고 한다.

Early sailors used *celestial* navigation to find their way around the oceans.
초기의 선원들은 대양에서 진로를 찾기 위해 천문 항법을 이용했다.

CEREMONY [sérəmòuni/-məni] n. a formal activity performed in honor of a specific occasion 의식, 식

The *ceremony* for the opening of the new supermarket was attended by the mayor, the supermarket manager, and five townspeople who had nothing better to do that day.
새로 문을 연 슈퍼마켓의 개장식에는 시장과 슈퍼마켓 점장, 그리고 그 날 별달리 할 일이 없는 마을 주민 다섯 명이 참석했다.

The wedding *ceremony* was going along very well until the groom's tuxedo caught on fire and had to be extinguished with the contents of the punch bowl.
결혼식은 아주 잘 진행이 되다가 신랑 턱시도에 불이 붙는 바람에 펀치 볼에 담겨 있던 물을 부어서 꺼야했다.

CHAR [tʃɑːr] v. to burn until reduced to charcoal or to burn a little 숯으로 만들다, 까맣게 태우다

The fire from the sentence above *charred* the groom's dress pants and transformed them into blackened dress shorts.
위의 문장에서 나온 불이 신랑의 예복 바지를 까맣게 태워서 새까만 예복 반바지로 바꾸어버렸다.

The hot dog had been *charred* so badly in the fire that I could eat it only after coating it in mustard.
핫도그가 불에 너무 심하게 타서 겨자를 바른 후에야 먹을 수 있었다.

CHARISMA [kərízmə] n. an exceptional ability to be liked and admired by a great number of people 카리스마, 남을 끌어당기는 강한 매력, 비범한 지도력

Once the employees learned that their pension money had been stolen by their boss, even his famous *charisma* could not save him from their wrath.
사장이 직원들의 연금을 횡령했다는 사실이 알려지자 그의 대단한 카리스마도 그들의 분노에서 그를 구해낼 수 없었다.

Even though she wasn't the smartest girl in school, Adelaide had such *charisma* that she easily won the election for student council president.
아들레이드는 학교에서 가장 똑똑한 여학생은 아니었지만 카리스마가 대단해 학생회 의장 선거에서 쉽게 당선됐다.

CHERISH [tʃériʃ] v. to value highly; to affectionately care for 애지중지하다, 고이 간직하다; 정성껏 돌보다

Although I had *cherished* my baseball card collection for many years, when a businessman offered me two million dollars for it, I sold it instantly.
나는 야구 카드 수집한 것을 수년 동안 고이 간직해 왔지만, 한 사업가가 내게 2백만 달러를 제의하자 즉시 팔았다.

Thelma and Louise *cherished* the friendship they had built by playing baseball together.
델마와 루이스는 함께 야구 경기를 하며 쌓아온 우정을 소중히 여겼다.

CHIDE [tʃaid] v. to scold 꾸짖다

Natalie *chided* her friend Rachel for setting her up with Teddy "The Spaz" Zubazz without first asking her if she was interested in him.
나탈리는 친구 레이첼을 나무랐는데, 자기한테 "스파즈"라고 불리는 테디 주바즈를 어떻게 생각하는지 물어보지도 않고 그와의 소개팅을 주선해줬기 때문이다.

When they finally saw his apartment at college, John's parents *chided* him for not cleaning the dishes in over three years.
존의 부모님은 마침내 존의 대학 아파트를 보시고는 그가 3년 넘도록 설거지를 하지 않은 것을 꾸짖으셨다.

CHRISTEN [krísn] v. to name at a Christian baptism; to name for the first time   세례명을 주다; 이름을 붙이다

Once the child had been dipped in the sacred water, the priest *christened* him "Newton Sigfrinnius IV."
신부는 아이가 성수에 몸을 담그고 나자 "뉴튼 지그프리니우스 4세"라는 세례명을 주었다.

Just before the freak hurricane wiped out the entire waterfront, the brand new yacht had been *christened* "The Invincible."
미친 듯한 허리케인이 해안 지역 전체를 휩쓸기 바로 직전 갓 들여온 요트에는 "무적"이라는 이름이 붙여졌다.

CHRONOLOGICAL [krɑ̀nəládʒikəl/krɔ̀nəlɔ́dʒ-] adj. arranged according to time of occurrence, from earliest to latest   연대순의, 시간 순의

Unless you read them in *chronological* order, the seven books in the Dark Lord of Emnon series can be very confusing.
'Dark Lord of Emnon' 시리즈는 일곱 권을 연대순으로 읽지 않으면 아주 혼란스러울 수 있다.

Once the detectives had figured out the *chronological* order of the night's events, they instantly knew who the real killer was.
탐정들은 그날 밤 사건들의 시간 순서를 밝혀내자 진짜 살인자가 누구인지 바로 알 수 있었다.

CINDERS [síndər] n. something burned down to the point where it can't be burned anymore; ashes   재

Following Dawn's cruel prank, all I had left of my Snooky Bear was a pile of *cinders* that I kept in jar.
돈의 잔혹한 장난을 따라하고 나니 내 스누키 베어에 남은 것은 병 속에 담겨진 잿더미뿐이었다.

We shoveled the *cinders* out of the fireplace and placed them in the garden as fertilizer.
우리는 벽난로의 재를 삽으로 떠다가 비료로 쓰려고 정원에 두었다.

CIRCULATE [sə́:rkjulèit] v. to move around freely or to spread widely   여기저기 돌아다니다; 널리 퍼지다

With my fake mustache, blonde wig, and dark sunglasses, I was able to *circulate* throughout the party without being recognized by my friends.
가짜 콧수염을 붙이고 금발 가발에 까만 선글라스를 쓰자 파티 내내 친구들한테 들키지 않고 맘껏 돌아다닐 수 있었다.

Rumors *circulated* throughout the town that the new mayor was actually an alien, but everyone soon learned that she was just a big Star Trek fan.
새로 부임한 시장이 사실은 외계인이라는 소문이 마을 전체에 퍼졌는데, 알고 보니 그녀는 그저 스타트렉의 열렬한 팬이었다.

CIRCUMSTANTIAL [sə̀:rkəmstǽnʃəl] adj. not of main importance   부수적인

I got a D on my essay about Albert Einstein because I focused on *circumstantial* facts like his crazy hairstyle and love of wontons and didn't mention any of his important scientific breakthroughs.
나는 알버트 아인슈타인에 대한 에세이에서 D를 맞았는데, 그의 미치광이 같은 머리 모양과 중국식 만두를 좋아했다는 등의 부수적인 사실에만 초점을 맞추고 그의 중요한 과학적 발견은 전혀 언급하지 않았기 때문이다.

[Note] *Circumstantial evidence* refers to facts offered as evidence in a trial from which jurors are supposed to draw conclusions and make decisions. Circumstantial evidence is not direct proof.
circumstantial evidence는 재판에서 결론이나 판단을 이끌어내는 간접적인 추정 증거, 즉 '정황 증거'를 말하며, 직접적인 증거는 아니다.

- The prosecution offered plenty of *circumstantial evidence* – such as the fact that Evans owned a shotgun and the victim had been killed by a shotgun – but the jury found him innocent because there was no solid proof that he was guilty.
  검찰 당국은 에반스가 엽총을 가지고 있고 희생자가 엽총으로 사살됐다는 등의 많은 정황 증거를 제시했지만, 배심원단은 그가 유죄라는 확실한 증거가 없기 때문에 무죄 평결을 내렸다.

CITE [sait] v. to quote as an example or to mention as a reward for honorable action 인용하다, 예증하다; 표창하다

In an attempt to lessen his punishment, Brandon *cited* his previous punishment for not doing the dishes, which was only one day without TV.
브랜든은 벌을 덜 받기 위해 지난 번 설거지를 안 해서 벌 받은 것을 인용했는데, 그때는 단 하루 TV를 보지 못했다.

The captain *cited* the brave sailor as having courageously wrestled the shark while the other crewmen swam for the lifeboats.
선장은 용감한 선원을 표창했는데, 다른 선원들은 모두 구명보트를 향해 헤엄쳐 가는데 그는 용감하게도 상어와 맞붙어 싸웠기 때문이다.

CLARIFY [klǽrəfai] v. to make something easier to understand; to explain in greater detail 명백하게 하다; 아주 자세히 설명하다

After our mother had *clarified* the directions for changing the oil in the car, the task became much easier to do and far less messy.
어머니가 자동차 오일 교환하는 방법을 아주 확실하게 설명해 주신 후로 그 일이 훨씬 더 쉽고 훨씬 덜 귀찮은 일이 됐다.

We asked our teacher to *clarify* his directions on the final exam because he had only written, "Tell me everything."
우린 선생님에게 기말 시험 문제를 자세히 설명해 달라고 요구했는데, 선생님은 "모든 걸 얘기하시오"라고만 써 놓았기 때문이다.

CLINCHER [klíntʃər] n. the final, decisive act or point 결정적인 행동이나 요인, 결정타

Several things led me to believe that Brandy had eaten my grape-flavored Popsicle, the fact that her tongue was purple was the *clincher*.
몇 가지 점으로 미루어 브랜디가 내 포도맛 아이스케이크를 먹었다고 믿게 됐는데, 그녀의 혀가 자주색인 것이 결정적 요인이었다.

The *clincher* in the Super Bowl was when DuPont "Scrappy" Carruthers returned a kickoff 97 yards.
수퍼볼에서의 결정타는 "스크래피"라 불리는 듀폰 캐러더스가 97야드의 킥오프를 되받아 찬 것이었다.

CLUTTER [klʌ́tər] n. a bunch of things scattered around in a mess or v. to fill up in a way that stops movement or action 어지러이 흩어져 있는 것, 난잡함 / 무질서하게 채우다, 메우다

I was unable to find my baseball glove in the *clutter* underneath my bed, but I did discover a three-year-old sandwich that I'd lost.
침대 밑 어질러져 있는 데서 야구 글러브를 찾을 수 없었지만, 3년 전에 잃어버렸던 샌드위치를 발견했다.

So many people were *cluttering* the exit to the movie theater that we decided to sit down and watch all the credits.
너무 많은 사람이 극장 출구를 메우고 있어서 우린 앉아서 클로징 크레딧 자막까지 다 보기로 했다.

COALITION [kòuəlíʃən] n. a group of people acting together for a specific goal 연합, 제휴

The sewer workers formed a *coalition* in order to demand higher pay and thicker boots.
하수 설비공들은 임금 인상과 더 두꺼운 부츠를 요구하기 위해 연합을 만들었다.

The *Coalition* for Better Education was an assortment of teachers, parents, and community leaders who demanded more funding for public education.
'나은 교육을 위한 연합'은 공교육에 더 많은 기금을 줄 것을 요구하는 교사, 학부모, 그리고 공동체 지도자의 모임이었다.

COAX [kouks] v. to gently persuade 구슬리다

After a week of discussion, I finally *coaxed* my parents into letting me go on a camping trip with my friends.
일주일간 토의한 끝에 마침내 부모님을 구슬려 친구들과 캠핑 여행가는 걸 허락받았다.

By placing cat treats in the middle of the room, I was able to *coax* the kitten out from under the sofa.
방 한가운데 고양이 스낵을 놓아서 새끼 고양이가 소파 밑에서 나오도록 꾀드길 수 있었다.

COHERENT [kouhíərənt] adj. easily understood; connected logically 분명한, 명쾌한; 조리가 서는

Once the gag had been removed from his mouth, the rescued prisoner was able to speak in a *coherent* manner.
입에 물려 있던 재갈을 빼자 구조된 포로는 알아듣게 얘기할 수 있었다.

The feverish patient kept blurting out sentences that were not *coherent*.
열이 오른 환자는 계속 조리가 서지 않는 말들을 했다.

COMBUSTION [kəmbʌ́stʃən] n. the act of burning 연소

The car's *combustion* problems were soon traced to the fact that it was out of gasoline.
차의 연소 문제는 알고 보니 휘발유가 떨어져서였다.

In an amateur science experiment, we learned that the *combustion* of firewood is not as smelly and nasty as the burning of plastic.
우리는 아마추어 과학 실험을 통해 장작의 연소는 플라스틱을 태우는 것만큼 냄새가 지독하고 고약하지 않다는 걸 알게됐다.

COMELY [kʌ́mli] adj. attractive and pleasant 미모의, 잘생긴

The *comely* and smiling faces of the Everly triplets soon made me happy that I was in Mrs. Willenbring's class.
내가 있던 윌렌브링 선생님 반에 잘 생기고 생긋 웃는 얼굴의 에벌리 가의 세 쌍둥이가 들어와서 금세 기분이 좋아졌다.

At our school's Thanksgiving dance, the *comely* lad had more than his fair share of willing dance partners.
학교 추수감사절 댄스파티에서 잘 생긴 녀석에게는 그와 댄스 파트너가 되려는 여학생들이 불공평할 정도로 많았다.

COMMISSION [kəmíʃən] v. to grant authority to someone or some group for a specific purpose or n. a group of people granted the authority to do something 위임하다, 권한을 주다 / 위원회

The president *commissioned* a panel of chefs to review the contents of all Italian foods after a plate of spaghetti attacked a group of waiters in Atlanta.
대통령은 애틀랜타에서 스파게티를 먹은 웨이터들이 탈이 난 이후로 요리사단을 위임해 모든 이탈리아 음식에 대해 내용물을 자세히 살피도록 했다.

The Italian Food *commission* soon discovered that the combination of low-fat cheese and garlic was bringing out a violent streak in several traditional dishes.
이탈리아 음식위원회는 곧 저지방 치즈와 마늘의 결합이 몇몇 전통 음식에서 잇따라 배탈을 일으켰다는 걸 알아냈다.

COMMUNAL [kəmjúːnl/kámju-/kɔ́mju-] adj. related to or serving every person in the community (공동체, 집단 등에서) 공동의

The waitstaff at the coffee shop had a *communal* tip jar, which they emptied and split evenly every night.
커피숍의 웨이터들은 공동의 팁 단지가 있었는데, 매일 밤 비워서 똑같이 나누어 가졌다.

On July Fourth, our town holds a huge *communal* picnic, for which everyone brings one dish of food.
우리 마을에서는 7월 4일에 성대한 전체 피크닉을 가는데, 각자 음식 한 그릇씩을 가져온다.

COMPATIBLE [kəmpǽtəbl] adj. able to exist or work together in the same system 양립할 수 있는, 잘 맞는; 호환성의

We quickly realized that the three-pronged electrical plug was not at all *compatible* with our two-pronged wall socket.
세 가닥 전기 플러그가 우리 집의 두 가닥 짜리 벽 소켓에는 맞지 않는다는 걸 금방 알게 됐다.

The software was not *compatible* with my computer, so when I tried to run it, the whole system crashed.
소프트웨어는 내 컴퓨터와 호환되지 않아, 실행시켜 보려고 하자 시스템 전체가 고장나 버렸다.

Sam and Sylvia were such *compatible* dance partners that they moved as a graceful unit.
샘과 실비아는 댄스 파트너로 너무나 잘 맞아서 한 몸처럼 우아하게 움직였다.

COMPUTE [kəmpjúːt] v. to work toward a solution through the use of math or a computer (수학이나 컴퓨터로) 계산하다, 산정하다

Using his knowledge of physics and gravity, the scientist was able to *compute* the location at which the satellite would hit the Earth.
과학자는 물리와 중력에 대한 지식을 이용해 인공위성이 지구와 충돌하게 될 지점을 산정해 낼 수 있었다.

The automated teller machine at my bank instantly *computes* how much money I have left in my account after each withdrawal I make.
은행의 현금인출기는 인출을 할 때마다 내 계좌에 잔고가 얼마 남았는지 즉시 계산해낸다.

CONCEDE [kənsíːd] v. to give in; to surrender or to grudgingly admit that something is true 양보하다, 포기하다; (마지못해) 인정하다

Our team was forced to *concede* the football game after our quarterback ran home bawling for his mommy.
우리 팀은 쿼터백이 엄마를 찾아 엉엉 울며 집으로 뛰어가 버려 미식축구 경기를 포기할 수밖에 없었다.

Seconds before the firing squad was going to shoot, the general *conceded* that he had made some mistakes during his career.
장군은 총살대가 사살하기 몇 초 전에 자신의 군 생활에서 몇 가지 실수를 했음을 인정했다.

CONCOCTION [kɑnkɑ́kʃən/kənkɔ́k-] n. a mixture of different ingredients 혼성, 조합

While in the kitchen, Herb made a *concoction* of olive oil, molasses, grape juice, and tobacco, and then served it to us claiming that it was cola.
허브는 부엌에서 올리브 오일, 당밀, 포도 주스, 담배를 섞은 다음, 콜라라고 하면서 우리에게 내놓았다.

The powerful chemical *concoction* destroys mildew on contact, but unfortunately it also eats through porcelain and enamel.
그 강력한 화학물질에 닿기만 하면 곰팡이는 죽지만 안타깝게도 자기와 에나멜까지 먹어치워 버린다.

CONDESCEND [kɑ̀ndəsénd/kɔ̀n-] v. to willingly do something that is beneath a person's dignity or to act in a way that shows you think you are better than others 자기를 낮추다, 겸손하게 굴다; 우월감을 갖고 대하다, 생색을 내다

The Nobel Peace Prize winner *condescended* to clean up the auditorium after the awards ceremony.
노벨평화상 수상자는 겸손하게도 시상식이 끝난 뒤 강당을 말끔히 청소했다.

Thurston is a great wrestler, but his teammates do not appreciate the way he *condescends* to them by constantly explaining what it means to be a champion.
서스턴은 훌륭한 레슬러긴 하지만, 같은 팀 사람들은 그가 끊임없이 챔피언이 어떤 것이냐에 대해 설명하면서 우쭐해 하는 걸 좋아하지 않는다.

CONFIDANT [kɑ́nfədænt/-dɑ̀:nt/kɔ́nfidæ̀nt] n. someone that you tell all your secrets to 절친한 친구

The Silencers Club was a group of *confidants* that met in my treehouse after school to discuss all the juicy gossip we had learned that day.
'침묵시키는 사람들 클럽' 은 방과 후에 그 날 들은 흥미진진한 가십들을 나누기 위해 나무 위의 집에 모였던 절친한 친구들의 모임이었다.

You can imagine my dismay when I learned that Sheryl, my *confidant* since grade school, had been selling all my deepest secrets to the *National Tattler*.
초등학교 때부터 절친한 친구였던 세릴이 내 가장 깊숙한 비밀을 '내셔널 태틀러' 에 모두 팔아 넘겼다는 걸 알고 내가 얼마나 당황했을지 상상이 갈 것이다.

CONFIGURATION [kənfìgjuréiʃən] n. the way in which the parts of an object are fitted together 형상, 구성, 배열

By rearranging the *configuration* of his hands and fingers, Robert made the "bunny" shadow figure on the wall transform into a terrifying "Tyrannosaurus Rex."
로버트는 손과 손가락 모양을 바꾸어 벽에 비친 "토끼" 그림자 형상을 무서운 "티라노사우루스 렉스" 로 바꾸었다.

Because of the careful *configuration* of the boulders at the ancient monument of Stonehenge, some scientists believe it was used as a tool for charting the stars and seasons.
일부의 과학자들은 고대 유적 스톤헨지에 있는 둥근 돌들의 면밀한 배열을 보고 그것이 별과 절기의 도표를 만드는 도구로 사용됐다고 믿는다.

CONFINES [kɑ́nfainz/kɔ́n-] n. the border or limits of a particular space 경계, 범위

A suspicious family, the Alvertons protected the *confines* of their garden by placing land mines around the entire area and patrolling it with watch dogs.
의심 많은 앨버튼 가족은 그들의 정원 둘레 전체에 지뢰를 매설하고 감시견들을 데리고 순찰을 돌며 보호했다.

Limited to the *confines* of his cell, the prisoner decided to give up his life of crime and violence and learn to paint with watercolors.
독방에 감금된 죄수는 범죄와 폭력의 삶을 포기하고 수채화를 배우겠다고 결심했다.

CONFIRMATION [kɑ̀nfərméiʃən/kɔ̀n-] n. something that provides proof 확증, 증거, 증언

When they received the battered royal crown through the mail, the police had *confirmation* that the kidnappers had taken King Muekus XIII.
그들에게 우편으로 박살난 왕관이 배달되어 오자, 경찰은 유괴범들이 무에커스 13세를 납치했다는 확증을 얻었다.

Sylvia's bright orange tongue *confirmed* that she ate the rest of the orange-flavored Blow Pops from the icebox.
실비아의 선명한 오렌지 빛 혀는 그녀가 냉장고에서 오렌지 맛 '블로우 팝스' 남은 걸 꺼내 먹었다는 증거였다.

CONFOUND [kənfáund] v. to puzzle, confuse, or bewilder 당황하게 하다, 어리둥절하게 하다, 난처하게 하다

By switching between English, German, Japanese, and Hungarian throughout her speech, the speaker completely *confounded* her audience.
연설자는 연설하는 내내 영어, 독일어, 일어에 헝가리어까지 섞어서 쓰는 바람에 청중들은 완전히 어리둥절했다.

The more I learn about politics, the more *confounded* I get.
나는 정치학에 대해 공부하면 할수록 더 어리둥절해진다.

CONFRONTATION [kànfrəntéiʃən/kɔ̀n-] n. a direct encounter, especially with an opponent 직면, 대결

After his *confrontation* with Mike "Crusher" Smith, Gerald "Yahoo" Johnson announced that he was retiring from boxing immediately.
"야후"라 불리는 제럴드 존슨은 "크러셔"라 불리는 마이크 스미스와 대결한 직후 복싱계를 떠나겠다고 발표했다.

Since the Mongols had a larger army, better fighters, and better equipment, their *confrontation* with the Chinese army was short.
몽고인들에게는 더 큰 군대와 더 뛰어난 전사들과 더 나은 장비들이 갖추어져 있어 중국군과의 대결이 오래가지 않았다.

CONGEAL [kəndʒí:l] v. to thicken; to change from a liquid to a solid 두껍게 하다; 응고되다

As it started to cool down, the top layer of the Thanksgiving gravy *congealed*.
추수감사절용 육즙이 식기 시작하자 맨 위층이 응고됐다.

The milk was left on the counter for a many days and eventually *congealed* into a chunky mass that looked like cottage cheese but smelled much worse.
우유를 카운터 위에 여러 날 두었더니 결국 한 덩어리로 굳어졌는데, 모양은 희고 연한 치즈 같았지만 냄새는 훨씬 더 지독했다.

CONGENIAL [kəndʒí:njəl] adj. pleasant, open, and friendly or having similar habits and tastes 쾌활하고 친절한; 취미가 같은, 마음이 맞는

The neighborhood tax collector was so *congenial* that everyone on the block was glad to see her and give her their money.
그 동네 세금 징수원은 워낙 쾌활하고 친절해 그 블록의 사람들은 모두 그녀를 보고 세금 내는 것이 즐거웠다.

The *congenial* roommates Magnus and Mahmoud shared a passion for Greek music, Jackie Chan movies, and hand grenade collections.
매그너스와 마무드는 마음이 맞는 룸메이트 사이로, 그리스 음악, 성룡의 영화, 수류탄 수집에 함께 열광했다.

CONGREGATE [káŋgrigèit/kɔ́ŋ-] v. to assemble; to come together and form a crowd 모으다; 모이다, 군집하다

The whole town *congregated* in the town square when they heard that the two candidates for mayor were going to arm wrestle at 2:00 p.m.
두 명의 시장 후보가 오후 2시에 팔씨름을 한다는 소식을 듣고 읍민 전체가 읍광장에 모였다.

Before the football game, the pastor asked all the members of his church to *congregate* in the east end zone and pray for a swift victory.
미식축구 경기가 열리기 전 목사는 모든 신도에게 동쪽 끝 지역에 모여 속전속결을 위해 기도해 달라고 부탁했다.

CONJECTURE [kəndʒékt∫ər] v. to make a guess; to form an opinion based on incomplete knowledge or n. statement or opinion based on guesswork 추측하다; 어림짐작하다 / 어림짐작, 추측

Judging by the huge number of feathers left at the crime scene, the detectives *conjectured* that the millionaire was killed by a flock of pillow-wielding ducks.
형사들은 범죄 현장에 엄청난 수의 깃털이 남아 있는 것으로 미루어 백만장자는 베개를 휘두르는 오리떼에 의해 살해당했다고 추측했다.

Early *conjectures* about life on the moon were proved false when astronauts landed there.
달에 생명체가 있을 거라는 초기의 어림짐작은 우주비행사들이 그곳에 착륙하자 잘못된 것임이 밝혀졌다.

CONNOISSEUR [kànəsə́:r/-súər/kɔn-] n. a person who is an excellent judge in a specific field; an expert in a particular subject 감정가, 감식가; 전문가

The immense Marcel Roussaeu, a *connoisseur* of desserts, declared that Mrs. Finstin's Chocolate Fudge Dip was the greatest food he had ever tasted.
디저트 감식가인 거구의 마르셀 루소는 핀스틴 부인의 '초콜릿 퍼지 딥'이 그가 이제껏 먹어 본 음식 중 최고라고 말했다.

The *connoisseur* of early European paintings was shocked to find a painting by Giotto at a garage sale in Poughkeepsie, New York.
초기 유럽 회화의 전문가는 뉴욕 퍼킵시의 어느 차고 세일에서 조토의 그림을 발견하고는 깜짝 놀랐다.

CONSENSUS [kənsénsəs] n. an opinion or belief held by the majority of a group 여론, 의견일치

The governor was hoping for support for his plan to become the first King of Vermont, but the *consensus* among voters seemed to be that he was a raving lunatic.
주지사는 최초의 버몬트 왕이 되려는 자신의 계획을 지지해 주기 바랐지만, 유권자 사이의 여론은 그를 미치광이로 보는 것 같았다.

Since I had more brothers than sisters, the *consensus* among the children was that we would go to the wrestling match instead of the symphony.
나한테는 여자 형제보다 남자 형제가 많아서 우리는 교향곡을 들으러 가는 것보다는 레슬링 경기를 보러 가는 쪽으로 의견일치가 됐었다.

CONTENTIOUS [kəntén∫əs] adj. argumentative; easily bothered and ready to disagree 논쟁적인; 논쟁하기 좋아하는, 따지기 좋아하는

The *contentious* man asked me what time it was and then argued with me about whether or not my watch was accurate.
논쟁하기 좋아하는 남자는 나한테 몇 시냐고 묻더니 내 시계가 정확한지 아닌지에 대해 나와 논쟁을 벌었다.

When she argued my statement that the Earth was round, I knew that Sheryl was a *contentious* woman.
지구가 둥글다는 내 말에 셰릴이 논쟁을 벌이려 할 때 그녀가 따지기 좋아하는 여자라는 걸 알았다.

CONTRADICT [kàntrədíkt/kɔn-] v. to express the opposite of a statement; argue against an earlier remark or belief 반대하다, 부정하다; 반박하다

Innis knew it was rude to *contradict* people, but he had to protest when his friend started telling a story about how he had driven from California to Hawaii.
이니스는 사람들 말에 반박하는 것이 무례하다는 걸 알았지만, 그가 캘리포니아에서 하와이까지 어떻게 차를 몰았는지에 대해 친구가 이야기하기 시작하자 이의를 제기할 수밖에 없었다.

Phillip claimed that he loved to eat any kind of food but cornbread, but when he smelled the delicious yellow bread coming out of the oven, he *contradicted* himself and demanded a piece.
필립은 자기가 옥수수 빵만 빼고는 뭐든 잘 먹는다고 말해 놓고서는, 오븐에서 구워지는 향기로운 노란 빵의 냄새를 맡더니 자기 말을 부인하면서 한 조각 달라고 했다.

CONTRARY [kántreri/kóntrə-] adj. completely different; exactly opposite or unfavorable 완전히 다른, 정반대의; 불리한, 부적합한

"On the *contrary*, Watson. Although you thought I was in London, I was in fact on the other side of the world!" exclaimed Holmes.
"정반대네, 왓슨. 자네는 내가 런던에 있다고 생각했지만, 사실 난 지구 정반대에 있었다구!" 홈즈가 소리쳤다.

Even though the hurricane was still two hundred miles away, it created weather conditions that were too *contrary* for us to sail in.
허리케인이 아직은 2백 마일 거리에 있었지만 항해를 하기에는 부적합한 기상 상태였다.

CONTRITION [kəntríʃən] n. deep regret for doing something wrong 깊은 후회

Hera doubted that her brother's *contrition* was real since he burst into giggles whenever he looked at her.
헤라는 오빠가 자신을 쳐다볼 때마다 낄낄거렸기 때문에 깊이 후회한다는 게 진심일까 의심스러웠다.

[Note] *Contrite* [kəntráit/kántrait/kóntrait] adj. means sorry or regretful
contrite는 '깊이 뉘우치는'

■ At his trial, the robber seemed *contrite* for having taken part in the holdup of 343 different banks.
강도는 재판을 받는 중에, 자신이 343건의 은행털이에 가담했던 걸 깊이 후회하는 듯했다.

CONTROVERSY [kántrəvə̀:rsi] n. a public dispute between two sides who have opposing views 논쟁, 논의

The city decided to hold an open debate with the hope that it would settle the *controversy* surrounding higher taxes.
시에서는 세금 인상을 둘러싼 논쟁이 해결되리라는 기대를 가지고 공개 토론을 열기로 결정했다.

Prince's album *Controversy* created a lot of controversy because of the racy lyrics in many of the songs.
프린스의 앨범 'Controversy' 는 여러 노래의 음란한 가사 때문에 많은 논쟁을 일으켰다.

CONVENE [kənví:n] v. to assemble in one place 회합하다, 모이다

When their cars were complete, the soapbox Derby racers agreed to *convene* at the top of the mountain at sunrise.
어린이용 조립차 경주 참가자들은 그들의 자동차가 완성되자 해뜰 때에 산꼭대기에서 모이기로 했다.

Most of our neighbors *convened* for the block party when they heard that our family was providing free barbecue.
우리 집에서 바비큐를 무상으로 제공한다는 소문을 듣고 이웃 사람들 대부분이 블록 파티에 모여들었다.

CONVEY [kənvéi] v. to take from one place to another or to make something known or understood 나르다; 알리다

Henry rented a pick-up truck to help me *convey* my furniture to my new apartment.
헨리는 내가 새 아파트로 가구 나르는 걸 도와주기 위해 소형 트럭을 빌렸다.

The ambassador *conveyed* the deepest sympathies of his nation when he spoke at the funeral of the famous war general.
대사는 유명한 장군의 장례식에서 연설하면서 자신의 나라를 대표하여 깊은 애도를 표했다.

CONVICTION [kənvíkʃən]   n. a deeply held belief or opinion or a guilty judgment from a judge or jury   신념, 확신; 유죄판결

It is my *conviction* that long hair and earrings are fine for men, but my mother disagrees.
나는 남자들이 머리 기르고 귀고리 하는 게 좋다고 생각하지만, 우리 어머니는 동의하지 않으신다.

Because the accused was so obviously guilty, the jury returned a *conviction* in under ten minutes.
피고인은 너무나 명백한 유죄라서 배심원단은 10분도 안돼 유죄판결을 내렸다.

CONVOLUTED [kánvəlù:tid/kɔ́n-]   adj. difficult or complicated due to many twists and turns   뒤얽힌, 복잡한

Adele's *convoluted* scheme to take over the school involved four pieces of string, eighty-two assault helicopters, some peanut butter, and an android robot named McGyver.
아델리의 복잡한 학교 인수 계획에는 실 네 가닥, 82대의 공격 헬기, 땅콩버터 약간, 맥가이버라는 로봇이 필요했다.

Sam's fifty-seven step method for making a peanut butter and jelly sandwich was too *convoluted* for me to follow.
땅콩버터와 젤리 샌드위치를 만드는 샘의 57단계 방법은 내가 따라하기엔 너무 복잡했다.

COPIOUS [kóupiəs]   adj. plentiful; large in number or quantity   풍부한; 막대한

Our family had prepared such a *copious* amount of food for the party that I knew my mother wouldn't mind if I gave a whole turkey to our dog.
우리 집에서는 파티 음식을 아주 넉넉하게 준비해서 내가 칠면조 한 마리를 통째로 개에게 준다 해도 어머니는 개의치 않으셨을 거다.

After I saved my little brother from drowning, newspapers and television news shows heaped *copious* praise on me for my bravery.
내가 물에 빠진 남동생을 구해 준 이후 신문과 TV 뉴스에서 나의 용감한 행동에 대해 엄청나게 칭찬해 줬다.

CORRELATION [kɔ̀(:)rəléiʃən/kɑ̀r-]   n. connection or relationship of different factors or events   상관성, 상호관계

Over thirty years ago, doctors noticed a *correlation* between cigarette smoking and lung cancer.
30년도 더 전에 의사들은 흡연과 폐암 사이의 상관성을 인지했다.

I learned in college that there is a definite *correlation* between the amount of time you spend studying and how well you do on tests.
나는 대학을 다니면서 공부에 들이는 시간과 시험 성적은 분명한 상호관계가 있다는 걸 알게 됐다.

CORROBORATE [kərábərèit/-rɔ́b-]   v. provide additional support for a statement by supplying new evidence to back it up   확실하게 하다, 확증하다

The researchers need to *corroborate* their latest findings with an additional series of tests before they go public with their astounding breakthrough.
연구원들은 놀랄 만한 새로운 발견을 공표하기 전에 추가적인 일련의 시험을 거쳐 최근의 조사 결과를 확증해야 한다.

CORRUPTION [kərʌ́pʃən]   n. wickedness, dishonesty or bad behavior   타락, 비행

The ace reporter finally uncovered the *corruption* in state government when she photographed the State Attorney accepting money from a gangster.
베테랑 기자는 마침내 주 법무장관이 갱 단원에게서 뇌물을 받는 장면을 사진으로 찍어 주 정부의 타락상을 폭로했다.

[Note] *Corrupt* [kərʌ́pt] v. means to cause to behave wickedly or immorally, adj. means wicked or immoral.

corrupt는 타락시키다 / 타락한, 부도덕한

- Mark had been a high school honor student, but he was corrupted by evil friends who encouraged him to take drugs.
  마크는 고등학교 때는 우등생이었는데, 나쁜 친구들 때문에 타락해 마약에 손을 댔다.

COVERT [kʌ́vərt/kóu-] adj. secret; concealed; kept hidden 비밀의; 숨겨진

Members of the CIA discussed their *covert* plan to replace the Libyan president with a cleverly designed cloth puppet.
CIA 요원들은 리비아 국왕을 교묘하게 만들어진 헝겊 꼭두각시로 대신하기 위한 비밀 계획을 논의했다.

The spy used the *covert* compartment of her briefcase to hide documents that she'd stolen from hostile countries.
스파이는 서류 가방의 숨겨진 칸막이를 이용해 적대 국가에서 훔쳐낸 서류들을 감추었다.

COW [kau] v. to scare by using force or threats 위협하다, 으르다

Jonathan gathered together his eight older brothers and *cowed* the bully into letting him play in the baseball game.
조나단은 자기 형 여덟 명을 모이게 한 다음 깡패를 겁주어 야구 경기를 하라고 시켰다.

Tales of the Night Stalker Who Ate Only Brains *cowed* the Boy Scout troop into staying inside their tents at night.
'뇌만 먹는 나이트 스토커' 에 대한 이야기를 들은 보이스카우트 단원은 겁을 먹어 밤 동안 텐트 안에서 꼼짝하지 못했다.

CRAFTY [kræfti/krɑ́:f-] adj. sneaky; sly; skilled in deception or trickery 교활한, 간사한

The *crafty* card player was able to deal himself any card he needed from his specially-rigged deck.
교활한 카드 플레이어는 자신이 특별히 섞은 카드에서 자기한테 필요한 카드 패는 뭐든지 가져올 수 있었다.

I admired my sister's *crafty* plan to fake illness and avoid school by putting on some of our leftover Halloween makeup.
나는 여동생이 할로윈에서 남은 화장품으로 분장을 해 꾀병을 부리고 학교에 빠지려는 간사한 계획에 감탄했다.

CRAG [kræg] n. a steep thrust of rock that forms part of a cliff 울퉁불퉁한 바위, 험한 바위산

The hang glider stepped off the *crag* and soared into the air above the canyon.
행글라이더가 험한 바위산에서 발을 떼더니 협곡 위 공중으로 날아올랐다.

Desmond stopped himself from rolling off the side of the cliff by grabbing onto a *crag* at the last possible moment.
데즈먼드는 절벽에서 굴러 떨어지려는 마지막 찰나에 울퉁불퉁한 바위를 움켜잡았다.

CREED [kri:d] n. a belief system that helps guide a person's decisions and actions; a formal statement of the main beliefs of a religion 신조, 신념; 주의, 강령

It was Lazy Larry's *creed* that chores and housework should be avoided at all costs.
집안의 자질구레한 일들은 어떻게 해서든 안 한다는 것이 레이지 래리의 신조였다.

According to a religion practiced only by himself and his parents, Sarfu's *creed* demands that he submerge himself in a vat of mustard during every full moon.

사푸와 그의 부모님만이 지키는 종교가 있는데, 그에 따라 사푸는 보름달이 뜰 때마다 겨자가 담긴 큰 통에 자신의 몸을 담근다.

CREVICE [krévis]   n. a narrow crack or opening, usually in a rock   (바위의) 갈라진 틈

While hiking, I lost my favorite watch when it fell so far down a deep *crevice* that there was no way I could retrieve it.

하이킹을 하는 동안 가장 아끼는 시계를 잃어버렸는데, 깊은 바위틈 속으로 빠져 버려서 되찾을 방법이 없었다.

We watched dumbfounded as the earthquake first created a *crevice* in our ceiling, and then neatly split the entire room in two.

지진이 일어나 처음에는 천장에 틈이 하나 생기고, 그런 다음 방 전체가 두 동강이 났는데, 우린 그저 멍하니 보고만 있었다.

CRUCIAL [krúːʃəl]   adj. of the greatest importance; highly decisive   중대한; 결정적인

With the score tied and two seconds left on the clock, the penalty kick against the Dragons became the *crucial* play in the soccer game.

동점에 2초를 남겨 둔 상황에서 드래곤스를 상대로 한 페널티킥이 축구 경기의 결정적 플레이가 됐다.

I thought it was *crucial* that we tell my sister that we were keeping our new pet lizard in her bathroom, but my older brother locked me in the closet before I could get to her.

우리의 새로운 애완 도마뱀이 여동생 욕실에 있다는 것을 그녀에게 말해야 한다고 생각했지만, 형이 날 옷장 안에 가두어 버려 동생에게 갈 수가 없었다.

CRUSADE [kruːséid]   n. a movement toward a specific goal or reform or a series of expeditions that took place during the Middle Ages in which European knights fought Muslims in an attempt to recover the Holy Land   개혁 운동; 십자군 운동

In the early seventies, Ralph Nader led a successful *crusade* for car safety when he demanded that seat belts be improved and used by everyone.

70년대 초반 랄프 네이더는 안전벨트의 개선과 모든 사람들의 착용을 요구하며 자동차 안전에 대한 성공적인 개혁 운동을 이끌었다.

Although in some people's opinion the *Crusades* were mainly a waste of human life, the travel and communication between Europe and the Middle East did foster an exchange of ideas.

일부의 사람들은 십자군 운동이 대체로 인간 생명의 허비였다고 생각하지만, 유럽과 중동 지역 간의 여행과 의사소통으로 아이디어의 교환이 촉진되기도 했다.

CUMULATIVE [kjúːmjulətiv/-leit-]   adj. adding up through a series of increases or additions   누적하는, 누가하는

Doctors warn that the *cumulative* effect of chewing tobacco is a tremendous increase in your chances for tongue disease.

의사들의 경고에 따르면, 씹는 담배의 영향이 누적되면 혀에 질병이 생길 가능성이 심각하게 증가한다.

Although one rotten tomato didn't hurt, the *cumulative* effect of all of them being thrown at him forced the lousy magician from the stage.

썩은 토마토 하나였다면 지장을 주지 못했겠지만, 야비한 마술사에게 던져진 썩은 토마토 전부의 누적된 영향력은 결국 그를 무대에서 끌어내렸다.

CUNNING [kʌ́niŋ]   adj. skilled at fooling people; sly   교묘한; 교활한, 간사한

By hopping on a streetcar and riding to the finish line, Rosie the marathon runner proved that *cunning* is sometimes more important than athletic training.

시내 전차에 올라타서 결승선까지 온 마라톤 주자 로지는 때로는 교묘함이 운동 연습보다 중요하다는 걸 보여주었다.

The *cunning* burglar avoided the police by impersonating a newspaper reporter rushing to the crime scene.

교활한 강도는 범죄 현장으로 달려온 신문기자 행세를 해서 경찰을 피했다.

CURDLE [kə́:rdl]   v. to spoil or turn sour or to thicken into clumps   상하다; 굳어지다

When the mummy trapped the star of the film in a room, terror made my blood *curdle* and I could barely breathe.

미라가 인기 영화배우를 방에 가두었을 때 난 공포로 피가 굳어 숨조차 쉴 수 없었다.

When they were really bored on weekend, the farm kids took a glass of milk and watched it *curdle* over a four-day period.

농장 아이들은 주말 동안 정말로 따분해 우유 한 잔을 가져다가 4일간 상하는 것을 지켜보았다.

CURFEW [kə́:rfju:]   n. a law or rule calling for a certain type of person to be indoors by a specific time   귀가 시간, 야간 통행금지

My parents let me stay out later than my midnight *curfew* as long as I call and tell them exactly where I am.

우리 부모님은 내가 전화해서 정확히 어디 있는지만 말씀드리면 귀가 시간인 자정이 넘어도 밖에 있게 해주신다.

Due to the recent spread of smashed mailboxes, the city proposed a 6:00 *curfew* for all teenagers and a freeze on baseball bat sales.

최근에 유행처럼 우편함들이 깨부숴진 일 때문에 시에서는 6시 이후 십대들의 통행금지와 야구방망이 판매금지를 제안했다.

CURRICULUM [kəríkjuləm]   n. the set of classes or courses offered at a particular school or by a specific department, like the math department   교과 과정, 이수 과정

The bold high school proposed a *curriculum* that replaced geography class with a class called "Game Show History."

과감한 고등학교는 지리 수업을 "게임 쇼 역사" 수업으로 대체하는 교과 과정을 제안했다.

The small private college did not offer as broad a *curriculum* as the large state university, but the classes were smaller and more personal.

소규모 사립대학은 큰 주립 대학만큼 폭넓은 교과 과정을 제공하지는 않았지만, 강의들이 사람 수가 더 적고 더 개인적이었다.

CURTSY [kə́:rtsi]   n. a show of respect made by slightly bending one's knee and then lowering the body a little, usually performed by women and girls   (한쪽 무릎을 굽히고 몸을 약간 숙이는 여자의) 인사

The princess gracefully *curtsied* toward the King and Queen, then gave the order for the jousting tournament to begin.

공주는 왕과 왕비에게 우아하게 인사를 한 뒤 마상 창시합의 개회를 명했다.

Not only did the uppity schoolgirl refuse to *curtsy* to Mrs. Baba, she also refused to call the teacher anything other than "Yo, Lady."

거만한 여학생은 바바 선생님에게 인사를 거부한 것은 물론이고, 선생님을 고집스럽게 "야아, 부인"이라고만 불렀다.

CYCLONE [sáikloun]   n. a violent spinning windstorm with a calm center, on land also known as a tornado and at sea, a hurricane   큰 회오리바람 (육지에서는 토네이도, 바다에서는 허리케인이라고도 한다)

The *cyclone* ripped through the trailer park on the edge of town and distributed the trailers over a five mile radius.

큰 회오리바람이 마을 변두리의 이동 주택 주차 구역을 휩쓸어 이동 주택들이 반경 5마일 이상으로 흩어졌다.

D

DAINTY [déinti] adj. attractive and beautiful in a fragile, delicate way or very choosy; fussy 우아한, 고운; 까다로운; 야단법석 떠는

Mother's collection of *dainty* blow-glass figurines is admired by all our neighbors, but it is a nightmare to dust.
어머니가 모으신 우아한 유리 입상들을 보고 모든 이웃 주민이 감탄하지만 먼지를 떨어내려면 보통 성가신 게 아니다.

The *dainty* young woman refused to eat anything that came out of a can, so the rest of the campers ate her ration of baked beans.
까다로운 아가씨는 통조림을 절대 안 먹으려고 해서 나머지 야영자들이 그녀 몫의 구운 콩을 먹었다.

DAUNT [dɔ:nt/dɑ:nt] v. to scare and discourage 위압하다, 겁주다, 기세를 꺾다

The steep 3,000 foot slope *daunted* the amateur climbers, who had only climbed up the side of their garage one time for practice.
아마추어 등산가들은 가파른 3천 피트의 비탈에 겁을 먹었는데, 그들은 연습으로 차고의 옆면을 한 번 올라봤을 뿐이었다.

Many of the tourists were *daunted* when the tour guide informed them that over half of the last tour never returned from the jungle.
관광객들은 지난 투어에서 반 이상의 관광객이 정글에서 돌아오지 못했다는 가이드의 말을 듣고 기가 죽었다.

DAWN [dɔ:n] n. the appearance of the first light in the morning; the beginning of specific event or activity or v. to begin to be understood or noticed (usually followed by "on") 새벽; 시초 / 이해되기 시작하다, 보이기 시작하다

As the light of *dawn* cleared away the fog, I began to see the faint outline of the city.
새벽빛이 안개를 걷어내자 도시의 희미한 윤곽이 보이기 시작했다.

It's easy for scholars to look back and say that the birth of Peter the Great marked the *dawn* of a great age in Russian history.
학자들이 과거를 돌아보며 표트르 대제의 탄생이 러시아 역사에서 위대한 시기의 도래를 알린 사건이었다고 말하는 것은 쉽다.

As I looked at my cat's wet paws and happy expression, the thought *dawned* on me that maybe she was responsible for the disappearance of my goldfish, Phil.
고양이의 젖은 발과 행복한 표정을 보자 내 금붕어 필이 사라진 책임이 고양이에게 있을 거라는 생각이 들기 시작했다.

DAZZLE [dǽzl] v. to momentarily blind with light or to astonish, amaze, or impress 눈부시다; 감탄시키다, 압도하다

The huge spotlights arching over the crowd *dazzled* fans who looked straight into them.
군중 위에 아치 모양으로 밝혀진 거대한 스포트라이트가 그것을 똑바로 쳐다보는 팬들을 눈부시게 했다.

The Soaring Demplewolfs *dazzled* the audience as they juggled bowling balls while performing high-wire acrobatics.

소링 뎀플울프 가족이 줄타기를 하면서 볼링공을 저글링하는 모습을 보며 관중들은 감탄했다.

DEBUNK [diːbʌ́ŋk] v. to prove or show that an exaggerated claim is false   정체를 폭로하다, 거짓임을 밝혀내다

Officials used video recordings of the race to *debunk* rumors that Willis had cheated by placing jet rockets on his shoes.

심판원들은 경주의 녹화 비디오를 이용해 윌리스가 신발에 제트 로켓을 달아 부정행위를 했다는 소문이 잘못됐음을 증명했다.

Hector's claim that he was the first man on the moon was *debunked* when NASA proved that he was participating in a state bowling championship on November 3, 1965 and was nowhere near outer space.

자신이 달에 착륙한 최초의 사람이라는 헥터의 주장은 거짓임이 밝혀졌는데, 그는 1965년 11월 3일에 주 볼링 선수권 대회에 참가한 상태였으며 우주 공간 근처에는 가지도 않았다는 걸 NASA에서 증명했다.

DECEPTION [disépʃən] n. a form of trickery; something done to fool someone into believing a lie   속임; 사기

Samer's neck brace and bandages were a *deception* that he hoped would convince the jury that he was badly injured when my shopping cart bumped his at the supermarket.

세이머의 목 버팀대와 붕대는 속임수로, 배심원단에게 슈퍼마켓에서 내 쇼핑 카트와 그의 것이 부딪쳤을 때 자기가 심하게 다쳤다고 믿게 하려는 것이었다.

[Note] *Deceive* [disíːv] v. means to trick or fool

deceive는 '속이다'

- "Your eyes can *deceive* you," warned Cherly, Master of Illusion, as she began to float off the floor.
  "당신의 눈에 속을지도 모릅니다." '환상의 대가' 셰릴이 바닥에서 위로 떠오르기 시작하면서 경고했다.

DECOMPOSE [dìːkəmpóuz] v. to decay and rot; to break up into smaller, simpler pieces   부패시키다; 분해 시키다

Remember that poor raccoon from the "carcass" definition? Well, you can bet that its flesh is *decomposing*.

"사체(carcass)" 정의에서 불쌍한 미국 너구리 생각납니까? 분명히 살이 부패되고 있을 겁니다.

The chicken wing began to *decompose* when it was placed in the vat of acid, and soon only bits of floating chicken meat remained.

닭날개가 산이 담긴 큰 통에 넣어지자 분해되기 시작해, 곧 떠다니는 닭고기 몇 점만 남게 되었다.

DECREE [dikríː] n. an order or command given by a person of authority or v. to order or command something   법령, 명령 / 명하다

In an effort to ease the effects of the drought that was sweeping the country, the government *decreed* that no person could waste water by showering.

정부는 나라를 휩쓸고 있는 가뭄의 영향을 줄이기 위해 누구도 샤워를 해 물을 낭비하지 말라고 명했다.

The citizens were in an uproar when they heard of the king's *decree* that every first-born child would be named after him, King Blenny Blenblenneher.

시민들은 모든 첫번째 태어난 아이의 이름을 자신의 이름, 블레니 블렌블렌네어를 따서 지어야 한다는 왕의 명령을 듣고 소란을 일으켰다.

DEFIANCE [difáiəns] n. open disobedience to authority   공공연한 반항, 도전

In an act of *defiance*, the citizens from the sentence above started naming their children anything but "Blenny Blenblenneher," which, if you think about it, isn't hard to do.
공공연한 반항의 행동으로, 앞서 말한 시민들은 아이들의 이름을 "블레니 블렌블렌네어"만 빼고 붙이기 시작했는데, 생각해보면 그것은 어려운 일이 아니었다.

The corporal was sentenced to five days in the army prison for his *defiance* of the direct order from the general.
상등병은 장군의 직속 명령 불복종에 대해 군대 감옥에서 5일간의 복역을 선고받았다.

DEFINITIVE [difínətiv] adj. conclusive; having the ability to remove all doubt and end any debate   결정적인, 최종적인

The *definitive* point in the championship boxing match came when Roberto slugged Al so hard that his teeth flew out into the fourth row of seats.
로베르토가 앨에게 강타를 날려 앨의 이가 관중석의 네 번째 줄까지 날아갔을 때가 복싱 결승전의 결정적인 순간이었다.

Taking the girl and tying her to the train tracks was the *definitive* action that convinced me that Dick Viper was a bad man.
딕 바이퍼가 여자를 데리고 가 철도 선로에 묶는 걸 보고 그가 나쁜 놈임을 확신하게 됐다.

DELUSION [dilú:ʒən] n. a false opinion or idea   환상, 착각, 망상

When Clark arrived at the Sahara Desert Motel with his snorkeling equipment, the staff realized that he had some *delusion* about the presence of an ocean nearby.
클락이 스노클 장비를 들고 사하라 사막 모텔에 도착했을 때 모텔 직원은 그가 근처에 바다가 있을 거라고 착각하고 있음을 알았다.

Brandon insisted that Cindy Crawford was his girlfriend and that he talked to her every hour, but his friends realized he was suffering from a *delusion* brought on by watching taped episodes of *House of Style*.
브랜든은 신디 크로포드가 자신의 애인이고 매시간 그녀와 이야기를 나눈다고 주장했는데, 친구들이 알고 보니 그는 '하우스 오브 스타일' 녹화편을 보고 망상을 일으키는 것이었다.

DEPLORE [diplɔ́:r] v. to strongly dislike and disapprove; to condemn and hate   몹시 싫어하다; 비난하다

As much as father *deplores* the violence going on in the world, he sure does love football.
아버지는 전 세계에서 행해지고 있는 폭력을 혐오하시는 것만큼이나 미식축구를 무지 좋아하신다.

The left-handed protesters *deplored* the new law which stated that only right-handed people could run for political office.
왼손잡이 항의자들은 오른손잡이들만이 행정 관청직에 입후보할 수 있다고 명시하는 새로운 법령을 비난했다.

DEPLOY [diplɔ́i] v. to spread out and position in a systematic or strategic way   (조직적으로 혹은 전략적으로) 전개하다, 배치하다

The search party *deployed* in a wide line across the field so that they could cover as much ground as possible.
연구팀은 가능한 한 많은 공간을 답파할 수 있도록 들판을 가로질러 넓은 열을 이루었다.

DERAIL [di:réil] v. to go off the tracks   탈선시키다, 탈선하다

The pickup truck that was stalled on the railroad tracks *derailed* the 8:23 northbound freight train, which was going too fast to stop in time.
철도 선로에서 시동이 꺼져 버린 소형 트럭은 8시 23분 북행 화물열차를 탈선시켰는데, 열차가 너무 빨리 달리고 있어 제 시간에 멈출 수가 없었다.

Father's attempt at a quiet family picnic was *derailed* when Jonathan came across a drum set standing alone in the wilderness.

조용한 가족 피크닉을 가지려는 아버지의 계획은 조나단이 황야에 덩그러니 놓여 있는 드럼 세트를 발견한 순간 어긋나고 말았다.

DERIDE [diráid] v. to laugh at and ridicule; to mock and scorn 비웃다, 조롱하다

Safe inside his house of brick, the third little pig *derided* the wolf for his wasted huffing and puffing outside the door.

안전한 벽돌집 속의 셋째 꼬마 돼지는 문밖에서 헐떡거리고 씩씩거리며 헛수고하는 늑대를 비웃었다.

At the school for geniuses, Natasha was constantly *derided* for her inability to understand how Boltzmann's Constant applied to an eight-dimensional geodesic spatial causality.

영재학교에 다니는 나타샤는 볼쯔만 상수가 8차원의 측지학 공간 인과관계에 적용되는 방법을 이해하지 못해 계속 조롱을 당했다.

DESOLATION [dèsəléiʃən/dèz-] n. a dreary condition or place where very little exists or is happening or a feeling of sadness and isolation 황량한 곳, 폐허; 쓸쓸함, 처량함

One can never truly understand *desolation* unless one travels to Enid, Oklahoma, and stays in that drab wasteland for at least a week.

오클라호마 에니드로 여행을 가서 그 칙칙한 황무지에서 최소 일주일간 머물러 보지 않은 사람은 황량함이 어떤 것인지 진정 이해할 수 없다.

The Cherokee people felt great *desolation* when they were forced to leave their native land and begin the long, difficult journey to the west.

체로키족 사람들은 그들의 본토에서 쫓겨나 서부로의 길고도 힘겨운 여행을 시작했을 때 말할 수 없는 처량함을 느꼈다.

DESPAIR [dispέər] n. a feeling of absolute hopelessness or v. to lose all hope 절망, 자포자기 / 절망하다, 단념하다

Our feelings of *despair* increased every day that we were stranded on that desert island, but we did have incredible fans.

무인도에서 꼼짝 못하는 신세가 됐을 때 우리의 절망감은 나날이 늘어 갔지만, 우리에게는 엄청난 팬들이 있었다.

After eight months in solitary confinement, the imprisoned writer *despaired* of ever seeing another human again.

수감된 작가는 8개월째 독방에 갇혀있게 되자 사람을 만나볼 수 없을것 같은 절망감이 들었다.

DESPERADO [dèspərá:dou/-pəréi-] n. a bold outlaw 무법자, 물불을 가리지 않는 사람

After he had held up the stagecoach armed only with a banana, the *desperado* quickly peeled his weapon and ate it as he rode away.

무법자는 바나나 하나로 무장한 채 역마차를 세우더니, 타고 달아나면서 곧바로 무기의 껍질을 벗겨 먹었다.

The two *desperadoes* decided that they didn't need additional help to take over the fort and steal the eighteen tons of gold that were inside.

두 명의 무법자는 요새를 차지해 안에 있는 18톤의 금을 훔쳐 가는 데 다른 도움은 필요없다는 결정을 내렸다.

DETERIORATE [ditíəriərèit] v. to lessen in value, condition, or character, to get worse (질, 가치, 상태 등을) 저하시키다, 나빠지다

Once the termites really got down to business, the condition of the log cabin *deteriorated* rapidly.

흰개미들이 본격적으로 일에 착수하자 통나무 오두막의 상태가 급속도로 나빠졌다.

The ancient portrait had *deteriorated* to such an extent that no one even knew whether the person shown in it was a man or a woman.

고대의 초상화는 그림 속의 인물이 남자인지 여자인지도 알아볼 수 없을 만큼 상태가 나빠져 있었다.

DEVASTATE [dévəstèit] v. to totally ruin or destroy; to lay waste 황폐시키다, 훼손시키다; 망연자실하게 하다

The bombing of Dresden, Germany, by the Allies in World War II *devastated* the city to the point where most of it had to be completely rebuilt.

제2차 세계대전 당시 연합군에 의한 독일 드레스덴 폭격은 도시를 초토화시켜 대부분을 완전히 다시 지어야 할 정도였다.

Nikka was so *devastated* that she didn't get picked to be a cheerleader that she crawled under her bed and did not come out for three days.

니카는 자신이 치어리더에 못 뽑혔다는 사실에 너무 망연자실해서 침대에 기어 들어가더니 3일 동안 나오지 않았다.

DIABOLICAL [dàiəbálikəl/-bɔ́l-] adj. concerning the devil; evil or wicked 악마의; 악마적인, 극악무도한

The church pastor insisted that rock music was all part of a *diabolical* plot to steal teenagers' soul, but he did admit that it was fun to dance to.

교회 목사는 록음악은 온통 십대의 혼을 앗아가기 위한 악마의 음모라고 주장했지만, 거기에 맞춰 춤추는 게 즐겁다는 사실은 인정했다.

The entire staff of the Humanes Society raided Mr. Wemberley's house when they learned of his *diabolical* treatment of canaries.

인도주의 협회의 전 직원은 웸벌리 씨가 카나리아들을 학대한다는 사실을 알고 그의 집으로 쳐들어갔다.

DIAGNOSE [dáiəgnòus/-nòuz] v. to study and examine carefully; to identify 자세히 관찰하다; 진단하다

The mechanic claimed that he would be unable to *diagnose* the problem until he could take the entire engine apart.

기계공은 전체 엔진을 해체해 보기 전까지는 문제가 뭔지 알 수 없다고 말했다.

The dentist, who lacked experience with large reptiles, could not *diagnose* the alligator's illness.

대형 파충류에 대해 경험이 부족한 치과의사는 악어의 병을 진단할 수 없었다.

DICTATE [díkteit] v. to say something out loud so that it can be recorded by another person or to establish a rule or law with authority 구술하다, 받아쓰게 하다; 규정하다, 명하다

While shaving at the sink in his office, the executive *dictated* his instructions for the day to his attentive secretary.

사장은 자신의 사무실 세면대에서 면도를 하는 동안, 경청하는 비서에게 그 날의 지시사항을 받아 적도록 불러줬다.

The queen *dictated* her new rules of government to the crowd of peasants below, who reacted by promptly storming the castle.

여왕이 성 아래에 모여 있는 농부들에게 정부의 새로운 법령을 발표하자 농부들은 당장 성을 공격하며 항거했다.

DIFFERENTIATE [dìfərénʃièit] v. to be able to tell the difference between two or more things; to make a distinction 구별하다, 식별하다

Whenever the Pontifract twins dressed alike, no one was able to *differentiate* between them.

폰티프랙트 쌍둥이가 똑같은 옷을 입으면 아무도 둘을 구별 해내지 못했다.

The snobby residents of Upper Roxbury Street *differentiated* themselves from the residents of Lower Roxbury by placing gold flamingoes in their lawns.

북부 록스베리 가의 배타적인 거주민들은 그들 잔디밭에 금색 플라밍고를 놓아두어 남부 록스베리 거주민들과 자신들을 구분지었다.

DILAPIDATED [dilǽpədèitid] adj. worn down and in a state of disrepair 황폐한, 무너져가는, 헐어 빠진

Just after the foreman of the demolition crew sneezed, the *dilapidated* building collapsed around him into a pile of rotten wood and dust.
철거반 주임이 재채기를 하자마자 그 주변의 허름한 건물이 썩은 나무와 먼지더미 속으로 무너져 내렸다.

The apartment building was so *dilapidated* that the landlord let me have the room for five dollars a month.
아파트 빌딩이 너무 헐어 빠져서 주인은 내게 5달러 월세로 방을 내주었다.

DILUTE [dilú:t/dai-] v. to lessen the strength of a liquid by adding an additional liquid, usually water; to weaken the force of something 묽게 하다, 희석하다; 약화시키다

We *diluted* the lemonade by adding more water, but drinking it still made our mouths pucker up.
우린 레모네이드에 물을 더 부었는데, 그래도 마시자 얼굴이 찡그려졌다.

There was so much static coming from the old speakers that the power of the song was *diluted*.
오래된 스피커에서 너무 심한 잡음이 나와 노랫소리가 잘 안 들렸다.

DIMENSION [dimén∫ən/dai-] n. the measurements of an object's length, width, and height or the overall extent or scope 치수; 범위, 정도

We misjudged the *dimensions* of the front door, and as a result we had to saw our new couch in half to get it inside.
앞문의 치수를 잘못 재는 바람에 새로 산 소파를 들이려면 반으로 잘라 내야 했다.

The professor's in-depth discussion of variable quantum physics was well beyond the *dimensions* of my understanding.
가변 양자 물리학에 대한 교수의 깊이있는 토론은 내 이해 영역을 훨씬 뛰어넘었다.

DIMINISH [dimíni∫] v. to reduce or decrease 줄이다, 감소되다

The noise from the plane's engines gradually *diminished* as it flew away from the airport.
비행기 엔진의 소음이 비행기가 공항에서 이륙하자 차츰 줄어들었다.

My love for Nora Birloom has not *diminished*, even though she stuck a sign on my back that said "Kick Me."
노라 벌룸에 대한 나의 애정은 그녀가 내 등에 "날 차버려"라는 문구를 붙여 놓았어도 식지 않았다.

DINGY [díndʒi] adj. dirty with grime or filth; dull and shabby 때 묻은, 더러운

After a good scrubbing, the *dingy* old lace curtains came out shining and white.
더럽고 오래된 레이스 커튼을 북북 문질러 빨았더니 반짝반짝 하얗게 되었다.

The mirror in the hallway was so *dingy* that I couldn't even tell if the face I saw in it was my own.
복도의 거울이 너무 더러워 거울 속의 얼굴이 내 얼굴인지조차 알아볼 수 없었다.

DIRECTIVE [diréktiv/dai-] n. an order issued by a central authority 지령

Immediately after taking over, the new principal issued the *directive* that all students and faculty would be required to attend an early morning yoga class each day.
새로 부임한 교장은 교장직을 인계한 직후 전 학생과 교직원들에게 매일 이른 아침 요가 수업을 들으라는 지령을 내렸다.

Once Central Command issued the *directive* that all guards were required to wear dresses, we knew someone was playing a joke on us.

지휘 본부에서 모든 호위병들에게 드레스를 입으라는 명령을 내리자 우린 곧 누군가 우릴 놀리고 있다는 걸 알았다.

DISCIPLE [disáipl] n. a person who trains with a specific teacher and spreads their particular beliefs 문하생, 제자

Kevin's quick method for doing long division in his head attracted many *disciples* who were eager to show the rest of the middle school the easier way.

케빈이 장제법으로 금세 암산을 하는 방법은 남은 중학교 시절을 쉽게 보내고 싶어 하는 많은 제자들을 끌어들였다.

Ziggy Zigmund, a world-famous snake charmer, advises his *disciples* to use non-poisonous snakes when teaching his techniques to others.

세계적으로 유명한 뱀 부리는 사람, 지기 지그먼드는 다른 이들에게 기술을 가르칠 때는 독 없는 뱀을 사용하라고 문하생들에게 조언한다.

DISCOURSE [dískɔːrs] n. conversation or a formal, written discussion 담화, 강연; 논설, 논문

By carefully listening to every bit of *discourse* during the embassy party, the spy was able to learn about the secret weapon.

스파이는 대사관 파티에서 담화를 한 마디도 빼놓지 않고 열심히 들어서 비밀 무기에 대해 알아낼 수 있었다.

Students recently complained that reading the ancient Greek philosopher Aristotle's *discourses* on nature was one of the most boring things they had ever done.

학생들은 최근에, 고대 그리스 철학자 아리스토텔레스의 자연에 대한 대화를 읽는 것은 지금까지 읽은 것 중 가장 지루한 글이라며 불평했다.

DISCRETION [diskréʃən] n. caution and self-restraint in behavior or freedom of choice 분별, 신중; 선택의 자유

Knowing that the floors in the house were old, the colonel showed *discretion* by making a lieutenant walk in front of him.

집의 마룻바닥이 오래됐다는 걸 안 대령은 신중하게도 중위에게 자기보다 앞서 걸어가게 했다.

This November, I will use *discretion* in voting for the next President of the United States.

올 11월에는 미국의 차기 대통령 선거에서 내 마음대로 투표할 것이다.

DISMAL [dízməl] adj. depressing and miserable; gloomy 우울한, 비참한; 음침한, 음산한

The *dismal* weather made the beach party a terrible flop.

음산한 날씨 때문에 해변 파티를 완전히 망쳤다.

Since she had not opened her textbooks all year, Janice knew that finals week would be a *dismal* time for her.

일년 내내 교과서를 열어보지도 않은 재니스는 기말시험을 치르는 주가 그녀에게 우울한 시간이 되리라는 걸 알았다.

DISMAY [disméi] n. a quick loss of confidence or courage in the face of difficulty or danger 당황, 놀람

The bullfighter's confidence turned to *dismay* when he realized that his shoelaces were tied together.

투우사는 그의 구두끈이 한꺼번에 묶여 있는 걸 보고는 자신감을 잃고 당황했다.

The babysitter could not hide his *dismay* when little Mikey Munson came out of the bathroom and announced that he had shaved his sister's head.

베이비시터는 꼬마 마이키 먼슨이 욕실에서 나와 누이의 머리를 밀었다고 말하자 당황함을 감출 수 없었다.

DISPENSE [dispéns] v. to distribute in parts; to deal out or to do without (usually followed by "with") 분배하다, 나누어주다; ~없이 해내다(주로 with를 동반)

The cool new plastic Pez head was able to *dispense* candy from both its mouth and eyes.
새로 나온 근사한 플라스틱 페즈 머리는 입과 눈 두 군데서 사탕이 나왔다.

The dictator *dispensed* with justice and had the prisoner sentenced to death without a trial.
독재자는 정의라는 것을 무시하고 재판 과정 없이 죄수에게 사형 선고를 내렸다.

DISPERSE [dispə́:rs] v. to scatter in different directions or to vanish and disappear 흩뜨리다, 흩뿌리다; 사라지게 하다

The mechanical seeder used a rotating arm to *disperse* wheat seeds over a large area of land.
자동 파종기는 회전 팔을 이용해 넓은 땅에 밀 씨앗을 흩뿌렸다.

The bright morning sunlight *dispersed* the fog that had been hanging over the bay.
화사한 아침 햇살이 만 위에 걸려 있던 안개를 걷어 냈다.

DISPOSITION [dìspəzíʃən] n. the way a person usually feels, their mood or an inclination or tendency 성질, 기질; 성향, 경향

Wilhelm's bad-tempered *disposition* often made him punch any animal, vegetable, or mineral that crossed his path.
빌헬름은 성미가 까다로워 종종 자신의 길을 막고 있는 건 동물이든 야채든 광물이든 가리지 않고 주먹질을 해댔다.

Although my sister is usually *disposed* toward green socks, that day she chose the black socks because it was almost Halloween.
여동생은 주로 녹색 양말을 좋아하지만 그 날에는 검은 양말을 골랐는데, 할로윈이 가까워 오기 때문이었다.

DISTEND [disténd] v. to expand or swell due to some form of internal pressure 팽창하다, 넓어지다

After the Alka-Seltzer eating contest, the stomachs of both boys *distended* quite a bit.
위장약 먹기 대회가 끝난 뒤 두 소년의 위가 불룩해졌다.

Filling up the balloon with too much water *distended* it, and soon it exploded in the bathroom sink.
풍선에 물을 너무 많이 채워 넣었더니 풍선이 팽창돼 곧 욕실 세면대에서 터져 버렸다.

DISTORT [distɔ́:rt] v. to bend or twist something out of its normal shape 비틀다, 뒤틀다

The weird mirrors in the carnival fun house *distorted* my reflection so it looked like I had a four-foot head and three-inch legs.
놀이 공원 유령의 집에 있는 이상한 거울에 내 모습이 뒤틀리게 비쳐 머리는 4피트, 다리는 3인치인 것 같았다.

DNA [dì: en éi] n. the molecule that is responsible for transmitting characteristics and traits in all life forms 디엔에이, 디옥시리보 핵산

The scientists used *DNA* samples from the orphan's blood to determine the identity of her real father.
과학자들은 고아의 친부를 확인하기 위해 그녀의 혈액에서 채취한 DNA 샘플을 이용했다.

The nuclear waste from the power plant damaged the *DNA* of the fish in a local stream, causing them to be born with no gills.
발전소의 핵폐기물이 지역 시내의 물고기 DNA를 손상시켜 아가미 없는 물고기가 태어나게 했다.

DOLEFUL [dóulfəl] adj. full of grief and sadness 슬픈, 수심에 잠긴

The *doleful* family stopped by the cemetery one last time to pay their respects to the recently-departed family cat.
수심에 잠긴 가족은 마지막으로 묘지 옆에 서서 최근에 헤어진 가족 고양이에게 안부를 전했다.

The moviegoers were laughing and joking on the way in to see *Get Out Your Handkerchiefs*, but they were *doleful* on the way out.
영화 팬들은 '손수건을 꺼내요'를 보러 갈 때는 웃고 농담을 하더니, 나올 때는 슬픔에 잠겨 있었다.

DOMINION [dəmínjən] n. the exercise of control over a specific area or n. the area under control by a specific ruler 지배(권), 통제; 영토

With the rebellion in the south successfully defeated, the emperor could once more claim *dominion* over the entire continent.
남쪽 지방의 반란을 성공적으로 진압한 황제는 다시 한 번 대륙 전체에 대한 지배권을 획득할 수 있었다.

Signs posted along the border warned all travelers to stay out of King Vlad's *dominion*, or they would regret it.
가장자리를 따라 붙어 있는 표지판에는 여행객들에게 블라드 왕의 영토에 들어가지 말 것과, 들어갈 경우 후회하게 될 거라는 경고문이 적혀 있었다.

DOUR [duər/dauər] adj. silent and ill-tempered; forbidding and harsh 시무룩한, 뚱한; 엄한, 험악한

When the schoolchildren began to taunt him, the *dour* woodsman picked up his axe and chased them.
초등학생들이 나무꾼을 놀리기 시작하자 뚱한 나무꾼은 도끼를 집어 들고 그들을 쫓아가기 시작했다.

I wanted to buy a cookie, but the *dour* expression of the woman behind the counter made me decide to go across the street for some ice cream instead.
난 쿠키 하나를 사고 싶었는데, 카운터 여자의 무서운 표정을 보고는 그 대신 아이스크림을 사러 길 건너에 가기로 마음먹었다.

DREAD [dred] n. a large amount of fear; utter terror or v. to greatly fear 공포, 무서움 / 무서워하다, 공포에 떨다

I *dread* going to sleep at night because for the past week I have been having a terrible nightmare about zombies who look like Frank Sinatra.
난 밤에 잠자리에 들기가 무서웠는데, 지난 주 내내 프랭크 시나트라처럼 생긴 괴짜들이 나오는 끔찍한 악몽에 시달렸기 때문이다.

A shy child, Helena *dreaded* the moment she would have to present her book report to the whole class; the idea of speaking in front of the class filled Helena with *dread*.
수줍음이 많은 헬레나는 반 아이들 앞에서 독후감을 발표할 순간이 오는 게 너무나 두려웠다. 교실 앞에 나가 말할 생각을 하자 헬레나는 두려움에 휩싸였다.

DREARY [dríəri] adj. dark and bleak or dull and boring 음산한, 쓸쓸한; 지루한, 따분한

The *dreary* look of the farm cellar was altered when we put in new light bulbs and hung bright streamers everywhere.
농장 지하실의 음산하던 모습이 백열전구를 갈아 끼우고 여기저기에 밝은 장식 리본을 달았더니 바뀌었다.

So many audience members had been put to sleep by the *dreary* play that you could hardly hear the actors over their snoring.
지루한 연극에 하도 많은 관객들이 잠에 빠져들어 그들의 코고는 소리 너머로 배우들의 목소리를 거의 들을 수 없을 지경이었다.

DRENCH [drentʃ] v. to soak thoroughly 흠뻑 적시다

After I was *drenched* in the rainstorm, I vowed to never again buy a five cent, paper umbrella.
나는 폭풍우에 흠뻑 젖고 난 뒤로 다시는 5센트짜리 종이우산을 사지 않으리라 맹세했다.

The escape artist managed to free herself from the iron chest that had been thrown into the sea, but she was *drenched* in the process.
곡예사는 바다 속에 던져진 철제 상자에서 가까스로 빠져나왔지만, 그러는 동안 몸이 흠뻑 젖었다.

DRONE [droun] v. to speak in a monotonous tone; to make a continuous, low humming noise 단조롭게 얘기하다; 낮게 윙윙거리다

My uncle would *drone* on about his experiences as a short order cook in the Gulf War until someone in the family changed the subject.
우리 삼촌은 가족 중 누군가 주제를 바꿀 때까지 걸프전 동안 패스트푸드 요리사로 일했던 경험을 단조로운 투로 얘기하곤 했다.

The farmhand would often go to sleep at night by listening to the steady *drone* of the cicadas outside.
농장 노동자는 밤이면 밖에 있는 매미가 한결같이 낮게 윙윙거리는 소리를 들으며 잠자리에 들곤 했다.

DUPLICITY [djuːplísəti/duː-] n. deliberate trickery or deception 계획적인 속임수, 사기

The man who impersonated the mayor and ordered that everyone pay him twenty dollars in city taxes was arrested and convicted for his *duplicity*.
시장의 흉내를 내며 모든 사람에게 시 세금으로 자기한테 20달러씩을 내라고 하던 남자가 체포되어 사기죄를 선고받았다.

Jane was a bully who terrorized everyone at school, but she had a knack for *duplicity* that helped her convince all the teachers that she was the victim.
제인은 전교생을 공포에 떨게 하는 깡패였는데, 속임수를 써서 모든 교사들로 하여금 자신은 피해자라고 믿게 만들었다.

DYNAMIC [dainǽmik] adj. exciting and vigorous or rapidly changing; constantly active 정력적인, 활동적인; 급변하는

The audience screamed for the *dynamic* performer to come back on stage and play some more.
청중들은 정력적인 연주자에게 무대에 다시 나와 연주를 더 해달라고 소리 질렀다.

The *dynamic* couple would often go on round-the-world vacations without a moment's notice.
활동적인 부부는 종종 말 한마디도 없이 세계 일주 여행을 떠나곤 했다.

E

EBULLIENT [ibʌ́ljənt/-búl-] adj. high spirited, bubbly, and full of enthusiasm 열정적인, 의욕적인

Although no one was seriously injured, the *ebullient* mood of the festival was lost once the roof collapsed onto the dance floor.
아무도 심하게 다치지는 않았지만 지붕이 댄스 플로어 위로 떨어지자 축제의 열정적인 분위기가 싹 가셨다.

Maxine's *ebullient* personality and charming smile made her the most popular girl at school.
열정적인 성격과 매력적인 미소로 맥신은 학교에서 가장 인기 있는 소녀가 되었다.

ECLECTIC [iklέktik/ek-] adj. coming from a variety of different sources; choosing from a variety of sources 절충적인; 취사선택하는

The Hammerboy's first album was an *eclectic* blend of Icelandic folk songs, Japanese heavy metal, and Brazilian samba music.
해머보이의 데뷔 앨범은 아이슬란드의 포크송, 일본의 헤비메탈, 브라질의 삼바 음악을 절충한 것이었다.

The restaurant's *eclectic* buffet featured eels dipped in peanut butter as well as roasted sheep's stomach filled with a frothy lime sauce.
식당의 골라 먹는 뷔페는 부글거리는 라임 소스를 듬뿍 바른 양의 위 구이와 땅콩버터에 적신 뱀장어가 특징이었다.

ECOSYSTEM [í:kousìstəm/ék-] n. a term used to describe the interactions between all living things and their particular environments 생태계

The oil spill caused massive damage to the Alaskan *ecosystem* by destroying countless birds and fish.
석유 유출은 무수한 새와 물고기를 죽게 함으로써 알래스카 생태계에 막대한 피해를 끼쳤다.

The fragile *ecosystem* of the swamp has been upset by acid rain and many types of frogs are dying off.
늪의 연약한 생태계가 산성비로 계속 망가져서 많은 종류의 개구리들이 죽어 가고 있다.

EDIBLE [édəbl] adj. fit for eating 먹을 수 있는, 식용의

We decided that the berries were *edible* after our dog ate some and did not get sick.
우리 집 개가 딸기류 열매를 먹고 아프지 않은 걸 보고 난 뒤 그것을 먹어도 된다는 결론을 내렸다.

Sally's mom quickly determined that the four-month-old sandwich she found under Sally's bed was no longer *edible*.
샐리의 엄마는 샐리의 침대 밑에서 발견한 4개월 된 샌드위치는 먹을 수 없다고 했다.

ELABORATE [ilǽbərət] adj. created with great attention to details; intricate or [ilǽbərèit] v. to explain ideas or thoughts in even greater detail than before 공들여 만든; 복잡한, 정교한 / 아주 상세하게 설명하다

The *elaborate* stitching and beading on the wedding dress took four seamstresses six months to complete.
재봉사는 웨딩드레스의 복잡한 바느질과 구슬 장식 때문에 드레스를 완성하는 데 6개월이 걸렸다.

Since Billy's answer to the Civil War question was rather short and vague, the teacher asked him to *elaborate* on his response.
남북전쟁에 대한 빌리의 대답은 다소 짧고 모호해서 교사는 좀더 자세하게 설명해 달라고 요구했다.

ELEGANCE [éligəns] n. grace and cultured beauty in appearance or style 우아, 고상

The small apartment was decorated with such taste and *elegance* that visitors hardly noticed that it only measured six feet by ten feet.
작은 아파트는 아주 감각 있고 우아하게 장식되어 있어서 방문객들은 그곳의 넓이가 폭 6피트, 길이 10피트밖에 안 된다는 걸 알아차리지 못했다.

When Odette, the Black Swan, appeared on the stage, her *elegance* and talent made the other ballerinas look like waddling penguins in comparison.
흑조 오데트가 무대에 나타났는데, 그녀의 우아함과 재능 때문에 다른 발레리나들은 상대적으로 뒤뚱거리는 펭귄처럼 보였다.

ELEMENT [éləmənt] n. one part of a whole or in chemistry, a substance that cannot be broken down into simpler substance 요소, 성분; 원소

A talented drummer is only one *element* of a good jazz band.
재능 있는 드러머는 훌륭한 재즈 밴드를 이루는 단 하나의 요소일 뿐이다.

Silicon, which is found in sand, is the second most abundant *element* on the Earth.
모래에서 발견되는 실리콘은 지구상에서 두 번째로 가장 풍부한 원소다.

ELITE [ilí:t/eilí:t] n. the very best or the highest group; what is thought to be the best or highest group or adj. made up of the very best; belonging to or made up of a small, privileged group 정예, 엘리트층, (사회의) 중추 / 엘리트의; 정선된

Now that he was a member of the *elite*, the recently appointed knight refused to talk to any of his old "commoner" friends.
최근에 나이트 작위를 받은 사람은 이제 엘리트층의 일원이 되었다며 오랜 "평민" 친구들과는 얘기하려 들지 않았다.

The *elite* country club only accepted millionaires as members.
엘리트 컨트리클럽에서는 백만장자들만 회원으로 받아들였다.

ELONGATE [iló:ŋgeit/í:lɔŋgeit] v. to stretch out or lengthen 늘이다, 연장하다

The wad of chewing gum *elongated* as Billy held a part of it in his teeth while stretching out the rest with his hand.
빌리가 껌의 일부는 입안에 넣은 채 나머지를 손으로 잡아당기자 껌 덩어리가 늘어졌다.

Time seemed to *elongate* as I listened to the speaker drone on about her favorite type of garden beetle.
강사가 자신이 가장 좋아하는 정원 딱정벌레에 대해 단조롭게 얘기하는 걸 듣고 있자니 시간이 늘어지는 것 같았다.

EMBED [imbéd/em-] v. to place something firmly within a surrounding mass 깊숙이 끼워 넣다, 파묻다

The explorer *embedded* the flagpole in the soil and proudly claimed this new land as part of France.
탐험가는 땅 속에 깃대를 깊숙이 끼워 넣더니 자랑스럽게 이 새로운 땅은 프랑스의 것이라고 주장했다.

The splinter was so deeply *embedded* in her palm that tweezers couldn't remove it.
가시가 그녀의 손바닥에 너무 깊숙이 박혀서 족집게로도 빼낼 수가 없었다.

EMBROIDER [imbrɔ́idər] v. to decorate an object using needlework 수놓다

The once plain rug was *embroidered* with fine pearls so that it would be beautiful enough for the princess' room.
평범했던 깔개가 공주의 방에 어울리도록 고운 빛깔의 진주들로 수놓아졌다.

The biker's denim jacket was *embroidered* in an odd pattern that appeared to be rows of animal skulls.
자전거 탄 사람이 입은 무명 재킷에는 이상한 무늬가 수놓아져서 동물 해골들이 늘어서 있는 것 같았다.

EMPATHY [émpəθi] n. the ability to understand another person's feelings or thoughts 공감

The teacher's *empathy* for Robert did not stop her from giving him a failing grade, but she did offer to help him study for the next test.
교사는 로버트에게 공감을 느낀다고 해서 그에게 낙제를 면해 주지는 않았지만, 다음 시험을 대비해 공부하는 걸 도와주겠다고 했다.

Van's *empathy* for the refugees in Rwanda is so intense that he cries whenever he reads about them in the newspaper.
밴은 르완다 난민들에 대해 아주 강한 공감을 느껴서 그들에 대한 신문 기사를 읽을 때마다 소리 내어 운다.

EMPHATIC [imfǽtik] adj. stressed with emphasis; forceful and striking 강조된; 힘 있는, 눈에 띄는

Kruschev made his declaration *emphatic* by taking off his shoe and pounding it into a table as he spoke.
후르시초프는 연설을 하는 동안 신발을 벗어 테이블에 내려치면서 자신의 선언을 강조했다.

EMULATE [émjulèit] v. to imitate someone in the hopes of equaling or exceeding their achievements (다른 사람에게 필적하려고) 열심히 흉내내다

Walt tried to *emulate* the astronauts on a space flight by living in his closet for almost three weeks.
월트는 우주 비행 중인 비행사들을 흉내내려고 거의 3주간을 옷장 속에서 지냈다.

When I was in junior high school I spent hours teasing my hair, and I cut off the sleeves of my T-shirts, in an attempt to *emulate* Madonna.
나는 중학교에 다닐 때 마돈나와 똑같아지려고 머리를 거꾸로 세우는 데 몇 시간을 들이고 티셔츠 소매를 잘라 냈다.

ENDEAVOR [indévər] n. a serious attempt or v. to attempt to do something 노력, 전력을 기울임 / 노력하다

After long months of sleepless nights, we succeeded in our *endeavor* to transmit psychic messages to Elvis Presley.
우리는 몇 달 동안 밤을 지새우던 끝에 엘비스 프레슬리에게 심령 메시지를 전송하는 데 성공했다.

The crew *endeavored* to please the captain, but nothing they did ever seemed to be good enough for him.
승무원들은 선장의 비위를 맞추려고 애썼지만, 그들이 어떻게 해도 그의 성에 차지 않는 것 같았다.

ENGAGING [ingéidʒiŋ] adj. likable and attractive; charming 마음을 끄는, 매력 있는

Soon everyone in the party had gathered around one *engaging* man who was telling hilarious stories.
파티에 찾아온 사람들은 이내 유쾌한 이야기를 하는 매력적인 한 남자 주위로 모여들었다.

The audience was delighted by the *engaging* piece of music Claudia played at her recital.
관객들은 클로디아가 독주회에서 선보인 매력적인 음악에 매료당했다.

ENHANCE [inhǽns/-hɑ́ːns] v. to increase 높이다, 강화하다

The boxer hoped to *enhance* his reputation as one bad dude by claiming he once beat up a supertanker full of African killer bees.
권투 선수는 자기가 한때 아프리카 살인 벌떼가 가득한 초대형 유조선을 박살냈다고 주장하면서 불량배라는 평판을 드높이고 싶어 했다.

The value of my Elvis Presley stamp was *enhanced* when all of the other Elvis Presley stamps in the world suddenly disappeared.
전 세계에 있는 다른 엘비스 프레슬리 우표들이 전부 갑자기 사라지자 내가 갖고 있는 엘비스 프레슬리 우표의 가치가 뛰어올랐다.

"Good lighting and good make-up *enhance* almost everyone's beauty," said the old movie star.
"조명발과 화장발은 거의 모든 사람을 더 아름다워 보이게 만든다." 고 나이든 영화배우가 말했다.

ENSURE [inʃúər] v. to make certain; to guarantee 확실하게 하다; 보증하다

Father *ensured* that our luggage would not fly off the top of the car by wrapping eight steel cables around the suitcases.
아버지는 여행 가방들을 여덟 줄의 쇠사슬로 칭칭 감아 짐이 차 밖으로 절대 빠져나가지 못하도록 하셨다.

The witch doctor *ensured* that the other team would lose the ball game by giving its entire starting offense the mumps.
마법사는 상대팀의 선발 공격 선수 전체를 유행성 이하선염에 걸리게 해 야구 경기에 지게 만들 거라고 장담했다.

ENTITLE [intáitl] v. to give the right or privilege to somebody 권리(자격)를 주다

The will clearly stated that the oldest sister was *entitled* to her mother's entire collection of sad-faced clown paintings but nothing else.
유언장에는 어머니가 모아 놓으신 울상의 어릿광대 그림 전부가 한 점도 빠짐없이 큰언니의 것이라고 분명히 명시돼 있었다.

Although Morgan was actually *entitled* to receive the car next, she passed the Gremlin on to her younger brother.
모건은 다음 번에 자동차를 받을 자격이 있었지만 그녀는 남동생에게 그렘린을 넘겨주었다.

ENTREPRENEUR [ɑ̀ːntrəprənə́ːr/ɔ̀n-] n. someone who starts his or her own business 기업가

The young *entrepreneur* lost all his money when a national coffee shop chain opened a huge restaurant across the street from his small coffee stand and stole all of his customers.
젊은 기업가는 그의 작은 커피 노점 건너편에 전국적인 커피숍 체인이 큰 가게를 열어 그의 고객들을 전부 빼앗아 가자 전 재산을 잃고 말았다.

The young *entrepreneur* soon transformed her tiny company into the worldwide leader in disposable bathtubs.
젊은 기업가는 금세 자그마한 회사를 일회용 욕조 분야에서 세계적인 리더로 바꾸어 놓았다.

ERA [íərə/érə] n. a period of time marked by certain conditions or events or a unit of time, usually hundreds or millions of years long, used by scientists to describe major stages in the Earth's development 연대, 시기; 대(代)

An *era* called "Reconstruction," which began after the end of the Civil War, saw many changes to the United States.
남북전쟁이 끝난 뒤 시작된 "재건"이라 불린 시기에는 미국에 많은 변화가 일어났다.

Geologist believe that all of the dinosaurs died off during the Mesozoic *era*.
지질학자들은 공룡이 중생대에 멸종했다고 믿는다.

EVACUATE [ivǽkjuèit] v. to leave or withdraw, usually from an area that is dangerous in some way 비우고 나가다, 피난하다, 대피하다

When the fire alarm sounded, the school was quickly *evacuated*.
화재 경보가 울리자 학교 학생들은 신속하게 대피했다.

Visitors were forced to *evacuate* the zoo when the alligators broke loose from their pond and began to roam freely.
방문객들은 악어들이 연못에서 도망쳐 나와 마음대로 돌아다니기 시작하자 동물원을 나와야 했다.

EVOKE [ivóuk] v. to summon or call forth or to come to mind because of some type of stimulation or suggestion 불러내다; 일깨우다, 환기시키다

The high priest of Kronhorst spoke the ancient chant that was supposed to *evoke* the spirit of the volcano god, but the spirit of Kronhorst's secretary answered instead.
크론호스트 제사장은 화산신의 신령을 불러낸다는 고대의 주문을 외웠지만 화산신 대신에 그의 비서의 영혼이 대답했다.

Looking at the water lilies in the pond *evoked* memories of the Monet paintings I saw while in France.
연못의 수련을 보고 있자니 프랑스에 있을 때 봤던 모네의 그림들이 떠올랐다.

EXASPERATE [igzǽspəreit/igzáːs-] v. to irritate greatly; to make impatient or angry 화나게 하다, 격분시키다

Bennie's inability to catch fly balls *exasperated* his teammates.
베니는 플라이 볼을 잡지 못해 팀원들을 화나게 했다.

The loud music from the apartment next door *exasperated* the student, who was trying to study.
아파트 옆집에서 나는 큰 음악 소리 때문에 공부하려던 학생은 화가 났다.

EXCLUSION [iksklúːʒən] n. the state of not being allowed to enter or to join 제외, 배제

The continued *exclusion* of non-male, non-white people from high-ranking positions in our country is one of the most serious problems we face today.
우리나라의 고위직에 아직도 남성, 그것도 백인만을 임용하는 것은 오늘날 우리가 직면한 가장 심각한 문제 중 하나다.

Rudolph the red-nosed reindeer felt very sad because of his constant *exclusion* from all of the games that were enjoyed by the other reindeer.
빨간 코의 순록, 루돌프는 다른 순록들이 즐기는 놀이에 자기는 계속 끼워 주지 않자 너무나 슬펐다.

EXEMPT [igzémpt] adj. excused; free from obligation or v. to release from obligation 면제된; 면제하다

Since she passed every one of her classes with an "A" average, Gia was *exempt* from final exams her senior year.
기아는 모든 과목을 평균 A로 통과했기 때문에 마지막 학년 기말시험을 면제받았다.

Phil's flat feet and partial blindness *exempted* him from having to serve in the army.
필은 평발에 부분 색맹으로 군복무를 면제받았다.

EXERTION [igzə́ːrʃən] n. strenuous effort or work 노력, 진력

It's hard to imagine the amount of *exertion* that must have gone into the building of the Egyptian pyramids.
이집트 피라미드를 짓는 데 얼마나 많은 애를 썼을지는 상상하기 힘들 정도다.

We started to build a four-story treehouse in our backyard, but the *exertion* of going up and down the tree soon wore us out.
우리는 뒤뜰에 4층짜리 나무 집을 짓기 시작했는데, 나무를 오르락내리락 하자니 금방 기진맥진해졌다.

EXILE [égzail/éks-] n. a person forced to live outside their native country or v. to banish someone from his or her native land 망명객, 유랑자 / 추방하다

While the *exile* yearned to return to his native Elvonia and continue the revolutionary struggle, he did admit that the television shows were much better in the United States.
망명객은 자신의 본국인 엘보니아로 돌아가 혁명 투쟁을 계속하기를 열망했지만, 미국의 TV 프로그램들이 훨씬 더 낫다는 것을 인정했다.

Having been convicted of treason, Napoleon was *exiled* to the tiny island of Elba.
반역죄 선고를 받은 나폴레옹은 엘바라는 조그마한 섬으로 유배당했다.

EXORBITANT [igzɔ́:rbətənt] adj. far beyond customary levels or bounds 엄청난, 과대한

I thought that $50,000 was a little *exorbitant* for a pair of shoes, although they did have cool Velcro fasteners.
멋진 벨크로 고정 장치가 달려 있다 해도 신발 한 켤레에 5만 달러는 좀 과한 것 같았다.

The forty-foot cake at movie star Tiffani Twinkle's wedding reception was *exorbitant* even by Hollywood standards.
영화배우 티파니 트윙클의 결혼 피로연에서 40피트 높이의 케이크는 할리우드 기준으로도 엄청난 것이었다.

EXOTIC [igzátik/-zɔ́t-] adj. from a foreign land or excitingly unusually and strange 외래의, 외국산의; 이국적인, 색다른

The *exotic* vine imported from Japan grew so quickly in America that it soon destroyed most of the local vegetation.
일본에서 들여온 외국산 덩굴식물이 미국 땅에서 너무 빨리 자라 순식간에 그 지역 식물 대부분을 없애 버렸다.

Though Kelly has very ordinary features, her *exotic* perfumes and unique clothing give her an air of mystery.
켈리는 아주 평범하게 생겼지만 이국적인 향수와 독특한 옷차림으로 신비스러운 분위기를 자아낸다.

EXPANSE [ikspǽns] n. a wide, open area 넓은 공간

Travelers with good vision could see for three miles in any direction across the grassy *expanse*.
시력이 좋은 여행객들은 드넓은 초원을 가로질러 어느 방향으로든 3마일을 볼 수 있었다.

Each year, huge herds of wildebeest travel across the African *expanse* in search of food and water.
해마다 어마어마한 누 영양떼가 먹이와 물을 찾아 넓디넓은 아프리카를 가로질러 여행한다.

EXPLETIVE [éksplətiv/iksplí:tiv] n. a curse or vulgar word; profanity 저주의 말, 속어; 신성을 모독하는 말

Lola's mother washed her mouth out with soap when she overheard all the *expletives* her daughter used during a phone conversation with her classmate.
롤라의 어머니는 딸이 친구와 전화 통화하며 상스럽게 말하는 것을 엿듣고는 그녀의 입을 비누로 씻어 냈다.

The sailor kept quiet in polite company because the only words he knew were *expletives*.
선원은 점잖은 일행 사이에서 침묵을 지키고 있었는데, 그가 아는 말은 욕설밖에 없었기 때문이다.

EXQUISITE [ikskwízit/ékskwi-] adj. having a beautiful and intricate design or intense; very powerful
아름다운, 정교한, 우아한; 강렬한

The microscopic brush strokes, some smaller than the eye can see, give an *exquisite* brilliance to the painting.
눈에 보이는 것보다 더 작은 극히 미세한 붓놀림은 그림에 정교한 광택을 더해 준다.

The joy of the eighty-story roller coaster drop was mixed with an *exquisite* sense of terror.
80층 높이에서 롤러코스터를 타고 떨어질 때 즐거움과 격렬한 공포감이 뒤섞였다.

EXTINCT [ikstíŋkt] adj. no longer alive anywhere on the Earth 절멸한, 사멸된

The flightless dodo bird, killed and eaten in great number by Dutch sailors, has been *extinct* for over three hundred years.
네덜란드 선원들이 다량으로 잡아먹었던 날지 못하는 도도새는 멸종된 지 3백년이 넘었다.

African elephants were in danger of becoming *extinct* until international laws were formed to protect them from ivory hunters.
아프리카 코끼리들은 국제적인 법규가 마련돼 상아 사냥꾼들로부터 그들을 보호해 주기까지 멸종 위기에 처해 있었다.

EXTRICATE [ékstrəkèit] v. to get out of a situation; to remove or set free 벗어나게 해주다, 제거하다, 구해 주다

Once the Mortons got the slide projector out, I knew it was time to *extricate* myself from their dinner party.
모튼 가족이 슬라이드 영사기를 꺼내자 난 그들의 저녁 파티에서 빠져나올 때라는 걸 알았다.

The famous magician, Harry Houdini, was able to *extricate* himself from handcuffs, straightjackets, and ropes with great ease.
유명한 마술사 해리 후디니는 수갑, 구속복, 밧줄에 매여서도 식은 죽 먹기로 풀려나올 수 있었다.

EXUBERANT [igzú:bərənt/igzjú:-] adj. overflowing with joy and happiness 즐거움(행복감)이 넘쳐 흐르는

The child was *exuberant* after receiving the Christmas gift she wanted most, a GI Hank Anti-Terrorist Guerrilla kit.
아이는 크리스마스 선물로 가장 갖고 싶어 했던 'GI 행크 반테러 게릴라' 조립품을 받자 행복에 겨웠다.

The *exuberant* feeling at the meeting of the Lucky People's Club disappeared when the comet crashed into the building.
'럭키 피플 클럽' 모임의 즐겁던 분위기가 혜성이 건물과 충돌하는 바람에 사라졌다.

EXUDE [igzú:d/iksú:d] v. to ooze out, give forth as if oozing; radiate 스며 나오다; 발산하다

The sap *exuded* by the rubber tree is used to make... you guessed it, rubber!
고무나무에서 스며 나오는 액즙은 짐작할 수 있듯이 콘돔을 만드는 데 쓰인다.

The salesman *exuded* a friendliness that caused many people to buy his products without even looking at them first.
판매원의 친절함은 많은 사람들로 하여금 물건을 먼저 보지도 않고 사도록 만들었다.

F

FATHOM [fǽðəm] v. to understand; to get the point or n. a unit of length that equals six feet and is used by sailors to measure the depth of water 이해하다; 간파하다 / 길(6피트, 1.83m에 해당하는 길이의 단위)

The professor's speech was so garbled and full of gaps in logic that I was unable to *fathom* what she was trying to tell the class.
교수의 말은 너무 왜곡되고 논리가 부족해 학생들에게 무슨 얘기를 하려는 건지 이해할 수 없었다.

Since the water near the left bank of the river was over three *fathoms* deeper than the water in the center, the steamship headed left.
강의 왼쪽 제방 부근의 물은 중심부의 수심보다 3길 이상 깊어서 기선은 왼쪽으로 방향을 틀었다.

FAWN [fɔːn] v. to try to please someone by excessive flattery; to seek favor by showing attention 아첨하다, 비위를 맞추다; 아양 떨다

The cheerleaders used to *fawn* over the star quarterback until one of them found out the hard way that he never brushed his teeth.
치어리더들은 인기 있는 쿼터백에게 아양을 떨곤 했는데, 그들 중 한 명이 그가 절대로 양치질을 안 한다는 사실을 어렵사리 알아냈다.

The three brothers *fawned* over the new babysitter, hoping that they could convince her to give them ice cream for dinner.
세 형제는 저녁으로 아이스크림을 얻어먹으려고 새로 온 베이비시터의 비위를 맞추었다.

FAX [fæks] n. a machine which uses telephone lines to send and receive exact copies of paper documents; the copy produced by a fax machine or v. to send someone a document by fax machine 팩스; 팩스로 온 문서 / 팩스로 보내다

The *fax* machine in our office received a copy of the important contract that was sent from our Michigan office only moments before lightning struck the building.
우리 사무실의 팩스로 미시건 사무소에서 보낸 중요한 계약서 사본이 들어왔는데, 번개가 건물을 강타하기 겨우 몇 분전이었다.

I photocopied my face and then *faxed* it to a friend of mine who lives in Alaska.
내 얼굴을 복사해서 알래스카에 사는 친구에게 팩스로 보냈다.

FELICITY [filísəti] n. joy and great happiness 커다란 행복

The *felicity* of the wedding reception was threatened when the bridesmaids got into a fist fight over the bouquet.
결혼 피로연의 행복한 분위기가 신부 들러리들이 서로 부케를 갖겠다고 주먹다짐을 하는 바람에 깨질 뻔했다.

The beautiful sunrise and a swarm of colorful butterflies added to the *felicity* we felt as we strolled through the park.
우리가 공원을 거닐고 있을 때 아름다운 일출과 한 떼의 화려한 나비들이 행복감을 더해 주었다.

FEND [fend] v. to hold off, especially an attack or to attempt to manage   방어하다; 꾸려 가다, 부양하다

By placing a wall of sandbags around the house, the Thompsons were able to *fend* off the rising flood waters for one more day.
톰슨 가족은 집 둘레에 모래주머니로 벽을 쌓아 점점 올라오는 홍수의 물을 하루 더 막아낼 수 있었다.

When our hiking guide went mad after eating those weird purple berries, we knew we would have to *fend* for ourselves on the way back to camp.
하이킹 가이드가 이상하게 생긴 자주색 열매를 먹고 나서 제정신을 잃자, 캠프로 돌아가는 길은 우리 힘으로 꾸려 가야 한다는 걸 알았다.

FICTION [fíkʃən] n. a piece of writing that is made up from the writer's imagination and is not factual; the category of writing that includes novels and short stories, but not plays, poems, or factual works or a lie   소설; 꾸민 이야기, 허구

Miranda's love of star-gazing and wild imagination help her write great *fiction* about visitors from other planets and travels through space.
미란다는 천문학에 대한 애정과 엉뚱한 상상력 덕분에 다른 행성에서 온 방문객들과 우주여행에 대한 근사한 소설을 쓸 수 있다.

My brother likes reading history books and biographies of famous people, but I think *fiction* is more interesting.
우리 오빠는 역사책과 유명 인사의 전기 읽는 것을 좋아하지만, 나는 소설이 더 재미있다.

Myron's story about a giant ostrich breaking into his bedroom and eating his homework turned out to be complete *fiction*.
거대한 타조가 자기 방에 쳐들어와 숙제해 놓은 걸 먹어 버렸다는 마이런의 얘기는 알고 보니 순전히 꾸며낸 것이었다.

FIGUREHEAD [fígjəhed/fígər-] n. someone who is the head of a group by title, but who actually has no real power or a carved figure, usually of a woman, on the front part (the prow) of a ship   명목상의 대표; 뱃머리에 놓는 조상(彫像)

After China lost its war with Japan, the once powerful Emperor of China became a *figurehead* controlled completely by the Japanese government.
중국이 일본과의 전쟁에서 패하자 강력했던 중국의 황제는 일본 정부에 철저히 지배당하는 꼭두각시가 되었다.

The *figurehead* on the pirate ship looked like an Amazon warrior, bravely facing the dangerous seas.
해적선 뱃머리의 조상은 위험한 바다에 용감히 맞서는 아마존 전사의 모습이었다.

FISCAL [fískəl] adj. concerning money or finances; concerning the government's treasury or finances   재정상의, 회계의; 국고의

Stan, who liked to shop and spent money freely, became cranky whenever his wife brought up *fiscal* matters or tried to set up a family budget.
쇼핑을 좋아해 돈을 맘껏 쓰고 다니는 스탠은 아내가 재정적인 문제를 들고 나오거나 가계 예산을 짜려고 할 때면 심기가 뒤틀렸다.

The government hoped to solve its *fiscal* problems by printing ten trillion dollars in new money.
정부는 십조에 달하는 새 화폐를 찍어내 국고 문제를 해결하고자 했다.

FISSURE [fíʃər] n. a long, thin split in a rock; any long, thin split   갈라진 틈

The horizontal *fissure* in the rock provided an excellent fingerhold during my climb up the face of Yosemite Cliff.
요세미티 절벽을 기어오를 때 가로로 벌어진 바위틈이 있어 손가락으로 잡고 오를 수 있었다.

As the days grew warmer, *fissures* and cracks began to appear in the layer of ice covering the lake.
날씨가 따뜻해지자 호수를 뒤덮고 있는 얼음 층에 틈이 생기기 시작했다.

FLABBERGAST [flǽbərgæst/-gɑ̀:st] v. to amaze, astonish, bewilder 깜짝 놀라게 하다, 어리둥절하게 하다

When the penguin at the zoo asked me for a cigarette, I was too *flabbergasted* to tell it I didn't smoke.
동물원의 펭귄이 내게 담배 한 개비를 달라고 했을 때 난 너무 놀라서 담배를 안 피운다는 말조차 할 수 없었다.

During the basketball game, when all the players started to float towards the ceiling, the referee was too *flabbergasted* to blow his whistle or call any penalties.
농구 경기 동안 모든 선수들이 천장을 향해 두둥실 떠다니기 시작하자 너무 당황한 레퍼리는 휘슬을 불지도, 반칙을 주지도 못했다.

FLAG [flæg] v. to lose strength; to weaken 축 늘어지다, 약해지다

As the malaria ran its course, the patient's health *flagged* dangerously.
말라리아가 진행되자 환자의 건강이 극도로 쇠약해졌다.

As they reached the twenty-mile point in the marathon, the pace of the runners started to *flag*.
주자들이 마라톤의 20마일 지점에 이르자 속도가 느려지기 시작했다.

FLAMBOYANT [flæmbɔ́iənt] adj. very flashy, over-the-top, exaggerated 대단히 화려한, 과장된, 과한

Although I didn't mind the diamond-studded suit and pants that Robert wore, I did think his eight-foot neon crown was a little *flamboyant*.
로버트가 입은 다이아몬드 박힌 정장은 그런대로 괜찮았지만 8피트 높이의 네온 왕관은 좀 심한 것 같았다.

The *flamboyant* actor liked to burst into a room, scream, run around, and kiss everyone, and only then would he sit down for the morning meeting.
오버하기 좋아하는 배우는 방으로 불쑥 들어와 소리를 지르고 뛰어다니고 모든 사람에게 입을 맞춘 다음에라야 아침 회의를 위해 자리에 앉곤 했다.

FLANK [flæŋk] v. to move around and attack the side of something; to be placed at the side of another object or n. the side of a body, just above the hip 측면을 공격하다; 측면에 위치하다 / 옆구리

By galloping around a hill to their left, the Huns were able to *flank* their opponents and attack them from two directions.
훈족은 왼쪽으로 언덕을 돌아 말을 몰고 질주해 적들을 두 방향에서 측면 공격할 수 있었다.

We decided that the two smaller stuffed bears should *flank* the larger Papa Bear which was in the middle of the bed.
우리는 두 개의 작은 곰 인형을 침대 가운데에 있는 커다란 아빠곰 옆에 놓기로 했다.

The racehorse's muscular *flank* rippled as he rounded the first turn in the track.
경주마가 트랙에서 첫 번째 바퀴를 돌 때 근육질 옆구리가 꿈틀거렸다.

FLATTERY [flǽtəri] n. excessive or insincere compliments 아첨

The reporters continued their *flattery* of the actress until she finally granted them an interview.
기자들은 여배우에게 계속 아첨을 해서 마침내 그녀에게서 인터뷰 허락을 얻어냈다.

I was certain that *flattery* would put my mother in a good enough mood that she wouldn't get mad about the missing sofa, but I was wrong.
나는 어머니한테 알랑거려 없어진 소파에 대해 화내지 않을 만큼 기분이 좋아졌다고 확신했는데, 잘못 생각한 것이었다.

FLEDGLING [flédʒliŋ] n. a baby bird that has just learned how to fly or adj. new and inexperienced 겨우 날 수 있게 된 아기 새 / 경험이 없는, 풋내기의

The alley cat stood watch below the bluejay's nest, hoping that one of the *fledglings* would fall as it was trying to fly for the first time.
도둑고양이는 아기새가 처음으로 나는 연습을 할 때 한 마리라도 떨어지기를 바라며 큰어치 둥지밑에 서 있었다.

When our *fledgling* tour guide had trouble even turning on the microphone, I knew I was in for a long day at the museum.
경험이 부족한 관광 가이드가 마이크를 켜는 데도 어려움을 겪자 나는 박물관에서 지루한 하루가 되리라는 걸 알았다.

FLEECE [fliːs] n. a sheep's coat of wool 양털

Fleece makes an excellent jacket liner, but only after you wash the smell of sheep out of it.
양털은 뛰어난 재킷 안감이 되지만, 그 전에 양의 냄새를 씻어 내야 한다.

Since they had some extra *fleece* left over after the shearing, the shepherds decided to knit warm gloves for everyone.
양치기들은 양털을 깎은 뒤 여분의 양털이 생기자 모두에게 따뜻한 장갑을 떠 주기로 했다.

FLOTSAM [flátsəm/flɔ́t-] n. floating wreckage and debris from a wrecked ship and its cargo (조난선의) 표류 화물

A jewelry box, a parasol, and some piano keys drifted among the *flotsam* from the sunken luxury ocean liner.
보석 상자, 양산, 피아노 건반 몇 개가 침몰된 호화 정기선의 표류 화물 사이에 떠다녔다.

FLOUT [flaut] v. to scorn and show contempt for; to treat with contempt 모욕하다, 업신여기다

Xander *flouted* his parents' authority by grabbing his father's car keys and speeding off to the Foo Fighters concert, even though he was supposed to be grounded.
잰더는 외출 금지를 당한 상태였는데, 아버지의 차 열쇠를 훔쳐서 '푸 파이터스' 콘서트에 몰고 감으로써 부모님의 권위를 무시했다.

The French waiter *flouted* my efforts to speak his language by calling my accent barbaric and covering his ears whenever I began to talk.
프랑스 출신 웨이터는 내가 말을 꺼낼 때마다 내 억양이 세련되지 못하다면서 두 귀를 막아 프랑스어를 해보려는 내 노력을 업신여겼다.

FLUCTUATE [flʌ́ktʃueit] v. to shift back and forth; to change irregularly 오락가락하다, 오르내리다; 불규칙하게 변하다

Fall weather in hill country *fluctuates* between eighty degrees and sunny one day to forty degrees and cloudy the next.
고지의 가을 날씨는 어느 날은 화씨 80도에 화창하다가, 다음 날엔 40도에 흐려지는 등 불규칙하게 변한다.

Pavel's weight *fluctuates* so wildly from month to month that he has to keep both extra-large and extra-small shirts in his closet.
패블의 몸무게는 한 달 간격으로 너무 심하게 오르내려서 옷장 속에 셔츠를 특대와 특소 두 가지 다 넣어 두어야 한다.

FLUENT [flúːənt] adj. able to express yourself smoothly; graceful 유창한, 말 잘하는; 우아한, 품위있는

Since she was *fluent* in many languages, the translator had no problem interpreting everything the four foreign diplomats said.
통역사는 여러 언어를 유창하게 말해서 서로 다른 나라의 외교관 네 명이 말하는 것을 전부 옮기는 데 아무 문제가 없었다.

Jordan's *fluent* movements on the basketball court make him a pleasure to watch.
농구 코트에서 조던의 우아한 움직임은 보는 즐거움을 준다.

FLUSTER [flʌ́stər] v. to shake up and make nervous or excited 흥분시키다, 정신을 못 차리게 하다

When told she was one of three finalists for the lottery, the woman was so *flustered* that she dropped the telephone.
여자는 자신이 최종 복권 당첨 가능자 세 명 중에 들었다는 얘기를 듣고 너무 흥분해 수화기를 떨어뜨렸다.

The 3:00 a.m. surprise visit from the king *flustered* the farmer and his wife.
새벽 세 시에 느닷없이 왕의 방문을 받은 농부와 아내는 정신을 차릴 수 없었다.

FLUX [flʌks] n. continuous change; flow 끊임없는 변화: 흐름, 유동

Chrissie's career plans are always in *flux*; last week she wanted to be a mail carrier, yesterday she decided to become a ballerina, and today she announced that she intended to play golf for a living.
크리시의 직업 계획은 끊임없이 변한다. 지난주에는 우편배달부가 되고 싶다더니, 어제는 발레리나가 되겠다고 하고, 오늘은 프로 골프 선수가 되겠다고 발표했다.

FOIL [fɔil] v. to prevent from being successful, to ruin 좌절시키다

The villain's plan to kill the heroine was *foiled* when Pokey Slim arrived just in time to untie her from the railroad track and carry her to safety.
여주인공을 없애려는 악한의 계획은 포키 슬림이 제때에 도착해 선로에서 그녀를 풀어 주고 안전한 곳으로 데려가자 좌절되었다.

Meg *foiled* my dreams of becoming student class president by convincing everyone that I was a teacher's pet who secretly wanted to lengthen the school day by two hours.
멕은 학급 회장이 되려는 내 꿈을 좌절시켰는데, 내가 선생님의 귀염둥이로, 수업이 두 시간씩 연장되는 걸 몰래 원하고 있다며 모든 아이들이 그걸 믿도록 설득시켰기 때문이다.

FOLIAGE [fóuliidʒ] n. a group of plant leaves (나무 한 그루의) 잎 전부

We stood next to the trunk of a tree so its dense *foliage* would shelter us from the rainstorm.
우리는 나무줄기 옆에 서서 빽빽한 잎들 밑에서 폭풍우를 피했다.

As they searched for the fabled Gold Howler Monkey, the explorers used machetes to hack away the *foliage* of the jungle.
탐험가들은 전설적인 금빛 짖는 원숭이를 찾을 때 칼을 이용해 정글의 잎을 베며 나아갔다.

FOLLY [fáli/fɔ́li] n. lack of good judgment; stupidity and foolishness 어리석음

Looking back, Edwin realized the *folly* of his plan to cross the Sahara Desert on rollerskates.
돌이켜 보면, 에드윈은 롤러스케이트를 타고 사하라 사막을 횡단하겠다는 자신의 계획이 어리석었음을 깨달았다.

The daredevil's attempt to go over Niagara Falls in a barrel filled with deadly snakes was *folly* for all concerned, including the snakes.
독사가 가득 담긴 통 속에 들어가 나이아가라 폭포를 건너겠다는 무모한 사람의 시도는 뱀을 포함해 모든 사람에게 어리석게 보였다.

FOOLHARDY [fú:lhàːrdi] adj. reckless and rash; bold without thinking 무모한, 앞뒤를 가리지 않는

As she plummeted through the sky, Gabriella realized that it was *foolhardy* to go skydiving without a parachute.
가브리엘라는 하늘에서 곤두박질칠 때 낙하산 없이 스카이다이빙을 하는 건 무모한 일임을 깨달았다.

The *foolhardy* soldier quickly volunteered to attack the German 7th Tank Regiment armed only with a spoon and an old muffin.
앞뒤를 가리지 않는 군인은 숟가락 하나와 오래된 머핀 하나로 무장한 채 독일의 제7전차 부대 공격에 서둘러 자원했다.

FORAGE [fɔ́(:)ridʒ/fɑ́r-] v. to hunt or search for something 찾아다니다

The raccoons that hang around our apartment complex love to *forage* for food in the dumpsters.
우리 아파트 단지 주변을 어슬렁거리는 미국 너구리들은 쓰레기통 속의 음식을 찾아다니기 좋아한다.

I *foraged* through my sock drawer looking for the one pair of tweed argyles that I wear whenever I need good luck.
나는 행운이 필요할 때마다 신는 트위드 마름모 색 무늬 양말 한 짝을 찾으려고 양말 서랍을 뒤적거렸다.

FOREBODING [fɔːrbóudiŋ] n. a feeling that something bad is about to happen (불길한 일에 대한) 육감, 예감

A certain *foreboding* fell over the football crowd as they watched the mean-looking aliens descend from the sky and beat up the school band.
미식축구 관중들은 심술궂게 생긴 외계인들이 하늘에서 내려와 학교 밴드를 두들겨 패자 불길한 예감에 휩싸였다.

Milt Haaspand was a superstitious man who always had a sense of *foreboding* when his left knee started to ache.
밀트 하스팬드는 미신에 사로잡힌 사람으로, 왼쪽 무릎이 욱신거리기 시작하면 늘 불길한 예감을 느꼈다.

FORGE [fɔːrdʒ] v. to form (usually metal) by heating then shaping; to shape or mold carefully or v. to head forward against resistance 쇠를 달구어 모양을 만들다; 정성 들여 모양을 만들다; 꾸준히 나아가다

Back in the old days, when peace returned to a country, black-smiths would gather up the soldiers' swords and *forge* them into farm tools, such as plowshares.
옛날 옛적에는 나라에 평화가 돌아오면 대장장이들이 군인들의 칼을 모아다가 보습 같은 농기구를 만들었다.

The skillful diplomat was able to *forge* a lasting peace between Israel and Egypt.
능숙한 외교관은 이스라엘과 이집트 사이에 지속적인 평화를 구축할 수 있었다.

The candidate was determined to *forge* ahead with his campaign, despite the opinion polls that showed he was trailing far behind his opponent.
후보자는 그가 상대 후보보다 훨씬 뒤떨어져 있다는 걸 보여주는 여론조사에도 아랑곳없이 선거운동을 계속해 나가기로 했다.

FORMIDABLE [fɔ́ːrmidəbl] adj. difficult to defeat; frightening or alarming; awe-inspiring 만만치 않은, 이기기 힘든; 무서운; 경외심을 일으키는

Lightning quick and over seven feet tall, Ed "Three Hands" Hroboski was one of the most *formidable* Ping-Pong players around.
번개같이 빠르고 신장이 7피트가 넘는 "세 손"이란 별명의 에드 흐로보스키는 가장 이기기 힘든 탁구 선수 중의 하나다.

I think of Glenda as a *formidable* person because I once saw her uproot an oak tree with one arm.
글렌다는 무서운 사람 같은데, 전에 그녀가 한 손으로 오크를 뿌리째 뽑는 걸 봤기 때문이다.

FORTHRIGHT [fɔ́ːrθrait] adj. honest and open; straightforward and direct 정직한; 솔직한

Voters loved the *forthright* governor who always kept her campaign promises and never once did anything unethical.
유권자들은 정직한 주지사를 좋아했는데, 그녀는 언제나 자신의 선거 공약을 지키고 윤리에 어긋나는 일은 절대 하지 않았다.

Because he was so *forthright* about his feelings for her, Karen agreed to go to the prom with Charles.
카렌은 찰스가 그녀에 대한 감정에 아주 솔직했기 때문에 그와 함께 댄스파티에 가겠다고 했다.

FOSSIL [fásəl/fɔ́səl] n. the bones or remains of an ancient life form 화석

A farmer in England found a *fossil* that appears to be the footprint of the largest dinosaur ever discovered.
영국의 한 농부가 화석을 발견했는데, 그것은 지금까지 발견된 것 중 몸집이 가장 큰 공룡의 발자국처럼 보인다.

In the Museum of Natural History, I saw *fossils* of ancient plants and fish.
자연사 박물관에서 고대 식물과 물고기의 화석들을 보았다.

[Note] *Fossil fuel* is any fossil material that burns. Coal, petroleum, and natural gas all came from fossils.
fossil fuel은 '화석연료' 로, 석탄, 석유, 천연가스 등을 말한다.

FRAIL [freil] adj. weak and easily broken 약한, 쉽게 깨지는

Surgery had left Francine very *frail*, so her doctors kept her in the hospital for an extra week to make sure she was strong enough to go home.
수술을 받은 프랜신은 아주 쇠약해져서 의사들은 그녀가 퇴원할 정도로 충분히 건강해질 때까지 한 주 더 입원해 있도록 했다.

It took only a mild gust of wind to smash the *frail* treehouse the boys had made out of toothpicks.
부드러운 바람이 겨우 한번 불었는데 아이들이 이쑤시개로 만들어 놓은 연약한 나무 위의 집이 부숴졌다.

FRANK [fræŋk] adj. open and direct; sincere 솔직한; 진심 어린

The queen liked *frank* advisers who pointed out her errors, not flatterers who always agreed with her and were afraid to speak their minds.
여왕은 언제나 그녀의 의견에 동의하고 자신들의 마음을 이야기하기 두려워하는 아첨꾼들 대신에 그녀의 잘못을 지적하는 솔직한 조언자들을 좋아했다.

[Note] *Frankness* [fræŋknis] n. means openness and directness
frankness는 '솔직함'

▪ I admire Carol's *frankness* because even though she sometimes says unpleasant things, I always know she's giving me her true opinion.
나는 캐롤의 솔직함을 아주 좋아하는데, 그녀가 가끔씩은 불쾌한 이야기를 하지만 언제나 진실된 의견을 내놓는다는 걸 알기 때문이다.

FRENZY [frénzi] n. a condition of wild excitement and agitation 격분, 광란

Jonas, a huge Tampa Bay fan since birth, went into a *frenzy* after the Buccaneer's last-second win in the Super Bowl.
태어날 때부터 탬파베이의 골수팬인 요나는 수퍼볼에서 바커니어스가 막판에 우승을 거두자 광란 상태가 됐다.

The townsfolk went into a *frenzy* when they learned that Mayor Snide had tried to raise taxes by eighty percent and rename the town Snidesville.
읍민들은 스나이드 읍장이 세금을 80%나 올리고 읍 이름을 스나이즈빌로 바꾸려고 한다는 걸 알고 격분했다.

FRINGE [frindʒ] n. the outer portion or margin; the edge or a decorative edge with dangling or hanging threads 가장자리, 언저리; 술 장식 / 술을 붙이다; 가장자리를 달다

Salt *fringed* the little pool of sea water that was drying in the sun.
바닷물이 담긴 작은 저수지가 햇볕에 말라가자 가장자리에 소금이 생겼다.

Teresa used tiny ribbons to create a *fringe* for her new dress.
테레사는 작은 리본들을 이용해 새로 산 드레스에 술 장식을 달았다.

FROCK [frɑk/frɔk] n. a large, loose outer garment, like a priest's robe; a woman's dress   (성직자복 같은) 길고 헐렁한 겉옷; 드레스

I tried to listen to the priest's sermon, but I was distracted by the incredible number of mustard stains all over the front of his *frock*.
신부님의 설교에 귀를 기울이려고 노력했지만 성직자복 앞에 잔뜩 묻어 있는 겨자 얼룩 때문에 주의가 산만해졌다.

Diane's party *frock* was so loose and formless that it made her look like a human tent.
다이안의 파티 드레스는 너무 헐렁하고 밋밋해서 마치 인간 텐트처럼 보였다.

FUNDAMENTAL [fʌ̀ndəméntl] adj. having to do with the basic level; primary or elemental   기초의; 근본적인, 중요한

One of the *fundamental* rules of soccer is to never touch the ball with your hands.
축구의 기본 규칙 가운데 하나는 절대 손으로 공을 건드리지 않는 것이다.

Obedience to their commander is a *fundamental* requirement of all soldiers.
지휘자에게 복종하는 것은 모든 군인들에게 중요한 요건이다.

A *fundamental* knowledge of math is all you need in order to balance your checkbook.
수학은 수표장을 결산하는 데 필요한 기본적 지식만 알면 된다.

FURTIVE [fə́ːrtiv] adj. done in a quiet, secretive way   은밀한, 몰래 하는

While her mother's back was turned, Sandy took a *furtive* peek inside the closet where she knew the Christmas presents were hidden.
샌디는 어머니가 등을 돌리자 옷장 속을 슬쩍 들여다봤는데, 거기에 크리스마스 선물이 숨겨져 있는 걸 알았기 때문이다.

Miguel had no hall pass, so he had to slide *furtively* along the wall and duck while passing the windows in the doors of classrooms so no teachers would see him.
미구엘은 외출증이 없어서 교실 문에 달린 창유리들을 지날 때 교사들에게 들키지 않도록 벽을 따라 살금살금 몰래 가면서 머리를 푹 숙여야 했다.

G

GALE [geil] n. an extremely strong wind or a loud outburst 질풍, 강풍; 요란한 폭발

The rainfall from the thunderstorm wasn't threatening, but the *gales* ripped apart houses and knocked people off their feet.
뇌우로 인한 강우는 심하지 않았지만, 강풍이 불어와 집들이 부서지고 사람들이 쓰러졌다.

Gales of laughter erupted from the club audience as the comedian went into his famous "Smashing Mushrooms" skit.
코미디언이 그의 유명한 촌극 "스매싱 머쉬룸스"를 시작하자 클럽의 관객들에게서 왁자지껄한 웃음이 터져 나왔다.

GALLEON [gǽliən] n. a large ship with sails, used especially by the Spanish in the 1400s, 1500s, and 1600s 갤리온선(1400년대 ~ 1600년대 스페인의 대범선)

The sunset glowed off the *galleon's* white sails as it glided into port at Montevideo.
갤리온선이 몬테비데오 항구로 미끄러져 들어올 때 하얀 돛에 저녁놀 빛이 타올랐다.

GARBLE [gɑ́:rbl] v. to mix up or distort 왜곡하다

The poem is beautiful in the original Spanish, but this bad translation *garbles* its meaning.
본래 스페인어로 쓰여진 그 시는 아름다운데, 형편없는 번역이 의미를 왜곡시킨다.

The principal interrupted our classes to make an important announcement, but the intercom *garbled* his voice so badly that it was impossible to tell what he was saying.
교장이 중대 발표를 하겠다며 수업을 중단시켰는데, 인터콤에서 나오는 목소리가 너무 일그러져서 무슨 얘기를 하는지 알아들을 수가 없었다.

GARLAND [gɑ́:rlənd] n. a string of flowers, leaves, or other materials woven together to form a crown or some other ornament 화환, 화관

I twisted the stems of the roses together to create a beautiful *garland*, but the thorns made wearing it a little painful.
장미 줄기를 한데 꼬아서 아름다운 화관을 만들었지만 가시 때문에 머리에 쓰면 좀 아팠다.

The Pattersons always hung a *garland* of mistletoe and holly on their front door to show their Christmas spirit.
패터슨 가족은 언제나 크리스마스 기분을 내기 위해 겨우살이와 서양 호랑가시나무로 만든 화환을 앞문에 걸어 두었다.

GARRISON [gǽrəsn]   n. a military fort or the group of soldiers stationed at that fort   요새, 주둔지; 수비대, 주둔군

The walls of the *garrison* had to be repaired after the fire started by the rebel soldiers burned most of them down.
반란군 병사들이 일으킨 화재로 요새의 벽 대부분이 전소돼 수리를 해야만 했다.

Reinforcements from Adleyville boosted the *garrison's* strength, but the soldiers were still badly outnumbered by their enemy.
아들리빌에서 도착한 지원군이 주둔군의 전력을 높여 주긴 했지만 적군에 비하면 아직도 훨씬 모자란 숫자였다.

GAUNT [gɔ:nt]   adj. bony and thin; undernourished or bleak and stark   여윈, 바짝 마른; 영양 부족의; 쓸쓸한, 황량한

The *gaunt* cat looked like it was made of nothing more than furry paper stretched over a rib cage.
비쩍 마른 고양이는 흉곽 위에 모피로 만든 종이를 펴놓은 것 같았다.

George Orwell's *gaunt* vision of the future in the book *1984* is enough to make anyone want to build a time machine and go live in the Paleozoic Era.
'1984년'이라는 책 속에서 미래에 대한 조지 오웰의 암울한 상상은 누구든지 타임머신을 만들어 고생대로 가서 살고 싶도록 만들기에 충분하다.

GENE [dʒi:n]   n. a particular section of DNA that determines a particular hereditary characteristic which is passed down from one generation to the next   유전자

The color of your eyes is determined entirely by the combination of your father's and mother's *genes*.
눈 색깔은 전적으로 아버지와 어머니의 유전자 조합으로 결정된다.

Scientists try to isolate the *genes* that cause hereditary diseases like diabetes so that they may some day be able to eliminate the disease.
과학자들은 당뇨병 같은 유전적 질병을 일으키는 유전인자를 분리하려고 하는데, 언젠가 그런 질병을 퇴치할 수 있기 위해서다.

GENRE [ʒɑ́:nrə]   n. a specific type of literature or music, like science fiction or heavy metal   장르, 양식

My father loves opera, but I think most of the music in that *genre* sounds like people screaming in some crazy language.
우리 아버지는 오페라를 좋아하시지만, 나한테는 그런 장르의 음악 대부분이 좀 미친 듯한 언어로 소리를 지르는 것처럼 들린다.

The writer Curly Pickins was a master of the Western *genre*, but critics hated his romances.
작가 컬리 피킨스는 서부물의 대가였지만 평론가들은 그의 소설을 싫어했다.

GIBBERISH [dʒíbəriʃ]   n. speech or writing that makes no sense; crazy talk   횡설수설, 말이 안 되는 말

Walking bananas Tom bluebird in the dufflebeak nosehair mackinute soapdish von *gibberish* nork nork nork. (This is just an example.)
말이 안 되는 소리의 예.

Foreign languages sound like *gibberish* unless you know how to speak them.
외국어는 말하는 방법을 모르면 말도 안 되는 소리처럼 들린다.

GIDDY [gídi] adj. dizzy; feeling an unsteady, whirling sensation or excited and light-headed 어지러운, 현기증 나는; 흥분한, 경솔한

Riding the Doomhills of Tharg rollercoaster nineteen consecutive times left Jim *giddy* and unable to remember his own name.
짐은 '둠힐스 오브 타그' 롤러코스터를 연달아 19번 탔더니 어지러웠고 자기 이름조차 생각나지 않았다.

I felt *giddy* as I rounded the bases after hitting my first home run ever in Little League game.
나는 리틀 야구 경기에서 처음으로 홈런을 때리고 베이스를 돌 때 흥분됐다.

GLARE [glɛər] v. to stare angrily or to shine very brightly or n. a long, angry stare or a bright, a blinding light 노려보다; 번쩍번쩍 빛나다 / 노려봄; 번쩍이는 빛, 눈부신 빛

The jealous student *glared* at Evelyn the whole time she was onstage accepting her award for being the Geography Student of the Year.
질투심 많은 학생은 에블린이 무대 위로 올라가 '올해의 지리학도 상'을 수여하는 내내 그녀를 노려보았다.

Evelyn noticed the *glare* of the jealous student, but she was too happy to care.
에블린은 질투심 많은 학생이 자신을 노려보는 걸 알아차렸지만 너무 기뻐서 개의치 않았다.

The sun *glared* down on the beach, making the sand look bright white.
태양이 해변에 눈부시게 쏟아져 모래가 새하얗게 보였다.

The *glare* of the sun, which was reflected off the sand, made it hard for me to see who was approaching my beach blanket.
눈부신 태양 빛이 모래에 반사돼 내 해변 담요 쪽으로 누가 걸어오는지 알아보기 힘들었다.

GLEAN [gliːn] v. to gather or find something out piece by piece 조금씩 모으다, 알아내다

After collecting and sorting through all the numerous fingerprints, the detectives began to *glean* the identity of the burglar.
형사들은 수많은 지문을 모두 모아 분류한 뒤 강도의 신원을 파악해내기 시작했다.

Staring at the eight maps of Paris, Humberto was able to *glean* some idea of where they were.
움베르토는 여덟 개의 파리 지도를 뚫어져라 쳐다보자 그들이 있는 곳이 어딘지 어느 정도 알 수 있었다.

GLISTEN [glísn] v. to shine with a sparkling light; to sparkle 반짝이다, 번쩍이다

The light coat of dew caused the grass to *glisten* in the morning sunlight.
아침의 태양 빛 속에서 이슬의 표면이 빛을 내자 잔디가 반짝였다.

The sunbather *glistened* with sweat and suntan oil.
일광욕을 즐기는 사람은 땀과 선탠오일로 몸이 번쩍거렸다.

GNASH [næʃ] v. to grind or strike teeth together 이를 갈다

The weightlifter *gnashed* his teeth as he tried to bench press 600 pounds.
역도 선수는 6백 파운드의 역기를 벤치 프레스(역도에서, 벤치에 누워 가슴 높이에서 양팔을 완전히 뻗어 들어올리는 것)하려고 애쓰며 이를 갈았다.

Hearing fingernails being raked across a chalk board makes me *gnash* my teeth in agony.
손톱이 칠판에서 긁히는 소리를 들으면 난 괴로움에 이가 갈린다.

GOAD [goud] v. to urge or prod   자극하다, 부추기다; 못살게 굴다

We finally went outside and sat down in the backyard after our father *goaded* us to get off the sofa and do something with our lives.
아버지가 우리에게 소파에서 일어나 활기차게 뭔가를 하라며 못살게 해서 우린 밖으로 나와 뒤뜰에 앉았다.

The bully tried to *goad* Casey into fighting by spitting on him and then making chicken noises.
깡패는 케이시에게 침을 뱉고 겁쟁이라는 표시로 시끄러운 닭소리를 내면서 그를 자극해 싸움을 붙이려고 했다.

GOBLET [gáblit/gɔ́b-] n. a drinking cup with a stem and a base and no handle   고블릿, (손잡이 없이) 굽이 높은 술잔

It took both of my hands wrapped tightly around the stem to lift the thick, gold *goblet* which weighed eighty pounds.
80파운드 무게의 두툼한 황금 고블릿을 들기 위해 양손으로 굽 둘레를 단단히 감쌌다.

The Stanley Cup Trophy, given to be best pro hockey team each year, is a large *goblet*.
해마다 최고의 프로 하키 팀에게 주어지는 스탠리컵 트로피는 커다란 고블릿이다.

GOVERNESS [gʌ́vərnis] n. a woman whose job is to teach the children of a specific household   여성 가정교사

The strict *governess* told the Hansen kids to be at bed by eight with their teeth brushed and their toys put away.
엄한 가정교사는 핸슨 씨네 아이들에게 이를 닦고 장난감을 치운 다음 8시까지는 잠자리에 들어야 한다고 말했다.

GRANDEUR [grǽndʒər/-dʒuər] n. the state of being magnificent or grand   장려, 웅장

The tourists were so impressed with the *grandeur* of the German castle atop the snowy hill that they forgot to take a picture of it.
관광객들은 눈 덮인 언덕 꼭대기에 자리 잡은 독일 성의 웅장한 모습을 보고 너무나 감명을 받아서 사진을 찍을 생각도 잊고 있었다.

The redwood forests of California have as much *grandeur* as the palaces of Europe.
캘리포니아의 아메리카 삼나무 숲은 유럽의 궁궐들만큼이나 장대하다.

GRANDIOSE [grǽndious] adj. having a huge scope or intent or being pompous; having a pretended grandeur   방대한, 웅장한; 뽐내는, 과시하는; 과장한

Kevin's editor explained that his plan to write a book called "The Entire History of the World from Day One Until Now" might be a bit *grandiose*.
케빈의 편집자는 "전 세계사, 첫날부터 지금까지" 라는 책의 집필 계획이 좀 방대할지 모르겠다고 설명했다.

When Steve struck oil and got rich, he built a *grandiose* mansion with solid gold toilets, diamond doorknobs, and wall-to-wall zebra skin carpet in every room.
스티브는 유전을 발견해 떼돈을 벌게 되자 순금으로 된 변기에 다이아몬드 문손잡이가 달리고, 모든 방마다 바닥 전체에 얼룩말 가죽 양탄자가 깔린 웅장한 대저택을 지었다.

GRAPPLE [grǽpl] v. to struggle to hold onto; to struggle to understand   꽉 붙잡다; 맞붙어 싸우다; 이해하려고 애쓰다

When she jumped into the cold water of the lake, Gina learned that *grappling* with an eel should be avoided whenever possible.
지나는 호수의 차가운 물속에 뛰어 들어갈 때 가능한 한 뱀장어와 맞붙어 싸우는 건 피해야 한다는 걸 알았다.

After *grappling* with the idea that maybe he wasn't the most attractive man in the world, Brady understood why Sheila had rejected him.

브래디는 어쩌면 자신이 세상에서 가장 매력적인 남자가 아닐 거라는 생각과 씨름한 뒤 쉴라가 자신을 왜 거절했는지 이해하게 됐다.

GRIDLOCK [grídlɑ̀k/-lɔ̀k] n. a complete stop of all traffic on a road; a complete halt in activity 교통 정체; 완전한 정지

The man turned off his car engine and started to read a book after being stuck in the *gridlock* downtown for two hours.

남자는 시내에서 두 시간 동안 교통 정체에 갇히게 되자 자동차 시동을 끄고 책을 읽기 시작했다.

Negotiations reached a *gridlock* when each side refused to concede to further demands.

양측에서 그 이상의 요구 사항을 받아들이기 거부하자 협상이 완전히 중단됐다.

GUARDED [gɑ́:rdid] adj. cautious or restrained 신중한, 절제된; 방어된

When asked if she knew anything about the secret missile base, the government spokesperson gave the *guarded* reply of "Maybe. No comment."

정부 대변인은 비밀 미사일 기지에 대해 아는 것이 있느냐는 질문에 "어쩌면요. 하지만 언급하지 않겠습니다." 라며 대답을 아꼈다.

Mr. Johnson raised one eyebrow and gave a *guarded* welcome to his daughter's prom date, who came to pick her up wearing a black leather biker outfit and six nose rings.

존슨 씨는 딸의 졸업파티 파트너에게 한쪽 눈썹을 치켜들며 방어적으로 맞이했는데, 그는 검정 가죽 차림에 여섯 개의 코걸이를 하고 딸을 데리러 왔다.

GURNEY [gə́:rni] n. a flat table with wheels used to transport patients around a hospital 환자 수송용 테이블

The emergency room nurses quickly placed the injured man on a *gurney* and wheeled him away from the ambulance and into surgery.

응급실 간호사들은 부상당한 남자를 재빨리 수송 침대에 눕힌 뒤 구급차에서 빼내 수술실로 밀고 갔다.

GURU [gúru] n. a person who is both teacher and leader to a group of followers (정신적) 지도자

Thousands of believers traveled from all over the world to hear the *guru* speak about love, religion, and her new diet plan.

수천 명의 신도들이 사랑, 종교, 새로운 다이어트 계획에 대한 지도자의 이야기를 듣기 위해 세계 각지에서 몰려왔다.

Zam Zamford, whose seminars and lectures are always packed full of farmers, is recognized as an agriculture *guru*.

세미나와 강연이 열릴 때마다 농부들이 발 디딜 틈 없이 몰려오는 잼 잼포드는 농업의 지도자로 인정받는다.

H

HAPHAZARD [hæphǽzərd] adj. marked by chance or luck; random 우연한; 되는 대로의

The blindfolded children took many *haphazard* swings at the piñata, but Elwood finally landed a lucky blow and tore it open.
눈을 가린 아이들이 공중에 매달린 피냐타에 대고 되는대로 막대기를 휘둘렀지만, 엘우드가 마침내 행운의 강타를 날려 부숴져 열리게 했다.

The librarian's *haphazard* approach to shelving and organizing books makes it difficult to find the materials you're looking for.
사서가 책들을 아무렇게나 꽂아서 정리해 놓아 필요한 자료를 찾기가 힘들다.

HAZE [heiz] v. to force someone to perform unpleasant tasks; usually in order for them to be qualified to join a club or fraternity (주로 신입생을) 괴롭히다, 골탕 먹이다.

The young sailor was *hazed* by the older seamen, who painted his face and shaved his head while he was sleeping.
젊은 선원은 나이든 선원들에게 신고식을 당했는데, 그가 자고 있는 동안 그들은 그의 얼굴에 그림을 그리고 머리를 밀어 버렸다.

The Kappa Gnu Sigma fraternity *hazed* first-year students by forcing them to run across campus totally naked.
남학생 자치 기숙사인 '카파 누 시그마'는 신입생들에게 신고식으로 알몸으로 캠퍼스를 뛰도록 했다.

HEIST [haist] v. to rob or steal or n. a burglary 훔치다 / 강도

The thief *heisted* the wallet from the lady's purse and ran away down the street.
도둑은 숙녀 핸드백에서 지갑을 훔쳐 도망갔다.

Once the train *heist* was over, the robbers split up and then met three weeks later at an abandoned farm to split up the goods.
일단 열차 강도를 끝낸 도둑들은 헤어졌다가 3주 후 물건을 나누기 위해 버려진 농가에서 만났다.

[Note] *Heist* is a slang term.
heist는 속어로 쓰이는 말이다.

HIDEOUS [hídiəs] adj. extremely ugly; disgusting and revolting 소름끼치는, 흉측한; 메스꺼운, 고약한

The face of Medusa was reportedly so *hideous* that people would turn to stone just from looking at her. Needless to say, she seldom had a date.
소문에 의하면 메두사의 얼굴은 너무나 흉측해 사람들이 그냥 쳐다보기만 해도 돌로 변했다고 한다. 말할 필요도 없이 그녀에겐 데이트 상대가 거의 없었다.

The piece of rotting lasagna under Michael's bed is so *hideous* that I would rather burn his room than have to pick it up to throw it away.
마이클 침대 밑에서 썩고 있는 라자냐 덩어리는 너무 끔찍해 그걸 집어서 버려야 하느니 차라리 방을 태우겠다.

HOARSE [hɔːrs]　adj.　having a low, gruff sound; husky　쉰 목소리의

My voice was *hoarse* after I spent the afternoon screaming for my team during the doubleheader baseball game.
오후에 야구 더블헤더를 보는 동안 우리 팀을 응원하느라 소리를 질렀더니 목소리가 쉬어 버렸다.

Bruce Springsteen's *hoarse* version of the song "Pink Cadillac" blared from car stereos all across New Jersey when it first came out.
브루스 스프링스틴의 노래 "핑크 캐딜락"이 처음 나왔을 때 그의 거친 목소리가 뉴저지 전역의 자동차 스테레오에서 울려 퍼졌다.

HOARY [hɔ́ːri]　adj.　gray or white because of age or very old　(늙어서) 흰, 백발의; 매우 늙은

Fleming's great-grandchildren loved to pull at his long, *hoary* beard, but I don't think Fleming thought it was much fun.
플레밍의 증손자들은 그의 기다랗고 하얀 턱수염을 잡아당기기 좋아했지만, 플레밍은 그걸 그리 재밌어 했던 것 같지 않다.

The *hoary* gold digger told stories about the Wild West to the children until he fell asleep and his head fell forward into a bowl of soup.
백발의 금광 갱부는 아이들에게 서부 개척 시대에 대한 이야기를 들려주다가 잠이 들어 머리를 수프 사발 속에 박았다.

HOBBLE [hábl/hɔ́bl]　v.　to walk with a limp or with difficulty or to slow something down or get in the way of something　절뚝거리다; 방해하다

Sylvia *hobbled* around for three days after the Alaskan King Crab attacked her foot.
실비아는 알래스카 대게에 다리를 물려 3일 동안 절뚝거렸다.

The heavy radio equipment and sleeping gear *hobbled* their efforts to reach the cabin before sunset.
무거운 무선 장비와 침구 장비 때문에 그들은 해가 떨어지기 전 오두막에 도착할 수가 없었다.

HOMELY [hóumli]　adv.　not good-looking; plain or simple　못생긴; 수수한, 검소한

Since they were both shy and *homely*, the Grinson girls didn't get many dates until they struck oil in their backyard.
그린슨 가의 딸들은 부끄럼도 많고 못생겨서 뒤뜰에서 유전을 발견할 때까지는 데이트 상대가 별로 없었다.

The shirt was warm and comfortable, but its design was rather *homely*.
셔츠가 따뜻하고 편안하긴 했지만 디자인이 좀 수수했다.

HOOPLA [hú(ː)plɑː]　n.　excitement and confusion　소동, 야단법석

The rock star's surprise performance at the small local nightclub caused a lot of *hoopla*.
지방의 작은 나이트클럽에서 록스타가 깜짝 공연을 해 커다란 소동이 일었다.

The players were quickly separated from each other in the locker room during the *hoopla* surrounding their amazing victory.
선수들은 그들의 굉장한 승리를 두고 야단법석이 일어나는 동안 라커룸에서 서둘러 헤어졌다.

HORRID [hɔ́ːrid/hár-]　adj.　extremely offensive; causing terror and disgust　아주 불쾌한; 무시무시한, 혐오스러운

The *horrid* display of bad table manners by the Embertons caused all of the other dinner guests to lose their appetites for several days.
엠버튼 부부가 보여준 아주 불쾌한 식사 예절 때문에 저녁 식사에 모인 다른 손님들 모두가 며칠 동안 식욕을 잃어버렸다.

Although my stomach was doing flip-flops and I wanted to run out of the theater, I just couldn't help watching the *horrid* film until it ended.

속이 울렁거려서 극장 밖으로 뛰어나가고 싶었지만 무시무시한 영화가 끝날 때까지는 보고 있을 수밖에 없었다.

HOVER [hʌ́vər/hʌ́v-/hɔ́v-] v. to float in one place in the air or to hang around close by 공중을 떠돌다, 공중 정지하다; 어슬렁거리다, 배회하다

The flying saucer *hovered* silently in the air over a crowd of amazed campers, then blazed off over the mountains in a flash of blinding light.

비행접시가 화들짝 놀란 야영객 무리 위에 고요히 떠 있다가 눈부신 빛을 번쩍이며 산맥 너머로 사라졌다.

My friend *hovered* eagerly outside the telephone booth while I called the radio station hoping to be the lucky listener who would win two backstage passes to the concert.

내가 콘서트의 분장실 출입증 두 장을 차지할 행운의 청취자가 되려는 희망으로 방송국에 전화를 거는 동안 친구는 전화박스 밖에서 흥분하며 왔다갔다했다.

HUE [hju:] n. the color of an object or the shade or tint of a specific color 빛깔; 색조

After it had been exposed to the air a while, the white flesh of the apple took on a distinctly brownish *hue*.

사과의 흰 과육이 공기 중에 잠깐 노출되자 뚜렷하게 갈색으로 바뀌었다.

The salesperson showed us "lime" and "winter pine," but we were actually looking for a *hue* of green closer to "emerald."

판매원은 우리에게 "라임"과 "겨울 소나무"를 보여줬지만, 우리가 찾는 건 "에메랄드"에 더 가까운 녹색이었다.

HUSKY [hʌ́ski] adj. strongly built and very sturdy or having a hoarse, deep quality (of the voice) 튼튼한, 건장한; 허스키한, 쉰 목소리의

Although the wooden casks each weighed two hundred pounds, the *husky* workers were able to lift two at a time off the barge.

나무통은 하나의 무게가 2백 파운드였지만 건장한 일꾼은 거룻배에서 한 번에 두 개를 들어올릴 수 있었다.

Actress Demi Moore is famous for her *husky* voice.

여배우 데미 무어는 허스키한 목소리로 유명하다

HYGIENE [háidʒiːn] n. practices related to good health, disease prevention, and cleanliness 위생

Albert was a brilliant student, but his personal *hygiene* was so bad that the other students would not sit next to him because he smelled horrible.

앨버트는 뛰어난 학생이었지만, 너무 지저분하게 다녀서 다른 학생들은 그의 지독한 냄새 때문에 옆자리에 앉기를 꺼렸다.

[Note] *Hygienic* [haidʒínik/-dʒé-] adj. means clean, sanitary, or related to good health.

hygienic은 '위생적인', '위생학의'

■ It is important to keep newborn babies in *hygienic* surroundings because they catch diseases more easily than adults and older children.

신생아들은 위생적인 환경에 두는 것이 중요한데, 그들은 성인이나 어린이들보다 질병에 더 쉽게 감염되기 때문이다.

HYPE [haip] n. exaggerated publicity or v. to deceive or swindle 사기 / 속이다

Braxo Detergent's claim that four out of five dentists use Braxo to clean their teeth as well as their laundry turned out to be nothing but *hype*.

치과의사 5명 중 4명이 세탁할 때 뿐 아니라 양치질을 할 때도 브락소를 사용한다는 브락소 세제 회사의 주장은 알고 보니 사기였다.

The small-time poker player continued to *hype* himself as the greatest player of his time, although in truth he could only play Solitaire and Go Fish.

3류의 포커 선수는 할 수 있는 거라고는 솔리테어(혼자 하는 카드 게임)와 고피쉬 밖에 없으면서 자신이 당대 최고의 선수라고 스스로를 기만했다.

HYPODERMIC [hàipədə́:*r*mik] adj. placed beneath the layer of skin or n. an injection given under the skin 피하의, 피하 주사용의 / 피하 주사

Using a *hypodermic* needle, the nurse was able to tap a vein directly to get a blood sample.

간호사는 피하 주사용 바늘을 바로 정맥에 찔러 넣어 혈액 샘플을 빼낼 수 있었다.

The patient was given *hypodermic* medication in her arm to settle her nerves.

환자는 신경을 안정시키기 위해 팔에 피하 주사를 맞았다.

IDEOLOGY [àidiɑ́lədʒi/ìdi-/-ɔ́l-] n. a set of beliefs shared by a group of people, such as a specific religion or political party 이데올로기

> The Green Party's *ideology* centers around the belief that we must devote more energy to protecting our environment from the effects of pollution.
> 녹색당의 이데올로기는 오염의 영향으로부터 우리의 환경을 보호하는 데 더 많은 에너지를 쏟아야 한다는 신조에 중점을 둔다.

> Non-violence is a central part of Christian *ideology*.
> 비폭력은 기독교 이데올로기의 중심적인 부분이다.

IMPEDIMENT [impédəmənt] n. something that blocks progress; an obstacle 방해물, 장애

> My inability to speak or read German is a serious *impediment* to my quest to become the next Chancellor of Germany.
> 독일어를 말하지도 읽지도 못한다는 것은 차기 독일 수상이 되고자 하는 내게 심각한 장애다.

> Commuters braved such *impediments* as icy roads and fog to make it to work today.
> 통근자들은 오늘 빙판길과 안개 같은 장애물들을 무릅쓰고 출근했다.

IMPEL [impél] v. to drive forward; to urge into action 추진하다; 재촉하다, 억지로 시키다

> Brandon *impelled* his two daughters to study by denying them any television privileges until they finished all their homework.
> 브랜든은 두 딸들에게 숙제를 끝마칠 때까지 TV를 못 보게 함으로써 억지로 공부를 시켰다.

> Ginsberg tried to *impel* his roommates to go play basketball, but they preferred to lie around instead.
> 긴스버그는 룸메이트들에게 농구하러 가자고 재촉했지만, 그들은 그냥 빈둥거리며 있겠다고 했다.

IMPERIOUS [impíəriəs] adj. behaving like royalty; arrogant and snooty 위엄 있는; 오만한, 거만한

> Although she was only twelve, the Princess fixed her *imperious* stare on the poor gardener and soon had him crying with fear.
> 공주는 겨우 12세였지만 가엾은 정원사를 위엄에 찬 표정으로 빤히 쳐다보자 정원사가 이내 두려움으로 울음을 터뜨렸다.

> The *imperious* club owner refused to let in anyone who earned less than one million dollars a year.
> 오만한 클럽 주인은 연수입이 백만 달러가 안 되는 사람은 들여보내지 않았다.

IMPLORE [implɔ́ːr]   v. to beg earnestly; to ask anxiously   간청하다, 애원하다

The kids got down on their knees and *implored* their parents to take them to Wally's World of Wondrous Ice Cream.
아이들은 무릎을 꿇더니 부모님에게 '월리의 놀라운 아이스크림 세상' 에 데려가 달라고 애원했다.

Realizing that it was Christmas Eve and they still had no tree, Mr. Dwiley called the Christmas Tree Store and *implored* them to stay open a few minutes later than usual.
크리스마스 이브인데 아직도 트리가 없다는 걸 깨달은 드윌리 씨는 크리스마스 트리 가게에 전화를 걸어 평소보다 몇 분만 더 늦게 문을 닫아 달라고 간청했다.

IMPORT [impɔ́ːrt]   v. to bring something in from a foreign country in order to sell it or [   ] n. significance or importance   수입하다 / 중요(성)

The United States *imports* most of its oil from the Middle East.
미국은 석유의 대부분을 중동에서 수입한다.

Every reporter agreed that the fact that the President punched out two foreign leaders was a news event of *import*.
기자들은 대통령이 두 명의 외국 지도자를 두들겨 팼다는 사실은 중요한 사건이라는 데 의견을 같이 했다.

IMPOSE [impóuz]   v. to force yourself upon others; to place a burden upon others   강요하다; (짐을) 지우다

Jonathan *imposed* on me by showing up on my doorstep and announcing that he was moving in with me.
조나단은 우리 집 현관 층층대에 나타나 자기가 우리집으로 이사하겠다고 말하면서 내게 동의하도록 강요했다.

The boss *imposed* on her secretary when she asked him to do her laundry for the rest of his natural life.
여사장은 자기 비서에게 살아있는동안 자기 빨래를 하라고 강요했다.

INAUGURATION [inɔ̀ːgjuréiʃən]   n. a formal gathering to install a person into a position or office   취임식

Heavy rains prevented Governor Jubjub's *inauguration* from being held outdoors.
폭우가 쏟아져 야외에서 열기로 한 주브주브 주지사의 취임식이 취소됐다.

The speech that the new mayor gave at his *inauguration* was so boring that many people fell asleep.
새로 부임한 시장의 취임 연설은 너무 지루해 많은 사람들이 잠들었다.

INCARNATE [inkáːrneit]   v. to embody in flesh, to put into or represent in concrete form or [inkáːrnit]   adj. given human form; given bodily form   육체를 부여하다, 구현시키다 / 사람의 모습을 한; 육체를 갖춘

Some readers of *The Adventures of Huckleberry Finn* feel that Huck *incarnates* the free-spirited independence of 19th-century America.
'허클베리 핀의 모험' 을 읽은 일부의 사람들은 허크가 19세기 미국의 자유 독립정신의 화신이라고 생각한다.

The cat was so mean to everyone that we were convinced it was evil *incarnate*.
고양이가 모든 사람에게 너무 심술궂게 굴어서 우린 그것이 악마의 화신이라 확신했다.

INCINERATE [insínərèit] v. to burn to ashes 태워서 재로 만들다, 소각하다

Once the semester was over, I gleefully built a bonfire and *incinerated* my history textbook.
학기가 끝나자 난 너무 기쁜 마음에 불을 지펴 역사 교과서를 불태웠다.

Although the kitchen fire *incinerated* almost everything in the room, amazingly enough the electric can opener was untouched by the blaze.
화재로 부엌에 있던 거의 모든 물건이 재가 됐지만, 놀랍게도 전기 깡통 따개는 불길에 닿지도 않았다.

INCOMPETENT [inkámpətənt/-kóm-] adj. unable to do things correctly 무능한, 능력이 없는

The *incompetent* waiter managed to forget our lunch order seven times and then served us food that we hadn't asked for.
무능한 웨이터는 우리의 점심 주문 내용을 7번이나 잊어버리고는 시키지도 않은 음식을 갖다 주었다.

The high school basketball team was so *incompetent* that their cheerleaders eventually had to suit up and play.
고등학교 농구팀은 너무 형편없어서 결국 치어리더들까지 유니폼을 차려입고 경기에 참가했다.

INCREMENT [ínkrimənt] n. an added amount; an increase 증가량, 증가액; 증가, 증대

The tax increase came in such small *increments* that we didn't even know it was happening until one year we ended up owing more money than we earned.
세금이 워낙 조금씩 인상되었기 때문에 우리는 인상되고 있는지도 모르다가, 일년 뒤 지출이 수입을 초과하게 되자 알게 됐다.

As victory seemed within reach, the noise of the crowd increased in *increments* from a low whisper to a huge roar.
승리가 임박한 것처럼 보이자 관중들의 소리가 작은 속삭임에서 엄청난 외침으로 점점 커졌다.

INCRIMINATE [inkrímənèit] v. to cause to appear guilty of some crime 죄를 씌우다, 유죄를 입증하다

The presence of eight large lumps of wax in his kitchen was enough to *incriminate* the museum guard in the wax statue robbery.
박물관 경비원의 부엌에서 발견된 8개의 커다란 밀랍 덩어리는 그를 밀랍상 약탈 사건의 범인으로 보기에 충분했다.

The presence of O'Malley's fingerprints all over the gun and the crime scene *incriminated* him.
총과 범죄 현장 전체에 찍혀 있는 오몰리의 지문이 그가 유죄임을 입증했다.

The defendant *incriminated* himself in the Bambi's Mom Trial when he admitted that he only liked to hunt deer out of season.
피고인은 '밤비 어미 재판' 에서 자신은 금렵기의 사슴 사냥을 좋아한다고 인정하면서 자신의 유죄를 입증했다.

INCUMBENT [inkámbənt] n. the person who currently holds a specific political office or adj. holding a position or office 현직자, 재직자 / 현직의, 재직의

Senator Morst, the 106-year-old *incumbent*, easily won a tenth term in office and vowed to run for an eleventh term in six years.
106세의 모스트 현 상원 의원은 거뜬하게 10선에 당선됐는데, 6년 뒤에 11선에 도전하겠다고 단언했다.

Most experts agreed that the *incumbent* lost the debate with her challenger when she started crying on stage and asking for her mommy.
전문가 대부분은, 현직자가 무대 위에서 울음을 터뜨리며 엄마를 찾자 도전자와의 토론에서 졌다는 데 의견을 모았다.

INDIFFERENT [indífərənt] adj. showing no concern or interest; not giving a hoot one way or the other or neither good nor bad; just so-so 무관심한; 개의치 않는, 상관없는; 좋지도 나쁘지도 않은; 그냥 그런

The fact that the general started playing his Gameboy during my story made me think that he was *indifferent* to its ending.
장군이 내 이야기를 듣는 동안 게임보이를 하기 시작하자 그는 이야기 결말에 관심이 없다는 생각이 들었다.

While the cast of the play was known for putting on an incredible show, tonight's performance was *indifferent* at best.
그 연극의 배우들은 대단한 연기를 보여준다고 알려졌지만 오늘밤의 공연은 기껏해야 그냥 그런 정도였다.

INDIGNANT [indígnənt] adj. feeling angry or upset about a perceived injustice or wrongdoing 분개한, 성난

Ms. Shropshire was *indignant* when the Health Department declared her pet mosquitoes a health hazard and ordered her to kill them.
슈롭셔 씨는 보건성에서 그녀의 애완 모기들이 건강에 해롭다며 죽이라고 하자 분개했다.

When the lawyer suggested that Judge Jaasma was part of the cover-up, the judge became *indignant* and had the lawyer tossed from the building.
변호사가 자스마 판사에게 음모에 가담하고 있다고 말하자 판사는 분개해 변호사를 건물 밖으로 내던져 버렸다.

INDUCE [indjú:s/-dú:-] v. to influence or lead on; to coax or to cause something to happen 영향을 끼치다; 꾀다, 구슬리다; 일으키다, 야기하다

We finally *induced* the cat to come out from under the couch by putting a plate of tuna on the floor in the middle of the room.
방바닥 한가운데 참치 접시를 놓아서 마침내 고양이를 소파 밑에서 나오게 했다.

Syrup of Ipecac *induces* vomiting when swallowed, which is good if you've just been poisoned and bad at any other time than that.
이페칵 시럽을 삼키면 구토 증세가 일어나는데, 독을 삼켰거나 그 외에 아플 때 마시면 도움이 된다.

INDULGENT [indʌ́ldʒənt] adj. characterized by giving in to needs or desires; pampering 하고 싶은 대로 하는, 관대한, 엄하지 않은

Unable to stick to his diet any longer, the *indulgent* clerk broke down and ate twenty chocolate bars in a row.
끈기가 약한 점원은 더 이상 다이어트를 계속할 수 없어서 포기하고 한번에 초콜릿 바 스무 개를 먹어 치웠다.

Even though he already worked at three jobs, seventy hours a week to support his family, the *indulgent* father told his ten children that he would buy them ponies.
응석을 다 받아 주는 아버지는 가족을 부양하기 위해 이미 세 가지 직업을 갖고 일주일에 70시간을 일하면서, 열 명의 아이들에게 조랑말을 사 주겠다고 말했다.

INDUSTRIOUS [indʌ́striəs] adj. hard working and consistent 근면한, 부지런한

The father in the sentence above is very *industrious*.
윗 문장의 아버지는 정말 부지런하다.

When told she would have to work through the entire Christmas break, the *industrious* employee merely grinned and started filing.
부지런한 사원은 크리스마스 연휴 내내 일해야 할 거라는 얘기를 듣고 그저 싱긋 웃더니 서류를 정리하기 시작했다.

INFERENCE [ínfərəns] n. the act of figuring something out by looking at all the facts or a conclusion drawn from looking at the facts in a situation   추리, 추론; 단정, 추정

The old detective preferred to figure out the identity of the bank robber by *inferring*, based on the clues at hand, but his young assistant simply watched the security video, which had recorded the whole crime.
나이든 형사는 은행 강도의 신원을 파악할 때 가까이 있는 단서를 기초로 추론하는 편이었지만, 젊은 조수는 그저 범죄 현장을 녹화해 놓은 보안 비디오를 볼 뿐이었다.

Pinkerton *inferred* that a man dressed as a pigeon must have robbed the bank because there were a few feathers at the crime scene.
핑커튼은 비둘기 차림을 한 남자가 은행을 털었을 거라고 추정했는데, 범죄 현장에 깃털이 몇 개 있었기 때문이다.

INFERNO [infɔ́ːrnou] n. a confusing, chaotic place, usually on fire; someplace that resembles hell   (화재로 인한) 아수라장; 지옥

When a gas valve exploded and everything caught on fire, the calm dining room of the ship was transformed into an *inferno*.
가스 밸브가 폭발해 도처에 불이 붙자 조용하던 배의 식당이 아수라장으로 변했다.

Working in the hot, windowless basement of the Department of Motor Vehicles was as close to an *inferno* as Joe wanted to get.
자동차 관리국의 무덥고 창문도 없는 지하에서 일하는 것은 조가 원하던 지옥 같은 환경이었다.

INFINITE [ínfənət] adj. having no end or limit; boundless   무한한, 끝없는

When I look up at the stars and think about how far away even the closest one is, I have no trouble believing that the universe is *infinite*.
별들을 올려다보고 가장 가까운 별조차도 얼마나 멀리 떨어져 있나를 생각하니 우주가 무한하다는 것에 의심이 가지 않았다.

I thought my mother had an *infinite* supply of patience until one day, when I was thirty-six years old, she finally lost her temper and yelled at me.
어머니는 무한한 인내심을 가지셨다고 생각했는데, 내가 서른여섯 살이던 어느 날 마침내 평정을 잃고 내게 소리를 지르셨다.

INFUSE [infjúːz] v. to fill or put into   붓다, 부어넣다

William *infused* a little humor into the annual Board of Directors meeting when he arrived dressed as a circus clown.
윌리엄은 연례 이사회 모임에 서커스 광대 차림을 하고 와 웃음을 자아냈다.

The coach *infused* some energy into his sagging football program by hiring seven new players.
코치는 점점 재미가 없어지는 야구 프로그램에 7명의 새로운 선수를 들여와 활력을 불어넣었다.

INGENUOUS [indʒénjuəs] adj. honest and open, without trickery or innocent and simple   솔직담백한; 순진한, 꾸밈없는

In the story "The Emperor's New Clothes," an *ingenuous* little boy points out that the emperor is naked while everyone else is pretending that he is wearing the finest outfit they have ever seen.
"벌거벗은 임금님"을 보면, 다른 사람들은 모두 임금이 지금껏 보지 못한 최고의 의상을 입고 있는 것처럼 연기하지만 솔직한 꼬마 아이는 그가 벌거벗고 있다고 지적한다.

The *ingenuous* country girl was easily tricked into giving her life savings to the fast-talking con artist from Chicago.
순진한 시골 아이는 시카고 출신의 사기꾼이 수작을 부리자 쉽게 속아 넘어가 평생 모은 저축을 주고 말았다.

INITIATIVE [iníʃətiv] n. the first step of an action; the lead or the ability to start your own projects 시작; 주도(권); 독창력

The boxer seized the *initiative* in the match when he ran over and started punching his opponent as soon as the bell rang.
권투 선수는 종이 울리자마자 상대 선수에게 뛰어가 주먹을 날리기 시작하면서 시합의 주도권을 잡았다.

Sandy's plan to build a rocket and travel to the moon on her sixteenth birthday required a lot of *initiative*.
로켓을 만들어 16세 생일에 달 여행을 가겠다는 샌디의 계획에는 많은 독창력이 필요했다.

INLET [ínlet/-lit] n. a body of water, like a bay, that points in toward land or a narrow passage of water between two islands 만, 후미; 섬 사이의 좁은 수로

The thin strip of land protected the *inlet* from many of the high waves caused by the ocean storm.
좁다랗고 긴 땅은 바다 폭풍이 일 때 높은 파도로부터 후미를 보호해 주었다.

The two boys, eager to see their girlfriends, built a makeshift raft to cross the *inlet* between Kwaje Island and Lein Island.
두 명의 소년은 자신들의 여자 친구가 너무 그리워, 콰제 섬과 레인 섬 사이의 좁은 수로를 건너갈 임시 뗏목을 만들었다.

INORDINATE [inɔ́:rdənət] adj. going way too far; excessive 지나친, 과도한

The Police Commissioner admitted that using two hundred armed officers to arrest one man who was speeding was an *inordinate* display of force.
경찰청장은 속도를 위반하는 한 남자를 체포하기 위해 2백 명의 무장 경관을 푼 것은 지나친 병력 과시라는 걸 인정했다.

Spending eighteen hours on the same math problem seemed like an *inordinate* waste of time to me, but I tried telling that to my teacher and was suspended from school.
수학 문제 하나를 푸는 데 18시간을 들인다는 것은 지나친 시간 낭비인 것 같았는데, 선생님에게 그렇게 얘기했다가 정학을 당했다.

INQUIRY [inkwáiəri/ínkwəri] n. a request for information or an in-depth search into a matter 질문, 문의; 조사, 탐구

Joan made an *inquiry* at the State Department about the whereabouts of her brother who was a diplomat, but officials there claimed he was still missing.
조안은 국무성에 외교관인 남동생의 행방을 문의했지만, 그 곳 공무원들은 그가 아직도 행방불명이라고 말했다.

The reporter's *inquiry* into the counterfeiting ring unearthed startling evidence that the entire city council was involved the crime.
기자는 위조 도당에 대한 조사를 해 시의회 전체가 범죄에 개입해 있다는 놀랄 만한 증거를 찾아냈다.

INSINUATE [insínjuèit] v. to suggest something in an indirect manner; to sneak something into conversation 넌지시 비치다, 둘러서 말하다; 교묘하게 끼워 넣다

Graham was constantly *insinuating* that Jeanne was mentally unbalanced; whenever she spoke in groups of people he would silently rotate his finger at his temple and roll his eyes.
그레이엄은 끊임없이 진이 정서 불안이라는 것을 넌지시 비쳤다. 그녀가 여러 사람 앞에서 얘기할 때마다 그는 관자놀이에 손가락을 대고 빙빙 돌리며 눈동자를 굴리곤 했다.

The mild accountant tried to *insinuate* himself into the local motorcycle club by wearing a leather jacket and army boots, but he had no luck.
암전한 회계사는 가죽 재킷에 군화를 신고 와 지역 오토바이 클럽에 슬쩍 들어가려고 했지만, 운이 따라 주지 않았다.

INSOLENT [ínsələnt] adj. boldly rude or disrespectful 건방진, 무례한

When asked to apologize, the *insolent* prisoner spat in the judge's face and then put a curse on the next three generations of his family.
건방진 죄수는 사과를 하라는 말을 듣더니 판사의 얼굴에 침을 뱉고는 그의 가족을 다음 3대까지 저주했다.

The *insolent* child walked through the front door six hours after her curfew and refused to answer any of her parents' questions.
무례한 아이는 귀가 시간에서 6시간이 지나 현관문을 열고 들어오더니 부모님의 질문에 어떤 대답도 하지 않았다.

INTEGRATE [íntəgrèit] v. to bring all different parts together 통합하다, 전체로 합치다

Researchers had to *integrate* the many pieces of clay into one single block before they could decipher the ancient message written on it.
연구원들은 그 위에 쓰여진 고대의 메시지를 판독하려면 여러 점토 조각을 하나의 덩어리로 합쳐야 했다.

The community leaders hoped to *integrate* the town, which had been severely racially divided.
지역사회 지도자들은 심한 인종 분규를 겪고있던 마을을 통합하고자 했다.

INTEGRITY [intégrəti] n. a person's moral character; honesty or togetherness and unity; completeness 덕성, 품성; 통일(체); 완전

Mr. Colright's *integrity* was damaged in our eyes when we learned that he was the one responsible for all of the illegal gun sales.
콜라이트 씨가 불법 총기 판매에 전적인 책임이 있다는 걸 알고 우리는 그의 품성에 실망했다.

The *integrity* of the ship's hull remained intact when the torpedo failed to detonate.
어뢰가 불발로 끝나서 선체 전부가 전혀 손상되지 않았다.

INTERVAL [íntərvəl] n. the amount of time between two events; the space between two things 시간 간격; 틈

There was such a brief *interval* between the first and second act of the play that I couldn't even get up to buy some popcorn.
연극의 1막과 2막 사이의 막간이 너무 짧아서 팝콘을 사러 갈 시간도 없었다.

INTRIGUE [íntri:g] n. a secret plot or scheme or [intrí:g] v. to fascinate and excite curiosity 음모 / 호기심을 돋우다

Movies in the fifties were full of drama and *intrigue* because filmmakers relied more on stimulating personal interactions and less on special effects.
50년대의 영화들은 극적인 사건과 음모로 가득한데, 영화제작자들이 특수 효과보다는 자극적인 개인의 상호작용에 더 의존했기 때문이다.

My father was so *intrigued* by the juggling bears that he didn't even notice when I slipped away and joined the high-wire act.
아버지는 저글링 하는 곰들에게 정신을 팔려서 내가 몰래 빠져나가 줄타기에 참가하는 것도 몰랐다.

INVARIABLE [invέəriəbl] adj. always the same; never changing 불변의

Few plants grow in the desert because it is *invariably* hot and dry.
사막에는 식물이 거의 없는데, 한결같이 무덥고 건조하기 때문이다.

Because of Victor's immense bad luck and utter lack of experience, something *invariably* went wrong whenever he tried to fly a helicopter.

빅터는 운도 지지리 없고 경험도 전무해 헬리콥터를 조종하려고 할 때마다 늘 뭔가가 잘못됐다.

J

JABBER [dʒǽbər] v. to speak rapidly but without making much sense; to chatter 별다른 의미 없이 지껄이다; 재잘거리다

The crazy man on the corner *jabbered* about whales and tuxedos living together until somebody threw him some money.
모퉁이의 미친 남자는 누군가 돈을 던져 줄 때까지 고래와 턱시도가 함께 사는 이야기를 정신없이 지껄였다.

The gossipy old women *jabbered* for so long at the coffee house that the waitress was certain their jaws were going to fall off.
수다스러운 할머니들이 커피숍에서 하도 오래 수다를 떨고 있어, 웨이트리스는 그들의 턱이 떨어져 나갈 거라고 생각했다.

JAR [dʒɑ:r] v. to have an irritating effect; to bother or to knock off balance; to frighten and upset 신경을 거슬리게 하다; 평정을 잃게 하다, 흔들다; 깜짝 놀라게 하다

The sound of fingernails being scraped down the chalkboard was horribly *jarring*.
칠판에 대고 손톱을 긁는 소리는 끔찍할 정도로 신경에 거슬렸다.

The news that I was about to speak in front of three million people *jarred* me out of my relaxed mood.
3백만 명 앞에서 그 소식을 이야기하려니 차분했던 마음이 흔들렸다.

JARGON [dʒɑ́:rgən/-gɑn] n. a specialized language for a specific trade or industry, like "computer jargon" or "medical jargon" or a mixture of several different languages 전문어; 횡설수설

The paint salesman used *jargon* like "coat factoring" and "color distortion effect" in the hopes that it would impress people and inspire them to buy paint.
페인트 판매원은 "칠 팩토링"과 "색 변형 효과" 같은 전문어를 써서 사람들이 거기에 감명 받아 페인트를 사게 하려고 했다.

The Caribbean sailor spoke *jargon* which was made up of French, English, and Dutch words all mixed together.
카리브 해의 선원은 프랑스어, 영어, 네덜란드어를 한데 뒤섞어 횡설수설을 했다.

JOSTLE [dʒásl/dʒɔ́sl] v. to bump or come into contact with roughly while you're in motion 밀치다, 부딪치다

I *jostled* my way through the crowd on the train in an attempt to reach the luggage compartment and look for my lucky suitcase.
나는 수하물 칸에 가서 애지중지하던 여행 가방을 찾으려고 열차에 탄 사람들을 밀치며 갔다.

The rude baseball fan used his elbows to *jostle* people out of his path and reach his seat.
무례한 야구팬은 사람들을 팔꿈치로 밀치면서 길을 만들어 자리를 찾아갔다.

K

KALEIDOSCOPE [kəláidəskòup] n. a series of changing events or ideas, or a little, telescope shaped object that you can look through to see a blend of changing colors   (사건, 아이디어 등의) 일련의 변화; 주마등, 만화경

The *kaleidoscope* of events that led up to the first World War has long been a hot topic among historians.
제1차 세계대전이 일어나도록 만든 일련의 사건들은 오랫동안 역사학자들 사이에서 뜨거운 논쟁거리였다.

KARMA [káːrmə] n. a belief put forward by certain religions that a person's conduct and actions during life determines his/her destiny in the world; a person's fate   업(業), 인과응보; 숙명

Natasha kept good *karma* by always helping sick animals and, according to her, because of this she won the lottery.
나타샤는 늘 병든 동물을 도와주면서 좋은 업을 쌓았는데, 그녀 말로는 이 때문에 복권에 당첨됐다고 한다.

Brent knew that it was bad *karma* when he broke his arm after stepping on a piece of gum, because at school he would always try to put gum in his classmates' hair.
브렌트는 껌 조각을 밟고 팔이 부러졌을 때 그것이 인과응보라는 걸 알았는데, 학교에서 자신이 늘 동급생들 머리에 껌을 붙이고 다녔기 때문이다.

KEEN [kiːn] adj. having a sharp edge; intense or very intelligent and bright   날카로운; 강렬한; 총명한

The *keen* scissors were able to cut through the thin piece of steel like it was butter.
날카로운 가위에 얇은 철 조각이 버터처럼 잘라졌다.

The Student of the Year award went to Adrian Gilcutty, who everyone agreed was one *keen* thinker.
'올해의 학생 상'은 아드리안 길커티에게 돌아갔는데, 그가 생각이 총명한 학생이라는 데 모두들 의견을 모았다.

KNOLL [noul] n. a small, rounded hill   작고 둥근 언덕

Jack and Jill started to climb up the *knoll* to fetch a pail of water, but then Jack said, "Hey, this doesn't rhyme, let's go up that hill over there instead."
잭과 질은 물을 한 들통 받아오려고 언덕을 오르기 시작했는데, 그때 잭이 말했다. "야, 여긴 운이 안 맞아. 대신 저쪽 언덕으로 가자."

The Zimberts built their house on top of a *knoll* so that they could go sledding in the winter.
짐버트 부부는 겨울에 썰매를 탈 수 있도록 언덕 꼭대기에 집을 지었다.

L

LADEN [léidn] adj. weighed down with a heavy load; burdened   짐을 실은; 괴로운, 고민하는

With a loud snap, one wheel of the cart, which was *laden* with crowbars, broke off under its weight.
쇠지레를 실은 짐마차의 한쪽 바퀴가 크게 툭 소리를 내며 무게를 못 이기고 부러졌다.

Mom walked in with her shoulders slumped and her face drooping, and we knew that she was *laden* with bad news.
엄마가 축 처진 어깨와 풀죽은 얼굴로 들어오자 우린 엄마가 나쁜 소식으로 괴로워한다는 걸 알았다.

LANGUID [læŋgwid] adj. slow-moving, usually because of a lack of energy; weak   기운이 없는, 느릿느릿한; 약한

My stupid older brother once took too much Nyquil by accident, and he moved *languidly* about for three days.
어리석은 우리 오빠는 전에 한번 실수로 감기약을 너무 많이 먹고서 3일간 흐느적거리며 돌아다녔다.

The film was shown in slow motion, and the Olympic sprinters were transformed into *languid* walkers out on a stroll.
영화가 슬로모션으로 나오자 올림픽 단거리 주자들이 산책 나와 느릿느릿 걷는 사람들처럼 변했다.

LARCENY [láːrsəni] n. a robbery; taking someone else's possessions unlawfully   절도, 도둑질

Police suspected that the *larceny* committed at the Peanut Storage Facility was the work of rogue elephants.
경찰은 땅콩 비축 기지에서 일어난 절도가 떠돌아다니는 코끼리들의 소행이 아닐까 생각했다.

Miles Keenan was convicted of *larceny* after police found thirty-two TV sets stamped with "Property of the Governor" in his living room.
마일즈 키난은 경찰이 그의 거실에서 "주지사 소유"라고 도장 찍힌 32대의 TV 세트를 발견한 뒤 절도로 유죄판결을 받았다.

LARGESS [lɑːrdʒés] n. generous giving and generosity   아낌없이 줌, 후함

Every Halloween the Hamiltons demonstrate their *largess* by giving each child in the neighborhood a chocolate-covered tricycle.
할로윈데이 때마다 해밀턴 부부는 동네의 모든 아이들에게 초콜릿으로 뒤덮인 세바퀴 자전거를 주면서 후하다는 걸 보여준다.

LARVA [lɑːrvə] n. the wormlike stage of an insect's development   애벌레, 유충

Caterpillars, which are *larva*, are the wormlike stage of development between egg and butterfly.
애벌레인 모충은 알과 나비 사이의 발달단계다.

I found the white, wriggling *larva* disgusting to look at, but the adult butterflies were quite beautiful to see.
하얀 색의 꿈틀거리는 애벌레는 쳐다보기에 구역질이 났지만, 성충이 된 나비는 매우 아름다웠다.

LINGER [líŋɡər]   v. to be slow in leaving or acting   꾸물거리다, 서성대다

Curious onlookers *lingered* at the scene of the crime, hoping to catch a look at the person that police arrested.
호기심 많은 구경꾼들은 경찰이 누굴 잡아가나 보려고 범죄 현장을 서성댔다.

Marcus *lingered* in the doorway in a final effort to get invited to the slumber party, but the cheerleaders ignored him.
마커스는 파자마 파티에 초대받으려고 마지막으로 애를 쓰며 현관에서 꾸물거렸지만, 치어리더들은 그의 존재를 무시했다.

LIVID [lívid]   adj. discolored and bruised or white or ashen from fright or very angry; furious   멍든; 하얗게 질린; 격노한, 노발대발한

Mom's left arm was *livid* after she accidentally dropped the large cooking pot on it.
엄마는 왼쪽 팔에 실수로 커다란 냄비를 떨어뜨려 팔이 퍼렇게 멍들었다.

Mom's face was *livid* as she watched the final scary scenes from the movie *Jaws*.
엄마는 영화 '죠스'에서 무서운 마지막 장면들을 볼 때 얼굴이 하얗게 질렸다.

Mom was *livid* when she found out we used her wedding dress to clean up the Coke we spilled on the floor.
엄마는 우리가 바닥에 쏟은 콜라를 엄마의 웨딩드레스로 닦았다는 걸 알고는 노발대발했다.

LOFT [lɔ(:)ft]   n. a large, open, upper floor of a building; an open space under a roof, like an attic   건물의 맨 위층; 지붕 밑 방, 다락방

Since the light was better in the *loft*, the artist climbed into it from the living room and placed her painting supplies there.
화가는 맨 위층의 빛이 더 밝아서 거실에서 올라가 화구를 그곳에 두었다.

Last night I climbed up the ladder and discovered that the odd noises coming from the *loft* in the garage were being made by a family of feisty raccoons.
어젯밤 사다리를 타고 올라가 보니 차고 다락방에서 나는 이상한 소음은 공격적인 너구리 가족이 내는 것이었다.

LOGO [lóuɡou]   n. a symbol or trademark designed for easy recognition of a specific company or group   로고, 심벌마크

When we saw McDonald's *logo*, which is the golden arches, appear on the horizon we knew that our prayers for fast food had been answered.
우리는 금빛 아치 모양의 맥도널드 로고가 지평선에 나타나는 걸 보고 패스트푸드를 먹게 해 달라던 우리의 기도가 응답됐다는 걸 알았다.

LOOM [lu:m]   v. to come into view, usually in a threatening way; to stand over someone threateningly   위협적으로 다가오다; 불쑥 나타나다, 갑자기 모습을 드러내다

The huge gym teacher *loomed* over the frightened second grade students and ordered them to start playing dodgeball.
거구의 체육 교사가 겁먹은 2학년 학생들에게 위협적으로 다가오더니 도지볼을 시작하라고 명령했다.

The entire ocean *loomed* up before us as we drove over the last sand dune.
우리가 마지막 모래 언덕으로 차를 몰고 갈 때 우리 앞으로 바다 전체가 불쑥 모습을 드러냈다.

LOPE [loup]　v.　to run using long, easy strides　껑충껑충 뛰다, 성큼성큼 걷다(뛰다)

The timberwolves *loped* across the snowy mountainside, while the trappers in pursuit of them struggled to keep from sinking into snowdrifts.
얼룩 이리를 쫓는 덫사냥꾼들이 바람에 불려 깊이 쌓인 눈 더미 속에 빠져 들어가지 않으려고 허우적거리는 사이, 얼룩 이리들은 눈 덮인 산허리를 가로질러 껑충껑충 뛰어가버렸다.

Gary changed his *lope* into a dead run when he saw that the student known only as Mucus Child was approaching to give him one of his famous "gifts."
게리는 성큼성큼 걷다가 '콧물 아이'라고만 알려진 학생이 그의 유명한 "선물" 하나를 주려고 다가오는 걸 보고는 죽을 힘을 다해 도망쳤다.

LOUT [laut]　n.　a stupid, awkward, foolish person　촌스러운 사람, 바보 같은 사람

Even members of Vince's own family considered him a *lout* and would cross the street so that they wouldn't have to stop and talk to him.
빈스의 가족들조차도 그를 바보라고 생각해서 걸음을 멈추고 그와 얘기하는 걸 피하기 위해 길을 건너곤 했다.

Darryl admitted that he was a *lout* for selling all of his sister's furniture so that he could raise the money to take a trip to the Bahamas.
대릴은 바하마 여행 경비를 벌기 위해 여동생의 가구를 전부 팔아 버리고는 스스로 어리석었다는 걸 인정했다.

LUG [lʌg]　v.　to carry something with great difficulty　힘들여 가져가다

The bellboy *lugged* Howard's two suitcases full of igneous rocks all the way from the car to the third floor room.
사환은 화성암이 가득 담긴 하워드의 여행 가방 두 개를 차에서부터 3층의 객실까지 겨우겨우 들고 갔다.

The workmen *lugged* the grand piano up one flight of stairs before they agreed to quit their jobs and join the French Foreign Legion.
노동자들은 일을 그만두고 프랑스군 외인부대에 입대하기로 뜻을 모으기 전에 그랜드 피아노를 들고 끙끙거리며 계단을 올라갔다.

LUSH [lʌʃ]　adj.　covered with a great amount of plant life or juicy and tender　풀이 많은, 무성한; 즙이 많고 연한

There were so many different plants and animals living in the *lush* jungle that destroying even one acre of it affected hundreds of species.
무성한 정글에는 갖가지 동식물들이 아주 많아서 1에이커의 땅만 파괴해도 수백 종의 동식물들에게 영향을 준다.

The *lush* bananas tasted even better than they looked and Weiss ate one hundred of them and then suffered potassium poisoning.
즙이 많고 연한 바나나가 보기보다 훨씬 맛이 좋아서 웨이스는 백 개를 먹고는 칼륨 중독으로 고생했다.

LUSTER [lʌ́stər]　n.　fame and glory or a soft reflection of light; gloss　영광, 명성; 광채; 광택

The general knew that the *luster* of victory would fade if he admitted that he had been in the bathroom during the final battle.
장군은 자신이 마지막 전투 때 화장실에 있었다는 걸 인정하면 승리의 영광이 사라질 것이란 걸 알았다.

The antique brass platter regained its beautiful *luster* after we polished it for an hour.
골동품인 놋쇠 접시를 한 시간 동안 닦았더니 아름다운 광택이 되살아났다.

M

MAGISTRATE [mǽdʒəstrèit/-trət] n. a civil servant with the authority to enforce the law 치안판사

Since the two neighbors couldn't agree about where one's yard ended and the other's began, they took their dispute to the *magistrate*.
두 이웃은 서로의 뜰 경계를 두고 합의를 보지 못해 그들의 논쟁을 치안판사에게 가지고 갔다.

Bob Pickle promised that if he was elected *magistrate* of Boone County, he would eliminate all unpaid parking tickets from everyone's record.
밥 피클은 자신이 분 카운티의 치안판사로 선출되면 모든 사람의 기록에서 미납된 주차 위반 요금을 지워 주겠다고 약속했다.

MAGMA [mǽgmə] n. liquid rock heated to great temperatures inside the Earth's core 마그마

After *magma* reaches the surface of the earth, it cools and forms new landscapes.
마그마는 지표면에 닿으면 열이 식어 새로운 풍경을 형성한다.

The miner boasted that he once drank *magma* and X-ray showed that his throat was indeed lined with rock.
광부는 자신이 이전에 마그마를 마셨다며 으스댔는데, X-레이를 찍어 보니 정말로 그의 목구멍의 안쪽 벽은 바위 성분으로 덮여 있었다.

MAHOGANY [məhágəni/-hɔ́g-] n. a tree with a hard, reddish-brown wood well-suited for furniture because of its strength; wood with such a tree 마호가니

Although the *mahogany* bow looked beautiful, no one was able to bend it because the wood was too stiff.
마호가니 활은 예뻐 보이긴 했지만, 나무가 너무 단단해 아무도 당길 수가 없었다.

While my baby brother wanted to make a desk out of spit, we ended up using *mahogany* since I thought it would last longer.
막내 남동생은 쇠꼬챙이로 책상을 만들고 싶어 했지만, 우린 결국 더 오래갈 것 같은 마호가니로 만들었다.

MANE [mein] n. the long hair which grows from the neck of certain animals 갈기

The long golden *mane* of the lion helps it to blend into the grassland, and protects its neck from injury during fights over territory and mates.
사자의 기다란 금빛 갈기는 초원 색깔과 어우러져 몸을 숨기는 걸 도와주고 영역이나 짝을 두고 싸움을 벌일 때 다치지 않도록 목을 보호해 준다.

Terrified by the knowledge that I was a city girl, I held on to the horse's *mane* for dear life as we galloped across the field.
우리가 들판을 가로질러 말을 타고 질주할 때 나는 내가 도시 아이라는 사실에 겁을 먹고 죽을 힘을 다해 말의 갈기를 붙들었다.

MANGY [méindʒi] adj. looking shabby; covered with bare spots and appearing worn and rundown 지저분한: 옴투성이의

The *mangy* dog inspired pity in every person who saw it because it lived in an alley and ate whatever scraps of food it came across.
지저분한 개는 보는 이들에게 동정심을 일으켰는데, 골목에 살면서 음식 찌꺼기를 닥치는 대로 먹었기 때문이다.

Henderson mistreated his cat to the point where it started looking so *mangy* that many people thought it was a rat with patches of heavy fur.
헨더슨은 자신의 고양이를 학대해, 사람들이 군데군데 털이 무성하게 자란 쥐라고 생각할 정도로 아주 지저분해 보이는 지경까지 만들었다.

MANIFEST [mǽnəfèst] adj. obvious and clear or v. to show or display or to be the physical proof of something 명백한, 분명한 / 표명하다; 증명하다

Gene's feelings toward Gwen *manifested* themselves on Valentine's Day, when Gwen received eight dozen roses from him.
그웬을 향한 진의 감정이 발렌타인데이에 드러났는데, 그 날 그웬은 진에게서 96송이의 장미를 받았다.

MANTLE [mǽntl] n. a loose, cape-like coat without sleeves or the layer of rock between the Earth's core and the upper crust 망토, 소매 없는 외투; 맨틀(중심핵과 지각의 중간)

Asmara put on her uncle's thick wool *mantle* and went out into the cold, driving rain.
아스마라는 삼촌의 두툼한 양모 망토를 걸치고 휘몰아치는 차가운 빗속으로 나갔다.

The explorers hoped to find the lost land of dinosaurs that they saw in an old space movie by mining the Earth's crust and boring into the *mantle*.
탐험가들은 옛날 우주 영화에서 본 공룡의 잃어버린 땅을 찾으려고 지각을 파내고 맨틀을 뚫으려 했다.

MAR [mɑ:r] v. to damage or ruin; to deface 훼손하다, 망쳐 놓다

Terrance *marred* the surface of the birthday cake when he raked his fingers through the icing.
터렌스는 생일 케이크의 크림을 손가락으로 헤집어서 케이크 모양을 망쳐 놓았다.

The large scratch marks all over the hood *marred* the beauty of the 1964 Corvette, which was otherwise in perfect condition.
후드 전체에 큼직하게 긁힌 자국들 때문에 1964년 형 코르벳의 멋진 외관이 손상됐는데, 그것만 빼고는 완벽한 상태였다.

MEDDLESOME [médlsəm] adj. interfering in others' business 참견하기 좋아하는

The entire town of Nash wrote and signed a letter that asked the *meddlesome* Mr. Banks to either sew his lips together or mind his own business.
내슈 읍민 전체가 참견하기 좋아하는 뱅크스 씨에게 그의 입을 꿰매든지 아니면 자기 일에나 신경 쓰든지 하라는 내용의 편지를 써서 서명했다.

The *meddlesome* dentist was constantly sneaking up to me at the mall and trying to floss my teeth.
참견하기 좋아하는 치과의사는 쇼핑몰에서 계속 나한테 몰래 다가와서는 내 이 사이에 낀 것을 빼려고 했다.

MEGAPHONE [mégəfòun] n. a funnel-shaped device through which people speak in order to amplify their voices 메가폰, 확성기

The cheerleaders held their *megaphones* to their mouths and began leading the crowd in the popular chant "Go, team, go!"
치어리더들은 확성기를 입에 대고 흔한 슬로건 "이겨라, 이겨라!"를 외치며 관중들을 이끌기 시작했다.

Even though his voice was terrible even at a normal volume, Principal Murdoch liked to stand in the halls every day and sing "Good Morning to You" through a *megaphone* as the students headed for their classes.

머독 교장은 목소리가 보통 크기일 때도 소름끼칠 정도였는데, 날마다 학생들이 교실로 향할 때 복도에 서서 확성기에 대고 "굿모닝 투 유"를 노래하기 좋아했다.

MELODRAMA [mélədrà:mə/-dræmə] n. a play, book, or movie characterized by exaggerated emotions and feelings; behavior or actions full of exaggerated emotions and feelings   멜로드라마; 멜로드라마 같은 행동

During the entire four-hour *melodrama*, not one moment passed where some actor or actress wasn't shrieking, crying, or shrieking and crying onstage.

4시간의 멜로드라마 동안 단 1분도 남자 배우나 여자 배우가 무대 위에서 소리 지르며 울고불고하지 않고서 지나가는 경우가 없었다.

Watch any episode of *Melrose Place* for dozens of examples of *melodrama*.

멜로드라마 같은 행동의 예가 많이 필요하면 몇 회든지 '멜로즈 플레이스'를 한번 봐라.

MERCURIAL [mə:kjúəriəl/mə:r-] adj. rapidly changeable in thought, feeling, or opinion; fickle   변덕스러운

That night, my *mercurial* roommate decided to leave for Guam, then changed his mind and decided to stay, and then left to become a priest in Ireland.

그날 밤 변덕스러운 룸메이트는 괌으로 떠나겠다고 하더니 마음을 바꾸어 그냥 있겠다고 했다가, 다음엔 성직자가 되겠다며 아일랜드로 갔다.

MIDST [midst] n. the center or middle position; right in the middle of something   중앙, 한가운데

As loyal Green Bay Packer fans, we were disappointed to learn that our seats were located in the *midst* of the Tampa Bay section.

우리는 충직한 그린베이 패커스의 팬인데, 우리 좌석이 탬파베이 구역 한가운데라는 걸 알고 실망했다.

In the *midst* of all of the confusion resulting from the fire in the banquet hall, the waiter sat down at a table and ate someone's ham sandwich.

연회장에 화재가 발생해 어수선한 가운데, 웨이터는 테이블에 앉아 다른 사람의 햄 샌드위치를 먹었다.

MINGLE [míŋgl] v. to combine by mixing together; to join with others   섞다; 교제하다, 어울리다

Trey and Kelly were worried that the party would be a flop, but Kelly's lawyer friends were easily able to *mingle* with Trey's friends, who were mainly ex-cons and toll booth operators.

트레이와 켈리는 파티가 엉망이 될까 봐 걱정했지만, 켈리의 변호사 친구들이 전과자와 고속도로 요금 징수소 직원이 대부분인 트레이의 친구들과 쉽게 어울렸다.

We *mingled* in the crowd standing at the front of the ferry since we wanted to get a good look at the Statue of Liberty as we passed it.

우린 자유의 여신상을 지나갈 때 제대로 쳐다보려고 나룻배 앞부분에 서 있는 사람들 사이에 함께 끼었다.

MINUTE [mínit] adj. incredibly small; insignificant or characterized by a close study of all small details   미소한, 미세한; 사소한, 하찮은; 상세한, 정밀한

Always a pig, Tommy ate an entire large pizza and left me only a *minute* portion that wouldn't even feed a starving cricket.

언제나 돼지같이 먹어 대는 토미는 피자 라지 한 판을 다 먹고 나한테는 눈곱만한 조각을 남겨 줬는데, 그건 배고픈 귀뚜라미도 먹일 수 없을 정도였다.

It was only after a *minute* inspection of the car that the police found a piece of hair that belonged to the kidnapped prize-winning hamster.

경찰은 자동차를 정밀하게 검사하고 난 뒤에야 납치당한 수상 햄스터의 털 한 가닥을 발견했다.

MIRTH [məːrθ] n. happiness and good cheer 행복, 환희, 즐거움

Even though it was quite cold, the group singing Christmas carols door-to-door was warmed by the general *mirth* of the season.

집집마다 크리스마스 캐롤을 부르고 다니는 이들은 날씨는 아주 추웠지만 시즌 동안 행복해하는 사람들을 보고 마음이 따뜻해졌다.

The *mirth* of the vacationing couple quickly ended when the real owners of the condo arrived and found strangers using all of their things.

휴가를 보내고 있던 부부는 콘도의 진짜 주인들이 나타나 그들의 물건을 쓰고 있는 걸 들키자 이내 행복이 사라졌다.

MODE [moud] n. a manner of style or the latest fashion or trend 양식, 방법; 유행

Brent's strange *mode* of speaking made it necessary for his friends to translate what he said to his teachers.

브렌트는 말하는 방법이 이상해서 그가 하는 말을 친구들이 선생님들에게 옮겨 주어야 했다.

The *mode* of traveling around town on rollerblades ended soon after the first winter storm covered the roads with a thin layer of ice.

롤러블레이드를 타고 마을을 돌아다니는 유행은 첫 겨울 폭설이 쏟아져 길에 얇은 빙판이 깔리자 이내 수그러들었다.

MOGUL [móugəl] n. a very rich and influential person 중요 인물, 거물

Every year, the *moguls* of the movie industry get together and decide who they want to make the next big star.

해마다 영화산업의 거물들이 모여서 다음번엔 누구를 빅스타로 만들지 결정한다.

A *mogul* of the car industry, Marlene once bought eight hundred Volkswagens and gave them away as stocking stuffers on Christmas.

자동차 산업의 거물인 말렌은 일찍이 한번 폴크스바겐 8백 대를 구입해서는 크리스마스에 양말 속에 넣는 선물처럼 나눠주었다.

MOLECULE [mǽləkjùːl/mɔ́l-] n. the smallest unit of a chemical that still maintains all of the properties of that chemical 분자

A long time ago, scientists learned that one atom of sodium combined with one atom of chlorine forms a *molecule* of ordinary table salt.

오래 전에 과학자들은 나트륨 원자 하나와 염소 원자 하나를 결합하면 평범한 식탁용 소금의 분자 하나가 만들어진다는 걸 알았다.

Diatomic oxygen makes up only twenty percent of the *molecules* found in ordinary air.

2원자 산소는 보통 공기 속의 분자 가운데 단지 20%만 차지한다.

MONSTROUS [mǽnstrəs/mɔ́n-] adj. abnormal and horrifying; frightening and shocking or really large 기괴한; 끔찍한; 거대한

The *monstrous* creature that rose up out of the radioactive tar sludge terrified everyone except Dan, who was hoping to write a great screenplay based on his experience.

방사능의 타르 진창에서 떠오른 괴물을 보고 댄만은 겁을 먹지 않았는데, 그는 그 경험을 바탕으로 근사한 시나리오를 쓰고 싶어 했다.

My older sister once had a pimple on her nose that was so *monstrous* that we needed a brace to support her head from falling forward under its weight.

누나가 한번은 코에 여드름이 났었는데, 정말 거대한 크기여서 무게를 못 이기고 머리가 앞으로 넘어지지 않게 지탱해줄 버팀대가 필요할 정도였다.

MOOR [muər] v. to secure or fasten something, usually a ship or n. a broad stretch of land with low-lying shrubs and patches of wetland (배를) 잡아매다, 정박시키다 / 습지

Sailors on the boat threw ropes to people waiting on the dock, who tied them around large wooden poles to *moor* the ship in place.

보트 위의 선원들이 선창에서 기다리고 있는 사람들에게 밧줄을 던졌더니, 그들은 배를 정박시키기 위해 커다란 나무 기둥에 밧줄을 감아 묶었다.

After wandering across the *moor* for hours, Heathcliff was forced to admit that he had lost his left contact lens for good.

히드클리프는 몇 시간 동안 황야를 헤매고 다닌 뒤 왼쪽 콘택트렌즈를 영영 잃어버렸다는 걸 받아들일 수밖에 없었다.

MOTIVATE [móutəvèit] v. to provide with an incentive for action; to get things moving 자극하다, 동기를 부여하다

Gavin *motivated* the normally lazy group by promising to pay each of them five thousand dollars if they would help him fix his car.

개빈은 게으른 무리에게 그의 자동차 고치는 걸 도와주면 5천 달러씩을 주겠다고 약속해 그들을 자극했다.

The opening band *motivated* the crowd to dance.

오프닝 밴드가 사람들을 춤추게 만들었다.

MUCK [mʌk] n. a moist, sticky pile of dirt, manure, rotting matter, or all three 오물

No amount of water or scrubbing got rid of the *muck* that was stuck to the bottom of my boots.

부츠 바닥에 달라붙은 오물은 물을 뿌려도 북북 문질러도 없어지지 않았다.

While most animals stayed away from the offensive pile of *muck*, the pigs enjoyed rolling in it and squealed happily.

대부분의 동물은 불쾌한 오물 더미에서 멀리 떨어져 있는데, 돼지들은 그 안에서 뒹굴며 행복의 비명을 질러 댔다.

MULTILINGUAL [mʌltilíŋgwəl] adj. able to speak more than one language well 여러 언어를 말하는

The *multilingual* diplomat was able to hold a conversation in Belgian, Swahili, Portuguese, and pig Latin all at the same time.

여러 언어를 말하는 외교관은 벨기에어, 스와힐리어, 포르투갈어, 피그 라틴어까지를 동시에 구사하며 대화할 수 있었다.

Donald needed to use his *multilingual* skills almost every day while working at the U.S. Immigration Service.

도널드는 미국 이민국에서 일하는 동안 거의 매일 다국어를 구사해야 했다.

MUNICIPAL [mju:nísəpəl] adj. relating to a municipality, which is just a fancy word for a town or city 자치도시의, 시의, 읍의

The *municipal* council worked closely with county and state officials to plan the construction of the new dam.

시의회는 신규 댐 건설을 계획하는 데 있어 카운티 공무원, 주 공무원들과 긴밀하게 공조했다.

A successful *municipal* council member, Maxine decided to be up the stakes and run for state senator.
성공한 시의회 의원인 맥신은 목표를 높여 주 상원 의원에 출마하기로 했다.

MURMUR [mə́:rmər] v. to speak in a low voice; to speak unclearly 속삭이다; 중얼거리다

The *murmurs* of discontent from the audience got much louder as the assembly about cardboard waste went on and on.
판지 쓰레기에 대한 집회가 계속될수록 청중들 사이에서 불평의 수군거림이 훨씬 더 커졌다.

"Speak up or shut up!" was what my brother would tell me whenever I started to *murmur*.
오빠는 내가 중얼거리기 시작하면 "크게 말해, 아니면 입을 다물든가!"라고 말했다.

MUSE [mjuːz] v. to consider for a long time; to meditate on a subject 숙고하다, 곰곰이 생각하다

The philosophy teacher *mused* about the student's research paper for almost an entire day, and then he gave the student an F.
철학 교사는 학생의 연구 보고서에 대해 거의 하루 종일 생각하더니 F학점을 주었다.

We *mused* for so long about how to spend our Saturday afternoon that it was nighttime before we had reached a decision.
우린 토요일 오후를 어떻게 보낼까에 대해 너무 오래 숙고한 탓에, 결론에 이르기도 전에 밤이 돼 버렸다.

MUSKET [mʌ́skit] n. a primitive shoulder firearm that was used before the modern rifle was invented. It was invented in the late 1500s and used into the 1900s 머스켓총

During the Battle of Bunker Hill, rebel soldiers were ordered not to fire their *muskets* until they could see the whites of the British soldiers' eyes.
벙커힐 전투 때 반란군 병사들은 영국 병사들 눈의 흰자위가 보일 때까지는 머스켓 총을 쏘지 말라는 명령을 받았다.

MUSTER [mʌ́stər] v. to bring together into one place; to call to come together, to summon 한데 모으다, 소집하다

The sounds of the morning trumpet solo *mustered* the sleeping troops together in the main plaza.
아침에 트럼펫 독주 소리가 들리면 자고 있는 군사들은 주 광장에 모였다.

We *mustered* all of the family members to the spring picnic by promising free hot dogs for everyone.
우리는 가족 모두에게 무료 핫도그를 주겠다고 약속해 전 가족들을 봄 소풍에 불러 모았다.

MUTILATE [mjúːtəlèit] v. to damage or ruin badly, usually by cutting off or destroying some part 절단하다, 불구로 만들다, 못쓰게 만들다

The lawn mower plowed over the toy monster truck and *mutilated* it beyond all recognition.
잔디 깎는 기계가 장난감 몬스터 트럭을 깔고 지나가 옛 모습을 전혀 알아볼 수 없을 정도로 망가뜨려 놓았다.

My jealous sister *mutilated* my G. I. Joe shaped Jello dessert by eating his arm.
질투심 많은 여동생이 내 젤로 디저트 모양의 G. I. 조의 팔을 뜯어먹어 못쓰게 만들어 버렸다.

MUZZLE [mʌ́zl] v. to prevent from speaking or expressing an opinion or n. a device that fits over an animal's nose and mouth to keep it from opening its mouth 입막음하다 / 재갈

When I see a dog walking down the street wearing a *muzzle*, I instantly feel sorry for it because it can no longer freely bite people.
입에 재갈을 물고 길을 가는 개를 보니, 더 이상 맘대로 사람을 물지 못할 것 같아 불쌍한 생각이 들었다.

MYSTIFY [místəfai] v. to confuse or stump 어리둥절하게 하다, 난처하게 하다

The complex string of mathematical equations written on the chalkboard totally *mystified* Earl, who had trouble even remembering his own age.
얼은 칠판에 쓰여진 한 줄의 복잡한 수학 방정식을 보고 어리둥절했는데, 그는 자기 나이조차 제대로 기억하지 못하는 아이였다.

The talking sheepdog *mystified* us with its incredible knowledge of history, although it did confuse the Battle of New Orleans with the Battle of Bunker Hill.
말을 할 줄 아는 양치기 개는 뉴올리언스 전투와 벙커힐 전투를 혼동하기는 했지만, 역사에 대한 놀라운 지식으로 우리를 어리둥절하게 만들었다.

N

NARRATOR [nəréitər/næréi-/nærei-] n. the person telling a particular story 나레이터, 이야기를 들려주는 사람

The comments made by the *narrator* of the book were much funnier than the things that were said by the main characters in the novel.
책 속의 나레이터가 들려주는 말이 소설 속 주인공들의 얘기보다 훨씬 더 재미있었다.

NAUGHT [nɔːt] n. zero; nothing 제로, 영; 무(無)

When we learned that the plane flight had been delayed for three hours, my family realized our mad dash to get to the airport on time had been for *naught*.
우리 가족은 비행기 운항이 3시간 동안 지연됐었다는 걸 알고 공항에 제시간에 도착하려고 미친 듯이 서둘러 온 게 헛수고였다는 걸 깨달았다.

Ron believed that wishing for something really hard would make it happen, but his efforts to become World Ruler in this way proved to be all for *naught*.
론은 뭔가를 정말 간절히 바라면 이루어진다고 믿었지만, 그런 식으로 세계의 지배자가 되려는 노력은 완전히 헛된 일이었다.

NAUTICAL [nɔ́ːtikəl] adj. related to ships or sailing 선박의, 항해의

Although he was eighty years old and blind, the old sailor's great store of *nautical* knowledge was extremely helpful to us on our voyage to the South Seas.
늙은 선원은 80세인데다 눈도 멀었지만, 항해에 대한 풍부한 지식을 갖고 있어서 우리가 남태평양으로 항해할 때 막대한 도움을 주었다.

The researcher read every book on *nautical* history that exists, in an attempt to learn who had constructed the first ship in a bottle.
연구원은 누가 병 속에 최초의 배를 건조했는지 알아내기 위해 항해 역사에 대한 책이란 책은 모조리 읽었다.

NIGH [nai] adj. or adv. near or close in some way 가까운 / 가까이

The fact that my stomach was growling indicated to me that the time was *nigh* for me to go and get some lunch.
뱃속에서 꼬르륵 소리가 나는 걸 듣고 점심 먹으러 갈 시간이 가까웠다는 걸 알 수 있었다.

It was *nigh* onto 7 o'clock at night when the AP English class decided that their teacher wasn't going to show up for class, and left reluctantly.
저녁 7시가 가까워지자 AP 영어 클래스 학생들은 교사가 오지 않을 거라고 결론짓고 마지못해 교실을 떠났다.

NIMBLE [nímbl] adj. quick and agile in movement or thought 재빠른, 민첩한

The *nimble* child was able to complete the obstacle course in a new world record time.
민첩한 아이는 세계기록을 수립하면서 장애물 코스를 완주했다.

Petra *nimbly* solved the question "What is three pi times seven-tenths minus eighty?" in less than thirty seconds.

페트라는 "3π×7/10−80은 얼마인가?"라는 문제를 30초도 안돼 재빨리 풀었다.

NONDESCRIPT [nɑ̀ndiskrípt/nɔ̀n-] adj. without any qualities that stand out, rendering something difficult to describe 특징이 없는, 막연한

The bank robber's *nondescript* clothing allowed her to fade into the crowd easily and escape detection by the police.

은행 강도는 특징 없는 옷을 입어서 사람들 속으로 쉽게 사라져 경찰에 발각되지 않았다.

Uncle Ted had such a *nondescript* face and appearance that most people would only refer to him as "You know, that guy."

테드 삼촌의 얼굴과 생김새는 하도 평범해서 대부분의 사람이 그를 가리켜 "있잖아, 그 친구"라고 말했다.

NOOK [nuk] n. a hidden spot or a corner or recess that is part of a larger room 비밀 장소; 구석

Billy kept all of his expensive baseball cards in a *nook* at the far end of the garage so that his little brother wouldn't find them and chew on them.

빌리는 값비싼 농구 카드를 차고 저쪽 끝의 비밀 장소에 두어 남동생이 찾아서 물어뜯지 못하게 했다.

The young couple always had coffee together before leaving for work, in the breakfast *nook* just off the kitchen.

젊은 부부는 항상 출근 전에 부엌 바로 옆의 아침 먹는 자리에서 함께 커피를 마셨다.

NOTION [nóuʃən] n. an idea of how something should be; an opinion 관념, 개념; 의견

A fanatic about American nationalism, the patriot had the *notion* that everyone should only wear red, white, and blue clothes.

그 애국자는 미국 민족주의의 광신자로, 모두가 빨강, 하양, 파랑의 옷만 입어야 한다고 생각했다.

I had a *notion* that I should call my sick girlfriend after eight of her friends cornered me and said, "Contact Becky at home or you won't make it to sixth period."

내 여자 친구의 친구들 여덟 명이 날 코너에 몰아 놓고 "베키 집으로 전화해. 안 그러면 넌 6교시에 못 들어갈 거야."라고 말한 뒤, 난 아픈 여자 친구에게 전화를 걸어야겠단 생각이 들었다.

NUANCE [njúːɑːns/núː-] n. a small, subtle change in something 뉘앙스, 미묘한 차이

Adding just a pinch of pepper gave a spicy *nuance* to the strawberry Jell-O.

후추를 아주 조금 넣었더니 딸기 젤로가 살짝 향긋해졌다.

The Australian boys' accent gave an interesting *nuance* to words like "shrimp" and "leather tuxedo" that I found quite exciting.

오스트레일리아 아이들의 억양은 "새우"나 "가죽 턱시도" 같은 단어에 재미있는 뉘앙스가 있는데, 내게 아주 흥미로웠다.

 O

OATH [ouθ]   n. a promise to behave in certain way, calling on God or using some sacred item as your witness   맹세, 서약, 선서

Placing his hand on the Bible, the witness gave his solemn *oath* that he would tell the whole truth and nothing but the truth.
증인은 성경에 손을 올려놓고 진실을 모두, 또한 진실만을 이야기하겠다는 엄숙한 선서를 했다.

With all nine of us holding onto our only baseball bat, our team made an *oath* that we would practice at least once before next season.
우리 팀의 아홉 선수 모두가 하나뿐인 야구 방망이를 붙잡은 채로 다음 시즌까지 적어도 한번은 연습하겠다는 맹세를 했다.

OBLIGE [əbláidʒ]   v. to do a favor for or to make thanks   은혜를 베풀다, 호의를 보이다; 고맙게 여기도록 하다

Father felt *obliged* to invite Timmy over for supper after he mowed our lawn every week during the summer that we were away.
아버지는 우리가 없는 여름 동안 매주 우리 집 잔디를 깎아 준 티미에게 고마움을 느껴 그를 저녁 식사에 초대했다.

The engaged couple felt *obliged* to listen to their parents' request not to have their wedding take place in zero gravity on the Space Shuttle.
약혼한 커플은 우주 왕복선의 무중력 상태에서는 결혼식을 올리지 말라는 부모님들의 요구를 듣고 고마움을 느꼈다.

OBSTINATE [ábstənət/ɔ́b-]   adj. stubborn; unwilling to change from a particular course or belief   고집 센, 완고한

Even though she didn't have a ticket for the seat that she was in, the *obstinate* woman refused to get up and go sit where she was supposed to.
고집 센 여자는 자기가 앉아 있는 자리의 티켓이 없으면서 일어나서 본래 자리로 가서 앉기를 거부했다.

The *obstinate* family was convinced that cars were just a fad and refused to give up their horse and carriage.
완고한 가족은 자동차는 일시적 유행에 불과하다고 확신해 말과 마차를 버리지 않으려 했다.

ODIOUS [óudiəs]   adj. disgusting and nasty; causing repulsion   역겨운, 더러운; 증오심을 일으키는, 혐오스러운

Several passengers on the train took out perfume bottle and sprayed furiously in order to cover up the *odious* smell from the dead skunk that had been found in the cargo area.
열차의 몇몇 승객은 짐칸에서 발견된 죽은 스컹크에서 나오는 악취를 막기 위해 향수병을 꺼내서 마구 뿌려 댔다.

Carlos had such an *odious* reputation as a student that most teachers failed him before he even reached their classroom door.
카를로스는 학생으로서 혐오할 만한 평판을 갖고 있어서 대부분의 교사는 그가 교실 문까지 오기도 전에 낙제시켰다.

OPTIMAL [áptəməl/ɔ́p-] adj. the best or most favorable   최상의, 최적의

Clear skies and a constant mild breeze are the *optimal* conditions in which to fly a kite.
맑은 하늘과 계속 불어오는 가벼운 미풍은 연을 날리기에 최상의 조건이다.

Lawrence soon learned that the *optimal* time to ask his Dad for some cash was just after he came home from work on every other Friday.
로렌스는 아빠에게 돈을 달라고 하기에 가장 좋은 때는 격주 금요일에 아빠가 퇴근하고 집에 오신 직후라는 걸 곧 알게 됐다.

OPULENT [ápjulənt/ɔ́p-] adj. characterized by great wealth and abundance; rich   풍부한; 부유한

When we stepped into the mansion we were immediately surrounded by incredible *opulence*; there were even huge, uncut diamonds being used as doorsteps.
우린 대저택에 발을 들여놓는 순간 엄청난 부유함에 둘러싸였다. 현관의 층층대가 거대한 한 덩어리의 다이아몬드로 이루어져 있었던 것이다.

OPUS [óupəs] n. an artistic work of some kind, usually musical   작품, 주로 음악 작품

My favorite *opus* of Beethoven's is probably his Ninth Symphony, which he wrote when he was deaf.
베토벤 작품 가운데 내가 가장 좋아하는 것은 제9번 교향곡인데, 베토벤이 귀가 먹었을 때 지은 곡이다.

After eight years of hard work, the writer finally completed her six hundred pages *opus* about a family who moves from Maine to Kuala Lumpur.
작가는 8년 동안의 고된 집필 끝에 메인 주에서 쿠알라룸푸르로 이민가는 가족에 대한 6백 페이지의 작품을 완성 지었다.

ORATION [ɔːréiʃən] n. a formal speech given at a special event   연설

During the Governor's *oration* at the black-tie dinner, he continually thanked Semartech's leaders for building their new plant in his city.
약식 예장 파티에서 주지사는 연설을 하는 동안 그의 시에 새 공장을 건설한 세마테크 지도자들에게 연신 감사를 표했다.

Mark Antony gave a brilliant *oration* at the funeral of Julius Caesar.
안토니우스는 시저의 장례식에서 훌륭한 연설을 했다.

ORCHESTRATE [ɔ́ːrkəstrèit] v. to arrange a performance of an orchestra; to arrange something that has many different parts   관현악으로 편곡하다; 배합하다, 배치하다

Adding kazoos and whistles made it harder to *orchestrate* Mozart's Great Symphony, but the conductor did the best she could.
카주피리와 호각을 더했더니 모차르트의 대교향곡을 편곡하기가 더 어려워졌지만, 지휘자는 최선을 다했다.

The travel agent tried to *orchestrate* the vacation plans of the four families so that they would all be in Paris at the same time.
여행사 직원은 네 가족이 동시에 파리에 머물도록 하기 위해 여행 계획을 잘 배치했다.

ORGANISM [ɔ́ːrɡənizm] n. a living thing of any kind   유기체, 생물

Scientists recently discovered small bacterial *organisms* that live at the bottom of the ocean and consume sulfur that rises up from underground vents.
과학자들은 최근 해저에 살면서 땅속 구멍에서 올라오는 유황을 섭취하는 작은 박테리아 유기체를 발견했다.

Insects make up over fifty percent of all the different kinds of *organisms* living on this planet.
곤충은 지구상에 생존하는 온갖 종류의 유기체 가운데 50% 이상을 차지한다.

OSTENTATIOUS [àstentéiʃəs/ɔ̀s-] adj. flashy or showy for the sake of being impressive 자랑삼아 드러내는, 화려한

Wearing fourteen brightly-colored glass rings on each hand is a little *ostentatious* for a trip to the local convenience store.

가까운 편의점에 가려고 양손에 눈에 띄는 색깔의 유리 반지 14개를 끼는 건 좀 화려하다.

Since the old man was blind, the *ostentatious* costumes worn by the parade-goers did not effect his belief that the parade was dull.

노인은 눈이 안 보였기 때문에, 퍼레이드를 보러 가는 사람들이 입은 화려한 의상이 퍼레이드는 재미없다는 그의 믿음에 영향을 주지 못했다.

P

PACT [pækt] n. a formal agreement between two countries; a bargain   (국가간의) 조약, 협정; 약속, 계약

The A.N.Z.U.S. *pact* between Australia, New Zealand, and the United States pledged that each country would come to the aid of the others in times of economic or political crisis.
오스트레일리아, 뉴질랜드, 미국 간에 체결한 앤저스 조약은 각국이 경제적 혹은 정치적 위기에 처한 다른 두 나라를 도와주기로 서약한 것이다.

I made a *pact* with my brother to stop calling him "four eyes" if he would stop telling Janine Strong that I loved her.
형이 재나인 스트롱에게 내가 그녀를 좋아한다고 말하는 걸 그만두면 나는 형을 "네 눈" 이라고 부르는 걸 그만두겠다고 약속했다.

PAINSTAKING [péinztèikiŋ/péins-] adj. involving great care and thoroughness   수고를 아끼지 않는, 정성을 들이는

The veterinarian took five *painstaking* hours to perform triple-bypass heart surgery on the hamster.
수의사는 햄스터의 심장에 3중 혈관 이식 수술을 하느라 5시간 동안 수고를 아끼지 않았다.

Our *painstaking* search of the entire house finally ended when we found Mom's lost ring in the clothes hamper.
집안 전체에 대한 우리의 철저한 수색은 엄마의 없어진 반지가 세탁물 바구니에서 나오자 마침내 끝이 났다.

PALPABLE [pǽlpəbl] adj. able to be touched or felt; very obvious   만질 수 있는, 느낄 수 있는; 명백한

There was a *palpable* bump on Tracy's head after she accidentally hit herself behind the ear with the baseball bat.
트레이시는 잘못해서 야구 방망이로 자신의 귀 뒤를 친 후 머리에 만지면 알 수 있는 혹이 생겼다.

The tension in the air between the two rivals was almost *palpable*.
두 경쟁자 사이에 흐르는 긴장감은 거의 만져질 것 같았다.

PANHANDLE [pǽnhæ̀ndl] n. a small strip of land extending like the handle of a pan from a large area of land (look at a map of Oklahoma or Texas) or v. to beg for handouts or money on the street   (프라이팬 손잡이처럼 생긴) 기다란 지역 / 길에서 구걸하다

Any good student of geography knows that the *panhandle* of Florida extends west all the way to Alabama.
지리학을 잘 아는 학생이라면 플로리다에서 길게 뻗어 나온 지역이 서쪽의 앨라바마로 뻗어 있다는 걸 안다.

The city council passed a law that made it illegal for beggars to *panhandle* on any public property.
시의회는 공유지에서 거지들의 구걸 행위를 금지하는 법안을 통과시켰다.

PANORAMA [pæ̀nərǽmə/-rɑ́ːmə] n. a view of everything over a wide area; a view of a long series of events or a period of time 전경; 개관, 광범위한 조사

The family pulled over at the scenic overlook in order to gaze at the *panoramic* view of the Valley of Sponges that sprawled below them.
가족은 그들 아래로 뻗어 있는 '스펀지 계곡'의 전경을 응시하기 위해 전망이 좋은 곳에서 차를 세웠다.

The historian wanted to write a book that viewed the entire *panorama* of World War II through the eyes of a common Russian soldier.
역사학자는 평범한 러시아 병사의 눈을 통해 제2차 세계대전의 전체적인 개관을 보여줄 책을 집필하고 싶어 했다.

PARADOX [pǽrədɑ̀ks/-dɔ̀ks] n. a statement that seems to contradict itself, but still might be true 역설, 패러독스

Some people might consider the phrase "military intelligence" a *paradox*, but if so they probably aren't in the military.
어떤 사람들은 "군인의 지성"이라는 표현이 패러독스라고 생각할지 모르지만, 그렇다면 그들은 아마 군대에 있는 사람이 아닐 것이다.

After I failed to make the cross-country skipping team, Dad comforted me with this rather meaningless *paradox*: Sometimes you have to fail in order to succeed.
내가 크로스컨트리 스키핑 팀에 떨어졌을 때 아빠는 "이따금은 성공하기 위해 실패해야 한다"는 좀 무의미한 패러독스로 날 위로하셨다.

PARCEL [pɑ́ːrsəl] n. a package; something bundled up to be sent for delivery or a section or piece 꾸러미; 소포; 부분, 조각

The post office representative claimed that the *parcel* from Aunt Bea containing her famous brownies was lost in the mail, but I could hardly understand him because his mouth was full at the time.
우체국 직원은 비 이모가 잘하기로 소문난 땅콩 초코케이크를 담아서 보낸 소포가 우편물 속에서 분실됐다고 했지만, 난 그의 말을 거의 이해할 수 없었는데, 그의 입에 뭔가가 가득 들어 있었기 때문이다.

The farmer bought the *parcel* of land between his property and the river so that he could take his cows down to the river to drink without trespassing on someone else's land.
농부는 다른 사람의 땅에 피해를 주지 않고 소들에게 강물을 먹일 수 있도록 자신의 소유지와 강 사이에 있는 땅을 사들였다.

PARCH [pɑːrtʃ] v. to make very thirsty and dry, usually by intense heat 바짝 마르게 하다, 목마르게 하다

Playing a soccer game without stopping in the July Texas sun makes my mouth so *parched* that I feel like I could drink an ocean.
7월에 텍사스의 태양 아래서 쉬지 않고 축구 경기를 하면 입이 바짝 말라서 바닷물을 다 마실 수 있을 것 같다.

Try eating eight saltines in one minute without water, and by the end of that minute your mouth will definitely be *parched*.
1분 안에 물 없이 소금 뿌린 크래커 8개를 먹어 봐, 그러면 다 먹고 났을 때 네 입이 바짝 말라 있을 게 틀림없어.

PARIAH [pəráiə/pǽriə] n. someone who has been kicked out of society; an outcast 쫓겨난 사람, 부랑자

Judy became a *pariah* at work when her fellow employees learned that every day she stole her lunch from someone.
주디는 그녀가 날마다 다른 사람의 점심을 훔쳐 간다는 사실을 동료 직원들이 알게 돼 직장에서 쫓겨났다.

The villagers tarred and feathered the *pariah* before throwing rocks at him and running him out of town.
마을 사람들은 부랑자에게 돌을 던지고 마을에서 쫓아내기 전에 그의 몸에 타르를 바르고 깃털을 달았다.

PARODY [pǽrədi] n. a comic piece that exaggerates the actions or characters of some other piece to the extent that it becomes absurd and ridiculous or a poor, weak imitation 풍자적인 개작품; 서투른 모방

While I thought my *parody* of principal Hawkins, which portrayed him as a ruthless dictator, was quite amusing, I changed my mind after he gave me ten hours of detention.
나는 호킨스 교장을 무자비한 독재자로 묘사한 내 패러디가 꽤 재미있다고 생각했는데, 그에게서 방과 후에 열 시간 동안 남아 있는 벌을 받은 뒤 마음을 바꾸었다.

The hearing before the Student Council was a *parody* of justice because the council slept through our explanations and then promptly ruled against us.
학생회에 앞에서 열린 청문회는 불공평했는데, 우리가 설명하는 내내 학생회는 잠을 자더니 그런 다음 즉석에서 우리에게 불리한 판결을 내렸기 때문이다.

PARSON [pá:rsn] n. a religious leader in charge of a specific area called a parish 교구 사제

Parson Collins had administered all of the weddings in Somerset County for the past thirty years.
콜린스 교구 사제는 지난 30년 동안 서머셋 카운티에서 열리는 모든 결혼식을 주재했었다.

The young couple went to the *parson* to find out what the sign that said "John 3:16" that they saw at the football game meant.
젊은 부부는 그들이 미식축구 경기에서 본 "요한복음 3장 16절"이란 표시가 무슨 의미인지 알아보려고 교구 사제를 찾아갔다.

PAWN [pɔːn] n. someone used and controlled by others 볼모, 인질

The foot soldiers knew that they were merely *pawns* used by the government for purposes that they couldn't understand, but at least it was a job.
보병들은 자신들이 알 수 없는 목적으로 정부에 이용당하는 볼모에 지나지 않다는 걸 알았지만, 어쨌든 그건 일이었다.

The boss of the huge corporation liked to give the "Employee of the Month" award to the lowly *pawn* who made the best coffee.
거대 기업의 사장은 "이 달의 직원"상을 커피를 가장 맛있게 타는 말단 사원에게 수여하고 싶어 했다.

PECULIAR [pikjú:liər] adj. strange or unusual; weird or belonging specifically to one area or region (usually followed by "to") 별난, 색다른; 이상한; 고유의, 특유의

Saul thought it was *peculiar* that he lost his pack of blueberry gum right before he saw his two younger brothers blowing huge purple bubbles from their mouths.
솔은 두 명의 남동생이 입으로 커다란 자주색 풍선을 부는 걸 보기 직전에 자신의 블루베리 껌 갑이 없어졌다는 게 이상했다.

Fortunately, the custom of greeting one's neighbors with a hard slap is *peculiar* to a very small southern region of France.
손바닥으로 세게 찰싹 때리면서 이웃과 인사를 나누는 풍습이 프랑스의 아주 작은 남부 지역 고유의 것이어서 다행이다.

PEDDLER [pédlər] n. someone who travels around selling goods 행상인

At first the *peddler* made fairly good money selling kitchen supplies to households in eastern Mississippi, but then people started ordering their supplies through catalogs.
처음에 행상인은 동부 미시시피의 가정에 부엌 용품을 팔아 꽤 많은 수입을 올렸지만, 그 이후로 사람들은 카탈로그를 보고 물건을 주문하기 시작했다.

On his way into town the farmer stopped a *peddler* and traded his basket of eggs for a new rake.
농부는 마을로 들어오는 길에 행상인을 멈추어 세우고는 자신의 달걀 바구니를 새 갈퀴와 바꾸었다.

PEEVISH [píːviʃ] adj. irritable; easily annoyed 화를 잘 내는, 까다로운

A single mosquito bite was enough to make the *peevish* child bawl for hours.
모기에 단 한번 물린 것도 투정부리는 아이에겐 몇 시간 동안 울부짖게 만들기에 충분했다.

The *peevish* roommate erupted in anger when he saw that his CD collection was no longer in alphabetical order.
까다로운 룸메이트는 자신의 CD 수집품이 알파벳순으로 안 되어 있는 것을 보고 화를 버럭 냈다.

PENICILLIN [pènəsílin] n. a compound found in a kind of mold that is used to cure a variety of bacterial diseases 페니실린

Although a shot of *penicillin* can cure strep throat, the administration of the shot makes it uncomfortable for the patient to sit down for several days.
페니실린 주사를 한방 맞으면 패혈성 인두염을 치료할 수 있지만, 그 주사를 맞은 환자는 며칠 동안 자리에 앉기가 불편해진다.

The doctors weren't certain what kind of a bacteria was causing the high fever, but they figured that *penicillin* would probably kill whatever it was.
의사들은 어떤 종류의 박테리아가 고열을 일으키는지 확신하지 못했지만, 어떤 것이든 아마 페니실린으로 없앨 수 있을 거라고 생각했다.

PERENNIAL [pəréniəl] adj. living indefinitely; perpetual; appearing again and again 영속적인; 반복해서 나오는

Until dams were built, flooding on the Colorado River was a *perennial* problem that prevented settlers from building anywhere near the river.
댐이 완공될 때까지는 콜로라도 강의 범람이 이주자들에게 강 가까이에 어떤 것도 못 짓게 만드는 풀리지 않는 문제였다.

Even though old Stasson was ninety, the *perennial* candidate ran for President for the twentieth consecutive time.
스태슨 노인은 90세였지만 잇따라 스무 번을 대통령 선거에 출마한 단골 후보자다.

PERPETRATOR [pə́ːrpətreitər] n. someone guilty of committing a crime 범인

The police knew that Gomez was the *perpetrator* of the tobacco store robberies when they saw that he was slowly building a house for himself out of cigars.
경찰은 고메즈가 느릿느릿 담배로 자기 집을 짓고 있는 것을 보고 그가 담뱃가게 절도범이라는 걸 알았다.

The *perpetrator* admitted to having stolen the puppies, but she claimed that the devil had been speaking to her through old show tunes, and had instructed her to do it.
범인은 자신이 강아지들을 훔쳤음을 인정했지만, 악마가 브로드웨이 뮤지컬에 나오는 옛날 노래들을 통해 자신에게 말을 걸었고, 그렇게 할 것을 지시했었다고 주장했다.

PERPLEX [pərpléks] v. to confuse or bewilder; to puzzle through excessive complication 당황하게 하다; 골치 아프게 하다

The strobe light, fog machine, and deafening music of the disco completely *perplexed* the simple goatherd who had never even seen a lightbulb before.
디스코의 플래시 라이트, 안개 분사기, 귀청이 터질 듯한 음악은 백열전구조차도 본 적이 없었던 순진한 염소지기의 정신을 완전히 빼놓았다.

The question of how the escape artist was able to free herself from the iron trunk that had been shot into space *perplexed* everyone in the audience.
곡예사가 어떻게 우주로 쏘아 올려진 철제 트렁크에서 빠져나올 수 있었느냐는 의문에 모든 관중은 당황했다.

PERSISTENT [pərsístənt] adj. refusing to give up; stubborn and undaunted 악착같은, 끈질긴; 고집 센, 겁 없는

Although they failed the first eighty-three times, the *persistent* movers tried once more to carry the grand piano up the stairs.
고집 센 이삿짐 운송업자들은 그랜드피아노를 계단으로 옮기는 데 83번 실패했으면서도 한 번 더 시도했다.

Shawna acknowledged the fact that Horatio was *persistent* when he asked her out every day for three years, but she still refused to go to the movies with him.
쇼나는 호라티오가 3년 동안 매일같이 자신에게 데이트 신청을 하는 걸 보고 그가 끈질기다는 걸 알았지만, 그래도 여전히 그와 영화관에 가는 걸 거절했다.

PETULANT [pétʃulənt] adj. ill-tempered and spoiled; bratty 성미가 급한; 어린애 같은, 철없는

Realizing he was no longer the center of attention, the *petulant* child screamed at the top of his lungs.
성마른 아이는 자신이 더 이상 관심을 받지 못한다는 걸 알고 목청이 터져라 소리를 질러 댔다.

The *petulant* child demanded that anyone who stayed overnight at her house address her as "your Highness."
철없는 아이는 자신의 집에서 묵고 가는 사람이면 누구든 자기에게 "전하"라고 부르라고 했다.

PHENOMENON [finámənɑn/-nən/-nɔ́minən] n. an unusual occurrence or event; something wacky that happens 이상한 사건, 별난 일

The *phenomenon* of the glowing lights over Farmer Ben's wheat field was explained when Benny was caught painting moths with glow-in-the-dark paint.
파머 벤의 밀밭에 시뻘건 빛이 타올랐던 사건은 베니가 야광 페인트로 나방을 칠하다가 붙잡혔을 때 해명이 됐다.

The *phenomenal* child wrote her first major symphony when she was only two years old.
놀라운 아이는 겨우 두 살 때 첫 번째 교향곡을 썼다.

PHILOSOPHY [filásəfi/-lɔ́s-] n. a study of the basic truths that govern the world and society or a value system by which you live 철학; 가치 체계

The college freshman chose to study ancient *philosophy* because she wanted to have a better understanding of why humans exist.
대학 신입생은 인간의 존재 이유에 대해 좀 더 잘 이해하고 싶어서 고대 철학을 공부하기로 했다.

It was against the rock star's *philosophy* to wake up before 2:00 in the afternoon.
오후 2시 이전에 잠자리에서 일어나는 것은 록스타의 가치 체계와 맞지 않았다.

PIGMENT [pígmənt] n. a specific substance that provides a characteristic color to an object, such as hemoglobin (red) in blood 색소

Chlorophyll converts sunlight into food in plants, and is also the *pigment* that makes them green.
식물 속의 엽록소는 햇빛을 양분으로 바꾸며, 식물을 초록색으로 만드는 색소기도 한다.

Determined to find the *pigments* that make Gummy bears different color, the amateur doctors took out their microscopes and a kitchen knife.
아마추어 의사들은 구미 베어를 여러 색깔로 만드는 색소를 알아내리라 굳게 결심하고 현미경과 부엌칼을 꺼내들었다.

PIT [pit] v. to set against in a competition or to mark with depressions   싸움을 붙이다, 경쟁시키다; 움푹 들어가게 하다

The opening round of the karate competition *pitted* Frank "Walking Pain" Fantos against Maurice "Choppy Dog" Smoot.
가라테 시합의 첫 판에서 "워킹 페인"이라 불리는 프랭크 판토스와 "초피 독"이란 별명의 모리스 스쿠트가 맞붙었다.

We used an icepick to *pit* the pumpkin with holes that made it look as though it had two eyes, a nose, and a very small mouth.
우리는 얼음 깨는 송곳으로 호박에 구멍을 내 두 눈, 코, 아주 작은 입이 있는 것처럼 보이게 했다.

PLAUSIBLE [plɔ́ːzəbl] adj. appearing to be reasonable and true   그럴 듯한, 정말 같은

Judging by the empty bed, open window, and missing car, the only *plausible* explanation for Angela's disappearance was that she sneaked out to see her friends.
텅 빈 침대, 열린 창문, 없어진 차로 판단해 보건대, 안젤라의 실종에 그럴 듯한 설명은 그녀가 친구들을 만나러 몰래 빠졌나갔다는 것 밖에 없다.

While my excuse that I was too lazy to do my homework was certainly *plausible* to my teacher, it didn't prevent her from giving me an F for the assignment.
내가 너무 게을러서 숙제를 못했다는 건 선생님에게 확실히 그럴 듯한 변명이 됐지만, 그렇다고 과제물 점수로 F 받는 것을 면할 수는 없었다.

PLUMAGE [plúːmidʒ] n. the feathers on a bird   깃털

The male peacock spread out its colorful *plumage* in an effort to attract a certain female peacock he had his eye on.
수컷 공작은 관심 있는 암컷 공작을 유혹하기 위해 화려한 깃털을 펼쳤다.

The brown *plumage* of the owl allowed it to blend well into the tree trunk.
올빼미의 갈색 깃털은 나무 줄기와 분간하기 힘들게 만들었다.

PONDER [pándər/pɔ́n-] v. to think about something for a while; to carefully consider   곰곰이 생각하다

Once I spent the whole afternoon *pondering* why cats and dogs don't get along, but then I realized that I would never be able to figure it out and that I didn't care anyway.
나는 이전에 왜 고양이와 개는 사이가 안 좋을까에 대해 반나절 동안을 곰곰이 생각했는데, 그 이유를 결코 알아낼 수 없다는 것과 어쨌든 나한테는 상관없는 일이라는 걸 깨달았다.

The coach *pondered* the score, the field position, and time remaining in the game before he signaled for a field goal attempt.
코치는 필드골을 시도하라고 신호를 보내기 전에 점수와 경기장 위치, 남아 있는 시간에 대해 곰곰이 생각했다.

PRECISE [prisáis] adj. exact in execution; direct and clear; right on the nose   정확한; 명확한

Walter's estimate of the baseball crowd at 32,743 people turned out to be *precise*.
월터가 야구장 관중을 3만2천743명이라고 어림잡은 것은 정확한 것으로 밝혀졌다.

The Space Shuttle pilot's calculations were so good that she landed the shuttle on the *precise* spot from which it had taken off six days before.
우주 왕복선 조종사의 계산은 아주 뛰어나서 6일 전 이륙했던 지점에 정확하게 우주선을 착륙시켰다.

PREDATOR [prédətər] n. an animal that hunts and eats other animals for its survival 포식 동물

Humans are the only *predators* that kill other animals for reasons other than survival.
인간은 생존 이외의 이유로 다른 동물을 죽이는 유일한 포식 동물이다.

Mountain lions are fierce *predators* that are becoming scarce as more of their natural habitat is being converted for human use.
쿠거는 사나운 포식 동물인데, 자연 서식지의 대부분이 인간의 용도로 전환됨에 따라 희귀해지고 있다.

PREDECESSOR [prédəsesər/príːd-] n. the person who came before another person in time, such as the former person to have a certain job 전임자

My *predecessor* had been fired so suddenly that a half-empty cup of his coffee was still on the desk when I arrived for my first day of work.
내 전임자는 너무 갑작스레 해고를 당해서 내가 출근 첫날 도착했을 때 그가 마시다 만 커피가 책상 위에 그대로 있었다.

PREDICAMENT [pridíkəmənt] n. a difficult, unpleasant situation that is hard for you get out of 곤경, 궁지

After my sister faked an illness, I knew there was no escaping the *predicament* of baby-sitting my eight cousins for the whole weekend.
여동생이 꾀병을 부리자 내가 주말 내내 여덟 명의 조카를 돌봐야 하는 곤경에서 헤어날 방법이 없다는 걸 알았다.

PREMISE [prémis] n. a fundamental fact or facts 전제

Once the witness admitted he was lying, the whole *premise* of the case against K.O. Hertz fell to pieces.
증인이 자신의 위증을 인정하고 나자 K.O. 허츠를 상대로 한 소송의 모든 전제가 엉망이 됐다.

The brother based his accusation of his little sister on the *premise* that a little kid was more likely than a dog to steal his last chocolate bar.
오빠는 개보다는 꼬마 아이가 자신의 마지막 초콜릿 바를 더 훔쳐 먹을 만하다는 전제 하에 자신의 여동생에게 혐의를 두었다.

PRESUME [prizúːm/-zjúːm] v. to assume that something is true; to take for granted or to do something without asking permission 가정하다; 여기다, 생각하다; 허가를 구하지 않고 하다, 감히 하다

When he heard the knock on the door, Derek *presumed* that it was his next-door neighbor returning the rake that he'd borrowed.
데릭은 문 노크 소리를 듣고 옆집 사람이 빌려 갔던 갈퀴를 되돌려 주려고 온 거라 생각했다.

Since I had finished all my chores and homework, I *presumed* that father wouldn't mind if I took the car. Boy, I was wrong.
난 집안일과 숙제를 다 마쳤기 때문에 차를 가지고 나가도 아버지가 뭐라고 안 하실 줄 알았지. 이런, 내가 잘못 생각했어.

"How could you *presume* to take my car without asking me?" Dad demanded.
"어떻게 감히 나한테 물어보지도 않고 내 차를 가지고 나갈 수 있는 거냐?" 라고 아빠가 물었다.

PRETENSE [priténs/príːtens] n. a false action or reason that's used to deceive; an unsupported claim 가식, 허위, 거짓 구실; 터무니없는 주장, 요구

Citing national security as his *pretense*, the brother stole his sister's diary and ran off to read it to his friends.
오빠는 국가 안보라는 거짓 구실을 들먹이며 여동생의 일기장을 친구들에게 읽어 주려고 훔쳐서 도망갔다.

Our mother used the *pretense* that she had to ask us a question in order to try and find out what we were talking about in our Secret Treehouse Club meeting.

어머니는 우리가 '비밀 트리하우스 클럽' 모임에서 무슨 얘기를 나누는지 알아내기 위해 뭘 좀 물어봐야겠다고 주장하셨다.

PRETENTIOUS [priténʃəs] adj. trying to assume a position of status or wealth that is false; showy without a reason to be   겉치레하는, 허세 부리는

The *pretentious* host took two tin statues, painted them with gold paint, and then told her guests that they were priceless works of art.

겉치레를 좋아하는 주인은 주석 동상 두 개를 가져다가 금색 페인트로 칠한 다음 손님들에게 아주 귀중한 미술품이라고 말했다.

The other customers felt that driving that limousine to the Stop-N-Drive to get a carton of eggs was a little *pretentious*.

다른 손님들은 달걀 한 판을 사려고 '스탑-앤-드라이브' 까지 리무진을 몰고 오는 것은 좀 허세를 부리는 것이라고 느꼈다.

PREVAIL [privéil] v. to triumph or to be most common or frequent   이기다; 유행하다, 보급되다

The Union *prevailed* over the Confederates during the Civil War because they had a greater number of troops and more supplies.

남북 전쟁 때 연방 정부 지지자가 남부 동맹 지지자를 이겼는데, 그들에게 더 많은 군대와 군량이 있었기 때문이다.

When the teacher took a survey of the class he learned that the *prevailing* desire was for there to be no homework assigned over the weekend.

교사는 학급에서 의견 조사를 했을 때 주말 동안 숙제가 없었으면 하는 바람이 우세하다는 걸 알았다.

PRIM [prim] adj. stiffly proper and correct in manner   점잔빼는, 새침한

The *prim* secretary was shocked when the boss announced that Friday would be shorts-and-T shirt wearing day at the bank.

새침한 비서는 사장이 금요일은 반바지와 티셔츠를 입고 은행에 나오라고 발표하자 깜짝 놀랐다.

Bridget offended some of her *prim* relatives when she hugged Grandpa Anka instead of curtsying to him.

브리지트가 앵카 할아버지를 뵙고 절을 하는 대신 포옹을 하자 점잔빼는 친척들은 불쾌해 했다.

PRINCIPAL [prínsəpəl] adj. first in rank or degree   제일의, 주요한

The manager discovered that the double overtime football game on Monday night was the *principal* reason that half of his workers were late to work on Tuesday.

과장은 월요일 밤에 방영된 미식축구경기가 두번이나 연장전에 들어간 것이 화요일에 직원의 절반이 지각한 주요한 이유라는 걸 알게 됐다.

Most of the nation agreed that the *principal* achievement of the Lunos 6 space probe was the discovery of the intelligent alien named Shamus.

국민의 대부분은 우주 탐사용 로켓 루노스 6호의 주요한 업적이 샤머스라는 지적인 외계인을 발견해낸 것이라는 데 동의했다.

PRISTINE [prísti:n] adj. remaining in a pure, original state, unspoiled by humanity   본래의, 자연 그대로의; 소박한, 청순한

After watching one week of daytime soap operas, the child was no longer *pristine*.

일주일 동안 주간 멜로드라마를 시청한 아이는 소박함을 잃어버렸다.

Sheldon quickly jumped into the *pristine* snow of the backyard and started making a snow angel.

셸던은 뒤뜰에 그대로 있는 눈 속에 뛰어 들어가 눈 천사를 만들기 시작했다.

PROCESSION [prəséʃən] n. a group of something that's moving forward together in an orderly line; the act of moving forward 행렬; 행진

The wedding *procession* walked gracefully up the aisle but then the bride tripped on her dress and fell forward into the priest.
결혼 행진이 복도까지는 우아하게 진행됐는데, 그 뒤에 신부가 드레스 자락에 발이 걸려 목사의 품에 넘어지고 말았다.

The problem with the ticket machine caused the *procession* of people waiting to see *Free Willy VIII* to halt.
티켓 발매기에 문제가 생겨 '프리 윌리 8'을 보려고 기다리는 사람들의 행렬을 멈추게 했다.

PROFESS [prəfés] v. to claim openly; to state out loud or to claim knowledge or skill in 공언하다, 분명히 말하다; 전문가라고 자칭하다, 직업으로 하다

Using a megaphone, Xavier stood on a table and *professed* his love for Claire to everyone at lunch.
재비어는 점심시간에 테이블 위에 서서 확성기에 대고 모든 사람들을 향해 클레어에 대한 자신의 사랑을 공언했다.

Although Morton had originally *professed* to be skilled at surgery, he later confessed that he had learned everything he knew through playing the game *Operation*.
모튼은 처음에 자신이 외과 수술을 잘한다고 자신했었지만, 나중에 고백한 바에 따르면, 알고 있는 건 모두 '오퍼레이션' 게임을 하면서 터득한 것이었다.

PROLIFERATE [prəlífərèit] v. to multiply and increase at a fast rate; to grow rapidly 증식하다, 번식하다; 급격히 증가하다

With no predators and unlimited food, a male and female rabbit would *proliferate* so fast that you'd be swimming in bunnies in no time at all.
포식자는 없고 먹이가 무한하다면 토끼들은 아주 빨리 증식해 순식간에 토끼들 사이에서 헤엄치고 다니게 될 것이다.

The idea of a rebellion *proliferated* in the countryside, where the people had been overtaxed by the government for decades.
반란을 일으키자는 아이디어가 그 지방에서 급속히 번졌는데, 그곳 사람들은 수십년 동안 정부로부터 지나친 과세를 강요당해 왔었다.

PROPHETIC [prəfétik] adj. predicting the future 예언하는

Harold started to think he was *prophetic* after he picked the winning team in ten basketball games in a row.
헤롤드는 열 번의 농구 경기에서 잇따라 우승 팀을 알아맞힌 뒤 자신에게 예언의 능력이 있다고 여기기 시작했다.

The flower salesman was *prophetic* when he told the man that his wife would be mad if he came home without a gift for her birthday.
꽃 판매원은 남자에게 아내 생일인데 선물도 없이 집에 들어가면 아내가 화낼 거라는 예언을 했다.

[Note] A *prophet* [práfit/prɔ́-] is someone who can tell the future.
prophet은 '예언자'

PROSPEROUS [práspərəs/prɔ́s-] adj. economically successful; enjoying success and good fortune 경제적으로 성공하는, 번영하는

During a gold rush, people who sell mining and digging equipment are virtually guaranteed to *prosper*.
골드러시 동안 채광 장비를 판매하는 사람들은 성공을 보장받는 거나 다름없다.

Every year on Valentine's Day, the *prosperous* rose seller thanked the huge number of romantics in the world.
해마다 밸런타인데이가 되면 큰 수익을 올리는 장미 판매상은 전 세계의 엄청난 낭만주의자들에게 고마움을 느꼈다.

PROTOTYPE [próutətaip] n. the first example of an object or idea, upon which later models are based
원형(原型), 시작품

Instead of using gasoline as fuel, the new engine *prototype* ran on sea water.
새로운 엔진 원형은 가솔린 연료를 사용하는 대신에 바닷물을 연료로 가동했다.

Once the rocket exploded on the launch pad, the scientists knew that their *prototype* fuel was a little too dangerous to use at that point.
로켓이 발사대 위에서 폭발을 일으키자 과학자들은 원형 연료를 그 단계에서 사용하는 것은 좀 위험하다는 걸 알았다.

PROVISIONS [prəvíʒənz] n. stockpiles of food or other supplies or measure taken to prepare for a certain event   식량, 저장품; 준비

A steady stream of supply boats from the mainland kept the tiny island stocked with *provisions* the whole year round.
끊임없이 이어지는 본토로부터의 공급선 덕분에 작은 섬에는 일년 내내 식량이 비축되었다.

Deepening the moat and adding more guards were the only *provisions* the king took to protect the castle from the invaders.
해자를 더 깊게 파고 파수꾼을 늘리는 것이 침입자들로부터 성을 보호하기 위해 왕이 취한 준비의 전부였다.

PRUDENT [prú:dnt] adj. sensible in handling common matters; level-headed and wise or careful about your own conduct; cautious   분별 있는, 신중한, 조심성 있는

Screaming "Fire!" in a crowded movie theater is only a *prudent* action when there actually is a fire.
복잡한 영화관에서 실제로 화재가 발생했을 때 취할 수 있는 분별 있는 행동은 "불이야!"하고 외치는 것뿐이다.

The college sophomore knew that it would not be *prudent* to date the fifty-year-old Dean of Admissions, even though she was cute.
대학 2학년생은 50세의 입학 담당 학장이 비록 귀엽긴 해도 데이트를 하는 것은 신중하지 못한 일이라는 걸 알았다.

PUNGENT [pʌ́ndʒənt] adj. a sharp, biting smell or taste   (냄새나 맛이) 자극적인, 혀나 코를 찌르는

The homemade cheese Wanda kept in her kitchen was so *pungent* that you could smell it as you walked up to the front door of her house.
부엌에 있는 완다가 직접 만든 치즈는 냄새가 너무 자극적이어서 집 현관문까지만 가도 냄새가 날 정도였다.

The *pungent* smell coming from the kitchen warned me that Jonathan's pizza would not be at all ordinary.
부엌에서 나오는 코를 찌르는 냄새는 조나단의 피자가 전혀 멀쩡하지 않다는 경고였다.

Q

QUAINT [kweint] adj. unfamiliar and odd or odd in an old-fashioned way 기이한; 고풍스러워 흥미를 끄는

One of the *quaint* things about the Dzudombi Sand People is their custom of shaking each other's ankles fiercely as a way of saying "hello."
'드주돔비 샌드 사람들'의 기이한 것 중 하나는 만날 때의 인사로 상대의 발목을 심하게 흔드는 풍습이다.

The time travelers from the 22nd Century thought that our use of calculators was incredibly *quaint*.
22세기에서 타임머신을 타고 온 사람들은 우리가 사용하는 계산기는 정말 골통품이라고 생각했다.

QUALIFY [kwɑ́ləfai/kwɔ́l-] v. to limit the meaning or to soften; to make less extreme 의미를 한정하다; 가라앉히다, 완화하다

The governor quickly *qualified* his remarks about a tax increase by stating that only the top 5% of all companies would be affected.
주지사는 세금 인상에 대해 발언을 한 뒤 재빨리 모든 기업 가운데 상위 5%에만 적용될 거라면서 그 의미를 한정시켰다.

QUELL [kwel] v. to stop by using force or to calm 진압하다; 가라앉히다

By quickly putting on heavy boots and stomping, the oil workers were able to *quell* the Great Mouse Riot of 1827.
석유 노동자들은 무거운 부츠를 신고 발을 쿵쿵 굴러서 1827년의 '쥐 대폭동'을 진압했다.

Valeria *quelled* our fears about walking into the haunted house by showing us the patented Ghost Zapper she bought through the mail.
발레리아는 우편으로 구입한 특허 받은 '유령 재퍼'를 보여주면서 흉가에 들어가는 데 대한 우리의 두려움을 가라앉혔다.

QUIBBLE [kwíbl] v. to complain about little things; to gripe for small reasons 사소한 것을 불평하다; 별일 아닌 것에 잔소리하다

Even though he was about to become the first person to walk on Mars, Morton kept *quibbling* about the unflattering color of his space suit.
모튼은 화성에 발을 내딛는 최초의 사람이 될 것이면서 우주복 색깔이 돋보이지 않는다며 계속 불평을 했다.

Everyone left the party when the Hendersons started to *quibble* about who had made the better bean dip.
헨더슨 부부가 누가 만든 콩 소스가 더 나은지에 대해 잔소리하기 시작하자 모두들 파티장을 떠났다.

R

RADIANT [réidiənt] adj. sending out light or heat or bright with happiness 빛(열)을 내는, 빛나는; 표정이 밝은

The *radiant* sign in the window glowed brightly on the dark street and indicated that the restaurant was open.
창문 속의 간판이 어두운 거리에서 환하게 빛나면서 식당이 영업 중이라는 걸 알렸다.

Salma flashed a *radiant* smile at her parents after she finished playing the difficult song on the piano without making any mistakes.
샐마는 어려운 곡을 아무 실수 없이 피아노로 연주하고 난 뒤 부모님에게 환한 미소를 지어 보였다.

RAMBLE [ræmbl] v. to walk around with no purpose or direction or to write or speak for a long time, constantly wandering off the topic 정처 없이 돌아다니다; 두서없이 오래 말하다(쓰다)

If I were to write a sentence that *rambles*, I would probably want to talk about that one time I was in Chicago, not the first time I was there but the second, because the first time I was there was really just a layover at the airport, and normally I wouldn't count that as a stop except the flight I was supposed to be on was delayed, I think they had engine problems, or maybe it was something wrong with the wing, and so I had to spend more time than usual, something like three hours, I think, and so...
두서없는 내용의 문장을 써야 한다면 아마도 내가 시카고에 있을 때를 말하고 싶을 것 같다 내가 거기에 처음 갔을 때가 아니라 두 번째였는데, 왜냐면 처음에 거기 갔을 때는 공항에서 도중하차를 한 거였고, 보통 내가 타기로 한 비행기가 연착된 것만 아니면 거길 정류소로 생각하지 않았을 건데, 내 생각에 그때 엔진 문제가 있었거나, 아니면 날개에 무슨 문제가 있었을 수도 있고, 그래서 난 예정보다 긴 시간을 보내야 했는데, 세 시간쯤이었을 건데, 그래서…

RANCID [rǽnsid] adj. having a nasty smell or taste due to rotting 썩는 냄새가(맛이) 나는

In February, Emile found that the *rancid* smell coming from the trunk of his car was caused by the leftover Thanksgiving turkey which they'd decided to take home from his mother's house.
2월에 에밀은 자동차 트렁크에서 나는 썩는 냄새가 어머니 집에서 자기 집에 가져가려고 싸왔던 추수감사절 칠면조 남은 것 때문이라는 사실을 알았다.

Remember that raccoon carcass from the "Carcass" sentence earlier? Well, you can bet that animal smelled *rancid*.
앞서 "사체"가 나오는 문장에서 너구리 시체 기억나죠? 그 동물에서 틀림없이 썩는 냄새가 났을 거예요.

RASCAL [rǽskəl/rɑ́:s-] n. someone who misbehaves in a playful way or a dishonest person 못된 장난을 하는 사람; 악한, 불량배

Although he was certainly a *rascal*, Noah had such a cute smile that most adults rarely punished him for his pranks.
노아는 분명 못된 장난을 치는 아이였지만, 미소를 지을 때면 너무 귀여워 어른들 대부분은 그가 짓궂은 장난을 쳐도 좀처럼 벌을 주지 않았다.

When the townsfolk learned that the *rascal's* scheme to form a high school band was all a fake, they quickly located him and demanded back their money.

마을 사람들은 고등학교 밴드를 만든다는 불량배의 계획이 모두 가짜라는 걸 알고서 재빨리 그를 찾아내 돈을 돌려 달라고 했다.

RASPY [ræspi/rɑ́:spi] adj. rough and grating 삐걱거리는, 귀에 거슬리는

The *raspy* sound coming from the shed told me that my father was scraping the barnacles off of the bottom of our boat.

창고에서 들리는 삐걱거리는 소리는 아버지가 우리 배의 선체바닥에 붙어 있는 조개 삿갓을 긁어 떼어내고 있다는 걸 알려주었다.

After smoking three packs of cigarettes a day for ten years, the singer's voice was so *raspy* that she could no longer perform her songs well.

10년 동안 하루에 담배를 세 갑씩 피워 온 가수는 목소리가 너무 거칠어져서 더 이상 노래를 잘 할 수 없었다.

RATION [rǽʃən/réi-] v. to make available in set amounts, especially during a time when a supply is scarce 정해진 양만큼 주다, 공급을 제한하다

The county started to *ration* everyone's water supply when the drought was in its third month.

군청에서는 가뭄이 석 달째 계속되자 모든 사람들에 대해 물 공급을 제한하기 시작했다.

After cunning thieves stole over 75 percent of the nation's rubber trees, the government had to start *rationing* car tire sales.

교활한 도둑들이 전국의 고무나무 75% 이상을 베어 가자 정부에서는 자동차 타이어 판매를 제한해야만 했다.

REBUFF [ribʌ́f] n. an unfriendly rejection; a snub or v. to reject briefly and rudely 거절, 퇴짜; 푸대접; (단번에 무례하게) 거절하다, 퇴짜 놓다

I received my *rebuff* from Anderson Industries in the form of a quick slap in the face from its owner, Wiley "Snapper" Anderson.

나는 앤더슨 인더스트리즈에서 퇴짜를 맞았는데, "스내퍼"라 불리는 경영주 윌리 앤더슨한테서 바로 거절을 당했다.

Natalie *rebuffed* my request for a date by screaming "No!" and throwing her sandwich in my face.

나탈리는 "싫어!"라고 소리치고 그녀의 샌드위치를 내 얼굴에 던지면서 내 데이트 신청을 단번에 거절했다.

RECEDE [risí:d] v. to move away; to become smaller 물러가다; 감소하다

As our annoying guests drove away down the road, we made sure that their car had *receded* far enough into the distance before we started to celebrate.

성가신 손님들이 차를 몰고 떠나자 우린 그들의 차가 충분히 멀리 갔는지 확인한 뒤에 환호성을 치기 시작했다.

Once my fear of the new neighborhood dog had *receded*, I was able to resume my paper route.

새로 온 이웃집 개에 대한 두려움이 줄어들자 신문배달을 재개할 수 있었다.

RECIPIENT [risípiənt] n. a person who receives something 수납자, 수령인

Although she was listed as the *recipient* of the package, Angela denied that she knew that there was stolen artwork inside it.

안젤라는 자신이 소포의 수령인으로 등록돼 있었지만 그 안에 도난당한 미술품이 있다는 걸 모른다고 했다.

RECKONING [rékəniŋ] n. the process of computing or calculating; the settling of all accounts, debts or otherwise 계산; 청산

Using only a compass and an old map for *reckoning*, the guide was able to locate the site of the ancient stone carvings for us.
가이드는 나침반과 낡은 계산용 지도만을 이용해 우리에게 고대 돌조각 유적의 위치를 알려줄 수 있었다.

After my *reckoning* with the debt collector, all I had left was one pair of blue jeans and twenty-three cents.
빚 수금 대행 업자에게 빚을 청산하고 난 뒤 내게 남은 것은 청바지 한 벌과 23센트가 전부였다.

RECUPERATE [rikjú:pəreit/-kú:-] v. to get healthier after an illness; to return to normal health 회복하다

I was able to *recuperate* from the chicken pox faster than my sister since I continued to take walks outside and get fresh air, while my sister refused to get out of bed.
여동생은 침대에서 꼼짝하지 않았지만 나는 계속 산책을 나가서 신선한 공기를 마셨기 때문에 내가 여동생보다 빨리 수두에서 회복될 수 있었다.

When he had *recuperated* from his eighty broken bones, the stunt man decided not to ever jump over twenty flaming buses again.
뼈가 80개 부러진 데서 회복한 스턴트맨은 다시는 20대의 불타는 버스 위로 점프하지 않겠다고 다짐했다.

REEDY [rí:di] adj. tall and thin, like a reed or sounding like a reed instrument 갈대처럼 호리호리한, 길고 가느다란; 갈대 피리 소리 같은

The giraffe's *reedy* neck allows it to reach branches that no other animal can get to for food.
기린은 길고 가느다란 목 덕분에 다른 동물은 먹이를 구하려고 할 때 닿을 수 없는 가지까지 이를 수 있다.

Malcolm's *reedy* voice could be heard above all of the other voices in the choir.
말콤의 갈대 피리 같은 목소리는 성가대의 다른 목소리들 사이에서도 들을 수 있었다.

REEL [ri:l] v. to be thrown off balance; to stagger or to pull inward using a winding motion 비틀거리다; 감다, 감아 끌어당기다

After spinning in place for over thirty minutes, I was *reeling* all over the park, bumping into slides and other kids as I attempted to regain balance.
나는 30분 이상 자리에서 빙빙 돌고 난 뒤 균형을 회복하려다가 미끄럼틀과 아이들한테 부딪치면서 공원 전체를 비틀거리고 다녔다.

Grandpa slowly *reeled* in the hooked fish, which we would see occasionally jump out of the lake about twenty yards from shore.
할아버지는 낚시에 걸린 물고기를 천천히 감아서 끌어당기셨는데, 해안에서 20야드 가량 떨어진 호수의 수면 위로 물고기가 이따금씩 튀어 오르는 게 보였다.

REFRACT [rifrǽkt] v. to deflect or bend light 굴절시키다

Swimming underwater at the pool's deep end, I saw how the water *refracted* the sunlight into wavy shapes along the bottom.
수영장의 깊은 바닥에서 수영하다가 물에 햇빛이 굴절돼 바닥을 따라 너울거리는 모양이 만들어지는 걸 보았다.

Anyone can use a prism to take a beam of sunlight and *refract* it into a rainbow.
누구든지 프리즘을 이용해 햇빛을 모아 굴절시키면 무지개를 만들 수 있다.

REFRAIN [rifréin]　v.　to hold back; to restrain or　n.　a phrase that is repeated throughout a song or poem　삼가다, 억누르다 / 후렴

I tried to *refrain* from causing a disturbance, but when they brought out the cat jugglers, I had to rush the stage to try to stop the performance.
난 소동을 일으키지 않으려고 했지만, 고양이 저글러들이 나오자 공연을 저지하기 위해 무대로 뛰어갈 수밖에 없었다.

A local disc jockey noted the Fweeb's new song, which was called "Cake Tango," repeated the *refrain* "dance on the icing" over seventy times in four minutes.
어떤 디스크자키 말로는, Fweeb의 새 노래 "케이크 탱고"에서 "얼음 위에서 댄스"라는 후렴이 4분 동안 70번 넘게 나온다.

REGAL [rí:gəl]　adj.　very fancy, beautiful, and expensive; kingly or queenly　예쁘고 값비싼; 왕다운, 여왕다운

Unlike most dresses, the *regal* gown had large diamonds for buttons, which made it sparkle brilliantly in the sunlight.
다른 드레스와 달리 예쁘고 비싼 가운에는 단추마다 커다란 다이아몬드가 박혀 있어서 햇빛을 받으면 화려하게 빛이 났다.

The *regal* manner in which the king addressed the merchant made him tremble out of fear and respect.
왕이 상인을 왕다운 태도로 부르자 상인은 경외감으로 벌벌 떨었다.

REGIMENT [rédʒəmənt]　n.　a group of soldiers or　v.　to conform to a highly-ordered system　연대 / 엄격히 조직화(통제)하다

During World War II, the 83rd *regiment* became famous for stopping over two divisions of German soldiers by themselves.
제2차 세계대전 동안 제83 연대는 독일군의 2개 사단 이상을 혼자 힘으로 격퇴해서 유명해졌다.

My life at the summer camp was so *regimented* that even the times at which I brushed my teeth were strictly regulated.
여름 캠프에서의 생활이 너무 엄격해서 이를 닦는 시간조차 철저하게 통제를 받았다.

REGRESS [rigrés]　v.　to go back to a previous state of development　되돌아가다; 퇴보하다

Although the talking chimp experiment was successful, the monkey soon *regressed* to its normal state once the scientists stopped the injections.
말하는 침팬지 실험이 성공적이긴 했지만 과학자들이 주사를 멈추자 원숭이는 곧 보통 상태로 되돌아갔다.

Even though he was a mature, forty-year-old businessman, Chan would occasionally *regress* into childlike fits of rage.
마흔 살의 사업가 챈은 성숙한 사람이었지만 이따금 어린아이처럼 미친듯이 화를 내곤 했다.

REIGN [rein]　n.　the time period during which a king or queen is in power or　v.　to rule as a king or queen (usually followed by "over")　치세, 군림 / 통치하다, 군림하다(뒤에 over와 함께 쓰여)

The *reign* of King Henry VIII of England spanned four decades.
영국 왕 헨리 8세는 40년에 걸쳐 군림했다.

Emperor Charlemagne *reigned* over much of what is now Europe.
샤를마뉴 대제는 지금의 유럽 땅 대부분을 통치했다.

RELISH [réliʃ] v. to greatly enjoy; to take immense pleasure in 대단히 즐기다, 아주 좋아하다

Even though the drive was over three hours, all the kids *relished* the chance to go to Six Flags over Bombay.
차를 타고 세 시간 넘게 가야 했지만 아이들은 모두 'Six Flags over Bombay'로 가는 기회를 대단히 반겼다.

Sigmund *relished* the thought of playing tennis against Jung, since Jung's serve was so weak that Sigmund knew he would win.
지그문트는 융의 서브가 너무 약해서 자신이 이길 줄을 알았기 때문에 융파의 테니스 시합을 아주 좋아했다.

REPARATION [rèpəréiʃən] n. something done or paid in order to repay a debt or earlier mistake 배상

The government paid over fifty million dollars in *reparations* for people who were wrongly imprisoned during the last war.
정부는 지난 전쟁 동안 착오로 수감되었던 사람들에게 5천만 달러의 배상금을 지불했다.

After testifying against them in the trial, the brother tried to make *reparations* to his family by offering them the best legal service money could buy.
형제는 재판에서 자신의 가족에게 불리한 증언을 한 뒤 돈으로 살 수 있는 가장 합법적인 서비스를 제공해 배상하려고 했다.

REPLENISH [ripléniʃ] v. to fill again; to restock or resupply 다시 채우다; 다시 공급하다

Luckily the thunderstorm *replenished* most of the water that had been lost from the pond during the days of the drought.
다행히도 뇌우가 찾아와 며칠 동안 가뭄으로 말라 버린 저수지에 물을 채워 주었다.

The parents knew they had to *replenish* their stock of batteries after Gerald bought a portable stereo that used sixteen C batteries at a time.
제럴드의 부모는 제럴드가 한번에 C배터리 16개를 사용하는 휴대용 스테레오를 구입한 후 배터리를 다시 사다 놓아야 한다는 걸 알았다.

REPOSE [ripóuz] n. a state of mental peace; freedom from anxiety or unrest 휴식; 평온

Once she had complete her eighth and final midterm exam, Maeve kicked back her chair and assumed a position of *repose*.
메이브는 여덟 번째이자 마지막 중간고사를 끝내고 나자 의자를 뒤로 물려 휴식의 자세를 취했다.

The quiet *repose* of the little fishing village was shattered when the army of sea monsters appeared with high tide.
만조가 되면서 은상어떼가 나타나자 조그만 어촌의 평온함이 깨졌다.

REPRESS [riprés] v. to hold back; to keep down or hidden away or to force out of the conscious mind
감추다; 억누르다; 무의식 속으로 억압하다

Government officials rapidly tried to *repress* the information that the President liked to wear women's clothes, but the photos had already been taken.
공무원들은 대통령이 여성복을 입기 좋아한다는 정보를 재빨리 감추려고 했지만, 이미 사진들이 찍혀진 후였다.

The three days I had to spend with smelly Uncle Stan were so horrible that I've *repressed* the entire event in my memory.
냄새가 고약한 스탠 삼촌과 보내야 했던 3일은 너무나 끔찍해서 난 기억 속에 있는 모든 사건을 떠올리지 않으려 했다.

REPROACH [ripróutʃ] v. to blame or criticize or n. blame or contempt; disgrace 꾸짖다, 비난하다 / 비난, 질책; 불명예, 망신

The boss *reproached* her secretary Ross for forgetting to mail paychecks out to any of the employees except himself.
사장은 비서 로스가 자신을 제외한 다른 직원들에게 급료 보내는 걸 잊어버렸다고 꾸짖었다.

After I burned down the house by trying to bake cigarettes, my wife gave me a dark look of *reproach*.
내가 잎담배를 구워 말리려다가 집을 태워 버리자 아내는 내게 어두운 질책의 표정을 지어 보였다.

REPUGNANT [ripʌ́gnənt] adj. highly disgusting; offensive 아주 역겨운, 불쾌한

The mixture of spam, bacon grease, motor oil, and vanilla sprinkles was so *repugnant* that I couldn't imagine why anyone would want to eat it for dessert.
스팸, 베이컨 기름, 모터오일, 바닐라 약간을 섞었더니 너무나 역겨워 누구도 디저트로 먹고 싶어 하지 않을 것 같았다.

Killeen's *repugnant* personal habits were attractive only to flies and a certain type of carrion beetle.
킬린은 아주 불쾌한 습관을 가지고 있었는데, 파리와 특정한 종류의 썩은 고기를 먹는 딱정벌레들이나 좋아할 만한 것이었다.

RESENT [rizént] v. to be angry about something unfair or unjust 분개하다, 화내다

Myra deeply *resented* the fact that her best friend Sheila had stolen her boyfriend Mehke away from her during the Valentine's Day dance.
미라는 가장 친한 친구 쉴라가 밸런타인데이 댄스파티에서 자신의 남자 친구 메케를 빼앗아 갔다는 사실에 분개했다.

Since they played Irish folk songs loudly until three a.m. every night, most of the Dwiskson's neighbors *resented* them.
드윅슨 가족이 매일 밤 3시까지 아일랜드 민요를 큰소리로 연주했기 때문에 이웃 사람 대부분이 그들에게 화를 냈다.

RESIDUE [rézədjuː/-duː] n. the remains for something after a larger part is removed 나머지, 잔여

One we removed the plant from its pot, all that remained was a tiny *residue* of the dirt.
화분에서 화초를 뽑아내고 나자 남은 거라고는 흙부스러기 조금뿐이었다.

The snail left a *residue* of slime as it traveled across my face while I was taking a nap in the garden.
내가 정원에서 낮잠을 자고 있을 때 달팽이가 내 얼굴을 지나가면서 점액 찌꺼기를 남겨 놓았다.

RETROSPECT [rétrəspèkt] n. the review of a past event or of past events; hindsight 회고, 추억; 뒷궁리

Now that I am old and very ill, in *retrospect* I realize that it was a bad idea to smoke two packs of cigarettes a day when I was younger.
이제 나이가 들고 병들어 되돌아보니, 젊은 시절 하루에 담배 두 갑씩을 피웠던 것이 나빴다는 걸 알겠다.

In *retrospect*, Dan realized that selling one of his legs for only $50 was a poor decision.
되돌아보면, 다리 한쪽에 겨우 50달러를 받고 판 것은 형편없는 결정이었다는 걸 댄은 깨달았다.

REVELATION [rèvəléiʃən] n. the act of revealing; a surprising disclosure 폭로

Our teacher Mr. Mieszkowski's *revelation* that he was a sheepdog trapped in a man's body came as quite a surprise to all of us.
우리 선생님 미즈코브스키 씨가 자신은 인간의 몸에 갇힌 양치기개라고 폭로하자 우린 모두 큰 충격을 받았다.

REVENUE [révənju:/-nu:] n. income; the money collected by the government for public expenses 수입; 정부의 세입

With the *revenue* from my international chain of lasagna restaurants steadily increasing, I could not help but become more and more wealthy.
라자냐 식당의 외국 체인점에서 들어오는 수입이 꾸준히 증가하자 나는 점점 더 부유해질 수밖에 없었다.

The state government created a tax on all pet goldfish in order to raise *revenue* for a new convention center.
주 정부에서는 새로운 컨벤션 센터 건립을 위한 세입을 늘리기 위해 모든 애완용 금붕어에 대한 세금을 제정했다.

REVERENCE [révərəns] n. a feeling of respect, admiration, and love 존경, 경의, 애정

Our *reverence* for the holy hermit diminished when we learned he had used church funds to buy a satellite TV dish for his cave.
경건한 은둔자가 그의 동굴에 위성 TV 안테나를 달려고 교회 기금을 사용했다는 사실을 알고 그에 대한 우리의 존경심이 사라졌다.

The old men talked about football with so much *reverence* and seriousness that you would have thought they were discussing philosophy.
노인들이 미식축구에 대해 워낙 대단한 애정으로 진지하게 얘기해서 철학을 논하고 있다고 생각될 정도였다.

REVILE [riváil] v. to denounce using abusive language 욕하다

Since he had wanted to fly forever, the pilot *reviled* his passengers for their pathetic desire to land the plane at the airport.
비행기 조종사는 영원히 날아다니고 싶어서 승객들이 공항에 비행기를 착륙시키라고 애원하자 욕을 했다.

The manager of the construction crew *reviled* his workers for falling asleep on the job and threatened to seal them in cement if it ever happened again.
건설반 감독은 일하다 잠이 든 인부들에게 욕을 하면서 또다시 그러면 시멘트 속에 가두어 버리겠다고 협박했다.

RHETORIC [rétərik] n. the study of how to use language persuasively and expertly or insincere, snobbish, and boorish speaking or writing 수사학; 성의 없고 상스러운 말(글)

Many of today's successful politicians study *rhetoric* so that their speeches and beliefs will affect a great number of people.
오늘날 성공하는 정치인 다수가 자신들의 연설과 소신이 많은 사람들에게 영향을 줄 수 있도록 수사학을 공부한다.

The student's self-evaluation was full of *rhetoric* and the teacher threw it away in disgust.
학생의 반성문은 상스러운 표현들로 가득 차서 교사는 혐오감을 느끼며 내버렸다.

RHEUMATISM [rú:mətizm] n. a disease that effects the muscles and joint, causing pain and disability 류머티즘

Now that my grandfather has *rheumatism*, he never goes to the second floor because the walk up the stairs is too painful.
우리 할아버지는 류머티즘에 걸리셔서 계단을 오르는 것이 너무 고통스러워 2층에는 못 올라가신다.

A daily massage and visit to the whirlpool helps my old aunt Bea cope with her *rheumatism*.
나이 많은 비 숙모는 매일 마사지를 받고 월풀에 다니면서 류머티즘을 관리한다.

RHYTHM [ríðm] n. a movement or action that occurs over and over again in a regular pattern 리듬, 규칙적인 반복 운동

The *rhythm* of the waves against the sides of the lifeboat eventually lulled me to sleep.
구명보트 측면에 부딪치는 파도의 리듬 때문에 난 잠에 빠져들었다.

Leo discovered that the pulsing *rhythm* of Cuban music made him want to dance.
레오는 쿠바 음악의 리듬감 있는 박자를 들으니 춤을 추고 싶어졌다.

RICOCHET [ríkəʃei] v. to bounce off at least one surface 튀어 나가다

Fortunately, the bullet *ricocheted* off of my belt buckle, bounced off a wall, and hit the robber in the foot.
다행히도 총알이 내 허리띠 버클에서 튀어 나가 벽을 튕긴 다음 강도의 발에 박혔다.

RIFT [rift] n. a narrow break, as in a rock; a split 갈라진 틈, 균열

A brown lizard that had been sunbathing on a boulder quickly ran into a *rift* in the rock when it saw us coming.
둥근 돌 위에서 일광욕을 즐기던 갈색 도마뱀이 우리가 오는 걸 보자 재빨리 바위 틈새로 도망쳐 들어갔다.

By flirting with both of them openly, Jeannie created a *rift* in Bob and Doug's friendship that never closed until they met the beautiful Klein twins.
지니는 밥과 덕 모두와 공공연하게 어울려 다니면서 그 둘의 우정을 갈라놓았는데, 어여쁜 클레인 쌍둥이를 만나자 그들의 우정이 회복됐다.

RITUAL [rítʃuəl] n. a ceremony; a specific procedure or method 의식; 특정한 절차

Only yellow candles made from the pollen of Siberian bees may be used in the ancient *ritual* of blessing Kronhorst the Rice God.
시베리아 벌의 꽃가루로 만들어진 노란 양초만이 곡식의 신 크론호스트를 찬미하는 고대 의식에 사용될 수 있다.

The purification *ritual* in Jed's church was so complicated that everyone received a twelve-page manual describing the procedure.
제드가 다니는 교회의 재계 의식은 너무 복잡해서 모두에게 12페이지짜리 절차 설명 안내서를 나눠주었다.

RIVALRY [ráivəlri] n. a competition between two parties 경쟁

Although the two colleges often worked together on academic projects, there was a fierce *rivalry* between their football teams.
두 대학은 종종 대학 프로젝트에 대해 공동 작업을 했지만 미식축구팀 사이에서는 사나운 경쟁을 벌였다.

The intense *rivalry* between the two soccer teams sometimes resulted in fights between their overly enthusiastic fans.
두 축구팀 사이의 격렬한 경쟁은 가끔씩 지나치게 열광적인 팬들 사이에 싸움을 일으킨다.

ROMP [rɑmp/rɔmp] v. to goof off and have fun in an energetic, lively way 신나게 뛰어놀다

Our playful *romp* in the nearby field ended once we realized that we were jumping around in poison ivy.
우리는 가까운 벌판에서 신나게 뛰어놀다가, 독담쟁이 덩굴에서 뛰어다니고 있다는 걸 알게 된 뒤 곧 그만두었다.

The three brothers were having such a fun *romp* in the local mall that security eventually threw them out for "disturbing the serious shoppers."
세 형제는 동네 상점에서 심하게 뛰어다니다가 경비원에게 "중요한 쇼핑객들을 방해한다"는 이유로 쫓겨났다.

ROUT [raut]   n. an overwhelming defeat; a blow-out or   v. to drive away; to scatter   완패 / 쫓아 버리다, 패주시키다

Once the other team hit its eighteenth home run in a row, the coach of the home team admitted that the softball game was a *rout*.
상대팀에서 잇따라 18번째 홈런을 날리자 홈팀의 코치는 소프트볼 게임에 완패했음을 인정했다.

Because of their superior weapons and technology, the Romans were able to *rout* the invading barbarians from their country.
로마인들은 뛰어난 무기와 기술 덕분에 그들 나라에 쳐들어오는 야만인들을 내쫓을 수 있었다.

ROVE [rouv]   v. to wander around a large area   헤매다, 배회하다

After *roving* around the valley for several hours, Jakob had to admit that his lucky picnic basket was lost for good.
제이콥은 몇 시간 동안 계곡을 배회한 뒤 행운의 피크닉 바구니를 영영 잃어버렸다는 걸 받아들여야 했다.

The cows spent the day peacefully *roving* around the west pasture until some high school kids showed up and tried to tip them over.
젖소들은 낮 동안 서쪽 목초지를 한가로이 돌아다니고 있었는데 고등학생 몇 명이 나타나 그들을 공격하려고 했다.

RUBBLE [rʌbl]   n. fragments of material left after a building collapses or is destroyed   파편, 조각

Volunteers searched through the *rubble* of the collapsed building, hoping to find some sign of the three people still missing.
자원봉사자들은 아직 실종 상태인 세 사람의 흔적을 찾길 바라며 붕괴된 건물의 파편을 뒤졌다.

In the spirit of recycling, the villagers used the *rubble* from the old castle to build a rock wall around their new town.
마을 사람들은 재활용의 정신으로 오래된 성에서 나온 돌조각을 새로운 읍 주변을 두르는 돌담을 쌓는 데 사용했다.

RUDDY [rʌdi]   adj. characterized by a healthy, reddish look   불그스레한, 혈색이 좋은

The mother's habit of making her kids eat only healthy foods was manifested in the *ruddy* faces of her three daughters.
어머니가 자신의 아이들에게 몸에 좋은 음식만을 먹인다는 것은 세 딸의 혈색 좋은 얼굴을 보면 분명히 알 수 있었다.

RUFFIAN [rʌfiən]   n. a thug or tough guy   악한, 무법자, 깡패

Ever since the two *ruffians* beat him up in an alley and took his wallet, Cuttrell never leaves the house without wearing a full suit of armor.
커트렐은 골목에서 두 명의 깡패에게 두들겨 맞고 지갑을 뺏긴 이래로 집밖으로 나갈 때 갑옷을 입는다.

Yesterday, the police arrested the *ruffian* who broke into the zoo and started a fight with the baboons.
어제 경찰이 동물원에 침입해 개코원숭이와 싸움을 일으킨 깡패를 체포했다.

RUMINATE [rú:məneit]   v. to spend time thinking about something   곰곰이 생각하다, 생각에 잠기다

While I was *ruminating* on which flavor of chewing gum I should buy, my friends left the store and went to play without me.
내가 어떤 맛의 껌을 사야 하나 곰곰이 생각하고 있는 동안 친구들은 가게를 나가 나를 빼놓고 놀러 갔다.

After three days of *ruminating* on his choice of colleges, Terrance decided he should just flip a coin and choose one that way.

터렌스는 어떤 대학을 갈까 3일 동안 심사숙고한 뒤 그냥 동전을 던져 나오는 대로 가야겠다고 결정했다.

RUSE [ruːz] n. a sneaky trick or deception 책략, 계략

By lowering my voice, I had convinced the principal that I was my father, but then my mom walked in and destroyed my *ruse*.

나는 목소리를 내리깔고 교장에게 내가 아버지라고 믿게 했지만, 그때 엄마가 들어와 나의 계략을 망쳐 버렸다.

Their *ruse* of getting into the movie as adults was foiled when the eight-year-old at the top fell off of the shoulders of his friend below.

어른 행세를 해서 영화관에 들어가려던 그들의 책략은 위에 올라타 있던 여덟 살짜리가 밑에 있는 친구 어깨에서 떨어지는 바람에 좌절되었다.

RUSTLE [rʌ́səl] v. to act quickly and energetically or to move with a soft, fluttering sound 서둘러 행동하다, 활발하게 움직이다; 펄럭거리며(살랑거리며) 움직이다

The pioneer had been forced to eat cactus for the two days he was lost in the desert, and when finally found his way home he *rustled* around in his kitchen in order to get some real food.

개척자는 사막에서 길을 잃은 이틀 동안 선인장을 먹을 수밖에 없었는데, 마침내 집으로 돌아가게 되자 진짜 음식을 먹기 위해 서둘러 부엌으로 들어갔다.

As I heard the *rustle* of the geography worksheets being handed back, I prayed that I had remembered the Capitol of the United States correctly.

지리 문제지가 펄럭거리며 걷히는 소리가 들리자 나는 미국의 국회의사당을 제대로 썼기를 기도했다.

S

SALLOW [sǽlou] adj. characterized by a sickly, yellowish color 누르스름한

> After eating one hundred bananas in five days, Brent's face was *sallow* and his vision was failing.
> 5일 동안 백 개의 바나나를 먹은 브렌트는 얼굴이 누르스름해지고 시력이 나빠졌다.

> The once-purple grapes in the refrigerator appeared *sallow*, so we threw them away.
> 우리는 냉장고에 있는 포도가 지줏빛에서 누르스름하게 변하자 내다버렸다.

SATURATE [sǽtʃəreit] v. to fill or load to capacity; to soak thoroughly 가득 채우다; 흠뻑 적시다

> The air had become so *saturated* with smoke from our fireplace that we had to leave the house and spend Christmas in a nearby hotel.
> 공기가 벽난로에서 나오는 연기로 가득 차는 바람에 우린 집을 나와 가까운 호텔에서 크리스마스를 보내야 했다.

> Tammar *saturated* his towel with pool water and then snapped it at people as though it were a whip.
> 태머는 수영장 물로 타월을 흠뻑 적신 다음 그게 채찍이라도 되는 양 탁탁 소리가 나도록 사람들을 향해 내리쳤다.

SAUNTER [sɔ́:ntər] v. to walk at a casual pace; to stroll or n. a leisurely walk 한가로이 거닐다, 산책하다 / 느긋한 걸음, 산책

> The newlyweds *sauntered* through the park at sunset without a care in the world.
> 신혼부부는 세상에 대한 걱정이랑 없이 해질녘에 공원을 한가로이 거닐었다.

> Once we realized that we'd be late for the game, we changed our pace from a *saunter* to a quick jog.
> 우린 경기에 늦으리라는 걸 깨닫고 발걸음을 느긋한 걸음에서 속보로 바꾸었다.

SCAMPER [skǽmpər] v. to run quickly and lightly 재빨리 뛰다

> The rabbit *scampered* through the bushes and disappeared into its den when it saw the fox coming toward it.
> 토끼는 자신에게 다가오는 여우를 보고 수풀을 헤치며 재빨리 뛰어가 굴속으로 사라졌다.

> The running back was only five feet tall but he was incredibly fast, so he was often able to *scamper* past all the defenders and score touchdowns.
> 러닝백은 키가 5피트밖에 안됐지만 놀랄 만큼 빨라서 모든 수비수를 뚫고 달려가 득점을 올릴 수 있었다.

SCARCE [skɛərs/skɛəs] adj. hard to find; rare; not enough 찾기 힘든, 드문; 부족한

> The fact that gold is so *scarce* means that many people go to great lengths in order to get their hands on it.
> 금이 아주 드물다는 것은 많은 사람들이 금을 얻기 위해서라면 무슨 일이든 한다는 의미다.

In a town completely filled with vegetarians, ham and turkey sandwiches are rather *scarce*.
채식주의자들만 사는 마을에서 햄과 칠면조 샌드위치를 구하기란 상당히 힘들다.

SCENARIO [sinέəriòu/-ná:r-] n. an outline of an expected series of events or the outline of a story or play 개요, 초안; 대본, 시나리오

A team of Pentagon generals worked overnight to come up with all the possible *scenarios* that might occur now that Kubekstan has declared war on Canada.
미 국방성의 장군들로 구성된 팀은 쿠벡스탄이 캐나다에 전쟁 선포를 한 이상 일어날 수 있는 모든 가상 시나리오를 생각해내느라 밤을 지새웠다.

Julia tried to write a *scenario* of the book, but since she'd only read the title and the jacket cover, she wasn't very successful.
줄리아는 책의 개요를 써 보려고 했지만 그녀가 읽은 거라고는 제목과 표지뿐이어서 잘 해낼 수가 없었다.

SCHOONER [skú:nər] n. a sailing ship with two or more masts 스쿠너선

Because of the strong wind that was blowing steadily from the east, the *schooner* made excellent time on its voyage to New Spain.
동편에서 끊임없이 불어오는 강풍 때문에 스쿠너선은 뉴 스페인으로의 항해 동안 멋진 시간을 가졌다.

I broke both of the masts on my model *schooner* when I tried to force the ship into a glass bottle.
나는 모형 스쿠너선을 유리병에 억지로 집어넣으려다가 양 돛대를 부러뜨렸다.

SCORCH [skɔ:rtʃ] v. to burn the surface of; to burn intensely 겉을 태우다; 심하게 태우다

Although the skin of the hot dog had been *scorched* in the barbecue, the insides were still edible.
핫도그를 통째로 굽다가 표면이 검게 탔지만 속은 그래도 먹을 수 있었다.

The toasted marshmallow was so badly *scorched* that it was just a black lump.
마시맬로 구이가 심하게 타서 그냥 검은 덩어리가 돼 버렸다.

SCORN [skɔ:rn] v. to treat something as unworthy or inferior or n. a strong feeling of dislike and contempt 경멸하다, 모욕하다 / 혐오; 경멸, 멸시

The governor *scorned* the salesman's offer by slapping him in the face and instructing the butler to beat him up.
주지사는 판매원의 따귀를 때리고 집사에게 그를 두들겨 패라고 시키면서 그의 제의를 모욕했다.

The *scorn* that Allison felt for Mrs. Taylor was obvious after she put her photograph on the dartboard and started playing.
앨리슨이 테일러 부인을 혐오한다는 것은, 그녀가 부인의 사진을 다트판에 붙여 놓고 화살을 던지기 시작할 때 분명하게 드러났다.

SCOUNDREL [skáundrəl] n. a villain; a wicked person 악당, 불량배

The *scoundrel* tried to escape by using puppy hostages; he strapped bombs onto them and threatened to detonate them.
악당은 강아지들을 인질로 삼아 도망치려 했는데, 강아지들 몸에 폭탄을 묶은 다음 폭파시키겠다고 협박했다.

When Edward stole a wallet from a sleeping priest, I knew that he was definitely a *scoundrel*.
에드워드가 잠자고 있는 성직자의 지갑을 훔쳤을 때 그가 확실히 불량배라는 걸 알게 됐다.

SCOUR [skauər] v. to clean by scrubbing vigorously or to search thoroughly; to search over a large area 박박 문질러 닦다; 철저히 찾다; 두루 찾아다니다

We had to *scour* the bathtub with heavy-duty cleaner after we gave our dog Rufus his annual bath.
우린 연례행사로 우리 집 개 루퍼스를 목욕시킨 뒤 강력 세제로 욕조를 박박 문질러 닦아야 했다.

The search party *scoured* the forest around the cottage for any sign of the woodsman.
조사팀은 나무꾼의 흔적을 찾기 위해 오두막 주변의 숲을 샅샅이 수색했다.

SCOURGE [skə:rdʒ] n. a cause for widespread loss and suffering, like a war or disease (전쟁이나 질병 등의) 재앙

The Hundred Years War was a *scourge* that left most of central Europe in ruin.
백년전쟁은 유럽 중심지 대부분을 폐허로 만든 재앙이었다.

Almost half the people in London died when the *scourge* of bubonic plague struck the city centuries ago.
수세기 전 페스트의 재앙이 런던을 덮쳤을 때 런던 시민의 절반 가까이가 숨졌다.

SCRAWNY [skrɔ́:ni] adj. very bony and thin, often due to lack of adequate food or exercise 바싹 마른, 수척한

The fierce wind actually knocked the *scrawny* dog off of its feet and into a ditch.
사나운 바람이 불어와서 수척한 개가 넘어져 도랑에 빠졌다.

Although he was too *scrawny* to play any other position, Harrison's incredibly long arms made him an excellent goalie.
해리슨은 너무 야위어서 다른 포지션은 맡을 수 없었지만, 놀랍도록 긴 팔 덕분에 뛰어난 골키퍼가 될 수 있었다.

SCUFFLE [skʌ́fl] n. a rough, unorganized fight in close quarters 격투, 난투

The *scuffle* in the bar started near the pool table in the back but soon spread to the karaoke stage near the front window.
술집의 난투는 뒤쪽의 당구대 부근에서 시작됐다가 이내 앞 창문 가까이의 가라오케 무대까지 번졌다.

The *scuffle* in the Boy Scouts' tent arose from a disagreement over who should have to go outside and fight the bear.
보이스카우트 텐트의 격투는 누가 밖으로 나가 곰과 싸울 것인가를 두고 논쟁이 벌어진 데서 시작됐다.

SCULLERY [skʌ́ləri] n. a room next to the kitchen where dish washing and other cooking-related chores are done 부엌 옆방, 식기실

The water used to clean dishes was so dirty that a fire started in the *scullery* when someone dropped a match into it.
설거지에 사용한 물이 너무 더러워서 누군가 거기에 성냥을 떨어뜨리자 식기실에서 화재가 발생했다.

The new owner of the house decided to convert the *scullery* into a cozy little breakfast nook.
새로운 집주인은 식기실을 아담한 아침 식사 자리로 개조하기로 했다.

SECRETE [sí:krit] v. to exude or produce a substance, usually a fluid 분비하다

Everyone for miles around knew that the Johnson's pet skunk had just *secreted* her warning scent.
몇 마일 부근의 사람이면 누구든 존슨 가족의 애완용 스컹크가 방금 경계용 냄새를 분비했다는 걸 알 수 있었다.

SENTIMENT [séntəmənt] n. a general emotion or attitude; an opinion or feeling 감정, 정서; 의견, 소감

Although the jury found J.O. Billson innocent, public *sentiment* held that he had indeed murdered the two people.
배심원단은 J.O. 빌슨에게 무죄판결을 내렸지만 여론은 그가 정말 두 사람을 살해했다는 쪽이었다.

My father's *sentiments* in baseball are still with the Chicago Cubs, even though they haven't won a World Series in a hundred years.
시카고 컵스는 백 년 동안 한번도 월드 시리즈에서 우승을 못했지만 아버지는 야구라면 아직도 시카고 컵스의 팬이시다.

SHARD [ʃɑːrd] n. a fragment, often of glass or metal or a broken piece of pottery like those found at archeological digs 파편; 고고학 발굴에서 나오는 깨어진 도기 조각

At a contest booth in the carnival, Donovan threw the tennis ball so hard that it smashed the milk bottles into *shards* of glass.
도노반은 놀이 공원의 콘테스트 부스에서 테니스공을 너무 세게 던져 우유병을 산산조각 냈다.

Once the *shard* was identified as Fourth Millennium Axumite clay, the two professors knew that they had made a major discovery.
도기 조각이 '4천년 악숨 왕국'의 진흙으로 확인되자 두 명의 교수는 자신들이 중요한 발견을 해냈다는 걸 알았다.

SHREWD [ʃruːd] adj. very clever and smart; tricky 영리한; 간사한

The *shrewd* coach had one of his players jump to the ground and bark like a dog to distract the other team while his teammates scored the winning basket.
영리한 코치는 다른 팀원들이 결승골을 넣는 동안 한 선수에게 경기장으로 뛰어가 개처럼 짖어서 다른 팀의 주의를 분산시키라고 시켰다.

By deftly evading the actual question, the *shrewd* politician avoided exposing his ignorance.
간사한 정치인은 실제적인 질문을 재치 있게 피하면서 자신의 무식함을 드러내지 않았다.

SHRILL [ʃril] adj. high-pitched and piercing 날카로운

When little Klaus throws a temper tantrum, everyone in the house puts cotton in their ears to muffle his *shrill* screams.
꼬마 클로스가 짜증을 내면 집안의 모든 사람들이 날카로운 비명을 안 들으려고 솜으로 귀를 막는다.

The farmer quickly put an end to the *shrill* cries of the bluejay outside his bedroom window by shooting it with a pellet gun.
농부는 침실 창문 밖에서 큰 어치가 날카롭게 짖어 대자 재빨리 공기총으로 쏘아 울음을 그치게 했다.

SHUN [ʃʌn] v. to avoid deliberately; to stay away from 피하다

Incredibly shy, Jonas *shunned* the company of other people and spent most of his free time talking with his pet fern.
조나스는 부끄러움이 너무 많아 다른 사람들과 어울리는 것을 피하고 자유 시간 대부분을 애완 양치류와 이야기하는 데 보냈다.

After her third bout with food poisoning, Frances decided to *shun* Ishmael's House of Raw Clams.
프랜시스는 식중독으로 세 번째 탈이 난 뒤 이슈마엘의 조개 횟집에는 가지 않기로 했다.

SIDLE [sáidl] v. to walk or move sideways; to move in a quiet, sneaky way 옆걸음질 하다; 조용히 움직이다

The repairman *sidled* around the corner of the building on a thin ledge to fix the drainpipe.
수리공은 배수관을 고치기 위해 좁은 선반을 타고 옆걸음질로 건물 모퉁이를 돌았다.

SIMPER [símpər] v. to smile in a goofy, self-conscious manner 바보같이 웃다

My little brother's *simpering* revealed to us who had actually cooked the mystery waffles that morning.
남동생의 바보 같은 웃음을 보고 우린 그날 아침 정체 모를 와플을 누가 만든 건지 알 수 있었다.

Horace continued to *simper* uncontrollably while the three supermodels thanked him for saving them seats on the plane.
호러스는 세 명의 수퍼모델이 비행기 좌석을 맡아준 것에 대해 고마움을 표하자 연신 바보처럼 웃어댔다.

SINGULAR [síŋgjulər] adj. being one of a kind; unique or remarkable; peculiar 남다른, 보기 드문; 유일한, 독특한; 주목할 만한

Historians agree that Abraham Lincoln was a man of *singular* courage and determination.
역사학자들은 아브라함 링컨이 남다른 용기와 결단력의 소유자였다는 데 의견을 같이한다.

Crossing the Swiss Alps with a brigade of war elephants was a *singular* experience for most of Hannibal's troops.
코끼리 전사단과 스위스 알프스 산맥을 횡단한 것은 한니발 군대에게 독특한 경험이었다.

SIPHON [sáifən] n. a U-shaped tube used to transfer liquid from one container to another or v. to draw off liquid by using a siphon; to drain in some way 사이펀 / 사이펀으로 빨다; 방수하다

Since I ran out of gas while mowing the front lawn, I *siphoned* some gas from the car into the lawn mower.
앞 잔디를 깎고 있을 때 기름이 떨어져서 차에서 기름을 빨아올려 잔디 깎는 기계에 옮겼다.

SKULK [skʌlk] v. to creep around so that no one notices you 살금살금 다니다

Looking for the best house to rob, the burglar *skulked* around the neighborhood peering into windows.
강도는 털기에 가장 좋은 집을 찾으러 동네를 몰래 돌아다니며 창문들을 들여다봤다.

Determined to become an international spy, Laura practiced *skulking* around the house and ambushing the poodle.
국제 스파이가 되기로 굳게 결심한 로라는 집 주변을 살금살금 다니고 숨어서 푸들을 기다리며 연습을 했다.

SLACKEN [slǽkən] v. to slow down; decrease; to make something less firm or tense 늦추다; 줄이다; 완화시키다

At the end of a long day of walking across the desert our pace had *slackened* from a brisk walk to a slow crawl.
기나긴 하루 동안 사막을 가로질러 걸어 다닌 뒤 우리의 발걸음은 활발한 걸음에서 느린 걸음으로 늦추어졌다.

As the kite plummeted toward earth, the tension on the kite string *slackened* considerably.
연이 땅으로 곤두박질치면서 팽팽하던 연줄이 상당히 느슨해졌다.

SPASM [spǽzm] n. a sudden involuntary twitch of a muscle or a sudden burst of activity 근육의 경련; 갑작스러운 행동

Before he realized that he was allergic to shellfish, Michael would eat oysters and then immediately have violent *spasms* in his arms and legs.
마이클은 조개류에 앨러지가 있다는 것을 알기 전에 굴을 먹고는 곧바로 팔과 다리에 격렬한 경련이 일어나곤 했다.

My brother cleaned the entire house and washed both cars during a brief *spasm* of activity one Saturday afternoon, and then he took a five hour nap.

오빠는 어느 토요일 오후 느닷없이 잠깐 동안 집안 대청소를 하고 세차를 하더니 다섯 시간 동안 낮잠을 잤다.

SPECTACLE [spéktəkl] n. a remarkably impressive sight; a grand public display or a regrettable display or action 광경, 볼만한 것; 호화로운 구경거리, 쇼; 애처로운(딱한) 광경

The July fourth fireworks display near the Washington Monument is truly an awesome *spectacle* of light and sound.

워싱턴 기념관 부근에서 미국 독립기념일에 하는 불꽃놀이는 빛과 소리의 정말 장엄한 광경이다.

Keith made a *spectacle* of himself at the wedding when he punched out the bride and then proceeded to leg wrestle the priest.

키이스는 신부를 때려눕히고는 목사와 발씨름을 하려고 가면서 스스로 딱한 광경을 연출했다.

SPECTRUM [spéktrəm] n. a band of colors that together make up visible light or a broad range of related ideas or qualities 스펙트럼, 분광; 광범위한 생각이나 특성

Our science teacher used a prism to break up a beam of white light into a *spectrum* of colors.

과학 선생님은 프리즘을 이용해 흰 광선을 쪼개어 분광을 만들었다.

Although the conference was designed only to discuss lasers, a broad *spectrum* of scientific topics came up in conversations.

회의는 레이저에 대해서만 토의하기로 돼 있었지만 광범위한 과학 주제에 대한 대화가 이루어졌다.

SPITE [spait] n. ill feelings that cause one person to harm or hurt another 악의, 심술

Widow Bellson was so full of *spite* for everyone that not a day passed when she didn't try to hit someone with her umbrella.

벨슨 미망인은 모든 사람에 대한 악의로 가득 차 하루도 빠짐없이 우산으로 누군가를 치려고 했다.

SPORADIC [spərǽdik] adj. happening infrequently or on an irregular basis; having no pattern or order 드물게 일어나는, 산발성의; 일정한 패턴이나 순서가 없는

Thunderstorms in this part of the country are so *sporadic* that no one's ever prepared for the rain when it comes.

이 지역에서는 뇌우가 아주 드물어 비가 올 때면 아무도 준비가 안 되어 있다.

Since their parents liked to look in on them *sporadically* at night, the kids were never able to sneak out.

아이들의 부모는 밤에 예고 없이 그들을 보러 들어오기 좋아해 아이들은 절대 몰래 빠져나갈 수가 없었다.

SPRAWL [sprɔːl] v. to sit or lie down with your body spread out in every direction; to spread out awkwardly 몸을 쭉 펴고 앉다(눕다); 꼴사납게 뻗어 있다

Sprawled all over the floor, the basketball team made the living room look a bird's nest built of thin human arms and legs.

농구 팀원들이 바닥 전체에 큰 대자로 뻗어 있으니 거실이 가느다란 인간 팔다리로 만들어진 새둥지 같았다.

Heather fell down the stairs and was *sprawled* on the second floor landing.

히더는 계단에서 떨어져 2층 층계참에 벌렁 나자빠졌다.

SPREE [spri:]   n. a carefree outing or the overdoing of a certain activity   신나게 즐김, 흥청거림; 과도한 열중

Our shopping *spree* at the Lego factory left us completely broke but with enough Legos to build ourselves a three-story ranch house.
레고 공장에서 신나게 쇼핑을 하고 난 우리는 3층짜리 랜치 하우스를 지을만한 레고만 든 채 빈털터리가 돼서 나왔다.

Father decided to go on a spending *spree* at the mall and buy three items from every single store.
아버지는 쇼핑몰에 실컷 돈을 쓰러 가서 각 상점마다 물건을 세 가지씩 사기로 했다.

SPRY [sprai]   adj. lively and active   활발한, 원기 왕성한

Over the weekend, the *spry* kids played hide-and-seek in the neighborhood for eighteen hours in a row.
원기 왕성한 아이들은 주말 동안 동네에서 연달아 18시간을 숨바꼭질 놀이를 했다.

Although he was fifteen years old and practically blind, the *spry* cat still liked to fight with rattlesnakes in the backyard.
활발한 고양이는 15세에 눈도 거의 안 보였지만 여전히 뒤뜰에서 방울뱀들과 싸우길 좋아했다.

SPURN [spə:rn]   v. to reject something with a scornful air; to refuse something with disdain   쫓아내다; 단번에 거절하다, 일축하다

Tomasson *spurned* the offer of a truce by ripping up the document and then force-feeding the paper to its messenger.
토마슨은 문서를 잡아 찢은 뒤 배달부에게 억지로 먹임으로써 휴전 제의를 일축했다.

Brad *spurned* my offer of a date and asked me never to come within fifty yards of him again.
브래드는 나의 데이트 제의를 단번에 거절하고 다시는 자신에게 50야드 이내로 접근하지 말아 달라고 했다.

SQUALID [skwǽlid/skwɔ́l-]   adj. appearing dirty and repulsive; wretched   지저분한, 불쾌한; 비참한, 형편없는

Even rats and cockroaches were disgusted by the things they saw in the *squalid* apartment.
쥐와 바퀴벌레조차도 지저분한 아파트의 물건들을 보고는 질색했다.

The refugees were forced to live in *squalid* conditions until the fighting in their homeland stopped.
망명자들은 고국에서의 전투가 끝날 때까지 비참한 환경에서 지낼 수밖에 없었다.

STAMINA [stǽmənə]   n. the ability not to get tired when working or laboring hard; endurance   체력; 끈기

It was a salute to the *stamina* of the troops that they were able to march for four days in a row and then start fighting immediately.
기병대가 4일을 쉬지 않고 행군한 뒤 곧바로 전투에 돌입하자 대단한 체력을 가졌다는 명성이 자자했다.

The police officer knew that it would take a lot of *stamina* to fingerprint the 10,000 criminals by the next afternoon.
경관은 다음 날 오후까지 만 명의 범죄자의 지문을 채취하는 데에 막대한 체력이 필요하리란 걸 알았다.

STAMMER [stǽmər]   v. to speak with involuntary pauses or repetitions, usually caused by nervousness   말을 더듬거리다

Frightened of gorgeous Russian women, the normally calm Stan would begin to *stammer* badly whenever Svetlana entered the room.
평소에는 침착한 스탠은 스베틀라나가 방에 들어올 때면 멋진 러시아 여성에게 겁을 먹고 말을 심하게 더듬곤 했다.

STARK [sta:rk] adj. bare; without any decoration or adornment or adv. completely and totally 꾸밈없는, 장식이 없는 / 아주, 완전히

The bachelor's *stark* two-bedroom apartment contained only a stereo system, a mattress, and a Rick Springfield poster.
총각의 꾸밈없는 방 두 칸짜리 아파트에는 스테레오 시스템과 매트리스, 릭 스프링필드의 포스터 밖에 없었다.

When our neighbor asked us to stop insulting cheese since it interfered with her psychic communication with goats, we knew she was *stark* raving mad.
이웃 사람이 염소와의 심령 소통을 방해받는다며 우리에게 치즈를 모욕하는 걸 그만두라고 했을 때 우린 그녀가 완전히 미쳤다는 걸 알았다.

STATELY [stéitli] adj. characterized by formality and dignity; impressive due to its size; majestic 위엄 있는, 웅대한, 장엄한

The *stately* opening ceremony consisted of a parade, several speeches, and a formal blessing.
장엄한 개막식은 퍼레이드와 몇 차례의 연설, 형식적인 축복의 말로 이루어졌다.

The nine-story mansion was even more impressive because of the *stately* mountain range that loomed behind it.
9층짜리 대저택은 뒤편으로 어렴풋이 보이는 웅대한 산맥 때문에 훨씬 더 인상적이었다.

STENCH [stentʃ] n. a very unpleasant smell 악취

We soon discovered that the *stench* coming from the closet was a mixture of dirty gym socks and a forgotten piece of pizza.
우린 곧 옷장에서 나는 악취가 더러운 운동 양말과 깜빡 잊어버린 피자 조각이 섞인 것임을 알게 됐다.

No amount of soap seemed able to get rid of the *stench* of our car after Billy filled the back seat with pig manure.
빌리가 우리 차 뒷좌석에 돼지의 배설물을 잔뜩 부어 놓은 뒤 아무리 비누로 씻어 내도 악취가 없어지지 않을 것 같았다.

STEREOTYPE [stériǝtaip/stíǝr-] n. a conventional and oversimplified idea, usually about a group of people 정형, 전형; 고정관념, 판에 박힌 생각

The teenager's *stereotypical* view of teachers as boring was shattered when Ms. Eubanks decided to introduce a class in bungee jumping.
선생님들은 지루하다는 십대 아이들의 고정관념은 유뱅크 씨가 번지점프 수업을 도입하겠다고 결정하자 완전히 깨졌다.

The beauty contestant who was unable to tie her own shoelaces was a perfect example of the dumb blonde *stereotype*.
자신의 구두끈도 맬 줄 모르던 미인대회 출전자는 멍청한 금발미인의 전형을 보여주는 완벽한 예였다.

STERN [stǝ:rn] adj. hard and severe in manner; firm and unwilling to change or n. the rear part of a ship 엄격한; 단호한 / 선미, 고물

The *stern* principal said that saving a busload of nuns from certain death was no excuse for being two minutes late to class.
엄격한 교장은 수녀들이 탄 버스를 죽음에서 구한 것이 학교에 2분 지각한 데 대한 변명이 될 수는 없다고 말했다.

The captain sent the prisoners back toward his cabin which was located between the middle mast and the *stern* of the ship.
선장은 죄수들을 중간 돛대와 배의 고물 사이에 위치한 자신의 선실로 돌려보냈다.

STIFLE [stáifl] v. to keep something in or hold something back or to smother by depriving of air or oxygen 억누르다, 꾹 참다; 숨 막히게 하다, 질식시키다

Everyone in the meeting had to *stifle* a laugh as the chairman stapled a bundle of documents to his tie.
의장이 서류 뭉치를 호치키스로 자신의 넥타이에 박을 때 회의 참석자들은 모두 웃음을 참아야만 했다.

The bully threatened to stick smelly socks into my mouth and nose and *stifle* me if I didn't give him my lunch money.
깡패는 내가 점심값을 내놓지 않으면 냄새나는 양말을 내 입과 코에 쑤셔 넣고 질식시켜 버리겠다고 협박했다.

STILTED [stíltid] adj. having an artificially formal quality; pompous 점잔 빼는; 뽐내는, 과시하는

Jeffrey's *stilted* speech showed how desperately he wanted to become part of the wealthy class.
제프리의 점잔 빼는 연설은 그가 얼마나 필사적으로 부유층에 속하고 싶어하는지 보여주었다.

The *stilted* manner of the announcer at the square dance showed how self-important he felt he was.
스퀘어 댄스에서 아나운서의 뽐내는 태도로 그가 얼마나 자부심이 강한지 알 수 있었다.

STOUT [staut] adj. sturdy and bold; bulky; strong and determined 튼튼한; 거대한; 단호한

It took four men to lift up the *stout*, unconscious sailor and carry him from the bar.
의식을 잃은 거구의 선원을 들어올려 술집에서 데리고 나가는 데 네 명이 필요했다.

The *stout* courage of the team members allowed them to rally and win the world hopscotch championship.
팀원들의 두둑한 배짱 덕분에 그들은 원기를 회복하고 세계 돌차기 선수권 대회에서 우승할 수 있었다.

STREAMLINED [strí:mlaind] adj. designed and built to offer the least resistance to air; modernized and more efficient 유선형의; 최신식의, 능률적인

The Edsel's new *streamlined* hood increases the car's mileage considerably.
에드셀의 새로운 유선형 후드는 차의 단위 연료당 주행거리를 상당히 증가시킨다.

The new, *streamlined* post office has faster jeeps and can deliver packages anywhere in the world in only three hours.
새로 생긴 최신식 우체국에는 더 빠른 지프차가 있어 겨우 세 시간이면 세계 어느 곳에든지 소포를 배달할 수 있다.

STRIDE [straid] v. to walk quickly and take long steps; to take a single long step over something in your path 성큼성큼 걷다; 성큼 넘어서다

The two children had to run to keep up with the long *strides* taken by their seven-foot tall father.
두 아이는 7피트 키의 아버지가 성큼성큼 걸어가는 데 보조를 맞추기 위해 뛰어야 했다.

Nancy was able to *stride* over the mud puddle with her long legs without getting any part of her shoes wet.
낸시는 진흙 웅덩이를 긴 다리로 성큼 넘어서서 신발 어디도 젖지 않았다.

STRIVE [straiv] v. to put in a great deal of effort and work; to struggle against 노력하다, 힘쓰다; 싸우다, 분투하다

Everyone in the village, even young children, *strove* to build the wall around the city before the invading tax collectors arrived.
마을 사람들은 모두, 어린아이들까지도 세금 징수원들이 쳐들어오기 전에 힘을 다해 도시 주변에 벽을 쌓았다.

Jim was forced to *strive* against a strong current for two miles in order to find his lost swim trunks.
짐은 잃어버린 수영복 팬티를 찾기 위해 강한 해류에 맞서 싸우며 2마일 거리를 헤엄쳤다.

SUBLIME [səbláim] adj. inspiring awe and admiration; supreme and without any equal 장엄한, 숭고한; 최고의, 탁월한

Salma's *sublime* ability to convince anyone to stop fighting made her the ideal person to head the peace party.
샐마는 누구든지 설득해 싸움을 그만두게 만드는 탁월한 능력 덕분에 평화 모임을 이끌기에 이상적인 사람이었다.

Many people consider the first major rock concert they see a *sublime* experience, especially if it was the Grateful Dead.
많은 사람들은 자신들이 처음 본 메이저 록 콘서트를 최고의 경험으로 치는데, 그게 '그레이트풀 데드'의 공연이라면 특히 그렇다.

SUBSIDY [sʌ́bsədi] n. financial assistance, like a loan from the government to a small company 보조금

The Florida sugar farmers would have been forced into bankruptcy years ago if they hadn't received a sizable government *subsidy*.
플로리다 설탕 농장주들은 몇 년 전에 정부로부터 상당한 보조금을 받지 않았더라면 파산에 이르렀을 것이다.

Pick, Inc. used the *subsidy* to buy new equipment that would allow them to build better, stronger toothpicks.
피크 사는 더 낫고 튼튼한 이쑤시개를 만들기 위한 새로운 장비를 구입하기 위해 보조금을 사용했다.

SUFFICE [səfáis] v. to adequately meet present needs; to satisfy; to be enough 필요를 충족시키다; 만족시키다; 충분하다

While I really wanted glow-in-the-dark moon boots, the vintage green army boots *sufficed* to keep my feet warm during the winter.
난 야광 달빛 부츠를 갖고 싶긴 했지만 겨울 동안 내 발을 따뜻하게 해주는 데엔 오래 됐지만 고급스러운 초록색 군화로 충분했다.

SULLEN [sʌ́lən] adj. characterized by ill-humored brooding; having a morose and sulky personality 뚱한, 샐쭉한; 음울한, 시무룩한

The *sullen* ex-cheerleader liked to go to football games and root against her own school.
샐쭉한 전 치어리더는 미식축구를 보러 가서 다른 학교 응원하는 걸 좋아했다.

Although everyone else could see that the sky was clear, the *sullen* child continued to believe that a huge comet was about to hit their town.
다른 사람은 모두 하늘이 맑다는 걸 알 수 있었지만, 음울한 그 아이는 계속 거대한 혜성이 자신들의 마을을 덮칠 거라고 믿었다.

SUMMIT [sʌ́mit] n. the highest point, usually the top of a mountain; the peak 정상, 꼭대기; 절정, 최고점

The hikers reached the *summit* of the mountain and looked down at the forest below them, which spread in all directions.
하이커들은 산꼭대기까지 올라가 그들 아래에 사방으로 뻗어 있는 숲을 내려다봤다.

Going to school for a summer at Oxford was the *summit* of my educational experience.
옥스퍼드에서 여름 동안 학교에 다닌 것은 나에게 최고의 교육 경험이었다.

SUPPLE [sʌ́pl] adj. easily bend and manipulated; moving easily; limber and adaptable 유연한; 순응하는

After it had been in the refrigerator for a week the *supple* stalk of celery could be tied into a knot.
셀러리를 냉장고에 일 주일간 넣어 두었더니 줄기가 유연해져 매듭을 지을 수 있을 정도가 되었다.

While many other trees were uprooted, the *supple* trunk of the coconut tree allowed it to withstand the hurricane's force.
다른 나무들은 다 뿌리째 뽑혔는데, 코코넛 나무는 유연한 줄기 덕분에 허리케인의 힘에도 견뎌낼 수 있었다.

SUPPLICATE [sʌ́pləkeit] v. to humbly ask; to earnestly appeal to 간청하다, 애원하다

The baseball fan *supplicated* himself in front of his boss in the hope that he would be allowed to leave work early to go watch the game.
야구팬은 야구 경기를 보러 가려고 일찍 퇴근할 수 있게 되길 바라며 상사 앞에서 간청했다.

SWAGGER [swǽgər] v. to walk with a boastful air; to strut about with excessive pride 뽐내며 걷다; 점잔빼며 걷다

After making the move that would win him the game, the nerdy chess player *swaggered* around the room like she had just gained world dominion.
우둔한 체스 경기자는 결정적인 수를 둔 다음 전 세계 지배권을 획득한 듯이 뽐내며 방안을 걸어 다녔다.

I thought that *swaggering* down the aisle would show my history classmates how cool I was, but then I tripped and dislocated my jaw.
나는 복도를 점잔빼고 걸으며 역사반 동급생에게 내가 얼마나 멋진지 보여주려고 했는데, 그만 발을 헛디뎌 턱이 깨졌다.

SWAY [swei] v. to move from side to side or to have influence over something 흔들다; 움직이다, 좌우하다

After riding in the Spinning Teacup Ride at the state fair, I found myself *swaying* back and forth as I attempted to regain my balance.
주립 놀이동산에서 회전 찻잔을 타고 난 뒤 균형을 회복하려고 하자 몸이 앞뒤로 흔들렸다.

Sylvia's persuasive speeches, when combined with her ability to entertain people by juggling, *swayed* all of the voters in the district in her favor.
실비아의 설득력 있는 연설은 저글링으로 사람들을 즐겁게 해주는 소질과 결합되어 선거구의 모든 유권자들의 마음을 자신에게 유리하도록 움직였다.

SWOON [swuːn] v. to lose consciousness; to faint 기절하다

Unable to overcome his stage fright, Sam *swooned* onstage and had to be carried off by a teacher.
샘은 무대 공포증을 이겨내지 못하고 무대 위에서 기절을 해 교사에게 실려 나가야 했다.

When the New Infants in the Community took the stage, many of the girls in the audience *swooned* with delight.
'New Infants in the Community' 가 무대에 나오자 관중석의 많은 여자아이들이 기뻐서 정신을 잃었다.

SYNCHRONIZE [síŋkrənaiz] v. to plan something so that it occurs at the same time; to happen at the same time 동시에 일어나게 하다, 똑같이 맞추다; 동시에 일어나다

The four police units surrounding the stadium *synchronized* their watches so that they would all move forward at exactly the same time.
경기장을 둘러싼 4개 부대의 경찰은 정확히 똑같은 시간에 전진할 수 있도록 시계를 똑같이 맞추었다.

The twins *synchronized* their dance movements so well that some people in the audience thought they were seeing double.

쌍둥이가 춤추는 동작을 아주 잘 맞추어서 관중 가운데 일부는 자신의 눈에 이상이 생겨 한사람이 둘로 보이는 것인 줄 알았다.

T

TANGIBLE [tǽndʒəbl]   adj. something real; something you can actually touch   실재하는; 만질 수 있는

Since Bronson could show us no *tangible* evidence of his friend Luke, we all agreed that Luke was probably imaginary.
브론슨은 자신의 친구 루크가 실재한다는 증거를 보여줄 수 없었기 때문에 우린 모두 루크가 가공의 인물일 거라고 생각했다.

While sadness is not *tangible*, tears are.
슬픔은 만질 수 없지만 눈물은 만질 수 있다.

TANTRUM [tǽntrəm]   n. a fit of anger in which you behave badly and sometimes even throw things   짜증을 내며 발끈거림

Kerri threw such a *tantrum* at the church picnic that it took six priests to subdue her.
케리가 교회 소풍에서 화를 내며 길길이 날뛰는바람에 성직자 여섯명이 합세해 그녀를 누그러뜨렸다.

Denied her yellow duck, the infant went into a *tantrum* that only a trip to the amusement park could stop.
자신의 노란 오리를 빼앗긴 아이는 짜증을 부렸는데 놀이 동산에 데려간다고 하자 그제서야 그쳤다.

TAPESTRY [tǽpəstri]   n. a large, heavy cloth decorated with a design or scene and then hung on the wall as decoration   태피스트리, 벽걸이 융단

Once the *tapestry* in the hallway caught fire, I knew I shouldn't have tried to barbecue inside the old castle.
복도의 태피스트리에 불이 붙자 오래된 성안에서 바비큐를 하지 말았어야 한다는 걸 깨달았다.

We found a secret doorway behind one of the *tapestries* in the hallway of the old mansion.
우린 오래된 대저택의 복도에서 한 태피스트리 뒤로 비밀 출입구가 나 있는 걸 발견했다.

TARPAULIN [tɑːrpɔ́ːlin]   n. a waterproof piece of fabric used to cover and protect something from getting wet   방수천; 방수 외투

After the grounds crew removed the *tarpaulin* that had covered the infield, game one of the Little League World Series was officially underway.
정비원들이 내야를 덮고 있던 방수천을 제거하고 난 뒤 리틀 야구 월드 시리즈 첫 경기가 정식으로 진행됐다.

Dad loved his new lawn furniture so much that he would cover it with a *tarpaulin* each night, despite the odd looks his neighbors gave him.
아빠는 새로 산 잔디 위의 의자를 너무 좋아해서 매일 밤 이웃 사람들의 시선도 아랑곳하지 않고 방수천으로 의자를 덮곤 했다.

TAUT [tɔːt] adj. pulled tight 팽팽한

The tug-of-war game between the ten rival weightlifters made the rope so *taut* that I was certain it was going to snap.
라이벌 역도 선수들 열명이서 줄다리기를 하자 밧줄이 너무 팽팽해져 툭하고 끊어질 것 같았다.

When I popped the paper bag behind her back, my sister's *taut* emotions finally snapped and she shrieked wildly.
내가 여동생 뒤에서 종이 봉지를 뻥하고 터뜨리자 동생은 팽팽하던 감정이 마침내 폭발해 사납게 소리를 질러댔다.

TEEM [tiːm] v. to be full of things; to abound 가득하다; 풍부하다

Holding the gun at my side, I looked in and saw that the barrel was *teeming* with fish. This was going to be easy, I thought.
옆구리에 총을 찬 채 안을 들여다보니 통 속에 물고기가 가득했다. 난 일이 쉽게 풀리겠구나 하고 생각했다.

The soup was *teeming* with bugs and I couldn't stick my spoon into it without hitting a fly.
수프에 벌레가 잔뜩 들어서 파리를 한 마리도 건드리지 않고는 숟가락을 댈 수가 없었다.

TEMPERAMENT [témpərəmənt] n. how a person acts; his/her attitude towards all events and situations 기질, 성미

I thought that the sight of his wrecked car would send my dad into a rage, but his *temperament* was more composed than I had predicted and he only cried.
나는 아빠가 망가진 차를 보고 노발대발할 줄 알았는데, 생각했던것보다 성질을 많이 죽이고 소리만 치셨다.

Charles' cat Loki had such a nervous *temperament* that simply slamming a door too hard would send her running under the bed for cover.
찰스의 고양이 로키는 겁이 너무 많아서 문을 쾅 닫기만 해도 침대 밑으로 뛰어 들어가 몸을 숨겼다.

TENDRIL [téndril] n. something long, slim, and curling, like a vine 덩굴손, 덩굴손 모양의 것

The *tendrils* of ivy that covered the sides of the buildings had completely changed their color from brick red to dark green.
건물들의 벽면을 뒤덮은 담쟁이 덩굴의 색깔이 붉은 벽돌색에서 진 초록색으로 완전히 바뀌었다.

Within days after planting the magic beans, the little *tendrils* of the plants had transformed into a huge forest of towering trunks.
요술 콩을 심은 지 며칠도 안돼서 작은 덩굴들이 자라나 줄기가 하늘로 우뚝솟은 거대한 숲으로 탈바꿈되었다.

TEPID [tépid] adj. neither hot nor cold; lukewarm 미지근한; 열의가 없는, 미온적인

The *tepid* water of the pond was not as satisfying as we'd thought it was going to be when we jumped in to escape the summer heat.
우리는 여름 더위를 피하기 위해 연못 속으로 뛰어 들어갔는데, 물이 미지근해서 생각했던 것만큼 만족스럽지 못했다.

Bill was able to chug down his entire mug of coffee once the liquid became *tepid*.
빌은 커피가 미지근해지자 머그 한 잔을 단숨에 마실 수 있었다.

TERRAIN [teréin/tə-] n. the surface characteristics of a specific piece of land 지형, 지세

The flat Oklahoma *terrain* allowed the farmers to set up an outdoor bowling lane that was 2,000 yards long.
오클라호마는 지형이 평평해 농부들은 2천 야드 길이에 달하는 야외 볼링장을 만들 수 있었다.

Since no cars could cross over the rocky *terrain*, we were forced to unload the supplies and start walking.

어떤 차도 바위투성이의 지형을 넘어갈 수 없어서 우린 어쩔 수 없이 짐을 내리고 걸어가기 시작했다.

TERRESTRIAL [təréstriəl] adj. originating from the planet Earth 지구의

Once the blue-skinned creatures started speaking some crazy moon language, I knew they were extra-*terrestrial*.

푸른 피부의 생물체들이 괴상한 달 언어로 말하기 시작하자 그들이 지구 출신이 아니라는 걸 알았다.

All *terrestrial* forms of life, from bugs to people to whales, share many of the same characteristics.

벌레에서부터 사람, 고래에까지 이르는 지구의 모든 생명체는 많은 특성을 공유한다.

TESTY [tésti] adj. irritable or impatient 성미가 급한, 참을성 없는

During a faculty meeting, the *testy* principal started screaming at a teacher for chewing his gum too loud.

교직원회의가 열리는 동안 성마른 교장이 큰소리로 껌을 씹는 교사에게 소리를 지르기 시작했다.

Since waiting in lines made my parents *testy*, we always went to the movies fifteen minutes late.

줄서서 기다리는 것을 못 참는 부모님 때문에 우린 언제나 영화관에 15분 늦게 갔다.

THATCH [θætʃ] n. roofing material made out of plant stalks or leaves (나무줄기나 잎으로 만든 지붕의) 이엉

Hurricane Jerry easily blew away the *thatch* roofs in the village, but the brick roofs remained intact.

허리케인 제리에 마을의 초가 지붕은 쉽게 날아갔지만 벽돌 지붕은 멀쩡했다.

Once the *thatch* roof got soaked and started rotting away, the smell convinced us that it was time to install a slate roof.

초가 지붕이 흠뻑 젖어 썩기 시작하자 지독한 냄새가 나 우린 슬레이트 지붕을 놓아야겠다고 생각했다.

THERAPY [θérəpi] n. a procedure used to heal people who are physically or mentally ill 요법, 치료

The daily *therapy* of a hot bath and a massage eventually cured the athlete of the muscle pains in her back.

매일 뜨거운 물에 목욕하고 마사지를 했더니 그 운동선수 등의 근육통이 다 나았다.

As part of my *therapy* to overcome a fear of heights, I have to climb a mountain each week and then stand at the edge and look off of the steepest cliff I can find.

나는 고소공포증을 극복하기 위한 치료의 일환으로 매주 산에 올라가 가장 가파른 절벽의 가장자리에 서서 먼산을 바라본다.

THRESHOLD [θréʃhould] n. the lowest level at which something can be heard or recognized or the place of beginning 시초, 발단

I knew I was near the *threshold* of understanding my weird dream that involved penguins at my Senior prom, but I still couldn't put it into words.

졸업반 댄스파티에서 펭귄이 등장하는 이상한 꿈을 막 이해하게 될 것 같았지만, 여전히 말로 표현할 수는 없었다.

As I opened the secret door leading into Queen Nuputoopoo's tomb, I was certain I was on the *threshold* of a great scientific discovery.

누푸투푸 여왕 무덤으로 들어가는 비밀 문을 열었을 때 내가 중대한 과학적 발견의 시초에 있다는 걸 확신했다.

THRIFT [θrift]　n.　the ability to handle money wisely　돈을 현명하게 쓰는 능력, 절약

Gwendolyn demonstrated her *thrift* by transforming her lemonade stand into a multimillion dollar company.
그웬돌린은 레모네이드 노점을 수백만 달러짜리 회사로 바꾸어 놓음으로써 돈을 현명하게 다루는 능력을 보여주었다.

Although she was from a poor family, Sophie's purchase of $10,000 socks showed that she lacked *thriftiness*.
소피는 가난한 집안 출신이었는데도 만 달러짜리 양말을 사 신었 던걸 보면 절약 정신이 부족했다는 것을 알 수 있었다.

THRIVE [θraiv]　v.　to grow vigorously　번영하다, 번성하다; 성공하다

With no predators and abundant flowers, the African bees *thrived* in the jungles of Central America.
포식자가 없고 꽃들이 풍부해 중앙아프리카 정글 속에서 아프리카 벌이 번성했다.

A born daredevil, Winston *thrived* in the high-speed, high-risk world of flaming motorcycles races.
천성적으로 물불을 안 가리는 윈스턴은 고속, 고위험의 세계이자 열기로 가득찬 오토바이 경주에 성공했다.

TIMID [tímid]　adj.　very shy; easily scared　수줍음 많은; 겁 많은, 소심한

The *timid* cat refused to leave her little box whenever strangers would enter the house.
겁이 많은 고양이는 낯선 사람이 집에 들어올 때는 작은 상자 밖으로 나오지 않았다.

By telling him that these vitamins pills were actually Instant Hero Capsules, we transformed *timid* Gary into a fearless football player.
우린 게리에게 이 비타민 알약이 사실은 '순간 영웅 캡슐'이라고 말해서 소심한 게리를 대담무쌍한 미식축구 선수로 바꾸어 놓았다.

TINGE [tindʒ]　n.　a slight hue, a little bit of color　엷은 색조

Although it was originally painted bright yellow, the car now had a *tinge* of red to it as small spots of rust started to become visible.
차를 원래 밝은 노랑으로 칠했었는데, 작은 녹 자국들이 눈에 띄기 시작하자 붉은 색조가 엷게 생겼다.

TORRENTIAL [tɔːrénʃəl, tɑr-/-tə-]　adj.　resembling a massive downpour of water　급류의, 억수의

As the *torrential* rainstorm showed no sign of letting up, I began to appreciate the fact that I worked in the canoe store.
억수 같은 폭풍우가 가라앉을 기미가 안 보이자 나는 카누 가게에서 일하고 있다는 사실에 감사한 마음이 들었다.

The *torrential* flow of information into the computer's circuits caused it to crackle, shoot sparks, and then shut down.
컴퓨터 회로 속으로 엄청난 양의 정보가 쏟아져 들어오자 컴퓨터에서 우지직 소리가 나고 불꽃이 튀기더니 꺼져 버렸다.

TRACT [trækt]　n.　a specific stretch of land or a document written to declare a political or religious viewpoint　넓이, 구역; 소책자, 팸플릿

The *tract* of land between the river and the dirt road was known throughout the county as Farmer Anse's famous turnip patch.
강과 진흙길 사이의 땅이 앤스 농부의 유명한 순무 밭이라는 것은 카운티 전체에 알려져 있었다.

In open defiance of the military leaders, Suu Kyi wrote a fiery *tract* outlining the reasons that democracy must prevail in her country.
아웅산 수키는 군부독재자들에 대해 공공연히 반항하며 자신의 나라에서 민주주의가 정착되어야하는 당위성을 역설한 논문을 썼다.

TRAIT [trei(t)] n. a recognizable characteristic of feature 특성

Oddly-colored hair and multiple body piercings are two *traits* that most Californian surfers have in common.
이상한 색깔의 머리와 몸 여러 곳에 구멍을 뚫은 것은 캘리포니아 서퍼들 대부분의 공통적 특성이다.

A common *trait* among all Mongolian types of clothing is a lack of pockets.
모든 몽고인 의상의 공통적인 특성은 주머니가 없다는 것이다.

TRAJECTORY [trədʒéktəri] n. the path of a moving object, like the arc of a ball through air 진로, 탄도, 궤도

By watching games that were recorded on film, the coaches were able to study the *trajectory* of their star pitcher's fastball, and then give advice to the other pitchers.
코치들은 녹화된 경기를 보면서 주전 투수가 던지는 속구의 진로를 연구해 다른 투수들에게 조언할 수 있었다.

The cannonball traced a graceful *trajectory* through the air before it smashed into the fortress wall.
포탄은 요새의 벽을 뚫고 들어가기 전에 공기를 가르며 우아한 탄도를 그렸다.

TRANQUIL [trǽŋkwil] adj. very calm and peaceful; without anxiety or stress 조용한, 평온한; 편안한, 걱정이 없는

Our *tranquil* day at the lake was destroyed by the four power boats that came roaring down the river.
우리는 호수에서 조용한 날을 보내고 있었는데 모터보트 네 대가 강을 요란하게 질주해가면서 평온을 깨고 말았다.

Although it didn't pay much, the job of snail babysitting was certainly very *tranquil*.
달팽이를 돌보는 일은 보수는 많지 않았지만 확실히 아주 편안했다.

TRANSFIX [trænsfíks] v. to pierce something firmly or to pin something so that it is unable to move 꿰뚫다, 찌르다; 고정시키다, 못 박다

Freddie would *transfix* the butterflies in his collection with a pin through the abdomen and then mount them on a board.
프레디는 자신이 수집한 나비들의 배를 핀으로 찔러서 칠판에 붙여 놓곤 했다.

I was so *transfixed* by the lead character's god-like looks that I barely blinked during the entire three-hour film.
나는 주인공의 위엄있는 모습에 완전히 매료당해서 세 시간짜리 영화를 보는 내내 눈도 거의 깜박이지 않았다.

TRANSGRESSION [trænsgréʃən/trænz-] n. a violation of a law or order 위반

After being caught asleep while on sentry duty, the White House guard was fined $50 for her *transgression* and demoted to the position of guard of the vice-president's dog.
백악관 호위병은 보초를 서는동안 잠든게 발각되자 임무일탈에 대해 50달러의 벌칙금을 부과받고 부대통령 개의 파수꾼으로 강등됐다.

I knew that staying out past my curfew was *transgression* of the rules, but since I had just won the lottery, I didn't really care.
나는 귀가시간이 지나도록 밖에 있는 것은 규율을 어기는 것임을 알았지만 막 복권에 당첨됐기 때문에 그다지 신경 쓰지 않았다.

TRAVAIL [trəvéil/trǽveil] n. difficult and painful work; a really tough task 노고, 수고; 노역, 힘든 일

Feeding liver soup to the six Mackenzie brats was hard enough, but my *travails* weren't over until I got them all to sleep.
매켄지 가의 버릇없는 아이들 여섯 명에게 간 수프를 먹이는 것은 정말 힘들었는데, 그들 모두가 잠들고나니 나의 노고는 끝이 났다.

The mountain climber knew that her *travails* were not over until she successfully climbed all the way back down the mountain.

등산객은 산 밑까지 무사히 내려갈 때까지는 고생이 끝난게 아니라는 걸 알았다.

TREND [trend] n. a current fashion or style or the general direction in which something seems to move
유행; 경향, 추세

The recent *trend* of dancing the Macarena finally ended once people realized just how idiotic they looked doing it.

최근 유행하던 마카레나 춤은 사람들이 그 춤을 출때 정말 바보같아 보인다는 걸 알게되자 마침내 그 유행이 끝났다.

The car dealer was forced to admit that there was a *trend* toward buying more compact vehicles.

그 자동차 딜러는 좀더 아담한 차를 구입하는 추세라는 걸 인정하지 않을 수 없었다.

TRIFLE [tráifl] n. a little thing that's not very important or v. to play around 사소한 일, 하찮은 일 / 장난하다

The color of the aliens' shoes was a *trifling* issue compared to the great scientific knowledge and many exotic board games they brought the Earth.

외계인의 신발 색은 그들이 가지고 온 대단한 과학적 지식과 여러 가지 색다른 보드 게임에 비하면 사소한 문제였다.

When I learned that Gladys had only gone out with me because of a one dollar dare, I knew she was just *trifling* with my feelings.

글래디즈가 나와 데이트한 것은 단지 1달러 때문이었다는 것을 알고난 후, 나는 그녀가 내 감정을 가지고 장난을 쳤다는 것을 깨달았다.

TUNDRA [tʌ́ndrə/tún-] n. a cold region of the earth, without trees and with only small, stunted shrubs and mosses for plant life 동토대(凍土帶), 툰드라 지방

While trekking across the open *tundra* of Siberia during our expedition, I couldn't help wishing for the warmth and comfort of my hometown shopping mall.

나는 탐험 여행 동안 시베리아의 드넓은 툰드라를 힘겹게 횡단하면서 고향 쇼핑몰의 따뜻함과 편안함을 그리워하지 않을 수 없었다.

The mouse hoped to hide from the swooping hawk, but the *tundra* offered nothing to shelter it.

쥐는 급습해오는 매에게서 숨고 싶었지만 툰드라에는 쥐가 몸을 피활만한 곳이 아무것도 없었다.

U

UNFURL [ʌnfə́ːrl] v. to open up or spread out 펴다

Before raising the flag, we *unfurled* it so that our drill sergeant could inspect the material to make sure that it was spotless.
우리는 기를 올리기 전에 거기에 흠이 없는지 훈련 담당 하사관이 검사하도록 기를 폈다.

The banner proclaiming the Houston Rockets as national champions was *unfurled* from the ceiling and everyone applauded wildly.
휴스턴 로케츠가 전국 챔피언임을 선언하는 기가 천장에서부터 펼쳐졌고 사람들이 모두 열광적으로 박수를 쳤다.

UNIFORM [júːnəfɔ̀ːrm] adj. always exactly the same; never changing 한결같은; 변함없는

Since all the tables were of *uniform* size and color, it didn't really matter where we sat to eat our Big Brother burgers.
테이블의 크기와 색깔이 모두 똑같아서 우리가 빅브라더 버거를 어디에 앉아서 먹을까는 아무 문제가 안됐다.

Every saxophone reed produced by the highly advanced machine was *uniform* in shape and size.
고도로 향상된 기계에서 생산하는 색소폰 리드는 모양과 크기가 한결같았다.

UNPRECEDENTED [ʌnprésədèntid] adj. with no previous example 전례 없는, 전에 없던

The ice skater's quadruple upside-down somersault with a twist was such an *unprecedented* move that the judges awarded her the gold medal instantly.
아이스 스케이터가 연속 네 차례 몸을 꼬며 수직으로 공중 돌기한 것은 전례 없는 동작이어서 심사위원들은 그 선수에게 즉시 금메달을 수여했다.

In an *unprecedented* move, the government spokesperson refused to answer any questions unless the reporter would agree to play "Charades."
전례 없는 조처로 정부 대변인은 기자가 "제스처 게임"을 하겠다고 안 하면 어떤 질문에도 답변하지 않으려 했다.

UTMOST [ʌ́tmoust] adj. of the greatest amount or degree 최대의, 최고의

This Friday, getting home in time to watch the season premiere of *The X-Files* is of the *utmost* importance, so I'm planning on leaving work two hours early.
이번 주 금요일에 제 시간에 집에 가서 X파일의 시즌 첫 회를 보는 것이 최고로 중요하기 때문에 난 두 시간 일찍 퇴근할 계획이다.

It took the *utmost* amount of courage for the spectator from the audience to place her head into the lion's open mouth.
관중석에서 나온 관객은 자신의 머리를 사자의 벌어진 입안으로 집어넣기 위해서 용기를 있는 대로 모아야 했다.

UTOPIA [juːtóupiə] n. a perfect, ideal place; a land where everything is perfect 유토피아, 이상향

Jimmy's idea of *utopia* was a really awesome couch in front of a television that had over two million sport programs playing every day.

지미가 꿈꾸는 유토피아는 날마다 스포츠 프로그램을 2백만 개 이상씩 보여주는 텔레비전이 있고, 그 앞에 정말 끝내 주는 소파가 놓여 있는 것이었다.

Listening to the radio announcer talk about pollution alerts and crime statistics serves to remind us of how far from *utopia* we really are.

오염 경보와 범죄 통계에 대한 라디오 아나운서의 얘기를 듣고 있으면 우리가 정말 유토피아로부터 얼마나 동떨어진 세계에 살고있나를 생각하게 된다.

V

VACCINE [vǽksiːn/væksíːn] n. a drug given before the onset of a specific disease that helps prevent the disease from occurring 백신

> In the United States, few people die from polio anymore since over ninety percent of the population now receives a *vaccine* against it when they're very young.
> 미국에서는 더 이상 소아마비로 사망하는 사람이 거의 없는데, 인구의 90% 이상이 아주 어렸을 때 예방 백신을 맞기 때문이다.

> Unfortunately, science has yet to create a *vaccine* that prevents people from acting like jerks in a movie theater.
> 불행히도 아직까지 과학은 극장에서 얼간이 짓을 못하게 하는 백신을 만들어내지 못했다.

VANTAGE [vǽntidʒ/váːn-] adj. having a superior position or state of events or n. an advantage of some kind 우세한 / 우세, 유리

> From our *vantage* point in the weather balloon, we could look down and see the entire countryside below.
> 우리는 기상 관측 기구의 유리한 위치에서 시골 전체를 내려다볼 수 있었다.

> The country of Hyborea used its *vantage* in trade to destroy the economy of its enemy, Emorial.
> 하이보리아는 무역에서의 이점을 이용해 적국인 에모리얼의 경제를 파괴했다.

VEHEMENT [víːəmənt] adj. forceful or intensely emotional; vigorous and energetic 격심한, 격렬한; 정력적인, 원기 왕성한

> In a *vehement* response to the reporter's question, Jacob hurled his microphone at the reporter and jumped into the crowd and attacked him.
> 제이콥은 기자의 질문에 격렬하게 대답하면서 기자에게 마이크를 내던지고는 군중 속으로 뛰어 들어가 그를 공격했다.

> It took four nurses and two doctors to hold down the patient after his *vehement* reaction to what he'd read in a tabloid while waiting for his appointment.
> 진료 약속을 기다리는 동안 타블로이드판 신문에서 기사를 읽고 격심한 반응을 보이는 환자를 진정시키는 데 간호사 네 명과 의사 두 명이 합세했다.

VENTRILOQUIST [ventríləkwìst] n. someone skilled at projecting his/her voice so that it sounds as if it were coming from someplace else 복화술사

> A skilled *ventriloquist*, Loren would often appear to be having a serious conversation with her lampshade.
> 솜씨 좋은 복화술사 로렌은 이따금 자신의 전등갓과 심각한 대화를 나누고 있는 듯이 보였다.

The prolonged case of laryngitis signaled bad times for the *ventriloquist* and his hopes for a national tour.
복화술사의 후두염이 오래가는 바람에 전국 투어를 하겠다는 그의 희망에 먹구름이 드리워졌다.

VENTURE [véntʃər] n. a risky undertaking or v. to take a risk; to guess 모험 / 모험하다; 위험을 무릅쓰고(감히) 추측하다

Diving into shark-infested waters was not a *venture* I was willing to make.
상어가 가득한 물 속으로 뛰어드는 모험은 하고 싶지 않았다.

With the polls showing that the two delegates were almost dead even, I would not *venture* to say who will win the election for dogcatcher.
여론조사에서 두 명의 대표가 거의 막상막하여서 집없는 개들을 잡는 사람을 뽑는 선거에서 누가 당선될지 도저히 장담을 못하겠다.

VERANDAH [vərǽndə] n. a covered porch that wraps around the outside of a house 베란다

Grandfather liked to sit out on the *verandah* of his home in Georgia, sip lemonade, and watch the sun set over the river.
할아버지는 조지아의 집에서 베란다에 나가 앉아 레모네이드를 홀짝이면서 강 위로 해 떨어지는 모습을 바라보는 걸 좋아하셨다.

While the plants inside our house always died, the ones we had on the *verandah* did quite well.
집안에 있는 식물들은 늘 죽어 버리는데 베란다에 있는 것들은 꽤 잘 자랐다.

VETO [víːtou] n. the right of the President to reject a bill that has been passed by Congress 거부권(대통령이 국회에서 통과한 법안을 거부하는 권리)

By law, Congress can override a Presidential *veto* if over two-thirds of Congress approve the bill.
법에 따르면 국회는 국회의원의 3분의 2 이상이 법안에 찬성할 경우 대통령의 거부권을 무효로 할 수 있다.

VEX [veks] v. to really irritate; to greatly annoy 안절부절 못하게 하다, 성가시게 하다, 괴롭히다

The constant buzzing of a fly near my ear *vexed* me so greatly that I couldn't get back to sleep all night.
귓전에서 끊임없이 윙윙거리는 파리에 너무 신경이 쓰여 밤새 다시 잠을 이룰수가 없었다.

The Mustard Game, which consisted of spraying mustard on every carpet in the house, *vexed* our parents greatly.
'머스터드 게임' 은 집에 있는 모든 카펫에 겨자를 뿌리는 것인데, 그 게임때문에 우리 부모님들은 매우 짜증이 났다.

VIABLE [vái əbl] adj. capable of success or continued growth; workable 성공 가능한, 성장 가능한; 실행할 수 있는

Although we had yet to win a game that season, our upbeat coach still believed that a shot at the playoffs was *viable*.
우리는 그 시즌에서 한 게임을 더 이겨야 했지만 낙관적인 코치는 여전히 우리의 플레이오프 진출이 가능하다고 믿었다.

The commission declared that only candidates without a prison record were *viable* choices for the office of police chief.
위원회는 전과 기록이 없는 후보만이 경찰서장에 뽑힐 수 있다고 언명했다.

VIGIL [vídʒəl]　n. guard or watch over something for an extended period of time　감시, 망보기

FBI agents maintained a constant *vigil* around the house of Stones "The Hammer" Pugolowski, key witness in the Kronhorst murder trial.
FBI 요원들은 크론호스트 살인 재판의 중요한 증인인 "해머"란 별명의 스톤즈 푸골로스키의 집 주변에서 불철주야 망을 봤다.

Despite my unending *vigil* in the kitchen, the pot of water that I had been watching started to boil.
부엌에서 한눈을 팔지 않았는데도 내가 지켜보고 있던 물 냄비가 끓어오르기 시작했다.

VINDICATE [víndəkeit]　v. to clear someone of wrongdoing by providing evidence that shows their innocence　정당함(결백함)을 입증하다, 혐의를 풀다

After the secret witness told her story, the defendant was immediately *vindicated*.
비밀 증인이 이야기를 하고 난 뒤 피고는 곧 혐의에서 풀렸다.

Finding my sister's lost ring in the crow's nest *vindicated* me of the crime of brotherly theft.
까마귀 둥지에서 여동생의 없어진 반지가 나오자 형제인 내가 훔쳤다는 혐의가 풀렸다.

VIRTUE [və́ːrtʃuː]　n. moral righteousness and excellence　덕, 덕행, 미덕

Our image of Mr. Ertel as a man of great *virtue* was destroyed when we learned that he had four different wives.
대단한 미덕을 갖춘 사람이라는 어텔 씨에 대한 이미지가 그에게 네 명의 아내가 있다는 것이 알려진 뒤 산산이 부서졌다.

Try as they might, the witches were unable to corrupt the *virtue* of the gallant knight.
마녀들이 아무리 애를 써도 용감한 기사의 고결함을 더럽힐 수 없었다.

VISTA [vístə]　n. a view, usually of things far away　원경, 멀리 내다보이는 경치

Standing on top of the island's highest mountain, we gazed with wonder at the endless *vista* of the Pacific Ocean.
우린 섬에서 가장 높은 산꼭대기에 올라서서 끝없이 펼쳐진 태평양의 모습을 감탄에 잠겨 바라보았다.

The mad dictator ordered all buildings over two stories destroyed because they were blocking the *vista* from his mansion's porch.
포악한 독재자는 3층 이상의 건물을 모두 파괴하라고 명령했는데, 그것들이 자신의 대저택 현관에서 내다보이는 풍경을 막았기 때문이다.

VIVID [vívid]　adj. very distinct and sharp; very realistic　선명한, 뚜렷한; 생생한, 눈에 보이는 듯한

The *vivid* use of red, black, and blue in the center of the painting greatly contrasted with the soft browns and yellows around the edge of the canvas.
그림 가운데에 빨간색, 검은색, 파란색을 선명하게 썼더니 캔버스 가장자리의 부드러운 갈색 및 노란색과 확연한 대조를 이루었다.

The experience of Smell-O-Vision was so *vivid* that I almost believed I had actually been walking inside the cheese factory myself.
스멜-오-비전(공기 순환 장치를 이용해 영화 속 냄새를 관객에게 실제로 전달하는 방식)의 체험이 너무 생생해 내가 실제로 치즈 공장 안을 걸어다니고 있는 것처럼 믿어질 지경이었다.

VOID [vɔid]　n. a place of nothingness, seemingly without end　빈곳, 빈틈, 무한한 공간

We dropped a pebble into the *void*, but we never heard it hit the bottom.
우린 빈틈 안에 조약돌을 떨어뜨렸는데, 바닥에 부딪히는 소리를 못 들었다.

506

Looking out into the *void* of space that surrounded the spacecraft, the astronaut was suddenly very glad that she had brought her lucky rabbit's foot.

우주선을 둘러싼 무한한 우주 공간을 내다보면서 우주 비행사는 문득 행운의 토끼 발을 가져와 정말 다행이라고 느꼈다.

VOLATILE [váletl/-til/vɔ́letail] adj. easily changeable; quick to explode   변덕스러운; 폭발하기 쉬운

The actor's *volatile* moods were such that he would sometimes laugh, cry, and then laugh again in the space of a minute.

그 배우는 감정의 기복이 너무 심해서 1분 사이에 웃다가 울다가 다시 웃곤 했다.

Nitroglycerin is such a *volatile* liquid that just looking at it the wrong way will sometimes cause it to explode.

니트로글리세린은 아주 불안정한 액체여서 잘못 쳐다보기만 해도 폭발을 일으킬 때가 있다.

VOLLEY [váli/vɔ́li] n. a group of shots fired at the same time   일제사격, 연발

The revolutionary soldiers waited until they could see the whites of the British troops' eyes before they released their *volley* of shots at them.

혁명군은 영국군의 모습이 확실히 보일때까지 기다렸다가 퍼부었다.

The candidate's statement that she was an alien caused a *volley* of questions to erupt from the gathered reporters.

후보자가 자신은 외계인이라고 말하자 모여든 기자들로부터 질문이 연신 쏟아졌다.

VOUCH [vaut∫] v. to provide support; to give supporting evidence   보증하다; 증거를 제시하다

Because his principal personally *vouched* for Leroy's commitment to learning, he was accepted as a student at Harvard Barber College.

교장이 직접 학문탐구에 대한 러로이의 열의를 보증해주어 러로이는 하버드 바버 대학에 합격하게 됐다.

Since no one but fish could *vouch* for her story that she had been at the lake, Gwendolyn was arrested by police on the charge of bank robbery.

물고기말고는 그웬돌린이 호수에 있었다는 이야기를 뒷받침해줄 증인이 없었기때문에 그웬돌린은 은행 강도 혐의로 경찰에 체포됐다.

W

WAFT [wɑːft/wæft] v. to float gently through the air or on water or n. a light breeze or scent 둥실둥실 떠돌다 / 산들바람; 떠도는 향기

The tiny leaf *wafted* slowly down from the tree until it reached the lava flow below and was burned to a crisp.
조그만 잎이 나무에서 두둥실 내려오더니 흘러나오는 용암에 이르자 바싹 탔다.

After having been stranded on the sea for ten days, the sailors cheered wildly when a *waft* of air struck the sails and began to slowly move the ship.
선원들은 바다 위에서 꼼짝 못하고 열흘을 보낸 뒤 한줄기 산들바람이 돛에 부딪쳐 천천히 배를 움직이기 시작하자 미친 듯이 환호했다.

WANE [wein] v. to decrease; to approach an end to something 작아지다, 적어지다; 끝이 가까워오다, 끝나다

My hope for a quick visit *waned* when the Hendersons brought out eighteen video cassettes that they filmed during their trip to Milwaukee.
헨더슨 가에 잠깐만 들르겠다는 내 기대는 그들이 밀워키 여행 동안 찍어온 18개의 비디오카세트를 꺼내는 순간 허물어졌다.

As the distance separating the two approaching clowns *waned*, each began to see distinct features of the other.
두 명의 광대가 가까이 다가와 서로간의 거리가 없어지자 상대방의 생김새를 뚜렷하게 볼 수 있었다.

WHET [wet] v. to sharpen; to stimulate 갈아서 날카롭게 하다; 자극하다

I *whet* the blade of my lucky knife by running it along the edge of a nearby rock.
내 행운의 칼을 가까이 있는 바위 끝에 갈아서 칼날을 날카롭게 만들었다.

Although the chips and salsa were only supposed to *whet* my appetite, I ate so many of them that I was full by the time the main course arrived.
살사소스를 곁들인 포테이토칩으로는 식욕을 돋우기만 해야 하는데 너무 많이 먹어서 본 요리가 나올 때는 이미 배가 불렀다.

WHIRL [hwəːrl/wəːl] v. to spin rapidly; to turn around suddenly or n. a state of confusion; a swift round of events 핑핑 돌다; 갑자기 돌다 / 혼란; 정신없이 돌아감

As the merry-go-round *whirled* faster and faster, the kids found it harder and harder to hold onto the bars.
회전목마가 점점 더 빨리 돌자 아이들은 막대기를 붙잡고 있기가 점점 더 힘들었다.

After the tear gas canister exploded by accident, events were in such a *whirl* at the police station that the criminal was able to walk out the front door.
최루탄이 우발적으로 터지자 경찰서가 온통 뒤죽박죽이 돼 그 범죄자는 정문으로 걸어나갈 수 있었다.

WILY [wáili] adj. crafty or cunning 교활한, 약삭빠른

Even though the coyote was *wily* and dangerous, he was never able to catch that speedy roadrunner.
코요테는 교활하고 위험했지만 날렵한 로드러너는 절대로 잡을 수가 없었다.

The *wily* general devised a plan to fool the enemy troops which involved placing uniforms on mannequins so that they looked like real soldiers.
약삭빠른 장군은 적군을 속이기 위해 마네킹에 제복을 입혀 진짜 군인처럼 보이게 만들 계획을 궁리했다.

WISTFUL [wístfəl] adj. full of hopeful wanting; mildly sad 탐내는, 몹시 바라는; 약간 슬픈

The kid with the broken leg had a *wistful* look on her face as she watched the marathon runners reach the finish line.
한쪽 다리가 부러진 아이가 마라톤 주자들이 결승선에 이르는 걸 지켜볼 때 그 얼굴에 부러움의 표정이 서렸다.

It was a *wistful* moment in the movie when we realized that Tinkerbell had always loved Peter Pan, but could never tell him.
영화에서 팅커벨이 피터팬을 늘 좋아해 왔다는 걸 알게 되지만 그에게 말해 줄 수 없는 장면은 애잔한 순간이었다.

WONDROUS [wʌ́ndrəs] adj. brilliantly remarkable; extraordinary 놀랄 만한, 아주 훌륭한

The *wondrous* movie won every Academy Award possible that year, and its lead actress was given the Nobel Peace Prize.
정말 뛰어났던 그 영화는 그 해에 모든 아카데미상을 휩쓸었고 주연 여배우는 노벨 평화상까지 받았다.

When the aliens showed up with free lottery tickets for everyone, I knew it was a *wondrous* time to be alive.
외계인들이 모든 사람에게 나눠줄 무료 복권을 가지고 나타났을 때 살아 있다는 것은 정말 놀라운 시간이라는 걸 알았다.

WRATH [ræθ/rɑ:θ/rɔ(:)θ] n. violent anger 격노, 분노

Rather than face the queen's *wrath*, most of the people in the castle jumped into the moat and started swimming for their lives.
성안의 사람 대부분이 분노에 찬 여왕과 마주하는 대신 해자로 뛰어들어 죽을 힘을 다해 헤엄치기 시작했다.

The *wrath* of the umpire was so great that he threw the entire baseball team out of the game, as well as their fans.
심판은 대단히 격노해 팬뿐만 아니라 야구팀 전체를 그 경기에서 퇴장시켰다.

WRETCHED [rétʃid] adj. very miserable and unhappy; hateful or inferior in quality 비참한, 불쌍한; 열등한, 형편 없는

I soon realized that working twenty hours a day making pickles in a cellar was a *wretched* way to live.
나는 곧 지하실에서 피클을 만들며 하루에 20시간 동안 일하는 것은 비참한 생활이란 걸 깨달았다.

The *wretched* car could not even be sold for scrap metal, so we dug a large hole and buried it.
형편없는 자동차는 고철 값에도 안 팔려서 우린 커다란 구멍을 파 그 안에 차를 묻어버렸다.

WRY [rai] adj. funny in an understated way or twisted into an expression of distaste; crooked or twisted 비꼬는, 빈정대는; 찡그린; 구부러진, 뒤틀린

The *wry* play produced a lot of chuckles from the audience, but no huge bouts of laughter.
그 풍자극을 보고 관객들은 낄낄대며 많이들 웃었지만 엄청난 폭소는 한 번도 터져 나오지 않았다.

Boundas's expression was *wry* after he ate the entire rotten lemon, skin and all.
분다스는 썩은 레몬을 통째로 껍질까지 먹고 난 뒤 표정을 찡그렸다.

Y

YEARN [jə:*r*n] v. to want something greatly; to feel deep concern or pity   열망하다; 불쌍히 여기다

Walter *yearned* to be an Air Force pilot so badly that he memorized every word of the movie *Top Gun*, even though we told him that it wasn't required.
월터는 너무나 간절히 공군 조종사가 되고 싶어 한 나머지, 우리가 그럴 필요까지는 없다고 하는데도 영화 '탑건'의 대사를 모두 암기했다.

While the townsfolk *yearned* for the poor prairie dogs whose homes would be ruined, the greedy developer continued with his housing project enthusiastically.
마을 사람들은 집을 잃게 될 가엾은 프레리도그들을 불쌍하게 생각했지만 탐욕스런 택지 개발업자는 자신의 주택 계획을 열광적으로 밀고 나갔다.

YONDER [jándər/jón-] adv. in or at a place indicated usually by pointing or adj. at a distance but within sight 저쪽에 / 저쪽의

"The town lies directly over *yonder* hill," replied the old man, pointing at a large, rocky hill directly ahead of us.
"마을은 저쪽 언덕 바로 너머에 있어요." 노인은 우리 바로 앞에 있는 커다란 바위 언덕을 가리키며 대답했다.

"I'll meet you over by that tree *yonder*," said the girl, pointing to a willow at the edge of the meadow.
"저기 저 나무 옆에서 만나자." 소녀가 초원 끝의 버드나무를 가리키며 말했다.

Seventh
Inning
Snatch

7회 때의 납치

1

Trinidad! That island paradise where the deep green water glistens in the sun so brightly that the eyes are dazzled by beauty and shine! Soon, soon I will be there, and Consuela and I will *cavort* on the beach, dancing, *prancing*, and swirling about until we fall down on the sand...

At least, that's what I kept telling myself as I sat within the dreary, depressing confines of waiting area 27B at one of New York City's airports. My flight was hours late because of the weather; the rainfall outside was heavy. No, it was worse than heavy, it was **torrential**; it was as if rivers were flowing from the sky. I tried to remain patient. After pacing back and forth for a couple of hours, I decided to **repose** under a chair, where I curled up into a ball and closed my eyes, with my long, black tail tucked safely under me. But as I awakened from my short nap, the strangest thing happened...

Ah, but I am getting ahead of myself as usual. Allow me to introduce myself. My name is Beauregard, and I am a traveling gentle-cat from South Carolina. I suppose you might call me unusually **burly** for a cat. I am quite muscular, and stand over four feet tall when I walk on my back legs. I consider myself elegant, tasteful, an well-mannered, and I hope you will agree with me after you've learned a bit more about me. Since I'll be telling you a lot of this story, you could call me your **narrator**. Well, it's such an interesting and exciting story that I don't mind the job one bit.

CAVORT v. to jump about excitedly 신나게 뛰다
Stop cavorting around and sit still, just for five minutes.
5분만이라도 뛰어다니지 말고 얌전히 앉아 있어 봐라.

PRANCE v. to move gaily or proudly 껑충거리다
The children pranced about in their new Halloween costumes.
아이들은 새 할로윈 복장을 입고 이리저리 껑충거리며 다녔다.

As I was saying, I was on my way to Trinidad to visit a lovely cat names Consuela. She is such an **exotic**, unusual beauty! Her dainty paws are perfectly shaped. But alas, I did not get to see Consuela. As I opened my eyes after my nap, I heard a loud "POP." Only one thing and one person can make that sound: Bridget. I crawled out from under the chair and sure enough, there was Bridget, in jeans and a New York Knicks *jersey*, *peeling* the remains of the giant gum bubble off of her face. A second later, her neat black *braids* were flying out from under her baseball cap as she quickly **scampered** like a kitten toward a crowd of people.

"Babette! Babette!" she yelled. "Over here! Are you blind?"

Babette and Bridget were back together again. That settled it for me. These **foolhardy** young friends of mine had a special talent for stumbling into trouble, and I wasn't about to let them try to **fend** off danger by themselves. Trinidad would have to wait—I had to protect them. Besides, I had been with them on more than one good adventure. Little did I know, this would be the biggest of them all.

"Bridget?" cried Babette, a tall young French girl, dressed fashionably in black from head to toe. She tilted her giant sunglasses down to get a better look around.

"Babette, I'm over here! Take those sunglasses off, you can't see a thing!" answered Bridget.

"Ah, there you are, *mon amie*. How are you?" Babette smiled, shoving her glasses firmly back in place.

"How am I? We haven't see each other in months! I'm excited!" exclaimed Bridget, as she hugged her friend. "I'm glad your flight finally made it. Man, do I have plans for us. You showed me Paris and now it's my turn to show you New York. By the way, do you hear that strange noise?"

JERSEY n. a close-fitting sweater or shirt that is pulled on over the head 몸에 꼭 맞는 스웨터나 셔츠
Put on the blue jersey.
그 파란색 셔츠를 입어라.

PEEL v. to take the skin off; to be removed 벗겨내다, 떼어내다
Would you peel me an orange?
제게 오렌지 좀 까주시겠어요?

BRAID n. a band formed by weaving together three or more strands of hair 땋은 머리
She wears her hair in braids.
그녀는 땋은 머리를 하고 있다.

"Yes, it's a quiet purring, or a motor running, but it's barely **audible**."

"Hey, Babette, look over there under that chair! Could that be...?"

"Absolutely! Beauregard, our old friend," Babette declared with delight.

The two girls ran toward the cat, which, pretending to sleep, tried to stay completely still.

"Wake up, *sleepyhead*! It's us!" demanded Bridget.

Beauregard opened one eye, look up at them, then closed his eye again.

"Now, Beauregard, do not be so **blasé**. Only the French can really pull that off, you know," *teased* Babette.

"Yeah," Bridget chimed in, "we know you're not completely **indifferent** to us. You like us a heck of a lot, or you wouldn't keep following us around. In fact, I think you're happy to see us."

Beauregard **murmured** something about "crazy kids" under his breath, came out from underneath the chair, and stretched.

"I couldn't quite make that out. Did he just say something?" Bridget asked. "Oh, I forgot, he doesn't talk—to us, anyway. Come on, Beauregard, we're going into town."

The long black cat blinked calmy and slowly **loped** along beside the girls, bouncing easily from paw to paw.

Outside the airport, Babette stood by the *curb* and began waving her arms.

"Taxi! Taxi!" she yelled. "Where are the taxicabs? This rain is **drenching** my new outfit. Soon it will be **saturated** with water; you'll have to *wring* me out!"

SLEEPYHEAD n. a sleepy, drowsy, or lazy person 잠꾸러기
Wake up the sleepyhead!
그 잠꾸러기를 깨워라!

TEASE v. to make fun of somebody in a playful or unkind way 놀리다
The other boys used to tease him because of his accent.
억양 때문에 다른 소년들이 그를 놀리곤 했다.

CURB n. a raised border along the edge of a pavement or sidewalk (인도와 차도 사이의) 연석
He parked his car close to the curb.
그는 인도 옆에 차를 주차했다.

WRING v. to twist and squeeze in order to remove liquid from it 비틀어 짜다
He wrung the clothes before putting them on the line to dry.
그는 옷을 짜서 빨랫줄에 널었다.

"Wait, Babette, we shouldn't take a taxi in this weather anyway," advised Bridget. "New York drivers seem to just forget how to drive when it rains. Every intersection gets jammed; there are **gridlocks** where traffic is stopped in all directions. We'll have to head underground: To the subways!"

Bridget led her friends to a shuttle bus that took them to the subway. Soon they were *zipping* along toward downtown New York. Babette and Bridget had a lot of catching up to do, so they **jabbered** happily, barely pausing for a breath, about school, their families—everything they'd done since they'd last met.

"Where are we going first?" asked Babette, finally. "I almost forgot to ask."

Bridget grinned. "It's a surprise. But don't worry, you won't have to wait long to find out. This is where we get off."

The subway train came to a stop and the friends got out and started making their way to the stairs that led outside.

"Uh oh, it's rush hour," remarked Bridget, as she looked around the crowded station. "All of these rain-soaked people are trying to get home. You may get **jostled** by the crowd, but just put your elbows out so you don't get hurt and meet me at the top of the stairs. Good luck!"

With that, Bridget began *wriggling* her way through the mass of people, with Babette and Beauregard following close behind. A few minutes later, they stood together on the street and Beauregard began licking and straightening his fur.

"You have to **muster** up a lot of strength and courage to make it through a crowd like that," remarked Babette. "How do you do it every day?"

"You get used to it," shrugged Bridget. "But what are we **lingering** around the subway station for? We have better things to do. Hey, I think it stopped raining!"

ZIP v. to move vigorously or quickly in the specified direction 힘차게 나가다
She's just zipped into town to buy some food.
그 여자는 음식을 사기 위해 방금 시내로 힘차게 나갔다.

WRIGGLE v. to make quick, short, twisting and turning movement 꿈틀거리며 빠져나가다
The eel wriggled out of my fingers.
뱀장어가 손가락 사이로 꿈틀거리며 빠져나갔다.

As Bridget held out her hand to make sure that no more drops were falling, a passing man dropped a quarter in her palm.

"Hey, mister, wait!" yelled Bridget, but the man had already disappeared into the crowd. "He thinks I'm a **panhandler**, begging for change. I guess I did have my hand out. Well, I needed a quarter for the pay phone anyway. Come on, there's one up ahead."

Bridget made a quick, secretive call, then gestured to her friends to follow her.

"We're heading in here," she said, pointing to a tall brick building.

The lobby of the building was quiet and fancy, the three friends walked across the smooth marble floor to the elevator and pushed the button for the top floor. When the doors opened, the scene before them looked like something out of a science fiction movie: A strange looking shiny metal ship about the size of a sailboat took up most of the large open room, and *scraps* of metal, bubbling test tubes, and piles of scribbled notes *littered* the floor. A **rustle**, like the sound of windswept leaves, came from the far corner. One of the piles of paper was moving toward them!

Beauregard, always on the lookout for danger, *crouched* and then pounced on the rustling paper. After a short **scuffle**, which Beauregard won easily, the paper cried out for mercy.

"Aaaargh!" screamed the pile. A huge, bushy head of very light blonde hair appeared. The owner of the hair stood up, brushed off his slightly stained lab coat, and straightened his glasses.

"Barnaby!" yelped Babette, rushing toward the young scientist. "Are you okay?"

"Babette! Wonderful to see you! Why, um, yes, quite, quite, um, huh?" stammered the confused boy. "What just happened?"

SCRAP n. small, unwanted piece; fragment 조각
Only a few scraps of news about the disaster have emerged.
그 재난에 대해서 단편적인 소식만 몇 가지 나와 있다.

LITTER v. to make untidy with scattered rubbish 어지럽게 널려 놓다
Newspapers littered the floor.
신문지들이 마루에 어지럽게 널려 있었다.

CROUCH v. to lower the body by bending the knees in fear or to hide 몸을 웅크리다
I crouched behind the sofa.
나는 소파 뒤에서 몸을 웅크렸다.

"Take a look in the corner by the window," replied Bridget with a jerk of her head. "Beauregard is **skulking** around like a hunter *stalking* his prey. I think he hopes that another one of these piles of paper starts moving so he can attack it."

"I should have known," said Barnaby, smiling. "Well here we are, together again. Excellent! The last time you visited my laboratory, when I lived in Paris, I believe we had a bit of an explosion, didn't we? Yes, most of my notes and samples were lost under the rocks and **rubble** of the science building after it blew up when my gym sock experiment went **awry**. Not every experiment goes as planned, I told the university, but the other professors were very upset. They wouldn't listen to reason or any of my apologies. Basically, they ran me out of town. Luckily this university here in New York offered me space to continue my work. I thought they might change their minds when I told them about the **catastrophe** in Paris, but they didn't **balk**. They not only gave me all of the equipment I needed, but they gave it to me so quickly that I was back in action in just a week's time!"

"Well, speaking of gym socks and terrible disasters, Barnaby, it smells like you are up to your old tricks," remarked Bridget. "What is that awful **stench**? It smells like something died and is starting to **decompose**." She held her nose in disgust.

Babette agreed, "Yes, and I believe I also notice the odor of old milk that's beginning to **curdle** and **congeal** into a thick, disgusting *blob*. It's a rather sharp and **pungent** odor, Barnaby, and one that's difficult to ignore."

"No, there's nothing rotting or **rancid** in here, Bridget, and nothing's curdling, Babette," insisted Barnaby. "What you both seem to think is a **horrid** odor is actually the sweet smell of success! I feel so **giddy** and excited when I think about it, I don't know whether to fall over or turn *cartwheels*."

STALK v. to approach or pursue without being seen or heard ~을 몰래 쫓다
The detective stalked the suspect only to lose him in a crowd.
수사관은 용의자를 뒤쫓았지만 군중 속에서 그를 놓치고 말았다.

BLOB n. small round mass; spot of color; drop of a liquid 둥그스름한 작은 덩이; 얼룩; 방울
Blobs of wax covered the candlestick.
촛대가 촛농으로 뒤덮혔다.

CARTWHEEL n. sideways somersault 옆으로 재주넘기
We saw the bears turning cartwheels.
우리는 곰들이 옆으로 재주넘기하는 것을 보았다.

Bridget rolled her eyes and thought about **chiding** her friend for stretching the truth, but she was used to Barnaby's wild inventions and grand claims. Most of them were just *kooky* ideas that never worked, but sometimes, she had to admit, the young scientist came up with something really amazing. The problem was, she could never tell what was **folly** and what was genius. She decided to bite her tongue and not scold him for now.

Barnaby took several long **strides** toward the metal ship.

"You see this?" he asked, pointing toward the craft. "This is my latest **prototype**—it's the first model of the first spaceship that can fly without using a **combustion** engine! That means that nothing gets burned. Whereas cars, airplanes, rockets, and space shuttles all burn incredible amounts of fuel, my new space shuttles doesn't burn any fuel at all. Humans are wrecking the planet when they dig for oil and gas and polluting the air when we burn those natural resources. But worse than that, combustion engines don't really work that well. I just can't believe that the world has put up with those dirty machines for so long!" The **indignant** inventor shook his fist in the air and then sighed with displeasure and continued.

"The new method of travel that I *envision* will make it possible for us to explore outer space and protect the world's environment at the same time. As you both have heard me say many times, the most **crucial** challenge that humans face is that of solving the problems and surpassing the limitations of our present means of transportation. If we don't try to do this, we are dooming ourselves to living in darkest ignorance."

Barnaby's speech was beginning to **exasperate** Babette. She stamped her foot with annoyance and impatience.

"Barnaby, please, enough **melodrama**. You're like one of those overly-emotional actors in the American soap operas," she snapped. "Just tell us about your invention!"

KOOKY adj. odd or silly 이상한, 미치광이의
Look at the kooky little turtle-neck sweater dresses.
저 이상하게 생긴 작은 터틀넥 스웨터 좀 봐.

ENVISION v. to see as if in a vision; envisage 상상하다
The mother envisioned her little girl as a prima ballerina.
어머니는 자신의 어린 딸을 발레의 주역으로 상상했다.

Barnaby blushed, and Babette was immediately sorry that she'd spoken so harshly.

"I'm just eager to hear what you've made," she said gently.

"Yes, well, as you know, I have always been **intrigued** by the thought of **celestial** exploration. Exploring the heavens—ah, how many nights have I stared at the stars and dreamed of visiting distant worlds! Oops, there I go again. Sorry. Anyway, I started studying modern rockets, and after careful **analysis** of their design, I came to the conclusion that those rocket scientists at NASA have been doing it all wrong. Then, out of the *blue*, the solution came to me: I could use a **nautical** model for my spaceship!"

"Nautical?" asked Bridget. "You mean stuff like boats and sails and anchors and all that? That's kind of **quaint**, isn't it? I mean it's nice but it seems very old-fashioned."

"The idea may seem old-fashioned, but it really turned out to be very effective," insisted Barnaby. "I based my calculations on the latest research into the magnetic qualities of space dust. I have designed special ionic outer space sails and a vacuum-valent anchor for normal planetary travel. Then there is the quasi-quantum quickener for time travel, but there are still some *kinks* in that. The strong smell you notice is from a very sticky, but highly conductive, plant mash I *concocted*. It took months for me to do all of this planning and construction, but finally I'm finished."

"Wow, Barnaby, that sounds great, but I'm afraid that most of what you said sounded like **gibberish** to me," sighed Bridget. "I just didn't understand a word. Vacuum, ionic, quantum, whatchamajiggy, huh? You'll have to sit down and explain it to me step by step sometime, but not now. Now, we have bigger fish to fry."

"Fish?" asked Babette, completely confused. Beauregard, who had been stretched out on top of Barnaby's notes, perked up his ears at the word.

BLUE n. (out of the blue의 형태로 쓰여) unexpectedly, without warning 느닷없이
She arrived out of the blue.
그녀는 느닷없이 도착했다.

KINK n. a hindrance; difficulty, obstruction 방해: 어려움, 장애
Some kinks are knotting up auto distribution.
몇 가지 난제 때문에 자동차 유통이 막혀 있다.

CONCOCT v. to make something by mixing ingredients 혼합해서 만들다
She concocted the drink out of sherry and lemon juice.
그 여자는 셰리주와 레몬주스를 섞어 그 음료를 만들었다.

"Not real fish," explained Bridget. "It's just an expression. It means that we have more important things to deal with right now, namely, the Yankees game. The evil Boston Red Sox are in town, and the **rivalry** between the Red Sox and Yankees is ancient! They've been battling each other in the ballpark since before we were even born! Now that it has stopped raining, we have to go try to get tickets for the game. The only problem is that tickets are as **scarce** as hens' teeth."

"Hens?" Babette asked, as Beauregard once again *cocked* an interested ear.

"She means that tickets are rare, they're hard to come by," explained Barnaby. "Not only that, but I'm sure that prices are getting **exorbitant**. We'd have to *cough* up ridiculous amounts of money in order to get decent seats. But I have the strange feeling that we might be able to lay our hands on some tickets. Hmmm. How could we get some?"

Barnaby began pacing around the room and scratching his bushy head. Babette *nudged* Bridget and smiled knowingly. Something exciting **invariably** happened when Barnaby starting scratching.

"Tickets, tickets, tickets," he murmured, scratching furiously. "Aha! I know! We can go to the box office and try to buy some!"

"Wait, Barnaby," Bridget said, "what is that thing that's stuck behind your glasses?"

"Oh. I wondered why I couldn't see out of my left eye," Barnaby said. "Let's see. Oh. Now that's interesting. It seems I have four tickets to tonight's Yankees game. Right above the home team dugout, too. They must have fallen out of my hair. I really should brush it from time to time."

"Don't you dare," said Bridget, as she hugged her friend. "Come on, we have to get back to the subway."

COCK v. to be upright or erect; to raise 세우다
The horse cocked up its ears when it heard the noise.
그 말은 소음을 듣고 귀를 세웠다.

COUGH v. to say or produce reluctantly 마지못해 말하거나 내놓다
He owes us money, but he won't cough it up.
그는 우리에게 줄 돈이 있는데 내놓으려 하지를 않는다.

NUDGE v. to touch or push with one's elbow to draw his attention (주위를 환기하기 위해) 팔꿈치로 쿡쿡 찌르다
I nudged her and pointed to the man across the street.
나는 팔꿈치로 그녀를 슬쩍 찌르며 길 건너편에 있는 남자를 보라고 가리켰다.

So Barnaby left his lab for the evening, and the friends scurried down to the subway with Beauregard trotting behind.

"Right above the dugout!" gasped Bridget excitedly, as they walked down into the station. "What a perfect **vantage** for catching foul balls. We couldn't be in a better position!"

A short while later, they were walking toward Yankee Stadium. The streets and parking lot were filled with excited, cheering fans and **peddlers** selling souvenirs, candy, and T-shirts from their carts. The sun was just beginning to set, and the late-summer evening was warm and pleasant.

"This crowd is so excited, Bridget," remarked Babette. "In France, we only see such a **hoopla** at soccer games. What a *commotion*!"

"I have to admit that even though I am a *whiz* at physics and chemistry, for some reason baseball **confounds** me," said Barnaby. "I love watching it, but I never understand what's going on. Bridget, Babbete and I are counting on you to explain everything."

"Have no fear," declared Bridget, laughing. "With me as your guide, baseball will never **mystify** or **bewilder** you again. Let's get a move on, though, my throat is parched; I could drink a bathtub full of soda. And I want you guys to see the field keepers roll up the giant plastic **tarpaulin** that keeps the rain off the field. It's really cool!"

Once she made sure that Babette and Barnaby were in their seats, Bridget took off for the snack stand to get some food. Beauregard followed her, which was lucky, since Bridget bought far too many treats to carry by herself. She and Beureagrd returned **laden** with drinks, popcorn, candy, and a dozen foot-long hot dogs that were fully loaded with dressings.

"You look like a couple of pack mules, all loaded down like that," joked Barnaby.

"Are you going to grab some of this, or what?" asked Bridget, who was struggling to keep it all balanced.

COMMOTION n. noisy confusion or excitement 시끄러움 ,소동
Suddenly, there was a great commotion next door.
갑자기 옆집에서 대단한 소동이 일어났다.

WHIZ n. a very clever person; expert 천재: 전문가
He is a whiz in mathematics.
그는 수학의 천재다.

Babette and Barnaby eagerly took the giant drinks off of the cardboard tray on Beauregard's back and unloaded the food from Bridget's arms.

"You can't enjoy a baseball game without the proper **provisions**," said Bridget. "And now we have all the supplies we could possible want: *Dig* in everyone! I bought every **edible** product that was available. You might argue that red *licorice* isn't fit to eat, but hey, I say if you can swallow it, it's edible."

They ate as if they hadn't had a meal in weeks; they only stopped *slurping* and chewing for long enough to cheer and *holler* for the Yankees. Bridget amazed everyone with her whistling abilities; she could stick two fingers in her mouth and produce a sound so loud and **shrill** that people at a distance of a hundred yards had to cover their ears.

"My, that is a piercing sound," said Babette, admiringly. "I just can't seem to do it."

"Don't feel bad, Babette," replied Bridget. "You have plenty of skills of your own. For example, you're **multilingual**. Exactly how many languages *do* you know?"

"Five," Babette said hurriedly, and then stood in her chair and yelled "*J'aime les* Yankees! *Victoire pour les* Yankees!" Bridget looked at her friend enviously.

"Uggh," groaned Barnaby. "I feel like I weigh a ton. My stomach is **bloated** to three times its normal size. In **retrospect**, I see that eating that fifth foot-long hot dog was a bad idea."

"No sense regretting it now, Barnaby," said Bridget. "You need to get active. Wave your arms. Clap your hands. Let's hear some noise! Hey battabattabatta, hey... Ouch!"

"What happened?" asked Babette.

"Ow, it looks like a **shard** of fiberglass is sticking out from this seat and it just stuck me in the *rear*."

DIG v. (dig in의 형태로 쓰여) to eat hungrily or enthusiastically 게걸스레 먹다
The food's ready, so dig in!
식사 준비됐으니 먹어라!

LICORICE n. plant that yields a sweet-tasting substance obtained from its roots 감초
Licorice is used as a flavoring in medicine, tobacco, soft drinks, and candy.
감초는 약, 담배, 청량음료, 사탕의 감미료로 쓰인다.

SLURP v. to make a loud noise with the lips as one eats or drinks 요란하게 소리내며 먹거나 마시다
He was slurping down his soup.
그는 요란한 소리를 내면서 수프를 먹었다.

HOLLER v. to shout; to yell 소리치다
He hollered to me that the boat was sinking.
그는 배가 가라앉고 있다고 나에게 소리쳤다.

REAR n. buttocks 엉덩이
He sat on his rear on the sofa.
그는 소파 위에 털썩 주저앉았다.

"How big a shard? Ooh, that's a pretty big splinter," remarked Barnaby, as he **sidled** over to Bridget with scientific interest. "There are probably *germs* all over these seats. We need to get you to the doctor for a shot of **penicillin** so you don't get an infection. That's the **prudent** thing to do; penicillin is great at killing germs."

"Slide back over to your seat, doc" laughed Bridget. "It only poked me, there's no blood."

"That's a relief," said Barnaby.

"Is it time for the **interval**?" asked Babette.

"Interval?" replied Bridget, confused.

"Yes, an interval, you know, a space between things. You said that there was an interval between innings in which we would stand up and sing."

"Oh, you mean the seventh inning stretch," said Bridget. "Oh yeah. Look, it's time right now! This is when we get up and sing 'Take Me Out to the Ball Game.' I'll tell you the words quickly, it's an easy song to learn."

But Bridget didn't sing. Something had caught everyone's attention. Just above the edge of the stadium a large object *loomed*, as big as a cloud. I couldn't make out exactly what it was. The last rays of the setting sun glared so brightly that I couldn't see very well. Whatever the object was, I didn't like it. I was filled with a dark sense of foreboding.

Bridget lost no time in making use of her famous gum-chewing talent. She started blowing a bubble, bigger and bigger and bigger until a gust of wind lifted her off the ground. Babette, Barnaby, and I knew exactly what to do. We grabbed on to her legs for dear life and went sailing into the air. Just as we were taking off, a booming voice from the sky thundered through the stadium.

"Your Yankees or your lives!" the voice demanded. Then we heard an evil **cackle**, a **diabolical** laugh, that made us *shiver* with **dread**.

GERM n. micro-organism, especially one capable of causing disease 세균
Disinfectant kills germs.
살균제는 세균들을 죽인다.

LOOM v. to appear in an indistinct and often threatening way 불쑥 나타나다
An enormous shape loomed up in the distance.
거대한 형상이 멀리서 불쑥 나타났다.

SHIVER v. to tremble from cold or fear 벌벌 떨다
She shivered at the thought of going into the dark house alone.
그 여자는 어두운 집에 혼자 들어갈 생각을 하고 벌벌 떨었다.

Q U I C K   Q U I Z

Relationships

Decide what relationship the following pairs of words have to each other. If they mean close to the same thing, make "S." If they have opposite meanings, mark "O."

1. scarce :: exorbitant
2. catastrophe :: disaster
3. rancid :: foul
4. rival :: ally
5. foolhardy :: prudent
6. bewilder :: confound
7. drench :: saturate
8. indifferent :: apathetic
9. giddy :: morose
10. celestial :: earthly
11. dread :: anxiety

Q U I C K   Q U I Z   2

Relationships

Decide what relationship the following pairs of words have to each other. If they mean close to the same thing, make "S." If they have opposite meanings, mark "O."

1. murmur :: shriek
2. crucial :: decisive
3. blasé :: exotic
4. mystify :: perplex
5. elegant :: refined
6. exasperate :: intrigue
7. indignant :: resentful
8. burly :: gaunt
9. parch :: drench
10. lope :: stride

Q U I C K   Q U I Z   3

Fill in the Blank

For each sentence below, choose the word that best completes the sentence.

1. Mrs. Finster had such an unpleasant _____ that people would only tell her jokes that weren't funny.

   a. muster   b. cackle   c. balk   d. jabber

2. After we thoroughly washed and waxed the 1972 Volkswagen, the car _____ like it was brand new.

   a. congealed   b. glistened   c. rustled   d. scuffled

3. The colored glass statue of a rose was beautiful, but even a slight wind was enough to knock the _____ artwork on its side.

   a. pungent   b. quaint   c. horrid   d. dainty

4. Hoping to get a free ice cream cone, the children continued _____ at the drug store counter for hours after they had finished their burgers.

    a. chiding   b. skulking   c. lingering   d. scampering

5. The _____ had no trouble selling his mini-refrigerators in California, but his trip to Alaska almost ruined him financially.

    a. panhandler   b. peddler   c. melodrama   d. hoopla

6. After three days of heavy thunderstorms, the main street of our town transformed into a _____ of rushing water.

    a. torrent   b. stench   c. gridlock   d. penicillin

7. The judge wanted to _____ the questions to the alleged burglary, but questions about the defendant's past continued to come up during the trial.

    a. confine   b. jostle   c. glare   d. narrate

8. Although the hurricane had downed some seats and soaked most of the countryside, the _____ over the baseball field kept the infield dirt relatively dry.

    a. analysis   b. rubble   c. combustion   d. tarpaulin

9. A cruel person, the chef uttered a(n) _____ laugh before placing the lobsters into the boiling water.

    a. audible   b. sidling   c. diabolical   d. multilingual

10. Nancy felt it necessary to _____ excitedly around the room every day before English class started.

    a. fend   b. loom   c. curdle   d. cavort

Q U I C K Q U I Z 4

Matching

Match each word on the right with a word on the left that has a meaning that's close to the same.

1. prototype	A. supplies
2. retrospect	B. ship related
3. provisions	C. stand over
4. gibberish	D. fragment
5. decompose	E. nonsense
6. loom	F. original model
7. dreary	G. act of stupidity
8. shard	H. hindsight
9. nautical	I. bleak
10. folly	J. decay

Matching

Match each word on the right with a word on the left that has a meaning that's close to the same.

1. awry	A. mental tranquillity
2. shrill	B. inevitably
3. bloat	C. wrong
4. foreboding	D. able to be eaten
5. repose	E. sense of disaster
6. vantage	F. astonish
7. dazzle	G. burdened with goods
8. invariably	H. high point
9. edible	I. distended
10. laden	J. high-pitched

Knuckleballs and Tentacles

너클볼과 촉수

2

Exactly what happened next, I'll probably never know. I remember that there was a bright light and a wave of sticky, hot air. For a minute it looked like the entire New York Yankees baseball team was flying through the air, like a band of athletic angels with mitts instead of harps. What a **spectacle**! You don't see things like that every day. Then I **swooned** and everything went black.

When I woke up, I found myself on a red velvet cushion on a chair at the head of a large *banquet* table. The room I was in was so expensively furnished that it looked fit for **regal** visitors. The **grandeur** of the heavy red *drapes* along the walls was made more *noticeable* by the gold thread that was **embroidered** around its edges. Such lovely decoration! Precious gems embedded in the gold dishes on the table, drinking goblets, and *platters* on the table, all sparkled in the candlelight. Every aspect of the room was delightful, but the part that really filled me with awe and admiration was the food. I hadn't seen a *spread* like that since the summer I spent at the court of the Sultan Subadai. That sultan really knew how to throw a party! I remember the time that he imported ten tons of caviar from Russia to fill his swimming pool, then hired the Spanish Olympic aqua-aerobics team to... but that's a story for another time. The question was what were we doing in a fancy banquet hall?

"Eek!" shrieked Bridget as she awakened from what must have been a *trance*. "What happened to my clothes?"

She stared down in horror at her pink satin dress, white lacy socks, and shiny, black, patent leather shoes. Babette and Barnaby laughed uncontrollably as their shocked friend examined her outfit. There were even ribbons in her hair!

BANQUET n. a formal dinner, often with speeches, prepared for a special occasion; feast 연회
We went to the wedding banquet.
우리는 결혼식 피로연에 갔다.

DRAPE n. cloth hung in folds; hanging; drapery 커튼
There are heavy drapes on the large windows in the living room.
거실 큰 창문에 무거운 커튼이 드리워져 있다.

NOTICEABLE adj. easily seen or noticed 눈에 띄는, 돋보이는
There's been a noticeable improvement in her handwriting.
그녀의 필체가 눈에 띄게 좋아졌다.

PLATTER n. large shallow dish for serving food 큰 접시
We need some platters to have a party.
파티를 열려면 큰 접시들이 필요하다

SPREAD n. meal spread out on a table 진수성찬
What a spread!
정말 진수성찬이구만!

TRANCE n. sleep-like state caused by being hypnotized 최면상태
She fell into a trance.
그녀는 최면상태에 빠졌다.

"I see no reason for such **mirth**," grumbled Bridget. "You'll quit your giggling when you get a load of the clothes you're wearing!"

"There's no need to be **testy**, Bridget. We did not mean to vex you by laughing, but... oh, no!" howled Babette, looking down with **dismay** as she realized that her stylish black outfit had been replaced by a serious, navy blue dress with a white sailor collar. "What a **prim** and proper, little girl dress! I feel like a school principal! This is horrible. I **abhor** dresses."

"I hate them, too," Bridget said. "I'd rather be dressed like Barnaby, even though he does look pretty *goofy*."

Barnaby's lab coat was gone, and in its place was a green satin jacket with black velvet *lapels*. A *dashing* silk scarf was tucked around his neck. Barnaby did not seem at all unhappy with his new clothes. After admiring himself in a large mirror that was hanging on the wall, he **swaggered** over to his friends with all the pride of a peacock.

"Yes, it seems there have been some *wardrobe* changes," announced Barnaby. "But what we need to know is *why*, and what's going on? What information can we **glean** from our surroundings? We must examine every detail for clues."

"Okay, Sherlock," joked Bridget. "I'd say that judging from the **opulent** furnishings and food, we are in the home of a very rich person."

"I think it's quite **ostentatious** and overdone," sniffed Babette with disapproval. "I think whoever brought us here is a **pretentious** *snob* without any taste or class. But we are definitely supposed to be impressed with the expense of all of this."

"Aren't you two forgetting something? Like the flying baseball players?" asked Barnaby.

"Oh, yeah," sighed Bridget. "Okay, so we're in the home of a very rich person who probably has a space ship that can make people hover above the ground. Great. Now what?"

Barnaby began poking around the curtains, looking for a way to open them.

GOOFY adj. silly 바보같은
Don't be goofy!
바보같이 굴지 마라!

LAPEL n. front part of the collar of a coat or jacket that is folded back over the chest 옷깃
What is that badge on your lapel?
옷깃 위에 있는 그 배지는 뭐니?

DASHING adj. showy or stylish 화려한
The men in the band wore bright and dashing uniforms.
밴드에 속한 사람들은 밝고 화려한 유니폼을 입고 있었다.

WARDROBE n. a stock of clothes 의상
She is shopping for her spring wardrobe.
그녀는 봄 의상을 사려고 쇼핑하고 있다.

SNOB n. a person who cares too much for rank, wealth, position, and the like, and too little for real merit 속물
He is a man of a fine old family, but a dreadful snob.
그는 유서 깊은 명문가 출신이긴 하지만, 끔찍한 속물이다.

"There has to be a way to look outside and see where we... ah, yes, here it is," Barnaby said as he pulled a long yellow cord. The curtains swung open to reveal the blackness of outer space to the right, and a swirling white mass of clouds to the left. Barnaby gasped, "What an **atmosphere!**"

"I'm so glad that you approve," boomed a deep voice. "I tried to make the room homey and comfortable, and like a room that you might see on your own planet."

Barnaby, Babette, and Bridget spun around to face the door at the end of the banquet hall. Standing there—or hovering, maybe—was the strangest looking creature that they'd ever seen. It had ten long **tentacles**, like the arms of an octopus, and a huge green head with *droopy* ears. It didn't have a nose as far as they could tell, and its mouth was just a tiny opening, but all around its head were a dozen eyes that blinked and winked. A short, black **mane** of hair, like a horse's, sprang from the top of its skull and extended a short way down its back. Around its shoulders (or what they thought were shoulders) the creature wore a little purple cape.

"That is the most **hideous**, frightful creature I have ever seen," whispered Babette, to no one in particular.

"Tut, tut, young lady," scolded the being. "How rude. You wouldn't catch me calling you **homely** or unattractive just because you look different from me, or because you dress like a principal." He turned to Barnaby and said, "Young man, you were admiring the room's atmosphere?"

"Umm, actually I was looking at Earth's atmosphere, you know, its protective layer of gasses, but the room is, umm, it's really, really nice as well," **stammered** Barnaby.

"Thank you, young man," said the strange being, holding out one arm toward the boy. "I hope you have been enjoying the food—but how rude of me, I have not even introduced myself. I am Gorgas, an explorer from another galaxy. And you are...?"

Barnaby was frozen in place.

DROOPY **adj.** hanging down; drooping 축 늘어진
Put on this droopy hat.
이 축 늘어진 모자를 써라.

"Come, lad, there's no need to be shy and **timid**, I only want to shake your hand," urged Gorgas.

Bridget broke in, "Pardon him, Gorgas," she sensed that Barnaby needed a few seconds to get a *grip* on himself. "He's a scientist and he isn't used to social events. My name is Bridget, and these are my friends Babette, Barnaby, and Beauregard. Beauregard is the cat over there that's enjoying your chicken pot pie. We are all pleased to make your acquaintance."

Beauregard licked his *whiskers*, gave a polite little nod toward their host, and continued eating. Bridget took Gorgas's tentacle into her hand, bent her knees slightly, and dipped into a perfect **curtsy**, just like her mother had told her she should when meeting royalty. Bridget wasn't sure if Gorgas was a king, but she figured that it couldn't hurt.

"My dear, what lovely manners!" remarked Gorgas with pleasure. "What a delight! In general I simply cannot **abide** ill-mannered people. I just cannot put up with them. And as for me, I would rather be torn limb from limb from limb from limb from limb than behave rudely. Might I add, Bridget, that you look quite comely in that **frock**. I knew you would look pretty in it."

"Thank you," said Bridget, since she knew that it would be impolite to give her real opinion of the outfit. "I hope I won't seem rude for asking, but we were wondering why exactly we were brought here."

"My apologies, Bridget, my dear, but it was an accident," said Gorgas. "You just *drifted* into my path. I had only meant to take possession of the baseball players, but once you arrived, I decided to try and make you feel welcome."

"Were you the one who said 'Your Yankees or your lives'?" asked Babette.

"That was just my idea of little joke," said Gorgas. "I'm afraid I'm a bit of a *prankster*."

GRIP n. (get a grip on oneself의 형태로 쓰여) to gain control of oneself and improve one's behaviour 스스로를 통제하다
I finally got a grip on myself.
마침내 내 자신을 통제했다.

WHISKERS n. long hair growing on a man's face 구레나룻, 수염
The old man's long beard was full of gray whiskers.
그 노인의 긴 턱수염은 회색 구레나룻로 꽉 찼다.

DRIFT v. to be carried along gently by a current of air or water 떠내려가다
The boat drifted down the river.
배는 강을 따라 떠내려갔다.

PRANKSTER n. person who plays playful or mischievous tricks 장난꾸러기
He is a cute prankster.
그는 귀여운 장난꾸러기이다.

"So you're saying that the **acquisition** of the Yankees was your goal," Bridget pressed on. "You seem to have quite a lot of money—one can't help but notice, so why didn't you just buy the team?"

"I don't want to own them forever, young lady," explained Gorgas. "You see, part of my mission as an explorer is to **accumulate** information about other worlds. I must **amass** as much knowledge as I can. At any rate, for the past couple of weeks I have been watching television *transmissions* of baseball on my TV here in the space ship. It's such a *fascinating pastime*! I must confess, though, that I am not confident that I truly understand all of the rules of the game."

"Oh, Bridget can **clarify** them for you. She's great at explaining things about baseball," said Barnaby, who had finally remembered how to talk.

Gorgas said *snootily*, "I'm sure Bridget has been a great help to *you*. How difficult it must have been for you to grasp those very complicated concepts."

"There is no need to **condescend** to Barnaby," snapped Babette. "You may think that you're super-intelligent because you've mastered intergalactic travel, but Barnaby is a brilliant inventor and scientist on the Earth, and..."

"Well, excuse me, I would never dare to put on airs in front of a brilliant scientist," interrupted Gorgas. "I **presume** that Barnaby is quite capable of understanding the sport of baseball."

"You presume correctly, Gorgas," Bridget said, and folded her arms across her chest.

"In any event," Gorgas proceeded, "the rules of the game no longer interest me. I have another, more scientific, question to ask the Yankees. My **inquiry** will be about a certain amazing ability that is possessed by Lefty Zambisi, the starting pitcher—I must ask him about a trick that he performs, which I believe is called the 'knuckle ball'..."

TRANSMISSION **n.** radio or TV broadcast 중계방송
It's a live transmission from Washington.
그것은 워싱턴으로부터의 생중계 방송이다.

FASCINATING **adj.** having great attraction or charm 매우 흥미 진진한, 매력적인
She has a fascinating voice.
그녀는 매력적인 목소리를 갖고 있다.

PASTIME **n.** thing done to pass the time pleasantly 오락, 심심풀이, 취미
Photography is her favourite pastime.
사진 촬영은 그녀가 가장 좋아하는 취미 활동이다.

SNOOTILY **adv.** contemptuously; conceitedly 거만하게, 잘난 체하는
She always speaks snootily to the neighbours.
그녀는 항상 이웃에게 거만하게 말한다.

"The knuckle ball is their secret weapon," Bridget said with excitement. "No other pitcher in the history of baseball has been able to throw a knuckle ball with such control and **precision**. The ball always goes exactly where Lefty wants it to, directly over the *plate*. The beauty of this pitch is that the **trajectory** of the ball as it travels to the plate is impossible to predict. As soon as it leaves Lefty's hand, it could curve to the left or right or it could dip or *wobble*, but every time it crosses the plate it's safely in the strike zone. Batters go nuts! Whenever Lefty starts throwing knuckle balls, you know that the game will end in a **rout**, with the other team running for cover!"

"I can see that Lefty was right when he said you might be interested in our little experiment," said Gorgas. "He told me that you were offering him quite a bit of loud advice from the stands during the game, and suggested I ask you for help. He has a most unpleasant **disposition**— what a quick-tempered and *gruff* man! And I have never met anyone quite so **obstinate**; despite all of my begging and pleading, he absolutely refuses to show me how he throws his famous pitch."

"I'm sure it's not because of **spite** or meanness. He probably thinks you're a spy from another team or something," said Bridget.

"Well, I don't mean to **impose** upon you, Bridget, because you are a guest aboard my ship, but would it be too much trouble for you and your friends to come to the practice room with me? You see, that pitch is a miracle, it doesn't follow any known laws of motion in the universe. I must uncover the secret, for, uh, for the good of science. Yes, that's it, for the good of science," said Gorgas.

"Of course I'll come," Bridget replied. "Lead the way."

Bridget followed Gorgas as he slipped through the doorway. Barnaby, on the other hand, was going to have to be **coaxed**. He and Babette hung behind for a moment.

PLATE n. (in baseball) home base of the batting side   본루
The base runner must reach the plate safely in order to score a run.
베이스 주자는 1점을 얻기 위해 안전하게 본루를 밟아야 한다.

WOBBLE v. to move from side to side unsteadily   흔들흔들하다
I was so terrified my legs were wobbling.
난 너무 겁이 나서 다리가 후들후들 떨렸다.

GRUFF adj. rough   거친
Beneath his gruff exterior he's really very kind-hearted.
거친 외모와는 달리 그는 정말 매우 친절하다.

"Now Barnaby, come on," urged Babette gently. "I'm sure Bridget has a plan to get us out of here. I don't like Gorgas any more than you do, I think his way of talking is **stilted** and *stuck up*, and I don't think he's up to any good."

"Did you notice that he **exudes** some sort of *slimy* liquid from his tentacles? That's why I didn't shake his hand. Plus, there was something *fishy* about his reason for wanting to learn about knuckle balls. I don't like this," added Barnaby.

"We'll discuss it later, but now we have to hurry; we don't want to lose them," said Babette.

She and Barnaby jogged through the doorway. Beauregard, his belly full from feasting, followed sluggishly. They caught sight of Gorgas's purple cape swishing around a corner ahead of them, and ran to catch up.

"Here we are!" announced Gorgas, stopping in the doorway of a huge gym.

In the gym some of the Yankees were playing casual games of catch. A couple of them were practicing their swings in batting cages. Lefty Zambisi, however, sat on the floor with his arms crossed and his back against the wall, and when Gorgas entered the room, he groaned.

"Listen, fella, I've talked myself **hoarse** trying to get this through that giant green head of yours," *rasped* Lefty, rubbing his tired throat. "You will never throw my pitch, understand? I can't show you how to do it. I can't, I can't, I can't!"

"He certainly is **vehement**," remarked Gorgas to Bridget. "You might be right about his suspecting that I'm a spy." To Lefty, he said, "Listen, I've had about enough of your **defiance**. You *must* do as I ask. It is rude to refuse me a simple favor."

"Look, mister, can't you see that my energy is **flagging**; I'm *tuckered* out. Why don't you just leave me alone?" he whined.

Bridget sat down on the ground next to Lefty with a look of concern on her face.

STUCK-UP adj. conceited and unwilling to mix with others; snobbish 거만한
We heard no more of the stuck-up boy's great strength after he lost the fight.
그 거만한 소년이 싸움에서 진 뒤 그의 대단한 힘에 대해서 우리는 더 이상 아무 말도 못 들었다.

SLIMY adj. covered with thick soft slippery liquid substance 미끌미끌한
She slipped on the slimy steps.
그녀는 미끌미끌한 계단에서 미끄러졌다.

FISHY adj. not probable; doubtful; unlikely; suspicious 수상한
His excuse sounds fishy; I don't believe it.
그의 변명은 수상하게 들려. 나는 안 믿어.

RASP v. to say in an unpleasant grating voice 귀에 거슬리는 소리로 말하다
He rasped out orders.
그는 귀에 거슬리는 소리로 명령했다.

TUCKER v. to tire or exhaust 지칠대로 지치게 하다
I'm fair tuckered out.
나는 정말 지칠 대로 지쳐 있다.

"Gorgas," she said, "Lefty does seem tired. Remember, he just pitched seven straight innings and he's getting kind of old; he doesn't have the **stamina** that he used to. Maybe if you went and got him a soda, I could see if I can bring him around to see your point of view. Don't worry, I'll **sway** him."

Gorgas strutted purposefully off and left them alone with Lefty.

"What is this, kid?" asked Lefty, narrowing his eyes at her. "I would never have suspected you of **duplicity**. I thought you were a *die-hard* Yankees fans, and here you are spying for the enemy. Pretty two-faced, isn't this? And by the way, I am not getting old, and I have just as much staying power as I used to."

"*Stow* it, Lefty, I'm no spy. I'm here to help you get off of this ship," snapped Bridget. "And I only made that 'old' comment to get Gorgas to leave us alone."

"Oh, yeah?" the pitcher said suspiciously, "Well, how do I know you're not lying?"

"We can **corroborate** her story, Mr. Zambisi," said Barnaby. "Babette and I can confirm that Bridget is the biggest Yankees fan around. Gorgas only transported us up here by accident, when he was transporting the team. Bridget is definitely not a spy."

"Bridget, I am so glad to hear that you have a plan to get us out of here. Gorgas is frightening me. He probably has plans to take over the world, enslave the human race, and declare himself Supreme Ruler of the Galaxy," said Babette.

"Come on, Babette, that's a **stereotype**. You've been watching too many sci-fi movies," scolded Bridget. "Not every *alien* with tentacles and a big green head wants to take over the world, you know. I think Gorgas is a little weird and I don't want to hang around here much longer, but I think he's pretty harmless, and I also think you're making too big of a deal out of this."

"I am not, I am not!" insisted Babette, with a **petulant** stamp of her foot.

STRUT v. to walk in an upright, proud way 점잔을 빼며 걷다
She strutted past us, ignoring our greeting.
그녀는 우리의 인사를 무시한 채 점잔을 빼며 우리 곁을 지나갔다.

DIE-HARD n. person who is stubborn in resisting change 골수분자
A few die-hards are trying to stop the reforms.
몇몇 골수분자들이 개혁을 중단시키려 하고 있다.

STOW v. (stow it의 형태로 쓰여) to stop 그만두다
Stow it!
그만 둬! 입 닥쳐!

ALIEN n. being from another world 외계인
Do you believe in aliens?
너는 외계인을 믿니?

"Easy, kid, no need to have a tantrum," joked Lefty. "If it makes you feel better, I agree with you: This Gorgas guy is trouble."

"I think so, too!" Barnaby blurted out.

Even Beauregard nodded his head slightly in agreement.

"Okay, okay. I know when I'm out-numbered," said Bridget. "I suppose we should figure out what to do next."

"I ought to confess that I never really thought Gorgas was a spy from another team," said Lefty. "But for some reason, I just don't want to explain my pitch to him. I realize that there's been a lot of **hype** in the media about my knuckle ball, and a lot of folks are interested in learning how I do it. But Gorgas, he seems a little *too* interested in it, and he's so **persistent**. He's been *pestering* me about it for hours; he just won't let up!"

"Wait a minute, something just **dawned** on me," Barnaby broke in. "First of all, I admit that I'm not a baseball expert, but it looks to me like Gorgas has an **impediment** that would prevent him from being able to throw a knuckle ball. He has no knuckles!"

"You sure *are* sharper than Gorgas," grinned Lefty. "For all of his brains, he didn't seem to understand that a person without knuckles can't throw a knuckle ball. That's exactly what I told him from the very start, but he still doesn't believe me."

"What are we going to do?" asked Bridget. "We don't have time to sit and **ponder** the situation for hours. We have to think fast. Gorgas will be back with the soda any minute."

"Whatever you do, don't try to strong-arm him," warned Lefty. "My teammates and I tried to **pit** our strength against him, and we got *licked*. He is a **formidable** fighter, and is nowhere near as easy to beat as the Red Sox. Those weird tentacles of his are strong, and they have *suckers* on them!"

PESTER v. to annoy or disturb with frequent requests 조르다
Don't pester me with foolish questions.
어리석은 질문으로 나를 조르지 마라.

LICK v. to defeat in a fight; to conquer; to overcome 물리치다
I could lick you with one hand tied behind me, if I wanted to.
원하기만 하면 한 손을 뒤로 묶고도 너를 물리칠 수 있다.

SUCKER n. organ of certain animals that enables them to stick to a surface by suction 흡반
An octopus has suckers on its tentacles.
문어는 촉수에 흡반이 달려 있다.

"Did you say suckers? Hmmm. Very interesting," remarked Babette. "No, we should not try to beat Gorgas with force. This situation requires **cunning** and **deception**. We must *outsmart* Gorgas and trick him into thinking that we're giving him everything he wants."

"What did you have in mind?" asked Barnaby, interested.

"Well, Gorgas seems to like Bridget very much, especially since she curtsied for him. Bridget, do you think you could continue to convince Gorgas that you are his **ally**?" asked Babette.

"Sure," said Bridget. "What do you think I should do?"

Babette quickly *outlined* her plan—and finished not a moment too soon. Gorgas returned with a large bottle of soda pop and plopped it at Lefty's feet.

"Well?" he boomed with the **imperious** tone of a powerful ruler. "Have you decided to tell me what I want to know? Or are you going to sit there **peevishly** refusing?"

"Go suck eggs, Gorgas," scoffed Lefty.

It would be hard to describe exactly how angry Gorgas got. He was **livid**, and his mouth, which was already little, tightened up until it was so **minute** it was barely even visible. Something was about to happen. The tension in that air was so thick that it seemed to have substance; it was nearly **palpable**. And suddenly Gorgas lost what little control he'd had. He threw a **tantrum** worthy of a three-year-old child who is deprived of dessert.

"You! You horrible, nasty, **odious** man!" howled Gorgas, waving his tentacles. "I have displayed an **inordinate** amount of patience with you. Much, much more patience than you have deserved. If you do not tell me how to throw a knuckle ball right this instant, I'll..."

"Gorgas!" shouted Bridget, so he would listen to her. "Let me have a word with you for a minute."

Gorgas heaved a great sigh, obviously disappointed that his outburst was interrupted, and took a few steps away with Bridget.

OUTSMART v. to use intelligence or a clever trick to defeat somebody or to gain an advantage 재치나 꾀로 이기다
The council outsmarted us by releasing their own press statement.
자기네 언론 문서를 풀면서 협회가 우리를 꾀로 이겼다.

OUTLINE v. to explain something in a general way, without giving all the details 개략적으로 설명하다
He listened as I outlined my reasons.
내가 이유를 설명할 때 그는 듣고 있었다.

"Pardon me for that rather excessive display, my dear," said Gorgas.

"Well, I have good news," said Bridget with a smile. "All I had to do was **cajole** him a little to get him to reveal his secret. You know, I used **flattery**; I told him what a great player he is and how much I admire him and a bunch of other nice things like that."

"Oh! you **crafty**, *sneaky* little thing, you. Good job. Oh, this is marvelous," squeaked Gorgas, bouncing up and down. "Please do go on."

"You'll never believe this, but he says he cheats. It has nothing to do with knuckles. He makes a little suction cup with his hand so that when he throws, the ball is delayed for a second before it comes loose. Batters can never figure out the timing so they can never hit the ball," Bridget explained.

"Did you say suction cup?" asked Gorgas.

"Yes, we could get a few suction cups for you and you could easily **emulate** hit pitch. You could even do it better than him if... but, Gorgas, look at your arms!" cried Bridget, pretending to be surprised. "They are covered in suckers! They're perfect!"

"Aren't they lovely?" laughed Gorgas. "I will unlock the secret of that pitch at last! There's no stopping me now! Surely having more than one sucker will **enhance** the effectiveness of the pitch. No longer will it be called the knuckle ball; we'll call it the Sucker Ball—the pitch for suckers!"

"What a great name," Bridget agreed enthusiastically, giggling to herself.

"My dear, I am greatly *indebted* to you. I am **obliged** to repay you for this fantastic favor you have done for me; my good manners simply prevent me from letting this pass unrewarded. What can I do for you?" Gorgas asked.

SNEAKY adj. done or acting in a secret or deceptive way 비열한, 남의 눈을 속이는
This sneaky girl was disliked by the rest of the class.
학급의 나머지 학생들은 남을 잘 속이는 이 여학생을 싫어했다.

INDEBTED adj. owing money or gratitude to somebody ~에게 빚을 진, ~에게 은혜를 입은
I am greatly indebted to him for his help.
나는 그의 도움에 크게 은혜를 입고 있다.

"Think nothing of it, Gorgas," Bridget said. "But if you insist on doing something for me, how about returning the Yankees to Yankee Stadium so that they can continue their game?"

"Of course I'll return the baseball players," agreed Gorgas.

"And while you're at it, my friends and I are ready to go back at any time," Bridget added. "In our regular clothes, too, if that's okay."

"Did you say at any time?" asked Gorgas, with what looked like a grin.

"Sure!" said Bridget.

"Very well, then. Children! Come here!" ordered the alien as he pulled a long stick that looked like a magic *wand* out from under his purple cape.

Babette, Barnaby, and Beauregard gathered around Bridget.

"You will now return to the Earth—at *any time*, as requested," giggled Gorgas, and he waved the wand around them.

The four friends were suddenly bathed in a bright, hot light. The air around them grew heavy and they began to feel *light-headed*. The spaceship around them *faded*, the light dimmed, and as darkness surrounded them, they heard Gorgas's terrible laugh.

"Enjoy the seventeenth century!" he thundered.

WAND n. slender stick or rod held in the hand   지팡이
The fairy godmother waved her magic wand.
그 요정 대모는 요술 지팡이를 흔들었다.

LIGHT-HEADED adj. feeling slightly faint or dizzy   머리가 어질어질한
A second glass of wine made him light-headed.
와인 두 잔을 마시고 그는 머리가 어질어질해졌다.

FADE v. to disappear gradually; to become indistinct   사라지다; 희미해지다
All memory of her childhood had faded from her mind.
어린 시절의 모든 기억이 그녀의 머리에서 사라졌다.

Relationships

Decide what relationship the following pairs of words have to each other. If they mean close to the same thing, make "S." If they have opposite meanings, mark "O."

1. timid :: vehement
2. prim :: casual
3. pretentious :: humble
4. accumulate :: hoard
5. stamina :: constitution
6. duplicity :: fraud
7. comely :: hideous
8. emulate :: copy
9. mirth :: dismay
10. flattering :: spiteful
11. ponder :: contemplate

Relationships

Decide what relationship the following pairs of words have to each other. If they mean close to the same thing, make "S." If they have opposite meanings, mark "O."

1. petulant :: pleasant
2. enhance :: intensify
3. cunning :: crafty
4. awe :: scorn
5. odious :: abominable
6. defiance :: obstinance
7. palpable :: unnoticeable
8. clarify :: obscure
9. flag :: signal
10. homely :: opulent
11. tantrum :: outburst

Fill in the Blank

For each sentence below, choose the word that best completes the sentence.

1. Joanie's _____ requests—she called Thomas every hour for two weeks straight—finally got her the date she wanted for the prom.
   a. condescending   b. persistent   c. formidable   d. peevish

2. The villagers _____ the bandits so thoroughly that most of the survivors never picked up a weapon again without starting to cry.
   a. exuded   b. coaxed   c. routed   d. abhorred

3. The gift of the mammoth _____ was very thoughtful, since the king enjoyed using ice cubes that were nine inches thick.
   a. goblet   b. frock   c. trajectory   d. curtsy

4. Since she always won, Katie _____ such a collection of marbles that it looked like she was carrying huge bunches of grapes in her pockets.

   a. swaggered   b. imposed   c. vexed   d. amassed

5. The clock used at the Naval Command Center was so _____ that it only lost a second for every two hundred years of use.

   a. minute   b. regal   c. precise   d. livid

6. Once my parents arrived home from vacation two days early, the _____ at my house party went from very good to very bad.

   a. tentacles   b. atmosphere   c. mane   d. ally

7. Toby asked such a(n) _____ amount of questions that the teacher eventually asked him to just sit on his hands and let her finish at least one sentence.

   a. testy   b. ostentatious   c. inordinate   d. obliging

8. Once he learned that he had just won the lottery, Morgan's sour _____ took a change for the better.

   a. acquisition   b. corroboration   c. deception   d. disposition

9. The large glowing rock was _____ too deeply in the side of the cave for me to pry it out with my hand alone.

   a. embedded   b. pitted   c. cajoled   d. gleaned

Q U I C K   Q U I Z   9

Matching

Match each word on the right with a word on the left that has a meaning that's close to the same.

1. impediment	A. oversimplified idea
2. stereotype	B. movement back and forth
3. spectacle	C. obstacle
4. imported	D. viewpoint
5. sway	E. the beginning
6. aspect	F. from another country
7. stilted	G. pompous
8. dawn	H. assume
9. presume	I. impressive display

Q U I C K   Q U I Z   10

Matching

Match each word on the right with a word on the left that has a meaning that's close to the same.

1. imperious	A. faint
2. stammer	B. live with
3. embroider	C. stutter
4. grandeur	D. gloriousness
5. inquiry	E. regal
6. swoon	F. gruff
7. hoarse	G. investigation
8. hype	H. exaggeration
9. abide	I. stitch

Popo the Bandicoot

주머니쥐 포포

Cats, as you probably already know, do not like being thrown into water. I am no different; I've noticed that having wet, matted fur strips you of every *shred* of your dignity. But wet fur was the least of our troubles. Gorgas had placed us in quite a **predicament**. Not only were we floating in the water off of the coast of what appeared to be Caribbean island, but there was a naval battle going on less than a hundred yards away from us. We were all pretty shaken up, and fortunately some **flotsam**, probably wreckage from another sea battle, came drifting along, and we were able to grab hold of some boards and float.

One strange thing that we noticed immediately was that the ships in the battle looked like *antiques*. One was a Spanish **galleon**, a big ship with several sails that sailed the seas at least two or three hundred years ago, and the other was a smaller ship called a **schooner** that was flying the British flag—the Union Jack, I believe they call it. The schooner was getting the worst of it. The galleon was bombarding it with frequent **volleys** of cannon fire, and one of its sails was in flames; it looked like the Spanish ship would **prevail** before long.

At what appeared to be the last possible moment, the schooner made a break toward a little **inlet** on the shore of the island. They raced for the *cove* at full speed, and we were directly in their path!

"Ouch, Beauregard, stop scratching me," complained Bridget, who had been floating silently, trying to figure out what to do next. "I said quit it! Hey, which way do you think that ship's heading?"

Barnaby looked up. "You mean that schooner?" he asked. "Considering its original **bearing**, and seeing its position now, I would say that it's headed straight in our direction!"

MAT v. to become thickly tangled or knotted 헝클어지다
The swimmer's wet hair was matted together.
수영 선수의 젖은 머리카락이 한데 뒤엉켜 있었다.

SHRED n. strip or piece torn, cut or scraped from something 조각, 파편
The jacket was torn to shreds by the barbed wire.
재킷이 철조망에 걸려 갈갈이 찢어졌다.

ANTIQUE n. belonging to the distant past 골동품
This carved chest is a genuine antique.
이 조각 장식된 궤짝은 틀림없는 골동품이다.

COVE n. small bay; mouth of a creek 후미, 내포
A bay is usually smaller than a gulf and larger than a cove.
만(bay)은 보통 gulf보다는 작고 cove보다는 크다.

"Beauregard, please watch your claws," said Babette, rubbing her head. "Oh! Oh! That flaming ship is about to hit us! *Paddle* everyone; kick your legs! Hurry!"

Bridget and Barnaby started kicking and paddling—and not a moment too soon; the schooner *whizzed* by them, missing them by only a few feet.

"Thank goodness we're safe," sighed Bridget, as she watched the ship race to shore.

"Argh, that's what *you* think, *matey*," came a voice from above.

Bridget spun around and looked up. Right above her, attached to the front of the huge Spanish ship, hung a painted **figurehead**, carved in the shape of a beautiful woman with flowing gowns.

"I must be dreaming," said Bridget. "Did that figurehead just talk? And did it have a man's voice?"

"No, you sea-soaked *nitwit*. I'm over here," demanded the voice.

Standing on the deck of the galleon was a tall **buccaneer** with a striped shirt, a *bandanna* tied around his head, and a large gold hoop dangling from his left ear. The pirate's face was **ruddy** from sunburn and sea air and he wore an eye patch over his right eye.

"Wow, this is just like being in the movies," said Barnaby.

"Movies? What is a 'movies'?" asked the pirate. "No, I've no time to waste chatting with you. My name's Keelhaul McCall. *You* will call me Captain Keel. This is my boat—the *Ruffian*. I named it after myself, for sure as you're born, I'm the toughest outlaw on the seven seas."

Barnaby, Babette, and Bridget stared at him in fear, quite convinced that Captain Keel was the meanest **desperado** that had ever lived.

PADDLE v. to move through the water using a short oar   노 저어 나가다
We paddles the canoe slowly upstream.
우리는 상류로 천천히 카누를 노 저어 가고 있다.

WHIZ v. to make a sound like that of an object moving very fast through the air   쌩하고 지나가다
A bullet whizzed past my ear.
총알이 내 귀 옆을 쌩하고 지나갔다.

MATEY n. mate; fellow worker   친구
He's an old matey of mine.
그는 내 오랜 친구이다.

NITWIT n. stupid or foolish person   바보
Why did you do that, you nitwit?
왜 그 짓을 했니, 이 바보야?

BANDANNA n. large handkerchief with coloured spots   (목 · 머리용의) 스카프
He tied a bandanna round the neck.
그는 목에 스카프를 맸다.

"My men will be taking you prisoner now. There must be some relations hereabouts who would pay a few sacks of gold to have them back," remarked the captain to his men, who were climbing down rope ladders toward the water. "And, mateys, bring me that **mangy** black cat, as well; we'll clean it up and add it to the collection."

Beauregard was deeply hurt. His fur was just wet, after all, it wasn't patchy, but his expression was not nearly as **doleful** as were Bridget's, Babette's, and Barnaby's.

"Argh, *buck* up there, my hearties," urged Captain Keel, his voice softening a little. "You're in for some real excitement. That schooner made a big mistake when it went to hide in that inlet; we're going to form a **blockade** and then **besiege** it until it hands over what's rightfully ours!"

"I thought it took a whole **armada** to surround and attack a ship in harbor," remarked Barnaby, as though he knew what he was talking about. "And you only have *one* ship."

"Aye lad, you're right, it would take a *fleet* of *most* sorts of ships," said the captain, "but the *Ruffian* is the finest ship I've ever commanded. The Spanish admiral I stole it from put up quite a fight, but like I told you, I am the **scourge** of the seven seas, and my reputation helps me win my fights; As soon as any captain sees the flag of my ship on the horizon his teeth start to chatter!"

"Pardon me, Captain Keel, but what is it exactly that you want from that schooner?" asked Bridget, with the **utmost** politeness and care. She didn't want to make the captain angry.

"The captain of that ship was the **perpetrator** of an outrageous **heist**! He stole from me!" thundered the *pirate*. "And he is the worst kind of thief—he's a pirate who steals from other pirates. He is the lowest of the low!"

"But that ship is flying the Union Jack, are you sure they're pirates?" asked Barnaby.

BUCK v. (cause somebody to) become more cheerful 기운나게 하다
The good news bucked us all up.
그 멋진 소식이 우리 모두를 기운나게 해주었다.

FLEET n. group of warships, submarines, etc. under one commander 함대
The sixth fleet is based in San Francisco.
제 6함대는 샌프란시스코에 기지를 두고 있다.

PIRATE n. a person who attacks and robs ships 해적
He became one of the most fearful pirates operating in the West Indies.
그는 서인도 제도에서 활동하는 가장 무서운 해적 중에 한 명이 되었다.

"Boy, don't you think I know what I'm talking about? Every pirate ship owns several different flags, and the one they fly depends on which people they want to trick. Sailing a pirate ship is all about **ruses**, you see? It so happens that there is a British colony in Trinidad. That **rascal** of a stealing pirate is hoping that the soldiers who live in that **garrison** there will think that a British ship is under attack and will send out a whole **regiment** to help them," explained Captain Keel. "Now boy, do I make sense to you, or do still think that you know more about pirating than old Captain Keel?"

Barnaby was forced to **concede** that Captain Keel did know more about pirating, and that in all the excitement over the battle, he'd just gotten a little carried away. But a disturbing new thought began to occur to him as he was calming down. He turned to whisper to Bridget and Babette. "Hey, what was the last thing that Gorgas said? You don't suppose that we're really..."

"In the 1600s?" whispered Babette. "I think we must be. The waters of the Caribbean are usually **teeming** with tourists and motorboats, and I don't see any! I don't see any large cities along that coast, and by the way, Trinidad used to be a British colony. It isn't anymore, or at least it isn't supposed to be."

Beauregard cast a **wistful** gaze toward the shore, thinking of Consuela and the vacation he had missed.

"It would seem that your friend the cat is **yearning** to go ashore," laughed the captain. "I don't blame him; there's great fun to be had in Trinidad, but all in good time. First, I have *proposition* to make. That ship in the harbor holds a few things that are mine, and if you will fight with me and my men to get them back, you can join as members of our crew and share in the bounty that we win, and then I will let you go ashore. If you refuse, you will be my prisoners until I can get a good price for you... in one way or another."

Babette, Barnaby, and Bridget exchanged quick glances and found themselves in agreement.

PROPOSITION n. offer or arrangement which it is suggested that someone might be interested in   제안
He came to me one day with an extraordinary proposition.
어느 날 그가 정말 보기 드문 제안을 들고 나한테 왔다.

"Under the circumstances we'll fight with you," said Bridget. "But just out of curiosity, what exactly are we trying to get back?"

"I supposed it's only fair to tell you the whole story." said the captain, who strolled along the deck. "It's like this. There's a secret place called Hanged Man's Island that only I know how to find. It's there I keep my **cache** of treasures, deep in an underground cave. I also store extra food and fresh water there, and whenever my men and I need to **replenish** our supplies, that's where we go. Ah, it's a lovely island. Sometimes, just sometimes, I would invite a couple of other pirates, who I *deemed* to be relatively good fellows, to join us there for fine food and entertainment at my **bungalow**. It's a simple cottage with a **thatch** roof that I made by myself from palm leaves, but you couldn't ask for a nicer place for a dinner party. There's even a **verandah** that wraps all the way around the house where you can sit outside and enjoy the beautiful **vista**. I may be a rough buccaneer, but I am also quite a **connoisseur** when it comes to good food and wine. I know how to entertain, and believe me, after all the ships we've raided, I can afford the very finest of everything."

"Aren't you afraid those other pirates will come back and take you *booty* while you aren't there?" asked Bridget.

"Well, little missy, I never was before. Have you never heard the old **adage...** now how did that one go, hmmm... oh, yes, 'there's honor among thieves'?" asked Captain Keel. "In my many years as a pirate, I always found that that was true. Pirates don't raid other pirates' islands or boats. Besides, before I ever brought anyone there, I made them make a **pact** saying that they would never to speak of the island to another soul, nor reveal its *whereabouts*. That's what makes Singapore Sam's **transgression** so much worse than mere thievery. He has sinned against a fellow pirate."

"Is Singapore Sam the captain of the schooner?" asked Babette.

DEEM v. to consider; to regard 생각하다
He deemed that it was his duty to help.
그는 도와주는 것이 자기의 의무라고 생각했다.

BOOTY n. things taken by thieves or captured from an enemy in war; loot; plunder 노획물; 약탈품
They loaded the carts with booty.
그들은 노획물을 손수레에 가득 실었다.

WHEREABOUT n. place where somebody/something is 소재
We are looking for a man whose whereabout is unknown.
우리는 소재가 알려져 있지 않은 한 남자를 찾고 있다.

"Aye, that he is," growled the captain. "He was my guest at Hanged Man's Island and he betrayed me. He stole something from me that is more precious than gold and rubies. And as soon as I get my treasure back, I'm going to completely smash his ship with my cannon fire. No, I'll do more than that, I'll **incinerate** it. There will be nothing left of it but **cinders** and ash!"

Barnaby was about to ask what the valuable treasure was, but Captain Keel had already started shouting orders to his men, rushing about the ship, and generally preparing for battle.

"All right, mateys, bring the *Ruffian* in as close as you can. I want her **nigh** onto that schooner; near enough that we can tie onto her and jump across to her decks and take back what's ours. Are you with me?" he demanded.

The band of pirates let out a cheer of enthusiasm and turned the ship into the cove. The wind filled the sails and in no time, the *Ruffian* was **adjacent** to the schooner. Captain Keel had **deployed** his men all along the length of the galleon and as soon as they tied on they began *charging* the deck of the other ship, waving their *sabers* and **muskets** and **bellowing** like bee-stung bulls. But the other crew was ready for them. The air was filled with the *clang* and clash of swords, angry shouts, and smoke from firing muskets.

The three friends found themselves in the **midst** of this furious battle.

Bridget ducked and shielded her head with her arms and yelled, "Run for cover!"

Barnaby followed Bridget into an empty water barrel, but Babette stood her ground and showed them all just how much damage an expert in karate, judo, and several other secret *martial arts* can do to a bunch of clumsy pirates. She started by *flipping* several men over her shoulder and into the water. The other pirates were **flabbergasted**.

CHARGE v. to rush forward and attack 돌진하다
The troops charged at the enemy lines.
그 부대는 적의 전투 부대를 향해 돌격했다.

SABER n. heavy cavalry sword with a curved blade 사브르, 기병도(刀)
He fought with a saber.
그는 기병도(刀)를 갖고 싸웠다.

CLANG n. loud ringing sound of metal being struck 뗑그렁 소리
We can hear the clang of the school bell.
학교 종이 뗑그렁하고 울리는 소리를 들을 수 있다.

MARTIAL ARTS n. fighting sports such as judo, taekwondo, and karate 무술
Be sure to do warm-up before you do martial arts.
무술을 하기 전에 반드시 준비운동을 해라.

FLIP v. to toss with a sharp movement 휙 던지다
I flipped a coin in the air.
나는 동전을 공중으로 휙 던져 올렸다.

"She's just a **scrawny** little skinny kid," complained a rather thick-skulled **lout**, scratching his head in confusion. "How can she do that?"

"Let's get her!" urged on the his crewman and, *snarling*, he charged toward her.

Babette quickly **hobbled** him with a sharp kick to his left leg. As he tried to *limp* away, she *back-flipped* toward him and delivered a powerful kick to his chin. He **reeled** backward from the blow and fell over the edge of the ship. As soon as they saw how easily Babette had dealt with him, most of the enemies **dispersed** in search of easier prey.

On *foul-mouthed* sailor, however, refused to be **daunted** by her amazing fighting abilities. He **gnashed** his teeth together so hard it seemed they might break, then he shouted out several **expletives** so shocking that Babette blushed.

"Please," she objected, "I find such terrible language **repugnant**."

"I don't care what you find," he shouted, "just as long as the shot of my musket finds you!"

With that, the pirate lifted the musket to his shoulder and took aim directly at Babette. As soon as they saw that this new confrontation involved a gun, Bridget and Barnaby, who had been cheering on their friend from their hiding place, came tumbling out of the barrel and ran toward the pirate to *tackle* him.

But they were too late; he had fired the gun. In what seemed like the blink of an eye, Babette calmly removed her sunglasses and held them up above her shoulder. The musket ball bounced off of the lens and **ricocheted** off of the figurehead, hit the main mast, and then *rebounded* to hit the pirate in the shoulder, which forced him to drop his musket.

SNARL v. to show the teeth and growl angrily 으르렁거리다
The dog snarled at the milkman.
개가 우유 배달원에게 으르렁거렸다.

LIMP v. to walk unevenly, as when one foot or leg is hurt or stiff 절뚝거리며 걷다
That dog must be hurt—he's limping.
저 개는 다친 게 틀림없어. 절뚝거리며 걷고 있잖아.

BACK-FLIP n. a backward somersault, as in fancy diving 뒤로 도는 공중제비
I jerked out of the forward somersault into a back-flip.
나는 앞으로 도는 공중제비에서 뒤로 도는 공중제비로 갑자기 바꾸었다.

FOUL-MOUTHED adj. using obscene and offensive language 입이 거친
Tom is a foul-mouthed child.
탐은 입이 거친 아이이다.

TACKLE v. to grip physically; to lay hold of; to fasten upon; to seize or attack 달려들다, 공격하다
The policeman tackled the thief and threw him.
경찰관은 그 도둑에게 달려들어 쓰러뜨렸다.

REBOUND v. to spring or bounce back after hitting something 되돌아가다, 되튀기다
The ball rebounded from the wall into the pond.
공이 벽을 맞고 되돌아 나와 연못으로 들어갔다.

"Ow!" he yelled, and turned to run.

"Those are some incredible sunglasses, Babette," remarked Bridget. "No wonder you always wear them."

Babette nodded mysteriously, and at the same time they heard a distant and enraged *yowl* that they recognized as coming from Beauregard. The three friends immediately ran over to see what was the matter. Captain Keel was **grappling** with a big man with a *peg leg* and Beauregard, who was stuck in-between them, was desperately trying to **extricate** himself from the fight by furiously clawing. To make matters more confusing, a beautiful parrot with bright green plumage, which was tied to the peg-legged pirate's shoulder, was flapping frantically about their heads.

"You monstrously nasty cat!" *wheezed* the peg-legged man in a **rasping**, gravely voice.

"Pieces of eight! Pieces of eight!" squawked the frightened parrot.

"Someone slap a **muzzle** on that bird's beak," grunted Captain Keel. "I'm tired of its talk. Say, young mateys, how about giving me a hand here? I'm running out of steam, and my back is killing me!"

Babette jumped in and made short work of the peg-legged pirate. After a couple of well placed kicks, he was tumbling into the sea with the rest of his crew.

"Ha, ha! you *lily-livered* cowards!" shouted Captain Keel in triumph, mocking and **flouting** at the swimming sailors. "That'll show you not to cross me, Sam! And I want you to know that I'm going to go over every inch of my galleon and make a careful **assessment** of the damages. You're going to pay **reparations** for all of your treachery!"

YOWL n. loud wailing cry   울부짖음
I can hear the dog's yowl.
개가 울부짖는 소리를 들을 수 있다.

Peg Leg n. artificial legs, usually wooden   의족
His left leg is a peg leg.
그의 왼쪽 다리는 의족이다.

WHEEZE v. to say while breathing noisily or with difficulty   씨근거리며 말하다
'I've got a sore throat,' he wheezed.
'나는 목이 아파' 라고 그가 힘들게 말했다.

LILY-LIVERED adj. cowardly   겁 많은
It was lily-livered of you not to admit your mistake.
네 실수를 인정하지 않았다니 겁이 많았구나.

Singapore Sam and his *soggy* crewmen shook their fists and shouted angry curses, but Captain Keel just ignored them and turned to Babette.

"Ouch," he grumbled, rubbing his back, "my **rheumatism** must be acting up. That always happened when a storm is about to blow through. I can feel the weather in my bones."

"Are you sure your back isn't just sore from fighting?" asked Barnaby.

"Look, child, a little **exertion** never hurt Keelhaul McCall," growled the captain. "Can't you feel the **gale** that's whipping the sails? The wind is really picking up; we'd better hurry and collect the treasure."

Barnaby stared out toward the great **expanse** of ocean, which stretched as far as he could see. Sure enough, in the distance there was a vivid sunset that filled the sky with deep red, bright purple and blue. The huge clouds glowed with such **radiance** that it almost hurt the eyes to look at them. Barnaby had read plenty of sailor stories and knew that a sunset like that meant trouble ahead.

"By the way, that was some job you did handling Sam's men," said Captain Keel to Babette. "I'd be proud to have you as a member of my crew."

"It wasn't really difficult," answered Babette *modestly*. "You see, their attack was so **haphazard** and disorganized. It's easy to defeat a group as *sloppy* as that one."

"Not so easy, my hearty," said the captain. "But let's discuss that another time. Now we must make sure that the *Ruffian* is safely **moored** so she won't blow away in the storm. Come with me—your friends, too. My men will secure the ship while we board the schooner. I think you'll be surprised at what we find there."

SOGGY adj. very wet 흠뻑 젖은, 물에 잠긴
The ground was soggy after heavy rain.
폭우가 내린 뒤에 운동장은 물에 잠겼다.

MODESTLY adv. not thinking too highly of oneself; not vainly; humbly   겸손하게
In spite of the honors he received, the scientist behaved modestly.
존경을 받고 있음에도 불구하고 그 과학자는 겸손하게 행동했다.

SLOPPY adj. careless and untidy in the way he does things   느슨한
We can clear up some of our own sloppy thinking on the subject.
우리는 그 문제에 대한 우리의 느슨한 생각을 고칠 수 있다.

Surprise was not the word to describe what they felt; sadness and **despair** were more like it. The schooner's cabins were packed full of rare and unusual animals that were being kept in **wretched** conditions. Every **berth** contained at least two creatures, and the floors were completely covered with straw and **muck**, and looked like they hadn't been cleaned in weeks. The poor animals, frightened by the fighting, were *bleating*, howling, crying, and scurrying around in a **frenzy**.

"Captain Keel," said Bridget with horror, "I can't even find the words to tell you how much I **deplore** what you've done to these poor animals."

"Child, I'm as **appalled** as you are," said the captain, shaking his head. "This little schooner is far too small to **accommodate** all of these animals comfortably. These animals were perfectly healthy when I kept them. I looks like these *cramped*, dirty conditions have caused their health to **deteriorate** *drastically*."

Beauregard had begun to walk through the cabins. He stopped to look at the dodo bird from Australia and the indri from Madagascar. He paused by the *bunk* of the duck-billed platypus and the three-toed sloth. Dangerous **predators** like the mountain lion and the polar bear welcomed him and didn't seem interested in eating him at all. The big black cat even walked to the kitchen to check on the butterflies who were shut in the scullery. The animals all seemed comforted by his presence.

"But why did you capture all of these animals?" asked Barnaby.

"Well, now, I'll tell you, but you probably won't believe me," the captain started. "You see, I was visited by a strange being from the heavens who came down and told me that many of these animals were being hunted and killed to the point that they were becoming nearly **extinct**. He told me that the environment was in danger of..."

"Keelhaul!" boomed a deep voice from the deck above. "Are you down there? Where are my animals?"

BLEAT v. to say, speak or cry feebly or plaintively   하소연하듯 말하거나 울다; 푸념하다, 우는 소리를 하다
What are you bleating about?
뭐라고 우는 소리를 하는 거야?

CRAMPED adj. narrow and restricted   비좁은
Our accommodations are rather cramped.
우리의 숙박 시설은 다소 비좁다.

DRASTICALLY adv. very seriously; extremely; vigorously   심하게, 과감하게
The police drastically took measures to put a stop to the wave of robberies.
경찰은 강력하게 강도 열풍을 근절시킬 대책을 취했다.

BUNK n. narrow bed built into a wall like a shelf   (벽에 부착된) 침대, 침상
Sailors sleep in bunks.
선원들은 벙크에서 잔다.

Bridget, Barnaby, and Babette exchanged **perplexed** glances. They were not sure what to think. Could it be Gorgas? Had he returned for them? What did he want with the animals?

"Quick, quick, now, let's all get up on deck," urged Captain Keel with fear in his voice.

The children followed the captain up the ladder and onto the deck. Standing or hovering near the mast was an alien with a huge green head, ten tentacles, and a dozen blinking eyes. The purple cape he wore flapped in the stiff evening breeze.

"Gorgas!" shouted Bridget. "What do you mean by sending us back three hundred years? That was not very polite!"

"Excuse me?" asked the alien. "Did you just call me Gorgas? How insulting. I am Vargas, a far wiser being. The fact that you have only two eyes must affect your ability to see clearly. Gorgas's hair is an unattractive black color, while mine, you will notice, is a fashionable and distinguished white."

The alien tilted his huge head to display a long mane of **hoary** hair.

"Vargas, sir, I was just explaining your plan to save the endangered ecosystems of the world to these crew members," offered the captain. "Why don't you tell them about all of the natural communities of animals and plants you will be *preserving*?"

"Ecosystem? What do I care about the Earth's... oh, yes, that," said Vargas. "Well, there's been a slight change of plans, old boy. I'll tell you what, I'll still pay you those bars of gold, if you hand over one platypus and one of those birds whose feathers have that odd, pink **pigment**. I think they're called flamingos? Yes, I'd like a flamingo please."

Captain Keel climbed below the deck and returned with the animals. Vargas *coiled* his tentacles tightly around them.

PRESERVE v. to make something remain the way it is, and protect it from changing or stopping   보존하다, 지키다
We are interested in preserving world peace.
우리는 세계평화를 지키는 데 관심이 있다.

COIL v. to curve into a continuous series of loops or into the shape of a ring   돌돌 감다
The cat coiled round his legs.
고양이는 다리를 모아 감았다.

"But what about the other animals, Vargas?" asked the captain.

"My dear fellow, that's your affair. I wouldn't dare tell you what to do with them," said Vargas. "Well, I hate to be **antisocial**—but I have more important things to do than sit around here chatting. Also, I need to use this boat, so I'm afraid you and all of the animals will have to jump overboard."

Vargas *slithered* over to Captain Keel and knocked him over the edge of the ship. He was heading toward Barnaby when a *stampede* of animals came rushing out from under the deck in a tidal wave of feathers and fur with Beauregard leading them! Vargas was so taken **aback** that he dropped the platypus and the flamingo.

Barnaby wasted no time. He jumped straight at the surprised alien's head!

Vargas was either sweating or **secreting** something slippery from his *scalp*, because he had a terrible time hanging on. But no matter. He only needed to keep his grip for a couple of seconds; just long enough for Popo the bandicoot to do his job.

A bandicoot, in case you don't know, is a rather large East Indian rat. And what, you might well ask, was I doing cheering on with a rat? Ordinary cats, I must admit, do not look fondly upon rats and their **brethren**, mice. But I am a free-thinking cat, and I try to view all animals equally. Even dogs. Besides, it was Popo who came up with the plan to steal Vargas's wand. Apparently, the little bandicoot had once seen Vargas pull a stick just like Gorgas's out from under his cape. My job was to *distract* the alien while Popo scrambled under his cape to fetch it.

SLITHER v. to slide or slip unsteadily 주르르 미끄러지다
The snake slithered into the grass as we approached.
우리가 다가가자 그 뱀은 풀속으로 스르르 미끄러지듯 들어갔다.

STAMPEDE n. sudden wild rush or mass movement of people 놀라서 우하고 달아남, 앞을 다투어 달아남, 우하고 몰려옴, 쇄도
There was a stampede towards the stage when the singer appeared.
가수가 나타나자 무대 쪽으로 우하고 군중들이 몰려 들었다.

SCALP n. skin of the head excluding the face 머리 가죽
His scalp is very smooth.
그의 두피는 아주 매끄럽다.

DISTRACT v. to draw away (the mind or attention) 분산시키다
Don't distract my attention—I'm trying to study!
내 주의를 분산시키지 마. 공부하려고 애쓰고 있잖아!

At first, Vargas was so upset that Barnaby was clinging to his head that Popo had no trouble scurrying under his cape in search of the wand, and he slipped off as soon as Popo had scrambled safely away. Babette, always quick and as **nimble** as an *acrobat*, flipped across the deck with lightning speed and sent Vargas flying into the sea with one of her kicks. As soon as we were free of the alien, Popo, who assured me that he knew exactly what he was doing, began waving the wand.

The schooner slowly rose out of the water and into the air. The strong winds from the coming storm blew around us, **circulating** faster and faster. Before we knew it, we were caught up in a *funnel* of wind. And there was no telling where the **cyclone** would drop us.

ACROBAT n. person who performs difficult or unusual physical acts   곡예사
The acrobat on the trampoline was performing somersaults.
그 곡예사는 트램폴린 위에서 공중제비를 하고 있었다.

FUNNEL n. tube or pipe that is wide at the top and narrow at the bottom, used for pouring liquids, powders, etc. into a small opening
깔때기
I need a funnel to pour petrol into the tank.
탱크 안에 휘발유를 넣기 위해서는 깔때기가 필요하다.

Q U I C K   Q U I Z   11

Relationships

Decide what relationship the following pairs of words have to each other. If they mean close to the same thing, make "S." If they have opposite meanings, mark "O."

1. ruffian :: desperado
2. disperse :: amass
3. appall :: please
4. musket :: rifle
5. connoisseur :: novice
6. perplex :: mystify
7. expletive :: curse
8. adage :: motto
9. deteriorate :: improve
10. brethren :: siblings
11. scourge :: savior
12. antisocial :: friendly

Q U I C K   Q U I Z   12

Relationships

Decide what relationship the following pairs of words have to each other. If they mean close to the same thing, make "S." If they have opposite meanings, mark "O."

1. regiment :: garrison
2. extinct :: thriving
3. wistful :: yearning
4. pact :: treaty
5. prevail :: fail
6. flabbergasted :: composed
7. predator :: prey
8. rasping :: scratching
9. muck :: slime
10. nimble :: clumsy
11. despair :: hopelessness
12. repugnant :: attractive

Q U I C K   Q U I Z   13

Fill in the Blank

For each sentence below, choose the word that best completes the sentence.

1. I thought the seaside cottage looked beautiful, although we did have to replace the _____ on the roof before we moved in.

    a. bungalow   b. verandah   c. thatch   d. scullery

2. Believing the fish to be swimming closer to the bottom than usual, the fishermen _____ their nets deeper than they would usually.

    a. confronted   b. deployed   c. exerted   d. grappled

3. Spending thirty minutes outside building a snowman with my family gave my face a _____ glow.

    a. ruddy   b. mangy   c. scrawny   d. hoary

4. Luckily for the bank teller, the _____ caused when the robber's bullet hit the bank vault, a camera, and a potted plant eventually ended up striking the burglar's own arm.

   a. volley   b. muzzle   c. ricochet   d. plumage

5. I had hope to _____ my new magazine all over the world, but unfortunately only my parents seemed interested in reading it.

   a. bombard   b. gnash   c. circulate   d. extricate

6. After the powder keg exploded, the only evidence left that there was once a raft at all were some pieces of torn sail and _____ .

   a. buccaneer   b. schooner   c. figurehead   d. flotsam

7. Since the vessels in the Lithuanian _____ outnumbered their enemy by nine to one, the Lithuanians were almost certain of their upcoming victory.

   a. galleon   b. armada   c. blockade   d. heist

8. Since the next convenience store was 173 miles away, my brother and I decided to _____ our supply of Twinkies for the road trip.

   a. replenish   b. besiege   c. flout   d. bellow

9. After the last-second touchdown, the _____ fans rushed the field and began tearing down the goalposts.

   a. vivid   b. wretched   c. adjacent   d. frenzied

10. Fearing high winds and a possible hurricane, we _____ our boat to the pier with the strongest rope we could find.

   a. incinerated   b. unfurled   c. conceded   d. moored

11. When Sally saw that her blind date was made of paper-mâche, she knew that she was the victim of a horrible _____ .

   a. ruse   b. lout   c. gale   d. midst

12. Chris was embarrassed by his sister at school because she _____ a horrible scent whenever someone made her angry.

   a. secreted   b. deplored   c. reeled   d. hobbled

Q U I C K   Q U I Z   14

Matching

Match each word on the right with a word on the left that has a meaning that's close to the same.

1. nigh	A. view
2. cinders	B. joint disease
3. vista	C. water passage
4. doleful	D. environment
5. ecosystem	E. violation
6. utmost	F. almost
7. rheumatism	G. manner
8. accommodate	H. ash
9. inlet	I. help
10. transgression	J. bind
11. bearing	K. bright glow
12. predicament	L. sad
13. radiance	M. greatest degree

Matching

Match each word on the right with a word on the left that has a meaning that's close to the same.

1. aback
2. cache
3. expanse
4. pigment
5. teem
6. haphazard
7. daunted
8. assessment
9. reparations
10. cyclone
11. perpetrator
12. berth
13. rascal

A. secret supply
B. cowed
C. twister
D. surprised
E. law breaker
F. swarm
G. ship bed
H. open space
I. analysis
J. prankster
K. dye
L. repayment
M. disorganized

Dr. Borges and the Library of the Infinite Fiction

보그스 박사와 무한한 허구의 도서관

Where we wound up was unlike any place or time I had ever seen. At first it looked like we had been sucked into a **void**. I thought we were back in outer space, but then I realized that there were no stars. We knew one thing for sure, and that was that we weren't anywhere on the Earth. There was nothing **terrestrial** about it.

The schooner was drifting through the black emptiness and we all waited in silence, wondering whether we had been plunged into a deep **abyss** or hurled to the absolute end of the universe. Then, in the distance, a large, glowing object appeared. It was a tower, a huge ivory tower that far exceeded any tower we'd ever seen in size. It was covered in **exquisitely** beautiful and elaborately detailed carvings of flowers, animals and historical scenes. Their detail was amazing; the art was more breathtaking than the work of the Earth's greatest masters. We were drifting right toward it, which caused us all great alarm; there didn't appear to be any door or other means of access to the tower, and I feared that we would just crash straight into it.

Everyone aboard the ship, including the animals, stood as still as statues, **transfixed** with wonder and fright. Just as we were about to smash into the tower, my tail began *twitching* in uncontrollable **spasms.** I tried unsuccessfully to stifle a yowl of fright that was threatening to escape my throat and there I stood, twitching and yowling rather embarrassingly while everyone else hit the deck and covered their heads.

But at the last moment a **rift** appeared in the tower. It was a narrow **fissure**, but its dimensions were such that we were just able to fit through it. I heaved a mighty sigh and stopped screeching. My terror was **quelled**—for the moment, that is.

TWITCH v. to move with a quick jerk   (손가락, 근육 따위가) 씰룩거리다
The dog's nose twitched as it smelt the meat.
개의 코가 고기 냄새를 맡으면서 씰룩거렸다.

"Whoa!" yelled Bridget, with relief. "I thought we were going to have to **evacuate** the ship!"

"What good would it have done to jump off?" asked Barnaby, who, like Bridget, was still lying down on the deck. "There would have been nowhere else to go!"

"On the **contrary**, young man!" echoed a strange voice.

Barnaby, Babette, and Bridget stood up and looked around them. They were in the most gigantic library they'd ever seen. There were shelves that spiraled like *corkscrews* along the walls as far up as they could see, but this library was not neat and orderly like any libraries they had visited before. The shelves were extremely **cluttered**; they were *crammed* with a random arrangement of papers, notes, magazines, postcards, and books. Creeping, flowering vines and other plants were growing out of the shelves themselves, and on some shelves the **foliage** was so thick that you couldn't even see what was on them. But the strangest thing of all was that the whole library was in **flux**, objects were changing and moving around them at all times. New papers appeared on shelves as others disappeared, some books became thinner while others grew fat, all of the contents of one shelf would suddenly move to another. A flower suddenly blossomed with amazing speed: The three friends felt dizzy just looking around.

"Uh, what do you mean, on the contrary?" asked Barnaby, determined to keep hold of himself this time.

"I mean that what you said before is quite wrong," replied the voice in a **peculiar** accent. "The reason that I **contradict** what you said is because if you *had* jumped off of the ship, there would have been somewhere to go, which is here! But I don't mean to be **contentious**. I do hate to **quibble** or argue."

"Who are you, where are you, and where are we?" asked Babette.

"Patience, please. I'm coming down," said the voice, which did sound a little closer.

CORKSCREW n. device for pulling corks from bottles 타래송곳 (코르크 마개 뽑는 용)
It's necessary to use a corkscrew to open the bottle.
그 병을 여는 데는 타래송곳이 필요하다.

CRAM v. to push, force too much of something into something 채워 넣다, 밀어 넣다, 쑤셔 넣다
The room's full; we can't cram anymore people in.
방이 가득 찼다. 더 이상 사람들을 안으로 밀어 넣을 수가 없다.

Babette looked up. Something was rustling along one of the shelves above her, and slowly circling down the spiral. Finally they saw a man rumbling toward them on a rolling library ladder, which was attached at the top to a smooth, shiny brass rail that was **burnished** by many years of use. It came to a halt beside the ship and the man jumped off.

At first glance, he looked very old. He had a long, pointy white beard and although his hairline had **receded**, he still *sported* a *shock* of bushy, white hair. He looked oddly familiar to Babette. He wore a *rumpled*, brown tweed jacket and thick glasses that were pushed down low on his nose. His face was wrinkled, but the way he jumped off the ladder and walked toward them was so **spry** that it seemed like he couldn't be as ancient as they had at first thought.

"My, my," he remarked, "I am surprised you could travel in such a **dilapidated** ship. You really should take better care of it. It's practically falling apart!"

"It's not really our ship," offered Bridget.

"Ah, yes, you're the pirates then," said the man, *stroking* his beard.

"Well, not exactly, but sort of, I guess," said Bridget, "My name is Bridget, and these are my friends, Babette, Barnaby, and Beauregard. I'm afraid I don't know any of the names of the other animals. We just rescued them."

"Lovely!" exclaimed the man. "My name is Dr. Borges, and this is my library. Do you mind if I come aboard and visit the animals? I so rarely get visitors."

Dr. Borges did not wait for permission. He climbed onto the deck with ease, and began to chatter, click, whinny, and hoot like a *lunatic* at every animal he saw. He kept it up for quite a while and the animals seemed to find him very amusing.

SPORT v. to have or wear proudly for others to see 뽐내다
She sported her diamond ring.
그녀는 자신의 다이아몬드 반지를 뽐냈다.

SHOCK n. rough untidy mass of hair on the head 엉클어진 털, 흐트러진 머리칼
He has a shock of red hair.
그는 빨간색 엉클어진 머리카락의 소유자다.

RUMPLE v. to make creased or untidy; to crumple 구겨지게 하다
Don't play in your new dress; you'll rumple it.
새 옷 입고 놀지 마라. 구겨질 거야.

STROKE v. to move the hand gently over 쓰다듬다
She likes to stroke her kitten.
그 여자는 자기 고양이 쓰다듬는 것을 좋아한다.

LUNATIC n. an insane person 미친 사람
Lunatics are often put in insane asylums.
미친 사람들은 종종 정신 병원에 보내진다.

"He seems to be **fluent** in the language of every animal!" remarked Babette with admiration. "It must have been hard to master so many languages."

"Wonderful!" laughed Dr. Borges as he approached the three children. "That little flamingo **fledgling** over there—that little one just old enough to fly—just told the funniest joke about a chicken crossing a road. It's amazing that he has such a sense of humor after what they've all been through. Those dragonfly **larvae** were **ailing** from sea sickness."

"How can you talk to larvae?" asked Barnaby. "They aren't even fully developed insects yet."

"You should be the last person to doubt that young creatures have opinions," replied Dr. Borges. "Most **organisms**, from tiny *bugs* to giant whales, have opinions. In any event, the main complaint from these fellows is that they've been taken from their homes and are finding their new surroundings uncomfortable. They're glad that you rescued them, of course, but they are still unhappy to be so far away from their homes."

"That polar bear, for example, is from the icy **tundra** of the arctic with its vast plains of snow. The Caribbean sun was melting him! And that poor sheep was beginning to shed all of her beautiful **fleece** in the heat."

"It is a lucky thing that we came along," agreed Barnaby. "I also noticed that the animals from **arid**, desert climates weren't reacting well to the dark and damp in the *hull* of the ship. It's very difficult for an animal to thrive outside of its normal climate."

Just then, a tiny canary **alighted** on Dr. Borges's shoulder and twittered something in his ear.

"Yes, I suppose you must be curious about the library," said the *librarian* in response.

"Curious? Yes, we are curious, too," Babette said eagerly. "Dr. Borges, just standing here in your library has been a very strange experience. I believe I am suffering from **delusions**. My eyes might be playing tricks on me, but it seems like your tower is growing and changing all around us!"

BUG n. a crawling insect with a pointed beak for piercing and sucking   벌레
There are a lot of bugs around here.
이 근처에는 벌레들이 많다.

HULL n. body of a ship   선체
The masts, yards, sails, and riggings are not part of the hull.
돛대나 활대, 돛, 삭구는 선체의 일부가 아니다.

LIBRARIAN n. a person in charge of or assisting in a library   사서, 도서관원
He is a good librarian.
그는 훌륭한 사서이다.

"I have noticed that as well," added Barnaby, "but I can't even begin to **fathom** what might be causing it."

Meanwhile, Bridget, who was always very easily distracted, had wandered off and was poking around in some of the bookshelves.

"Hey, Doc!" she called. "This is quite a **copious** collection you have. I've never seen so many different kinds of books; you have very **eclectic** taste in literature; there are *biographies*, histories, medical books, essays, college term papers, letters, and tons of great **fiction**. I think fiction is my favorite **genre**. I mean, poetry and plays and factual books are fine and all, but made-up stories are the best kind."

"Well, my collection might seem eclectic, but this is actually not an accurate representation of my tastes," explained Dr. Borges. "This library is just a **cumulative** collection from my lifetime."

"You mean that stuff keeps getting added to it?" asked Bridget.

"That's exactly what you see going on around you," he said, nodding. "Additions are being made to some volumes when new knowledge is gained, and information that has been proved to be inaccurate is being removed from other volumes. The **philosophy** section is always growing the fastest. It seems people never tired of writing about the meaning of life and truth and all that. New volumes might be added to a series, a new chapter **appended** to an old book. Most things seem to get longer and more detailed—rarely are things **abridged**. Actually, that introduces an interesting **paradox**, which I have wondered about for ever so long."

"What kind of paradox?" asked Bridget with interest.

MEANWHILE adv. while a particular thing is happening   그동안
She ate an olive and tried to sit still. Nick, meanwhile, was talking about Rose.
그녀는 올리브를 먹고 조용히 앉아 있으려고 했다. 그동안 닉은 로즈에 대해 이야기를 했다.

BIOGRAPHY n. an account of somebody's life that has been written by someone else   전기
I have been asked to write a biography of Dylan Thomas.
나는 딜런 토마스의 전기를 써달라는 부탁을 받았다.

"You see, this is the Library of the **Infinite** Fiction. It's infinite because it's endless; it goes on forever. It has existed forever, here on the edge of time and space, and contains a record of all the thoughts and experiences that have ever occurred in the whole universe. Everything that has ever been written, everything that you can even imagine being written, is here. Even things that haven't been written yet are here," said the librarian. "And yet, it keeps growing."

"Hey, it can't be infinite *and* be growing at the same time," Barnaby said, thinking out loud, "because something that's infinite already extends far beyond the realm of the imagination in size."

"That's the paradox! An infinite, yet growing library—it contradicts itself," exclaimed Bridget. "It's a paradox just like that old song that goes, '*You've got to be cruel to be kind.*'"

Bridget began singing the song and dancing around wildly, and Dr. Borges immediately joined her, singing in a **reedy** voice that squeaked like a clarinet. Bridget started in on the second verse while running and doing cartwheels, but Borges begged her to stop.

"Please, I **implore** you, no more." gasped the librarian, who was turning red in the face. "Not that I don't like your singing, but I'm afraid I find it impossible to **repress** the urge to dance whenever I hear music. I just can't stop myself. The problem is, I'm not used to dancing anymore. Whew! Give me a couple of minutes to **recuperate**. I'm *beat*."

Bridget stopped her **romping**. She was still giggly and excited about the paradox, but out of respect for the old librarian, she tried to appear **tranquil**. After a few seconds, however, her curiosity got the better of her.

"Dr. Borges, what did you mean when you called this the Library of the Infinite *Fiction*? There's a lot more than fiction here," asked Bridget.

BEAT adj. tired out; exhausted 지친
I'm dead beat.
나는 완전히 지쳤다.

"The explanation is a bit complicated, but I'll try to make it clear," he began, as his face started to become a normal color again. "You see, the history of time and all of the events in the universe are like a big story. And, in a way, we all make it up as we go along. Or, if you look at it another way, we are all characters in the story that's unfolding. Either way, it's an unending tale."

"You're right, that is a **convoluted** explanation," said Barnaby suspiciously. "Is that another one of your paradoxes? We are characters and authors at the same time? Why don't you tell us what's really going on?"

"Barnaby, there is no need to be **insolent**," whispered Babette. "Show a little respect for your elders. A man as smart as he is deserves some **reverence**."

Dr. Borges smiled an **indulgent** smile, as if Barnaby's little outburst amused him more than it offended him.

"It seems I would have a hard time making a **disciple** out of you!" laughed the librarian. "You wouldn't want to be a follower of an old man who can't even provide a **coherent** explanation of how his own home operates. Such a sharp scientific mind you have! However, young man, there are more ways to study the universe than merely looking at tiny **molecules** of matter under microscopes."

"There are no events so strange, no facts so odd, no **phenomena** so weird that science can't come up with a *workable* explanation for them," **asserted** Barnaby with confidence, even stomping his foot to make his point more **emphatic**.

"Well, now, Barnaby, I'd have to agree that scientists can come up with **viable** explanations for a lot of things," smiled Dr. Borges. "I'm sure you can **cite** many examples to prove your point— as you see it. I admire the strength of your **convictions**. It's good to have strong beliefs, and I wouldn't want to be accused of trying to **debunk** yours. You know you remind me of a boy I once knew, long, long ago."

WORKABLE adj. that can be worked; that can be used or put into effect; practicable   그럴듯한
It's a workable plan.
그것은 그럴듯한 계획이다.

Dr. Borges sighed and shook his bushy head.

"Anyway, why don't we just call my explanations **avant-garde**, okay? I am, after all, always slightly ahead of my time," he said. "For the sake of simplicity, let's just say that some of the books in this library are **prophetic**. They tell of events that have not happened yet. I was just reading one a little while ago, which is how I found out that a pirate ship was heading my way. That's how I knew to open the tower. But the book contained other **revelations** that I must tell you about. For example, the book revealed that you and your friend Beauregard must rescue the Earth from destruction! More than once, in fact."

"Wait a minute, now, Dr. Borges," said Bridget. "We're just kids. I can't imagine a possible **scenario** that would involve us saving the world. Are you sure that revelation was *reliable*?"

"I am absolutely certain of its **authenticity**," replied Dr. Borges. "Do you, or do you not, know of a couple of ten-armed travelers names Gorgas and Vargas?"

"Uh oh," said Barnaby. "I'm almost afraid to hear this."

"Maybe we should have gone to the Metropolitan Museum of Art instead of the Yankees game," groaned Bridget.

The librarian continued, "You see, Gorgas and Vargas are the bitterest of rivals. They used to be private investigators back on their home planet of Smeltvlat. People from planets all around would hire them to track down lost people and property. But what started as simple professional competition turned into a **monstrous**, horrible battle that has spread ruin and **devastation** across many planets. They began *betting* with each other, challenging each other with impossible tasks that were designed to prove which one was the best at *tracking down* rare and unique things; they would stop at nothing to win these bets. The people of Smeltvlat finally got sick of their games and kicked them off of the planet. Now these dangerous **pariahs** are looking for a new world to call home."

RELIABLE adj. consistently good in quality or performance, and so deserving trust; dependable 믿을 만한
My memory's not very reliable these days.
내 기억력은 요즘 믿을 만한 것이 못된다.

BETTING n. the act of making a wager or bet 내기
Betting was very fashionable in the 18th century.
내기는 18세기에 꽤 유행이었다.

TRACK v. (track down의 형태로 쓰여) to find somebody/something by searching 찾아내다
I finally tracked down the reference in a dictionary of quotations.
나는 마침내 인용 사전에서 인용문을 찾아냈다.

Babette, Bridget, and Barnaby listened with horror.

"Sure, at first their little *scavenger* hunts were harmless," Dr. Borges went on. "But gradually, Gorgas and Vargas both developed a state for power and wealth, as you have already seen. Unfortunately for the people of the Earth, they've decided that your planet is full of the weirdest plants, animals, sports, food, clothes, and customs in the whole universe. They have agreed that the one who can capture the most *bizarre* specimens in the shortest amount of time will win the right to rule Earth."

"I told you that Gorgas was after world **dominion**!" shrieked Babette.

Bridget and Barnaby were too shocked to speak.

"I know that this is a lot to chew on," said the librarian. "You must believe that Gorgas and Vargas would never give up this battle. Either of them would rather destroy your planet than turn it over to his rival. But you will have a hard time stopping them. Yes, a very hard time. Most, most difficult..."

Dr. Borges scratched his head and paced.

"It is a good thing that Popo thought to steal that wand from Vargas," he said, still pacing and scratching. "You'll need a way to travel back and forth through time. They could be anywhere. Let's see, I had something around here that might help you. Maybe I left it in this **nook** over here. Let me see..."

"How can there be a hidden corner in a circular building?" asked Babette.

Barnaby just shrugged. He wasn't about to start worrying about contradictions again.

"Nope," mumbled the librarian. "Hey, maybe I... ouch! My foot!"

SCAVENGER n. animal that searches for decaying flesh as food 썩은 고기를 먹는 청소 동물
Vultures, jackals, and some snails and beetles are scavengers.
대머리수리, 재칼, 달팽이, 딱정벌레는 썩은 고기를 먹는 동물이다.

BIZARRE adj. strange in appearance or effect; grotesque; eccentric 기괴한
The frost made bizarre patterns on the windowpanes.
서리가 창문에 기괴한 무늬를 만들었다.

Babette and Bridget almost fell over with surprise. A long metal tube, shining with a soft golden **luster**, had just fallen out of Dr. Borges's hair and hit his foot.

"Hey, I know how you feel," laughed Barnaby, patting his own *mop* of hair as the librarian hopped on one foot.

"Aha! Here it is," said Dr. Borges, stooping down to pick up the tube. "It's a **kaleidoscope**, you see, but not an ordinary one. With most kaleidoscopes, you look in one end and twist the tube and see beautiful shapes and colors shifting around together. But this one shows you different places and people shifting around together. It shows you the future, and sometimes the shapes and colors aren't that beautiful. Here, give it a try!"

He handed the tube to Barnaby, who held it up to the light and twisted the bottom. At first, he saw nothing but smoke and clouds. But slowly a figure began to **manifest** itself. It was Gorgas! He was slithering up the side of a steaming volcano. But he wasn't the only big green monster that the kaleidoscope showed.

"I don't know if this will sound **plausible** to you," said Barnaby, placing the tube on a shelf, "but you have to believe me because it's true. Gorgas is back in the time of the dinosaurs. I have no idea what he's up to, but we'd better stop him!"

Beauregard, who had been having a wonderful deck party with his animal friends, picked up the kaleidoscope and looked for himself. He returned to visit with Popo the bandicoot briefly, then returned to his human friends.

And in his mouth was Popo's magic wand.

MOP n. (a mop of hair의 형태로 쓰여) a thick, tangled, or unruly hair 더벅머리
Look at the mop of curly red hair.
저 곱실거리는 빨간색 더벅머리를 봐라.

QUICK QUIZ 16

Relationships

Decide what relationship the following pairs of words have to each other. If they mean close to the same thing, make "S." If they have opposite meanings, mark "O."

1. recede :: ebb
2. elaborate :: plain
3. plausible :: likely
4. thrive :: devastate
5. stifle :: repress
6. fiction :: reality
7. contentious :: congenial
8. assert :: contend
9. dilapidated :: exquisite
10. contrary :: stubborn

QUICK QUIZ 17

Relationships

Decide what relationship the following pairs of words have to each other. If they mean close to the same thing, make "S." If they have opposite meanings, mark "O."

1. pariah :: outcast
2. ailing :: recuperating
3. infinite :: boundless
4. quibble :: bicker
5. tranquil :: agitated
6. coherent :: chaotic
7. fissure :: rift
8. insolent :: courteous
9. reverence :: disgust
10. avant-garde :: innovative

QUICK QUIZ 18

Fill in the Blank

For each sentence below, choose the word that best completes the sentence.

1. The scientists hoped their new invention could use electricity to extract all the _____ of gold from sea water.

   a. molecules   b. organisms   c. foliage   d. fleeces

2. Although many researchers had already _____ his idea as pure make-believe, Professor Strock still insisted his Gravity-is-a-Lie theory was true.

   a. implored   b. abridged   c. debunked   d. transfixed

3. Difficult as it was, climbing out of the north side of the canyon was the only _____ option for escape, since the enemy army was advancing from the other three directions.

   a. convoluted   b. indulgent   c. spry   d. viable

4. Once the little red dots began to _____ themselves all over Tina's face, the doctors knew for certain that she had the chicken pox.

   a. manifest   b. romp   c. cite   d. burnish

5. Police _____ the initial riot that began in the plaza, but by the end of the day the mob had come to life again and overrun the entire city.

a. alighted   b. quelled   c. appended   d. contradicted

6. All the lights in the building continued to flicker on and off due to the _____ in the city's electrical supply.

a. genre   b. tundra   c. flux   d. abyss

7. After retiring in 1987, Viola started playing racquetball for eight hours a day to fill the _____ created in her daily routine.

a. dimension   b. paradox   c. void   d. phenomena

8. We packed an extra trio of canteens since we knew we were about to hike across one of the most _____ regions of the country.

a. terrestrial   b. copious   c. eclectic   d. arid

9. "Do as little as you possibly can" is Brannart's _____ about work, which explains why he has been fired from over 2,000 jobs.

a. scenario   b. philosophy   c. dominion   d. larvae

Q U I C K   Q U I Z   **19**

Matching

Match each word on the right with a word on the left that has a meaning that's close to the same.

1. clutter	A. admittance
2. kaleidoscope	B. shifting series of events
3. luster	C. gigantic
4. fledgling	D. forceful
5. access	E. pupil
6. fluent	F. sudden insight
7. monstrous	G. gloss
8. revelation	H. baby bird
9. emphatic	I. graceful
10. disciple	J. mess

Q U I C K   Q U I Z   **20**

Matching

Match each word on the right with a word on the left that has a meaning that's close to the same.

1. spasm	A. odd
2. peculiar	B. adding up
3. authentic	C. misconception
4. cumulative	D. guessing the future correctly
5. reedy	E. beliefs
6. prophetic	F. muscle twitch
7. fathom	G. genuine
8. convictions	H. leave
9. evacuate	I. understand
10. delusion	J. thin

Volcano of Doom

운명의 화산

While Dr. Borges was meeting and mingling with the animals on the deck of the schooner, I overheard him telling them that all their **travails** were over. He assured them that he would put an end to their hardship and return them all to their rightful times and places—after throwing a big party for them, that is. Popo was happy to let us have the wand, even though it was actually his. He's such an **altruistic** bandicoot and is always putting the need of others before his own.

Barnaby took Vargas's wand from my hand, picked up the kaleidoscope, and turned to thank Dr. Borges for all his help—but that crazy librarian was busy dancing on the deck with a bunch of songbirds. He kind of reminded me of my Uncle Bojangles. When Bojangles heard music, he couldn't **refrain** from dancing either. I remember one time at a Christmas party back in South Carolina, he *jitterbugged* for nine hours straight, and everyone thought he must have drunk some of the water from under the tree. But actually, the band leader had... well, that's a story for another time.

As I was saying, Bridget, Babette, and I gathered around Barnaby while he moved the wand in small circles. We weren't exactly sure how to work the stick, so we all just concentrated on traveling back to the Mesozoic era, which was a period of time that took place over 180 million years ago. The *Mesozoic* era! Just thinking about it **evoked** pictures of terrifying dinosaurs roving aimlessly across a **stark**, *grim* land. Actually, I must admit, I didn't know what type of **terrain** to expect, but for some reason, I expected a lot of rocks and no trees.

JITTERBUG v. to dance the jitterbug(=a lively dance for couples, featuring rapid twirling movements and acrobatic maneuvers, usually done to swing music) 지르박을 추다
Jitterbug was especially popular in the 1940's.
지르박은 특히 1940년대에 유행했다.

MESOZOIC n. the geological era before the present era 중생대
Mesozoic era was characterized by the development of mammals, flying reptiles, birds, and flowering plants, and the appearance and death of dinosaurs.
중생대는 포유동물과 날아다니는 파충류, 새, 꽃피는 식물의 진화와 공룡의 등장 및 멸종으로 특징지워졌다.

GRIM adj. horrible; frightful; ghastly 으스스한
I don't like grim jokes about graves, worms and epitaphs.
나는 무덤이나 벌레, 그리고 비문 같은 것에 대한 으스스한 농담을 좋아하지 않는다.

But what I didn't expect was that traveling back in time would be so completely unsettling. At first, we just felt the hot, sticky air that we usually felt when the wand was doing its magic, and everything went black. But then we found ourselves flying in circles amidst a swirl of color and light, as a *blaring* noise, like jet engines and jack hammers, nearly deafened us. Every few seconds, a weird, ghost-lie **apparition** of a person or animal would pop out of the swirl, look at us, and disappear. After that, things really got strange. It looked like Bridget, Babette, and Barnaby were being stretched like *taffy*. Their head and legs started to **elongate**, then their chests started to **distend** and swell outward. I saw that my tail had stretched out several yards below me. Just as I was thought we had been stretched until we would *snap*, something went "Pop!" and we found ourselves falling through the sky toward the Earth.

"Bridget, I sure hope you are still chewing that gum of yours!" yelled Barnaby. "Because I clearly don't know how to work this wand, so we won't be getting any help right now from it!"

But Bridget was way ahead of him. She was already blowing a huge, pink bubble and waving her arms to tell her friends to grab on to her. Within seconds, the four of them were drifting downward at a comfortable speed under Bridget's bubble balloon.

"That settles it," huffed Babette as she grasped Bridget's left foot with both hands. "After this is over, no more traveling backward in time. I want to live in **chronological** order, so that the past is the past and the future is the future and we all know in which direction we're heading."

"I don't mind mentally **regressing** to my early childhood and playing with toys from time to time," agreed Barnaby, holding tight to Bridget's right leg. "That's fun. But really going back one or two hundred million years is not fun at all."

BLARE v. to make a loud, harsh sound like a trumpet 쾅쾅 울리는 소리를 내다
The trumpets blared out.
트럼펫들이 쾅쾅 울리는 소리를 냈다.

TAFFY n. a kind of chewy candy made of brown sugar or molasses boiled down, often with butter 엿가락
I like taffies.
나는 엿가락을 좋아한다.

SNAP v. to break suddenly with a sharp noise 툭 끊어지다
Suddenly the branch that he was standing on snapped off.
갑자기 그가 서 있던 나무 가지가 툭 끊어졌다.

HUFF v. to puff; to blow (숨을) 훅훅 불다, 숨을 헐떡이며 말하다
I'll huff and I'll puff till I blow your house down!
네 집을 넘어뜨릴 때까지 계속 훅훅 불거야!

The unhappy travelers **slackened** their grips as they approached the ground and let themselves slip to the grass. Beauregard, who had been *draped* around Bridget's neck, came tumbling after them.

"Oof!" *grunted* Bridget, falling on top of the pile of her friends and sucking her gum back into her mouth.

She wiped her jeans off, put her hands on her hips, and scolded her friends gently.

"Complaining like this isn't going to get us anywhere, so you'd both better start thinking positively," she **admonished**. "Dr. Borges said we had to save the world, so let's get our acts together."

"Bridget is right," said Babette, who *fluffed* her hair and looked as fashionable as usual. "We have a serious mission, and we must **strive** with all our might to complete it."

"You know, this place is kind of odd," remarked Barnaby, as he looked around. "Do you notice anything?"

Babette and Bridget carefully looked over the **panorama** that presented itself to them. The view certainly was unusual. In the distance was an ocean. The land right around them was **lush**; it was absolutely covered in grass and flowering plants. They stood at the **summit** of a high hill and could see a long way in every direction. In the direction of the ocean they could see smoke rising from a *volcanic* island. On land to their left, rose another mountain that was also smoking. Beneath them the ground rumbled softly.

"It seems like there are several volcanoes nearby," noted Bridget. "But we knew that already. I don't see any dinosaurs, but I can't say I'm unhappy about that."

DRAPE v. to hang loosely on something 대충 매달다
Dust-sheets were draped over the furniture.
먼지 막이 커버가 가구 위에 대충 매달려 있었다.

GRUNT v. to say with a deep, hoarse sound; to groan; to grumble 퉁명스럽게 말하다, 툴툴대다
The sullen boy grunted his apology.
부루퉁한 소년은 퉁명스럽게 사과했다.

FLUFF v. to shake something into a soft full mass 부풀리다
The bird fluffed (out) its feathers.
그 새는 깃털을 부풀렸다.

VOLCANIC adj. of like volcano 화산의, 화산 같은
The French Revolution was a volcanic upheaval in European history.
프랑스 혁명은 유럽 역사에 있어 화산 같은 대 변동이었다.

"I know it's probably a small point, but volcanic activity was very common in the early part of the Mesozoic era, about 200 million years ago," explained Barnaby. "If I remember the latest scientific research, flowering plants and giant dinosaurs like the ones I saw in the kaleidoscope don't show up until much later: Like twenty or thirty million years later. But, hey, I'm more of a chemist that a dinosaur expert. I could be wrong."

"Let me ask you this, Barnaby," began Bridget. "Were scientists ever able to travel into the past to get **confirmation** of their *hunches*? Are they absolutely certain? Can they even give a **definitive** explanation for why the dinosaurs died out?"

"Well, there are some popular ideas about what happened. For example, we know that the climate changed dramatically and the dinosaurs couldn't adjust to it," replied Barnaby. "But we don't really know what caused that. Most explanations that scientists have are just **conjecture**; there's just not enough proof to support any one theory."

"It would seem that you're in a fine position to make some theories of your own," laughed Babette. "But you'll never get any of those **academic** friends of yours back at the university to believe that you actually traveled back in time and saw things for yourself."

Barnaby sighed, "Yes, those professors and scholars already consider me either insane or dangerously **incompetent** because I keep blowing things up. I tell them over and over that I know exactly what I'm doing and that I'm perfectly capable of conducting an experiment, but sometimes, in the name of science, risks must be taken in order for the common good to be served and the people of the world to be able to advance. It's like in kindergarten when Mrs. Chiz said…"

"Barnaby?" said Babette, nudging him with her elbow. "You're starting to **ramble** again."

HUNCH n. idea based on intuition or instinct and not on evidence   예감
He had a hunch that she was lying.
그는 그녀가 거짓말을 하고 있다는 예감이 들었다.

"Sorry. I do tend to go on and on and get off track when I'm talking about my experiments," apologized Barnaby. "I really am sorry."

"Come on, Barnaby, there's no need for **contrition**," chirped Bridget. "We usually love listening to you *yak*. The only problem is that right now we have no time to lose. Something's terribly wrong here; there should be dinosaurs running all over the place. And for some reasons, that volcano over there seems like the key to the mystery; something is **impelling** me to go check it out."

"Not some*thing*," giggled Babette, pointing. "Some*one*."

Bridget looked behind her to discover that Beauregard was indeed *butting* his head into her back to push her toward the volcano.

"Okay, I get the picture," said Bridget. "Let's get a move on."

Babette, Bridget, Beauregard, and Barnaby began a quick march over the hills toward the smoking volcano. As they drew closer, the smell of burning earth came **wafting** toward them on the wind. The beautiful greenery of the hills was **marred** here and there by long, ugly, black strips of **charred** land. The further they walked, the more the hills and smaller **knolls** were burned and **scorched**, and the warmer the air grew.

"That volcano must have blown its top pretty recently," remarked Barnaby. "Let's hope the *eruptions* are only **sporadic** and not regular."

"I'm with you," agreed Bridget nervously. "We have plenty to worry about, but I have to admit that my **principal** fear is that we're going to get blasted by this volcano."

"I have heard that they do start to rumble before they... hey!" said Babette, as they reached the top of another hill. "Do you see that down in the valley?"

YAK v. to laugh or cause to laugh heartily 웃거나 웃게 하다, 재잘거리다
His minions are yaking here.
그의 부하들이 여기에서 재잘거리고 있다.

BUTT v. to hit (one's head) on something 부딪치다, 대다
He butted his head against the shelf as he was getting up.
그는 일어나면서 머리를 선반에 부딪쳤다.

ERUPTION n. outbreak of a volcano; outburst (화산의) 폭발; 발생
A careless smoker may cause the eruption of a disastrous forest fire.
조심성 없는 흡연가가 끔찍한 산불을 발생시킬 수 있다.

In the valley below them and *spilling* up into the hills, hundreds of dinosaurs of all types had **congregated**. There were tyranosaurs and brontosaurs, and pterodactyl were *swooping* and *perching* all over the place. Every giant *reptile* for miles around must have been gathered there. They were making a lot of noise, but they seemed fairly peaceful, for dinosaurs.

"It doesn't look like they're in this valley to **forage** for food. Or to fight each other, either," observed Barnaby. "What on earth could they be doing here?"

His question was answered immediately. High on a rocky **crag**, just at the other end of the valley, Gorgas appeared, mane and purple cape flapping proudly in the breeze. The dinosaurs quieted quickly and looked at him.

"**Yonder** mountain is the Volcano of Doom!" his voice rang out across the crowd as he gestured with one tentacle to the volcano behind him.

His booming voice was so frightening that even the giant meat-eaters were **cowed** into respectful silence. Gorgas cleared his throat and blinked his many eyes thoughtfully.

"Uh oh, I think he's about to launch into an **oration**," said Bridget.

"Maybe his speech will give us a clue about what he's up to," added Babette. "Why don't we *sneak* around this side of the crowd and come up behind him and then take him by surprise?"

Bridget and Barnaby agreed. They began to make their way around the edge of the dinosaur mob as carefully and quietly as possible.

"Mighty dinosaurs," shouted Gorgas, "this pure, **pristine**, and untouched land is yours. Do you not want to keep it that way? You live in a blooming paradise of peace. But your **utopia** will become an **inferno** and you will all be burned to crisps, unless you listen to me. I have seen the future, and I see a great **cataclysm**, a horrible disaster, coming that will wipe out your entire population—unless you stop it, unless you do as I say!"

SPILL v. to run or fall over the edge of a container 흘러나오다
The ink spilt all over the desk.
잉크가 책상 위에 흘러 나와 있었다.

SWOOP v. to come down suddenly with a rushing movement 내리 덮치다, 달려들다
The owl swooped down on the mouse.
부엉이가 쥐를 내리 덮쳤다.

PERCH v. to come to rest or stay 자리를 잡고 앉아 있다
The birds perched on the television aerial.
새들이 텔레비전 안테나 위에 자리를 잡고 앉아 있었다.

REPTILE n. any of the class of cold-blooded, egg-laying animals including lizards, tortoises, crocodiles, snakes, etc. 파충류
Reptiles were the dominant form of life during the Mesozoic.
파충류는 중생대 동안 주종을 이룬 생명체였다.

SNEAK v. to go quietly and secretly in the direction specified 몰래 가다
He stole the money and sneaked out of the house.
그는 돈을 훔쳐 집을 몰래 빠져나갔다.

A low roar came from the crowd.

"Do as I say, or the creatures of the future will burn your remains for fuel!" he *thundered* again. "Your dead **carcasses** will be buried deep beneath the ground and millions of years from now these creatures, which are called humans, will call you **fossils** and use the oil and gas you turned into to fill their gas tanks and heat their homes. You will make for a rather nasty fuel, too, if you ask me, and messy, but, whoops, oh, no offense, that was not the point I wanted to **convey** at all. What am I trying to get across, again?"

"Looks like Gorgas rambles, too," whispered Barnaby as they *tip-toed* along. "He'd better get to the point, these dinosaurs are already starting to look confused. Their brains are not very large, and they have trouble following complicated instructions."

"Oh, yes, yes," continued Gorgas, clearing his throat again. "Do you not wish to **proliferate** and multiply in number, spreading young dinosaurs across the globe? If so, hear my plan. See that bright, glowing, orange river of hot, melted rock trickling down the side of the mountain?" He pointed behind him enthusiastically, "Well, that is the **magma** that will destroy you sooner or later unless we all work together to construct a large tube, like a U-shaped drinking straw. We'll stick one end in the volcano and the other end in the ocean and **siphon** all of the magma into the water! It could work! Or, if you think that's too hard, we could just **bore** a big hole in the side of the mountain and let most of the magma just spill out. Of course, that could get kind of messy. Anyway, the important thing is that you dinosaurs must take charge of this situation immediately. Yes, take the **initiative**! Bore the hole! Bore it today!"

The dinosaurs seemed **flustered**, nervous, and confused. Grunts of "Huh?" and "What is he talking about?" rose from the crowd. Ordinarily, Gorgas had the **charisma** and personality that was necessary to stir up a crowd. He had clearly studied the art of **rhetoric**, because his speech was well-structured and usually quite convincing, but this crowd just didn't seem to get his drift. Finally, a **stately**, dignified older brontosaur stepped forward and tried to clear things up.

THUNDER v. to say something loudly and forcefully, especially because you are angry   화나서 큰 소리로 강하게 말하다
'Get out of my house!' he thundered.
'내 집에서 나가!' 그가 큰 소리로 말했다.

TIP-TOE v. to walk very quietly on one's toe   발끝으로 조심조심 걷다
He knocked softly on the door and tip-toed into the room.
그는 조용히 문을 두드리고 나서 까치발로 방에 들어갔다.

"Dinosaurs, bore?" asked the huge, gentle creature.

Before Gorgas could think of a reply, Barnaby, Bridget, Babette, and Beauregard scrambled up onto the crag behind him.

"Hold it right there, Gorgas," warned Bridget. "Just what do you thik you're doing?"

"Oh! Well, my dear, what a surprise!" yelped Gorgas. "Um, I was just doing a small experiment. I had heard that dinosaurs were not the most **industrious** reptiles, and I wanted to see what it would take to make them better, harder workers. I call it my Mesozoic **motivation** project— I really want to get the reptiles going, give them something to do. All for the sake of science, of course."

"Aw, come off it, Gorgas," scoffed Bridget. "We know all about your competition with Vargas. What we can't figure out is why you are trying to **induce** these dinosaurs to *drain* the volcano into the ocean. Don't you realize what kind of disaster that would cause?"

"Vargas? Vargas is a **scoundrel** and a villain and a cheat!" insisted Gorgas. "Whatever he told you is a lie. What did he tell you?"

"He told us nothing. We found out on our own," said Babette. "We discovered your plans to gather strange specimens and rule the world, and we know why you and Vargas were **exiled** from the planet Smeltvlat. There's no sense in denying it. And we are here to tell you that you might as well give up. We will make sure that you never succeed!"

In the valley below, the dinosaurs grumbled impatiently.

"Dinosaurs, bore?" repeated the old brontosaur slowly, but loudly.

DRAIN v. (cause liquid to) flow away   빼내다
The mechanic drained all the oil from the engine.
그 기계공은 엔진에서 기름을 모두 빼냈다.

"My goodness, such **meddlesome** children," said the alien, shaking his head and taking no notice of the crowd of reptiles. "Why can't you stay out of my affairs? Well, if you must know, Vargas was ahead of me in gathering odd creatures, so I knew I had to do something out of the ordinary. I decided to do a little research into the DNA of you the Earth creatures. DNA, you see, is like a tiny handbook made out of chemicals. It's inside each and every one of the cells in your body. **DNA** explains how you developed and how you work. I knew that giant reptiles once roamed this planet, and I figured that these ancient reptiles were the **predecessors** of all modern Earth creatures. I just couldn't understand why so few of you had reptile **traits**, like cold blood and *scaly* skin. Then I took apart the DNA and looked at the **genes**. Your genes come from your parents and grandparents. And eventually it was pretty clear to me that dinosaurs had nothing to do with humans, or cats, or polar bears. Or bandicoots, for that matter."

"All I can figure, the only reasonable **inference** I can make about why you are talking to these dinosaurs, is that you want to save them from dying out so that their genes will *survive* into modern times. If dinosaurs survive into modern times, then there's no telling what might happen," said Barnaby, scratching his head in puzzlement. "But why drain the volcano? What good would that do, unless... oh! I see! Scientists know that a shift in climate wiped out the dinosaurs. You think that these volcanic eruptions are *spewing* enough dust and ash into the air to cause that shift! And you want to stop the volcanoes to keep the dinosaurs alive!"

"It doesn't take a super-intelligent being to know that there is a **correlation** between high volcanic activity and large changes in climate," remarked Gorgas. "Any fool would notice the connection."

"Gorgas, I certainly don't mean to be rude, but you have come up with the silliest **notion** I have ever heard of," said Bridget, rolling her eyes. "How did you think of such a half-baked idea? If you drain all the magma into the seas, the sea creatures will die, the water will dry up, all of the plants will die so that the dinosaurs will have nothing to eat, and then they'll all die, and the... then... then the Earth will be nothing but a dried up *hunk* of rock!"

SCALY adj. covered with scales; having scales like a fish 비늘로 덮여 있는, 비늘이 있는
The iron pipe is scaly with rust.
그 쇠파이프는 녹으로 덮여 있다.

SURVIVE v. continue to live or exist 살아남다
Of the six people in the plane that crashed, only one survived.
추락된 비행기 안에 있던 여섯 사람 중 한 사람만 살아남았다.

SPEW v. to vomit; to send out in a stream 내뿜다
The volcano spewed molten lava.
그 화산은 유동 상태의 용암을 내뿜었다.

HUNK n. large piece cut from a larger piece 덩어리
She gave us a hunk of bread.
그녀는 우리에게 빵 덩어리를 주었다.

Bridget's eyes opened wide as she realized how horrible Gorgas's plan really was. Gorgas noticed her shock and laughed his threatening, **baleful** chuckle.

"But, Gorgas, this must not be!" wailed Babette. "Earth is a beautiful planet filled with so much life! You must not destroy it!"

"Calm yourself, my dear, there is no need to get all **sentimental** and emotional just yet," said Gorgas. "Bridget does not know for sure that the oceans will dry up. Perhaps there will be enough water, and the dinosaurs will live on. In that case, strange new creatures will appear in the future, and I will win the contest. If the planet does dry up, well, that's a pity. But at least Vargas won't win, either."

Barnaby kept scratching his head and thinking as he whispered to Bridget, "We need a plan, and fast. These dinosaurs are getting *cranky*, and Gorgas doesn't seem to have control of them at all. Wait! That's it! Now if only we had a loudspeaker or a **megaphone** so that they could all hear me."

"Um, Barnaby," whispered Bridget. "What is that big cone-shaped thing sticking out of your hair?"

Barnaby patted his hair and, sure enough, discovered a megaphone sticking out of it.

"Great! I thought I had one of these around somewhere!" said Barnaby. "Quick, Bridget, Babette, Beauregard, jump down into that deep **crevice**. That crack in the rocks is the perfect place to hide. I think we're going to need some protection."

All of the friends quickly followed Barnaby and huddled together.

CRANKY adj. bad-tempered 심기가 뒤틀리는
He was cranky when I came home.
내가 집에 왔을 때 그는 심기가 뒤틀려 있었다.

"Now," explained the young scientist. "I hope this works. Have you noticed that the dinosaurs are nervous and excited? They don't understand what Gorgas said, but I think they are ready for some kind of action. All that brontosaur seemed to get out of Gorgas's speech was the word 'bore'. It looks like the dinosaurs think that Gorgas is calling them *boring*."

"That's not very nice," remarked Babette.

"No, it isn't," agreed Barnaby. "But I think I can use that misunderstanding to get the dinosaurs to take care of Gorgas for us. All I need is a simple message that they can understand. But I'll have to be a pretty good **ventriloquist** to pull this one off."

"Is that what the megaphone is for? You are going to say something and make it look like it's Gorgas who's talking?" asked Babette.

"That's the idea," he said. "I just hope I can do a good enough job *faking* his voice. Well, here goes..."

Barnaby cleared his throat, paused for a moment to think, then held the megaphone to his mouth.

"Dinosaurs! Dinosaurs hear me!" boomed Barnaby. "Dinosaurs bad. Dinosaurs stupid. Dinosaurs boring. Hate dinosaurs. Dinosaur bore! Dinosaur bore!"

A chorus of roars rang out in the valley. The dinosaurs began to get the message. And as far as they were concerned, Gorgas was *insulting* them. The giant brontosaur, no longer gentle, moved forward and hip-checked the crag with his tough **flank**. Barnaby, Babette, Bridget, and Beauregard covered their heads as rocks and dirt fell around them. Again the brontosaur *rammed* his side into the crag and this time, the rock was **jarred** so violently that Gorgas went tumbling into the crowd of angry reptiles. It looked like he was done for.

BORING adj. uninteresting; dull; tedious   따분한, 지루한
I don't like this boring conversation.
나는 이런 지루한 대화를 좋아하지 않는다.

FAKE v. to pretend; to feign; to make so that it seems genuine   ~인 척하다; 흉내내다, 위조하다
He faked that he was surprised.
그는 놀란 척 했다.

INSULT v. to speak or act in a way that hurts or is intended to hurt the feelings or dignity of (somebody); to be extremely rude to (somebody)   모욕하다
I felt most insulted when they made me sit at a little table at the back.
그들이 나를 뒤에 있는 작은 탁자에 앉게 했을 때 나는 극도로 모욕감을 느꼈다.

RAM v. to crash against something; to strike or push something with great force   들이받다
The ice skater rammed into the barrier.
그 스케이트 선수는 벽에 들이받았다.

The children and Beauregard had to sit still for some time while the angry roars and stomping continued. Barnaby even had time to **ruminate**, which was one of his favorite activities. The thing he was **musing** about this time was the *fate* of the poor dinosaurs.

"You know," he began, "I feel sorry for these dinosaurs. Maybe they understood a little more of what Gorgas said than we think they did. Maybe they know now that some day—millions of years from now, but still some day—their kind will disappear. I do feel some **empathy** for them. After all, for a while there, I knew just what it felt like to worry about disappearing. It was like I felt what they felt."

"I feel kind of bad, too," said Bridget. "But in all of the science fiction movies I watch, the most important **directive** time travelers get is that they should not change the things that happen in the past, because there's no telling how it will affect the future. Speaking of which, we should get out of here before we accidentally change history."

Barnaby nodded sadly and pulled the wand out of his pocket, but he didn't get a chance to use it. Before he could even wave it in once circle, Babette, Bridget, Beauregard and he were caught up in a whirlwind of light and noise like the one they'd traveled in before. And they had a pretty good idea of who was controlling this one.

FATE n. a power that is believed to control and decide everything that happens 운명
The fate was against my will.
운명은 나의 의지와는 어긋나 있었다.

Relationships

Decide what relationship the following pairs of words have to each other. If they mean close to the same thing, make "S." If they have opposite meanings, mark "O."

1. scoundrel :: rogue
2. academic :: uneducated
3. cataclysm :: devastation
4. lush :: stark
5. motivate :: discourage
6. muse :: ruminate
7. proliferate :: decrease
8. charisma :: appeal
9. bore :: burrow
10. pristine :: marred

Relationships

Decide what relationship the following pairs of words have to each other. If they mean close to the same thing, make "S." If they have opposite meanings, mark "O."

1. elongate :: distend
2. char :: scorch
3. industrious :: lazy
4. stately :: humble
5. oration :: speech
6. congregate :: scatter
7. fluster :: soothe
8. empathy :: identification
9. rhetoric :: eloquence
10. contrite :: proud

Fill in the Blank

For each sentence below, choose the word that best completes the sentence.

1. Despite all his kind requests, Farmer Jones was unable to _____ his sheep into leaving the north meadow.

   a. impel   b. mingle   c. slacken   d. cow

2. Since a fine layer of moss covered all the tiny pebbles along the riverbank, we were extra careful when crossing the slippery _____ .

   a. utopia   b. panorama   c. terrain   d. inferno

3. A professor at the local university told Wilhelm that the _____ he found in the cave was the leg bone of Tyrannosaurus Rex.

   a. fossil   b. carcass   c. gene   d. DNA

4. The walls of the city, which were four hundred feet high and twenty feet deep, were the _____ line of defense against foreign invaders.

   a. chronological   b. principal   c. sentimental   d. altruistic

5. Since the twenty-four ounce strawberry smoothie tasted so good, it was difficult for Jim to _____ from drinking it all at once.

   a. jar   b. convey   c. flank   d. refrain

6. Since it was his favorite topic, my father would _____ about the weather for hours until mom hushed him.

   a. strive   b. ramble   c. rove   d. exile

7. It was a hard climb, but when we reached the _____ of Mount Fuji, the view from the top was worth it.

   a. crag   b. knoll   c. summit   d. crevice

8. The _____ look from the class bully scared Christian so much that he decided to beat himself up rather than face the bully on the playground.

   a. incompetent   b. sporadic   c. meddlesome   d. baleful

9. Although the lawn mower was out of fuel, we used a _____ to get gas out of pickup's tank so we could mow the front lawn.

   a. predecessor   b. megaphone   c. ventriloquist   d. siphon

Q U I C K   Q U I Z   **24**

Matching

Match each word on the right with a word on the left that has a meaning that's close to the same.

1. magma	A. ghost
2. conjecture	B. lava
3. yonder	C. cause to happen
4. induce	D. guess
5. apparition	E. idea
6. definitive	F. go backward
7. notion	G. characteristic
8. regress	H. at a distance
9. inference	I. conclusion
10. trait	J. conclusive

Q U I C K   Q U I Z   **25**

Matching

Match each word on the right with a word on the left that has a meaning that's close to the same.

1. forage	A. connection
2. travail	B. first step
3. era	C. period of time
4. waft	D. order
5. correlation	E. proof
6. evoke	F. float gently
7. confirmation	G. criticize
8. initiative	H. search for food
9. admonish	I. difficult task
10. directive	J. summon

Judge, Jury, and Jailer

재판관, 배심원 그리고 교도관

Traveling through time must not be something you ever get used to. You would think that on the third time around, the process wouldn't stretch and **distort** our bodies so much, and maybe we wouldn't feel quite as dizzy. But the side effects of time travel did not diminish. If anything, they got worse.

When we came out of our *tailspin*, Bridget, Babette, Barnaby, and I found ourselves sitting in a big wooden *jury box* in an old-fashioned courtroom. It looked like we were the only ones there. I can't tell you how relieved I was to see sunlight streaming through the glass windows. At least it seemed like we were on the Earth at some time in the recent past. I took a *peek* outside to see if I could get any clues about where we were, and almost yelped with joy to see a tall magnolia tree with branches abounding in big, creamy, white blossoms. In fact, the blossoms were so plentiful that you could barely see the dark green *waxy* leaves. I knew there was something about the sunlight that reminded me of the South, but the magnolia tree was the clincher. There is practically no surer way to know you are in the South than to see a magnolia tree.

The kids were starting to come to their senses, and I was about to push them toward the door of the courtroom, when a terrible wail sprung up from across the room. There, in the prisoner's box, sat Gorgas. Several of his eyes were blackened, his mane was tangled, and his purple cape, usually bright and fresh, was *dingy* and dirty. His tentacles were chained together. He looked so **frail**, weak, and helpless, it was almost enough to make you feel sorry for him. Of course, we didn't care much for Gorgas. But Vargas—now he could really hold a *grudge*, as we were about to find out.

TAILSPIN n. spiral dive of an aircraft in which the tail makes wider circles than the front 나선형 급강하
We saw the tailspin of the plane.
우리는 비행기의 나선형 급강하를 보았다.

JURY BOX n. enclosure where a jury(=group of people in a law court who have been chosen to listen to the facts in a case and to decide whether the accused person is guilty or not guilty) sits in a court 배심원 석
Seven men and five women sat on the jury box.
배심원 석에는 남자 7명과 여자 5명이 앉아 있었다.

PEEK v. to look quickly and often secretively 살짝 들여다보다, 엿보다 **n.** a quick or sly look 흘끗 봄
No peeking!
엿보지 말 것!

WAXY adj. having a surface or texture like wax 매끈한
I envy her waxy skin.
그녀의 매끈한 피부가 부럽다.

DINGY adj. dirty-looking; not cheerful or bright 때 묻은
Dingy curtains covered the windows of the dusty old room.
먼지 쌓인 낡은 방의 창문들에 때 묻은 커튼이 쳐져 있었다.

GRUDGE n. feeling of ill-will, envy, resentment, spite, etc. 원한, 악감, 유감
He has a grudge against me.
그는 나에게 유감이 있다.

"All rise for the Honorable Judge Vargas," announced Vargas, as he entered through the doors of the courtroom.

The alien wore a powdered, white *wig* on top of his already white mane. The wig kind of looked like George Washington's hair. Instead of his cape, he wore a long, black robe. He **sauntered** up to the front of the room as slowly and casually as his tentacles would carry him, as if he had not a care in the world. Behind Vargas came a **procession** of furry little creatures who looked like coconuts with arms and legs, walking in a straight line as if they were in a parade. Gorgas let out another wail. Apparently, Vargas leading a **cavalcade** of walking coconuts was the last thing he wanted to see. Bridget, Babette, and Barnaby, who were too confused to do anything else, stood up.

"Not you, Gorgas," snarled Vargas as he passed the prisoner. "Don't stand up. **Sprawl** face down on the floor, with your tentacles spread wide, like a sorry criminal should."

"But Vargas, I am chained! I cannot spread my arms to show you the respect you deserve," *whimpered* Gorgas, reaching out to Vargas as best he could through the bars of the prisoner's box. "Oh, mighty one, come here and let me touch the *hem* of your robe so I can kiss the **fringe**. You are so wise and great! Please, be merciful!"

"Enough!" barked Vargas, whipping his robe away and **rebuffing** Gorgas's efforts to come near him. "Don't **fawn** over me. You'll get no special favors by praising me, and your prayers and **supplications** disgust me."

"But how can you **spurn** me this way? We have known each other for so long!" continued Gorgas, *rattling* his chains. "What have I done to deserve such **scorn**?"

"I'm glad you asked," replied Vargas, with a **wry**, crooked smile. "Ladies and gentlemen of the jury—hey, you Vizwatts; sit down and be quiet! Remember, you're at the trial of the century!"

WIG n. covering for the head made of real or artificial hair, worn to hide baldness, or in a law court, or by actors as part of a costume 가발
She disguised herself with a blonde wig and dark glasses.
그 여자는 금발 가발과 검은색 안경으로 변장했다.

WHIMPER v. to whine or cry softly, especially with fear or pain; to say in this way 흐느끼다
'Please don't leave me alone,' he whimpered.
'제발 날 혼자 두지 말아요' 그가 흐느끼며 말했다.

HEM n. edge of a piece of cloth which has been turned under and sewn or fixed down 옷자락, 옷단
I took the hems of my dresses up to make them shorter.
나는 드레스들의 단을 올려서 짧게 만들었다.

RATTLE v. to make short sharp sounds quickly, one after the other; (cause something to) shake while making such sounds 덜거덕거리다
The windows were rattling in the wind.
창문들이 바람에 덜거덕거리고 있었다.

The little coconut creatures had been tumbling and rolling around the *aisle*, but they jumped to attention when the judge spoke and they took their seats.

"That's better. Now then, ladies and gentlemen of the jury, this person, one Gorgas by name, stands accused of the most unheard of crime in the galaxy," Vargas began. "In fact, some of his crimes are truly **unprecedented**, which means that this evil creature was the first to *mastermind* and perform the horrible crimes. Hopefully, we will be able to punish him in a measure that is equal to the evilness of the crimes he has committed."

"But, **magistrate**, sir, if these crimes are totally new and so are unknown to the justice system, how can you be sure that they're against the law?" asked Bridget, who had learned a lot about the law by watching *re-runs* of L.A. *Law* while she was sick in bed with the *chicken pox*. Not that she wanted Gorgas to go free, but she was curious.

"Fine, fine, I will list some of the more common charges against Gorgas. We will deal with his stranger crimes later," sighed Vargas. "And please, don't call me a magistrate. Magistrates only deal with small trials. This, as I have said, is the trial of the century! I am an important judge."

"Sorry, your honor," said Bridget.

"See that you remember that. As I was saying, even long ago, when he was a child on Smeltvlat, Gorgas had a criminal mind. He had a fine, rich family who hired the best Karloffian **governess** to take care of him and teach him. Karloffian *nannies* are as strict as they come, but even when Gorgas was a very young Smeltvlatian, he did everything he could to disobey her. He refused to clean up his room, he never ate anything on his plate, and he refused to stop reading his comic books when it was time to go to bed. Horrifying, isn't it?" asked Vargas.

"Well, lack of tidiness isn't exactly a crime on the Earth..." began Barnaby.

AISLE n. a passage between rows of seats in a hall, theater, or school 통로, 복도
Don't run in the aisle.
복도에서 달리지 마라.

MASTERMIND v. to plan and/or direct (a scheme, etc.) 주모자 노릇하다
He masterminded the huge fraud.
그가 그 거대한 사기의 주모자 노릇을 했다.

RE-RUN n. film or program that is shown or broadcast again; repeat 재방송
We don't want a re-run of Monday's fiasco.
우리는 월요일에 있었던 큰 실수를 재현하고 싶지 않다.

CHICKEN POX n. disease, especially of children, with a mild fever and itchy red spots on the skin 수두
My daughter caught chicken pox last week.
내 딸은 지난 주에 수두에 걸렸다.

NANNY n. child's nurse 유모
He cross-examined her on the subject of nannies.
그는 유모 문제에 대해 그녀를 힐문했다.

"No, of course not," snapped Vargas. "I'm only trying to show you what a bad sort of person he is. He never possessed any of the **virtues** that you might hope to find in a child, like cleanliness, respectfulness, or generosity. In fact, aside from fairly good manners, I don't think he has developed any positive qualities at all. But he did not commit his first real crime until he was a teenager. You see, by law, all youngsters on our planet had a curfew. They had to be at home and indoors by the time the third moon rose above the horizon. Of course, Gorgas thought that the law wasn't meant for him. He would break **curfew** and stay out at the *arcade*, *whooping* it up with his friends until the fifth or sixth moonrise."

"My, that is *naughty*," remarked Babette.

"But that's only the beginning," insisted Vargas. "The rest of his life can only be described as a crime **spree**. He committed crime after crime, all with great enjoyment. While he was a private investigator, his favorite crime was larceny."

"I was not a thief!" shouted Gorgas. "I never stole anything from my clients. Back then, I had **integrity**. I would never lie, cheat, or do anything dishonest."

"Oh, no?" boomed Vargas. "How about all of the clients you stole from me? Now that's larceny, pure and simple. Then, of course, there were the charges of **corruption** brought against you while you were mayor of Tralala. Apparently, Gorgas was a very wicked mayor who could be paid to do almost anything. What do you have to say about that? Well? Can you defend yourself?"

The Vizwatts excitedly *chittered* like monkeys and rolled themselves around on the hard, wooden benches.

ARCADE n. covered passage or area, especially one with an arched roof and shops along one or both sides 아케이드
She went to a shopping arcade.
그녀는 쇼핑 아케이드에 갔다.

WHOOP v. (whoop it up의 형태로 쓰여) to take part in noisy celebrations 떠들며 놀다
After their victory they were whooping it up all night long.
승리한 후에 그들은 밤새 떠들며 놀고 있었다.

NAUGHTY adj. disobedient; bad; causing trouble 순종하지 않는, 나쁜
He's a terribly naughty child.
그는 아주 나쁜 아이이다.

CHITTER v. to twitter; to chirp 찍찍거리다
Rats chitter behind the curtain.
쥐들이 커튼 뒤에서 찍찍거린다.

"Order! Order in the court! Stop that, you crazy Vizwatts!" demanded Vargas. "Well, Gorgas? I also seem to remember a certain election year. You were the **incumbent**, trying to get reelected mayor. And the **candidate** you were running against—Welmok, I think it was—mysteriously disappeared. Kidnapped, so the rumor went, by a bunch of *thugs* you hired. You thought you had it made. You won the election, of course, but then, at your **inauguration**, just at the point in the **ceremony** when you are supposed to swear to obey the law, Welmok showed up, all *roughed* up and dusty. And he had quite a story to tell; it was amazing how fast you tried to get out of town!"

"Did he get caught?" asked Bridget. "What happened?"

"Oh, the usual," complained Vargas. "A committee was formed to look into the whole affair. There were people from both political parties, Gorgas's and Welmok's, on the committee, so it was **bipartisan**. But bipartisan doesn't always mean fair. The committee met for months, but nothing was ever decided. They couldn't seem to come to a **consensus** about what should be done. The members would gather, some person would **drone** on and on about how we needed to get to the bottom of this, and then everyone would fall asleep. Then the next day, the same people would **convene** again, and the same thing would happen. Finally, Gorgas decided to hire people, his so-called "friends," to come in and **vouch** for his honesty. These well-paid witnesses swore up and down that Gorgas was innocent. And the committee believed them! They let Gorgas go free!"

"I was innocent!" shrieked Gorgas. "It was you who kidnapped Welmok, but you wanted it to look like I was the criminal! You did everything you could to **incriminate** me and get me thrown in jail. You're the kidnapper!"

Boos and hisses echoed through the courtroom as the Vizwatts showed their displeasure with Gorgas.

THUG n. a ruffian or cutthroat; a violent criminal or hooligan   부랑아, 무뢰한, 자객
One thug with a pistol struck the druggist on the head.
총을 든 한 피한이 약제사의 머리를 쳤다.

ROUGH v. to treat somebody roughly, with physical violence   거칠게 다루다, 학대하다
The angry mob roughed up the suspected traitor.
화난 폭도는 배신자로 의심이 가는 사람을 거칠게 다루었다.

"Be careful what you **allege**, Gorgas," warned Vargas. "You know that you have no proof to back up that claim."

But Gorgas continued, pleading to the children, "I know I have no proof of the *allegation* I just made, but who else could it have been? My evidence against him is only **circumstantial**, it's true. There were no witnesses, no hard facts. But Vargas hates me. He practically led a **crusade** against me to have me thrown out of the office when I was first elected. He was like a soldier with a *mission*; he even had an army, so to speak. It was a **coalition** of ice-cream truck drivers, butterfly collectors, and *welders*. Why such different groups would want to make friends in order to form and **alliance** against me is, to this day, a mystery. But Vargas got them to work together and they did everything they could to drag me down."

"Um, Gorgas and Vargas, I must admit, this is all very interesting," began Bridget politely, "but, if it's all the same to you, we'll be on our way. This seems to be a private matter between you two."

Bridget, Babette, Barnaby, and Beauregard had not set foot out of the jury box before Vargas stood up and bellowed. "Stay where you are! The trial has not even begun. You, with the braids, do you know how to use a *stenography* machine?"

"A what?" asked Bridget.

"No matter, no matter," said Vargas. "Come sit down here by this machine and type down everything anyone in this room says. That's the official way to do things here on the Earth, correct? You, with the sunglasses, how do you feel about swearing in the witness? He must take an **oath** saying that he will tell the truth. It probably won't do any good to ask him to promise, but he must anyway. Here's a Bible for him to put his tentacle on."

Vargas had slithered off of the judge's chair and was busily **bustling** around the room like a last-minute holiday shopper trying to get everything ready.

ALLEGATION n. statement made without proof; act of alleging   (충분한 증거가 없는) 주장
These are serious allegations.
이것들은 위험한 주장들이다.

MISSION n. particular task or duty undertaken by an individual or a group   사명
My mission in life is to help poor people.
내 인생의 사명은 불쌍한 사람을 돕는 것이다.

WELDER n. person whose job is making welded joints   용접공
The welder works at the car factory.
그 용접공은 자동차 공장에서 일한다.

STENOGRAPHY n. method of writing rapidly, using special quickly-written symbols   속기
Sometimes it is possible to make actual notes in stenography.
속기로 실제 기록을 하는 것이 가능할 때가 있다.

"Well, don't you have to be a **parson** or *preacher* to do that? Swear someone in, I mean?" asked Babette.

"Nonsense. Regular humans do it all the time. I have seen it on your television programs," said Vargas.

"He's right," said Bridget.

"Okay, then," said Babette, taking the Bible and shrugging her shoulders.

"What about me?" asked Barnaby. "What should I do?"

"Oh, yes. Here, take this legal pad. I might need to **dictate** a letter or something. If I do, I'll say, 'Take a letter,' and then you must write down everything I say. Got it?" asked Vargas.

Barnaby nodded.

"Right. Very well, then, swear in the witness," commanded the wig-wearing alien.

Babette stepped up to Gorgas and held out the Bible. Gorgas placed on tentacle on top of it, but he did not look happy.

"Do you swear to tell the truth, the whole truth, and nothing but the truth?" asked Babette.

"What do you mean by the truth?" asked Gorgas, narrowing his eyes in a **guarded**, cautious way. "You cannot be too careful about making these things clear up front. I must say, Vargas, this does not look like it will be a fair, balanced trial. You hate me, and these children, I fear, are none too fond of me either. In fact, I suspect that in this courtroom there is a general **bias** against me. So much, alas, for the fair lady, Justice! My heart overflows with sadness. It is a true, true shame."

PREACHER n. person who preaches, especially a clergyman who preaches sermons 목사
He is a preacher famous for his inspiring sermons.
그는 영감을 불러일으키는 설교로 유명한 목사이다.

"I will tell you what the shame is, Gorgas," snapped Babette. "The shame is the **affected** manner you have. Quit putting on airs. You sound like a character in an old, British play."

The Vizwatts giggled and bounced in the aisles with amusement. Babette stared coldly at them, then returned her attention to Gorgas.

"Now, Gorgas, you must be **forthright**. Come straight to the point and say what you have to say. **Frankness** is the key, so you must be straightforward and hide nothing." Babette explained. "Do you swear?"

"Oh, very well," huffed Gorgas, a little put out by Babette's comments.

"Thank you," said Vargas, who was just shuffling out from under a table. "I will now explain the case against Gorgas."

"Hey, isn't that a new wig?" asked Barnaby. "That one seems a lot curlier than the last one. And it seems to have every color in the **spectrum**. Are judges supposed to wear rainbow-colored clown wigs?"

"What a **keen** eye you have! Such sharp powers of observation. You notice every **nuance** of my clothing," remarked Vargas, obviously pleased with Barnaby's comment.

"There aren't many nuances to a clown wig," replied Barnaby. "The fact that you're wearing one isn't a subtle detail; it would be pretty hard to miss. But why the change?"

"You see, I am the lawyer now," explained the alien. "The other wig is for when I am the judge. And I have a nice, blond *page-boy* wig for when I'm a *jailer*."

"This is not a trial!" yelled Gorgas, struggling against his chains. "It's a **parody** of a trial. A rotten, weak imitation of the real thing. Vargas, you *filthy*, *stinking*, *oozy*-headed..."

PAGE-BOY n. a boy or manservant; person who carries parcels, delivers messages, and runs errands; bellboy 시종, 급사
The page-boys at hotels usually wear uniforms.
호텔에 있는 급사들은 대개 제복을 입는다.

JAILER n. the keeper of a jail 교도관
He has been a jailer for three years.
그는 3년 동안 교도관으로 일해 왔다.

FILTHY adj. disgustingly dirty 더러운
We ran into a beggar dressed in filthy rags.
우리는 더러운 누더기를 걸친 거지를 우연히 만났다.

STINKING adj. very bad or unpleasant; horrible 악취가 나는, 코를 찌르는, 비열한
I don't want your stinking money.
나는 너의 비열한 돈을 원하지 않는다.

OOZY adj. (of thick liquids) coming or flowing out slowly 줄줄 흘러나오는, 질벅질벅 나오는
It was a big oozy creature.
그것은 액체가 줄줄 흘러나오는 거대한 생물이었다.

"Tut, tut!" scolded Vargas. "There's no reason why we can't keep the **discourse** in this court polite. Please **endeavor** to watch your language and *converse* nicely. I know it is hard for you, but please try as hard as you can."

Gorgas had been bearing Vargas's insults well, but his patience was wearing thin. By the way he was scowling, it was clear that his fear had given way to **wrath**. The angry alien was planning something.

"Vargas, come on. I know we have had our differences. Why don't we just settle this fairly?" he offered. "Since we cannot seem to come to an agreement, let's ask these children to **arbitrate**. They will listen to our arguments and make a decision, and we will do what they think is the fairest thing. If it turns out that I have certain, um, **assets**—money, property, or anything of value—that should belong to you, well, I will gladly **bestow** them upon you, along with a thousand apologies."

"I admire your proposed **largess**, Gorgas," sniffed Vargas. "I have never known you to give gifts so generously. So, are you saying that you trust the humans, who dislike you even more than they dislike me, to do our **reckoning** for us? You think that they can settle our accounts and figure out who owes who, what?"

"I trust their **discretion** completely," claimed Gorgas. "They are free to make their own decision. And I'm sure it will be wise."

"Hah!" snorted Vargas. "Then you are a bigger fool than I thought you were. No way. What a laugh. You, little girl with the braids. Read back what Gorgas just said. I want to hear it again."

Bridget looked down at the roll of paper coming from the stenography machine. She had been trying to type down everything, but, of course, she didn't know how to type. And besides, a stenography machine is not like a typewriter.

"Uh, Vargas, I'm afraid it's a little **garbled** and *jumbled* up," confessed Bridget. "It doesn't make much sense. I'm not much of a typist."

CONVERSE **v.** to talk 이야기하다
She sat conversing with the President.
그녀는 대통령과 이야기하면서 앉아 있었다.

JUMBLE **v.** to mix in a confused way 뒤범벅을 만들다, 뒤죽박죽이 되다
Toys, books, shoes and clothes were jumbled on the floor.
장난감, 책, 구두, 옷들이 바닥 위에 뒤죽박죽 있었다.

"Well, I suppose the memory of his idiocy will have to **suffice**," sighed Vargas. "Yes, the memory will have to do. Sorry to **foil** your little plan, Gorgas, but I am looking forward to playing the part of the **dynamic** lawyer, full of fire and excitement. The lawyers on the television programs from the Earth are so *thrilling* and impressive, don't you think?"

Gorgas grumbled, stared at the ground, and refused to answer.

"Come, now, there's no use acting **sullen**," teased the alien lawyer. "I know you too well. Usually when you're angry, you have a lot to say. In fact, I'd miss all the goofy things you say if you weren't around. That's why I'm not going to execute you or *banish* you when I become Ruler of the Earth. My **reign** over this planet will be kind and generous. No, I just intend to shave your head."

Gorgas howled with anger and struggled against his chains. Vargas laughed and swirled around so that his robe flew up around him. All the little Vizwatts jumped up and started spinning around with him until they fell down from dizziness.

"Yes, when I am Ruler of the World, my first **decree** will be that all criminals must have their heads shaved. A shaved head is the worst shame a Smeltvlatian can suffer. Calm down, Gorgas, you're acting like I mean to **mutilate** you or something. It's not like I'm going to cut off your tentacles. It's just your silly, little, black mane!"

Gorgas stopped struggling for a split second and cast a quick, **furtive** glance toward Vargas. He did not want anyone to notice that he had seen Vargas's spare wand and keys underneath his robe.

"Vargas, I'm not sure all of this carrying on is good for your **karma**," remarked Bridget. "You know, doing bad things damages your life force. And in your next life, you could come back as a cockroach or something really horrible. If you believe in that sort of thing, anyway."

"Karma, schmarma," said Vargas. "I'm a Smeltvlatian, so I'm **exempt** from your human rules of behavior. They don't apply to me, and I don't have to go along with them. You have too many rules anyway, for a..."

THRILLING adj. affecting with a thrill of emotion 스릴 있는
I like thrilling movies.
나는 스릴 있는 영화를 좋아한다.

BANISH v. to send somebody away from of the country, as a punishment 추방하다
He was banished from his homeland.
그는 고향에서 추방당했다.

Suddenly a wail and a loud *thump* came from the prisoner's box. Gorgas had *collapsed*!

"Oh, dear, this is no fun," whined Vargas. "If he faints, terrorizing him just isn't as fun. You, science boy, put down that notepad. Can you **diagnose** him for me?"

"Well, I'm not a doctor, so I don't really think I can figure out what's wrong," explained Barnaby. "Besides, he's an alien, and I know nothing about alien health problems."

"Fine, then. I'll try to deal with him. The rest of you, see if one of these tables has wheels on its legs. Maybe we can use it as a **gurney**, you know, one of those rolling beds that they have in hospitals," said Vargas, as he bent over Gorgas. "Let's see, what seems to be the pro..."

Gorgas moved like lightning, and Vargas learned too late that his enemy's fainting spell was only a **pretense**, a **shrewd** and clever act to *lure* him into a position so that the keys and the wand could easily be taken out from underneath his robe. They **bandied** blows for a few seconds, knocking each other around with their tentacles. But Gorgas had the benefit of surprise. In a few seconds, he was free and holding Vargas at *bay* with his own wand.

Gorgas paused for a moment to **relish** his victory and enjoy the sight of Vargas with his clown wig all tangled up. Then he began his speech.

"Vargas, I **resent** the insulting way you have treated me and all the lies you have told," he began. "I am most displeased. But I will be **vindicated**. Oh, yes, my name will be cleared. Once the people of Smeltvlat find out what a dangerous criminal you are, they will **shun** you forever. No Smeltvlatian will ever speak to you again. Then they will forget about all of the little things I did, and welcome me home."

Bridget, Barnaby, Babette, Beauregard, and all the Vizwatts had hoped that the battling Smeltvlatians would not notice them sneaking toward the door. No such luck.

"Hold it right there!" commanded Gorgas. "You silly Vizwatts can go. But you kids are coming with us, and bring that cat. We have some scores to settle."

THUMP n. heavy blow; noise made by this 탁 때림; 쿵하는 소리
We heard the thump as he fell.
우리는 그가 넘어지면서 내는 쿵 소리를 들었다.

COLLAPSE v. to fall down 넘어지다
He collapsed in the street and died on the way to hospital.
그는 거리에서 넘어졌는데 병원으로 가는 길에 죽었다.

LURE v. to attract or tempt (a person or an animal) 불러들이다, 유혹하다
Bees are lured by the scent of flowers.
꽃향기에 벌들이 모여들었다.

BAY (hold at bay의 형태로 쓰여) to prevent an enemy, pursuer, etc. from coming near 다가오지 못하게 하다
I'm trying to hold my creditors at bay.
나는 채권자들이 다가오지 못하도록 애쓰고 있다.

Relationships

Decide what relationship the following pairs of words have to each other. If they mean close to the same thing, make "S." If they have opposite meanings, mark "O."

1. resentment :: ire
2. oath :: pledge
3. keen :: blunt
4. cavalcade :: procession
5. bustle :: saunter
6. wrath :: animosity
7. shun :: embrace
8. frank :: covert
9. spurn :: rebuff
10. dingy :: immaculate

Q U I C K   Q U I Z   **27**

Relationships

Decide what relationship the following pairs of words have to each other. If they mean close to the same thing, make "S." If they have opposite meanings, mark "O."

1. consensus :: accord
2. alliance :: coalition
3. largess :: philanthropy
4. fringe :: center
5. shrewd :: candid
6. relish :: distaste
7. furtive :: guarded
8. integrity :: virtue
9. bias :: fairness
10. dynamic :: lethargic

Q U I C K   Q U I Z   **28**

Fill in the Blank

For each sentence below, choose the word that best completes the sentence.

1. While everyone agreed that Doug's _____ of Principal Evans during the talent show was funny, it didn't stop Doug from getting two days of detention.

   a. crusade   b. inauguration   c. parody   d. ceremony

2. Since the _____ was also a big *Star Trek* fan, he enjoyed dressing up as a Klingon to perform Lulu and Frank's wedding.

   a. magistrate   b. parson   c. candidate   d. governess

3. The Secretary of State hoped to _____ a peaceful settlement between the two sides before a full-scale war erupted.

   a. arbitrate   b. vindicate   c. incriminate   d. endeavor

4. Once Jim Halbof, regarded by everyone as the most honest person in the world, _____ for Romero's character, Romero was elected Mayor by a landslide.

   a. alleged   b. vouched   c. distorted   d. diminished

5. Sent to his room and hour earlier than usual, the boy's _____ mood quickly changed to joy when he discovered his new train set waiting for him there.

   a. forthright   b. bipartisan   c. sullen   d. discreet

6. Since Shelby was born and raised in Palestine, Texas, it was obvious to everyone that her English accent was _____ .

   a. affected   b. circumstantial   c. wry   d. unprecedented

7. When the evening paper ran a picture of the governor accepting a million dollar bribe, the citizens knew that the _____ in the government was everywhere.

   a. larceny   b. corruption   c. curfew   d. karma

8. The king had a revolution on his hands after he _____ that all peasants had to work an extra three hours a day to build his new castle.

   a. bandied   b. decreed   c. sprawled   d. diagnosed

9. When she became a world famous singer, Glydia hoped to _____ a great gift of money to the Juilliard, Ohio School of Music, where she was first trained.

   a. dictate   b. garble   c. reckon   d. bestow

Q U I C K   Q U I Z   (29)

Matching

Match each word on the right with a word on the left that has a meaning that's close to the same.

1. assets	A. gather
2. mutilate	B. deform
3. suffice	C. fun outing
4. nuance	D. flatter
5. convene	E. band of colors
6. fawn	F. subtle difference
7. incumbent	G. personal resources
8. drone	H. holder of office
9. spectrum	I. satisfy
10. spree	J. continuous low hum

Q U I C K   Q U I Z   (30)

Matching

Match each word on the right with a word on the left that has a meaning that's close to the same.

1. exempt	A. unsupported claim
2. clincher	B. movable hospital table
3. abounding	C. weak
4. gurney	D. excused
5. reign	E. plentiful
6. supplication	F. begging
7. frail	G. conversation
8. pretense	H. rule
9. discourse	I. decisive act

Showdown
2026

최후의 대결 2026

I probably don't have to tell you that I wasn't looking forward to another trip through time and space. The last couple of *jaunts* had left my head *fuzzy* and my eyes **bleary**. To tell the truth, I'm not sure that the whole process is even **hygienic**—it certainly did nothing to promote my health or cleanliness. After each time jump, I was left with a strange, sticky **residue** on my fur, as if I had been dipped in oil. I noticed it on Babette, Barnaby, and Bridget, too. They looked sweaty, but the sweat had an odd, greenish tinge to it that made their healthy faces take on a sickly **hue**. I remember wishing I had a *scrub brush* so I could scour that green mess off their faces. After that, perhaps, a nice **astringent** to make sure every last bit of *slime* was gone and leave their skin fresh and **taut**. Nice tight skin is the key to a good *complexion*, you know. But, the situation being what it was, I was forced to try to lick them clean.

As it turned out, we had been in the Sacajabogue City courthouse in Louisiana, in the year 1926. It was a small, pretty town in the southern swamps. Too bad we didn't get a chance to really take a look around. I have often wondered what the natives thought of the crazy little alien coconut creatures. The courtroom Vizwatts took Gorgas at his word and ran away as fast as they could. I noticed them rolling through the bushes and blackberry bramble to get away. Perhaps they got caught in some dark **bog** on the edge of town. The earth in south Louisiana is so wet and spongy that whole horses used to get stuck in it. Or maybe the Vizwatts made friends and settled down. I guess we'll never know.

JAUNT n. short journey, made for pleasure   여행, 소풍
She's gone on a jaunt into town.
그 여자는 시내로 소풍을 갔다.

FUZZY adj. blurred or indistinct   흐린, 희미한
This photograph is too fuzzy for me to identify the people in it.
이 사진은 너무 흐려서 사진에 있는 사람이 누구인지 알 수가 없다.

SCRUB BRUSH n. stiff brush for scrubbing floors, etc.   세탁솔, 수세미
Use the scrub brush when you clean the floor.
바닥을 청소할 때 세탁솔을 사용해라.

SLIME n. thick soft slippery liquid substance, especially mud   미끌미끌한 것, 더러운 것
There was a coating of slime on the unwashed sink.
씻지 않은 싱크대에는 더러운 때가 입혀져 있었다.

COMPLEXION n. the color, quality, and general appearance of the skin, particularly of the face   안색, 혈색
The fisherman had a rough complexion from the weather.
그 어부는 악천후로 인해 거친 안색을 드러냈다.

We, on the other hand, got dragged forward in time about one hundred years. At least, that's what Gorgas told us. When I came to, I was in the corner of what used to be called an artist's loft, a big, open room on the top floor of a building. For some reason, it looked familiar, but I couldn't tell why. The room looked like a science lab. *Strewn* everywhere were bottles full of bubbling liquids, sheets of metal, and scribbled notes. But it was much fancier than most labs I'd seen. In a corner, by one of the tall windows, was a beautiful wooden desk—probably **mahogany**, judging from its rich, reddish-brown color. Fine furniture and rugs filled the room. The skyline that I saw through the windows looked familiar, too. Familiar, but different; I couldn't quite place it.

In the center of the room stood a tall man with a long, thin nose and pale hair. He was so **gaunt** that it looked like he must not have eaten for a month. His skin was dull, yellowish, and **sallow**. He wore a lab coat, sort of like Barnaby's, and seemed to be having some sort of argument with Gorgas, who was standing close by.

"What do you mean, it's not ready?" demanded Gorgas. "Didn't I make you rich? Before I came along, you were a poor, struggling scientist. Now you are a **prosperous entrepreneur**, owner of your own successful company."

"Yes, I agree, the **revenues** my business has enjoyed have been large. I could never have tried such as **venture** without the large, cash **subsidy** you gave me," said the skinny scientist. "I was very honored to be the **recipient** of such a big gift. But, please, let me explain. I didn't say the Death Ray wasn't ready. I just said that I wasn't sure I could give it to you."

Bridget, Babette, and Barnaby, who had been rolling around on the floor dizzily, pushed themselves up to their feet, looked around, and tried to get their *bearings*. Vargas, his clown wig now gone, was still unconscious.

"Hey," whispered Barnaby. "I feel like I've been here before."

"I know what you mean," said Bridget, nodding.

Babette jerked her head toward Gorgas and asked, "What do you think is going on?"

"You had better have a good explanation for this, Niels," growled Gorgas.

STREW v. to scatter; to cover with scattered things; sprinkle 흩뿌리다; 흩뿌려 덮다
His desk is strewn with journals.
그의 책상은 잡지들로 어수선하게 뒤덮여 있다.

BEARING n. (get one's bearings의 형태로 쓰여) to find out where one is by recognizing landmarks, etc. 현재 위치를 알아내다
They got their bearings in a violent snowstorm.
그들은 거친 폭풍우 속에서 현재 있는 위치를 파악했다.

Niels, the scientist, blinked calmly and replied, "Well, of course. You see, you have another one of your kind with you here. I hope you are not upset, but I really cannot **differentiate** between the two of you. You both have a dozen eyes, ten legs, moist heads. Aside from your hair, which could easily be dyed and cut, and I can't tell you apart. I have to be very careful about handing over my inventions. How do I know you are the one who **commissioned** me to build the Death Ray? How do I know it wasn't him, the one with white hair, who hired me?"

"So, you think all Smeltvlatians have a **uniform** appearance? Well, I suppose I can't **reproach** you for your poor skills of observation, because you aren't to blame. Humans do tend to miss a lot of details," sighed Gorgas. "But, no matter. I forgive you. Now hand over the keys to the Death Ray."

"Wait one second!" groaned Vargas, untangling his tentacles and standing up. "Niels, he is lying. It was I who paid you. I'll prove it, too. Remember how I visited you that time when you were *stumped*? You couldn't figure out a certain problem, and you were about to give up. You told me that science really wasn't for you, and that all your life, you really wanted to be a tap dancer. But you had to give up your dream because you had no sense of **rhythm** so you couldn't dance in time to any music. Right?"

"Yes, how glad I was to have a **confidant**. I needed someone to tell my secrets to, someone to trust," said Niels sadly. "I thought all my work had been for **naught**, but you helped me by showing me that my work was worth something. So who is this other guy and what should I do?"

"What should you do?" snapped Gorgas. "Don't listen to this fellow. I am your employer. Listen, remember how you lost your lucky pen in this huge room, and I helped you do a **painstaking** search of the entire place, crawling across every inch of the floor, even though I had no idea what your lucky pen looked like?"

Niels seemed confused.

STUMP v. to pay (a sum of money); to make somebody penniless (돈을) 지불하다; 무일푼으로 만들다
Finally I was stumped, so I decided to find a job.
마침내 무일푼이 되어서 나는 일자리를 찾기로 결정했다.

"Yes, yes, I remember that, too," he agreed. "You couldn't find it. It didn't turn up again for months. Hmm. I'm afraid I don't know exactly what to do, here. Which one is the real you?"

"I almost hate to get involved in this **controversy**," began Bridget, "but isn't it possible that they both hired you to create a Death Ray?"

"Who are you and what exactly do you mean?" snapped the scientist.

"My name is Bridget, and these two are Babette and Barnaby. I can't say we're happy to be here, but we might as well help you out if we can," she replied. "What I was suggesting was that Gorgas and Vargas, without realizing what the other had done, may have both hired you to create a Death Ray. You couldn't tell them apart, so you thought it was only one alien. I can tell you one thing—unless you made two Death Rays, we're probably going to have trouble."

Niels nodded. "I think you may be onto something. Gorgas and Vargas, eh? I never knew his, uh, their names. But, say, what are you doing here?"

"We should ask you the same thing," chimed in Babette. "Do you realize what kind of aliens you are mixed up with? The two of them are responsible for some of the most **abominable** crimes in the galaxy. In fact, they nearly destroyed the Earth for the sake of sport. And you're making a Death Ray—whatever that is—for them?"

Vargas did his best to look sad and helpless. A *twisty* little **tendril** of white hair fell over a couple of his eyes, making him look almost boyish.

"How can you believe that, Niels?" asked Vargas sadly. "Can't you see that these children and I are being held prisoner by that terrible creature?"

"That doesn't make any difference," said Barnaby. "They may be two separate aliens, but they have the same **mode** of action, the same way of doing things. They are both **wily**, crafty, and sneaky through and through. And bad to the bone—if they have bones, that is. I'd call them evil **incarnate**."

TWISTY **adj.** full of twists and turns; winding 꾸불꾸불한
The road was very twisty.
그 길은 정말 꾸불꾸불했다.

"Those are strong words, Barnaby," commented Niels. "You really think they *embody* all that is evil?"

"Look, he's not kidding around," Bridget jumped in. "They are competing with each other to rule the world, and they would rather destroy the planet than lose the game, We have to stop them."

Niels stroked his chin and thought. He did not appear to be convinced. Gorgas stood by patiently.

"I'm not sure. I'd like some **tangible** proof—something I can touch and see and hold in my hands," he said. "I'm sorry, but I have a cautious **temperament**. That's just the way I am."

"We don't have time to argue about this," insisted Babette, stomping her foot. "I tell you, every time we see these aliens something bad happens. It is an alarming trend. I feel certain that the pattern will continue if one of them gets a Death Ray. You must not hand it over."

Gorgas heaved a sigh and held up his wand.

"My dear, you base your argument on a *shaky* **premise**," he said. "You act as if Niels here has a choice. I'm afraid he doesn't. Niels, I am bored with this discussion. Let us **dispense** with the *chit chat* and get down to business."

Gorgas shook a couple of his tentacles threateningly. Niels stroked his chin and shook his head.

"It looks like you kids were right," said the scientist. "It does seem that he would be **apt** to use the Death Ray for evil. Such mood *swings* he has! One minute he's acting like my friend, and the next he wants to beat me up."

"Yes, you're right, Niels," urged Vargas, inching closer. "Gorgas is a **volatile** being; he could *lash* out at any time. Give the Death Ray to me."

EMBODY v. to put into a form that can be seen; to express in definite form 구현하다, 구체화하다
A building embodies the idea of the architect.
건물은 건축가의 이념을 구현한다.

SHAKY adj. not firm and steady; not safe and reliable 불안정한; 믿을만 하지 않은
My French is a bit shaky.
나는 불어를 잘하지 못한다.

CHIT CHAT n. chat; gossip 잡담
We were enjoying chit chat at the hotel lobby.
우리는 호텔 로비에서 잡담을 하고 있었다.

SWING n. a change or shift in attitude, opinion, behavior, etc. 동요, 변동; 변경
I did the job without any swings of attitude.
나는 태도에 아무런 변화 없이 그 일을 했다.

LASH v. (lash out의 형태로 쓰여) to make a sudden violent attack with blows or words 덥석 덤벼들다
He lashed out at the opposition's policies.
그는 상대편의 정책을 공격했다.

"That's enough, Vargas!" boomed Gorgas. "Niels, you disappoint me. But no matter. I will punish you later. The Death Ray is around here somewhere. I will find it myself."

Gorgas slithered over to the lab area and began *snooping* around, opening drawers, looking behind curtains, and *overturning* piles of paper. Vargas, no longer guarded by his enemy, quietly sneaked over to the desk and began searching as well. The Two Smeltvlatians were so focused on finding the invention first that neither of them took any notice of the humans.

"I owe you kids an apology. It's true, these aliens are *creeps*," Niels huffed. "I was feeling guilty about cheating them, but now I'm glad."

"Cheating them?" asked Bridget, confused. "You mean that..."

"That's right. There isn't any Death Ray," he explained. "Oh, I tried to design one, but I guess I'm just not good at weapons. I used the money they gave me to create a **vaccine** that prevents nonrhythmitis, which is the condition that kept me from being a tap dancer. I wanted to make sure that no child would ever again suffer from the *devastating* lack of rhythm that cost me my dream."

"That's definitely better than a Death Ray," said Bridget. "Is the vaccine a pill? What's it made of?"

"No, it's not a pill," explained Niels. "You have to shoot it under the skin with a **hypodermic** needle. As far as what it's made of, it's a pretty complicated **concoction**. I don't want to bore you with a lot of medical **jargon**, so I won't list all of the ingredients."

"No offense, Niels, but do you think we could discuss this later?" asked Barnaby. "I'd really like to hear about it, but Gorgas and Vargas are going to get tired of searching soon, and they'll be coming back to you for answers. We need a plan."

SNOOP v. to try to find out things that do not concern oneself; to pry into   기웃거리다, 간섭하다
The old lady snooped into everybody's business.
그 노인은 모든 사람들의 일에 간섭했다.

OVERTURN v. to turn over or upside-down; to upset   뒤집다, 뒤집어지다, 들추어 보다
The boat overturned.
배가 뒤집어졌다.

CREEP n. an undesirable, unpleasant, or worthless person   소름끼치는 녀석
What a creep he is!
얼마나 소름끼치는 녀석이냐!

DEVASTATING adj. causing severe shock   심각한, 지독한, 형편없는
It's a devastating news.
그것은 심각한 뉴스다.

"I think I have an idea," said Babette, "but we'll have to **orchestrate** our actions carefully; we're going to have to act as a team to pull this off. Bridget, do you still have your gum?"

"Naturally," grinned Bridget.

"Niels, is that your lucky pen in the pocket of your lab coat?" asked Babette.

"Er, yes..." replied Niels.

"Okay, here's what we're going to do," began Babette.

The humans gathered in a huddle and whispered frantically as the aliens continued to search. Gorgas tore at the tape on an unopened **parcel** that was sitting on the **threshold** only to discover it was a package of chocolate chip cookies that had been sent by Niels's mother. Vargas had even overturned a filing cabinet, but they'd found nothing. Finally, Niels interrupted their search with a laugh.

"Look at you two!" he cried. "Scrambling around on the floor. You won't find what you're looking for, you know. You'll never find it. Not in a million years."

"Niels, I've had enough of you," warned Gorgas, moving threateningly toward the tall scientist. "I'm going to *sock* you in the jaw."

"W-wait!" cried Niels, nervously backing away. "I mean, you won't find it because I have it. It's right here!"

Niels reached into his pocket and pulled out his lucky pen. It was a **nondescript** ballpoint pen, nothing special or unusual about it. It was black and it had one of those little buttons on the top that you push to bring the tip in and out. The only mark on it was a tiny picture of a *skull*, which was the **logo** of a local chemical company. It was just an ordinary pen, but the aliens were fascinated.

SOCK v. to give (somebody) a strong blow 때리다, 날려주다, 충격을 주다
Sock him on the jaw!
그 녀석 턱을 날려줘라!

SKULL n. bony framework of the head under the skin 두개골
The fall fractured his skull.
추락으로 그의 두개골이 부서졌다.

"Ah, so small and elegant!" cooed Vargas. "It is the perfect **covert** weapon—dreadfully destructive, yet so easily hidden. Please, Niels, give it to me."

"Nope, Since I can't decide between you, you will have to decided for yourselves," said Niels, tossing the pen to the middle of the room. "Fight for it. Come on, fight for it. What are you *chickens*?"

Niels did not have to **goad** the aliens for long. In an instant, they were in the center of the loft, circling carefully around the pen on the floor, waiting for a chance to bend over for it without getting knocked in the head by a tentacle. Vargas, who had taken a letter opener from the desk, seemed to have an advantage. But Gorgas was quicker. He distracted Vargas by waving one of his left tentacles and made a grab for the Death Ray with a right.

"Ha, ha!" he *crowed* with triumph. "Here we are at last, Vargas. And it is I who have the Death Ray and you only have a letter opener!"

"Curses!" shouted Vargas, backing away.

Gorgas pointed the pen at Vargas and began hitting the button. Click. Click. Click, click. Click, click, click. Nothing happened. He tried again. Click. Click. Still nothing. Vargas seized his chance and charged at Gorgas full speed. They fell to the floor, a big oozy ball of tentacles.

"Now, Bridget!" urged Babette.

Bridget ran toward the fighting pair, pulling her gum in a long string from between her teeth. Working like lightning, she began to wrap the gum like a rope around and around the aliens. Before they knew what was happening they were tied up tightly with gum, unable to even *wiggle* one tentacle. Babette and Barnaby relieved the aliens of their wands, their *back-up* wands, and their weapons—the pen and the letter opener.

CHICKEN n. coward 겁쟁이
I won't play with such a chicken.
나는 그런 겁쟁이하고는 놀지 않을 거다.

CROW v. to express gleeful triumph (about one's success, etc.) 환성을 울리다
She won the competition and won't stop crowing.
그녀는 시합에서 이겨서 환성을 멈추지 못했다.

WIGGLE v. to move from side to side with rapid short movements 움직이다
The baby was wiggling its toes.
그 아기는 발가락을 움직이고 있었다.

BACK-UP n. support; reserve 지원; 대응(품), 예비
The police had military back-up.
경찰은 군사적인 지원을 받았다.

"My dear!" objected Gorgas. "Please release me! Didn't you see, Vargas was the **assailant**. I was just the victim of his attack."

"Ooh, Gorgas, how I **revile** you!" growled Vargas. "You never stop. Please, children, do what you want with us, but don't leave me tied to someone I hate so much."

"You know, guys, I'm a nice person," said Bridget. "I have this personal **creed** I like to live by, which is that on a **fundamental** level, everyone is good. At their core, no one is evil. Sure, they may develop some bad habits and do some bad things, but everybody deserves a second chance."

"That's a lovely **ideology**, my dear," agreed Gorgas eagerly. "What a beautiful belief system. You'll see. Vargas and I will **forge** an agreement and become friends. I swear, we will reach an **accord**, or my name isn't Gorgas!"

"You didn't let me finish," replied Bridget, shaking her head. "I have always held that idea dear. I **cherish** the belief that people will do the right thing, if only you show them how. But my experience with you two has **infused** me with a deep mistrust for aliens on scavenger hunts. I have no faith in you."

Vargas *squirmed* and objected, "You are right to dislike us, after all the things we've done. I don't know how it happened. I used to be the most **ingenuous** young Smeltvlatian, just as open and honest as I could be. Then, because of Gorgas and all that he did to me, my honesty began to **atrophy** and my sense of fair play *withered* away."

Vargas tried to smile at Bridget, but it came off looking more like a silly **simper**.

"Perhaps, here on the Earth, there is some sort of **therapy** I could go through, some treatment to restore my better qualities," he continued. "You see, I can be made well again, unlike some people I know."

SQUIRM v. to move by twisting the body about; to wriggle; to writhe 몸부림치다
He was squirming (around) on the floor in agony.
그는 고뇌에 차서 바닥에서 몸부림치고 있었다.

WITHER v. to become dry, shrivelled or dead 사라지다, 시들다
Their hopes gradually withered away.
그들의 희망은 서서히 사라졌다.

"I see what you are hinting at!" growled Gorgas. "But if you're trying to **insinuate** that I cannot be cured, you are wrong! My dear Bridget, Vargas may **profess** a desire to reform, but his claim is false. I, however, truly want to fly right from now on."

"You just don't get it," said Barnaby. "We are not going to believe you. The things you have done are not **trifles**, they are serious crimes! We're not going to let you get away with them. Niels, why don't you **whet** the razor so it will be nice and sharp?"

"Actually, Barnaby, it's an electric razor. Straight razors are too dangerous," whispered Niels.

"Oh. Well, whatever," said Barnaby. "Gorgas, Vargas, you'd better get ready. We're going to shave your heads and send you back to Smeltvlat!"

"No! Not that!" shrieked the aliens.

"Yes, that," said Barnaby. "Niels, do you want to do the honors?"

"Why, certainly," said Niels, stepping forward with his battery-driven razor. "Get ready, you two."

It was a good thing Bridget's gum was so carefully wrapped around the two aliens. They screamed and yelled as Niels shaved their heads, but they could not move. After it was over, the aliens, who never were very attractive in the first place, were *downright* ugly. The **dour**, gloomy expressions on their faces did not improve their appearances.

"You will pay for this!" they both shouted.

Babette stepped forward and held out one of the wands she'd taken from Gorgas.

DOWNRIGHT adv. frankly; straightforwardly   정말로
He is downright rude.
그는 정말로 무례하다.

"Barnaby has explained to me that using this wand is simple," she began. "I only have to concentrate on what I want your *destination* to be, and it will do the rest. But first, Bridget, please pin the note on them."

Bridget came forward and taped a note to the tied up aliens. It read, "People of Smeltvlat: Please **ensure** that these criminals are punished to the full extent of the law." Once the note was attached, Babette closed her eyes and began moving the wand in slow circles. The aliens howled like wolves and in a matter of seconds, they were gone. They left behind nothing but their shaved hair and a small, oozy puddle.

"All right!" cried Bridget, happily exchanging high fives with everyone. "That was some plan, Babette. It was perfect—the **optimal** solution to our problems."

"I'm not so sure," sighed Babette. "These wands worry me. They are so powerful, I fear what would happen if they fell into the wrong hands. I think we should destroy them."

"Destroy them? But how are we supposed to get home? Niels, what year is this and where exactly are we?" asked Bridget.

"It's 2026 and we're in New York City. I guess you come from the past, huh?" he responded.

"Yes," sighed Bridget, as she sadly sunk into a chair and gazed out the window. "At least we're in New York. My family is probably out there somewhere. I can't go back to them now. They probably think I've been missing for years! But Babette is right. Those wands should be destroyed."

The look of **desolation** on Bridget's face moved Niels deeply. She looked so lost and miserable. He was about to hug her when a terrible crash came from across the room.

"Beauregard!" shouted Bridget, jumping out of her chair. "What are you doing?"

DESTINATION n. the place to which somebody is going or being sent   목적지
I reached my destination around half-past two.
두시 반쯤 목적지에 도착했다.

The giant black cat had been trying to climb a large **tapestry** that was hanging on the far wall. The thick, wool drape was carefully stitched with a picture of the Earth as seen from outer space. Unfortunately, the tapestry did not hold his weight, and it came *toppling* down on top of him. But instead of a wall behind the curtain, there was an **alcove**, a little curved room that dipped back about a dozen feet. Inside the alcove was a metal space ship about the size of a sail boat.

"Hey, wait a second… that's my ship!" cried Barnaby, clapping and running toward it. "I knew this place looked familiar. This is my old laboratory! And that's the space ship I was showing you before we went to the Yankees game!"

"You designed that ship?" asked Niels with surprise. "It was here when I rented this space. I have spent years trying to figure it out. It's so advanced!"

"Why, thank you! Bridget, don't you see? Our troubles could be over," Barnaby explained. "This ship is capable of time travel."

"Really?" asked Bridget, *perking* up.

"Absolutely. Hey, Babette. Hand me those wands. I'll hold them while you, you know, karate kick them or something," said Barnaby.

Babette gathered the Smeltvlatian wands and Barnaby held them bunched up in front of him. Babette took a moment to center herself, then with one mighty "Hiyah!" chopped them all in two with the edge of her hand.

"So much for that," said Barnaby. "Now then, everybody help me **lug** that ship out here. It's so heavy that it'll take all of us to drag it out. I need to examine it and see if I can get it going."

Bridget, Babette, Barnaby, Niels, and even Beauregard pulled the ship into the middle of the loft, and Barnaby jumped in the *hatch* on top and got right to work. After a few minutes, he jumped out with a puzzled look on his face.

TOPPLE v. to be unsteady and fall 떨어지다
The pile of books toppled over onto the floor.
책더미가 바닥 위로 떨어졌다.

PERK v. to become more cheerful, lively or vigorous 기운을 차리다
He looked depressed but perked up when his friends arrived.
그는 우울해 보였는데 친구들이 도착하자 생생해졌다.

HATCH n. an opening in a ship's deck; door in an aircraft or a space craft 승강구 뚜껑
They closed the hatch purposely.
그들은 고의로 승강구 뚜껑을 닫았다.

"Remember how I told you that there were some problems with the quasi-quantum quickener?" asked Barnaby. "Well, there still are. The **configuration** of the controls is a little messed up and laid out wrong. I put all the buttons in reverse order. But that's not a big problem. I can't seem to **synchronize** the steering clock with the probe clock. They should always show the same time and tick together exactly the same way, but the probe clock is running fast. Finally, there seems to be some sort of **fluctuation** in the engine system; one minute I have plenty of power and the next, the power **wanes** and I'm left with almost nothing."

"I hope you won't think I'm intruding," said Niels, "but as I said, I have spent years studying your ship and the notes you left behind. I think I might have solved your power problem."

"Oh?" asked Barnaby, hopefully.

"Yes, I did several experiments to find out what you were using to fuel the ship," began Niels. "You were using a *mash* made of bananas, correct? The sugar from the fruit was released slowly as the fruit decayed, and the ship **derived** its energy from the sugar. Well, that's fine for normal planetary travel, but for time travel you need something with more kick than just fruit sugars. Happily, I was able to discover that the **element** you were missing was chocolate."

Niels walked over to the threshold of the loft, picked up the box Gorgas had opened, and brought it to Barnaby.

"I had my mother bake these up special," he explained. "They are chocolate chip cookies that are designed to **integrate** into the system the exact amounts of sugar and chocolate that you need to travel through time. Just set up a reserve tank for the cookies and keep the fruit mash for space travel. What do you think?"

"Niels, you're the greatest!" cried Barnaby, hugging his fellow scientist around the waist. "I'm glad you believe in my project. No one in my time takes me seriously; they all think I'm crazy. Ah, well. Now, if only I could figure out how to get these clocks to run correctly."

MASH n. any substance made by crushing something into a soft mass 짓이긴 것
He beat the potato into a mash before eating it.
그는 감자를 짓이겨 먹었다.

620

"Let me at them," said Babette, rolling up her sleeve. "I have a way with machines."

Barnaby led her into the ship. And sure enough, one good *whack* was all those clocks needed to straighten up and tick and tock together. The friends were finally ready to go home.

Bridget, Barnaby, Babette, and Beauregard gathered around to say farewell to Niels. He seemed a little sad that they were leaving.

"I am sorry to see you go," sighed the scientist. "I get so little company. It's lonely. I wonder what will become of me, now that the aliens aren't funding my research."

"I think I can help you with that," said Barnaby, pulling his kaleidoscope out of his pocket. "Here, look through this and tell me what you see."

"Wow!" said Niels. "I see myself wearing a **garland** of roses around my neck. Someone is giving me an award for my vaccine! And now, now I see an invitation to join the most **elite** science club in the world, the Geneva Group. Only the finest, most respected scientists are asked to join. And now, but this is *hazy*, I think I see... no... wait... yes! I see myself dancing, tap dancing in a musical production! This is great!"

"That's your future, Niels," said Bridget, smiling warmly. "See? You have nothing to worry about."

Niels handed the kaleidoscope back to Barnaby and hugged all of the kids good-bye. He even patted Beauregard on the head. They all piled into the ship and Niels opened one of the large windows.

"Thanks for your help!" chirped Bridget as she climbed in. "We have to go now, we have a Yankees game to finish."

Barnaby fastened the hatch and strapped everyone in, then he sat down behind the controls and heaved a deep sigh.

"Keep your *fingers* crossed," he cautioned. "Let's hope that those cookies *pack* a serious punch!"

WHACK n. heavy blow 쾅 치기
I'll give you such a whack!
너를 한방 때려 주겠다.

HAZY adj. misty; not clear; vague 안개 낀; 흐릿한
We couldn't see far because it was so hazy.
너무 흐려서 우리는 멀리까지 볼 수 없었다.

FINGERS n. (cross one's fingers의 형태로 쓰여) to hope that one's plans will be successful 행운을 빌다
Keep your fingers crossed!
행운을 빌어요!

PACK v. to have a very powerful effect (위력 등을) 갖추고 있다
Those cocktails pack quite a punch!
저 칵테일들은 꽤 위력이 있다.

Relationships

Decide what relationship the following pairs of words have to each other. If they mean close to the same thing, make "S." If they have opposite meanings, mark "O."

1. fundamental :: trifling
2. integrate :: fuse
3. nondescript :: usual
4. cherish :: despise
5. wane :: wax
6. tendril :: sprout
7. wily :: devious
8. covert :: overt
9. reproach :: praise
10. assailant :: mugger
11. prosperous :: impoverished

Relationships

Decide what relationship the following pairs of words have to each other. If they mean close to the same thing, make "S." If they have opposite meanings, mark "O."

1. tangible :: actual
2. jargon :: lingo
3. revile :: adore
4. forge :: fabricate
5. abominable :: commendable
6. optimal :: worst
7. hue :: tone
8. volatile :: inert
9. bog :: mire
10. taut :: tense
11. hygienic :: sanitary

Fill in the Blank

For each sentence below, choose the word that best completes the sentence.

1. The tents within the rebel camp were of such _____ appearance that it was almost impossible to tell them apart.

    a. dour   b. bleary   c. uniform   d. rhythmic

2. Normally an easily frightened person, Nigel was _____ into taking skydiving lessons by the ceaseless taunts of his older sister.

    a. derived   b. insinuated   c. goaded   d. orchestrated

3. Since the assault team all had to reach the perimeter of the enemy base at exactly the same time, everyone worked to _____ their movements as closely as possible.

    a. fluctuate   b. concoct   c. differentiate   d. synchronize

4. Vincent's love of cruel practical jokes and vicious _____ earned him more bloody noses than any other person on the planet.

   a. creed   b. logo   c. premise   d. temperament

5. The new _____ was so fast and powerful that I could actually watch the pimples vanish into nothingness.

   a. vaccine   b. astringent   c. hypodermic   d. residue

6. With no visible landmarks for miles, it was easy to believe that the _____ grasslands stretched on forever.

   a. sallow   b. desolate   c. elite   d. gaunt

7. The _____ who invented the world's first disposable car (costing only $300) became a millionaire overnight.

   a. entrepreneur   b. recipient   c. revenue   d. subsidy

8. After watching the entire NBA basketball season without ever leaving his house, Robert realized that his leg muscles had begun to _____ .

   a. infuse   b. atrophy   c. whet   d. lug

9. We placed the _____ on our front door to show all carolers that they were welcome to come sing to us.

   a. alcove   b. mahogany   c. parcel   d. garland

10. Luckily, an _____ was reached between the fourth grades before the spitwad fight got too out of hand.

   a. ideology   b. controversy   c. accord   d. trend

Q U I C K   Q U I Z   34

Matching

Match each word on the right with a word on the left that has a meaning that's close to the same.

1. commission	A. claim knowledge
2. incarnate	B. nothing
3. profess	C. point of entering
4. bramble	D. thorny shrub
5. naught	E. scrub thoroughly
6. configure	F. grant authority
7. loft	G. space under a root
8. element	H. distribute
9. threshold	I. given human form
10. dispense	J. part of a whole
11. scour	K. fit parts together

Q U I C K   Q U I Z   35

Matching

Match each word on the right with a word on the left that has a meaning that's close to the same.

1. painstaking	A. likely
2. confidant	B. tiny amount
3. apt	C. honest
4. mode	D. decorated cloth

5. tinge
6. ensure
7. tapestry
8. simper
9. ingenuous
10. therapy
11. venture

E. trusty companion
F. counsel
G. manner
H. treatment
I. smirk
J. great thoroughness
K. guarantee

Like the Cheshire Cat...

체셔 고양이처럼

Bridget is the most naturally adventurous of the children, but she is also the first to grow tired of her travels. I remember her telling me once that she thought the best part of visiting new places was coming home. Not that she didn't like exploring. She just liked home most. As soon as Barnaby closed the hatch, Bridget started beaming as though it were her birthday.

I wasn't so sure that there was a reason to be smiling just yet. This was, after all, the first voyage the ship had ever made. It hadn't even been properly **christened**. Traditionally, there is a **ritual** that new ships go through before they sail. Someone declares the ship's name and then smashes a bottle of champagne across the bow. I decided that if we actually made it back to our correct time and place, I would personally christen the ship "Mr. Lucky."

I had no idea what to expect from time travel in Barnaby's boat. Gorgas and Vargas, for all their faults, had at least tried out their wands before they started *zapping* us around in time. To use an analogy that I learned while traveling through Asia with the Peking circus, what we were about to do was like *juggling* knives blindfolded. We didn't know what we were doing, and we had no idea where we might get stuck.

Barnaby did seem to have good control of the ship at first. He *eased* us out through the open window, which was luckily of the right *proportion* to let us through. We hovered in the air, just hanging out for a second, as Barnaby tried to compute our route with the help of the ship's *calculator*. He twisted a few *knobs*, punched a couple of buttons, and eased a lever forward.

ZAP v. to move very fast   재빨리 움직이다
Have you seen him zapping around town on his new motor bike?
그가 새 오토바이를 타고 시내를 급히 돌아다니는 것을 본 적이 있니?

JUGGLE v. to throw (a number of objects) up into the air, catch them and throw them into the air again and again, keeping one or more in the air at the same time   저글링을 하다
When did you learn to juggle?
언제 저글링 하는 것을 배웠니?

EASE v. (ease out의 형태로 쓰여) to dismiss from or leave quietly (a job, an office, or other position or place)   사직하다, 추방하다
The old player was about to ease himself out of the game.
그 나이든 선수는 그 경기에서 물러날 참이었다.

PROPORTION n. relation of one thing to another in quantity, size, etc.; ratio   비율
The proportion of imports to exports is worrying the government.
수출에 대한 수입의 비율을 보고 정부는 걱정을 하고 있다.

CALCULATOR n. small electronic device for making mathematical calculations   계산기
The bookkeeper used a desk calculator to help keep the accounts.
부기 계원은 경리 일을 돕기 위해 탁상용 계산기를 사용했다.

KNOB n. round handle (of a door, drawer, etc.)   손잡이
Open it with the knob of the drawer.
서랍 손잡이로 그것을 열어라.

Then, things got really weird.

"Whoa! What's going on?" gasped Barnaby, looking down.

It didn't seem as if the ship had moved at all, but for a minute all the light around them was **refracted**, so that the white light was split into a rainbow of color that swirled in circles. Then it stopped. The building they had just flown out of was still standing, but everything else was different. There were horses and carriages instead of cars in the dusty street below and the buildings were all made of wood and brick. The shining skyscrapers were gone.

"Umm, I think we went too far back," said Bridget, looking down through a window.

"Can you fix it?" asked Babette.

"Oh, I see," said Barnaby, *tinkering* with his controls. "We were moving in **increments** of ten years instead of one-year. We went back centuries instead of *decades*. Let's see, now. Okay, I think I have us back on track. Is everyone ready?"

Barnaby eased back on a lever and the light swirled again. This time, when they could see clearly again, Bridget almost *squealed* with joy. They were hovering outside the same building, but everything around her looked like the New York City she grew up in.

"This looks right!" she said clapping.

"Babette, what does the *probe* clock say?" asked Barnaby hopefully.

"It says we're back," smiled Babette. "We can even make it to the Yankees game—but we might be a little late."

TINKER v. to work in a casual or inexpert way, especially trying to repair or improve something 어설프게 만지작거리다, 서투르게 수선하다
He likes tinkering with computers.
그는 컴퓨터를 어설프지만 이리저리 만지작거리기를 좋아한다.

DECADE n. period of ten years 10년
I traveled Europe two decades ago.
나는 20년 전에 유럽을 여행했다.

SQUEAL v. to make a long, sharp, high-pitched cry or sound 비명을 지르다
He squealed like a pig.
그는 돼지 같은 비명을 질렀다.

PROBE n. unmanned spacecraft which obtains information about space and transmits it back to earth 우주 탐사기
We obtained the information about Venus from the Russian probes.
우리는 러시아 우주 탐사기로부터 금성에 관한 정보를 얻었다.

"Great! I'm going to have to crash through the window of my laboratory," warned Barnaby. "I don't want to land this ship on the street. Hold on!"

Barnaby rammed his ship into the window and the glass gave way with a crash. The boar slid across the floor, knocking over tables and cabinets until it finally came to a stop in a huge pile of paper. Bridget quickly unfastened the hatch and jumped out. Her eyes shone brightly as she danced around clapping.

"We're back! The world is safe from Smeltvlatian scavengers and we can still catch the Yankees game," she said excitedly. "What could be better?"

Just as she asked the question, there was a knock at the door.

"Open up, Barnaby, it's *Dean* O'Malley," called a rough, hoarse voice.

"Uh oh," groaned Barnaby. "Not the dean! I'm really in trouble now. He's in charge of my department. Wait until he sees this mess!"

"Don't worry, we'll think of something," said Bridget, too happy to worry about anything.

She skipped over to the door and flung it open.

"Welcome, welcome, Dean O'Malley!" cried Bridget. "My name is Bridget and this is Babette. The cat's name is Beauregard. We are friends of Barnaby's. Please come on in, because we have so much to tell you."

"My, what an **ebullient** personality you have," said the dean in a **husky** voice. "Are you always so *bubbly* and excited?"

DEAN n. a head of a division or school in a college or university   학장
He is the dean of the Law School.
그는 법학 대학원 학장이다.

BUBBLY adj. lively; vivacious; animated   생기가 넘치는
She is a bubbly personality.
그녀는 생기가 넘치는 인물이다.

The dean was not what Bridget expected. He was a short man, and so **stout** that he almost looked round. Most professors and scientists she knew wore simple clothing, but Dean O'Malley was wearing a **flamboyant** outfit that made him look more like a big, important movie **mogul** from the 1920s. He wore a long, silvery gray **mantle** over his *plump* shoulders, which was fastened at the neck with a glistening jeweled *clasp*. He carried a walking cane with a golden *tip* and wore sparkling rings on all of his fingers. His white hair and beard were carefully combed and styled. He had a friendly, pink face and a warm smile. Bridget could not help smiling at him.

"So, you have a lot to tell me, eh?" he asked, winking. "Splendid. But first, I have to tell Barnaby something. Barnaby? Where are you?"

Barnaby peeked out from behind the spaceship and then nervously came forward.

"Y-y-yes, sir?" he said.

"Barnaby! Didn't you get my **fax**? I've been trying to send you a note for hours! I finally decided that there must be something wrong with your phone line and that the message wasn't being received, so I came over myself. I see now that you probably just couldn't find the fax machine," said Dean O'Malley, looking around at the piles or paper and broken glass.

"Please do not be angry," urged Babette. "Let us explain. You see, we have just been traveling through time in order to save the world from destruction. Barnaby made an important scientific discovery that allowed us to return home from the future. We had to break the window to get in. I know you may not believe me, but it's..."

"It's true. I know," said the dean. "You see, I just got a visit from a scientist named Niels, who came from several decades in the future. He explained that it was Barnaby's research that allowed him to come, and he urged me to *nominate* Barnaby for membership in the Geneva Group. I am a member, you see, so I can invite new scientists to join."

PLUMP adj. having a full rounded shape; fleshy 포동포동한
The baby with plump cheeks is really cute.
포동포동한 빰을 가진 그 아기는 정말 귀엽다.

CLASP n. device for fastening things (e.g. the ends of a belt or a necklace) together 걸쇠, 버클
The clasp of my brooch is broken.
내 브로치의 걸쇠가 부러졌다.

TIP n. pointed or thin end of something 끝 부분
Put the tips of your fingers in the water.
손가락 끝 부분을 물속에 넣어라.

NOMINATE v. to appoint somebody to an office 지명하다
The board nominated her as the new director.
위원회에서 그녀를 새 이사로 지명했다.

Barnaby, Bridget, and Babette gazed at the stylish dean in amazement.

"Come, come, don't look so surprised!" laughed O'Malley. "Niels went over your notes with me and explained everything. I must say, I am impressed. You are certainly **entitled** to join the club. Yes, you definitely have earned the right. The **exclusion** of someone as brilliant as you are would be *unpardonable*."

"I am honored, Dean O'Malley," said Barnaby, blushing.

"Way to go, Barnaby!" said Bridget, slapping him on the back.

"That's wonderful!" agreed Babette.

Even Beauregard, who was stretched out on the floor, nuzzled Barnaby's foot fondly.

"Yes, congratulations, young man," continued the dean, taking on a look of seriousness. "In fairness, however, I should **qualify** my congratulations by warning you that the Geneva Group is pretty rough on its new members. There are some tasks that you will be forced to perform if you want to join."

Barnaby looked confused. "You mean the Geneva Group **hazes** its new members? I thought college students were the only ones childish enough to demand people to complete embarrassing tasks in order to qualify for clubs."

A smile crept across O'Malley's face as he reached into his vest pocket.

"Oh, no. I'm afraid you have to come with me right now. Your friends, too. And see if that *languid* cat has enough energy to stand up. If you want to be a member of the Geneva Group, you must come to tonight's Yankees game. And we have to see just how many hot dogs we can all eat," laughed the dean, waving several tickets in front of Barnaby.

UNPARDONABLE adj. not pardonable; that cannot be pardoned   용서받을 수 없는
According to the Bible, the sin of blasphemy against the Holy Ghost is the unpardonable sin.
성경에 의하면 성령에 대한 불경죄는 용서받을 수 없는 죄이다.

Barnaby laughed. "Come to think of it, I am hungry," he said. "What do you say, guys?"

Bridget and Babette nodded eagerly, and Beauregard stood up *grudgingly*.

"Marvelous!" said O'Malley. "Oh! The **felicity** of this occasion almost made me forget my other news. Happy occasions always make me forgetful. Barnaby, I know you don't like to think about money matters, but luckily for you, I do like to consider the **fiscal** side of things. A **singular** invention like a time-traveling space ship will bring a lot of *donations* to the university, and of course, you will share in the **bounty** you create. I have arranged to get you a new laboratory with all of the latest equipment. Something so fancy that it'll make this lab look **squalid** in comparison. Although I must say, this lab is so dirty, it is approaching *squalor*. Is that a half-eaten sandwich I see on the floor?"

Dean O'Malley poked at an old tuna sandwich with his cane. Barnaby blushed again.

"I know, I'm messy," agreed Barnaby sadly. "Maybe I don't deserve a new lab."

"Nonsense!" said the dean. "It's already settled. I decorated the new lab myself, and it's quite impressive, if you don't mind my saying so. I only hope you don't think I've gone *overboard* and made it too **grandiose**."

Barnaby laughed. "I'm sure you've done a **sublime** job. Your great taste in furniture and clothes is well-known in the department. Everyone is always in awe at how grand you make any room that you decide to redecorate. Of course, no one could accuse you of exercising **thrift**."

"No, I've never been one to *pinch* pennies in interior decoration, that's for sure," chuckled the dean. "It's a good thing I'm such a **canny** investor of money. I believe in investing carefully. As far as keeping your new lab neat, well, we'll leave that up to your students and your research team."

GRUDGINGLY adv. unwillingly; reluctantly 마지못해, 억지로
The boss grudgingly raised my salary.
사장은 마지못해 내 월급을 올려주었다.

DONATION n. a gift; contribution 기부(금)
He makes the same donation to the church each year.
그는 해마다 교회에 똑같은 기부를 한다.

SQUALOR n. misery and dirt; filth 누추함
By modem standards people in medieval Europe lived in indescribable squalor.
현대적 기준에서 볼 때 중세 유럽 사람들은 말도 못할 정도로 누추한 삶을 살았다.

OVERBOARD adv. (go overboard의 형태로 쓰여) be very or too enthusiastic (about something/somebody) 극단적으로 나가다, ~에 열중하다
He goes overboard about every young woman he meets.
그는 만나는 젊은 여자들마다 열중한다.

PINCH v. to be stingy; to live in a very miserly way 인색하게 굴다; 몹시 절약하다
Her parents pinched so that she could study singing abroad.
그녀가 외국에서 노래 공부를 할 수 있도록 부모님은 굉장히 절약하셨다.

"Research team? Students?" asked Barnaby.

"Of course! And furthermore, I want you to design a new **curriculum** for the science department," said O'Malley. "Come up with a whole new set of science classes that will help students think about science in the truly unique way that you do. You will soon be recognized as a time-travel **guru**, the wisest and most knowledgeable in your field, and people everywhere will expect you to teach them and to set an example. But let's worry about that tomorrow. Today we're off to Yankee Stadium!"

Dean O'Malley turned dramatically on his heel and marched out the door, followed closely by Bridget, Barnaby, Babette, and Beauregard. Out on the street, the dean waved the children toward a shiny black van. It was not *boxy*, like old vans, but was **streamlined** to perfection, all of its slopes and angles were designed to help it cut through the air. Traffic, for once, was a *breeze*. None of New York's major **arteries** were *clogged* with honking cars, and they arrived at the ballpark in what seemed like no time at all.

This time, their seats were right behind home plate. The fans around them were mostly local police officers, firefighters, and other **municipal** workers still in their uniforms.

"All right!" said Bridget, when she saw the crowd near their seats. "They must have come straight from work. People who work for the city are the most **exuberant** fans there are. They really put a lot of energy into cheering for the Yankees. We're going to have some fun today!"

"Yes, those screaming men over there who have 'Go Yankees' and 'Kill the Red Sox' painted on their chests do seem to be **ardent** fans," agreed Babette.

"Yep, they really put their hearts into it," said Bridget.

BOXY adj. shaped like a box; square 네모진
There are lots of boxy houses around here.
이 근처에는 네모진 집들이 많이 있다.

BREEZE n. thing that is easy to do or enjoy 수월한 것
Some people think learning to drive is a breeze.
운전 배우는 것이 수월한 일이라고 생각하는 사람들도 있다.

CLOG v. to become blocked with thick or sticky material 막히다
The pipes are clogging up.
파이프들이 막히고 있다.

"I am very glad the **dismal** weather cleared. Baseball weather should be cheery, not dreary," commented Dean O'Malley. "Come, Barnaby. Let's go to the snack stand. We need fuel."

The dean and Barnaby took off in search of food and returned a few minutes later with armloads of it. Even Bridget was impressed with the amount.

"Now then, this five-gallon *tub* of popcorn is for our **communal** enjoyment. We must all be polite and share it," explained the plump scientist. "I got each of us a separate super-giant soda. Mine is the grape drink without ice. I prefer my soda **tepid**, not cold. If the drink is just slightly warm, it is easier for me to smell it and enjoy its sweet, fruity **bouquet**. Besides, I hate it when the ice melts and **dilutes** my drink. I'm afraid the snack seller would only sell me fifty hot dogs at one time. We will have to **ration** our supply if we want to make it through the game. So only eat one per inning, okay? Dig in!"

The game began, and the fans were swept away with excitement. The Yankees fought hard, and managed to build a two-run lead early in the game. Before they knew it, the seventh inning arrived.

"The seventh inning already," remarked Dean O'Malley. "Time for that timeless, **perennial** favorite, 'Take Me Out to the Ballgame.' That's an old song that will stay popular forever."

"It's quite an **opus**," Bridget agreed, as she stood up and got ready to sing. "Not quite a symphony or opera or anything, but I do think it's a nice work. Hey, Babette, Barnaby, are you ready to sing? I sure hope we stay on the ground this time!"

Barnaby, Babette, Bridget, and Dean O'Malley joined arms and *belted* out the song with great energy. They were so happy and excited about Barnaby's good fortune, so glad to be home, and so caught up in the game, they didn't even notice the big, black cat quietly sneaking away into the gathering shadows of the evening.

TUB n. a small container of plastic for food, etc.; a small cask or keg containing about four gallons 통
She eats three tubs of ice-cream at a time.
그 여자는 한번에 아이스크림 세 통을 먹는다.

BELT v. (belt out의 형태로 쓰여) to sing or play loudly and forcefully 노래를 부르다
She can belt out popular songs very well.
그녀는 팝송을 아주 잘 부를 줄 안다.

What can I say? I hate good-byes. All I wanted to do was make sure that they made it safely through the seventh inning without being kidnapped by aliens. But I wasn't too worried—I think they had their fill of adventures for a while. There was no need for me to keep such a careful **vigil** over them. O'Malley seemd like the sort who could keep three kids out of trouble.

Besides, I had a plane to catch. Ah, Trinidad! Ah, Consuela! Such a lovely time I had there! Consuela is a wonderfully **mercurial** cat—lively, high-spirited, and always keeping me *guessing*. She was such a **congenial** companion, with a personality so **engaging** and charming, most of the tomcats on the island were in love with her. We were so **compatible**; we were made for each other! I got so comfortable with my life there that I almost bought a **tract** of beach front property and settled down.

Almost. But then, along came a mysterious Siamese, with magical blue eyes and a mysterious past, who **derailed** my plans and put the whole island in an uproar. You see, she was a spy for a Burmese *warlord* named Chow who was trying to take over the *sugar cane* market in the Caribbean. And I became an unwilling **pawn**, completely under her control, in a plot to take over Trinidad and set up a secret outpost for Chow. Consuela tried to stop me, but I was caught in a web of lies, and Bridget, Barnaby, and Babette had to... well, perhaps we should save the details for later.

That's a story for another time.

GUESS n. (keep somebody guessing의 형태로 쓰여) to keep somebody uncertain about one's plans, etc. 마음 졸이게 만들다
My son's marriage was keeping me guessing a lot.
내 아들 결혼이 내 마음을 무척 졸이게 했었다.

WARLORD n. a military commander or commander in chief 장군, 군사 지도자
He was a brave warlord.
그는 용감한 장군이었다.

SUGAR CANE n. tall tropical grass from which sugar is made 사탕수수
Sugar cane is one of the chief sources of manufactured sugar.
사탕수수는 공장에서 제조되는 설탕의 주된 원료 중 하나이다.

QUICK QUIZ ⬤36

Relationships

Decide what relationship the following pairs of words have to each other. If they mean close to the same thing, make "S." If they have opposite meanings, mark "O."

1. ebullient :: exuberant
2. mogul :: tycoon
3. refract :: straighten
4. flamboyant :: grandiose
5. thrift :: extravagance
6. tepid :: scalding

QUICK QUIZ ⬤37

Relationships

Decide what relationship the following pairs of words have to each other. If they mean close to the same thing, make "S." If they have opposite meanings, mark "O."

1. congenial :: engaging
2. dismal :: squalid
3. guru :: prophet
4. dilute :: strengthen
5. stout :: lanky

QUICK QUIZ ⬤38

Fill in the Blank

For each sentence below, choose the word that best completes the sentence.

1. The _____ teacher soon learned that not everyone in the world liked to spend eighteen hours a day researching cockroaches like he did.
   a. singular   b. ardent   c. compatible   d. languid

2. Unfortunately, Ben was unable to complete his two-hour _____ on the harmonica, "Schoolyard Blues," before his mother made him come inside for supper.
   a. mantle   b. vigil   c. opus   d. tract

3. The new portable phone network used by the train engineers and station managers helped _____ the workings of the railroad and reduce commuter time by ten percent.
   a. derail   b. hover   c. beam   d. streamline

4. Since they had no idea how long they would be shipwrecked, the crew decided to start _____ supplies immediately.
   a. rationing   b. christening   c. excluding   d. entitling

5. The _____ singer would often start a concert in a sad mood, leave halfway through in a rage, and then come back at the end as happy as can be.
   a. perennial   b. mercurial   c. municipal   d. communal

6. In our house, the making of the first cup of coffee was an elaborate _____ that involved multiple grinders, four different kinds of beans, and purified water.
   a. analogy   b. pawn   c. curriculum   d. ritual

Matching

Match each word on the right with a word on the left that has a meaning that's close to the same.

1. fax
2. sublime
3. increments
4. haze
5. canny
6. bouquet
7. felicity

A. electronic document transfer
B. shrewd
C. increases
D. pleasant smell
E. supreme
F. joy
G. fog

Q   U   I   C   K   Q   U   I   Z   40

Matching

Match each word on the right with a word on the left that has a meaning that's close to the same.

1. arteries
2. fiscal
3. bounty
4. compute
5. husky
6. qualify

A. specify the meaning
B. financial
C. sturdy
D. blood vessels
E. calculate
F. plentiful wealth

Translation & Answer

해석 및 정답

1 7회 때의 납치

p.514

트리니다드! 진초록 물이 햇빛 속에서 너무나 환하게 빛나 아름다움에 눈이 부신 낙원 같은 섬! 곧, 곧 나는 그곳에 갈 거야. 그래서 콘수엘라와 해변 위에서 춤추고 껑충거리고 빙글빙글 돌며 신나게 뛰어노는 거야. 그리고는 모래 위로 몸을 던져서...

뉴욕시티의 한 공항에서 쓸쓸하고 답답한 대기 구역 27B 안에 앉아 있을 때 적어도 난 계속 이렇게 혼잣말을 지껄였지. 내가 탈 비행기는 날씨 때문에 몇 시간이 연착됐는데, 밖에서는 비가 심하게 오고 있었어. 아니, 심한 정도가 아니라 억수로 퍼붓고 있었지. 마치 하늘에서부터 강들이 흘러내리고 있는 것 같았어. 난 느긋하게 기다리려고 애썼어. 두어 시간 동안 왔다갔다하고 난 뒤 의자 밑에서 휴식을 취해야겠다 마음먹었어. 의자 밑으로 들어가 길다랗고 검은 꼬리를 몸 밑으로 안전하게 밀어 넣은 뒤 몸을 공처럼 둥글게 말고 두 눈을 감았지. 하지만 선잠에서 깨어났을 때 정말 이상한 일이 벌어졌어...

아, 내가 또 평소처럼 앞서가고 있군. 내 소개를 할게. 내 이름은 보리가드고, 사우스 캐롤라이나 출신의 여행을 다니는 신사 고양이지. 아마 내가 고양이치고는 유별나게 한 체격한다고 생각할 거야. 난 근육도 꽤 발달돼 있고, 뒷다리로 서면 키가 4피트가 넘어. 내가 생각해도 난 우아하고 고상하고 예의가 바른데, 너희도 나에 대해 좀 알게 되면 내 말에 고개를 끄덕일 거야. 내가 너희한테 이런 식으로 얘기를 많이 하니까 날 나레이터라고 불러도 돼. 이야기가 아주 재미있고 흥미진진하기 때문에 이 정도 일은 기꺼이 할 수 있지.

p. 515

아까 말했듯이 난 콘수엘라라는 사랑스러운 고양이를 방문하러 트리니다드에 가는 길이었어. 그녀는 이국적이고 색다른 아름다움을 지녔어! 그녀의 우아한 발은 완벽하게 모양이 잡혔지. 하지만 애통하게도 콘수엘라를 보러 갈 수 없게 됐어. 선잠에서 깬 눈을 떴을 때 크게 "뻥"하는 소리가 났어. 그런 소리를 낼 수 있는 사람은 오직 하나, 바로 브리지트였어. 난 의자 밑에서 기어 나왔는데, 아니나 다를까 브리지트가 있었어. 청바지에 뉴욕 닉스 셔츠를 입은 채 얼굴에서 거대한 풍선껌의 찌꺼기를 떼어내고 있었어. 잠시 후 그녀가 사람들이 몰려 있는 쪽으로 새끼 고양이처럼 잽싸게 뛰어가자 야구 모자 밑에서 깔끔하게 땋은 검은 머리가 나와 팔랑거렸어.

"바베트! 바베트!" 브리지트가 소리쳤다. "이쪽이야! 너 눈이 멀었니?"

바베트와 브리지트가 다시 만난 것이다. 그것으로 내 일은 결정이 났다. 앞뒤를 안 가리는 이 친구들은 걸핏하면 사고를 치는 특별한 재능을 갖고 있었고, 난 얘네들이 자기네들끼리 위험을 감당하도록 내버려 둘 수가 없었어. 트리니다드는 좀 미뤄야겠어. 난 그들을 보호해야 했다. 거기다 난 그들과 여러 번 근사한 모험을 했었다. 잘 모르긴 해도 이번이 가장 대단한 모험이 될 것 같았다.

"브리지트?" 머리에서 발끝까지 검은색으로 멋지게 차려입은 큰 키의 프랑스 여자아이, 바베트가 소리쳤다. 그녀는 주위를 더 잘 둘러보기 위해 커다란 선글라스를 비스듬하게 내려 썼다.

"바베트, 이쪽이야! 선글라스를 벗어, 하나도 안 보이겠어!" 브리지트가 대답했다.

"아, 거기 있구나, 내 친구. 잘 지냈니?" 바베트가 선글라스를 제대로 다시 쓰며 미소지었다.

"잘 지냈냐고? 우리 이게 몇 달만이야! 흥분되는 걸!" 브리지트가 친구를 포옹하며 소리쳤다. "네 비행기가 결국 무사히 도착해서 다행이야. 너랑 같이 할 계획들을 세워놨어. 네가 나한테 파리 구경을 시켜줬으니, 이젠 내가 너한테 뉴욕을 보여줘야지. 그건 그렇고, 저 이상한 소음 들려?"

"응, 그르렁거리는 소리 같아, 아니면 모터 돌아가는 소리든가, 그런데 제대로 안 들려."

"이봐, 바베트, 저기 의자 밑을 봐! 저거 혹시...?"

"맞아! 보리가드, 우리의 옛친구잖아." 바베트가 기뻐하며 선포하듯 말했다.

두 명의 여자아이는 고양이가 있는 쪽으로 달려갔는데, 고양이는 자는 척하면서 꼼짝하지 않으려고 애썼다.

"일어나, 잠꾸러기야! 우리란 말야!" 브리지트가 말했다.

보리가드는 한쪽 눈을 떠서 그들을 올려다보고는 다시 눈을 감았다.

"자, 보리가드, 그렇게 무관심하게 굴지 마. 그런 건 프랑스 사람만이 잘하는 거라구." 바베트가 놀리듯 말했다.

"그래," 브리지트가 끼어들었다. "넌 우리한테 전혀 무관심하지 않아. 넌 우릴 무지 좋아하잖아. 아니면 우릴 계속 따라오지 않았겠지. 사실은 너도 우릴 만나서 기쁠 거야."

보리가드는 입 속에서 "정신나간 아이들" 어쩌고 툴툴거리더니 의자 밑에서 나와 기지개를 켰다.

"무슨 소린지 모르겠는데. 쟤가 방금 뭐라고 그랬니?" 브리지트가 물었다. "아, 맞다, 쟤는 말을 못하잖아, 어쨌든 우리한테는 말야. 자, 보리가드, 우린 시내로 갈 거야."

큰 키의 검은 고양이는 가만히 눈을 깜박이더니 여자애들을 따라 발을 성큼성큼 내딛으며 여유롭게 걸어갔다.

공항 밖으로 나오자 바베트가 인도 끝에 서서 두 팔을 흔들기 시작했다.

"택시! 택시!" 바베트가 소리쳤다. "택시들이 어딨지? 비 때문에 새 옷이 젖고 있잖아. 곧 빗물에 흠뻑 젖게 될 거야. 그럼 네가 날 비틀어 짜줘야 할 거라구!"

"잠깐, 바베트, 이런 날씨에 택시를 잡을 수는 없어." 브리지트가 조언했다. "뉴욕 운전기사들은 비가 오면 운전하는 법을 잊어버리는 모양이야. 교차로가 전부 꽉 막혔어. 각 방향에서 전부 차가 막혀 완전히 마비 상태야. 지하로 내려가야 되겠다. 지하철로 말야!"

브리지트는 친구들을 이끌고 지하철역까지 운행되는 셔틀버스를 탔다. 곧 그들은 뉴욕 시내를 향해 힘차게 나아가고 있었다. 바베트와 브리지트는 할 얘기가 너무 많아서 거의 한숨도 쉬지 않고 학교나 가족 얘기 등 지난 번 만났던 이후로 있었던 모든 일에 대해 신나게 재잘거렸다.

"제일 먼저 어딜 가는 거야?" 마침내 바베트가 물었다. "물어보는 것도 잊어버릴 뻔했어."

브리지트가 싱긋 웃었다. "깜짝 놀라게 해줄 거야. 하지만 걱정 마, 곧 알게 될 거야. 여기서 내리자."

지하철이 멈추자 친구들은 차에서 내려 밖으로 나가는 계단으로 걸어가기 시작했다.

"이런, 러시아워구나."브리지트가 혼잡한 역을 둘러보며 말했다. "비에 흠뻑 젖은 이 사람들은 모두 집에 가려는 거야. 사람들한테 부딪칠 수도 있는데, 다치지 않도록 팔꿈치를 밖으로 내밀고 계단 위에서 만나자. 행운을 빌어!"

그러면서 브리지트가 사람들 무리를 헤치고 요리조리 빠져나가기 시작했고, 바베트와 보리가드가 뒤를 바짝 따라갔다. 몇 분 후에 그들은 함께 거리에 서 있었고, 보리가드는 자신의 털을 혀로 핥으며 정돈하기 시작했다.

"그렇게 많은 사람들을 헤치고 나오려면 힘과 용기를 있는 대로 모아야겠어." 바베트가 말했다. "어떻게 날마다 그렇게 하니?"

"너도 익숙해질 거야." 브리지트가 어깨를 으쓱했다. "그런데 우리가 왜 지하철 역 주변에서 꾸물거리고 있지? 더 좋은 일이 많은데. 야, 비가 멈췄나봐!"

브리지트가 더 이상 빗방울이 안 떨어지는지 확인하려고 팔을 내뻗었을 때 지나가는 남자가 그녀의 손바닥에 25센트 짜리 동전 하나를 떨어뜨렸다.

"어, 아저씨, 잠깐만요!" 브리지트가 소리쳤지만, 남자는 이미 군중 속으로 사라진 뒤였다. "저 사람이 내가 잔돈을 달라고 구걸하는 거지인 줄 아네. 내가 손을 내밀었나보지. 뭐, 어쨌든 공중전화를 걸려면 동전이 필요했는데. 가자, 저기 앞에 전화가 있어."

브리지트는 비밀스러운 통화를 단숨에 끝낸 후 친구들에게 따라오라는 몸짓을 했다.

"우린 여기엘 가는 거야." 브리지트가 커다란 벽돌 건물을 가리키며 말했다.

건물의 로비는 조용하고 화려했다. 세 친구는 부드러운 대리석 바닥을 가로질러 엘리베이터로 걸어가 꼭대기 층 버튼을 눌렀다. 엘리베이터 문이 열리자, 그들 앞에 나타난 광경은 마치 SF영화에 나오는 장면과도 같았다. 범선만한 크기의 이상하게 생긴 금속 배가 번쩍거리며 커다란 방의 거의 대부분을 차지하고 있었고, 금속 조각, 부글거리는 시험관, 휘갈겨쓴 메모지 더미들이 바닥에 어지러이 널려 있었다. 바람에 나뭇잎이 바스락거리는 듯한 소리가 저쪽 구석에서 들렸다. 종이 더미 하나가 그들을 향해 오고 있었다!

항상 만일의 위험에 경계태세를 하고 있던 보리가드가 몸을 웅크려 바스락거리는 종이로 와락 덤벼들었다. 잠깐 동안의 격투 끝에 보리가드가 손쉽게 이겼고, 종이는 살려달라고 애걸복걸했다.

"아야!" 종이 더미가 소리쳤다. 밝은 금발의 커다랗고 텁수룩한 머리가 나타났다. 그 머리의 주인공이 일어서서 약간 더러워진 실험실 가운을 털어내고 안경을 고쳐 썼다.

"바너비!" 바베트가 젊은 과학자에게 뛰어가며 크게 소리쳤다. "너 괜찮아?"

"바베트! 또 만나다니 놀랍다! 어째, 어, 그래, 아주, 어, 응?" 어리둥절한 소년은 말을 더듬었다. "방금 무슨 일이었지?"

p. 519

"창문 옆의 구석을 봐." 브리지트가 고개를 홱 돌리며 대답했다. "보리가드가 먹이를 쫓는 사냥꾼처럼 살금살금 돌아다니고 있어. 또 다른 종이 더미가 움직이길 바라나봐. 공격할 수 있게 말야."

"보리가드인 줄 알았어야 했는데." 바너비가 미소지으며 말했다. "이렇게 다시 만났구나. 굉장해! 너희가 내 실험실을 찾아왔던 게 내가 파리에 있을 때였지. 폭발 사고가 좀 있었던 것 같은데, 그렇지? 맞아, 내 노트와 샘플 대부분이 과학관 건물이 무너져내린 돌더미와 파편 속으로 사라졌지. 내 운동 양말 실험이 실패로 돌아가서 건물이 폭파된 뒤로 말야. 난 학교측에 모든 실험이 계획대로 되는 건 아니라고 말했지만, 다른 교수들은 단단히 화가 났어. 그들은 내게서 정당한 이유라든가 사과 따위는 들으려고도 하지 않았지. 근본적으로 그들은 날 쫓아냈어. 하지만 다행히도 여기 뉴욕에 있는 대학에서 내게 연구를 계속할 자리를 제공해줬지. 내가 파리에서의 대실패에 대해 얘기하면 그들이 마음을 바꿀지도 모르겠다고 생각했는데, 꺼려하지 않고 받아 주더군. 그들은 내게 필요한 장비를 전부 제공해줬을 뿐 아니라 그것도 아주 빨리 줘서 고작 일주일만에 다시 작업할 수 있게 됐어!"

"바너비, 운동 양말과 끔찍한 참사에 대해 얘기하니까, 어쩐지 옛날의 그 장난에 계속 매달리고 있는 것 같은데." 브리지트가 말했다. "이 끔찍한 악취는 뭐야? 뭔가가 죽어서 부패가 시작되는 냄새 같아." 그녀는 메스꺼워하며 코를 잡았다.

바베트가 동의했다. "그래, 오래된 우유가 두껍고 메스꺼운 덩어리로 응고하기 시작하는 냄새 같아. 코를 찌르는 지독한 냄새야, 바너비, 못 참겠어."

"아니, 여기엔 썩고 있는 것도, 썩은 냄새가 나는 것도 없어, 브리지트. 응고하는 것도 없어, 바베트." 바너비가 주장했다. "너희 둘이 지독한 냄새라고 생각하는 건 사실 달콤한 성공의 냄새라구! 난 그 생각을 할 때마다 너무 흥분이 돼서 앞으로 굴러야 할지, 옆으로 재주를 넘어야 할지 모르겠어."

p. 520

브리지트는 눈동자를 굴렸고 진실을 왜곡하는 데 대해 친구를 나무랄까 생각했지만, 그녀는 바너비의 엉뚱한 발명품과 거창한 주장에 익숙해져 있었다. 그것들 대부분이 효과도 없는 미치광이 같은 생각이긴 했지만, 가끔은 젊은 과학자가 정말 놀라운 것을 생각해낸다는 걸 인정해야만 했다. 문제는, 뭐가 바보 같은 것이고 뭐가 천재적인 것인지 구분할 수 없다는 것이었다. 브리지트는 지금 당장은 꾹 참고 꾸짖지 않기로 마음먹었다.

바너비는 금속 배가 있는 쪽으로 몇 걸음 성큼성큼 걸어갔다.

"이거 보여?" 그가 배를 가리키며 물었다. "이건 가장 최근의 내 시작품이야. 연소 엔진을 사용하지 않고 비행할 수 있는 최초 우주선의 최초 모델이지! 그 말은 아무 것도 태우지 않는다는 거야. 자동차와 비행기, 로켓, 우주선은 모두 엄청난 양의 연료를 태우지만, 내가 만든 새로운 우주선은 어떤 연료도 전혀 연소시키지 않는다구. 인간은 석유와 가스를 얻으려고 땅을 파헤치면서 지구를 파괴하고 있고, 그런 천연자원들을 태우면서 공기를 오염시키고 있어. 하지만 그보다 더한 것은, 연소 엔진이 실제로 그렇게 잘 작동되지 않는다는 거야. 전세계가 그렇게 형편없는 엔진을 그렇게 오랫동안 참아왔다니 어처구니가 없어!" 분개한 발명가는 공중에 대고 주먹을 휘두르더니 불쾌함으로 한숨을 쉬고는 말을 이었다.

"내가 상상하는 새로운 여행수단은 우리가 우주를 탐험하면서 동시에 지구의 환경을 보호하는 것을 가능하게 해줄 거야. 너희도 내 말을 여러 번 들었듯이, 인류가 직면한 가장 중대한 도전은 문제점들을 해결하고 현재 교통수단의 한계를 능가하는 거야. 이 일에 노력을 기울이지 않으면 우린 결국 극도의 무지 속에서 살아가게 되는 거야."

바너비의 연설에 바베트는 슬슬 짜증이 나기 시작했다. 그녀는 짜증이 나고 조바심이 나서 발을 쿵쿵 굴렸다.

"바너비, 제발, 멜로드라마는 그만해. 마치 미국 드라마에 나오는 감정을 오버하는 배우 같아." 바베트가 땍땍거리며 말했다. "네 발명품 얘기나 하라구!"

p. 521

바너비가 얼굴을 붉히자, 바베트는 곧 너무 심하게 얘기한 것을 후회했다.

"난 그저 네가 뭘 만들었는지 너무 듣고 싶어서." 그녀가 부드럽게 말했다.

"그래, 뭐, 너도 알 듯이, 난 늘 천체 탐험을 한다는 생각에 호기심을 느껴왔어. 하늘을 탐험하는 건, 아, 얼마나 많은 밤 동안 내가 별들을 바라보며 머나먼 세상의 여행을 꿈꿔왔는지! 이런, 내가 또 그러네. 미안. 어쨌든, 난 현대 로켓을 연구하기 시작했고, 그것들의 설계를 꼼꼼히 분석해 본 결과 미 항공우주국의 로켓 과학자들은 완전히 잘못해왔다는 결론에 도달했어. 그러다 느닷없이 내게 해결책이 떠오른 거야. 선박 모델을 이용해 우주선을 만들 수 있겠구나 하고 말야!"

"선박이라구?" 브리지트가 물었다. "그러니까 보트며 돛, 닻, 그런 거 말야? 그것 좀 이상하지 않니? 내 말은, 좋긴 하지만 너무 구식인 것 같아."

"아이디어는 구식처럼 생각될지 몰라도, 알고 보면 아주 능률적이야." 바너비가 주장했다. "나의 추측은 우주 먼지의 자기적 특성에 대한 최근의 연구에 바탕을 뒀어. 특별한 이온 우주 돛과 전형적인 행성 여행에 이용되는 진공가 닻을 설계했어. 그러면 시간여행에 필요한 준양자 가속기가 생기지만, 거기엔 아직 몇 가지 문제가 있어. 너희가 느끼는 지독한 냄새는 식물을 섞어 짓이겨 만든 것인데, 아주 끈적거리지만 전도성이 강해. 이 모든 걸 계획하고 만드는 데 몇 달이 걸렸지만 마침내 완성했지."

"와, 바너비, 대단하다. 그런데 네가 한 말 대부분이 어려워서 이해가 안돼." 브리지트가 한숨을 쉬며 말했다. "말뜻을 모르겠어. 진공이니 이온이니 양자니 그런 게 무슨 소리니, 어? 언젠가 앉아서 차근차근 설명해줘야겠어, 지금은 말고. 지금 우린 더 큰 생선을 튀겨야 하니까."

"생선이라구?" 완전히 어리둥절한 바베트가 말했다. 바너비의 노트 더미 위에서 기지개를 켜던 보리가드는 생선이라는 말에 귀를 쫑긋 세웠다.

p. 522

"진짜 생선이 아니야." 브리지트가 설명했다. "그냥 표현이 그렇다는 거야. 우리에겐 지금 당장 해결해야 할 더 큰 문제가 있다는 얘기야. 그러니까, 양키스 경기를 말하는 거지. 사악한 보스턴 레드삭스가 여기 와 있어. 레드삭스와 양키스 사이의 경쟁은 아주 오래됐어! 두 팀은 우리가 태어나기 전부터 야구장에서 싸워댔다구! 이제 비가 그쳤으니까 우린 가서 경기장 입장권을 얻어야 해. 문제는 입장권이 암탉의 이빨만큼 드물다는 거야."

"암탉이라구?" 바베트가 묻자, 보리가드는 다시 한번 흥미로워하며 귀를 세웠다.

"브리지트 말은 입장권이 별로 없어서 구하기가 힘들다는 얘기야." 바너비가 설명해줬다. "그뿐 아니라 가격도 엄청나게 올라가고 있을 거야. 우린 어지간한 자리에 앉으려면 터무니없이 많은 돈을 내야 할 거야. 하지만 우리가 입장권을 구할 수나 있을지 의심스러운데. 음. 어떻게 입장권을 구할 수 있을까?"

바너비는 방안을 왔다갔다하며 텁수룩한 머리를 긁적이기 시작했다. 바베트는 브리지트를 슬쩍 찌르더니 알겠다는 듯이 미소지었다. 바너비가 머리를 긁적이기 시작하면 언제나 흥미진진한 일이 일어났다.

"입장권, 입장권, 입장권." 바너비가 심하게 긁적이며 중얼거렸다. "아하! 그래! 우린 매표소에 가서 입장권을 사는 거야!"

"잠깐, 바너비," 브리지트가 말했다. "네 안경 뒤에 끼워져 있는 게 뭐야?"

"아. 왼쪽 눈이 왜 안 보이나 했어." 바너비가 말했다. "어디 보자. 아, 이거 재미있는데. 오늘밤 양키스 경기 입장권 네 장인 것 같아. 거기다 홈팀 선수대기소 바로 윗자리야. 내 머리카락 속에서 나왔나봐. 정말 가끔씩 빗질을 해줘야겠어."

"넌 정말..." 브리지트가 바너비를 껴안으며 말했다. "자, 지하철 타러 가자."

p. 523

그렇게 해서 바너비는 그날 밤 실험실을 떠났고, 친구들은 허둥지둥 지하철역으로 뛰어갔으며 보리가드도 부지런히 뒤따라갔다.

"선수대기소 바로 위라구!" 다같이 지하철역 안으로 들어갈 때 브리지트가 흥분하며 헐떡거렸다. "파울볼을 잡기에 완벽한 자리야. 그보다 더 좋은 자리는 없다구!"

잠시 후 그들은 양키스 구장을 향해 걷고 있었다. 거리와 주차장에는 흥분으로 환호하는 팬들과 기념품이나 사탕, 티셔츠를 수레에 놓고 파는 행상인들이 가득했다. 태양이 막 지기 시작했고, 늦여름 밤은 따뜻하고 쾌적했다.

"이 사람들 정말 들떠 있다, 브리지트." 바베트가 말했다. "프랑스에서 이런 야단법석을 볼 수 있는 곳은 축구 경기장뿐인데. 정말 난리야!"

"솔직히 난 물리나 화학에는 신동이지만 어쩐지 야구는 뭐가 뭔지 모르겠어." 바너비가 말했다. "보는 건 좋지만 뭐가 어떻게 되는 건지 하나도 모르겠어. 브리지트, 바베트와 난 너만 믿을 테니 다 설명해줘."

"걱정 마." 브리지트가 웃으며 말했다. "내가 너희를 가이드해주면 야구 때문에 다시는 어리둥절하거나 당황하지 않을 거야. 하지만, 어서 가자, 너무 목말라. 소다를 한 욕조라도 마시겠어. 너희들, 필드 관리인들이 운동장에 비가 안 떨어지게 하는 거대한 플라스틱 방수 천을 말아올리는 것도 봐야 해. 얼마나 멋진데!"

바베트와 바너비를 자리에 앉힌 브리지트는 먹을 것을 사러 매점으로 갔다. 보리가드도 다행히도 브리지트 뒤를 따라갔는데, 그녀가 혼자 들고 오기에는 너무 많은 것을 샀기 때문이다. 브리지트와 보리가드는 음료수, 팝콘, 사탕, 그리고 드레싱이 듬뿍 발라져 있는 1피트 길이만한 핫도그를 12개 들고 돌아왔다.

"그렇게 잔뜩 들고 오니까 짐 나르는 노새 두 마리 같다." 바너비가 익살을 부렸다.

"이것 좀 잡을래?" 브리지트가 균형을 유지하려고 애쓰며 물었다.

p. 524

바베트와 바너비는 보리가드 등 위의 판지 쟁반에서 커다란 음료수를 잽싸게 집어들고 브리지트 양팔에 들려 있는 음식을 내려놓았다.

"먹을 것이 적당하지 않으면 야구 경기를 즐길 수가 없지." 브리지트가 말했다. "이제 우리에게 필요할 만한 건 뭐든 다 있어. 어서들 먹어! 먹을 수 있는 건 모조리 다 사왔어. 빨간 감초는 못 먹겠다고 할지 모르겠는데, 삼킬 수 있으면 먹을 수 있는 거라구."

그들은 몇 주 동안 쫄쫄 굶었던 것처럼 먹어댔다. 양키스에게 환호하며 소리칠 동안만 요란하게 먹는 걸 멈추었다. 브리지트는 휘파람을 부는 재주로 모두를 놀라게 했다. 그녀는 손가락 두 개를 입 속에 집어넣어 아주 크고 날카로운 소리를 내서 백 야드 떨어져 있는 사람들도 귀를 막아야 할 정도였다.

"세상에, 그 소리 정말 날카롭다." 바베트가 감탄하며 말했다. "난 못할 것 같아."

"속상해하지 마, 바베트." 브리지트가 대답했다. "너한테만 있는 재주가 많잖아. 예를 들면, 넌 여러 나라 말을 하잖아. 넌 정확히 몇 개 언어를 아는 거야?"

"다섯 개." 바베트는 황급히 얘기하더니, 의자에서 일어나 소리를 질렀다. "양키스 사랑해요! 양키스 이겨라!" 브리지트는 친구를 부러움의 눈길로 바라봤다.

"어어." 바너비가 끙끙거렸다. "몸무게가 1톤은 나가는 것 같아. 배가 평소 크기의 세 배로 부풀어 올랐어. 1피트짜리 핫도그를 다섯 개째 먹는 게 아니었는데."

"지금 후회해봐야 소용없어, 바너비." 브리지트가 말했다. "넌 좀 움직여야겠다. 팔을 흔들어봐. 박수도 치고. 시끄러운 소리를 들어보자구! 헤이 바타바타바타, 헤이... 아얏!"

"왜 그래?" 바베트가 물었다.

"이 의자에서 유리섬유 파편이 삐져나와 있나봐. 그게 내 엉덩이를 찔렀어."

"얼마나 큰 파편인데? 야, 상당히 큰 조각이야." 바너비가 과학적인 흥미를 느끼고 브리지트쪽으로 가만히 다가가며 말했다. 의자들에 온통 세균이 득시글거릴 거야. 병원에 가서 페니실린 주사를 맞아야겠어. 감염되지 않게 말야. 그러는 게 좋겠어. 페니실린은 세균을 죽이는 데 탁월하니까."

"네 자리로 돌아가, 의사 선생." 브리지트가 웃으며 말했다. "엉덩이를 쿡 찔렸을 뿐이야. 피는 안 났다구."

"그럼 다행이구." 바너비가 말했다.

"쉬는 시간이니?" 바베트가 물었다.

"쉬는 시간?" 브리지트가 어리둥절해서 물었다.

"그래, 쉬는 시간, 그러니까 중간의 틈 말야. 매회가 끝날 때마다 일어나서 노래하는 틈이 있다고 했잖아."

"아, 7회 기지개 시간을 말하는구나." 브리지트가 말했다. "어 그래. 봐, 지금이 바로 그 시간이야! 다같이 일어나서 '날 야구장에 데려가줘' 라는 노래를 부르는 거야. 내가 금방 가사를 알려줄게. 배우기 쉬운 노래야."

하지만 브리지트는 노래를 부르지 못했어. 뭔가가 모든 사람들의 주목을 끌었어. 경기장의 가장자리 바로 위에서 커다란 물체가 불쑥 나타났는데, 구름만한 크기였어. 그게 뭔지 정확히 보이지 않았어. 떨어지는 태양의 마지막 빛이 너무 환해서 잘 보이지 않았거든. 그게 뭐든지 간에 맘에 들지 않았어. 난 뭔가 불길한 예감에 휩싸였거든.

브리지트는 한시도 지체하지 않고 그 유명한 껌 씹는 능력을 발휘했지. 그녀는 풍선을 불기 시작했는데, 점점 더 크게 불어서 돌풍이 불어와 그녀를 땅에서 들어올렸어. 바베트, 바너비, 그리고 나는 어떻게 해야 하는지 정확히 알고 있었지. 우린 죽일 힘을 다해 그녀의 다리를 붙잡았고 대기 속으로 날아갔어. 우리가 이륙하자마자 하늘로부터 우렁찬 소리가 천둥치듯 경기장에 울려퍼졌어.

"양키스를 내놓을 테냐, 너희 목숨을 내놓을 테냐!" 목소리가 요구했어. 그러더니 사악하게 깔깔거리는 악마의 웃음소리가 들렸는데, 우린 두려움에 벌벌 떨었어.

QUICK QUIZ 1
관계 짓기
아래의 단어 쌍들이 서로 어떤 관계를 갖는지 판단하세요. 비슷한 의미면 "S" 반대 의미면 "O"를 하세요.

1. 드문, 진기한 :: 엄청난, 과대한
2. 대참사, 큰 재앙 :: 재앙, 재난
3. 썩은 냄새가 나는 :: 악취가 나는
4. 경쟁자, 적수 :: 동맹국
5. 무모한 :: 분별있는, 신중한
6. 당황하게 하다 :: 어리둥절하게 하다
7. 흠뻑 적시다 :: 흠뻑 적시다
8. 무관심한 :: 냉담한
9. 흥분한, 들떠 있는 :: 뚱한, 샐쭉한
10. 하늘의, 천체의 :: 지구의
11. 공포, 불안 :: 걱정, 근심

QUICK QUIZ 2
관계 짓기
아래의 단어 쌍들이 서로 어떤 관계를 갖는지 판단하세요. 비슷한 의미면 "S" 반대 의미면 "O"를 하세요.

1. 중얼거리다, 낮게 속삭이다 :: 소리를 지르다
2. 중대한, 결정적인 :: 결정적인
3. 지루한, 무관심한 :: 이국적인, 색다른
4. 어리둥절하게 하다 :: 당황하게 하다
5. 우아한 :: 품위있는
6. 짜증나게 하다 :: 흥미를 돋우다
7. 성난 :: 분개한
8. 체격이 우람한 :: 야윈, 바짝 마른
9. 바짝 말리다 :: 물에 흠뻑 적시다
10. 성큼성큼 걷다 :: 큰 걸음으로 걷다

빈칸 채우기

아래에 있는 각각의 단어들 중에서 가장 완벽한 문장을 만들어주는 단어를 고르세요.

1. 핀스터 부인이 불쾌할 정도로 (   ) 사람들은 그녀에게 웃기지 않은 농담만 하려고 했다.
   a. 소집해서   b. 깔깔거리며 웃어서   c. 방해해서   d. 재잘거려서

2. 우리가 1972년형 폴크스바겐을 완전히 세차하고 왁스칠을 하고 나자 최신형처럼 (   ).
   a. 얼었다   b. 번쩍거렸다   c. 살랑거렸다   d. 격투했다

3. 색유리로 만든 장미상은 아름답긴 했지만, 바람만 살짝 불어도 그 (   ) 수공예품은 쓰러져버릴 것 같았다.
   a. 날카로운   b. 기묘한   c. 무시무시한   d. 우아한

p. 527

4. 아이들은 공짜 아이스크림 콘을 얻어먹으려는 기대로 버거를 다 먹고 난 뒤에도 몇 시간 동안 약국 카운터 옆에서 (   ).
   a. 잔소리했다   b. 살금살금 걸어다녔다   c. 서성거렸다   d. 재빨리 달렸다

5. (   )은/는 캘리포니아에서는 미니 냉장고를 파는 데 아무 어려움이 없었는데, 알래스카로 옮기자 거의 파산할 지경에 이르렀다.
   a. 거지   b. 행상인   c. 멜로드라마   d. 야단법석

6. 3일 동안 엄청난 강풍이 휘몰아친 뒤 우리 마을의 메인 가는 세차게 흐르는 (   )(으)로 변해버렸다.
   a. 급류   b. 악취   c. 교통정체   d. 페니실린

7. 판사는 질문을 강도 혐의에 대한 것으로 (   ) 싶었지만, 재판 동안 피고의 과거에 대한 질문들이 계속 제기됐다.
   a. 제한하고   b. 밀치고   c. 번쩍이고   d. 이야기하고

8. 허리케인으로 좌석 일부가 내려앉고 주민 대부분이 물에 흠뻑 젖었지만 야구 경기장 위의 (   ) 때문에 내야의 흙은 비교적 건조하게 유지됐다.
   a. 분석   b. 파편   c. 연소   d. 방수 천

9. 무자비한 요리사는 바닷가재들을 끓는 물에 집어넣기 전에 (   ) 웃음을 터뜨렸다.
   a. 들리는   b. 옆걸음질하는   c. 사악한   d. 여러 언어의

10. 낸시는 매일 영어 수업이 시작되기 전에 교실 주변에서 기를 쓰고 (   ) 필요가 있다고 생각했다.
    a. 방어할   b. 어렴풋이 나타날   c. 응고할   d. 신나게 뛰어놀

짝짓기

오른쪽의 단어를 비슷한 의미의 왼쪽 단어와 짝지으세요.

1. 원형, 시제품	A. 양식, 보급품
2. 지난 일을 되돌아본	B. 배와 관련된
3. 식량, 저장품	C. 저쪽에 서 있다
4. 영문 모를 말, 횡설수설	D. 조각
5. 부패시키다, 분해시키다	E. 말도 안 되는 소리
6. 불쑥 나타나다, 어렴풋이 나타나다	F. 원형, 최초의 모델
7. 음산한, 황량한	G. 어리석은 짓
8. 조각	H. 지나고 나서 깨닫게 된
9. 선박의, 항해의	I. 황량한
10. 어리석은 짓	J. 부패시키다

p. 528

짝짓기

오른쪽의 단어를 비슷한 의미의 왼쪽 단어와 짝지으세요.

1. 비틀어져, 잘못돼	A. 정신적인 고요함
2. 소리가 날카로운	B. 피할 수 없이, 어김없이
3. 부풀게 하다	C. 잘못하여, 틀리게
4. 예감, 불길한 전조	D. 먹을 수 있는
5. 평온	E. 불길한 예감

6. 유리한 위치　　　　　　　　　　F. 깜짝 놀라게 하다

7. 감탄하게 하다　　　　　　　　　G. 물건을 실은

8. 늘, 반드시　　　　　　　　　　 H. 최고점

9. 식용의　　　　　　　　　　　　I. 팽창된

10. 짐을 실은　　　　　　　　　　 J. 소리가 날카로운, 소리 톤이 높은

2 너클볼과 촉수

p. 530

그 다음에 정확히 무슨 일이 일어났는지는 앞으로도 절대 알 수 없을 거야. 생각나는 건, 밝은 빛이 났었고 끈적거리는 뜨거운 공기가 너울거렸다는 거야. 잠깐 동안 뉴욕 양키스 야구팀 전체가 하늘로 날아오른 것 같았어. 하프 대신 미트를 든 운동하는 천사들 무리처럼 말야. 정말 장관이었지! 좀처럼 보기 힘든 광경이었어. 그리고 나서 난 정신을 잃었고 모든 게 깜깜해졌어.

깨어나 보니 난 커다란 연회용 테이블의 윗자리에 놓인 의자의 빨간 벨벳 쿠션 위에 있었어. 내가 있는 방은 아주 화려하게 장식되어 있어서 왕 같은 방문객을 맞기 위한 곳 같았어. 벽을 따라 처 있는 진붉은 커튼의 웅장함은 가장자리에 수놓아진 금색 실로 더욱 돋보였지. 정말 멋진 장식이었어! 테이블 위에 놓인 황금 접시에 박힌 값비싼 보석, 받침 달린 잔, 테이블 위의 큰 접시, 모든 것들이 촛불 안에서 번쩍이고 있었지. 방의 모든 면이 매혹적이었지만, 나를 정말 두려움과 감탄에 사로잡히게 한 건 음식이었어. 술탄 수바다이의 궁정에서 보냈던 여름 이후로 그런 진수성찬은 처음이었어. 그 술탄은 파티를 어떻게 여는 건지 제대로 알고 있었지! 생각나는 건, 그가 러시아에서 10톤의 캐비어를 수입해서 자신의 수영장을 가득 채운 다음 스페인의 올림픽 수중에어로빅 팀을 불러다가... 그 얘긴 다음에 하지 뭐. 문제는, 화려한 연회홀에서 우리가 뭘 하고 있는 것이냐 였지.

"아이쿠!" 최면상태에 빠졌던 게 분명한 브리지트가 깨어나면서 소리질렀다. "내 옷이 어떻게 된 거지?"

그녀는 공포에 질려 자신의 핑크빛 새틴 드레스와 하얀 레이스 양말, 번쩍이는 검은 에나멜 가죽 구두를 내려다봤다. 바베트와 바너비는 깜짝 놀란 친구가 자신의 차림을 쳐다보고 있는 모습에 웃음을 참지 못했다. 브리지트 머리에는 리본까지 달려 있었다!

p. 531

"뭐가 그리 즐거운지 모르겠네." 브리지트가 투덜거렸다. "네 옷차림을 본다면 낄낄거리는 웃음이 뚝 그칠걸!"

"화낼 필요 없어, 브리지트. 우린 널 괴롭히려고 웃은 게 아니라... 어, 안돼!" 바베트는 자신의 멋진 검은색 차림이 하얀 세일러 칼라가 달린 딱딱한 분위기의 짙은 남색 드레스로 바뀌어 있는 걸 내려다보고는 어쩔 바를 몰라 소리쳤다. "이게 웬 점잔빼며 단정한 꼬마숙녀 드레스야! 교장이 된 것 같잖아! 끔찍해. 드레스는 질색이란 말야."

"드레스는 나도 싫어해." 브리지트가 말했다. "차라리 바너비 차림이 낫겠어. 바보 같아 보이긴 하지만."

바너비의 실험실 가운은 온데 간데 없고, 그 자리에 검은 벨벳 옷깃이 달린 초록색 새틴 자켓이 입혀져 있었다. 목 둘레에는 화려한 실크 스카프가 끼워져 있었다. 바너비는 자신의 새 옷차림에 불만이 전혀 없는 것 같았다. 벽에 걸린 커다란 거울 속의 자신을 보고 감탄하더니 있는 대로 뽐내며 친구들 쪽으로 걸어왔다.

"그래, 의상의 변화가 좀 있었나봐." 바너비가 말했다. "하지만 우리가 알아야 하는 건 '이유'가 뭐냐는 거지, 대체 지금 무슨 일이 일어나고 있는 거냐구? 주변 상황에서 어떤 정보를 알아낼 수 있을까? 단서가 될 만한 모든 세부사항을 꼼꼼히 살펴야 해."

645

"좋아, 명탐정." 브리지트가 조롱했다. "이렇게 많은 가구와 음식으로 판단해 보건대, 우린 아주 부유한 사람의 집에 와 있는 것 같아."

"이건 아주 허식적이고 지나친 것 같아." 바베트가 불만스러운 듯 콧방귀를 뀌며 말했다. "내 생각엔, 우릴 여기에 데려온 게 누구든 멋이나 품위 없이 허세부리기 좋아하는 속물인 것 같아. 하지만 이 모든 것들의 비용을 생각하면 충분히 깊은 인상을 받을 만하지."

"너희들 뭐 잊어버린 거 없니? 하늘을 나는 야구 선수들 같은 것 말야." 바너비가 물었다.

"아, 그래." 브리지트가 한숨지으며 말했다. "좋아, 그럼 우리는 사람을 공중에 붕 떠있게 만드는 우주선을 가진 아주 부유한 사람의 집에 와 있나봐. 좋아. 이제 어쩌지?"

바너비는 출구를 찾으며 커튼 주변을 어슬렁거리기 시작했다.

p. 532

"바깥을 내다봐서 나가서 여기가 어딘지 알 수 있는 방법이 있을 거야... 아, 그래, 여기다." 바너비가 길다란 노란 색 끈을 잡아당기며 말했다. 커튼이 휙 열리더니 오른쪽으로는 암흑의 우주공간이, 왼쪽으로는 소용돌이치는 하얀 구름 덩어리가 드러났다. 바너비가 깜짝 놀라 가슴을 헐떡이며 말했다. "굉장한 대기(분위기)다!"

"인정해주니 기쁘구나." 장중한 목소리가 쿵하고 울렸다. "방을 집처럼 편안하게 만들려고 애썼다. 너희 지구에서 볼 수 있는 방처럼 말이다."

바너비, 바베트, 브리지트는 몸을 돌려 연회홀 끝에 있는 문을 쳐다봤다. 거기에는 그들이 생전 처음 보는 정말 이상하게 생긴 생물체가 서, 아니 공중에 떠 있는 것 같았다. 문어발처럼 생긴 길다란 촉수가 열 개 달려 있었고, 거대한 초록색 머리에 축 늘어진 귀가 달려 있었다. 그들이 알아볼 수 있는 한 코는 없었고, 입은 그저 작은 구멍이 뚫려 있는 정도였지만, 머리 주변으로 온통 열두 개의 눈이 달려서 깜박거렸다. 말의 갈기처럼 생긴 짧고 검은 머리털이 머리 위에서부터 나와 등쪽으로 짧게 드리워져 있었다. 어깨(어쩌면 어깨 같은 것) 둘레에는 작은 자줏빛 망토를 걸치고 있었다.

"이렇게 끔찍하고 소름끼치는 생물은 처음 봐." 바베트가 특히 누구에게랄 것 없이 속삭였다.

"쯧쯧, 꼬마 아가씨." 그 생물이 꾸짖었다. "참 무례하군. 네가 나와 다르게 생겼다거나 괴장 차림을 했다고 해서 널 보고 못생겼다거나 매력없다고 하면 넌 내 말을 이해하지 못할 거다." 그는 바너비 쪽으로 고개를 돌리고 말했다. "젊은 친구, 자넨 방의 분위기에 감탄했지?"

"어, 사실 난 지구의 대기를 보고 있었어요, 그러니까, 보호 가스층 말이죠. 하지만 방은, 어, 정말, 역시 정말 좋아요." 바너비가 더듬거리며 말했다.

"고맙네, 젊은 친구." 이상한 생물이 바너비에게 한쪽 손을 내밀며 말했다. "음식이 맛있었길 바라네, 이런 내가 이렇게 무례하다니, 아직 내 소개도 안 했군. 내 이름은 고르가스로, 다른 은하계에서 온 탐험가지. 자넨...?"

바너비는 그 자리에 움츠리고 있었다.

p. 533

"자, 젊은이, 부끄럽거나 겁낼 것 없네. 악수를 하자는 것뿐이니까." 고르가스가 재촉했다.

브리지트가 끼여들었다. "죄송해요, 고르가스." 그녀는 바너비에게 스스로를 추스릴 시간이 필요하다는 걸 알아차렸다. "이 아인 과학자인데, 사교적인 일에 익숙하지 않아서요. 제 이름은 브리지트고, 이쪽은 제 친구들 바베트, 바너비 그리고 보리가드예요. 보리가드는 저쪽에서 당신의 치킨 파이를 먹고 있는 고양이죠. 당신을 알게 돼서 저희 모두 기뻐요."

보리가드는 수염을 핥고는 주인을 향해 공손하게 고개를 살짝 끄덕이고 나서 먹기를 계속했다. 브리지트는 손으로 고르가스의 촉수 하나를 잡고 무릎을 약간 구부리고 머리를 숙여 완벽한 여자의 인사를 했는데, 왕족을 만나면 그렇게 하라고 어머니가 일러주신 대로였다. 브리지트는 고르가스가 왕인지는 확신할 수 없었지만 그렇게 해서 손해볼 건 없다고 생각했다.

"아가씨, 정말 근사한 예절이군!" 고르가스가 즐거워하며 말했다. "이렇게 기쁠 수가! 난 보통 예의없는 사람은 그냥 참지 못하지. 그런 사람들은 두고 볼 수가 없어. 나로서는 버릇없이 행동하느니 차라리 사지가 찢기고 찢기고 또 찢기고 계속 찢기고 하나 더 찢기고 말겠어. 하나 더 말하자면, 브리지트, 그렇게 드레스를 입으니까 아주 예쁘구나. 그렇게 입으면 예뻐 보일 줄 알았어."

"고마워요." 브리지트는 옷차림에 대해 진심을 얘기하는 건 버릇없는 일이 되리라는 걸 알고 이렇게 말했다. "이렇게 여쭤보는 게 무례해 보이지 않았으면 하는데요, 우리가 여기에 정확히 왜 오게 된 건지 모르겠어요."

"미안하구나, 브리지트, 그건 사고였단다." 고르가스가 말했다. "너희는 내 진로에 그냥 떠밀려 들어오게 된 거야. 난 야구선수들만 데려오려고 했었는데, 너희가 온 이상 환대해줘야겠다고 생각했지."

"당신이 '양키스를 내놓을 테냐, 너희 목숨을 내놓을 테냐!'라고 말했던 사람인가요?" 바베트가 물었다.

"그건 그냥 장난으로 생각해낸 거였어." 고르가스가 말했다. "내가 좀 장난꾸러기거든."

p. 534

"그럼 양키스를 데려가는 게 당신의 목적이었다는 거네요." 브리지트가 계속 채근하듯 말했다. "당신은 돈도 아주 많은 것 같은데, 누가 봐도 알 수 있을 정도로 말예요. 그럼 팀을 돈으로 사지 그러셨어요?"

"난 그들을 영원히 소유하고 싶진 않아, 꼬마 아가씨." 고르가스가 설명했다. "탐험가로서 나의 임무 중 일부는 다른 세계들에 대한 정보를 모으는 거야. 가능한 한 많은 지식을 모아야 하지. 어쨌든 지난 2주 동안 난 여기 우주선에 있는 TV로 야구 중계방송을 보았어. 정말 재미있는 오락이었지! 하지만 고백하건대, 야구경기의 룰을 모두 이해하지는 못하겠더라."

"아, 브리지트가 당신을 위해서 명확하게 설명해줄 수 있어요. 브리지트는 야구에 대한 걸 설명하는 데엔 도사예요." 마침내 말하는 방법을 되찾은 바너비가 말했다.

고르가스는 잘난 체하며 말했다. "브리지트는 너한테도 큰 도움을 줬을 거야. 네가 그렇게 복잡한 개념들을 이해하는 게 얼마나 어려웠겠니."

"바너비에게 그렇게 우쭐하실 필요 없어요." 바베트가 툭 말했다. "당신은 은하계 우주간의 여행을 맘대로 하실 수 있다고 스스로를 대단히 똑똑하다고 생각하시나 본데, 바너비는 지구에서 훌륭한 발명가이자 과학자예요. 그리고..."

"그래, 미안하다, 훌륭한 과학자 면전에서 감히 으스댈 수는 없지." 고르가스가 말을 가로막았다. "그럼 바너비는 야구 경기를 아주 잘 이해하겠구나."

"맞아요, 고르가스." 브리지트가 말하더니 팔짱을 끼었다.

"어쨌든," 고르가스가 말을 이었다. "난 야구경기의 룰에는 더 이상 관심없다. 난 양키스에게 다른 질문, 좀더 과학적인 걸 물어볼 거야. 내가 궁금한 건, 선발투수인 레프티 잼비시가 갖고 있는 어떤 놀라운 능력에 대한 거야. 그가 보여주는 재주에 대해 물어봐야겠어. 그걸 '너클볼'이라고 부르는 것 같은데..."

p. 535

"너클볼은 그 팀의 비밀 무기예요." 브리지트가 흥분하며 말했다. "야구 역사상 다른 어떤 선수도 그만한 제구력과 정확도를 가지고 너클볼을 던지지 못했어요. 공은 언제나 레프티가 원하는 곳으로 날아가 본루 위로 곧장 꽂혀요. 이 투구의 특징은 공이 본루 쪽으로 날아올 때 공의 진로를 예측할 수 없다는 거예요. 공이 레프티의 손을 떠나자마자 왼쪽이나 오른쪽으로 휘어질 수도 있고 밑으로 내려가거나 흔들흔들할 수도 있지만, 본루를 가로지를 때마다 예외없이 안전하게 스트라이크 존에 들어가죠. 타자들은 미치는 거예요! 레프티가 너클볼을 던지기 시작하면 경기는 완패로 끝나고 상대팀은 숨을 곳을 찾아 뛰어가는 거죠!"

"네가 우리의 작은 실험에 관심이 있을지도 모른다고 레프티가 말한 게 옳았구나." 고르가스가 말했다. "그 친구 말이, 네가 경기가 열리는 동안 관람석에서 큰소리로 조언을 준다면서, 네게 도움을 구해보라고 하더라. 그 친구는 성질이 아주 불쾌해. 얼마나 성급하고 거친 녀석인지! 그렇게 고집센 사람은 만나보질 못했어. 내가 그렇게 애걸복걸을 하는데도 그 유명한 투구법을 보여달라는 걸 단칼에 거절하더라구."

"그건 악의가 있거나 야비해서가 아니에요. 그는 아마 당신이 다른 팀이나 어디서 온 스파이라고 생각하나봐요." 브리지트가 말했다.

"브리지트, 난 네가 내 배에 승선한 승객이라고 해서 강요를 하려는 건 아니지만, 너와 네 친구들이 나와 함께 연습실로 가줄 수 있겠니? 있지, 그 투구는 기적이야. 우주상의 어떤 운동 법칙으로도 설명이 안돼. 난 그 비밀을 밝혀내야 해, 어, 과학의 발전을 위해서 말야. 그래, 그거야, 과학의 발전을 위해서라구." 고르가스가 말했다.

"같이 가고 말고요." 브리지트가 대답했다. "앞장서세요."

브리지트는 고르가스가 출입구로 미끄러져 나가자 뒤따라갔다. 그와 달리 바너비는 좀 구슬러야 할 것 같았다. 그와 바베트는 잠깐 동안 뒤에서 머뭇거렸다.

p. 536

"자, 바너비, 가자." 바베트가 부드럽게 설득했다. "브리지트에겐 분명 우리를 여기서 나가게 해줄 계획이 있을 거야. 나도 고르가스가 너만큼 싫어. 말투는 점잔을 빼고 거만한 것 같고, 어떤 계교를 꾸미고 있는 것 같아."

"그의 촉수에서 미끌미끌한 액체가 나오는 거 봤니? 그래서 내가 악수를 안 한 거야. 거기다, 너클볼을 배우고 싶어 하는 이유에 뭔가 수상한 게 있었어. 맘에 안 들어." 바너비가 덧붙였다.

"나중에 얘기하자. 지금은 서둘러야 해. 그들을 놓치면 안돼." 바베트가 말했다.

바베트와 바너비는 가볍게 뛰어 출입구를 나섰다. 배가 잔뜩 부른 보리가드도 느릿느릿 뒤를 따랐다. 그들은 고르가스의 자줏빛 망토가 앞쪽의 구석에서 휙 움직이는 걸 보았고 따라잡으려고 뛰어갔다.

"바로 여기다!" 고르가스가 거대한 체육관의 출입구에서 멈춰서며 큰소리로 말했다.

체육관에서는 양키스 선수 몇 명이 늘 하던 식으로 볼캐치를 하고 있었다. 두어 명의 선수는 배팅 케이지에서 스윙 연습을 하고 있었다. 하지만 레프티 잼비시는 팔짱을 끼고 벽에 기댄 채 바닥에 앉아 있었는데, 고르가스가 방에 들어서자 통명스럽게 말했다.

"이봐요, 저 거구의 초록색 머리들한테 이걸 이해시키려고 애쓰느라 내 목이 다 쉬었어요." 레프티가 피곤한 목을 문지르며 귀에 거슬리는 소리로 말했다. "당신들은 절대 나처럼 못 던져요, 알겠어요? 투구법을 보여줄 수가 없다구요. 안돼요, 안돼!"

"정말 격렬하군." 고르가스가 브리지트에게 말했다. "나를 스파이라고 의심한다는 자네 말이 맞을지 모르겠네." 고르가스는 레프티를 보며 말했다. "이것 봐, 자네가 공공연하게 반항하는 건 참을 만큼 참았네. 자넨 내가 요구하는 대로 해야 하네. 나의 간단한 부탁을 거절하는 건 무례지."

"이봐요, 선생님, 내 에너지가 바닥나고 있는 것 모르겠어요? 난 지칠대로 지쳤어요. 날 좀 그냥 내버려줘요." 그가 쉰 목소리로 말했다.

브리지트는 레프티 옆으로 가서 바닥에 주저앉았는데, 얼굴에는 근심이 서려 있었다.

p. 537

"고르가스." 브리지트가 말했다. "레프티는 지친 것 같아요. 그는 연달아 7이닝을 던졌고, 이젠 나이도 들고 있잖아요. 예전만큼의 체력이 없다구요. 가서 소다수 한 잔을 갖다주시면 제가 설득해서 당신의 견해를 이해하도록 할 수 있나 볼게요. 걱정 마세요, 제가 움직여 볼게요."

고르가스는 씩씩하게 점잔을 빼며 걸어갔고, 레프티와 친구들만 남게 됐다.

"이게 뭐니, 얘야?" 레프티가 브리지트를 보고 눈을 가늘게 뜨며 물었다. "난 네가 사기를 치는 애라고는 생각 못했는데. 넌 양키스 골수팬인 줄 알았는데, 여기서 적군을 위해 스파이 노릇을 하다니. 안팎이 아주 다르구나, 응? 그건 그렇고, 난 나이 들어가고 있지 않아, 예전과 다름없는 지구력을 갖고 있다구."

"그만하세요, 레프티, 난 스파이가 아니에요. 내가 여기 온 건 당신이 이 배에서 나가는 걸 도와주기 위해서라구요." 브리지트가 톡 쏘며 말했다. "그리고 '나이 든다'고 말한 건 그저 고르가스가 우릴 내버려두도록 만들기 위해서였어요."

"어, 그래?" 투수는 의심스러운 듯 말했다. "네 말이 거짓말이 아니란 걸 어떻게 믿지?"

"우리가 그녀의 얘기를 증명할 수 있어요, 잼비시 씨." 바너비가 말했다. "바베트와 제가 장담하건대, 브리지트는 가장 열렬한 양키스 팬이라구요. 고르가스가 우릴 여기 데려온 건 실수였어요. 그가 양키스 팀을 끌어갈 때 말예요. 브리지트는 절대 스파이가 아니라구요."

"브리지트, 너한테 우릴 여기서 탈출시킬 계획이 있다니 정말 다행이야. 고르가스 때문에 너무 무서워. 그는 아마 세계를 지배해서 인간을 노예로 만들고 자신을 은하계의 최고 지배자라고 선포할 계획이 있는 것 같아." 바베트가 말했다.

"이봐, 바베트, 그건 고정관념이야. 넌 공상과학 영화를 너무 많이 봤다구." 브리지트가 꾸짖듯 말했다. "촉수와 커다란 녹색 머리가 달린 외계인이라고 모두 세계를 지배하려 드는 건 아니야. 고르가스는 좀 이상한 것 같고 나도 여기서 더 오래 있고 싶지 않지만, 그가 해를 끼치는 사람 같지는 않아. 그리고 넌 이 상황을 너무 심각하게 생각하는 것 같아."

"난 아니야, 아니라구!" 바베트는 이렇게 주장하며 화가 나 발을 쾅쾅 굴렀다.

p. 538

"진정해라, 얘야, 화낼 필요까진 없어." 레프티가 놀렸다. "네 기분이 좀 나아진다면 나도 네 말에 동의하겠어. 이 고르가스란 녀석은 골칫덩어리지."

"내 생각도 그래!" 바너비가 불쑥 말했다.

보리가드조차도 동의한다며 고개를 살짝 끄덕였다.

"좋아, 좋아. 내가 졌어." 브리지트가 말했다. "우린 이제 어떻게 할지 궁리해야 할 것 같아."

"솔직히 말해서, 난 고르가스가 다른 팀에서 보낸 스파이라고는 전혀 생각 안 했어." 레프티가 말했다. "그런데 어쩐지 그에게 내 투구를 설명해 주고 싶지 않아. 매스컴에서 내 너클볼에 대해 떠들썩하게 많이들 얘기했고, 많은 사람들이 내 투구법을 배우고 싶어한다는 걸 알아. 하지만 고르가스는 거기에 좀 지나칠 정도로 관심이 있는 것 같고, 너무 고집이 세. 그는 몇 시간 동안 날 들볶아왔어. 그만두려고 하질 않아!"

"잠깐만요, 이제 뭔가를 알 것 같아요." 바너비가 끼어들었다. "우선 난 야구 전문가가 아니지만, 고르가스에겐 너클볼을 던지지 못하게 만드는 장애가 있는 것 같아요. 그에겐 너클, 즉 손가락 관절이 없어요!"

"넌 확실히 고르가스 보다는 똑똑하구나." 레프티가 히죽거렸다. "그는 아무리 머리를 써도 관절이 없는 사람은 너클볼을 던질 수 없다는 걸 이해 못하는 것 같았어. 처음 시작할 때부터 그렇게 말했지만 그는 도통 내 말을 믿지 않아."

"우린 어떻게 해야 하죠?" 브리지트가 물었다. "몇 시간 동안 앉아서 상황을 곰곰이 생각하고 있을 여유가 없어요. 빨리 생각해야 한다구요. 고르가스가 곧 소다수를 가지고 돌아올 거예요."

"너희가 뭘 하든 그에게 완력을 쓰려고 하지 마라." 레프티가 경고했다. "우리 팀원 전체가 그에 맞서 힘을 겨뤄보려고 했다가 된통 당했어. 그는 무시무시한 투사인데다가, 레드삭스 만큼 손쉽게 이길 수 있는 상대가 아니야. 그에게 달린 이상한 촉수들은 힘이 강한데다 거기엔 흡반도 달렸다구!"

p. 539

"흡반이라구요? 음. 정말 재미있는 걸." 바베트가 말했다. "고르가스를 무력으로 이길 생각은 하면 안되겠어. 이런 상황에는 교활함과 속임수가 필요해. 우린 고르가스를 꾀로 이겨야 하고, 그가 원하는 모든 걸 우리가 줄 거라고 믿게 만들어야 해."

"무슨 생각을 하는 건데?" 바너비가 흥미를 느끼며 물었다.

"글쎄, 고르가스는 브리지트를 아주 좋아하는 것 같아, 특히 브리지트가 그에게 인사를 한 뒤부터 말야. 브리지트, 고르가스에게 네가 그의 편이라고 계속 안심시킬 수 있겠니?" 바베트가 물었다.

"물론이지." 브리지트가 말했다. "내가 뭘 할 수 있을 것 같은데?"

바베트는 재빨리 자신의 계획을 대략 설명했고, 마침 제때에 끝마쳤다. 고르가스가 큼지막한 소다수 병을 들고 돌아와 레프티의 발에 풍덩 떨어뜨렸다.

"그래서?" 그가 강력한 지배자의 위엄있는 톤으로 우렁차게 말했다. "내가 알고 싶어하는 걸 말해주기로 했나? 아니면 거기 앉아서 까다롭게 굴며 거절할 건가?"

"저리 꺼져, 고르가스." 레프티가 비웃었다.

고르가스가 얼마나 화가 났는지 정확히 설명하기는 어려울 것이다. 그는 노발대발했는데, 안 그래도 조그만 입을 단단히 다무는 바람에 너무 작아져서 거의 보이지도 않았다. 무슨 일이 곧 일어나려고 했다. 공기 속에 긴장감이 팽팽해져 마치 실체가 있는 것 같았다. 거의 손으로 만져질 것 같았다. 그때 갑자기 고르가스는 얼마 되지도 않던 통제력을 완전히 잃어버렸다. 그는 디저트를 빼앗긴 세 살 짜리 아이처럼 버럭 화를 냈다.

"야! 이 끔찍하고 더럽고 역겨운 자식!" 고르가스가 촉수들을 흔들며 악을 썼다. "내가 널 너무 많이 참아줬어. 그럴 자격도 없는 너한테 너무도 많이 참았어. 지금 당장 너클볼 던지는 법을 알려주지 않으면, 내가..."

"고르가스!" 브리지트가 소리치자 고르가스가 그녀에게 귀를 기울였다. "잠깐만 제가 한 마디 할게요."

고르가스는 자신의 감정 폭발이 방해를 받은 것에 실망한 빛이 역력해 깊은 한숨을 쉬더니 브리지트로부터 몇 걸음

물러섰다.

p. 540

"미안하다, 내가 좀 지나쳤구나." 고르가스가 말했다.

"저한테 좋은 소식이 있어요." 브리지트가 미소를 지으며 말했다. "그를 좀 달콤한 말로 속였더니 그의 비밀을 들추어낼 수 있었어요. 그러니까, 아첨을 한 거예요. 그가 얼마나 훌륭한 선수고 내가 그를 얼마나 우러러보는지, 그런 달콤한 말들을 잔뜩 한 거예요."

"아! 간사하고 비열한 것. 잘했다. 아, 훌륭하구나." 고르가스가 펄쩍펄쩍 뛰며 찍찍거렸다. "어서 계속하렴."

"절대 못 믿으시겠지만, 그 사람 말로는 자기가 속이는 거래요. 그건 관절하고는 아무 상관이 없어요. 그는 손으로 조그만 흡각을 만들어서 공을 던질 때 공이 나가기 전 잠깐 동안 늦춰지게 하는 거예요. 타자들은 절대 그 타이밍을 알 수 없기 때문에 공을 못 치는 거구요." 브리지트가 설명했다.

"흡각이라구?" 고르가스가 물었다.

"네, 우리가 당신을 위해 흡각을 몇 개 얻어올 수 있어요. 그러면 당신은 쉽게 레프티의 투구를 흉내낼 수 있을 거예요. 그보다 더 잘할 수도 있어요... 그런데 고르가스, 당신 팔 좀 봐요!" 브리지트가 놀라는 척하며 소리쳤다. "팔들이 흡반으로 뒤덮였네요! 완벽해요!"

"멋지지 않니?" 고르가스가 웃었다. "난 마침내 그 투구의 비밀을 알아낼 거야! 이젠 날 가로막을 게 아무 것도 없어! 흡반을 하나 이상 가지고 있으니 틀림없이 투구의 효과를 높여줄 거야. 더 이상 너클볼이라고 부르지 않겠어. 우린 그걸 흡반볼이라고 부를 거야. 흡반을 이용한 투구 말야!"

"대단한 이름이에요." 브리지트가 속으로 낄낄거리며 열렬히 동의했다.

"얘야, 이게 다 네 덕분이다. 이렇게 엄청난 호의를 베풀어주다니 보답을 해야겠어. 예의범절을 갖춘 내가 보답도 없이 그냥 지나칠 순 없지. 내가 뭘 해주면 될까?" 고르가스가 물었다.

p. 541

"아니에요, 고르가스." 브리지트가 말했다. "하지만 정 뭔가를 해주시겠다면 양키스가 계속 경기를 할 수 있도록 양키스 구장으로 돌려보내는 건 어때요?"

"당연히 야구 선수들을 돌려보내야지." 고르가스가 동의했다.

"그래주신다면 저와 제 친구들은 언제라도 돌아갈 준비가 돼 있어요." 브리지트가 덧붙였다. "원래 입고 있던 옷으로도요, 괜찮다면 말예요."

"언제라도라고 했니?" 고르가스가 싱긋 웃으며 물었다.

"그럼요!" 브리지트가 말했다.

"그렇다면 아주 좋아. 얘들아! 이리 와라!" 외계인이 자줏빛 망토 밑에서 요술 지팡이처럼 생긴 길다란 막대기를 끄집어내며 명령했다.

바베트, 바너비, 보리가드가 브리지트 옆으로 모였다.

"너희는 이제 지구로 돌아가는 거다. 원하기만 하면 언제라도." 고르가스가 낄낄거리더니 그들 둘레로 지팡이를 흔들었다.

네 명의 친구들은 갑자기 환하고 뜨거운 빛에 감싸였다. 그들 주변의 공기가 무거워졌고 그들은 머리가 어질어질해지기 시작했다. 그들 주위에 있던 우주선이 사라졌고 빛이 희미해졌으며, 암흑이 그들을 둘러쌀 때 고르가스의 소름끼치는 웃음소리가 들려왔다.

"즐거운 17세기를 보내거라!" 그가 큰소리로 말했다.

p.542

QUICK QUIZ 6

관계 짓기

아래의 단어 쌍들이 서로 어떤 관계를 갖는지 판단하세요. 비슷한 의미면 "S" 반대 의미면 "O"를 하세요.

1. 소심한 :: 정력적인
2. 점잔빼는, 새침한 :: 격의없는
3. 잘난 체하는 :: 겸손한
4. 모으다 :: 저장하다
5. 정력, 체력 :: 체질
6. 표리부동, 사기 :: 사기, 속임수
7. 미모의 :: 끔찍한
8. 흉내내다 :: 모방하다
9. 환희, 즐거움 :: 당황, 놀람
10. 아첨하는, 칭찬하는 :: 짓궂은, 악의에 찬
11. 곰곰이 생각하다 :: 심사숙고하다

QUICK QUIZ 7

관계 짓기

아래의 단어 쌍들이 서로 어떤 관계를 갖는지 판단하세요. 비슷한 의미면 "S" 반대 의미면 "O"를 하세요.

1. 성미 급한, 까다로운 :: 쾌활한, 명랑한
2. 강화하다, 향상시키다 :: 강화하다
3. 교활한 :: 간사한
4. 두려움, 경외: 경멸, 멸시
5. 밉살스러운, 불유쾌한 :: 혐오스러운
6. 공공연한 반항, 도전 :: 생각의 고수
7. 촉지할 수 있는 :: 눈에 띄지 않는
8. 명백하게 하다 :: 모호하게 하다
9. 기 :: 신호
10. 검소한, 수수한 :: 부유한, 풍부한
11. 발끈거림 :: 감정의 폭발

QUICK QUIZ 8

빈칸 채우기

아래에 있는 각각의 단어들 중에서 가장 완벽한 문장을 만들어주는 단어를 고르세요.

1. 조니는 2주 동안을 꼬박 날마다 토마스에게 전화를 걸어 (   ) 부탁을 한 끝에 마침내 댄스파티에 같이 가고 싶은 데이트 상대를 얻었다.
   a. 겸손한   b. 끈질긴   c. 무서운   d. 투정부리는

2. 마을사람들은 산적들을 완전히 (   ) 생존자 대부분이 울음을 터뜨리지 않고서는 무기를 들어올릴 수가 없었다.
   a. 발산해서   b. 구슬려서   c. 때려눕혀서   d. 질색해서

3. 거대한 (   )을/를 선물한 것은 대단히 사려 깊었는데, 왕은 9인치 두께의 각얼음을 즐겨 사용했기 때문이다.
   a. 받침 달린 잔   b. 드레스   c. 궤도   d. 무릎을 살짝 굽혀 존경의 뜻을 나타내며 고개를 숙이는 여자의 인사

p. 543

4. 케티는 번번이 이겼기 때문에 구슬을 하도 많이 (   ) 주머니에 거대한 포도송이를 담고 있는 것 같았다.
   a. 뽐내며 걸어서   b. 강요해서   c. 성가시게 해서   d. 모아서

5. 해군 사령부에서 사용하는 시계는 워낙 (   ) 2백 년 동안 사용하면서 단 1초가 늦었다.
   a. 미세해서   b. 제왕다워서   c. 정확해서   d. 노발대발해서

6. 부모님이 휴가에서 이틀 일찍 집에 돌아오시자 우리집 파티의 (   )이/가 아주 좋은 상태에서 아주 나쁜 상태로 변했다.
   a. 촉수   b. 분위기   c. 갈기   d. 동맹국

7. 토비의 질문은 너무 (   ) 교사는 결국 그에게 그냥 가만히 앉아서 한 문장이라도 끝내게 해달라고 부탁했다.
   a. 성미가 급해서   b. 화려해서   c. 지나치게 많아서   d. 친절해서

8. 모건은 자신이 막 복권에 당첨됐다는 걸 알게 되자 삐딱한 (   )이/가 변해서 좋아졌다.
    a. 획득   b. 확증   c. 속임   d. 성질

9. 커다란 시뻘건 바위가 동굴 옆면에 너무 깊숙이 (   ) 내 손만으로는 빼낼 수가 없었다.
    a. 박혀 있어서   b. 얽은 자국이 있어   c. 부추겨져서   d. 주워 모아져서

QUICK QUIZ 9

짝짓기

오른쪽의 단어를 비슷한 의미의 왼쪽 단어와 짝지으세요.

1. 방해, 장애	A. 실제로 중요한 사실을 간과한 채 문제를 단순화시킨 생각
2. 고정관념, 실제로 옳진 않지만 조직 내 다수가 선호하는 생각	B. 흔들거림
3. 광경, 볼거리	C. 장애(물)
4. 수입된	D. 견해
5. 동요, 진동	E. 시작
6. 관점	F. 타국에서 들여온
7. 뽐내는	G. 과시하는
8. 시초, 조짐	H. 추측하다
9. 추측하다	I. 인상적인 모습

QUICK QUIZ 10

짝짓기

오른쪽의 단어를 비슷한 의미의 왼쪽 단어와 짝지으세요.

1. 위엄있는, 거만한	A. 졸도하다
2. 말을 더듬다	B. 같이 살다
3. 수놓다	C. 말을 더듬다
4. 장려, 웅장	D. 영예로움, 장려함
5. 조사	E. 제왕다운, 당당한
6. 기절하다	F. 쉰 목소리의
7. 쉰 목소리의	G. 연구
8. 과대선전	H. 과장
9. 머물다, 살다	I. 꿰매다, 수놓다

3 주머니쥐 포포

p. 546

아마 벌써 알고 있겠지만 고양이들은 물 속에 빠지는 걸 싫어하지. 나도 다르지 않아. 물에 젖어서 헝클어진 털은 품위를 완전히 떨어뜨린다는 걸 알거든. 하지만 젖은 털은 우리에게 큰 문제라고 할 수도 없었어. 고르가스는 우릴 아주 난처한 곳에 떨어지게 했던 거야. 우린 카리브 해의 어느 섬처럼 보이는 곳의 해안에서 떨어진 바다 속에 둥둥 떠 있었을 뿐 아니라 우리가 있는 데서부터 백 야드도 안 되는 곳에서 해군 전투가 벌어지고 있었던 거야. 우리 모두는 잔뜩 긴장을 했는데, 다행히도 다른 해전에서 나온 것 같은 표류물이 우리 옆에 떠다니고 있어서 우린 판자와 떠다니는 물건을 꼭 붙잡을 수 있었지.

우린 곧 이상한 점 하나를 발견했는데, 전투용 배들이 골동품처럼 보였어. 하나는 스페인의 갤리온선, 즉 최소한 2, 3백 년 전에 항해했던 돛이 여러 개 달린 커다란 선박이었고, 다른 하나는 스쿠너선이라는 좀더 작은 배였는데, 유니

652

언 잭이라는 영국 국기를 휘날리고 있었어. 스쿠너선이 패하고 있었지. 갤리온선은 스쿠너선을 향해 대포로 일제사격을 퍼부었고 스쿠너선의 돛 하나가 불길에 휩싸였는데, 오래지 않아 스페인 함선이 이길 것 같았어.

갈 때까지 간 것 같은 순간에 스쿠너선은 섬 해안의 작은 후미를 향해 돌진했어. 전속력으로 후미를 향해 달려오는데, 글쎄 우리가 바로 그 진로에 있었지 뭐야!

"아야, 보리가드, 날 할퀴지 좀 마." 이제 어떻게 해야할 지 궁리하려고 애쓰며 조용히 떠 있던 브리지트가 투덜거렸다. "그만하라고 했잖아! 이봐, 저 배가 어느 쪽으로 오는 것 같니?"

바너비를 고개를 들고 쳐다봤다. "저 스쿠너선 말야?" 그가 물었다. "원래의 방위를 고려해보고 지금 위치를 보면, 곧장 우리가 있는 쪽으로 오고 있잖아!"

p. 547

"보리가드, 네 발톱 좀 조심해." 바베트가 머리를 문지르며 말했다. "아! 아! 저 불타는 배가 우리랑 부딪치겠어! 모두들 노 저어. 다리를 차라구! 어서!"

브리지트와 바너비가 다리를 차며 노를 젓기 시작했는데, 바로 그 순간에 스쿠너선이 그들 옆을 씽하고 지나갔는데, 불과 몇 피트 차이로 그들을 비켜갔다.

"다행이다, 우린 살았어." 브리지트가 해안으로 질주하는 배를 보며 한숨을 내쉬었다.

"그건 네 생각이지, 친구." 위에서 어떤 목소리가 들려왔다.

브리지트는 몸을 돌려 위를 올려다봤다. 그녀 바로 위로, 거대한 스페인 함선 앞에 하늘하늘한 가운을 입은 아름다운 여인의 형상을 조각한 색칠된 조상이 매달려 있었다.

"이건 꿈일 거야." 브리지트가 말했다. "저 조상이 말을 했단 말야? 그것도 남자의 목소리로?"

"아니, 물에 빠진 바보야. 난 이쪽에 있다." 그 목소리가 말했다.

갤리온선의 갑판 위에 줄무늬 셔츠를 입고 머리에 화려한 큰 손수건을 매고 왼쪽 귀에 큼직한 금색 링을 매단 큰 키의 해적이 서 있었다. 해적의 얼굴은 햇볕에 타고 바닷바람을 맞아 불그스레했으며 오른쪽 눈에 안대를 하고 있었다.

"와, 이거 마치 영화에 나오는 것 같네." 바너비가 말했다.

"영화라구? '영화'가 뭐냐?" 해적이 물었다. "아니, 너희랑 잡담하면서 낭비할 시간 없다. 내 이름은 킬홀 맥콜이다. 너희는 날 킬 선장이라 부르면 된다. 이건 내 배 '무법자'다. 내 이름을 따서 지은 거지. 난 틀림없이 7개 바다에서 가장 강인한 무법자니까."

바너비, 바베트, 브리지트는 킬 선장이 역사상 가장 비열한 무법자라는 걸 확신하면서 공포에 질려 그를 빤히 쳐다봤다.

p. 548

"이제 내 부하들이 너희를 포로로 잡아갈 거다. 금 몇 자루도 내놓고 저 애들을 되찾아가려고 할 친척이 근처 어디에 틀림없이 있을 거다." 바닷물 쪽으로 줄사다리를 타고 내려가는 부하들에게 선장이 말했다. "그리고 친구들, 저 지저분한 검은 고양이도 데려와. 깨끗이 씻겨서 수집품에 추가할 거야."

보리가드는 깊은 상처를 받았다. 그의 털은 그저 젖어 있는 것이었지, 어쨌든 누더기처럼 된 건 아니었다. 하지만 그의 표정은 결코 브리지트나 바베트, 바너비의 표정만큼 수심에 잠겨 있진 않았다.

"여보게들, 기운내라구." 킬 선장이 목소리를 좀 누그러뜨리며 재촉했다. "너희는 정말 흥분되는 일을 보게 될 거다. 스쿠너선이 숨으려고 저 후미로 들어간 건 큰 실수를 한 거야. 우린 거길 봉쇄해서 포위공격을 할 거라구. 그럼 당연히 우리 차지가 되는 거지!"

"항구에 있는 배를 포위해 공격하려면 전 함대가 필요할 줄 알았어요." 바너비가 무슨 얘기를 하는지 아는 것처럼 말했다. "그런데 당신은 배가 한 척뿐이잖아요"

"그렇지, 네 말이 맞다. 최대한 많은 종류의 배로 이루어진 함대가 필요할 거다." 선장이 말했다. "하지만 '무법자'는 내가 여태껏 지휘해본 배 중 가장 뛰어난 배지. 스페인 제독에게서 이 배를 뺏느라고 싸움까나 했지. 하지만 내가 말했듯이 난 7개 바다에서 재앙 같은 존재고, 내 명성은 싸울 때 도움을 주지. 어떤 선장이든 수평선에 내 배의 깃발이 떠 있는 걸 보는 순간 턱을 덜덜 떨기 시작하거든!"

"죄송한데요, 킬 선장님, 저 스쿠너선에서 정확히 뭘 얻으려는 거죠?" 브리지트가 최대한 예의를 갖추어 조심스게 물었다. 그녀는 선장을 화나게 하고 싶지 않았다.

"저 배의 선장은 포악한 강도짓을 한 자야! 내 물건을 훔쳐갔다구!" 해적이 고함을 쳤다. "저 자는 가장 악랄한 도둑놈으로, 다른 해적한테서 물건을 훔치는 해적이라구. 저 자는 가장 저급한 인간이야!"

"하지만 저 배는 유니언 잭을 휘날리고 있는데, 정말 해적이 맞나요?" 바너비가 물었다.

p. 549

"얘야, 넌 내가 무슨 소리를 하는지도 모르는 줄 아냐? 모든 해적선에는 몇 가지 다른 깃발이 있고, 어떤 깃발을 올리느냐는 누구를 속이려고 하느냐에 달렸지. 해적선을 띄우는 데는 다 계략이 있는 거라구, 알겠냐? 마침 트리니다드에는 영국의 식민지가 있지. 도둑 해적선의 저 못된 놈은 그쪽 요새에 있는 군인들이 영국 선박이 공격을 받고 있다고 생각해서 연대 전체를 도와주러 보낼 거라고 기대하고 있는 거야." 킬 선장이 설명했다. "얘야, 이제 알아듣겠냐, 아니면 네가 아직도 이 늙은 킬 선장보다 해적 행위에 대해 더 많이 안다고 생각하나?"

바너비는 어쩔 수 없이 킬 선장이 해적 행위에 대해 더 많이 안다는 것과, 자신이 전투에 대해 흥분을 해 정신을 좀 잃었었다는 걸 인정해야 했다. 하지만 그의 마음이 가라앉자 불안한 생각이 새롭게 떠오르기 시작했다. 그는 브리지트와 바베트에게 몸을 돌려 귓속말을 했다. "있지, 고르가스가 맨 마지막에 한 말이 뭐였지? 설마 우리가 진짜..."

"1600년대에 있다구?" 바베트가 속삭였다. "정말 그런 것 같아. 카리브 해는 늘 관광객들과 모터보트로 넘쳐나는데, 하나도 못 봤어! 해안을 따라 큰 도시가 있는 것도 전혀 못 봤고, 그것도 그렇지만 트리니다드가 영국의 식민지였던 건 옛날 일이지. 더 이상은 아니잖아, 적어도 그렇지 않을 거야."

보리가드는 콘수엘라와 놓쳐버린 휴가를 생각하면서 슬픈 듯 해안을 뚫어져라 응시했다.

"너희 친구 고양이가 해변으로 몹시 가고 싶은 모양이구나." 선장이 웃었다. "그럴 만도 하지. 트리니다드에 있으면 참 즐거울 텐데, 하지만 때가 되면 그렇게 되겠지. 우선 내가 제안을 하겠다. 항구에 있는 저 배에는 내 물건이 몇 가지 있는데, 그걸 되찾아오기 위해 너희가 나와 내 부하들과 같이 싸운다면 우리의 선원으로 받아들여 우리가 얻어낸 하사품을 나누어 가질 수 있고, 그런 다음 해변으로 보내주겠다. 너희가 거절한다면 내 포로가 되는 거고, 난 너희를 상당한 가격에 팔아 넘기는 거지... 이렇게 하든지 저렇게 하든지."

바베트, 바너비, 브리지트는 재빨리 서로를 흘긋 쳐다본 뒤 의견을 모았다.

p. 550

"사정이 이렇게 됐으니 아저씨와 함께 싸우겠어요." 브리지트가 말했다. "하지만 그냥 궁금해서 여쭤보는 건데 우리가 되찾아오려는 게 정확히 뭔가요?"

"전체 얘기를 다 해주는 게 공평할 것 같구나." 선장이 갑판을 따라 어슬렁거리며 말했다. "얘기가 이렇단다. 핸드맨 아일랜드라는 비밀 장소가 있는데, 그곳에 찾아가는 방법을 아는 사람은 나뿐이지. 그곳에 지하 동굴 속 깊숙이 내 보물들을 숨겨놓았어. 거기에 여분의 음식과 신선한 물도 저장해 놓았고, 나와 내 부하들은 우리의 비축물을 채워놓아야 할 때마다 그곳에 가지. 아, 정말 아름다운 섬이야. 이따금, 정말 이따금씩 비교적 괜찮은 친구들이라고 생각되는 다른 해적들을 두어 명씩 내 방갈로에 초대해서 근사한 음식과 오락을 함께 즐긴단다. 그곳은 짚으로 지붕을 인 조그만 오두막으로 내가 야자나무 잎으로 직접 만들었는데, 디너 파티를 열기에 그보다 더 좋은 장소는 없을 거야. 집 전체가 베란다로 둘러싸여 있어서 밖에 앉아 아름다운 경치를 즐길 수 있어. 내가 거친 해적일지 몰라도 근사한 음식과 포도주에 관해서라면 상당한 전문가라고 할 수 있지. 난 어떻게 하면 즐거운지 아는 사람이고, 온갖 배를 급습했기 때문에 어떤 것이든 제일 좋은 것을 갖고 있다구."

"다른 해적들이 아저씨가 없는 동안 돌아와서 아저씨 노획물을 가져가 버리면 어떡해요?" 브리지트가 물었다.

"꼬마 아가씨, 그런 걱정은 안 해봤다. 옛날 격언 못 들어봤니... 그게 뭐냐면, 어... 아, 그래, '도둑들간에 의리가 있다'란 얘기 말이다." 킬 선장이 물었다. "내가 수년 간 해적 생활을 해왔는데 그 말은 언제나 맞더라. 해적은 다른 해적의 섬이나 배를 약탈하지 않는다. 거기다, 난 거기에 누굴 데려오기 전에 그 섬에 대해서 누구에게든지 얘기하지도 않고, 그 소재를 폭로하지도 않을 거라는 내용의 계약을 맺도록 했지. 그래서 싱가포르 샘이 계약을 위반한 건 단순한 도둑질보다 훨씬 더 나쁜 짓이야. 그는 동료 해적에게 죄를 지었다구."

"싱가포르 샘이 스쿠너선의 선장인가요?" 바베트가 물었다.

"그렇지, 바로 그 자다." 선장이 으르렁거렸다. "그 자는 핸드맨 아일랜드에 초대받은 손님이었는데 날 배신했어. 그 자는 금이나 루비보다 더 귀한 내 물건을 훔쳐갔지. 난 내 보물을 되찾자마자 그 자의 배를 대포로 완전히 박살낼 거라구. 아니, 그보다 더 심하게 할 거야. 태워서 잿더미로 만들어 버리겠어. 오로지 재만 남게 할 거라구!"

바너비는 귀중한 보물이라는 게 뭔지 물어보려고 했지만, 킬 선장은 이미 자신의 부하들에게 소리쳐 명령을 내리고 배로 돌진하면서 총전투 태세를 갖추기 시작했다.

"좋아, 친구들, '무법자'를 최대한 바짝 들이라구. 저 스쿠너선에 가깝도록 말야. 스쿠너선에 끈을 묶어서 갑판으로 뛰어올라가 우리 물건을 가져올 수 있도록 가깝게. 알겠어?" 그가 명령을 내렸다.

해적떼는 열광적으로 환호성을 지르며 배의 방향을 후미 안으로 틀었다. 바람이 돛에 가득 불어와 금새 '무법자'는 스쿠너선과 가까워졌다. 킬 선장은 갤리온선 전체에 부하들을 배치해 놓았는데, 부하들은 배에 끈을 묶자마자 사브르와 머스켓총을 휘두르고 벌에 쏘인 황소처럼 소리를 지르며 스쿠너선의 갑판으로 돌격하기 시작했다. 하지만 스쿠너선의 선원들도 그들을 맞이할 준비가 돼 있었다. 칼이 부딪히는 철커덩 소리와 땡그렁 소리, 성난 외침, 머스켓총을 발사하며 나오는 연기가 공기를 가득 메웠다.

세 친구들은 이 격렬한 전투의 한복판에 있었던 것이다.

브리지트는 몸을 확 구부리고 두 팔로 머리를 가리면서 소리쳤다. "숨을 곳을 찾아 뛰어!"

바너비는 브리지트를 따라 속이 빈 물통 속으로 들어갔지만, 바베트는 그 자리에 서서 카라테와 유도, 그 밖의 다른 몇 가지 비밀 무술을 겸비한 전문가가 형편없는 해적 떼거리에게 얼마나 많은 피해를 입힐 수 있는지 보여주고 있었다. 그녀는 서너 명의 해적을 어깨 너머로 들어올려 물 속으로 내던지기 시작했다. 다른 해적들은 깜짝 놀랐다.

"그저 바싹 마른 꼬마에 불과한데." 머리가 좀 둔한 바보가 어리둥절한 채로 머리를 긁적이며 투덜거렸다. "어떻게 저럴 수가 있지?"

"저 애를 잡자!" 선원 중의 하나가 으르렁거리며 말하고는, 그녀를 향해 돌진해왔다.

바베트는 잽싸게 그의 왼쪽 다리를 세게 걷어차 절뚝거리게 만들었다. 그가 절뚝거리며 가려고 하자 바베트는 그의 뒤에서 공중제비를 해 턱을 세게 걷어찼다. 그는 일격을 당해 뒤로 휘청거리더니 배의 가장자리 위로 털썩 넘어졌다. 상대편 해적들은 바베트가 얼마나 손쉽게 그를 다루었는지 보자마자 대부분 좀더 쉬운 상대를 찾아 흩어졌다.

하지만 입이 거친 선원 하나는 그녀의 놀라운 전투력을 보고도 기가 꺾이지 않았다. 그는 부러질 듯이 아주 세게 이를 갈더니 큰소리로 몇 마디 욕을 내뱉었는데 너무 소름이 끼쳐 바베트는 얼굴을 붉혔다.

"그만해요." 바베트가 항의했다. "그런 끔찍한 말은 정말 싫어요."

"네가 어떻든 난 상관없다." 그가 소리쳤다. "내 머스켓총으로 널 쏘기만 한다면 말이다!"

그렇게 말하면서 해적은 머스켓총을 어깨 높이로 들어 바베트를 똑바로 겨누었다. 숨어 있는 곳에서 친구를 응원하고 있던 브리지트와 바너비는 이 새로운 대결에 총이 개입되어 있다는 걸 알자 곧 허둥지둥 통 밖으로 나와 해적에게 달려들었다.

하지만 그들은 너무 늦었고, 해적은 이미 총을 쏜 뒤였다. 눈 깜짝할 사이가 지나 바베트는 조용히 자신의 선글라스를 벗더니 어깨 위로 치켜들었다. 머스켓총 탄환은 선글라스 렌즈에 튕긴 다음 이물의 조상에 맞고 튕겨나가 큰 돛대를 쳤고, 그런 다음 해적에게 되돌아와 그의 어깨에 맞았고, 그러자 그는 머스켓총을 떨어뜨렸다.

"아야!" 그가 소리치더니 뒤돌아서 도망쳤다.

"그거 놀라운 선글라스다, 바베트." 브리지트가 말했다. "어쩐지 항상 쓰고 다닌다 했지."

바베트는 알 수 없는 표정으로 고개를 끄덕였고, 바로 그 순간 멀리서 분노에 찬 울부짖음이 들려왔는데, 그것은 보리가드에게서 나오는 소리였다. 세 친구는 즉시 무슨 일인지 알아보려고 그쪽으로 뛰어갔다. 킬 선장이 나무 의족을 한 큰 남자와 맞붙어 싸우고 있었고, 그 틈바구니에 낀 보리가드는 미친 듯이 발톱으로 할퀴며 싸움에서 빠져 나오려고 안간힘을 쓰고 있었다. 거기서 더 정신이 없게, 밝은 초록색 깃털을 한 아름다운 앵무새 한 마리가 나무 의족을 한 해적의 어깨에 묶인 채 두 사람의 머리 사이에서 미친 듯이 날개를 퍼덕거리고 있었다.

"이 끔찍하게 더러운 고양이!" 의족을 한 남자가 씨근거리며 말했는데, 귀에 거슬릴 정도로 근엄한 목소리였다.

"여덟 조각! 여덟 조각!" 겁에 질린 앵무새가 꽥꽥거렸다.

"누구 저 새 부리 좀 한대 쳐." 킬 선장이 툴툴거렸다. "더 이상 못 들어주겠어. 이봐, 젊은 친구들, 여기 나 좀 도와주 겠나? 난 힘이 다 빠져가고, 등이 아파 죽겠어!"

바베트가 뛰어들어가더니 의족을 한 해적을 재빨리 해치웠다. 두어 번 제대로 발차기를 하자 해적은 나머지 선원들과 함께 바다 속으로 굴러 떨어졌다.

"하하! 이 겁쟁이들!" 킬 선장이 헤엄치는 선원들을 놀리고 조롱하면서 의기양양해서 외쳤다. "날 방해하면 안 된다 는 거 알겠지, 샘! 그리고 내 갈리온선의 구석구석을 조사해서 모든 손해를 철저하게 평가할 거라는 걸 알아둬. 네 놈 이 저지른 모든 배신 행위에 대해 배상을 하게 될 거라구!"

p. 554

싱가포르 샘과 물에 잠긴 그의 선원들은 주먹을 휘두르고 험한 욕설을 퍼부었지만, 킬 선장은 그들을 그냥 무시하고 바베트 쪽으로 몸을 돌렸다.

"아얏," 그가 등을 문지르며 투덜거렸다, "류머티즘이 도지고 있나봐. 폭풍이 몰려오려고 하면 꼭 쑤신다니까. 난 뼛 속에서 날씨를 안다구."

"아저씨 등은 정말 싸우다가 다친 게 아니에요?" 바너비가 물었다.

"얘, 꼬마야, 그 정도 힘을 써서 킬홀 맥콜을 다치게 할 순 없지." 선장이 으르렁거렸다. "돛을 세차게 두드리는 강풍 을 못 느끼겠니? 바람이 정말 불어오고 있어. 우린 서둘러 보물을 모아야 해."

바너비는 넓디넓은 대양을 응시했는데, 대양의 끝이 보이지 않았다. 아니나 다를까, 멀리서 뚜렷한 저녁놀이 하늘을 짙은 빨강, 밝은 자주, 그리고 파랑으로 가득 물들였다. 거대한 구름이 너무나 밝은 빛을 내 쳐다보기에 눈이 부실 정 도였다. 바너비는 선원에 관한 이야기를 많이 읽었기 때문에 저런 식의 일몰은 곤란한 일이 생긴다는 의미라는 걸 알 고 있었다.

"그건 그렇고, 네가 샘의 부하들을 처리한 건 대단한 일이었다." 킬 선장이 바베트에게 말했다. "널 우리 승무원의 일 원으로 맞게 돼 자랑스럽구나."

"별로 어려운 일도 아니었어요." 바베트가 겸손하게 대답했다. "그들의 공격은 정말 제멋대로에 엉터리였잖아요. 그 렇게 느슨한 사람들은 처부수기 쉽죠."

"그렇게 쉬운 일이 아니었다, 얘야." 선장이 말했다. "하지만 그 얘긴 다음에 하자꾸나. 지금은 '무법자'를 단단히 잡 아매서 폭풍에 쓸려가지 않도록 해야 해. 이리 오너라, 친구들도 함께. 우리가 스쿠너선에 타고 있는 동안 내 부하들 이 배를 안전하게 할 거다. 우리가 거기서 찾아내는 걸 보면 너희는 놀랄 거야."

p. 555

놀라움이라는 단어로는 그들의 감정을 표현할 수 없었다. 그보다는 슬픔과 절망이라는 단어가 더 적절했다. 스쿠너선 의 선실에는 드물고 진귀한 동물들이 꽉 들어차 있었는데, 모두들 비참한 상태로 갇혀 있었다. 모든 침대마다 최소한 두 동물이 들어 있었고, 바닥은 짚과 오물로 뒤덮여 있었는데, 몇 주 동안 청소를 안 한 것 같았다. 싸우는 소리에 겁 을 먹은 불쌍한 동물들은 힘없이 울부짖고 흐느끼고 격분하여 이리저리 돌아다니고 있었다.

"킬 선장님," 브리지트가 겁에 질려 말했다, "선장님이 이 불쌍한 동물들한테 하신 일을 보니 말로 표현할 수 없이 개 탄스러워요."

"얘야, 나도 너만큼 오싹하다." 선장이 머리를 저으며 말했다. "이 조그만 스쿠너선은 이 모든 동물들을 편안하게 수 용하기엔 턱없이 작아. 내가 이 동물들을 데리고 있을 때는 동물들이 아주 건강했어. 이렇게 비좁고 더러운 환경 때문 에 건강이 심하게 악화된 것 같다."

보리가드는 선실들 사이를 걸어다니고 있었다. 그는 오스트레일리아산 도도새와 마다가스카르산 인드리원숭이를 보 고는 걸음을 멈추었다. 그는 또 주둥이가 오리 같은 오리너구리와 세발가락나무늘보가 있는 침대 옆에서 잠시 멈추었 다. 쿠거와 북극곰 같은 위험한 포식자들이 그를 보고 반겼는데, 고양이를 잡아먹는 데엔 전혀 관심이 없는 것 같았 다. 커다란 검은 고양이는 부엌으로도 걸어가더니 식기실에 갇혀 있는 새들도 점검했다. 모든 동물들은 보리가드가 나타나자 안심하는 것 같았다.

"하지만 왜 이 동물들을 모두 잡으셨죠?" 바너비가 물었다.

"그래, 얘기해주마, 하지만 아마 내 말을 못 믿을 거다." 선장이 말하기 시작했다. "하늘에서 어떤 이상한 존재가 내려오더니 날 찾아왔는데, 그는 내게 이 동물들의 많은 수가 사냥되고 있고 거의 멸종될 지경까지 죽임을 당하고 있다고 했다. 그의 말로는 환경이 위험에 처해서..."

"킬홀!" 위쪽의 갑판에서 장중한 목소리가 쿵하고 울렸다. "거기 있느냐? 내 동물들은 어디 있나?"

p. 556

브리지트, 바너비, 바베트는 어리둥절해서 서로를 흘깃 쳐다봤다. 그들은 어떻게 생각해야 할지 몰랐다. 저 목소리는 고르가스란 말인가? 그가 그들을 잡으러 돌아왔단 말인가? 그가 동물들을 어쩌려는 거지?

"자, 어서, 모두 갑판으로 올라가자." 킬 선장이 두려움이 섞인 목소리로 재촉했다.

아이들은 선장을 따라 사다리를 타고 갑판으로 올라갔다. 돛대 근처에 서 있는 건지 떠 있는 건지 커다란 초록 머리와 열 개의 촉수, 그리고 열두 개의 눈을 깜박거리는 외계인이 있었다. 그가 입은 자줏빛 망토가 거센 저녁 바람에 펄럭거렸다.

"고르가스!" 브리지트가 소리쳤다. "왜 우릴 3백 년 전으로 보낸 거죠? 정말 무례한 짓이었어요!"

"뭐라구?" 외계인이 물었다. "날 보고 고르가스라고 했나? 이렇게 모욕적일 수가. 난 바르가스다. 훨씬 더 지혜로운 존재지. 눈이 두 개 밖에 없으니 제대로 볼 수가 없나보군. 고르가스의 머리카락은 멋없는 검은색이지만, 내 머린 보다시피, 멋지고 품위있는 하얀색이다."

외계인은 커다란 머리를 기울여 하얀 털에 덮인 길다란 갈기를 보여주었다.

"바르가스, 선생님, 전 막 이 선원들에게 위험에 처한 지구 생태계를 구하려는 선생님의 계획을 설명하는 중이었습니다." 선장이 말했다. "선생님이 보호하시려는 동식물들의 자연 공동체에 대해 이들에게 전부 말씀해 주시죠."

"생태계? 나랑 무슨 상관이냐, 지구의... 아, 그래." 바르가스가 말했다. "계획이 약간 변경됐다. 그러니까, 여전히 너한테 저 금괴들은 줄 거다. 네가 오리너구리 하나와 깃털에 이상한 분홍빛 색소가 있는 새들 중 한 마리를 건네준다면 말이다. 저게 플라밍고 맞지? 그래, 플라밍고 한 마리를 줘라."

킬 선장은 갑판 아래로 내려가서 동물들을 데리고 돌아왔다. 바르가스는 동물들을 자신의 촉수로 단단히 감았다.

p. 557

"하지만 다른 동물들은 어떻게 하나요, 바르가스?" 선장이 물었다.

"이봐, 그건 네가 알아서 해. 그걸 어떻게 처리하는지까지 말해줄 순 없지." 바르가스가 말했다. "어, 같이 어울리고는 싶지만, 여기 앉아 잡담하는 것보단 더 중요한 일들이 있어서. 그리고, 이 보트는 내가 써야겠으니, 안됐지만 너와 동물들은 다 물 속으로 뛰어들어가야겠다."

바르가스는 킬 선장 쪽으로 미끄러지듯 와서는 배 가장자리 위로 그를 때려눕혔다. 그가 바너비 쪽으로 다가오고 있을 때, 놀라서 앞을 다투어 달아나려는 동물들이 그들을 인도하는 보리가드와 함께 깃털과 모피의 파도를 이루며 갑판 아래에서부터 쏟아져 나왔다! 바르가스는 너무나 깜짝 놀라서 오리너구리와 플라밍고를 떨어뜨리고 말았다.

바너비는 지체하지 않았다. 그는 깜짝 놀란 외계인의 머리를 향해 곧장 뛰어들었다!

바르가스의 머리 가죽에서 끈적거리는 뭔가가 스며나오고 있었는데, 바너비가 낑낑거리며 매달려 있었기 때문이야. 하지만 그건 별일 아니었어. 그는 단 몇 초 동안만 꽉 붙잡고 있으면 됐어. 오래지 않아 주머니쥐 포포가 그 일을 맡게 됐으니까.

혹시 모를까봐 하는 말인데, 주머니쥐는 몸집이 다소 큰 동인도 쥐를 말해. 또 혹시 궁금해할지 모르겠는데, 내가 쥐 편을 들다니 어떻게 된 거냐고? 그래, 일반적으로 고양이는 쥐나 그 형제들인 생쥐를 다정하게 쳐다보지 않지. 하지만 난 자유사상을 지닌 고양이고, 모든 동물을 평등하게 보려고 노력하지. 개까지도 말야. 거기다, 바르가스의 요술 지팡이를 훔쳐내는 계획을 생각해낸 건 바로 포포였거든. 어린 주머니쥐는 바르가스가 그의 망토 밑에서 고르가스의 것과 똑같이 생긴 지팡이를 끄집어내는 걸 봤던 모양이야. 내가 맡은 일은, 포포가 그 외계인의 망토 속으로 기어 들어가 지팡이를 가져오는 동안 그의 주의를 분산시키는 거였어.

처음에 바르가스는 바너비가 자신의 머리에 매달리자 정신을 못 차려서 포포가 지팡이를 찾아 그의 망토 속으로 들어가는 데 어려움이 없었지. 그리고 포포가 무사히 기어 나오자마자 바너비는 미끄러져 떨어졌어. 언제나 재빠르고 곡예사처럼 민첩한 바베트는 번개처럼 갑판을 휙 가로질러 가서는 바르가스를 한방에 걷어차 물 속으로 날려버렸지.

우리가 외계인으로부터 벗어나자마자 포포는 자신이 뭘 하고 있는지 정확히 안다고 날 안심시키더니 요술 지팡이를 흔들기 시작했어.

스쿠너선은 천천히 물 밖으로 나와 공중으로 떠올랐어. 밀려오는 폭풍의 강한 바람이 우리 둘레로 불어와서는 점점 더 빨리 빙빙 돌았어. 우린 순식간에 깔때기 모양의 바람 속에 갇히게 된 거야. 그 회오리바람이 우릴 어디로 데려갈지는 알 수 없었어.

QUICK QUIZ 11

관계 짓기

아래의 단어 쌍들이 서로 어떤 관계를 갖는지 판단하세요. 비슷한 의미면 "S" 반대 의미면 "O"를 하세요.

1. 무법자 :: 무법자
2. 흩뜨리다 :: 모으다
3. 오싹하게 하다 :: 즐겁게 하다
4. 머스켓총 :: 라이플총
5. 전문가 :: 풋내기, 초보자
6. 당황하게 하다 :: 어리둥절하게 하다
7. 속어, 악담 :: 악담, 독설
8. 격언 :: 금언
9. 저하시키다, 악화시키다 :: 향상시키다
10. 형제 :: 형제
11. 천벌, 재앙 :: 구세주
12. 비사교적인 :: 정다운, 친절한

QUICK QUIZ 12

관계 짓기

아래의 단어 쌍들이 서로 어떤 관계를 갖는지 판단하세요. 비슷한 의미면 "S" 반대 의미면 "O"를 하세요.

1. 연대 :: 수비대, 주둔군
2. 절멸한, 사멸된 :: 번영하는, 번성하는
3. 동경하는 :: 열망하는
4. 조약, 약속 :: 조약
5. 이기다, 우세하다 :: 실패하다
6. 깜짝 놀란 :: 침착한
7. 포식자 :: 먹이, 밥
8. 긁는, 긁는 소리를 내는 :: 긁는
9. 쓰레기, 오물 :: 더러운 것
10. 민첩한 :: 서투른
11. 절망 :: 절망
12. 아주 싫은 :: 매력적인

QUICK QUIZ 13

빈칸 채우기

아래에 있는 각각의 단어들 중에서 가장 완벽한 문장을 만들어주는 단어를 고르세요.

1. 내가 보기엔 해변의 오두막이 아름다웠다. 비록 우리가 이사 들어가기 전에 지붕의 (   )을/를 교체해야 했지만 말이다.
   a. 방갈로　　　　　　b. 베란다　　　　　　c. 이엉　　　　　　d. 식기실

2. 낚시꾼들은 물고기가 평소보다 더 깊은 곳에서 헤엄치고 있다고 생각해서 그들의 그물을 평상시보다 더 깊게 (   ).
   a. 직면했다　　　　　b. 배치했다　　　　　c. 썼다　　　　　　d. 꽉 잡았다

3. 가족들과 눈사람을 만드느라 밖에서 30분을 있었더니 내 얼굴이 (   ).
   a. 벌겋게 됐다   b. 옴투성이가 됐다   c. 수척해졌다   d. 하얗게 됐다

p. 560

4. 은행 직원에게 다행히도, 강도의 총탄은 (   )을/를 해서 은행금고, 카메라, 화분에 차례로 맞은 뒤 결국 강도의 팔에 꽂혔다.
   a. 일제사격   b. 재갈   c. 스쳐날기   d. 깃털

5. 나의 새로운 잡지가 전세계에 (   ) 바랬지만, 안타깝게도 우리 부모님만이 흥미있게 보시는 것 같았다.
   a. 포격하길   b. 이를 갈길   c. 널리 퍼지길   d. 구해내길

6. 화약통이 폭발하고 난 뒤 전에 뗏목이 있었다는 걸 보여주는 유일한 증거는 찢어진 돛 조각과 (   )뿐이었다.
   a. 해적   b. 스쿠너선   c. 이물의 조상   d. 표류화물

7. 리투아니아 (   )의 배가 적군보다 9대 1로 많았기 때문에 리투아니아인은 그들의 승리를 거의 확신했다.
   a. 갤리온선   b. 함대   c. 봉쇄   d. 강도

8. 다음 번 편의점은 173마일이 떨어져 있어서 오빠와 나는 도로 여행중에 먹을 트윙키의 비축량을 (   ) 했다.
   a. 채워넣기로   b. 포위하기로   c. 모욕하기로   d. 고함치기로

9. 마지막 터치다운이 끝나자 (   ) 팬들이 운동장으로 몰려와 골포스트를 잡아 찢기 시작했다.
   a. 발랄한   b. 불쌍한   c. 이웃의   d. 격분한

10. 세찬 바람과 허리케인이 닥칠지 모른다는 두려움에 우린 가장 튼튼한 밧줄로 보트를 부두에 (   ).
    a. 소각했다   b. 폈다   c. 양보했다   d. 잡아맸다

11. 샐리는 자신의 미팅 상대가 종이 모형으로 만들어진 걸 보고는 자신이 끔찍한 (   )의 희생양임을 알았다.
    a. 계략   b. 촌스러운 사람   c. 질풍   d. 한복판

12. 크리스는 학교에서 여동생 때문에 부끄러웠는데, 동생은 누군가 자기를 화나게 만들면 끔찍한 냄새를 (   ) 때문이다.
    a. 발산했기   b. 개탄했기   c. 감았기   d. 절뚝거렸기

QUICK QUIZ 14

짝짓기

오른쪽의 단어를 비슷한 의미의 왼쪽 단어와 짝지으세요.

1. 가까이, 거의	A. 경치, 전망
2. 재	B. 관절 질병
3. 원경, 전망	C. 수로
4. 서글픈	D. 환경
5. 생태계	E. 위반
6. 최대한도	F. 거의
7. 류머티즘	G. 태도
8. 편의를 도모하다, 도와주다	H. 재
9. 후미, 좁은 수로	I. 도와주다
10. 위반	J. 곤경, 딱한 처지
11. 태도	K. 환한 빛
12. 곤경, 궁지	L. 슬픈
13. 발광, 광채	M. 최대한도

p. 561

QUICK QUIZ 15

짝짓기

오른쪽의 단어를 비슷한 의미의 왼쪽 단어와 짝지으세요.

1. 놀라서	A. 감추어둔 물건
2. 은닉처의 저장물	B. 검먹은
3. 넓은 공간	C. 회오리바람
4. 색소	D. 놀란
5. 풍부하다	E. 범법자
6. 아무렇게나 하는	F. 많다, 들끓다

7. 기가 꺾인, 겁먹은   G. 배의 침대
8. 평가   H. 넓은 곳
9. 배상   I. 분석
10. 회오리바람   J. 장난꾸러기
11. 범인   K. 염료, 물감
12. 배나 기차의 침대   L. 보상
13. 장난꾸러기   M. 질서없는, 엉터리의

4 보그스 박사와 무한한 허구의 도서관

p. 564

우리가 있게 된 곳은, 내가 생전 가보지도 않은 장소에 겪어보지도 않은 시간 같았어. 처음에 우린 끝이 없는 빈 공간 속으로 빨려 들어간 것 같았지. 난 우리가 우주공간으로 되돌아온 줄 알았는데, 가만 보니 별이 없더라구. 우린 한 가지는 확실히 알았는데, 그건 우리가 있는 곳이 지구의 어디도 아니라는 거였어. 어디를 봐도 지구 같은 구석이 없었지.

스쿠너선은 암흑의 텅 빈곳을 뚫고 표류했으며, 우리 모두는 우리가 깊은 심연에 빠졌거나 우주의 완전한 끝으로 내던져진 게 아닌지 의심하면서 아무 말없이 잠자코 있었어. 그러다가 멀리서 커다랗고 이글거리는 물체가 나타났어. 그건 탑이었는데, 지금껏 보았던 어떤 탑보다도 훨씬 큰 거대한 상아색 탑이었어. 탑에는 온통 꽃과 동물과 역사적인 장면들이 더없이 아름답고 정교하게 조각돼 있었어. 놀라울 정도로 세밀했어. 지구의 위대한 대가들의 작품보다도 뛰어난 예술품이었어. 우린 곧장 그 탑을 향해 나아가고 있었는데, 모두들 화들짝 놀랐어. 탑에는 문도 없었고 달리 들어갈 방법도 없는 것 같았는데, 난 우리가 그대로 쿵하고 충돌하는 게 아닌가 하는 두려움에 떨었어.

동물들을 포함해 배에 타고 있는 모두는 놀라움과 두려움으로 꼼짝 못한 채 동상처럼 그대로 서 있었어. 우리가 막 탑을 들이받으려던 찰나, 내 꼬리가 걷잡을 수 없이 경련을 일으키며 씰룩거리기 시작했어. 나는 목구멍에서 공포의 울부짖음이 새어나오려는 걸 억누를 수가 없었고, 다른 이들 모두 갑판에 부딪쳐 머리를 감싸쥐고 있을 때 나는 가만히 서서 경련을 일으키고 울부짖으면서 쩔쩔매고 있었지.

하지만 마지막 순간에 탑 속에 틈 하나가 나타났어. 그것은 좁은 틈이었지만 우리가 딱 맞추어 뚫고 갈 수 있을 만큼의 크기였어. 난 크게 한숨을 내쉬고 소리지르던 것을 멈추었지. 공포가 가라앉은 거야, 그 순간 동안은 그랬어.

p. 565

"와와!" 브리지트가 안도하며 소리쳤다. "배에서 도망쳐 나가야 하는 줄 알았어!"

"뛰어나간다고 무슨 도움이 됐겠니?" 바너비가 물었는데, 그 역시 브리지트처럼 갑판에 그대로 누운 채였다. "달리 갈 만한 데도 없었을 거야!"

"그 반대지, 청년!" 이상한 목소리가 울려 퍼졌다.

바너비, 바베트, 브리지트는 일어서서 주변을 둘러보았다. 그들은 전에 본 적이 없는 정말 거대한 도서관 안에 있었다. 벽을 따라 위로 그들의 눈이 닿는 곳까지 나선형의 책꽂이들이 세워져 있었는데, 그들이 전에 가보았던 도서관들과 달리 깔끔하지도 질서정연하지도 않았다. 책꽂이들은 심할 정도로 아무렇게나 채워져 있었고, 신문, 노트, 잡지, 엽서, 책들이 아무 순서 없이 마구 쑤셔 넣어져 있었다. 덩굴 꽃식물과 다른 식물들이 책꽂이에서 저절로 자라 나오고 있었고, 어떤 책꽂이에서는 잎이 너무 두꺼워 무엇이 꽂혀 있는지 안 보일 정도였다. 하지만 그 중에서 가장 이상한

것은, 도서관 전체가 계속해서 움직여 물건들이 그들 주위에서 쉴새 없이 바뀌고 움직이는 것이었다. 책꽂이에서는 다른 신문이 사라지면 새로운 신문이 나타났고, 어떤 책은 두꺼워지는 반면 어떤 책은 더 얇아졌으며, 한 책꽂이의 내용물 모두가 느닷없이 다른 책꽂이로 이동하곤 했다. 한 꽃이 갑자기 놀랄 만한 속도로 피어났다. 세 친구는 그저 둘러보면서 현기증을 느꼈다.

"어, 무슨 말이에요, 그 반대라뇨?" 이제 정신을 차려야겠다고 생각한 바너비가 물었다.

"그러니까 네가 전에 한 말이 전혀 틀렸다는 얘기란다." 기묘한 억양의 목소리가 대답했다. "네가 한 말을 내가 부정하는 이유는, 네가 배 밖으로 뛰어나갔더라면 갈 곳이 있었을 것이기 때문인데, 그게 바로 여기지! 하지만 난 논쟁할 생각은 없단다. 사소한 걸로 말다툼하고 다투는 건 싫으니까."

"아저씬 누구시고, 어디 계시는 거고, 또 여긴 어디죠?" 바베트가 물었다.

"기다려라. 내가 내려갈 테니." 목소리가 말했는데, 이번엔 좀더 가깝게 들렸다.

p. 566

바베트는 위를 쳐다봤다. 그녀 위에 있는 책꽂이 하나를 따라 뭔가가 살랑거리며 움직이더니 천천히 나선형의 책꽂이를 돌면서 내려왔다. 마침내 회전하는 도서관 사다리를 타고 그들 쪽으로 덜컹거리며 다가오는 남자가 보였는데, 사다리는 수년 동안 사용해서 반질반질해진 부드럽고 번쩍거리는 놋쇠 가로대 꼭대기에 부착돼 있었다. 그것은 배 옆에서 멈추었고 남자는 뛰어내렸다.

얼핏 보니 그는 대단히 늙어 보였다. 길다랗고 끝이 뾰족한 흰 수염을 기르고 있었고, 이마가 벗겨지긴 했지만 여전히 숱이 많고 하얀 엉클어진 머리카락을 뽐내고 있었다. 그는 바베트에게 이상하게도 친숙해 보였다. 그는 구겨진 갈색 트위드 재킷을 입고 두꺼운 안경을 코 아랫부분에 걸치고 있었다. 얼굴엔 주름이 가득했지만, 사다리에서 뛰어내려 그들 쪽으로 걸어오는 모습이 너무 원기왕성해 처음 생각했던 것처럼 나이든 사람 같지가 않았다.

"이런, 이런." 그가 말했다. "이렇게 헐어빠진 배를 타고 여행하다니 놀랍구나. 더 잘 손질을 해야겠는걸. 부서지고 있는 거나 다름없잖니!"

"사실 저희의 배가 아니에요." 브리지트가 말했다.

"아, 그래, 그럼 너희는 해적이구나." 남자가 수염을 쓰다듬으며 말했다.

"뭐, 꼭 그렇진 않지만 어느 정도는 그렇다고 할 수 있겠죠." 브리지트가 말했다. "전 브리지트고, 이쪽은 제 친구들, 바베트, 바너비 그리고 보리가드예요. 안타깝게도 다른 동물들의 이름은 전혀 모르겠어요. 우린 구해준 것 뿐이거든요."

"멋지구나!" 노인이 소리쳤다. "난 보그스 박사고, 여긴 내 도서관이지. 내가 배에 올라타서 동물들을 만나봐도 되겠니? 여긴 누가 찾아오는 일이 거의 없거든."

보그스 박사는 허락이 떨어지길 기다리지도 않았다. 그는 손쉽게 갑판에 오르더니 보는 동물마다 미친 사람처럼 새 울음소리, 딸깍거리는 소리, 말 울음소리, 부엉이 울음소리를 내기 시작했다. 한참 동안을 그렇게 했는데, 동물들은 그를 보고 아주 즐거워하는 것 같았다.

p. 567

"할아버지는 모든 동물의 말을 유창하게 하시는 모양이야!" 바베트가 감탄하며 말했다. "그렇게 많은 언어를 마스터하기 어려울 텐데."

"놀랍구나!" 보그스 박사가 세 아이들에게 다가오며 웃었다. "저쪽에 있는 플라밍고 아기 새가, 이제 겨우 날 만큼 자란 어린 새가 길을 건너는 병아리에 대해 정말 웃긴 얘기를 해줬다. 그렇게 많은 일을 겪고 나서도 저런 유머감각을 가졌다니 놀랍구나. 잠자리 애벌레들은 배멀미로 고생하고 있더구나."

"어떻게 애벌레와 얘길 하세요?" 바너비가 물었다. "아직 곤충으로 완전히 자라지도 않았잖아요."

"어린 생물도 생각이 있다는 걸 의심하면 안되지." 보그스 박사가 대답했다. "대부분의 유기체는, 작은 벌레에서부터 거대한 고래에 이르기까지 모두 생각이 있단다. 어쨌든 이 녀석들의 주요한 불평은, 자기들이 강제로 고향을 떠났는데 새로운 환경은 불편하다는 거야. 물론 너희가 구해준 건 다행이지만, 그래도 고향에서 이렇게 멀리 떠나온 건 슬프다는 거란다."

"예를 들면, 저 북극곰은 광활한 눈의 평원으로 이루어진 북극의 차가운 툰드라에서 왔지. 카리브 해의 태양이 곰을

녹이고 있었어! 그리고 불쌍한 양은 열 때문에 아름다운 양털이 벗겨지고 있었단다!"

"우리가 때 맞춰 오길 잘했네요." 바너비가 동의했다.

"또 보니까, 메마른 사막 지방에서 온 동물들은 선체의 어둠과 습기에 잘 적응하지 못 하더라구요. 동물이 정상적인 기후를 벗어나 잘 자라기란 너무 어려워요."

바로 그때, 자그마한 카나리아가 보그스 박사 어깨 위에 내려앉더니 그의 귀에 대고 뭔가를 지저귀었다.

"그래, 네가 도서관에 대해 궁금한 모양이구나." 도서관원이 대답했다.

"궁금하다구? 그래요, 저희도 궁금해요." 바베트가 간절히 말했다. "보그스 박사님, 박사님의 도서관에 그냥 서 있기만 해도 정말 색다른 경험이었어요. 망상을 일으키는 것 같아요. 제 눈이 장난을 치는 건지 모르겠는데, 박사님의 탑이 우리 주변에서 온통 점점 커지고 변하고 있는 것 같아요!"

p. 568

"제가 봐도 그랬어요." 바너비가 덧붙였다. "하지만 왜 그러는지는 도무지 모르겠어요."

그러는 동안 언제나 쉽게 주의가 산만해지는 브리지트는 저쪽으로 걸어가더니 책꽂이에 있는 것들을 이리저리 쑤셔보았다.

"박사님!" 그녀가 불렀다. "정말 많은 걸 모으셨네요. 이렇게 많은 종류의 책은 처음 봤어요. 박사님은 아주 다양한 문학적 취미를 가지셨네요. 전기도 있고, 역사서, 의학서적, 에세이, 대학 학기논문, 편지, 훌륭한 소설들도 굉장히 많아요. 전 소설을 제일 좋아해요. 그러니까, 시나 수필, 사실에 입각한 책들도 좋지만, 만들어낸 이야기가 가장 좋아요."

"글쎄, 내가 모아놓은 책들이 다양할지는 모르지만, 이건 사실 내 취향을 정확히 보여주는 건 아니란다." 보그스 박사가 설명했다. "이 도서관은 내가 평생동안 계속 모아놓는 것에 불과해."

"그럼, 그게 계속 보태진다는 말씀인가요?" 브리지트가 물었다.

"그게 바로 네가 본 것처럼 네 주변에서 계속 일어나고 있는 거란다." 그가 고개를 끄덕이며 말했다. "새로운 지식이 습득되면 어떤 책에 내용이 추가되는 거고, 부정확한 것으로 판명된 정보는 다른 책에서 없어지고 있는 거다. 철학 부분이 언제나 가장 빨리 늘어나지. 사람들은 인생과 진실 같은 것들의 의미를 얘기하는 데엔 절대 지칠 줄 모르는 것 같더구나. 새로운 권이 시리즈에 더해질 수도 있고, 새로운 장이 옛날 책에 추가되기도 한단다. 대부분의 것이 더 길어지고 자세해지고, 줄어드는 건 거의 없는 것 같다. 사실 그건 흥미로운 역설을 가져오는데, 내가 아주 오랫동안 궁금하게 생각해온 것이지."

p. 569

"어떤 종류의 역설인데요?" 브리지트가 흥미를 느끼며 물었다.

"여긴 무한한 허구의 도서관이란다. 끝이 없기 때문에, 영원히 계속되기 때문에 무한한 것이지. 이 도서관은 이곳, 시간과 공간의 끝에서 영원토록 존재해왔고, 전 우주에서 일어났던 모든 사고와 경험의 기록을 보관하고 있지. 여태껏 쓰여졌던 모든 것, 네가 쓰여질 거라고 상상할 수 있는 모든 것이 이곳에 있단다. 여기엔 아직 쓰여지지 않은 것들까지도 있지." 도서관원이 말했다. "그리고 아직도 계속 늘어나고 있다."

"에이, 무한하면서 동시에 늘어날 수는 없잖아." 바너비가 머릿속의 생각을 소리내어 말했다. "왜냐면 뭔가가 무한하다는 것은 이미 그 크기를 상상할 수 없다는 거니까."

"그러니까 역설이지! 무한한, 그렇지만 늘어나는 도서관, 그 자체가 모순이잖아." 브리지트가 소리쳤다. "마치 '친절하려면 무정해야죠'라는 옛날 노래 같은 역설이지."

브리지트는 그 노래를 부르며 미친 듯이 춤을 추고 돌아다녔는데, 보그스 박사도 곧 그녀와 합세해 클라리넷처럼 삑삑거리는 새된 목소리로 노래를 불렀다. 브리지트는 뛰어서 재주넘기를 하며 2절을 부르기 시작했지만 보그스는 그녀에게 그만하라고 간청했다.

"제발 그만하렴." 도서관원은 얼굴이 벌개지면서 숨을 헐떡거렸다. "네 노래가 싫진 않지만, 난 음악을 들을 때마다 춤추고 싶은 충동을 억제할 수 없단다. 문제는, 난 더 이상 춤추는 것에 익숙하지 않다는 거지. 휴! 잠깐 숨돌릴 시간 좀 주렴. 난 완전히 지쳤다."

브리지트는 장난치며 뛰어다니는 걸 멈추었다. 그녀는 그 역설에 대해 여전히 깔깔거리며 흥분한 상태였지만, 늙은 도서관원을 존중하는 뜻에서 조용히 있으려고 애썼다. 하지만 몇 초 후 그녀는 호기심을 이기지 못했다.

"보그스 박사님, 무슨 뜻으로 여길 '무한한 허구의 도서관'이라고 하셨나요? 여긴 허구(소설) 말고 다른 게 더 많잖아요." 브리지트가 물었다.

p. 570

"설명을 하자면 좀 복잡하지만, 한번 해보도록 하지." 안색이 정상으로 돌아오자 그가 입을 열었다. "있잖니, 시간의 역사와 우주의 모든 사건은 하나의 대단한 이야기와 같단다. 어떤 면에서는 우리 모두가 살아가면서 그 이야기를 만들어내는 거지. 또는 다른 식으로 보자면, 우리 모두가 전개되고 있는 이야기의 주인공들이지. 어느 쪽으로든 그건 끝없는 이야기란다."

"맞아요, 그건 복잡한 설명이네요." 바너비가 의심스러워하며 말했다. "그게 박사님 역설의 또 다른 하나인가요? 우리는 주인공이자 동시에 작가라구요? 진짜 무슨 일이 일어나고 있는 건지 말해주세요."

"바너비, 무례하게 굴 필요는 없어." 바베트가 귓속말을 했다. "연장자에게는 존경심을 좀 보이라구. 저 정도로 현명한 사람은 존경받을 자격이 있다구."

보그스 박사는 관대한 미소를 지어 보였는데, 마치 바너비가 좀 분격한 것이 그를 화나게 만들었다기 보다 기분좋게 한 것 같았다.

"널 문하생으로 만들기는 힘들 것 같구나!" 도서관원이 웃으며 말했다. "자기 집이 어떻게 작동하는지에 대해서도 명쾌한 설명을 못해주는 노인의 제자가 되고 싶지는 않을 테니까. 정말 날카로운 과학적 사고를 지녔구나! 하지만 젊은이, 우주를 연구하는 방법에는 단순히 현미경으로 사물의 자그마한 미립자를 들여다보는 것 이상의 많은 방법이 있다네."

"과학이 그럴 듯한 설명을 내놓지 못할 정도로 그렇게 색다른 사건이나 그렇게 이상한 사실이나 그렇게 기묘한 현상이란 없어요." 바너비가 확신에 차서 단언했는데, 자신의 요점을 강조하기 위해 발을 쿵쿵 구르기까지 했다.

"자, 바너비, 과학자들이 많은 것들에 대해서 가능성 있는 설명을 내놓을 수 있다는 데엔 나도 동의할 수 밖에 없구나." 보그스 박사가 미소지었다. "넌 틀림없이 네 요점을 입증해줄 예를 많이 인용할 수 있을 거야. 네가 보는 바로는 말이다. 네 강한 신념은 감탄할 만하다. 강한 확신을 갖는다는 건 좋은 거고, 난 네 신념이 거짓임을 밝히려고 든다는 비난은 듣고 싶지 않구나. 그런데, 널 보니 내가 전에 알았던, 아주 아주 오래 전에 알았던 한 소년이 생각난다."

p. 571

보그스 박사는 한숨을 짓더니 부시시한 머리를 흔들었다.

"그건 그렇고, 내 설명을 그냥 전위적이라고 부르는 게 어떨까, 괜찮지? 아무튼 난 늘 내 시간을 좀 앞질러 가니까." 그가 말했다. "간단하게 이 도서관에 있는 책 일부를 예언이라고 해두자. 그 책들은 아직 일어나지 않은 일들을 얘기해주지. 좀전에 한 권을 읽고 있었는데, 그걸 보고 해적선이 여기로 오고 있다는 걸 알았단다. 그래서 내가 탑을 열어두었던 거지. 하지만 그 책에는 다른 얘기도 있었는데 말해줘야겠구나. 예를 들어 책에서 밝히는 바로는, 너희와 너희의 친구 보리가드는 지구를 멸망의 위험에서 구해내야 해! 그것도 사실, 몇 번씩이나."

"잠깐만요, 보그스 박사님." 브리지트가 말했다. "우린 어린애들에 불과해요. 우리가 지구를 구하는 일에 개입되다니, 그런 시나리오는 상상할 수도 없어요. 그런 얘기가 정말 믿을 만한 건가요?"

"그건 절대적으로 믿을 수 있지." 보그스 박사가 대답했다. "고르가스와 바르가스라는 팔이 열 개 달린 여행자들에 대해서 아니?"

"이런." 바너비가 말했다. "듣기가 겁나는 걸."

"우린 양키스 경기 대신 메트로폴리탄 미술관에 갔어야 했나봐." 브리지트가 괴로워하며 말했다.

도서관원이 말을 이었다. "고르가스와 바르가스는 가장 지독한 라이벌이지. 그들은 자신들의 고향인 스멜트블랏 행성에서는 사설탐정이었단다. 다른 모든 행성의 사람들이 잃어버린 사람이나 재산을 추적해 달라고 그들을 고용하곤 했지. 하지만 그저 직업적인 경쟁관계로 시작된 것이 끔찍하고 소름끼치는 싸움으로 바뀌어 여러 행성을 오가며 파괴와 훼손을 일삼게 됐어. 그들은 누가 진귀하고 독특한 것들을 찾아내는 데 최고인가를 입증하기 위해 불가능한 일에 도전하면서 서로 내기를 하기 시작했지. 이런 내기에 이기기 위해서라면 물불을 가리지 않으려 했어. 스멜트블랏의 사람들은 마침내 그들의 시합에 염증이 났고 그들을 행성에서 쫓아내 버렸어. 이제 이 위험한 부랑자들은 고향이라

부를 새로운 세계를 찾고 있는 거란다."

p. 572

바베트, 브리지트, 바너비는 전율을 느끼며 듣고 있었다.

"물론 처음에는 사소한 육식동물 사냥이 해로울 게 없었지." 보그스 박사는 계속 말을 이었다. "하지만 점점 고르가스와 바르가스는 둘 다 권력과 부에 맛을 들였단다. 너희가 벌써 본 것처럼 말이다.

지구 사람들에게는 불행하게도, 그들은 전 우주에서 너희들의 행성이 가장 이상한 식물과 동물, 스포츠, 음식, 옷, 관습이 가득하다는 결론을 내렸어. 그리고는 가장 짧은 시간에 가장 많은 기괴한 표본을 차지하는 자가 지구에 대한 지배권을 따낸다는 데 뜻을 같이 했지."

"고르가스가 세계의 지배권을 차지하려 한다고 내가 그랬잖아!" 바베트가 소리쳤다.

브리지트와 바너비는 너무 놀라서 뭐라 할 말이 없었다.

"그래, 이건 깊이 생각해볼 게 많다." 도서관원이 말했다. "너흰 고르가스와 바르가스가 이 싸움을 절대 그만두지 않으리라는 걸 믿어야 한다. 그들 중 누구라도 자신의 적수에게 지구를 내주느니 차라리 파괴해 버리려 할 거다. 하지만 너희가 그들을 막으려면 힘들 거야. 그래, 정말 어려울 거다. 가장, 가장 어려운 건..."

보그스 박사는 머리를 긁적이면서 왔다갔다했다.

"포포가 바르가스에게서 요술 지팡이를 훔칠 생각을 한 건 잘한 일이야." 그는 계속 걸어다니면서 머리를 긁적였다. "너희에겐 시간을 초월해 여행하는 방법이 필요할 게다. 그들은 어디에도 있을 수 있으니까. 보자, 여기 도움이 될 만한 게 있었는데. 아마 여기 이 구석에 두었나보다. 자..."

"어떻게 빙빙 도는 건물에 숨겨진 구석이 있을 수 있어요?" 바베트가 물었다.

바너비는 그저 어깨를 으쓱했다. 그는 다시는 모순에 대해 고민하지 않으려고 했다.

"아니." 도서관원이 중얼거렸다. "아마 내가... 아얏! 내 발!"

p. 573

바베트와 브리지트는 깜짝 놀라 엎어질 뻔했다. 은은한 금색으로 빛나는 길다란 금속 튜브가 보그스 박사의 머리카락 속에서 나와 그의 발 위로 떨어졌다.

"박사님 심정을 알겠어요." 도서관원이 한쪽 발로 껑충거리자 바너비가 자신의 더벅머리를 쓰다듬으며 웃었다.

"아하! 여기 있구나." 보그스 박사가 허리를 구부려 튜브를 집으며 말했다. "만화경인데, 보통 것과는 다르단다. 보통 만화경은 한쪽 끝을 들여다보고 튜브를 비틀어 돌리면 아름다운 모양과 색깔이 한꺼번에 바뀌지. 하지만 이건 갖가지 장소와 사람들이 바뀌는 거란다. 이건 너희에게 미래를 보여주는데, 가끔은 그리 아름답지 않은 모양과 색깔을 보여주지. 자, 한번 보거라!"

그는 튜브를 바너비에게 주었고, 바너비는 그것을 들어 빛에 대고 바닥을 비틀어 돌렸다. 처음에는 아무 것도 안 보이다가 연기와 구름이 나왔다. 하지만 서서히 한 형상이 분명하게 보이기 시작했다. 그것은 고르가스였다! 그는 김이 푹푹 나는 화산의 옆면을 미끄러져 올라가고 있었다. 하지만 만화경에 나타난 초록색의 거대한 괴물은 그뿐이 아니었다.

"이게 사실처럼 들릴지 모르겠지만," 바너비가 튜브를 책꽂이에 놓으며 말했다. "내 말을 믿어야만 해. 왜냐면 사실이니까. 고르가스는 공룡이 살던 시대로 돌아가 있어. 그가 뭘 하려는 건지 모르겠지만, 우린 그를 저지해야 해!"

동물 친구들과 근사한 갑판 파티를 벌이고 있던 보리가드가 만화경을 집어들더니 자기 모습을 들여다봤다. 그는 돌아가 주머니쥐 포포와 잠깐 이야기를 나누더니, 그런 다음 인간 친구들에게 돌아왔다.

그의 입에는 포포의 요술 지팡이가 들려 있었다.

QUICK QUIZ 16

관계 짓기

아래의 단어 쌍들이 서로 어떤 관계를 갖는지 판단하세요. 비슷한 의미면 "S" 반대 의미면 "O"를 하세요.

1. (힘 따위가) 점점 약해지다 ∷ (힘 따위가) 쇠해지다
2. 공들여 만든, 복잡한: 검소한, 간소한
3. 그럴 듯한 ∷ 있음직한
4. 번영하다, 무성해지다 ∷ 황폐시키다
5. 억누르다 ∷ 억압하다
6. 소설, 허구 ∷ 진실
7. 논쟁하기 좋아하는, 이론이 분분한 ∷ 마음이 맞는
8. 단언하다, 강력히 주장하다 ∷ 강력히 주장하다
9. 황폐한, 초라한 ∷ 더없이 훌륭한
10. 반대의, 외고집의 ∷ 완고한

QUICK QUIZ 17

관계 짓기

아래의 단어 쌍들이 서로 어떤 관계를 갖는지 판단하세요. 비슷한 의미면 "S" 반대 의미면 "O"를 하세요.

1. 천민, 부랑자 ∷ 부랑자, 추방당한 사람
2. 병든 ∷ 회복하는, 건강해지는
3. 무한한 ∷ 끝없는
4. 사소한 일로 불평하다, 다투다 ∷ 사소한 일로 말다툼하다
5. 조용한, 차분한 ∷ 흥분한
6. 질서있는, 조리가 서는: 무질서한, 혼란한
7. 틈 ∷ 틈, 균열
8. 건방진, 오만한 ∷ 예의바른
9. 존경, 숭상 ∷ 싫음, 혐오
10. 전위적인, 첨단적인 ∷ 혁신적인

QUICK QUIZ 18

빈칸 채우기

아래에 있는 각각의 단어들 중에서 가장 완벽한 문장을 만들어주는 단어를 고르세요.

1. 과학자들은 그들의 새로운 발명품으로 바닷물에서 금 ( )을/를 모두 추출하는 데에 전기를 이용할 수 있길 기대했다.
   a. 분자   b. 유기체   c. 잎   d. 양털
2. 많은 연구원들이 이미 스트록 교수의 아이디어가 순전히 거짓임을 ( ), 그는 여전히 자신의 '중력은 거짓말' 이라는 이론이 사실이라고 주장했다.
   a. 간청했지만   b. 요약했지만   c. 밝혀냈지만   d. 꿰뚫었지만
3. 협곡의 북쪽 면으로 기어 나오는 것은 어려운 일이었지만 다른 세 방향으로부터 적군이 진격해오고 있었기 때문에 ( ) 도피를 위해서는 유일한 선택이었다.
   a. 복잡한   b. 관대한   c. 원기왕성한   d. 성공적인
4. 티나의 얼굴 전체에 붉은 반점이 ( ) 시작하자 의사들은 그녀가 수두에 걸렸다는 걸 확실히 알 수 있었다.
   a. 분명히 나타나기 b. 뛰어놀기   c. 인용하기   d. 윤내기

5. 경찰은 광장에서 시작된 맨 처음의 폭동을 ( ), 그날 늦게 폭도가 다시 일어나 도시 전체에 들끓었다.
   a. 내려앉았지만   b. 진압했지만   c. 덧붙였지만   d. 부인했지만
6. 도시의 전기 공급에 ( )이/가 발생해 건물의 모든 전기가 들어왔다 나갔다를 반복했다.
   a. 장르   b. 툰드라   c. 계속적인 변화   d. 심연
7. 비올라는 1987년 은퇴한 뒤로 일상에서 생긴 ( )을/를 메우기 위해 하루에 8시간씩 라켓볼을 치기 시작했다.
   a. 치수   b. 역설   c. 빈틈   d. 현상
8. 우리는 나라에서 가장 ( ) 지역 중 하나를 가로질러 하이킹한다는 걸 알고 세 개 짜리 물통 한 벌을 짐에 더 보탰다.
   a. 지구의   b. 풍부한   c. 절충적인   d. 건조한

9. "가능한 한 조금 일해라"가 브래너트의 (　　　　　)인데, 그걸 보면 왜 그가 2천 개가 넘는 일자리에서 해고당했는지 알 수 있다.
　　a. 시나리오　　　　b. 철학　　　　　c. 지배권　　　　d. 애벌레

QUICK QUIZ 19

짝짓기

오른쪽의 단어를 비슷한 의미의 왼쪽 단어와 짝지으세요.

1. 난잡, 혼란	A. 입장
2. 일련의 변화	B. 일련의 변화
3. 광택	C. 거대한
4. 아기새	D. 힘있는
5. 접근, 출입	E. 학생, 제자
6. 우아한, 품위있는	F. 갑작스러운 간파
7. 거대한, 괴물같은	G. 윤
8. 폭로, 발각	H. 아기새
9. 힘있는	I. 우아한
10. 문하생, 제자	J. 혼란, 뒤죽박죽

QUICK QUIZ 20

짝짓기

오른쪽의 단어를 비슷한 의미의 왼쪽 단어와 짝지으세요.

1. 근육의 경련	A. 이상한
2. 기묘한, 색다른	B. 계속 더해지는
3. 진짜의, 믿을 만한	C. 오해, 잘못된 생각
4. 누적하는	D. 미래를 제대로 추측하는
5. 갈대같은, 호리호리한	E. 믿음, 확신
6. 예언하는	F. 근육경련
7. 이해하다, 간파하다	G. 진짜의
8. 신념, 확신	H. 떠나다
9. 비우고 나가다	I. 이해하다
10. 망상, 착각	J. 살이 없는

5 운명의 화산

---

p. 578

보그스 박사가 스쿠너선의 갑판에서 동물들과 어울리고 있는 동안 그가 동물들에게 그들의 노고가 이제 끝났다고 말하는 소리를 우연히 들었어. 그는 동물들에게 자신이 책임지고 그들의 고통을 끝나게 해줄 것이고 적당한 때와 장소로 보내주겠다고 했지. 그러니까 그들을 위해 성대한 파티를 열어준 후에 말야. 포포는 행복에 겨워 요술 지팡이를 우리한테 주었어. 실제로 자기 것인데도 말이지. 그는 정말 이타적인 주머니쥐로, 언제나 다른 사람의 필요를 자기의 필요보다 우선하지.

바너비는 내 손에서 바르가스의 요술 지팡이를 가져가고 만화경을 집어든 다음 보그스 박사에게 몸을 돌려 도와주어서 고맙다고 했는데, 그 정신나간 도서관원은 한떼의 우는 새들과 갑판에서 춤을 추느라 정신이 없었어. 그를 보니 어딘지 우리 보쟁글스 삼촌이 생각나더군. 삼촌도 음악을 들으면 저절로 춤이 나왔거든. 한번은 사우스 캐롤라이나에서

크리스마스 파티를 할 때였는데, 삼촌이 9시간 동안 쉬지 않고 지르박을 추셨고, 모두들 삼촌이 나무 밑에서 나오는 물을 마신 게 틀림없다고 생각했지. 하지만 사실, 밴드 리더가... 뭐, 그 얘긴 다음에 하기로 하지.

하던 얘기로 돌아가서, 바너비가 요술 지팡이를 움직여 조그만 원을 만드는 동안 브리지트, 바베트, 그리고 나는 그 둘레에 모여 있었어. 우린 지팡이를 어떻게 사용하는지 잘 몰랐고, 그래서 우린 다같이 정신을 집중해 중생대로 거슬러 가려고 했는데, 중생대는 1억8천만 년도 더 전에 일어났던 시기야. 중생대라니! 그냥 생각만 해봐도 황량하고 으스스한 땅을 가로질러 정처없이 떠돌아다니는 무서운 공룡들의 모습이 떠올랐지.

사실 난 솔직히, 어떤 종류의 지역을 기대해야 할지 몰랐지만 어쩐지 바위가 많고 나무는 없는 곳일 것 같았어.

p. 579

하지만 난 시간을 거슬러 여행하는 것이 그렇게 불안하기만 할 줄은 미처 몰랐어. 처음에 우린 요술 지팡이가 마술을 부릴 때 느끼는 것처럼 뜨겁고 끈적끈적한 공기를 느꼈는데, 그러더니 모든 게 까맣게 됐어. 그러다가 우리가 어디 있나 봤더니, 우린 원 안, 색과 빛이 소용돌이치는 한가운데서 날고 있었는데, 제트엔진과 수동 착암기 같은 소리가 쾅쾅 울려서 귀가 먹을 지경이었지. 단 몇 초 간격으로 이상하고 무시무시한 어떤 사람 혹은 동물의 환영이 소용돌이에서 튀어나와 우릴 쳐다본 다음 사라지곤 했어. 그런 다음 모든 게 정말 이상해졌어. 브리지트, 바베트, 바너비는 엿가락처럼 늘어져 있는 것 같았어. 그들의 머리와 다리가 길게 늘어지기 시작하더니, 가슴이 부풀어오르기 시작했어. 내 꼬리를 보니까 밑으로 몇 야드 늘어져 있었어. 이렇게까지 늘어졌으니 툭 끊어지겠구나 생각할 찰나, 어디선가 "뻥!" 하는 소리가 났고, 우린 하늘을 뚫고 지구를 향해 곤두박질치고 있었던 거야.

"브리지트, 너 아직 그 껌을 씹고 있겠지!" 바너비가 소리쳤다. "이 요술 지팡이를 어떻게 작동시키는지 모르겠어. 지금 당장은 지팡이한테서 어떤 도움도 받을 수 없다구!"

하지만 브리지트는 그를 훨씬 앞서가고 있었다. 그녀는 벌써 커다란 분홍빛 풍선을 불고 있었고, 팔을 흔들어 친구들에게 자신을 붙잡으라고 했다. 몇 초 사이에 그들 네 명은 브리지트의 풍선 밑에서 안정적인 속도로 내려가고 있었다.

"이젠 됐어." 바베트가 양손으로 브리지트의 왼쪽 발을 붙잡은 채 숨을 헐떡이며 말했다. "이게 끝나면 더 이상 시간을 거슬러 여행하지 않을 거야. 난 연대순으로 살고 싶어. 과거는 과거고, 미래는 미래고, 우리가 어디로 가고 있는 건지 다 알 수 있도록 말야."

"가끔씩 마음속으로 어린 시절로 돌아가서 장난감을 가지고 노는 건 괜찮아." 바너비가 브리지트의 오른쪽 다리를 단단히 붙잡은 채 맞장구를 쳤다. "그건 재미있지. 하지만 정말로 1, 2억 년 전까지 거슬러 가는 건 전혀 재미없어."

p. 580

불행한 여행자들은 땅에 이르러 잔디 위로 미끄러지자 잡고 있던 손을 느슨하게 풀었다. 브리지트의 목에 대충 매달려 있던 보리가드는 그들을 뒤따라 넘어졌다.

"이크!" 브리지트가 친구들 더미 위로 떨어지면서 껌을 입 속으로 다시 빨아들이며 투덜거렸다.

그녀는 진바지를 털고 나서 엉덩이에 양손을 대고 친구들을 점잖게 꾸짖었다.

"이렇게 불평한다고 우리가 어딜 갈 수 있는 게 아냐. 그러니 너희 둘 다 긍정적으로 생각하도록 해." 그녀가 주의를 줬다. "보그스 박사님이 우리가 세계를 구해야 한다고 하셨잖아. 그러니 다같이 힘을 모으자구."

"브리지트 말이 맞아." 바베트가 이렇게 말하면서 머리를 부풀리자 평소처럼 멋진 모습이 됐다. "우리에겐 중대한 사명이 있으니 전력을 기울여 그 일을 완수해야 해."

"그런데, 여긴 좀 이상하다." 바너비가 주위를 둘러보며 말했다. "뭐라도 보이니?"

바베트와 브리지트는 조심스레 그들 앞으로 펼쳐져 있는 전경을 살펴보았다. 정말 이상한 경치였다. 멀리에 대양이 있었다. 그들 바로 주변의 땅은 무성했는데, 풀과 꽃식물들로 완전히 뒤덮여 있었다. 그들이 서 있는 곳은 높은 언덕의 꼭대기로, 사방으로 멀리까지 바라다 보였다. 대양 쪽을 보니 화산섬에서 연기가 피어오르고 있었다. 왼편의 땅에는 또 다른 산이 솟아 있었는데, 역시 연기가 피어올랐다. 그들 아래의 땅에서는 조용히 우르르 소리가 났다.

"이 근처에 화산이 몇 개 있나봐." 브리지트가 말했다. "하지만 우린 벌써 그걸 알고 있었잖아. 공룡은 안 보이지만 그래서 불만이라고 할 수는 없지."

p. 581

"사소한 점일지 모르지만, 중생대 초기, 그러니까 2억 년 전쯤에는 화산 활동이 아주 활발했어." 바너비가 설명했다. "최근의 과학적 조사를 한 기억으로는, 꽃식물과 만화경에서 본 것 같은 거대한 공룡들은 훨씬 이후에야 나타나는 거야. 2, 3천만 년쯤 후에 말야. 하지만 난 공룡 전문가보다는 화학자니까. 내가 틀릴 수도 있겠지."

"궁금한 게 있어, 바너비." 브리지트가 입을 열었다. "과학자들이 자신들의 예감에 대한 확증을 얻기 위해 과거로 여행했던 적이 있니? 그들은 절대적으로 확신하는 거야? 공룡이 왜 멸종됐는지에 대해 그들이 명확한 설명을 할 수 있는 거야?"

"글쎄, 어떤 일이 일어났는지에 대해 몇 가지 대중적인 견해가 있어. 예를 들어, 우린 기후가 급격하게 변화해서 공룡들이 거기에 적응할 수 없었다는 걸 알잖아." 바너비가 대답했다. "하지만 무엇 때문에 그렇게 됐는지는 모르지. 과학자들이 내놓는 설명의 대부분은 추측에 불과하고, 어떤 한 가지 이론을 뒷받침해줄 만한 증거는 충분하지 않아."

"너도 이제 네 고유의 이론을 만들 수 있을 것 같은데." 바베트가 웃었다. "하지만 대학 친구들 중에 네가 정말 과거를 여행하면서 직접 이것저것을 봤다고 하면 믿어줄 사람이 없을 걸."

바너비가 한숨지었다. "그래, 교수와 학자들은 내가 계속 일을 망쳐놓는다고 날 이미 미쳤거나 위험할 정도로 쓸모없는 사람이라고 생각하니까. 난 그들에게 내가 뭘 하는 건지 제대로 알고 있고 완벽하게 실험을 수행할 수 있다고 계속 얘기하지만, 가끔은 과학이라는 이름으로 공익에 이바지하고 세상 사람들의 진보를 도모하려면 모험을 감수해야만 하지. 그건 마치 유치원에서 치즈 선생님이..."

"바너비?" 바베트가 팔꿈치로 바너비를 슬쩍 찌르며 말했다. "너 또 횡설수설하기 시작하는구나."

p. 582

"미안. 난 실험에 대해 얘기할 때면 말을 계속하다가 옆길로 빠지기 일쑤야." 바너비가 사과했다. "정말 미안해."

"됐어, 바너비, 뉘우칠 것까진 없어." 브리지트가 명랑하게 말했다. "우린 평상시엔 네가 재잘거리는 걸 듣는 게 좋아. 문제는, 지금 당장은 낭비할 시간이 없다는 거지. 여기서 뭔가가 크게 잘못됐어. 여기저기에서 공룡들이 뛰돌아야 하는데. 어쩐지 저쪽의 화산이 미스터리를 푸는 열쇠인 것 같아. 뭔가가 계속 나한테 가서 확인해 보라고 재촉하고 있어."

"뭔가가 아니야." 바베트가 지적하며 낄낄거렸다. "누군가지."

브리지트는 뒤를 돌아보고는, 보리가드가 정말로 그의 머리를 브리지트 등에 대고는 화산 쪽으로 가보라고 재촉하고 있음을 알았다.

"좋아, 알았어." 브리지트가 말했다. "어서 가보자."

바베트, 브리지트, 보리가드, 바너비는 연기가 나오는 화산을 향해 언덕 위로 서둘러 걸어가기 시작했다. 그들이 가까이 가자 흙이 타는 냄새가 바람에 실려 그들 쪽으로 날아왔다. 언덕의 아름다운 푸른 나무들이 여기저기서 새까맣게 탄 길다랗고 흉한 땅 때문에 훼손돼 있었다. 그들이 더 걸어갈수록 언덕과 그보다 작은 언덕들이 더 많이 타서 그을려 있었고 공기는 점점 후끈해졌다.

"저 화산은 아주 최근에 힘을 잃은 게 틀림없어." 바너비가 말했다. "화산 폭발이 규칙적이 아니라 산발적이어야 할 텐데."

"그러게 말야." 브리지트가 초초해하며 맞장구를 쳤다. "우린 걱정할 게 많지만, 솔직히 난 우리가 있을 때 이 화산이 폭발해 버릴까봐 제일 걱정이야."

"내가 듣기로, 화산은 먼저 우르르 울리기 시작해서... 얘들아!" 그들이 다른 언덕의 꼭대기에 이르렀을 때 바베트가 말했다. "저 아래 계곡 보이니?"

p. 583

그들 아래, 언덕들로 물이 흘러 들어오는 계곡 속에 수백 마리에 달하는 온갖 종류의 공룡이 모여 있었다. 티라노사우루스, 브론토사우루스, 익룡이 도처에서 뛰어다니거나 자리잡고 앉아 있었다. 몸둘레가 수 마일에 이르는 거대한 파충류들이 모두 그곳에 모여 있는 것 같았다. 그들은 대단히 시끄러운 소리를 냈지만 공룡들치고는 아주 평화로워 보였다.

"저들이 이 계곡에 온 건 먹이를 찾기 위해서가 아닌 것 같아. 서로 싸우기 위해서도 아니고." 바너비가 말했다. "대체 저들이 여기서 뭘 하는 거지?"

그의 질문에 바로 답이 나왔다. 계곡의 맞은 편 끝, 울퉁불퉁한 바위 위에 고르가스가 모습을 드러냈는데, 갈기와 자줏빛 망토를 산들바람 속에 뽐내듯이 펄럭거리고 있었다. 공룡들은 곧 조용해졌고 그를 쳐다봤다.

"저쪽의 산은 운명의 화산이다!" 그가 촉수 하나를 들어 뒤쪽의 화산을 가리킬 때 그의 목소리가 공룡들 사이에 울려 퍼졌다.

그의 우렁찬 목소리는 너무 무서워서 거대한 육식동물들조차 겁을 먹고 공손하게 침묵을 지켰다. 고르가스는 목소리를 가다듬더니 생각에 잠긴 듯 많은 눈을 깜박거렸다.

"연설을 시작하려나봐." 브리지트가 말했다.

"아마 저 사람의 연설을 들으면 무슨 꿍꿍이인지 실마리를 얻을 수 있을 거야." 바베트가 덧붙였다. "우리가 무리들 이쪽으로 몰래 돌아가서 저 사람 뒤로 간 다음, 불시에 덮치는 게 어떨까?"

브리지트와 바너비가 찬성했다. 그들은 모여 있는 공룡들 가장자리를 돌아 가능한 한 조심스럽고 조용하게 나아가기 시작했다.

"강력한 공룡 여러분," 고르가스가 소리쳤다. "이 순수하고 자연 그대로의 때묻지 않은 땅은 여러분의 것입니다. 이곳을 그대로 유지하고 싶지 않습니까? 여러분은 평화가 가득한 꽃피는 낙원에 살고 있습니다. 하지만 여러분이 내 말에 귀를 기울이지 않으면 여러분의 유토피아는 지옥이 될 것이고 여러분 모두 바싹 타버릴 것입니다. 난 미래를 보았는데, 끔찍한 재앙, 여러분 전부를 없애버릴 만한 무시무시한 재난이 닥쳐오고 있습니다. 여러분이 그걸 막지 않으면, 내 얘기대로 하지 않으면 말입니다!"

p. 584

군중으로부터 낮게 으르렁거리는 소리가 나왔다.

"내가 얘기하는 대로 하십시오. 그렇지 않으면 미래의 생물들이 여러분의 유골을 연료로 태워버릴 겁니다!" 그가 또 다시 큰소리로 말했다. "여러분의 시체는 땅속 깊숙이 매장될 것이고, 지금부터 수백만 년 후에 인간이라고 하는 새로운 생물들이 여러분을 화석이라 부르면서 여러분이 변해서 만들어진 석유와 가스를 사용해 자신들의 연료 탱크를 채우고 집을 따뜻하게 할 겁니다. 여러분은 좀 더러운 연료로도 이용될 겁니다. 지저분하고, 이런, 기분 나빠하지 마십시오. 내가 하려는 얘기는 그게 아니었습니다. 내가 하고자 하는 얘기가 뭐냐구요?"

"고르가스도 횡설수설하는 것 같아." 그들이 발끝으로 걸어갈 때 바너비가 속삭였다. "요점으로 들어가는 게 낫겠어. 공룡들이 벌써 혼란스러워하기 시작했어. 그들의 뇌는 별로 크지 않아서 복잡한 지시는 따르기 힘들어."

"아, 네, 네." 고르가스가 목소리를 가다듬고 다시 말을 이었다. "여러분은 지구 전체에 새끼 공룡을 퍼뜨리며 번식하고 증식하고 싶지 않습니까? 그렇다면 내 계획을 들으십시오. 산에서 흘러 내려오는 뜨거운 녹은 바위로 이루어진 저 빛나고 이글거리는 오렌지색 강물이 보입니까?" 그는 열광적으로 뒤를 가리켰다. "저건 마그마인데, 우리 모두 힘을 합쳐 U자 모양의 빨대처럼 생긴 커다란 튜브를 만들지 않으면 저것이 머지 않아 여러분을 멸망시킬 겁니다. 우린 튜브의 한쪽 끝을 화산 속에 꽂고 다른 쪽 끝을 바다 속에 집어넣어 마그마를 전부 물 속으로 옮겨야 합니다! 그러면 됩니다! 혹시 그게 너무 어렵다고 생각한다면, 그냥 산의 옆면에 커다란 구멍을 뚫어 마그마가 쏟아져 나오도록 할 수도 있습니다. 물론 그러면 좀 지저분해질지도 모릅니다. 어쨌든 중요한 건, 공룡 여러분이 당장 이 상황을 떠맡아야 한다는 겁니다. 자, 어서 하십시오! 구멍을 파십시오(bore)! 오늘 파야 합니다!"

공룡들은 흥분하고 불안하고 어리둥절한 것 같았다. 무리로부터 "어?"와 "지금 무슨 얘길 하는 거지?"라는 투덜거림이 나왔다. 보통 고르가스에겐 군중을 선동하는 데 필요한 카리스마와 개성이 있었다. 그의 연설은 짜임새가 있고 대개 상당한 설득력이 있어서 수사학을 공부한 게 틀림없어 보였는데, 이 군중은 그의 말뜻을 못 알아듣는 것 같았다. 마침내 위엄있고 기품있는 나이든 브론토사우루스가 앞으로 나오더니 상황을 정리해 보려고 했다.

p. 585

"공룡 여러분, 땅을 파라구요?" 거구의 점잖은 공룡이 물었다.

고르가스가 대답을 생각해내기도 전에 바너비와 브리지트, 바베트, 보리가드가 뒤편의 울퉁불퉁한 바위로 기어올라 왔다.

"거기서 꼼짝 마, 고르가스." 브리지트가 경고했다. "지금 뭘 하고 있는 거예요?"

"아! 어, 얘야, 놀랐잖니!" 고르가스가 소리를 질렀다. "어, 그냥 작은 실험을 하고 있었어. 공룡들이 그리 부지런한 파충류가 아니라고 하길래, 그들을 더 훌륭하고 부지런한 일꾼으로 만들려면 어떻게 해야 하는지 궁금해서. 그걸 중 생대 동기부여 프로젝트라고 한단다. 난 정말 파충류들을 움직이게 하고 뭔가 할 일을 주고 싶어. 물론 오로지 과학을 위해서지."

"아, 그만둬요, 고르가스." 브리지트가 비웃었다. "당신이 바르가스와 경쟁하고 있다는 거 다 알아요. 우리가 알 수 없는 건 왜 이 공룡들을 구슬려서 화산을 바다로 빼내려고 하는지예요. 그러면 어떤 재난이 일어날지 모르나요?"

"바르가스? 바르가스는 불량배에 악한이고 사기꾼이야!" 고르가스가 주장했다. "그 놈이 너희한테 무슨 얘기를 했든 다 거짓말이야. 그가 너희한테 뭐라고 했는데?"

"아무 말도 안 했어요. 우리가 직접 알아낸 거예요." 바베트가 말했다. "우린 이상한 표본들을 모아서 세계를 지배하 려는 당신의 계획을 알게 됐고, 당신과 바르가스와 스멜트블랫 행성에서 왜 추방당했는지도 알아. 부인해봐야 소용 없어요. 우린 당신이 포기하는 게 좋을 거라고 말하려고 온 거예요. 당신이 절대 성공하지 못하도록 하겠어요!"

아래 계곡에서는 공룡들이 조바심을 내며 으르렁거렸다.

"공룡 여러분, 땅을 파라구요?" 늙은 브론토사우루스는 느리게, 그러나 큰 소리로 반복했다.

p. 586

"세상에, 정말 참견하기 좋아하는 애들이로군." 외계인은 머리를 가로저으며 파충류에게는 신경도 안 쓰고 얘기했다. "내 일에서 좀 빠져줄 수 없겠니? 뭐, 너희가 알아야겠다면 말해주지. 바르가스가 이상한 생물을 모으는 데 나보다 앞섰어. 그래서 난 보통과 다른 뭔가를 해야만 한다는 걸 알았지. 난 너희 지구 인간들의 디엔에이를 연구해 보려고 했어. 디엔에이는 화학물질로 만들어진 조그만 안내책자 같은 거지. 너희 몸 속의 모든 세포에 들어 있는 거야. 디엔 에이는 너희가 어떻게 성장했고 어떻게 기능하는지 알려주지. 난 저 거대한 파충류들이 한때 이 행성에서 어슬렁거렸다 는 걸 알고 이 고대 파충류가 모든 현대 지구 생물체의 전임자라고 판단한 거야. 그런데 너희에겐 왜 냉혈이나 비늘 모양의 피부 같은 파충류의 특성이 거의 없는지 이해가 안 갔어. 그래서 디엔에이를 분리해 유전자를 들여다보았지. 너희 유전자는 네 부모와 조부모에게서 받은 거야. 결국 공룡은 인간이나 고양이 혹은 북극곰과는 아무 관계가 없다 는 게 분명해졌지. 주머니쥐와도 마찬가지고."

"내 생각엔, 당신이 이 공룡들에게 말을 거는 이유에 대해 그럴 듯한 추론을 해보면, 당신은 이들이 멸종되지 않게 해 서 그들의 유전자가 현대까지 살아남도록 하기 위해서예요. 공룡들이 현대까지 살아남게 되면 어떤 일이 일어나게 될 지는 아무도 알 수 없어요." 바너비가 어리둥절한 채 머리를 긁적이며 말했다. "하지만 화산을 빼내는 건 왜죠? 그게 무슨 소용이에요, 만일... 아! 알겠다! 과학자들은 기후의 변화가 공룡을 멸종시켰다고 알고 있어요. 당신은 이 화산 폭발이 먼지와 재를 공기 중으로 내뿜어 그런 변화를 일으키고 있다고 생각하는 거예요! 그래서 화산폭발을 멈추게 해 공룡들을 살리려는 거라구요!"

"이해력이 특별히 뛰어나지 않더라도 격심한 화산활동과 커다란 기후변화 사이에 상관관계가 있다는 정도는 알 수 있지." 고르가스가 말했다. "바보라도 그 관계는 알 수 있을 거라구."

"고르가스, 무례하게 굴려는 건 절대 아니지만, 당신이 이끌어낸 견해는 내가 지금껏 들어본 것 중 제일 어리석어요." 브리지트가 눈동자를 굴리며 말했다. "어쩜 그렇게 미숙한 아이디어를 생각할 수 있죠? 마그마를 전부 바다 속으로 빼버리면 바다 생물들이 죽을 거고, 물은 말라버릴 거고, 모든 식물이 죽어버려 공룡들은 먹을 게 없을 거고, 그럼 공 룡도 전부 죽을 거고, 그리고... 그러면... 지구도 말라빠진 바위 덩어리가 될 거라구요!"

p. 587

브리지트는 고르가스의 계획이 얼마나 끔찍한가를 깨닫고는 눈이 휘둥그레졌다. 고르가스는 그녀가 충격받은 걸 알 아차리고는 위협하는 듯이 낄낄거리며 웃었다.

"하지만 고르가스, 이렇게 하면 안돼요!" 바베트가 울부짖듯이 말했다. "지구는 아주 많은 생명체들로 가득한 아름다 운 행성이에요! 멸망시키면 안 된다구요!"

"조용히 해라, 얘야, 아직은 그렇게 감상에 젖을 필요 없다." 고르가스가 말했다. "브리지트는 바다가 말라버릴 거라 고 확실히 알고 있는 게 아냐. 아마 물은 충분할 거고, 공룡들은 계속 살아갈 거다. 그렇게 되면, 미래에는 새로운 이 상 생물체가 나타날 거고, 난 경쟁에서 이기는 거지. 지구가 말라버린다면, 글쎄, 그건 유감이지. 하지만 최소한 바르 가스도 이기지 못하는 거다."

바너비는 계속 머리를 긁적이며 생각하다가 브리지트에게 귓속말을 했다. "우린 계획을 세워야 해, 그것도 빨리. 이 공룡들이 점점 심기가 뒤틀리고 있고, 고르가스는 저들을 전혀 제어하지 못하는 것 같아. 잠깐! 바로 그거야! 지금 공룡들이 내 말을 잘 들을 수 있도록 확성기가 있으면 좋겠는데."

"어, 바너비." 브리지트가 속삭였다. "네 머리에서 삐져나와 있는 커다란 원뿔 모양의 물건이 뭐야?"

바너비는 머리를 두드렸는데, 아니나 다를까 머리에서 삐져나와 있는 확성기를 발견했다.

"좋았어! 어딘가에 이런 게 하나 있을 줄 알았지." 바너비가 말했다. "자, 브리지트, 바베트, 보리가드, 저 깊은 틈 속으로 뛰어내려. 저 바위틈새가 몸을 숨기기에 안성맞춤이야. 우린 보호를 좀 해야할 것 같아."

친구들 모두 서둘러 바너비를 따라 한데 모였다.

p. 588

"자." 젊은 과학자가 설명했다. "이게 효과가 있어야 할텐데. 공룡들이 초조해하고 흥분돼 있는 것 봤지? 그들은 고르가스의 말은 못 알아들었지만 뭔가 행동할 준비가 돼 있는 것 같아. 브론토사우루스가 고르가스 말에서 알아들은 건 'bore'가 전부인 것 같아. 공룡들은 고르가스가 자기들 보고 지겹다고(boring) 하는 줄 아는 것 같아."

"그렇다면 곤란한데." 바베트가 말했다.

"그래, 맞아." 바너비가 동의했다. "하지만 내가 그런 오해를 이용해 공룡들이 우리 대신 고르가스를 처리하도록 할 수 있을 것 같아. 내게 필요한 건 그들이 이해할 수 있는 간단한 메시지 뿐이야. 하지만 이 일을 잘 해내려면 훌륭한 복화술사가 되어야 해."

"그래서 확성기가 필요한 거야? 네가 하는 말이 고르가스가 말하는 것처럼 들리게 만들려고?" 바베트가 물었다.

"바로 그렇지." 그가 말했다. "그의 목소리를 잘 흉내내야 할텐데. 아무튼, 자 이제..."

바너비는 목청을 가다듬고 잠깐 생각하더니 확성기를 입으로 가져갔다.

"공룡 여러분! 내 말을 들으십시오!" 바너비가 우렁차게 말했다. "공룡은 나빠요. 공룡은 멍청해요. 공룡은 지겨워요. 공룡이 싫어요. 공룡은 지겨워! 공룡은 지겨워!"

일제히 으르렁거리는 소리가 계곡에 울려 퍼졌다. 공룡들이 알아듣기 시작한 것이다. 그들이 이해하는 한 고르가스가 자신들을 모욕하고 있는 것이었다. 이젠 더 이상 점잖지 않은 거구의 브론토사우루스가 앞으로 나오더니 튼튼한 옆구리로 울퉁불퉁한 바위를 막아섰다. 바너비, 바베트, 브리지트, 보리가드는 바위와 먼지가 그들 주위로 떨어지자 머리를 감쌌다. 또다시 브론토사우루스가 옆구리로 바위산을 들이받았는데, 이번에는 바위가 너무 심하게 흔들려서 고르가스가 성난 파충류 무리 속으로 굴러 떨어지고 말았다. 이제 고르가스는 끝장난 것 같았다.

p. 589

아이들과 보리가드는 성난 으르렁거림과 쿵쿵거림이 계속되는 동안 가만히 앉아 있어야 했다. 바너비에겐 생각에 잠길 시간이 생겼는데, 그것이 그가 가장 좋아하는 일이었다. 그가 이번에 곰곰이 생각한 것은 불쌍한 공룡들의 운명이었다.

"있잖아," 그가 말하기 시작했다, "이 공룡들이 불쌍해. 저들은 우리가 생각했던 것 이상으로 고르가스의 말을 이해한 모양이야. 아마 저들은 언젠가, 지금부터 수백만 년 후지만 그래도 언젠가는 자신들의 종이 사라지리라는 걸 아는 것 같아. 저들의 심정을 좀 알 것 같아. 어쨌거나 저기 잠깐 있으니까 사라지는 것에 대한 걱정이 어떤 건지 알겠더라. 나도 저들과 똑같은 심정이 되는 것 같았어."

"나도 기분이 안 좋아." 브리지트가 말했다. "하지만 공상과학 영화들을 보면 시간 여행자들에게 주어지는 가장 중요한 명령은, 과거에 일어나는 일을 바꾸지 말라는 거야. 그게 미래에 어떤 영향을 줄지 알 수 없으니까. 그 얘기가 나와서 말인데, 우리가 실수로라도 과거를 바꾸기 전에 여기서 빠져나가야겠어."

바너비는 슬픔에 잠겨 고개를 끄덕이더니 주머니에서 요술 지팡이를 꺼냈는데, 미처 사용할 기회를 얻지 못했다. 그가 지팡이를 휘둘러 원 하나를 채 그리기도 전에, 바베트와 브리지트, 보리가드, 바너비는 전에 들어가 본 듯한 빛과 소음의 회오리바람 속에 갇히게 됐다. 그리고 그들은 누가 이것을 통제하고 있는지 충분히 알 수 있었다.

QUICK QUIZ 21

관계 짓기

아래의 단어 쌍들이 서로 어떤 관계를 갖는지 판단하세요. 비슷한 의미면 "S" 반대 의미면 "O"를 하세요.

1. 악당, 불량배 :: 건달, 악한
2. 대학의, 학구적인 :: 무교육의, 무식한
3. 끔찍한 재난, 격변 :: 황폐화시킴
4. 무성한 :: 황량한
5. 동기를 주다, 흥미를 유발하다 :: 낙담시키다, 단념시키다
6. 곰곰이 생각하다 :: 심사숙고하다
7. 증식하다 :: 감소하다
8. 카리스마 :: 마음을 움직이는 힘, 매력
9. 뚫다 :: 파다
10. 자연 그대로의 :: 훼손된

QUICK QUIZ 22

관계 짓기

아래의 단어 쌍들이 서로 어떤 관계를 갖는지 판단하세요. 비슷한 의미면 "S" 반대 의미면 "O"를 하세요.

1. 늘이다 :: 넓히다
2. 태우다 :: 태우다
3. 부지런한 :: 게으른
4. 위엄있는 :: 비천한
5. 연설 :: 연설
6. 모으다 :: 흩뿌리다
7. 어리둥절하게 하다 :: 진정시키다
8. 공감, 감정이입 :: 동일시
9. 수사학, 웅변술 :: 수사법, 능변
10. 죄를 뉘우치는 :: 의기양양한

QUICK QUIZ 23

빈칸 채우기

아래에 있는 각각의 단어들 중에서 가장 완벽한 문장을 만들어주는 단어를 고르세요.

1. 존스 농부는 아무리 친절하게 간청해도 그의 양을 북쪽 초원에서 (   ) 떠나게 할 수 없었다.
   a. 억지로   b. 섞여서   c. 늦추어서   d. 위협해서

2. 강둑을 따라 놓인 모든 작은 조약돌 위에 미세한 이끼층이 덮여 있어서 우린 미끄러운 그 (   )을/를 건널 때 특별히 조심했다.
   a. 유토피아   b. 파노라마   c. 지역   d. 지옥

3. 지방 대학의 교수는 빌헬름에게 그가 동굴에서 발견한 (   )은/는 티라노사우루스 렉스의 다리뼈라고 말했다.
   a. 화석   b. 시체   c. 유전자   d. 디엔에이

4. 4백 피트 높이, 20피트 깊이에 달하는 도시의 벽은 외국의 침략자들을 막는 (   ) 방어선이었다.
   a. 연대기적인   b. 주요한   c. 감상적인   d. 이타적인

5. 짐은 24온스 딸기 음료가 너무 맛있어서 한번에 다 마시는 것을 (   ) 힘들었다.
   a. 깜짝 놀라게 하기가   b. 나르기가   c. 측면을 공격하기가   d. 억제하기가

6. 날씨는 아버지가 가장 좋아하시는 주제였기 때문에 아버지는 엄마가 그만하라고 할 때까지 몇 시간이고 날씨에 대해 (   ) 하셨다.
   a. 얻으려고 애쓰곤   b. 두서없이 얘기하곤   c. 배회하곤   d. 추방하곤

7. 후지 산에 오르는 것은 힘들었지만 산의 (   )에 도달하고 나서 꼭대기에서 경치를 내려다보니 충분히 올라올 만했다.
   a. 울퉁불퉁한 바위   b. 작고 둥근 언덕   c. 정상   d. 틈

8. 자기 반 깡패의 (   ) 표정에 잔뜩 겁을 먹은 크리스찬은 운동장에서 그와 마주하느니 차라리 두들겨 맞기로 했다.
   a. 무능한   b. 산발적인   c. 지겹도록 참견하는   d. 악의에 찬

9. 잔디 깎는 기계에 기름이 다 떨어졌지만 우린 앞 잔디를 깎을 수 있도록 (   )을/를 이용해 픽업트럭의 탱크에서 기름을 퍼
   왔다.
   a. 전임자   b. 확성기   c. 복화술사   d. 사이펀

QUICK QUIZ 24
짝짓기
오른쪽의 단어를 비슷한 의미의 왼쪽 단어와 짝지으세요.

1. 마그마	A. 유령
2. 어림짐작, 추측	B. 용암
3. 저쪽에	C. 일으키다
4. 야기하다	D. 추측
5. 환영, 유령	E. 생각, 관념
6. 결정적인	F. 되돌아가다
7. 관념, 개념	G. 특징
8. 되돌아가다	H. 떨어져서
9. 추정, 결론	I. 결론
10. 특성	J. 결정적인, 최종적인

QUICK QUIZ 25
짝짓기
오른쪽의 단어를 비슷한 의미의 왼쪽 단어와 짝지으세요.

1. 먹이를 찾아다니다, 약탈하다	A. 연결, 관계
2. 노역, 힘든 일	B. 첫 단계
3. 시대, 시기	C. 시대, 시기
4. 둥둥 떠다니다	D. 명령
5. 관계, 상관성	E. 증거, 입증
6. 불러내다, 일깨우다	F. 가볍게 떠다니다
7. 확정, 증거	G. 비평하다, 비난하다
8. 처음	H. 먹이를 찾아다니다
9. 훈계하다, 주의를 주다	I. 어려운 일
10. 지령	J. 소환하다, 불러일으키다

6 재판관, 배심원 그리고 교도관

p. 594

시간을 통과하여 여행하는 것은 익숙해지는 게 아닌가봐. 이번으로 세 번째니까, 여행하는 과정이라도 우리 몸이 그리 심하게 잡아 늘어지거나 뒤틀리지 않을 거고, 그렇게 어지럽지도 않을 거라고 생각하겠지. 하지만 시간여행의 부작용은 줄어들지 않았어. 심하다면 더 심했지.

나선형 급강하를 하고 나와보니 브리지트, 바베트, 바너비, 그리고 나는 고풍스러운 법정에서 커다란 목조 배심원석에 앉아 있었어. 거기 있는 사람은 우리뿐인 것 같았어. 유리창을 통해 햇빛이 비치는 걸 보고 내가 얼마나 안도했는지 몰라. 최소한 우린 지구에, 최근의 과거 어느 때에 있는 것 같았지. 난 우리가 있는 곳이 어디인지 실마리라도 좀 얻을 수 있나 보려고 바깥을 살짝 내다봤는데, 커다랗고 크림같이 하얀 꽃이 만발해 있고 가지가 무성한 커다란 목련

나무를 보고는 기쁨으로 소리를 지를 뻔했어. 사실 꽃들이 너무 많아서 진초록의 매끈한 잎들은 거의 보이지도 않았지. 햇빛을 보고 남부가 아닐까 싶었지만, 목련나무를 보니 확실히 알 수 있었어. 사실, 남부에 있다는 걸 아는 방법 중에서 목련나무를 보는 것보다 더 확실한 건 없으니까.

아이들이 정신을 차리기 시작했고, 난 애들을 떠밀어 법정의 문 쪽으로 가려고 했는데, 그때 갑자기 끔찍한 통곡소리가 방을 가로질러 터져 나왔어. 거기, 죄수석에 고르가스가 앉아 있었어. 그의 눈 몇 개는 시커멓게 돼 있었고, 갈기는 뒤엉켜 있었으며, 밝고 깨끗하던 자줏빛 망토는 때묻고 더러워져 있었어. 그의 촉수들은 사슬로 한데 묶여 있었어. 그는 너무나 허약하고 기운없고 무기력해 보여서, 불쌍한 생각이 들 정도였어. 물론 우린 고르가스를 그리 신경쓰지 않았지. 하지만 바르가스는 달랐어. 이젠 그가 정말 원한을 품을 수 있으니까. 우리가 찾아내려고 하면 말이지.

p. 595

"존경하는 바르가스 재판장님을 위해 일동 기립." 바르가스가 법정의 문을 열고 들어오면서 큰소리로 말했다.

외계인은 안 그래도 하얀 갈기 위에 분을 바른 하얀 가발을 쓰고 있었다. 가발은 어딘지 모르게 조지 워싱턴 머리처럼 보였다. 그는 망토 대신에 길다란 검은 옷을 입고 있었다. 그는 촉수가 이끌어주는 대로 천천히 격식을 차리지 않고 법정 앞으로 느릿느릿 걸어왔는데, 세상에 걱정 하나 없는 것 같았다. 바르가스 뒤로는 팔다리가 달린 코코넛처럼 생긴 털복숭이의 작은 동물들의 행렬이 이어졌는데, 마치 퍼레이드를 하는 듯 일직선으로 걸어왔다. 고르가스는 또 통곡을 했다. 걸어 다니는 코코넛의 행렬을 이끄는 바르가스의 모습만큼은 절대 보고 싶지 않은 것 같았다. 너무나 어리둥절해 달리 어떻게 할 수 없는 브리지트, 바베트, 바너비는 자리에서 일어났다.

"넌 아니야, 고르가스." 바르가스가 죄수를 지나가면서 호통쳤다. "일어서지 마. 촉수를 넓게 펴고 얼굴을 바닥에 내리깔아. 딱한 죄수가 하는 것처럼."

"하지만 바르가스, 난 사슬에 묶여 있어! 자네한테 존경을 표시할래도 팔을 펼 수가 없다구." 고르가스가 죄수석의 빗장 사이로 몸을 내밀어 가능한 한 바르가스에게 가까이 가려고 하면서 흐느꼈다. "아, 강력한 재판장님, 이리 오셔서 당신 옷자락이라도 만지고 술장식에 입맞춤을 하게 해주세요. 당신은 정말 현명하고 위대하십니다! 제발, 자비를 베푸소서!"

"됐다!" 바르가스가 호통을 쳤고, 자신의 옷을 홱 끌어가면서 자신에게 다가오려는 고르가스의 노력을 단번에 거절했다. "나한테 아양떨지 마라. 네놈이 날 추켜세운다고 특별한 호의를 얻을 줄 아나, 네놈의 간청과 애원은 역겹다."

"하지만 어떻게 이런 식으로 내 청을 거절할 수가 있나? 우린 오랫동안 아는 사이였잖아!" 고르가스가 사슬을 덜거덕거리며 말을 이었다. "내가 뭘 어쨌길래 이렇게 멸시를 당해야 하나?"

"질문 잘했다." 바르가스가 얼굴을 찡그리며 억지 웃음을 지었다. "배심원단 여러분, 거기 비즈워트들, 앉아서 입 다물어! 명심해, 너희들은 지금 세기의 재판을 보고 있는 거라구!"

p. 596

작은 코코넛 모양의 동물들은 통로에서 이리저리 굴러다니고 있었는데, 재판장이 말하자 벌떡 정신을 차리고는 자리에 앉았다.

"좋아. 자 이제, 배심원단 여러분, 고르가스라는 이 사람이 은하계에서 전대미문의 죄를 짓고 이 자리에 나왔습니다." 바르가스가 말하기 시작했다. "사실 이 자의 범죄 중 몇 가지는 정말로 전례가 없는 것으로, 이 말인즉슨, 이 사악한 자가 끔찍한 죄들을 주모하고 실행에 옮긴 최초의 자라는 겁니다. 우린 이 자를 그가 저지른 사악한 죄와 똑같은 정도로 처벌할 수 있길 바랍니다."

"하지만, 치안판사님, 이 죄들이 완전히 새롭고, 그래서 법조계에 알려져 있지 않은 거라면 그게 법을 거스르는 건지 어떻게 확신하실 수 있죠?" 브리지트가 물었는데, 그녀는 수두에 걸려 침대에 누워 있는 동안 'LA Law'의 재방송을 보면서 법에 대해 많이 알게 됐다. 그녀는 고르가스를 석방시키고 싶었던 게 아니라 그냥 궁금했던 것이다.

"좋소. 고르가스가 저지른 좀더 일반적인 죄들을 목록에 올리도록 하겠소. 이상한 죄들은 나중에 다루기로 하고." 바르가스가 한숨을 지었다. "그리고 날 치안판사라 부르지 마시오. 치안판사는 작은 재판을 다룰 뿐이오. 이건, 내가 말했듯이, 세기의 재판이오! 난 중요한 재판장이오."

"죄송합니다, 재판장님." 브리지트가 말했다.

"알고 있군. 하던 얘기를 계속하자면, 고르가스는 훨씬 오래 전부터, 스멜트블랏에서 어린아이였을 때부터 범죄자의 마음을 갖고 있었소. 그의 집안은 세련되고 부유해서 최고의 칼로피안 여자 가정교사를 고용해 그를 돌보게 하고 가르치게 했소. 칼로피안 유모들은 엄격하기로 유명하지만, 고르가스는 아주 어린 나이였을 때부터 온갖 짓을 다해 유모에게 반항을 했소. 그는 방청소도 안 하려 했고, 접시도 깨끗이 비우지 않았고, 잠잘 시간이 돼도 만화책을 덮지 않으려고 했소. 끔찍하지 않소?" 바르가스가 물었다.

"뭐, 깔끔하지 못한 게 지구에서는 꼭 죄가 되지는 않는데..." 바너비가 입을 열었다.

p. 597

"그야 물론 죄는 아니오." 바르가스가 날카롭게 말했다. "단지 그가 얼마나 나쁜 자인지 보여주려는 것이오. 그는 어린아이에게서 기대할 수 있는 청결함, 공손함, 관용 같은 덕목을 하나도 갖고 있지 않았소. 사실 훌륭한 예의범절은 제쳐두고라도, 그에게는 어떤 긍정적인 자질이라고 할 게 하나도 없는 것 같소. 하지만 그가 처음으로 진짜 범죄를 저지른 건 십대에 이르러서였소. 법에 따라 우리 행성의 모든 청소년들에겐 야간 통행금지가 있소. 세 번째 달이 지평선 위에 떠오를 때까지 모든 청소년들은 집에 와 있어야 했소. 물론, 고르가스는 그런 법이 자신에겐 상관없다고 생각했소. 그는 야간 통행금지를 어기고 아케이드 밖에 나가서 친구들과 어울려 다섯 번째, 여섯 번째 달이 뜰 때까지 떠들며 놀았소."

"그러면 못쓰죠." 바베트가 말했다.

"하지만 그건 시작에 불과하오." 바르가스가 강조했다. "그의 나머지 인생은 신나는 범죄행각이라고 표현할 수밖에 없소. 그는 끊임없이 범죄를 저질렀고, 그때마다 대단히 즐거워했소. 사설탐정으로 일하는 동안에 가장 즐겨했던 범죄는 절도였소."

"난 도둑이 아니었어!" 고르가스가 소리쳤다. "의뢰인들한테 아무 것도 훔치지 않았네. 그 당시엔 덕성을 갖추고 있었다구. 거짓말도 안 했고 사기도 안 쳤고 부정직한 일은 아무 것도 안 했단 말야!"

"어, 아니라구?" 바르가스가 우렁차게 말했다. "나한테서 훔쳐간 그 의뢰인들은 다 뭔가? 그게 바로 절도지. 물론 자넨 트랄랄라의 시장으로 있을 때 비행을 저지른 죄로 고발됐었소. 고르가스는 어떤 일을 하든 돈을 받아낼 수 있는 아주 사악한 시장이었소. 거기에 대해 뭐 할 말 있나? 자기변호를 할 텐가?"

비즈워트들은 딱딱한 나무 의자 위에서 원숭이들처럼 기를 쓰고 찍찍거리면서 이리저리 굴러다녔다.

p. 598

"질서를 지키시오! 법정에서는 질서를 지키라구! 그만해, 미친 비즈워트들아!" 바르가스가 말했다. "어때, 고르가스? 선거가 있던 어떤 해가 생각나는군. 자넨 현 시장이면서 재선되려고 했었지. 자네와 겨루던 후보자가, 웰목이었던 것 같은데, 이해할 수 없이 사라져버렸지. 소문대로 자네가 고용한 한패의 자객에게 납치당했던 거야. 자넨 성공했다고 생각했지. 물론 자네가 선거에서 당선됐어. 하지만 취임식때, 자네가 법에 따를 것을 맹세하기로 되어 있는 식순에서 온통 얻어맞고 먼지투성이가 된 웰목이 나타난 거야. 그는 굉장한 이야기를 들려줬지. 자네가 그렇게 잽싸게 마을을 빠져나가려고 한 건 정말 놀라웠네!"

"그가 붙잡혔나요?" 브리지트가 물었다. "어떻게 됐어요?"

"아, 뻔하게 됐소." 바르가스가 투덜거렸다. "전체 사건을 조사할 위원회가 구성됐소. 두 개의 정당, 곧 고르가스의 당과 웰목의 당에서 나온 사람들이었소. 즉 2대 정당이었소. 하지만 2대 정당이 늘 공정한 것은 아니오. 위원회는 몇 달간 소집됐지만 어떤 결론도 나지 않았소. 그들은 어떻게 해야 할지에 대해 의견일치를 못 보는 것 같았소. 의원들이 모이면 어떤 사람이 나와서 어떻게 해야 사건의 진상을 밝힐 수 있는지 단조롭게 이야기하고, 그러면 모두들 잠이 들었소. 그리고 나서 다음 날 똑같은 사람들이 다시 모이고, 또 똑같은 일이 벌어진 거요. 마침내, 고르가스는 와서 자신의 정직함을 보증해줄 사람들, 소위 '친구들'을 고용하기로 마음먹었소. 보수가 좋은 이 증인들은 고르가스가 결백하다고 단호하게 맹세를 했소. 위원회는 그들 말을 믿은 거요! 그들은 고르가스를 풀어주었소!"

"난 결백해!" 고르가스가 소리쳤다. "웰목을 납치한 건 자네였으면서, 날 범죄자처럼 만들려고 한 거잖아! 무슨 수를 써서라도 나에게 죄를 씌워 감옥에 집어넣으려고 했어. 유괴범은 자네라구!"

비즈워트들이 고르가스에게 불쾌감을 드러내자 법정 전체에 우우 하는 소리와 쉿쉿 하는 소리가 울려 퍼졌다.

"함부로 주장을 하면 안되지, 고르가스." 바르가스가 경고했다. "그 주장을 뒷받침해줄 증거도 없잖나."

하지만 고르가스는 아이들에게 간청하며 계속 말을 이었다. "그래, 내가 방금 주장한 것에 대해 증거는 없지만, 달리 그럴 사람이 누가 있겠나? 그에 대한 내 증거는 단지 정황적인 거지만 사실이네. 목격자도 없었고 확실한 사실도 없었지. 하지만 바르가스는 날 미워해. 그는 내가 처음 시장에 당선되자 사무실에서 날 쫓아내려고 나에 대항해 십자군을 일으킨 거나 다름없어. 그는 사명을 띤 군인 같았지. 군대까지 있었어, 말하자면 말야. 그건 아이스크림 트럭 운전수들, 나비 수집가들, 용접공들의 연합이었어. 왜 그렇게 다른 부류의 사람들이 나에게 맞서는 동맹을 맺기 위해 친해지려고 했는지는 오늘까지도 미스테리야. 하지만 바르가스는 그들을 함께 일하게 만들었고, 그들은 날 끌어내리는 일이라면 뭐든 다했지."

"어, 고르가스와 바르가스, 솔직히 이건 정말 재미있네요." 브리지트가 공손하게 말하기 시작했다. "하지만 두 분한테 상관없다면 우린 갈 길을 가야겠어요. 아저씨 두 분들 사이의 개인적인 문제인 것 같아요."

브리지트, 바베트, 바너비, 보리가드가 배심원석 밖으로 발을 내딛기도 전에 바르가스가 일어서더니 고함을 질렀다.

"거기 그대로 있거라! 재판은 아직 시작도 안됐다. 거기, 머리 땋은 아이, 속기 기계 작동하는 법 아나?"

"뭐라구요?" 브리지트가 물었다.

"상관없다." 바르가스가 말했다. "여기 기계 옆에 앉아서 이 방에 있는 누구든 말하는 내용을 타이프로 치거라. 그게 지구에서 일을 처리하는 공식적인 방법이다, 그렇지? 너, 선글라스 낀 아이, 너는 증인 선서를 시키는 게 어떠냐? 저 놈은 진실만을 말하겠다고 맹세해야 돼. 저 놈한테 약속하라고 해봐야 별 소용은 없겠지만, 어쨌든 하긴 해야지. 여기 성경책 있으니 가져가서 촉수를 올려놔라."

바르가스는 재판장 의자에서 주르르 미끄러져 나와 만반의 준비를 하려고 애쓰는 마지막 휴일 쇼핑객처럼 법정을 이리저리 바쁘게 돌아다녔다.

"어, 교구사제나 목사여야지 그렇게 하는 거 아닌가요? 그러니까, 누군가한테 맹세를 시키려면요." 바베트가 물었다.

"말도 안되는 소리. 보통 사람들도 늘상 그렇게 한다. 너희 텔레비전에서 봤는걸." 바르가스가 말했다.

"그 말이 맞아." 브리지트가 말했다.

"좋아요, 그렇담." 바베트가 이렇게 말하더니 성경책을 가져가며 어깨를 으쓱했다.

"나는요?" 바너비가 물었다. "난 뭘 해야 하죠?"

"어, 그래. 자, 이 법률 용지철을 가져가라. 편지 같은 걸 받아쓰게 해야 할지도 모르니까. 그럴 경우 내가 '서한을 작성하시오'라고 할 거고, 그러면 넌 내가 말하는 걸 전부 기록해야 한다. 알겠나?" 바르가스가 물었다.

바너비는 고개를 끄덕였다.

"좋아. 아주 좋아, 그러면 증인 선서를 하시오." 가발을 쓴 외계인이 지시했다.

바베트는 고르가스에게로 걸어가 성경책을 내밀었다. 고르가스는 촉수 하나를 성경 위에 올려놓았지만 만족스러운 표정은 아니었다.

"증인은 진실을, 모든 진실을, 오로지 진실만을 말할 것을 맹세합니까?" 바베트가 물었다.

"진실이라는 게 뭔가?" 고르가스가 신중하고 조심스럽게 눈을 가늘게 뜨며 물었다. "이런 것들을 숨김없이 분명하게 하는 건 아무리 주의해도 지나치지 않아. 바르가스, 이건 공정하고 균형잡힌 재판이 아닌 것 같네. 자넨 날 미워하고, 이 아이들도 날 그리 좋아하지 않지. 사실 이 법정에는 나에 대한 편견이 가득해. 슬프도다, 공정한 여인, 정의의 여신이여! 내 마음은 슬픔으로 가득 찼네. 정말 정말 안타까워."

"정말 안타까운 게 뭔지 얘기해 줄게요, 고르가스." 바베트가 느닷없이 말했다. "안타까운 건 아저씨의 꾸미는 태도예요. 으스대지 좀 마세요. 꼭 옛날 영국 연극에 나오는 인물 같아요."

비즈위트들은 재미있는지 낄낄거리며 통로를 펄쩍펄쩍 뛰어다녔다. 바베트가 그들을 쌀쌀맞게 노려보고는 다시 고르가스를 쳐다봤다.

"자, 고르가스, 정직해야 돼요. 요점만 얘기해요. 솔직한 게 중요해요. 정직하게 얘기해야지 아무 것도 숨기면 안돼요." 바베트가 설명했다. "맹세하나요?"

"아, 좋다 좋아." 바베트의 얘기에 심기가 좀 불편해진 고르가스가 화를 냈다.

"고맙소." 바르가스가 말했는데, 막 탁자 밑에서 발을 질질 끌며 나오고 있었다. "이제 고르가스에 대한 소송사건을 설명하겠소."

"저거 새 가발이잖아?" 바너비가 물었다. "전의 것보다 훨씬 더 곱슬거리는 것 같아. 게다가 모든 색깔이 스펙트럼으로 나오나봐. 재판장들은 무지개 색깔의 광대 가발을 써야 하나?"

"보는 눈이 정말 날카롭구나! 정말 예리한 관찰력이다. 내 의상의 모든 미묘한 차이를 알아보다니." 바르가스가 말했는데, 바너비 말에 기분이 좋아진 게 확연했다.

"광대 가발에 미묘한 차이가 많았잖죠." 바너비가 대답했다. "당신이 광대 가발을 쓰고 있다는 건 알아보기 힘든 세부적인 게 아니에요. 모르고 지나치기가 아주 어려운 거죠. 그런데 왜 바꿔 쓴 거예요?"

"그건, 내가 이번엔 변호사거든." 외계인이 설명했다. "아까 그 가발은 내가 재판장일 때 쓰는 거고. 교도관일 때 쓰는 멋진 금발의 급사용 가발도 있단다."

"이건 재판이 아니야!" 고르가스가 사슬을 풀려고 몸부림치며 소리쳤다. "이건 재판을 어설프게 흉내내는 거야. 진짜를 서툴고 불충분하게 모방하는 거지. 바르가스, 이 더럽고 비열하고 질벅거리는 머리의..."

p. 602

"쯧쯧!" 바르가스가 혀를 찼다. "우린 이 법정에서 공손한 말을 써야 하오. 언어에 주의하고 예의바르게 이야기하도록 애써주시오. 당신에겐 어려운 일이겠지만, 가능한 한 그렇게 노력해 주시오."

고르가스는 그 동안 바르가스의 모욕을 잘 참아왔지만, 이젠 인내심이 바닥을 드러내고 있었다. 얼굴을 찌푸리고 있는 걸 보면 그의 두려움이 분노로 바뀐 게 분명했다. 성난 외계인은 뭔가를 궁리하고 있었다.

"바르가스, 그러지 말고. 그래, 우린 그 동안 불화를 일으켜 왔지. 그냥 이걸 공정하게 해결하는 게 어떤가?" 그가 제안했다. "우리가 의견일치를 본다는 건 어려워 보이니까 이 아이들에게 중재를 부탁하세. 이 애들이 우리가 주장하는 걸 듣고 결론을 내리려면, 우린 애들이 가장 공정하다고 생각하는 대로 하는 걸세. 만약 내가 자네가 가져야 마땅한 어떤, 어, 자산, 그러니까 돈이나 토지나 가치가 있는 어떤 걸 갖고 있다고 판명되면, 난 기꺼이 그것들을 자네에게 주겠네. 천 번의 사과도 곁들여서 말야."

"그렇게 아낌없이 주겠다니 감탄할 지경이군, 고르가스." 바르가스가 코방귀를 뀌었다. "내가 알기로 자넨 그렇게 후하게 선물을 줄 사람이 아니네. 그러면 자넨, 나보다 자넬 더 싫어하는 인간들을 믿고서 우리의 계산을 맡기겠다는 얘기가? 자넨 인간들이 우리 사이의 계산을 끝내고 누가 누구한테 빚이 있는지 결론내줄 수 있다고 생각하는 건가?"

"난 전적으로 그들의 분별력을 믿네." 고르가스가 말했다. "그들은 자유롭게 스스로 결정을 내리는 거야. 그리고 난 그게 현명한 일이라 확신하네."

"하!" 바르가스가 코웃음쳤다. "자넨 내가 생각했던 것보다 더 바보로군. 말도 안돼. 정말 웃기는군. 너, 머리 땋은 여자애. 고르가스가 방금 한 말을 다시 읽어봐. 다시 듣고 싶다."

브리지트는 속기 기계에서 나오는 동그랗게 말린 종이를 내려다봤다. 그녀는 모든 말을 받아치려고 노력은 했지만, 물론 타이프하는 방법을 몰랐다. 거기다 속기 기계는 타이프라이터와 달랐다.

"어, 바르가스, 그게 좀 왜곡되고 뒤죽박죽이 됐는데요." 브리지트가 솔직히 털어놓았다. "별로 말이 안돼요. 제가 타이피스트의 소질은 별로 없거든요."

p. 603

"그의 바보같은 짓은 충분히 기록해 두어야 할텐데." 바르가스가 안타까워했다. "그래, 그건 충분히 기록해야지. 자네의 하찮은 계획을 좌절시키는 건 미안하네만, 고르가스, 난 정력적인 변호사, 정열과 흥분으로 가득한 변호사의 역할을 맡을 기대에 부풀어 있다네. 지구의 텔레비전에 나오는 변호사들은 아주 스릴 만점에 인상적이던데, 안 그런가?"

고르가스는 바닥을 응시한 채 투덜거리며 대답하기를 거부했다.

"자, 시무룩하게 그래봐야 소용없네." 외계인 변호사가 놀리듯 말했다. "난 자넬 너무 잘 알지. 보통 때 자넨 화가 나면 말이 많아지지. 사실 자네가 없다면 자네의 바보같은 말이 그리울 걸세. 그래서 내가 지구의 지배자가 되도 자넬 처형하거나 추방하지 않으려는 거네. 난 이 행성을 친절하고 관대하게 다스릴 거네. 단지 자네 머릴 밀기만 할 거야."

고르가스는 분노로 악을 썼고 사슬을 풀려고 몸부림쳤다. 바르가스는 웃더니 소용돌이치듯 빙 돌아 옷자락을 높이 나부꼈다. 조그만 비즈위트들도 펄쩍 뛰어올라 그와 함께 빙빙 돌다가 어지러워서 푹 쓰러졌다.

"그래, 난 세계의 지배자가 되면 맨 처음 모든 범죄자들의 머리를 삭발시키라는 명령을 내릴 거네. 삭발한 머리는 스멜트블랏에서 가장 치욕스런 일이지. 진정하게, 고르가스, 내가 자넬 불구로 만들기라도 하려는 것처럼 행동하는군. 자네의 촉수를 자르거나 하진 않을 거네. 그건 자네의 바보같고 초라하고 시키면 갈기에 불과해!"

고르가스는 순간 몸부림을 멈추더니 바르가스를 재빨리 아무도 모르게 흘깃 쳐다봤다. 그는 자신이 바르가스 옷 밑에 있는 여분의 요술 지팡이와 열쇠를 본 걸 아무도 눈치채지 못했길 바랬다.

"바르가스, 이렇게 하는 것이 당신의 업보에 도움이 될지 모르겠어요." 브리지트가 말했다. "나쁜 일을 하는 건 당신의 생명력에 손상을 줘요. 당신은 내세에 바퀴벌레나 정말 끔찍한 뭔가로 환생할 수도 있어요. 어쨌든 그런 걸 믿는다면 말예요."

"업보라, 슈마르마" 바르가스가 말했다. "난 스멜트블랏에서 왔다. 그래서 너희 인간의 행동규정에서 면제를 받는다구. 그것들은 나한테는 적용이 안 되는 거고, 그러니 따를 필요가 없지. 아무튼 너희들한텐 규정이 너무 많아..."

p. 604

그때 갑자기 죄수석에서 통곡소리와 함께 크게 쿵 하는 소리가 났다. 고르가스가 넘어진 것이다!

"아, 이런, 이러면 재미없지." 바르가스가 푸념했다. "그가 기절해 버리면 겁주는 게 별로 재미가 없어지지. 너, 과학하는 아이, 그 메모지철 내려놓아라. 나 대신 진단해 줄 수 있겠나?"

"어, 난 의사가 아니라서 뭐가 잘못됐는지 알아낼 수 없을 것 같아요." 바너비가 설명했다. "게다가 그는 외계인인데, 난 외계인의 건강 문제에 대해선 아무 것도 몰라요."

"그렇다면 좋다. 내가 처리하도록 해보지. 너희 나머지는 이 탁자 중에 다리에 바퀴달린 게 있나 봐라. 환자 수송용 테이블로 쓸 수 있을 거다. 병원에서 쓰는 굴러다니는 침대 있잖아." 바르가스가 고르가스에게 몸을 굽히며 말했다. "보자, 뭐가 문제인지..."

고르가스는 번개처럼 몸을 움직였고, 바르가스가 그의 적이 기절한 것은 그를 불러들여 옷 속에서 열쇠와 요술 지팡이를 쉽게 빼갈 수 있는 위치를 잡기 위한 구실이자 간사하고 영악한 행동이었다는 걸 알았을 때는 이미 늦은 뒤였다. 그들은 잠깐 동안 촉수로 서로를 때리며 치고 받았다. 하지만 고르가스가 기습의 덕을 보았다. 몇 초 후 그는 사슬에서 풀려나 자신의 요술 지팡이로 바르가스를 꼼짝 못하게 하고 있었다.

고르가스는 잠깐 멈추어 자신의 승리를 대단히 기뻐했고 광대 가발이 완전히 뒤엉킨 바르가스의 모습을 보고 즐거워했다. 그리고 나서 말하기 시작했다.

"바르가스, 네가 나를 모욕적으로 대한 것과 온통 거짓말을 한 것에 정말 화가 난다." 그가 입을 열었다. "난 정말 불쾌하다. 하지만 나의 결백함은 입증될 것이다. 아, 그래, 난 오명을 벗게 될 거야. 스멜트블랏 사람들이 네가 얼마나 위험한 범죄자인지 알게만 되면 그들은 너를 영원토록 피할 거라구. 스멜트블랏의 누구도 다신 너와 말하지 않을 거야. 그러면 그들은 내가 저지른 사소한 일들은 모두 잊어버릴 거고 나의 귀향을 반겨줄 거다."

브리지트, 바너비, 바베트, 보리가드, 그리고 비즈위트 전부는, 그들이 문쪽으로 몰래 가고 있는 것을 싸우고 있는 두 스멜트블랏인이 눈치채지 못하길 바랬다. 하지만 그런 행운은 없었다.

"거기 서라!" 고르가스가 명령했다. "멍청한 비즈위트들은 가도 돼. 하지만 너희 꼬맹이들은 우리랑 같이 가야 돼. 그 고양이도 데려와. 우린 계산할 게 좀 남았다구."

p. 605

QUICK QUIZ 26

관계 짓기

아래의 단어 쌍들이 서로 어떤 관계를 갖는지 판단하세요. 비슷한 의미면 "S" 반대 의미면 "O"를 하세요.

1. 분개 :: 분노
2. 맹세 :: 서약
3. 날카로운 :: 무딘

4. 행렬, 퍼레이드 :: 행진

5. 서두르다 :: 한가로이 거닐다

6. 격노, 분노 :: 원한, 증오

7. 피하다 :: 포옹하다

8. 솔직한 :: 은밀한

9. 쫓아내다, 거절하다 :: 거절하다

10. 거무죽죽한, 때묻은 :: 오점없는, 깨끗한

QUICK QUIZ 27

관계 짓기

아래의 단어 쌍들이 서로 어떤 관계를 갖는지 판단하세요. 비슷한 의미면 "S" 반대 의미면 "O"를 하세요.

1. 일치 :: 일치

2. 결연, 동맹 :: 연합

3. 아낌없이 줌 :: 박애, 자선

4. 언저리, 가 :: 중앙

5. 약삭빠른 :: 솔직한

6. 흥미, 취미 :: 혐오, 싫어함

7. 은밀한, 남몰래 하는 :: 조심성 있는, 신중한, 입이 무거운

8. 덕성, 품성 :: 덕, 미덕

9. 편향, 치우침 :: 공평

10. 활동적인 :: 무기력한

QUICK QUIZ 28

빈칸 채우기

아래에 있는 각각의 단어들 중에서 가장 완벽한 문장을 만들어주는 단어를 고르세요.

1. 탤런트 쇼에서 덕이 에반스 교장을 (   )한 것은 모두들 재미있다고 인정했지만, 그에 대한 벌로 이틀 동안 방과후 학교에 남는 것을 피할 수는 없었다.
   a. 십자군   b. 취임   c. 패러디   d. 의식

2. (   ) 역시 '스타트렉'의 대단한 팬이어서 룰루와 프랭크의 결혼식을 거행하는 데에 클링온처럼 차려입기를 좋아했다.
   a. 치안판사   b. 교구사제   c. 후보자   d. 여자 가정교사

3. 장관은 전면전이 터지기 전에 양측 사이에 평화적인 화해를 (   ) 희망했다.
   a. 중재하길   b. 입증하길   c. 고발하길   d. 노력하길

4. 세계에서 가장 정직한 사람이라고 모두가 인정하는 짐 핼보프가 로메로의 품성을 (   ) 로메로는 압도적 표차로 시장에 당선되었다.
   a. 단언하자   b. 보증하자   c. 왜곡하자   d. 감소하자

p. 606

5. 소년은 평소보다 1시간 일찍 방으로 보내져서 기분이 (   ), 방에서 그를 기다리고 있는 새로운 기차 세트를 발견하자 금새 기뻐했다.
   a. 솔직했는데   b. 2등이었는데   c. 시무룩했는데   d. 신중했는데

6. 셸비는 텍사스 주 팔레스타인에서 태어나 자랐기 때문에 그녀의 영어 액센트가 (   ) 것을 대번에 알 수 있었다.
   a. 영향받았다는   b. 부수적이라는   c. 찡그렸다는   d. 전례없다는

7. 석간 신문에 백만 달러의 뇌물을 수수한 주지사의 사진이 실리자 시민은 정부의 (   )이/가 만연해 있다는 걸 알았다.
   a. 절도   b. 부패   c. 야간 통행금지   d. 인과응보

8. 왕은 자신의 새로운 성을 건설하기 위해 모든 소작인들이 하루에 3시간씩 더 일해야 한다고 (   ) 뒤 혁명을 맞이했다.
   a. 주고받은   b. 명령을 내린 뒤   c. 팔다리를 쭉 편   d. 진단한

9. 글리디아는 세계적으로 유명한 가수가 되자 자신이 처음 교육을 받은 줄리어드, 오하이오 음악학교에 거금을 (   ) 싶어했다.
   a. 구술하고   b. 왜곡하고   c. 계산하고   d. 주고

짝짓기

오른쪽의 단어를 비슷한 의미의 왼쪽 단어와 짝지으세요.

1. 재산	A. 모으다
2. 못쓰게 만들다	B. 볼품없게 하다
3. 만족시키다	C. 신나는 소풍
4. 미묘한 차이	D. 아첨하다
5. 소집하다	E. 빛깔의 띠
6. 아양떨다	F. 미묘한 차이
7. 현직자, 현직의원	G. 개인의 자산
8. 단조로운 저음, 윙윙거림	H. 현공직자, 현직관료
9. 스펙트럼, 분광	I. 만족시키다
10. 신나게 즐김	J. 계속적인 낮은 윙윙거림

QUICK QUIZ 30
짝짓기

오른쪽의 단어를 비슷한 의미의 왼쪽 단어와 짝지으세요.

1. 면제된	A. 지지되지 않은 주장
2. 결정타	B. 이동식 병원 테이블
3. 풍부한	C. 약한
4. 환자 수송용 테이블	D. 면제된
5. 통치하다	E. 풍부한
6. 탄원, 간청	F. 간청, 구걸
7. 연약한	G. 대화
8. 구실, 터무니없는 주장	H. 지배하다
9. 이야기, 담화	I. 결정적인 행위

7 최후의 대결 2026

p. 608

내가 시공을 초월한 여행을 또 하고 싶어하지 않았다는 건 굳이 말 안 해도 알 거야. 지난 두 번의 여행으로 머리는 멍하고 두 눈은 흐릿해졌어. 사실, 그 전 과정이 위생적인지 조차 모르겠어. 내 건강이나 청결함을 증진시켜줄 만한 일은 전혀 없었으니까. 매번 여행을 하고 나면 기름에 몸을 담그고 있었던 것처럼 털에는 이상하고 끈적거리는 게 남아 있었거든. 그건 바베트, 바너비, 브리지트도 마찬가지였어. 그들은 땀범벅이 된 듯 했는데, 땀에는 이상하게 옅은 초록빛이 있어서 건강한 얼굴에 병색이 돌았어. 난 그들의 얼굴을 북북 문질러서 초록색 때를 씻어내주고 싶었어. 그런 다음엔 아마, 더러운 것을 깨끗이 닦아주고 피부를 밝고 탱탱하게 만들어줄 좋은 아스트린젠트가 있었으면 좋겠다고 생각했어. 탱탱한 피부가 좋은 안색의 비결이잖아. 하지만 상황이 그렇다보니 내가 그들을 핥아서 깨끗하게 해보는 수 밖에 없었지.

알고 보니 우린 1926년의 루이지애나 사카자보그 시 법원에 있었던 거였어. 그곳은 남부 습지에 있는 작고 예쁜 마을이었어. 안타깝게도 제대로 둘러볼 기회는 없었어. 그곳 원주민들이 정신나간 조그만 코코넛 동물들을 어떻게 생각했을지 모르겠어. 법정의 비즈워트들은 고르가스의 말을 그대로 믿고 있는 힘을 다해 도망쳤어. 보니까, 그들은 덤불과 검은딸기를 헤치며 굴러서 도망가더라구. 아마 마을 어귀에서 시커먼 늪 속에 빠졌을 거야. 남부 루이지애나의 땅은 아주 축축하고 폭신폭신해서 말떼도 빠져서 꼼짝 못하곤 했지. 아니면 친구들을 사귀고 정착을 했을지도 모르고. 그거야 우리로선 모를 일이지.

p. 609

한편 우리는 약 백 년의 시간을 앞질러 가게 됐어. 적어도 고르가스 말로는 그랬지. 정신을 차려보니까, 화가의 다락방이라고 부르는 건물 꼭대기층의 커다랗고 탁 트인 방의 구석에 있더라구. 어쩐지 그곳은 낯이 익었는데, 이유는 말할 수 없었어. 그 방은 과학 실험실 같았어. 온통 부글거리는 액체가 담긴 병과 금속판, 마구 갈겨쓴 메모들이 널려 있었지. 하지만 내가 지금껏 본 가장 멋진 실험실이었어. 높다란 창문 옆의 한 구석에는 아름다운 목조 책상이 있었는데, 선명한 적갈색으로 봐서 마호가니 같았어. 방안 가득 멋진 가구와 융단이 있었지. 창문 너머로 보이는 지평선도 친숙한 모습이었어. 친숙하지만 같지는 않았는데, 생각이 잘 안 났어.

방 한가운데엔 길고 가느다란 코에 허연 머리를 한 키 큰 남자가 서 있었어. 그는 너무나 수척해서 한달 동안 쫄쫄 굶은 사람 같았어. 피부는 우중충하고 누르스름했어. 바너비가 입던 것과 비슷한 실험실 가운을 입고 있었고, 옆에 서 있는 고르가스와 뭔가 논쟁을 벌이고 있는 것 같았지.

"무슨 뜻이지, 준비가 안됐다니?" 고르가스가 물었다. "내가 자넬 부자로 만들어 줬잖소? 내가 오기 전에 자넨 가난하고 생활고에 시달리는 과학자였어. 이제는 잘나가는 회사를 소유한 부유한 기업가고 말야."

"그래, 맞소. 내 사업으로 벌어들인 수입이 상당했소. 당신이 준 상당한 보조금이 없었다면 그런 모험은 꿈도 못 꾸었을 거요." 바싹 마른 과학자가 말했다. "난 정말 영광스럽게도 그런 큰 선물을 받았소. 하지만 내 말 좀 들어보시오. 난 살인광선이 준비되지 않았다고 한 게 아니오. 내 말은, 당신한테 줄 수 있을지 모르겠다는 거요."

바닥에서 어지럽게 이리 뒹굴 저리 뒹굴 하고 있던 브리지트, 바베트, 바너비는 일어서서 주위를 둘러보고는 자기들이 있는 곳이 어딘지를 알아내고자 했다. 광대 가발을 벗은 바르가스는 여전히 의식이 없었다.

"이봐." 바너비가 속삭였다. "전에 여기 와본 것 같아."

"무슨 얘긴지 알겠어." 브리지트가 고개를 끄덕이며 말했다.

바베트는 고개를 고르가스 쪽으로 홱 돌리더니 물었다. "무슨 일이 일어나고 있는 거죠?"

"자네가 제대로 설명을 해보시지, 닐스." 고르가스가 으르렁거렸다.

p. 610

과학자 닐스는 말없이 눈을 깜박이더니 대답했다. "뭐, 그러죠. 그런데 당신과 똑같은 종류가 여기 또 있군요. 화내지 않았으면 좋겠는데, 정말 둘을 분간하지 못하겠소. 둘 다 눈이 12개에 다리가 10개고, 머리가 축축하잖소. 머리카락은 쉽게 염색하고 자를 수 있으니까 그렇다 치고, 당신들을 구분하지 못하겠소. 내 발명품을 넘겨주는 데도 정말 조심해야겠소. 내게 살인광선 만드는 일을 위임한 사람이 누군지 어떻게 알겠소? 하얀 머리를 한 그 자가 날 고용한 게 아니라는 걸 내가 어떻게 알겠소?"

"그러니까, 자넨 스멜트블랏 사람이 다 똑같이 생겼다고 생각하는 건가? 관찰력이 형편없다고 나무랄 수는 없을 것 같군. 그럴 만도 하니까. 인간들은 곧잘 세부적인 것들을 많이 놓치더군." 고르가스가 한숨을 지었다. "하지만 상관없어. 용서해 주지. 자, 살인광선의 열쇠를 넘기게."

"잠깐만 기다려!" 바르가스가 자신의 촉수를 풀고 일어서며 신음했다. "닐스, 저 자는 거짓말을 하는 거야. 자네한테 돈을 준 건 바로 나야. 증명할 수도 있다구. 자네가 무일푼이었을 때 내가 자넬 찾아왔던 거 기억나나? 자넨 어떤 문제를 해결할 수 없었고, 막 포기하려고 했지. 과학은 정말 자네한테 맞지 않는다고 하고선, 평생토록 정말 되고 싶은 건 탭댄서라고 했잖나. 하지만 자넨 리듬감각이 없어서 어떤 음악에 맞춰서도 춤출 수 없기 때문에 꿈을 포기할 수밖에 없었지. 안 그런가?"

"그렇소, 나에게 절친한 친구가 생겨 얼마나 기뻤던지. 난 내 비밀을 털어놓을 만한 사람, 믿을 만한 사람이 필요했소." 닐스가 슬픈 듯이 말했다. "난 내 연구가 모두 헛된 것이었다고 생각했는데, 당신이 날 도와주어 내 연구는 상당한 가치가 있다는 걸 보여주었소. 그럼 이 자는 누구고 난 어떻게 해야 하는 거요?"

"어떻게 해야 되냐고?" 고르가스가 잽싸게 끼어들었다. "이 자의 말은 들을 것 없어. 내가 자넬 고용한 거야. 자, 자네가 이 커다란 방에서 행운의 펜을 잃어버렸고, 내가 자넬 도와서 바닥 구석구석을 기어다니며 방 전체를 살살이 뒤졌던 거 기억나나? 난 자네의 행운의 펜이 어떻게 생겼는지도 몰랐는데 말야."

닐스는 어찌할 바를 모르는 것 같았다.

"그래, 그래, 그것도 기억나오." 그가 동의했다. "당신은 그걸 찾을 수 없었소. 그건 몇 달 동안 보이지 않았었소. 음. 뭘 어떻게 해야 할지 모르겠군. 어느 쪽이 진짜 당신이오?"

"웬만해서 이런 논쟁에 휘말리는 건 싫은데." 브리지트가 말을 꺼냈다. "하지만 저 사람 둘 다 당신을 고용해 살인광선을 만들게 했을 수도 있지 않나요?"

"넌 누구고, 또 그게 무슨 말이냐?" 과학자가 날카롭게 말했다.

"제 이름은 브리지트고, 이쪽은 바베트와 바너비예요. 저희가 여기 온 게 기쁜 일은 아니지만 가능하다면 도와드리는 게 낫겠어요." 브리지트가 대답했다. "제 얘기는 고르가스와 바르가스가 상대방이 그런 줄은 모르고 둘 다 할아버지를 고용해 살인광선을 만들라고 했을지도 모른다는 거예요. 할아버지는 그들을 분간하지 못하시니까 한 명의 외계인이라고 생각하신 거구요. 한가지 말씀드릴 수 있는 건, 할아버지가 살인광선을 두 개 만들지 않으셨다면, 우린 아마 곤란해질 거예요."

닐스가 고개를 끄덕였다. "네가 뭔가를 알고 있나 보구나. 고르가스와 바르가스라구? 난 그 자, 어, 그들의 이름은 몰랐다. 그런데 너희는 여기서 뭘 하고 있는 거냐?"

"저희도 똑같은 걸 여쭤야겠어요." 바베트가 끼어들었다. "할아버지는 어떤 종류의 외계인들과 어울리고 계신 건지 아시나요? 저 둘은 은하계에서 가장 끔찍한 범죄의 책임자들이에요. 사실 저들은 재미삼아서 하마터면 지구를 파괴할 뻔했다구요. 할아버지는 저들을 위해 살인광선을, 그게 뭔지는 간에, 아무튼 그걸 만들고 계신 건가요?"

바르가스는 어떻게든지 슬프고 절망적인 표정을 지으려 애썼다. 꾸불꾸불한 작은 덩굴손 같은 흰머리가 눈 두 개에 드리워져 있었는데, 그것 때문에 거의 소년처럼 보였다.

"어떻게 그런 말을 믿을 수가 있지, 닐스?" 바르가스가 슬프게 물었다. "이 애들과 내가 저 무시무시한 녀석한테 죄수로 붙잡혀 있는 걸 모르겠나?"

"그래봐야 소용없어요." 바너비가 말했다. "저들이 각각 다른 외계인이라 해도 행동 양식이 똑같고 하는 일이 똑같아요. 둘 다 철두철미하게 교활하고 간사하고 비열해요. 뼛속까지 나빠요, 만약 뼈라는 게 있다면요. 난 저들을 사람의 탈을 쓴 악마라고 부르겠어요."

"그건 말이 좀 심하구나, 바너비." 닐스가 말했다. "넌 정말 저들이 사악한 모든 일을 구체화한다고 생각하니?"

"할아버지, 바너비 말은 정말이에요." 브리지트가 끼어들었다. "저들은 서로 세상을 지배하려고 경쟁하고 있는 거고, 게임에서 지느니 지구를 멸망시켜 버리려고 해요. 우린 저들을 막아야 해요."

닐스는 턱을 쓰다듬더니 생각에 잠겼다. 그는 확신을 얻지 못한 것 같았다. 고르가스가 끈기있게 기다리고 있었다.

"모르겠구나. 좀 확실한 증거가 있어야지. 만질 수 있고 눈에 보이고 손에 잡을 수 있는 것 말이다." 그가 말했다. "미안하지만 내가 좀 신중한 성격이라서. 내가 원래 그렇다."

"우린 지금 논쟁할 시간이 없어요." 바베트가 발을 쿵쿵 구르며 강조했다. "할아버지, 저희가 이 외계인들을 볼 때마다 꼭 안 좋은 일이 생겨요. 그건 심상치 않은 경향이에요. 저들 중 하나가 살인광선을 갖게 되면 틀림없이 계속 그렇게 될 거라구요. 할아버지는 그걸 넘겨주시면 안돼요."

고르가스는 한숨을 내쉬더니 요술 지팡이를 들어올렸다.

"얘야, 네 주장은 불확실한 전제에 기반을 두고 있어." 그가 말했다. "넌 마치 지금 닐스에게 선택권이 있는 것처럼 그러는구나. 안됐지만 그게 아니란다. 닐스, 이런 식의 토론은 지겹군. 잡담은 그만하고 본론에 들어가자구."

고르가스는 촉수 두 개를 위협하듯이 흔들었다. 닐스는 턱을 어루만지고 고개를 저었다.

"너희들 얘기가 맞는 것 같구나." 과학자가 말했다. "저 자는 살인광선을 악한 일에 사용하려는 것 같다. 감정의 동요가 심하구나! 한때는 내 친구인 것처럼 행동하더니, 그 다음엔 날 때려눕히려고 한다."

"그래, 맞네, 닐스." 바르가스가 가까이 다가오더니 역설했다. "고르가스는 변덕스러운 녀석이야. 아무 때라도 덥석 덤벼들 수 있지. 살인광선은 나한테 주게."

"그만둬, 바르가스!" 고르가스가 우렁차게 말했다. "닐스, 자네한테 실망이군. 하지만 상관없네. 벌은 나중에 주지. 여기 어디에 살인광선이 있겠지. 내가 직접 찾아내겠네."

고르가스는 실험실 쪽으로 주르르 미끄러져 가더니 여기저기를 기웃거리며 서랍을 열어보고 커튼 뒤를 보고 서류더미를 들추어보기 시작했다. 더 이상 적의 감시를 받지 않게 된 바르가스는 조용히 책상 쪽으로 슬그머니 가서는 역시 뒤지기 시작했다. 두 명의 스멜트블랏인은 먼저 발명품을 찾아내는 데 너무 집중하느라 인간들에 대해서는 신경을 쓰지 않았다.

"너희한테 사과를 해야겠다. 정말 이 외계인들은 소름끼치는 녀석들이구나." 닐스가 벌컥 화를 냈다. "저들을 속여서 죄책감이 들었었는데 이젠 다행이구나."

"속이다니요?" 브리지트가 어리둥절해하며 물었다. "할아버지 말씀은..."

"그래. 살인광선이란 건 없다." 그가 설명했다. "하나를 설계하려고 해봤지만 난 무기 만드는 데엔 소질이 없는 모양이다. 난 그들이 준 돈으로 무리듬염을 방지하는 백신을 개발하는 데 썼지. 무리듬염이란 내가 탭댄서를 못하게 만드는 증상이지. 어떤 아이들도 내 꿈을 희생시킨 것처럼 리듬감이 심각하게 부족해 고통당하는 일이 없도록 하고 싶었다."

"그건 확실히 살인광선보다는 낫네요." 브리지트가 말했다. "그 백신이란 게 알약인가요? 뭘로 만들어진 건데요?"

"아니, 알약은 아니란다." 닐스가 설명했다. "피하주사기로 피부 속에 주사를 맞아야 한단다. 뭘로 만들어졌는가 하면, 상당히 복잡한 조합이란다. 전문 의학용어로 널 따분하게 하고 싶진 않으니 성분을 모두 열거하진 않겠다."

"기분 나쁘게 듣진 마세요, 닐스 할아버지, 그런데 이 얘기는 나중에 해도 되지 않을까요?" 바너비가 물었다. "정말 듣고 싶긴 하지만, 고르가스와 바르가스는 수색작업에 곧 지쳐버릴 테고, 할아버지한테 돌아와 답을 구하려고 할 거예요. 우린 계획을 세워야 해요."

"나한테 무슨 수가 있긴 한데," 바베트가 말했다, "우리가 행동을 조심스럽게 결집해야 해. 이걸 훌륭히 해내려면 한 팀처럼 움직여야 해. 브리지트, 너 아직도 껌 있지?"

"물론이지." 브리지트가 싱긋 웃었다.

"닐스, 할아버지 실험실 가운 주머니에 있는 꽂혀 있는 그게 행운의 펜인가요?" 바베트가 물었다.

"어, 그래..." 닐스가 대답했다.

"좋아요, 우린 이렇게 하는 거예요." 바베트가 얘기하기 시작했다.

외계인들이 계속 수색을 벌이고 있는 동안 인간들이 허둥지둥 모여서 정신없이 속삭여댔다. 고르가스는 입구에 놓여 있는 개봉되지 않은 소포를 보고 테이프를 잡아뜯었는데, 열어보니 닐스 어머니가 보낸 초콜릿칩 쿠키 꾸러미일 뿐이었다. 바르가스는 서류 정리용 캐비넷을 뒤집어 엎었지만, 아무 것도 없었다. 마침내 닐스가 웃으며 그들의 수색을 중단시켰다.

"뭣들 하는 거요!" 닐스가 소리쳤다. "바닥도 기어다녀 보시오. 그래도 못 찾아낼 거요. 절대 못 찾을 거요. 백만 년이 지나도 안 될 거요."

"닐스, 더 이상 못 참겠다." 고르가스가 키 큰 과학자를 향해 위협하듯 다가오면서 경고했다. "네 놈 턱을 날려주겠다."

"자-잠깐!" 긴장한 닐스가 뒷걸음질치며 소리쳤다. "그러니까, 그게 나한테 있으니까 못 찾을 거란 얘기요. 바로 여기 있소!"

닐스가 주머니 속으로 손을 집어넣어 자신의 행운의 펜을 꺼냈다. 그건 별다른 특징이 없는 볼펜으로 특별하거나 특이한 게 없었다. 검은 색 펜으로, 맨 위에 흔히 있는 조그만 버튼이 달려서 그걸 눌러 심을 뺐다 넣었다 하는 것이었다. 유일한 특징은 조그만 두개골 그림으로, 지방의 한 화학회사의 로고였다. 그건 그냥 평범한 펜이었는데, 외계인들은 넋을 잃었다.

"아, 정말 작고 멋지다!" 바르가스가 킥킥거리며 좋아했다. "그건 완벽한 비밀무기군. 무시무시한 파괴력이지만 아주 쉽게 숨길 수가 있겠군. 자, 닐스, 이리 주게."

"아니. 난 당신들 중 하나를 결정할 수 없으니 당신들이 직접 결정하시오." 닐스가 펜을 방 한가운데로 던지면서 말했다. "싸워서 차지하시오. 자, 싸우라니까. 당신들, 겁쟁이요?"

닐스가 외계인들을 오래 부추길 필요도 없었다. 눈 깜짝할 사이에 그들은 방 가운데로 가서 바닥에 떨어진 펜 주위를 조심스럽게 돌면서 촉수에 머리를 맞지 않고 몸을 구부려 펜을 집을 수 있는 기회를 노렸다. 책상에서 종이 자르는 칼을 가져온 바르가스가 유리한 것 같았다. 하지만 고르가스가 더 빨랐다. 그는 왼쪽 촉수를 하나 흔들어 바르가스를 방해하면서 오른쪽 촉수로 살인광선을 잡았다.

"하하!" 고르가스가 승리의 환성을 올렸다. "드디어 우리가 여기까지 왔군, 바르가스. 살인광선을 차지한 건 나고, 자넨 겨우 종이 자르는 칼을 가졌군!"

"제기랄!" 바르가스가 뒤로 주춤하며 소리쳤다.

고르가스는 바르가스에게 펜을 들이대고는 버튼을 누르기 시작했다. 톡, 톡, 톡, 톡, 톡, 톡, 톡, 아무 일도 일어나지 않았다. 그는 다시 한번 시도했다. 톡, 톡, 역시 아무 일이 없었다. 바르가스는 기회를 포착하고 전속력으로 고르가스에게 달려들었다. 그들은 촉수 달린 축축한 큰 공처럼 바닥에 나뒹굴어졌다.

"자, 브리지트!" 바베트가 재촉했다.

브리지트는 이 사이에서 길다란 줄 모양의 껌을 잡아당기며 싸우고 있는 한 쌍에게 뛰어갔다. 그녀는 번개처럼 재빨리 껌을 가지고 밧줄처럼 외계인들을 칭칭 감았다. 그들은 무슨 일이 일어나고 있는지를 알아차리기도 전에 껌으로 꽁꽁 묶여 촉수 하나도 움직일 수가 없게 됐다. 바베트와 바너비는 외계인들에게서 요술 지팡이와 예비 지팡이, 그리고 무기인 펜과 종이 자르는 칼을 빼앗았다.

"얘야!" 고르가스가 항의했다. "날 좀 풀어줘! 못 봤니, 바르가스가 날 공격한 거야. 난 이 녀석한테 공격을 당한 거라구."

"우, 고르가스, 이 나쁜 놈!" 바르가스가 으르렁거렸다. "넌 끝이 없구나. 얘들아, 너희들 마음대로 하는 건 좋은데, 내가 끔찍하게 싫어하는 녀석과 묶어두진 말아줘."

"이것 봐요, 난 좋은 사람이에요." 브리지트가 말했다. "내겐 지키며 살고 싶은 개인적인 신조가 있는데, 그건 바로 기본적으로 모든 사람은 착하다는 거예요. 마음속을 들여다보면 나쁜 사람은 아무도 없다는 거죠. 물론 나쁜 버릇을 키울 수도 있고 나쁜 짓을 할 수도 있지만, 모든 사람에겐 두 번째 기회를 줘야 해요."

"그거 멋진 이데올로기구나, 얘야." 고르가스가 열렬히 맞장구쳤다. "정말 멋있는 신조로구나. 알게 될 거다. 바르가스와 난 합의를 보고 친구가 될 거야. 맹세코 우린 합의에 도달할 거야. 그렇지 않으면 내가 고르가스가 아니다!"

"내 얘긴 아직 안 끝났어요." 브리지트가 고개를 저으며 말했다. "난 언제나 그런 생각을 가지고 있었어요. 난 사람들에게 그 방법만 알려준다면 옳은 일을 할 거라는 믿음을 소중히 간직하고 있어요. 하지만 당신 둘을 겪고 보니 육식동물 사냥대회를 하는 외계인들에 대해 깊은 불신이 생겼어요. 당신들을 믿을 수 없어요."

바르가스는 몸부림치며 이의를 제기했다. "우리가 한 일을 보면 우릴 미워할 만하지. 일이 어떻게 그렇게 됐는지 모르겠다. 난 스멜트블랏에서 정말 꾸밈없는 젊은이였어. 최선을 다해 솔직하고 정직하게 살았지. 그런데 고르가스와 그가 내게 한 일 때문에 내 정직함은 위축되기 시작했고 페어플레이 정신이 사라져버리고 말았어."

바르가스는 브리지트에게 미소를 지어 보이려고 애썼지만, 바보처럼 웃는 표정이 됐다.

"어쩌면 여기 지구에 내가 해볼 만한 치료법이 있을지도 모르겠다. 더 나은 자질을 회복시키는 치료 말이야." 그가 말을 이었다. "있지, 난 다시 좋아질 수 있을 거다. 내가 아는 다른 사람들과는 다르게 말야."

"무슨 암시를 하는 건지 알겠다!" 고르가스가 으르렁거렸다. "하지만 난 고쳐질 수 없다고 넌지시 빗대려는 거라면 네 놈이 틀렸어! 브리지트야, 바르가스가 개심하고픈 바람을 분명하게 말할지 모르지만, 이 놈의 주장은 틀렸어. 하지만 난 정말 지금부터 착해지고 싶어."

"말뜻을 이해하지 못하는군요." 바너비가 말했다. "우린 당신들을 안 믿을 거예요. 당신들이 저지른 일은 사소한 게 아니라 심각한 범죄예요! 우린 당신들이 거기에서 벗어나지 못하게 할 거예요. 닐스, 면도칼을 아주 날카롭게 가시겠어요?"

"바너비, 사실 그건 전기 면도날이란다. 곧은 면도날은 너무 위험해." 닐스가 속삭였다.

"아. 뭐, 어떻든지 간에요." 바너비가 말했다. "고르가스, 바르가스, 각오하세요. 당신들 머리를 밀어서 스멜트블랏으로 돌려보내겠어요!"

"안돼! 그건 안돼!" 외계인들이 비명을 질렀다.

"그렇게 할 거예요." 바너비가 말했다. "닐스, 할아버지가 명예로운 일을 하시겠어요?"

"암, 물론이지." 닐스는 이렇게 말하며 전기 면도날을 들고 앞으로 나아갔다. "각오해라, 너희 둘 다."

다행히도 브리지트의 껌이 두 외계인을 아주 꼼짝 못하게 감고 있었다. 그들은 닐스가 머리를 밀자 소리를 질러댔지만, 움직일 수가 없었다. 모든 일이 끝나자 워낙에 그리 매력적이지 못한 외계인들이었지만 정말로 흉측해졌다. 시무룩하고 침울한 표정으로도 모습이 나아지지 않았다.

"너희는 벌받게 될 거다!" 그들이 함께 소리쳤다.

바베트는 앞으로 나가더니 고르가스에게서 빼앗은 요술 지팡이 하나를 내밀었다.

p. 618

"바너비가 설명해 줬는데, 이 요술 지팡이 사용법은 간단하더라구요." 그녀가 입을 열었다. "정신을 집중해서 당신들의 행선지로 원하는 곳을 생각하기만 하면 나머지는 알아서 되는 거예요. 하지만 먼저, 브리지트, 저들 몸에 쪽지를 붙여줘."

브리지트가 앞으로 나오더니 꽁꽁 묶인 외계인들 몸에 쪽지를 붙였다. 이렇게 써 있었다. "스멜트블랏 사람들: 반드시 이 범죄자들을 법이 미치는 내에서 최대한 처벌하세요." 쪽지를 붙인 뒤 바베트는 두 눈을 감고 요술 지팡이를 움직여 작은 원을 그리기 시작했다. 외계인들은 이리처럼 울부짖더니 몇 초 후에 사라졌다. 그들이 남긴 것은 깎여나간 머리카락과 조그맣게 고여 있는 축축한 액체가 전부였다.

"됐어!" 브리지트가 소리지르더니 모든 사람과 유쾌하게 손뼉을 마주쳤다. "멋진 계획이었어, 바베트. 완벽했어. 우리 문제에 대한 최선의 해결책이었다구."

"난 잘 모르겠어." 바베트가 한숨을 쉬었다. "이 요술 지팡이가 걱정이야. 지팡이가 너무 강력해서 그것들이 엉뚱한 손에 들어가면 어떤 일이 생길지 걱정돼. 우리가 없애버려야 할 것 같아."

"없애버린다구? 그러면 우린 집에 어떻게 돌아가라구? 닐스, 지금이 몇 년도고, 여긴 정확히 어디죠?" 브리지트가 물었다.

"지금은 2026년이고, 여긴 뉴욕 시티란다. 너흰 과거에서 온 것 같구나, 그렇지?" 그가 대답했다.

"네." 브리지트가 한숨을 지으며 슬픈 표정으로 의자에 주저앉아 창 밖을 내다봤다. "그래도 우린 뉴욕에 있잖아. 우리 가족이 저기 어디쯤에 있을 텐데. 지금 가족한테 돌아갈 순 없어. 내가 몇 년 동안 실종됐다고 생각할 거야. 하지만 바베트 말이 옳아. 저 요술 지팡이들은 없애버려야 해."

브리지트 얼굴에 나타난 쓸쓸한 표정에 닐스는 마음이 몹시 흔들렸다. 그녀는 아주 넋이 나가고 가엾어 보였다. 그가 그녀를 막 안아주려고 할 때 끔찍하게 쿵하는 소리가 방 전체에 울렸다.

"보리가드!" 브리지트가 의자에서 벌떡 일어나며 소리쳤다. "너 뭐하는 거야?"

p. 619

거구의 검은 고양이는 저쪽 벽에 걸려 있는 커다란 태피스트리를 기어오르려 했던 것이다. 두툼한 양모 천에 우주에서 본 듯한 지구의 그림이 꼼꼼하게 수놓아져 있었다. 불행히도 태피스트리는 고양이의 무게를 감당하지 못하고 보리가드 위로 떨어졌다. 하지만 커튼 뒤에는 벽 대신에 반침이 있었는데, 뒤로 12피트 정도가 파여 있는 곡선 모양의 방이었다. 반침 안에는 범선만한 크기의 금속 우주선이 놓여 있었다.

"어, 잠깐만... 그거 내 배잖아!" 바너비가 소리치더니 손뼉을 치며 그쪽으로 뛰어갔다. "어쩐지 이곳이 눈에 익는다 했어. 이건 내 옛날 실험실이잖아! 그리고 저건 우리가 양키스 경기 보러 가기 전에 내가 너희한테 보여줬던 우주선이야!"

"네가 저 우주선을 설계했다고?" 닐스가 놀라며 물었다. "저건 내가 이 곳을 임대할 때부터 여기 있었다. 난 저걸 이해하느라 몇 년을 보냈어. 저건 정말 진보적이야!"

"아이, 별 말씀을요! 브리지트, 모르겠니? 우리의 걱정이 끝날지도 몰라." 바너비가 설명했다. "이 배는 시간여행을 할 수 있어."

"정말?" 브리지트가 기운을 차리며 물었다.

"물론이지. 이봐, 바베트. 요술 지팡이들 좀 줘. 내가 들고 있을 테니 네가, 그 가라테로 발차기를 하든지 해." 바너비가 말했다.

바베트는 스멜트블랏인의 요술 지팡이를 모아주었고 바너비는 그것들을 한데 모아 앞에 들었다. 바베트가 잠시 정신을 집중하더니 힘차게 "하이야!"를 외치면서 손끝으로 지팡이 모두를 두 동강이씩 잘라냈다.

"그만하면 됐어." 바너비가 말했다. "자 이젠 모두 날 도와서 저 배를 꺼내오자. 아주 무거워서 다같이 끌어내야 될 거야. 내가 살펴보고 작동할 수 있는지 봐야겠어."

브리지트, 바베트, 바너비, 닐스 그리고 보리가드까지 합세해 우주선을 방 한가운데로 끌어왔고, 바너비가 맨 위에 있는 승강구 뚜껑으로 뛰어들어가 곧바로 작업을 시작했다. 몇 분 후 그는 어리둥절한 표정을 하고 뛰어나왔다.

p. 620

"내가 준양자 가속기에 문제가 좀 있다고 말했던 거 기억나니?" 바너비가 물었다. "그 문제가 그대로 있어. 제어장치가 좀 뒤죽박죽으로 잘못 구성돼 있어. 모든 버튼을 반대 순서로 놓았거든. 하지만 큰 문제는 그게 아냐. 조타 시계와 우주 탐사기 시계를 똑같이 맞출 수가 없는 것 같아. 그것들은 언제나 똑같은 시간을 표시하고 정확히 똑같은 방식으로 재깍거려야 하는데, 우주 탐사기 시계가 빨리 가고 있어. 마침내는 엔진 체계에 불규칙한 변동이 생기는 것 같아. 어떤 때는 동력이 빵빵하다가 그 다음엔 동력이 줄어들고 거의 아무 것도 남질 않아."

"내가 참견한다고 생각진되지 않았으면 좋겠는데," 닐스가 말했다, "아까 말한 대로 난 네 배와 네가 남겨놓은 기록을 연구하느라 몇 년을 보냈단다. 내가 네 동력 문제를 풀었을지도 모르겠구나."

"그래요?" 바너비가 기대에 부풀어 물었다.

"그래, 몇 가지 실험을 통해 네가 우주선에 연료를 공급하는 데 무얼 이용했는지 알아냈지." 닐스가 입을 열었다. "바나나 짓이긴 걸 사용했더구나, 그렇지? 바나나가 썩으면서 그 안의 당분이 천천히 빠져 나왔고, 그래서 우주선은 당분으로부터 에너지를 얻은 거지. 글쎄, 그건 보통의 행성 여행에는 좋지만, 시간 여행을 하려면 과일 당분보다는 힘이 더 센 뭔가가 있어야 하지. 다행히도 난 네가 빠뜨린 성분이 초콜릿이라는 걸 알 수 있었단다."

닐스는 방 출입구 쪽으로 걸어가더니 고르가스가 아까 열었던 박스를 집어서 바너비에게 가져다주었다.

"어머니께 부탁해서 이 초콜릿을 특별히 구워달라고 했지." 그가 설명했다. "이건 시스템 안에 네가 시간여행을 하는 데 필요한 설탕과 초콜릿의 정확한 양이 합쳐지도록 만든 초콜릿칩 쿠키란다. 쿠키를 담을 보관 탱크를 하나 만들고 시간여행에 필요한 과일 짓이긴 것은 그대로 두면 되지. 어떻게 생각하니?"

"닐스, 정말 대단하세요!" 바너비가 동료 과학자의 허리를 감싸안으며 소리쳤다. "제가 설계한 걸 믿어주셔서 기뻐요. 제가 살고 있는 시대엔 아무도 제 일을 진지하게 생각하지 않아요. 모두들 제가 미쳤다고 생각하죠. 아, 어쩌겠어요. 이젠 이 시계들을 제대로 가게 하는 방법만 알아내면 되겠어요."

p. 621

"내가 한번 볼게." 바베트가 소매를 말아 올리며 말했다. "내가 기계를 좀 다룰 줄 알거든."

바너비는 그녀를 데리고 우주선에 들어갔다. 그리고 아니나 다를까, 한번 세게 쾅 치는 것만으로 시계들이 한꺼번에 똑딱똑딱하며 가게 됐다. 친구들은 마침내 집에 갈 준비가 된 것이다.

브리지트, 바너비, 바베트 그리고 보리가드는 한데 모여 닐스에게 작별인사를 했다. 그들이 떠나려고 하자 그는 좀 슬픈 것 같았다.

"너희들이 간다니 섭섭하구나." 과학자가 한숨을 내쉬었다. "나한텐 친구가 별로 없는데. 외롭단다. 이제 외계인들이 내게 연구 기금을 대주지 않으니 난 어떻게 될지 모르겠구나."

"그 문제는 제가 도와드릴 수 있을 것 같아요." 바너비가 주머니에서 만화경을 꺼내며 말했다. "자, 이걸 들여다보시고 뭐가 보이는지 말씀해 보세요."

"와!" 닐스가 말했다. "내가 목에 장미 화환을 두르고 있구나. 누군가 내 백신에 대해 상을 주고 있네! 그리고 이젠, 세계에서 최고의 엘리트들만 모이는 과학 클럽인 제네바 클럽에 들어오라는 초대장을 받았구나. 가장 뛰어나고 훌륭한 과학자들만 참가요청을 받는데 말야. 그리고 지금은, 그런데 흐릿해서 보이는 게... 아니... 잠깐만... 그래! 내가 춤을 추고 있네, 뮤지컬 공연에서 탭댄스를 추고 있구나! 굉장하다!"

"그건 할아버지의 미래예요." 브리지트가 따뜻한 미소를 지으며 말했다. "아시겠어요? 할아버지는 걱정하실 게 없다구요."

닐스는 만화경을 바너비에게 돌려주고 아이들 모두에게 작별의 포옹을 했다. 그는 보리가드의 머리도 토닥거려 주었다. 그들 모두 우주선으로 우르르 들어갔고 닐스는 커다란 창문 하나를 열었다.

"도와주셔서 감사해요!" 브리지트가 기어 들어가며 명랑하게 말했다. "이제 저희는 가봐야겠어요. 양키스 경기도 마저 봐야 하거든요."

바너비는 승강기 뚜껑을 잠그고 모두에게 벨트를 매준 다음, 제어장치 뒤에 앉아 깊은 한숨을 내쉬었다.

"행운을 빌어줘." 그가 주의를 주었다. "저 쿠키에 상당한 효과가 있기를 바라자!"

p. 622

QUICK QUIZ 31

관계 짓기

아래의 단어 쌍들이 서로 어떤 관계를 갖는지 판단하세요. 비슷한 의미면 "S" 반대 의미면 "O"를 하세요.

1. 근본적인, 중요한 :: 하찮은, 사소한
2. 통합하다 :: 녹이다, 융합시키다
3. 특징이 없는, 막연한 :: 흔한, 평범한
4. 소중히 하다 :: 경멸하다
5. 감소하다, 약해지다 :: 커지다, 증대하다
6. 덩굴손 :: 싹, 어린 가지
7. 교활한 :: 사악한
8. 은밀한 :: 명백한, 공공연한
9. 꾸짖다 :: 칭찬하다
10. 공격자, 적 :: 폭력 강도
11. 번영하는, 부유한 :: 가난해진

QUICK QUIZ 32

관계 짓기

아래의 단어 쌍들이 서로 어떤 관계를 갖는지 판단하세요. 비슷한 의미면 "S" 반대 의미면 "O"를 하세요.

1. 실체적인, 현실의 :: 현실의
2. 횡설수설 :: 알아들을 수 없는 말
3. 욕하다 :: 숭배하다
4. 위조하다 :: 위조하다
5. 지긋지긋한, 혐오스러운 :: 칭찬할 만한, 훌륭한
6. 최상의 :: 최악의
7. 빛깔, 색조, 경향 :: 음조, 음색, 풍조
8. 변덕스러운, 불안정한 :: 둔한, 완만한
9. 습지, 늪 :: 진흙, 진창
10. 팽팽한 :: 긴장된
11. 위생적인 :: 청결한

QUICK QUIZ 33

빈칸 채우기

아래에 있는 각각의 단어들 중에서 가장 완벽한 문장을 만들어주는 단어를 고르세요.

1. 반란군 캠프의 텐트가 아주 (   ) 생겨서 구분하기가 거의 불가능했다.
   a. 시무룩하게   b. 흐릿하게   c. 똑같이   d. 율동적으로

2. 나이젤은 평상시에 쉽게 깜짝 놀라는 사람인데, 누나의 끊임없는 놀림에 (   ) 스카이다이빙 레슨을 받기로 했다.
   a. 끌어내져   b. 넌지시 비추어져   c. 자극을 받아   d. 잘 배합되어

3. 돌격부대는 전원이 정확히 똑같은 시간에 적군 기지의 방어선에 닿아야 했기 때문에 모두 움직임을 가능한 한 가깝게 (   ) 나아갔다.
   a. 오르내리며   b. 섞어 만들어서   c. 구별해서   d. 맞추어

p. 623

4. 빈센트는 악의적인 농담을 즐겨하고 (   )이/가 고약해서 행성의 다른 누구보다도 코피를 많이 쏟았다.
   a. 신조   b. 모토   c. 전제   d. 성미

5. 새로운 (   )은/는 정말 빠르고 강력해서 여드름이 정말로 싹 없어졌다.
   a. 백신   b. 아스트린젠트   c. 피하주사   d. 찌꺼기

6. 몇 마일을 가도록 경계표가 보이지 않아서 (   ) 목초지가 끝없이 펼쳐져 있다고 믿을 만했다.
   a. 누르스름한   b. 황량한   c. 엘리트의   d. 수척한

7. 세계 최초로 일회용 자동차(겨우 3백 달러)를 고안해낸 (   )은/는 하룻밤 사이에 백만장자가 됐다.
   a. 기업가   b. 수납자   c. 세입   d. 보조금

8. 로버트는 NBA 내내 집밖으로 전혀 나가지 않고 TV만 보고 난 뒤 다리 근육이 (   ) 시작했다는 걸 알았다.
   a. 우러나기   b. 위축되기   c. 자극하기   d. 끌어당기기

9. 우리는 현관에 (   )을/를 놓아서 캐럴 부르는 사람이 우리에게 와서 노래 불러주는 것을 환영한다고 표시했다.
   a. 받침   b. 마호가니   c. 소포   d. 화환

10. 4학년 아이들의 종이 뱉기 시합이 손을 쓸 수 없을 정도가 되기 전에 그들 사이에 (   )이/가 이루어졌다.
    a. 이데올로기   b. 논쟁   c. 합의   d. 경향

QUICK QUIZ 34
짝짓기
오른쪽의 단어를 비슷한 의미의 왼쪽 단어와 짝지으세요.

1. 위임하다	A. 학식이 있다고 주장하다
2. 육체를 갖춘	B. 무
3. 전문가라고 자처하다	C. 시작하는 지점
4. 가시나무	D. 가시 돋친 관목
5. 무, 제로	E. 북북 문지르다
6. 형성하다, 배열하다	F. 권한을 주다
7. 지붕 밑 방, 다락방	G. 지붕 밑의 공간
8. 요소, 성분	H. 배분하다
9. 문지방, 발단	I. 사람 모습을 한
10. 분배하다	J. 전체의 부분
11. 문질러 닦다	K. 부분들을 한데 맞추다

QUICK QUIZ 35
짝짓기
오른쪽의 단어를 비슷한 의미의 왼쪽 단어와 짝지으세요.

1. 수고, 공들임	A. ~할 것 같은
2. 절친한 친구	B. 작은 양
3. ~하기 쉬운	C. 정직한
4. 방법, 양식	D. 장식된 천

p. 624

5. 엷은 색조, 기미	E. 믿을 만한 벗
6. 확실히 하다	F. 조언하다, 권고하다
7. 태피스트리	G. 방법, 태도
8. 선웃음, 바보같은 웃음	H. 치료
9. 꾸밈없는	I. 능글맞은 웃음
10. 치료, 요법	J. 철저함
11. 감히 표명하다, 과감히 말하다	K. 보증하다

p. 626

브리지트는 아이들 중에서 가장 타고난 모험가지만, 여행다니는 것에 가장 먼저 싫증을 내는 아이이기도 해. 한번은 나한테, 새로운 곳을 찾아다니면서 가장 좋은 건 집에 돌아오는 일 같다고 말한 적이 있어. 그렇다고 탐험을 좋아하지 않았던 건 아냐. 그 애는 그저 집을 제일 좋아했던 거지. 바너비가 승강구 뚜껑을 닫자마자 브리지트는 자기 생일이라도 되는 듯이 기뻐하기 시작했어.

난 아직까진 미소를 지을 만한 이유가 있는 줄 모르겠더라. 어쨌든 우주선이 첫 항해를 하는 거였으니까. 우주선엔 아직 적당한 이름조차 붙여지지 않았어. 전통적으로 새로운 배가 출항하기 전에 거쳐야 할 의식이란 게 있지. 누군가 배의 이름을 선포하고, 그런 다음 샴페인 한 병을 뱃머리에 던져 부수지. 난 우리가 정말 정확한 시간과 장소로 돌아가는 데 성공한다면 개인적으로 그 배를 "미스터 럭키"라고 이름 붙여 주기로 마음먹었어.

바너비의 우주선을 타고 시간여행을 하면 어떤 일이 벌어질지 몰랐어. 고르가스와 바르가스는 많은 잘못을 저질렀지만 적어도 우릴 이 시간 저 시간으로 데리고 다니기 전에 자신들의 요술 지팡이를 충분히 시험해 보았어. 내가 베이징 곡예단과 함께 아시아를 돌아다니면서 배운 유추법을 사용해 보니까, 우린 막 눈을 가린 채 칼을 들고 저글링을 하려는 것 같았어. 우린 우리가 뭘 하고 있는 건지도 몰랐고, 어디서 꼼짝 못하게 될지도 몰랐지.

처음에는 바너비가 우주선 조종을 잘 하는 것 같았어. 그는 열려진 창문을 통해 조심스럽게 우릴 데리고 나갔는데, 다행히도 창문은 우릴 내보내기에 딱 적당한 비율이었어. 우린 잠깐 동안 서성거리며 공중에서 정지한 채로 있었는데, 바너비가 우주선의 계산기를 이용해 우리의 항로를 어림잡아 보려고 했어. 그는 손잡이 몇 개를 비틀어 돌리고 단추 두어 개를 쿵 누른 다음 레버를 앞쪽으로 풀었어.

p. 627

그런 다음, 상황이 정말 이상하게 돼버렸어.

"어어! 어떻게 된 거지?" 바너비가 아래를 내려다보며 숨을 헐떡였다.

우주선이 옴짝달싹을 안 하는 것 같았는데, 잠깐 동안 그들 주변의 모든 빛이 굴절되어서 하얀빛이 나누어지더니 무지개 색이 되어 원을 그리며 빙빙 돌았다. 그러더니 뚝 멈추었다. 그들이 막 빠져나온 건물은 그대로 서 있었지만, 그 외의 모든 것은 달랐다. 밑으로 보이는 먼지투성이 거리엔 자동차 대신 말과 마차가 있었고 건물들은 모두 나무와 벽돌로 지어져 있었다. 번쩍이던 고층빌딩들은 온데 간데 없었다.

"음, 우리가 너무 거슬러 온 모양이야." 브리지트가 창문을 통해 내려다보며 말했다.

"바로잡을 수 있겠니?" 바베트가 물었다.

"아, 알겠다." 바너비가 제어장치를 만지작거리며 말했다. "우린 1년이 아니라 10년의 증가비율로 움직이고 있었어. 그래서 몇 십 년이 아닌 몇 세기를 거슬러 온 거야. 자, 어디 보자. 좋아, 항로로 돌아온 것 같아. 모두들 준비됐어?"

바너비가 레버를 다시 느슨하게 했고 빛이 다시 빙빙 돌았다. 이번에는, 다시 분명하게 볼 수 있게 되자 브리지트가 기쁨으로 비명을 지르다시피 했다. 그들은 전과 똑같은 건물밖에 떠 있었지만, 브리지트 주변의 모든 것은 그녀가 성장한 뉴욕 시티와 같은 모습이었다.

"이젠 제대로 된 모습이야!" 그녀가 박수를 치며 말했다.

"바베트, 우주 탐사기 시계에 뭐라고 돼 있어?" 바너비가 기대에 부풀어 물었다.

"우린 돌아왔다고 써 있어." 바베트가 미소지었다. "우린 양키스 경기에도 갈 수 있겠다. 하지만 좀 늦을지도 몰라."

"좋았어! 내 실험실 창문을 부수고 들어가야겠다." 바너비가 경고했다. "이 우주선을 길거리에 착륙시키고 싶진 않아. 꽉 잡아!"

바너비는 창문에 우주선을 부딪쳤고 창유리가 와장창 깨졌다. 우주선은 바닥을 가로질러 미끄러지면서 테이블과 캐비넷을 덮쳤고 마침내 거대한 종이 더미 속에서 멈추었다. 브리지트가 재빨리 승강구 뚜껑을 열고는 뛰어나왔다. 그녀는 두 눈을 반짝거리며 손뼉을 치면서 춤을 추고 다녔다.

"우린 돌아왔어! 세상은 스멜트블랏 사냥꾼들로부터 안전해졌고, 우린 아직 양키스 경기를 볼 수 있다구." 그녀가 흥분하며 말했다. "이보다 더 좋은 일이 뭐가 있겠니?"

그녀가 그렇게 물어보는 순간, 문에서 노크 소리가 났다.

"문 열어, 바너비, 오몰리 학장이다." 거칠고 허스키한 목소리가 소리쳤다.

"이런." 바너비가 괴로워했다. "학장은 안돼! 이거 정말 큰일났는 걸. 학장은 우리 학과를 담당하고 있어. 이렇게 엉망진창된 걸 보여줄 순 없다구!"

"걱정하지 마, 우리한테 좋은 수가 있을 거야." 행복에 겨워 아무 걱정도 할 수 없는 브리지트가 말했다.

그녀는 문으로 뛰어가더니 문을 확 열어 젖혔다.

"어서 오세요, 오몰리 학장님!" 브리지트가 소리쳤다. "전 브리지트고 이쪽은 바베트예요. 고양이 이름은 보리가드랍니다. 저희는 바너비의 친구들이에요. 들어오세요, 드릴 말씀이 너무나 많아요."

"아, 정말 의욕에 넘치는군." 학장은 쉰 목소리로 말했다. "자넨 언제나 그렇게 생기가 넘치고 활발하나?"

학장의 모습은 브리지트의 예상과 달랐다. 그는 키가 작은 남자로, 너무 뚱뚱해서 거의 둥그렇게 보일 정도였다. 그녀가 알고 있는 교수와 과학자 대부분은 옷차림이 간소했지만, 오몰리 학장은 화려한 옷을 입고 있어서 학장이라기 보다는 1920년대의 영화계 거물처럼 보였다. 그는 포동포동한 어깨 위에 길다란 은회색 망토를 걸치고 있었는데, 목에서 번쩍거리는 보석 버클로 잠겨져 있었다. 그는 끝부분이 금색으로 된 지팡이를 쥐고 있었고, 손가락마다 반짝거리는 반지를 끼고 있었다. 하얀색의 머리와 턱수염은 세심하게 빗질되어 스타일이 잡혀 있었다. 친근한 얼굴에는 핑크빛이 돌고 따뜻한 미소를 짓고 있었다. 브리지트는 그를 보고 웃음을 참을 수가 없었다.

"그래, 자네가 나한테 할 얘기가 많다고?" 그가 눈을 깜박이며 물었다. "좋네. 하지만 우선 난 바너비에게 할 얘기가 있다네. 바너비? 어디 있는 건가?"

바너비가 우주선 뒤에서 슬쩍 내다보더니 긴장한 채로 나왔다.

"...네, 선생님?" 그가 말했다.

"바너비! 내가 보낸 팩스 못 받았나? 자네한테 편지를 보내려고 몇 시간을 끙끙거렸다네! 마침내 자네 전화선에 틀림없이 문제가 있어서 내 메시지 수신이 안 되는 거라고 결론짓고, 이렇게 직접 온 거라네. 이제 보니 팩스 기계를 못 찾았던 것 같구만." 오몰리 학장이 말하며 종이 더미와 깨진 유리를 둘러보았다.

"화내지 말아주세요." 바베트가 몰아대듯 말했다. "저희가 설명할게요. 저희는 막 지구를 멸망의 위험에서 구해내기 위해 시간을 지나서 여행하고 왔어요. 바너비가 중요한 과학적 발견을 해서 저희는 미래에서부터 집에 돌아올 수 있었어요. 저희는 유리창을 깨고 들어올 수 밖에 없었어요. 제 말을 믿지 않으시겠지만, 그건..."

"사실이네. 나도 안다네." 학장이 말했다. "방금 닐스라는 과학자가 날 찾아왔는데, 몇 십 년 후의 미래에서 온 사람이더군. 그는 바너비의 연구 덕분에 자신이 여기 올 수 있었다고 설명하면서, 바너비를 제네바 그룹의 회원으로 지명해야 한다고 역설하더군. 내가 그곳 회원이라서 새로운 과학자들에게 가입을 권할 수 있지."

바너비, 브리지트, 바베트는 놀라서 맵시있는 학장을 빤히 쳐다봤다.

"자, 자, 그렇게 놀라지들 말게!" 오몰리가 웃었다. "닐스가 나와 함께 자네 노트를 훑어보면서 모든 걸 설명해줬지. 난 감명을 받았다네. 자넨 클럽에 들어올 자격이 충분해. 그래, 자넨 그럴 만하고 말고. 자네같이 뛰어난 사람을 배제한다면 용서받을 수 없는 일이 될 걸세."

"영광입니다, 오몰리 학장님." 바너비가 얼굴을 붉히며 말했다.

"잘됐다, 바너비!" 브리지트가 그의 등을 찰싹 치며 말했다.

"정말 대단해!" 바베트도 동의했다.

바닥에 큰 대자로 뻗어 있던 보리가드마저도 바너비의 발에 코를 다정스레 비벼댔다.

"그래, 축하하네, 젊은이." 학장이 진지한 표정으로 말을 이었다. "하지만 공정을 기하기 위해, 제네바 그룹에선 새로운 회원에게 상당히 거칠다는 걸 미리 알려주어 내 축하를 좀 자제해야겠군. 자네가 들어오길 원한다면 치러야 할 일이 좀 있다네."

바너비는 어리둥절한 표정이었다. "제네바 그룹에서 새 회원들을 골탕먹인다는 말씀인가요? 클럽에 들어올 자격을 갖추기 위해 무안한 일을 끝마치게 할 정도로 유치한 건 대학생들뿐인 줄 알았는데요."

오몰리가 조끼 주머니에 손을 집어넣을 때 그의 얼굴에 미소가 번졌다.

"아, 아닐세. 안됐지만 지금 당장 나와 같이 가야겠네. 자네 친구들도 함께. 저 기운없는 고양이도 일어설 힘이 있는지 보게. 자네가 제네바 그룹의 일원이 되려면 오늘밤 양키스 경기를 보러 가야 한다네. 우리 모두가 핫도그를 얼마나 많이 먹을 수 있는지 봐야 하거든." 학장이 바너비 앞에서 입장권 몇 장을 흔들며 웃었다.

p. 631

바너비도 웃었다. "생각해 보니까 배가 고픈 걸." 그가 말했다. "너희는 어떠니?"

브리지트와 바베트는 열렬히 고개를 끄덕였고, 보리가드는 마지못해 일어섰다.

"좋았어!" 오몰리가 말했다. "아! 이 얘기를 하느라 너무 좋아서 다른 소식을 잊을 뻔했네. 난 행복한 일만 있으면 건망증이 생기지. 바너비, 자네가 돈 문제에 대해선 생각하기 싫어하는 걸 아네만, 다행스럽게도 난 여러 가지 일들의 재정적인 면을 고려하는 걸 좋아하지. 시간여행 우주선처럼 주목할 만한 발명품은 대학에 많은 기부금이 들어오게 해 줄 테고, 물론 자넨 자네 덕분에 들어온 상여금을 나누어 갖게 될 걸세. 내가 자네한테 최신 장비로 가득찬 새 실험실을 주도록 준비해 두었네. 너무나 근사해서 비교해보면 이 실험실은 형편없어 보일 걸세. 말을 안 할 수가 없겠는데, 이 실험실은 정말 지저분하군. 누추하다고 할 정도야. 저 바닥에 있는 건 먹다 남은 샌드위치인가?"

오몰리 학장은 지팡이로 오래된 참치 샌드위치를 쑤셨다. 바너비는 또 얼굴을 붉혔다.

"네, 전 지저분해요." 바너비가 슬픈 표정으로 동의했다. "새 실험실을 가질 자격이 없을지도 몰라요."

"말도 안 되는 소리!" 학장이 말했다. "그건 벌써 결정된 거네. 내가 직접 새 실험실을 장식했고, 상당히 인상적이네. 그렇게 말해도 괜찮다면 말일세. 내가 좀 지나쳐서 너무 웅장하게 만들었다고 생각하지 않길 바랄 뿐이네."

바너비는 웃었다. "틀림없이 최고로 하셨을 거예요. 가구와 옷에 대한 학장님의 탁월한 감각은 학과에서 유명하니까요. 학장님이 다시 장식하기로 마음 먹으면 어떤 방이라도 얼마나 멋지게 만들어 놓으시나를 보고 모두들 경외감을 느낄 정도죠. 물론 아무도 학장님이 절약정신을 발휘한다고 비난할 수는 없었어요."

"그렇지, 난 절대 실내장식을 하는 데 돈을 아끼는 사람은 아니었네. 정말 그래." 학장이 킬킬 웃었다. "다행히도 난 아주 신중한 투자자라네. 조심스럽게 투자하는 것이 좋다고 생각하지. 자네의 새 실험실을 깔끔하게 유지하는 것에 대해선 자네의 학생들과 연구팀에게 맡기겠네."

p. 632

"연구팀이오? 학생들이오?" 바너비가 물었다.

"물론이지! 거기다 자네가 과학과를 위한 새 교과과정을 짜주었으면 하네." 오몰리가 말했다. "학생들이 자네처럼 정말 독특한 방식으로 과학을 생각하게끔 도와줄 완전히 새로운 과학 수업을 만들어주게. 자넨 곧 시간여행의 권위자, 자네 분야에서 가장 총명하고 식견있는 사람으로 인정받게 될 테고, 도처의 사람들이 자네의 가르침과 본보기를 기대할 걸세. 하지만 그 문제는 내일 걱정하기로 하세. 오늘은 양키스 구장으로 가세!"

오몰리 학장은 갑자기 확 돌아서서 문 밖으로 걸어나갔고, 그 뒤로 바짝 브리지트, 바너비, 바베트, 보리가드가 따라갔다. 거리에 나온 학장은 아이들에게 번쩍이는 검은색 밴을 가리켜 보였다. 구식 밴처럼 네모진 것이 아니라 완벽한 유선형으로, 모든 사면과 모서리가 공기를 가르며 갈 수 있도록 설계되어 있었다. 이번만은 교통도 수월했다. 뉴욕의 주요 도로 어느 곳도 빵빵거리는 자동차로 막혀 있지 않았고, 그래서 그들은 눈 깜짝할 사이에 야구장에 도착했다.

이번에는 그들의 자리가 본루 바로 뒤였다. 그들 주변의 팬들은 대부분 지역 경찰관, 소방관, 그 밖의 시 직원들이었는데 여전히 제복 차림이었다.

"좋아!" 브리지트가 그들 자리 근처에 있는 사람들을 보고는 말했다. "저 사람들은 퇴근하고 바로 왔나봐. 시를 위해 일하는 저 사람들이 가장 행복한 팬들이야. 정말 많은 에너지를 쏟아서 양키스를 응원하는구나. 오늘 우리도 재미있 겠는걸!"

"그래, 저쪽에 가슴에다 '잘해라 양키스', '레드삭스를 없애버려' 라고 페인트칠하고 소리지르는 남자들은 대단한 팬 인가봐." 바베트가 동의했다.

"그래, 저 사람들 정말 열광적이다." 브리지트가 말했다.

p. 633

"음산하던 날씨가 개어서 정말 다행이구나. 야구할 때는 날씨가 좋아야지, 음산하면 안되지." 오몰리 학장이 말했다. "자, 바너비. 매점에 가자. 뭘 좀 먹어야지."

학장과 바너비는 먹을 것을 사러 갔고 몇 분 후에 한아름의 음식을 안고 돌아왔다. 브리지트조차 그 양을 보고 놀랐 다.

"자 그럼, 이 5갤론 통에 든 팝콘은 다함께 먹는 거다. 모두들 예의바르게 나눠 먹어야 한다." 포동포동한 과학자가 말했다. "각 사람마다 초대형 소다수를 하나씩 사왔단다. 내 건 얼음 없는 포도 음료. 난 차갑지 않고 미지근한 소 다수가 더 좋거든. 음료수가 약간 따뜻하면 냄새를 맡고 달콤한 과일향을 즐기기가 더 쉬우니까. 게다가 난 얼음이 녹 아서 음료수가 묽어지는 게 싫단다. 안타깝게도 스낵 판매원이 핫도그를 한번에 50개밖에 안 팔더구나. 경기가 끝날 때까지 먹으려면 배급량을 제한해야겠구나. 그러니 한 회에 하나씩만 먹는 거다, 알겠지? 먹어라!"

경기가 시작되었고, 팬들은 흥분에 휩싸였다. 양키스는 열심히 싸웠고, 경기 초반에 2점을 앞서갔다. 그들이 알지도 못하는 사이에 7회가 되었다.

"벌써 7회구나." 오몰리 학장이 말했다. "영원한 인기곡 '날 야구장에 데려가줘' 를 부를 시간이다. 그건 옛날 노래지 만 그 인기가 식을 줄 모르지."

"대단한 작품이죠." 브리지트가 동의하면서 일어나 노래할 준비를 했다. "대단한 교향곡이나 오페라 같은 건 아니지 만 좋은 곡인 것 같아요. 이봐, 바베트, 바너비, 노래할 준비 됐어? 이번엔 꼭 그라운드로 나갔으면 좋겠다!"

바너비, 바베트, 브리지트, 오몰리 학장은 서로서로 팔짱을 끼고 힘차게 노래를 불렀다. 그들은 바너비의 행운에 너무 나 행복하고 흥분했고, 집에 돌아온 게 너무나 기뻤으며, 경기에 정신이 온통 팔려서 커다랗고 검은 고양이가 슬그머 니 빠져나가 점점 커져가는 저녁의 그림자 속으로 사라지는 것을 알아차리지도 못했다.

p. 634

내가 무슨 할 말이 있겠어? 헤어지는 건 싫어. 내가 바랐던 건 그들이 외계인들에게 납치당하는 일 없이 7회를 무사 히 마치는 거였어. 하지만 그렇게 걱정되진 않았어. 얼마 동안은 모험을 실컷 한 것 같으니까. 내가 계속 그렇게 주의 깊게 감시할 필요는 없었어. 오몰리가 세 아이들을 곤경에 처하지 않도록 돌볼 수 있을 것 같았어.

게다가 난 비행기를 타야 했거든. 아, 트리니다드! 아, 콘수엘라! 그곳에서 정말 멋진 시간을 보냈지! 콘수엘라는 놀 랄 만큼 활달한 고양이야. 명랑하고 씩씩하고 언제나 날 마음 졸이게 만들지. 그녀는 나와 마음이 아주 잘 맞는 친구 였는데, 성격이 참 매력적이어서 그 섬에 있는 수코양이 대부분이 그녀에게 반할 정도였지. 우린 너무나 잘 맞았어. 천생연분이었다니까! 그곳에서의 내 생활은 너무나 안락해서 해변의 땅 한 구역을 사서 정착할 뻔했었지.

거의 그럴 뻔했어. 하지만 그때, 신비한 푸른 눈에 알쏭달쏭한 과거를 지닌 수수께끼같은 시암고양이가 와서는 내 계 획을 빗나가게 하고 섬 전체를 소란스럽게 만들었어. 그녀는 차우라는 미얀마의 장군 밑에서 일하는 스파이였는데, 차우는 카리브 해안에서 사탕수수 시장을 떠맡으려고 했지. 트리니다드를 정복해 차우를 위한 비밀 전초기지를 세우 려는 음모 속에서 난 뜻하지 않게 볼모로 붙잡혀 철저히 그녀의 통제 아래 놓이게 됐어. 콘수엘라는 날 저지하려고 했 지만, 난 거짓말투성이의 이야기 속에 꼼짝없이 붙들렸고, 브리지트, 바너비, 바베트가... 뭐, 자세한 얘기는 다음 기 회를 위해 남겨둬야겠군.

그 얘긴 다음에 하자고.

QUICK QUIZ 36

관계 짓기

아래의 단어 쌍들이 서로 어떤 관계를 갖는지 판단하세요. 비슷한 의미면 "S" 반대 의미면 "O"를 하세요.

1. 넘쳐흐르는 :: 풍부한
2. 중요 인물 :: 거물
3. 굴절시키다 :: 똑바르게 하다
4. 화려한 :: 웅장한
5. 절약 :: 사치, 낭비
6. 미지근한 :: 뜨거운

QUICK QUIZ 37

관계 짓기

아래의 단어 쌍들이 서로 어떤 관계를 갖는지 판단하세요. 비슷한 의미면 "S" 반대 의미면 "O"를 하세요.

1. 마음이 맞는 :: 마음을 끄는
2. 음침한, 황량한 :: 누추한, 황폐한
3. 정신적 지도자 :: 예언자, 선지자
4. 희석하다 :: 강화하다
5. 튼튼한, 뚱뚱한 :: 호리호리한

QUICK QUIZ 38

빈칸 채우기

아래에 있는 각각의 단어들 중에서 가장 완벽한 문장을 만들어주는 단어를 고르세요.

1. (   ) 교사는 곧 세상 사람 모두가 자기처럼 바퀴벌레를 연구하느라 하루에 18시간씩 들이는 것을 좋아하지는 않는다는 걸 알게 됐다.
   a. 둘도 없는   b. 열심인   c. 모순 없는   d. 나른한

2. 안타깝게도 벤이 자신의 두 시간 짜리 하모니카 (   ) "교정 블루스"를 완성하기 전에 어머니가 그에게 저녁을 먹으러 오라고 했다.
   a. 망토   b. 철야   c. 작품   d. 넓이

3. 열차 기관사와 역장이 사용하는 새로운 휴대용 전화 네트워크 덕분에 철도 운행이 (   ) 통근시간이 10%까지 줄었다.
   a. 탈선하고   b. 공중 정지하고   c. 빛을 발하고   d. 능률화되고

4. 선원들은 난파된 채로 얼마나 오래 있게 될지 몰라서 즉시 비축물을 (   ) 했다.
   a. 제한적으로 배급하기로 b. 기독교도로 만들기로 c. 배제하기로   d. 권리를 주기로

5. (   ) 가수는 종종 공연을 하면서 시작은 슬픈 기분으로 하고, 중간까지는 화를 내면서 하다가 끝에 가서는 최고로 기분이 좋은 상태가 됐다.
   a. 계속적인   b. 변덕스러운   c. 지방자치의   d. 공동사회의

6. 우리 집에서 첫 잔의 커피를 만드는 것은 공을 들이는 (   )이어서, 여러 가지 분쇄기에, 4종류의 다른 원두, 정화시킨 물을 이용했다.
   a. 유사   b. 전당   c. 교과과정   d. 의식

QUICK QUIZ 39

짝짓기

오른쪽의 단어를 비슷한 의미의 왼쪽 단어와 짝지으세요.

1. 팩시밀리	A. 전기 서류 전송기
2. 탁월한	B. 약삭빠른
3. 증대	C. 증가
4. 아지랑이, 안개	D. 좋은 냄새
5. 영리한, 빈틈없는	E. 최고의
6. 향기	F. 기쁨, 즐거움
7. 다시없는 기쁨	G. 안개

짝짓기

오른쪽의 단어를 비슷한 의미의 왼쪽 단어와 짝지으세요.

1. 동맥   A. 뜻을 명기하다
2. 국고의 재정상의   B. 재정적인
3. 풍부한 재산   C. 튼튼한
4. 계산하다   D. 혈관
5. 건장한   E. 계산하다
6. 제한하다   F. 많은 재산

QUICK QUIZ 정답

QUICK QUIZ 1

1. O 2. S 3. S 4. O 5. O 6. S 7. S 8. S 9. O 10. O 11. S

QUICK QUIZ 2

1. O 2. S 3. O 4. S 5. S 6. O 7. S 8. O 9. O 10. S

QUICK QUIZ 3

1. B 2. B 3. D 4. C 5. B 6. A 7. A 8. D 9. C 10. D

QUICK QUIZ 4

1. F 2. H 3. A 4. E 5. J 6. C 7. I 8. D 9. B 10. G

QUICK QUIZ 5

1. C 2. J 3. I 4. E 5. A 6. H 7. F 8. B 9. D 10. G

QUICK QUIZ 6

1. O 2. O 3. O 4. S 5. S 6. S 7. O 8. S 9. O 10. O 11. S

QUICK QUIZ 7

1. O 2. S 3. S 4. O 5. S 6. S 7. O 8. O 9. S 10. O 11. S

QUICK QUIZ 8

1. B 2. C 3. A 4. D 5. C 6. B 7. C 8. D 9. A

QUICK QUIZ 9

1. C 2. A 3. I 4. F 5. B 6. D 7. G 8. E 9. H

QUICK QUIZ 10

1. E 2. C 3. I 4. D 5. G 6. A 7. F 8. H 9. B

QUICK QUIZ 11

1. S 2. O 3. O 4. S 5. O 6. S 7. S 8. S 9. O 10. S 11. O 12. O

QUICK QUIZ 12

1. S 2. O 3. S 4. S 5. O 6. O 7. O 8. S 9. S 10. O 11. S 12. O

QUICK QUIZ 13

1. C 2. B 3. A 4. C 5. C 6. D 7. B 8. A 9. D 10. D 11. A 12. A

QUICK QUIZ 14

1. F 2. H 3. A 4. L 5. D 6. M 7. B 8. I 9. C 10. E 11. G 12. J 13. K

QUICK QUIZ 15

1. D 2. A 3. H 4. K 5. F 6. M 7. B 8. I 9. L 10. C 11. E 12. G 13. J

QUICK QUIZ 16

1. S 2. O 3. S 4. O 5. S 6. O 7. O 8. S 9. O 10. S

QUICK QUIZ 17

1. S 2. O 3. S 4. S 5. O 6. O 7. S 8. O 9. O 10. S

QUICK QUIZ 18

1. A 2. C 3. D 4. A 5. B 6. C 7. C 8. D 9. B

QUICK QUIZ 19

1. J   2. B   3. G   4. H   5. A   6. I   7. C   8. F   9. D   10. E

QUICK QUIZ 20

1. F   2. A   3. G   4. B   5. J   6. D   7. I   8. E   9. H   10. C

QUICK QUIZ 21

1. S   2. O   3. S   4. O   5. O   6. S   7. O   8. S   9. S   10. O

QUICK QUIZ 22

1. S   2. S   3. O   4. O   5. S   6. O   7. O   8. S   9. S   10. O

QUICK QUIZ 23

1. A   2. C   3. A   4. B   5. D   6. B   7. C   8. D   9. D

QUICK QUIZ 24

1. B   2. D   3. H   4. C   5. A   6. J   7. E   8. F   9. I   10. G

QUICK QUIZ 25

1. H   2. I   3. C   4. F   5. A   6. J   7. E   8. B   9. G   10. D

QUICK QUIZ 26

1. S   2. S   3. O   4. S   5. O   6. S   7. O   8. O   9. S   10. O

QUICK QUIZ 27

1. S   2. S   3. S   4. O   5. O   6. O   7. S   8. S   9. O   10. O

QUICK QUIZ 28

1. C   2. D   3. A   4. B   5. C   6. A   7. B   8. B   9. D

QUICK QUIZ 29

1. G   2. B   3. I   4. F   5. A   6. D   7. H   8. J   9. E   10. C

QUICK QUIZ 30

1. D   2. I   3. E   4. B   5. H   6. F   7. C   8. A   9. G

QUICK QUIZ 31

1. O   2. S   3. S   4. O   5. O   6. S   7. S   8. O   9. O   10. S   11. O

QUICK QUIZ 32

1. S   2. S   3. O   4. S   5. O   6. O   7. S   8. O   9. S   10. S   11. S

QUICK QUIZ 33

1. C   2. C   3. D   4. D   5. B   6. B   7. A   8. B   9. D   10. C

QUICK QUIZ 34

1. F   2. I   3. A   4. D   5. B   6. K   7. G   8. J   9. C   10. H   11. E

QUICK QUIZ 35

1. J   2. E   3. A   4. G   5. B   6. K   7. D   8. I   9. C   10. H   11. F

QUICK QUIZ 36

1. S   2. S   3. O   4. S   5. O   6. O

QUICK QUIZ 37

1. S   2. S   3. S   4. O   5. O

QUICK QUIZ 38

1. B   2. C   3. D   4. A   5. B   6. D

QUICK QUIZ 39

1. A   2. E   3. C   4. G   5. B   6. D   7. F

QUICK QUIZ 40

1. D   2. B   3. F   4. E   5. C   6. A